RIGVEDA BRAHMANAS:

THE AITAREYA AND KAUSITAKI BRAHMANAS OF THE RIGVEDA

Owing to the antiquity and rarity of this book, certain pages are regrettably absent, and readability is compromised due to the blurring of the original text. If you possess any insights regarding the availability of these missing sections, kindly inform us. Your assistance is crucial in ensuring the completion of this significant work for the benefit of future generations.

RIGVEDA BRAHMANAS:

THE AITAREYA AND KAUSITAKI BRAHMANAS OF THE RIGVEDA

TRANSLATED FROM THE ORIGINAL SANSKRIT

BY

ARTHUR BERRIEDALE KEITH,

D.C.L., D.LITT.

GYAN

Published by

Gyan Publishing House
5, Ansari Road
Daryaganj, New Delhi-110002
Phone: 011-47034999, 9811692060
E-mail: books@gyanbooks.com

Distribution Network
gyanbooks.com
India, USA, Canada, UK, Australia

ISBN: 978-93-6280-486-0 (HB)
First Published, 1920

2nd Impression 2024

Printed at: Gyan Press, Delhi.

RIGVEDA BRAHMANAS: THE AITAREYA AND KAUSITAKI BRAHMANAS OF THE RIGVEDA
Translator: ARTHUR BERRIEDALE KEITH

RIGVEDA BRAHMANAS:

THE AITAREYA AND KAUṢĪTAKI BRĀHMAṆAS OF THE RIGVEDA

TRANSLATED FROM THE ORIGINAL SANSKRIT

BY

ARTHUR BERRIEDALE KEITH, D.C.L., D.LITT.

OF THE INNER TEMPLE, BARRISTER-AT-LAW

REGIUS PROFESSOR OF SANSKRIT AND COMPARATIVE PHILOLOGY

AT THE UNIVERSITY OF EDINBURGH

LATE OF HIS MAJESTY'S COLONIAL OFFICE

TRANSLATOR OF THE VEDA OF THE BLACK YAJUS SCHOOL

CAMBRIDGE, MASSACHUSETTS

Harvard University Press

1920

IN MEMORIAM

FRATRIS

R. C. STEUART KEITH, I.C.S.

(1876-1919)

PREFACE

THIS translation of the Brāhmaṇas of the Rigveda was prepared in the winter of 1914–15, and in the following autumn Professor C. R. Lanman added to the many obligations which I owe to him by undertaking to find a place for it in the Harvard Oriental Series. Interruption of correspondence, due to submarine activity, delayed arrangements for printing, but substantial progress was made in 1917. Thereafter, however, the increasing pressure of war conditions rendered work difficult, and when, on the conclusion of the armistice, an active resumption of printing took place, my absence in London, while serving on Lord Crewe's Committee on the Home Administration of Indian Affairs, postponed for a considerable period the correction of the proofs.

The plan followed in this work is that adopted in the case of the translation of the *Taittirīya Saṁhitā*, vols. xviii and xix in this series, and it gives me sincere pleasure to express once more my indebtedness to the works of Professors A. A. Macdonell; T. Aufrecht and J. Eggeling, my predecessors at Edinburgh; W. Caland, V. Henry, A. Hillebrandt, H. Oldenberg, W. D. Whitney, and, last but not least, C. R. Lanman. Dr. F. W. Thomas, as ever, facilitated the use of the resources of the Library of the India Office, including the MS. of Vināyaka's commentary on the *Kauṣītaki Brāhmaṇa*, from which are derived the renderings ascribed in my translation to the commentary. My wife shared with me the task of correcting the proofs and preparing the indexes. To Mr. Frederick Hall and his staff my best thanks are due for the care which they have taken in the production of the work.

A. BERRIEDALE KEITH.

EDINBURGH,
October 10, 1919.

CONTENTS

	PAGE
INTRODUCTION	1–103
1. Comparison of Contents of the two Brāhmaṇas	1–21
2. The Relations of the two Brāhmaṇas	22–28
3. The Composition of the Aitareya Brāhmaṇa	28–36
4. The Composition of the Kauṣītaki Brāhmaṇa	36–42
5. The Dates of the two Brāhmaṇas	42–50
Relation to Pāṇini	42
Relation to Yāska	42
Relation to Çākalya	43
Relation to Āçvalāyana and Çāṅkhāyana	44
Absence of reference to Metempsychosis	44
Political references	44
Relation to other Brāhmaṇa texts	45
Relation to Āpastamba	48
Astronomical data	49
Date of later part of the Aitareya	49
Date of Metrical Portions of the Aitareya	50
6. The Ritual	50–68
The Çāṅkhāyana Çrauta Sūtra	50
The Āçvalāyana Çrauta Sūtra	51
The Soma Sacrifice	53
The Rājasūya and the Story of Çunaḥçepa	61
7. Language, Style, and Metre	68–101
Language of the Mantras	68
Language of the Prose	70
Style	96
Metre	98
8. Commentaries and Editions	101–103
TRANSLATION OF THE AITAREYA BRĀHMAṆA	105–344
TRANSLATION OF THE KAUṢĪTAKI BRĀHMAṆA	345–530
GENERAL INDEX	531–546
SANSKRIT INDEX	547–555

ADDITIONS

Introduction. P. 42. S. K. Belvalkar (*Systems of Sanskrit Grammar*, pp. 15–19) defends the view which places Pāṇini in the seventh century B.C., but without adding any argument of weight. K. P. Jayaswal (*Ind. Ant.* xlvii. 138) holds that Kātyāyana's date may be ascribed to 248–200 B.C., on the ground of his Vārttika on ii. 1. 60 (*çākapārthivādīnām upasaṁkhyānam*), and argues that, as Pāṇini holds (vi. 3. 21) that the genitive case-ending is retained in compounds in a disparaging sense, he cannot have known the imperial title *devānāmpriya*, which Açoka attributes to his predecessors. The cogency of the argument is imperfect, since there is no real proof that the title was actually used before Açoka's time as an imperial title. On the other hand, S. Lévi's effort (*Journal Asiatique*, sér. 8, xv. 234–240) to bring down Pāṇini's date to *c.* 300 B.C. on the strength of his mention of Sāṁkala, Bhagāla, and Takṣaçilā, and of the occurrence of Āmbhi in the *Gaṇapāṭha* equally lacks cogency.

P. 45. P. D. Gune (*Bhandarkar Commemoration Volume*, pp. 46, 50, 51) inclines to favour the view of the priority of the *Gopatha Brāhmaṇa* to Yāska, but adduces no new evidence of weight, the similarity of *Nirukta* iv. 27 to *Gopatha* v. 5 being one of substance alone.

P. 46. The publication by W. Caland of *Das Jaiminīya-Brāhmaṇa in Auswahl* (Amsterdam, November 1919), renders available proof of the posteriority of the *Jaiminīya* to both the *Aitareya* and *Kauṣītaki Brāhmaṇas.* Thus the account of the Gavām Ayana (ii. 374) is plainly later than AB. iv. 17, and that of the consecration of Keçin (ii. 53, 54) than KB. vii. 4. Many proper names in the *Jaiminīya* have parallels in the other two texts, the former presenting some of these names in inferior forms; of special interest are Vāsiṣṭha Sātyahavya, Aikādaçākṣi, Ṛjīçvan Vātavāta, Nagarin Jānaçruteya, Saujāta Ārāḍi, Vṛṣaçuṣma Ārjīçvana, Somaçuṣma Sātyayajñi, Hiraṇyadant Veda, Buḍila Āçvatarāçvi, Kratujit Jānaki, and the Ābhipratāraṇas. The comparative epoch of the *Jaiminīya* is suggested by such names as Yājñavalkya, Janaka Vaideha, Çvetaketu Āruṇeya, Kahoḷa Kauṣītakeya, Kṣatra Prātardana the confusion of Keçin Dārbhya and Keçin Sātyakāmi, &c.

Aitareya Brāhmaṇa. iii. 43. That the verse was early unintelligible is shown by JB. i. 258, where a quite irrelevant story of one Çakala Gaupāyana is told in order to illustrate it.

iv. 17. In the parallel in JB. ii. 374: *tāsāṁ dvādaçe māsi çṛṅgāṇi prāvartanta* Caland renders 'Deren Hörner begannen (erst) im zwölften Monate hervorzukommen', but this sense of *prāvartanta* is in itself unlikely, and, what is more important, is not consistent with the following phrase: *tasmāt sattriṇo dvādaçe māsy api çikhāḥ pravapante*, where the parallelism of *pra-* proves that the *Brāhmaṇa* understood *prāvartanta* as 'fell off'; the horns existed as the result of the first ten months, but were lost through the next two, just as the *çikhāḥ* are removed. But that this was the original sense is most implausible.

vi. 1. Caland (ZDMG. lxxii. 23) suggests *evopodāsarpan*, a correction already made by O. Böhtlingk (*Chrestomathie*[2], p. 21) to eliminate *ha sma* with the imperfect; at its second occurrence he omits *sma* rather than adopt Delbrück's suggestion (Böhtlingk, p. 350) *sa ha sma yenopodāsarpati*. But these conjectures do too much violence to the text, and it must be remembered that in vii. 16 is found *ha sma . . . mumuce* and at v. 30 *ha sma . . . uvāca*, which is not probably to be taken with Delbrück (*Altind. Synt.* p. 503) as equivalent to the normal *ha smāha*.

vi. 35. The conjectures of Weber as to the end of the Devanītha are borne out by JB. ii. 116, where the reading is *ahā ned asann apurogavāṇi, yajñā ned asann avicetanāsaḥ*.

vii. 18. The Udantyas here are clearly the same as the Udantas in JB. i. 197, as Caland (JB. p. 80) rightly suggests. His further suggestions (pp. 99, 104) that the Udantas include the Kurus and Pañcālas, or the Kurus only (JB. i. 256, 262) and are northerners generally is quite inconsistent with his first identification. Nor are the Kurus and Pañcālas northerners proper; cf. *Vedic Index*, i. 168.

Kauṣītaki Brāhmaṇa. vii. 4. There is a variant in JB. ii. 53, 54, where the text as it stands does not make sense. The same *Brāhmaṇa* (i. 285) converts Keçin Dārbhya from a king into a Purohita of Keçin Sātyakāmi, which contradicts its own version elsewhere, and is doubtless a product of secondary tradition.

x. 2 and xvii. 9. Caland (ZDMG. lxxii. 1, 2) suggests 'eindringen' for *anvavapātoḥ*, but this is not necessary; for *yadi na* cf. ÇĀ. i. 8.

xxi. 1. Caland (ZDMG. lxxii. 24) conjectures for *nānvavāyanāya* the more natural *'nanvavāyanāya*.

xxiii. 2. Caland reads *hatvāyantam*, which is an improvement, though *yantam* is unobjectionable unless referred to Indra's attack on Vṛtra.

xxiii. 5. Caland accepts M's reading of *Paruchepāt* in the second clause, and restores it in the first; this makes the sentence so simple as to render the corruption unaccountable, and M, while often showing a good tradition, is also not without obvious efforts at correction. In this case the correction, unfortunately, ruins the meaning of the passage; the one-day form has no Parucchepa hymn.

xxv. 10. For *saṁsthāpayiṣeyuḥ* Caland suggests *saṁtiṣṭhāpayiṣeyuḥ*; very possibly *saṁsthāpayeyuḥ* is correct.

xxv. 13. Caland suggests that for *ned . . . antariyām* should be read *antarayāma*, since there is a variant *antaryāma*, and the subjunctive is required. But the injunctive would be correct (Delbrück, *Altind. Synt.* p. 360), and the conjecture is therefore needless. The plural, however, is a difficulty, though not impossible; *antarayam*, injunctive of the verb found in xii. 4 and xxiii. 4, may be read, and would explain the divergent readings, since it would be a rare and easily misunderstood form. If *iyām* is correct, then the passage is comparable with AB. viii. 23.

xxvi. 4. Caland deduces from xvi. 9 and xxv. 14 the suggestion *hīyate* in lieu of *dhīyate*, but from PB. xvi. 1. 2: *kartapatyaṁ taj jīyate vā pra vā mīyate* concludes that *jīyate* is original. But *dhīyate* can stand.

xxvi. 7. Caland's suggestion to omit *smāha* is open to the objection that its insertion is not easy to explain, and the text can be translated.

xxviii. 1. Caland reads *etāvate*, 'so wichtig sind'.

xxviii. 2. Caland suggests that *apajajñire* is a misprint for *apajaghnire*. The Ānand. ed., however, has the same reading, but the sense must be as rendered below.

INTRODUCTION

§ 1. Comparison of Contents of the Two Brāhmaṇas.

A. THE AITAREYA BRĀHMAṆA

Pañcikā I.

The Soma Sacrifice.

Adhyāya I.

The Consecration rites.

i. 1 =	i. 1.	The consecration offering.	KB. vii. 1
2 =	2.	The origin of the terms Āhuti and Hotṛ.	
3 =	3.	The rebirth of the consecrated man in the rite.	
4 =	4.	The verses recited at the sacrifices of the consecration offering.	vii. 2
5 =	5.	The verses for the Sviṣṭakṛt rite.	
6 =	6.	The choice of Virāj verses.	

Adhyāya II.

The Introductory Sacrifice.

7 =	ii. 1.	The deities of the introductory sacrifice.	vii. 5, 8
8 =	2.	The fore-offerings.	
9 =	3.	The metres used in verses of the introductory sacrifice.	
10 =	4.	The Virāj metre in the Sviṣṭakṛt verses.	
11 =	5.	The use of the fore- and after-offerings.	
		The offerings to the wives of the gods.	vii. 9
		The introductory and the concluding sacrifices.	vii. 7, 9

Adhyāya III.

The buying and bringing of the Soma.

12 =	iii. 1.	The bringing of the Soma.	vii. 10
13 =	2.	The bringing forward of the Soma.	vii. 10
14 =	3.	The unyoking of the Soma cart.	vii. 10
15 =	4.	The guest-offering to Soma.	viii. 1
16 =	5.	The production of fire by friction.	viii. 1
17 =	6.	The remaining rites of the guest reception.	viii. 2

Adhyāya IV.

The Pravargya.

i. 18 = iv. 1.	The origin of the Pravargya.	KB. viii. 3
19 = 2.	The first twenty-one verses of the Hotṛ.	viii. 4
20 = 3.	The Pāvamānī and other verses.	viii. 5
21 = 4.	The completion of the first section of the Mantras	viii. 5, 6
22 = 5.	The second section of the Mantras.	viii. 7
23 = 6.	The Upasads.	viii. 8
24 = 7.	The Tānūnaptra rite.	
25 = 8.	The Upasads (continued).	viii. 9
26 = 9.	The fore- and after-offerings omitted in the Upasads. The Tānūnaptra and Nihnavana.	

Adhyāya V.

The carrying forward of the fire, Soma, and the offerings to the High Altar.

27 = v. 1.	The purchase of Soma by speech and her return.	ix. 1
28 = 2.	The carrying forward of the fire.	ix. 2
29 = 3.	The bringing forward of the oblation receptacles.	ix. 3, 4
30 = 4.	The Mantras for the bringing forward of Agni and Soma.	ix. 5, 6

Pañcikā II.

THE SOMA SACRIFICE (*continued*).

Adhyāya I = VI.

The Animal Sacrifice.

ii. 1 = vi. 1.	The erecting of the sacrificial post.	x. 1
2 = 2.	The anointing of the sacrificial post.	x. 2
3 = 3.	The symbolic value of the post and of the sacrifice.	x. 3
4 = 4.	The fire offerings with the Āprī verses.	
5 = 5.	The carrying of fire round the victim.	
6 = 6.	The formulae for the slaying of the victim.	x. 4
7 = 7.	The formulae for the slaying of the victim (continued).	x. 5
8 = 8.	The sacrificial animals.	
9 = 9.	The relation of the cake and animal offerings. The sanctity of the consecrated man.	
10 = 10.	The offering of the portions for Manotā.	x. 6

Adhyāya II = VII.

The Animal Sacrifice (continued) and the Morning Litany.

ii. 11 = vii.	1. The reason for carrying fire round the victim.	
12 =	2. The offering of the drops from the omentum.	KB. x. 5
13 =	3. The offerings to the calls of Hail!	x. 5
14 =	4. The offering of the omentum.	x. 5
15 =	5. The time for the repetition of the morning litany.	xi. 3
16 =	6. The beginning of the litany.	xi. 4
17 =	7. The number of the verses.	xi. 7
18 =	8. The mode of reciting the verses.	xi. 2, 6
	The deities addressed.	xi. 4, 6

Adhyāya III = VIII.

The Aponaptrīya and other ceremonies.

19 = viii.	1. Story of the seer Kavaṣa.	xii. 3
20 =	2. The mixing of the Vasatīvarī and Ekadhanā waters.	xii. 1, 2
21 =	3. The Upāṅçu and Antaryāma cups.	xii. 4
22 =	4. The Bahiṣpavamāna Stotra.	xii. 5
23 =	5. The cake offerings at the three pressings.	xiii. 3
24 =	6. The offering of five oblations.	xiii. 2

Adhyāya IV = IX.

The Various Cups.

25 = ix.	1. The cups for Indra and Vāyu, Mitra and Varuṇa, and the Açvins	xiii. 5
26 =	2. The symbolism of these cups.	xiii. 5
27 =	3. The drinking of the Hotṛ from these cups.	xiii. 6
28 =	4. The two offering verses for these cups.	
29 =	5. The offerings to the seasons.	xiii. 9
30 =	6. The eating and drinking of the Hotṛ.	xiii. 7
31 =	7. The silent praise.	
32 =	8. The symbolism of the silent praise.	

Adhyāya V = X.

The Ājya Çastra.

33 = x.	1. The call and the Nivid (Puroruc).	xiv. 3
34 =	2. The words of the Nivid (Puroruc).	
35 =	3. The recitation of the hymn of the Ājya.	xiv. 2
36 =	4. The altars of the priests.	
	The Çastra of the Achāvāka.	

ii. 37 = x. 5. The correspondence of the Stotras and Çastras.
38 = 6. The muttering of the Hotṛ.
39 = 7. The silent praise, the Puroruc, and the hymn.
40 = 8. The hymn. KB. xiv. 1
41 = 9. The hymn (continued). xiv. 1

Pañcikā III.

The Soma Sacrifice (*continued*).

Adhyāya I = XI.

The Praüga Çastra, the Vaṣaṭ call, and the Nivids.

iii. 1 = xi. 1. The seven triplets of the Praüga Çastra. xiv. 4
2 = 2. The meaning of the triplets. xiv. 5
3 = 3. The power of the Hotṛ to ruin the sacrificer.
4 = 4. Agni as the real deity of the Çastra.
5 = 5. The *vaṣaṭ* call and the secondary *vaṣaṭ* call.
6 = 6. The meaning of the *vaṣaṭ* call.
7 = 7. The three kinds of *vaṣaṭ* call.
8 = 8. The Anumantraṇa of the *vaṣaṭ* call.
9 = 9. The meaning of Praiṣa, Puroruc, Vedi, Nivid, and Graha.
10 = 10. The place of the Nivids.
11 = 11. The mode of repeating the Nivids.

Adhyāya II = XII.

The Marutvatīya and the Niṣkevalya Çastras.

12 = xii. 1. The call and the response. KB. xiv. 3
13 = 2. The Anuṣṭubh at the beginning of the Çastra.
14 = 3. The mode in which Agni escaped death in the several Çastras. xv. 5
15 = 4. The beginning of the Marutvatīya Çastra. xv. 2
16 = 5. The Pragātha to invoke Indra. xv. 2
17 = 6. The Pragātha to Brahmaṇaspati. xv. 2
18 = 7. The inserted verses. xv. 3
19 = 8. The Marutvatīya Pragātha and the hymn. xv. 3
20 = 9. The origin of the Çastra for the Maruts.
21 = 10. Indra's claim to the Niṣkevalya Çastra. xv. 4
22 = 11. Prāsahā, the wife of Indra, and the inserted verse.
23 = 12. The four parts of the Sāman and of the Çastra.
24 = 13. The strophe, antistrophe, inserted verse, Sāma-Pragātha, and hymn. xv. 4

Adhyāya III = XIII.

The Vaiçvadeva and the Āgnimāruta.

iii. 25 =	xiii. 1.	The fetching of Soma by the metres.	
26 =	2.	The success of the Gāyatrī and the loss of her nail.	
27 =	3.	The origin of the three pressings.	
28 =	4.	The syllables of the Triṣṭubh and Gāyatrī.	
29 =	5.	The share of the Ādityas, Savitṛ, Vāyu, and sky and earth.	KB. xvi. 1–4
30 =	6.	The share of the Ṛbhus.	xvi. 3, 4
31 =	7.	The hymn to the All-gods and the inserted verses.	xvi. 3, 4
32 =	8.	Offerings to Agni, Soma, and Viṣṇu.	xvi. 5
33 =	9.	The legend of Prajāpati and his daughter and the origin of Bhūtapati.	
34 =	10.	The propitiation of Rudra.	
35 =	11.	The hymns to Vaiçvānara and the Maruts and	xvi. 7
		the strophe and antistrophe of the Āgnimāruta.	xvi. 7
36 =	12.	The hymn to Jātavedas.	
37 =	13.	The offerings to the wives of the gods, to Yama and the Kāvyas.	xvi. 7
38 =	14.	The share of Indra, and verses to Viṣṇu, Varuṇa, and Prajāpati.	

Adhyāya IV = XIV.

General considerations regarding the Agniṣṭoma.

39 =	xiv. 1.	The origin of the term Agniṣṭoma.	
40 =	2.	The comprehensive character of the Agniṣṭoma.	iv. 4, 5
41 =	3.	The Ukthya and Atirātra as dependent on the Agniṣṭoma. The number of Stotriya verses in the Agniṣṭoma.	
42 =	4.	The four Stomas of the Agniṣṭoma.	
43 =	5.	The names Agniṣṭoma, Catuṣṭoma, and Jyotiṣṭoma.	
44 =	6	The mode of performing the ceremony in accordance with the course of the sun.	

Adhyāya V = XV.

Certain Details regarding the Sacrifice.

45 =	xv. 1.	The recovery of the sacrifice by the gods.	
46 =	2.	Errors in the selection of priests.	
47 =	3.	The offerings to Dhātṛ and the minor deities.	
48 =	4.	The offerings to the goddesses as alternative or additional rites.	
49 =	5.	The origin and form of the Ukthya and its Sāmans.	xvi. 11
50 =	6.	The Çastras of the Hotrakas at the evening pressing.	xvi. 11

Pañcikā IV.

The Soma Sacrifice (*continued*).

Adhyāya I = XVI.

The Ṣoḍaçin and the Atirātra Sacrifices.

AB.		KB.
iv. 1 = xvi. 1.	The nature of the Ṣoḍaçin.	KB. xvii. 1
2 = 2.	The mode of reciting the Ṣoḍaçin Çastra.	
3 = 3.	The intermingling of the metres.	xvii. 2, 3
4 = 4.	The additions from the Mahānāmnīs.	xvii. 4
5 = 5.	The origin of the Atirātra	xvii. 5
6 = 6.	The Çastras of the Atirātra at the three rounds and the Sandhi Stotra.	xvii. 6

Adhyāya II = XVII.

The Āçvina Çastra and the Gavām Ayana.

AB.		KB.
7 = xvii. 1.	The Āçvina Çastra as Prajāpati's gift to Sūryā.	
8 = 2.	The race of the gods for the Çastra.	xviii. 1
9 = 3.	The steeds of the gods in their race.	
10 = 4.	The verses to Sūrya, Indra, the Rathantara Sāman, &c.	xviii. 3
11 = 5.	The conclusion of the Çastra.	xviii. 4, 5
12 = 6.	The Caturviñça day of the Gavām Ayana.	xix. 3
13 = 7.	The two Sāmans of the Sattra and the order of the parts of the Sattra.	
14 = 8.	The modification of the Niṣkevalya Çastra on the Caturviñça and Mahāvrata days.	xix. 9

Adhyāya III = XVIII.

The Ṣaḍahas and Viṣuvant.

AB.		KB.
15 = xviii. 1.	The composition of the Ṣaḍaha.	xx. 1
16 = 2.	The five Ṣaḍahas in the month.	xxi. 5
17 = 3.	The Gavām and other Ayanas.	
18 = 4.	The Ekaviñça Viṣuvant day.	
19 = 5.	The Svarasāmans, Abhijit and Viçvajit, and Viṣuvant.	xxiv. 1–9; xxv. 7
20 = 6.	The Dūrohaṇa in the Tārkṣya hymn.	xxv. 7
21 = 7.	The mode of repeating the Dūrohaṇa.	xxv. 7
22 = 8.	The distinctive characteristics of the Viṣuvant day.	

Adhyāya IV = XIX.

The Dvādaçāha rite.

AB.		KB.
23 = xix. 1.	The origin of the Dvādaçāha rite.	
24 = 2.	The parts of the Dvādaçāha.	
25 = 3.	Prajāpati and the Dvādaçāha.	

iv. 26 = xix. 4. The consecration for the Dvādaçāha, the victim for Prajāpati, and the cake for Vāyu.
27 = 5. The transposed Dvādaçāha.
28 = 6. The Sāmans of the Pṛṣṭhas.

Adhyāya V = XX.

The first two days of the Dvādaçāha.

29 = xx. 1. The Çastras of the morning and midday pressings of the first day. KB. xxii. 1
30 = 2. The remaining Çastras. xxii. 1
31 = 3. The Çastras of the morning and midday pressings of the second day. xxii. 2
32 = 4. The remaining Çastras. xxii. 2

Pañcikā V.

The Soma Sacrifice (*continued*).

Adhyāya I = XXI.

The third and fourth days of the Dvādaçāha.

v. 1 = xxi. 1. The Çastras of the morning and midday pressings of the third day. xxii. 3, 4
2 = 2. The remaining Çastras. xxii. 4, 5
3 = 3. The Nyūñkha in the fourth day. xxii. 3
4 = 4. The characteristics of the morning and midday pressings of the fourth day. xxii. 6–8
5 = 5. The remaining Çastras. xxii. 8, 9

Adhyāya II = XXII.

The fifth and sixth days of the Dvādaçāha.

6 = xxii. 1. The Çastras of the morning and midday pressings of the fifth day. xxiii. 1
7 = 2. The Çakvara Sāman and the Mahānāmnī verses and the Niṣkevalya Çastra. xxiii. 2
8 = 3. The remainder of the Niṣkevalya Çastra and the other Çastras. xxiii. 3
9 = 4. The season offerings on the sixth day.
10 = 5. The use of the Parucchepa verses before the Yājyās of the Prasthita offerings. xxiii. 4, 5
11 = 6. The origin of these verses. xxiii. 4
12 = 7. The Çastras of the morning and midday pressings of the sixth day. xxii. 6, 7
13 = 8. The remaining Çastras. xxiii. 7, 8
14 = 9. The Nābhānediṣṭha hymn of the Vaiçvadeva.
15 = 10. The special Çastras of the third pressing.

Adhyāya III = XXIII.

The seventh and eighth days of the Dvādaçāha.

v. 16 = xxiii. 1. The Çastras of the morning and midday pressings of the seventh day. KB. xxvi. 7, 8
17 = 2. The remaining Çastras. xxvi. 9, 10
18 = 3. The Çastras of the morning and midday pressings of the eighth day. xxvi. 11, 12
19 = 4. The remaining Çastras. xxvi. 12, 13

Adhyāya IV = XXIV.

The ninth and tenth days of the Dvādaçāha.

20 = xxiv. 1. The Çastras of the morning and midday pressings of the ninth day. xxvi. 14, 15
21 = 2. The remaining Çastras. xxvi. 16, 17
22 = 3. The tenth day. xxvii. 1-3
23 = 4. The Mantras of the Serpent Queen and the Caturhotṛs. xxvii. 4
24 = 5. The breaking of silence by the priests. xxvii. 6
25 = 6. The text of the Caturhotṛs, the bodies of Prajāpati, and the riddle. xxvii. 5

Adhyāya V = XXV.

The Agnihotra and the Brahman Priest.

26 = xxv. 1. The Agnihotra offering. ii. 1
27 = 2. Expiations for accidents to the Agnihotra cow (= vii. 3).
28 = 3. The symbolism of the Agnihotra.
29 = 4. The time of offering the Agnihotra before or after sunrise. ii. 9
30 = 5. The arguments for offering after sunrise. ii. 9
31 = 6. The conclusion. ii. 9
32 = 7. The expiations for errors in the sacrifice. vi. 10, 12
33 = 8. The office of the Brahman priest. vi. 13
34 = 9. The work done by the Brahman priest. vi. 12, 13

Pañcikā VI.

THE ÇASTRAS OF THE HOTRAKAS.

Adhyāya I = XXVI.

The office of the Grāvastut and Subrahmaṇyā.

vi. 1 = xxvi. 1. The origin of the midday Mantras of the Grāvastut. KB. xxix. 1
2 = 2. The manner and mode of reciting these Mantras. xxix. 1
3 = 3. The Subrahmaṇyā formula and the priest.

Adhyāya II = XXVII.

The Çastras of the Hotrakas at Sattras and Ahīnas.

vi. 4 = xxvii. 1. The origin of the Çastras of the Hotrakas.
5 = 2. The strophes and antistrophes at the morning pressing of Ahīnas. KB. xxviii. 10
6 = 3. The opening verses of these Çastras.
7 = 4. The concluding verses of these Çastras.
8 = 5. The two kinds, Ahīna and Aikāhika, of concluding verses. The recitation of verses additional to those of the Stoma. xxviii. 10

Adhyāya III = XXVIII.

Miscellaneous points as to the Hotrakas.

9 = xxviii. 1. The number of verses used for the filling of the Soma goblets. xxviii. 8
10 = 2. The offering verses for the Prasthita libations. xxviii. 8
11 = 3. The filling of the goblets and the Prasthita libations at the midday pressing. xxix. 2
12 = 4. The filling of the goblets and the Prasthita libations at the third pressing. xxx. 1
13 = 5. The Hotrakas with and without Çastras.
14 = 6. The substitute for the Çastras of the Agnīdh, Potṛ and Neṣṭṛ. The Praiṣa formulae of the Maitrāvaruṇa. xxviii. 1 The discrepancies between the Stotras and Çastras at the third pressing.
15 = 7. The Jagatī hymn to Indra, the hymn of the Achāvāka and the concluding verses of the Hotrakas at the third pressing. xxx. 2, 3
16 = 8. The omission of Nārāçaṅsa verses in the Achāvāka's Çastra at the third pressing.

Adhyāya IV = XXIX.

The Sampāta Hymns, the Vālakhilyās, and the Dūrohaṇa.

17 = xxix. 1. The strophes and antistrophes at the morning pressings. xxix. 2–3 The continuity of the sacrifice.
18 = 2. The Sampāta hymns of the Ṣaḍaha at the midday pressing. The Ahīna hymns of the separate days at the midday pressing. xxix. 3
19 = 3. The order of the Sampāta hymns in the Ṣaḍaha. xxix. 5

vi. 20 = xxix. 4. The hymns recited daily.
21 = 5. The Pragāthas recited daily. **KB. xxix. 4**
The Triṣṭubhs recited daily. **xxix. 4**
22 = 6. The texts of the Triṣṭubhs. **xxix. 4**
23 = 7. The daily and general connecting and disconnecting of the Ahīnas.
24 = 8. The Vālakhilyās recited by the Maitrāvaruṇa.
25 = 9. The Dūrohaṇa recitation and the hymn in which it occurs. **xxx. 5**
26 = 10. The recitation of the Dūrohaṇa by itself.

Adhyāya V = XXX.

The Çilpa Çastras of the Third Pressing.

27 = xxx. 1. The Nābhānediṣṭha and Nārāçaṅsa of the Hotṛ. **xxx. 4**
28 = 2. The Vālakhilyās of the Maitrāvaruṇa. **xxx. 4**
29 = 3. The Sukīrti and Vṛṣākapi of the Brāhmaṇācchaṅsin. **xxx. 5**
30 = 4. The Evayāmarut of the Achāvāka. **xxv. 12, 13; xxx. 8**
31 = 5. The arrangement of hymns on the Viçvajit day. **xxv. 12, 13**
32 = 6. The Kuntāpa hymns. **xxx. 5, 7**
33 = 7. The Kuntāpa hymns (continued): the Aitaçapralāpa. **xxx. 5**
34 = 8. The Kuntāpa hymns (continued): the Devanītha. **xxx. 6**
35 = 9. The Kuntāpa hymns: the Devanītha, the Ādityas and Añgirases. **xxx. 6**
36 = 10. The Kuntāpa hymns (concluded): the Pāvamānī verses. **xxx. 7, 8**

Pañcikā VII.

The Animal Offering, Expiations, and the Royal Consecration.

Adhyāya I = XXXI.

vii. 1 = xxxi. 1. *The Distribution of the Portions of the Victim.*

Adhyāya II = XXXII.

Expiations of Errors in the Sacrifices.

2 = xxxii. 1. Expiations in the case of the death of an Agnihotrin.
3 = 2. Expiations for accidents to the Agnihotra cow (= v. 27).
4 = 3. Expiations for the spilling of the Sāṁnāyya.
5 = 4. Expiations for the spilling of the Agnihotra and the extinction of the Gārhapatya.
6 = 5. Expiations for the mingling of the fires with other sacrificial fires.
7 = 6. Expiations for the mingling of the fires with non-sacrificial fires.

viii. 22 = xxxix. 8. The kings for whom the great anointing was performed: stanzas on Añga and Udamaya.

23 = 9. The kings for whom the great anointing was performed: stanzas on Bharata, and legends of Durmukha and Sātyahavya and Atyarāti.

Adhyāya V = XL.

The Office of Purohita.

24 = xl. 1. The need of a king for a Purohita.
25 = 2. The protection of Agni secured by having a Purohita.
26 = 3. The evidence of the Ṛgveda as to the Purohita.
27 = 4. The qualification of a Purohita.
28 = 5. The spell for the slaying of the king's enemies.

B. THE KAUṢĪTAKI BRĀHMAṆA

Adhyāya I.

The Establishment of the Fires.

i. 1. The offerings to the forms of Agni.
2. The attainment of the fore- and after-offerings by Agni.
3. The time of the re-establishment of the fires.
4. The fore- and after-offerings and the butter portions.
5. The Vibhaktis and the offering to Aditi.

Adhyāya II.

The Agnihotra.

ii. 1. The preparation of the milk. AB. v. 26
2. The libations.
3. The making of the offering in the Āhavanīya fire.
4. The reverence paid to the fires and the releasing of the vow.
5. The homage paid to the fires by one when about to be or having been absent. vii. 12
6. The placing of the fire on the fire sticks.
7. The relation of speech and the other senses.
8. The result of the true knowledge of the Agnihotra.
9. The time of the offering. v. 29–31

Adhyāya III.

The New and Full Moon Offerings.

iii. 1. The time of commencing the full moon offering.
2. The kindling verses and the Ārṣeya.
3. The invitation of the gods.
4. The fore-offerings.
5. The butter portions.
6. The chief oblations of the sacrifices.
7. The invocation of the sacrificial food.
8. The after-offerings, the Sūktavāka, and the Çaṁyuvāka.
9. The joint sacrifices to the wives of the gods.

Adhyāya IV.

Special Sacrifices.

iv. 1. The Anunirvāpyā.
2. The Abhyuditā.
3. The Abhyuddṛṣṭā.
4. The Dākṣāyaṇa. AB. iii. 40
5. The Iḍādadha. AB. iii. 40
6. The Çaunaka.
7. The Sārvaseniya.
8. The Vasiṣṭha.
9. The Sākaṁprasthāyya.
10. The Munyayana.
11. The Turāyaṇa.
12. The offering of first-fruits of millet.
13. The offering of first-fruits of bamboo seeds.
14. The offering of first-fruits of rice and barley.

Adhyāya V.

The Four-Monthly Sacrifices.

v. 1. The time and purpose of the Vaiçvadeva.
2. The deities of the Vaiçvadeva.
3. The rites of the Varuṇapraghāsas.
4. The deities of the Varuṇapraghāsas.
5. The Sākamedhas.
6. The offering to the fathers.
7. The omission at the Sākamedhas of the offerings to the strew.
8. The Çunāsīrya offering.
9. The performance of the expiations and substitutions.
10. The laying to rest of the sacrificer with his own fires.

Adhyāya VI.

The Brahman Priest.

vi. 1–9. The activity of Prajāpati.
10–14. The part of the Brahman priest. — AB. v. 32–34
15. General remarks on the Haviryajñas.

Adhyāya VII.

The Soma Sacrifice.

vii. 1. The consecration offering. — i. 1
2. The verses recited. — i. 4
3. The position of the consecrated man.
4. The consecration according to Keçin Dārbhya.
5. The introductory sacrifice. — i. 7
6. The discernment of the quarters by the gods.
7. The relation of the introductory and the concluding sacrifices. — i. 11
8. The deities of the introductory sacrifice. — i. 7
9. The relation of the introductory and the concluding sacrifices. — i. 11
The offerings to the wives of the gods.
10. The buying and bringing forward of the Soma. — i. 12–14

Adhyāya VIII.

The Soma Sacrifice (continued).

viii. 1. The guest reception of Soma. — i. 15, 16
2. The conclusion of the guest reception. — i. 17
3. The significance of the Mahāvīra pot in the Pravargya. — i. 18
4. The first part of the Mantras. — i. 19
5. The first part of the Mantras (continued). — i. 20, 21
6. The first part of the Mantras (concluded). — i. 21
7. The second part of the Mantras. — i. 22
8. The Upasads. — i. 23
9. The verses used in the Upasads. — i. 25

Adhyāya IX.

The Soma Sacrifice (continued).

ix. 1. The bringing forward of the fire, and the share of speech. — i. 27
2. The verses for the bringing forward. — i. 28
3, 4. The bringing forward of the oblation receptacles. — i. 29
5, 6. The Mantras for the bringing forward of Agni and Soma. — i. 30

Adhyāya X.

The Animal Sacrifice.

x. 1.	The erection of the sacrificial post.	AB. ii. 1
2.	The anointing of the sacrificial post. The use of the post for a number of victims.	ii. 2
3.	The symbolic value of the sacrifice.	ii. 3
4.	The formulae for the slaying of the victim.	ii. 6, 7
5.	The offerings of the drops, to the calls of Hail!, and of the omentum.	ii. 12–14
6.	The offering of the portions for Manota.	ii. 10

Adhyāya XI.

The Soma Sacrifice (continued).

xi. 1.	The recitation of the Prātaranuvāka.	
2.	The various metres used.	ii. 18
3.	The attaining of cattle.	
4.	The deities of the Prātaranuvāka.	ii. 16, 18
5.	The nature of the Praṇava.	
6.	The metres and the Ekaviñça Stoma.	ii. 18
7.	The number of verses to be recited.	ii. 17
8.	The place and time of the recitation.	ii. 15

Adhyāya XII.

The Soma Sacrifice (continued).

xii. 1, 2.	The performance of the Aponaptrīya.	ii. 20
3.	The legend of Kavaṣa.	ii. 19
4.	The Upāñçu and Antaryāma Cups.	ii. 21
5.	The Bahiṣpavamāna Stotra.	ii. 22
6.	The deities who share the victim and the Soma.	ii. 18
7.	The invitations to the gods when eleven victims are offered.	
8.	The offering of the eleven victims.	

Adhyāya XIII.

The Soma Sacrifice (continued).

xiii. 1.	The creeping to the Sadas.	
2.	The offering of five oblations.	ii. 24
3.	The cakes.	ii. 23
4.	The Soma shoots symbolized.	
5.	The cups for two deities.	ii. 25
6.	The Hotṛ's share in the offering.	ii. 30
7.	The invocation of the sacrificial food.	
8.	The response of the Achāvāka.	
9.	The season cups.	ii. 29

Adhyāya XIV.

The Soma Sacrifice (continued).

xiv. 1.	The Ājya Çastra.	AB. ii. 40, 41
2.	The mode of reciting the hymn.	ii. 35
3.	The call.	ii. 38; iii. 12
4.	The Praüga Çastra.	iii. 1
5.	The Praüga Çastra (continued).	iii. 2

Adhyāya XV.

The Soma Sacrifice (continued).

xv. 1.	Preliminary Rites	
2.	The Marutvatīya Çastra.	iii. 15–17
3.	The Marutvatīya Çastra (continued).	iii. 18, 19
4.	The Niṣkevalya Çastra.	iii. 21, 24
5.	The mode in which Agni evaded death in the several Çastras.	iii. 14

Adhyāya XVI.

The Soma Sacrifice (continued).

xvi. 1.	The Āditya cup.	iii. 29
2.	The Sāvitra cup.	iii. 29
3.	The Vaiçvadeva Çastra.	iii. 29–31
4.	The meaning of the Çastra.	iii. 29–31
5.	The offerings to Agni, Soma, and Viṣṇu.	iii. 32
6.	The Pātnīvata cup.	
7.	The Āgnimāruta Çastra.	iii. 35–37
8.	The five syllables.	
9.	The conclusion.	
10.	The Sautrāmaṇī.	
11.	The Ukthas of the Ukthya.	iii. 49, 50

Adhyāya XVII.

The Soma Sacrifice (continued).

xvii. 1.	The Ṣoḍaçin.	iv. 1
2, 3.	The mode of reciting the Sodaçin Çastra.	iv. 3
4.	The non-use of the Mahānāmnīs.	iv. 4
5.	The result of the Atirātra.	iv. 5
6, 7.	The connexion of Sāman and Çastra.	iv. 6
8, 9.	The mode of recitation.	

Adhyāya XVIII.

The Soma Sacrifice (continued).

xviii. 1. The origin of the Āçvina Çastra. AB. iv. 8
2. The beginning of the Çastra.
3. The composition of the Çastra. iv. 10, 11
4, 5. The conclusion of the Çastra. iv. 11
6. The Hāriyojana.
7. The Çakalas.
8. The conclusion of the Jyotiṣṭoma.
9, 10. The concluding bath.
11–14. The offering of the final victim.

Adhyāya XIX.

The Soma Sacrifice (continued).

xix. 1. The preparation for the consecration.
2. The deity of the cake in the sacrifice of an animal to Prajāpati. The date of the consecration.
3. The date of the consecration.
4. The consecration offering of five oblations in the fire piling.
5. Offerings to the divine instigators.
6. Offering to Tvaṣṭṛ.
7. The offerings to the minor deities.
8. The Çastras of the Caturviñça. iv. 12
9. The Çastras of the Caturviñça (continued). iv. 14
10. The form of the rite when all the Stomas are used.

Adhyāya XX.

The Soma Sacrifice (continued).

xx. 1. The results of the performance of the Abhiplava Ṣaḍaha. iv. 15
2. The Jyotis day.
3. The Go day.
4. The Āyus day.

Adhyāya XXI.

The Soma Sacrifice (continued).

xxi. 1. The value of the second set of three days.
2. The Go day.
3. The Āyus day.
4. The Jyotis day.
5. The Abhiplavas and Pṛṣṭhya Ṣaḍahas in the Sattra. iv. 16
6. The origin of the term Abhiplava.

Adhyāya XXII.

The Soma Sacrifice (continued).

xxii. 1. The first day of the Pṛṣṭhya Ṣaḍaha. AB. iv. 29, 30
2. The second day of the Pṛṣṭhya Ṣaḍaha. iv. 31, 32
3. The third day: Ājya and Praüga Çastras. v. 1
4. The third day: Marutvatīya and Niṣkevalya Çastras. v. 1, 2
5. The third day: Vaiçvadeva and Āgnimāruta Çastras. v. 2
6. The fourth day: general characteristics. v. 4
7. The fourth day: Ājya, Praüga, and Marutvatīya Çastras. v. 4
8. The fourth day: Marutvatīya Çastra and Nyūṅkha. v. 3–5
9. The fourth day: Vaiçvadeva and Āgnimāruta Çastras. v. 5

Adhyāya XXIII.

The Soma Sacrifice (continued).

xxiii. 1. The fifth day of the Pṛṣṭhya Ṣaḍaha: Ājya, Praüga, and Marutvatīya Çastras. v. 6
2. The fifth day: Marutvatīya and Niṣkevalya Çastras. v. 7
3. The fifth day: Vaiçvadeva and Āgnimāruta Çastras. v. 8
4, 5. The use of the Parucchepa verses on the sixth day. v. 10, 11
6. The sixth day: Ājya, Praüga, and Marutvatīya Çastras. v. 12
7. The sixth day: Marutvatīya and Niṣkevalya Çastras. v. 12, 13
8. The sixth day: Vaiçvadeva and Āgnimāruta Çastras. v. 13

Adhyāya XXIV.

The Soma Sacrifice (continued).

xxiv. 1. The Abhijit: Ājya and Praüga Çastras. iv. 19
2. The Abhijit: the remaining Çastras.
3, 4. The origin of the Svarasāman days. iv. 19
5. The Ājya, Praüga, and Marutvatīya Çastras.
6. The Marutvatīya and Niṣkevalya of the first day and the Pragātha of the second.
7. The Marutvatīya and Niṣkevalya of the second day and the Pragātha of the third.
8. The Marutvatīya and Niṣkevalya of the third day.
9. The Vaiçvadeva and Āgnimāruta Çastras.

Adhyāya XXV.

The Soma Sacrifice (continued).

xxv. 1. The Viṣuvant day: Ājya and Praüga Çastras.
2. The Viṣuvant day: Praüga Çastra.

xxv. 3. The Viṣuvant day: alternative Ājya, Praüga, Marutvatīya.
4. The Viṣuvant day: the Pṛṣṭha as Bṛhat or Mahādivākīrtya.
5. The Viṣuvant day: the Pṛṣṭha as Bṛhat or Mahādivākīrtya.
6. The Viṣuvant day: the Pṛṣṭha as Bṛhat or with neither Bṛhat nor Rathantara.
7. The Viṣuvant day: the Dūrohaṇa and the 101 verses. AB. iv. 19–21
8. The Viṣuvant day: the form approved by Kauṣītaki.
9. The Viṣuvant day: the Vaiçvadeva and Āgnimāruta Çastras.
10. The Viṣuvant day: the Prātaranuvāka.
11. The Viçvajit: the Çastras of the first two pressings.
12, 13. The Viçvajit: the two modes of its performance as regards the Çilpas. vi. 30, 31
14. The Viçvajit: as an Agniṣṭoma and Atirātra.
15. The Viçvajit: the verses of the Hotrakas.

Adhyāya XXVI.

xxvi. 1. The order of the Gavām Ayana.
2. The Go and Āyus days.
3–6. Prāyaçcittas.
7. The Chandomas generally. v. 16
8. The first Chandoma: Ājya and Praüga Çastras. v. 16
9. The first Chandoma: Marutvatīya and Niṣkevalya Çastras. v. 17
10. The first Chandoma: Vaiçvadeva and Āgnimāruta Çastras. v. 17
11. The second Chandoma: Ājya and Praüga Çastras. v. 18
12. The second Chandoma: Marutvatīya and Niṣkevalya Çastras. v. 18, 19
13. The second Chandoma: Vaiçvadeva and Āgnimāruta Castras. v. 19
14. The third Chandoma: Ājya Çastra. v. 20
15. The third Chandoma: Praüga Çastra. v. 20
16. The third Chandoma: Marutvatīya and Niṣkevalya Çastras. v. 21
17. The third Chandoma: Vaiçvadeva and Āgnimāruta Castras. v. 21

Adhyāya XXVII.

The Soma Sacrifice (continued).

xxvii. 1. The tenth day and the Anuṣṭubh. v. 22
2. The Çastras of the tenth day. v. 22
3. The number of verses and the Anuṣṭubh character. v. 22
4. The verses of the Serpent Queen, the offerings to Prajāpati. v. 22, 23
5. The bodies of Prajāpati and the riddle. v. 25
6. The releasing of speech. v. 24
7. The metres of the three pressings in the Daçarātra.

Adhyāya XXVIII.

The Soma Sacrifice (continued).

xxviii. 1. The Praiṣas, Anupraiṣas, and Nigadas. AB. vi. 14
2. The invitatory verses of the Maitrāvaruṇa for the cups.
3. The verses for the filling of the goblets and the Prasthita libations at the morning pressing. vi. 9, 10
4–7. The activity of the Achāvāka.
8. The Praiṣas of the season offerings.
9. The general characteristics of the recitation of the Hotrakas.
10. The verses of the Hotrakas at the morning pressing. vi. 5, 8, 17

Adhyāya XXIX.

The Soma Sacrifice (continued).

xxix. 1. The function of the Grāvastut at the midday pressing. vi. 1, 2
2. The filling of the goblets and the Prasthita libations. vi. 11
3. The litanies of the Hotrakas at the midday pressing.
4. The Pragāthas and the Triṣṭubh verses. vi. 21, 22
5. The triplets on the fourth, fifth, and sixth days. vi. 19
6. The Brāhmaṇācchaṅsin's verses.
7. The Achāvāka's verses.
8. The numbers of hymns used by the Hotrakas on the special days of the Chandomas. vi. 18

Adhyāya XXX.

The Soma Sacrifice (continued).

xxx. 1. The preliminary rites of the third pressing.
2. The litanies of the Ukthyas.
3. The invitatory and offering verses at the third pressing.
4. The Nābhānediṣṭha, Nārāçaṅsa, Vālakhilyās. vi. 27, 28
5. The Tārkṣya and the Dūrohaṇa of the Maitrāvaruṇa. vi. 25
The Sukīrti, the Vṛṣākapi and the Kuntāpa of the Brāhmaṇācchaṅsin: the Aitaçapralāpa. } vi. 29, 32 vi. 33
6. The Kuntāpa: the Ādityas and the Aṅgirases. vi. 34
7. The Kuntāpa: the remainder of the Çastra. vi. 32, 33, 36
8. The Dadhikrā verse, the Evayāmarut and Vālakhilyās. vi. 36, 30
9. The invitatory and offering verses on certain days.
10. Certain peculiarities in the Chandomas.
11. Certain points regarding the Atirātra, Vājapeya, Aptoryāma.

§ 2. The Relations of the two Brāhmaṇas.

It is certainly the case[1] that the two *Brāhmaṇas* represent for us the development of a single tradition, and that there must have been a time when there existed a single Bahṛvca text.[2] The detailed account of the contents of the two Brāhmaṇas shows clearly how considerable is their difference. Not only does the *Kauṣītaki Brāhmaṇa* contain much less material than the *Aitareya*, but it has a wider scope. It includes all the Çrauta sacrifices of the first rank, omitting the less normal offerings such as the Rājasūya and the Açvamedha. Thus the first four Adhyāyas cover fully enough for a Brāhmaṇa the Agnyādhāna, the Agnihotra, the new and full moon sacrifices, the special sacrifices, and the four-monthly sacrifices, and then follows a section on the function of the Brahman priest before the seventh Adhyāya carries us to the discussion of the Soma sacrifice which occupies the rest of the book. In the case of the *Aitareya*, on the other hand, the Soma sacrifice alone forms the real subject of the book, for the remarks on the Agnihotra, found in the *Aitareya* v. 26–34, are clearly a later addition to the main text, and the whole of Adhyāyas vii and viii, which carry us into the field of the Rājasūya under a special and peculiar aspect, are also certainly later than the first twenty-four Adhyāyas (i–v. 25).

In the parts which they have in parallel versions the normal rule is that the *Kauṣītaki* is at once far more closely and carefully arranged, and much less discursive than the *Aitareya*, which never shows any desire to cultivate brevity and is rather fond of excursions into legends. A striking instance of this tendency can be seen in the accounts of the function of the Grāvastut priest and the origin of his use of the Arbuda hymn as contained in the *Aitareya* (vi. 1) and the *Kauṣītaki* (xxx. 1). In the former case the story is told for its own sake as well as for its bearing on the ritual, in the latter as little as possible is made of the episode. Or again, in the account of the prattle of Aitaça the *Aitareya* (vi. 33) is far more detailed than the *Kauṣītaki* (xxx. 5), while the long account of the conflict of the Añgirases and the Ādityas over the question of sacrificing first in the *Aitareya* (vi. 34 and 35) shrinks into an almost unintelligible version in the *Kauṣītaki* (xxx. 6). Or again, while the *Aitareya* (v. 14) has a long account of Nābhānediṣṭha Mānava and the mode in which after his unfair treatment by his brothers in the division of the joint property in the lifetime of their father, and the recovery of prosperity by his connexion with the Añgirases,

[1] See Max Müller, *Anc. Sansk Lit.* p. 346.

[2] For traces of another Brāhmaṇa see Keith, JRAS. 1915, pp. 593–598.

the *Kauṣītaki* (xxviii. 4) has a bare allusion to the fact of his application to the Añgirases, showing that, while the story was well known, it was not desired to develop the idea in detail. Nor is the distinction less marked in the parts of the two texts which have no point of contact. Thus the elaborate tale of Rāma Mārgaveya and Janamejaya which is found in the *Aitareya* (vii. 27–34), the legend of Çunaḥçepa (vii. 13–18), the list of anointed kings (vii. 34), and the list of those who performed the great anointment of Indra (viii. 21–23) are in perfect keeping with the spirit of the older part of the text, but have nothing similar in the *Kauṣītaki*.

While again the *Aitareya* does contain a good deal of information in detail as to the Çastras of the priests, the main object of the text is not to enumerate, but to explain, as is the proper function of a Brāhmaṇa. On the other hand the *Kauṣītaki* is specially careful to enumerate and the explanation often dwindles indefinitely. Moreover, in its enumeration the *Kauṣītaki* is far more complete than the *Aitareya* and is more definitely systematic. The best instance of this perhaps is the detailed treatment of the Abhiplava Ṣaḍaha in Adhyāyas xx and xxi. But there are many other cases, such as the detailed treatment of the cups for Āditya and Savitṛ which prelude the Vaiçvadeva Çastra at the third pressing (xvi. 1–3), the Pātnīvata cup which follows it (xvi. 6), the concluding rite of the Soma sacrifice such as the Hāriyojana (xviii. 6), the Çākalas (xviii. 7), the concluding bath (xviii. 9), and the offering of a barren cow (xviii. 11–14). The Abhijit (xxiv. 1, 2), the Svarasāmans (xxiv. 3–9), the Viçvajit (xxv. 11–15) are treated in far greater fullness than in the *Aitareya*, while the Viṣuvant (xxv. 1–10) though not ignored by the *Aitareya* is yet comparatively briefly treated.

In its character as a systematic treatise the *Kauṣītaki* makes almost interminable use of the phrase *tasyoktaṁ brāhmaṇam*, by which it avoids the need of giving over again an explanation, while on the other hand it recites the texts and thus makes its exposition more satisfactory and complete. This phrase is foreign to all the older part of the *Aitareya* and is alien to its spirit, which takes no exception to repetition of explanation on the one hand, and on the other makes no attempt to mention all the texts for the Çastras, thus adhering to the true Brāhmaṇa as against the Sūtra style of composition.

The more catholic nature of the *Aitareya* is further indicated by its frank acceptance of the magic powers of the priest and his right to exercise them by way of punishment on his employer, the sacrificer, if he sees fit, as well as in procuring for him benefits. Thus in the description of the powers of the *vaṣaṭ* call (iii. 5–8), a passage which has no parallel in the *Kauṣītaki* as it is not in any way necessary for the exposition of the rite, we learn how the priest can injure the sacrificer by the mode in which he pronounces the call (iii. 7). Again the Hotṛ can ruin the sacrificer by misplacing the parts of the Praüga Çastra at the morning pressing (iii. 3), and can deprive a Kṣatriya of his lordly power by placing the hymn at the first or Ājya Çastra of the morning pressing within the Nivid instead of *vice versa* (ii. 33). Nor even in its most original portion (iii. 22) does the *Aitareya* refrain from giving an amusing spell for the defeat by a king of an enemy army by means of the employment of the natural shyness of a daughter-in-law before her husband's father, while the very last chapter of the work (viii. 28) uses as a spell for a king against his enemy an application of the mystic doctrines of the disappearance of fire, the sun, the moon, rain and lightning, and of their rebirth.

It is a matter of some interest to wonder whether this difference in the outlook of the two texts is merely due to the greater system of the *Kauṣītaki* in which the spells would be out of place and needless, or whether it reflects a moral difference of tone. For the latter theory may be set the fact that the *Çāñkhāyana Çrauta Sūtra* (xvii. 6. 2) expressly reprobates [1] as *purāṇam utsannaṁ na kāryam* a certain fertility rite which the *Aitareya Āraṇyaka* mentions without hint of disapproval. Nor is there *a priori* the slightest ground to doubt the probability of moral differences in the attitude of the schools. It is notorious that Āpastamba in his *Dharma Sūtra* is strenuously puritanical in practically all the questions involved in marriage, such as adoption of sons, the levirate, and so forth.

Finally, as an outstanding point of distinction must be noted the fact that the *Aitareya* unlike the *Kauṣītaki* does not cite authorities. The name Aitareya never occurs in its whole text, whereas the *Kauṣītaki Brāhmaṇa* constantly cites Kauṣītaki, and twice the *Kauṣītaka*, while though much less often it cites the views of the parallel school of Paiñgya.[2] It is one of the many clear proofs of the unauthenticity of a brief chapter (vii. 11) of the *Aitareya* that it cites the authority of Paiñgya and Kauṣītaki. It is impossible of course to decide the question whether these views were already expressed in formal text-books, whether committed to writing as suggested by Roth,[3] or merely handed down by oral tradition as is more probable,[4] or whether the views were merely current as views on the several

[1] Cf. Friedländer, *Der Mahāvrata Abschnitt des Çāñkhāyana Āraṇyaka*, p. 18.

[2] Kauṣītaki is cited in ii. 9; vii. 4, 10; viii. 9; xi. 5, 7; xiv. 2, 4; xv. 2; xvi. 9; xviii. 5; xxii. 1, 2; xxiii. 1, 4; xxiv. 8, 9; xxv. 8, 10, 14, 15; xxvi. 3, 4, 5, 8, 9, 11, 14; xxvii. 1, 6; xxviii. 2, 7; xxx. 11; the *Kauṣītaka* in iii. 1; xix. 9; Paiñgya in viii. 9; xvi. 9; xxvi. 3, 4, 14; xxviii. 7; the *Paiñgya* in iii. 1; xix. 9; xxiv. 8; Paiñgī *sampad* occurs in xxv. 7.

[3] *Nirukta*, p. ix.

[4] *Ind. Stud.* i. 393; cf. ii. 298; reff. in Oertel, JAOS. xxiii. 325, n. 4.

points raised. But there is nothing inherently improbable that the text of the Brāhmaṇa represents a work based on existing Brāhmaṇas, and the constant citation of authorities rather suggests that this was the case.

On the other hand the resemblances of the two texts are in many respects fundamental. The Çastras differ according to the two schools repeatedly in minor and meaningless details, the one taking certain verses for a special portion, the other different verses. But the fact remains that the essential similarity of the Brāhmaṇas is so great that it cannot be doubted that they both represent the tradition of one school, but that the tradition has received different handling by the branches of that school. Nor can we derive the two versions directly from the one source, for the evidence of the *Kauṣītaki* shows clearly that it is only a branch of a school which divided into the Paiñgya and the Kauṣītaka sub-schools, so that if a title of descent is to be drawn up we must place in it as a common ancestor of these two versions the tradition from which the two are offshoots. In the case of the *Aitareya* no such intermediate stage is capable of proof. The common source no doubt contained the same sort of material as is given in the extant texts, for it is significant that the legends shared by the two texts contain much similarity of wording. Thus in the *Kauṣītaki* (xxx. 5) in the tale of Aitaça we have *yad vai me jālma mukhaṁ nāpy agrahīṣyaḥ çatāyuṣaṁ gām akariṣyaṁ sahasrāyuṣaṁ puruṣam*, while the *Aitareya* (vi. 33) has *alaso 'bhūr yo me vācam avadhīḥ. çatāyuṁ gām akariṣyaṁ sahasrāyuṁ puruṣam* where the sense is precisely the same. The tale of Kavaṣa as given in the *Kauṣītaki* (xii. 3) and the *Aitareya* (ii. 19) illustrates very well both the degree of similarity due to the use of one source, and the different mode of developing the topic followed by the two schools.

Another important sign of the homogeneous character of the tradition of the school is the attitude of both texts to the gods. Beside the formal pantheon is found clear proof of the great importance of the figure of Rudra. In the *Aitareya* (iii. 33) we hear of the incest of Prajāpati and the determination of the gods to punish him, which led to the decision to create from their most dread forms the figure of Bhūtapati, who pierced Prajāpati and for his act received the name of Paçupati. To avoid mention of his name, Rudra, even a Ṛgvedic verse (ii. 33. 1) must be altered, or if not altered omitted (iii. 34). A man in a black garment appears on the scene of sacrifice when Nābhānediṣṭha was given a share by the Añgirases, and claims as his own all that is left on the place of sacrifice, a claim allowed to be valid by the father of Nābhānediṣṭha (v. 14). The *Kauṣītaki* contains a long section (vi. 1–9) where we find the distinctive names of Rudra as Bhava, Çarva, Paçupati, Ugra Deva, Mahān Deva, Rudra, Īçāna, and Açani. There is therefore no doubt that Aufrecht[1] is right in his declaration that the period of the Brāhmaṇas was one when the old polytheism was in a condition of decline and the new faith which presents itself in Indian religious history as Çaivism was gaining ground. It is impossible not to feel in both Brāhmaṇas, as also in the *Çatapatha*, that the figure of Rudra has a very different reality from that possessed by the more normal members of the pantheon, or by Prajāpati as creator, with whom as lord of creatures he successfully contends.

Moreover, on the whole, the order of exposition of the two texts agrees. There are a good many minor alterations, but the chief difference only arises in the treatment of the Sattras; the *Aitareya* proceeds from the Caturviñça day to an account of the general composition of the Gavām Ayana Sattra as consisting of sets of days and certain special days, the Abhijit, Svarasāmans, Viṣuvant, Svarasāmans, and Viçvajit (iv. 15–22) and then takes up the Dvādaçāha as a general type of Sattras and as incidentally giving the details of the Pṛṣṭhya Ṣaḍahas of the Gavām Ayana. The *Kauṣītaki*, on the other hand, while dealing with the Caturviñça proceeds to the Ṣaḍahas and deals in detail with the Abhiplava (xx and xxi) to which the *Aitareya* devotes only a brief mention (iv. 15), and then with the Pṛṣṭhya Ṣaḍaha (xxii and xxiii) and only then does it turn to the special days which make up the Gavām Ayana, the Abhijit, Svarasāmans, Viṣuvant, Viçvajit (xxiv and xxv), and the Chandomas are reserved for xxvi.

The **comparative age** of the two *Brāhmaṇas* is suggested by the facts above set out. The *Kauṣītaki* is essentially the more scientific composition; its arrangement alone is a token of that, as the arrangement which it chooses is the logical one of setting out the various elements, single days, and sets of days of which the Dvādaçāha as the model of the Sattra is composed, and of which the longer Sattras may be made up. The *Aitareya*, on the other hand, takes the opposite and more naïve course of dealing serially with the Gavām Ayana, and thus the Abhiplava Ṣaḍaha escapes full and due treatment. The condensation and completeness with which the Çastras are given and the dislike of diverging into legends for their own sake all tend to point to a more recent origin. Another consideration which points in the same direction is the fact of the citation of authorities as diverging, pointing clearly to a prolonged school tradition.

This general reasoning can be strengthened by other considerations. The position of Rudra in the *Aitareya* is one of high importance, but more significance attaches to the names given to the god in the *Kauṣītaki*. There are two of these of special importance, Mahān Deva and Īçāna, which, as

[1] *Aitareya Brāhmaṇa*, p. vi.

Weber[1] long ago pointed out, involves quite a special prominence of the deity as compared with the other gods and indeed indicates a sectarian worship The names occur in the *Vājasaneyi Saṁhitā* (xxxix. 8 and 9), but not in the Çatarudrīya in Adhyāya xvi of that text, nor in the *Taittirīya Saṁhitā* (iv. 5. 1). It is true that Mahādeva occurs in the *Maitrāyaṇī Saṁhitā* but only in a passage[2] which von Schroeder[3] long ago pointed out as spurious. The names further occur in the *Atharvaveda* (xv. 5) in the Vrātya hymn, but that also is late, so that it is clearly legitimate to treat their occurrence in the *Kauṣītaki* as a sign of later date than the *Aitareya*. Nor is there any ground on which we can assume that these names are an addition to the text of the *Kauṣītaki*, as Weber[4] suggested. The view that there is no connexion between the passage and the following is an error, as the creative activity of Prajāpati and its results is the common bond of connexion, and therefore the passage is quite in place. Nor is it the case that Rudra is not elsewhere prominent in the text, as passages like iii. 4, 6; v. 7 clearly show his importance.

A further sign of the advanced religious view of the *Kauṣītaki* is seen in the occurrence in it, and not in the *Aitareya*, of the term *punarmṛtyu*,[5] implying the conception of repeated deaths from which the idea of transmigration in due course comes to full development. The idea is another link between the *Kauṣītaki* and the *Çatapatha Brāhmaṇa*, which has, like the *Kauṣītaki*, the names of Rudra as Īçāna and Mahādeva.[6] Possibly also as signs of later date are to be reckoned the indications noted above of the more puritanic character of the *Kauṣītaki*, and while both texts are very sparingly supplied with materials affecting normal life it may be significant that *rājamātra*[7] is found in the *Kauṣītaki*, but not in the *Aitareya*. Importance also attaches to the occurrence in the *Kauṣītaki* of the personal Brahman,[8] while the *Aitareya* has only the neuter.

In language the two texts stand broadly speaking on the same level. There are several matters in which the *Aitareya* has more variety of form than the *Kauṣītaki*; thus it has more varied uses of the infinitive in a greater variety of forms and so forth, but the different extent of the texts of the two works must duly be borne in mind; similarly the *Aitareya* has a fuller list of subjunctives, but that is natural in its greater use of narrative form. What is however significant is the use of the perfect and the imperfect in the narrative sense.[9] The *Kauṣītaki* has according to the

[1] *Ind. Stud.* ii. 302.
[2] ii. 9. 1; cf. KS. xvii. 11; TĀ. x. 1. 5.
[3] *Maitrāyaṇī Saṁhitā*, ii. p. viii.
[4] *Ind. Stud.* ii. 303.
[5] xxv. 1.
[6] vi. 1. 3. 10–17.
[7] xxvii. 6; cf. ÇÇS. xvii. 5. 3, 4; 15. 3.
[8] xxi. 1; also in TB. and ÇB.
[9] Cf. Whitney, PAOS. May 1891, pp. lxxxv *seq.*

reckoning of Whitney 263 narrative imperfects to 149 perfects, or say 5 : 3; the *Aitareya* as a whole has 1080 to 266, or say 4 : 1, but these figures are misleading without qualification. In the original part of the *Aitareya* (i–v), roughly speaking, the proportions are 34 : 1 (viz. 929 to 27), and it is absolutely clear that the use of the perfect is normally in it motived. It is therefore a reasonable conclusion that the *Kauṣītaki* is the younger in style as in content. It is significant in this connexion that all the older texts, such as the Brāhmaṇa portions of the *Taittirīya Saṁhitā*, the *Maitrāyaṇī Saṁhitā*, the *Kāṭhaka Saṁhitā*, and the *Pañcaviṅça Brāhmaṇa* have little evidence of the narrative use of the perfect,[1] while the *Çatapatha* has in i–v, xi, xii, xiv a large use of perfects. What is also of interest is that the last three books of the *Aitareya*, which are no doubt later in origin, show a free use of perfects which in the narrative of Çunaḥçepa exceed by far the imperfects. It is also worthy of note that the last chapter of the fifth book of the *Aitareya*, which begins to show a marked use of the narrative perfect and which is probably a later addition to that book, contains in its account (v. 29) of the views of Vṛṣaçuṣma and the maiden seized by a Gandharva on the time of performance of the Agnihotra what is clearly a superior and more correct version than that of the *Kauṣītaki* (ii. 9).

§ 3. The Composition of the Aitareya Brāhmaṇa.

The whole of the present text of the *Aitareya Brāhmaṇa* is recognized by tradition as handed down to us by Sāyaṇa as the work of one man, to whom alone the tradition ascribes the composition of the *Aitareya Āraṇyaka*. This legendary author is Mahidāsa Aitareya, who like another seer recorded in both Brāhmaṇas, Kavaṣa Ailūṣa, is stated to have been disregarded, in this case by his father who preferred sons of other wives to the son given him by Itarā. The devotion of that lady to the goddess earth secured her son's elevation to due honour. The story is, of course, worthless, but the name of Mahidāsa Aitareya is preserved for us in the *Aitareya Āraṇyaka* (ii. 1. 7; 3. 8), the *Chāndogya Upaniṣad* (iii. 16. 7), and the *Jaiminīya Upaniṣad Brāhmaṇa*. There is no reason to doubt that to him may be ascribed the redaction of the present *Brāhmaṇa*, but there is no conclusive reason to make us accept the tradition to that effect; and it is open to the obvious objection that it cannot be treated as perfectly accurate, since the *Āraṇyaka* which cites him is a very composite work, and it is most improbable that the editor of it would cite himself as is done twice in the

[1] Keith, *Taittirīya Saṁhitā*, I. lxxi, lxxxii *seq.*, ci.

second book. Still it is not improbable that if the *Brāhmaṇa* were redacted by him, he would have ascribed to him the *Āraṇyaka* also.

What is really important is that, whoever the redactor was, the work is not of one hand or time. The contents and comparison with the *Kauṣītaki Brāhmaṇa* show clearly that the Soma sacrifice is the real theme of the text, and anything that does not concern that sacrifice and has no parallel in the *Kauṣītaki* is certainly suspect. This at once leads us to regard as later such parts as Pañcikās vii and viii, which deal in the main with the anointing of the king at the royal consecration and the drink ascribed to him in place of the Soma, reserved for the priests. The chapters which deal with the rite commence with the legend of Çunaḥçepa (vii. 13–18), which is appropriate because it is recited to the king after his anointing, then it is elaborately proved (vii. 19–26) that the royal power is dependent on the priestly power and that the king must not drink the Soma, and finally (vii. 27–34) the proper drink for his use is explained by means of a legend emphasizing the dependence of kings on the priesthood. Then come, after a description of the Stotras and Çastras of the Soma day (viii. 1–4), a description of the anointing of the king (viii. 5–11), a description of the great anointing of Indra (viii. 12–14), and of its application to kings (viii. 15–23), ending with an exaltation of the office of Purohita (viii. 24–28). The whole passage is full of a spirit of Brahmanical self-assertion, which is at any rate not prominent in the rest of the *Aitareya*, and it is also marked by the important part played by Janamejaya, who is mentioned in vii. 27, 34; viii. 11, 21, and whose pre-eminence in the eyes of the composer is perfectly obvious. The account of the consecration, it should be noted, has really nothing parallel in the other texts dealing with the subject, but the ascription of the great consecration of Indra to certain kings[1] is parallel to the description in the *Çatapatha Brāhmaṇa*[2] of the Açvamedha as performed by these kings. The whole rite stands in no real relation to the *Brāhmaṇa* as a whole.

In the *Çāñkhāyana Çrauta Sūtra*[3] there is a parallel version of the story of Çunaḥçepa, which is introduced without any connexion whatever with the context and which diverges merely in a few words from the version of the *Aitareya*. It is not altogether easy to see how the passage came to be received in that text without even the slight modification necessary to make it fit in, but the fact of its presence is probably simply due to the desire of the Çāñkhāyana school to have within its text-books so splendid a narrative, and the slight changes are no doubt merely due to the natural alteration in form of a story when transferred from

[1] See viii. 21–23 with the notes.

[2] xiii. 5. 4; cf. ÇÇS. xvi. 9. 1.

[3] xv. 17–27.

one school to another. It is clearly the case that the changes are not signs of earlier, but of later date. Thus the Çāñkhāyana version adds a seventh year to Rohita's wanderings and a new verse (xv. 19); in another passage (xv. 24) it has tried to improve the simple *asaṁdheyam iti Viçvāmitra upapapāda* into *asaṁdheyam iti vā avocad iti Viçvāmitra upapapāda*, while it has completely altered the sense of the last of the Gāthās (xv. 27). It has indeed been ingeniously[1] argued that the occurrence twice of *āmantrayām āsa* as a periphrastic perfect is a sign of an incorrect and modern version, since the *Çāñkhāyana* has *cakre*, but the whole force of the argument disappears when it is borne in mind that the *Çāñkhāyana* has *īkṣām āsa*[2] in place of *īkṣāṁ cakre*.[3] It is therefore necessary either to assert, as Liebich, had he observed the forms *īkṣāṁ cakre* and *īkṣām āsa*, presumably would have done, that both forms were incorrectly handed down, or as is much more probable that the use of *āsa* was a careless innovation which was creeping into use. The text is in other respects marked by bad forms like *sāṁnāhukaḥ* (for *saṁnāhukaḥ*) in vii. 14; *açanayāparītaḥ*, vii. 15; *niniyoja* (ÇÇS. has *niyuyoja*), and *niḥçāna* in vii. 16.

With the last section (viii. 24–28) the *Brāhmaṇa* passes to a quasi-philosophical doctrine of the resolution of the deities, lightning, rain, moon, sun, fire, in Brahman, here conceived (viii. 28) as Vāyu, but the doctrine is degraded to a mere practical device for enabling the Purohita to overcome the king's enemies. This combination is doubtless a sign of comparatively recent origin.

With the rest of Pañcikā vii must be classed as late the first twelve sections. The first section, which in a manner unparalleled in the rest of the text, consists of the whole of the first Adhyāya, is made up of an account of the due division of the sacrificial animal among the priests and their assistants; it commences *athātaḥ paçor vibhaktis tasya vibhāgaṁ vakṣyāmaḥ*. The new form is wholly unparalleled, and the possibility of its being original is disposed of by the occurrence of the whole passage in the *Āçvalāyana Çrauta Sūtra*.[4] The division of the victim may conceivably have once stood in the text, but not as it now is handed down.

The second Adhyāya of the Pañcikā deals with the occurrence of mishaps of one sort or another to an Agnihotrin. It contains within it two passages of later and clearly non-genuine character. The first (vii. 10) deals with the question how the offerings of a man whose wife dies are to be carried on; it is far from clear in sense, and doubtless corrupt.

[1] Liebich, *Pāṇini*, pp. 80, 81.
[2] xv. 21.
[3] vii. 16.
[4] xii. 9.

That the second passage is corrupt (vii. 11) does not rest, as in the former case, on mere reasoning; it is proved by the fact that it is obviously and palpably a mere working over of a passage in the *Kauṣītaki*.[1] Finally there is the conclusive evidence that Sāyaṇa in his commentary admits that in certain places the texts had not these passages and that the passages had not been explained by previous commentators.

The other chapters are more of the Sūtra type, and in point of fact vii. 3 which repeats v. 27 is largely found in the *Āçvalāyana Çrauta Sūtra* iii. 11, and of the other sections portions have parallels in that book (iii) of the Sūtra. They have no real connexion with the rest of the texts, and the same remark applies to the last Adhyāya of the fifth Pañcikā, which (v. 26–34) deals with the Agnihotra and the time of its being performed (v. 26, 28–31), with expiations of mishaps in it (v. 27 = vii. 3), and with the office of the Brahman priest. These sections in themselves have no real connexion with the Soma offering; they have however some affinities in the *Kauṣītaki Brāhmaṇa*, which discusses the time of the Agnihotra (ii. 9) and the duties of the Brahman priest (vi. 10–14), and no doubt they represent the Aitareya tradition of the performance of these rites in their school. Indeed, as has already been noted, the language of the *Aitareya* (v. 29) account of the disputes over the time of offering the Agnihotra is clearly older than that of the *Kauṣītaki* (ii. 9). The portion regarding the Brahman also shows no trace of later origin than the corresponding *Kauṣītaki* text. But the section cannot really have been originally part of the Brāhmaṇa of the Soma sacrifice.

The doubtful authenticity of even **Pañcikā vi** is suggested by the fact that it obviously is merely a supplement to the main text, which deals with the duties of the Hotṛ and which ignores his assistants. This argument was recognized by Haug[2] and accepted by Weber,[3] who added to the general consideration the particular observation that in the first twenty-four Adhyāyas of the *Aitareya* the formula adopted for rejecting unapproved opinions is *tat tan nādṛtyam*[4] and once only[5] *tat tathā na kuryāt*. The rule in the rest of the text[6] is to use the latter phrase with a variant[7] of *tad u punaḥ paricakṣate*, although the root *ā-dṛ* is found elsewhere in the sixth book.[8] But this is the only special point adduced by Weber in support of his theory.

The theory is however, no doubt, correct and it can be supported by other evidence than that adduced by Weber. The character of Pañcikā vi

[1] iii. 1.
[2] *Aitareya Brāhmaṇa*, i. 65.
[3] *Ind. Stud.* ix. 372 *seq.*
[4] i. 4, 11; ii. 3 (*bis*), 22, 23 (*bis*), 26; iii. 18, 37; iv. 7, 9 (*bis*), 22.
[5] iii. 32.
[6] vi. 9, 21; vii. 26.
[7] viii. 7.
[8] vi. 17, 24.

as of a supplementary character is indicated by its internal composition, which is much inferior to that of the first twenty-four Adhyāyas. Thus in vi. 5 and 17 there is repeated the rule of the use of the Stotriya verses of one day as the Anurūpa verses of the preceding day, and it is impossible to see any justification for the repetition of the statement, though there is no inconsistency in it. Again in vi. 26 there is a discussion of the question whether the Maitrāvaruṇa should combine the Dūrohaṇa with the normal Çastra, and the reply is in the negative; in vi. 36. 15 *seq.* the same question is put regarding the Brāhmaṇācchaṅsin, the repetition being very clumsily carried out. In these cases there is no contradiction and in the second case the subject-matter actually is slightly different, but in vi. 8 and 23 there is direct contradiction. In the former we are told *ekāṁ dve na stomam atiçaṅset*, and *aparimitābhir uttarayoḥ savanayoḥ*, and in the latter *ekāṁ dve na dvayoḥ savanayoḥ stomam atiçaṅset* and *aparimitābhir tṛtīyasavane*, statements which no ingenuity will reconcile.

The treatment of the Vālakhilyās is also confused and muddled. The natural place of treatment is in vi. 28 after the Nābhānediṣṭha and Nārāçaṅsa of the Hotṛ, and *de facto* the hymns are there fully dealt with. But in vi. 24 they appear, and are followed by the description of the Dūrohaṇa as performed after them (vi. 25), and a discussion whether the ordinary Çastra is, or is not, to be omitted with the Dūrohaṇa. The matter is further complicated by the fact that the Vālakhilyās in the first case (vi. 24) are to be recited in one (the Mahābalabhid manner of Āçvalāyana), in the second case in yet another manner. Nor is there any hint of the use of the two manners on distinct occasions either in the Brāhmaṇa or even in the *Āçvalāyana Çrauta Sūtra* (viii. 2). It is therefore impossible to avoid the conclusion that there is repetition and confusion. The same conclusion follows from the fact that in vi. 16 we have an odd chapter dealing with the Achāvāka's Çilpa Çastra and its lack of relation to the Nārāçaṅsa. There is no conceivable reason for its appearance at that place, while it clearly should come somewhere in vi. 30 and 31 where the Achāvāka's work is dealt with, and subsequent to the mention of the Nārāçaṅsa in vi. 27. The treatment of the Achāvāka is also decidedly confused in both vi. 30 and 31, the essential distinction of the use of the Çilpas at the evening pressing on an Ukthya and at the midday pressing on an Agniṣṭoma day not being made at all clear.

These are all signs of internal defects of construction, and have validity in so far as they show a much poorer workmanship than is to be found in the rest of the Soma books. What is still more convincing is the fact that the mention of the Çilpas and their treatment in vi. 27–30 is quite inconsistent with the treatment of the question of the Hotṛ's recitations in

v. 15. The two passages cannot possibly have stood in one work without some effort to bring them into at least intelligible relationship. Sāyaṇa evades the difficulty by his usual happy power of not referring in either case (v. 15 or vi. 27 *seq.*) to the problem, for which neither *Āçvalāyana* nor the *Çāṅkhāyana Çrauta Sūtra* has any solution to offer. Therefore we can conclude with certainty that Pañcikā vi was really an addition to the main text. Presumably it was the first addition, and the insertion at the end of v of the portion dealing with the Brahman (v. 32–34) was an effort to make complete the account of the Hotṛ's sacrifice by adding to the account of the Hotrakas' work that of one who, like the Brahman, was to aid the sacrificer, but mainly by silence, and therefore in a way not recorded naturally in a full text as was done for the Adhvaryus and the Sāman singers in their text-books. The interpolation before the Brahmatva in v. 26–31 and the addition after vi in vii. 2–12 (omitting 10 and 11 which were never really parts of the text) of an account of the Agnihotra are only to be explained, if at all, on logical grounds by the fact that the Agnihotra is not to be omitted, even when the Soma sacrifice is being performed, while to the work thus filled up Pañcikās vii and viii were doubtless added on the strength of the fact that the rite was connected with the Soma sacrifice and was of special importance. vii. 1, which is borrowed from the *Āçvalāyana Çrauta Sūtra*, may have been interpolated at almost any time. It differs from vii. 10 and 11 in so far that the latter sections never obtained like it full citizenship in the text.

There remains one further passage, which lies open to doubt. Weber points out that the 14th Adhyāya (iii. 39–44), which handles the Agniṣṭoma in general, is in no way closely or naturally fitted into its context. Moreover, what is more significant is that the text (iii. 41), in place of the three Saṁsthās, Ukthya, Ṣoḍaçin, and Atirātra, mentions the Ukthya, Vājapeya, Atirātra, and Aptoryāma, while the Vājapeya and Aptoryāma are never again mentioned in the *Brāhmaṇa*. It may be added that even the *Kauṣītaki Brāhmaṇa* knows them only in the last chapter (xxx. 11). Moreover, in iii. 44 we have a somewhat novel account of the sun's apparent progress when the word *nimrocati* is used, and again that word occurs nowhere else in the *Aitareya*. The evidence is not, and cannot be, conclusive, but it is reasonably effective, and it should be noted that the *Kauṣītaki* has nothing parallel, so that the case against the chapter is practically certain. It is perhaps a point to note that the proverb of a horse *sudhāyāṁ ha vai vājī suhito dadhāti* (iii. 39) occurs also in iii. 47.

The conclusions which are based on considerations of content and context are supported by certain facts of usage. There is no doubt that in the first twenty-four Adhyāyas (i–v. 25) the only tense of narration is the imperfect, and that perfects are extremely rare in any narrative sense. On the contrary, from v. 26 to the end the proportion of perfects grows steadily, and in the Çunaḥçepa narrative the perfect prevails. But even the narrative in vi. 1 and 2 is adequate to show the complete change of style, which cannot possibly be accounted for by anything save a change in taste. That the perfect in prose is a later development is beyond reasonable doubt, and on the strength of this the last sixteen Adhyāyas can be safely ascribed to a later period than the first twenty-four, to the period of the *Kauṣītaki* and the *Çatapatha Brāhmaṇas*.

Again difference in time is suggested by the use, as in the Sūtras, of the term *brāhmaṇa* in the phrase *tasyoktaṁ brāhmaṇam*, vi. 25. 1, and *iti brāhmaṇam udāharanti*, vii. 12. There is nothing to compare with the first phrase in the earlier part of the AB., though *brāhmaṇa* is used as 'explanation' in AB. i. 25, but it is in constant use in the *Kauṣītaki*.

Difference of authorship are also shown by the repeated use in vi (10. 1; 12. 1; 14. 1; 15. 1, &c.) of the phrase *athāha*, raising a series of points of discussion. The plural is used elsewhere, both earlier and later in the text.

On the other hand books vii and viii show a common hand in the curious phrase *tat-tad itī 3* ऩ to assert a doctrine; it is found in vii. 22. 6; 25. 8; viii. 6. 5; 9. 18, and it is clear that it serves to prove unity in all the great section from vii. 19 to the end of viii, which deals with the consecration of the king.

A further difference of recension noted by Weber is that in vii. 2 is read *haviṣṣu*; vii. 5 *niṣṣicya*; viii. 23 *Dauṣṣantiḥ*, while in i. 25 we find *catuḥsaṁdhiḥ*,; iii. 48 *catuḥṣaṣṭim*; ii. 29 *duḥṣamam*. But the point seems to be without adequate foundation, as Aufrecht reads *duṣṣamam* and *Dauḥṣantiḥ*, and the MSS. do not show enough consistency to justify any conclusion being built upon them.

It is perhaps worth noting that the tradition of the last three Pañcikās appears somewhat inferior to that of the first five. Even in v. 30 we find *so jahāra* for *yo jahāra*; vi. 1 has *apinahyuḥ*; vii. 13: *iti ha smā ākhyāya* for *iti hāsmā* (or *iti ha smāsmā*); 14: *sāṁnākukaḥ*; 15: *açanayāparītaḥ*; 16: *niḥçānaḥ*; *niniyoja*; 5: *vyapanayitum*; viii. 15: *ajāyethāḥ*; *vṛñjīyam*; 23: *avapadyeyam*; 28: *prajighyati, prajighyatu*; *jāgriyāt*. Some of these cannot be real forms, even if others are.

There are other minor points in which the texts vary, but it would be idle to rely upon any of them as decisive, and the evidence above cited is ample to show that the text consists of the following strata:

(1) i–iv; v. 1–25, on the Soma sacrifice, with the possible exception of iii. 39–44.

(2) v. 26–34; on the Agnihotra (26–31) and on the Brahman priest (32–34)

(3) vi on the Hotrakas' performance at the Soma rite.

(4) vii. 1; the division of the sacrificial victim, in its present form apparently borrowed from the *Āçvalāyana Çrauta Sūtra*, xii. 9.

(5) vii. 2–12; on the Agnihotrin's errors and mishaps in sacrifice (10 and 11 being interpolations, 11 from the *Kauṣītaki*, iii. 1).

(6) vii. 13–18; the tale of Çunaḥçepa.

(7) vii. 19–viii. 28; the royal consecration and the Purohitaship (viii. 24–28).

The question which presents itself is whether the *Brāhmaṇa* ever consisted of a collection of the first thirty Adhyāyas (i–vi). This view has the authority of Aufrecht,[1] who points out that this is not at all inconsistent with the fact that Pāṇini (v. 1. 62) is generally held to have known of the forty Adhyāyas of the *Aitareya*. For that view may be set the fact that it explains in a reasonable manner the fact that there is a certain community of subject-matter between v. 26–31 and vii. 2–12, v. 27 and vii. 3 being identical, save for the addition of a sentence in the former and the prefixing of *tad āhuḥ* to the clauses of the latter. If the *Brāhmaṇa* were a fixed whole when the new matter came in, the fact is more naturally explained than if we have to invent a reason for the separation of matter essentially of one kind. This would accord also with the fact that the use of the narrative perfect is yet restrained in vi as compared with vii or viii (roughly in vi 1 : 2; in vii 4 : 1; in viii 5 : 3). There would be thus an intermediate stage in the composition of the text when it was extended and brought up to thirty Adhyāyas, and a final stage, still early, when it became forty Adhyāyas.

Another small point tells in the same direction; the *Kauṣītaki Brāhmaṇa* in ii. 9 has a parallel to the discussion of the time of the Agnihotra in the *Aitareya* (v. 29–31), which seems clearly later in redaction. Moreover, if the *Aitareya* was fixed in its compass of thirty Adhyāyas before the *Kauṣītaki* was redacted we have a good and significant cause for the exact number of Adhyāyas chosen.[2] On the other hand, it is most unlikely that the *Aitareya* in its extended form was redacted before the *Kauṣītaki*, for then it would be very difficult to account for the fact that the Çunaḥçepa story was placed in the *Sūtra* only. The order of redaction seems therefore to have been (1) *Aitareya*, i–vi; (2) the *Kauṣītaki*; (3) the

[1] *Aitareya Brāhmaṇa*, p. v.

[2] Cf. Keith, *Aitareya Āraṇyaka*, pp. 32–34.

complete *Aitareya*; but even the latest form of the *Aitareya* must antedate the *Çāñkhāyana Çrauta Sūtra.*

It is significant that in both cases the *Brāhmaṇas* leave alone the Mahāvrata day and its special rites, which must be looked for in the *Çāñkhāyana Çrauta Sūtra* in its two supplementary books (xvii and xviii) and in the *Çāñkhāyana Āraṇyaka* (i and ii), and in the *Aitareya Āraṇyaka* (i and v). It is practically certain that the *Çāñkhāyana* in this case also represents a later version than the *Aitareya.* The cause of this discrimination of the treatment of the day is not certain, but it is at least possible that it is due to the fact that the Mahāvrata ceremony with all its special features[1] was only later taken up into the full Brahmanical system. There is nothing in either *Āraṇyaka*, *Aitareya*, or *Çāñkhāyana* to render this theory improbable.

The question naturally presents itself whether in the fact of the increase in size of the *Aitareya* we have an explanation of the term Mahaitareya which occurs with Mahākauṣītaka in the *Āçvalāyana Gṛhya Sūtra* (iii. 4. 4) and the *Çāñkhāyana Gṛhya Sūtra* (iv. 10; vi. 1). The suggestion is a possible one, but naturally it cannot be offered for more than a conjecture for which there is not, and is never likely to be, any independent evidence.

Nor have we any idea when the division of the text into Pañcikās was made; it is clearly not a natural division in any way, as the text does not fall into sets of five Adhyāyas, and it is unfortunate that the Pañcikā division should have become usual in citations.[2]

It is of course possible that here and there slight additions were made to the original text of Adhyāyas i–xxiv in the course of the increase of the work. This is suggested by the occurrence of groups of perfects, unmotived, in narration at i. 16 and iii. 48. 9 respectively; in both cases the passage may easily have been added in the final redaction, but it is dangerous to press such a point.

§ 4. The Composition of the Kauṣītaki Brāhmaṇa.

The composition of the *Kauṣītaki Brāhmaṇa* presents none of the complications of that of the *Aitareya.* It is, as we have it, a single, homogeneous text, which by its constant phrase *tasyoktaṁ brāhmaṇam* indicates its purpose of avoiding repetitions and of carrying out its task in a simple and definite manner.

It has been suggested by Weber[3] that the passage vi. 1–9, which describes the might of Rudra, is an interpolation, on the two grounds that there is

[1] See Keith, *Çāñkhāyana Āraṇyaka*, pp. 72 *seq.*

[2] As, however, it is now established, the citation by Adhyāya in Lévi's *Doctrine du sacrifice dans les Brāhmaṇas* is to be regretted.

[3] *Ind. Stud.* ii. 301 *seq.*; cf. above, p. 27.

no obvious connexion between the rest of the text and this passage, and that there is no special prominence of Rudra or Agni in the rest of the text. These arguments are, however, both inadequate, and neither is quite effective. In the first place the first nine chapters are linked with the rest, which deal with the activity of the Brahman priest, by their common concern with the activity in creation of Prajāpati; the passage regarding the Brahman cannot be disregarded as needless, as it has a parallel in the *Aitareya* (v. 32–34), and its insertion rendered it easy to place before it what is no doubt intended deliberately as a glorification of Rudra in his various forms. The second argument is equally incomplete, for we know that the *Aitareya Brāhmaṇa* treats Rudra as the great deity *par excellence*, and on the other hand the *Kauṣītaki Brāhmaṇa* has several points of contact with the *Çatapatha Brāhmaṇa*, which is clearly like the *Aitareya* inclined to set a very high value on the Rudra cult. It is true that the stories of Rudra in the *Aitareya* and in the *Kauṣītaki* are drawn in bodily, and are no necessary parts of the whole texts, but that is merely to say that the new religion was pervading the old traditional worship; it does not show that the texts ever stood as they now are, but without those particular passages.

Much of the material of the *Kauṣītaki*, and especially the legends, has been taken over by the *Brāhmaṇa* from a source common to it and the *Aitareya*, but the whole has been worked up into a harmonious unity which presents no such irregularities as are found in the *Aitareya*. It is clearly a redaction of the tradition of the school made deliberately after the redaction of the *Aitareya* in its first thirty Adhyāyas (i–vi), and embracing in it the views of the schools of Kauṣītaki and Paiñgya, but with a preference in any case of dispute for the views of Kauṣītaki. Whether written texts or texts orally transmitted or mere views were used by the compiler we cannot know, for the quotation of a *Paiñgi Brāhmaṇa* by Sāyaṇa[1] tells us nothing of its comparative age.

That the *Brāhmaṇa* is not actually the product of a Kauṣītaki is proved by the mode in which he is referred to therein; his views are authentic and accepted, but it is not conceivable that he actually himself composed in this style. The MSS. of the book which show the title *Kauṣītaki Brāhmaṇa* as the normal title have as a variant here and there *Çāñkhāyana* (*Çāñkhyāyana* is a bad variant) *Brāhmaṇa*; the most exact version, that preserved in the MSS. in the Bodleian Library,[2] is *Kauṣītakimatānusāri Çāñkhāyana Brāhmaṇa*. There is no mention of *Çāñkhāyana* in the text, and Vināyakabhaṭṭa, the commentator on the *Brāhmaṇa*, never mentions

[1] Weber, *Ind. Lit.* p. 46. The Paiñgi Kalpa is known in the *Mahābhāṣya*, Weber, *Ind. Stud.* xiii. 455.

[2] *Bodleian Catal.* ii. 42.

it under the title *Çāñkhāyana*, but we cannot reasonably deny that this is a case where tradition should be respected, and where we must admit that in all probability the version of the doctrines of the Kauṣītaki school is preserved for us in a Çāñkhāyana tradition. This view receives solid support from the fact that the *Çāñkhāyana Çrauta Sūtra* is so closely connected with the *Brāhmaṇa*. Nothing, however, turns on the fact, except the explanation of the title given in many of the MSS.

The *Brāhmaṇa*, though in itself complete, does not represent the whole of the Brāhmaṇa tradition associated with the Çāñkhāyana school. That tradition appears in the Mahāvrata section of the *Çāñkhāyana Āraṇyaka* (i and ii), which stands in the same relation to the *Kauṣītaki Brāhmaṇa* as does book i of the *Aitareya Āraṇyaka* to the *Aitareya Brāhmaṇa*, and there is indeed some slight evidence, that of the commentary of Vināyaka,[1] that the two books were sometimes regarded as two books of the *Kauṣītaki Brāhmaṇa*. There can be no doubt that these were not normally so reckoned, since Pāṇini (v. 1. 62) doubtless knew the *Kauṣītaki* as consisting of thirty Adhyāyas only, but it is possible that it was the presence of such additions which gave rise to the tradition of a Mahākauṣītaka as recorded in the *Āçvalāyana Gṛhya Sūtra* (iii. 4. 4) and the *Çāñkhāyana Gṛhya* (iv. 10; vi. 1). The relation of the *Āraṇyaka* (i and ii) to the *Brāhmaṇa* is probably one of a slightly later date; and it is difficult otherwise to see why it should have not been included in the principal text, for it has no special claim to secrecy in character, though the *Āraṇyaka* of the *Aitareya* in its Sūtra portion claims for it a special sanctity and importance, and the *Çāñkhāyana* (i. 1) contains a notice to the same effect.

A second quasi-supplement to the *Kauṣītaki* is contained in the *Çāñkhāyana Çrauta Sūtra*. That Sūtra is normally a well-arranged Sūtra text without pretensions to any other quality, but it contains in books xiv, xv, and xvi passages of a quasi-Brāhmaṇa character dealing with certain Savas and including the story of Çunaḥçepa.

Now these passages are quite out of harmony with the normal style of the *Çāñkhāyana Çrauta Sūtra* and cannot possibly be brought into agreement with that style. It is indeed in a special form of its own; it is not in the proper and full Brāhmaṇa style, which does not seek to give in full the details of the sacrifice, though in the course of its exposition it often does so. But these books of the Sūtra are set on expounding the sacrifice in the details of its composition as regards recitations as well as giving the motives and explanations of the rites, and this combination is a new note, and one which can equally be seen in portions of the *Baudhāyana*

[1] On *Kauṣītaki Brāhmaṇa*, v. 5.

and the ***Mānava Çrauta Sūtras***. We have in fact a form of literature, anterior in development, in all probability, to the normal Sūtra of the type of Āpastamba and Kātyāyana, in which exposition and comment are much more blended than in the case of the Brāhmaṇas, whereas the Sūtras proper have lost this comment practically altogether.

The nature of the content of these books of the *Sūtra* suggests at once a later date than the *Kauṣītaki Brāhmaṇa*, just as in the case of the *Baudhāyana Çrauta Sūtra* the many new Savas described represent, beyond doubt, developments of the ritual beyond the period of the *Saṁhitās* of the Black Yajurveda. Nor otherwise is it easy to see why these rites should not be noticed in any way in the *Brāhmaṇa*. The same conclusion is strengthened when it is noted that in xiv. 40 there is a version of the conflict of the Añgirases and the Ādityas which differs from that given in the *Aitareya Brāhmaṇa* (vi. 34 and 35) and the *Kauṣītaki* (xxx. 6). The important point is that, after a long introductory paragraph in the Brāhmaṇa style, there comes *trivṛt stomaḥ*; *rathantaraṁ pṛṣṭham*; *tṛcaklptaṁ çastram*; *agniṣṭomo yajñaḥ*; *yavorvarā vediḥ*; *yavakhala uttaravediḥ*; *lāñgaleṣā yūpaḥ*, *yavakalāpiç caṣālam*; *ijānasya kulād vasatīvaryaḥ*. This sort of style is not that normal in a Brāhmaṇa. The same phenomenon occurs repeatedly; thus in xiv. 32 after a Brāhmaṇa narrative of the gods and the Asuras comes *aparapakṣe saurīṣṭiḥ pūrvāhṇe*; *cāndramasī sāyam*, *vidhuṁ dadrāṇaṁ navo navaḥ*; *sauvarṇaḥ çatavalo dakṣiṇā pūrvasyām*, *rājata uttarasyām*; *Bhāradvājaṁ pṛṣṭham*; *tathā sūkte*. The same phenomenon recurs constantly in these books, and is quite unparalleled in the Brāhmaṇa. The real question of difficulty is whether the Sūtra was compiled by the use of a Brāhmaṇa text which was used to make up a complex result in these cases where there was nothing in the *Kauṣītaki Brāhmaṇa*, or whether it generally represents a style of composition intermediate between Sūtra and Brāhmaṇa. While there is no adequate evidence to prove the correctness of either of these obvious alternatives as to the origin of this form, it is at least probable that the latter is the correct view of the facts. There seems no conceivable reason why the Sūtra-maker should have adopted this form in the last three books (xiv–xvi) if he did not find it necessary in the rest of the text where, as in most of xiii, there was no Brāhmaṇa preserved in the *Kauṣītaki*. xvi is really in the same position as xiv and xv, though in the case of the last book the proportion of Brāhmaṇa is small, owing to the elaboration of the rites to be described. These three books form a single whole, an account of a development of the ritual with its explanations.

The special character of these books is borne out by their contents: xiv begins with an account of the Haviryajñas, the Agnyādheya, the

Punarādheya, the new and full moon sacrifices, the four-monthly sacrifices, as Soma sacrifices; chapter 11 deals with the Pratyavarohaṇīya; 12 and 13 the Sautrāmaṇī; 14 the Udbhid; 15 the Gosava; 16 the Ṛtapeya; 17–19 the *bhūḥ*, *bhuvaḥ* and *svar* offerings; 20 the Çukrastoma; 21 the Tīvrasava; 22 the Sūtasava; 23 the Ṛṣabha; 24 the Vyoman; 25 the Virāj; 26 the Svarāj; 27 the first Uçanastoma; 28 the second Uçanastoma; 29 the Indrāgnyoḥ Kulāya; 30 the Virāṭsvarāj; 31 the Jyeṣṭhastoma; 32 the Durāça; 33 the Apiciti; 34 the Tviṣi; 35 the Vṛṣṭi; 36 the Āditya; 37 the Svarga; 38 the Vinutty-Abhibhūtī; 39 the Rāçimarāyau; 40 the Sādyaḥkra; 41 the Nṛjit; 44 the Pṛtanājit; 45 the Satrājit; 46 the Dhanajit; 47 the Svarjit; 48 the Sarvajit; 49 the Ujjit; 50 the Upahavya; 51 the Agniṣṭut (described in great detail); 58 the Indrastut; 59 the Sūryastut; 60 the Vaiçvadevastut; 61 the Gotamasya Caturuttarastoma; 62 the Pañcaçāradīya; 63 the Ṛṣistomas of Gotama; 64 of Bharadvāja; 65 of Atri; 66 of Vasiṣṭha; 67 of Jamadagni; 68 of Prajāpati; 69 the Vrātyastomas; 71 the Utkrānti; 74 the tenth day; 75 the Ṛtustomas; 76 the Māsastomas; 77 the Ardhamāsastomas; 78 the Nakṣatrastomas; 79 the Ahorātrastomas; 80 the Muhūrtastomas; 81 the Nimeṣastomas; 82 the Dhvaṅsistomas; 83 the Diçāṁ stomāḥ; 84 the Avāntaradiçāṁ stomāḥ. Book xv contains in 1–3 the Vājapeya; 4 the Bṛhaspatisava; 5–8 the Saṁsthās with especial stress on the Aptoryāma; 9, 10 the Yamastoma; 11 the Vācaḥstoma; 12–16 the Rājasūya, and 17–27 the Çunaḥçepa legend. Book xvi contains in 1–9 the Açvamedha; 10–14 the Puruṣamedha; 15 and 16 the Sarvamedha; 17 the Vājapeya; 18 points regarding the Rājasūya and the Açvamedha including the expulsion of a scapegoat; 19–30 other Ahīnas.

There is a good parallel to the style of the Sūtra in the *Baudhāyana Çrauta Sūtra*,[1] which in xvii. 55 to xviii. 53 contains matter parallel to the *Çāṅkhāyana* book xiv, and which is couched in a similar style. In both cases also that style on its verbal side is of a more recent type than the Brāhmaṇa style, though it is based on that style and therefore differs entirely from the style of the Sūtras in its passage of comment, while on the other hand in its enumeration of the Çastras it is precisely of the Sūtra type. Such a style is a perfectly natural development of the Brāhmaṇa style which here and there in the *Kauṣītaki* approaches to that of the Sūtras without ever going so far as in the books xiv–xvi of the Sūtra.

In these books xv. 17–27, which have the legend of Çunaḥçepa, have a special place and significance. They do not fit into the Rājasūya in the place where they occur, and they are equally not in place in the Puruṣamedha where a Çunaḥçepa narrative is prescribed by the *Çāṅkhāyana Çrauta Sutra*

[1] There is a good deal of similar matter in point of style in the *Mānava Çrauta Sūtra*; cf. Garbe, *Āpastamba Çrauta Sūtra*, III, xxii–xxiv.

(xvi. 11. 1). There can be no doubt that the legend was recorded in the *Aitareya* text after the *Kauṣītaki Brāhmaṇa* was completed, and that then the Çāñkhāyana school, determined to save the masterpiece, took it over with a slight change here and there (including the addition of one more year of wandering and one more Gāthā), and stuck it in the Sūtra where least it seemed out of place, after a passage dealing with the Rājasūya, though not in a suitable place.

There is a point of some interest in the content of the Sūtra which shows that the Kurus had suffered a severe reverse of some sort. The episode is narrated of the King Vṛddhadyumna Ābhipratāriṇa, who made the error of sacrificing with the *Kṣattrasya dhṛti* with three Stomas instead of four, and because of that a Brahman cursed him saying the Kurus *Kurukṣetrāc cyoṣyante* (xv. 16. 10 *seq.*). No such disaster is recorded in the Brāhmaṇas, and it is probably a sign of a later date than the Brāhmaṇa period.

It is possible as asserted by Ānartīya in his commentary on xiv. 2. 3 that these books may have in some cases been reckoned as part of the *Mahākauṣītaki Brāhmaṇa*, but there is no other proof of this and the quotations of that Brāhmaṇa in Vināyaka's commentary on the *Kauṣītaki Brāhmaṇa*[1] seem to throw no light on the matter.

It must also be noted that the *Çrauta Sūtra* had before it a wider range of opinions of Kauṣītaki than are recorded in the *Brāhmaṇa*. Thus there are citations of Kauṣītaki in the Sūtra at vii. 21. 6; ix. 20. 33; xi. 11. 3, 6, and of the Kauṣītaka at xi. 14. 20, all of which are at once recognizable in the *Brāhmaṇa*. But at iv. 2. 13 the Kauṣītaka and at iv. 15. 7 Kauṣītaki are cited. In the former case the passage is significant; it deals with the rite of the Anvādhāna and cites the views on one point of Prāgahi, Paiñgya, Kauṣītaki, and Āruṇi (iv. 2. 10–14). This collection of authorities is parallel to the grouping in the *Kauṣītaki Brāhmaṇa* (xxvi. 4), nor can there be the least doubt that the Sūtra had before it a Brāhmaṇa text to this effect; the Sūtras do not, we may safely conclude, in such cases collate opinions. In iv. 15. 7 there is actually a verbal quotation *nāghāhāni vardhayeyuḥ* from Kauṣītaki. No doubt these notices refer to the *Mahākauṣītaki Brāhmaṇa*, and from it may come varied notices in the commentary of Ānartīya on the *Çāñkhāyana Çrauta Sūtra* which are not ascribed to any defined source.

It is uncertain whether any portion of the *Kauṣītaki Brāhmaṇa* as we have it can be assigned to a later period than the completion of the whole work. The sixth Adhyāya certainly is not open to suspicion on any

[1] iii. 4, 5, 7; x. 4; xviii. 14; xxiv. 1, 2; xxvi. 1. According to Eggeling (SBE. XLIV. xvi, n. 1) the 15th and 16th books of the ÇÇS. are reckoned as part of the Mahākauṣītaka. For Ānartīya's note see Weber, *Rājasūya*, p. 122.

reliable grounds, but the last chapter (xxx. 11) of the work may be suspicious in that it mentions the Vājapeya and Āptoryāma rites elsewhere unknown to the Brāhmaṇa, just as the occurrence of these names in the *Aitareya* (iii. 41) helps to indicate the later date of the fourteenth Adhyāya of that text.

The *Kauṣītaki* seems for some reason or other not to have been a popular text-book.[1] We are expressly told by Agnisvāmin in his commentary on the *Lāṭyāyana Çrauta Sūtra* (i. 1. 6) that the Kauṣītakins did not fulfil the requisite of being able to answer rightly any difficult problem, as exemplified by their inability to deal with the curse of Luçākapi Khārgali recorded in the *Pañcaviñça Brāhmaṇa* (xvii. 4. 3), and Dhānaṁjayya, as reported in the *Nidāna Sūtra* (vi. 12), declared that he considered the Kauṣītakis *akuçalān* and *vyāhatān*.

The geographical position of the Kauṣītaki school seems to have been in the west in later times, for the account of the location of the school in the *Mahārṇava* cited by Bühler[2] places the *Kauṣītaki Brāhmaṇa* and the *Çāṅkhāyana Çākhā* in northern Gujarat. It is not impossible that in this fact of location lies the explanation of the comparatively little use made of the text by other schools.

§ 5. The Dates of the two Brāhmaṇas.

(a) *Relation to Pāṇini.*

There can be no real doubt that the *Kauṣītaki* is a later work than the *Aitareya Brāhmaṇa.* But it is clear that the *Kauṣītaki Brāhmaṇa* and the *Aitareya* were both known to Pāṇini, who in his grammar (v. 1. 62) mentions the formation of the names of Brāhmaṇas with thirty and forty Adhyāyas, a fact which cannot but be brought into connexion as was done by Weber[3] with the two Brāhmaṇas as known to us in their complete form. The same conclusion as to their relation to Pāṇini is clearly proved by their language which is decidedly older than the Bhāṣā of Pāṇini, as Liebich[4] has shown in detail for its verbal forms, and as is not disputed by any scholar. This gives us a latest date of before 300 B.C.[5]

(b) *Relation to Yāska.*

The date can be carried further back by the undoubted fact that Yāska knew both the Brāhmaṇas. In the *Nirukta*, i. 9, he cites and explains the phrase *paryāya iva tvad āçvinam* occurring in the *Kauṣītaki* (xvii. 4).

[1] See Weber, *Ind. Stud.* x. 145, n. 2.

[2] SBE. II. xxiii.

[3] *Ind. Lit.* p. 45. The view has been accepted by Haug and Aufrecht.

[4] *Pāṇini*, pp. 18–28, 72–82.

[5] Keith, *Aitareya Āraṇyaka*, pp. 22 *seq.*

Though Yāska does not actually cite the *Aitareya* textually, he clearly knew it well as Aufrecht[1] shows. Thus in iv. 27: *pañcartavaḥ saṁvatsarasyeti ca brāhmaṇaṁ hemantaçiçirayoḥ samāsena*, there is a clear echo of AB. i. 1. 14: *pañcartavo hemantaçiçirayoḥ samāsena*; in iv. 27: *sapta ca vai çatāni viṅçatiç ca saṁvatsarasyāhorātrāḥ* is exactly copied from AB. ii. 17. 4; in viii. 22: *yasya devatāyai havir gṛhītaṁ syāt tāṁ manasā dhyāyed vaṣaṭkariṣyan* follows, save for the insertion of *manasā*, the text of AB. iii. 8. 1, while the *Gopatha Brāhmaṇa* (viii. 4) has *tāṁ manasā dhyāyan vaṣaṭkuryāt*; i. 16 is exactly as i. 4. 9; the remarks on Anumati and Rākā in the *Nirukta*, xi. 29, and on Sinīvālī and Kuhū in xi. 31, which are attributed to the Yājñikas are borrowed from vii. 11, or more probably perhaps its real source, the *Kauṣītaki* (iii. 1). In *Nirukta*, viii. 4, *āprībhir āprīṇātīti ca brāhmaṇam* is cited no doubt from AB. ii. 4. 1.

Other citations are less clear; in *Nirukta*, xii. 8, occurs *savitā sūryāṁ prāyachat somāya rājñe prajāpataye veti brāhmaṇam*, with which compare KB. xviii. 1: *savitā sūryāṁ prāyachat somāya rājñe yadi vā prajāpateḥ*. The reading there is odd and abnormal, but it is not clear that the citation is of the KB. In *Nirukta*, xii. 14, we read *andho bhaga ity āhur anutsṛpto na dṛçyate prāçitram asyākṣiṇī nirjaghāneti ca brāhmaṇam*. In KB. vi. 13, speaking of the *prāçitra*, we are told *tad bhagāya parijahrus tasyākṣiṇī nirjaghāna tasmād āhur andho bhaga iti*. In *Nirukta*, vi. 31, it is said *adantakaḥ pūṣeti ca brāhmaṇam*, while the KB. vi. 13 has *tasmād āhur adantakaḥ pūṣā karambhabhāga iti*.

With the priority of the Brāhmaṇas to Yāska is in keeping the style of that author which is later than that of the Brāhmaṇas, as is seen for instance in his free use of the narrative perfect and of the conditional, and his developed use of grammatical terminology. The date of Yāska is clearly a good deal anterior to that of Pāṇini, for there must have been a great development of grammar between the two authorities.

(c) *Relation to Çākalya.*

Further evidence of date can be deduced from the mention of the number of syllables in the phrase in AB. iii. 12: *ukthaṁ vācīndrāya* where the number is given as seven, though the text is written as six. In the same passage *ukthaṁ vācīndrāya devebhyaḥ* is given as eleven syllables. In KB. xiv. 3 we have *uktham avāci* as five syllables, *uktham avācīndrāya* as eight syllables, *avācīndrāyokthaṁ devebhyaḥ* as nine syllables. The conclusion from the AB. evidence, added to the fact that the *Aitareya Āraṇyaka* (i. 3. 4) recognizes the absence of Sandhi in what is given with Sandhi in

[1] *Aitareya Brāhmaṇa*, p. 432.

the text of the *Ṛgveda Saṁhitā*, is that the *Aitareya* was redacted before the period of the orthoepic diaskeuasis of the *Ṛgveda* carried out before Çākalya, which doubtless was done in accordance with a growing demand for the adaption of the text of the *Ṛgveda* to the theory of Sandhi, which again doubtless represented a real tendency of speech developed and elaborated. The evidence in the case of the *Kauṣītaki*, if it is not to be taken as by Oldenberg as merely due to liturgical convenience, points rather to the period of transition when either mode of use was acceptable enough. It is significant also that the AB. seems to contemplate *devebhyaḥ* as pronounced of four syllables, as against the three of the *Kauṣītaki*.[1]

Çākalya is clearly anterior to Çaunaka whose *Prātiçākhya* cites him, to Pāṇini who also cites him, and to Yāska who quotes in the past tense and criticizes his Pada text (vi. 28). His date therefore is reasonably fixed about the sixth century B.C.[2]

(*d*) *Relation to Āçvalāyana and Çāñkhāyana.*

This evidence is supported by the priority of the two Brāhmaṇas to the *Çrauta Sūtras* of Āçvalāyana and Çāñkhāyana respectively. There must have been a considerable interval of time in each case, for the Sūtras clearly contemplate a ritual more developed and extended and more definitely fixed than the ritual of the period of the Brāhmaṇas.

The Sūtra of Āçvalāyana is probably to be dated by its author's connexion with Çaunaka[3] and his being referred to in the *Bṛhaddevatā*,[4] facts which suggest for him a date in the vicinity of 400 B.C.[5] There is no reason[6] to seek an earlier date for the Sūtra of Suyajña Çāñkhāyana, and the result therefore is to support the date already obtained for the Brāhmaṇas on other evidence.

(*e*) *Absence of reference to Metempsychosis.*

Again the two texts are free of all reference to metempsychosis in any form. This fact is significant and legitimately may be taken as placing them before the period of the Buddha and probably not later than 600 B. C. The *Kauṣītaki*, however, is rather the younger in its philosophic aspect, as it does contain the concept, *punarmṛtyu* (xxv. 1).

(*f*) *Political references.*

The early date thus arrived at for the texts is in perfect harmony with their references to contemporary and earlier priests and persons. There is

[1] See Oldenberg, *Prolegomena*, pp. 373–376.

[2] Keith, *Aitareya Āraṇyaka*, pp. 239, 240; Oldenberg, op. cit. pp. 383–386.

[3] Proved by his *Çrauta Sūtra*.

[4] iv. 139 (B recension).

[5] Cf. Macdonell, *Bṛhaddevatā*, I. xxii–xxiv.

[6] See Keith, JRAS. 1907, pp. 410–412; 1908, p. 337.

abundant evidence of the milieu which produced the *Aitareya Brāhmaṇa*: it was that of the Bharatas in the middle country, and a time when the fame of Janamejaya was at its height. The Bharatas, the Kuru-Pañcālas with the Vaças and the Uçīnaras are the inhabitants of the middle country (AB. viii. 14), and we hear of the raids of the Bharatas upon the Satvants, and the custom of their cattle, and their practice in ritual matters, all as authoritative. We are told of the consecration of Bharata Dauḥṣanti (viii. 22), but the great king is Janamejaya Pārikṣita and his priest is Tura Kāvaṣeya, who anointed him (viii. 21), who proclaimed to him the proper drink at the royal consecration (vii. 34), and who talked with him on the nature of pasturage (iv. 27), and it is of him that the story of the Asitamṛgas is told (vii. 27). There is less evidence of place in the *Kauṣītaki Brāhmaṇa* as is natural in its condensation, but it knows of Daivodāsi Pratardana,[1] whose name connects him with the Tṛtsus and the Bharatas, and of the Naimiṣīyas,[2] whose name points to the Kuru country. Now the period of Janamejaya is doubtless that of the close of the earlier Vedic period of the Saṁhitās, and thus accords well with the position he holds in the *Aitareya*. The political references do not hint at any great kingdoms, but at a large number of petty princes, who despite their titles and claims to sovereignty were doubtless rulers of limited portions of territory. The social conditions are in full accord with this view, nor does it seem possible with Weber to see the conception of a real empire in the great consecration of Indra in the *Aitareya*. The *Aitareya* contains the first reference (vii. 18) to the Andhras and other tribes, but as outside the Aryan sphere of action.

(g) *Relation to other Brāhmaṇa texts.*

The relation of the two Brāhmaṇas to other texts of the same type does not throw any light of a decisive character on their date. Both texts are known to the *Gopatha Brāhmaṇa*,[3] but the importance of that fact is diminished greatly by the doubt as to whether that text really is older than Yāska, as to which there is no certain evidence available.[4]

The *Kauṣītaki*, however, by its mention of Īçāna and Mahān Deva as names of Rudra is clearly on a footing of equality with the *Çatapatha Brāhmaṇa*, vi, and this view is borne out by the fondness of either text for the use of the narrative perfect, and the occurrence in both of the doctrine of *punarmṛtya*. It is fair therefore to class these two texts together, especially as they often agree on points of doctrine.

On the other hand the *Aitareya* at least in Adhyāyas i–xxiv seems to be of an earlier date than the Brāhmaṇa portion of the *Taittirīya Saṁhitā*.

[1] xxvi. 5.
[2] xxvi. 5; xxviii. 4.
[3] See Bloomfield, *Atharvaveda*, pp. 102 seq.
[4] See Keith, *Taittirīya Saṁhitā*, I. clxix, clxx.

This is a conclusion which rests on a comparison of a large number of passages (especially from the sixth book of the *Taittirīya*), and no absolutely conclusive result can be expected, but that the borrowing is by the *Taittirīya* seems to me most probable.[1] Similarly there is some evidence of the dependence of the *Pañcaviṅça Brāhmaṇa* (iv. 1. 1 *seq.*) on the *Aitareya* (iv. 17).[2] The *Aitareya* will then stand as one of the oldest of the Brāhmaṇas, and doubtless it is older than the *Jaiminīya* or the *Çatapatha*.

It is right however to note that a different opinion on this point has been expressed by Wackernagel,[3] who has set above it the *Taittirīya Brāhmaṇa* (and of course the Brāhmaṇa portions of the *Saṁhitā*) and the *Pañcaviṅça*, and even the *Jaiminīya*. The evidence is extremely feeble; it consists of the following points. In the first place there is the use of the narrative perfect which however applies only to the last sixteen Adhyāyas of the text, and which therefore proves nothing for the later date of the main text: on the contrary the argument is a proof against the placing of the *Aitareya* after the *Jaiminīya*. In the second place the use of *āmantrayām āsa* is quoted; that occurs only in vii. 17. 7 and again proves nil for the older text: it is doubtful if it even proves much for the later text as the form is isolated and the ÇÇS. has *cakre*. In the third place stress is laid on the potential in *īta* from *a* verbal bases; this is however a natural assimilation to the verbs of the second class, and is not capable of indicating date. In the fourth place *saṁlokete* in iv. 15. 6, where the *k* is noteworthy, but it comes from the *k* seen in *roka* and that is Ṛgvedic and therefore no date can be deduced from the word. Fifthly reference is made to the Prākritism *lajjamāna*, iii. 22. 4, but the word cannot be relied upon, for as *lajj* is regularly used later on the change of *lajyamāna* to *lajjamāna* was inevitable, if the derivation from *laj* = *raj* is accepted,[4] and if not there is no evidential value at all in the word. Sixthly, *saciva* stands in the same position as *lokete*: it is a legitimate formation and its occurrence in the AB. alone of early texts has no decisive value. Similarly, *āvām* in the AB. is not a valid criterion of date. Or again, if a compound like *unmūla* occurs first in the AB., still, as it is a legitimate and natural form, it cannot be used as a proof of later date. The same considerations apply to the use of expressions like *anyo 'nya* which occurs in AB. iv. 27 of *chandāṅsi* as in the *Taittirīya Saṁhitā*.[5] So in KB. xxvii. 7; xxvi. 2 and ii. 8; in none of these cases is the further step taken which is found in the *Çatapatha* when *anyonya* can be used without a nominative in apposition (xi. 6. 2. 2). The development of use in the *Çatapatha* is indeed important, for it is a sign of

[1] See Keith, *op. cit.* I. xcvii–xcix.
[2] Keith, p. c.
[3] *Altindische Grammatik*, I. xxx; II. i. 189. Cf. Keith, *Aitareya Āraṇyaka*, p. 172.
[4] Wackernagel, *op. cit.* II. i. 282.
[5] See Wackernagel, pp. 322, 323.

the complete stereotyping of the phrase, and it is significant that it is not found until the *Çatapatha* which is certainly later than the *Aitareya*. But the use of *anyonya* of other than masculine subjects is natural in any text. Similarly *ekaika* is common to the two Brāhmaṇas with the *Taittirīya Saṁhitā*. Another case worth mention is the use of *dvandvaṁ samāsyan* in KB. xxvi. 7, which has a parallel in the *Maitrāyaṇī Saṁhitā* (i. 7. 3), while the *Taittirīya* carries the matter further by using the plural *dvandvāni* (i. 6. 9. 4).[1] But it would be unwise to deduce from this any chronological result, though it is right to set it off against the evidence telling for a later date for the *Aitareya*.

There is, however, an occurrence in the KB. (ii. 2) which would be valuable if correct: the text of Lindner has *prāgudīcīm* and *prāgudīcīḥ* which would be significant, as the rule in the literature before the Sūtras is to have not compounds[2] but the two adjectives, and the variation of the compound is first seen in cases like MÇS. i. 1. 1. 12. But the reading of the MS. M is *prācīm* and *prācīr* in each case, not *prāg*, and this should be inserted in the text.

It is of course the case that both Brāhmaṇas expressly mention the existence of the *trayī vidyā*, and it may be thought that this supposes the existence of the Black Yajurveda in its present form of prose and verse intermingled. This, however, would be a complete error, as what is recognized as the *trayī vidyā* is not any prose Brāhmaṇa passages, but the Ṛces, the Sāmans and the Yajus verses and formulae, the Brāhmaṇas dealing in both cases with the appropriate mode of correcting errors in the performance of those parts of the service. It is therefore quite natural that the *Kauṣītaki Brāhmaṇa* should in one passage (iii. 6) cite a Mantra preserved for us only in the *Maitrāyaṇī Saṁhitā* (iv. 10. 3), for the Mantras of the Black Yajurveda are clearly far older than the prose, and existed independently as a collection before the prose was brought into existence.[3] Neither text recognizes in any way the existence of the *Atharvaveda*[4]: the Kuntāpa hymns cited by both doubtless were taken from the *Khilas* of the *Ṛgveda*.

For the date of the *Kauṣītaki* the evidence already cited suggests a period prior to the extension of the *Aitareya Brāhmaṇa*. It stands in point of view of style as regards the use of the narrative perfect on much the same level as the *Çatapatha Brāhmaṇa* and it agrees with that text in its doctrine of *punarmṛtyu*. It also agrees with it in its mention

[1] Wackernagel, *Altindische Grammatik*, II. i. 29.

[2] Ibid. II. i. 171, where this passage is not noted.

[3] Oldenberg, *Prolegomena*, pp. 220 *seq.*

[4] Contrast TB. iii. 12. 8. 2; 9. 1; TĀ. ii. 9. 2; 10. 7. 8; 11. 2; viii. 3. 3. Cf. TS. vii. 5. 11.

of Āruṇi and Çvetaketu as authorities, and thus is brought into the sphere of the remark of Āpastamba that Çvetaketu was an Avara. The *Aitareya* has no allusion to Çvetaketu or the more famous Āruṇi, and therefore we have another suggestion in favour of its comparatively older date.

It is also worth mention that the *Çatapatha*, without indicating its source, opposes (x. 4. 1. 19) the use of a seventeenth priest at the sacrifice. This seems a clear reference to the practice of the Kauṣītakins, which is formally recorded for us by Āpastamba[1] and elsewhere referred to,[2] of having a seventeenth priest, the Sadasya, who was an overseer of the whole offering, and never left the Sadas alone.[3] This priest is known to the *Kauṣītaki Brāhmaṇa*, as he is incidentally referred to in the Prāyaçcitta section of that text.[4]

(*h*) *Relation to Āpastamba.*

Some information of interest as to the date of the *Kauṣītaki* might be obtained from the *Āpastamba Çrauta Sūtra* if it were true that, as Garbe[5] states, that text,[6] in one case at least, cites the *Kauṣītaki*.[7] But this statement is hardly borne out by facts. The *Āpastamba Çrauta Sūtra* nine times cites a Bahvṛcabrāhmaṇa; in six of these cases the notices do not agree with the *Kauṣītaki*, in two[8] they resemble but differ from statements in that text, and in one only is the correspondence almost but not quite complete.[9] The evidence therefore points to a source for Āpastamba in another Brāhmaṇa of the *Ṛgveda*, but not the *Aitareya*. But there is not the slightest reason to doubt that Āpastamba knew the *Kauṣītaki Brāhmaṇa*, though there is no evidence that he actually cites from it, since he knows of the usage of the Kauṣītakins in one special regard and deems it worthy of mention.

Āpastamba's date is unknown, but is indicated by his remarkable fondness[10] for forms which are unauthorized by Pāṇini whether Vedic (such as the ablative genitive *ai*; locative in *an*; potential in *īta* for *eta*; tmesis of prefixes) or Prākritic. This characteristic is not really consistent with a date after the full influence of Pāṇini became felt, and probably causes it to be necessary to place Āpastamba not later than 250 B.C. or 300 B.C. In favour of this fact it may be mentioned that Kātyāyana, the author of the *Çrauta Sūtra* of the White Yajurveda, who for the same reason has been

[1] x. 1. 10, 11.

[2] See a Mantra in ÇÇS. v. 1. 8; ĀGS. i. 23. 5; comm. on KÇS. vii. 1. 7; Weber, *Ind. Stud.* x. 144.

[3] See Chandoga cited in Anartīya on ÇÇS. *l. c.*

[4] xxvi. 5.

[5] See his edition, III. xxvii.

[6] xii. 17. 2.

[7] xii. 8.

[8] xii. 17. 2 and vi. 18. 9 (= KB. ii. 8).

[9] xi. 2. 9 = KB. viii. 3.

[10] See Garbe's edition, III. vi *seq.*

placed before Pāṇini by Professor Macdonell,[1] was probably known to Pāṇini,[2] and that his rule as to *ekaçruti*[3] seems to have been borrowed by Pāṇini.[4] In style and condensation of expression Kātyāyana is certainly more developed than Āpastamba, and this argument helps to give him a latest date of the third century B.C. and even probably the fourth century B.C. Garbe,[5] with Bühler, indeed, does not hesitate to assign Āpastamba to the fifth century B.C.; but this seems to me to go beyond the necessities of the case.

(*i*) *Astronomical data.*

Note should finally be made of the statement in the *Kauṣītaki* (xix. 3) that the winter solstice took place at the new moon of Māgha. This notion is, however, clearly nothing more or less than the datum of the *Jyotiṣa* and thus yields us no date of any assured value for the period in question; Weber[6] places the limits of the date of the initial fixing of the series of Nakṣatras in the *Jyotiṣa* at 1820 B.C.–860 B.C., and there is no reason to show for how long the order would be kept after it had ceased to represent the facts, apart altogether from any other considerations as to the origin of the Nakṣatras. If, as is most probable, the Nakṣatras were not an Indian invention at all, but were derived from some foreign—perhaps Semitic—source, it is clear that the date of their fixation would not have the slightest value, save as an upper date, for the Brāhmaṇas. At most the Māgha datum tends to render 800 B.C. a reasonable maximum date for the composition of the Brāhmaṇa literature.

(*j*) *Date of later part of the Aitareya.*

Of the date of the later parts of the *Aitareya* there is little further to be said. It is most probable that all of vii and viii were added after the completion of the *Kauṣītaki Brāhmaṇa.* The use of the narrative perfect points to a period similar to that of the *Çatapatha Brāhmaṇa*, and other affinities with that text may be seen in the resemblances of the Prāyaçcitta section in vii. 2–12 and the corresponding section in the later *Çatapatha*, book xii (4. 1 *seq.*); and of the account of the Açvamedhins in viii. 21–23 and the *Çatapatha* (xiii. 5. 4). That the two books were not added to the *Brāhmaṇa* before the *Kauṣītaki Brāhmaṇa* was complete would be proved by the fact that vii. 11 is a bad version of the *Kauṣītaki*, iii. 1, but that

[1] *Bṛhaddevatā*, I. xxii–xxiv.

[2] See Weber, *Ind. Stud.* v. 64.

[3] i. 18. 19. Cf. VPr. i. 131.

[4] i. 2. 33, 34; see Weber, *Ind. Stud.* x. 423–426.

[5] *Op. cit.* III. xv. It is, of course, possible that Pāṇini borrows from Kātyāyana's source: hence this argument is not proof.

[6] *Ind. Stud.* x. 234 *seq.* Whitney suggests that even these limits cannot be fixed as correct.

section is probably enough not an old addition to the main text. No stress can be laid on the nature of the Rājasūya as described in the *Aitareya* as being more primitive in certain details (e.g. the amount of materials required for the anointing) than the versions of the Yajurveda, a point noted by Weber,[1] as pointing to a greater age than the Yajus texts: the development of the ritual in different schools doubtless was very uneven.

(k) *Date of Metrical Portions of the Aitareya.*

The Gāthās of the *Aitareya* and the occasional odd verses found therein are of decidedly antique form: the Çloka metre shows a form unquestionably later than that of the *Ṛgveda*, but equally clearly older than that of the metrical portions of the Upaniṣads, for instance the *Kaṭha*, *Kena* or *Īçā*, as has been fully shown by Oldenberg.[2] Unhappily this gives us no definite date: the *Kaṭha Upaniṣad*, for instance, cannot certainly be dated before the Buddha, because its context is obviously the reflex of a period when the views of the prose Upaniṣads such as the *Bṛhadāraṇyaka* and the *Chāndogya* had become a matter of common knowledge and could be summed up in allusive and epigrammatic verse. That this period antedated Buddhism cannot be safely assumed, and we must be content with the conclusion that the metre of even the latest parts of the *Aitareya* is old and tends to confirm the general impression of antiquity of the work, though it directly proves nothing, since it is open to argue that it was much older than the prose with which it is found.

§ 6. The Ritual.

(a) *The Çāṅkhāyana Çrauta Sūtra.*

The ritual for the *Brāhmaṇas* is given in the *Çrauta Sūtras* of Āçvalāyana and Çāṅkhāyana, which are works of probably the fourth century B.C. There is not the slightest doubt that both these Sūtras knew the Brāhmaṇas and based their exposition on those texts. But in both cases the Sūtras go far beyond the present Brāhmaṇa texts, and it is not open to question that allowance must be made for a considerable development of practice between the Brāhmaṇas and the Sūtras.

The *Çāṅkhāyana Çrauta Sūtra* coincides more completely with the *Kauṣītaki* than the *Āçvalāyana* with the *Aitareya*. Thus the *Çāṅkhāyana* contains in—

i. The New and Full Moon sacrifices = *Kauṣītaki Brāhmaṇa*, iv.
ii. 1–5. The Agnyādheya and Punarādheya = *Kauṣītaki Brāhmaṇa*, i.

[1] *Rājasūya*, pp. 111 *seq.*
[2] GGN. 1909, pp. 219 *seq.*; ZDMG. xxxvii. 66 *seq.*

ii. 6–17. The Agnihotra = *Kauṣītaki Brāhmaṇa*, ii.
iii. 1–12. The special offerings = *Kauṣītaki Brāhmaṇa*, iii.
iii. 13–18. The four-monthly sacrifices = *Kauṣītaki Brāhmaṇa*, v.
iii. 19–21. Prāyaçcittas; cf. *Kauṣītaki Brāhmaṇa*, xxvi. 3–6.
iv. Minor points including the Piṇḍapitṛyajña and the Çūlagava.
v–viii. The Agniṣṭoma = *Kauṣītaki Brāhmaṇa*, vii–xvi, xviii. 6–14.
ix. The Ukthya, Ṣoḍaçin, and Atirātra = *Kauṣītaki Brāhmaṇa*, xvi. 11–xvii. 9; xviii. 1–5.
x. The Dvādaçāha = *Kauṣītaki Brāhmaṇa*, xx, xxi, xxvi. 7–17; xxvii.
xi. The Caturviñça, Abhiplava Ṣaḍaha, Abhijit, Svarasāmans, Viṣuvant and Viçvajit = *Kauṣītaki Brāhmaṇa*, xix, xxii, xxiii, xxiv, xxv.
xii. The Çastras of the Hotrakas = *Kauṣītaki Brāhmaṇa*, xxviii–xxx.
xiii. 1–13. Certain Prāyaçcittas, conflicting sacrifices.
xiii. 14–29. Sattras, Gavām and other Ayanas.

With xiv a new section of the Sūtra opens, which is partly Brāhmaṇa in style, and of which full details have been given above. xvii and xviii are no real part of the Sūtra: they deal with the Mahāvrata ceremony and are really supplements to the *Çāñkhāyana Āraṇyaka* i and ii, which represent the Brāhmaṇa of that text.

It is somewhat striking that the order of the sections should be so different in some respects from that of the Brāhmaṇa. The essential features are the placing in the forefront of the new and full moon sacrifices, which are the real model of Iṣṭis, and which therefore in a logical arrangement should come first. The second point is the bringing together in book x of the whole elements of the Dvādaçāha, the Pṛṣṭhya Ṣaḍaha, the Chandomas, and the tenth day: the Brāhmaṇa has the material in books xxii and xxiii, xxvi. 7–17, and xxvii respectively. Again the Sūtra very naturally deals with the final rites of the Agniṣṭoma before the Ukthya, not as in the Brāhmaṇa after the Atirātra. These changes explain the altered order of the two texts, and all of these prove the improved order of the Sūtra.

(*b*) *The Āçvalāyana Çrauta Sūtra.*

The *Āçvalāyuna Çrauta Sūtra* contains a great deal more than the *Aitareya Brāhmaṇa*. Thus for the first three books which deal with the new and full moon sacrifices, the Agnihotra, the Agnyādhāna, the four-monthly sacrifices, the Prāyaçcittas and the animal sacrifice, there are but few real parallels in the *Aitareya* except the section (ii. 1–14) regarding the animal sacrifice, and that relating to the Agnihotra (v. 26–31), and the section on Prāyaçcittas (vii. 2–12) which is very closely connected with the *Çrauta Sūtra* (iii. 10 and 11). The rest of the *Aitareya* agrees with books iv. 1–viii. 13 of the *Sūtra*. The arrangement is briefly as follows:

iv. The preparations for the Soma pressing day = *Aitareya Brāhmaṇa*, i. 1–ii. 18.
v. The Agniṣṭoma proper = *Aitareya Brāhmaṇa*, ii. 19–iii. 48.
vi. 1. The Ukthya = *Aitareya Brāhmaṇa*, iii. 49, 50.
vi. 2, 3. The Ṣoḍaçin = *Aitareya Brāhmaṇa*, iv. 1–4.
vi. 4–6. The Atirātra = *Aitareya Brāhmaṇa*, iv. 5–11.
vi. 7–10. The Prāyaçcittas and rites in case of death or disease.
vi. 11–14. The concluding rites of the Agniṣṭoma = *Aitareya Brāhmaṇa*, iii. 47, 48.
vii. 1. General observations.
vii. 2–4. The Caturviñça = *Aitareya Brāhmaṇa*, iv. 12, 14.
vii. 5–9. The Abhiplava Ṣaḍaha, &c. = *Aitareya Brāhmaṇa*, iv. 13, 15, 16.
vii. 10–12. The Pṛṣṭhya Ṣaḍaha = *Aitareya Brāhmaṇa*, iv. 13, 15, 16, 27–v. 15.
viii. 1–4. The Çastras of the Hotṛ and the Hotrakas on the sixth day = *Aitareya Brāhmaṇa*, vi.
viii. 5. The Abhijit and Svarasāmans = *Aitareya Brāhmaṇa*, iv. 19.
viii. 6. The Viṣuvant = *Aitareya Brāhmaṇa*, iv. 19–22.
viii. 7. The Viçvajit and Svarasāmans = *Aitareya Brāhmaṇa*, iv. 19.
The Abhiplava forms.
The Chandomas in the *samūḍha* form.
viii. 8. The *vyūḍha* Dvādaçāha = *Aitareya Brāhmaṇa*, iv. 27.
viii. 9–11. The Chandomas = *Aitareya Brāhmaṇa*, v. 16–21.
viii. 12. The tenth day = *Aitareya Brāhmaṇa*, v. 22–25.
viii. 13. The concluding rites of the tenth day.
viii. 14. The rules for recitation.
ix–xii. Ahīnas and Sattras.

To the last four books there is hardly anything in the *Aitareya* to correspond. x. 5 contains an account of the Dvādaçāha; xi. 7 of the Gavām Ayana, and xii. 9 is verbally the same as AB. vii. 1, which seems to be derived from it. On the other hand the concluding words of the Çunaḥçepa episode (vii. 18) are repeated as a Sūtra in ix. 3, and in this case the borrowing must be from the *Aitareya*.

The *Āçvalāyana Çrauta Sūtra* is by no means so well arranged as the *Çāñkhāyana*, and its superiority to the Brāhmaṇa is not very marked. It is very much less comprehensive than the *Çāñkhāyana* as it contains nothing really corresponding to book xiv. It has an account of the Açvamedha in x. 6–10, but it has nothing of the Puruṣamedha or the

Sarvamedha, and its account of the Rājasūya (ix. 3 and 4) is very brief compared to that of the Çāñkhāyana text, and it is always strictly a Sūtra text. Of its twelve books only about half are really represented in the *Aitareya Brāhmaṇa* as against about twelve out of sixteen in the case of the *Çāñkhāyana*.

The *Çāñkhāyana* has one great merit in comparison with the *Āçvalāyana*; it gives Mantras in cases where the *Āçvalāyana* is silent, as for example the Nivids for the Agniṣṭoma hymns, and it sets out in detail the complicated Çilpa Çastra of the Brāhmaṇācchaṅsin at the third pressing on the sixth Pṛṣṭhya day, which the *Aitareya* mentions and the *Āçvalāyana* also merely mentions.

(c) *The Soma Sacrifice.*

The two Brāhmaṇas agree in treating of only four forms of the Jyotiṣṭoma, the Agniṣṭoma, the Ukthya, the Ṣoḍaçin, and the Atirātra, distinguished by the possession of twelve Çastras and Stotras, fifteen, sixteen, and twenty-eight or twenty-nine respectively.

Of the **Ukthya** form of sacrifice fairly complete accounts are given in both the Brāhmaṇas. Its essential feature is the three Uktha Stotras and the three Uktha Çastras of the Hotrakas, and from this feature possibly its name is borrowed, as suggested by Eggeling[1] in view of the remarks in AB. vi. 13. There is also a he-goat to Indra and Agni as a second victim in addition to the ordinary victim for Agni and Soma prescribed on the day before the pressing day, and the victim for Agni on that day. The Ukthya cup is also drawn at the third pressing.

The **Ṣoḍaçin** adds a third victim, a ram to Indra, and another cup with an extra Stotra and Çastra. As pointed out in the *Aitareya Brāhmaṇa* (iv. 1), the name is derived very probably from the sixteen Stotras and Çastras used, but the Çastra is also specially developed in a peculiar manner described in iv. 2, where also the name is appropriate.

The **Atirātra** adds twelve Stotras and Çastras in three rounds, chanted through the night and accompanied by libations and potations; these are followed by the Sandhi Stotra (*Sāmaveda*, ii. 99–104) chanted at daybreak, and followed by the recitation by the Hotṛ of the Āçvina Çastra. The difficulty arises whether the Ṣoḍaçin is included in the Atirātra. The view of the *Çāñkhāyana Çrauta Sūtra* (ix. 1. 10) is clearly that it is; there is nothing to contradict this in the *Kauṣītaki Brāhmaṇa*, and it is assumed by the *Āçvalāyana Çrauta Sūtra* (v. 11. 1) that an Atirātra contains a Ṣoḍaçin.[2] This is also the view of the *Kātyāyana Çrauta Sūtra* (ix. 8. 5), while the *Pañcaviñça Brāhmaṇa* (xx. 1. 1) recognizes both modes of

[1] SBE. xli. xv seq.

[2] So AB. iii. 41, which is late (p. 88).

usage.[1] The *Aitareya* (iv. 6) clearly contemplates only the form without, i.e. with twenty-eight Stotras, or as it reckons them, by making three out of the Sandhi Stotra, thirty Stotras. It is clear also that to the *Aitareya* (iv. 1) the Ṣoḍaçin is essentially only a rite used as part of a Dvādaçāha or similar rite, for it is expressly stated that on the fourth day is the Ṣoḍaçin used, i.e. on the fourth day of the Pṛṣṭhya Ṣaḍaha which follows the Atirātra.[2] Similarly the Ukthya from its position is doubtless mentioned mainly because it is an essential feature of the Pṛṣṭhya Ṣaḍaha. The Atirātra has a victim for Sarasvātī as a fourth victim.

The two combinations of days which they dwell upon are the **Dvādaçāha** and the Gavām Ayana, as these two act as models for the other prolonged Soma rites.

The **Atyagniṣṭoma** is not mentioned in either of the *Brāhmaṇas* nor is the tenth day treated as being of this class.[3] Its real existence as a sacrifice (being a Ṣoḍaçin minus the Ukthyas) is very doubtful, its main purpose being doubtless to fill up the number of forms of the Jyotiṣṭoma to seven. But in the extra Uktha of the tenth day of the Dvādaçāha in the school of Çāñkhāyana may be seen a form analogous to the Atyagniṣṭoma.

The **Vājapeya** and **Aptoryāma** receive a brief allusion in the *Aitareya* (iii. 41) and the *Kauṣītaki* (xxx. 11),[4] in either case no other notice being taken of them in the texts. It is very doubtful if these references can be treated as primitive, and it is perfectly clear that neither rite was really considered as of importance by the Brāhmaṇas. But there are notices of the latter in the *Āçvalāyana* (ix. 11) and the *Çāñkhāyana Çrauta Sūtras*, the latter of which (xv. 5) calls it Āptoryāman. It is distinguished by having four extra (*atirikta*) Stotras and Çastras over and above those of the Atirātra. Moreover it is marked by having all the six Pṛṣṭhas distributed among the four Pṛṣṭha Stotras and the Mādhyaṁdina and Ārbhava Pavamāna Stotras, and in the case of all the Stotras save the three Pavamānas the performance conforms to the true Pṛṣṭha form, i.e. with one Sāman enclosed in two others. The Vājapeya is a special rite, preliminary to the Bṛhaspatisava, which is for the Brahman much the same thing as the Rājasūya for the king, and to the Rājasūya; it shows clear traces of a popular origin and once was available for Vaiçyas, but the ritual (*Āçvalāyana*, ix. 9; *Çāñkhāyana*, xvi. 17) is not evidently known to the Brāhmaṇas or at least accepted by them. Both the Vājapeya and the Aptoryāma are not normally used as anything but independent rites; in *Çāñkhāyana* (xvi. 15. 6 and 7) they are made the models of the sixth and seventh days of the mythical

[1] So MÇS. ii. 5. 3; Āp. xiv. 3. 8 is obscure; see Rudra *ad loc*; BÇS. xvii. 1 *seq.* seems to assume the Ṣoḍaçin.

[2] ÇÇS. x. 2. 11.

[3] Cf. Weber, *Ind. Stud.* ix. 120–121.

[4] Āptoryāma; so ÇÇS. xv. 5. 18; xvi. 15. 7.

Sarvamedha. Similarly in the *Mānava Çrauta Sūtra* (ii. 5. 3) the only forms given are the Ukthya, Ṣoḍaçin and Atirātra; in the *Baudhāyana Çrauta Sūtra* (xvii. 1, 2) these three only are mentioned, and it remains for the *Āpastamba Çrauta Sūtra* (xiv. 1. 1) to add the Aptoryāma. On that passage Rudradatta has an elaborate comment from which he deduces the fact that the omission arises from the fact that the Atyagniṣṭoma and the Vājapeya are not the models on which any other offerings are based, for the Sūtra does not even know the name of the Atyagniṣṭoma.

While the greater part of both the Brāhmaṇas is devoted to the Agniṣṭoma as model of the Soma sacrifice, they do not contemplate its use merely as a one-day rite.

The **Dvādaçāha** consisted of a period of ten days with an introductory and a concluding Atirātra. Within this period of ten days three elements are to be distinguished, the first six days, which can be divided into two sets of three, the seventh to ninth days, the Chandomas, and the tenth or Avivākya day, to which the name was applied, because, according to the Brāhmaṇas, the day was one on which corrections of errors were not in place.

In the careful analysis of the *Çāñkhāyana*[1] the Dvādaçāha is thus constituted as regards the period of ten days (Daçarātra):—

I. The Pṛṣṭhya Ṣaḍaha, consisting of—

1st day. Agniṣṭoma type; Trivṛt Stoma; Rathantara as Pṛṣṭha Stotra.
2nd day. Ukthya type; Pañcadaça Stoma; Bṛhat as Pṛṣṭha Stotra.
3rd day. Ukthya type; Saptadaça Stoma; Vairūpa as Pṛṣṭha Stotra.
4th day. Ṣoḍaçin type; Ekaviñça Stoma; Vairāja as Pṛṣṭha Stotra.
5th day. Ukthya type; Triṇava Stoma; Çākvara as Pṛṣṭha Stotra.
6th day. Ukthya type; Trayastriñça Stoma; Raivata as Pṛṣṭha Stotra.

II. The Chandomas.

7th day. Ukthya type; Caturviñça Stoma; both Sāmans with Bṛhat as Pṛṣṭha Stotra.
8th day. Ukthya type; Catuçcatvāriñça Stoma; Rathantara as Pṛṣṭha Stotra.
9th day. Ukthya type; Aṣṭācatvāriñca Stoma; Bṛhat as Pṛṣṭha Stotra.

III. The Tenth Day.

10th day. Agniṣṭoma type; Caturviñça Stoma with Trayastriñça in the Agniṣṭoma Sāman; the Rathantara or the base of the Vāmadevya as Pṛṣṭha Stotra.

[1] x; cf. ĀÇS. x. 5; vii. 10–viii. 4. That the tenth day is an Atyagniṣṭoma (Eggeling, SBE. xxvi. 412) is not in accord with these authorities, nor BÇS. xvi. 6; ĀpÇS. xxi. 9. 1; but ÇÇS. and KB. allow an *atiriktokatha* (p. 54).

While the Dvādaçāha served as a model for all the other Ahīna rites (that is, from two up to twelve days) and the Sattras (for twelve days upwards), the model of the year rite was the Gavām Ayana, which in both texts is constituted as follows[1]:—

1. Prāyaṇīya Atirātra.

2. Caturviñça day; Agniṣṭoma or Ukthya type; Caturviñça Stoma; both Sāmans with Bṛhat as Pṛṣṭha.

1st month. 4 Abhiplava Ṣaḍahas = 24 days.
1 Pṛṣṭhya Ṣaḍaha = 6 days.

2nd month. 4 Abhiplava Ṣaḍahas.
1 Pṛṣṭhya Ṣaḍaha.

3rd month. 4 Abhiplava Ṣaḍahas.
1 Pṛṣṭhya Ṣaḍaha.

4th month. 4 Abhiplava Ṣaḍahas.
1 Pṛṣṭhya Ṣaḍaha.

5th month. 4 Abhiplava Ṣaḍahas.
1 Pṛṣṭhya Ṣaḍaha.

6th month. 3 Abhiplava Ṣaḍahas.
1 Pṛṣṭhya Ṣaḍaha.
Abhijit; Agniṣṭoma, with all the Stomas, both Sāmans, and Rathantara or Bṛhat as Pṛṣṭha Stotra.
3 Svarasāman days; Ukthyas or Agniṣṭomas; with the Svaras as Pṛṣṭhas.

Viṣuvant day; Agniṣṭoma type; Ekaviñça Stoma; Bṛhat or Mahādivākīrtya as Pṛṣṭha.

7th month. 3 Svarasāmans reversed.
Viçvajit, Agniṣṭoma, with all the Stomas and Pṛṣṭhas.
1 Pṛṣṭhya Ṣaḍaha reversed.
3 Abhiplava Ṣaḍahas reversed.

8th month. 1 Pṛṣṭhya Ṣaḍaha reversed.
4 Abhiplava Ṣaḍahas reversed.

9th month. 1 Pṛṣṭhya Ṣaḍaha reversed.
4 Abhiplava Ṣaḍahas reversed.

10th month. 1 Pṛṣṭhya Ṣaḍaha reversed.
4 Abhiplava Ṣaḍahas reversed.

11th month. 1 Pṛṣṭhya Ṣaḍaha reversed.
4 Abhiplava Ṣaḍahas reversed.

[1] ÇÇS. xiii. 19.

12th month. 3 Abhiplava Ṣaḍahas reversed.
Āyus day.
Go day.
Daçarātra.

Mahāvrata day.
Atirātra day as Udayanīya.

The account of the Gavām Ayana given in the *Āçvalāyana Çrauta Sūtra*[1] differs in that it expressly places the Go and Āyus days in the normal order in the last month, though this offends against the rule that the last month should like the preceding months after the Viṣuvant be reversed in order of performance. But it is in harmony with the normal order, and the Divādaçāha itself according to Āpastamba is not reversed in performance. It is expressly stated that the sixth month is completed by adding the first two days, and the seventh by adding the last two days. Other possible arrangements are mentioned by Āçvalāyana, including the placing of the Go and Āyus in different positions and the alteration of allowing only the Ṣaḍaha or the Svarasāman days to be reversed and not as usual both. It is also suggested that the seventh month can be made complete, leaving four days over, that these can be added to the last month, giving 30 + 2 + 4 and that then twelve days, the Go and Āyus and the Daçarātra, can be deducted, and an Abhiplava added, giving 30 in all.[2]

The version of Baudhāyana[3] agrees generally with that of the Aitareyins, but it makes the seventh month complete with a Pṛṣṭhya and four Abhiplavas and composes the last month of

2 Abhiplava Ṣaḍahas	= 12 days
Go and Āyus	= 2 days
3 Svarasāmans and Viçvajit	= 4 days
Daçarātra	= 10 days
Mahāvrata and Udayanīya	= 2 days.

He explains that in the inserted Pṛṣṭhya the Trayastriñça Stoma and Āgrayaṇa cup begin and so on, while in the Abhiplava the Āyus and Go days are transposed and the Sāmans alternate as Bṛhat and Rathantara.

In Āpastamba[4] the scheme is more elaborate. Three forms are distinguished. In the Çāṭyāyanaka the first six months agree with Çāñkhāyana and Āçvalāyana's accounts; the second with Baudhāyana. The Tāṇḍaka agrees with the Çāñkhāyana. The Bhāllavika agrees with the Çāṭyāyanaka save that it places the Abhijit and Viçvajit before the last and after the first Pṛṣṭhya Ṣaḍaha in the two parts of the year respectively.

[1] xi. 5.
[2] See ĀÇS. xi. 5. 19 with the comm. The above must be the sense but the ed. is incorrect.
[3] xvi. 14 and 15.
[4] xxi. 15 and 16.

According to the *Aitareya Brāhmaṇa*[1] the Ayanas of the Ādityas and the Añgirases differ from the Gavām Ayana in that the former type has all its Ṣaḍahas in the Abhiplava and the latter all in the Pṛṣṭhya form. This account is found also in the Sūtra of Baudhāyana,[2] but both the *Āçvalāyana Çrauta Sūtra*[3] and the *Çāñkhāyana Çrauta Sūtra*[4] have elaborate accounts of these Ayanas which give other points of difference and not this one. The same remark applies to the *Āpastamba Çrauta Sūtra.*[5]

The **Abhiplava Ṣaḍaha** is composed of six days of which the first and last are Agniṣṭomas, the rest Ukthyas. Further, the characteristic Pṛṣṭha Stotra, which corresponds to the second Çastra of the Hotṛ at the midday pressing, is on the alternative days made up of the Rathantara and the Bṛhat Sāmans respectively, and not of a different Sāman each day as in the case of the Pṛṣṭhya Ṣaḍahas. Moreover, whereas in the case of the Pṛṣṭhya Ṣaḍaha the Stomas vary from day to day, but only one applies each day, in the Abhiplava the usual four Stomas occur daily but in a divergent manner, which results in the description of the days as Jyotis, Go, and Āyus, thus:

Stotra.	Jyotis.	Go.	Āyus.
Bahiṣpavamaña	Trivṛt	Pañcadaça	Trivṛt
Ājya Stotras	Pañcadaça	Trivṛt	Pañcadaça
Mādhyaṁdinapavamāna	Pañcadaça	Saptadaça	Saptadaça
Pṛṣṭha Stotras	Saptadaça	Saptadaça	Saptadaça
Ārbhavapavamāna	Saptadaça	Ekaviñça	Ekaviñça
Agniṣṭoma Sāman	Ekaviñça	Ekaviñça	Ekaviñça
Uktha Stotras		Ekaviñça	Ekaviñça

In the **Pṛṣṭhya Ṣaḍaha** the sixth day is of quite special importance, and at its third pressing in its full form the Hotṛ, the Maitrāvaruṇa, the Brāhmaṇācchaṅsin and the Achāvāka have to recite elaborate Çastras, viz. the Nābhānediṣṭha and Nārāçaṅsa; the Vālakhilyās; the Sukirti and Vṛṣākapi and the Kuntāpa; and the Evayāmarut, full details of which are given in the two Brāhmaṇas.[6] The Brāhmaṇas also give the **Çastras** of the **Hotrakas** on other occasions; the most important are those performed by them at the midday pressing. On these occasions, whether the Ṣaḍaha be Pṛṣṭhya or Abhiplava, the Çastra begins with

(1) strophe and antistrophe; then follow
(2) the *kadvant* Pragātha,
(3) the Ārambhaṇīya,
(4) the daily hymn (*aharahaḥçasya*),
(5) the Saṁpāta

[1] iv. 17.
[2] xvi. 16.
[3] xii. 1 and 2.
[4] xiii. 21 and 22.
[5] xxiii. 9.
[6] AB. vi. 24-36; KB. xxx.

in the case of the Maitrāvaruṇa, (4) and (5) being reversed in the other two cases.[1] The Saṁpātas are nine hymns, three for each Hotraka, which he recites one by one, day by day.

In the case of the days other than the Ṣaḍahas, viz. the Caturviṅça, Abhijit, Viṣuvant, Viçvajit, and the Mahāvrata, for the Saṁpāta hymns are substituted others called Ahīnas. The name is confusing, as it is not of course really appropriate, since those days can hardly be said to be Ahīnas as opposed to Aikāhikas, and the two Brāhmaṇas both derive the word from *a-hīna*, thus showing that they desired to obviate confusion with the ordinary Ahīnas (from *ahas*).

One point in the use of the Saṁpātas is the employment of insertions on the fourth, fifth, and sixth days, consisting of Virāj verses and verses by Vimada on the fourth, Paṅkti verses on the fifth, and Parucchepa's verses on the sixth day. For the Chandomas with their long Stomas other special verses are prescribed.

In the recitation of the Hotrakas special attention is given to the rule of *atiçaṅsana* of the Stotra; apparently the practice was to restrict this *atiçaṅsana* to one or two extra verses at the first two pressings, but to use an indefinite number at the third pressing, but the passages (vi. 8 and 23) of the *Aitareya* which deal with the rule somewhat conflict.

The other chief points regarding the Hotrakas which are dealt with are their opening and concluding verses, their use at the morning pressing in Ahīna rites of the Stotriyas of the one day as the Anurūpas of the preceding, and the verses used by them as offering verses for the Prasthita libations, which are given in connexion with the Hotṛ's verses for the filling of the goblets from which all drink after libations have been duly made. There are also given in full the Çastras of the Hotrakas at the Ukthya at its third pressing.

The **Dvādaçāha** is complicated by the fact that it is not merely performed in a simple (*samūḍha*) form, but in a *vyūḍha* form, that is, one in which the 'metres' are *vyūḍha*, 'transposed'. These terms which occur in the Ṛgvedic texts do not receive explanation there, but the sense of *vyūḍhachandas* appears from the discussion in the *Çatapatha Brāhmaṇa* (iv. 5. 9) of the question of differing arrangements of the cups which are drawn on the several days of the Dvādaçāha. According to that version the cups begin with the Aindravāyava (after the Upāṅçu and the Antaryāma) on the first three, the fifth, the eighth, tenth, eleventh, and twelfth days, the Āgrayaṇa on the fourth and ninth, and the Çukra on the sixth and seventh,

[1] Haug, *Aitareya Brāhmaṇa*, ii. 412, n. 8, gives a different account, but clearly it cannot be reconciled with the two Brāhmaṇas or the Sūtras. See ĀÇS. vii. 5. 20–22; 4. 8, 9; 10. 2, cf. *Vait.* xxxi. 25.

the Āgrayaṇa being the first of the cups of the third and the Çukra of those of the midday pressing. This rule is entirely disapproved of by the *Çatapatha*, which does not think any variation of the order of the cups is needed although the metres be changed.[1]

In the *Āpastamba Çrauta Sūtra* (xxi. 14) there is a distinction made between the *tryaṇīkā* form if *avyūḍha* and if not; in the first case the order is—

Aindravāyava on 1st, 2nd, 5th, 8th, 11th, 12th;
Çukra on 3rd, 6th, 9th;
Āgrayaṇa on 4th, 7th, 10th;

in the second case the order is—

Aindravāyava on 1st, 2nd, 6th, 10th, 11th, 12th;
Çukra on 3rd, 7th, 8th;
Āgrayaṇa on 4th, 5th, 9th.

In the *Baudhāyana Çrauta Sūtra* (xvi. 10) the order is given as—

Aindravāyava on 1st, 2nd, 6th, 10th, 11th, 12th;
Çukra on 3rd, 7th, 8th;
Āgrayaṇa on 4th, 5th, 9th,

thus agreeing with the account of Āpastamba of the *vyūḍha* form. Here it is expressly coupled with the corresponding change of the Stotras and Çastras under which the Daçarātra consists of three sets of three days which have respectively at the three pressings—

(1st) Gāyatrī, Triṣṭubh, Jagatī;
(2nd) Jagatī, Gāyatrī, Triṣṭubh;
(3rd) Triṣṭubh, Jagatī, Gāyatrī.

It is clear that the change of order of the metres in the Savanas does not correspond with that of the order of the cups, and that therefore the terms *vyūḍha* and *avyūḍha* cannot be explained adequately in the sense that they correspond to any arrangement of the cups, or of the metres, so far as their use in the *Kauṣītaki Brāhmaṇa* (xxii) and the *Çāṅkhāyana Çrauta Sūtra* (x) are concerned. In the *Aitareya Brāhmaṇa* the term *vyūḍha* of *dvādaçāha* appears in the compound *vyūḍhachandas* and the sense (iv. 27) is simply that of the change of metres according to which the days are arranged in sets of three. But in the *Kauṣītaki* there are two variant forms for the first six days and the tenth day given in detail as *vyūḍha* and *samūḍha*, showing clearly a futher development of distinctions of form beyond that of the *Aitareya*.

In the case of the tenth day, contrary to the usage in certain other texts,

[1] The reference in this is clearly to the variation of the order of the metres at the pressings, a fact which explains the term *vyūḍhachandas* better than the view in Eggeling, SBE. xxvi. 416, n. 1, 421, n. 2.

there is in the *Çāñkhāyana Çrauta Sūtra* (x. 13. 25) and in the *Brāhmaṇa* an *atiriktoktha*, which really makes the number of the Çastras (and doubtless of the Stotras) up to thirteen, the same number as that prescribed for the Atyagniṣṭoma, but without its characteristic, the Ṣoḍaçin Çastra and Stotra.

The *Āçvalāyana Çrauta Sūtra* on the other hand very clearly uses the terms *samūḍha* and *vyūḍha* in the sense that they correspond with the variations of the form of the three sets of days in the Daçarātra; this is to be seen with perfect clearness from the description of the *samūḍha* form of the Daçarātra given in viii. 7 and the variants of the *vyūḍha* in viii. 8 for the second three days, and 9–11 for the three Chandomas. The tenth day on the contrary has no variation of form as *vyūḍha* and *samūḍha* but is common to both forms of the Daçarātra. According to the commentary on x. 5. 4 the *samūḍha* is the model of the Ahīnas, the *vyūḍha* for the Sattras.

In addition to the normal Dvādaçāha with its sets of three days each closely united, the *Āçvalāyana Çrauta Sūtra* (x. 5. 8–11) recognizes one in which there is no such connexion and the days are each taken separately as (1) Atirātra; (2) Agniṣṭoma; (3–10) Ukthyas; (11) Agniṣṭoma; (12) Atirātra, and this form is alluded to in the *Aitareya Brāhmaṇa* (iv. 23). It is ignored in the *Çāñkhāyana Çrauta Sutra*, and a different rite of twelve Agniṣṭomas with the Rathantara Sāman is given in the *Āpastamba Çrauta Sutra* (xxi. 14. 14 and 15).

(*d*) *The Rājasūya and the Story of Çunaḥçepa.*

The ritual of the Rājasūya as presented in the *Aitareya Brāhmaṇa* is peculiar to it and is not recorded elsewhere, except to the limited extent that the *Āçvalāyana Çrauta Sūtra* (ix. 3) repeats textually the directions at the end of vii. 18 and the *Çāñkhāyana Çrauta Sūtra* (xv. 17–27) has a parallel to the Çunaḥçepa legend. But otherwise there is complete silence in the texts of the Rājasūya as to the mode of the preparation of the drink for the king, and the mode of the anointing of the king and the spells by which his success is secured. On the other hand the *Aitareya* is silent regarding the more normal features of the Rājasūya, such as they appear in the *Çāñkhāyana* (xv. 12–16; xvi. 18). The *Aitareya* version shows further its peculiar character by its being brought into connexion with the Açvamedha, the great kings who are celebrated in viii. 21–23 corresponding with the list of Açvamedhins in the *Çatapatha Brāhmaṇa* (xiii. 5. 4), and it is clear that the Açvamedha was the original source of their fame and that the connexion of the Açvamedhins with the consecration is secondary, and probably induced by the desire of the redactor of the *Aitareya* to include in it as much as possible of the deeds of kings, which form the theme of all of vii. 13–viii. 23.

The most important part of the account is undoubtedly the story of Çunaḥçepa, and its occurrence in the Rājasūya is claimed by Hillebrandt [1] as proof that once human sacrifice marked that event. It is of interest to note that its occurrence in this use rests ultimately on the *Aitareya Brāhmaṇa*, for the other mention of the use of the legend in the *Kātyāyana Çrauta Sūtra* (xv. 6. 1 *seq.*) is simply derived from the *Aitareya*, as an examination of the passage at once shows. It is, however, prescribed in the *Çāñkhāyana Çrauta Sūtra* (xvi. 11. 1) as recited in the Puruṣamedha, though the story as there recited seems to have been merely a portion of the tale as it occurs in the Rājasūya. But the argument from the Puruṣamedha use is not significant for the question of human sacrifice, for the Puruṣamedha as depicted in the *Çāñkhāyana* and in the *Vaitāna Sūtra* (xxxvii. 10 *seq.*) has every appearance of being a theoretic and not a real sacrifice.[2]

But as evidence of a real human sacrifice at the royal consecration no stress can possibly be laid on the Çunaḥçepa tale. Its motive is inexplicable on such a theory, for it does not enjoin or approve a sacrifice of this sort, but expressly relates that the sacrifice was not carried out, and that the priest Ajīgarta who was willing to sacrifice his son was deprived of him as a punishment. Moreover, the mere fact that the great priests alleged to have been engaged in the offering would not perform the slaying is a proof that the rite was not an approved one. If the rite was ever one practised at the royal consecration, the moral sense of the priests had repudiated it, and had expressed their repudiation in a striking form in the shape of the use of a narrative as a part of the Rājasūya intended to show that such a sacrifice was not to be performed. The most attractive theory [3] of the rite from this point of view is that there once existed a practice of slaying the first-born sons of kings at their consecration, and that the Çunaḥçepa tale is a record of the removal of the practice of the slaying by the mercies of the gods, and for such a fanciful hypothesis we have not the slightest ground.

A further peculiarity of the legend is that it is employed as a device for obtaining sons as the two versions both assert. The legend itself deals with the obtaining by Hariçcandra of a son, and the adoption by Viçvāmitra of a son, but the means by which Hariçcandra obtained his are peculiar, as they consist of a promise to sacrifice what he obtains, a process of peculiar inutility, though not altogether unintelligible. Moreover, the hostility against the priest Ajīgarta is seen perhaps in his very name which indicates his beggared condition, and in the names of his sons which cannot be called complimentary, and in his connexion with the Añgirases who were

[1] *Rituallitteratur*, p. 145.

[2] Eggeling, SBE. XLIV. xli–xlv.

[3] Hillebrandt, *Ved. Myth.* iii. 32, which is criticized by Keith, JRAS. 1908, p. 846.

responsible as it would seem for the use of a human head in the ceremony of the piling of the fire altar may perhaps be found, as suggested by Eggeling, the explanation of his appearance in this legend. In that case the legend would show nothing as to a practice of slaying a man at the Rājasūya, and it may possibly be considered a polemic against any form of human sacrifice even at the Agnicayana, worked up into a story in connexion with other motives, one of which at any rate was presumably the dependence of the royal power on the efforts of the priests, and the importance of Viçvāmitra and his family.

The *Aitareya* version claims to follow the text of the *Ṛgveda* and to find in the hymns the situation which it describes in its Gāthās and its prose. The version distinctly describes itself as being of 100 Ṛc verses and Gāthās beside, and this is the form in which it is handed down. The question arises whether this form is its original form.

In the view of Roth[1] the version depends on an older metrical version, whereas Oldenberg[2] thinks that we have in the Gāthās and the prose a real example of the Ākhyāna type which he believes to exist. Two distinct questions are involved in the matter, (1) the relation of the narrative to the *Ṛgveda* and (2) the relation of the prose to the Gāthās.

In the *Ṛgveda* there are references to the case of Çunaḥçepa in the group of hymns associated with his name and in the fifth Maṇḍala. Varuṇa is implored in i. 24. 12 to release the singer, Varuṇa *Çúnaḥçépo yám áhvad gṛbhītáḥ*. In the next verse we read *Çúnaḥçépo hy áhvad gṛbhītás triṣv ādityáṁ drupadéṣu baddháḥ*. In v. 2. 7 occurs *çúnaç cit chépaṁ níditaṁ sahásrād yū́pād amuñcaḥ*, addressed to Agni.

Now neither of these passages seems in any way to accord with the account of the *Aitareya* which has three main points at least, (*a*) the episode of Varuṇa, Hariçcandra, and Rohita; (*b*) the episode of Çunaḥçepa and Ajīgarta; (*c*) the episode of Viçvāmitra's sons and Çunaḥçepa. In the first passage, which purports at least to treat Çunaḥçepa as a figure of the present, there is no hint of anything but that Çunaḥçepa was bound to three pieces of wood (*dru-pada*). That these made up the sacrificial post, a sort of tripod, as suggested by Griffith in his translation, is the best mode of reconciling the *Ṛgveda* and the *Brāhmaṇa*, but it is wholly without any support from the passages where the sacrificial post is mentioned, always as a single post, never as a real tripod. Roth therefore seems clearly justified in taking it that Çunaḥçepa was tied to the three pieces of wood in preparation for martyrdom or punishment, much as Prometheus

[1] *Ind. Stud.* ii. 112 *seq.* *Contra*, Oldenberg, ZDMG. xxxvii. 79–81.

[2] See GGN. 1911, pp. 461 *seq.*, in reply to Keith, JRAS. 1911, pp. 989 *seq.*

was bound to the rock so as to be helpless to avoid the vulture's onslaught.

In v. 2. 7 the reference to a *yūpa* does occur, but the phrase *sahasrāt* at once takes it into the sphere of the metaphorical. Griffith evades this difficulty by taking the sense as 'bound for a thousand' as the price, but, apart from the fact that the figure is inaccurate, the construction is rejected by every consideration of probability and has not even the authority of Sāyaṇa.

Of Hariçcandra, of Rohita, of Ajīgarta, and, in this connexion, of Viçvāmitra we have no information in the *Ṛgveda*. In the face of these facts we can only dismiss the whole narrative as a later invention than the *Ṛgveda*, and ascribe its utilization of the Ṛgvedic verses, 100 in all, to a time when it was desired to find recitations for the Hotṛ at the Rājasūya in connexion with the tale of Çunaḥçepa. In the opinion of Roth[1] the legend grew up into its present content during the period when the collection of the *Ṛgveda* was in process of being carried out, and it was due to it that the series of hymns in the first book to various deities was ascribed to the authorship of Çunaḥçepa. He lays stress on the argument that the arrangement of the hymns in part depends on the theory of authorship. On the other hand, in the view of Aufrecht,[2] the authorships ascribed by the *Anukramaṇī* are compiled from the notices of the Brāhmaṇas, and, while this view is not altogether tenable, it would be impossible to come to any definite conclusion regarding the period of growth of the legend from the order of hymns in the *Saṁhitā* or the attribution to Çunaḥçepa of the hymns in question.

But it is clear from the Gāthās of the *Aitareya* that there came into existence a legend of the saving of Çunaḥçepa and his transfer to the family of Viçvāmitra. This is clearly preserved to us in the text, and from vii. 17. 8 to the end of the verses it runs as a perfectly simple narrative requiring only the names of the speakers to be supplied to make it clear, just as they are supplied in the epic. The *Aitareya*, however, does make one very considerable addition to the verses; it tells us that only half the sons of Viçvāmitra accepted the new position of Çunaḥçepa. This is not told us by the verses, and seems to be inconsistent with the verses. For Viçvāmitra addresses Madhuchandas and all his brothers, and the reply of Madhuchandas is that they accept his wishes, and three times *sarve* is applied to them in the following Gāthās, with never a hint at any division of opinion. Moreover, why should Viçvāmitra have addressed the midmost of his sons to the omission of the older ones, when he wished to place Çunaḥçepa not in the middle—perhaps his most

[1] *Ind. Stud.* ii. 118.

[2] *Aitareya Brāhmaṇa*, p. 422.

natural place as he was the midmost of Ajīgarta's sons—but at the very head? The explanation of the idea of two sets of Viçvāmitra's sons may quite possibly be the fact that Viçvāmitra says to them

> *te vai putrāḥ paçumanto vīravanto bhaviṣyatha*
> *ye mānaṁ me 'nugṛhṇanto vīravantam akarta mām.*

Of course *te* and *ye* do not mean 'those of you who', but 'ye because', but this point may easily have been lost, and have assisted the framing of the fiction of the origin of the Andhras, Pulindas, &c., from the rebellious sons of Viçvāmitra.

It appears to me that, since, in the first place, the prose adds nothing to the verses that is necessary for the sense, and since, in the second place, it contains a notice which is not in harmony with the verses, it is only reasonable to conclude that the prose is later, and that there was once a metrical version in Gāthās of this episode. But can we go further and believe that this episode included in it all the Brāhmaṇa story, including Hariçcandra and Rohita? Roth evidently hesitated on this question, and there seems to me to be no evidence on which we can find a positive answer. The verses in chapters 13 and 15 are quite different from those in chapters 17 and 18, which are full of references to an individual and clear action, while those in the first two chapters are general in the extreme. Indeed, so inappropriate is the exhortation to the king to obtain a son in chapter 13 that it is addressed to Brahmans! There can therefore be only one logical conclusion, that the verses are not chosen out of a narrative made up apropos of Hariçcandra, but are mere general maxims fitted into such a story. The same remark applies to the verses in chapter 15 on the benefits of energy, with the solitary exception that Rohita appears in one verse. This is of course capable of three explanations: (1) the verses may really belong to a narrative of Rohita and Hariçcandra, as Oldenberg urges; (2) the name Rohita for the king's son may be borrowed from an older verse where Rohita denoted some other person altogether; (3) the name may have been put in place of some other word in a verse, in order to fit it more closely into the story. There is no evidence in favour of any of these views which is at all conclusive, and therefore the question must remain undecided whether the verses ever formed part of the narrative of Çunaḥçepa.

It will be seen therefore that the present text is composite, and probably not primitive, and that an Ākhyāna in the sense of Oldenberg cannot be found in it. An Ākhyāna essentially requires to fulfil the type postulated that there should be a prose narrative explaining verses, which give the chief points and moments of the narrative, including especially the speeches of the parties.[1] The verses in chapters 17 and 18 would be an Ākhyāna if they really were accompanied by prose which did explain and connect them, but this as we have seen is not the case. The narrative in the preceding chapters stands in no such relation to the Gāthās; they are gnomic verses, not narrative, not dialogue proper, and they therefore are precisely like the form of literature common later in the *Pañcatantra* and allied literature, but that form of literature is not the Ākhyāna of Oldenberg.

The legend of Çunaḥçepa therefore presents itself in the following stages: (1) Çunaḥçepa is rescued from some great danger and stands as a specimen of the results of divine favour (RV. i. 24. 12, 13; v. 2. 7). (2) This tale is developed into the narrative of the proposal to sacrifice Çunaḥçepa and his rescue and adoption by Viçvāmitra, the latter being a very important element in the narrative. This stage is represented by the Gāthās in the *Aitareya Brāhmaṇa*, vii. 17 and 18.

(3) This story is brought to completion by the narrative of Hariçcandra and Rohita which explains the reason for the intended sacrifice of Çunaḥçepa, as it appears in the *Aitareya Brāhmaṇa*, vii. 13–16. It is impossible to say whether this narrative is presupposed by the Gāthās and whether it ever existed in Gāthā form. It is of course obvious that some reason must have existed for the offering of Çunaḥçepa, but that may merely have been an ordinary tale of the performance of the human sacrifice and not a tale of the extraordinary and almost ludicrous action of Hariçcandra and Nārada. Very probably the two stories of Hariçcandra and his son and Çunaḥçepa have been allowed to mingle, as they seem to belong to different strata of tradition, the first falling among the many stories of the sacrifice of children among the Semitic and other races, and the latter reprobating the practice of human sacrifice as a custom, perhaps one specially favoured by the Añgiras family, which was opposed by other Vedic families.

The Hariçcandra and Çunaḥçepa legend, as we possess it, has no trace of hostility between Vasiṣṭha and Viçvāmitra, who appear amicably as Brahman and Hotṛ, at the sacrifice; it is left for later texts from the *Harivaṅça* onwards to find in the legend of Triçañku, which is a pale reflection of the fact of Çunaḥçepa's binding to these *drupadas*, an account of the growth of contention between the two sages.[2] But to these legends no possible faith can be given. What is, however, of interest is that we already find here traces of the royal character[3] attributed to Viçvāmitra,

[1] Cf. Pischel, *Oriental. Literaturen*, pp. 167, 168; for a criticism see Keith, JRAS. 1911, pp. 979 *seq.*; 1912, pp. 428 *seq.*

[2] See Roth, *Ind. Stud.* ii. 121–123; Keith JRAS. 1914, pp. 118–126.

[3] PB. xxi. 12. 2; *Vedic Index*, 310–312.

since the young Çunaḥçepa is said to succeed to the lordship of the Jahnus as well as the divine lore of the Gāthinas. Without accepting the view that this idea of Viçvāmitra is primitive, it is clearly to be connected with the mention of Viçvāmitra as a king of the Jahnus in the *Pañcaviñça Brāhmaṇa*.

According to the ritual as given in the *Āçvalāyana Çrauta Sūtra*[1] the sacrifice begins with a Pavitra Agniṣṭoma before the Phālgunī full moon, followed by a year in which the four-monthly rites are duly performed. Then follow the Abhiṣecanīya and the Daçapeya. The former is an Ukthya with the Bṛhat as Pṛṣṭha Stotra and both Sāmans (i. e. the Rathantara in the Pavamāna), and it is after the Marutvatīya on that day has been recited that the story of Çunaḥçepa is narrated to the king surrounded by his children and ministers. This is followed by seven days of Saṁsṛpeṣṭis, and then by the Daçapeya. Then in the bright half of Vaiçākha occurs the Keçavapanīya, an Atirātra with the Bṛhat as Pṛṣṭha. Then in the bright half of Aṣāḍha the Dvyaha called Vyuṣṭi, the first day an Agniṣṭoma, the second an Atirātra with all the Stomas. Finally a month later comes the Kṣatrasya Dhṛti, an Agniṣṭoma.

Much the same account with detailed differences is given by the *Çāṅkhāyana Çrauta Sūtra*[2] which however interpolates a Sautrāmaṇī before the Keçavapanīya. The *Baudhāyana Çrauta Sūtra*[3] also follows the same general outline, but places the narrative of Çunaḥçepa during the cooking of an *odana*.[4] Similarly the *Āpastamba Çrauta Sūtra*[5] and the *Kātyāyana Çrauta Sūtra*[6] include the episode in their texts. There is no mention of it in the account in the *Kauçika Sūtra*.[7]

The *Aitareya* confines its whole matter to the solitary Abhiṣecanīya day and adds a new form to those of the Adhvaryu texts. Hence the Abhiṣeka is called the Punarabhiṣeka (viii. 5) and an account is given in vii. 19–viii. 4 of the drink of the king on the occasion of the Abhiṣeka and of the litany of the day. Then comes an alternative form (viii. 12–20) of the Abhiṣeka, an account of those so anointed (viii. 21–23), and the text concludes (viii. 24–28) with the Purohita and his functions. It may be taken as certain that it was from the Aitareya that the Adhvaryu texts took their account of the Çunaḥçepa episode: all of them mention the response of the Adhvaryu, and Āpastamba characteristically fills out the story by allowing the Ākhyāna to have over a 100 or 1,000 verses, possibly

[1] ix. 3 and 4; Weber, *Rājasūya*, pp. 119–123. The plural *Rājasūyāḥ* clearly indicates various forms as possible.

[2] xv. 12–16.

[3] xii.

[4] 15 and 16.

[5] xviii. 19. 10.

[6] xv. 5. 1.

[7] xvii; Weber, *Rājasūya*, pp. 140–142; Caland's view (*Altind. Zaub.* p. 40, n. 6) of *sarvasvajainam* (xvii. 18) as containing a Vṛddhi form of *ji* is quite impossible.

by a tenfold recitation. The ceremony in the Aitareya (viii. 5–11) is in many respects less elaborate than that of the Yajurveda, but a conclusion as to a temporal relation would be risky.

§ 7. Language, Style, and Metre.

A. *Language of the Mantras.*

The two Brāhmaṇas present in essentials a common language, a living prose considerably anterior to the stage of the language presented in the grammar of Pāṇini. There are many distinctions in the use of phrases in the two works, and even between the different parts of the *Aitareya*, but these are of minor importance. On the other hand, the Mantra material must be carefully distinguished; it is comparatively brief in extent, and falls into two distinct divisions. The first of these is Ṛgvedic citations, which are normally short, merely the first few words (Pratīka) of the verse meant being alluded to, though both texts to emphasize a point at issue do not hesitate to cite the whole of a verse. The second division is that of the prose formulae and the metrical formulae, which appear in a limited degree, and in the case of the *Aitareya* the Gāthās, of which there are a considerable number, mainly in the story of Çunaḥçepa, but also in the account of the Agnihotra, the great consecration, &c. There is no reasonable ground to doubt that this material is normally, if not absolutely always, older than the prose text, and it is certain that it yields a very large number of unusual and archaic forms.[1] Thus the Gāthās of the Çunaḥçepa episode are perfectly clearly from their content older than the prose text appended, and in their forms they show a prodigality of rarities compared with the prose text. The *Kauṣītaki* in keeping with the brevity of its style quotes very few verses indeed, and of these one (xxvii. 1) has long been treated by the editors as prose, and a similar fate has befallen some verses in the *Aitareya* (viii. 25 and 27).

Here and there in the prose of the account of the Purohita in the *Aitareya* (viii. 25, 27) can be detected signs of a metrical account, from which the prose has freely borrowed, but there is no possibility of recovering more than an occasional line of such verses. Prose Mantras are not numerous or important with the exception of those regarding the actual cutting up of the victim which are given in the *Aitareya* (ii. 6 and 7) with greater completeness than in the *Kauṣītaki*.

The forms in Ṛgvedic verses need not here be noted, but in the other Mantra material mention should be made of the verbal forms *smasi* (AB.

[1] Cf. Keith, *Taittirīya Saṁhitā*, I. clxi.

vii. 18. 3); *vidmasi* (ib. 7); *sthana* (ib. 17. 7); *çere* (ib. 15. 2); and of the infinitives and subjunctives *abhiçastāt* and *apaharāt* (v. 30. 11) in a main clause and *kṛṇavātha* after *yat* (ii. 7). In AB. vii. 15. 3 the use of *carāti* with a number of presents is regarded as suspicious by the commentators, and Aufrecht goes so far as to suggest a metrical ground for the change, but the passage really allows or even requires a futural form. In vii. 17. 6 *jñapayā* is regarded normally as an imperative with *a* lengthened, but this sense is very doubtful. On the other hand, the prose of the direction for the cutting up of the victim provides a large number of examples of the use of °*tāt* as an imperative ending of the second person, including *nidhattāt*, *gamayatāt*, *anvavasṛjatāt*, *āchyatāt*, *utkhidatāt*, *kṛṇutāt*, *uccyāvayatāt*, *khanatāt*, *sammṛjatāt*. This passage (AB. ii. 6) presents also the rare form *vārayadhvāt* for °*tāt*. In the second plural we have in AB. vii. 17. 7 *çṛṇotana*. The AB. has the irregular optative *vṛñjīyam* (cf. *avapadyeyam* in viii. 23) and the impossible *ajāyethaḥ* (viii. 15).

The aorist is represented by *akarta* (vii. 18. 5) and *adarçuḥ* (vii. 17. 3) for which the Çāñkhāyana version has *adrākṣuḥ*, and perhaps by *alapsata* (vii. 17. 3).

The second future appears in *upetā* (vii. 18. 7), a variant of *upaitā* rather than a second plural, for which the context presents no legitimate use.

The perfect appears in *çuçruma* (vii. 15), a use which is never in the first person common and in Pāṇini is proscribed in normal cases.

The desiderative yields the form *didāsitha* (viii. 21. 10) for which the *Çatapatha Brāhmaṇa* substitutes *manda āsitha*, but which the *Çāñkhāyana Çrauta Sūtra* confirms. It also gives *prasiṅkṣāṇi* (after *no*) in KB. xxvii. 1 (Aufrecht[1] conjectures *sisakṣāṇi*).

Most interesting of all, perhaps, is the colloquial form *yām-ak-i* found in the last cited passage of the *Kauṣītaki*, which is a diminutive form of the verbal form *yāmi*.

The constructions of note are *purā nābhyā apiçasaḥ* (AB. ii. 6), and *mā rāviṣṭa . . . ned vas toke tanaye ravitā ravat* (ii. 7) where the first verb is from the root = 'cut', and the second from that = 'cry' and where the use of the negatives is of interest. In AB. v. 30 is found the use, frequent later, of the optative in similes: *yathā ha vā sthūrinaikena yāyāt . . . evaṁ yanti*, and the regular verse use of the perfect in narrative in *apa yo jahāra* (v. 30. 11).

The normal forms offer some of interest such as *janāsaḥ* in AB. v. 30. 6, and the very curious form in AB. ii. 6 *praçasā bāhū çalā doṣaṇī kaçyapevāñçāchidre çroṇī kavaṣorū parṇasrekāṣṭhīvantā*. These forms are very

[1] ZDMG. xxxiv. 175, 176; Keith, JRAS. 1915 pp. 502, 503.

striking in their **antiquity** and show [illegible] that the prose Mantras are not recent. The Gāthās, however, yield ([illegible]B. vii. 18. 9) the remarkable form *Gāthinām* which the occurrence of *Gā*[illegible]*thināḥ* just before leads us to recognize as a real genitive plural in *ām*, for which, as for the duals in *ā* of the prose Mantras, the Brāhmaṇa text offers nothing parallel.[1]

The case uses are not remarkabl[illegible]e for novelty: the root *sthā* is found in close proximity with the locative in the sense of 'adhere to', 'accept' (AB. vii. 18. 3), and with the dative [illegible] 'acknowledge' (ib. 8). The ablative with *vṛ* has the natural sense of 'prefer to' in AB. vii. 17. 3. In AB. vii. 17. 7 *saṁjñānāneṣu vai brūyāt* would present difficulties, but *brūyāt* occurs in the ÇÇS. and the conjecture *s*[illegible]*aṁjñānam* is essential as the form *saṁjñānāneṣu* is quite impossible.

B. *Language of the Prose.*

In the case of the Ṛgvedic verses cited not rarely the prose repeats them in the text while explaining the verse. It is impossible to regard the forms thus quoted as being valid examples of what the prose would use, and the point though obvious is not unimportant as it has in some measure misled Liebich in his account of the irregularities, i. e. deviations from Pāṇini, of the *Aitareya Brāhmaṇa*, although he himself quite properly treats the Gāthās as *sui generis*, and older than the prose. Thus we must not credit the Brāhma[illegible]a with *mumugdhi* (iii. 19. 17) for it comes straight from the verse RV. x[illegible] 73. 11. Nor is *saṁçiçādhi* (i. 13. 28) any value for the Brāhmaṇa as it is from RV. viii. 42. 3. Again in ii. 2. 21 we have *kṛdhī na ūrdhvāñ carat*[illegible]*āya jīvase* explained in the identic words, but with *caraṇāya*; are we to believe that this shows that *kṛdhī* was a form approved by the Brāhmaṇa for prose? The answer is clearly no, but that the only word chang[illegible]ed in the version is the obscure one *carathāya* which is made simple by *caraṇa* being substituted, *kṛdhī* being far too well known to need explanation, and the Brāhmaṇa not aiming at a philological commentary. The same phenomenon meets us again in iii. 22. 4 where *yad īm uçmasi kartave karat tat* (RV. x. 74. 6 *d*) is explained as *yad evaitad avocāmākarat tat*; whatever we may think of this version it seems that the *Aitareya* took the text as *kartave 'karat*, but in any case to take *akarat* as a Brāhmaṇa form on the strength of this passage cannot be justified. Another illustration of the importance of discrimination is to be seen in ii. 2. 5, when *yad ūrdhvas tiṣṭhā draviṇeha dhattāt yad vā kṣayo mātur asyā upasthe* (RV. iii. 8. 1) becomes in free rendering

[1] In PB. xviii. 1[illegible] *bharatām prati*[illegible]*janāḥ brāhmaṇāḥ* probably *bharatām* can be taken as meant, governed by the effect of *prati* in the compound.

yadi ca tiṣṭhāsi yadi ca çayyāsai draviṇam evāsmāsu dhattāt. It is idle to treat these as Brāhmaṇa forms; it would else be incomprehensible that the forms should never occur in any Brāhmaṇa passage proper: the use of a subjunctive with *yadi* and the use of the imperative in *tāt* are not found elsewhere in the *Aitareya*, but they show that the compiler of the text knew the correct full forms of the subjunctive, and could replace them in the text.

Of the forms that are really characteristic of the Brāhmaṇa prose the most conform, of course, to the norms of Pāṇini; there are certain regular deviations, and also a small number of forms which cannot be regarded as anything but wholly irregular, and open perhaps to suspicion as being mere errors of a tradition which allowed almost any irregularity in the sacred text.

(1) Euphonic Combination.

1. The Sandhi of *au* is *āv* before vowels other than *ū* and *ā* before *ū* in both Brāhmaṇas as also in the *Aitareya Āraṇyaka* (i. 3. 5; 4. 2; 5. 1; iii. 2. 4, 6): so the AB. has *açvinā udajayatām açvināv āçnuvātām* (iv. 8. 4); *açvināv indram* (iv. 8. 2); *açvinā ūcatuḥ* (vii. 16); *dvā ubhayoḥ* (viii. 5). The KB. has *barhiṣmantā utsṛjati* (v. 7); *tā uktau* (vii. 2); *vyūḍhasamūḍhā upayanti* (xxvii. 7); *devā upāhvayante* (viii. 7), &c.

2. The Sandhi of *ā* with *ṛ* is *ă*; thus in AB. *prathama ṛk*, iii. 35; *pita ṛbhūn*, vi. 12; *yatha ṛṣabham*, vi. 18, 21, 22; *yatharṣi*, ii. 4; iv. 26; in the KB. there is only *neṣṭa ṛtvijām*, xxviii. 3. The ÇÇS. i. 4. 5 has,[1] however, *praçāsta ātmanā* and it is conceivable that in *vacasa ubhe*, KB. xxvi. 14, we have a case of Sandhi of *ā* = *a*, for the MS. M reads *vacasā*.

3. The Sandhi of *a* with *ṛ* is *ar*, but sometimes *ṛ* stands; thus *ca ṛṣayaḥ*, AB. i. 27; ii. 1, 13; iii. 25; vi. 17, 32; *asya ṛcam*, iii. 17; *nāma ṛk*, iii. 23; *Çrautarṣiḥ*, vii. 1; *sarparṣiḥ*, vi. 1. On the other hand, as Aufrecht[2] points out, in the Gāthā (vii. 17) *Bharatarṣabha* is written but must be pronounced *Bharatarṣabha*.

4. The effect of *r* in lingualizing *n* is seen in AB. i. 13 and 30 in the phrase *brahmaivāsmā etat purogavam akar ṇa vai.* The use is very strange and Sāyaṇa does not comment on it. Parallel to this silence of Sāyaṇa's is his silence regarding *mahāṇagnī* in i. 30, which is read by the

[1] See Hillebrandt, *Çāṅkhāyana Çrauta Sūtra*, i. 246.

[2] *Aitareya Brāhmaṇa*, p. 427; Weber (*Ind. Stud.* ix. 308, 309) exaggerates the frequency of the use of *a* + *ṛ*.

great weight of authority, though not by the Bibl. Ind. ed. and the Ānand. ed. (which admits it as read in five of its MSS.), but in the latter case the lingualizing has no excuse, and is really parallel to the forms *niṇyuḥ*, a *v. l.* in KB. xxx. 6, and *pariṇiṇyuḥ*, a *v. l.* in xxviii. 2.

5. In *yaças kīrtim* in AB. vii. 23 and 24 the retention of *s* is noteworthy, but the phrase is taken from a prose Mantra and proves nothing for the Brāhmaṇa which does not use that Sandhi elsewhere. Similarly the forms *urūkam* and *bahura* in AB. ii. 7 and 18 cited by Aufrecht[1] for *l* being in place of *r* occur only in Mantras. But the other cases cited by him, *romāṇi*, ii. 9, and *çithirāṇi*, iii. 31, are clear cases.

6. The lengthening of final vowels of particles survives in the AB. in *atī tu tam arjātai*, iii. 42, where emphasis is meant; *vy ū muñcante*, vi. 23, and *nī vīva nardet*, vi. 32, where doubt as to the reading is needless. KB. has nothing parallel. Internally the lengthening is found in *pratyavarūhya*, AB. viii. 9; *parīçeṣa*, vii. 5, and in a compound in *uttaravedīnābhi*, i. 28, which contrasts with *vedi* regularly in the text. In KB. xxiii. 5 *pratīvedram* occurs.

7. The forms *avākṣam*, AB. i. 28, and *enkṣva*, viii. 9, show *k* for *t* and are anomalous. The first is a verbal play on *vāc*,[2] the second possibly an incorrect restoration of a Prākritism for *entsva*.

8. In AB. iv. 17 *paryāṇa* is found, and in iv. 5 *paryat* in some MSS. In KB. xvi. 5 *paryajet* is a *v. l.*

(2) Accidence.

1. From **stems** in **a** is found in AB. iv. 15. 1 *stomebhiḥ*. This is an extraordinary form for prose.

2. From **stems** in **ā** the ablative and genitive are as in other Brāhmaṇas found in *ai*; but the normal forms in *āḥ* also occur; thus in the gen. *apūtāyai*, AB. vii. 27, but *pathyāyāḥ svasteḥ*, i. 9; and the abl. *asyāḥ*, i. 23; *pratiṣṭhāyāḥ*, iii. 14. So the KB. has *jīrṇāyai* (abl.) xviii. 7; *vidyāyai* (abl. or gen.), vi. 10; *vidyāyai* (gen.), vi. 11, and *etasyai* similarly.

The AB. has in vi. 15 the apparently contracted instrumental *jagatkāmyā*, which is a very rare form in prose. Aufrecht[3] cites a parallel *mitrakṛtyā* in iii. 4, but this is naturally taken as from *mitrakṛti*; KB. has no parallel form of this kind.

3. The **stems** in **i** and **ī** present as usual *ai* as the normal ablative and genitive form, but not the exclusive form of ablative and genitive. So *abhibhūtyai rūpam*, AB. viii. 2; *gāyatryai ca jagatyai ca* (gen.), iv. 27;

[1] *Op. cit.* p. 428; cf. Wackernagel, *Altind. Gramm.* i. 216.

[2] Böhtlingk, BKSGW. 15 Dec. 1900, p. 425, denies even this.

[3] *Aitareya Brāhmaṇa*, p. 428.

tatyai, vi. 20; but *gāyatryāḥ, jagatyāḥ* (gen.), vi. 32; *nirṛtyāḥ*, iv. 10. The KB. has *prajātyai* (gen.), iv. 6; v. 4; xv. 4; *abhikrāntyai*, viii. 2; *apracutyai*, xxii. 1; *bṛhatyai* (abl.), xxiv. 5; but according to Lindner in xii. 1 *iṣṭyāḥ* (abl.), but this is a very doubtful reading. In vi. 10 and 11 *trayyai* is abl. or gen. and gen. respectively.

4. The **datives of stems** in ĭ always have *ai* in both Brāhmaṇas; as in *dhṛtyai, guptyai, abhijityai, apahatyai, avaruddhyai, āptyai, upāptyai, saṁtatyai, samaṣṭyai* and others; rarer forms are *asaṁmugdhyai*, KB. xxiii. 4; *spṛṣṭyai*, xxiv. 8.

5. **Stems** in ĭ when feminine vary as to the use of the feminine endings in cases other than the dative; thus the AB. has as gen. *svasteḥ*, i. 9, as abl. *vedeḥ*, vi. 3; vii. 27; *devayonyai*, iii. 19; and as loc. not only *āhutyām, kīrtyām, yonyām*, but also *iṣṭau*, (*svayonau*, KB. xxv. 8); while *bhūmyām* in viii. 8 is followed by *bhūmau* in viii. 9. The KB. has *ātmasaṁskṛteḥ* and *prāṇasaṁskṛteḥ* (abl.), xx. 3; *çriyaḥ* (gen.), xxiv. 9; *çriyaḥ* (abl.) with *çriyām* (loc.) in iii. 17; *çriyām*, xviii. 9; xxix. 5; *vedyām*, iii. 9, and *apracyutyām*, xxv. 7 and often.

6. Other abnormalities in the ī declension are few; *tiraçcīḥ* (nom.) in AB. iv. 25. 10 has a parallel in vi. 32. 3 and *iṣṭīḥ* in KB. vi. 15. In AB. ii. 4. 2 *āpriyaḥ* is the nom. of *āprī* as elsewhere; in iii. 27 *samāvajjāmībhyām* and *samāvajjāmibhiḥ* both occur. In KB. v. 7 *patnyaḥ* is accusative in all MSS.; *akṣarapaṅktayaḥ*, xvi. 8; but *paṅktīḥ* nom. in xviii. 3; *dyāvāpṛthivī* in AB. iv. 27 is traditional; *dyāvā* there seems used as a nom. fem.

7. **Stems** in ŭ yield only *iṣvai saṁçityai*, AB. i. 27; *tanvaḥ* as acc. in AB. i. 24 and ii. 4.

8. Of **consonantal stems** may be noted the fact that *vichandāḥ* is used as a neuter in AB. v. 4, and that in iii. 10 *peças* and *peça* alternate as bases, indicating the constant tendency of confusion between them. Similarly, while in KB. xxx. 5 the age of the cow and man contemplated by Aitaça are fixed at *çatāyus* and *sahasrāyus*, in AB. vi. 33 the terms are *çatāyu* and *sahasrāyu*. In AB. viii. 17 *āpaḥ* is as often accusative.

9. In **stems** in an the locative has either *an* or *ani* on no clear principle. Thus, beside *ahan* (especially with adjectives) as in *samāne 'han*, iii. 47; *caturviṅçe 'han*, vi. 23; *parame vyoman, ātman, çīrṣan, sāman*, occurs *ahani*, iv. 31, 32; v. 2. So the KB. has *ātman*, iii. 7; v. 4; vii. 1; ix. 6, and often, especially in the phrase *ātman dhā*; *ahan*, ii. 8; xxv. 9; xxvi. 7, and elsewhere, but also *ahani*; *çīrṣan*, ii. 8; *parvan parvan* (*bis*), xxiii. 4. But beside *ātman* occurs *brahmaṇi*.

The neuter occurs in the masculine form in AB. iv. 2, when *bhrātṛvyahā* is applied to the Sāman.

10. From **stems** in **añc** the one form of note is the neuter *parāñ* as

often, in AB. iii. 46 (*ter*). The proposal of Liebich to take it as an adverb in AB. viii. 28 in the phrase *parāñ jighyati* is not, however, probable. Both Brāhmaṇas use *parāñcin* as well as *parāñc*.

11. The **superlative** with double ending occurs in *baliṣṭhatama* in AB. iii. 46, whereas *baliṣṭha* alone appears in ii. 36 and vii. 16. Noteworthy are the comparatives *upāptatarāṇi*, KB. xv. 5; *abhidhānatare*, xiii. 5.

12. In **numerals** occur the irregularities *trayastriṅçatyā*, AB. v. 32; *ṣaṭtriṅçatam ekapadāḥ*, vii. 1. Here may also be noted the readings of the MSS., *catuḥṣaṣṭiṁ kavacina āsuḥ*, AB. iii. 48, and *parṇaçaraḥ ṣaṣṭis triṇi ca çatāny āhṛtya*, vii. 2, where the base *parṇaçar* is very unusual and where the syntax is impossible.[1] Weber naturally suggests the necessary alteration in each case, and no doubt this is correct. The KB. has *dvāpañcāçyau* in xviii. 3 = 51st and 52nd as usual, and *saptatim anuṣṭubhaḥ saptatiṁ paṅktīḥ* as a nom.

13. The **pronoun** shows few anomalies. *yuvam* occurs in AB. ii. 22. 10, and *asmāka* in *kaḥ svit so 'smākāsti vīraḥ*, vii. 27. 2, where there is no metrical necessity.[2] But elsewhere *āvām* only appears. *enat* occurs as a nominative in AB. vii. 22: *tad enat prītaṁ kṣatrād gopāyati*, and also in KB. xxii. 1: *tasmād enau prathamau çasyete*; in both cases of course perhaps erroneously.[3]

14. In the **classes of verbs** the chief irregularities are the use of *tāṣṭi*, AB. ii. 4. 13, in an etymology of Tvaṣṭṛ as a verb of the second class; the same is the treatment of *kṣeti*, v. 21. 2, 17, and *parikṣeti*, vi. 32. 11, 14. Possibly here must be reckoned *prajighyati* in AB. viii. 28, but Böhtlingk reads *jigāti* and Liebich[4] desires to take the form as a third plural of *hi* as a third class verb. *nihnavate* in AB. i. 26 is a mere misreading for *nihnuvate*, but *nihnave* occurs in a Gāthā in vii. 17, where Liebich[5] would read *nihnuve*.

15. The **omission of the augment in the imperfect** is fairly common in the *Aitareya* and is also found in the *Kauṣītaki*. The examples are *īkṣata*, AB. iii. 21. 4; 45. 8; *nyubjan*, vii. 30. 3; *anvavayuḥ*, vi. 14. 10; *prajanayan*, ii. 38; *pratyuttabhnuvan*, iv. 18. 5, 6; *saṁsthāpayan*, ii. 31. 4; *visraṅsata*, iii. 27. 1; *viharanta*, ii. 36. 2. Two other cases are not real examples, namely in vii. 1 for *uccakrāmat* must be read *uccakrāma*, and in iii. 30 for *vāci kalpayiṣan* must be replaced *avācikalpayiṣan*. In one case the augment is wholly misplaced, *udaprapatat* in iii. 33, where, however, Aufrecht's

[1] Böhtlingk, BKSGW. 15 Dec. 1900, p. 414, insists on reading *catuḥṣaṣṭiḥ* and *ṣaṣṭim*, on the ground that Sāyaṇa ignores the irregularities; but this is not at all conclusive.

[2] Böhtlingk, BKSGW. 15 Dec. 1900, p. 419, reads *asmāko*.

[3] Böhtlingk, *ibid*. p. 418, reads *etat*.

[4] *Pāṇini*, p. 76.

[5] *Op. cit.* p. 77.

correction *udapatat* seems essential.[1] The KB. has *vimadan*, xxii. 6 (*v. l.*); *pratyudkramata*, xxiii. 4 (*v. l.*); *apaspṛṇvata*, xxiv. 3; *naṁnamuḥ*, as a *v. l.* in xii. 1 (*anaṁnamuḥ*, AB. ii. 20).

16. **In the present indicative** the AB. has the common forms *īçe*, i. 16. 4; 30. 3; and *duhe*, vi. 3. 2; it has also *çere* (for *çerate*) in v. 28, a form occurring also in a Gāthā in vii. 15. *anusmasi* in AB. iv. 5. 5 is a very odd form for prose, though it occurs with *vidmasi* in Gāthās. In v. 2 the KB. has *īçe*.

17. **In the imperfect indicative** there are more anomalies. The tendency to transfer roots to the first class is seen in *upaprāyata*, iii. 39. 2; *abhyahanat*, iv. 3. 2; *açayat*, iii. 15. 1. From the third class come *adīdet*, iii. 34. 1, in an etymology and therefore not to be pressed; *abhyasuṣavuḥ*, iii. 32. 3. In the ninth class *gṛh* has *bh* in *pratyagṛbhṇan*, vi. 35. 8, 9; *samagṛbhṇāt*, iii. 26. 2; 27. 1; *upasamagṛbhṇāt*, 26. 2. The KB. has *ahṛṇāt* in a doubtful passage, xxiv. 1. The AB. text has the extraordinary form *apāhata*, iv. 25. 3, for the proper *apāghnata* found elsewhere in the AB. In AB. viii. 15 *ajāyethāḥ* in a quasi-Mantra is impossible. In v. 11 *praupyanta* occurs awkwardly as a passive for *prāvapan*.

18. **In the optative** the tendency to carry over the roots to the first class is seen in *prāṇet*, *abhyapānet*, AB. ii. 21. 3; *pratirundhet*, vi. 34. 4, and in *mimet*, KB. x. 1. In AB. viii. 15 the most improbable Mantra forms *vṛñjīyam* and in viii. 23 the prose *avapadyeyam* occur. Both Brāhmaṇas agree in the use of *ī* for *e* in the verbs of the first conjugation, especially in the causative form; the occurrences are *āhvayīta*, AB. iv. 7. 3; *vyāhvayīta*, iii. 19. 10; vi. 21. 12; *kāmayīta*, iii. 45. 7; *āpayīta*, KB. iv. 4; *kalpayīta*, xix. 10. They also agree in the use of *īyuḥ* for *iyuḥ* in AB. v. 9. 5; KB. xxx. 6. The precative proper is seen in *bhakṣīṣṭa*, AB. vii. 18; *udyāsam*, KB. xxviii. 1. In AB. viii. 28 *jāgriyāt* is read for *jāgṛyāt*, which Böhtlingk insists on reading.

19. **Of the subjunctive** there are a considerable number of forms, but those in the KB. are in comparison few. Those in the prose of AB. are *tiṣṭhāsi*, ii. 2, which is, however, as noted above, merely a paraphrase of *tiṣṭhāḥ* in the RV.; *prajānātha*, i. 7; *juhavātha*, v. 32; *asat*, ii. 37; 11. 12; 13. 8; iii. 43. 6; viii. 1. 5; 4. 5; *atikrāmāt*, i. 24; *pratitiṣṭhāt*, iv. 25; *gachān*, ii. 12; *nirhaṇan*, viii. 6; *çayāsai*, ii. 2; *arjātai*, iii. 42; *saṁgachātai*, i. 24; *saṁtiṣṭhātai*, viii. 9; *haratai*,[2] v. 34; *asyāthāḥ*, vi. 30; for *arjasi*, iii. 42, Aufrecht suggests *arjāsi*.[3] To this list, from which the Gāthā forms are omitted, should be added *adan*, viii. 22. 4. The KB. has *asat*, viii. 9;

[1] Böhtlingk, p. 416, prefers the view of Weber, *Ind. Stud.* ix. 270, °*apravata*. *prajanayan* renders *çaṁsan* and is prob. injunctive.

[2] Böhtlingk, BKSGW. 14 Dec. 1900, p. 414, restores *harātai*.

[3] Or *arjasva*, Böhtlingk, p. 416.

xxvii. 6; *vañchān*, xxv. 15; *udyachāte*, xviii. 5; *pravartantai*,[1] viii. 5; *asataḥ*, viii. 8.

20. The **injunctive** is rare in its use; it is normally used with *mā*, *bibhīta*, ii. 16; *yātayan*, i. 13. 12 (the only imperfects); *anuvocaḥ*, *pracārīḥ*, i. 13. 12; *vadiṣuḥ*, ii. 31. 4; *parigāta*, vi. 33; *bhūt*, vi. 1; *hiṅsīḥ*, KB. xii. 3; *mandhvam*, xxx. 5; *anupravadiṣma*, AB. ii. 15. 13; *anuvādiṣma*, v. 22. 5, where the difference of quantity in *vad'* is noteworthy. Where the clause is positive the only probable case is *anuparyāguḥ*, iii. 28. 1, and *prajanayan*, ii. 38. 8, merely represents *çaṅsan* in the Mantra.

21. The **aorists** are numerous and mainly regular; the following are in point of form noteworthy; *ayāṅsi*, AB. ii. 40. 3; *ajñāsam*, vi. 34. 3; *pratyarautsi*, vi. 34. 4; *asakthāḥ*, vi. 33. 4; *ajñata*, vii. 14. 5, 7; *prāvṛkṣīḥ*, vii. 26. 6; *adrukṣaḥ*, viii. 23. 10 (perhaps a misreading); strange are *ajagrabhaiṣam*, vi. 35. 21; *paryagrahaiṣam*, vi. 24. 16,[2] in which the use of *ai* for *ī* is strange, while the use of *bh* for *h* is paralleled by the imperfect forms noted above. In AB. i. 20. 3 *nābheḥ* is given as a derivation for *nābhi*: it cannot really be regarded as a genuine form for the AB., and the sense is uncertain. The KB. has *asicāmahai*, vi. 1, which is an impossible form. *āpati*, xiv. 2, may be noted. In the earlier part of the AB., while the irregular forms common later do not occur freely, there are found *akar*, i. 13. 4; 30. 5; ii. 38. 5; *akrata*, i. 23. 1; ii. 23. 3; iii. 33. 3; *adrāk*, i. 6. 11; in vi. 24. 13 *akar* by its parallelism with *avadhīḥ* is shown to be second person. In accordance with its later character is the fact that KB. shows hardly any of these short forms of the aorist in *s* without *ī* (Whitney, *Sansk. Gramm.* § 888).

22. The **perfect** is not very common in the AB. i–v but is frequent thereafter and is very common in the KB. Rare or unusual forms are very rare; but the AB. has *sam . . . vidre*, i. 17. 15; *saṁjabhruḥ*, i. 18. 1; *apinahyuḥ*, vi. 1[3]; *niniyoja*,[4] vii. 16. 1; the last phrase is impossible; and *āmantrayām āsa*, vii. 14. 8; 17. 7 (where the ÇÇS. has *cakre*). Further, for the absurd *prāpat*, vii. 14. 8, *prāpa* is necessary, and for *uccakrāmat*, vii. 1, *uccakrāma*. The AB. has *dādhāra*, iv. 12. 8; v. 4. 15; 5. 3; 6. 12 and often; *bibhāya*, v. 25. 17; *dīdhāya*, i. 28. 9; ii. 40. 2; 41. 4; iii. 8. 2; iv. 11. 8.

23. Of **participial** forms are noteworthy *çocatyaḥ*, AB. iii. 36; *vadatyaḥ*, vi. 27. 10; 32. 3; *siṣāsatyaḥ*, iv. 17. 2.[5] In AB. vii. 16 *nihçāna* is recorded, but is clearly wrong. Of perfect participles are noteworthy beside *cakruṣe*,

[1] Cf. *karātai* above; Whitney, *Sansk. Gr.* § 787.

[2] Cf. Böhtlingk, ZDMG. liv. 511, who reads *agṛbhāyann eṣām* (cf. TB. i. 8. 27) and *paryagrahīṣam*.

[3] *apinahuḥ* is read by Böhtlingk, BKSGW. 15 Dec. 1900, p. 414.

[4] *niyuyoja*, Weber, *Ind. Stud.* ix. 315.

[5] Böhtlingk restores the missing *n*.

AB. v. 24. 3, *ohuṣī*, KB. xxvii. 1; *sasṛjānam*, AB. iv. 28. 1; *vividānaḥ*, v. 28. 5; *riricānaḥ*, KB. x. 3; *vijigyānāḥ*, AB. iv. 31. 1; *abhiṣiṣicāna*, viii. 6. 11. In *gṛbhītaḥ*, AB. ii. 1, *bh* appears for *h*.

24. The **infinitive** in *tum* occurs in both texts, but not freely; that in *toḥ* is common in the AB. and occurs in the KB. That in *tavai* is found in three forms only; the AB. has *etavai*, v. 15; *startavai*, ii. 6, 35; iii. 7; the KB. *uddhartavai*, iv. 14. The AB. has *āsade*, i. 29. 7, but *purā* . . . *apiçasaḥ*, ii. 6, is only in a Mantra. One irregular form is *vyapanayitum*, vii. 5, which Böhtlingk[1] corrects on the ground that Sāyaṇa does not note it, but without adequate ground.

25. The **gerunds** and **gerundives** show few new forms; Weber[2] cites as cases of the long vowel for the short *udūhya*, vii. 6; *nirūhya*, vii. 5; *anūtsāram*, iii. 45, but in the last case Aufrecht's correction *anutsāram* is obviously correct, and in the two former *ūh* may be the root, not *vah*. *pratyavarūhya*, viii. 9, is different but doubtful. As usual there are many cases of the gerund in *am*, of which *nyūṅkham*, KB. xxx. 5; *pratīsāram*, xxiii. 5; *abhigrāsam*, xxii. 8; *yathopapādam*, xxv. 10, may be noted. The gerundive is seen in *çaṅstavya*, ii. 32; iii. 24, 35–37; iv. 2, like *çaṅstvā*, iii. 20. 2, where, however, the correct reading is *çastvā*. The KB. has *pratiṣṭhānīyaḥ*, xvi. 7. To *yathākāmaprayāpyaḥ* in AB. vii. 29 Haug and Weber accord an active sense which is impossible.

26. The **second future** appear in a large variety of forms without irregularities. The first future shows the unique form *klapsyete*, AB. ii. 26. 4.

27. The **passive** is marked by two strange forms in the AB., *pariçriyete*, i. 29. 21, and *pravlīyeran*, iv. 19. 2, where the *ī* is unaccountable, and perhaps a mere error. Perfects are *atimumuce*, *atimumucire*, KB. xiii. 3; *atimumucānaḥ*, xv. 5.

28. The **secondary conjugations** offer some peculiarities. **Causatives** include *avajyotayati*, KB. ii. 1, a *v. l.* for *avadyotayati*, found also in the AV. and MS. The MSS. differ also as to *prasrāvayanti* and *prasrāpayanti* in KB. ii. 2, and this text gives *ninartayanti*, xvii. 8, and the **denominative** *utpāthayati*, iv. 3, if the reading is accepted. The AB. has *nābhayanti*, iii. 24; *svadayati*, ii. 9. 10; *iḍayati*, v. 25. 17, and both texts have *nyūṅkhayati*. The KB. seems also to have converted the normal *antar-i* into a denominative in *antarayanti*, xxiii. 4.

The **desiderative** is not rare and offers the abnormal form *līpsitavyam*, AB. ii. 3; *jijyūṣitaḥ*, vii. 29. The KB. besides more or less normal forms

[1] BKSGW. 15 Dec. 1900, p. 414.

[2] *Ind. Stud.* ix. 267. Böhtlingk reads *pratyavaruhya*.

like *jigīṣitam*, xxiii. 6; *tustūrṣamāṇa*, iv. 7 (as in ĀpÇS. vi. 6. 2), has in ii. 9 *parijigrahīṣyan*, which is a monstrous form, and probably incorrect for °*hīṣan*; in AB. vi. 35. 21 *ajigrabhīṣan* perhaps is necessary.

The **desiderative** of the **causative** presents in AB. v. 3 the form *pravibhāvayiṣyanti* which Sāyaṇa read and explains. Nevertheless Aufrecht's[1] restoration of *prabibhāvayiṣyanti* is certainly correct. In AB. iii. 30 *'vācikalpayiṣan* is now read for *vāci kalpayiṣan*. It also gives the subjunctive form *ālulobhayiṣāt*, AB. i. 24, and three optatives in KB. xxv. 10.

The form *atimokṣamāṇah* is found in KB. xvi. 7; it must be either changed with the MS. M to °*mokṣyamāṇaḥ* or taken as a denominative from *mokṣa*, which is not improbable.

29. Contrary to the rule of Pāṇini (i. 4. 80) **prefixes** are normally and regularly separated from their verbs in both Brāhmaṇas, examples being very numerous. But in AB. vii. 6 the traditional reading, kept even in the Ānand. ed., *yady anānupaçyet*, is clearly nonsense,[2] and Aufrecht's emendation *yady u nānupaçyet* puts all in order.

30. **Adverbial forms** are normal; there may be noted *pratyakṣatamāt*, AB. iv. 20. 18; *udāyitatarām* should, it seems, be read with the MS. M in KB. xv. 4, where *udāyi nitarām* is kept by Lindner. In the AB. *paçcā* regularly occurs before vowels only, i. 7; ii. 36 (*bis*); iii. 2; iv. 17. Adverbs in comparative and superlative forms are *uttarām*, AB. vii. 20; *abhitarām*, iii. 44; *nīcaistarām*, iii. 24; *çanaistarām*, 45; *pratamām*, i. 9; iii. 47; *jyoktamām*, ii. 8. None of the neuter forms used later, as in the *Gṛhya Sūtras*, are found.

(3) Compounds, Vocabulary, and Word Formation.

1. There are few anomalies in the formation of compounds. Both texts have the fully developed compounds *ekaika* (*ekaikena*, AB. iii. 42; *ekaikayā*, iii. 18; *ekaikām*, KB. xxx. 7; *ekaikasyai*, xvii. 1) and *anyonya* (*anyonyasya*, AB. iv. 27. 1; KB. xxvii. 7; *anyonyasmin*, xxvi. 2; apparently *anyonye*, ii. 8).

2. With forms of *kṛ* the KB. has *krūrīkṛtam*, vi. 4; *tīvrīkārāya*, xiii. 2; *pragāthīkṛtya*, xix. 10. In AB. i. 3 are found *muṣṭīkurute* and *muṣṭī vai kṛtvā*.

3. The making of a word from a grammatical phrase is illustrated by *yeyajāmahaḥ*, *yeyajāmahasya* in KB. iii. 5. The same text has in xxviii. 3

[1] *Aitareya Brāhmaṇa*, p. 326, n. 1.

[2] There is no case of the negative prefix to a verb in the Vedic literature, and any effort to find one in it is wholly illegitimate; Keith, JRAS. 1906, p. 495; Aufrecht, ibid. 998.

the odd phrase *āgnipātnivatī*, which is uncertain of interpretation. The term *abrāhmaṇokta* (AB. i. 16) is obscure in sense. In KB. ii. 1 *supratyūḍhān aṅgārān pratyūhet*, the use of *su* is noteworthy and common in the Sūtras.

4. The AB. vii. 15 has the irregular *açanāyāparītaḥ*, for which either *açanāyayā parītaḥ* or *açanāyāparītaḥ* would be normally expected;[1] an old haplology is quite possible.

5. In KB. xxvi. 1 is found the normal but rare *katiṣaḍahaḥ*, 'containing how many periods of six days?' In AB. ii. 9 occurs the strange *yat kiṁcitkam*, which Weber[2] would alter to *yat kiṁcit kaṁsāram*, but this is improbable. In AB. viii. 26 *manuṣyarājñām* is abnormal. In KB. xxv. 15 *aphālakṛṣṭān pratigṛhṇan* is as often (Wackernagel, *Altind. Gramm.* II. i. 78, 79) really equivalent to *phālakṛṣṭān apratigṛhṇan*. In xviii. 10 *ṛtebarhiṣkān* is a compound. *yāvadaham* occurs twice in the KB. In KB. xxvi. 2 *godyuṣī* as a compound is retained even when the order is inverted, as often. In AB. viii. 17. 5 *rajakartāraḥ* is a late form.

6. **Word Formation** offers few novelties; in KB. xxv. 13 is found *nyūṅkhamānaka*, the *ka* being added to a present participle, and in AB. iv. 27 in Janamejayaka it is added to a king's name, on the analogy of *putraka* (AB. vi. 32; KB. xxx. 5). The KB. also has the curious *nediyastā*, viii. 2, &c.; *akūdrīcyaḥ*, viii. 5, as a name of verses, and *devatyā* or *devakyā*, both equally rare forms in xxvii. 3. The AB. in vii. 14 has *sāṁnāthuka* with double Vṛddhi.[3] In KB. xxvii. 3 *vyakṣara* is corrupt.

7. The names of **hymns** are variously given, but one common form is to substitute the author for the work; thus the hymn by Arbuda is regularly called Arbuda (KB. xvi. 1), and the hymn RV. x. 61 Nābhānediṣṭha (AB. vi. 29 *seq.*; KB. xxx. 5 *seq.*); the hymn RV. x. 86 is called Vṛṣākapi, the hymn RV. x. 62 Nārāçaṅsa, the hymn RV. v. 29 Evayāmarut. This use explains the reading of all the MSS. in KB. xxv. 8 *Pataṅgas tisraḥ* where *pataṅgam iti* is needlessly conjectured by Lindner. So also Bṛhaddiva in AB. iv. 14, and Baru in vi. 25 to denote RV. x. 120 and x. 96 respectively. The KB. in xi. 8 uses *aporevatyai* as ablative to denote the hymn beginning *apo revatīḥ*; in xxv. 10 as genitive. In xxiii. 5 Parucchepa occurs as a name of a set of verses, and possibly with a play on the word in the plural to denote the users of these verses. The KB. also has *sarvahari*, xxv. 8, a name of RV. x. 96. To RV. i. 120. 1–9 the term *akūdhrīcyaḥ* is applied in KB. viii. 5.

8. Certain grammatical terms appear, of which the most important are

[1] See Böhtlingk, BKSGW. 16 Dec. 1900, p. 418. Both ÇB. xi. 7. 8. 3 and CU. vi. 8. 3 point to *açanā* as a variant base.

[2] *Ind. Stud.* ix. 247.

[3] Böhtlingk, p. 414, denies the possibility of this.

the terms for the three tenses, which in the AB. iv. 29; 31; v. 1 are *kariṣyat*, *kurvat*, and *kṛta*, and in the KB. xxii. 1, 2, 3 *kariṣyat*, *kurvat*, and *cakṛvat*.[1] The AB. v. 32 resolves *om* in the three latter *a-kāra*, *u-kāra*, and *ma-kāra*, a passage not paralleled in the KB. Both use *akṣara* as a syllable and *varṇa* as a letter. *punarnivṛttam* and *punarninṛttam* occur in AB. v. 1. 3, and it appears clear that the former refers to repetition of words or portions of words while the latter refers to what is normally called alliteration, the recurrence of similar sounds in different words, especially of vowels,[2] as Sāyaṇa, who gives two different renderings, takes it, in the first of which he vainly seeks to find some direct connexion with dancing, whereas the point is clearly the regular recurrence of a sound which is comparable with rhythm in dancing. The AB. has also in a clear grammatical sense *vṛṣan* and *yoṣan*, vi. 3, although Max Müller[3] thinks that the distinction first appears in Pāṇini, and *bahu* as 'plural', v. 2, 15. In KB. xxvi. 5 *pada* and *varṇa* denote 'word' and 'letter' respectively. AB. has *pragrāham*, vi. 32; *padāvagrāham*, 33.

9. In this connexion interest attaches to the numerous devices adopted in order to indicate the sense 'containing a form of the root', which are found in the two texts. The past participle passive is frequently so used as in *ratavat*, 'containing a form of *ram*' in AB. v. 1 and 12, where KB. xxii. 3 has *rathavat*.[4] *paryastavat*, AB. v. 1. 16, is supposed to be justified by *pary . . . āsa* (RV. vii. 32.10); *vṛdhanvat*, AB. iv. 31. 8, is more strange, and is perhaps based on the preceding *vṛṣaṇvat*. On the other hand, in AB. iv. 29. 3 is found *pibavat*. The KB. in xxii. 1 has *eṣavat*, *arṣavat*, *yuktavat*, *yuñjānavat*; in xxvi. 15, *çritavat*; 17, *kṣitavat*; in xxii. 3 *gatavat*, *sthitavat*, and many more. Another point of interest is *yad viriphitam* in AB. v. 3 where the reference is apparently grammatical, to the special pronunciation of the passage in question.

In other cases *vat* denotes certainly the word specified, or an equivalent idea, but usually the former is meant. *antavat* in AB. v. 1 is not, however, a case of the second sense as suggested by Weber[5]; his correction of Haug is necessary, but overlooks the fact that *antarūpam* also occurs in AB. v. 1, and gives the necessary explanation of the passages misunderstood by Haug. In some cases, however, the possession of the word is disclosed not by the possession of anything like it, but merely by the presence of the actual letters in some word or words in the text, a phenomenon interesting in the

[1] Unlike the AB. the KB. explains the meaning of these terms.

[2] Not, as Weber (*Ind. Stud.* ix. 285), 'with different vowels': *svaraviçeṣeṇa* can have either sense, but Sāyaṇa's meaning is clearly shown by his examples. So *nivṛtti* in KB; see xxii. 4 and 5.

[3] *Anc. Sansk. Lit.* p. 163.

[4] Weber (*Ind. Stud.* ix. 284) doubts *ratavat* as a misreading of *rathavat*.

[5] *Loc. cit.*

history of the attitude adopted by the Brāhmaṇas towards language and its analysis.

10. In KB. xv. 4 we find *pratikāminam annādyam* in all the MSS. The form may be a development from the *in* declension to *ina*,[1] or a difference of gender, as is not rare in later Vedic texts.[2]

(4) Syntax.

The syntax of the AB. has received full treatment by Delbrück in his *Altindische Syntax*, but that of the KB. he was unable to deal with save in a few points, the text only becoming available to him when his work was practically finished. Therefore in the following account of the most striking features of that syntax special attention is given to the latter text.

1. The rules of concord are normally observed with the usual care of Sanskrit. In KB. vii. 1 is found *etayā saha stotriyaḥ ṣaḍ anuṣṭubhaḥ saṁpadyante* where the predicate may be *ṣaḍ anuṣṭubhaḥ* or *stotriyaḥ*. In the case of attributive concord we have the usual abnormalities of *īçvara*; thus the AB. has *īçvaro hāsya vitte devā arantoḥ* iii. 48; *īçvaro hotāraṁ yaço 'rtoḥ* ii. 20; i. 25; ii. 7; the KB. has twice *īçvarā yadi nāsurarakṣāṅsy anvavapātoḥ*, x. 2; xvii. 9. These are really distinct from the other cases adduced by Aufrecht[3] such as *parāñ, bhrātṛvyahā*, and *vichandāḥ* as neuter forms.

In AB. iv. 9 occurs *vāhanānāṁ anāçiṣṭhaḥ*.

The *pluralis majestatis* occurs in *vaktā smaḥ* in AB. v. 29; KB. ii. 9; so probably in AB. vi. 30 *mā . . . çaṅsiṣṭa*. The generic plural is common in *āhuḥ*.

2. The use of the cases is on the whole normal in character. The nominative seems to occur in an anacoluthon in AB. vii. 5. 6, where *prāñ udāyan* is taken by Weber[4] as being nominative, but where that use is distinctly hard to justify as *yasya*, which precedes, seems clearly to refer to the same person. In KB. viii. 2 the reading *Viṣṇur iti yajati* is, no doubt, a mere error for *Viṣṇum iti*, the *iti* of enumeration being constantly used in both Brāhmaṇas. In AB. vi. 35 occurs the not unusual construction *açvaḥ çveto rūpaṁ kṛtvā*, while in v. 7 the nominative appears used as predicate *vice* the accusative, *Indro vā etābhir mahān ātmānaṁ niramimīta*. In ii. 6 we have the natural anacoluthon *paçur vai nīyamānaḥ sa mṛtyuṁ prāpaçyat*. The nom. alone as introducing a topic of discussion is seen in KB. xviii. 9 *avabhṛthaḥ*; 11 *anubandhyā*; xxiv. 1 *abhijit* (bis).

3. The **accusative** shows some special uses. The ordinary *inner* or

[1] Whitney, *Sansk. Gr.* § 441 *b*, 1209 *a*.
[2] Keith, JRAS. 1912, p. 774.
[3] *Op. cit.* p. 428.
[4] *Ind. Stud.* ix. 311.

cognate use is seen in *sarvaṁ javaṁ dhāvati*, KB. xviii. 1; the phrase *gartapatyaṁ dhīyate*, xvi. 9; xxv. 14, however, is prob. a nominative; *sarvān kāmān ṛdhnuvanti*, xxv. 2; xxvi. 1, 15; xxvii. 6; by a bolder use the AB. has *devān ṛdhnuvanti*, i. 1. 5, where the sense is not 'worship' as Sāyaṇa, or 'make to prosper' as Haug, or 'genügen' as BR. In the active *bhuñjanti* has the acc., KB. i. 5; in the middle the instr., xi. 3. In *hitaṁ manyamānaḥ*, KB. xviii. 2, the nom. would be legitimate and more normal, but cf. *Kaṭha Upaniṣad*, i. 19. The accusative in an *exclamation* is seen in all probability in AB. ii. 13: *te 'bhitaḥ paricaranta ait paçuṁ nirantraṁ çayānam*, where Aufrecht[1] sees an irregularity for *āyan*, but Weber[2] the particle *et* (misread *ait*). This leaves an anacoluthon, but not a very grave one. In *ekaṁ dve na stomam atiçaṅset*, AB. vi. 8. 7; 23. 10 there is a conflict between the grammar which demands that the sense should be '(he should recite) one or two verses; he should not overrecite the Stoma' and the sense which as already understood by the *Açvalāyana Çrauta Sūtra* (vii. 12. 3) is that the Stoma is to be overrecited by one or two.

An accusative in *apposition* to a sentence seems clearly found in AB. vi. 21. 8: *kṣatrāyaiva tad viçaṁ pratyudyāminīṁ kuryuḥ pāpavasyasam*; *tām anukṛtiṁ*, ii. 35, 37; *tadanukṛti*, vi. 1. 2, 4.

4. The **instrumental** though freely used shows no special irregularities; in KB. xxvii. 1 *nandati . . . viduṣāgachatā* the stress is as not rarely on the participle, 'in the coming of a learned man.' In xviii. 4 *dhāpayet* appears used without an acc. but with an instr.

5. The **dative** as used in Brāhmaṇa texts serves very freely to denote the purpose of the action, being much oftener thus used than for any other purpose and surviving even in Pāli. Instances of this use of less common order are *amoghāya*, KB. x. 6; *anāvraskāya*, xi. 8; *saṁçaṅsāyai*, xxviii. 7; *asyai bubhūṣāyai syāt*, xxv. 15; with double dative, *sarvasmā eva çāntyai*, AB. ii. 34. 7. The same use is seen with *sthā* is AB. iv. 25; *tasmai . . . jyaiṣṭhyāya . . . atiṣṭhanta* (so in a Gāthā in vii. 18), and Weber[3] seeks in vi. 5 to read, for *tasmai na tatsthānāni yad . . . kuryuḥ*, *tasthānāni* the second dative being represented by a *yad* clause. But the correctness of the text is proved by KB. xxvi. 8: *na . . . etatsthāne . . . çasyāya*.

The dative as *indirect object* appears with *ā-vṛç* in KB. xi. 4, and with *praṇayanti* and a locative in the sense of 'give a lead to', used of the Sāman singers from whom the Stotriya is borrowed by the priests in KB. xvi. 11 and several times in xxx.

A double dat. is found with *abhisaṁjñā*, KB. xxvi. 9.

A *dativus commodi* with a term of space is found in KB. ix. 4: *tasmā ardhāyābhayaṁ bhavati*.

[1] *Op. cit.* p. 430. [2] *Ind. Stud.* ix. 249. [3] Ibid. 295

6. The **ablative** shows no special use; the occurrence of it with *vṛ* in a Gāthā (AB. vii. 17. 3) has been above noted.

7. The **genitive** is freely used in the KB. in the headings of chapters as in iv. 1: *athāto 'bhyuditāyai*; 2: *athāto 'bhyuddṛṣṭāyai* and so on. The use is found in AB. viii. 5. Other uses are *pavamānasya kīrtayati*, KB. i. 4; iii. 8; *dvidevatyānām anuvaṣaṭkuryāt*, AB. ii. 28. 2, and with *bhakṣayati*, KB. xiii. 6. The person for whom a sacrifice is being carried on is often put in the genitive; in AB. ii. 17: *anūcyāny abrāhmaṇoktasya* may be used thus or less probably as a genitive of agency. The genitive is also used with *juṣ* in KB. xxvi. 3; *ava-vad* in AB. v. 22; *prati-vadh*, vii. 28.

The *possessive* genitive in the predicate appears with *brū* in KB. vi. 2, and in a special use in AB. ii. 9. 6: *na dīkṣitasyāçnīyāt* where, of course, there is no question of eating the consecrated man.

In AB. vii. 15. 7 *tasya ha çataṁ dattvā tasya* may be 'for him' not 'to him', as usually taken. With *upālambhya* it means 'in addition to', AB. iv. 19, 22; KB. xxv. 10.

8. The **locative** denotes measure of *distance* in *time* in *paçcā . . . ṣaṣṭyāṁ vā varṣeṣu*, AB. iv. 17. 5; in the sense 'at the end of' in *saṁvatsare*, KB. xix. 9; and of distance in *sahasrāçvīne vā itaḥ svargo lokaḥ*, AB. ii. 17. 8; *sahasrayojane*, KB. viii. 3. The common use of *thing for which* is illustrated in the KB. by *asmint sahasre*, xviii. 1; that of *thing in which* in *na paçau na some*, iii. 5. The person with whom one lives (*vas*) is expressed in the loc. in KB. xxv. 15. The dat. and loc. are found with *saṁjñā* in *sam asmai svāḥ çreṣṭhatāyāṁ jānate*, AB. iv. 25. 9; the acc. and loc. with *ṛdh* in KB. xxv. 2; xxvi. 1, &c.

The locative absolute is found, but not the genitive absolute.

9. The **prepositions** do not appear in many new uses. There is as usual often doubt to what extent prepositions or prefixes are meant and whether the case governed is governed by the preposition alone or the whole phrase. Thus in KB. ix. 2: *tā gāyatrīm abhisaṁpadyante* it is clear that *abhi* causes the accusative and perhaps, as in the AB. on Aufrecht's plan, *abhi* here should be written separately. So *abhi dīkṣate*, vii. 3, 4.

The AB. has *ā* in iv. 24. 1: *ā daçamam āhar ā dvāv atirātrau*, where Sāyaṇa hesitates between the two senses of exclusion and inclusion, the former of which seems to be meant. In iii. 45 *āntam* can be taken as a compound, and so in *ājarasam*, iii. 19. 16; *āratam*, KB. xv. 4; xvi. 3. With the abl. *ā* is common in KB., as in *ā haviṣkṛta udvādanāt*, vi. 13; *aṣṭamāt puruṣāt*, vi. 9; *mūlāt*, x. 2; xxvii. 6; ii. 4., &c.

ati in AB. iv. 11. 6 has a personal object, *atīva vānyān*; in KB. ii. 1 an impersonal, *namaskāram*, said of the gods, who are not above receiving it.

adhi has the acc. in *adhi . . . paçūn tiṣṭhati*, KB. xxvi. 17; the abl. in

Agner evādhi gṛhapater Ādityaṁ kāṣṭhām akurvata, AB. iv. 7. 6, where perhaps *Ādityam* conceals *ā* but not probably. In KB. ii. 2 for *ātmano 'bhi* it seems necessary to read *ātmano 'dhi*.

abhi appears in *yad etad bhūtam ivābhi*, KB. xxi. 4, &c.

anyatra has the abl. in KB. xxv. 14; xxix. 5.

arvāk occurs in *arvāk sahasrāt*, KB. xviii. 3.

purā with the abl. occurs in KB. ii. 5; xviii. 3; in *purā vāco visargāt*, xi. 8, the modern tendency to use an abstract noun in the place of the infinitive is noteworthy.

prāg daçamāt ahnaḥ is found in KB. xxix. 5.

10. The **pronouns** show few anomalies of use. There is, however, a tendency for the demonstrative *sa* to lose its full force and to become a mere particle. The placing of *sa* before a relative or particle is natural and is sometimes carried to other parts of the word, as in *tā yā agnāv āhutayo hūyante tābhir āhutibhāgāḥ prīṇāti*; AB. ii. 18. 4. Hence the use extends to cases like *sa yaḥ . . . vidyāt kathaṁ taṁ veder utthāpayanti*, AB. vii. 28. 1; *sa yaḥ . . . tādṛk tat*, v. 31. 1; *sa yaḥ . . . yathā . . . tādṛk tat*, i. 17. 14. So probably *sa yadi somam*, AB. vii. 29. 2, where possibly the second person is the subject, though Sāyaṇa supplies for *sa* a priest, and vii. 5. 1: *sa yady ekasminn unnīte yadi dvayor eṣa eva kalpaḥ*. In KB. xxv. 10 *sa yas taṁ nirbrūyād yas taṁ tatra brūyāt* shows *sa* without construction.

11. The **interrogative pronoun** shows one or two interesting forms; in AB. vii. 27. 2 is found *kaḥ svid . . . asti vīraḥ*, and in KB. xxi. 4: *kadriyañ hi tata iyāt* and so often. In AB. iv. 5. 1 is found *kaç cāhaṁ ca* with a dual first person verb as usual.

12. The **indefinite pronoun** shows certain peculiar forms. In AB. iii. 22. 5: *yā no 'smin na vai kam avidat*, which Weber[1] renders 'welche hiebei keinen von uns genommen hat', and in which he takes *na vai kam* as = *na kam api* or a Sandhi for *na vā* (= *vai*) *ekam* as in AB. iv. 11. 6 *vānyan* has the sense of *vai anyān*. Liebich,[2] however, reads *yā no 'sminn avaikam avidat* but without regard to the sense, which seems to be 'who has not obtained any (share) in this of ours' rather than as taken by Weber.

kaç cit occurs absolutely as 'some one' in AB. vi. 26. 5: *kaç cid vai svarge loke sameti*. The AB. has *kim iva ca*, vi. 16; the KB. *bahu kiṁ ca kiṁ cid iva*, ii. 2; *etad vai kiṁ cid iva rcām*, xviii. 3; and *na kā cana riṣṭiḥ*, viii. 1 and often. The adjectival *yat kiṁcitkam*, AB. ii. 9, has been noted above.

13. As regards the use of the voices it is clear[3] that there is a consider-

[1] *Ind. Stud.* ix. 263.

[2] *Pāṇini*, p. 72, n. 2.

[3] See Liebich, *op. cit.*, pp. 72 *seq.*

able degree of distinction between the Brāhmaṇas and the rules of Pāṇini. It is only necessary to note that in both texts *apahate* is normal; *ā hvayate* regularly means 'say the call (*āhāva*)'; the AB. also has an interesting distinction in its use of *ā-pad*, which is active in the future, but middle in imperfect and aorist, e.g. ii. 6. 1; iv. 7. 7. The KB. has the future in the middle also. In AB. iv. 30. 2 *sampibasva* is used with the instr. of those with whom drinking takes place. The neat distinction of *yajati* and *yajate* is seen in AB. ii. 24 where *yajate yajatīti ca* seems deliberately intended by the use of *iti* to mark out the use.

14. The **present indicative** has no abnormal uses. It repeatedly occurs and it is only necessary to note the use with *ha sma* of the habitual past, as in *ha sma . . . tapanti*, AB. vii. 34. In some cases the form is strengthened by *purā*; *ha sma vai purā . . . gopāyanti*, KB. xii. 1; xxvii. 2. Or again *purā* alone is used as in KB. xxviii. 4: *purā . . . pariharāmaḥ*.

15. The **imperfect indicative** is overwhelmingly the tense of *narration* in AB. i–v, but in vi it becomes less prominent, and in vii and viii yields to the perfect. In the KB. it is used frequently but the perfect is also freely used. On the other hand it is naturally not used freely in speeches, where the aorist is the natural tense for the past. It is however so used in AB. iii. 48. 9: *amādayam*, no stress being laid on the recent character of the action; so in KB. vii. 4: *sakṛd ayaje tasya kṣayād bibhemi*; ÇÇS. xiv. 12. 2: *agacham*. In AB. iii. 18. 8 *abhivyajānīma* is curious especially as Aufrecht prints it as if it were *abhivyājānīmaḥ*, but as it governs *çasyamānām*, a present participle, the imperfect may be used to show that the action of the participle is past. The form *anamnamuḥ*, AB. ii. 20. 12; KB. xii. 1, in a quasi-Mantra is unexpected, but aorists of intensives are few, and hence an imperfect may be excused; in AB. it follows *aveḥ*: the Mantra usage was probably less strict than the later prose.[1] In AB. viii. 7. 9 the sentence runs *sarvam āpnod vijayena . . . yam . . . abhiṣiñcanti*, but this is really impossible and *āptor* or *āpnoti jayena* can stand instead. Cf. in ÇB. iii. 7. 4. 2 the difficult *adhṛṣṇot*.

The imperfect implies *attempt* clearly in AB. iv. 26: *anvayuñjata*. The sense of continuous action is seen in *ha sma . . . udasarpat* in KB. vi. 1 (*bis*) in contrast with the perfect. In AB. vii. 14. 8 for the imperfect *prāpnot* the aorist is necessary.

16. The **aorist** is very freely used of the proximate past and naturally usually in speeches where it occurs often both in the AB. and in the KB. (e.g. ii. 7: *prāṇiṣam, apāniṣam, adrākṣam, asprākṣam, açrauṣam, acīkḷpam*). There remain only a few passages where the aorist occurs outside speech. Thus in AB. vi. 36. 8 and 11 occurs *idaṁ vā idaṁ vyāhanasyāṁ vācam*

[1] It is paraphrased by *avidaḥ* in the prose, which is significant.

avādīt tat devapavitreṇa vācaṁ punīte. Here the English 'he has said' is an exact equivalent, the time being the proximate past from the point of view of *punīte.*[1] So AB. iii. 32. 3: *avadhiṣur vā etat somam yad abhyasuṣavuḥ*; *tasmād enaṁ punaḥ saṁbhāvayanti*; where *abhyasuṣavuḥ* is an odd form, though apparently a regular imperfect of the root *su* in the third class. In AB. ii. 23. 3: *puro vā tān devā akrata yat puroḷāçās tat puroḷāçānāṁ puroḷāçatvam* is less easy but still can be so taken. In the KB. this use appears in a different form in xiii. 4: *atha soma iti vai paçum avocāma*, which may be compared with *yatra . . . anvavocat*, ix. 7; *yad . . . prāvocāma*, ix. 10 in M's reading, against *prāg aikṣāma* of the other MSS. Here may be classed the *yad . . . avocāma* of AB. iii. 22. 4 where it paraphases a Ṛgvedic verse. So KB. xiv. 3: *gāyatryā savanaṁ pratipadya gāyatryāṁ pratyaṣṭhātām*, where the aorist approximates to the present sense. In xxiv. 8 *aspṛkṣan* is odd, but is perhaps used deliberately.

17. The **perfect** is used in two ways, as a present in sense, and as a narrative tense; it does not denote the proximate past. In the present sense it has often a heavy reduplication; thus *dādhāra*, AB. iv. 12. 8 and often; *bībhāya*, v. 25. 17; *dīdhāya*, i. 28. 9; ii. 40. 2; 41. 4; iii. 8. 2; iv. 11. 8; but this is not essential; so *bibhāya*, v. 15. 9, has the same sense as *bībhāya*. So regular is the present use that *ha sma* is regularly used with it, as indicating a repeated past, thus in AB. and KB. alike *iti ha smāha* means (the authority) 'used to say'.

The special character of the narrative use of the perfect in comparison with the imperfect is seen in the following figures[2] for the two Brāhmaṇas:—

AB.	Imperfects.	Perfects.	KB.	Imperfects.	Perfects.
i.	116	6	xi.	0	0
ii.	183	5	xii.	18	16
iii.	347	7	xiii.	0	6
iv.	186	8	xiv.	9	0
v.	97	6	xv.	20	8
vi.	92	49	xvi.	6	5
vii.	30	189	xvii.	1	0
viii.	29	51	xviii.	7	1
			xix.	8	0
KB.			xx.	8	0
i.	11	4	xxi.	8	1
ii.	12	4	xxii.	9	1
iii.	5	1	xxiii.	8	15
iv.	7	2	xxiv.	18	8
v.	8	1	xxv.	5	6
vi.	68	15	xxvi.	4	6
vii.	25	10	xxvii.	0	2
viii.	4	2	xxviii.	2	29
ix.	7	0	xxix.	2	9
x.	1	6	xxx.	2	17

[1] Cf. Delbrück, *Vergl. Synt.* ii. 284, 285.

[2] See Whitney, PAOS. May, 1891, pp. lxxxviii *seq.*

But the significance of the figures is in the case of the AB. strengthened when the cases of the perfect are scrutinized. In v the six cases occur in the twenty-fifth Adhyāya, and that Adhyāya is no doubt later; they are *uvāca*, v. 29 (*bis*); 30. 15; *babhūva*, 30. 15; *āsa*, 36. 3 (*bis*). In the cases in iv. in 8. 3 *dadhṛṣatuḥ* is clearly intended to be differentiated from the preceding *abrūtām* as it explains why they said as they did, as they had not the daring to say something else. In iv. 17. 5 the loss of *jagmuḥ* occurs with *pūrve*, but the reason for its use is not at all obvious, unless it be to convey the precise sense 'arrived first'.

In iii there is a group of three perfects in iii. 48. 9, *saṁniruvāpa*, *uvāca*, and *āsuḥ*, in iii. 20. 1 occur *āsatuḥ* and *abhyanūvāca*; in iii. 18 *yatra yatra* ... *nirajānan* is followed by *apidadhuḥ* which may well be taken as an unaugmented imperfect. In iii. 49. 5 *āsa* is clearly differentiated from the surrounding imperfects.

In ii there occur *āsa*, differentiated, and *abhyanūvāca* in 33. 5; *abhyanūvāca* in 25; *parisasāra* in 19 is probably not past but present in sense; in 36 *nirvāpayāṁ cakruḥ* is pluperfect in contrast with *viharanta* following it.

In i all the perfects in narrative occur in one chapter (18), viz. *vimethire*, *parābabhūva*, *ūcuḥ* (*bis*), *saṁjabhruḥ*, *āhatuḥ*. This is a very peculiar feature, comparable to the group in iii. 48. 9. Possibly in both cases interpolation is present.

In the KB. and in the last three books of the AB., while of course here and there differences of tense can be read into the text naturally enough, the constant use of the perfect in a narrative sense shows that that tense had acquired a regular narrative use in prose as always in verse, for in the Vedic verse, including the Gāthās, and in the epic as well as in classical poetry the perfect is an established narrative tense.

18. The **future** tense shows little of note. Chiefly to be remarked is the frequent use of the periphrastic future which is marked in both texts and normally with distinct definiteness of time allusion. The simple future and still more the second future convey the idea of purpose or resolve quite as much as that of mere futurity. Thus in AB. v. 29 and KB. ii. 9 alike *vaktā smaḥ* expresses the fixed and definite intention of the speakers, not mere futurity.

19. The **subjunctive** finds its place in speech, not in narrative, and therefore hardly ever occurs except in clauses terminating in *iti*. The only exception in either Brāhmaṇa is AB. iii. 42: *yaç cainam evaṁ vedātī tu tam arjātai*. In other cases the sense is normally imperative or a strong assertion of purpose or of desire, in all of which uses its occurrence is quite common. Thus the optative sense is clear in *devā me 'nnam adann*

iti, AB. viii. 24. 2, with which the optative *açnīyuḥ* in KB. iii. 1 is a precise parallel. So often *asat* ii. 8. 7; 11. 12; 13. 8; iii. 43. 6; viii. 1. 5; 4. 5; KB. viii. 9; *udyachāte*. xviii. 5; *vāñchān*, xxv. 15 (with a *v. l. vāñchantu*). Probably injunctive is *prajanayan*, AB. ii. 38. 8, by which is paraphrased *çaṅsan* of the RV. *haratai*, AB. v. 34. 1, is a case of the subjunctive used in a question. *prajānātha*, AB. i. 7. 4, and *juhavātha*, v. 32. 5 (*bis*), are imperatives. In AB. i. 24. 5: *saṁgachātai yaḥ . . . atikrāmāt . . . yaḥ . . . ālulobhayiṣāt* the use of the subjunctive in a relative clause is noteworthy. In a conditional clause in AB. ii. 2. 5 *yadi ca tiṣṭhāsi yadi ca çayāsai . . . dhattat* the forms are paraphrases of the Ṛgvedic verse. In AB. iii. 42 *arjasi* seems an error for *arjāsi* or *arjasva*, while in vii. 16 *hantāham upadhavāmi* is probably a blunder for °*dhavāni*, as usual with *hanta*.

20. The optative occurs freely in the sense of wish, and in the sense of direction. But it shows no peculiarity of usage in main clauses.

21. The injunctive is rare and is practically confined to the use with *mā* in which it occurs in AB. i. 13. 12; ii. 16 (imperf.); vi. 1 and 33, &c.; KB. xii. 13; xxx. 5. That the augmented imperfect is used in AB. vi. 14 is most improbable. In AB. iii. 28. 1 *anuparyāguḥ* may be an injunctive.[1] With the first person plural *mā* occurs in AB. ii. 15. 13; v. 22. 5. *prajanayan*, AB. ii. 38. 8, has been noted above: it is not independent of *çaṅsan* which it explains.

22. The infinitive in the two Brāhmaṇas has a very limited use. The infinitive in *tum* is found with *akāmayata*, AB. iii. 39; *veda*, vi. 23. 5; *arhati*, vi. 23. 4; *dadhṛṣatuḥ*, iv. 8; and the root *çak*, i. 7. 3; iii. 14. The KB. has the infinitive with *çak*, iii. 6; xv. 2; xxiii. 2; *arh*, viii. 6; *dṛ*, xxv. 13. More unusual is *yanti vācaṁ çikṣitum*, vii. 6.

The form in *toḥ* is found with *īçvara* in *aitoḥ*, *paraitoḥ*, AB. viii. 7; *abhyupaitoḥ*, vii. 29; *pratyetoḥ* (without *īçvara*), vi. 30; *anṛṇākartoḥ*, i. 14; *glāvo janitoḥ*, i. 25; *vāco rakṣobhāṣo janitoḥ*, ii. 7; *ni vā roddhor vi vā mathitoḥ*, i. 10; *pratyavahartoḥ*, vii. 33; *hiṅsitoḥ*, i. 30; with a negatived infinitive, *arantoḥ*, iii. 48; *avarṣṭoḥ*, iii. 18. It is also found with *ā*, *ā çarīrāṇām āhartoḥ*, vii. 2, and with *purā*, *purā vācaḥ pravaditoḥ*, ii. 15. The KB. has no case with *ā* or *purā*, with which it uses only abstract nouns; it has *īçvara* with *kartoḥ*, vii. 8; *īçvaro vivaktāraṁ bhreṣo 'nvetoḥ*, xxvii. 1; there occurs, however, the rare use *īçvarā yadi nāsurarakṣāṅsy anvavapātoḥ*, x. 2; xvii. 9.

The AB. has *taṁ harati vadhaṁ yo 'sya stṛtyas tasmai startavai* ii. 6, 35; iii. 7; *tenedaṁ sarvam etavai kṛtam*, v. 15. The KB. has only *āgrayaṇīyān uddhartavā āha*, iv. 14.

Finally the AB. has *āsade 'cīkḷpat* i. 29. 7.

[1] If so, it is overlooked by Delbrück, *Altind. Synt.* p. 359.

In AB. ii. 7 it is possible that *vāco rakṣobhāṣo janitoḥ* is a case of the attr. gen. as taken by BR. But the accusative is at least as probable; the nominative is unlikely as *janitoḥ* is active.

23. The **participles** show no special peculiarities of use. The apparent use of the **gerund** as a finite verb seen by Aufrecht[1] in *ya āhitāgnir jīve mṛtaçabdaṁ çrutvā*, AB. vii. 9, cannot be correct, and the obvious solution is to read *jīven mṛtaçabdam* which would be written as *jīveṁ*, and the *ṁ* would easily disappear. The frequent use of the gerund in *am* is noteworthy in both Brāhmaṇas; it perhaps should be read in KB. viii. 9.

There also is an apparent use of the participle as a finite verb in *te abhitaḥ paricaranta ait paçum*, AB. ii. 7, but there is in that case an anacoluthon, or possibly a misreading.

Participles are governed by *man*, and by *abhivijñā* in AB. iii. 18. 8.

Gerunds followed by *atha* occur in KB. xi. 8 and probably in AB. vii. 13. Past participles passive without copula are never historical in sense.

The past *aprāptāḥ* may be active in KB. xii. 2, where the usual periphrastic tenses with *āsīt*, *āsan* occur.

24. **Adverbs** show little of interest in syntactic use. In KB. xxvi. 5 occurs *tūṣṇīm āsuḥ*. The indefinite forms *yata eva kutaç ca*, AB. vii. 2. 5, and *yataḥ kutaç ca*, ii. 24, occur without verbs, and with these may be compared the use of adverbial phrases like *yāvatkāmam*, AB. vi. 33. 7; *yāvanmātram eva*, KB. iv. 5, and *yathāyatham*.

In the relation of **prefixes** to the verb is to be noted the separation of *anu* from the infin. in AB. iii. 39.

25. In the use of the **particles** of assertion certain points require notice.

iva is often used in the sense practically of *eva*, or more accurately as a sort of modification of the sense of the plain assertion; thus *pṛṣṭhata ivāgnīdhraṁ kṛtvā*, AB. i. 30; *yadi ha vā api bahava iva yajante*, ii. 2; *so 'je jyoktamām ivāramata*, ii. 8, besides many other places where the sense is less certain.

vā here and there clearly has the sense of *vai* as in *atīva vānyān*, AB. iv. 11. 6; *ṣaṣṭyāṁ vā varṣeṣu*, 17. 5; *yathā vā*, 6; *iti bahūni vāha*, vi. 12. 17; in KB. xii. 4 and xvi. 9 are possible cases.

nvai occurs in both texts, AB. ii. 22. 3; KB. xiii. 4; xxvi. 14; xxviii. 2. The normal *iti nu* is strengthened to *iti nvai* in KB. xii. 4.

vāva is frequent in the earlier portion of the AB., while *vai* is normal in the latter portion, in comparisons as *yathā vāva*; it is found in KB. xxiv. 1 as a *v. l.*

Combinations with *vai* include *ha vā api*, AB. ii. 2; KB. i. 1; ii. 8;

[1] Cf. Weber, *Ind. Stud.* ix. 249.

xiv. 3 (wrongly printed by Lindner as *iha vā api*); *u ha vā api*, ii. 8; *ha va u*, vi. 12; xxviii. 1, 2; *u ha vai*, xi. 5; AB. vii. 26. 5, &c.

aha occurs in *upāha . . . āpnoti*, AB. vii. 26. 4; *atrāhaiva*, vi. 23. 7; and in a verse in KB. xxvii. 1: *nāhaiva*. *aho* occurs in KB. vii. 4.

uta is found in AB. iv. 26. 10: *yad anyadevatya uta*.

nu is specially frequent in the phrase *iti nu* terminating a description, e.g. AB. i. 21; iii. 19. 7; 41; 47. 13; KB. x. 2; xxii. 1; xxiii. 1. 3.

çaçvat in addition to its function in the AB. in the apodosis of conditional clauses occurs in that text absolutely in iii. 48. 9: *catuḥṣaṣṭiḥ kavacinaḥ çaçvad dhāsya putranaptāra āsuḥ*.

u is found with *tv* in KB. xviii. 13: *u tv eva*; with *kim* in viii. 8.

atha after an absolute form is perhaps[1] to be seen in AB. vii. 13: *iti hāsmā ākhyāyāthainam uvāca*, and clearly in KB. xi. 8.

26. The **repetition of particles** is seen in a few cases, namely, *hy eva hi* twice repeated in AB. ii. 12; *naivaiva*, vi. 32; and according to Weber, *nī vīva*, vi. 32, should be taken as *ni iva iva*. *atho . . . u vai* occurs in KB. xvii. 1.

27. **Negative particles** are normal, except that *net* occurs as a simple negative in *net tu pragāthāḥ kalpante*, AB. vi. 28. The emphatic *no eva* is found in AB. vi. 2. 6; KB. ix. 1. The indefinite negative *cana* is found in both texts after *na*, KB. ii. 1; vi. 2.

In a question in AB. vi. 34. 3: *no hi na pratyajñāsthāḥ* the sense is, 'Surely you did not promise?' Normally *na* is used to ask a simple negative question without implication of the answer.

28. **Connective and disjunctive particles** are as normal in the Brāhmaṇas duplicated. In no case is a particle used with the first member only. Examples of the use are, for *vā*, *uta vā . . . uta vā*, AB. iii. 46. 2; *kena vā nu kena vā*, KB. xiii. 3; *vāpi vā*, AB. vii. 5. 6. In KB. ix. 4 *u ha . . . u ha* occurs. *vā* alone without a preceding *vā* is found in AB. ii. 17: *abrāhmaṇoktasya yo vā . . . yajeta*; perhaps in KB. xvi. 9; xxv. 14; in KB. xviii. 1 is found *yadi vā Prajāpateḥ* as a contrast to *sūryām*; *vā* with an independent clause occurs in AB. vii. 9; KB. xvi. 10.

29. In **questions** when simple no particle is normally used at all. In a double question in AB. v. 36 *kiṁ svid . . . nīyante* is followed by *akṛtvāho svid . . . haratai*. *kim u* in KB. viii. 8 seems to raise an objection, rather than to carry on a previous clause.

30. In the **compound sentence** in many cases the use of **parataxis** supplies the place of hypotaxis. Of this there is an excellent example in AB. vi. 31: *katham atrāçasta eva nābhānediṣṭho bhavaty atha maitrāvaruṇo*

[1] See Weber, *Ind. Stud.* ix. 314; Böhtlingk, BKSGW. 15 Dec. 1900, p. 417, in place of Aufrecht's emendation (p. 431) *iti ha smāsmā*.

vālakhilyāḥ çaṅsati te prāṇā reto vā agre 'tha prāṇāḥ . . . katham atra yajamānasya prajāteḥ kathaṁ prāṇā aviklptā bhavanti. This clause is further noteworthy as it depends on a *yad* clause, and contains within it an elaborate parenthesis applying the same principle to the Brāhmaṇāc-chaṅsin.

This is a specially elaborate case but other instances occur *passim*: *prāyaṇīyam iti nirvapanti prāyaṇīyam iti caranti prayanty evāsmāl lokāt*, i. 11; *samayāviṣitaḥ sūryaḥ syād atha vācaṁ visṛjeraṅs tāvantam eva tad dviṣate lokaṁ pariçiṅṣanti*, v. 24. 11; *cakṣuṣī vimṛjīta cakṣur-evāsya tad gopāyati*, KB. xvi. 5; *adhīyann upahanyād anyaṁ vivaktāram ichet*, A.B. iii. 35; ii. 33. 1; iii. 5. 1, &c.; KB. x. 5, &c.

31. **Relative clauses** have certain special characteristics. The use of such a clause as precisely parallel to an adjective is seen in *abrāhmaṇok-tasya yo vā . . . yajeta*, AB. ii. 17.

In the *causal* sense relative clauses occur very markedly in *alaso 'bhūr yo me vācam avadhīḥ*, AB. vi. 33. 4; *yo . . . asakthāḥ*, ibid.; *tvaṁ vai naḥ çreṣṭho 'si yaṁ tvā . . . anveti*, AB. iii. 22. 5.

The use of the relative in *comparison* is noteworthy in *bhūyāṅsaḥ . . . yac ca*, AB. iii. 29. 6; *samānaṁ . . . yac ca*, iv. 30. 15.

The *indefinite* use of the relative is common and the indicative is frequently the tense employed, as in *yāvatāṁ vai . . . veda . . . bhavanti, yeṣām u na veda kim u te syuḥ*, AB. ii. 39. 11. The same use still more definitely *conditional* appears in *sarvajyānir haiva sā yaḥ . . . dadāti*, KB. xxv. 14 ('if a man give'); *yaḥ . . . veda tat suviditam*, AB. ii. 29. 11. But the optative tends also to appear; thus *yasya tat kāmāya tathā kuryāt prāṇasya ca vācaç cātraiva tad upāptam*, AB. ii. 26; *yaḥ . . . yajeta . . . āpnoti*, KB. xvi. 10; *yat kiṁcic chandaḥ . . . yujyeta*, xxvi. 8 (no verb). Still more natural is *çaṅsed yat . . . çaṅseyuḥ*, AB. vi. 8. 9, in view of the influence of the preceding optative; *anūcyāni . . . yo vā . . . yajeta*, AB. ii. 17, shows a participle of necessity as equivalent to an optative but *yām . . . utsarpet* in KB. iii. 1 in a definition is more clearly merely generic.

In another set of cases the optative occurs in both clauses, the conditional sense being perfectly clear: of this character is the constant phrase *ya evaṁ tatra brūyāt vācā vajreṇa yajamānasya prāṇān vyagāt prāṇa enaṁ hāsyatīti çaçvat tathā syāt*, AB. ii. 21. 2. There is no anacoluthon proper as *yaḥ* is really felt as 'if any one', and the clause may be further elaborated by a still extra conditional relative clause as in *yaḥ . . . iyāt yas . . . taṁ tatra brūyāc cyoṣyata iti tathā ha syāt*, KB. ix. 4. Normally *brūyāt* means 'speak of' a person, but occasionally 'speak to' as in *ya enaṁ tatra brūyād vācaḥ kūṭena yajamānāt paçūn niravadhīr apaçum enam akar iti çaçvat tathā syāt*, AB. vi 24. 13. The use is found in the KB. always with *tathā ha syāt,* never *çaçvat* as in the AB.; see vii. 19; xii. 7; xiii. 9; xiv. 2; xvii. 1; xxiii. 6; xxv. 10. In the AB. *çaçvat* occurs once also in another form of clause *yat saumyātithimatī syāt çaçvat sā syāt,* AB. i. 17. 3. The optative also occurs in a clause without *çaçvat* in *jāmi ha syād ya etaṁ nigadaṁ brūyāt,* KB. viii. 8. In the place of the apodosis there may be a question without a verb as in a series of sentences in AB. vii. 2 *seq.,* commencing *yasya* . . . (opt.) *kā tatra prāyaçcittiḥ.*

32. The **conditional sentence** runs parallel with the relative clause. The normal form has the optative in both protasis and apodosis, but the apodosis may take another form. The apodosis may be an expression which can be regarded as a potential, thus *yad* . . . *saṁnirvaped īçvarā hāsya vitte devā arantor,* AB. iii. 48; so 18. 8; ii. 7. 6, *īçvara* being an expression approximately future in sense. Or again, *yadi* . . . *kuryuḥ* . . . *çaṅstavyaḥ,* AB. iv. 2, where the participle of necessity serves as an optative. In other cases the verb of the apodosis is not expressed, as *te yadi tathā kuryur etāv eva stotriyānurūpau,* KB. xxiv. 5; 26; xxv. 6; xxvi. 4; AB. iv. 13. 5; so with the interrogative form *ya āhitāgnir yadi kapālaṁ naçyet kā tatra prāyaçcittiḥ,* AB. vii. 9. 2; v. 32. 5.

A further development is when the optative in the protasis is accompanied by an indicative in the apodosis; *yad* . . . *vyācakṣīta* . . . *gamayati,* AB. v. 23. 10; *yadi* . . . *abhyābhavet* . . . *asti,* iii. 46; *yadi* . . . *budhyeta* . . . *bhavati,* KB. xxvi. 4; *yadi svarāṇi pṛṣṭhāni bhavanti* . . . *tarhi* . . . *kurvanti, yady u* . . . *syātāṁ tarhi* . . . *kurvanti,* KB. xxiv. 8; cf. xxv. 5. These are on the whole rare and slightly irregular; on the other hand *yad* . . . *juhoti* . . . *anubrūyāt,* KB. ix. 5, is of a normal type.

The protasis may be of course abbreviated; so *sattram u cet,* AB. iv. 29. 13; KB. xxv. 14; *na cet svayonau,* xxv. 6; AB. vii. 5. 1.

In AB. iii. 46. 10 occurs *api yadi*; *api ha yadi,* iii. 16. 2.

The conditional is found in a full condition of what was not realized in AB. iv. 30. 6; in KB. xxx. 5 and in the apodosis of the same condition in AB. vi. 33, and in *kuto hy anyam āhariṣyan,* KB. xxvi. 7.

33. Clauses of **comparison** are frequent, and very often show an optative in the dependent clause. In that case the apodosis takes two types, either the indicative stands or it is reduced to a mere *evaṁ tat* or *tādṛk tat.* Of the first type is *yathā* . . . *praplaverann evaṁ haiva te praplavante,* AB. vi. 21. 10 (*bis*); iii. 19; KB. i. 5; vii. 7; xi. 4, 8; xvii. 8; xviii. 7; xxvii. 6; *āhvayanti yathā* . . . *āhvayet,* AB. vi. 3. 1. Of the latter are *yathā* . . . *kuryāt evaṁ tat,* KB. x. 3; v. 5; vii. 3, 9; viii. 2, 9; xii. 3, 6; xiv. 4; xviii. 4; xxii. 10; xxv. 10; xxvi. 1; AB. iii. 47; iv. 4; v. 32; so *yathā* . . . *syād evam eva* . . . *saṁçleṣiṇyaḥ,* KB. vi. 12. In the

AB. the normal form in the main clause is *tādṛk tat*, i. 17. 12; iii. 10; 20. 21; iv. 9. 9; v. 28 (*bis*), 31; vi. 23. 8; KB. ii. 9. In AB. v. 15 *tat* is explained by a clause *yad . . . çaṅsati*; in vi. 23. 7 the opt. occurs with *yathā* in a clause where there are optatives in protasis and apodosis.

In KB. xxii. 6 the relative and comparative forms are merged in *yathā yas taptaṁ ninayet evaṁ tat.*

34. In the case of **sentences** of **time** and **place** there are no special peculiarities in either text. But both use **yatra** somewhat freely in clauses of **occasion**. Thus is found in AB. vii. 28 *yatra . . . tatra* with imperfects, and in iv. 20. 21 *yatra* is so used without any correlative. In vii. 33 *yatra* and *tat* with the opt. are found and in iv. 20. 19 *yatra* without correlative with the opt. In iii. 18 *yatra . . . nirajānan . . . apidadhuḥ* the apparent perfect is probably an unaugmented imperfect. In the KB. *yatra . . . tad* with imperfect occurs in xviii. 1; *yatra* with perfects, xxviii. 3, 4; xvi. 1; *yatra* with imperfect and a perfect in the main clause, vi. 13.

35. **Clauses** denoting the **purpose** with which an action is done or the result it is desired to avert are normally expressed not by subordinate clauses proper, but by *oratio recta* with *iti*. If the purpose is positive the subjunctive or optative is used without any particle, if negative the optative normally is not used, but *ned*, occasionally *na*, with the subjunctive and *mā* with the injunctive.

Moreover, the sentence may be not merely a simple one, but a complex one, giving a reason for the action arrived at, or to be averted: and thus the building up of larger complexes becomes possible.

Examples of the positive form are *āhutī juhoti mahacchastraṁ vāk ca manaç ca prīte udyachāte iti*, KB. xviii. 5; iv. 14, *uttamaṁ vartmopaniçrayetāyaṁ vai loko dakṣiṇaṁ havirdhānaṁ pratiṣṭhā vā ayaṁ lokaḥ pratiṣṭhāyām anucchinno 'sānīti.* In this case and in similar cases, such as xxv. 15; xii. 5 it is open to argue that the reason is given by the Brāhmaṇa, and that a new clause begins with the clause of purpose, but this seems needless and not very natural. Besides the subjunctive occurs the precative (*udyāsam*) in KB. xxviii. 1, and a future (*atsyāmi*) is used in iv. 14.

Instances of the negative form are *tasmād u nānūttiṣṭhen ned ṛcaṁ svād āyatanāc cyavayānīti ned ṛcaṁ sāmno 'nuvartmānaṁ karavāṇīti*, KB. xii. 5; *tān avagṛhyāste net pravartantā iti* xiii. 5; xvii. 7; *tasmāt . . . çilpāni çasyante net prāṇebhya ātmānam apādadhānīti*, xxv. 12; xxvii. 6; *na pāpaḥ puruṣo yājyo dvādaçāhena ned ayaṁ mayi pratitiṣṭhād iti*, AB. iv. 25. 5, 7; quite exceptional is *tasmāt . . . na kṣatriyo druhyen ned rāṣṭrād avapadyeyaṁ ned vā mā prāṇo jahad iti*, viii. 23. 11. The complex type is seen in *naite viparyasyati pratiṣṭhe vai saṁyājye net pratiṣṭhe vyatisajānīti*, KB. vii. 9; iii. 4, 5; vii. 9; ix. 6; x. 4; xi. 8; xiii. 5 (*bis*), 6, 7, 9; xiv. 3 (*ned* . . . *gāma*); xvi. 1, 2, 6; xviii. 10; xix. 6; *tad avivākyaṁ bhavati na hi tad addhā veda kaçcana ned avidvān nirbravāṇīti*, xxvii. 1; AB. iii. 29. 3–4; vi. 3. 9.

ned is not essential in this use; in AB. viii. 6. 9–11 is found *athainam abhiṣekṣyann apāṁ çāntiṁ vācayati* . . . *naitasyābhiṣiṣicānasyāçāntā āpo vīryaṁ nirhaṇann iti*. In AB. v. 22. 5 *tasmād daçamam ahar avivākyaṁ bhavati mā çriyo 'vavādiṣmeti*. In both cases the sense is precisely as with *ned*, and the origin of the use of *ned* through its equivalence to *na* is obvious. In accented texts the verb with *ned* is regularly accented because of the logical relation of the *ned* to the principal clause, but it is unnecessary with Weber[1] and Delbrück[2] to insist on translating by 'Lest' like Latin *ne*, for in prose as opposed to verse and prose Mantra (AB. ii. 7. 10: *mā rāviṣṭha* . . . *ned* . . . *ravitā ravat*) the clauses always are flung into *oratio recta* and can well be rendered 'Let me not',

ned occurs once with the optative and with a form (*jahat*) which can be subj. or inj. in parallel clauses in AB. viii. 23. 11, quoted above; the former use is unique.

36. In these cases the clause with *iti* is clearly dependent on a main clause; in another set of instances the *iti* clause instead forms the main clause, expressing the view or thought of the actors. These clauses take several forms. In the first place the clause may stand somewhat isolated: thus *yathā hy evāsya prāyaṇam evam udayanam asad iti*, AB. iii. 43. 6; *brahmapurastān ma ugraṁ rāṣṭram avyathyam asad iti*, viii. 1. 5; 4. 5.

In the second place the clause follows one in *yad*, as in *tad yat somaṁ rājānaṁ krīṇāty asau vai somo rājā vicakṣaṇaç candramā abhiṣuto 'sad iti*, KB. vii. 10; xvii. 7; *yad eva vāco jitā3ṁ tan ma idam anu karma saṁtiṣṭhātā iti*, AB. viii. 9. 11; *yad v evaitaçapralāpā3ḥ*: *ayātayāmā vā aitaçapralāpo 'yātayāmā me yajñe 'sad akṣitir me yajñe 'sad iti* vi. 33. 11.

In the third place the clause with *iti* may be negatived by *ned*; thus *yad* . . . *nāha ned yajamānaṁ pravṛṇajānīti*, KB. v. 6; 7; xviii. 4; *yat stokāḥ çcotanti sarvadevatyā vai stokā nen ma ime 'nabhiprītā devān gachān iti*, ii. 12. 3. The same effect as *ned* is produced by *mā* in *tad yat purā çakunivādād anubrūyān mā yajñiyāṁ vācaṁ proditām anupravadiṣmeti*, ii. 15. 13.

37. In comparison with clauses with *iti* other forms of indicating purpose are very rare. In KB. ix. 4 occurs *yathā hotar abhayam asat tathā kuru*; in AB. viii. 10. 6: *tathā me kuru yathemāṁ senāṁ jayāni*; in

[1] *Ind. Stud.* ix. 249.

[2] *Altind. Synt.* p. 316.

KB. xxvii. 3: *yathā sahasraṁ pañcadaça cānuṣṭubhaḥ syus tathā . . . saṁpādayet.*

38. Just as in the case of clauses with *iti*, after a preceding clause with *yad*, a clause with *vai* intervenes giving a ground,[1] so when the main clause has *eva* or *tasmāt* a clause with *vai* frequently intervenes. It is usual[2] to take such clauses as giving the reason for the preceding clause in *yad*, but the real force is rather to add a further train in the reasoning, and the main clause is not that in *vai* but rather that in *eva*. Such clauses are common in both texts, e.g. *yad eva gāyatrībhir abhiṣṭauti gāyatraṁ vai prātaḥsavanaṁ tena prātaḥsavane (abhiṣṭutaṁ bhavati)*, AB. vi. 2. 8; *atha yad agniṁ prathamaṁ devatānāṁ yajaty agnir vai devānāṁ mukhaṁ mukhata eva tad devān prīṇāti*, KB. iii. 6; 7; 8; v. 8; viii. 6 (*ter*), &c. Or with *tasmāt*, *atha yad aparāhṇe pitṛyajñena caranty apakṣayabhājo vai pitaras tasmād aparāhṇe pitṛyajñena caranti*, KB. v. 6; *yad agniṁ kāvyavāhanam antato yajaty etat sviṣṭakṛto vai pitaras tasmād enam antato yajati*, v. 7. The *yad* clause states the fact to be explained, the *vai* clause the reason for it, and the *eva* or *tasmāt* clause the necessary conclusion. In any case the clause with *vai* is a parenthesis rather than an apodosis, and how exactly it was felt by the users of the phrase cannot now be determined.

39. By an illogical, if natural, use the fact to be explained is sometimes stated in the *yad* clause and the cause given in a clause with *hi*, and not as oftener *vai*. Thus *atha yad vyavagrāhaṁ devatā āvāhayati nānā hy ābhyo havīṅṣi gṛhītāni bhavanti*, KB. iii. 3; iv. 12; v. 5.

40. **Clauses of reported speech** stand regularly and very commonly in *oratio recta* with *iti*. But the *iti* may be, and not very rarely is, omitted, especially when *tad āhuḥ* or a similar expression has been used, and the extent of the quotation is left to the context to show. There are clear cases of this in AB. iii. 8; 22; KB. x. 1, 3; xii. 7; xvii. 1; xxiv. 8.

This omission is very natural, where in any case there occurs an *iti* at the end of the passage quoted, as in AB. iv. 25. 5; no case of a double *iti* occurs in the AB. There is room therefore for uncertainty in AB. v. 29. 1: *uvāca Jātūkarṇyo vaktā smo vā idaṁ devebhyo yad vai tad agnihotram ubhayedyur ahūyatānyedyur vāva tad etarhi hūyata iti* whether the *iti* belongs to *uvāca* or *vaktā smo* or to both, and also whether *yad* serves a double function as relative and particle = 'that'. Cf. also AB. i. 25. 15.

In one case cause seems to be expressed by both *yad* and *iti*, namely *içvaro hāsya vitte devā arantor: yad vā ayam alam ātmane 'maṅsteti*, AB. iii. 48. 8.

41. A distinctive feature of the prose is the free use of **prolongation**

[1] Cf. Eggeling, SBE. xxvi. 15.

[2] E.g. Delbrück, *Altind. Synt.* p. 573. Of course when, as often, the *vai* clause is the only apodosis, this view is correct.

of vowels for purposes of emphasis. It is thus in place in the asking of a question: thus in AB. vi. 26. 10: *vihṛtā3ṁ stotrā3m avihṛtā3m iti*; vi. 34. 3: *prāvocā3ḥ iti . . . no hi na pratyajñāsthā3ḥ iti* and so often. Another characteristic use is that at the conclusion of a *yad* clause giving the topic of discussion, as *yad eva na saṁ çaṁsati 3 ī ātmā vai stotriyaḥ*, vi. 26. 5; *yad eva çilpānī 3 ī ātmasaṁskṛtir vāva çilpāni*, vi. 27. 4, and so often. Thirdly it is used merely as emphatic to bring out the full importance of a word, as in *tad āhur mahāvādā3ḥ*, AB. v. 33. 1.

42. The order of words in the texts presents few points of note. The regular practice of placing the subject after the predicate is adhered to freely, but there are of course exceptions, and in many cases which is subject or predicate must remain doubtful.[1] Occasionally a deliberate change of order is found, as in AB. ii. 28. 5: *prāṇā vai dvidevatyā āgūr vajraḥ*. In many cases the distinction of predicate and subject is expressly made by the use of *yad* to introduce the subject, as in AB. ii. 28. 3: *saṁsthā vā eṣā yad anuvaṣaṭkāraḥ*.

43. The text as preserved is unaccented. It is no doubt the case that it originally was duly accented, but the accents have not been preserved by the tradition. So in the case of the *Pañcaviṅça Brāhmaṇa* we have a formal record that it was once accented in the style of the *Çatapatha* and was still so extant at the time of the *Bhāṣikasūtra* (ii. 32),[2] but by Kumārila's time it had ceased to bear accents.[3]

C. *Style.*

It is impossible to place the *Brāhmaṇas* in any respectable position as regards their style. The *Kauṣītaki* is distinctly inferior to the *Aitareya*, as the former text is everywhere so seriously condensed as to be needlessly and notoriously hard to understand. The *Aitareya* has all the demerits common to the Brāhmaṇas, but it does not suffer normally from excessive brevity. This is one of the reasons which would in any case have thrown doubt on the genuineness of vii. 10 and 11; it would be impossible in the whole of the rest of the text to discover any similar abbreviation of the arguments, whereas in the *Kauṣītaki* the passage (iii. 1) on which the second of the spurious passages is based is perfectly normal and in place. Similarly in all the legends narrated the brevity of the *Kauṣītaki* is excessive, and illustrates that tendency to abandon literary composition for mnemonic phraseology which finds its full development in the monstrosities of the philosophical Sūtras.

[1] Cf. Eggeling, SBE. xxvi. 211, n. 2.

[2] Kielhorn, *Ind. Stud.* x. 421.

[3] See Burnell, *Sāmavidhāna Brāhmaṇa*, p. vi. Cf., however, his *Saṁhitopaniṣad Brāhmaṇa*, p. xiii.

While the *Aitareya*, by its lack of exclusive devotion to brevity, avoids none of the obscurity of the *Kauṣītaki*, it would be idle to assert that it is simple or clear in style. A good deal of it is fairly easy to understand, but there remains much that can never have been anything but obscure. Doubtless this is due in no small degree to the nature of the subject-matter; the pseudo-profundity of the texts reflects itself in the vagueness of their language. But this defect is also, in part at least, accounted for by the fact that the texts were the subjects of oral transmission and explanation, and that, therefore, it was sufficient to mention a matter allusively, leaving the meaning to be made clear by the teacher. A good instance of this defect is the phrase *ā caturaṁ vai dvandvaṁ mithunaṁ prajananaṁ prajātyai*, which occurs in the *Kauṣītaki* (iii. 9; vii. 10; xxix. 3). What it actually means we are reduced to guessing; it is not more than a brief mnemonic of a fact which is regarded as known to those who listened to the Brāhmaṇa.

The language of the Brāhmaṇas, as has been seen, is very definitely restricted in its grammatical forms, and thus a certain precision is never wanting, but it is only fair to the compilers of these texts to admit that they do all that is possible to lessen the advantage thus conferred upon them. This they accomplish by the constant practice of ellipsis, by the rapid and bewildering change of subject, and by the undue straining of the force of single words and cases. The word *iti* helps them indefinitely in this struggle to avoid definiteness; it is much more often than not allowed to stand alone to show that the sentence it ends contains either a fact stated, or a purpose set forth as explaining the action mentioned in the preceding clause. A further aid is the repeated use of interpolated clauses with the particle *vai* which supply the place of statements in parentheses in English, but which are used not here and there, but everywhere. Another support is the use of the demonstrative pronouns without any feeling for discrimination, and the dative of end contemplated repeatedly saves a sentence.

In a style of this kind ornament would doubtless be out of place, and at any rate it is carefully avoided. An interesting or novel metaphor or simile cannot be found in either Brāhmaṇa, and in both of them similes are distinctly rare. The few that occur are merely taken from the most normal aspects of life, such as the movement of a chariot, or the speed of horses.

The structure of the sentences is drearily monotonous; parataxis is wearisomely frequent, and the chief form of subordinate clause is the explanatory which begins with a *yad* clause, is often followed by a clause in *vai*, and then concludes with a clause in *eva*, a form even more affected by the *Kauṣītaki* than by the *Aitareya*. There is no objection to a chapter consisting, as does the *Aitareya*, v. 8, of a series of sentences precisely the same in shape and form, and in this, as in many other respects, it is easy to see the genesis in the Brāhmaṇas of the style which disfigures so many of the Pāli texts.

On the other hand in some things the style of the Brāhmaṇas remains natural and simple and reminds us that it represents the only natural Sanskrit prose, save to a very much less degree that of the fable literature. It is free from the worst features of the nominal style of classical Sanskrit; if it overworks the dative of end, it has hardly developed the ablative of cause, which is a leading feature of the philosophical Sūtras. It is free in its use of verbal forms, and has no preference for passive constructions. Gerunds and passive participles are quite rare, and are used in strictly reasonable proportions. Even more important perhaps is the fact that the long compound, which has all the possible disadvantages of any form of speech, has not come into being.

The result is that in a few passages the *Aitareya* is really satisfactory. The narrative of Çunaḥçepa is not a model of style but it is a competent piece of work, and reads easily enough. But it must be admitted that most of its merit it does not owe to the Brāhmaṇa at all, but to the inserted verses, without which the prose would show little enough to praise. It is indeed a really astonishing fact that while verse could show very real qualities of style the prose should fall so lamentably short, but the same phenomenon is familiar in other branches of literature, and notably in that of the drama. Of these verses the best is one which expresses with simplicity and felicity the philosophy of human and divine effort:

caran vai madhu vindati caran svādum udumbaram
sūryasya paçya çremāṇaṁ yo na tandrayate caran.

But this verse and its fellows are alien to the Brāhmaṇa and but serve to mark the distinction which exists between the literary form of the gnomic poetry of the day and the stiffness and lack of beauty of the theosophic prose style.

D. *Metre.*

There are twenty-nine Çlokas in the narrative of Çunaḥçepa (AB. vii. 13–18) and their metrical form is decidedly interesting. Of the fifty-eight half-verses all but one end in an iambus, and all but two in a di-iambus, and the former line is one which has the unparalleled occurrence of di-iambi at the first and third Pādas:

Madhuchandaḥ çṛṇotana Ṛṣabho Reṇur Aṣṭakaḥ
ye ke ca bhrātara sthana asmai jyaiṣṭhyāya kalpadhvam.

Kalpadhvam is a strange expression for which Böhtlingk conjectures *tiṣṭhata*, but that is not necessary. The other line ends in *tu dvāparaḥ*. Moreover the rule which forbids ⏓ ⏑ ⏑ ⏓ in any foot is rigidly adhered to to the extent of resulting in the use of the subjunctive *carāti* for *carati* in *carāti carato bhagaḥ*, though the sense of *carāti* suits well enough, but *kiṁ nu malam* is found in a prior Pāda.

In the odd Pādas the pervading form is that known later as the Pathyā ending in ⏑ – – ⏓, but only fifteen out of fifty-eight Pādas end in it, whereas later on it is the normal form. The variants are:

⏓ – – – ⏑ – – ⏓ 6 ⏓ – – ⏑ ⏑ – – ⏓ 2
– – ⏑ – ⏑ – – ⏓ 3 – ⏑ – ⏑ ⏑ – – ⏑ 1
⏓ ⏑ – – ⏑ – – ⏓ 3

The short at the end is found nine times.

The form ending in ⏑ ⏑ ⏑ ⏓, later a common variant (the first Vipulā), occurs only four times:

⏓ – – – ⏑ ⏑ ⏑ ⏑ 3 – ⏑ ⏑ – ⏑ ⏑ ⏑ ⏑ 1

Neither of these forms is allowed in classical metre; in every case ⏑ is found at the end.

The form ending in – ⏑ ⏑ ⏓ occurs six times (the second Vipulā):

⏑ – ⏑ – – ⏑ ⏑ ⏓ 2 ⏑ ⏑ – – – ⏑ ⏑ ⏑ 1
– ⏑ – ⏑ – ⏑ ⏑ ⏑ 1 – – – – – ⏑ ⏑ ⏑ 2

In one case only – is found.

The form ending in – – – ⏓ occurs twelve times, nearly as often as the Pathyā (the third Vipulā):

– – ⏑ – –, – – ⏓ 4 – – – ⏑ – – – ⏓ 2 ⏑ ⏑ – – – – – – 1
– – – – – – – ⏓ 4 – – ⏑ ⏑ – – – ⏑ 1

At the end ⏑ and – balance.

The form ending in – ⏑ – ⏓ occurs six times (the fourth Vipulā):

– ⏑ ⏑ – – ⏑ – ⏑ 1 ⏑ – ⏑ ⏑, – ⏑ – ⏑ 1
⏑ – – – – ⏑ – ⏑ 1 – – – ⏑ – ⏑ – – 1
⏑ ⏑ – – – ⏑ – ⏑ 1

one irregular (*sarve rādhyāḥ stha putrāḥ*). The last syllable is normally short.[1]

The form ending in – – ⏑ ⏓ occurs four times:

⏑ – – – – – ⏑ – 2 – – ⏑ – – – ⏑ ⏓ 2 (one ⏑ at end).

The form ending in ⏑ ⏑ – ⏓ occurs three times:

– – – – ⏑ ⏑ – ⏑ 2 ⏑ – ⏑ – ⏑ ⏑ – ⏑ 1

The form ending in ⏑ – ⏑ ⏓ occurs eight times:

⏓ – – – ⏑ – ⏑ ⏓ 3 ⏑ – – ⏑ ⏑ – ⏑ ⏑ 2
– – ⏑ – ⏑ – ⏑ ⏑ 2 – ⏑ – – ⏑ – ⏑ ⏑ 1

The last three forms are wholly alien to classical versification, and it is

[1] Thus in Vipulās 1, 2, and 4 the short ending markedly prevails.

significant that the di-iambic ending is found in 15·5 per cent. of the verses, and that the forbidden forms are nearly 28 per cent. of the whole. But the figure is really far higher, for the only forms allowed in the later poetry are in all twenty-five in number, viz. fifteen in the Pathyā form, two in – ⏑ ⏑ ⏓, five in –, – – ⏓, and three in – ⏑ – ⏓.

Further, in arriving at these results, it is necessary to take into consideration various contractions which must be resolved, while again some contractions must be made. Thus *na apāgāḥ* is necessary; *yāvanto apsu* must stand (*o* no doubt short), *ābhūtir eṣābhūtir* must be resolved; *rādhyāḥ* and *sauhardyāya* made into *rādhi(y)āḥ* and *sauhardi(y)āya*; *syāt* at the end of a line made *si(y)āt*; *cādhipatye* read *ca ādhipatya*, and also *yathaivāñgirasaḥ* must be read *yathaiva āñgirasaḥ*. On the other hand *sa irāvaty atitāriṇī* must be read as *serāvaty*, and *ma upetā* as *mopetā*. These are, of course, phenomena which cannot be paralleled even in the epic save to a very limited degree. The Upaniṣads of the older type (e.g. *Kaṭha* and *Īçā*) have similar phenomena.

In the verses in the account of the consecration of the kings (AB. vii. 21–23) are twelve Çlokas; none of these ends in anything save a di-iambus except one which terminates with *āḍhyaduhitṛṇām*, where *duhi* counts as but one syllable, as also in a Triṣṭubh verse in vii. 13. In these verses again are found a resolution like *niṣkakaṇṭhi(y)aḥ* for *°kaṇṭhyaḥ* and *medhi(y)ān* for *medhyān*, and a contraction like *martyeva* for *martya iva*.

Nevertheless the appearance of the verses from the metrical standpoint is different in a marked degree from that of the Çunaḥçepa episode. The Pathyā form occurs fifteen times out of twenty-four as contrasted with fifteen out of fifty-eight; the forms are ⏓ – – – ⏑ – – ⏓ 5; – – – ⏑ ⏑ – – ⏓ 4; ⏓ – ⏑ – ⏑ – – ⏓ 3; ⏑ ⏑ – ⏑ ⏑ – – ⏓ 2; ⏑ ⏑ – – ⏑ – – ⏓ 1. The form in ⏑ ⏑ ⏑ ⏓ is found once (– – – ⏑ ⏑ ⏑ ⏑ ⏑); that in – ⏑ ⏑ ⏓ in – – – ⏑ – ⏑ ⏑ ⏑; that in – – – ⏓ three times (in – – ⏑ – –, – – ⏓ 2; – – – – – – – – 1). The form – – ⏑ – occurs in – – ⏑ – –, – ⏑ ⏓, and that in ⏑ ⏑ – ⏑ in ⏑ – – ⏑ ⏑ ⏑ – ⏑. The di-iambus occurs in ⏓ – – ⏑ ⏑ – ⏑ ⏓ twice, and this in one verse. But of the nine irregular forms eight are not allowed in classical Sanskrit, and this significantly indicates the nature of the verse.

The same phenomena recur in the verses in AB. viii. 25 and 27 (printed as prose in the editions); there are in all only four different half-verses, but of these one ends in ⏑ ⏑ ⏑ ⏑, which is a very rare ending, and the odd Pādas show

– – – – – ⏑ ⏑ ⏑; – – – – – – ⏑ ⏑;
– ⏑ – – – – – ⏓[1]; – – ⏑ – – – ⏑ –

A Yajñagāthā in AB. vii. 9. 15 is still more irregular.

[1] *tasya rājā mitraṃ bhavati* (*bhavati* = *hoti* as often in the epic and in the Upaniṣads).

In the AB. there occur also four Yajñagāthās in Triṣṭubh metre. Of these sixteen lines two are irregular in v. 30, the first having thirteen syllables, the latter ten, both with trochaic endings. The other fourteen lines all end in a double trochee, and the scheme of the verse is normally ⏑ – ⏑ –, ⏓ ⏑ ⏓ – ⏑ – ⏓. The proportion of the length in the several syllables are, long to short, as follows: (1) 5:9; (2) 10:4; (3) 7:7; (4) 13:1; (5) 6:8; (6) 2:12; (7) 8:6. The fourth syllable is normally followed by a diaeresis. There is no case of the similar composition of the whole four lines of the stanza, nor indeed are any two lines of any stanza the same, throughout, though in two cases two, and three in one case, are the same in the last seven syllables.

There are also four stanzas not Yajñagāthās; of these one (AB. viii. 21. 10) has lines of 12+12+10+13 syllables, the rhythm of the first, second, and fourth being iambic, the third being trochaic. Another is in Triṣṭubh, with *vyoman* as *vi(y)oman* and *duhitā* as disyllabic (vii. 13. 8); the last three lines are ⏓ – ⏑ – –, ⏑ ⏑ – ⏑ – ⏓, and the first only differs by having a long on the third syllable. The next verse (vii. 13. 13) is, on the other hand, quite irregular, the third line having a di-iambic instead of a trochaic conclusion. The fourth verse (v. 30. 11) is also irregular, the second line having only ten syllables.

These verses are therefore all definitely older than the epic in their metrical construction, and older even than the verses of the *Bṛhaddevatā*[1] and the *Ṛgvidhāna*,[2] works which, in all probability, fall about the beginning of the fourth century B.C.

The KB. contains a couple of verses of the Yajñagāthā type (xviii. 3; xxvii. 1), which differ greatly from the normal Çloka metre: the first has di-iambic endings with ⏑ – – – ⏑ ⏑ ⏑ ⏓ and – – – – ⏑ – – ⏓ for the odd Pādas; in the second the even Pādas end in ⏑ – – ⏓, and the odd Pādas are – – – ⏑ ⏑ ⏑ – – – and – – – – ⏑ – ⏑ ⏑.

§ 8. Commentaries and Editions.

For the *Aitareya Brāhmaṇa* there is available the commentary of Sāyaṇa, which is preserved, as Aufrecht has shown, in two divergent versions. Sāyaṇa's text of the AB. is that which is read in all the available MSS., and there are practically no variations of reading and certainly none of

[1] See Keith, JRAS. 1906, pp. 1 *seq.* For the Çloka metre see Oldenberg, GGN. 1909, pp. 219 *seq.*; comparison with Pāli texts, however, seems to me methodologically unsound. Oldenberg's use of the AB. in his account of the Triṣṭubh (ZDMG. xxxvii. 52–61) arrives at somewhat too definite results by ignoring the variety of forms actually found.

[2] Keith, JRAS. 1912, pp. 770–772.

any real meaning. This is seen by the fact that the other editions of the text subsequent to Aufrecht's, that in the *Anandāçrama* series, No. 32 (2 parts, Poona, 1896), by Kāçinātha Sāstry Āgāçe, that of the Nirṇaya Sāgara press, by Vāsudevaçarman Paṇaçikara and Kṛṣṇaṁbhaṭṭa Gore (Bombay, 1911), and that in the *Bibliotheca Indica*, by Satyavrata Sāmaçramī, agree in the text. The edition of Haug (Bombay, 1863) is indeed different in several points, but these changes cannot be regarded as more than mere blunders, many being due to the difficulty of early printing.

Sāyaṇa's commentary is admittedly much superior in value to his commentary on the Ṛgveda. As in the case of the *Taittirīya Saṁhitā* it shows real knowledge of the ritual, the Sūtras of Āçvalāyana, Āpastamba, and Baudhāyana being used with special frequency. Moreover he often cites real parallels from the *Taittirīya Saṁhitā* and the *Taittirīya Brāhmaṇa*, a fact which illustrates his familiarity, as commentator, with these two texts. He cites an earlier commentator, Govindasvāmin, by name[1] and mentions others.[2]

Aufrecht's text is of the greatest possible accuracy: apart from slight errors as at iii. 18. 9, there are but two clear errors, both of word division; in vii. 12. 3 *vāçvā(ḥ)* is a mistake for *vā çvā*, as is proved by the syntax and the parallel versions; in iv. 6. 5 *manorathāḥ* is an error for *anorathāḥ*. His excerpts from Sāyaṇa are excellently chosen, and admirably edited. The other editions have only a value as containing a fuller text of the commentary.

Haug's edition is accompanied by a translation, the first ever made into English of any Brāhmaṇa text. It is a work for its time of very great merit, and its chief defects are due to its being based on a defective text and to insufficient use of the commentary. The review of it by A. Weber in *Indische Studien*, ix (1865), is of considerable importance and corrects many of the errors of Haug, but unfortunately it does not deal with the more serious difficulties of interpretation arising from the contents, as contrasted with mere errors of translation. A very valuable series of grammatical criticisms is contained in an article of Böhtlingk's.[3]

The *Kauṣītaki Brāhmaṇa*, as opposed to the *Aitareya*, has received little attention; though it was early known in manuscript and described elaborately by Weber in an article in the second volume of the *Indische Studien* (1853), that account was never completed, and the text was not edited until 1887, when appeared the edition by B. Lindner (Jena, 1887): the second volume of the edition, which was to have contained a translation

[1] On AB. vi. 33. 16, where Aufrecht notes that he is cited in the *Dhātuvṛtti* under the root *valh*.

[2] On AB. vii. 10 (11).

[3] BKSGW. 15 Dec. 1900, pp. 418 *seq.*

and notes, has never appeared. Lindner's edition does not include the commentary of Vināyakabhaṭṭa, son of Mādhavabhaṭṭa, as the important work could not be edited from the available MSS. Some extracts from it are given by Weber in his article cited above, and it has been used by other scholars; the comment on Adhyāya x has been edited by R. Löbbecke[1] in 1908.

Unlike the *Aitareya* the *Kauṣītaki* shows two distinct MS. traditions, one that preserved in Vināyaka's commentary and most MSS.,[2] and one in a MS. (M in Lindner) in Burnell's collection in Malayālam script. The latter is clearly a MS. with a good, but not perfect, tradition, and Lindner might profitably have adopted many more of its readings than he has done. Thus in ii. 2, M has *adhi* for the impossible *abhi* of the other MSS., and *prācīm udīcīm* and *prācīr udīcīḥ* for the later forms *prāgudīcīm* and *prāgudīcīḥ* of the other MSS.; in iv. 6 *āpayīta* must replace the absurd *āpaiti*. On the other hand the MS. is clearly one interpolated and fond of glosses; in i. 2 *triṣu* for *eṣu* before *lokeṣu* is not at all probable; in ii. 1 *avadyotayati* is merely, it seems, a correction of *avajyotayati*; in iv. 12 *yasmin kalyāṇe nakṣatre* is no improvement on *yasmin nakṣatre*, and so often. The translation here given rests on Lindner's text, but also takes account of the Burnell MS.[3] There is also an edition in the *Ānandāçrama* series No. 65 (Çaka, 1832, A. D. 1911), by Gulābarāya Vajeçaṁkara Chāyā, but it has only the value of a very mediocre manuscript, from which doubtless it has been printed, with occasional corrections. It is practically, as opposed to Lindner's text, of no value whatever. Neither is punctuated.

[1] Caland, VOJ. xxiii. 68.

[2] Lindner used an India Office MS. (L), two of Wilson's Collection in the Bodleian (W and w), two other Bodleian MSS. (O and o), three Berlin MSS. (B, b, and K), and one of Max Müller's. Some readings from another Bodleian MS. are given in Winternitz and Keith, *Bodleian Catal.*, p. 48. That MS. has the same tradition as the Vulgate.

[3] See his *Catalogue of Vedic Manuscripts*, p. 7 (no. viii). The collation of Lindner as reported in his edition is very defective: thus in the difficult passage xxvii. 1 he omits to note the readings *tad etan* (which is infinitely superior to the difficult *tad enām* of his text), *prasisṛkṣāmi* (superior to *prasisṛkṣāṇi*), *puṅçcalyāyanam* (approaching (*āyanam*) a *puṅçcalī*, a better reading) and *saṁpādayati*. The superiority of M as a MS. is decisively shown in just such a case. Unhappily it has many lacunae and many errors, and could not be used as a basis for an edition. For some corrections of Lindner see Caland, VOJ. xxiii. 61–64; Keith, JRAS. 1915, pp. 498–504, and in the notes to the translation. M agrees with the Vulgate in the curious forms *cyavayati*, xii. 5 (for which there is some parallel), *añjati*, x. 1 (perhaps excused by *añjanti* in a quotation in x. 2), and *apajighnāte*, xxviii. 8, for which Gaastra suggests °*jaghnāte*, doubtless correctly.

TRANSLATION OF THE

AITAREYA BRĀHMAṆA

PAÑCIKĀ I

The Soma Sacrifice

ADHYĀYA I

The Consecration Sacrifice.

i. 1. Agni[1] is the lowest[2] of the gods, Viṣṇu the highest; between them are all the other deities. A cake to Agni and Viṣṇu on eleven potsherds they offer in connexion with the consecration; verily thus they offer it without omission to all the deities. All the deities are Agni; all the deities are Viṣṇu; Agni and Viṣṇu are the two terminal forms of the sacrifice. In that they offer the cake to Agni and Viṣṇu, verily thus at the ends they prosper as regards the gods.[3] They say 'In that the cake is on eleven potsherds, and Agni and Viṣṇu are two, what is the arrangement here for the two, what the division?' That for Agni is on eight potsherds; the Gāyatrī has eight syllables; the metre of Agni is the Gāyatrī. That for Viṣṇu is on three potsherds, for thrice did Viṣṇu stride across this. This is the arrangement here for the two, this the division. A pap in ghee should he offer, who considers himself unsupported; in this (earth) does he not find support who does not find support. Ghee is the milk of the woman, the rice grains that of the man; that is a pairing; with a pairing verily thus does he propagate him with offspring and cattle, for generation; he is propagated with offspring and with cattle who knows thus. He has grasped the sacrifice, he has grasped the deities, who offers the new and full moon sacrifices. Having sacrificed with the new moon or full moon oblation he should consecrate

[1] AB. i. 1-6, corresponding to KB. vii. 1-4, deals with the consecration sacrifice which according to different authorities precedes or follows the consecration proper. For the ritual see ĀÇS. iv. 2. 1-8; ÇÇS. v. 3. 1-9; Caland and Henry, *L'Agniṣṭoma*, pp. 15, 16.

[2] Sāyaṇa refers these terms to the place of the deities in the litanies of the Agniṣṭoma, the Ājya Çastra being addressed to Agni, and the last Çastra, the Āgnimāruta, containing a verse to Viṣṇu, while Haug insists that the terms are of locality in the universe, and hence only secondarily correspond with the position of the gods at the sacrifice. Both sides of the relation are clearly present to the Brāhmaṇa. Cf. RV. iv. 1. 5; ÇB. iii. 1. 3. 1; v. 2. 3. 6; KB. vii. 2; TS. v. 5. 1. 4 cited by Aufrecht, who, for Agni as all other gods, cites TS. vi. 2. 2. 6; TB. iii. 2. 3. 10.

[3] In Haug's view the sense of *rdh* with acc. is 'make to prosper', rather than 'satisfy' as taken in BR., or 'worship', as in Sāyaṇa's *paricaranti*. Rather the accusative is one of reference; see Keith, *Taittirīya Saṁhitā*, p. 100, n. 3.

himself in the same oblation, the same strew; this is one consecration.[4] Seventeen[5] kindling verses should he recite; Prajāpati is seventeenfold; the months are twelve, the seasons five through the union of winter and the cool season[6]; so great is the year; Prajāpati is the year. With these (verses) which abide in Prajāpati does he prosper who knows thus.

i. 2. The sacrifice went away from the gods; it they sought to start up with offerings; in that they sought to start it up with offerings that is why offerings have their name. They found it; he prospers having found the sacrifice who knows thus. The libations (*āhuti*) are callings by name, for by them the sacrificer calls to the gods; that is why libations have their name. Ways[1] (*ūti*) rather are they called by which the gods come to the call of the sacrificer; paths and passages are ways; verily thus are they the roads to heaven of the sacrificer. They say, 'Since another pours the libation, then why do they style Hotṛ him who recites (the invitatory verses) and says the offering verses?' In that he here according to their portion invites the deities, (saying[2]) 'Bring hither N. N., bring hither N. N.', that is why the Hotṛ has the name. A Hotṛ becomes he, a Hotṛ they call him who knows thus.

i. 3. Him whom they consecrate the priests make into an embryo again. With waters they sprinkle; the waters are seed; verily having made him possessed of seed they consecrate him. With fresh butter they anoint; to the gods appertains melted butter, to men fragrant ghee, slightly melted butter to the fathers, fresh butter to embryos.[1] In that they anoint with fresh butter, verily thus they make him successful with his own portion. They anoint him completely; ointment is the brilliance in the eyes; verily thus having made him possessed of brilliance they consecrate him. With twenty-one handfuls of Darbha they purify him; verily thus purified and pure they consecrate him. They conduct him to the hut of the consecrated; the hut of the consecrated is the womb of the consecrated; verily thus they conduct him to his own womb; therefore (in and) from a firm womb he stands and moves; therefore (in and) from a firm womb embryos are placed and grow forth. Therefore the sun should not rise or set on the consecrated

[4] The rule is laid down by ĀÇS. iv. 1. 1 that the new and full moon sacrifices should precede the Agrayaṇa, the Nirūḍhapaçu, the Cāturmāsyas, and the Soma sacrifice, but he admits (iv. 1. 2) that the reverse order was possible and the other Sūtras leave the order undecided. The sacrifice here laid down for the consecration is in fact a mere variant of the full moon rite.

[5] i.e. the usual fifteen, ĀÇS. i. 2. 7, and two Dhāyyās, iv. 2. 1. On the other hand, fifteen only are prescribed in ÇÇS. v. 8. 3 and in KB.

[6] Cf. Macdonell and Keith, *Vedic Index*, i. 110, 111.

[1] As Aufrecht points out, this derivation is not intended as grammatically correct.

[2] See AÇS. i. 2. 6; ÇÇS. i. 4. 22 seq.

i. 3. [1] Cf. TS. vi. 1. 1.4; ÇB. iii. 1. 3.8; and for §§ 9 and 10, 11, 15 and 16, 19, cf. TS. vi. 1. 2. 1; 2.5.5; 1. 3. 2; 4. 3; Lévi, *La doctrine du sacrifice*, pp. 103–105.

elsewhere than in the hut of the consecrated, nor should they call out to him. With a garment they cover him; the garment is the caul of the consecrated; verily thus they cover him with a caul. Above that is the black antelope skin; the placenta is above the caul; verily thus they cover him with the placenta. He closes his hands[2]; verily closing its hands the embryo lies within; with closed hands the child is born. In that he closes his hands, verily thus he clasps in his hands the sacrifice and all the deities. They say, 'There is no competing pressing[3] for him who is first consecrated; the sacrifice is grasped by him, the deities are grasped; no misfortune is his as there is of him who is not consecrated first.' Having loosened the black antelope skin, he descends to the final bath; therefore embryos are born freed from the placenta; with the garment he descends; therefore a child is born with a caul.

i. 4. 'Thou, O Agni, art extending' and 'O Soma, thy wondrous' should he recite as invitatory verses[1] for the butter portions for him who previously has not sacrificed; 'with thee they extend the sacrifice' (he says[2]); verily thus for him he extends the sacrifice. 'Agni with ancient thought' and 'O Soma, with verses thee' (he should use[3]) for him who has sacrificed before; in the word 'ancient' he refers to the former offering. This is not to be regarded. 'May Agni slay the foe' and 'Thou, O Soma, art very lord' (these should he recite and) make (the butter portions) contain a reference to the slaying of Vṛtra.[4] Vṛtra he slays to whom the sacrifice condescends; therefore should they be made to contain a reference to the slaying of Vṛtra. 'Agni the head, the first of the deities' and 'With Agni, O Viṣṇu, the highest great penance' are the invitatory and offering verses of the oblation for Agni and Viṣṇu[5]; they are perfect in form as being addressed to Agni and Viṣṇu; that in the sacrifice is perfect which is perfect in form, that rite which as it is performed the verse describes. Agni and Viṣṇu are the guardians of consecration of the gods; they are lords of the consecration; in that the oblation is for Agni and Viṣṇu, (it is because they desire[6]) 'May those who are the lords of the consecration, being delighted, confer consecration, may those who consecrate consecrate.' They are Triṣṭubh verses, to secure power.

[2] See ApÇS. xi. 18. 7.

[3] i.e. a sacrifice instituted at the same time and place by another sacrificer; a mountain or stream constitutes a sufficient local differentiation; see ĀÇS. vi. 6. 11.

[1] RV. v. 13. 4 and i. 91. 9. These are the *sadvantau* which are used in the ordinary Iṣṭi; see KB. i. 1; ÇÇS. ii. 2. 13.

[2] RV. v. 13. 4 c.

[3] RV. viii. 44. 12 and i. 91. 11

[4] RV. vi. 16. 34 and i. 91. 5.

[5] Not in RV. and therefore given in full in ĀÇS. iv. 2. 3.

[6] The correct sense of the use of *iti* is realized by Sāyaṇa; it is very common in the AB. and KB., especially the latter, but is normally disregarded by Haug.

i. 5. Gāyatrī verses[1] should he use as the invitatory and offering verses of the Sviṣṭakṛt, who desires brilliance or splendour; the Gāyatrī is brilliance and splendour; brilliant and resplendent does he become who knowing thus uses Gāyatrī verses. Uṣṇih verses[2] should he use who desires life; the Uṣṇih is life; he lives all his days who knowing thus uses Uṣṇih verses. Anuṣṭubh verses[3] should he use who desires the heaven; of two Anuṣṭubhs there are sixty-four syllables; three worlds each twenty-onefold are there stretching upwards; with twenty-one (verses) each he mounts these worlds; with the sixty-fourth he finds support in the world of heaven; support he finds who knowing thus uses Anuṣṭubh verses. Bṛhatī verses[4] should he use who desires prosperity and glory; the Bṛhatī is prosperity and glory among the metres; verily prosperity and glory he places in himself who knowing thus uses Bṛhatī verses. Pañkti verses[5] should he use who desires the sacrifice; the sacrifice is fivefold; verily the sacrifice condescends to him who knowing thus uses Pañkti verses. Triṣṭubh verses[6] should he use who desires strength; the Triṣṭubh is force, power, and strength; possessed of force, power, and strength does he become who knowing thus uses Triṣṭubh verses. Jagatī verses[7] should he use who desires cattle; cattle are connected with the Jagatī; he becomes possessed of cattle who knowing thus uses Jagatī verses. Virāj verses[8] should he use who desires proper food; the Virāj is food; therefore he who here has most food is most glorious in the world; that is why the Virāj has its name (the glorious). Glorious among his own is he, best of his own does he become who knows thus.

i. 6. Now the Virāj is a metre of five strengths; in that it has three Padas, it is the Uṣṇih and Gāyatrī; in that its Padas have eleven syllables, it is the Triṣṭubh; in that it has thirty-three syllables, it is the Anuṣṭubh, for metres are not different by reason of one syllable, nor yet by two; in that it is the Virāj, that is its fifth (strength). The strength of all the metres he wins, the strength of all the metres he attains, unity with and identity of form and world with all the metres he attains, an eater of food, a lord of food he becomes, with his offspring he attains proper food, who knowing thus uses Virāj verses. Therefore should Virāj verses[8] be used, namely 'Kindled, O Agni' and 'These, O Agni'. The consecration is holy order, the consecration is truth; therefore by one who is consecrated should truth alone be spoken. Rather they say, 'What man ought to speak all truth; the gods are

[1] RV. iii. 11. 2 and 1. For *saṁyājye* see AÇS. ii. 1. 21. The term is not used in ÇÇS.
[2] RV. i. 79. 4 and 5.
[3] RV. i. 45. 1 and 2.
[4] RV. vii. 16. 1 and 3.
[5] RV. v. 6. 1 and 2.
[6] RV. i. 95. 1 and 2.
[7] RV. v. 11. 1 and 2.
[8] RV. vii. 1. 3 and 18.

of truth compact,[1] but men of untruth compact.' He should speak with (the word[2]) 'discerning'; 'the discerning is the eye, for by it he sees distinctly' (they say). Now the eye is truth deposited among men; therefore to him who narrates they say, 'Hast thou seen?' If he replies 'I have seen', then him they believe. But if a man himself sees, he believes not even many others. Therefore should he speak with (the word) 'discerning'; his speech is uttered as essentially true.[3]

ADHYĀYA II

The Introductory Sacrifice.

i. 7 (ii. 1). In[1] that there is the introductory (sacrifice), thereby they advance to the world of heaven; that is why the introductory (sacrifice: Prāyaṇīya) has its name (advancing). The introductory (sacrifice) is expiration, the concluding (sacrifice) is out-breathing, the Hotṛ is common, for expiration and out-breathing are common, for the arrangement of the breaths, for the discrimination of the breaths. The sacrifice went away from the gods; the gods could do nothing, they could not discern it. They said to Aditi, 'Through thee let us discern the sacrifice.' She said, 'So be it, but let me choose a boon from you.' 'Choose' (they replied). This boon she choose, 'Let the sacrifices begin from me and end with me.' 'So be it' (they replied). Therefore there is a pap to Aditi as introductory (offering), (a pap) to Aditi as concluding (offering), for as a boon by her was this chosen. Moreover she chose this boon, 'Through me shall ye know the eastern quarter, through Agni the southern, through Soma the western, through Savitṛ the northern.' He says the offering verse for Pathyā[2]; in that he says the offering verse for Pathyā, therefore does yonder (sun) arise in the east and set in the west, for it follows Pathyā. He says the offering verse for Agni[3]; in that he says the offering verse for Agni, therefore from the south the plants come first ripe, for the plants are connected with Agni. He says the offering verse for Soma[4]; in that he says the

[1] Cf. ÇB. i. 1. 1. 4: *satyam eva devā anṛtaṁ manuṣyāḥ.*

[2] The point is that he is to add in his addresses the word *vicakṣaṇa* to the proper name or (according to ĀpÇS. x. 12. 7, 8) *canasita* in the case of a Brahman. The passage is borrowed in GB. vii. 23.

[3] So Sāyaṇa; the compound can be reduced into *satyā uttarā*, the rest of his speech is made true by using *vicakṣaṇa*. For the superiority of sight to hearing cf. TB. i. 1. 4. 2; ÇB. i. 3. 1. 27; below AB. ii. 40.

i.7. [1] AB. i. 7-11 contains the introductory sacrifice as in KB. vii. 5-9; for the ritual see ĀÇS. iv. 3. 1-8; ÇÇS. v. 5. 1-7; Caland and Henry, *L'Agniṣṭoma*, pp. 28, 29. For §§ 2 and 3 cf. KB. vii. 5, 6, 8; for § 3 TS. vi. 1. 5. 1; MS. iii. 7. 1; ÇB. iii. 2. 3. 1 *seq.*; Lévi, *La doctrine du sacrifice*, pp. 49, 50.

[2] RV. x. 63. 15 and 16 are the verses used at the sacrifice.

[3] RV. i. 189. 1; x. 2. 3. The use of *āyanti* suggests rice brought north from S. India.

[4] RV. i. 91. 1 and 4.

offering verse for Soma therefore westward flow many rivers, for the waters are connected with Soma. He says the offering verse for Savitṛ[5]; in that he says the offering verse for Savitṛ, therefore on the north-west he that blows blows most, for he blows instigated by Savitṛ. For Aditi[6] last he says the offering verse; in that he says the offering verse for Aditi last, therefore yonder (sky) wets this (earth) with rain and snuffs it up. For five deities does he say the offering verses; the sacrifice is fivefold; all the regions are in order, the sacrifice also is in order, for that people is (all) in order, where there is a Hotṛ knowing thus.

i. 8 (ii. 2). He who desires brilliance and splendour should turn towards the east with the libations of the fore-offerings; the eastern quarter is brilliance and splendour; brilliant and resplendent does he become who knowing thus goes to the east. He who desires proper food should turn towards the south with the libations of the fore-offerings; Agni is eater of food and lord of food; he becomes an eater of food, a lord of food, with his offspring he attains proper food who knowing thus turns to the south. He who desires cattle should turn west with the libations of the fore-offerings; the waters are cattle; he becomes possessed of cattle who knowing thus turns west. He who desires the drinking of Soma should turn north with the libations of the fore-offerings; Soma the king is in the north; he obtains the drinking of Soma who knowing thus turns north; the upward region is heavenly; in all the quarters he prospers. These worlds are turned towards one another[1]; turned towards him these worlds shine for prosperity for him who knows thus. For Pathyā he says the offering verse; in that he says the offering verse for Pathyā, verily thus at the beginning of the sacrifice he gathers speech together. Agni and Soma are expiration and inspiration, Savitṛ (serves) for instigation, Aditi for support. Verily for Pathyā he says the offering verse; in that he says the offering verse for Pathyā, verily thus with speech he leads the sacrifice to the path. Agni and Soma are the eyes; Savitṛ (serves) for instigation, Aditi for support. By the eye the gods discerned the sacrifice; by the eye that is discerned which cannot be discerned; therefore even after wandering in confusion, when a man perceives with the eye immediately,[2] then he discerns indeed. In that the gods discerned the sacrifice, in this (earth) they discerned, in it they gathered together; from[3] it is the sacrifice extended, from it is it performed, from it is it gathered

[5] RV. x. 82. 7 and 9.

[6] RV. x. 63. 10 and the verse *mahīm ū ṣu*, AV. vii. 6. 2.

[1] The sense is uncertain; Sāyaṇa has *svocitabhogaprada*, Haug 'linked together'.

[2] *Anuṣṭhyā* is rendered 'successively' by Haug, which agrees generally with *kenāpi yatnaviçeṣeṇa*.

[3] Sāyaṇa has the loc. as the explanation; so Haug, but abl. or dat. alone can be meant.

together, for Aditi is this (earth). Thus he says the offering verse for Aditi last; in that he says the offering verse for Aditi last, it is for the discernment of the sacrifice, for the revealing of the world of heaven.

i. 9 (ii. 3). 'The subjects of the gods should be brought into order,' they say; 'as they are brought into order, the subjects of men come into order.' All the subjects come into order, the sacrifice comes into order also, (all) is in order for that people where there is a Hotṛ knowing thus. He recites,[1]

> 'Prosperity to us in the ways, in the deserts,
> Prosperity in the waters, in the abode which hath the light,
> Prosperity to us in the wombs that bear children,
> Prosperity for wealth do ye, O Maruts, bestow.'

The Maruts are the subjects of the gods; verily thus at the beginning of the sacrifice he brings them into order. 'With all the metres should he say the offering verse,' they say; having sacrificed with all the metres, the gods conquered the world of heaven; verily thus the sacrificer having sacrificed with all the metres conquers the world of heaven. 'Prosperity to us in the ways, in the deserts' and 'The highest safety in the way' are the Triṣṭubh verses for Pathyā Svasti.[2] 'O Agni, lead us by a fair path to wealth' and 'We have come to the path of the gods' are the Triṣṭubh verses for Agni.[3] 'Thou, O Soma, skilled in thought' and 'Thine abodes in the sky, on the earth' are the Triṣṭubh verses for Soma.[4] 'The god of all, the lord of the good' and 'Who all these beings' are the Gāyatrī verses for Savitṛ.[5] 'The good protector, the earth, sky unequalled' and 'The great one, the mother of those of good vows' are the Jagatī verses for Aditi.[6] These are all the metres, Gāyatrī, Triṣṭubh, and Jagatī, the others are dependent (on them), for these are used most prominently in the sacrifice. By means of these metres the sacrificer has sacrificed with all metres, who knows thus.

i. 10 (ii. 4). The invitatory and offering verses of this oblation contain the words[1] 'forward', 'lead', 'path', and 'prosperity'; having sacrificed with them the gods won the world of heaven; verily thus also the sacrificer having sacrificed with them wins the world of heaven. In them there is the line, 'Prosperity for wealth do ye, O Maruts, bestow'; the Maruts, as subjects of the gods,[2] occupy the atmosphere; whoever without notification to them goes to the world of heaven they are likely to obstruct him or to crush him. In that he says, 'Prosperity for wealth do ye, O Maruts, bestow,' he announces the sacrificer to the Maruts the subjects of the gods;

[1] RV. x. 63. 15.
[2] RV. x. 63. 15 and 16.
[3] RV. i. 189. 1 and x. 2. 3.
[4] RV. i. 91. 1 and 4.
[5] RV. v. 82. 7 and 9.
[6] RV. x. 63. 10 and AV. vii. 6. 2.

i. 10. [1] The word *netṛ* occurs only in the form *naya*, but the way of denoting roots varies greatly in AB. and KB.; cf. p. 80.
[2] Cf. KB. vii. 8; TS. vi. 1. 5. 3.

the Maruts, the subjects of the gods, do not obstruct him as he goes to the world of heaven, nor do they crush him. Prosperously they speed him to the world of heaven who knows thus. The invitatory and offering verses of the oblation for Sviṣṭakṛt should be the two Virāj[3] verses of thirty-three syllables, 'May Agni here be above the other Agnis' and 'The Agni who guardeth from the foe'. Having sacrificed with the two Virāj verses, the gods won the world of heaven; verily thus also the sacrificer having sacrificed with two Virāj verses wins the world of heaven. They are of thirty-three syllables; the gods are thirty-three, eight Vasus, eleven Rudras, twelve Ādityas, Prajāpati, and the *vaṣaṭ* call. Thus at the very beginning of the sacrifice he makes the deities sharers in the syllables; verily thus syllable by syllable he delights a deity; verily thus by a vessel for the gods he gladdens the deities.

i. 11 (ii. 5). 'The introductory (sacrifice) should be performed with the fore-offerings but without the after-offerings' they say;[1] 'in that there are after-offerings in the introductory (sacrifice), there is deficiency as it were, and delay as it were.' That is not to be regarded. It should be performed with the fore-offerings and also with the after-offerings;[2] the fore-offerings are the breaths, the after-offerings offspring; if he were to omit the fore-offerings he would omit the breaths of the sacrificer; if he were to omit the after-offerings, he would omit the offspring of the sacrificer; therefore should it be performed with the fore-offerings and also with the after-offerings. He should not perform the joint sacrifices for the wives (with the gods), nor should he offer with the concluding Yajus. By so much is the sacrifice incomplete. He should preserve the scrapings of the introductory (sacrifice) and mingle them with the concluding (sacrifice), for the continuity of the sacrifice, to prevent a breach in the sacrifice. Or rather in the pot in which he throws the introductory (sacrifice) into that he should throw the concluding (sacrifice). By so much the sacrifice becomes continuous and without a breach. 'Thereby they prosper in yonder world, not in this,' they say, 'in that it is introductory (advancing); as introductory they offer, as introductory they proceed; verily the sacrificers advance away from this world.' In ignorance verily they say thus. He should intertwine the invitatory and the offering verses; the invitatory verses of the introductory (sacrifice) he should make the offering verses of the concluding (sacrifice); the invitatory verses of the concluding (sacrifice) he should make the offering verses of the introductory (sacrifice). Thus he intertwines for success in both worlds, for support in both worlds; in both worlds is he successful, in

[3] RV. vii. 1. 14 and 15.

[1] For this discussion see TS. vi. 1. 5. 3.

[2] For the former see ĀÇS. i. 5. 5 *seq.*; ÇÇS. i. 6. 16 *seq.*; for the latter ĀÇS. i. 8. 7; ÇÇS. i. 12. 13 *seq.*

both worlds he finds support. He finds support who knows thus. There is a pap for Aditi at the introductory, and one for Aditi at the concluding (sacrifice), for the support of the sacrifice, for the tying of the knots of the sacrifice, to prevent the slipping of the sacrifice. Just as then, he used to say, one ties the knots at both ends of a rope to prevent slipping, so at both ends of the sacrifice he ties knots to prevent slipping, in that there is a pap for Aditi at the introductory and also one for Aditi at the concluding sacrifice. With Pathyā Svasti hence they advance, in Pathyā Svasti they end; prosperously hence they advance, prosperously they end.

ADHYĀYA III

The Buying of the Soma

i. 12 (iii. 1). In[1] the eastern quarter the gods bought Soma the king; therefore in the eastern quarter is he bought. Him from the thirteenth month they bought; therefore the thirteenth month is not known; the Soma seller is not known, for the Soma seller is evil. The strengths and powers of him when bought and going towards men went away to the quarters; them they sought to win with one verse; they could not win them; them with two, with three, with four, with five, with six, with seven they could not win; with eight they won, with eight they obtained; that is why eight has its name. Whatever he desires he attains who knows thus. Therefore in these rites eight (verses) each are repeated, to win powers and strengths.

i. 13 (iii. 2). 'For Soma when bought and being brought forward, do thou say the invitatory verse' the Adhvaryu says. 'From good to better do thou come forward' he says;[1] this world is good; than it yonder world is better; verily thus he causes the sacrificer to go to the world of heaven. 'Let Bṛhaspati be thy harbinger' (he says); Bṛhaspati is the holy power; verily thus he makes the holy power precede him; what has the holy power come to no harm. 'Do thou stay on the chosen spot of earth' (he says). The chosen spot of earth is the place of sacrifice to the gods; verily thus he settles him on the chosen spot of earth. 'Do thou drive afar the foes, with all powers' (he says); verily thus he drives away the evil rival who hates him, and brings him low. 'O Soma, thy wondrous' this triplet to Soma[2] in Gāyatrī

[1] AB. i. 12-14, like KB. vii. 10, treats briefly of the ceremony of carrying forward the Soma when bought. For the ritual see ĀÇS. iv. 4. 1-8; ÇÇS. v. 6. 1-8; Caland and Henry, *L'Agniṣṭoma*, pp. 50, 51.

i. 13. [1] This verse which is found in the same form as here in the Yajus recension is also found at AV. vii. 8. 1 with the bad variants *áthemám asyā́ çátrum* and *sárvavīram*. For § 1 cf. KB. vii. 10.

[2] RV. i. 91. 9-11.

he recites when Soma the king is being brought forward; verily thus with his own deity, his own metre he makes him successful. 'All rejoice in the glory that hath come' he recites;[3] Soma the king is glory; every one rejoices in his being bought, both he who is to gain something in the sacrifice and he who is not. 'The comrades in the comrade strong in the assembly, (he says); Soma the king is the comrade, strong in the assembly, of the Brahmans. 'Saving from sin' (he says); he indeed is a saviour from sin. He who is successful, he who attains pre-eminence, becomes sinful; therefore they say,[4] 'Do not recite, do not proceed; let them not have sin to requite.' 'Winner of nourishment' (he says); nourishment is food; nourishment is the sacrificial fee; thereby he wins it; verily thus he makes him a winner of food. 'Ready is he for manly force' (he says); manly force is power and strength; manly force is not lost by him up to old age who knows thus. 'The god hath come' (he says[5]), for he has come now; 'With the seasons may he prosper the dwelling' (he says). The seasons are the royal brothers of Soma the king, as of a man; verily thus with that he causes him to come. 'May Savitṛ bestow upon us fair progeny and sap' this benediction he invokes. 'May he quicken us with nights and days' (he says); the days are days, the nights are nights; verily then for him with the days and the nights he invokes this benediction. 'Wealth with offspring may he accord to us' this benediction he invokes. 'Thine abodes which they worship with oblation' he recites;[6] 'All these of thine be encompassing the sacrifice; conferring wealth, accomplishing with good heroes' (he says); verily thus he says 'Be thou a conferrer of cattle on us and an accomplisher.' 'Slayer of heroes, O Soma, go forward to the doors' (he says); the doors are the house; the house of the sacrificer is afraid of Soma the king as he advances; in that he recites this (verse), verily thus he calms him; he calmed injures not his offspring or cattle. 'This prayer of thy suppliant, O god', with (this verse) to Varuṇa he concludes; so long as he is tied up, Varuṇa is his deity, so long as he proceeds to the closed places; verily thus with his own deity, his own metre, he makes him successful. 'Of thy suppliant, O god' (he says[7]); he who sacrifices is a suppliant. 'Insight and skill, O Varuṇa, do thou quicken' (he says); verily thus he says, 'Do thou, O Varuṇa, quicken strength and knowledge.' 'Let us mount that ship fair crossing by

[3] RV. x. 71. 10.

[4] The version of Sāyaṇa takes *mā pracārīḥ* as addressed to the Adhvaryu and *yātayan* as *prāpnuvantaḥ*, but this seems unduly to minimize *yātayan*. The idea is that in too great prosperity danger of sin is near at hand.

[5] *Āgan* is taken as past by the Brāhmaṇa, though Sāyaṇa renders it as imperative. The verse is RV. iv. 53. 7.

[6] RV. i. 91. 19.

[7] RV. viii. 42. 3.

which we may pass over all evils' (he says); the ship fair crossing is the sacrifice; the ship fair crossing is the black antelope skin; the ship fair crossing is speech; verily thus having mounted upon speech with it he crosses over to the world of heaven. These he recites eight in number, perfect in form; that in the sacrifice is perfect which is perfect in form, that rite which as it is performed the verse describes. Of them he recites the first thrice, the last thrice; they make up twelve; the year has twelve months; Prajāpati is the year; verily with those whose abode is Prajāpati he prospers who knows thus. Thrice he recites the first, thrice the last; verily thus he ties the ends of the sacrifice, for firmness, for might, to prevent slipping.[8]

i. 14 (iii. 3). One of the two oxen should be yoked,[1] the other unloosened; then they should take down the king; if they were to take down when both were unloosed, they would make the king have the fathers as his deity; if when yoked, lack of peace and rest would come on offspring; offspring would scatter. The ox which is unyoked is the symbol of offspring who sit in the house; the yoked one is that of those on a journey. Those who take down when one is yoked and one unyoked, produce both peace and rest. The gods and the Asuras strove for these worlds; they contended for this eastern quarter; the Asuras conquered them thence; they contended for the southern quarter; the Asuras conquered them thence; they contended for the western quarter; the Asuras conquered them thence; they contended for the northern quarter; the Asuras conquered them thence. They contended for the north-eastern quarter; they were not conquered thence. This is the unconquered quarter; therefore in this quarter one should strive or cause striving;[2] for he has power to dispose of debts. The gods said, 'Through our lack of a king they conquer us; let us make a king.' 'Be it so' (they said). They made Soma king; with Soma as king they conquered all the quarters. He who sacrifices has Soma as king. While (the cart) stands facing east, they place on (the Soma); thereby he conquers the eastern quarter; him they carry round to the south; thereby he conquers the southern quarter; him they turn round to the west; thereby he conquers the western quarter; him they take down from (the cart) facing north; thereby he conquers the northern quarter. By Soma the king he conquers all the quarters who knows thus.

[8] Cf. TS. ii. 5. 7. 1.

[1] Cf. TS. vi. 2. 1. 1; MS. iii. 7. 9; ÇB. iii 4. 1. 4 disagrees with TS., MS., and AB. See Caland and Henry, *L'Agniṣṭoma*, p. 54.

[2] The sense of *yat* is probably no more definite than this.

The Guest Reception of Soma

i. 15 (iii. 4). The[1] oblation of the guest reception is offered, when Soma the king has come; Soma the king comes to the house of the sacrificer; to him this oblation of the guest reception is offered; that is why the guest reception has its name. It is offered on nine potsherds; the breaths are nine; (it serves) to arrange the breaths, to recognize the breaths. It is for Viṣṇu; the sacrifice is Viṣṇu; verily thus with his own deity, his own metre, he makes him successful. All the metres and the Pṛṣṭhas follow Soma the king when bought. As many as follow Soma the king, to all these is the guest reception performed. They kindle the fire, when Soma the king has come. Just as in the world when a human king has come, or another deserving person, they slay an ox or a cow that miscarries; so for him they slay in that they kindle the fire, for Agni is the victim of the gods.

i. 16 (iii. 5). 'Recite for Agni being kindled' the Adhvaryu says; 'To thee, O god Savitṛ,' (this verse) to Savitṛ he recites. They say 'Since it is for Agni being kindled that he recites by order, then why does he recite (a verse[1]) to Savitṛ?' Savitṛ is lord of instigations; verily thus on the instigation of Savitṛ they kindle him; therefore he recites (a verse) to Savitṛ. 'May the two great ones, sky and earth, for us,' (this verse) to sky and earth[2] he recites; they say, 'Since it is for Agni being kindled that he recites by order, then why does he recite (this verse) to sky and earth?' By means of sky and earth him when born the gods grasped; by these two even to-day is he grasped; therefore he recites (this verse) to sky and earth. 'Thee, O Agni, from the lotus' this triad in Gāyatrī to Agni[3] he recites when the fire is being kindled; verily thus with his own deity, his own metre he makes him successful. 'Atharvan kindled forth' is perfect in form; that in the sacrifice is perfect which is perfect in form, that rite which as it is performed the verse describes. If he is not born, if he is long in being born, then should be repeated Gāyatrī verses,[4] Rakṣas slaying, namely, 'O Agni strike down the foe' for the smiting away of the Rakṣases. The Rakṣases seize them when he is not born and is long in being born. If he is born when one only has been recited, or when two, then he should recite an appropriate (verse[5]) containing (the word) 'born', 'Let men say' for him when born. That which in the sacrifice is appropriate is perfect. 'Whom with the hand like a quoit' (he says[6]), for with the hands they kindle him.

[1] AB. i. 15–18 describe the guest reception of Soma; cf. KB. viii. 1 and 2. For the ritual see ĀÇS. iv. 5; ÇÇS. v. 7. For § 2 cf. TS. vi. 2. 1. 2. See also Caland and Henry, *L'Agniṣṭoma*, pp. 53, 57–60.

i. 16. [1] RV. i. 24. 3. For §§ 1 and 20 cf. TS. vi. 3. 5. 3; for § 2 KB. viii. 1.

[2] RV. iv. 56. 1.

[3] RV. vi. 16. 13–15.

[4] RV. x. 188.

[5] RV. i. 74. 3.

[6] RV. vi. 16. 40.

'The child born' (he says); Agni is a first-born child as it were; 'Like (it) they bear, Agni of the folk, good sacrificer' (he says); *om* is for them what *na* is for the gods. 'Forward bear the god to the feast for the gods, best winner of wealth' is the appropriate (verse [7]) for him when being taken forward; that which in the sacrifice is appropriate is perfect. 'Let him seat himself in his own place of birth' (he says); he is his own place of birth in that Agni is Agni's. 'Born in the all-knower' (he says [8]); one is born, one is the all-knower. 'Quicken the dear guest' (he says); he is his dear guest in that Agni is Agni's. 'On a smooth (place) the lord of the house' (he says); verily thus he places him in health. 'By Agni is Agni kindled, the sage, the lord of the house, the youthful, bearer of the oblation, with the ladle in his mouth' is the appropriate (verse [9]); that which in the sacrifice is appropriate is perfect. 'For thou, O Agni, by Agni, sage by the sage, good by the good' (he says [10]); one is a sage, the other a sage; one is good, the other good. 'Friend with friend thou art enkindled' (he says); he is his own friend in that Agni is Agni's. 'Him they make bright, the skilled, the victor in contests, the mighty one in his own dwellings' (he says [11]); he is his own house in that Agni is Agni's. 'With the sacrifice the sacrifice the gods sacrificed', with the last [12] he concludes; with the sacrifice the gods sacrificed the sacrifice in that with Agni they sacrificed to Agni; they went to the world of heaven. 'These laws were first; these greatnesses resort to the sky, where are the ancient Sādhya gods' (he says [12]); the Sādhya gods are the metres; they first sacrificed to Agni with Agni; they went to the world of heaven. The Ādityas and the Añgirases were here; they first sacrificed with Agni to Agni; they went to the world of heaven; the libation to Agni is a heavenly libation. Even if he who sacrifices is not a Brāhmaṇa [13] or is wrongly spoken of, nevertheless his libation goes to the gods and is not united with evil; his libation goes to the gods, and is not united with evil, who knows thus. These thirteen he recites perfect in form; that in the sacrifice is perfect which is perfect in form, that rite which as it is performed the verse describes. Of these he recites the first thrice, the last thrice. They make up seventeen; Prajāpati is seventeenfold,

[7] RV. vi. 16. 41.

[8] RV. vi. 16. 42.

[9] RV. i. 12. 6.

[10] RV. viii. 43. 14.

[11] RV. viii. 84. 8.

[12] RV. i. 164. 50; see ĀÇS. ii. 16. 7, 8; cf. ÇÇS. v. 15. 5.

[13] Sāyaṇa gives two views of *abrāhmaṇa*, either as one who is not instigated by a Brāhmaṇa or one who is declared to be a non-Brahman as explained by Çātātapa in his Smṛti. On the whole the use is probably in each case the same, 'one who is said to be not a Brahman', a non-Brahman (opposed to *subrāhmaṇa*, Wackernagel, *Altind. Gram.* II. i. 261) or *durukta*. The alternative is to take *ukta* as 'instigated', 'directed by' one who is not a Brahman or is ill-spoken of. See AB. ii. 17. Lévi (*La doctrine du sacrifice*, p. 123) has 'on sacrifice sans l'avis d'un brahmane ou si on est diffamé,' which is difficult.

the months are twelve, the seasons five; so great is the year; Prajāpati is the year; verily thus with these which have their abode in Prajāpati he prospers who knows thus. He recites the first thrice, the last thrice; verily thus he ties the ends of the sacrifice, for steadiness, for might, to prevent slipping.

i. 17 (iii. 6). 'With the kindling-stick honour Agni' and 'Swell up; be there gathered for thee' are the invitatory verses[1] of the two butter portions, referring to the guest reception and perfect in form; that in the sacrifice is perfect which is perfect in form, that rite which as it is being performed the verse describes. (The verse) to Agni contains (the word) 'guest', not that to Soma; if (the verse) to Soma contained (the word) 'guest', it would clearly[2] be (the verse to be used); but it does contain (the word) 'guest' as it contains (the word) 'made fat'; when they serve him with food, then does he become fat. For them he says as offering verses[3] 'Delighting'. 'Over this Viṣṇu strode' and 'To his beloved place may I win' are (two verses) to Viṣṇu.[4] Having used (a verse) of three Padas as invitatory verse, he says one of four as offering verse, there are seven Padas; the guest reception is the head of the sacrifice; there are seven breaths in the head; verily thus he places breaths in the head. 'The Hotṛ of the sacrifice with brilliant car' and 'Famed far is the Agni of Bharata' are the invitatory and offering verses of the Sviṣṭakṛt,[5] referring to the guest reception and perfect in form; that in the sacrifice is perfect which is perfect in form, that rite which as it is being performed the verse describes. They are Triṣṭubh verses, to secure power. (The sacrifice) ends with the sacrificial food; the gods prospered by means of the guest reception ending with the sacrificial food; therefore should it be performed ending with the sacrificial food. In this case they offer the fore-offerings, not the after-offerings. The fore-offerings and the after-offerings are the breaths; the fore-offerings are those breaths in the head, the after-offerings those below. If in the case one were to offer the after-offerings, that would be as if one were to break off those breaths and seek to place them in the head. That would be superfluous; these breaths, both those and those, are united together;[6] verily thus in that they offer the fore-offerings, not the after-offerings, they obtain their desires in the fore-offerings and in the after-offerings.

[1] RV. viii. 44. 1 and i. 91. 16.

[2] This seems here the sense of the ambiguous word *çaçvat*, which is common in AB. in this form. Cf. Eggeling SBE. xxvi. xxx.

[3] i. e. the usual verses *juṣāṇa agnir ājyasya vetu* and *juṣāṇaḥ soma ājyasya haviṣo vetu*, ĀÇS. i. 5, 29; ÇÇS. i. 8. 8 with *haviṣo* in the first also.

[4] RV. i. 22. 17 and i. 154. 5.

[5] RV. x. 1. 5 and vii. 8. 4.

[6] Sāyaṇa takes this as a potential and as explaining *atiriktam*, but it seems necessary to use it as explaining the next sentence, the breaths are united and so are in a sense one, *ime* ... *ime* because gestures are used.

ADHYĀYA IV

The Pravargya.

i. 18 (iv. 1). The[1] sacrifice went away from the gods (saying), 'I shall not be your food.' 'No', replied the gods, 'Verily thou shalt be our food.' The gods crushed it; it being taken apart was not sufficient for them. The gods said 'It will not be sufficient for us, being taken apart; come, let us gather together the sacrifice.' (They replied) 'Be it so'. They gathered it together; having gathered it together they said to the Açvins, 'Do ye two heal it', the Açvins are the physicians of the gods, the Açvins the Adhvaryus; therefore the two Adhvaryus gather together the cauldron. Having gathered it together they say, 'O Brahman, we shall proceed with the Pravargya offering; O Hotṛ, do thou recite.'

i. 19 (iv. 2). With 'The holy power born first in the east' he begins;[1] Bṛhaspati is the holy power; verily thus with the holy power he heals him. 'This royal one goeth in front to the father' (he says[2]); the royal one is speech; verily thus he places speech in him. 'The great one hath established the two great ones, when born' is addressed to Brahmaṇaspati;[3] Bṛhaspati is the holy power; verily thus with the holy power he heals him. 'Towards the god Savitṛ in the bowls' is addressed to Savitṛ;[4] Savitṛ is breath; verily thus he places breath in him. With[5] 'Sit thou down; thou art great' they make him sit down. 'Whom they anoint, the sages, as it were extending' is (the verse[6]) appropriate for the anointing; that which is appropriate in the sacrifice is perfect. 'The bird anointed by the skill of the Asura', 'The foe who secretly may attack us, O Agni', and 'Be thou well disposed to us, O Agni, at our approach' are sets of two appropriate (verses[7]); that which in the sacrifice is appropriate is perfect. 'Make thou thy brilliance like a broad net', (these) are

[1] AB. i. 18-22 and KB. viii. 3-7 describe the Pravargya as a necessary preliminary to the Soma sacrifice. For the ritual see ĀÇS. iv. 6 and 7; ÇÇS. v. 9 and 10; BÇS. ix. 1-16; MÇS. iv; ĀpÇS. xv. ÇÇS. does not require it for a first sacrifice. GB. vii. 6 borrows this. KB. viii. 3 allows it for a first sacrifice in certain cases. ÇB. xiv. 2. 2. 44, 45; KÇS. viii. 2. 16; xxvi. 7. 58 forbid it in any case; TĀ. v. 6. 8, however, allows it generally, and MÇS. iv. 1. 3, 4; Āp. in certain cases. For it cf. Hillebrandt, ZDMG. xxxiv. 319 *seq.*; Keith, *Taittirīya Saṁhitā*, I. cxxiii–cxxv. For the death of the sacrifice, cf. Lévi, *La doctrine du sacrifice*, p. 80.

i. 19. [1] Given in Āçv. and Çāñkh. as not in the Saṁhitā; see RVKh. iii. 22 (Scheftelowitz, pp. 107–109); AV. iv. 1. 1; KB. viii. 4. Cf. Oldenberg, *Prolegomena* pp. 363 *seq.*

[2] Also in Āçv. and Çāñkh.

[3] Also in Āçv. and Çāñkh.

[4] Also in Āçv. and Çāñkh.

[5] RV. i. 36. 9.

[6] RV. v. 43. 7.

[7] RV. x. 177. 1; v. 5. 4; iii. 18. 1 with the next verse in each case.

five (verses[8]) referring to the slaying of Rakṣases, for the smiting away of the Rakṣases. 'Round thee, O singer, the songs', 'In the two hast thou placed the word of praise', 'Pure is one of them, worthy of sacrifice one' and 'I saw the guardian never resting' are four isolated (verses[9]). They make up twenty-one; man here is twenty-onefold, ten fingers, ten toes, and the body as the twenty-first; this twenty-onefold self he prepares.

i. 20 (iv. 3). 'They of the sounding deep have sounded at the rim' are nine (verses[1]) for Soma the purifying; the breaths are nine; verily thus he places the breaths in him. 'May Vena impel those born of Pṛçni' (he says[2]); Vena is (this breath) here; above this here some breaths circulate (*venanti*), below others; therefore is it Vena; 'the breath being here hath not feared (*nābheḥ*)' (they say); therefore is it the navel; that is why the navel has its name; verily thus he places breath in him. 'Thy strainer is outspread, O lord of holy power', 'The strainer of the scorcher is outspread in the expanse of sky' and 'What time the Dhiṣaṇās spread out the strainer' (he says[3]); these breaths are connected[4] with (the word) 'strained'; those breaths below are connected with seed, urine, and excrement; them verily thus he places in him.

i. 21 (iv. 4). 'Thee lord of hosts we invoke' is addressed to Brahmaṇaspati;[1] Bṛhaspati is the holy power; verily thus with the holy power he heals him. 'Of which extending and far extending are the names' are the bodies of the cauldron;[2] verily thus he makes him possessed of body and form. 'The Rathantara Vasiṣṭha hath brought'; 'Bharadvāja hath fetched the Bṛhat of Agni' (he says[3]); verily thus he makes him possessed of the Bṛhat and the Rathantara. 'I saw thee deep in thought' (he says[4]); it contains (the word) 'offspring' and is addressed to Prajāpati; verily thus he confers offspring upon him. 'What offering will win your favour, O Açvins' are nine (verses[5]) in different metres; that is the entrails of the sacrifice; the entrails are mixed as it were, some smaller some thicker; therefore are they in different metres. With these Kakṣīvant went to

[8] RV. iv. 4. 1–5.

[9] RV. i. 10. 12; 88. 8; vi. 58. 1; x. 177. 3.

[1] RV. ix. 73. 1. Cf. KB. viii. 5.

[2] RV. x. 123. 1. The explanation is purely artificial, like *nābheḥ* below, which is probably best taken as a third, not second person. It is not to be pressed as a piece of grammar, being an etymology; cf. Liebich, *Pāṇini*, p. 27, who, with Sāyaṇa (Aufrecht has *na*), treats *nā* as *mā*.

[3] RV. ix. 83. 1, 2, and given in full in Āçv. and Çāñkh.

[4] The sense is that those breaths below being in need of purification obtain it *via* these three verses.

i. 21. [1] RV. ii. 23. Cf. KB. viii. 5.

[2] RV. x. 181. 1–3.

[3] RV. x. 181. 1 *d*; 2 *c* and *d*.

[4] RV. x. 183. 1–3; the hymn is attributed to Prajāvant Prājāpatya, and the words here are therefore taken even by Aufrecht as the name of the author, but the trans. adopted seems less unlikely.

[5] RV. i. 120. 1–9.

the dear home of the Açvins; he won the highest world; he goes to the dear home of the Açvins, he wins the highest world who knows thus. 'Agni shineth as the forefront of the dawns' is a hymn.[6] 'O Açvins, to the swelling cauldron' is appropriate; that which in the sacrifice is appropriate is perfect. It is in Triṣṭubh verses; the Triṣṭubh is strength; verily then he places strength in him. 'Like the two pressing-stones for the one purpose ye sing' is a hymn[7]; by enumerating the members in 'Like the two eyes, like the two ears, like the two nostrils', verily thus he places the senses in him. It is in Triṣṭubh verses; the Triṣṭubh is strength; verily thus he places strength in him. 'I praise sky and earth for first inspiration' is a hymn[8] and 'Agni, the cauldron, the shining, for hastening on the way' is appropriate; that which in the sacrifice is appropriate is perfect. It is in Jagatī verses; cattle are connected with the Jagatī; verily thus he confers cattle upon him. 'By which ye did help N. N., by which ye did help N. N.' (he says); so many desires do the Açvins see in it; them verily thus does he place in him; verily thus with them he makes him successful. 'The tawny one, the chief, hath made the dawns to glow' is (a verse[9]) containing (the word) 'glow'; verily thus he confers glowing upon him. 'With days and with nights guard us around', with the last (verse[10]) he concludes, 'With those unharmed and bringing good fortune, O Açvins; may this Mitra and Varuṇa accord us; Aditi, Sindhu, earth and sky'; verily thus with these desires he makes him successful. Such is the first section.

i. 22 (iv. 5). Then comes the second (section). 'I hail this fair milking cow', 'Making *hiñ*, the lady of riches', 'Towards thee, O god Savitṛ', 'Like a calf with the mothers', 'With the mothers like a calf', 'Thy teat, exhaustless spring of pleasure', 'The cow hath lowed after the blinking young one', 'With homage approach', 'In unison have they sat down kneeling', 'By the ten of Vivasvant', 'Seven milk one', 'Enkindled Agni, O Açvins', 'Enkindled Agni by the strong, the harbinger of heaven', 'This is his most evident deed', 'The living cloud is milked of ghee and milk', 'Rise up, O Brahmaṇaspati', 'He hath milked the swelling drink', 'Come up with the milk, milker of cows, swiftly', 'In the passed pour the admixture', 'Assuredly of the Açvins the seer', and 'Together these mighty waters' are twenty-one[1] appropriate (verses), that which in the

[6] RV. v. 76.

[7] RV. ii. 39; the expressions cited are from vv. 5 and 6.

[8] RV. i. 112. Cf. for cattle and the Jagatī TS. vi. 1. 6. 2.

[9] RV. ix. 83. 3. Cf. KB. viii. 6.

[10] RV. i. 112. 25.

[1] RV. i. 164. 26, 27; i. 24. 8; ix. 104. 2; 105. 2; i. 164. 49, 28; ix. 11. 1; i. 72. 5; viii. 72. 8; 7; two verses only in ĀÇS. iv. 7. 4; RV. i. 62. 6; ix. 74. 4; i. 40. 1; viii. 72. 16; in ĀÇS. iv. 7. 4; RV. viii. 72. 13; 9. 7; 7. 22. Cf. KB. viii. 7; ÇÇS. v. 10.

sacrifice is appropriate is perfect. With[2] 'Up this god Savitṛ with the golden' he rises up after (the others); with[3] 'Let Brahmaṇaspati move forward' he follows after; with[4] 'The Gandharva here guardeth his abode' he looks at the Khara; with[5] 'The eagle flying in the vault' he takes his place; in the forenoon he uses as offering verses[6] 'The heated cauldron reacheth you, self-offerer' and 'Both drink, O Açvins'. At 'O Agni, enjoy' he says the second *vaṣaṭ*, taking the place of the Sviṣṭakṛt. 'The ghee the milk offered in the cows' and 'Drink of this, O Açvins' he uses as offering verses[7] in the afternoon; at 'O Agni, enjoy' he says the second *vaṣaṭ*, taking the place of Sviṣṭakṛt. Of these three oblations they do not take portions for the Sviṣṭakṛt, Soma, the cauldron, and the strengthening drink. In that he says the second *vaṣaṭ*, (it is) to avoid omitting Agni Sviṣṭakṛt. 'Through all the regions, seated in the south' the Brahman[8] mutters; 'The pure cauldron among the gods over which the call of Hail! is uttered', 'From the ocean the wave Vena sendeth forth', 'The drop that goeth over the ocean', 'O friend, do thou turn towards the friend', 'Upright to our aid', 'Upright do thou protect us from tribulation', and 'Him indeed his worshippers' are appropriate[9] (verses); that which in the sacrifice is appropriate is perfect. With 'O thou of pure brilliance, around thy dwelling' he desires food.[10] With 'The oblation offered, the sweet oblation, on the fire that is most full of Indra, may we eat of thee, O divine cauldron, full of sweetness, full of nourishment, full of strength, full of the Aṅgirases; homage to thee; harm me not' he partakes of the cauldron. 'Like an eagle its nest, the seat wrought with prayer' and 'In which the seven Vāsavas' he recites[11] for him when being deposited. 'The oblation, O thou rich in oblation, the great divine seat' (he says[12]) on the day on which they are going to remove (the cauldron). 'From the good pasture mayst thou be of good fortune', with the last (verse[13]) he concludes. The cauldron is a divine pairing; the cauldron is the member, the two handles the testicles, the spoon the thigh bones, the milk the seed; this seed is poured in Agni as the birthplace of the gods, as generation; the birthplace of the gods is Agni; he comes into existence from Agni as the birthplace of the gods, from the libations; having come into existence as composed of the Ṛc,

[2] RV. vi. 71. 1.
[3] RV. i. 40. 3.
[4] RV. ix. 83. 4.
[5] RV. ix. 85. 11.
[6] Only in ĀÇS. iv. 7. 4 (cf. AV. vii. 73. 5) and RV. i. 46. 15.
[7] Only in AÇS. iv. 7. 4 (cf. AV. vii. 73. 4) and RV. viii. 5. 14.
[8] In ĀÇS. iv. 7. 4.
[9] In ĀÇS. iv. 7. 4; RV. x. 123. 2, 8; iv. 1. 3; i. 36. 13, 14; viii. 69. 17.
[10] RV. iii. 2. 6.
[11] RV. ix. 71. 6 and ĀÇS. iv. 7. 4.
[12] RV. ix. 83. 5.
[13] RV. i. 164. 40.

the Yajus, and the Sāman, and of the Veda, and of the holy power, and as immortal, he attains to the deities who knows thus and who knowing thus sacrifices with this sacrificial rite.

The Upasads.

i. 23 (iv. 6). The[1] gods and the Asuras strove for these worlds; the Asuras made these worlds as citadels, just as those who are more mighty and forceful. They made this (earth) an iron (citadel), the atmosphere one of silver, and the sky one of gold; thus they made these worlds as citadels. The gods said, 'The Asuras have made these worlds as citadels, let us make these worlds as citadels in opposition.' 'Be it so' (they replied). They made out of this (earth) as a counterpoise the Sadas, the Agnīdh's altar from the atmosphere, the two oblation holders from the sky. Thus they made these worlds as citadels in opposition. The gods said, 'Let us have recourse to the Upasads; by siege (Upasad) they conquer a great citadel.' 'Be it so' (they replied). With the first Upasad which they performed they repelled them from this world; with the second from the atmosphere, with the third from the sky. Thus from these worlds they repelled them.[4] The Asuras, repelled from these worlds, had recourse to the seasons. The gods said, 'Let us have recourse to the Upasads.' 'Be it so' (they replied). These three Upasads they performed one by one twice each; they made up six; the seasons are six; them they repelled from the seasons; they, repelled from the seasons, the Asuras, had recourse to the months. The gods said, 'Let us have recourse to the Upasads.' 'Be it so' (they replied). These Upasads being six they performed one by one twice each; they made up twelve; the months are twelve; them they repelled from the months. The Asuras, repelled from the months, had recourse to the half-months. The gods said, 'Let us have recourse to the half-months.' 'Be it so' (they replied). These Upasads being twelve they performed one by one twice each; they made up twenty-four; the half-months are twenty-four them they repelled from the half-months. The Asuras, repelled from the half-months, had recourse to day and night. The gods said, 'Let us have recourse to the two Upasads.' 'Be it so' (they replied). With the Upasad which they performed on the forenoon they repelled them from the day, by that on the afternoon, from the night; thus from both they excluded them. Therefore one should proceed with the first Upasad early

[1] AB. i. 23–26 and KB. viii. 8 and 9 deal with the Upasads; cf. TS. vi. 2. 3. 1; ÇB. iii. 4. 4. 3. For the ritual see ĀÇS. iv. 8; ÇÇS. v. 11; Caland and Henry, *L'Agniṣṭoma*, pp. 67–70. For the varying number of Upasads cf. ĀÇS. iv. 8. 18; TS. vi. 2. 5. 1.

in the forenoon, with the second early in the afternoon. So much only of space does he leave to his enemy.

i. 24 (iv. 7). The Upasads are called victories; by them the gods won an unrivalled victory; an unrivalled victory does he win who thus knows. The victory which the gods won over these worlds, the seasons, the months, the half-months, the day and night, that victory he wins who knows thus.

The[1] gods were afraid, 'Through our disagreement the Asuras will wax great here.' Having gone apart they took council; Agni went out with the Varus, Indra with the Rudras, Varuṇa with the Ādityas, Bṛhaspati with the All-gods. Having thus gone apart they took council; they said, 'Come, our dearest bodies let us deposit in the house of king Varuṇa; with them may he not be united who shall transgress this, who shall seek to cause trouble.' 'Be it so' (they replied). They deposited their bodies in the house of king Varuṇa; that became their bodily covenant; that is why the bodily covenant (Tānūnaptra) has its name. Therefore they say, 'One should not show treachery to one united by the bodily covenant.' Therefore the Asuras do not wax great here.

i. 25 (iv. 8). The guest reception is the head of the sacrifice, the Upasads the neck; they are performed on the same strew, for the head and the neck are the same. In the Upasads the gods fashioned an arrow; of it the point was Agni, the socket Soma; the shaft Viṣṇu, the feathers Varuṇa.[1] It they discharged, using the butter as a bow; with it they kept piercing the citadels; therefore these have butter as the oblation. At the Upasads he has first recourse to four teats for the fast milk, for the arrow is composed of four elements, point, socket, shaft, and feathers; three teats he has recourse to for the fast milk in the Upasads, for the arrow is composed of three elements, point, socket, and shaft; two teats he has recourse to for the fast milk in the Upasads, for the arrow is composed of two elements, the socket and the shaft only; one teat he has recourse to for the fast milk in the Upasads, for it is called the one thing 'arrow', by one is strength exercised. These worlds are broader above and narrower below; he performs the Upasads from the top downwards, for the conquering of these worlds. 'To the generous to be adored', 'This kindling stick of mine, O Agni, this waiting upon thee do thou accept' are sets of three kindling

[1] For this rite see ĀÇS. iv. 5. 3; ÇÇS. v. 7. 1, 2; LÇS. v. 6. 6; KÇS. viii. 1. 23–26. Cf. TS. i. 2. 10. 2; vi. 2. 2. 1; MS. iii. 7. 10; GB. vii. 2; ÇB. iii. 4. 2. 9; Caland and Henry, *L'Agniṣṭoma*, pp. 61, 62. The ÇB. assigns the Rudras to Soma. Cf. Lévi, *La doctrine du sacrifice*, p. 78.

i. 25. [1] Cf. TS. vi. 2. 3. 1; ÇB. iii. 4. 4. 14; and for § 4 KB. viii. 9; TS. vi. 2. 5. 2. For the parts of the arrow cf. *Vedic Index* i. 8; Eggeling, SBE. xxvi. 108, n. 2, who takes *çalya* as 'barb'; Muir, OST. v. 381, 383.

verses,[2] perfect in form; that in the sacrifice is perfect which is perfect in form, that rite which as it is being performed the verse describes. He should use (verses[3]) containing (the word) 'slay', as invitatory and offering verses, 'Let Agni slay the foes,' 'Who is dread, as it were, a slayer with darts,' 'Thou, O Soma, art very lord,' 'Bestowing prosperity, slayer of disease,' 'Over this Viṣṇu strode,' 'Three steps he strode apart,' these are they. He sacrifices in the afternoon with (the verses) inverted. With these in the Upasads the gods kept slaying and destroying the citadels. They should be of the same metre, not of different metres; if he were to make them of different metres, he would cause swelling on the neck; he would produce boils; therefore should they be made of the same metre, not of different metres. Now as to this Upāvi Jānaçruteya used to say, that is in his explanation of the Upasads, 'In that[4] the face of even an ugly Çrotriya is seen as joyous as it were and as singing, (it is) because the Upasads have butter as the oblation, and (it is) a face placed on the neck'; therefore was he wont to say this.

i. 26 (iv. 9). The[1] fore-offerings and the after-offerings are divine armour; (this rite) is without fore-offerings and after-offerings, to sharpen the arrow and to prevent rending. Having once stepped over he makes (him) proclaim, to master the sacrifice and to prevent its departure. They say, 'A cruel thing do they in the neighbourhood of Soma the king,[2] in that they offer the ghee in his neighbourhood, for by ghee as a thunderbolt Indra slew Vṛtra,' in that they make the king to swell, (saying) 'May every shoot of thine, O god Soma, swell for Indra who obtaineth the chief share; may Indra swell for thee; do thou swell for Indra; make us as comrades to swell; with gain, with insight, prosperously may I attain the conclusion in the pressing of thee, O God Soma'; verily thus they make whole whatever cruel as it were they do in his neighbourhood; moreover they cause him to grow. Soma the king is the embryo of sky and earth; in that, (saying) 'Sought by sacrifice is wealth, sought are good things, for strength, for prosperity; holy order to the speakers of holy order; homage to sky,

[2] RV. vii. 15. 1–7 and ii. 6. 1–7.

[3] RV. vi. 16. 34, 39; i. 91. 5, 12; i. 22. 17, 8.

[4] The sense is uncertain, as, if *iti* in *rebhatīvety* is taken as ending the quotation, then the sentence is hard to construe, unless it is made to mean 'From whatever (side) the face is seen', which is harsh. On the other hand *yasmāt* . . . *hi* contrast well and the omission of *iti* as in AB. iii. 8. 4 is not difficult. Yet *tasmāt* points to a reason given by the text, not by Upāvi. Weber takes it as 'In the Brāhmaṇa is to be found the reason that, &c.'. For Brāhmaṇa in this sense cf. ÇB. iv. 1. 5. 14; iii. 2. 4. 1. The sage is called Aupāvi in ÇB. v. 1. 1. 5, 7. *janitoḥ* must be active, not pass., as Delbrück, *Altind. Synt.* p. 480.

[1] The chief point of this chapter is the Nihnavana, for which see ĀÇS. iv. 5. 7; ÇÇS. v. 8. 5; Caland and Henry, *L'Agniṣṭoma*, pp. 63, 64. The Mantras occur in TS. i. 2. 11 and its parallels. For *devavarmā* cf. TS. ii. 6. 1. 5.

[2] Cf. TS. vi. 2. 2. 4.

homage to earth!' they make (their amends) on the strew,[3] verily thus they pay homage to sky and earth; moreover they cause them to grow.

ADHYĀYA V

The Bringing forward of the Soma and the Fire.

i. 27 (v. 1). Soma[1] the king was among the Gandharvas; the gods and the seers meditated on him, 'How shall Soma the king come hither to us?' Speech said, 'The Gandharvas love women; with me as a woman do ye barter it.' 'No,' replied the gods, 'how could we be without you?' She replied, 'Still do ye buy; when ye will have need of me,[2] then shall I return to you.' 'Be it so' (they replied). With her as a great naked one they bought Soma the king. In imitation of her they bring up a young immaculate cow to buy Soma; with her they buy Soma the king. Her he may repurchase again, for (speech) went back to them. Therefore one should speak inaudibly when Soma the king had been bought, for then speech is among the Gandharvas; when the fire is again brought forward, she returns again.

i. 28 (v. 2). 'Recite for Agni as he is being brought forward,' the Adhvaryu says.

'Forth the god with the thought divine,
Do ye bear the all-knower,
May he bear our libations daily,'

this Gāyatrī verse[1] should he recite for a Brahman; the Brahmin is connected with the Gāyatrī; the Gāyatrī is brilliance and splendour; verily thus with brilliance and with splendour he makes him prosper. 'To him the mighty, meet for assembly, the strengthening hymn,' this Triṣṭubh he should recite for a Rājanya; the Rājanya is connected with the Triṣṭubh; the Triṣṭubh is force, power, and strength; verily thus with force, power, and strength he makes him prosper. 'Ever uttering they have brought forward to the one worthy of praise' (he says); verily, thus he makes him attain pre-eminence over his own people. 'Let him bear

[3] *nihnavate* is clearly wrong: *nihnuvate* must be read as pointed out by Aufrecht (AB. p. 429); but *nihnave* in AB. vii. 17 is supported by *nihnavante* in ĀÇS. iv. 5. 7; viii. 18. 27, where, however, there is difference of reading, *nihnuvante* occurring in some MSS. (see Weber, *Ind. Stud.* ix. 221). Cf. ÇB. iii. 4. 3. 19–21.

[1] AB. i. 27 and 28 and KB. ix. 1 and 2 deal with the carrying forward of the fire to the high altar from the old Āhavanīya which now takes the place of the Gārhapatya; see ĀÇS. iii. 7. 8; ii. 17. 8; ÇÇS. iii. 14. 8–14; Schwab, *Das altindische Thieropfer*, pp. 80–88. For this legend cf. TS. vi. i. 6. 5; 10. 4; ÇB. iii. 2. 4. 8.

[2] Or possibly 'when your object shall be (accomplished) through me', but this is less likely.

i. 28. [1] RV. x. 176. 2. Cf. KB. ix. 2; ÇB. iii. 5. 2. 2.

[2] RV. iii. 54. 1.

us with the splendours of his home; let Agni hear us immortal with his divine (splendour); until old age on him he shines immortal, who thus knows.' 'He here first hath been set down by the ordainers', this Jagatī verse[3] should he recite for a Vaiçya; the Vaiçya is connected with the Jagatī; cattle are connected with the Jagatī; verily thus with cattle he makes him prosper. 'Variegated in the woods, manifested for every people' is an appropriate (verse[4]); that which in the sacrifice is appropriate is perfect. 'Here the godly', in this Anuṣṭubh[5] he utters speech; the Anuṣṭubh is speech; verily thus in speech he utters speech. In that he says 'Here', verily thus speech declares 'Here am I come who aforetime have dwelt with the Gandharvas.' 'Agni protecteth here' (he says[6]), Agni here protects; 'As from the immortal race'; verily thus he confers immortality upon him. 'Stronger than the strong the god made for life' (he says), for Agni is a god made for life. 'Thee in the footstep of the sacrificial food, on the navel of the earth' (he says[7]); the navel of the high altar is the footstep of the sacrificial food. 'O All-knower, we deposit thee' (he says), for they about to deposit him. 'O Agni, to carry the oblation' (he says), for he is about to carry the oblation. 'O Agni of fair face, with all the gods, sit first on the birthplace rich in wool' (he says[8]); verily thus he makes him sit with all the gods. 'Making a nest, rich in ghee, for Savitṛ' (he says); a nest as it were is made in the sacrifice by the enclosing sticks of Pītudāru wood, bdellium, the wool tufts, and the fragrant grasses. 'Lead the sacrifice well for the sacrificer' (he says); verily thus he establishes straight the sacrifice. 'Sit, O Hotṛ, in thine own place, discerning' (he says[9]); the Hotṛ of the gods is Agni; the navel of the high altar is his own place. 'Do thou place the sacrifice in the birthplace of good deeds' (he says); the sacrifice is the sacrificer; verily thus for the sacrificer he invokes this benediction. 'Seeking the gods, do thou sacrifice to the gods with oblation, O Agni, do thou accord great power to the sacrificer' (he says); power is breath; verily thus he places breath in the sacrificer. 'The Hotṛ in the Hotṛ's seat, well knowing' (he says[10]); the Hotṛ of the gods is Agni; the navel of the high altar is his Hotṛ's seat. 'Shining, resplendent, he hath sat, the well skilled' (he says), for he is seated here. 'With vows and foresight undeceived, most bright' (he says); Agni is the most bright of the gods. 'Bearing a thousand, Agni, of pure tongue' (he says); for this is his character of bearing

[3] RV. iv. 7. 1.

[4] RV iv. 7 1 *d*.

[5] RV. x. 176. 3. *avākṣam* is merely a play on *vāc*, not a genuine form; see Liebich, *Pāṇini*, p. 27. Cf. AB. viii. 9; above, p. 72.

[6] RV. x. 176. 4.

[7] RV. iii. 29. 4.

[8] RV. vi. 15. 16.

[9] RV. iii. 29. 8.

[10] RV. ii. 9. 1.

a thousand, that him being but one they carry apart in many directions; prosperity a thousandfold he obtains who knows thus. 'Thou art a herald, thou also our protector from afar,' with this last (verse[11]) he concludes. 'Thou, O strong one, art the leader to greater wealth; O Agni, for ourselves, our children and offspring, be thou the guardian, resplendent and never failing' (he says); Agni is the guardian of the gods; verily thus does he place Agni as a guardian on all sides for himself and for the sacrificer, when one knowing thus concludes with this (verse); moreover, thus he produces prosperity for a year. Eight he recites, perfect in form; that in the sacrifice is perfect which is perfect in form, that rite which as it is being performed the verse describes. Of these he recites the first thrice, the last thrice; they make up twelve; the year has twelve months; Prajāpati is the year; verily thus with those that have their abode in Prajāpati he prospers who knows thus. He repeats the first thrice, the last thrice; verily thus he ties the two ends of the sacrifice, for firmness, for might, to avoid slipping.

i. 29 (v. 3). 'Recite[1] for the two oblation holders being brought forward' the Adhvaryu says. 'I yoke your ancient holy power with praises' he recites;[2] with the holy power the gods yoked the two oblation holders; verily thus with the holy power he yokes the two; what has the holy power come to no harm. 'Let the two come forward with weal for the sacrifice,' this triplet[3] to sky and earth he recites. They say, 'Seeing that he recites by order for the two oblation holders being brought forward, then why does he recite a triplet to sky and earth?' Sky and earth were the oblation holders of the gods; even to-day also are they the oblation holders, for within these is here all oblation and whatever there is; therefore he recites a triplet to sky and earth. 'What time ye came like twins striving' (he says[4]), for moving like twins they come in an even line. 'Pious men bore you forward' (he says), for pious men bear them forward. 'Sit down in your own place, well knowing; be of secure abode for our Soma drop' (he says); the drop is Soma the king; verily thus he makes the two for Soma the king to sit on. 'In the two thou hast placed the word of praise' (he says[5]), for on the two the third, the covering, is deposited. In that he says 'The word of praise', and the word of praise is the sacrificial rite, verily with it he makes the sacrifice prosper. 'Who in union with

[11] RV. ii. 9. 2. The sense of *tokasya nas tane tanūnām* and its construction is uncertain.

[1] AB. i. 29 and KB. ix. 3 and 4 deal with the bringing forward of the two Soma carts to the high altar; see ĀÇS. iv. 9; ÇÇS. v. 13; Caland and Henry, *L'Agniṣṭoma*, pp. 82–93. Cf. ÇB. iii. 5. 3. 16.

[2] RV. x. 13. 1.

[3] RV. ii. 14. 19–21; cf. AB. ix. 3.

[4] RV. x. 13. 2.

[5] RV. i. 83. 3: 'restrain' is used in *yatasrucā*.

uplifted ladle pay honour; unrestrained he dwelleth in thine ordinance, he doth flourish' (he says); the line containing the word 'restrain' which he yonder first said, that with this he appeases, for appeasement. 'May thy strength be favouring to the sacrificer who poureth (oblation)', he invokes this benediction. 'All forms the sage doth assume,' this 'All form' (verse[6]) he recites; he should recite looking at the fronton, for the fronton has as it were all forms, white as it were, and black as it were. Every form he wins for himself and for the sacrificer when one knowing thus recites the verse while looking at the fronton. 'Around thee, O singer, the songs', with this last (verse[7]) he concludes. When he thinks that the oblation holders are covered, he should conclude then. The wives of the Hotṛ and the sacrificer are not likely to become naked, when one knowing thus concludes with this (verse) when the oblation holders have been covered. By a Yajus[8] are the oblation holders covered; verily thus with a Yajus they cover the two. When the Adhvaryu and the Pratiprasthātṛ strike in the posts on both sides, then should he conclude; for then are the two covered. Eight he recites, perfect in form; that in the sacrifice is perfect which is perfect in form, that rite which as it is being performed the verse describes. Of them he recites the first thrice, the last thrice; they make up twelve; the year has twelve months; Prajāpati is the year; verily thus with those whose abode is Prajāpati he prospers who knows thus. He recites the first thrice, the last thrice; verily, thus he ties the two ends of the sacrifice for firmness, for might, to prevent slipping.

The Bringing forward of Agni and Soma.

i. 30 (v. 4). 'Recite for Agni and Soma being brought forward' the Adhvaryu says.[1] 'Do thou pour forth, O god, for the first the father', (this verse[2]) to Savitṛ he recites. They say, 'Since he recites by order for Agni and Soma being brought forward, then why does he recite a verse to Savitṛ?' Savitṛ is lord of instigation; verily thus instigated by Savitṛ they bring them forward; therefore he recites (a verse) to Savitṛ. 'Let Brahmaṇaspati move forward', (this verse) to Brahmaṇaspati he recites[3] they say, 'Since he recites by order for Agni and Soma being brought forward, then why does he recite (a verse) to Brahmaṇaspati?' Bṛhaspati is the holy

[6] RV. v. 81. 2. *rarāṭyā* is a variant form of *rarāṭi*, not loc. as Sāyaṇa.

[7] RV. i. 10. 12.

[8] See TS. i. 2. 13 *k*.

[1] AB. i. 30 and KB. ix. 5 and 6 deal with the bringing forward of Agni and Soma and the placing of Soma in the right oblation holder; see AÇS. iv. 10; ÇÇS. v. 14; Caland and Henry, *L'Agniṣṭoma*, pp. 110–116. Cf. ÇB. iii. 6. 3. 9.

[2] Not in RV.: given in ĀÇS. iv. 10. 1; ÇÇS. v. 14. 9; cf. AV. vii. 14. 3; KS. xxxvii. 9; TB. ii. 7. 15. 1; KB. ix. 5

[3] RV. i. 40. 3.

power; verily thus he makes the holy power their harbinger; that which contains the holy power comes not to harm. 'Let the goddess move forward, the bounteous (he says); verily thus he makes the sacrifice possessed of bounteousness; therefore does he recite (a verse) to Brahmaṇaspati. 'The Hotṛ, the god, the immortal', this triplet[4] to Agni he recites, when Soma, the king, is being brought forward. Soma the king the Asuras and the Rakṣases sought to slay as he was being brought forward between the Sadas and the oblation holders; Agni by his cunning led him past. 'He goeth before by cunning' he says, for he led him past by cunning; therefore in front of him they carry Agni. 'To thee, O Agni, day by day' and 'To the dear the adorable' these three[5] and one[6] he recites; these two, coming together, are liable to injure the sacrificer, he that was formerly taken out and he whom after they bring forth. In that he recites three and one, verily thus he unites them in unison; verily thus he establishes them in security, to prevent injury to himself or the sacrificer. 'O Agni, rejoice; be glad in this prayer' he recites[7] when the libation is being offered; verily thus he causes the libation to gladden Agni. 'Soma goeth, who knoweth the way', this triplet[8] in Gāyatrī to Soma he recites, when Soma the king is being brought forward; verily thus with his own deity, his own metre, he makes him prosper. 'Soma hath sat him on his place' he says; for he is going to take his seat here; having gone beyond and placing the Agnīdh's altar at his back as it were should he recite. 'This of him King Varuṇa, this the Açvins', (this verse[9]) to Viṣṇu he recites; 'Attend the insight of him with the Maruts, the ordainer; he doth support the strength, the highest, that knoweth the day; the stall doth Viṣṇu with his comrades reveal' (he says); Viṣṇu is the door guardian of the gods; verily thus he opens the door to him. 'When within thou hast come forward, thou shalt be Aditi' he recites[10] when he is being put in place. 'Like an eagle his nest, the seat wrought with devotion' (he says[11]) when he has been put in place. 'To the golden to sit on the god hasteneth' (he says); golden as it were he spreads thus for the gods as a cover the black antelope skin. Therefore does he recite this (verse). 'He hath established the sky, the Asura, all-knower'[12], with (this verse) to Varuṇa he concludes; so long as he is tied up he has Varuṇa as his deity, so long as he is approaching the covered (places); verily thus with his own deity, his own metre, he makes him prosper. If they should run up to him or seek safety, he should conclude with the following (verse[13]), 'Do thou welcome Varuṇa the great.' For so many as

[4] RV. iii. 27. 7–9.
[5] RV. i. 1. 7–9.
[6] RV. ix. 67. 29.
[7] RV. i. 144. 7.
[8] RV. iii. 62. 13–15. Cf. KB. iv. 4.
[9] RV. i. 156. 4.
[10] RV. viii. 48. 2.
[11] RV. ix. 71. 6.
[12] RV. viii. 42. 1.
[13] RV. viii. 42. 2.

he desires freedom from fear, for so many as he contemplates freedom from fear, to so many is freedom from fear accorded, when one knowing thus concludes with this (verse). Seventeen (verses) he recites, perfect in form; that in the sacrifice is perfect, which is perfect in form, that rite which as it is being performed the verse describes. Of them he recites the first thrice, the last thrice; they make up twenty-one; Prajāpati is twenty-onefold; twelve months, five seasons, these three worlds, yonder Āditya as twenty-first, the highest support. This is the divine field, this prosperity, this is overlordship, this the expanse of the tawny one, this the abode of Prajāpati, this self-rule. Verily thus he prospers as regards him [14] with these twenty-one (verses).

[14] For the construction see above i. 1, n. 3. For *akar ṇa vai* above, which Böhtlingk condemns, may be cited MS. i. 6. 10; 10. 10, 18; 11. 10; iii. 6. 10; iv. 2. 1; perhaps i. 8. 7 (Caland, VOJ. xxiii. 58); JUB. i. 5. 1; TB. i. 208. 6; Oertel, *Trans. Connecticut Acad.* xv. 68; Bloomfield, JAOS. xxvii. 77; Wackernagel, *Altind. Gramm.* i. 191. *mahāṇagnyā* is apparently the MS. tradition in i. 27, but may be a later Prakritism.

PAÑCIKĀ II

THE SOMA SACRIFICE (*continued*).

ADHYĀYA I

The Animal Sacrifice.

ii. 1 (vi. 1). By[1] means of the sacrifice the gods went upwards to the world of heaven; they were afraid, 'Seeing this of us men and seers will track us.' Them they obstructed by means of the sacrificial post; in that they obstructed them by means of the post, that is why the post has its name. Having fixed it point down, they went upwards. Then men and seers came to the place of sacrifice of the gods, 'Let us seek something to track the sacrifice.' They found the post only, established with point downwards. They perceived, 'By this the gods have blocked the sacrifice.' Having dug it out they fixed it upwards; then did they discern the world of heaven. In that the post is fixed upright, (it is) to track the sacrifice, to reveal the world of heaven. The post is a thunderbolt; it should be made of eight corners; the bolt is eight-cornered. This he hurls as a weapon at the rival who hates him, to lay him low who is to be laid low by him. The post is a bolt; it stands erect as a weapon against the foe. Therefore also to him who hates there is displeasure in seeing, 'This is N. N.'s post, this is N. N.'s post.' Of Khadira wood should he make the post who desires heaven; by means of a post of Khadira the gods won the world of heaven; thus verily also the sacrificer by a post of Khadira wins the world of heaven. Of Bilva should he make the post, who desires proper food and desires prosperity. Year by year is Bilva taken; this is the symbol of proper food. It should be covered with branches up to the root, this is (the symbol) of prosperity. He prospers in offspring and cattle who knowing thus makes the post of Bilva. Now as to (his using) Bilva,[2] they say 'Bilva is light'; a light he becomes among his own people, he becomes the chief of his own people, who knows thus. Of Palāça should he make the post, who desires brilliance and desires splendour. The Palāça is the brilliance and splendour of the trees[3]; brilliant and resplendent he becomes

[1] AB. ii. 1–14 and KB. x deal with the animal sacrifice. The Sūtras (ĀÇS. iii. 1 *seq.*; ÇÇS. v. 15) are cited in full in Schwab, *Das altindische Thieropfer*. For § 1 cf. TS. vi. 3. 4. 7; Schwab, p. 2.

[2] The Pluti here accentuates the word. For Bilva cf. TS. ii. 1. 8. 1.

[3] For the Parṇa cf. TS. iii. 5. 7. 2, whence its name of *brahmavṛkṣa* like *çrīvṛkṣa* for the Bilva.

who knowing thus makes the post of Palāça. As to (his using) Palāça, the Palāça is the birthplace of all trees; therefore they speak with the word 'Palāça' of foliage generally, as 'the foliage of N. N.; the foliage of N. N.' The desire in all trees is obtained by him who knows thus.

ii. 2 (vi. 2). 'We are anointing the post; do thou recite' the Adhvaryu says. 'They anoint thus at the sacrifice, pious men' he recites,[1] for at the sacrifice pious men anoint him. 'O tree, with divine sweetness'; the butter is the divine sweetness. 'What time thou dost stand aloft, then give us riches, or what time thou dost dwell in the lap of the mother' (he says); 'if thou shalt stand or thou shalt lie, bestow wealth upon us' he says in effect. 'Rise erect, O lord of the forest' is the appropriate (verse [2]) for it being raised; that which in the sacrifice is appropriate is perfect. 'On the surface of the earth' (he says); that is the surface of the earth where they set up the post. 'Being set up with careful setting, do thou bestow radiance on the bearer of the sacrifice,' this benediction he invokes. 'Rising before the kindled' (he says [3]), for it is erected before the kindled (fire). 'Winning the holy power unaging, with good heroes', this benediction he invokes. 'Driving misfortune far from us' (he says); misfortune is hunger, the evil; verily thus he drives it away from the sacrifice and from the sacrificer. 'Rise erect for great good fortune,' this benediction he invokes.[4] 'Aloft to our aid do thou arise like the god Savitṛ [5]'; 'the *na* of the gods is their *om*' (they say); verily thus he says 'stand like the god Savitṛ'. 'Aloft as the gainer of booty' (he says); verily thus he gains it as a gainer of booty and winner of riches. 'What time with skilled singers we vie in calling' (he says); the skilled singers are the metres; by means of them the sacrificers vie in calling the gods; 'To my sacrifice come ye, to my sacrifice.' Even if many as it were sacrifice, the gods come to the sacrifice of him where one knowing thus recites this (verse). 'Aloft protect us from tribulation, with thy beams do thou consume every devourer' (he says [6]); the devourers are the Rakṣases, the evil; verily thus he says, 'Burn the Rakṣases, the evil.' 'Make us erect for motion, for life,' in that he says thus, verily he says 'Make us erect for moving, for life.' Even if the sacrificer is seized as it were, verily thus he gives him to the year. 'Find our worship among the gods', this benediction he invokes. 'Born he is born in the fairness of the days' (he says [7]), for born he is thus born. 'Waxing great in the mortal ordinance' (he says); verily thus they make

[1] RV. iii. 8. 1. Cf. KB. x. 2; ÇB. iii. 7. 1. 9 *seq.*; Schwab, *Das altindische Thieropfer*, pp. 70, 71, 73.
[2] RV. iii. 8. 3.
[3] RV. iii. 8. 2.
[4] RV. iii. 8. 2 d.
[5] RV. i. 36. 13; see Schwab, p. 71.
[6] RV. i. 36. 14.
[7] RV. iii. 8. 5.

it grow. 'They purify him, the clever, the busy, with skill' (he says); verily thus they purify it. 'The sage uttereth his speech desirous of the gods' (he says); verily thus he announces it to the gods. 'The youth, well clad, covered round, hath come', with this last (verse[8]) he concludes; the youth well clad is the breath; it is enclosed with the bodily parts. 'Better he becometh being born' (he says), for ever better he becomes being born. 'Him the wise sages raise up, the prudent, the pious with their minds' (he says); the sages are the learned ones; verily thus they raise it up. Seven (verses) he repeats, perfect in form; that in the sacrifice is perfect which is perfect in form, that rite which as it is being performed the verse describes. Of them he says the first thrice, the last thrice; they make up eleven; the Triṣṭubh has eleven syllables; the thunderbolt of Indra is the Triṣṭubh; verily thus with those whose abode is Indra he prospers who knows thus. He recites the first thrice, the last thrice; verily thus he ties the ends of the sacrifice, for firmness, for might, to prevent slipping.

ii. 3 (vi. 3). 'Should the post stand? Or should he throw it (into the fire)?' they say. It should stand for one desiring cattle. Cattle would not serve the gods for slaying as food. They having departed kept disputing; 'Ye shall not slay us, not us.' Then the gods saw this post as a thunderbolt; they raised it up against them; fearing it they came back; verily even to-day they come up to it. Thereafter the cattle served the gods for slaying as food. Cattle serve for slaying as food him who knows thus and for whom knowing thus the post continues standing. He should throw (it) after for one who desires heaven; the ancients used to throw it after, (thinking) 'the post is the sacrificer, the strew the sacrificer; Agni is the birthplace of the gods; he, having come into existence from Agni as the birthplace of the gods from the oblation, with a body of gold will go aloft to the world of heaven.' Then those who were later than they saw this chip as a fragment of the post[1]; it should be thrown after at this time; thence is obtained the desire in the throwing after, thence the desire is obtained which is in the standing. Himself to all the deities he offers who consecrates himself; all the deities are Agni; all the deities are Soma; in that he offers a victim to Agni and Soma, verily thus the sacrificer redeems himself from all the deities.[2] They say, 'As victim for Agni and Soma should be offered one of two colours,[3] for it is for two deities.' That is not to be regarded. It should be offered as fat; cattle are characterized by fat; the sacrificer becomes emaciated as it were; in that the victim is fat, verily thus he makes the sacrificer prosper with his own fat. They say, 'He should not eat of the

[8] RV. iii. 8. 4.

[1] Cf. TS. vi. 3. 4. 9; KS. xxvi. 6; MS. iii. 9. 4; ÇB. iii. 7. 1. 32.

[2] Çf. TS. vi. 1. 11. 6; KB. x. 3.

[3] Cf. ÇB. iii. 3. 4. 28; KB. x. 3; Lévi, *La doctrine du sacrifice*, p. 132.

victim for Agni and Soma; of a man he eats who eats of the victim for Agni and Soma, for thereby the sacrificer redeems himself.' That is not to be regarded.[4] (The victim) for Agni and Soma is an oblation connected with the slaying of Vṛtra; by means of Agni and Soma Indra slew Vṛtra; they said to him, 'Through us two thou hast slain Vṛtra; let us choose a boon from thee.' 'Choose' (he said). They chose this boon, the victim on the pressing day of to-morrow. This is regularly performed for those two, for it is chosen as a boon for them. Therefore should the victim be partaken of, and one should be fain to take it.

ii. 4 (vi. 4). With the Āprī verses he delights;[1] the Āprī verses are brilliance and splendour; verily thus with brilliance and splendour he causes him to prosper. He says the offering verses for the kindling-sticks; the kindling-sticks are the breaths, for the breaths enkindle all that there is here; verily thus he delights the breaths, he places the breaths in the sacrificer. He says the offering verse for Tanūnapāt; Tanūnapāt is the breath, for he protects bodies; verily thus he delights the breath, he places the breath in the sacrificer. He says the offering verse for Narāçaṅsa[2]; men are offspring; praise is speech; verily thus he delights offspring and speech; offspring and speech he confers upon the sacrificer. He says the offering verse for the sacrificial food; the sacrificial food is food; verily thus he delights food; food he confers upon the sacrificer. He says the offering verse for the strew; the strew is cattle; verily thus he delights cattle; cattle he confers upon the sacrificer. He says the offering verses for the doors; the doors are rain; verily thus he delights rain; rain and proper food he bestows upon the sacrificer. He says the offering verse for dawn and night; dawn and night are day and night; verily thus he delights day and night; in day and night he places the sacrificer. He says the offering verse for the divine Hotṛs; the divine Hotṛs are expiration and inspiration; verily thus he delights expiration and inspiration; expiration and inspiration he confers upon the sacrificer. He says the offering verse for the three goddesses; the three goddesses are expiration, inspiration, and cross-breathing; verily thus he delights them; them he confers upon the sacrificer. He says the offering verse for Tvaṣṭṛ; Tvaṣṭṛ is speech, for speech creates[3] all this as it were; verily thus he delights speech; he confers speech on the sacrificer. He says the offering verse

[4] Cf. TS. vi. 1. 11. 6.

[1] The literal sense is of course intended as well as the derivate 'say the Aprīs'. For the verses see ĀÇS. iii. 2. 5 *seq.*; ÇÇS. v. 16. 5–7. Cf. KB. x. 3, and for §§ 1 and 4 ÇB. iii. 8. 1. 2; ix. 2. 3. 44. Cf. also Schwab, *Das altindische Thieropfer*, pp. 90–92; Max Müller, *Anc. Sansk. Lit.* pp. 463 *seq.*

[2] According to ĀpÇS. xxiv. 12. 16 Narāçaṅsa is invoked by the Vasiṣṭhas and Çunakas only, the other families keep to the offering to Tanūnapāt as the second of the eleven fore-offerings; see ĀÇS. i. 5. 21; Weber, *Ind. Stud.* x. 88 *seq.*

[3] Cf. RV. x. 180. 1; Wackernagel, *Altind. Gramm.* i. 175, 274; Oldenberg, *Ṛgveda-Noten*, ii. 365.

for the lord of the forest; the lord of the forest is the breath; verily thus he delights the breath; the breath he places in the sacrificer. He says the offering verse for the calls of Hail!; the calls of Hail! are a support; verily thus on a support at the end he establishes the sacrificer. For these should he use (verses) by the ancestral seer; in that he uses (verses) by the seer, verily thus he does not set loose the sacrificer from his connexion.

ii. 5 (vi. 5). 'Recite for the carrying round of fire' the Adhvaryu says. 'Agni, the Hotṛ, at our sacrifice', this triplet[1] to Agni in Gāyatrī he recites when the carrying round of fire is being performed; verily thus with his own deity, his own metre, he makes him prosper. 'Being a steed he is carried round' (he says), for him being as it were a steed they carry round. 'Thrice round the sacrifice Agni goeth like a charioteer' (he says), for he like a charioteer goes round the sacrifice. 'The lord of strength, the sage' (he says), for he is the lord of strength. 'Do thou give the supplementary direction, O Hotṛ, for the oblations for the gods' the Adhvaryu says. 'Agni hath conquered,[2] he hath won strength', thus the Maitrāvaruṇa begins the supplementary direction. They say, 'Since the Adhvaryu gives the order for supplementary directions to the Hotṛ,[3] then why does the Maitrāvaruṇa begin the supplementary direction?' The Maitrāvaruṇa is the mind of the sacrifice; the Hotṛ is the voice of the sacrifice; instigated by mind voice speaks, for the speech which one speaks with his mind elsewhere, that speech is demoniacal and not acceptable to the gods. In that the Maitrāvaruṇa begins the supplementary direction, verily thus with mind he sets speech in motion; with speech set in motion by mind he provides the oblation for the gods.

ii. 6 (vi. 6). 'O divine slayers and O human (slayers) make ready' he says; the slayers of the gods and those of man, them thus he instructs. 'Bring ye (it) to the doors of sacrifice,[1] ordaining the sacrifice for the lords of the sacrifice' (he says). The sacrifice is the victim; the lord of the sacrifice the sacrificer; verily thus he makes the sacrificer prosper with his own sacrifice. Or rather they say, 'To whatever deity the victim is slaughtered, that is the lord of the sacrifice.' If the victim be for one deity, 'for the lord of the sacrifice' he should say; if for two deities, 'for the two lords of the sacrifice'; if for many deities 'for the lords of the sacrifice'. That is the rule. 'Forward for him bear Agni' (he

[1] RV. iv. 15. 1-3; see ĀÇS. iii. 2. 9. Cf. KB. x. 3; ÇB. iii. 8. 1. 6; ÇÇS. v. 16. 8; Schwab, *Das altindische Thieropfer*, p. 93.

[2] ĀÇS. iii. 2. 20; ÇÇS. v. 16. 9.

[3] In this case Hotṛ is addressed to the Maitrāvaruṇa, the generic term being used for the specific.

ii. 6. [1] The phrase Sāyaṇa takes as *havirmārgān* or *viçasanakeṭiḥ*. Cf. ĀÇS. iii. 3. 1; KB. x. 4; ÇÇS. v. 11; TB. iii. 6. 6. 1; KS. xvi. 21; MS. iv. 13. 4; BÇS. v. 2. 9; Scheftelowitz, *Die Apokryphen des Ṛgveda*, p. 154; Schwab, *Das altindische Thieropfer*, pp. 102 *seq.*; Roth, *Nirukta*, pp. xxxviii. sq.

says); the victim as it was borne along saw death before it, and was not willing to go to the gods; the gods said to it, 'Come; we shall make you go to the world of heaven.' It replied 'Be it so; but let one of you go before me.' 'Be it so' (they replied). Before it went Agni; it followed after Agni. Therefore they say, 'Every animal is connected with Agni, for after Agni it followed.' Therefore also they bear Agni before it. 'Spread the strew' (he says); the victim has plants as its body; verily thus he makes the victim have its full body. 'May its mother approve it, its father, its brother from the same womb, its comrade from the same flock' (he says); verily thus they slay it with the approval of its generators.[2] 'Place its feet north; make its eye go to the sun; let loose its breath to the wind, its life to the atmosphere, its ear to the quarters, its body to earth' (he says); verily it he thus places in these worlds. 'Flay off its skin in one piece; before cutting the navel force out the omentum; keep its breath within' (he says); verily thus he places the breaths in cattle. 'Make[3] its breast an eagle, its two front legs hatchets, its two fore feet spikes, its shoulders two tortoises as it were, its loins uncut, its thighs two door leaves, its knees oleander leaves; its ribs are twenty-six; them in order remove; make each limb of it perfect' (he says); verily thus its members and its limbs he delights. 'Make a hole in the earth to cover the offal' he says; the offal is connected with plants; this (earth) is the support of plants; verily thus at the end he establishes it in its own support.

ii. 7 (vi. 7). 'Unite the Rakṣases with the blood' he says.[1] With the husks and the polishings the gods deprived the Rakṣases of the offerings of oblations (of cereals, &c.), with blood of the great sacrifice. In that he says 'Unite the Rakṣases with the blood', with their own share he excludes the Rakṣases from the sacrifice. They say 'He should not at the sacrifice make mention of Rakṣases; what Rakṣases are there? The sacrifice is without Rakṣases.' They say, however, 'He should make mention; if a man deprive one with a portion of his portion, he revenges himself on him, or if he does not revenge himself on him, then on his son, or on his grandson, but he does revenge himself on him.' If he make mention he should do so inaudibly; the inaudible part of speech is hidden as it were, the Rakṣases are hidden as it were. If he were to make mention audibly he would make his speech the speech of the Rakṣases.

[2] An interesting example of the common practice of deprecating the anger of the relatives of the dead victim.

[3] The details of the cutting up are obscure; Sāyaṇa has for *praçasā prakṛṣṭachedanau*, for *çalā çalākākārau*. *kavaṣorū* is rendered *kavapākārau* and for this cf. *kavaṣ* of doors in MS. iii. 16. 2; VS. xxix. 5.

[1] Cf. ÇB. xi. 7. 4. 2. See ĀÇS. iii. 3. 1–4, ÇÇS. v. 17. 3 *seq.* *rakṣobhāgaḥ* is taken as acc. by Sāyaṇa, as gen. by BR., *cf.* i. 25. For *dṛp* cf. Oertel, *Connect. Acad.* xv. 159.

He who speaks the speech of the Rakṣases (speaks) that speech which a proud person or a man distraught speaks; that is the speech of the Rakṣases. He does not himself become proud, nor in his offspring is a proud son born who knows thus. 'Its entrails[2] do not cut deeming them an owl (in that shape), lest in your family and offspring a howler may howl, O slayer' (he says); to the divine and the human slayers verily thus he hands it over. 'O Adhrigu, toil, carefully toil; toil, O Adhrigu' thrice should he say and 'O free from sin';[3] the slayer of the gods is the Adhrigu, the Nigrabhītṛ the one free from sin; verily thus he hands it over to the slayers and the Nigrabhītṛs. 'O slayers, whatever here shall be well done, to us that; whatever ill done, elsewhere that' (he says); Agni was the Hotṛ of the gods; with speech he dissected it; by speech the Hotṛ dissects it. Whatever they cut below or above,[4] whatever is done to excess or defectively, verily thus he indicates it to the Nigrabhītṛs and the slayers; prosperously verily is the Hotṛ set free with full life for fullness of life; all his life he lives who thus knows.

ii. 8 (vi. 8). The gods slew man as the victim. When he had been slain his sap went out; it entered the horse; therefore the horse became fit for the sacrifice, and him whose sap had departed they dismissed; he became a monkey.[1] They slew the horse; it went away from the horse when slain; it entered the ox; therefore the ox became fit for sacrifice, and it whose sap had departed they dismissed; it became a Gauramṛga.[2] They slew the ox; it departed from the ox when slain; it entered the sheep; therefore the sheep became fit for sacrifice, and it whose sap had departed they dismissed; it became the Gayal. They slew the sheep; it departed from the sheep when slain; it entered the goat; therefore the goat became fit for sacrifice, and it whose sap had departed they dismissed; it became the camel. It dwelt for the longest time in the goat; therefore the goat is of these animals the most often employed. They slew the goat; it departed from the goat when slain; it entered this (earth); therefore this (earth) became fit for sacrifice, and it whose sap had departed they dismissed; it became a Çarabha.[3] These animals whose

[2] Sāyaṇa takes *rāviṣṭa* as 'cut' but *ravat* as 'make a noise', i.e. weep for a cause of grief, and this must be right. Schwab (*Das altindische Thieropfer*, p. 105) thinks *urūka* = *gudda* and renders *ned* = 'and not'. *ru* = 'cut'; BR. take *ru* = 'cry' both times.

[3] Cf. TB. iii. 6. 6. 4; Schwab, p. 106, n.

[4] I.e. too low or too far up; there must be an error, not merely a description here as in Sāyaṇa; Haug has 'too soon' and 'too late'.

[1] *kimpuruṣaḥ* is of very doubtful sense, but 'monkey' seems much more likely than 'dwarf' suggested by Haug. Cf. ÇB. i. 2. 3. 6–9; iii. 3. 3. 1; Weber, *Ind. Stud.* ix. 246.

[2] Of uncertain nature; 'white deer', Haug. Sāyaṇa says 'whose horns even are hairy'; *Bos gaurus* is the accepted version.

[3] Of uncertain nature; mentioned in AV. ix. 5. 9 (*çalabha* in Ppp.); VS. xiii. 51, &c.; an eight-footed lion-killer is Sāyaṇa's version.

sap is departed are unfit for sacrifice; therefore one should not eat of them. It they followed in this (earth); it, followed, became rice; in that they offer also a cake in the animal sacrifice (it is because they think) 'Let our sacrifice be with a victim with sap, let our sacrifice be with a victim whole.'[4] His sacrifice is performed with a victim with sap, his sacrifice is performed with a victim whole who knows thus.

ii. 9 (vi. 9). The cake (which is offered) is the victim which is killed; the chaff[1] of it is the hairs, the husks the skin, the polishings the blood, the pounded grains and fragments the flesh, whatever is substantial the bone. With the sap of all animals he sacrifices who sacrifices with the cake. Therefore they say, 'The cake offering is the people's sacrificial session.'

'Ye two, Agni and Soma, of joint power, have placed
These constellations in the sky;
Ye too the rivers from unspeakable misfortune,
O Agni and Soma, set free when fast held;'

this offering verse[2] he says for the omentum. By all these deities is he seized who becomes consecrated. Therefore they say 'He should not eat (the food) of one consecrated.' In that he says as offering verse for the omentum 'O Agni and Soma ye set free when fast held', verily thus from all the deities he sets the sacrificer free. Therefore they say 'One should eat when the omentum has been offered, for he then becomes the sacrificer.' 'Another from the sky Mātariçvan bore' he says as offering verse[3] for the cake. 'Another from the mountain the eagle pressed out', (he says) for hence as it were is he, hence is the sap gathered. 'Make ready the oblations, shape food forth' he uses as offering verse[4] for the Sviṣṭakṛt of the cake (offering). Verily thus he makes ready the oblation for him and places sap and strength in himself. He invokes the sacrificial food;[5] the sacrificial food is cattle;[6] verily thus he invokes cattle; he confers cattle on the sacrificer.

ii. 10 (vi. 10). 'Recite for the oblation being cut off for Manotā' the Adhvaryu says. He recites the hymn[1] 'For thou, O Agni, are the first thinker.' They say 'Since the victim is for other deities also, then why

[4] For this idea see the next sentence, ii. 9; 'whole sacrificial essence', Haug.

[1] The senses of the words are not all clear, but Sāyaṇa's views seem reasonable. Aufrecht maintains *yat kiṁcitkam* against PW. and Weber, *Ind. Stud.* ii. 9; *lokyam* must have some such sense as rendered, not merely = *prokṣaṇīyam*.

[2] RV. i. 93. 5; ĀÇS. iii. 8. 1; ÇÇS. v. 18. 11. For the gen. *dīkṣitasya* cf. KÇS. xxv. 8. 16; TB. i. 8. 2. 7; KS. xiv. 5; JUB. i. 57. 1.

[3] RV. i. 93. 6; see ĀÇS. i. 6. 1 *ad fin.*

[4] RV. iii. 54. 22; see ĀÇS. iii. 5. 9. Cf. Schwab, *Das altindische Thieropfer*, p. 138.

[5] ĀÇS. i. 7. 7; ÇÇS. i. 12. 1; though Sāyaṇa gives TB. iii. 5. 8. 1 as an alternative.

[6] Sāyaṇa cites for this TS. i. 7. 2. 1.

ii. 10. [1] RV. vi. 1. Cf. KB. x. 6; ÇB. iii. 8. 3. 14; ĀÇS. iii. 6. 1; ÇÇS. v. 19. 13. The Maitrāvaruṇa says it; Schwab, *Das altindische Thieropfer*, p. 137.

does he recite (verses) to Agni alone for the oblation being cut off for Manotā?' Three are the Manotās of the gods, for in them are their minds woven. Speech is the Manotā of the gods; for in it are their minds woven. The cow is the Manotā of the gods, for in it are their minds woven. Agni is the Manotā of the gods, for in him are their minds woven. Agni is all the Manotās; in Agni the Manotās unite. Therefore he recites (verses) to Agni only for the oblation being cut off for Manotā. 'O Agni and Soma, of the oblation set forward' he uses as offering verse[2] for the oblation. In 'of the oblation' it is (appropriate and) perfect in form, as 'set forward' it is perfect in form. Made perfect with all perfections his oblation goes to the gods who knows thus. He says the offering verse for the lord of the forest;[3] the lord of the forest is the breaths; with life his oblation goes to the gods when one knowing thus says the offering verse for the lord of the forest. He says the offering verse of the Sviṣṭakṛt;[4] the Sviṣṭakṛt is a support; verily thus on a support at the end he establishes the sacrifice. He invokes the sacrificial food;[5] the sacrificial food is cattle; verily thus he invokes cattle; he confers cattle upon the sacrificer.

ADHYĀYA II

The Animal Sacrifice (continued).

ii. 11 (vii. 1). The gods performed the sacrifice; towards them as they performed it came the Asuras, (saying) 'We shall make a disturbance of their sacrifice.' When over the victim had been said the Āprīs, before as it were the circumambulation with fire they attacked the post from the east. The gods, perceiving, placed around three forts consisting of citadels made of Agni, to protect themselves and the sacrifice. These Agni-made citadels kept shining and blazing. The Asuras, in terror, ran away; verily with Agni before and Agni behind they smote away the Asuras and the Rakṣases. Verily then also the sacrificers in that they perform the circumambulation with fire place around three forts, consisting of citadels made of Agni, to protect the sacrifice and themselves. Therefore they carry fire round; therefore for the carrying round of fire he recites. The victim over which the Āprīs have been said and round which fire has been carried they lead northwards.[1] They carry a torch before it, (thinking) 'The victim is in essence the sacrificer; by this light the sacrificer with light before him will go to the world of heaven.' By

[2] RV. i. 93. 7; ÇÇS. v. 19. 16.

[3] See ÇÇS. v. 19. 18–20. The verse is RV. x. 70. 10.

[4] See ÇÇS. v. 19. 21–23. There is no Nigada.

[5] See ÇÇS. v. 19. 24. Cf. AB. ii. 9. 11.

[1] Cf. TS. iii. 1. 3. 2.

this light the sacrificer with light before him goes to the world of heaven. When they are about to kill it, then the Adhvaryu throws the strew below. In that they lead it outside the altar when over it has been said the Āprīs and round it fire has been carried, verily thus they make it sit on the strew. They dig a hole for the offal; the offal is connected with plants; this (earth) is the support of plants; verily thus in its support it at the end they establish. They say, 'This animal is the oblation; now much of it goes away, hair, skin, blood, dewclaws, hooves, the two horns, the raw flesh falls away; by what is this made up?' In that they offer a cake also at the animal sacrifice, thereby is this made up for it. The saps went away from animals; becoming rice and barley were they born; in that in the animal sacrifice they offer also a cake, (it is because they think) 'Let our sacrifice be with a victim with sap; let our sacrifice be with a victim whole.' His sacrifice is performed with a victim with sap; his sacrifice is performed with a victim whole who knows thus.

ii. 12 (vii. 2). Having forced out its omentum they bring it up; the Adhvaryu covering it with butter from the dipping ladle says, 'Recite for the drops.' In that the drops are dropped, (it is because he thinks) 'The drops are connected with all the deities; let these not, undelighted by me, go to the gods.' 'Rejoice in the most extending' he recites.[1] 'This speech most pleasing to the gods, offering the oblations in thy mouth' (he says); verily thus he offers them in the mouth of Agni. 'This our sacrifice place among the immortals', this hymn[2] he recites. In 'Rejoice in these oblations, O all-knower' he invokes rejoicing in the oblations. 'Of the drops, O Agni, of fat, of ghee' (he says), for they are of fat and of ghee. 'O Hotṛ, eat first seated' (he says); Agni is the Hotṛ of the gods; verily thus he says 'O Agni, eat, first seated.' 'Rich in ghee, O purifying one, for thee the drops of fat are dropped' (he says),[3] for they are of fat and of ghee. In 'Bestow upon us in thy wont that most worthy thing meet for the enjoyment of the gods' he invokes a benediction. 'To thee, the sage, the drops drop ghee, O Agni, who art to be appeased' (he says),[4] for they drop ghee. In 'As best seer art thou kindled; do thou become the helper of the sacrifice' he invokes the perfecting of the sacrifice. 'For thee they drop,[5] O Adhrigu, O mighty one, the drops, O Agni, of fat and of ghee' (he says), for they are of fat and of ghee. 'Praised by the poet with great blaze hast thou come; rejoice in the oblations, O wise one', with this he invokes rejoicing in the oblations.

[1] RV. i. 75. 1; see Schwab, *Das altindische Thieropfer*, pp. 114, 115.
[2] RV. iii. 21.
[3] RV. iii. 21. 2.
[4] RV. iii. 21. 3.
[5] RV. iii. 21. 4.

'For thee from the middle the best fat is taken out,
We give it forth unto thee;
For thee, O bright one, the drops drop on the skin,
Taste of them among the gods'

(he says);[6] verily thus he says the *vaṣaṭ* call over them, just as in 'O Agni, taste the Soma.' In that the drops are dropped, and the drops are connected with all the deities, therefore the rain comes divided into drops.

ii. 13 (vii. 3). They say,[1] 'What are the invitatory verses of the calls of Hail! What the direction? What the offering verse?' These which he recites are the invitatory verses, the direction is the direction; the offering verse the offering verse. They say, 'What is the deity of the calls of Hail!?' 'The All-gods' he should reply. Therefore they use as offering verse 'May the gods eat the oblation over which has been said the call of Hail!' The gods by the sacrifice, by zeal, by fervour, by the libations went to the world of heaven; when the omentum had been offered the world of heaven was discerned by them; having offered the omentum, disregarding the other rites they went aloft to the world of heaven. Then the men and the seers came to the place of sacrifice of the gods, 'We shall seek something of the sacrifice for discernment.' They went round, and lo the victim lying without entrails![2] They perceived 'The victim is just so much as the omentum.' The victim is just so much as the omentum. In that having cooked it they offer it at the third pressing, (it is because they think) 'Let our sacrifice be performed with many libations; let our sacrifice be with the victim whole.' His sacrifice is performed with many libations; his sacrifice is with the victim whole who knows thus.

ii. 14 (vii. 4). The libation of the omentum is a libation of ambrosia; the Agni libation is a libation of ambrosia; the libation of butter is a libation of ambrosia; the libation of Soma is a libation of ambrosia. These are the incorporeal libations; with those libations which are incorporeal the sacrificer conquers immortality. The omentum is seed; seed disappears as it were, the omentum disappears as it were; seed is white, the omentum is white; seed is incorporeal, the omentum is incorporeal. The blood and the flesh are the body. Therefore should he say 'As much as is bloodless,

[6] RV. iii. 21. 5.

[1] The Puronuvākyās are those given above in AB. ii. 12; the Praiṣa is that of the fore-offering *hotā yakṣad agnim svāhājyasya*; and the Yājyā is that of the last Āprī verse. The first ten fore-offerings take place before the circumambulation with fire; the last fore-offering after the drops are offered and before the omentum is offered. See Schwab, *Das altindische Thieropfer*, pp. 115, 116.

[2] *ait* is changed by Weber to *ed* = *ā* + *id*, as often in ÇB. i. 6. 2. 3; ii. 2. 3. 3; iii. 4. 2. 2, &c.; KS. viii. 10; Caland, VOJ. xxiii. 61.

so much do thou cut off.' (The offering) is made in five portions;[1] even of the sacrifice is a four-portioner, still the omentum is made into five portions. He makes a basis of butter, a fragment of gold (comes next), the omentum, a fragment of gold; above he makes a layer of butter. They say 'If there is no gold, how shall it be?' Having made two bases of butter, having made a portion of the omentum, then he makes two layers of butter on the top; butter is ambrosia; gold is ambrosia; therein he obtains the desire which is in the butter, therein he obtains the desire which is in gold. They make up five; man is fivefold and disposed in five parts, hair, skin, flesh, bone, marrow. Having made ready the sacrifice in the same extent as is man, he offers in Agni as the birthplace of the gods; Agni is the birthplace of the gods; he having come into being from Agni as the birthplace of the gods, from the libation, with a body of gold, he goes aloft to the world of heaven.

The Morning Litany.

ii. 15 (vii. 5). 'For[1] the gods that move at morn recite, O Hotṛ' the Adhvaryu says. Agni, Uṣas, and the Açvins are the gods that move at morn; they come with seven metres each; the gods that move at morn come to the call of him who knows thus. When Prajāpati himself as Hotṛ was about to recite the morning litany, both the gods and the Asuras resorted to the sacrifice, (thinking) 'For us will he recite, for us.' He recited for the gods alone; then did the gods prosper, the Asuras were defeated. He prospers himself, the evil rival who hates him who knows thus is defeated. In the morning he recited it for the gods; in that he recited in the morning, that is why the morning litany has its name. It should be recited in the deep of the night, to secure the whole of speech, the whole of the holy power. If a man prospers or attains pre-eminence, his speech as uttered others repeat; therefore should it be recited in the deep of the night; before the utterance of speech must it be recited. If he should recite, when speech has been uttered, verily he would make him a repeater of what has been said by another; therefore in the deep of night should it be recited. Before the speaking of the fowls[2] should he recite; the birds, the fowls, are the mouth of Nirṛti;

[1] For this see Schwab, *Das altindische Thieropfer*, pp. 119, 120. Bhār. vi. 16. 4 and 5 are an obvious quotation from this passage. The omentum is not divided, but the offering is made of five portions. For the Avadānas see also Hillebrandt, *Neu- und Vollmondsopfer*, pp. 108 seq.

ii. 15. [1] For the morning litany see KB. xi. For the ritual see AÇS. iv. 13; ÇÇS. vi. 2; Caland and Henry, *L'Agniṣṭoma*, pp. 180–182.

[2] Cf. TS. vi. 4. 3. 1 as further explained by ĀpÇS. xii. 3. 14, 15, *purā vā vayobhyaḥ pravaditoḥ*.

now as to his reciting before the speaking of the fowls (it is because they think), 'Let us not speak after speech has been uttered unconnected with the sacrifice.' Therefore it should be recited in the deep of the night. Or rather when the Adhvaryu begins, then he should recite; when the Adhvaryu begins, verily with speech he begins, at speech the Hotṛ recites, for speech is the holy power. Herein is the desire obtained which is in speech and in the holy power.

ii. 16 (vii. 6). When Prajāpati himself as Hotṛ was about to recite the morning litany, all the deities expected 'With me will he begin; with me.' Prajāpati pondered, 'If I shall begin with one specified deity, then by what means shall I obtain the other deities?' He saw this verse,[1] 'O waters, the rich ones'; the waters are all the deities; the rich ones are all the deities. With this verse he began the morning litany. All these deities were delighted, 'With me has he begun; with me!' All the deities delight in him beginning the morning litany. By him who knows thus the morning litany is provided with all the deities. The gods were afraid, 'The Asuras will take from us this morning sacrifice, just as those that have more force and might.' To them said Indra 'Fear not; against them in the morning shall I hurl my thunderbolt thrice made perfect.' This verse did he speak; it is a thunderbolt, in that it is addressed to the son of the waters; it is a thunderbolt, in that it is a Triṣṭubh; it is a thunderbolt in that it is speech. It he hurled against them; with it he slew them; thus indeed the gods prospered, the Asuras were defeated. He prospers himself, the evil rival who hates him is defeated, who knows this. They say 'He indeed would be a Hotṛ who in this verse could produce all the metres'; this thrice repeated supports all the metres; this is the generating of the metres.

ii. 17 (vii. 7). A hundred (verses) should be recited for one desiring life; man has a hundred (years of life), a hundred strengths, a hundred powers; verily thus he confers upon him life, strength, and power. Three hundred and sixty should be recited for one desiring the sacrifice; three hundred and sixty are the days of the year; so great is the year; Prajāpati is the year; the sacrifice is Prajāpati. To him the sacrifice condescends, for whom one who knows thus recites three hundred and sixty. Seven hundred and twenty should be recited for one desiring offspring and cattle. Seven hundred and twenty are the days and nights of the year; so great is the year; Prajāpati is the year; he through whose propagation all this is propagated; verily thus through Prajāpati being propagated he is propagated with offspring and cattle for propagation; he is propagated with offspring and cattle who knows thus. Eight hundred should be recited for

[1] RV. x. 30. 12. Cf. KB. xi. 4; ĀÇS. iv. 13. 6.

one who is called not a Brahman[1] or who being ill-spoken of and seized with defilement sacrifices; the Gāyatrī has eight syllables; by means of the Gāyatrī the gods smote away the evil, the defilement; verily thus by the Gāyatrī he smites away the evil, the defilement. A thousand should be recited for one desiring heaven; the world of heaven is at a distance of a thousand journeys[2] of a horse hence; (they serve) for the attainment of the world of heaven, the securing, the going to (the world of heaven). An unlimited number should be recited; Prajāpati is unlimited; the morning litany is the litany of Prajāpati; in it are all desires obtained. In that he recites an unlimited number, (it serves) to win all desires; all desires he wins who knows thus. Therefore should an unlimited number be recited. In seven metres he recites for Agni; seven are the worlds of the gods; in all the worlds of the gods he prospers who knows thus. In seven metres he recites for Uṣas; seven are the tame animals; he wins the tame animals who knows thus. In seven metres he recites for the Açvins; in seven ways spoke speech; so much spoke speech; (they serve) to secure the whole of speech, the whole of the holy power. To three deities he recites; three are these threefold worlds; verily (they serve) to conquer these worlds.

ii. 18 (vii. 8). They say 'How is the morning litany to be recited?' The morning litany is to be recited according to the metres; the metres are the limbs of Prajāpati; the sacrificer is Prajāpati; that is meet for the sacrificer. The morning litany should be recited by feet; cattle have four feet, for the winning of cattle. By half-verses should it be recited, just as one usually recites it, for support; man has two supports, cattle four feet; verily thus the sacrificer with two supports he establishes among four-footed cattle; therefore should it be recited by half-verses. They say 'Since the morning litany is transposed,[1] how does it become not transposed?' 'Since the Bṛhatī does not depart from the middle of it,' he should reply, 'For this reason.' Some deities have the libations as their portion, others the Stomas and the metres. The libations which are offered in the fire, by them he delights those whose portion is the libations; in that they sing and recite, thereby those whose portion is the Stomas and the metres. Both sets of deities are delighted and sacrificed to by him who knows thus. Thirty-three are the gods that drink Soma, thirty-three that do not drink Soma; eight Vasus, eleven Rudras, twelve Ādityas, Prajāpati and the *vaṣaṭ* call are

[1] Cf. also AB. i. 16, n. 13.

[2] For other estimates see Weber, *Ind. Stud.* ix. 360; cf. *Vedic Index*, i. 70.

ii. 18. [1] This refers to the order of the metres on the morning litany, viz. Gāyatrī, Anuṣṭubh, Triṣṭubh, and Bṛhatī; Uṣṇih, Jagatī, and Paṅkti, not the normal (*avyūḍha*) order by fours upwards, which is given in the enumerations in the *Anukramaṇī*, ÇÇS. v. 27, &c.

the deities that drink Soma; the eleven fore-offerings, the eleven after-offerings, the eleven subordinate[2] offerings, are those that do not drink the Soma and have the victim as their portion; by Soma he delights the Soma drinkers, by the victim those that do not drink Soma. Both sets of deities are delighted and sacrificed to by him who knows thus. 'Uṣas with her ruddy kine hath appeared', with this last (verse[3]) he concludes. They say 'In that he recites for three rites, to Agni, to Uṣas, and to the Açvins, how are all these rites concluded by him when he concludes with one verse only?' 'Uṣas with her ruddy kine hath appeared' is the characteristic of Uṣas; 'Agni in due season hath been placed' of Agni; 'Your chariot hath been yoked, O ye of great wealth, wonder-workers, the immortal, lovers of sweetness, hear ye my call' of the Açvins. So all three rites are concluded by him when he concludes with one verse only.

ADHYĀYA III

The Aponaptrīya.

ii. 19 (viii. 1). The[1] seers performed a sacrificial season on the Sarasvatī; they drove away Kavaṣa Ailūṣa from the Soma, 'The child of a slave woman, a cheat, no Brahman; how has he been consecrated in our midst?' They sent him out to the desert, (saying) 'There let thirst slay him; let him drink not the water of the Sarasvatī.' He sent away to the wilderness, afflicted by thirst, saw the 'child of the waters' hymn,[2] 'Forth among the gods let there be speeding for the Brahman.' Thereby he went to the dear abode of the waters; him the waters welled out after; all around him Sarasvatī hastened. Therefore they call it here Parisāraka, in that Sarasvatī went all around him. The seers said 'The gods know him; let us summon him.' 'Be it so' (they replied). They summoned him; having summoned him they performed this 'child of the waters' (hymn), 'Forth among the gods let there be speeding for the Brahman'; therewith they went to the dear home of the waters, of the gods. He goes to the dear home of the waters, of the gods; he conquers the highest world who knows thus, and he who knowing thus performs the 'child of the waters' (hymn). It he should recite continuously; Parjanya comes to rain continuously[3] for

[2] For these see TS. i. 3. 11.

[3] RV. v. 75. 9.

[1] AB. ii. 19 and 20 and KB. xii. 1 and 2 deal with the recitation for the drawing of the water for the Soma; see ĀÇS. v. 1; Eggeling, SBE. xxvi. 232, n. 2; Caland and Henry, *L'Agniṣṭoma*, pp. 189 *seq.* For Kavaṣa cf. KB. xii. 3; Lévi, *La doctrine du sacrifice*, p. 150.

[2] RV. x. 30. The sense of the verse is doubtful: Caland and Henry render 'Que, pour le service divin, la marche (du sacrifice) aille aux dieux'.

[3] Not *jīmūtavarṣī*, i.e. 'from passing clouds' (Sāyaṇa absurdly 'on the mountains').

offspring when one knowing thus recites this continuously. If he were to recite with divisions, then Parjanya would rain with clouds for offspring; therefore should it be recited continuously only. Of it he recites the first (verse) thrice continuously; verily thereby the whole is continuously recited.

ii. 20 (viii. 2). These nine (verses) he recites without omission. 'Send forth our sacrifice with divine offering' (he says) as tenth.[1] 'Winding hitherward those of two streams' (he says[2]), when the Ekadhanā (waters) are turned hitherward; 'What time the waters are seen coming forward' (he says[3]) when they are being seen; 'May the cows with milk, eager for the end' (he says[4]), when they are coming up; 'Some come together, others come up' (he says[5]) when they come together. The waters were in conflict, 'we shall first bear the sacrifice; we'; both these Vasatīvarī waters, which are drawn on the previous day and the Ekadhanā (waters which are drawn) in the morning.

These Bhṛgu saw, 'These waters are in conflict.' Them with this verse he brought into harmony, 'Some come together, others come up.' They came into harmony; in harmony they support his sacrifice who knows thus. 'Like the waters divine they come up to the vessel of the offering' he recites[6] when they are being poured together into the Hotṛ's goblet, both the Vasatīvarī and the Ekadhanā (waters). 'Hast thou seen the waters, O Adhvaryu?' the Hotṛ asks the Adhvaryu; the sacrifice is the waters; verily thus he says 'Hast thou seen the sacrifice?' 'Yea, they have indeed condescended' the Adhvaryu replies; verily thus he says 'Look upon them.' 'In these, O Adhvaryu, shalt thou press for Indra the Soma rich in honey, full of rain, bitter at the end, thick meanwhile,[7] for him with the Vasus, the Rudras, the Ādityas, the Ṛbhus, the Vibhus, with Vāja, with Bṛhaspati, with the All-gods, of which having drunk, Indra shall slay the foes; he shall overcome their tribes'; (so saying) he rises to meet (them); the waters are to be met; men rise to meet a superior when he comes; therefore is he to rise to meet them. He must turn round behind them[8]; they turn round behind a superior; therefore must he turn round behind them. As he recites he should move after them; for even if another be the sacrificer

[1] RV. x. 30. 11. Cf. KB. xii. 1.

[2] RV. x. 30. 10. *āvṛttāsu* must be read.

[3] RV. x. 30. 13.

[4] RV. v. 43. 1.

[5] RV. ii. 35. 3.

[6] RV. i. 83. 2. The *na* is very curious and apparently untranslatable; Caland and Henry suggest 'Les déesses incarnées en eaux', but cf. Oldenberg, *Ṛgveda-Noten*, i. 83.

[7] So BR. v. 55 against Sāyaṇa. Oldenberg (on RV. x. 42. 8) takes the contrast to be not of the plant but the Savanas, the last being of *tīvra* Soma. *Vājavate* may mean 'full of strength. For the passage above cf. TS. vi. 4. 3. 4.

[8] Sāyaṇa tries to make *anu-* and *pary-āvṛtyāḥ* into two categories, which is impossible.

still fame will fall to the Hotṛ; therefore should he move after them as he recites. Reciting this (verse[9]), 'The mothers go with the paths,' should he move after. 'The sisters of those that sacrifice, mixing the milk with honey' (he says) who being without taste of the honey drink desires to win fame. 'Those that are in the sun or with which is the sun' (he says[10]) who desires brilliance and splendour. 'I invite the waters, the goddesses, where our kine drink' (he says[11]) who desires cattle. Reciting all these should he move after, to win these desires. These desires he wins who knows thus. 'They have come rich with living gifts' he recites[12] as the Vasatīvarī and the Ekadhanā waters are being set down; 'They have come, the waters, eager to this strew,' when[13] they have been set down. With this he concludes.

The Upāñçu and Antaryāma Cups.

ii. 21 (viii. 3). The[1] morning litany is the head of the sacrifice; the Upāñçu and Antaryāma (cups) are expiration and inspiration; speech verily is a thunderbolt. Before the Upāñçu and Antaryāma (cups) have been offered the Hotṛ should not utter speech; if, before the Upāñçu and the Antaryāma (cups) have been offered, the Hotṛ should utter speech, with speech as a thunderbolt he would interrupt the breaths of the sacrificer. If one were to say then of him, 'With speech as a thunderbolt he has interrupted the breaths of the sacrificer, breath will forsake him,' it would assuredly be so. Therefore the Hotṛ should not utter speech before the Upāñçu and Antaryāma (cups) have been offered. With 'Support expiration; hail! thee, O easy to invoke, to the sun!' he should accompany the Upāñçu (cup)[2]; towards it he should breath forth with 'O expiration, support my expiration.' With 'Support inspiration; hail! thee, O easy to invoke, to the sun!' he should accompany the Antaryāma (cup); towards it he should breath in with 'O inspiration, support my inspiration'; 'To cross-breathing thee!' with this he utters speech, having touched the stone for pressing (the Soma for) the Upāñçu. Verily thus the Hotṛ, having placed the breaths in the body, utters speech, with the whole of life, for the whole of life; a full life he lives who knows thus.

[9] RV. i. 23, 16.
[10] RV. i. 23. 17.
[11] RV. i. 23. 18.
[12] RV. x. 30. 14.
[13] RV. x. 30. 15.
[1] AB. ii. 21 and KB. xii. 4 deal with the first two cups offered, the Upāñçu and Antaryāma; see AÇS. v. 2; ÇÇS. vi. 8; Caland and Henry, *L'Agniṣṭoma*, pp. 155–157, 160–162.
[2] 'Restrain' is also possible as a rendering; 'O well-calling one' is Eggeling's version (SBE. xxvi. 254, n. 4).

The Sarpaṇa.

ii. 22 (viii. 4). They[1] say 'Should he creep? Should he not creep?' 'He should creep' hold some, saying 'The Bahiṣpavamāna is the food of both gods and men; therefore they go together towards it.' That is not to be regarded. If he were to creep, he would make the Ṛc a follower of the Sāman. If one here were to say of him, 'This Hotṛ has become a follower of the Sāman singer; he has conferred glory on the Udgātṛ; he has fallen from his place; she will fall from her place,' it would certainly be so. Therefore seated here he should recite,

'The Soma drink of the gods here,
At the sacrifice, on the strew, on the altar,
Of this, we are eating.'

So his self is not excluded from the Soma drinking. Moreover he should say, 'Thou art the mouth; may I become the mouth'; the Bahiṣpavamāna is the mouth of the sacrifice; the head among his own he becomes, the chief of his own he becomes, who knows thus. An Asura woman,[2] named Long Tongue, licked the morning pressing of the gods; it became drunk. The gods sought to remedy it; they said to Mitra and Varuṇa, 'Do ye remove this (intoxication).' They replied, 'Be it so; let us choose a boon from you.' 'Choose' (they said). They chose this boon, the milk mess of the morning pressing. This is their fixed portion, for it is chosen as a boon by the two. Thus what by her was made intoxicated, as it were, is made perfect by this (milk mess), for by it the two removed what was intoxicated as it were.

The Cakes.

ii. 23 (viii. 5). The[1] pressings of the gods were not firm. They saw these cakes; they offered them at each pressing, to support the pressings; then indeed were their pressings made firm. In that the cakes are offered at each pressing, (they serve) to support the pressings, for so are those of them made firm. The cakes the gods made citadels,[2] that is why the Puroḍāças

[1] AB. ii. 22 and KB. xii. 5 deal with the *sarpaṇa* of the priests for the Bahiṣpavamāna Stotra; see ĀÇS. v. 2. 4. 5; Caland and Henry, *L'Agniṣṭoma*, pp. 171, 172. The Mantra is spoiled in metre by the insertion of *iha*. Cf. also ÇB. iv. 2. 4. 7; Eggeling, SBE. xxvi. 249, n. 2. As the Sāman tune is based on the Ṛc (CU. iii. 6. 1), it is secondary.

[2] The legend explains the use of a milk mess at the Bahiṣpavamāna. The tale of the Āsurī is found in the Talavakāra tradition referred to here by Sāyaṇa, and published by Oertel, JAOS. xix. 120; cf. Lévi, *La doctrine du sacrifice*, p. 155.

ii. 23 [1] AB. ii. 23 and KB. xiii. 3 deal with the cakes for the three pressings of Soma. For the rule of eleven potsherds see TB. ii. 5. 11. 4; Caland and Henry, *L'Agniṣṭoma*, p. 184.

[2] *puraḥ* is presumably the noun rather than the prefix, cf. AB. i. 23. 1.

have their name. They say 'He should offer the cakes at each pressing, one on eight potsherds at the morning pressing, one on eleven potsherds at the midday pressing, one on twelve potsherds at the third pressing, for such is the characteristic of the pressings, such of the metres.' That is not to be regarded. The cakes at each pressing are all offered to Indra; therefore he should offer them on eleven potsherds. They say 'From that part of the cake should he eat where it is not anointed with ghee, to protect the Soma drink; for by ghee as a thunderbolt Indra slew Vṛtra.' That is not to be regarded. That which is purified is the oblation; what is purified is the Soma drink; therefore should he eat from any part whatever of it. From all sides these oblations, butter, fried grains, mush, the pap, the cake, and the milk mess flow up to the sacrificer as delights; on all sides delights flow up to him who knows thus.

The Sacrifice of Five Oblations.

ii. 24 (viii. 6). He[1] who knows the sacrifice with five oblations prospers with the sacrifice of five oblations; the sacrifice of five oblations is made up of fried grains, mush, the pap, the cake, and the milk mess; this is the sacrifice of five oblations; he who knows thus prospers with the sacrifice of five oblations. He who knows the sacrifice of five syllables prospers with the sacrifice of five syllables; the sacrifice of five syllables is *su mat pad vag de*; he prospers with the sacrifice of five syllables who knows thus. He who knows the sacrifice of five Narāçansas[2] prospers with the sacrifice of the five Narāçansas; the morning pressing has two Narāçansa (cups); the midday pressing two Narāçansas; the third pressing one Narāçansas; this is the sacrifice of five Narāçansas; he prospers with the sacrifice of five Narāçansas who knows thus. He who knows the sacrifice of five pressings prospers with the sacrifice of five pressings; the sacrifice of five pressings is the victim on the fast day, three pressings, the concluding victim; he prospers with the sacrifice of five pressings who knows thus. 'With the bay steeds let Indra eat the fried grains; with Pūṣan the mush; with Sarasvatī, with Bhāratī, the pap (is for Indra); for Indra the cake' is the offer-

[1] AB. ii. 24 and KB. xiii. 2 deal with the sacrifice of five oblations, and AB. adds speculations on other fivefold elements in the sacrifice; see Caland and Henry, *L'Agniṣṭoma*, pp. 134, 135. See also TS. vi. 5. 11. 4 which very closely agrees.

[2] This refers to the fillings of the goblets, two for the first two pressings and once at the third. For the sense see AB. vii. 34.

[3] The Mantra is defective as regards the milk mess (*payasyā*) and the construction is broken, the *parivāpa* being meant for Indra with Sarasvatī and Bhāratī. It is apparently older than the ritual to which it is accommodated. Cf. PB. i. 5. 11; ÇÇS. v. 4. 3.

ing verse for the five oblation (sacrifice); the two bays are the Ṛc and the Sāman; Pūṣan is cattle; mush is food; 'With Sarasvatī, with Bhāratī' (he says); Sarasvatī is speech, Bharata is the breath; 'the pap, for Indra the cake' (he says); the pap is food, the cake is power; verily thus he makes the sacrificer attain union and identity of form and world with these deities he is united with a stronger, he obtains pre-eminence who knows thus. 'Enjoy, O Agni, the oblation' he says as offering verse for the Sviṣṭakṛt of the cake at each pressing. Thereby did Avatsāra go to the dear home of Agni; he conquered the highest world. He goes to the dear home of Agni; he conquers the highest world, who knows thus and who knowing thus sacrifices with this (sacrifice of) five oblations and who says the offering verse.[4]

ADHYĀYA IV

The Cups for two Deities.

ii. 25 (ix. 1). The[1] gods could not agree in the drinking first of Soma, the king; 'Let me drink first; let me drink first' they desired. They said seeking agreement, 'Come, let us run a race; he who of us wins shall drink first of the Soma.' 'Be it so' (they replied). They ran a race; of them running the race when they had started Vāyu first took the lead, then Indra, then Mitra and Varuṇa, then the Açvins. Indra perceived of Vāyu 'He is winning.' He ran up after him (saying) 'Let us share together; then let us win.' He answered, 'No; I alone shall win.' 'A third for me; then let us win' (he said). 'No,' he answered, 'I alone shall win.' 'A fourth for me; then let us win' (he said). 'Be it so' (he replied); he admitted him to a fourth share; therefore Indra has a quarter as his portion, Vāyu three-quarters. Indra and Vāyu won together, then Mitra and Vāruṇa, then the Açvins. Their feeding is in accord with their winning; first for Indra and Vāyu, then for Mitra and Varuṇa, then for the Açvins. The Indra-Vāyu cup is drawn with a quarter for Indra. Seeing this the seer declares[2] 'With the teams, with Indra as charioteer.' Therefore now also (when) the Bharatas attack the property of the Satvants,

[4] *Yajate yajatīti ca* is very curious, though the sense is clear. Presumably *iti* here is used to point the contrast of *yajate* and *yajati*. For the use of *na* cf. perhaps the Kāṇva text of ÇB. iv. 2. 1. 7: *naty u tac cakāra*. Cf. AB. ii. 30. 5: *samavanayati* and °*nayate*.

[1] AB. ii. 25–28 and 30 and KB. xiii. 5–8 (cf. ÇB. iv. 1. 3. 11) deal with the cups for two deities, those for Indra and Vāyu, Mitra and Varuṇa, and the Açvins; see ĀÇS. v. 5; ÇÇS. vii. 2. 1–3. 5; Caland and Henry, *L'Agniṣṭoma*, pp. 199–208; for the race motive cf. Oertel, *Trans. Conn. Acad.* xv. 174; AB. iv. 7.

[2] RV. iv. 46. 2 *b* or 48. 2 *b*.

the charioteers claim a fourth (of the booty) by force of the example since then Indra becoming a charioteer as it were conquered.[3]

ii. 26 (ix. 2). The cups for two deities are the breaths; that for Indra and Vāyu is speech and breath; that for Mitra and Varuṇa eye and mind; that for the Açvins ear and self. Now some make the invitatory verses for that for Indra and Vāyu Anuṣṭubhs, and the offering verses Gāyatrīs (saying), 'The cup for Indra and Vāyu is speech and breath; thus will the two be in accord with metres also.' This is not to be regarded. Imperfection is produced in the sacrifice when the invitatory verse is longer than the offering verse; when the offering verse is the longer, that is perfect, and so also when they are equal. For whatever desire in speech or breath he thus acts, that is herein obtained. The first invitatory verse is addressed to Vāyu, the second to Indra and Vāyu[1] and so with the offering verses.[2] With the one addressed to Vāyu, he puts breath in order, for breath is Vāyu; then with the Indra line of (the verse) to Indra and Vāyu he puts speech in order, for speech is connected with Indra. He obtains the desire in breath and speech; he makes no unevenness in the sacrifice.

ii. 27 (ix. 3). (The cups) for two deities are the breaths; they are drawn in one vessel; therefore the breaths have one name. They are offered in two vessels[1]; therefore the breaths are in pairs. With the Yajus with which the Adhvaryu offers, the Hotṛ accepts. With 'This the wealthy one, of much wealth; here the wealthy, of much wealth; in me the wealthy, of much wealth; protector of speech, protect my speech' he partakes of (the cup) for Indra and Vāyu. 'Invoked is speech together with breath; may speech together with breath invoke me; invoked are the seers, divine, guardians of the body, born of fervour; may the seers, the divine, invoke me, guardians of the body, born of fervour' (he says); the seers, divine, guardians of the body, born of fervour are the breaths; verily thus he invokes them. With 'This the wealthy, finding wealth; here the wealthy, finding wealth; in me the wealthy, finding wealth; guardian of the eye, guard mine eye' he partakes of (the cup) for Mitra and Varuṇa. 'Invoked is the eye together with mind; may the eye together with mind invoke me; invoked are the seers, divine, guardians of the body; born of fervour' (he says); the seers, divine, guardians of the body, born of fervour are the

[3] That Satvant and Bharata are proper names is only to be believed, though Sāyaṇa does not recognize either. This involves the change of *Satvanām* to *Satvatām* as in ÇB. xiii. 5. 4. 21. Cf. below AB. viii. 14; Weber, *Ind. Stud.* ix. 253, 254; *Vedic Index*, ii. 421.

[1] RV. i. 2. 1 and 4. Cf. KB. xiii. 15.

[2] RV. iv. 46. 1 and 2. Haug has misinterpreted this chapter as allowing, and not as forbidding inequality, not observing that the verses used are in Gāyatrī.

ii. 27. [1] I.e. by the Adhvaryu and Pratiprasthātṛ; see Caland and Henry, *L'Agniṣṭoma*, p. 199. Cf. for the chapter TS. vi. 6. 9. 3, 4; ÇB. iv. 3. 1.

breaths; verily thus he invokes them. With 'This the wealthy, collecting wealth; here the wealthy, collecting wealth; in me the wealthy, collecting wealth; guardian of the earth, guard mine ear' he partakes of (the cup) for the Açvins. 'Invoked is the ear together with the self; may the ear together with the self invoke me; invoked are the seers, divine, guardians of the body, born of fervour; may the seers, divine, guardians of the body, born of fervour, invoke me' (he says); the seers divine, guardians of the body, born of fervour, are the breaths; verily thus he invokes them. He partakes of (the cup) for Indra and Vāyu front to front[2]; therefore expiration and inspiration are in front; he partakes of (the cup) for Mitra and Varuṇa front to front; therefore the eyes are in front; he partakes of (the cup) for the Açvins carrying it all round; therefore both men and beasts hear speech speaking on all sides.

ii. 28 (ix. 4). (The[1] cups) for two deities are the breaths; without taking in breath he should say the offering verses for (the cups) for the deities, for the continuity of the breath and to avoid splitting the breaths. (The cups) for two deities are the breaths; he should not say the second *vaṣaṭ* for (the cups) for two deities. If he were to say the second *vaṣaṭ* for those for two deities, he would bring to rest the unresting breaths; the second *vaṣaṭ* call is the ending. If one were then to say of him 'He has brought to rest the unresting breaths; breath will forsake him,' it would certainly be so. Therefore he should not say the second *vaṣaṭ* for (the cups) for two deities. They say 'Having twice expressed approval the Maitrāvaruṇa twice gives directions; having once expressed approval the Hotṛ twice says *vaṣaṭ*; what is the expression of approval of the Hotṛ?' (The cups) for two deities are the breaths; the expression of approval is the thunderbolt; if the Hotṛ were to express approval between, with the expression as a thunderbolt he would pierce the breaths of the sacrificer. If one were then to say of him, 'With the expression of approval as a thunderbolt he has pierced the breaths of the sacrificer,' it would certainly be so. Therefore the Hotṛ should not express approval between (the two offering verses). Moreover the Maitrāvaruṇa is the mind of the sacrifice, the Hotṛ is the voice of the sacrifice. Impelled by mind speech speaks, for the speech which he speaks with mind elsewhere is demoniacal and not welcome to the gods; verily thus in that the Maitrāvaruṇa twice utters the expression of approval, this is the expression of approval of the Hotṛ.

[2] I. e. the mouth of the cup is placed opposite his mouth, and he does not drink promiscuously from any part.

[1] This chapter explains the omission of the *anuvaṣaṭkāra* in the offering and the fact that there is only one *āgur* as there is no space to intervene between the two offering verses; see ĀÇS. v. 5. 4, and 21, where a memorial verse is cited on the *anuvaṣaṭkāra*. The latter peculiarity is again referred to in AB. iii. 5.

The Seasonal Cups.

ii. 29 (ix. 5). The offerings to the seasons[1] are the breaths; in that they proceed with the offerings to the seasons, verily thus they place the breaths in the sacrificer. Six (priests) offer (saying) 'With the season'; verily thus they place expiration in the sacrifice; four with 'With the seasons' offer; verily thus they place inspiration in the sacrifice; twice with 'With the season' later; verily thus they place cross-breathing in the sacrificer. This breath is divided in three ways, expiration, inspiration, and cross-breathing. In that they offer (saying) 'With the season,' 'with the seasons,' 'with the season,' (it is) for the continuity of the breaths, to avoid splitting the breaths. The offerings to the seasons are the breaths; he should not say the second *vaṣaṭ* for the offerings to the seasons; the seasons are unresting; each (follows) each. If he were to say the second *vaṣaṭ* for the offerings to the seasons he would bring to rest the unresting seasons; the second *vaṣaṭ* is an ending. If one were then to say of him 'He has brought to rest the unresting seasons; it will be an ill season', it would certainly be so. Therefore he should not say the second *vaṣaṭ* for the offerings to the seasons.

The Cups for two Deities (continued).

ii. 30 (ix. 6). (The cups[1]) for two deities are the breaths; the sacrificial food is cattle. Having partaken of (the cups) for two deities he invokes the sacrificial food; the sacrificial food is cattle; verily thus he invokes cattle; he confers cattle upon the sacrificer. They say 'Should he eat first the subdivided sacrificial food? (Or) should he partake of the Hotṛ's goblet?' First should he eat the subdivided[2] sacrificial food, and then should he partake of the Hotṛ's goblet. In that he partakes first of (the cups) for two deities, thereby is the Soma drink first partaken of by him; therefore should he first eat the subdivided sacrificial food, and then partake of the Hotṛ's goblet; then on both sides he envelopes food with Soma drinkings, to envelope food. (The cups) for two deities are the breaths; the Hotṛ's

AB. ii. 29 and KB. xiii. 9 deal with the offerings of cups to the Ṛtus; see ÇB. iv. 3. 1; ĀÇS. v. 8; ÇÇS. vii. 8; Caland and Henry, *L'Agniṣṭoma*, pp. 224–229. Cf. TS. vi. 5. 3. 2; GB. viii. 7 borrows from AB. as usual. The cups are drawn by the Adhvaryu and Pratiprasthātṛ for the seasons and offered to the various deities by the different priests, the gods being invited to partake 'with the seasons (season)'; Eggeling, SBE. xxvi. 319.

ii. 30. [1] Cf. TS. vi. 4. 9. 3.

[2] The *avāntareḍā* is a portion of the *iḍā* which is itself subdivided, and held by the Hotṛ from before his recitation to before he partakes of the *iḍā* proper; see ĀÇS. i. 7 ÇÇS. i. 10–12; Weber, *Ind. Stud.* ix. 225, 226.

goblet is the body; the remains of (the cups) for two deities he pours down into the Hotṛ's goblet; verily thus the Hotṛ places the breaths in the body, with full life for fullness of life; a full life lives he who knows thus.

The Silent Praise.

ii. 31 (ix. 7). What[1] the gods did at the sacrifice, that the Asuras did; they were of even strength and were not discriminated. Then indeed the gods saw this silent praise; that of them the Asuras could not follow. The silent praise is a silent essence. Whatever weapon the gods raised against the Asuras that the Asuras perceived and countered; then the gods saw this silent praise as a thunderbolt; they raised it against them; it the Asuras did not counter; it they hurled at them; with it not countered they smote them; then indeed the gods prospered, the Asuras were defeated. He prospers himself, the wicked rival who hates him is defeated, who knows thus. The gods, regarding themselves as victors, were performing the sacrifice; to it the Asuras came (thinking) 'We will make a confusion of the sacrifice.' They saw them ranged round on all sides, daring; they said, 'Let us conclude this sacrifice; let not the Asuras injure our sacrifice.' 'Be it so' (they replied). They concluded it in the silent praise. With '*Bhūḥ*, Agni, light, light, Agni' they concluded the Ājya and Praüga (Çastras). With 'Indra, light, *bhuvaḥ*, light, Indra' they concluded the Niṣkevalya and Marutvatīya (Çastras). With 'Sūrya, light, light, *svar*, Sūrya' they concluded the Vaiçvadeva and Āgnimāruta (Çastras). So they concluded it in the silent praise; having thus concluded it in the silent praise they attained the end with it uninjured. Then indeed does the sacrifice come to a conclusion, when the Hotṛ recites the silent praise. If any person should after the recitation of the silent praise reproach him or curse him, he should say of him, 'He will fall into this misfortune (he invokes[2]). Early to-day we complete this when the silent praise is recited. Just as one may attend upon one come to his house with due performance, even so now do we attend upon this.' He falls into this misfortune who knowing thus, after the silent praise is recited, either reproaches or curses. Therefore one who knows thus should not reproach or curse when the silent praise has been recited.

ii. 32 (ix. 8). The silent praise is the eyes of the pressings. '*Bhūḥ*, Agni, light, light, Agni' is the eyes of the morning pressing. 'Indra, light,

[1] AB. ii. 31 and 32 contain the treatment of the silent praise, which is part of the Ājya Çastra; see Caland and Henry, *L'Agniṣṭoma*, p. 282. Cf. KB. xiv. 1; ĀÇS. v. 9. 1; ÇÇS. vii. 9. 1.

[2] This seems to be the force of *ā́m*.

bhuvaḥ, light, Indra' is the eyes of the midday pressing. 'Sūrya, light, light, *svar*, Sūrya' is the eyes of the third pressing. He prospers with pressings possessed of eyes; with pressings possessed of eyes he goes to the world of heaven who knows thus. The silent praise is the eye of the sacrifice. The exclamation being one is said twice; therefore the eye being one is (manifested) twice. The silent praise is the root of the sacrifice: if he desire of a man 'May he be homeless', he should not recite the silent praise at his sacrifice; verily thus he comes to ruin along with the sacrifice which being without a root falls to ruin. They say 'He should certainly recite; it is not good for the priest, if the Hotṛ does not recite the silent praise, for on the priest rests the whole sacrifice, on the sacrifice the sacrificer; therefore must it be recited.'

ADHYĀYA V

The Ājya Çastra.

ii. 33 (x. 1). The[1] call is the holy power, the Nivid the lordly power, the hymn the people; he calls, then he inserts the Nivid; verily thus he makes the lordly power dependent on the holy power. Having inserted the Nivid he recites the hymn; the Nivid is the lordly power, the hymn the people; verily, thus he makes the people dependent on the lordly power. If he desire of a man, 'Let me deprive him of the lordly power,' he should recite the hymn in the middle of the Nivid; the Nivid is the lordly power, the hymn the people; verily thus he deprives him of the lordly power. If he desire of a man, 'Let me deprive him of the people,' he should recite a Nivid in the middle of the hymn; the Nivid is the lordly power, the hymn the people; verily thus he deprives him of the people. But if he desire of a man 'May all be in due and proper order and correct for him,' he should call, then insert the Nivid, and then recite the hymn. Thus is the ordering of all. Prajāpati was here being one only in the beginning. He desired 'May I be propagated and become greater'; he practised fervour; he restrained speech; at the end of the year he uttered twelve times. The Nivid has twelve clauses; it was just the Nivid that he uttered; after it were all beings created. Beholding this the seer declares[2]—

'He at the call aforetime of Āyu with his wisdom
Brought into being these sons of man.'

[1] AB. ii. 33–41 and KB. xiv. 1–3 deal with the Ājya Çastra; see ĀÇS. v. 2; ÇÇS. vii. 9; Caland and Henry, *L'Agniṣṭoma*, pp. 230–234.

[2] RV. i. 96. 2.

In that he inserts the Nivid before[3] the hymn (it serves) for propagation; he is propagated with offspring, with cattle who knows thus.

ii. 34 (x. 2). 'Agni god-kindled' he recites; Agni yonder is god-kindled, for the gods kindle him; verily thus he establishes him in that world. 'Agni man-kindled' he recites; Agni here is man-kindled, for men kindle him; verily thus he establishes him in this world. 'Agni the good kindler' he recites; Agni the good kindler is Vāyu, for Vāyu himself kindles himself, himself all this whatever there is here; Vāyu verily thus he establishes in the world of the atmosphere. 'The Hotṛ god-chosen' he recites; the Hotṛ god-chosen is yonder (sun), for he is chosen on all sides by the gods; verily thus he establishes him in that world. 'The Hotṛ chosen by man' he recites; the Hotṛ chosen by man is Agni here, for he is chosen on all sides by men; verily thus he establishes him in this world. 'Leader of the sacrifices' he recites; the leader of the sacrifices is Vāyu, for, when he breathes forth, then there is the sacrifice, then the Agnihotra; verily thus he establishes Vāyu in the world of the atmosphere. 'The charioteer of the offerings' he recites; the charioteer of the offerings[1] is yonder (sun), for he as he wanders yonder is as it were a charioteer; verily thus in yonder world he establishes him. 'The Hotṛ uncrossed' he recites; the Hotṛ uncrossed is Agni here; no one whatever crosses him; verily thus he establishes Agni in this world. 'The crosser, the bearer of the oblation' he recites; the crosser, the bearer of the oblation is Vāyu, for Vāyu at once crosses all that whatever there is here, Vāyu carries the oblation to the gods; verily thus he establishes Vāyu in the world of the atmosphere. 'May the god bring hither the gods' he recites; yonder god brings the gods; verily thus he establishes him in that world. 'May Agni, the god, offer to the gods' he recites. Agni here as a god sacrifices to the gods; verily thus he establishes Agni in this world. 'Let him perform the sacrifices, All-knower' he recites; the All-knower is Vāyu, for Vāyu makes all that whatever there is here; verily thus he establishes Vāyu in the world of the atmosphere.

ii. 35 (x. 3). 'Forward to your god Agni' are Anuṣṭubh (verses[1]). He separates the two first Padas;[2] therefore a woman separates her thighs. He creates the last two Padas; therefore a man unites his thighs. That is a pairing; verily thus he makes a pairing at the beginning of the litany, for generation; he is propagated with offspring, with cattle, who knows thus.

[3] Hence it is called a Puroruc, Weber, *Ind. Stud.* x. 354, n. 3. So AB. ii. 41.

[1] Cf. TS. ii. 5. 9. 2; Eggeling, SBE. xxvi. 326, n. 1.

ii. 35. [1] RV. iii. 13; *anuṣṭubhaḥ* may be genitive or nom. pl.

[2] Cf. KB. xiv. 2; Lévi, *La doctrine du sacrifice*, p. 107.

'Forward to your god Agni' are Anuṣṭubh (verses). He separates the first two Padas, verily thus he makes a thunderbolt broader below; he unites the last two Padas; at the beginning a thunderbolt is narrow, and so of a club and of an axe; verily thus he hurls a thunderbolt at the foe who hates him, as a weapon to lay low whom he has to lay low.

ii. 36 (x. 4). The gods and the Asuras fought over these worlds;[1] the gods made the Sadas their refuge; they conquered them from the Sadas; they went to the Agnīdh's altar; they were not conquered thence. Therefore they spend the fast day at the Agnīdh's altar, not in the Sadas, for they were supported at the Agnīdh's altar; in that they were supported at the Agnīdh's altar that is why the Agnīdh's altar has its name. The Asuras made a scattering of the fires of those gods in the Sadas; the gods drew off the fires in the Sadas from the Agnīdh's altar; with them they repelled the Asuras and the Rakṣases; verily thus also the sacrificers draw off the fires in the Sadas from the Agnīdh's altar; verily thus they repel the Asuras and the Rakṣases. In the morning they kept conquering by the Ājyas; in that they kept conquering (*ājayanta āyan*) by the Ājyas that is why the Ājyas have their name. Of the Hotṛ offices which continued conquering, that of the Achāvāka was left out; in it Indra and Agni took their place; Indra and Agni are the most forcible, mighty, strong, rich, and effective of the gods; therefore (a hymn) to Indra and Agni the Achāvāka[2] recites at the morning pressing, for Indra and Agni took their place in it. Therefore the other Hotrakas creep to the Sadas in front, the Achāvāka behind, for being left behind as it were he is anxious to follow after. Therefore a Brahman, skilled in the Ṛc verses and strong, should perform the Achāvāka's part; thereby it does not become neglected.

ii. 37 (x. 5). The sacrifice is a chariot of the gods; the Ājya and the Praüga Çastras are its inner reins;[1] in that with the Ājya he follows in recitation the Pavamāna, with the Praüga the Ājya (Stotra), verily thus he separates the inner reins of the chariot to prevent confusion; in imitation thereof they separate the inner reins of the chariot of men to prevent confusion. His chariot, whether of the gods or men does not become confused who knows thus. They say 'As is the Stotra, so the Çastra;

[1] Cf. TS. vi. 3. 1. 1; ÇB. iii. 6. 1. 27–29.

[2] For the Çastra of the Achāvāka see ĀÇS. v. 10. 28; ÇÇS. vii. 18. 1–4; Caland and Henry, *L'Agniṣṭoma*, pp. 262, 268.

ii. 37 [1] The sense seems clearly to be that there are four reins, two for each horse, the outer being the Pavamāna and Ājya Stotras, the inner the Ājya and Praüga Çastras; the two Ājyas if joined would mean thus that the two reins (outer and inner) of the horse would be held together, whereas by having Pavamāna and Ājya, Ājya and Praüga, the result is that one hand holds outer and inner, another inner and outer, so that the two inner do not fall together. Sāyaṇa misses the point by not seeing that four reins are referred to.

the Sāman singers sing to verses for Soma, the purifying; the Hotṛ recites the Ājya to Agni; how then does he follow in recitation the verses to Soma, the purifying?' Soma, the purifying, is Agni; that is declared by a seer.[2] 'Agni, the seer, the purifying'; therefore although he proceeds with verses to Agni, still he follows in recitation the verses to Soma, the purifying. They say 'As is the Stotra so the Çastra; the Sāman singers sing to verses in Gāyatrī; the Hotṛ recites the Ājya in Anuṣṭubhs; how then by him are Gāyatrīs followed in recitation.' 'By conversion' he should reply. There are seven Anuṣṭubhs; they become eleven through the first being repeated thrice and the last thrice; the twelfth is the Virāj offering verse; not by one syllable do metres change, nor yet by two. These make up sixteen Gāyatrī verses. Thus by him although he proceeds with Anuṣṭubhs are Gāyatrīs followed in recitation. 'O Agni with Indra, in the home of the generous one', (this verse[3]) to Agni and Indra he uses as offering verse. These two as Indra and Agni did not conquer; being Agni and Indra they did conquer; in that he uses (a verse) for Agni and Indra as offering verse (it serves) for conquest. The Virāj is of thirty-three syllables; the gods are thirty-three, eight Vasus, eleven Rudras, twelve Ādityas, Prajāpati, and the *vaṣaṭ* call. Thus in the very beginning of the litany he makes the deities sharers in the syllables; syllable by syllable the gods drink in order; verily thus the gods delight in the vessel for the gods. They say, 'As is the Çastra so the offering verse; the Hotṛ recites the Ājya to Agni, then how does he use (a verse) to Agni and Indra as offering verse.' Be it to Agni and Indra or to Indra and Agni, the litany is connected with both Indra and Agni through the cup and the silent praise; with[4]

> 'O Indra and Agni come hither to the pressed (drink)
> The delightful cloud, for our prayers;
> Of it do ye drink, impelled by our desire'

the Adhvaryu draws the cup for Indra and Agni. '*Bhūḥ*, Agni, light, light, Agni; Indra, light, *bhuvaḥ*, light, Indra; Sūrya, light, light, *svar*, Sūrya;' the Hotṛ recites as silent praise; therefore as is the Çastra, so is the offering verse.

ii. 38 (x. 6). He mutters the muttering of the Hotṛ;[1] thus he pours seed; inaudibly he mutters; inaudible as it were is the pouring of seed. Before the call he mutters; whatever there is after the call, that belongs to the Çastra. To him he calls as he lies on all fours with averted face; therefore turning their backs quadrupeds pour seed; when he faces him who

[2] RV. ix. 66. 20.

[3] RV. iii. 25. 4.

[4] RV. iii. 12. 1.

[1] The Japapraiṣa is laid down in ĀÇS. v. 9. 1; ÇÇS. vii. 2. 1; TS. v. 6. 8. 1, which differ considerably in text; see Scheftelowitz, *Die Apokryphen des Ṛgveda*, p. 154.

faces him he becomes two-footed; therefore bipeds facing (each other) emit seed.[2] 'Father Mātariçvan,' he says; the father is the breath; Mātariçvan is the breath; seed is the breath; thus he pours seed. 'Make the lines unbroken' (he says); what is unbroken is seed, for hence he arises unbroken. 'May the poets sing unbroken litanies'; the poets are the learned; 'May they propagate this unbroken seed,' he says, in effect. 'May Soma, All-knower, guide the songs, Bṛhaspati recite the litanies and the exclamations!' (he says); Bṛhaspati is the holy power, Soma the lordly power, the songs and the litanies with the exclamations are the Stotras and the Çastras. Verily thus instigated by the holy power divine and the lordly power divine he recites the litanies. These two are the lords of instigation of all this whatever there is here. What he does without instigation by these two that is not done; 'He has done what is not done,' they say, in blame. What is done is done, what is done is not undone by him who knows thus. 'Speech, life, of all life, all life' he says; life is the breath; seed is the breath; the womb is speech; thus having created a womb he pours seed. 'Who (*ka*) will recite this? He will recite this,' he says; Prajāpati is who; verily thus he says 'Prajāpati will propagate this.'

ii. 39 (x. 7). After the call, he recites the silent praise; thus he develops the seed poured; first is then pouring, then development. Inaudibly he recites the silent praise; inaudible as it were is the pouring of seed. Secretly as it were he recites the silent praise;[1] secretly as it were are seeds developed. Of six sentences he recites the silent praise; sixfold is man, with six members;[2] verily thus he develops the self as sixfold and of six members. Having recited the silent praise he recites the Puroruc; thus he propagates the seed when developed; first there is development, then birth. Aloud he recites the Puroruc, verily openly he propagates him. He recites the Puroruc in twelve sentences; the year has twelve months; Prajāpati is the year; he is the propagator of all this. He who is the propagator of all this propagates him with offspring and cattle, for generation. He is propagated with offspring, with cattle, who knows thus. He recites the Puroruc to Jātavedas, with an allusion to Jātavedas. They say, 'Since the morning pressing is the abode of Jātavedas, then why at the morning pressing does he recite a Puroruc to Jātavedas?' Jātavedas is the breath, for he knows of born creatures. Of so many creatures as he knows, they become; for how could they exist of whom he knows not? If one knows the making of the self in the Ājya, that is well known.

[2] Cf. Lévi, *La doctrine du sacrifice*, p. 107.

[1] See ĀÇS. v. 9. 11: there is a pause after each *jyotiḥ* in the middle of the three as well as at the end, when six are to be used.

[2] Cf. TS. v. 6. 9. 1.

ii. 40 (x. 8). 'Forward to your god, Agni,' he recites.[1] 'Forward' is the breath, for all these creatures advance following after the breath; verily thus he creates the breath, he makes breath perfect. 'Radiant, unparalleled,' he recites;[2] mind is radiant, for there is nothing prior to mind; verily thus he creates mind, he makes mind perfect. 'He for us protection for our enjoyment,' he recites;[3] protection is speech; therefore of one following him in speech he says, 'I have accorded him what has a protection'; verily thus he creates speech, he makes speech perfect. 'Do thou aid us, O Brahman' he recites[4]; the holy power is the ear, for by the ear the holy power hears, in the ear does the holy power find support; verily thus he creates the ear, he makes the ear perfect. 'He is the holder, the sage, of them' he recites;[5] the holder is inspiration, for expiration here is restrained by inspiration and departs not; verily thus he creates inspiration, he makes inspiration perfect. 'The righteous, of whom the two worlds' he recites;[6] the right is the eye; therefore when two contend, whichever says 'I actually have seen it with my eye,' him men believe; verily thus he creates the eye, he makes the eye perfect. 'Do thou accord us wealth with a thousand, with offspring, with prosperity', he recites[7] the last (verse) as concluding verse; the self when put together is possessed of a thousand, offspring, and prosperity; verily thus he creates the self as a complex, he makes the self as a complex perfect. He sacrifices with an offering verse; the offering verse is acquisition, prospering destiny; verily thus he creates a prospering destiny, he makes a prospering destiny perfect. He knowing thus, having come into being as composed of the metres, the deities, the holy power, immortality, goes to the gods, he who knows thus. If one knows how having come into being as composed of the metres, the deities the holy power, immortality, he goes to the gods, that is well known. So with regard to the self; now with regard to the deities.

ii. 41 (x. 9). He recites the silent praise as of six clauses; the seasons are six; verily thus he places the seasons in order; he goes to the seasons. He recites the Puroruc as of twelve clauses; the months are twelve; verily thus he places the months in order; he goes to the months. 'Forward to your god, Agni' he recites[1]; 'forward' is the atmosphere, for all these creatures advance following the atmosphere; verily thus he places the atmosphere in order; he goes to the atmosphere. 'Radiant, unparalleled' he recites;[2] he who yonder gives heat is radiant, for there is nothing that is

[1] RV. iii. 13. 1.
[2] RV. iii. 13. 5.
[3] RV. iii. 13. 4. *ásmā ayáṅsi* read by Aufrecht is clearly right though Sāyaṇa had *āyáṅsi*. So also Weber (*Ind. Stud.* ix. 255).
[4] RV. iii. 13. 6.
[5] RV. iii. 13. 3.
[6] RV. iii. 13. 2.
[7] RV. iii. 13. 7.

ii. 41. [1] RV. iii. 13. 1.
[2] RV. iii. 13. 5.

before him; verily thus he places him in order; he goes to him. 'He for us protection for our enjoyment' he recites;[3] Agni accords protection as proper foods; verily thus he places Agni in order; he goes to Agni. 'Do thou aid us, O Brahman' he recites;[4] the holy power is the moon; verily thus he places the moon in order; he goes to the moon. 'He is the holder, the sage, of them' he recites;[5] the holder is Vāyu, for this atmosphere held by Vāyu does not fall in; verily thus he places Vāyu in order; he goes to Vāyu. 'The righteous of whom the two worlds' he recites;[6] the two worlds are sky and earth; verily thus he places sky and earth in order; he goes to sky and earth. 'Do thou accord us wealth with a thousand, with offspring, with prosperity', with the last (verse[7]) he concludes; the year as a complex possesses a thousand, offspring, and prosperity; verily thus he places the year as a complex in order; he goes to the year as a complex. He sacrifices with an offering verse; the offering verse is rain and lightning, for lightning here gives rain and proper food; verily thus he places lightning in order; he goes to the lightning. He who knows this becomes thus composed, composed of the deities.

[3] RV. iii. 13. 4.
[4] RV. iii. 13. 6.
[5] RV. iii. 13. 3.
[6] RV. iii. 13. 2.
[7] RV. iii. 13. 7.

PAÑCIKĀ III

The Soma Sacrifice (*continued*).

ADHYĀYA I

The Praüga Çastra.

iii. 1 (xi. 1). The[1] Praüga is a litany of the cups; nine cups are drawn in the morning; with nine (verses) do they sing in the Bahiṣpavamāna (Stotra); when the Stoma has been performed, he draws the tenth; the sound *hiñ* of the other (verses) is the tenth; thus is there equality. (A triplet[2]) to Vāyu he recites; thereby has the Vāyu (cup) its litany. (A triplet[3]) to Indra and Vāyu he recites; thereby has (the cup) for Indra and Vāyu its litany. (A triplet[4]) for Mitra and Varuṇa he recites; thereby has (the cup) for Mitra and Varuṇa its litany. (A triplet[5]) for the Açvins he recites; thereby has (the cup) for the Açvins its litany. (A triplet[6]) for Indra he recites; thereby have (the cups) Çukra and Manthin litanies. (A triplet[7]) for the All-gods he recites; thereby has Āgrayaṇa cup its litany. (A triplet[8]) for Sarasvatī he recites; there is no cup for Sarasvatī, but Sarasvatī is speech; whatever cups are drawn with speech, they have all litanies recited for him, they become possessed of litanies for him, who knows thus.

iii. 2 (xi. 2). By the Praüga he wins proper food; now various deities are celebrated in the Praüga, different litanies are performed in the Praüga, different kinds of food are placed in the cups of him who knows thus. Now the Praüga is the most related to the self of the litanies for the sacrificer as it were; 'therefore it is most to be perfected as it were by him, they say, 'for by it the Hotṛ makes him perfect.' (A triplet[1]) to Vāyu he recites; therefore they say 'The breath is Vāyu, seed is the

[1] AB. iii. 1–4 and RB. xiv. 4 and 5 deal with the Praüga or second Çastra of the Hotṛ at the morning pressing; see ĀÇS. v. 10; ÇÇS. vii. 10; Caland and Henry, *L'Agniṣṭoma*, pp. 239–241.

[2] RV. i. 2. 1–3.

[3] RV. i. 2. 4–6.

[4] RV. i. 2. 7–9.

[5] RV. i. 3. 1–3.

[6] RV. i. 3. 4–6.

[7] RV. i. 3. 7–9.

[8] RV. i. 3. 10–12.

iii. 2. [1] RV. i. 2. 1–3.

breath; seed comes into existence first when man comes into existence.' In that he recites (a triplet) to Viṣṇu, verily thus he makes his breath perfect. (A triplet [2]) to Indra and Vāyu he recites; where there is expiration, there is inspiration; in that he recites (a triplet) to Indra and Vāyu, verily thus his expiration and inspiration he makes perfect. (A triplet [3]) to Mitra and Varuṇa he recites; therefore they say 'The eye comes into existence first when man comes into existence.' In that he recites (a triplet) to Mitra and Varuṇa, verily thus he makes his eye perfect. (A triplet [4]) to the Açvins he recites; therefore they talk of a child born 'He is trying to listen; he is taking notice.' In that he recites (a triplet) to the Açvins, verily thus he makes his ear perfect. (A triplet [5]) to Indra he recites; therefore they talk of a child born, 'He is holding erect his neck, and also his head'; in that he recites (a triplet) to Indra, verily thus he makes his strength perfect. (A triplet [6]) to the All-gods he recites; therefore a child born crawls on all fours, for the limbs are connected with the All-gods; in that he recites (a triplet) to the All-gods, verily thus he makes his limbs perfect. He recites (a triplet [7]) to Sarasvatī; therefore to a child born speech comes last, for Sarasvatī is speech; in that he recites (a triplet) to Sarasvatī, verily thus he makes his speech perfect. He being born is born from all these deities, from all the litanies, from all metres, from all Praügas, from all pressings, who knows thus and for whom knowing thus they recite thus.

iii. 3 (xi. 3). The Praüga is a litany of the breaths; seven deities he celebrates; seven are the breaths in the head; verily thus he places the breaths in the head. 'Should he consider the good or evil of the sacrificer' he used to say,[1] 'whose Hotṛ he is?' He should do to him at this point as he may desire. If he desire of a man 'Let me deprive him of expiration', he should recite (the triplet) to Vāyu for him in confusion; a verse or a line he should pass over; thereby is it confused; verily thus does he deprive him of expiration. If he desire of a man 'Let me deprive him of expiration and inspiration, he should recite for him (the triplet) to Indra and Vāyu in confusion; he should pass over a verse or a line; thereby is it confused; verily thus he deprives him of expiration and inspiration. If he desire of a man 'Let me deprive him of the eye', he should recite for him (the triplet) to Mitra and Varuṇa in confusion; he should pass over a verse or a line; thereby is it confused; verily thus

[2] RV. i. 2. 4–6.
[3] RV. i. 2. 7–9.
[4] RV. i. 3. 1–3.
[5] RV. i. 3. 4–6.
[6] RV. i. 3. 7–9.
[7] RV. i. 3. 10–12.
[1] For the references see above AB. iii. 1 and 2. For the sentiment cf. Lévi, *La doctrine du sacrifice*, p. 128. The teacher is meant.

he deprives him of the eye. If he desire of a man 'Let me deprive him of the ear', he should recite for him (the triplet) to the Açvins in confusion; he should pass over a verse or a line; thereby is it confused; verily thus he deprives him of the ear. If he desire of a man 'Let me deprive him of strength', he should recite for him (the triplet) to Indra in confusion; he should pass over a verse or a line; thereby is it confused; verily thus he deprives him of strength. If he desire of a man 'Let me deprive him of limbs', he should recite for him (the triplet) to the All-gods in confusion; he should pass over a verse or a line; thereby is it confused; verily thus he deprives him of limbs. If he desire of a man 'Let me deprive him of speech', he should recite for him (the triplet) to Sarasvatī in confusion; he should pass over a verse or a line; thereby is it confused; verily thus he deprives him of speech. But if he desire of a man 'With all his members, with all the self, let me make him to prosper', verily let him recite for him thus in due and proper order; verily thus he makes him prosper with all his members, with all his self. With all his members, with all his self, he prospers who knows thus.

iii. 4 (xi. 4). They say 'As is the Stotra, so the Çastra; the Sāman singers sing to (verses to) Agni;[1] the Hotṛ starts with one to Vāyu; how does he follow in recitation (verses) to Agni?' These deities are all forms of Agni; in that Agni burns forward as it were that is his form as Vāyu; thereby he follows in recitation that (form) of his.[2] Again in that making two as it were he burns and Indra and Vāyu are two, that is his form as Indra and Vāyu; thereby he follows in recitation that of his. Again in that he leaps up and down, that is his form as Mitra and Varuṇa; thereby he follows in recitation that of his. Again in that Agni is dread of contact, that is his form as Varuṇa; in that him being dread of contact they serve with friendliness, that is his form as Mitra; thereby he follows in recitation that of his. Again in that they kindle him with both arms from the two fire sticks and the Açvins are two, that is his form as the Açvins; thereby he follows in recitation that of his. Again in that with loud noise, thundering, and making the sound *ba ba bā* he burns, whence creatures shudder away, that is his form as Indra; thereby he follows in recitation that of him. Again in that him being one they carry apart in many places, that is his form as the All-gods; thereby he follows in recitation that of him. Again in that he burns, roaring and uttering speech as it were, that is his form as Sarasvatī; thereby he follows in recitation that of his. So though he begins with (a verse) to Vāyu, in

[1] I. e. the Ājya Stotra on RV. vi. 16. 10–12. For the rule of consonance see TB. ii. 2. 6. 3.

[2] This version is possibly correct, or *tad* = 'thus'; 'thus with this (form) of his he imitates in recitation'.

each triplet through these deities he follows in recitation (the triplet) of the Stotra. Having recited the Vaiçvadeva litany[3] he uses (a verse) to the All-gods as[4] offering verse.

'With all the sweet Soma drink,
O Agni, with Indra, with Vayu,
Do thou drink according to Mitra's laws.'

According to their portion he thus delights the deities.

The Vaṣaṭ Call.

iii. 5 (xi. 5). The[1] *vaṣaṭ* call is a vessel of the gods; he says the *vaṣaṭ* call; verily thus with a vessel of the gods he delights the deities. He says a second *vaṣaṭ*.[2] Just as in this world men delight horses or cows by renewed attention, verily so they delight the deities by renewed attention in that he says the second *vaṣaṭ*. 'These fires they worship' they say, 'the Dhiṣṇyas; then why do they offer in the former (fire), and say *vaṣaṭ* in the former?' In that with 'O Agni, enjoy the Soma' he says the second *vaṣaṭ* call, thereby he delights the Dhiṣṇyas. 'They partake of the Soma draughts when incomplete,' they say 'for whom he does not say the second *vaṣaṭ* call;[3] what now is the portion for Sviṣṭakṛt of the Soma?' In that with 'O Agni, enjoy the Soma' he says the second *vaṣaṭ* call, thereby they partake of the Soma draughts when complete; this is the Sviṣṭakṛt portion of the Soma. He says the call *vaṣaṭ*.

iii. 6 (xi. 6). The *vaṣaṭ* call is a thunderbolt; he should think of him whom he hates when about to say the *vaṣaṭ* call; verily in him he places the thunderbolt. In the *vaṣaṭ* call he says (the word) 'six'; the seasons are six; verily thus he puts in order the seasons; the seasons he establishes; all this whatever there is here finds support through the seasons finding support. He finds support who knows thus. As to this Hiraṇyadant Baida[1] used to say 'These six thereby he establishes; sky is established on the atmosphere; the atmosphere on the earth; the earth on the waters; the waters on truth; truth on the holy power; the holy

[3] Probably *uktham* here merely refers to the fact that the Praüga Çastra includes all the gods; so the Ājya Stotra is called *kṣullaka-vaiçvadeva*, the full term Vaiçvadeva belonging to the Çastra and Stotra of the evening pressing.

[4] RV. i. 14. 10.

[1] GB. viii. 1–6 follow AB. iii. 5–8.

[2] The term means that there is said a second *vauṣaṭ* with the words *somasyāgne vihi 3* (see Hillébrandt, *Rituallitteratur*, p. 102; Caland and Henry, *L'Agniṣṭoma*, p. 234). Cf. AÇS. v. 5. 19; ÇÇS. vii. 3. 6; *Vait.* xviii. 10; ĀpÇS. xix. 3. 1. The repetition of the *vauṣaṭ* follows from ĀÇS. i. 5. 5; ÇÇS. i. 1. 39, and the words above are not the *anuvaṣaṭkāra*. It is correctly explained by BR. vi. 824.

[3] See above AB. ii. 28.

iii. 6.[1] Cf. AĀ. ii. 1. 5 with Keith's note.

power on fervour.' All this whatever there is here finds support in these supports finding support. He finds support who knows thus. He says *vauṣaṭ* as the *vaṣaṭ* call; *vau* is yonder (sun), *ṣaṭ* (six) the seasons; verily thus he places him in the seasons, he establishes him in the seasons; whatever as it were he does to the gods, that as it were the gods do to him.

iii. 7 (xi. 7). There are three *vaṣaṭ* calls, the thunderbolt, the hider of his abode, the empty. The *vaṣaṭ* call which he makes aloud and forcibly is the thunderbolt; it he hurls as a missile at the rival who hates him to lay him low whom he should lay low. Therefore is it the *vaṣaṭ* to be said by one with rivals. That which is even, continuous, and without loss of (part of) the verse,[1] is the hider of his abode; on it depend offspring and cattle; therefore it is the *vaṣaṭ* to be said by one desiring offspring and cattle. That one wherein the *ṣaṭ* fails[2] is the empty; he empties himself, he empties the sacrificer; the sayer of *vaṣaṭ* becomes worse, he becomes worse for whom he says *vaṣaṭ*. Therefore he should not desire it. 'Should he consider the good and evil of the sacrificer', he used to say, 'whose Hotṛ he is?' He should do to him herein as he may desire. If he desire of a man 'As he has been before sacrificing, so let him be after sacrificing', he should say the *vaṣaṭ* call for him as he recites the Ṛc for him; verily thus he makes him the same. If he desire of a man 'Let him be worse', having recited the Ṛc for him in a more raised tone he should say the *vaṣaṭ* call in a more depressed tone; verily thus he makes him worse. If he desire of a man 'May he be better', having recited the Ṛc for him in a more depressed tone, he should say the *vaṣaṭ* call in a more raised tone; from[3] prosperity he places him in prosperity. The *vaṣaṭ* is said continuously with the Ṛc,[4] for continuity; he is united with offspring and cattle who knows thus.

iii. 8 (xi. 8). He should meditate on the deity for whom the oblation is taken when about to say the *vaṣaṭ*; verily thus openly he delights the deities; before all eyes he sacrifices to the deity. The *vaṣaṭ* call is a thunderbolt; it shines when hurled if not appeased. Of it not every man as it were knows the appeasing nor the support. From it even now there is often as it were death. The appeasing of it, the support is 'Speech[1]'.

[1] I. e. without the loss of the last syllable of the Ṛc merged in the *om*. See n. 4.

[2] Sāyaṇa says that *ṣaṭ* = *vaṣaṭ* and the loss is in a low pronunciation. The sense seems to be that the *ṣaṭ* is lost through imperfect utterance.

[3] *çriye* Sāyaṇa, but *çriyaḥ* seems at least as probable. For the mode of pronunciation see ĀÇS. i. 5. 6; ÇÇS. i. 1. 34, 35 (which allows *samo vā*).

[4] Whether with Pluti or not, ÇÇS. i. 1. 42, 43.

iii. 8. [1] ĀÇS. i. 5. 17: *vāg ojaḥ saha ojo mayi prāṇāpānau*; ÇÇS. i. 1. 39 has a slightly different form.

Therefore after each *vaṣaṭ* call he should recite as accompaniment 'Speech'; appeased it injures him not. With 'O *vaṣaṭ* call, do not injure me; let me not injure thee; with the great I invoke mind, with cross-breathing body; thou art a support; win support; make me attain support' he should accompany the *vaṣaṭ* call. As to that he[2] used to say 'That is long, yet it is impotent. With "Force, strength, force" he should accompany the *vaṣaṭ* call; force and strength are the two dearest forms of the *vaṣaṭ* call; verily thus he unites it with its abode; with a dear abode does he prosper who knows thus.' The *vaṣaṭ* call is speech and expiration and inspiration; they depart when each *vaṣaṭ* call has been said. Them he should accompany with 'Speech, force, strength, force, in me expiration and inspiration'; verily doth the Hotṛ establish speech and expiration and inspiration in the self, with a full life, for fullness of life; a full life he lives who knows thus.[3]

iii. 9 (xi. 9). The sacrifice went away from the gods; they sought to start it up with the directions; in that they sought to start it up with the directions, that is why the directions have their name (*praiṣa*). It they made radiant with the Puroruces; that is why the Puroruces have their name. It they found on the altar; in that they found it on the altar, that is why the altar has its name (*vedi*). It, when found, they drew off with drawing (cups); in that they drew it off with drawing (cups), that is why the cups have their name (*graha*). Having found it they made it known by Nivids; in that having found it they made it known (*nyavedayan*) by Nivids, that is why Nivids have their name. He who seeks what is lost desires something great or small; of the two he who desires the greater has the better desire; he who knows the directions as ever greater, knows them better, for the directions are a seeking for what is lost; therefore standing bent forward[1] he gives directions.

The Nivids.

iii. 10 (xi. 10). The Nivids are the embryos of the litanies; in that they are inserted before the litanies at the morning pressing, therefore embryos are deposited at the back and come into being at the back. In that they are inserted in the middle at the midday, therefore embryos are held in the middle. In that they are placed at the end at the third pressing,

[2] I. e. as Kauṣītaki is often cited in the KB., so Aitareya is thus meant in the AB. There is no *iti* to end the quotation.

[3] The beginning of the chapter is found also in Yāska, *Nirukta*, viii. 22.

[1] The reason given by Sāyaṇa is (1) in respect as to a father or teacher or (2) as a mode of concealment in finding a lost article: obviously (3) stooping to seek what is lost is possible.

therefore offspring are born downward thence, for generation. He is propagated with offspring and cattle who knows thus. The Nivids are the ornaments[1] of the litanies; in that they are inserted at the morning pressing before the litanies, that is as if one were to make a decoration in the upper part of the warp; in that they are inserted in the middle at the midday, that is as if one were to make a decoration in the middle; in that they are inserted at the end at the third pressing, that is as if one were to make a decoration in the lower part of the warp. On all sides he shines with the decoration of the sacrifice who knows thus.

iii. 11 (xi. 11). The Nivids are deities connected with the sun; in that they are inserted before the litanies at the morning pressing, in the middle at the midday pressing, at the end at the third pressing, verily thus they follow the course of the sun. By quarters the gods gathered together the sacrifice; thereby by sentences are the Nivids recited. In that the gods gathered together the sacrifice, therefore the horse came into being; therefore they say 'A horse should he give to the reciter of Nivids'; that boon indeed do they give. He should not pass over a sentence of the Nivid; if he were to pass over a sentence of the Nivid, he would make a break in the sacrifice; as the break in the sacrifice grows the sacrificer becomes worse. Therefore should he not pass over a line of the Nivid. He should not invert two sentences of the Nivid; if he were to invert two sentences of the Nivid, he would confuse the sacrifice; the sacrificer would be confused. Therefore he should not invert two sentences of the Nivid. He should not unite two sentences of the Nivid; if he were to unite two sentences of the Nivid, he would contract the life of the sacrifice, the sacrificer would be likely to die. Therefore he should not unite two sentences of the Nivid. 'Forward this holy power; forward this lordly power,' these two only should he unite, to unite the lordly power with the holy power; therefore are the lordly and the holy powers united. He should not go beyond (a hymn) of three or four verses for inserting a Nivid; each single sentence of a Nivid is a counterpart[1] to a verse, (even) to a hymn; therefore one must not go beyond (a hymn) of three or four verses for inserting a Nivid, for by the Nivid in itself the Stotra is exceeded in recitation. Having left one (verse) over should he insert a Nivid at the third pressing; if he were to insert having left two over, he would injure the propagative power; thus he would deprive people of embryos; therefore having left one only over, he should insert a Nivid at the third pressing. He should not go past the Nivid with the

[1] *peçāḥ* and *peças* in one passage are curious, but no doubt the desire to represent *nividaḥ* more accurately is the cause.

iii. 11. [1] Haug against Sāyaṇa takes that the sense must be that he is to use no hymn of 3 or 4 verses for a Nivid. This cannot be correct. Sāyaṇa holds that no shorter hymn is to be used.

hymn; if with a hymn he goes past the Nivid, he should not return there; verily that stays in its place; having taken another hymn of the same deity and metre he should insert in it the Nivid. 'Let us depart not from the way' he recites[2] before the hymn; he goes from the way who is confused at the sacrifice. 'Not from the sacrifice with Soma, O Indra' (he says); verily thus he falls not away from the sacrifice. 'May not evil spirits stand within us' (he says); verily thus he smites away those who plot evil.

'That which accomplisheth the sacrifice
The web spread out among the gods,
May we accomplish, when offered'

(he says[3]). The web is offspring; verily thus he secures offspring for him (he says[3]). 'Mind we invoke with Soma for Narāçaṅsa' (he says[4]); by mind the sacrifice is carried on, by mind it is performed. This here is the expiation.

ADHYĀYA II

The Marutvatīya Çastra.

iii. 12 (xii. 1). 'The[1] subjects of the gods must be brought into order' they say, 'The metre must be made to rest on the metre.' 'Let us two praise' is his call of three syllables at the morning pressing; 'Let us recite, O divine one' is the Adhvaryu's response in five syllables; that makes up eight syllables; the Gāyatrī has eight syllables; verily they place the Gāyatrī in front at the morning pressing. 'The hymn hath been recited' he says, having recited, in four syllables; 'Yes, reciter of hymns' replies the Adhvaryu in four syllables; that makes up eight syllables; the Gāyatrī has eight syllables; verily thus they place the Gāyatrī on both sides at the morning pressing. 'O Adhvaryu, let us two recite' is his call of six syllables at midday; 'Let us recite, O divine one' the Adhvaryu replies in five syllables; that makes up eleven syllables; the Triṣṭubh has eleven syllables; verily thus they place the Triṣṭubh in front at the midday (pressing). 'The hymn hath been uttered to Indra' he says, having recited, in seven syllables; 'Yes, reciter of hymns' replies the Adhvaryu in four syllables; that makes up eleven syllables; the Triṣṭubh has eleven syllables; verily thus they place

[2] RV. x. 57.

[3] RV. x. 57. 2.

[4] RV. x. 57. 3.

[1] For the calls and replies see KB. xiv. 3; Caland and Henry, *L'Agniṣṭoma*, p. 232; Weber, *Ind. Stud.* x. 36. They are to be 8, 11, and 12 syllables at the three pressings in order. The calls are all clearly mutilated forms from *çaṅs* with *om*. Cf. also TS. iii. 2. 9; GB. viii. 10 imitates as usual. Hillebrandt (*Ritual-litteratur*, p. 104) sees in *daiva* a corruption of *modava*.

the Triṣṭubh on both sides at the midday (pressing). 'O Adhvaryu, so let us two recite' is his call of seven syllables at the third pressing; 'Let us recite, O divine one' the Adhvaryu replies in five syllables; that makes up twelve syllables; the Jagatī has twelve syllables; verily thus they place the Jagatī in front at the third pressing. 'The hymn hath been uttered to Indra, to the gods' he says, having recited, in eleven [2] syllables; 'Yes' replies the Adhvaryu in one syllable; that makes up twelve syllables; the Jagatī has twelve syllables; verily thus they place the Jagatī on both sides at the third pressing. Seeing this the seer declares it a verse,[3]

> 'That the Gāyatrī is deposited on the Gāyatrī,
> Or that they fashioned the Triṣṭubh from the Triṣṭubh,
> Or that the Jagatī Pada is placed on the Jagatī,
> They who know this obtain immortality.'

Verily thus metre on metre he establishes. The subjects of the gods he sets in order who knows thus.

iii. 13 (xii. 2). Prajāpati assigned to the gods the sacrifice and the metres in portions. He allotted the Gāyatrī at the morning pressing to Agni and the Vasus, the Triṣṭubh to Indra and the Rudras at the midday (pressing), the Jagatī to the All-gods, and the Ādityas at the third pressing. Now, the metre that was his own, the Anuṣṭubh, he pushed out to the end to the office of the Achāvāka; she, the Anuṣṭubh, said to him 'Assuredly thou art the worst of the gods whose own metre I am and who yet hast pushed me to the end to the office of the Achāvāka.' This he recognized; he took his own Soma offering; he brought the Anuṣṭubh round to the very beginning in his own Soma offering; therefore the Anuṣṭubh is employed at the very beginning of all the pressings. The very first does he become, pre-eminence doth he attain, who knows thus. He arranged this in his own Soma offering; therefore whenever it falls under the power of the sacrificer the sacrifice is in order; (all) is in order for that people when a sacrificer knowing thus has power.

iii. 14 (xii. 3). Agni was the Hotṛ of the gods [1]; for him death waited in the Bahiṣpavamāna (Stotra); he began the Ājya (Çastra) with an Anuṣṭubh; verily thus he evaded death. For him it waited in the Ājya (Stotra); he began with the Praüga; verily thus he evaded death. For him it waited in the Mādhyaṁdina Pavamāna; he began the Marutvatīya with an Anuṣṭubh; verily thus he evaded death. For him it could not wait in the Bṛhatī verses in the midday (pressing); the Bṛhatī verses are the breaths; verily thus it

[2] But there are only ten, even with the necessary break of Sandhi. *avāci* may be read, but far more probably (see Oldenberg, *Prolegomena*, p. 376) *devebhi(y)aḥ*.

[3] RV. i. 164. 23.

[1] Cf. KB. xv. 5.

could not penetrate the breaths. Therefore at the midday pressing Hotṛ begins with a strophe in Bṛhatī; the Bṛhatī verses are the breaths; verily thus he begins with reference to the breaths. For him it waited in the third Pavamāna; he began the Vaiçvadeva (Çastra) with an Anuṣṭubh; verily thus he evaded death. For him it waited in the Yajñāyajñīya; he began the Āgnimāruta (Çastra) with (a triplet) for Vaiçvānara; verily thus he evaded death. That for Vaiçvānara is a thunderbolt, the Yajñāyajñīya is a support; verily thus by the thunderbolt he drives away death from the support. He having unloosened all the nets, all the posts, of death, was released in safety; in safety verily is the Hotṛ released with full life, for fullness of life; a full life he lives who knows thus.

iii. 15 (xii. 4). Indra[1] having slain Vṛtra, thinking 'I have not laid (him) low', went to the further distances; to the very furthest distance he went; the very furthest distance is the Anuṣṭubh; the Anuṣṭubh is speech. He, having entered speech, lay there; him all creatures severally searched for. Him on the previous day the fathers found, on the second day the gods. Therefore on the previous day is offering made to the fathers, on the second day they sacrifice to the gods. They said, 'Let us press; so assuredly most quickly will he come to us.' They pressed; with[2] 'Thee like a car for aid' they turned him towards (them); at (the verse[3]) praising the pressed (drink), 'This drink, O bright one, is pressed' he became revealed to them. With[4] 'O Indra, come nearer' they brought him into the midst; with a sacrifice to which Indra has come he sacrifices, with a sacrifice possessing Indra he prospers, who knows thus.

iii. 16 (xii. 5). When Indra had slain Vṛtra all the deities left him, thinking 'He has not laid (him) low'; the Maruts only, his true comrades, did not leave; the Maruts, true comrades, are the breaths; the breaths did not then leave him. Therefore this unchanging Pragātha[1] containing (the word) 'true friend' is recited, 'Hither, O true friend, with true friends.' Even if here onwards a recitation to Indra is recited, the whole is the Marutvatīya, if this unchanging Pragātha is recited, containing (the word) 'true friend', 'Hither, O true friend, with true friends.'

iii. 17 (xii. 6). He recites a Pragātha[1] to Brahmaṇaspati; with Bṛhaspati as Purohita the gods conquered the world of heaven, and conquered in the

[1] AB. iii. 12–14 contains introductory matter; 15–21 and KB. xv. 2 and 3 deal with the Marutvatīya Çastra, the first of the midday pressing; see ĀÇS. v. 14; ÇÇS. vii. 6–25; viii. 16; Caland and Henry, *L'Agniṣṭoma*, pp. 299–304. For this chapter cf. TS. ii. 5. 3. 6; ÇB. i. 6. 4. 1.

[2] RV. viii. 68. 1.

[3] RV. viii. 2. 1.

[4] RV. viii. 53. 5.

iii. 16. [1] RV. viii. 53. 5 and 6.

iii. 17. [1] The Pavamāna is composed of 3 Gāyatrī verses, SV. ii. 22–24; 2 Bṛhatī, ii. 25, 26; and 3 Triṣṭubh, ii. 27–29. The Bṛhatī and Gāyatrī verses are made up to 6 each, 2 Bṛhatīs as usual being made to give 3.

world. Verily so also the sacrificer with Bṛhaspati as Purohita conquers the world of heaven and conquers in the world. These two Pragāthas, though not being chanted, are recited with repetitions. They say 'Seeing that nothing which is not chanted is recited with a repetition, then how are these two Pragāthas, which are not chanted, recited with repetitions?' The Marutvatīya is the litany of the Pavamāna (Stotra); there they chant to six Gāyatrī verses, six Bṛhatī verses, and three Triṣṭubh verses; this is the midday Pavamāna, in the Pañcadaça (Stoma), with three metres. They say 'How is this midday Pavamāna, in the Pañcadaça, with three metres followed in recitation?' The two last verses of the strophe are in Gāyatrī, the antistrophe is in Gāyatrī[2]; by these the Gāyatrī verses are followed in recitation; by the two Pragāthas the Bṛhatī verses are followed in recitation. In these Bṛhatī verses the Sāman singers chant with repetitions with the Raurava and Yaudhājaya (Sāmans);[3] therefore these two Pragāthas, though not chanted, are recited with repetitions; thus with the Çastra he follows the Stotra. By the inserted verses in Triṣṭubh[4] and the Triṣṭubh Nivid insertion[5] the Triṣṭubh verses by him are followed in recitation. Thus indeed is the midday Pavamāna in the Pañcadaça with three metres followed in recitation by him who knows thus.

iii. 18 (xii. 7). He recites the inserted verses; by the inserted verses Prajāpati milked from these worlds whatever desire he desired; by means of the inserted verses he milks from these worlds whatever he desires, who knows thus. Now as to these inserted verses, whenever the gods observed a breach in the sacrifice that they closed up by the inserted verses; that is why the inserted verses have their name. With a sacrifice without breach does he sacrifice who knows thus. Now as to these inserted verses, the inserted verses are the sewing of the sacrifice; just as one continues putting together a garment with a needle, so does he continue with these putting together the breach in the sacrifice who knows thus. Further as to the inserted verses, the inserted verses are the recitations for the Upasads; 'Agni is the leader' (he says[1]); the first Upasad is connected with Agni; of that this is the recitation. 'Thou with insight, O Soma' (he says[2]); the second Upasad is connected with Soma; of that this is the recitation. 'They swell the waters' (he says[3]); the third Upasad is connected with Viṣṇu; of that this is the recitation. So much space as by sacrifice with the Soma sacrifice he

[2] RV. viii. 68. 1-3, and 2. 1-3 for antistrophe. The two Pragāthas are RV. viii. 53. 5, 6; i. 40. 5, 6.

[3] These are those to which SV. ii. 25 and 26 are sung; cf. Simon, *Puṣpa Sūtra*, p. 759.

[4] See AB. iii. 13.

[5] See AB. iii. 19.

[1] RV. iii. 20. 4. In §§ 3, 5, 6 *ad fin.* new clauses should begin with *yad* and not as in Aufrecht.

[2] RV. i. 91. 2.

[3] RV. i. 64. 6.

conquers, that he conquers with each Upasad who knows thus and who knowing thus recites the inserted verses. As to this some hold 'You the great' should he recite;[4] saying 'We know that this (verse) is recited among the Bharatas.' That is not to be regarded. If he were to recite it, Parjanya would be liable not to rain.[5] 'They swell the waters' only he should recite; that line has rain in it; it mentions the Maruts in 'Maruts', and contains (the word) 'lead' in 'Like a steed to make rain they lead about'; that which has (the word) 'lead' has the word 'stride'; that which has 'stride' is connected with Viṣṇu; 'The strong one' (he says); the strong one is Indra. In this (verse) there are four clauses, referring respectively to rain, the Maruts, Viṣṇu, and Indra. This verse which has its place in the third pressing is recited at the midday (pressing); therefore the cattle of the Bharatas now spend the evening in the cattle-ground, and at the midday come up to the cattle-shed.[6] It is in Jagatī, for cattle are connected with the Jagatī; the midday is the self of the sacrificer; thus he confers cattle on the sacrificer.

iii. 19 (xii. 8). He recites a Pragātha[1] to the Maruts; the Maruts are cattle; the Pragātha is cattle; (it serves) to win cattle. 'Thou hast been born dread, for impetuous strength', this hymn[2] he recites. This hymn is a propagation of the sacrificer; the sacrificer by it he propagates from the sacrifice as the birthplace of the gods. It is a bringer of victory; he gains victory and is victorious. It is by Gaurivīti. Gaurivīti Çāktya went nearest to the world of heaven; he saw this hymn; with it he conquered the world of heaven. Verily so also the sacrificer with this hymn conquers the world of heaven. Having recited half its (verses), leaving half over, he places a Nivid in the middle; the Nivid is a mounting to the world of heaven; the Nivid is a ladder to the world of heaven. It he should recite climbing up as it were; and he should take hold[3] of the sacrificer who is dear to him. So for one desiring the heaven. Now for one practising witchcraft. If he desire 'May I smite the people by the lordly power' thrice should he here separate with the Nivid the recitation of the hymn; the Nivid is the lordly power, the hymn the people; verily thus by the lordly power he smites the people. If he desire 'May I smite the lordly power by the people', thrice should he here divide the Nivid in recitation by the hymn; the Nivid is the lordly power, the hymn the people; verily thus he smites the lordly power by the people. But if he desire 'On both sides let me

[4] RV. ii. 34. 11. Read *abhivyā°*; cf. p. 85.

[5] The constr. is as in AB. iii. 48; PB. xvi. 15. 9.

[6] Against the time of heat, as Sāyaṇa explains; see *Vedic Index*, i. 282.

[1] RV. viii. 89. 3 and 4.

[2] RV. x. 73. The word is really inserted after v. 6 of the 11 verses; ĀÇS. v. 14. 20.

[3] I. e. he should hold him while imitating the climbing of a ladder, by puffing vigorously as Sāyaṇa says.

sever him from the people', he should here on both sides of the Nivid utter the call; on both sides thus he cuts him off from the people. So for one practising witchcraft, but the other way for one desiring heaven. 'The birds, fair winged, have approached Indra', with this last (verse[4]) he concludes; 'the Priyamedhas, the seers, seeking aid; do thou unroll the darkness' (he says). The darkness by which he deems himself surrounded that should he approach in mind; that from him is removed. 'Fill the eye', with this he should rub his eyes; possessed of sight until old age becomes he who knows thus. 'Release us that are bound as it were with a net' (he says); a net is snares; verily thus he says 'Release us being bound from a snare as it were'.

iii. 20 (xii. 9). Indra[1], being about to slay Vṛtra, said to all the deities 'Do ye support me; do ye call to me.' 'Be it so' (they replied). They ran forward to slay. He perceived 'They are running hither to slay me; well, let me terrify them.' Against them he breathed forth; before his snorting in haste all the gods ran away, but the Maruts did not abandon him; saying 'Smite, O blessed one; strike, show thy strength' they supported him. Seeing this the seer declares[2]

'Before the snorting of Vṛtra in haste,
All the gods, thy comrades, abandoned thee:
With the Maruts, O Indra, be there friendship for thee;
Then shalt thou conquer every foe.'

He perceived 'These indeed are my friends; they showed me love; well, let me give them a share in this litany.' He gave them a share in this litany; to that time both litanies were his only. He draws the cup for the Maruts, he recites the Pragātha to the Maruts, he recites the hymn to the Maruts, he inserts the Nivid to the Maruts; this is the portion of the Maruts. Having recited the litany to the Maruts, he uses (a verse) to the Maruts as offering verse; thus in due portion he delights the deities.

'Those who magnified thee, O bounteous one, at the slaying of the serpent,
Those who, O lord of the bays, at the affair with Çambara, the cattle foray,
Those who now, the sages, rejoice with thee,
In union with the Maruts, drink, O Indra, the Soma'

(he says[3]). Wherever with them he conquered, wherever he showed his strength, thus by mentioning that also he makes them share the Soma drink with Indra.

[4] RV. x. 73. 11.
[1] Cf. KB. xv. 2.
[2] RV. viii. 96. 7.
[3] RV. iii. 47. 4.

iii. 21 (xii. 10) Indra,[1] having slain Vṛtra, having won all victories, said to Prajāpati 'Let me be what thou art; let me be great.' Prajāpati replied, 'Then who am I?' 'Even that which thou hast said' he answered; then indeed did Prajāpati become Who by name; Prajāpati is Who by name.[1] In that Indra became great, that is why Mahendra has his name.[2] He having become great said to the deities 'Assign me a choice portion', just as one desires here, who prospers, who attains pre-eminence, who becomes great.[3] The gods said to him 'Claim thyself what is to be for thee.' He claimed this cup for Mahendra, the midday of pressings, the Niṣkevalya of litanies, the Triṣṭubh of metres, the Pṛṣṭha of Sāmans; this choice portion they assigned to him. They assign a choice portion to him who knows thus. To him the gods said 'All hast thou asked; let us have a share here also.' 'No', he replied, 'how can you have a share also?' They answered 'Let us have a share also, O bounteous one.' He merely looked at them.

The Niṣkevalya Çastra.

iii. 22 (xii. 11). The[1] gods said 'Here is the dear wife, the favourite of Indra, Prāsahā by name; from her let us seek (our desire).' 'Be it so' (he said). From her they sought; she said to them 'In the morning shall I tell you.' Therefore wives seek from a husband, therefore a wife seeks from her husband in the night. To her they went in the morning; she replied with (the verse[2]):

'Since many a time he hath conquered, enduring,
Indra hath made good his name as slayer of Vṛtra;
The mighty lord of strength hath been perceived:'

the mighty lord of strength is Indra.

'What we desire of him to do, let him perform that,'

verily thus she said to them 'What we have said, that he has done.' The gods said 'Let her have a share also, since she has not yet obtained one[3] in

[1] Sāyaṇa quotes TB. ii. 2. 5. 2.

[2] Cf. TS. vi. 5. 5. 3.

[3] These words as Aufrecht points out destroy the sentence in form; yo would save this.

iii. 22. [1] AB. ii. 22–24 and KB. xv. 4 and 5 deal with the Niṣkevalya Çastra of the Hotṛ at the midday pressing; see ĀÇS. v. 15; ÇÇS. vii. 20; viii. 17; Caland and Henry, *L'Agniṣṭoma*, pp. 310–318.

[2] RV. x. 74. 6. The interesting episode of the shame of the daughter-in-law is dealt with by Liebich, VOJ. xxvii. 474–477. For magic in the Brāhmaṇas cf. Lévi, *La doctrine du sacrifice*, p. 189. For *vāvātā* cf. *Vedic Index*, i. 478; ii. 290. For Indra as son of Prajāpati Sāyaṇa cites TB. ii. 2. 10. 1; for *senā*, ii. 2. 8. 1.

[3] Liebich (*Pāṇini*, p. 72, n. 2) suggests *yā no 'smin avaikam avidat*, easier syntax but different if possible sense.

this of ours.' 'Be it so' (they said). They gave her a share then; therefore herein is recited (the verse) 'Since many a time he hath conquered, enduring.' The dear wife, the favourite, Prāsahā by name, of Indra, is his host; her father-in-law is Prajāpati named Who. Therefore he who desires the victory of a host standing away from it at half distance, should cut a grass blade at both ends, and throw it towards the other host, saying 'Prāsahā, Ka seeth thee.' Then, just as in this world, a daughter-in-law keeps hiding in modesty before her father-in-law, so also the host keeps shrinking away in confusion, where one knowing thus, having cut a grass blade at both ends, hurls it against the other host (saying) 'Prāsahā, Ka seeth thee.' To them said Indra 'You may have a share here also.' The gods replied[4] 'Let the Virāj of thirty-three syllables be the offering verse of the Niṣkevalya.' The gods are thirty-three, eight Vasus, eleven Rudras, twelve Ādityas, Prajāpati and the *vaṣaṭ* call; he makes the gods share the syllables; syllable by syllable the gods drink in turn; verily thus with a vessel of the gods the gods are satisfied. If he desire of a man 'Let him be without an abode', let him use for him as offering verse a Gāyatrī, a Triṣṭubh or some other metre, not a Virāj, and say the *vaṣaṭ* call; verily thus he makes him without an abode. If he desire of a man 'Let him have an abode', he should use for him as offering verse[5] a Virāj 'Drink the Soma, O Indra; let it delight thee'; verily thus with it he makes him have an abode.

iii. 23 (xii. 12). The Ṛc and the Sāman were here in the beginning. The Ṛc was called 'she', the Sāman 'he'.[1] The Ṛc said to the Sāman 'Let us be united for generation.' 'No', replied the Sāman, 'my greatness is above thine.' She becoming two spoke (to him); he did not at all consent. Having become three she spoke; with three he united. In that with three he united, therefore with three they chant, with three sing, for with three is the Sāman commensurate. Therefore one (husband) has many wives, but not one (woman) at once many husbands. In that thus he and she were united, thus came into being the Sāma (*sā-ama*); that is why the Sāman has its name. He becomes[2] fair who knows thus; he who prospers, who attains pre-eminence, he becomes fair, for as 'unfair' men reproach (a man).

[4] No *iti* to make the end of the quotation clear, so above iii. 8.

[5] RV. vii. 22. 1.

[1] The same derivation in CU. iii. 6. 1–6. SB. viii. 20 and 21 follows AB.

[2] *sāman bhavati* can only be construed as a loc. but apparently the sense is as taken by Sāyaṇa on its second occurrence. Weber (*Ind. Stud.* ix. 268) offers no translation, and on its first Sāyaṇa renders *sarvair abhyarhitaiḥ sadṛço bhavati.* BR. (vii. 929) has 'er sitzt in der Fülle' (from *sā*), and Deussen (*Sechzig Upanishads*, p. 85) sees in CU. ii. 1. 1–3 a play on these senses of Sāman, those of richness, friendliness, and the Sāman. Probably all are in essence one, resting on the root idea 'conciliate', 'please'.

They came into order becoming one five, the other five; (namely) the call and the *hiñ* call, the prelude and the first Ṛc, the principal part and the middle Ṛc, the response and the last Ṛc, the finale and the *vaṣaṭ* call. In that the two came into order becoming one five, the other five, therefore they say 'The sacrifice is fivefold; cattle are fivefold.' In that, further, they made up, as a set of ten, the Virāj, therefore they say 'In the Virāj, as a set of ten, the sacrifice finds support.' The strophe is the self, the antistrophe offspring, the inserted verses the wife, the Pragātha cattle, the hymn the house. He in this and in yonder world abides with offspring and cattle in his home who knows thus.

iii. 24 (xii. 13). He recites the strophe[1]; the strophe is the self; it he recites with a middle tone; verily thus he makes the self perfect. He recites the antistrophe[2]; the antistrophe is offspring; the antistrophe is to be recited in a louder tone; verily thus he makes his offspring better than himself. He recites the inserted verse[3]; the inserted verse is the wife; the inserted verse must be recited in a lower tone as it were; in his house his wife is not likely to answer back, when one knowing thus recites the inserted verse in a lower tone. He recites the Pragātha[4]; it is to be recited with sonorous voice; sound is cattle, the Pragātha is cattle; (it serves) to win cattle. He recites the hymn[5] 'I shall declare the mighty deeds of Indra.' Thus is the hymn devoted only to and dear to Indra, by Hiraṇyastūpa. By the hymn Hiraṇyastūpa Āñgirasa went to the dear abode of Indra, he won the highest world. He goes to the dear abode of Indra, he wins the highest world who knows thus. The hymn is a house, a support. Therefore it should be recited in the most firm tone. Therefore even if a man gets cattle at a distance as it were, he desires to bring to his house; for a house is the support of cattle.

ADHYĀYA III

The Vaiçvadeva and the Āgnimāruta.

iii. 25 (xiii. 1). Soma[1] the king was in yonder world, on him the gods and the seers reflected 'How shall Soma the king come to us?' They said to the metres 'Do ye fetch for us this Soma the king.' 'Be it so' (they replied). Having become birds they flew up. In that having become birds they flew up, that (tale) those who know stories call the Sauparṇa; thus

[1] RV. vii. 32. 22, 23.
[2] RV. viii. 3. 7, 8.
[3] Above AB. iii. 22.
[4] RV. viii. 3. 12, 13.
[5] RV. i. 32.
iii. 25. [1] AB. iii. 25-32 and KB. xvi. 4 and 5 deal with the Vaiçvadeva Çastra of the Hotṛ at the evening pressing; see ĀÇS. v. 18; ÇÇS. viii. 3; Caland and Henry, *L'Agniṣṭoma*, pp. 354-361. For the legend cf. TS. vi. 1. 6. 2; PB. viii. 4. 1; ÇB. iv. 3. 2. 7; Bloomfield, JAOS. xvi. 1 seq.

the metres went towards Soma, the king. The metres then were of four syllables each only. The Jagatī being of four syllables first flew up; she having flown up and having gone half of the way felt weary; having laid aside three syllables, and becoming of one syllable, she flew back down again, bearing consecration and fervour. Therefore by him is consecration obtained, is fervour obtained, who has cattle, for cattle are connected with the Jagatī, for the Jagatī brought them back. Then the Triṣṭubh flew up. She having flown up and having gone more than half the way felt weary; she having laid aside one syllable, having become of three syllables, came back again, bearing the sacrificial fees. Therefore at the midday the sacrificial fees are taken, in the place of the Triṣṭubh, for the Triṣṭubh brought them back.

iii. 26 (xiii. 2). The gods said to the Gāyatrī 'Do thou fetch the Soma, the king, for us.' 'Be it so,' she replied, 'do ye accompany me with the recitation of the whole (formula for a) safe passage.' 'Be it so' (they said). She flew up; her the gods accompanied with the recitation of the whole (formula for a) safe passage, containing the words 'forward' and 'hither'. (The words) 'forward' and 'hither' are the whole (formula for a) safe passage; therefore him who is dear to him he should accompany with this (recitation) containing 'forward' and 'hither'; verily safely he goes, safely he returns. She, having flown and having terrified the guardians of the Soma, grasped with foot and mouth Soma the king, and also grasped the syllables which the other two metres had dropped. Having shot at her, Kṛçānu, a Soma guardian,[1] cut off the nail of her left foot; that became a porcupine; therefore is it like a nail. The fat that flowed became the barren cow[2]; therefore is it the oblation as it were. The socket and the point became a serpent, not biting; from its swiftness (came) the viper; the feathers became flying foxes, the sinews earthworms, the shaft the blind snake. Thus became the arrow.

iii. 27 (xiii. 3). What she grasped with her right foot became the morning pressing; the Gāyatrī made it her own abode; therefore they regard it as the most perfect of all the pressings. The very first he becomes, he attains pre-eminence who knows thus. What she grasped with her left foot became the midday pressing; it slipped; having slipped it did not match the former pressing. The gods sought to remedy this; in it they placed the Triṣṭubh of metres, Indra of deities; thereby it became of equal strength with the former pressing; with the two pressings of equal strength and of similar quality he prospers who knows thus. That which she grasped with her mouth became the third pressing. Flying she sucked its sap; having

[1] See TS. i. 2. 7; vi. 1. 10. 4; ÇB. i. 7. 1. 1 *seq.*; iii. 3. 4. 10.

[2] See TS. ii. 1. 2. 3.

its sap sucked,[1] it did not equal the two former pressings. The gods sought to remedy this; they saw it in cattle. In that they pour in an admixture (of milk), and proceed with the (offering of) butter[2] and the animal (offering), thereby it became of equal strength with the previous pressings. With all the pressings of equal strength and of similar quality he prospers who knows thus.

iii. 28 (xiii. 4). The other two metres said to the Gāyatrī 'Our property, the syllables have come round with (you).' 'No,' replied the Gāyatrī; 'ours are they as they were found (by us).' They disputed before the gods; the gods said 'They are yours as they were found (by you).' Therefore even now in a question of property they say 'It is ours by right of finding.' Then the Gāyatrī was of eight syllables, the Triṣṭubh of three, the Jagatī of one. The eight-syllable Gāyatrī supported the morning pressing; the Triṣṭubh with three syllables could not support the midday pressing; to her the Gāyatrī said 'Let me come; let there be a portion for me here also.' 'Be it so,' replied the Triṣṭubh, 'Do thou unite me with these eight syllables.' 'Be it so' (she said); her she united; thus to the Gāyatrī at the midday belong the last two (verses) of the strophe of the Marutvatīya and the antistrophe.[1] She, having become of eleven syllables, supported the midday pressing. The Jagatī having one syllable could not support the third pressing; to her the Gāyatrī said 'Let me come; let there be a portion for me here also. 'Be it so,' replied the Jāgatī, 'Do thou unite me with these eleven syllables.' 'Be it so' (she said); her she united; thus to the Gāyatrī at the third pressing belong the last two verses of the strophe of the Vaiçvadeva and the antistrophe. Having become of twelve syllables she supported the third pressing. Then indeed the Gāyatrī became of eight syllables, the Triṣṭubh of eleven syllables, and the Jagatī of twelve syllables. With all the metres of equal strength and of similar quality he prospers who knows thus. That which was one became three; therefore they say 'It should be given to one who knows thus'; for being one it became three.

iii. 29 (xiii. 5). The gods said to the Ādityas 'With you let us support this pressing.' 'Be it so' (they replied). Therefore the third pressing begins with the Ādityas; the cup for the Ādityas[1] is before it. He uses (a verse[2]) containing (the word) 'be drunk' and so perfect in form, as offering verse, 'Let the Ādityas and Aditi be drunk'; that which contains (the word) 'be drunk' is a characteristic of the third pressing. He does not say the second

[1] See TS. vi. 1. 6. 8.

[2] All things connected with cattle.

iii. 28. [1] See AB. iii. 17. 5.

iii. 29. [1] For this cup see KB. xvi. 1; ĀÇS. v. 17. 1–8; ÇÇS. viii. 1. 8–7; Caland and Henry, *L'Agniṣṭoma*, pp. 332, 338.

[2] RV. viii. 51. 2.

vaṣaṭ, nor eat (thinking) 'The second *vaṣaṭ* call is a conclusion; eating is a conclusion; the Ādityas are the breaths; let me not bring the breaths to a conclusion.' The Ādityas said to Savitṛ 'With thee let us support this pressing.' 'Be it so' (he replied). Therefore the strophe[3] of the Vaiçvadeva is addressed to Savitṛ, the cup for Savitṛ is before it. He uses (a verse[4]) containing (the word) 'be drunk', and so perfect in form, as offering verse, 'God of the home Savitṛ the delectable'; that which contains (the word) 'be drunk' is a symbol of the third pressing. He does not say the second *vaṣaṭ* nor eat, (thinking) 'The second *vaṣaṭ* call is a conclusion; eating is a conclusion; Savitṛ is the breath; let me not bring the breath to a conclusion.' Savitṛ drinks of both these pressings, the morning pressing and the third pressing. In that there is in the beginning of the Nivid[5] to Savitṛ a sentence containing (the word) 'drink' and at the end one containing (the word) 'be drunk', verily thus he gives him a share in both pressings, the morning pressing and the third pressing. Many verses to Vāyu are recited in the morning, but one[6] only at the third pressing; therefore the upward breaths of a man are more numerous than the lower. He recites (a hymn[7]) to sky and earth; sky and earth are supports; this (earth) is a support here, yonder (sun) yonder. In that he recites (a hymn) to sky and earth, verily thus he establishes him on a pair of supports.

iii. 30 (xiii. 6) He recites (a hymn) to the Ṛbhus[1]; the Ṛbhus by fervour among the gods won the drinking of Soma. For them they desired to arrange it at the morning pressing; them Agni with the Vasus repelled from the morning pressing. For them they sought to arrange it at the midday pressing; them Indra with the Rudras repelled from the midday pressing. For them they desired to arrange it at the third pressing; them the All-gods energetically repelled, (saying) 'They shall not drink here, not here.' Prajāpati said to Savitṛ 'These are thy pupils; do thou drink together with them.' 'Be it so,' replied Savitṛ, 'Do thou drink round them on both sides.' Prajāpati drank round them on both sides; these two inserted verses[2] without mention (of the deity), intended for Prajāpati, are recited round (the hymn) for the Ṛbhus, 'The maker of fair forms for aid' and 'Let Vena here impel those born of Pṛçni'; verily thus does Prajāpati drink on both sides of them. Therefore does one of high rank honour at his table him whom he desires. The gods had loathing of those because of the human

[3] RV. v. 82. 1–3.

[4] For the cup see KB. xvi. 2 and 3; ĀÇS. v. 18. 1, 2; ÇÇS. viii. 3. 1–4; Caland and Henry, pp. 352–354.

[5] In *somasya pibatu* and *somasya matsat* respectively.

[6] Not in the Saṁhitā.

[7] RV. i. 159.

[1] RV. i. 111. The reading *'vācikalpayiṣan* is given by Caland, VOJ. xxiii. 64; Weber, *Ind. Stud.* ix. 264.

[2] RV. i. 4. 1; x. 123. 1.

scent; they interposed these inserted verses[3] 'In whom the mother' and 'To the father'.

iii. 31 (xiii. 7). He recites (a hymn[1]) to the All-gods; as are peoples, so is the Vaiçvadeva. As are the peoples within, so are the hymns; as the wastes so the inserted verses. On both sides of the inserted verse he utters the call; 'therefore these being wastes seem not to be such by reason of the beasts and birds' he used to say. As is a man, so is the Vaiçvadeva; as are his members within, so are the hymns; as his joints, so the inserted verses. On both sides of the inserted verse he utters the calls; therefore the joints of a man being slack are made firm, for they are made firm by the holy power. The inserted verses and the offering verses are the root of the sacrifice; if they were to use different inserted verses and offering verses, they would uproot the sacrifice; therefore they should be the same. The Vaiçvadeva litany is connected with the five folks; it is the litany of all the five folks, gods and men, Gandharvas and Apsarases, serpents and fathers; of these five folks is it the litany; all the five folks know him; to him from the fivefold folk sacrificers go who knows thus. He who recites the Vaiçvadeva is the Hotṛ connected with all the gods. Of all the quarters should he think when about to recite; verily thus in all the quarters he places sap. He should not think of that quarter in which there is one whom he should hate; by omitting it he appropriates his strength. He concludes with the last (verse[2]) 'Aditi is the sky, Aditi the atmosphere'; Aditi is this (earth); the sky this (earth), the atmosphere this (earth). 'Aditi is mother, is father, is son' (he says); the mother is this (earth), the father this (earth), the son this (earth). 'Aditi is the All-gods, the five folks' (he says); in this are the All-gods, in this the five folks. 'Aditi is what is born, Aditi is what is to be born' (he says); what is born is this (earth); what is to be born is this (earth). He recites twice by lines the concluding (verse); cattle are four-footed; (verily it serves) to win cattle; once by half verses, for support. Man has a double support, cattle have four feet; verily thus he causes men with his double support to find support in four-footed cattle. He should always conclude with (a verse) connected with the five folks; touching the earth should he conclude. Thus in the very place where he brings together the sacrifice in that at the end he establishes it. Having recited the Vaiçvadeva litany he uses (a verse) to the All-gods as offering verse,[3] 'O All-gods, harken to this my call'; thus according to their portions he delights the deities.

iii. 32 (xiii. 8). The[1] first offering verse for the ghee is addressed to Agni,

[3] RV. x. 63. 3; iv. 50. 6.

[1] RV. i. 89. [2] RV. i. 89. 10.

[3] RV. vi. 52. 13.

iii. 32. [1] This chapter deals with the offering of a pap to Soma between libations of ghee to Agni and Viṣṇu; see ĀÇS. v. 19. 1–6;

the offering verse for (the pap for) Soma is addressed to Soma, the offering verse for the ghee is addressed to Viṣṇu. For (the pap for) Soma he uses as offering verse[2] 'Thou, O Soma, in unison with the fathers,' which contains (the word) 'fathers'. They slay the Soma in that they press it; for it they perform (the offering of) a barren cow in the form of (the pap) for Soma; the barren cow is for the fathers; therefore (a verse) containing (the word) 'fathers' he uses as offering verse for (the pap for) Soma. They have killed Soma in that they pressed it; thus do they again bring it into being; they swell it up again with the symbol of the Upasads, these deities, Agni, Soma, and Viṣṇu are the symbol of the Upasads. Having taken (the pap) for Soma before the Sāman singers the Hotṛ should look into it; some indeed give it first to the Sāman singers, but that he should not do. 'The sayer of *vaṣaṭ* eats first all foods', he used to say; in this way therefore the sayer of *vaṣaṭ* should first look into it, then they give it to the Sāman singers.

The Āgnimāruta Çastra.

iii. 33 (xiii. 9). Prajāpati[1] felt love towards his own daughter, the sky some say, Uṣas others. Having become a stag he approached her in the form of a deer. The gods saw him, 'A deed unknown Prajāpati now does.' They sought one to punish him; they found him not among one another. These most dread forms they brought together in one place. Brought together they became this deity here; therefore is his name containing (the word) Bhūta; he prospers who knows thus his name. To him the gods said 'Prajāpati here hath done a deed unknown; pierce him.' 'Be it so,' he replied, 'Let me choose a boon from you.' 'Choose' (they said). He chose this boon, the overlordship of cattle; therefore does his name contain the word 'cattle'.[2] Rich in cattle he becomes who knows thus this name of his. Having aimed at him he pierced him; being pierced he flew upwards;[3] him they call 'the deer'. The piercer of the deer is he of that name. The female deer is Rohiṇī; the three-pointed arrow is the

ÇÇS. viii. 4. 1-6; Caland and Henry, *L'Agniṣṭoma*, pp. 362-364.

[2] RV. viii. 48. 13.

[1] AB. iii. 33-38 and KB. xvi. 7 deal with the Āgnimāruta Çastra of the Hotṛ at the evening pressing; see ĀÇS. v. 20; ÇÇS. viii. 6; Caland and Henry, *L'Agniṣṭoma*, pp. 372-380. The astronomical data here given afford Tilak the source of his work *Orion*; cf. Whitney, JAOS. xvi. xcii, xciii. For the legend cf. ÇB. i. 7. 4. 1; RV. x. 61. 5-9.

[2] The two names are Bhūtapati and Paçupati according to Sāyaṇa, and this is more plausible than Weber's vaguer reference to Bhava (*Ind. Stud.* ix. 269, 270).

[3] *udaprapata* of the MSS. of Haug and Weber, whence the latter conjectured *udapravata* is to be read with Aufrecht as *udaprapatat* before *tam*. The form is so irregular that Aufrecht suggests *udapatat*, Böhtlingk (BKSGW. 15 Dec. 1900, p. 417) prefers *udapravata*.

three-pointed arrow. The seed of Prajāpati outpoured ran; it became a pond. The gods said 'Let not this seed of Prajāpatī be spoiled.' It became 'not to be spoilt;' that is why 'not to be spoilt' (*māduṣa*) has its name; connected with man is called 'not to be spoilt'; that being 'not to be spoilt' they call mystically 'connected with man (*mānuṣa*)', for the gods are lovers of mystery as it were.

iii. 34 (xiii. 10). It they surrounded with Agni; it the Maruts blew upon; Agni could not make it move; they surrounded it with Agni Vaiçvānara; the Maruts blew upon it; then Agni Vaiçvānara caused it to move. The first part of the seed that was kindled up became yonder Āditya; the second became Bhṛgu; him Varuṇa took; therefore is Bhṛgu descended from Varuṇa.[1] The third (part), that was brilliant (*adīdet*) as it were, became the Ādityas. The coals became the Aṅgirases; in that the coals after being quenched blazed forth again, Bṛhaspati came into being. The extinguished coals became black cattle; the reddened earth ruddy (cattle). The ash which there was crept about in diverse forms, the buffalo, the Gayal, the antelope, the camel, the ass, and these ruddy animals. To them this god said 'Mine is this, mine is what remains.'[2] Him they deprived of a claim by this verse which is recited as addressed to Rudra,[3]

> 'O father of the Maruts, let thy goodwill approach us;
> Do thou not sever us from the sight of the sun;
> Do thou, hero, be merciful to our steeds';

so should he say, not 'Towards us' (in the last line); this god is not likely to attack offspring then;

> 'May we be multiplied with children, O thou of Rudra,'

so he should say, not 'O Rudra', to avoid the use of the actual name. Or rather he should recite[4] 'Weal for us let him make'; with 'weal' he begins, for weal for all. 'For men, for women, for cows' (he says); men are males, women are females; (verily it serves) for weal for all. This verse, being without mention (of the name of the deity)[5] though addressed to Rudra, is appeased; with full life, for fullness of life, a full life he lives who knows thus. It is a Gāyatrī; the Gāyatrī is holy power; verily thus with the holy power he honours him.

iii. 35 (xiii. 11). He begins the Āgnimāruta with (a hymn[1]) to Vaiçvānara; Vaiçvānara caused to move the seed when poured; therefore with a

[1] The sense 'adopted' is supported by Sāyaṇa and the declaration of relation of father and son in TU. iii. 1. The preceding passage may be referred to in ÇB. i. 7. 4. 4; iv. 5. 1. 8; Eggeling, SBE. xxvi. 337, n. 4.

[2] So TS. iii. 1. 9. 5.

[3] RV. ii. 33. 1, with *tvām* for *abhi* in c and *rudriya* for *rudra* in d.

[4] RV. i. 43. 6.

[5] So Aufrecht for *so nirukta* of the MSS. which Weber (*Ind. Stud.* ix. 271) reads.

iii. 35. [1] RV. iii. 3. Cf. KB. xvi. 7.

hymn to Vaiçvānara he begins the Āgnimāruta. Without taking in breath the first verse is to be recited. He who recites the Āgnimāruta keeps quenching the fires which have not been appeased, the blazing flames; verily thus with the breaths he crosses the fires. In reciting he may err; he should seek another to point out; verily thus making him a bridge he crosses. Therefore at the Āgnimāruta he should not himself correct, a correcter (of errors) should be found. He recites (a hymn[2]) to the Maruts; the Maruts by blowing caused to move the seed when poured; therefore he recites (a hymn) to the Maruts. 'At each sacrifice to Agni' and 'The god wealth gives to you', the basis[3] (of the Stotra) and the antistrophe[4] he recites in the middle; in that in the middle he recites the basis (*yoni*) and the antistrophe, therefore is the womb placed in the middle. In that he recites after reciting two hymns, verily thus he places the organ of propagation above the two supports for generation. He is propagated with offspring and cattle who knows thus.

iii. 36 (xiii. 12). He recites (a hymn[1]) to Jātavedas; Prajāpati created offspring; they created went away and returned not. Them he surrounded with Agni; they came up to Agni; to him to-day even they come up. He said 'Offspring born by him I have found.' In that he said 'Offspring born by him I have found', that became (the hymn) to Jātavedas; that is why Jātavedas has his name. They, surrounded by Agni, and controlled, kept scorching and blazing; them he sprinkled with water. Therefore after (the hymn) to Jātavedas he recites the Āpohiṣṭhīya;[2] therefore should it be recited by one who is appeasing. Having sprinkled them with water he thought that he had destroyed them; in them by means of the dragon of the deep[3] he mysteriously placed brilliance. Agni Gārhapatya is the dragon of the deep; verily thus by Agni Gārhapatya mysteriously he places brilliance in them. Therefore they say 'He who offers is more brilliant than he who does not offer.'

iii. 37 (xiii. 13). He celebrates the wives of the gods[1] after Agni, the lord of the house; therefore the wife sits behind the Gārhapatya. They say 'Let him celebrate Rākā first; a sister has the first drink.' That is not to

[2] AV. i. 87.

[3] RV. i. 168. 1 and 2; the translation is doubtful.

[4] RV. vii. 16. 11 and 12. These are the connecting links with the Sāman, the *yoni* being the Stotriyapragātha corresponding to the Yajñāyajñīya Sāman, SV. ii. 53 and 54.

[1] RV. i. 143.

[2] RV. x. 9.

[3] RV. vi. 50. 14 is the verse referred to. *nijāsyaiva* cannot be taken as *svakīyāḥ* as by Sāyaṇa; the sense must be something like 'destroy' or 'injure' and the *Dhātupāṭha* root (xxvi. 102) *jas* in its causative form is clearly meant. Cf. Weber, *Ind. Stud.* ix. 272.

iii. 37. [1] RV. v. 46. 7 and 8. Probably *pañs* may here simply have its normal sense of 'praise', or the terms may be used as brief descriptions of the verses recited.

be regarded; the wives of the gods he should celebrate first. Agni Gārhapatya places seed in the wives; verily thus in these wives with Agni Gārhapatya openly he places seed, for propagation. He is propagated with offspring and cattle, who knows thus. Therefore a sister, though of the same womb, lives as inferior to a wife, though of a different womb. He celebrates Rākā;[2] Rākā is it that sews this suture in man which is in the organ. Male sons are born for him who knows thus. He celebrates Pāvīravī;[3] Pāvīravī is speech, Sarasvatī; verily thus he places speech in speech. They say 'Should he recite (the verse) to Yama first? Or that for the fathers?' That to Yama should he recite first. 'This strew, O Yama, do thou sit upon'; the first drink is the king's; therefore should he recite (the verse[4]) to Yama first. 'Mātalī with the sages, Yama with the Añgirases', he recites[5] after (it) for the sages. The sages are inferior to the gods, but above the fathers; therefore he recites it after (the verse to Yama). 'Let them arise, the lower, the higher', (these verses[6]) to the fathers he recites. 'The midmost fathers, loving the Soma' (he says); the lowest, the highest and the midmost, all these without omission he delights. 'I have found the kindly fathers' he recites as the second (verse). 'Who sitting on the strew (the drink) pressed with the call' (he says); 'sitting on the strew' is a reference to their dear abode (the strew); verily thus with their dear home he makes them prosper. With a dear home he prospers who knows thus. 'May there be this homage to the fathers to-day' he recites, containing the making of homage, at the end; therefore at the end is homage paid to the fathers. They say 'Should he recite (the verses) to the fathers separating (them) with the call? Or without separating (them) with the call.' He should recite separating (them) with the call; the good of the sacrifice to the fathers is incomplete[7]; he who recites separating (them) with the call completes the incomplete sacrifice to the fathers; therefore it is to be recited separating (them) with the call.

iii. 38 (xiii. 14). 'Sweet indeed is he, full of honey is he', he recites (verses[1] to) Indra for the drinking after of Indra; by these Indra drank after (the other gods) the third pressing; that is why (the verses) for the drinking after have their name. The deities become drunk as it were in that the Hotṛ recites these verses; therefore in their case the response (of the

[2] RV. ii. 32. 4.

[3] RV. vi. 49. 7.

[4] RV. x. 15. 4.

[5] RV. x. 14. 3.

[6] RV. x. 15. 1–3, but 2 is recited before 3.

[7] This is curious: Sāyaṇa and Haug take *sādhu* as 'is to be made complete'. Weber (*Ind. Stud.* ix. 278) renders 'The incomplete is suitable for the sacrifice to the fathers; he who recites without the call ('*vyāhāvam*).' But this is doubtful, and the rendering above given is preferable in any case as giving more accurately the sense of *vyā—hve*.

[1] RV. vi. 47. 1–4. *Cf.* KB. xvi. 8.

Adhvaryu) should contain[2] (the word) 'be drunk'. 'By whose might the regions are established', this verse[3] to Mitra and Varuṇa he recites; Viṣṇu guards what is ill offered in the sacrifice, Varuṇa what is well offered; verily (it serves) to appease them both. 'I will proclaim the mighty deeds of Viṣṇu', (this verse[4]) to Viṣṇu he recites. As is a roller, so is Viṣṇu to the sacrifice. Just as one may keep making well ploughed and well rolled what has been ill ploughed and ill rolled, so, in that the Hotṛ recites this verse, he keeps making well sung and well recited what has been ill sung and ill recited in the sacrifice. 'Weaving the web from the darkness follow to the light', (this verse[5]) to Prajāpati he recites; the web is offspring; verily thus he weaves the web of offspring for him. 'Guard the paths, full of light, wrought by prayer' (he says); the paths full of light are those that go to the gods; verily thus he extends them for him. With 'Weave without a flaw the works of the singers; be Manu, bring to birth the divine folk' verily he extends him with the offspring of Manu, for generation. He is propagated with offspring and cattle who knows thus. 'Do thou to us, the generous one, Indra, the resplendent', with this last (verse[6]) he concludes; the generous one, Indra, the resplendent, is this (earth); 'May he make true (blessings), supporter of the folk, the unequalled' (he says); the true, supporter of the folk, the unequalled is this (earth); 'Do thou, king of beings, confer upon us' (he says); the king of beings is this (earth). 'The great fame that is a singer's' (he says); great is this (earth); fame is the sacrifice; the singer is the sacrificer; verily thus he invokes this benediction for the sacrificer. Touching the earth should he say the conclusion; verily thus in the very same place in which he gathers together the sacrifice, in that he establishes it at the end. Having recited the Āgnimāruta litany he recites (a verse[7]) to Agni and the Maruts as offering verse 'O Agni with the Maruts brilliant and resounding'; thus according to their portions he delights the gods.

ADHYĀYA IV

The Characteristics of the Agniṣṭoma.

iii. 39 (xiv. 1). The[1] gods undertook battle with the Asuras, for conquest; them Agni was not willing to accompany. To him the gods said

[2] I.e. *madāmo daivom* in place of *çaṅsāmo daivom*; see ĀÇS. v. 20.

[3] Not in the *Saṁhitā*, but also in AV. vii. 25. 1.

[4] RV. i. 154. 1.

[5] RV. x. 53. 6.

[6] RV. iv. 17. 20. The AB. takes *satyā* as fem, which is quite impossible.

[7] RV. v. 60. 8.

[1] AB. iii. 39–44 contains miscellaneous remarks on the Agniṣṭoma and its relation to other rites. The passage seems a later addition; cf. Weber, *Ind. Stud.* ix. 275.

'Do thou come too; thou art one of us.' He replied 'I shall not follow you if I am not sung to; sing now to me.' They, having risen, and having returned, praised him; them praised he followed. Becoming in three rows, he went to battle for conquest with the Asuras in three columns; 'in three rows' (he says); verily he made the metres rows; 'in three columns' (he says); the pressings (he made) the columns. Them he defeated invincibly; then indeed the gods prospered, the Asuras were defeated. He prospers himself, the evil rival who hates him is defeated, who knows thus. The Agniṣṭoma is the Gāyatrī; the Gāyatrī has twenty-four syllables; there are twenty-four Stotras and Çastras in the Agniṣṭoma. This is why they say 'A horse well loaded gives (its rider) comfort.[3] This is the Gāyatrī; the Gāyatrī is not content with the earth; taking with it the sacrificer it goes aloft to the sky.' This is the Agniṣṭoma; the Agniṣṭoma is not content with the earth; taking with it the sacrificer it goes aloft to the sky. The Agniṣṭoma is the year; the year has twenty-four half-months; there are twenty-four Stotras and Çastras in the Agniṣṭoma. As in the ocean all streams, so in it all the sacrificial rites are resolved.

iii. 40 (xiv. 2). The consecration offering[1] is performed; all those offerings after it verily are resolved in the Agniṣṭoma. He invokes the sacrificial food; the sacrifices of cooked (food) have the form of the sacrificial food; all the sacrifices of cooked (food) are resolved in the Agniṣṭoma. At evening and morning they offer the Agnihotra; evening and morning they gave the fast (milk); with the call of Hail! they offer the Agnihotra; with the call of Hail! they gave the fast (milk). Through the call of Hail! the Agnihotra is resolved in the Agniṣṭoma. Fifteen kindling verses he recites at the introductory (offering), fifteen in the new and full moon sacrifices; through the introductory (offering) the new and full moon sacrifices are resolved in the Agniṣṭoma. They buy Soma, the king; Soma, the king, is connected with plants; with plants they heal whom they heal; therefore through the purchase of Soma, the king, whatever medicines there are, all these are resolved in the Agniṣṭoma. They kindle Agni by friction at the guest reception, Agni at the four-monthly sacrifices; through the guest reception the four-monthly sacrifices are resolved in the Agniṣṭoma. With milk they proceed at the Pravargya, with milk at the Dākṣāyaṇa sacrifice[2]; verily through the Pravargya the Dākṣāyaṇa sacrifice is resolved in the Agniṣṭoma. There is a victim on the fast day; verily

[3] So also TS. v. 5. 10. 7, and below, AB. iii. 47; cf. Keith, *Taittirīya Saṁhitā*, I. xcviii. The omission of any express object is natural enough in a proverb.

[1] For the Pākayajñas see ĀÇS. i. 1. 1, and for their connexion with the sacrificial food, TS. i. 7. 1. 1. Cf. Weber, *Ind. Stud.* ix. 227, 228.

[2] For this see ĀÇS. ii. 14. 7; KB. iv. 4; TS. ii. 5. 5. 4.

through it all animal sacrifices are resolved in the Agniṣṭoma. There is a sacrificial rite called the Iḍādadha;[3] it they perform with curds; with curds they perform the pot of curds; verily through the pot of curds the Iḍādadha is resolved in the Agniṣṭoma.

iii. 41 (xiv. 3). So now as to previous (rites) and next as to subsequent (rites). There are fifteen Stotras in the Ukthya, fifteen Çastras; that makes up a month; by months is the year arranged; Agni Vaiçvānara is the year; the Agniṣṭoma is Agni; verily through the year the Ukthya is resolved into the Agniṣṭoma. Through the resolution of the Ukthya the Vājapeya is resolved, for it is an Ukthya. There are twelve night rounds,[1] all in the Pañcadaça Stoma; taking these by two they make up thirty. The Ṣoḍaçin Sāman is the Ekaviṅça, the Sandhi (Sāman) is the Trivṛt; these are thirty, the month; the nights of the month are thirty; the year is arranged by months; Agni Vaiçvānara is the year; the Agniṣṭoma is Agni; verily through the year the Atirātra is resolved in the Agniṣṭoma; through the resolution of the Atirātra the Aptoryāma is resolved, for it is Atirātra. Thus all the sacrificial rites previous to and subsequent to (the Agniṣṭoma) are resolved into the Agniṣṭoma. Of it, taking the Stotras together, in all there are a hundred and ninety[2] Stotriya verses. The ninety corresponds to ten Trivṛt (Stomas); then the (next) ninety to ten more; of the ten (that remain) one Stotriya verse is in excess, a Trivṛt is left over; it yonder gives heat as the twenty-first placed over (the rest). It is the midmost[3] of the Stomas; before it are ten Trivṛts, after it ten; in the middle this twenty-first gives heat placed over on both sides. The Stotriya verse over is incorporated in this; it is the sacrificer; it is the divine lordly power, might and strength; he attains the divine lordly power, might and strength, he attains union and identity of form and world with it, who knows thus.

iii. 42 (xiv. 4). The gods having defeated the Asuras went aloft to the world of heaven. Agni arose aloft touching the sky: he opened the door of

[3] For this see ĀÇS. ii. 14. 11; KB. v. 5. For the pot of milk offering of the Agniṣṭoma see ĀÇS. v. 18; ÇÇS. vii. 18; Caland and Henry, *L'Agniṣṭoma*, p. 283.

[1] The Atirātra after the Ṣoḍaçin Graha adds four rounds, headed by the goblets of the Hotṛ, Maitrāvaruṇa, Brāhmaṇācchaṅsin, and Achāvāka respectively These are, of course, accompanied by recitations and Stotras and the later are Pañcadaça in Stomas, each of which doubled = 30 verses. The Ekaviṅça and Trivṛt Sāmans similarly have 21 + 9 verses.

[2] Thus made up: the morning pressing has a Trivṛt and four Pañcadaças = 69; the midday pressing has a Pañcadaça and four Saptadaças = 83; the evening pressing has a Saptadaça and Ekaviṅça = 38; viz. 190 = 10 × 9 + 10 × 9 + 10 (= 9 + 1).

[3] As Ekaviṅça Stoma. For the sun as *ekaviṅça* see AB. i. 30. The forms of these Stomas are given in PB. ii. 1. 1 (Trivṛt); 4. 1 (Pañcadaça); 7. 1 (Saptadaça); 14. 1 (Ekaviṅça).

the world of heaven; Agni is the overlord of the world of heaven. To him first came the Vasus; they said to him 'Let us through[1]; make room for us.' He replied 'Unless I am praised, I shall not let you through; praise me now.' 'Be it so' (they said); they praised him with the Trivṛt Stoma; being praised he let them through; they went to their due place. To him came the Rudras; they said to him 'Let us through; make room for us.' He replied 'Unless I am praised, I shall not let you through; praise me now.' 'Be it so' (they said); they praised him with the Pañcadaça Stoma; being praised, he let them through; they went to their due place. To him came the Ādityas; they said to him 'Let us through; make room for us.' He replied 'Unless I am praised, I shall not let you through; praise me now.' 'Be it so' (they said); they praised him with the Saptadaça Stoma; being praised, he let them through; they went to their due place. To him came the All-gods; they said to him 'Let us through; make room for us.' He replied 'Unless I am praised, I shall not let you through; praise me now.' 'Be it so' (they said); they praised him with the Ekaviñça Stoma; being praised, he let them through; they went to their due place. With each Stoma the gods praised him; them praised he let through; they went to their due places. So he who sacrifices praises him with all these Stomas, and he who knows thus him will he let pass; him he lets pass to the world of heaven who knows thus.

iii. 43 (xiv. 5). The Agniṣṭoma is Agni; in that they praised him, therefore is it the praise of Agni (*agnistoma*); it, being the praise of Agni, they call Agniṣṭoma mystically, for the gods love mystery as it were. In that four sets of gods praised him with four Stomas, therefore is it of four Stomas (*catu-stoma*); it being of four Stomas they call it Catuṣṭoma mystically, for the gods love mystery as it were. Again in that they praised him when aloft and having become light (*jyotis*), therefore is it the Jyotiṣṭoma; it being the Stoma of light, they call it the Jyotiṣṭoma mystically, for the gods love mystery as it were. This is the sacrificial rite without beginning or end; the Agniṣṭoma is like a chariot wheel endless; as is its beginning so is its end; as to this a sacrificial verse is sung:

'That which is its beginning is also its end,
That again which is its end is also its beginning,
Like the creeping of a snake is the movement of the Çakala[1] (ritual),
They discern not which of the two is the subsequent';

[1] Aufrecht (p. 480) conjectures *arjāsi* or *arjasva*, the latter of which Böhtlingk (BKSGW. 15 Dec. 1900, p. 416) approves.

iii. 43. [1] A kind of snake (Sāyaṇa) is absurd. The reference to the Çakala is seen by Weber (*Ind. Stud.* ix. 277), and though not apparently accepted by Aufrecht or others appear to me correct.

for (they say) 'As the beginning, so should be the end.' As to this they say 'Seeing that the beginning has the Trivṛt, the end the Ekaviñça, how are the two alike?' 'For the reason', he should reply, 'that the Ekaviñça is threefold and moreover that both consist of repeated triplets.

iii. 44. (xiv. 6). The[1] Agniṣṭoma is he who gives heat here; it is one to be finished in the day; with the day should they complete it; its name is what is finished with the day. They should proceed with it without haste; as at the morning pressing, so at the midday, so at the third pressing. So the sacrificer is not likely to perish. In that they proceed without hastening at the two former pressings, therefore here the villages of the east are densely populated; in that they proceed hastening at the third pressing, therefore here to the west there are long forests. Thus the sacrificer is likely to perish. Therefore without hastening they should proceed; as at the morning pressing, so at the midday, so at the third pressing. So the sacrificer is not likely to perish. He should follow in recitation the movement of this (sun); when he rises in the morning, then he gives a gentle heat; therefore he should recite in a gentle tone at the morning pressing. Then when he comes forward, he gives stronger heat; therefore at the midday should he recite with a stronger tone. Then when he comes still further forward, he gives his strongest heat; therefore he should recite at the third pressing with the strongest tone. So should he recite if he be lord of speech, for the Çastra is speech. He should begin in the tone in which he can complete, increasing in height; that is the best way of reciting. The (sun) never really sets or rises. In that they think of him 'He is setting', verily having reached the end of the day, he inverts himself; thus he makes evening below, day above. Again in that they think of him 'He is rising in the morning', verily having reached the end of night he inverts himself; thus he makes day below, night above. He never sets; indeed he never sets, union with him and identity of form and world he attains who knows thus.[2]

ADHYĀYA V

Miscellaneous Points regarding the Sacrifice.

iii. 45 (xv. 1). The sacrifice as food departed from the gods; the gods said 'The sacrifice as food hath left us; this sacrifice, food, let us search for.' They said 'How shall we search?' 'By the Brahman and the metres, they said.' They consecrated the Brahman with the metres; for him they performed the sacrifice up to the end; they also performed the joint offerings to the

[1] Copied in GB. ix. 10. For the forests of the west cf. ÇB. ix. 3. 1. 18.

[2] For this theory of the sun's motion see Speyer, JRAS. 1906, p. 723; *Vedic Index*, ii. 466; MS. iv. 6. 3; KS. xxvii. 8; TS. vi. 4. 10. 2, 3; ÇB. iv. 3. 1. 18; Caland, VOJ. xxvi. 119.

wives (of the gods). Therefore now also in the consecration offering they perform the sacrifice right up to the end, they also perform the joint offerings to the wives. According to this rule did they proceed. They performed the introductory (offering); to him with the introductory (offering) they came nearer; they hastened with the performance. They made it end in the Çaṁyu. Therefore now also the introductory (offering) ends in the Çaṁyu. According to this rule did they proceed. They performed the guest reception; to him with the guest reception they came nearer; they hastened with the performance. They made it end in the sacrificial food. Therefore now also the guest reception ends in the sacrificial food. According to this rule did they proceed. They performed the Upasads; to him with the Upasads they came nearer; they hastened with the performance; having repeated three kindling verses, they offered to three deities. Therefore now also in the Upasads having repeated three kindling verses,[1] they offer to three deities. According to this rule did they proceed. They performed the fast day; him on the fast day they obtained; having obtained him they performed the sacrifice; they also performed the joint offerings to the wives. Therefore now also on the fast day they perform the sacrifice to the end; they also perform the joint offerings to the wives. Therefore in these previous rites he should recite more and more gently; for they followed him creeping after.[2] 'Therefore with whatever voice he desires, he should recite on the fast day, for he is then obtained' (they say). Having obtained him they said 'Serve us for food'; 'No,' he replied, 'how can I serve you?' Them he only looked at. To him they said 'With the Brahman and the metres becoming united do thou serve us as food.' 'Be it so' (he replied). Therefore now also the sacrifice becoming united with the Brahman and the metres bears the sacrifice to the gods.

Errors in the choice of Priests.

iii. 46 (xv. 2). Three things are performed at the sacrifice, eating, swallowing, and vomiting. What is eaten is when he makes as priest one that expects 'May he give to me, or may he choose me.' That is remote like something eaten; that does not profit the sacrificer. Again what is swallowed is when fearing he chooses a priest, 'Let him not either oppress me, nor let him make confusion in the sacrifice for me.' That is remote like something swallowed; that does not profit the sacrificer. Again what is vomited is when he chooses as priest one who is spoken ill of. Just as here men are disgusted by what is vomited, so therefore the gods. That is

[1] ÄÇS. iv. 8. 5.

[2] *anutsāram* conjectured by Aufrecht is clearly right.

remote like something vomited; that does not profit the sacrificer. He should not desire these three. If against his desire he should have one of these three, there is in the Stotra of the Vāmadevya[1] an expiation for it. The Vāmadevya (Sāman) is this, the world of the sacrificer, the world of ambrosia, the world of heaven. It is three syllables short; having crept up for the chanting of the (Sāman), he should divide the self into three, *pu*, *ru*, and *ṣa*. He places the self in these worlds, in this world of the sacrificer, in this world of ambrosia, in the world of heaven; he overcomes all errors in sacrifice. 'Even if the priests are perfect,' he used to say, 'he should mutter this.'

The Offerings to the Minor Deities.

iii. 47 (xv. 8). The[1] metres having carried the oblation to the gods being wearied stand at the back part of the sacrifice; just as if a horse or a mule stands having carried (its load). He should offer to them the oblations to the minor deities after the cake of the animal (offering) to Mitra and Varuṇa, To Dhātṛ (he should offer) a cake on twelve potsherds; Dhātṛ is the *vaṣaṭ* call. To Anumati (he should offer) a pap; Anumati is the Gāyatrī. To Rākā (he should offer) a pap; Rākā is the Triṣṭubh. To Sinīvālī (he should offer) a pap; Sinīvālī is the Jagatī. To Kuhū (he should offer) a pap; Kuhū is the Anuṣṭubh. These are all the metres; Gāyatrī, Triṣṭubh, Jagatī, Anuṣṭubh; on (them) the others (depend), for these are performed most prominently at the sacrifice. By means of these metres the sacrificer sacrifices with all the metres, who knows thus. This is why they say 'A horse, well loaded, gives (its rider) comfort[2]'; this is the metres; the metres place him in comfort. A world which misses nothing he wins who knows thus. Now some say 'To Dhātṛ in front of each of these (deities) should he offer with butter; thus in all of them he makes pairing.' As to this they say 'There is tediousness in the sacrifice when on the same day he uses the same verses as offering verses.' Even if there are many wives as it were, one husband is a pair with them. In that before them all he offers to Dhātṛ,[3] he makes pairing in all of them. So now for the minor deities.

[1] SV. ii. 82–84; RV. iv. 81. 1–3; the last verse has three Pādas of seven syllables, acc. to Sāyaṇa, but Oldenberg (*Prolegomena*, p. 378) more correctly takes the shortage to lie in the words *madānām*, *sakhīnām*, and *jaritṝṇām*, leaving *bhavāsi ūtibhiḥ* in the last verse uncontracted; hence the insertion of *puruṣa*. The practice is not given in ĀÇS., though the verses are often rubricated (v. 16. 1; vii. 4. 2; viii. 12. 18; 14. 18).

iii. 47. [1] For the rites on the conclusion of the sacrifice, viz. the barren cow to Mitra and Varuṇa and the oblations to the Devikās see ĀÇS. vi. 14; ÇÇS. viii. 12; Caland and Henry, *L'Agniṣṭoma*, pp. 407–409.

[2] Above AB. iii. 39. 5.

[3] For the Mantra see ĀÇS. vi. 14. 16.

iii. 48 (xv. 4). Now as regards the goddesses.[1] To Sūrya (he should offer) a cake on eleven potsherds; Sūrya is Dhātṛ, and he is also the *vaṣaṭ* call. To sky (he should offer) a pap; the sky is Anumati; she is also the Gāyatrī. To Uṣas (he should offer) a pap; Uṣas is Rākā; she is also the Triṣṭubh. To the cow (he should offer) a pap; the cow is Sinīvālī; she is also the Jagatī. To earth (he should offer) a pap. Earth is Kuhū; she is also the Anuṣṭubh. These are all the metres; Gāyatrī, Triṣṭubh, Jagatī, Anuṣṭubh; on (them) the others (depend), for these are performed most prominently at the sacrifice. By means of these metres the sacrificer sacrifices with all the metres, who knows thus. This is why they say 'A horse, well loaded, gives (its rider) comfort'; this is the metres; the metres place him in comfort. A world which misses nothing he wins who knows thus. Now some say 'To Sūrya before each of these he should offer with butter; thus in all of them he makes pairing'. As to this they say 'There is tediousness in the sacrifice when on the same day he used the same verses as offering verses.' Even if there are many wives as it were, one husband is a pair with them. In that before all of them he offers to Sūrya, he makes pairing in all of them. Those here are those yonder; those yonder are those here; by either set he obtains the desire which is in both. Both sets he should offer for one desiring propagation who has attained prosperity, but not for one who is seeking it. If he were to offer them together for one who is seeking only, the gods would be liable[2] to be ill pleased in his gains since 'he has thought he has enough'. Çucivṛkṣa Gaupalāyana offered both together at the sacrifice of Vṛddhadyumna[3] Ābhipratāriṇa. He (Çucivṛkṣa Gaupalāyana) having seen his skilled charioteer plunging (in the water) said 'Here for this king I have delighted together at the sacrifice both the minor deities and the goddesses in that his skilled charioteer plunges.' Sixty-four armed warriors assuredly were his sons and grandsons.

The Ukthya

iii. 49 (xv. 5). In[1] the Agniṣṭoma the gods took refuge, in the Ukthas the Asuras; they were of equal strength; they could not be discriminated. These Bharadvāja among the seers saw 'These Asuras are resting in the Ukthas; them no one of these (gods) sees.' He called to Agni[2] 'Come, I shall proclaim to thee, O Agni, other words.' Other words are those of the Asuras. Agni, rising up, said 'What does this lean, tall, grey-haired

[1] See ĀÇS. vi. 14. 17; ÇÇS. ix. 28. 4 *seq.*

[2] The construction is not rare, e.g. ÇB. i. 1. 2. 22; v. 1. 1. 9; xiii. 8. 4. 11.

[3] For him cf. ÇÇS. xv. 16. 10; Weber, *Rājasūya*, p. 27, n. 2. The reference is perhaps to the final bath of the Açvamedha.

iii. 49. [1] For the Ukthya and the three additional Uktha Stotras and Çastras see KB. xvi. 11; ĀÇS. vi. 1; ÇÇS. ix. 1–4; MÇS. ii. 5. 8; ĀpÇS. xiv. 1–4. Cf. also PB. viii. 8.

[2] RV. vi. 6 16.

one desire to say to me?' Bharadvāja was lean, tall, and grey haired. He replied 'These Asuras are resting in the Ukthas; them no one of you sees.' Agni, becoming a horse, rushed to and beyond them; in that Agni, having become a horse, rushed to and beyond them, that was the origin of the Sākamaçva Sāman;[3] that is why the Sākamaçva has its name. They say 'He should begin the Ukthas with the Sākamaçva; the Ukthas have no proper beginning other than the Sākamaçva.' 'With the Pramaṅhiṣṭhīya[4] he should begin,' they say. By means of the Pramaṅhiṣṭhīya the gods repelled the Asuras from the Ukthas. Thus he may begin with the Pramaṅhiṣṭhīya, or with the Sākamaçva.

iii. 50 (xv. 6). The Asuras took refuge in the litany of the Maitrāvaruṇa; Indra said 'Who with me will repel hence these Asuras?' 'I too' replied Varuṇa. Therefore the Maitrāvaruṇa recites (a litany) to Indra and Varuṇa[1] at the third pressing, for Indra and Varuṇa drove them thence. Being driven thence, the Asuras took refuge in the litany of the Brāhmaṇācchaṅsin; Indra said 'Who with me will repel these Asuras hence?' 'I too' replied Bṛhaspati. Therefore the Brāhmaṇācchaṅsin recites to Indra and Bṛhaspati[2] at the third pressing, for Indra and Bṛhaspati drove them thence. Being driven thence, the Asuras took refuge in the litany of the Achāvāka; Indra said 'Who with me will repel them hence?' 'I too' replied Viṣṇu. Therefore the Achāvāka recites to Indra and Viṣṇu[3] at the third pressing, for Indra and Viṣṇu drove them thence. Jointly with Indra the deities are celebrated; a couple is a pairing; therefore from a couple a pairing is produced, for propagation; he is propagated with offspring and cattle who knows thus. There are four offerings to the seasons of the Potṛ and the Neṣṭṛ, and six verses;[4] they make up the tenfold Virāj; thus in the tenfold Virāj they establish the sacrifice.[5]

[3] SV. ii. 55–57; the other two are Saubhara (ii. 58, 59) and Nārmedhasa (ii. 60–62); ĀÇS. vi. 1. 2; ÇÇS. ix. 2. 1, 2; 3. 1, 2; 4. 1, 2.

[4] SV. ii. 228, 229. Uktha here probably means Uktha Stotra as taken by Sāyaṇa, or perhaps rather includes both Stotra and Çastra (see AB. iii. 50), since the latter adopts the former as usual. The option here is not in the Sūtras.

[1] RV. vii. 82. Cf. KB. xvi. 11. It follows RV. iii. 51. 1–3; viii. 42. 1–3; ĀÇS. vi. 1. 2; ÇÇS. ix. 2. 3, 4.

[2] RV. x. 68 and x. 43, following RV. i. 57; ĀÇS. vi. 1. 2; ÇÇS. ix. 3. 3, 4 differs.

[3] RV. vi. 69. It follows ii. 13; vii. 100; i. 156; ĀÇS. vi. 1. 2; ÇÇS. ix. 4. 3–5 differs.

[4] I. e. the 2nd and 3th and 3rd and 9th of the Ṛtuyājas (AB. ii. 29) and the six offering verses of the two priests at the *prasthita* offerings.

[5] The Çastras of the Hotrakas at the evening pressing of the Ukthya are thus:—
(1) Maitrāvaruṇa: RV. vi. 16. 16–18, 19–21; iii. 51. 1–3; viii. 42. 1–3; vii. 82, 84; vi. 68. 11.
(2) Brāhmaṇācchaṅsin: RV. viii. 21. 1, 2, 9, 10; i. 57; x. 68, 43; vii. 97. 10.
(3) Achāvāka: RV. viii. 98. 7; viii. 13. 4; ii. 13; vii. 100; i. 156; vi. 69; vi. 69. 3.
So ĀÇS. vi. 1. 2. ÇÇS. differs in detail (ix. 2–4).

PAÑCIKĀ IV

THE SOMA SACRIFICE (*continued*)

ADHYĀYA I

The Ṣoḍaçin.

iv. 1 (xvi. 1). The[1] gods by the first day collected the thunderbolt for Indra; by the second day they dipped it; by the third day they presented it; it he hurled on the fourth day. Therefore on the fourth day he recites the Ṣoḍaçin. The Ṣoḍaçin is a thunderbolt; in that on the fourth day he recites the Ṣoḍaçin, verily thus he hurls at the rival who hates him the thunderbolt as a weapon to lay him low who is to be laid low by him. The Ṣoḍaçin is a thunderbolt, the litanies cattle; putting it round after the litanies he recites. In that putting it round after the litanies he recites, verily thus with the Ṣoḍaçin as a thunderbolt he surrounds cattle. Therefore cattle, being surrounded by the Ṣoḍaçin as a thunderbolt, come up to man. Therefore a horse or a man or a cow or an elephant being surrounded, led by itself, comes up when bidden by the voice; by merely seeing the Ṣoḍaçin as a thunderbolt, he is surrounded by the Ṣoḍaçin as a thunderbolt, for the thunderbolt is speech, the Ṣoḍaçin speech. They say 'Why has the Ṣoḍaçin this name?' Of the Stotras it is the sixteenth; the sixteenth of the Çastras; with sixteen syllables he commences; with the (next) sixteen he says *om*; he inserts a Nivid of sixteen sentences; that is why the Ṣoḍaçin has its name. Two syllables are left over[2] when the Ṣoḍaçin is made into an Anuṣṭubh; these are the two breasts of speech; these are truth and falsehood; truth aids him, falsehood harms him not, who knows thus.

iv. 2 (xvi. 2). He who desires brilliance and splendour should use as the Ṣoḍaçin Sāman the Gaurivīta;[1] the Gaurivīta is brilliance and splendour; brilliant and resplendent he becomes who knowing thus uses the Gaurivīta as Ṣoḍaçin Sāman. 'The Nānada[2] should be used as the Ṣoḍaçin Sāman'

[1] AB. iv. 1–4 and KB. xvii. 1–4 deal with the Ṣoḍaçin rite; see ĀÇS. vi. 2 and 3; ÇÇS. ix. 2 *seq.*; ĀpÇS. xiv. 2; KÇS. xii. 5. 20 *seq.* The Ṣoḍaçin is treated here as performed on the fourth day of a Ṣaḍaha; cf. TS. vi. 6. 11. 1 where a distinct and independent rite of that name is denied. For § 5 cf. GB. ix. 19.

[2] See SV. ii. 302.

iv. 2. [1] SV. ii. 302–304; ĀÇS. vi. 3. 1. This is the *vihṛta* form of the Ṣoḍaçin.

[2] SV. i. 352–354 according to Sāyaṇa. Cf. KB. xxiii. 2; Nārāyaṇa on ĀÇS. vi. 3. 2.

they say; Indra lifted up his thunderbolt against Vṛtra; he hurled it at him; he smote him. He, being smitten, cried aloud; in that he cried aloud, the Nānada Sāman came into existence; that is why the Nānada has its name. That is a Sāman without rivals, one that destroys rivals, the Nānada; without rivals, a destroyer of rivals, he becomes who, knowing thus, uses the Nānada as the Ṣoḍaçin Sāman. If they use the Nānada, the Ṣoḍaçin must be recited without intermingling;[3] for they chant to the (verses) without intermingling. If it is the Gaurivīta, the Ṣoḍaçin must be recited with intermingling, for they chant to them with intermingling.

iv. 3 (xvi. 3). Then he intertwines the metres. In 'Let the bay steed carry thee hither' and 'Do thou hearken to our words' he intertwines Gāyatrī[1] and Pañkti[2] verses; man is connected with the Gāyatrī; cattle are connected with the Pañkti; verily thus he intertwines man with cattle, in cattle he makes him find support. The Gāyatrī and the Pañkti are two Anuṣṭubhs; thereby he does not depart from the symbol of speech, the symbol of the Anuṣṭubh, and the symbol of the thunderbolt. In 'What time, O Indra, in the conflict' and 'Let this delightful one be to you' he intertwines Uṣṇih[3] and Bṛhatī[4] verses; man is connected with the Uṣṇih, cattle with the Bṛhatī; verily thus he intertwines man with cattle, in cattle he makes him find support. The Uṣṇih and the Bṛhatī are two Anuṣṭubhs; thereby he does not depart from the symbol of speech, the symbol of the Anuṣṭubh, and the symbol of the thunderbolt. In 'On the yokes for him' and 'O Brahman, O hero, rejoicing in the making of holy power' he intertwines (a verse[5]) of two Padas and a Triṣṭubh;[6] man has two feet, the Triṣṭubh is strength; verily thus he intertwines man with cattle; in strength he makes him find support; therefore man, being established in strength, is the strongest of all cattle. In that (the verse) of two Padas has twenty syllables and there is a Triṣṭubh, there are two Anuṣṭubhs; thereby he does not depart from the symbol of speech, the symbol of the Anuṣṭubh, and the symbol of the thunderbolt. In 'This Brahman' and 'I shall declare to thee the bay steeds in the great assembly' he intertwines (verses) of two Padas[7] and Jagatīs;[8] man has two feet; cattle are connected with the

[3] The *viharaṇa* is described in ĀÇS. vi. 3; it consists of mixing up the verses by reciting their Pādas interlaced, that is, of 3 Gāyatrī Pādas and 5 Pañkti Pādas (RV. i. 16. 2 and 82. 3) is made up a verse form of Gāyatrī + Pañkti thrice and then two Pañkti Pāda verses. According to ĀÇS. vi. 2. 2 the *avihṛta* form has RV. i. 84. 1–6 (SV. i. 347 *seq.*) as its strophe and antistrophe, and this may really be meant as the Nānada.

[1] RV. i. 16. 1–3; ĀÇS. vi. 2. 3.

[2] RV. i. 82. 1 (and vv. 3 and 4); ĀÇS. vi. 2. 4.

[3] RV. viii. 12. 25–27; ĀÇS. vi. 2. 5.

[4] RV. iii. 44. 1–3; ĀÇS. vi. 2. 5.

[5] RV. vii. 34. 4; ĀÇS. vi. 2. 5.

[6] RV. vii. 29. 2; ĀÇS. vi. 2. 6.

[7] Only in ĀÇS. vi. 2. 6; SV. i. 433, etc.

[8] RV. x. 96. 1–3.

Jagatī; verily thus he intertwines man with cattle; in cattle he makes him find support. Therefore man, being established in cattle, both eats them and masters them; and these are in his power. In that (the verse) of two Padas has sixteen syllables, and there is a Jagatī, there are two Anuṣṭubhs; thereby he does not depart from the symbol of speech, the symbol of the Anuṣṭubh, and the symbol of the thunderbolt. In 'In the bowls the buffalo the barley-mixed' and 'Forward for him, with his chariot forward' he recites Atichandas verses;[9] the sap of the metres that flowed over, that flowed over to the Atichandas verse; that is why the Atichandas has its name. The Ṣoḍaçin is fashioned out of all the metres. In that he recites Atichandas verses, verily thus he fashions it out of all the metres. With the Ṣoḍaçin fashioned out of all the metres he prospers who knows thus.

iv. 4 (xvi. 4). He adds the additions of the Mahānāmnīs.[1] The first Mahānāmnī is this world, the second the world of the atmosphere, the third yonder world. The Ṣoḍaçin is fashioned out of all the worlds; in that he adds the additions of the Mahānāmnīs, verily thus he fashions it from all the worlds. With the Ṣoḍaçin fashioned out of all the worlds he prospers who knows thus. In 'Forward for you the Triṣṭubh sap', 'Praise, praise forth', and 'He who hath made to bound the steeds' he recites as normal Anuṣṭubhs.[2] As one who has wandered here and there out of his path comes back to the path, so it is in that he recites normal Anuṣṭubhs. He who considers himself complete and at the height of prosperity should make him recite the Ṣoḍaçin without intermingling, (thinking) 'Let me not fall, through the misery of the metres.' But he, who is desirous of removing evil, should make him recite the Ṣoḍaçin with intermingling; man is, as it were, intertwined with evil; verily thus he smites away the evil stain which is intertwined for him; evil he smites away who knows thus. 'When up to the place of the bright one', with this last[3] he concludes; the place of the bright one is the world of heaven; verily thus he causes the sacrificer to go to the world of heaven. 'Thou hast drunk of the ancient draughts, O lord of the bays' he uses as offering verse[4]; the Ṣoḍaçin is fashioned out of all the pressings; in that he uses as offering verse 'Thou hast drunk of the ancient draughts, O lord of the bays', and the morning pressing contains (the word) 'drink', verily thus he fashions it out of the morning pressing. 'Now let this pressing be thine only' (he says); the midday pressing (is Indra's) only; verily thus he fashions it from the midday pressing. 'Be drink with the Soma, rich in honey, O Indra' (he says); the third pressing contains (the words) 'be drunk'; verily thus he fashions it out of the third pressing.

[9] RV. ii. 22. 1–3; x. 133. 1–3; ĀÇS. vi. 2. 6.

[1] I. e. the verses in AĀ. iv; ĀÇS. vi. 2. 6 *seq.*

[2] RV. viii. 69. 1–3; 8–10; 13–15; ĀÇS. vi. 2. 9.

[3] RV. viii. 69. 7; ĀÇS. vi. 2. 12.

[4] RV. x. 96. 13; ĀÇS. vi. 2. 12.

'Do thou ever, O courser, press into thy belly' (he says); that which contains (the word) 'courser' is a symbol of the Ṣoḍaçin; the Ṣoḍaçin is fashioned out of all the pressings; in that he uses as offering verse 'Thou hast drunk of the ancient draughts, O lord of the bays', verily thus he fashions it out of all the pressings. With the Ṣoḍaçin fashioned out of all the pressings he prospers who knows thus. He adds five-syllable additions[5] of the Mahānāmnīs to Pādas of eleven syllables; the Ṣoḍaçin is fashioned out of all the metres; in that he adds four-syllable additions of the Mahānāmnīs to Pādas of eleven syllables, verily thus he fashions it out of all the metres. With the Ṣoḍaçin fashioned out of all the metres he prospers who knows thus.

The Atirātra.

iv. 5 (xvi. 5). In[1] the day the gods took refuge, in the night the Asuras; they were of equal strength; they could not be discriminated. Indra said 'Who with me will attack (to drive) hence these Asuras through the night?' He found no one among the gods, they were afraid of night, the darkness, death. Therefore now also in the night if one has gone away any distance whatever, he is afraid, for the night is darkness as it were, death as it were. The metres alone followed him; in that the metres alone followed him, therefore Indra and the metres bear the night. No Nivid is recited, nor Puroruc nor inserted verse, nor is any other deity celebrated; for Indra and the metres alone bear the night. They repelled them by going round in rounds; in that they repelled by going round in rounds, that is why the rounds have their name. Them they repelled from the first part of the night by the first round, from the middle of the night by the second, from the last part of night by the last. 'Up from the night do we follow' they said. 'Bordering on night are these metres' he used to say; for these rescued Indra when afraid from night, the darkness, death; that is why the Apiçarvaras have their name.

iv. 6 (xvi. 6). 'Drink of the Soma juice' with this Anuṣṭubh[1] containing (the word) 'Soma juice' he begins the night; the night is connected with the Anuṣṭubh; this is the symbol of night. The offering verses contain (the words) 'Soma juice', 'drink' and 'be drunk', and are appropriate; what in the sacrifice is appropriate is perfect. They chant the first round; they repeat the first Padas; their horses and cows, thereby they take from them.

[5] I. e. *evā hy eva*; *evā hīndra* (as 5 *hi indra*); *evā hi çakro*; *vaçī hi çakraḥ*; ĀÇS. vi. 2. 12 and 8. 16.

[1] AB. iv. 5 and 6 and KB. xvii. 5–9 deal with the Atirātra form of the Jyotiṣṭoma; see ĀÇS. vi. 4. The characteristic of this rite is the addition of four Paryāyas of three Çastras each. GB. x. 1–8 follow AB. iv. 5 and 6. Cf. JB. i. 208; Oertel, *Trans. Conn. Acad.* xv. 170.

iv. 6.[1] RV. viii. 92. 18; ĀÇS. vi. 4. 10; ÇÇS. ix. 7. 1.

They chant the second round; they repeat the middle Padas; their carts[1] and chariots,[2] thereby they take from them. They chant the last round; they repeat the last Padas; their clothes, their gold, the jewels on their bodies, thereby they take from them. He takes the property of his foe, he repels him from all these worlds, who knows thus. 'The day has Pavamāna (Stotras)', they say, 'the night has no Pavamānas; how have both Pavamānas, and through what have they equal portions?' In that 'To Indra, the drunken, the pressed (drink)', 'This Soma juice hath been pressed, O bright one', and 'This hath been pressed with might' they chant[3] and recite, thereby the night has Pavamānas; thereby the two become possessed of the Pavamānas; thereby they become of equal portions. 'The day has fifteen Stotras', they say, 'the night has not fifteen Stotras; how have both fifteen Stotras and through what have both equal portions?' The Apiçarvaras are twelve Stotras; they sing the Sandhi (Sāman)[4] to the Rathantara with three deities; thereby the night has fifteen Stotras; thereby both have fifteen Stotras; thereby they become of equal portions. They chant a limited amount, they recite an unlimited amount, (thinking) 'What has been is limited, what is to be is unlimited, (it serves) to win what is unlimited.' He recites more than the Stotra; offspring is beyond the self, cattle are beyond. In that he recites beyond the Stotra, verily thereby he wins whatever in him there is beyond the self.

ADHYĀYA II

The Āçvina Çastra.

iv. 7 (xvii. 1). Prajāpati[1] gave his daughter to Soma, the King, even Sūryā Sāvitrī; for her all the gods came as groomsmen; for her wedding ceremony he made this thousand (of verses) which they call the Āçvina (Çastra). What is less than a thousand is not the Āçvina; therefore he should recite a thousand or more. Having eaten of ghee, he should recite. Just as in this world a cart or a chariot, when oiled, goes (well), so he when oiled goes. He should call (making a posture) as of an eagle about to fly up. The gods did not agree as to this, 'Let this be mine; let this be mine.' They said coming to agreement 'Let us run a race for it; his who

[2] *manorathāḥ* in Aufrecht is clearly a slip.

[3] RV. viii. 92. 19–21; 2. 1–3; iii. 51. 10–12; ĀÇS. vi. 4. 10; ÇÇS. ix. 10. 1; 14. 1; 15. 1.

[4] See SV. ii. 99–104; to Agni, Uṣas, and Açvins, two verses being turned into three.

[1] AB. iv. 7–11 and KB. xviii. 1–5 deal with Āçvina Çastra which follows up the Sandhi Stotra of the Atirātra and is characterized by litanies for Agni, Uṣas, and the Açvins. See ĀÇS. vi. 5 and 6; ÇÇS. ix. 20. For the race cf. PB. ix. 1. 35, 36; JB. i. 218; Lévi, *La doctrine du sacrifice*, p. 72; Oertel, *Trans. Conn. Acad.* xv. 174.

wins shall it be'. They made the course from Agni, the lord of the house, to the sun; therefore the beginning[2] (verse) is addressed to Agni in the Āçvina, 'Agni is the Hotṛ, the lord of the house, he the King.' As to this some say '"Agni, O dear father, Agni friend" with this[3] should he begin; "In the sky the pure, the sacrificial, of the sun" with this as first verse he reaches the goal.' This is not to be regarded. If one were now to say of him 'He has had recourse to "Agni" and "Agni", he will fall into the fire', it would certainly be so. Therefore should he begin with 'Agni is the Hotṛ, the lord of the house, he the King.' It contains (the words) 'lord of the house' and 'generation', and is propitious; with full life for fullness of life, a full life he lives who knows thus.

iv. 8 (xvii. 2.) As these deities were running the race, and had started, Agni took the lead first; the Açvins followed him; to him they said 'Give way; we two will win this.' 'Be it so', he replied, 'Let me have a share here.' 'Be it so' (they said). For him they made a share herein; therefore at the Āçvina (Çastra) (a litany) to Agni is recited. They followed after Uṣas; to her they said 'Give way; we two will win this.' 'Be it so', she replied, 'Let me have a share here.' 'Be it so' (they said). For her they made a share herein; therefore at the Āçvina (a litany) to Uṣas is recited. They followed after Indra; to him they said 'We will win this, O generous one'; they did not dare to say to him 'Give way'. 'Be it so', he replied, 'Let me have a share herein.' 'Be it so' (they said). For him they made a share herein; therefore at the Āçvina (a litany) to Indra is recited.[1] The Açvins won the race; the Açvins attained it. In that the Açvins won the race the Açvins attained it, therefore they call it the Āçvina. He attains whatever he desires who knows thus. They say 'In that there are here recitations to Agni, to Uṣas, to Indra, then why do they call it the Āçvina?' (It is) because the Açvins won the race, the Açvins attained it. In that the Açvins won the race, the Açvins attained it, therefore they call it the Āçvina. He attains whatever he desires, who knows thus.

iv. 9 (xvii. 3). By means of a mule chariot Agni ran the race; as he drove on he burned their wombs; therefore they conceive not. With ruddy cows Uṣas ran the race; therefore, when dawn has come, there is a ruddy glow; the form of Uṣas. With a horse chariot Indra ran the race; therefore it as neighing aloud and resounding is the symbol of lordly power; for it is connected with Indra. With an ass chariot the Açvins won, the Açvins attained; in that the Açvins won, the Açvins attained, therefore is his speed outworn, his energy spent; he is here the least swift of all beasts of burden; but they did not take the strength of his seed; therefore has he virility and

[2] RV. vi. 15. 13; AÇS. vi. 5. 6; ÇÇS. ix. 20. 7.

[3] RV. x. 13. 3.

[1] See ĀÇS. vi. 5. 18 for his share; it follows the verses to Sūrya. So ÇÇS. ix. 20. 24.

possesses a double seed. 'Seven metres should he use in reciting to Sūrya', they say, 'as in (the recitations) to Agni, Uṣas, and the Açvins; the worlds of the gods are seven; he prospers in all the worlds of the gods.' That is not to be regarded. Three only should he use in recitation; three are these threefold worlds; (they serve) to win these worlds. They say 'He[1] should begin those for Sūrya with "Up this all-knower".' That is not to be regarded. That would be as if one having gone should miss the goal. He should begin[2] with 'Let Sūrya protect us from the sky'; that is as if one having gone should reach the goal. He recites second 'Up this all-knower'. 'The radiant countenance of the gods hath come forth' is a Triṣṭubh[3]. Yonder (sun) rises as the radiant one of the gods; therefore he recites this. 'Homage to the eye of Mitra and Varuṇa' is in Jagatī[4]; this has a Pada containing a benediction; verily thus he invokes a benediction for himself and the sacrificer.

iv. 10 (xvii. 4.) They say 'Sūrya should not be passed over in recitation; the Bṛhatī should not be passed over; if he were to pass over Sūrya, he would pass over splendour; if he were to pass over the Bṛhatī, he would pass over the breaths.' 'O Indra bear to us inspiration' he recites as a Pragātha to Indra.[1] 'Guide us, O much invoked, in this way; alive may we attain the light' (he says); the light is yonder (sun); thereby he does not pass over Sūrya. Moreover in that it is a Pragātha in Bṛhatī, thereby he does not pass over the Bṛhatī. In[2] 'Towards thee, O hero, we utter praise' he recites the basis of the Rathantara (Sāman); they chant to the Rathantara the Sandhi for the Āçvina; in that he recites the basis of the Rathantara, it is to provide the Rathantara with its basis. 'Lord of this world, beholding the light' (he says); yonder (sun) is he who beholds the light; thereby he does not pass over Sūrya. Moreover, in that it is a Pragātha in Bṛhatī, thereby he does not pass over the Bṛhatī. In[3] 'Many, sun-eyed' he recites a Pragātha to Mitra and Varuṇa; Mitra is the day, Varuṇa the night; both day and night does he lay hold on, who undertakes the Atirātra. In that he recites a Pragātha to Mitra and Varuṇa, verily thus he establishes him in day and night. 'Sun-eyed' (he says); thereby he does not pass over Sūrya. Moreover, in that it is a Pragātha in Bṛhatī, thereby he does not pass over the Bṛhatī. In 'May the two great ones, sky and earth, for us' and 'For they, sky and earth, all weal-producing' he recites (two verses[4]) to sky and earth; sky and earth

[1] RV. i. 50; ĀÇS. vi. 5. 18; ÇÇS. ix. 20. 21, which omits RV. x. 158.

[2] RV. x. 158; ĀÇS. vi. 5. 18.

[3] RV. i. 115; ĀÇS. vi. 5. 18; ÇÇS. ix. 20. 22.

[4] RV. x. 37; ĀÇS. vi. 5. 18; ÇÇS. ix. 20. 23.

iv. 10. [1] RV. vii. 32. 26, 27; ĀÇS. vi. 5. 18; ÇÇS. ix. 20. 24.

[2] RV. vii. 32. 22 and 27; ĀÇS. vi. 5. 18.

[3] RV. vii. 66. 10 and 11; ĀÇS. vi. 5. 18.

[4] RV. i. 22. 13 and 160. 1; ĀÇS. vi. 5. 18; ÇÇS. ix. 20. 25 has i. 22. 13-15.

are supports; this (earth) is a support here, yonder (sun) yonder. In that he recites (two verses) to sky and earth, verily thus he establishes him in sky and earth. 'The god, the goddess, according to the law, Sūrya, the pure' (he says); thereby he praises Sūrya. Moreover, in that (the two verses) Gāyatrī and Jagatī make up two Bṛhatīs, thereby he does not pass over the Bṛhatī. In

> 'Goddess of all the perishable kind
> Who shall not be wrath, nor seize (us),'

he recites (a verse) of two Padas[6]. The Āçvina they used to call a litany in which (the funeral) pyre is piled. Nirṛti with her noose used to await (thinking) 'When the Hotṛ concludes, then shall I let loose my nooses against him.' Then indeed Bṛhaspati saw (this verse) of two Padas. 'Who shall not be wrath, nor seize (us)'; therewith he cast below the nooses of Nirṛti with the nooses; in that the Hotṛ recites (this verse) of two Padas, verily thus he casts below the nooses of Nirṛti with the nooses; verily thus in safety the Hotṛ is released, with full life, for fullness of life; a full life he lives who knows thus. 'Of all the perishable kind' (he says); yonder (sun) causes to perish as it were; thereby he does not pass over Sūrya. Moreover in (the verse) of two Padas is man's metre; it includes all the metres; thereby he does not pass over the Bṛhatī.

iv. 11 (xvii. 5). He concludes with a verse to Brahmaṇaspati; Bṛhaspati is the holy power; verily thus at the end he establishes him in the holy power. With[1] 'To the father, with all the gods, the strong' should he conclude who desires offspring and cattle. 'O Bṛhaspati, with good offspring, with heroes' (he says); by offspring he has good offspring and heroes. 'Let us be lords of wealth' (he says); he becomes possessed of offspring, of cattle, of wealth, of heroes, when one knowing thus concludes with this (verse). With[2] 'O Bṛhaspati, that which may surpass the foe' he should conclude, who desires brilliance and splendour; beyond all others he deserves splendour. 'Brilliant' (he says); 'Brilliantly splendour shines' (they say); splendour shines as it were. 'That shall shine with radiance, O thou born of holy order' (he says); splendour is brilliant. 'Upon us do thou confer varied wealth' (he says); splendour is radiant as it were. Resplendent and glorious becomes he, when one knowing thus concludes with this (verse). Therefore he who knows thus should conclude with this (verse). (It is addressed) to Brahmaṇaspati; thereby he does not pass over Sūrya. In that he recites thrice (this) Triṣṭubh and it includes all the metres, thereby he does

[6] Not in RV.; ĀÇS. vi. 5 18; ÇÇS. ix. 20. 26, which has *mṛçayasya* and *grabhaḥ*.

[1] RV. iv. 50. 6.

[2] RV. ii. 23. 15; ĀÇS. vi. 5. 19; ÇÇS. ix. 20. 27.

not pass over the Bṛhatī. With a Gāyatrī and a Triṣṭubh he should say the *vaṣaṭ* call; the Gāyatrī is the holy power, the Triṣṭubh is strength; verily thus he unites the holy power with strength. Resplendent and glorious and full of strength does he become, when one knowing thus with a Gāyatrī[3] and a Triṣṭubh[4] says the *vaṣaṭ* call, 'O Açvins, skilled ones, with Vāyu' and 'Do ye both drink, O Açvins'. With a Gāyatrī and a Virāj he should say the *vaṣaṭ* call; the Gāyatrī is the holy power; the Virāj is food; verily thus he unites proper food with the holy power. Resplendent and glorious he becomes, he eats food made edible by the holy power, when one knowing thus says the *vaṣaṭ* call with the Gāyatrī and the Virāj. Therefore he who knows thus should say the *vaṣaṭ* call with the Gāyatrī and the Virāj,[5] with these (verses), 'For you the Soma juice is ready to be drunk' and 'Do ye both drink, O Açvins'.

The Caturviñça and Mahāvrata Days.

iv. 12 (xvii. 6). Now[1] they proceed to the Caturviñça day as the beginning, by it they grasp the year, by it the Stomas and the metres, by it all the deities. Not grasped in that metre, not grasped that deity, which is not grasped on this day. That is why the Ārambhaṇīya has its name. The Stoma is the Caturviñça; that is why the Caturviñça has its name; the half-months are twenty-four; verily thus by half-months they grasp the year. It is an Ukthya; the Ukthas are cattle; (it serves) for the winning of cattle. It has fifteen Stotras, fifteen Çastras; it is the month; verily thus by months they grasp the year. These are in the three hundred and sixty Stotriya verses; so many are the days of the year; verily thus by days they grasp the year. 'The day should be an Agniṣṭoma,' they say, 'the year is the Agniṣṭoma; no other than an Agniṣṭoma supports the day or discriminates it.' If it is an Agniṣṭoma, the three Pavamānas should be Aṣṭācatvāriñças, the other Stotras Caturviñças. Here also there are three hundred and sixty Stotriya verses; so many are the days of the year; verily thus by days they grasp the year. It should be an Ukthya; the sacrifice is made perfect by the animal (offering), the Sattra is made perfect by the animal (offering); all the Stotras are Caturviñças, for this is openly the Caturviñça day; therefore let it be an Ukthya.

[3] RV. i. 46. 15; ÇÇS. ix. 20. 34 (optional).

[4] RV. iii. 58. 7; ÇÇS. ix. 20. 32.

[5] RV. vii. 68. 2; ĀÇS. vi. 5. 24; ÇÇS. ix. 20. 32.

[1] AB. iv. 12-14 and KB. xix deal with the Caturviñça as the opening day of the Gavām Ayana Sattra, corresponding to the Mahāvrata at the end; see ĀÇS. vii. 1-4; ÇÇS. xi. 2 *seq.*

iv. 13 (xvii. 7). The Sāmans are the Bṛhat and the Rathantara.[1] These are the two ships which carry across the sacrifice; verily thus by them they cross over the year. The Bṛhat and the Rathantara are the two feet, this day the head; verily thus by the two feet they approach the head which is prosperity. The Bṛhat and Rathantara are the two wings, this day the head; verily thus with the two wings they unite the head, which is prosperity. The two are not both to be laid aside; if they were to lay them both aside, just as a vessel which has parted from its fastening floats moving to either bank, so the performers of Sattras would float, moving to either bank, if they were to lay aside both together. If they were to lay aside the Rathantara, then by the Bṛhat both are not laid aside; if they were to lay aside this Bṛhat, then by the Rathantara both are not laid aside. The Vairūpa is the Rathantara; the Vairāja is the Bṛhat; the Çākvara is the Rathantara; the Raivata is the Bṛhat. So these two become not laid aside both together. Those who knowing thus perform this day (rite), having obtained by the days the year, having obtained it by the half months, having obtained it by the months, having obtained the Stomas and the metres, having obtained all the deities, practising fervour, partaking of the Soma drink, continue pressing (Soma) all the year. Those who straight on[2] from the day perform the year (rite) they lay upon themselves a heavy burden, the heavy burden crushes them. He, who having obtained it with the rites straight forward approaches it (with the rites) reversed, attains in safety the other side of the year.[3]

iv. 14 (xvii. 8). The Mahāvrata is the Caturviñça; by means of the Bṛhaddiva (hymn[1]) the Hotṛ pours seed on this day; it on that day with the Mahāvrata day he propagates; in a year seed poured is born. Therefore the Bṛhaddiva is the common Niṣkevalya (Çastra). He having obtained it with the rites straight forward approaches it (with the rites) reversed, who knowing thus approaches this day. In safety he attains the other side of the year who knows thus. He, who knows this side and the other side of the year, in safety attains the other side of the year. The introductory Atirātra is this side, the concluding (Atirātra) is the other side. In safety he attains the other side of the year who knows thus.

[1] This chapter is intended to show that in every case one or other of those Sāmans is used whether in Abhiplava or Pṛṣṭhya Ṣaḍahas. The six Sāmans are based on the following verses: Rathantara, SV. ii. 30, 31; Bṛhat, SV. ii. 159, 160; Vairūpa, ii. 212, 213; Vairāja, ii. 277-279; Çākvara, ii. 1151-3; Raivata, ii. 434-436. Cf. AB. iv. 15, n. 1.

[2] I. e. without change of order according to Sāyaṇa; Haug treats it as merely meaning 'proceed with', and takes *abhi nidadhate* as 'lay down'. The point is as in n. 3.

[3] The second six months are intended to be a reverse of the first six. For the ship metaphor cf. AB. vi. 6. 6; ÇB. iv. 2. 5. 10; Lévi, *La doctrine du sacrifice*, p. 88.

iv. 14. [1] RV. x. 120. For the year cf. Keith, JRAS. 1917, p. 137.

He, who knows the descent and ascent[2] of the year, obtains in safety the other side of the year. The introductory Atirātra is the descent, the concluding (Atirātra) the ascent. In safety he attains the other side of the year who knows thus. He, who knows the expiration and the ending[3] breath of the year, attains in safety the other side of the year. The introductory Atirātra is the expiration, the concluding (Atirātra) the ending breath. In safety he reaches the other side of the year, who knows thus.

ADHYĀYA III

The Sadahas and the Viṣuvant.

iv. 15 (xviii. 1). They proceed with the Stomas, Jyotis, Go, and Āyus; the Jyotis is this world, the Go the atmosphere, the Āyus yonder world. There is the same second set of three days; there are three days, Jyotis, Go, and Āyus; there are three, Go, Āyus, and Jyotis. The Jyotis is this world, the Jyotis is yonder world. These two Jyotis (days) look together on both sides; thereby they proceed with this set of six days with a Jyotis on either side. In that they proceed with this set of six days with a Jyotis on either side, verily thus they continue to find support on both sides in these two worlds; in this world and in that world, both. The Abhiplava Ṣaḍaha is a circling wheel of the gods. The Agniṣṭomas on the two sides of it are the felloes; the four Ukthyas in the middle are the nave. He goes with it turning wherever he desires; thus in safety he attains the other side of the year who knows thus. He, who knows the first set of six days, in safety attains the other side of the year; (so) he who knows the second, he who knows the third, he who knows the fourth, he who knows the fifth.[1]

iv. 16 (xviii. 2). They perform the first set of six days,[1] there are six days; the seasons are six; verily thus by the seasons they obtain the year; by the seasons they continue finding support in the year. They perform the second set of six days; these are twelve days; the months are twelve; verily thus by months they obtain the year; by months they continue finding support in the year. They perform the third set of six days; they are eighteen days; these are twofold, one set of nine, one set of nine. There are nine

[2] *Ava°* and *udrodhanam* clearly have this sense, from *ruh*, not *rudh*, as Sāyaṇa and Haug. The contrast is as in *parastāt* and *avastāt*.

[3] The *udāna* here must be the *apāna*, but used for *udanīya* as suggested by Sāyaṇa.

[1] The Abhiplava Ṣaḍaha is dealt with in ĀÇS. vii. 5-7 and the Pṛṣṭhya in vii. 10-12; viii. 1-4; in ÇÇS. the order is reversed, viz. xi. 4-9 and x. 1-8. See also BÇS. xvi. 4, 5; ĀpÇS. xxi. 1-8.

iv. 16. [1] See ĀÇS. xi. 7; ÇÇS. xiii. 19.

breaths, nine worlds of heaven; verily thus they obtain the breaths and the worlds of heaven; verily thus they continue finding support in the breaths and the worlds of heaven. They perform the fourth set of six days; these are twenty-four days; the half-months are twenty-four; verily thus by half-months they obtain the year; by half-months they continue finding support in the year. They perform the fifth set of six days; they are thirty days; the Virāj has thirty syllables; proper food is the Virāj; verily thus they continue producing the Virāj month by month. Desiring proper food they performed the sacrificial session.[2] In that they continue producing the Virāj month by month, verily thus they continue winning proper food month by month, for the world and for that, for both.

iv. 17 (xviii. 3). They proceed with the way of the cows;[1] the Ādityas are the cows; verily thus they proceed with the way of the Ādityas. The cows performed a sacrificial session seeking to win hoofs and horns; in the tenth month their hoofs and horns came into being. They said 'That desire for which we have consecrated ourselves we have obtained; let us cease.' Those that ceased are those possessed of horns. Those who performed, (thinking) 'We will complete the year', they had only mock horns, these are the hornless; but they produced[2] strength. Therefore they having made up all the seasons, then cease, for they produced strength. Dear to all are cows, beloved by all. Dear to all, beloved by all, does he become who knows thus. The Ādityas and the Añgirases contended for the world of heaven,[3] 'We will go first, we'; the Ādityas went first to the world of heaven, behind the Añgirases by sixty years. The way of the Ādityas is thus,[4] an introductory Atirātra, the Caturviñça Ukthya, all the Abhiplava Ṣaḍahas, other Ākṣyant[5] days; the way of the Añgirases is thus, an

[2] *Āsata* would seem more natural, but the imperfect may convey the view in the minds of those performing the Sattra when they undertook it.

[1] For this see TS. vii. 5. 1. 2; PB. iv. 1. Aufrecht considers that *na* must be read as apparently by Sāyaṇa; the alternative is to read *açraddhayā çṛñgāṇi* as one term as suggested by BR. or to take *prāvartanta* as = 'fell off'. Cf. Keith, *Taittirīya Saṁhitā*, I. xcviii, xcix. Lévi (*La doctrine du sacrifice*, p. 111) renders the TS. passage without commenting on the sense.

[2] *asanvan* is obvious (as in TS.) but needless as *asunvan* makes sense.

[3] Cf. ÇB. xii. 2. 2. 9.

[4] *yathā vā* is odd; *vā* = *vai* has just before occurred, but *yathā* seems needless and in clause 7 is not inserted, but it can easily be taken in its usual sense. Sāyaṇa's attempt to make it allude to the mode of the Gavām Ayana is absurd. The Sattras are quite different in ĀÇS. xii. 1. 1; ÇÇS. xiii. 21, 22.

[5] This word is doubtful. Aufrecht takes it as 'stättige umwandelbare Tage' (= *ākṣiyanti*). Sāyaṇa cites Baudhāyana as restricting it to the Abhijit, Viṣuvant, Viçvajit, the tenth day (of the Dvādaçāha), the Mahāvrata and the concluding Atirātra; Çālika as including in it all save the Ṣaḍahas, and Aupamanyava as including in it all save the Ṣaḍahas and the tenth day. Cf. ĀpÇS. xxiii. 9. 16; ÇB. xii. 2. 3. 1; Eggeling, SBE. XLIV. 155, 156; Weber, *Ind. Stud.* ix. 282.

introductory Atirātra, the Caturviñça Ukthya, all the Pṛṣṭhya Ṣaḍahas, other Ākṣyant days. The Abhiplava Ṣaḍaha is the path that leads straight to the world of heaven; again the Pṛṣṭhya Ṣaḍaha is a great circuitous route to the world of heaven. In that they proceed with both, and going by both he comes to no ill, (it serves) to obtain both desires, that in the Abhiplava Ṣaḍaha and that in the Pṛṣṭhya.[6]

iv. 18 (xviii. 4). They perform the Ekaviñça day, the Viṣuvant,[1] in the middle of the year; by the Ekaviñça the gods raised up the sun to the world of heaven; it is here the Ekaviñça; below this Divākīrtya are ten days, ten above; in the middle is the Ekaviñça resting on both sides in the Virāj, for on both sides does he find support in the Virāj. Therefore he going between these worlds does not shake. The gods were afraid of this Āditya falling down from the world of heaven; him with three worlds of heaven from below they propped up; the three worlds of heaven are the Stomas. They were afraid of his falling away up; him with three worlds of heaven from above they propped up; the three worlds of heaven are the Stomas. Thus below there are three Saptadaça (Stomas), three above; in the middle is the Ekaviñça on both sides supported by the Svara Sāmans, for he is supported on both sides by the Svara Sāmans.[2] Therefore he going between these worlds does not shake. The gods were afraid of this Āditya falling from the world of heaven;[3] him with the highest worlds of heaven they propped up from below; the highest worlds of heaven are the Stomas. They were afraid of his falling away up; him with the highest worlds of heaven they propped up from above; the highest worlds of heaven are the Stomas. Thus there are three Saptadaça (Stomas) below, three above. Making them up by twos they are three Catustriñças; the Catustriñça is the highest of the Stomas. Placed over these it gives heat, for he placed over these gives heat. He is higher than all this that has been and will be; he shines over all this whatever there is here; he is higher; thus he becomes who knows thus higher than he than whom he desires to be higher.

iv. 19 (xviii. 5). They perform the Svara Sāmans; the Svara Sāmans are these worlds. They saved these worlds with the Svara Sāmans; that is why

6 The Gavām Ayana has a mixture of four Abhiplavas and a Pṛṣṭhya in the month; see ĀÇS. xi. 7. 1 *seq.* It is Prāyaṇīya; Caturviñça; 5 months of 4 Abhiplavas and 1 Pṛṣṭhya Ṣaḍaha; 3 Abhiplavas, 1 Pṛṣṭhya, Abhijit, 3 Svara Sāmans; Viṣuvant; 3 Svara Sāmans, Viçvajit, 1 Pṛṣṭhya, 3 Abhiplavas; 4 months of 1 Pṛṣṭhya and 4 Abhiplavas; 3 Abhiplavas, Go, Āyus, a Daçarātra; the Mahāvrata and Udayanīya, with variants.

1 AB. iv. 18–22 and KB. xxv. 1–10 deal with the Viṣuvant and connected rites; see ĀÇS. viii. 5–7; ÇÇS xi. 13.

2 For these as Saptadaças see TB. i. 2. 2. 1. *Cf.* ĀÇS. viii. 5. 10 *seq.*; ÇÇS. xi. 11, 12.

3 *Cf.* PB. iv. 5. 8 which has *avapādāt*.

the Svara Sāmans have their name. In that they perform the Svara Sāmans, they give him a share in these worlds. The gods were afraid of the sinking down of these Saptadaças, 'The Stomas are alike and unprotected; let them not sink down.' They secured them with all the Stomas from below, with all the Pṛṣṭhas from above; in that the Abhijit with all the Stomas is below, the Viçvajit with all the Pṛṣṭhas above, thus they secure the Saptadaças on both sides for security and to prevent sinking down.[1] The gods were afraid of this Āditya falling from the world of heaven, they fastened him up with five ropes; the Divākīrtya (Sāmans) are the ropes; the Pṛṣṭha is the Mahā-Divākīrtya,[2] the Sāman of the Brāhmaṇācchaṅsin is the Vikarṇa,[3] the Agniṣṭoma Sāman is the Bhāsa,[4] the Bṛhat and Rathantara are those of the Pavamānas; thus they fasten up Āditya with five ropes, for support, to avoid falling down. When the sun has arisen, he should recite the morning litany, for all the day (rite) is to be performed during the day time. They should offer as the victim to Sūrya (an animal) without blemish and white, in addition to (the victim) for the pressing, for this day has Sūrya as its deity. He should recite twenty-one kindling verses,[5] for this day is openly the Ekaviñça. Having recited fifty-one or fifty-two[6] he places a Nivid in the middle; so many after he recites. Man has a hundred (years of) life, a hundred powers, and a hundred strengths; verily thus he confers upon him life, strength, and power.

iv. 20 (xviii. 6). He mounts the difficult mounting; the difficult mounting is the world of heaven; verily thus he mounts the world of heaven who knows thus. As to its being the difficult mounting, he that gives heat yonder is hard to mount, and whoever goes there, in that he mounts the difficult mounting, verily thus he mounts him. He mounts (with a verse[1]) containing (the word) 'gander', 'The gander seated in purity'; he is the gander seated in purity. 'The Vasu seated in the atmosphere' (he says); he is the Vasu seated in the atmosphere. 'The Hotṛ seated at the altar' (he says); he is the Hotṛ seated at the altar. 'The guest seated in the house' (he says); he is the guest seated in the house. 'Seated among men'

[1] The Viṣuvant day is preceded by (1) the Abhijit, (2) the Svara Sāmans, and followed by (1) Svara Sāmans, (2) the Viçvajit.

[2] On RV. x. 170. 1. 3; SV. ii. 802–804; ĀÇS. viii. 6. 7, 8; contrast ÇÇS. xi. 13. 24.

[3] On RV. vi. 8. 1–3; ĀrS. iii. 8–10.

[4] The same verses as in n. 3 are used according to Sāyaṇa and ĀÇS. viii. 6. 22; ÇÇS. xi. 13. 28.

[5] See AÇS. viii. 6. 3; RV. iii. 27. 5–10.

[6] I. e. RV. i. 31 is to be divided either after the 8th or 9th verse; see ĀÇS. viii. 6. 13 with comm.

iv. 20. [1] RV. iv. 40. 5. Cf. KB. xxv. 7; Lévi, *La doctrine du sacrifice*, pp. 88, 89. For the mode of recitation see ĀÇS. viii. 2. 13–15; 6. 14, 15; it is first by Pādas, then by half-verses, then by three Pādas, then by the whole verse, and then in descending order. Cf. ÇÇS. xi. 14. 18; xii. 11. 12. The recitation of the Tārkṣya takes place at the end of the Niṣkevalya.

(he says); he is seated among men. 'Seated in the best (abode)' (he says); he is seated in the best (abode); the best of abodes is that in which seated he gives heat. 'Seated in holy order' (he says); he is seated in truth. 'Seated is the sky' (he says); he is seated in the sky; the sky is that seat in which seated he gives heat. 'Born of the waters' (he says); he is born of the waters; from the waters he rises in the morning, into the waters he enters at evening. 'Born of the cow' (he says); he is born of the cow.' Born of holy order' (he says); he is born of truth. 'Born of the mountain' (he says); he is born of the mountain. 'Holy order' (he says); he is truth. He is all these things. In the metres this (verse) is most manifestly as it were a symbol of him. Therefore, whenever he performs the difficult mounting, should he mount with (the verse) containing (the word) 'gander'. With the Tārkṣya[2] (hymn) should he mount for one desiring the heaven. Tārkṣya aforetime made the journey when yonder the Gāyatrī in the form of an eagle brought the Soma. Thus, just as one makes one knowing the place a guide on a journey, so is it in that (he mounts) with the Tārkṣya: he who blows is Tārkṣya; he is the bearer to the world of heaven. 'This steed, god-strengthened' (he says); he is the steed, god-strengthened. 'Enduring, the bearer of the cars' (he says); he bears across enduring, for he at once crosses these worlds. 'With chariot rim unharmed, the warrior, swift' (he says); he is the one with chariot rim unharmed, the warrior, swift. 'For safety' (he says); he invokes safety. 'Tārkṣya let us summon hither' (he says); verily thus he summons him. With 'Invoking by sacrifice the favour as of Indra for safety' he invokes safety. 'Like a ship let us mount' (he says); verily thus he mounts it for the attainment, the winning, the arrival at the world of heaven. 'Like the two broad ones, wide, large, deep, may we not be harmed at your going and coming' (he says); verily thus he recites for these two, when going to and returning.[3]

'He who at once with his glory over the five peoples
Like Sūrya with his light over the waters extendeth'

(he says); openly he mentions the sun.

'A thousandfold, a hundredfold bestowing, is his onset;
They cannot stay him like a young dart'

(he says); verily thus he invokes a benediction for himself and the sacrificers.

[2] RV. x. 178: it has 3 verses; here cited in full.

[3] The root here in *meṣyan* explains *Dhātupāṭha*, xxxiv. 18, *mī* 1 or 10.

iv. 21 (xviii. 7). Having uttered the call, he mounts the difficult mounting; the difficult mounting is the world of heaven; the call is speech; speech is the holy power; in that he calls, thus with the call as the holy power he mounts the world of heaven. He mounts by Padas first; thus he obtains this world; then by half-verses; thus he obtains the atmosphere; then by three Padas; thus he obtains yonder world; then with the whole (verse); thus he who gives heat here finds support in this (world). By three Padas he descends as one holding a branch;[1] thus he finds support in yonder world; by half-verses (he descends; thus he finds support) in the atmosphere; by Padas (he descends; thus he finds support) in this world. Thus, having obtained the world of heaven, the sacrificers find support in this world. For those who desire one only, (the world of) heaven, he should mount in the forward direction only; they will conquer the world of heaven, but they will not have long to live in the world. Pairing hymns are recited, Triṣṭubh and Jagatī; cattle are pairing; the metres are cattle; (verily they serve) to win cattle.

iv. 22 (xviii. 8). The Viṣuvant is like a man; the first half of the Viṣuvant is like the right half of a man; the second half of the Viṣuvant is like[1] the left half; therefore they call it the latter. The Viṣuvant is the head of a man standing on the level; man is composed of (two) sections; thus there is seen in the middle of his head a suture as it were. They say 'On the Viṣuvant alone should he perform (the recitations of) the day; the Viṣuvant is the Uktha of Ukthas; (holding that) "The Viṣuvant is that which has the Viṣuvant (Çastra)" they become the head, they attain preeminence.' That is not to be regarded. He should recite it only in the year; verily thus they keep holding the seed for a year. Whatever seeds are born before the year, of five months or six months, these wither; they do not profit by them; those that are born in ten months or a year, by these they profit. Therefore should he recite it in the year, for the year contains this day; as the year they obtain this day. He smites away evil by the year, by the Viṣuvant; from the limbs he drives away evil by the months, from the head by the Viṣuvant. He smites away evil by the year, by the Viṣuvant, who knows thus. As additional to (the victim)[2] for the pressing, they should offer to Viçvakarman a bull of two colours, variegated on both

[1] Cf. PB. xviii. 10. 10: *yathā çākhāyāḥ çākhām ālambham upāvaroheḍ evam etenemaṁ lokam upāvarohati pratiṣṭhāyai.*

iv. 22.[1] The first view, here rejected, must have held that the Viṣuvant rite might be performed always as a special rite on that day and not merely as part of a Sattra. The second view of the text appears to allow its use at a Sattra only (*eva*), the Viṣuvant having its full meaning only as the middle day of such a rite. So Sāyaṇa who, however, takes *viṣuvān viṣuvān iti* merely as saying that the *tulāmeṣasaṁkrānti* is thus called.

[2] Nārāyaṇa on ĀÇS. viii. 6. 4 makes this an additional, Sāyaṇa has a substituted victim.

sides, on the Mahāvrata day. Indra having slain Vṛtra became Viçvakarman; Prajāpati having created offspring became Viçvakarman; Viçvakarman is the year; verily thus Indra whose self it is, Prajāpati, the year, Viçvakarman, they obtain; verily thus in Indra whose self it is, Prajāpati, the year, Viçvakarman, they find support at the end. He finds support who knows thus.

ADHYĀYA IV

The Dvādaçāha.

iv. 23 (xix. 1). Prajāpati felt desire 'May I be propagated, may I become greater.' He practised fervour; he, having practised fervour, saw the twelve-day (rite) in the limbs and the breaths of his self; he meted it out from the limbs and the breaths of his self twelvefold; he grasped it, and sacrificed with it. Then indeed he prospered himself, he was propagated with offspring and cattle. He prospers himself, he is propagated with offspring and cattle who knows thus. He felt desire, 'How can I now, having encircled the twelve-day (rite) with the Gāyatrī on all sides, prosper with all prosperity?' It he encircled in front with brilliance, in the middle with the metres, at the last with the syllables; having encircled the twelve-day (rite) with the Gāyatrī on all sides he prospers with all prosperity. With all prosperity he prospers, who knows thus. He who knows the Gāyatrī as possessed of wings, of eyes, of light, and[1] of brilliance, goes to the world of heaven with the Gāyatrī as possessed of wings, of eyes, of light, and of brilliance; the twelve-day (rite) is the Gāyatrī as possessed of wings, of eyes, of light, and of brilliance. The two Atirātras on either side are the wings;[2] the two Agniṣṭomas within are the two eyes; the eight Ukthyas in the middle are the body. With the Gāyatrī as possessed of wings, of eyes, of light, and of brilliance, he goes to the world of heaven, who knows thus.

iv. 24 (xix. 2). The twelve-day (rite) consists of three sets of three days, the tenth day and two Atirātras.[1] For twelve days is he consecrated;[2] verily through them he becomes fit for sacrifice. He performs Upasads for twelve nights; verily with them he shakes clear his body. Having pressed for twelve days continuously, having become born anew, having shaken clear his body, pure and purified, he goes to the gods who

[1] For the Dvādaçāha see ĀÇS. x. 5; ÇÇS. x. For the beginning cf. TS. vii. 2. 9. 1.

[2] See ĀÇS. x. 5. 10: *atirātram agre 'thāgniṣṭomam athāṣṭā ukthyān athāgniṣṭomam athātirātram.*

iv. 24. [1] *Ā* according to Sāyaṇa is used here either in the sense of exclusion or limit (*maryādā*); it is accepted as exclusive by Delbrück, *Altind. Synt.* p. 452, n. 1.

[2] Cf. Eggeling, SBE. xxvi. 442, n. 1.

knows thus. The twelve-day (rite) is one of thirty-six days; the Bṛhatī has thirty-six syllables; the twelve-day (rite) is the way of the Bṛhatī; by means of the Bṛhatī the gods attained these worlds. They attained this world with ten syllables, the atmosphere with ten, the sky with ten, the four quarters with four; with two they found support in this world. He finds support who knows thus. They say 'Seeing that other metres are greater and have more syllables, then why do they call it the Bṛhatī?' Since by it the gods attained these worlds. They attained this world with ten syllables, the atmosphere with ten, the sky with ten, the four quarters with four; verily with two they found support in this world; therefore do they call it the Bṛhatī. He attains whatever he desires who knows thus.

iv. 25 (xix. 3). The twelve-day (rite) is a sacrifice of Prajāpati; Prajāpati at first sacrificed with this twelve-day (rite). He said to the seasons and to the months 'Make sacrifice for me with the twelve-day (rite).' Having caused him to consecrate himself, having made him move where he could not depart, they said to him 'Give to us; then shall we sacrifice for thee.' To them he gave sap and strength; sap is deposited in the seasons and in the months; they made sacrifice for him when giving; therefore should sacrifice be made for one when giving; they made sacrifice for him when receiving; therefore should sacrifice be made by one receiving. Both prosper, those who knowing thus sacrifice and make sacrifice. These seasons and months thought themselves heavy having received (gifts) at the twelve-day (rite); they said to Prajāpati 'Make sacrifice for us with the twelve-day rite.' 'Be it so', he replied, 'Do you consecrate yourselves.' Those of the first half consecrated themselves first; they smote away evil; therefore they are the daylight as it were, for the daylight as it were are those who have smitten away evil. Those of the second half consecrated themselves next; they did not at all smite away evil; therefore they are darkness as it were, for darkness as it were are those who have not smitten away evil. Therefore one who knows thus should ever seek to be first consecrated when men consecrate themselves. He smites away evil who knows thus. Prajāpati as the year found support in the seasons and the months; these seasons and months found support in Prajāpati as the year; these find support in one another. So he who sacrifices with the twelve-day (rite) finds support in the priest. Therefore they say 'No evil man should be sacrificed for with the twelve-day (rite), (thinking) "Let not this one find support in me."' The twelve-day (rite) is the oldest sacrifice, for the oldest of the gods it was who in the beginning sacrificed with it. The twelve-day (rite) is the best sacrifice, for it was the best of the gods who in the beginning sacrificed with it. The oldest and the best should sacrifice; here there becomes a good season. No evil man should be sacrificed for with the twelve-day (rite), (thinking) 'Let not this one find support in me.' The gods did not admit the seniority and superiority of Indra; he said to Bṛhaspati 'Make sacrifice for me with the twelve-day (rite).' For him he made sacrifice; then indeed did the gods admit his seniority and superiority. His superiority and seniority they admit, and his pre-eminence his own (people) accord, who knows thus. The first set of three days is in ascending order, the middle transverse, the last in descending order.[1] In that the first set of three days is in ascending order, therefore Agni here is kindled upwards, for his quarter is upwards; in that the middle is transverse, therefore Vāyu here blows transversely, the waters flow transversely, for his quarter is the transverse; in that the last is in descending order, therefore yonder sun gives heat downward, it rains downward, and the constellations (shine) downward, for his region is downward. These worlds are in unison; these sets of three days are in unison; in unison for him these worlds shine with prosperity, who knows thus.

iv. 26 (xix. 4). Consecration departed from the gods; it they sought to grasp with the two months of spring; it they could not obtain with the two months of spring. It they sought to grasp with the two months of summer, of the rainy season, of autumn, of winter; it they could not obtain with the months of winter. It they sought to grasp with the two months of the cool season; it they obtained with the two months of the cool season. He obtains whom he seeks to obtain, his enemy obtains him not, who knows thus. Therefore he to whom the consecration for the sacrificial season may condescend[1] should consecrate himself when these two months of the cool season have arrived. Obviously thus does he consecrate himself, when consecration has arrived; manifestly he encircles consecration. Therefore in these months of the cool season the cattle of the village and of the wild become thin and shaggy; verily thus they acquire the form of consecration. Before the consecration he offers a victim to Prajāpati; first he should recite seventeen kindling verses; Prajāpati is seventeenfold; (they serve) to obtain Prajāpati. The Āprīs verses for it are by Jamadagni.[2] They say 'Seeing that in the case of the other victims the Āprīs are according to the (ancestral) seer, then why

[1] The metres for the three pressings vary from (1) Gāyatrī, Triṣṭubh, and Jagatī to (2) Jagatī, Gāyatrī, and Triṣṭubh and (3) Triṣṭubh, Jagatī, and Gāyatrī.

iv. 26. [1] The Dvādaçāha is here treated as a Sattra.

[2] RV. x. 110. *Cf.* Max Müller, *Anc. Sansk. Lit.* p. 466; Weber, *Ind. Stud.* x. 88 *seq.*; ĀÇS. vii. 2. 6–8; ÇÇS. v. 16. 5, 6.

in this case are the verses by Jamadagni used by all?' The verses by Jamadagni are of all forms, all perfect; the victim is of all forms, all perfect; in that they are verses by Jamadagni (they serve) to secure the possession of all forms, all perfections. The cake offering for the victim is for Vāyu. They say 'Seeing that the victim is for other deities also, then why is the cake offering for the victim performed for Vāyu.' 'The sacrifice is Prajāpati, to prevent the exhaustion of the sacrifice' he should reply. In that it is for Vāyu, thereby he does not depart from Prajāpati, for Prajāpati is Vāyu. It is declared by the seer[3] 'Prajāpati, the blowing.' If it is a sacrificial session, they should offer after depositing the fires together, all should be consecrated, all should press. With spring he ends; spring is strength; verily thus he ends with sap and strength.

iv. 27 (xix. 5). The metres desired one another's abode; the Gāyatrī desired the abode of the Triṣṭubh and the Jagatī, the Triṣṭubh that of the Gāyatrī and the Jagatī, and the Jagatī that of the Gāyatrī and the Triṣṭubh. Then indeed did Prajāpati see this twelve-day (rite) with the metres transposed; he grasped it and sacrificed with it. Thereby he made the metres attain all their desires. He attains all desires who knows thus. He transposes the metres to avoid exhaustion. Verily he transposes the metres. Just as in the world men go with relays of fresh horses or oxen, so with relays of fresh metres they go to the world of heaven, in that he transposes the metres. These two worlds were together; they went apart; no rain fell, there was no heat; the five folks were not in harmony.[1] The gods brought them together; they uniting performed the divine marriage. By means of the Rathantara this (earth) quickens yonder (sky); by the Bṛhatī yonder (sky) this (earth); by the Naudhasa[2] this quickens that; by the Çyaita that this. With smoke this quickens that; with rain that this. This placed in that the place of sacrifice to the gods; cattle that in this. In that this placed the place of sacrifice to the gods, in that there is dark as it were in the moon. Therefore on the waxing fortnights they sacrifice as they desire to win that.[3] Yonder (sky) placed salt in the (earth); as to this Tura Kāvaṣeya said 'Salt is nutriment, O my dear Janamejaya.'[4] Therefore here also men considering a place for cattle ask 'Are there salts there?' for salt is nutriment. Yonder

[3] RV. ix. 5. 9.

[1] Cf. PB. vii. 10. 1, and for the *vyūha* of the metres KB. xxvii. 1.

[2] These are, according to Sāyaṇa, SV. ii. 299–301; ii. 163, 164.

[3] I.e. to see more distinctly as the moon waxes the black spot.

[4] *Ka* Sāyaṇa takes as an interrogation, and is followed by Haug.

world turned to this world; then were sky and earth born; neither from the atmosphere (comes) the sky,[5] nor from the atmosphere earth.

iv. 28 (xix. 6). In the beginning there were here the Bṛhat and the Rathantara; they were speech and mind; the Rathantara speech, the Bṛhat mind; the Bṛhat as first born despised the Rathantara; the Rathantara conceived and produced the Vairūpa; having become two, the Rathantara and the Vairūpa, they despised the Bṛhat. Then the Bṛhat conceived and produced the Vairāja; having become two, the Bṛhat and the Vairāja, they despised the Rathantara and the Vairūpa. Then the Rathantara conceived and produced the Çākvara; these having become three, the Rathantara and the Vairūpa and the Çākvara, despised the Bṛhat and the Vairāja. The Bṛhat conceived and produced the Raivata. These three and those three were the Pṛṣṭhas. The three metres were not enough for six Pṛṣṭhas. The Gāyatrī conceived and produced the Anuṣṭubh; the Triṣṭubh conceived and produced the Pañkti; the Jagatī conceived and produced the Atichandas. These three and those three others were the six metres; the Pṛṣṭhas were six; thus they came into order. The sacrifice is in order; (all) is in order for that folk where one knowing thus this ordering of the metres and the Pṛṣṭhas consecrates himself.

ADHYĀYA V

The Pṛṣṭhya Ṣaḍaha.

iv. 29 (xx. 1). Agni[1] as deity bears the first day, the Trivṛt Stoma, the Rathantara Sāman, the Gāyatrī metre. With it according to the deity, the Stoma, the Sāman, the metre, he prospers who knows thus. That which has (the words) 'hither' and 'forward' is a symbol of the first day. That which contains (the word) 'yoke', (the word) 'car', (the word) 'swift', (the word) 'drink', (the fact) that the deity is mentioned in the first Pada, that this world is referred to, that which is connected with the Rathantara, which is connected with the Gāyatrī, the future tense, these are the symbols of the first day. 'Advancing forward up to the sacrifice' is the Ājya[2] of the first day; (the word) 'forward' on the first day is a symbol of the first day. 'O Vāyu, come hither, O lovely one' is the Praüga[3]; (the word) 'hither'

[5] *dyāvā* is here probably merely = 'sky', and not as usual 'sky and earth'. The use is natural, as it is merely an analysis of *dyāvāpṛthivī*.

[1] AB. iv. 29–v. 15 and KB. xxii and xxiii describe in detail the Çastras of the Pṛṣṭhya Ṣaḍaha. Cf. ĀÇS. vii. 10–12; viii. 1–4; ÇÇS. x. 1–8.

[2] RV. i. 74; ĀÇS. vii. 10. 3; ÇÇS. x. 2. 2.

[3] RV. i. 2 and 3; ĀÇS. v. 10. 5; ÇÇS. vii. 10. 9.

on the first day is a symbol of the first day. 'Thee like a car forward' and 'This Soma juice, O bright one, hath been pressed' are the strophe and antistrophe [4] of the Marutvatīya; that which contains (the words) 'car' and 'drink' on the first day is the symbol of the first day. 'O Indra come nearer' is the Pragātha [5] invoking Indra; in the first Pada the god is mentioned, on the first day it is a symbol of the first day. 'Let Brahmaṇaspati move forward' is (the Pragātha) to Brahmaṇaspati [6]; (the word) 'forward' on the first day is a symbol of the first day. 'Agni the leader', 'Thou, O Soma, with inspiration' and 'They swell the waters' are the inserted verses [7]; in the first Padas the deities are mentioned; on the first day it is a symbol of the first day. 'Forward to Indra, the great' is the Marutvatīya Pragātha [8]; (the word) 'forward' on the first day is a symbol of the first day. 'Let Indra come hither for help to us' is the hymn [9]; (the word) 'hither' on the first day is a symbol of the first day. 'Towards thee, O hero, we utter praise' and 'Towards thee for the first drink' are the Rathantara as Pṛṣṭha [10], on the Rathantara day, the first day, it is a symbol of the first day. 'Since many a time he hath conquered, enduring' is the inserted verse; [11] in 'Indra hath made good (*ā ... aprāḥ*) his names as slayer of Vṛtra', (the word) 'hither (*ā*)' on the first day is a symbol of the first day. 'Drink of the pressed juice full of sap' is the Pragātha [12] of the Sāman; containing (the word) 'drink' on the first day it is a symbol of the first day. In 'This steed, god-strengthened' he recites the Tārkṣya [13] (hymn) before the hymn; Tārkṣya is safe passage; (verily it serves) to secure safety. Verily he secures a safe journey, he attains the other side of the year who knows thus.

iv. 30 (xx. 2). 'Hither to us, O Indra, hither to us, from afar, from near' is the hymn.[1] (The word) 'hither' on the first day is a symbol of the first day. In the Niṣkevalya and Marutvatīya (Çastras) (the hymns) in which Nivids are inserted are contiguous. Vāmadeva saw those worlds; to them he flew up with the Sampātas; because he flew up with the Sampātas, that is why Sampātas have their name. In that he repeats the two Sampātas on the first day, (it is) for the attaining, the securing, the union with, the world of heaven.

4 RV. viii. 68. 1-3 and 2. 1-3; ĀÇS. v. 14. 4; ÇÇS. vii. 19. 8.

5 RV. viii. 58. 5 and 6; ĀÇS. v. 14. 5; ÇÇS. vii. 19. 10.

6 RV. i. 40. 3 and 4; ĀÇS. v. 14. 6; ÇÇS. vii. 19. 11.

7 RV. iii. 20. 4; i. 91. 2; i. 64. 6 (already cited in AB. iii. 18); ĀÇS. v. 14. 17.

8 RV. viii. 89. 3 and 4; ĀÇS. v. 14. 18.

9 RV. iv. 21; ĀÇS. vii. 5. 18; ÇÇS. x. 2. 4.

10 RV. vii. 32. 22 and 23; viii. 3. 7 and 8; ĀÇS. v. 15. 2 as applied by vii. 5. 2 seq.; ÇÇS. vii. 20. 3.

11 RV. x. 74. 6 (already cited in AB. iii. 22); ĀÇS. v. 15. 21; ÇÇS. vii. 20. 5.

12 RV. vi. 46. 9 and 10; ĀÇS. vii. 3. 19; ÇÇS. x. 4. 10.

13 RV. x. 178 (cited above in AB. iv. 20); ĀÇS. vii. 1. 13.

1 RV. iv. 20; ĀÇS. vii. 5. 18; ÇÇS. x. 2. 5.

'That of Savitṛ we choose' and 'To-day for us, O god Savitṛ' are the strophe and antistrophe of the Vaiçvadeva[2]; on the Rathantara day, on the first day, (it is) a symbol of the first day. 'They yoke their mind, they also yoke their thoughts' is (the hymn) to Savitṛ[3]; containing (the word) 'yoke' (it is) on the first day a symbol of the first day. 'Forward sky and earth, increasing holy order, with the sacrifices' is (the hymn) to sky and earth[4]; "forward" on the first day is a symbol of the first day. 'Here, here, in mind is your relationship, O heroes' is (the hymn) to the Ṛbhus[5]; (the words) 'hither' and 'forward' are symbols of the first day; 'if (the word) "forward" had been used throughout, the sacrificers would have gone out forward from this world' (they say). In that on the first day he recites as (hymn) to the Ṛbhus, 'Here, here, in mind is your relationship, O heroes', and 'here, here' is this world, verily thus he makes them remain in this world. 'The gods I invoke of great fame for safety' is (the hymn) to the All-gods[6]; in the first Pada the gods are mentioned; on the first day (this is) a symbol of the first day. A long journey are they about to go who perform the year (session) or the twelve-day (rite). In that he recites as (the hymn) to the All-gods on the first day 'The gods I invoke of great fame for safety', (it serves) to secure safety. Verily thus he secures a safe passage; in safety he attains the other side of the year who knows thus and those for whom one as Hotṛ knowing thus recites on the first day as (the hymn) to the All-gods 'The gods I invoke of great fame for safety'. 'To Vaiçvānara, with broad radiance, bard' is the beginning of the Āgnimāruta;[7] in the first Pada the deity is mentioned; on the first day (this is) a symbol of the first day. 'Forward pressing, mighty, and resounding' is (the hymn) to the Maruts[8]; (the word) 'forward' on the first day is a symbol of the first day. 'To Jātavedas let us pour the Soma', (this verse) to Jātavedas[9] he recites before the hymn. The verses to Jātavedas are a benediction; (verily it serves) to secure safety. Verily thus he secures a safe passage; in safety he attains the other side of the year who knows thus. 'Forward the strong, new, hymn to Agni' is (the hymn) to Jātavedas[10]; (the word) 'forward' on the first day is a symbol of the first day. The Āgnimāruta is the same as in the Agniṣṭoma; through that which is performed the same in the sacrifice, offspring breathe together. Therefore the Āgnimāruta is the same.

[2] RV. v. 82. 1–3 and 4–6; ĀÇS. v. 18. 5; ÇÇS. viii. 3. 3.

[3] RV. v. 8. 1; ĀÇS. vii. 5. 23; ÇÇS. x. 2. 7.

[4] RV. i. 159; ĀÇS. v. 18. 5; ÇÇS. viii. 3. 11.

[5] RV. iii. 60; ĀÇS. vii. 5. 23 (*iti catasraḥ*); ÇÇS. x. 2. 7.

[6] RV. x. 66; ĀÇS. vii. 5. 23.

[7] RV. iii. 3; ĀÇS. v. 20. 6; ÇÇS. viii. 6. 2.

[8] RV. i. 87; ĀÇS. v. 20. 6; ÇÇS. viii. 6. 4.

[9] RV. i. 99. 1; ĀÇS. vii. 1. 14.

[10] RV. i. 143; ĀÇS. v. 20. 6; ÇÇS. viii. 6. 6.

iv. 31 (xx. 3). Indra as deity supports the second day, the Pañcadaça Stoma, the Bṛhat Sāman, the Triṣṭubh metre. With it according to the deity, the Stoma, the Sāman, the metre, he prospers who knows thus. That which has not either 'hither' or 'forward', that which has (the word) 'stand' is a symbol of the second day. That which contains (the word) 'upright', (the word) 'towards', (the word) 'between', (the word) 'strong', (the word) 'grow', (the fact) that in the middle Pada the deity is mentioned, that the atmosphere is referred to, that which is connected with the Bṛhat, that which is connected with the Triṣṭubh, the present tense, these are the symbols of the second day. 'Agni we choose as envoy' in the Ājya [1] of the second day; the present tense on the second day is a symbol of the second day. 'O Vāyu, thy thousands' is the Praüga [2]; as containing (the word) 'grow' on the second day [3] in 'The Soma hath been pressed, O ye that make holy order to grow', it is a symbol of the second day. 'Lord of all men' and 'Indra is the Soma drinker alone' are the strophe and antistrophe of the Marutvatīya [4]; as containing (the words) 'grow' and 'between' on the second day it is a symbol of the second day. 'O Indra, come nearer' is the normal Pragātha [5]; 'Arise up, O Brahmaṇaspati' is that for Brahmaṇaspati [6]; as containing (the word) 'upright' it is on the second day a symbol of the second day. 'Agni, the leader', 'Thou, O Soma, with inspiration', and 'They swell the waters' are the normal inserted verses.[7] 'Sing aloud to Indra' is the Marutvatīya Pragātha [8]; as containing (the word) 'grow' on the second day in 'Wherewith men, making holy order to grow, produced the light', it is a symbol of the second day. 'O Indra, lord of the Soma, drink this Soma' is the hymn [9]; as containing (the word) 'strong' on the second day in [10] 'In unison with the Rudras, show thyself strong,' it is a symbol of the second day. 'Thee we invoke' and 'Do thou come to the worshipper' are the Bṛhat as Pṛṣṭha [11]; on the Bṛhat day, the second day, (it is) a symbol of the second day. 'Since he hath conquered' is the normal inserted verse.[12] 'Both let him hear for us' is the Pragātha of the Sāman;[13] as containing 'What here to-day and what was yesterday' on the Bṛhat day, the second day, (it is)

[1] RV. i. 12; ĀÇS. vii. 10. 3; ÇÇS. x. 3. 2.

[2] RV. ii. 41; ĀÇS. vii. 6. 2; ÇÇS. x. 3. 5.

[3] RV. ii. 41. 4.

[4] RV. viii. 68. 4–6; 2. 4–6. *antar* is in viii. 2. 5; *vṛdh* in 68. 5; ĀÇS. vii. 6. 6; ÇÇS. x. 3. 6.

[5] RV. viii. 53. 5 and 6 (already cited in AB. iv. 29).

[6] RV. i. 48. 1 and 2.

[7] RV. iii. 20. 4; i. 91. 2; i. 64. 6 (already cited in AB. iii. 18); ĀÇS. v. 14. 17.

[8] RV. viii. 98. 1 and 2; ĀÇS. vii. 8. 2; ÇÇS. x. 13. 10.

[9] RV. iii. 32; ĀÇS. vii. 6. 4; ÇÇS. x. 3. 8.

[10] RV. iii. 32. 2.

[11] RV. iv. 46. 1 and 2; viii. 61. 7 and 8; ĀÇS. v. 15. 8; ÇÇS. vii. 20. 4. Probably as shown in iv. 29 (cf. v. 1, 4) by *rathantaram* the reading should be *bṛhat pṛṣṭham* here and elsewhere, not as a compound.

[12] RV. x. 74. 6 (already cited in AB. iii. 22).

[13] RV. viii. 61. 1 and 2; ĀÇS. vii. 8. 18; ÇÇS. vii. 20. 7.

a symbol of the second day. 'This steed, god-strengthened' is the normal Tārkṣya [14] (hymn).

iv. 32 (xx. 4). 'Thy nearest, furthest help' is the hymn;[1] as containing (the word) 'strong' on the second day in 'Slay the strong ones, make them depart', it is a symbol of the second day. 'Let every man of the god that leadeth', 'That desirable of Savitṛ' and 'Lord of all, lord of the good' are the strophe and antistrophe of the Vaiçvadeva [2]; on the Bṛhat day, the second day, they are a symbol of the second day. 'Up the god Savitṛ with the golden' is (the hymn) to Savitṛ [3]; as containing (the word) 'upright' on the second day it is a symbol of the second day. 'They, sky and earth, all weal producing' is (the hymn) to sky and earth [4]; as containing (the word) 'between' on the second day in 'Between the two bowls of high birth he moveth', it is a symbol of the second day. 'They have wrought the car, well rounded, whose skill is known' is (the hymn) to the Ṛbhus [5]; as containing (the word) 'strong' on the second day in 'They have wrought the two bay steeds that draw Indra, with strong wealth', it is a symbol of the second day. 'The charioteer of the sacrifice, the lord of the folk' is (the hymn) to the All-gods;[6] as containing (the word) 'strong' on the second day in 'The strong beacon, the holy one, hath attained the sky' it is a symbol of the second day. This hymn is by Çāryāta. The Añgirases were performing a sacrificial session for the world of heaven; whenever they came to the second day they used to go wrong. Them Çāryāta Mānava made to recite this hymn on the second day; then indeed did they discern the sacrifice, the world of heaven. In that he recites the hymn on the second day, (it serves) to discern the sacrifice, to reveal the world of heaven. 'The might of the swift, strong, ruddy one' is the beginning of the Āgnimāruta [7]; that which contains (the word) 'strong' on the second day is a symbol of the second day. 'To the strong host, the majestic, the wise' is (the hymn) to the Maruts [8]; that which contains (the word) 'strong' on the second day is a symbol of the second day. 'To Jātavedas let us pour the Soma' is the normal verse to Jātavedas.[9] 'With the sacrifice make Jātavedas to grow' is (the hymn) to Jātavedas;[10] that which contains (the word) 'grow' on the second day is a symbol of the second day.

[14] RV. x. 178 (already cited in AB. iv. 20); ĀÇS. vii. 1. 18.

[1] RV. vi. 25; v. 3 is that cited below; ĀÇS. vii. 6. 4; ÇÇS. x. 8. 9.

[2] RV. v. 50. 1 and iii. 62. 10 and 11; v. 82. 7–9; ĀÇS. vii. 6. 6; ÇÇS. x. 3. 11–18.

[3] RV. vi. 71. 1–3; AÇS. vii. 4. 12; ÇÇS. x. 4. 14.

[4] RV. i. 160; AÇS. vii. 4. 12; ÇÇS. x. 8. 14.

[5] RV. i. 111; ĀÇS. v. 18. 5; ÇÇS. viii. 3. 14.

[6] RV. x. 92; ĀÇS. vii. 4. 12; ÇÇS. x. 3. 14. For Çāryāta see *Vedic Index*, ii. 375.

[7] RV. vi. 8; ĀÇS. vii. 4. 18; ÇÇS. x. 3. 15.

[8] RV. i. 64; ĀÇS. vii. 4. 18; ÇÇS. x. 3. 15.

[9] RV. i. 99. 1 (already cited in AB. iv. 30); ĀÇS. vii. 1. 14.

[10] RV. ii. 2; ĀÇS. vii. 4. 18.

PAÑCIKĀ V

The Soma Sacrifice (*continued*).

ADHYĀYA I

The Pṛṣṭhya Ṣaḍaha (*continued*).

The Third and Fourth Days.

v. 1 (xxi. 1). The All-gods as deities support the third day, the Saptadaça Stoma, the Vairupa Sāman, the Jagatī metre. With it according to the deity, the Stoma, the Sāman, the metre, he prospers who knows thus. That which has the same endings is a symbol of the third day; that which contains (the word) 'horse', (the word) 'end', that which is repeated, that which is alliterated; that which contains (the word) 'stay', the word 'surpass', (the word) 'three', that which is a symbol of the end, (the fact) that the deity is mentioned in the last Pada, that yonder world is referred to, that which is connected with the Virūpa, that which is connected with the Jagatī, the past tense, these are the symbols of the third day, 'Yoke thou those best fitted to invoke the gods, thy steeds, O Agni, like a charioteer' is the Ājya [1] of the third day. By the third day the gods went to the world of heaven; the Asuras and the Rakṣases sought to hinder them. They kept prospering (saying) 'Become misshapen, become misshapen'; in that they kept prospering (saying) 'Become misshapen, become misshapen,' the Vairūpa Sāman came into existence; that is why the Vairūpa has its name (misshapen). They followed after them; they were united with them; them, having become horses, they smote away with their hoofs. In that, having become horses, they smote them away with their hoofs, that is why horses have their name. He attains whatever he desires who knows thus. Therefore a horse is the swiftest of animals; therefore a horse strikes backwards with his foot. He smites away evil who knows thus. Therefore this Ājya contains (the word) 'horse'; on the third day it is a symbol of the third day. 'O Vāyu, come for enjoyment', 'O Vāyu, come from the sky, auspicious', 'With Indra Vāyu, of these pressed draughts', 'Indra and

[1] RV. viii. 75. Cf. KB. xxii. 3–5 for the third day. See ĀÇS. vii. 10. 4; ÇÇS. x. 4. 2. The derivation of the Vairūpa is remarkable, but no other version is really possible.

Varuṇa we', 'O Açvins come hither', 'Come to that pressed with the stones', 'In unison with the All-gods', 'Dear for us among the dear' is the Praüga[2] in Uṣṇih verses; that which has similar endings on the third day is a symbol of the third day. 'It for great gain' and 'Three Soma draughts for Indra' are the strophe and antistrophe of the Marutvatīya[3]; that which has alliteration and contains (the word) 'three' on the third day is a symbol of the third day. 'O Indra come hither' is the normal Pragātha[4]. 'Forward now Brahmaṇaspati' is (the Pragātha) to Brahmaṇaspati[5]; as containing an alliteration on the third day it is a symbol of the third day. 'Agni, the leader', 'Thou, O Soma, with inspiration', 'They swell the waters' are the normal inserted verses.[6] 'No one hath surpassed the chariot of Sudās, nor caused it to pause' is the Marutvatīya Pragātha[7]; as containing (the word) 'surpass' at the third pressing, it is a symbol of the third pressing. 'Three friendships hath man's worship' is the hymn[8]: that which contains (the word) 'three' on the third day is a symbol of the third day. 'If a hundred skies, O Indra, were thine' and 'If, O Indra, as many as thou' are the Vairūpa as Pṛṣṭha[9]; on the Rathantara day, the third day, this is a symbol of the third day. 'Since he hath conquered' is the normal inserted verse.[10] In 'Towards thee, O hero, we utter praise' he brings back the basis of the Rathantara,[11] for this day is connected with the Rathantara in its place. 'O Indra, threefold protection' is the Pragātha of the Sāman[12]; as containing (the word) 'three' on the third day it is a symbol of the third day. 'This steed, god-strengthened' is the normal Tārkṣya[13] (hymn).

v. 2 (xxi. 2). 'Who is born first the thinker' is the hymn[1]; that which has the same endings on the third day is a symbol of the third day. It has (the words) 'He, O men'; (the hymn) with (the words) 'He, O men' is the power of Indra; on it being recited power enters Indra. As to this the Sāman singers say 'On the third day those of many verses recite the power of Indra'. It is by Gṛtsamada. By it Gṛtsamada went to the dear abode of Indra; he conquered the highest world; he goes to the dear abode

[2] RV. v. 51. 8 with viii. 26. 28–25; v. 51. 6–8; 72. 1–8; 75. 7–9; 40. 1–8; vii. 34. 15–17; vi. 61. 10–12; ĀÇS. vii. 10. 5; ÇÇS. x. 4. 5.

[3] RV. viii. 68. 7–9; 2. 7–9; ĀÇS. vii. 10. 8; ÇÇS. x. 4. 6.

[4] RV. viii. 58. 5 and 6 (already cited in AB. iv. 29).

[5] RV. i. 40. 5 and 6 (already cited in AB. iv. 29).

[6] RV. iii. 20. 4; i. 91. 2; i. 64. 6 (already cited in AB. iii. 18; iv. 81).

[7] RV. vii. 32. 60. Here is found a form of *ram* which explains *ratavat*; ĀÇS. vii. 8. 2.

[8] RV. v. 29; ĀÇS. vii. 7. 1; ÇÇS. x. 4. 8.

[9] RV. viii. 70. 5 and 6; vii. 32. 18 and 19; ĀÇS. vii. 10. 8.

[10] RV. x. 74. 6 (already cited in AB. iii. 22); AÇS. v. 15. 21; ÇÇS. vii. 20. 5.

[11] RV. vii. 32. 22 and 23; see above AB. iv. 29.

[12] RV. vi. 46. 9 and 10; ĀÇS. vii. 8. 19; ÇÇS. x. 4. 10.

[13] RV. x. 170; ĀÇS. vii. 1. 18.

[1] RV. ii. 12; ĀÇS. vii. 7. 1; ÇÇS. x. 4. 11.

of Indra, he conquers the highest world who knows thus. 'That of Savitṛ we chose' and 'To-day for us, O god Savitṛ' are the strophe and antistrophe of the Vaiçvadeva[2]; on the Rathantara day, on the third day, it is a symbol of the third day. 'That desirable greatness of Savitṛ the god' is (the hymn) to Savitṛ[3]; greatness is the end; the third day is the end; on the third day it is a symbol of the third day. 'With ghee sky and earth enveloped' is (the hymn) to sky and earth[4]; in 'Mixed with ghee, dropping ghee, ghee anointed' there is repetition and alliteration; on the third day this is a symbol of the third day. 'Born without steed, without reins, worthy of praise' is (the hymn) to the Ṛbhus[5]; as containing (the word) 'three' on the third day in 'The chariot of three wheels', it is a symbol of the third day. 'Those who from afar would assume kinship' is (the hymn) to the All-gods[6]; from afar is the end; the third day is the end; on the third day it is a symbol of the end. That is by Gaya; by it Gaya Plāta went to the dear abode of the All-gods; he conquered the highest world; he goes to the dear abode of the All-gods; he conquers the highest world who knows thus. 'To Vaiçvānara, the praise, increasing holy order' is the beginning of the Āgnimāruta[7]; the praise is the end; the third day is the end; on the third day it is a symbol of the end. 'Pouring showers, the Maruts, of daring might' is (the hymn) to the Maruts[8] with much to be recited; what is much is the end; the third day is the end; on the third day it is a symbol of the third day. 'To Jātavedas let us pour the Soma' is the normal (verse) to Jātavedas.[9] 'Thou, O Agni, the first Añgiras, the Ṛṣi' is (the hymn) to Jātavedas[10]; that with the same beginning on the third day is a symbol of the third day. In 'Thou' and 'Thou' he refers to the several sets of three days, for continuity. With sets of three days, uninterrupted and continuous, they proceed who proceed knowing this.[11]

v. 3 (xxi. 3). The Stomas are fully obtained, the metres obtained on the third day; verily this only is left over, namely speech alone.[1] This one element is three syllables; speech is one element, element is three syllables; this is the third set of three days, speech one, Go one, Dyo one. Therefore indeed

[2] RV. v. 82. 1–3 and 4–6; see also AB. iv. 30.
[3] RV. iv. 53. 1–3; ĀÇS. vii. 7. 2.
[4] RV. vi. 70. 4–6; ĀÇS. vii. 7. 2.
[5] RV. iv. 36; ĀÇS vii. 7. 2.
[6] RV. x. 63; ĀÇS. vii. 7. 2.
[7] RV. iii. 3; ĀÇS. vii. 7. 2.
[8] RV. ii. 34; ĀÇS. vii. 7. 2.
[9] RV. i. 99. 1; above AB. iv. 30; ĀÇS. vii. 1. 14.
[10] RV. i. 31; ĀÇS. vii. 7. 2.
[11] *ninṛtta* is clearly the alliteration produced by repetitions of one vowel or consonant; Sāyaṇa shows this in his definition (though he gives another) as *svaraviçeṣāṇām akṣarāṇām* . . . *āvartanena* where *viçeṣa* = especially, not 'with a difference' as Weber (*Ind. Stud.* ix. 285, 286) thinks, a view which does not suit RV. vi. 70.
[1] Cf. ÇB. vi. 3. 1. 43.

speech supports the fourth day. In that on the fourth day they utter the sound *o*[2], they extend this syllable, they make it to grow, they magnify[3] it, to support the fourth day. The sound *o* is food; when the farmers run about shouting, thus does food come into existence; in that on the fourth day they say the sound *o*, verily thus they produce food; (it serves) for the production of food. Therefore the four days contain (the word) 'born'. 'With the first four syllables should he say *o*' they say; cattle are four-footed; (verily it serves) to win cattle. 'With three syllables should he say *o*' they say; there are three threefold worlds; (verily it serves) to conquer these worlds. 'With one syllable should he say *o*' used Lāṅgalāyana Brahman Maudgalya to say; 'Speech has one syllable; he says *o* in truth now who says *o* with one syllable'. With two syllables should he say *o*, for a support; man has two supports, cattle four feet; verily thus he makes the sacrificer with two supports to find support in fourfooted cattle. Therefore should he say *o* with two syllables. At the beginning in the morning litany he says *o*; by the mouth offspring eat food; at the beginning of proper food he places the sacrificer. In the middle in the Ājya Çastra he says *o*; in the middle food quickens offspring; verily thus in the middle of proper food he places the sacrificer. At the beginning[4] in the midday he says *o*; by the mouth offspring eat food; verily thus at the beginning of proper food he places the sacrificer. Thus on both sides he grasps the saying of *o* with the pressings, to grasp proper food.

v. 4 (xxi. 4). Speech as deity supports the fourth day, the Ekaviṅça Stoma, the Vairāja Sāman, the Anuṣṭubh metre. With it according to the deity, the Stoma, the Sāman, the metre he prospers who knows thus. That which has 'hither' and 'forward' is a symbol of the fourth day, for the fourth day is the first day over again. That which contains (the word) 'yoke', (the word) 'chariot', (the word) 'swift', (the word) 'drink', (the fact) that the deity is mentioned in the first Pada, that this world is referred to, that which contains (the word) 'born', (the word) 'call', (the word) 'bright', that which is the symbol of speech, that which is by Vimada, that which is sounded, that which has various metres, that which is deficient, redundant, that which is connected with the Vairāja, that which is connected with the

[2] The Nyūṅkha is dealt with at length in ĀÇS. vii. 11. It is in the morning litany to take place at the second syllable of each halfverse and consists in altering the vowel of that syllable to *o 3 ooooo o 3 ooooo o3 ooo*, with accents on the three protracted *o* sounds. In the Ājya it is used in the third Padas, save in the last verse, ĀÇS. vii. 11. 8.

[3] The monstrous *pravibhāvayiṣanti* was read by Sāyaṇa whose explanation is *prabhūtvaṁ vibhūtvaṁ vākparasya kartum ichanti*, and it is kept in the Ānand. ed.

[4] See ĀÇS. vii. 11. 28. The Nyūṅkha is appropriate to the fourth day. Cf. KB. xxii. 7.

Anuṣṭubh, the future, that which is a symbol of the first day; these are the symbols of the fourth day. 'With offerings for ourselves Agni'[1] is the Ājya of the fourth day; it is by Vimada and is sounded[2]; being of the seer who is sounded, on the fourth day it is a symbol of the fourth day. It is of eight verses in Paṅkti; the sacrifice is fivefold, cattle are fivefold; (verily it serves) to win cattle. These are ten Jagatī verses; this set of three days has the Jagatī at the morning pressing; thereby is there a symbol of the fourth day. They are fifteen Anuṣṭubhs, for the day is connected with the Anuṣṭubh; thereby is there a symbol of the fourth day. They are twenty Gāyatrī verses, for this day is a repeated introduction; thereby is there a symbol of the fourth day. This hymn, unsung, unrecited, unexhausted, is the sacrifice made manifest. In that this is the Ājya of the fourth day, verily thus from the sacrifice they extend the sacrifice; verily thus they revert again to speech for continuity. With sets of three days, uninterrupted and continuous, they proceed who proceed knowing thus, 'O Vāyu, for thee the pure hath been prepared', 'Enjoy the fresh offerings', 'O Vāyu, a hundred bay steeds', 'With Indra, O Vāyu, of these pressed draughts', 'O wise one, those of good insight', 'Hither to us with all aids'. 'This for you I have sent forth', 'Away the wicked foe', and 'O best of mothers, O chief of streams', are the Praüga[3] in Anuṣṭubhs; (the words) 'hither', 'forward', and 'pure' on the fourth day are symbols of the fourth day. 'Thee with the sacrifices we invoke' is the beginning[4] of the Marutvatīya; as regards 'we invoke', this day is to be secured as it were; thereby is there a symbol of the fourth day. 'This Soma juice hath been pressed, O bright one', 'O Indra, come nearer', 'Let Brahmaṇaspati move forward' 'Agni the leader' 'Thou, O Soma, with inspiration' 'They swell the waters', 'Forward to Indra, the great' are the continuation[5] (of the Marutvatīya) being the same as that of the first day; on the fourth day this is a symbol of the fourth day. 'Hear our call, O Indra, harm us not' is the hymn[6]; as containing (the word) 'call' on the fourth day, it is a symbol of the fourth day. 'Indra with the Maruts, the bull, for joy' is the

[1] RV. x. 21; ĀÇS. vii. 11. 14, 17; ÇÇS. x. 5. 2. For this day see KB. xxii. 6–9.

[2] Doubtful in sense: Sāyaṇa connects, but no doubt wrongly, with the Nyūṅkha, which is indeed used in both x. 21 and 22 (see below AB. v. 5), but also in the morning litany, which is not by the sage Vimada. Possibly the reference is to the fact that both hymns begin with rough sounds (*suvṛktibhiḥ* and *kuha çruta indraḥ*). Weber (*Ind. Stud.* ix. 286) renders 'the seer distinguished by (Wohl-) Klang', comparing *viribhita* in comm. on Pāṇ. vii. 2. 18. Haug's view is 'contained in an alliteration in it (*vi vo made*)'.

[3] RV. iv. 47. 1; 48. 1, 5; 47. 2–4; v. 66. 1–3; vii. 24. 4–6; vi. 44. 4–6; 51. 13–15; ii. 41. 1–3; ĀÇS. vii. 11. 22; ÇÇS. x. 5. 4.

[4] RV. viii. 68. 10–12; ĀÇS. vii. 11. 24; ÇÇS. x. 5. 6.

[5] RV. viii. 2. 1–3; 53. 5, 6; i. 40. 3, 4; iii. 20. 4; i. 91. 2; 64. 6; viii. 39. 3; ĀÇS. vii. 2. 24; ÇÇS. x. 5. 6, 7; above AB. iv. 29.

[6] RV. ii. 11; ĀÇS. vii. 11. 25; ÇÇS. x. 5. 8.

hymn[7]; as containing (the word) 'call' in[8] 'Dread, giver of strength, let us call him' on the fourth day, it is a symbol of the fourth day. This is in Triṣṭubh. With this (hymn), with its feet supported, he maintains the pressing; verily thereby it leaves not its place. 'Him the cunning I call' is the conclusion[9]; as containing (the word) call on the fourth day it is a symbol of the fourth day. These are Gāyatrī verses; the Gāyatrī support the midday (pressing) of this set of three days; that metre is a support in which a Nivid is inserted; therefore in the Gāyatrī verses he inserts a Nivid, 'Drink the Soma, O Indra, let it gladden thee' and 'Hear the call of the much drinking stone' are the Vairāja as Pṛṣṭha[10]; on the Bṛhat day, the fourth day, it is a symbol of the fourth day. 'What he hath conquered' is the normal inserted verse[11]. In 'Thee we invoke' he makes to follow the basis[12] of the Bṛhat, for the day is connected with the Bṛhat in place. 'Thou, O Indra, in the conflicts' is the Pragātha of the Sāman[13]; as containing (the word) 'born' in 'slaying imprecation, cause of birth' on the fourth day, it is a symbol of the fourth day. 'This steed, god-strengthened' is the normal Tārkṣya[14] (hymn).

v. 5 (xxi. 5). 'Where is Indra famed, in what to-day?' is the hymn[1] by Vimada, which is sounded; being of the seer who is sounded, on the fourth day it is a symbol of the fourth day. 'Of thee the roarer, the bull self-ruling' is the hymn[2]; as containing (the word) 'born' on the fourth day in 'Dread, deep, by birth, to the dread' it is a symbol of the fourth day. It is a Triṣṭubh; with it with its feet supported he maintains the pressing;[3] thereby it leaves not its place. 'Him of you ever enduring' is the conclusion. 'Secured in all speech' (he says); this day is to be secured as it were; thereby is there a symbol of the fourth day. They are Gāyatrī verses; the Gāyatrī verses support the midday (pressing) of this set of three days: that metre is a support in which a Nivid is inserted; therefore in the Gāyatrī verses, he inserts a Nivid. 'Let each man of the god that leadeth'; 'That desirable of Savitṛ', and 'God of all, lord of the good' are the strophe and antistrophe of the Vaiçvadeva[4]; on the Bṛhat day, the fourth day, it is a symbol of the fourth day. 'Let the god, Savitṛ, with fair jewels come hither' is (the hymn) to Savitṛ[5]; (the word) 'hither' on the fourth day is a symbol of the fourth day. 'Forward the sky and earth

[7] RV. iii. 47; ĀÇS. vii. 11. 25; ÇÇS. x. 5. 8.

[8] RV. iii. 47. 5.

[9] RV. viii. 76. 18; ĀÇS. viii. 8. 2; ÇÇS. x. 5. 8.

[10] RV. vii. 22. 1–3 and 4–6; ĀÇS. vii. 11. 27; ÇÇS. x. 5. 9.

[11] RV. x. 74. 6; see above AB. iv. 29.

[12] RV. vi. 46. 1 and 2; see AB. iv. 31.

[13] RV. viii. 99. 5; ĀÇS. vii. 8. 19.

[14] RV. x. 178; ĀÇS. vii. 1. 18.

[1] RV. x. 22; ĀÇS. vii. 11. 28; ÇÇS. x. 5. 20.

[2] RV. iii. 46; ĀÇS. vii. 11. 28; ÇÇS. x. 5. 20.

[3] RV. viii. 92. 7–9; ĀÇS. viii. 8. 2; ÇÇS. x. 5. 20.

[4] RV. v. 50. 1; iii. 62. 10, 11; v. 82. 7–9; see above AB. iv. 32.

[5] RV. vii. 45; ĀÇS. viii. 8. 4; ÇÇS. x. 5. 23.

with sacrifices, with homage' is (the hymn) to sky and earth[6]; (the word) 'forward' on the fourth day is a symbol of the fourth day. 'Forward to the Ṛbhus like a messenger shall I speed my speech' is (the hymn) to the Ṛbhus[7]; (the words) 'forward' and 'Shall I speed my speech' are symbols of the fourth day. 'Forward the pure, the divine, hymn' is (the hymn) to the All-gods[8]; (the words) 'forward' and 'pure' on the fourth day are symbols of the fourth day. These are in varied metres, there are verses of two Padas, there are verses of four Padas; thereby is there a symbol of the fourth day. 'Let us enjoy the loving kindness of Vaiçvānara' is the beginning of the Āgnimāruta[9]; as containing (the word) 'born' in 'Born hence' on the fourth day it is a symbol of the fourth day. 'Who are these heroes revealed, of one home?' is (the hymn) to the Maruts[10]; as containing (the word) 'birth' in 'No man knoweth their place of birth', on the fourth day it is a symbol of the fourth day. These are in varied metres; there are verses of two Padas, there are verses of four Padas; thereby is there a symbol of the fourth day. 'To Jātavedas let us pour the Soma' is the normal (verse) to Jātavedas[11]. 'Agni men with devotion from the fire sticks' is (the hymn) to Jātavedas[12]; as containing (the word) 'born' in 'By movements of the hands have made to be born' on the fourth day it is a symbol of the fourth day. These are in different metres; there are Virāj verses, there are Triṣṭubh verses; thereby is there a symbol of the fourth day.

ADHYĀYA II

The Pṛṣṭhya Ṣaḍaha (continued).

The Fifth and Sixth Days.

v. 6 (xxii. 1). The cow as deity supports the fifth day, the Triṇava Stoma, the Çākvara Sāman, the Pañkti metre. With it according to the deity, the Stoma, the Sāman, the metre, he prospers who knows thus. That which has not (the words) 'hither' and 'forward', that which has (the word) 'stand', is a symbol of the fifth day, for the fifth day is a repetition of the second day. That which contains (the word) 'upright', (the word) 'to', (the word) 'between', (the word) 'strong', (the word) 'grow', (the fact) that the deity is mentioned in the middle Pada, (the fact) that the atmosphere is referred to, that which contains (the word), 'milk', (the word)

[6] RV. vii. 53; ĀÇS. viii. 8. 4; ÇÇS. x. 5. 23.

[7] RV. iv. 33; ĀÇS. viii. 8. 4; ÇÇS. x. 5. 23.

[8] RV. vii. 34; ĀÇS. viii. 8. 4; ÇÇS. x. 5. 23.

[9] RV. i. 98: ĀÇS. viii. 8. 4; ÇÇS. differs.

[10] RV. vii. 56; ĀÇS. viii, 8. 4; ÇÇS. x. 5. 24.

[11] RV. i. 99. 1; ĀÇS. vii. 1. 14.

[12] RV. vii. 1; ĀÇS. viii. 8. 4; ÇÇS. differs.

'udder', (the word) 'cow', (the word) 'dappled', (the word) 'be drunk', that which is a symbol of cattle, that which has an addition,—for cattle are as it were of varied size—that which is connected with the Jagatī—for cattle are connected with the Jagatī—, that which is connected with the Bṛhat—for cattle are connected with the Bṛhat—, that which is connected with the Pañkti—for cattle are connected with the number five—, that which is desirable—for cattle are desirable, that which contains (the word) 'oblation'—for cattle are the oblation—, that which contains (the word) 'form'—for cattle are form—, that which is connected with the Çākvara, that which is connected with the Pañkti, the present tense, that which is a symbol of the second day; these are symbols of the fifth day. 'This guest of yours waking at dawn' is the Ājya[1] of the fifth day; it is in Jagatī, contains an addition, is a symbol of cattle and so on the fifth day it is a symbol of the fifth day. 'Hither to us the sacrifice, touching the sky', 'Hither to us, O Vāyu, to the great rite', 'With the chariot of broad radiance', 'The many, sun-eyed', 'These morning offerings you', 'Drink the pressed draught, rich in sap', 'Each god for grace', and 'A great speech dost thou sing' are the Praüga[2] in Bṛhatī; on the fifth day it is a symbol of the fifth day. 'When with the folk of the five peoples' is the beginning of the Marutvatīya[3]; (the word) 'of the five peoples' on the fifth day is a symbol of the fifth day. 'Indra is the Soma drinker alone', 'O Indra, come near', 'Rise up, O Brahmaṇaspati, 'Agni the leader', 'Thou, O Soma, with inspiration', 'They swell the waters', and 'Sing aloud to Indra' are the continuation[4], being the same as that of the second day; on the fifth day it is a symbol of the fifth day. 'Thou art the helper of him who presseth, who plucketh the grass' is the hymn[5]; as containing (the word) 'be drunk', and being in the Pañkti metre, and of five Padas, on the fifth day, it is a symbol of the fifth day. 'Thus in the Soma, in the drink' is the hymn[6]; as containing (the word) 'be drunk' and being in the Pañkti metre and of five Padas, on the fifth day it is a symbol of the fifth day. 'O Indra, drink; for thee is it pressed to be drunk' is the hymn[7], containing (the word) 'be drunk' and in the Triṣṭubh metre; with it with its feet supported he maintains the pressing; thereby it departs not from its abode. 'O Indra with the Maruts, O bounteous one' is the conclusion[8]. It has neither (the word) 'hither' nor

[1] RV. vi. 15; ĀÇS. vii. 12. 6; ÇÇS. x. 6. 2. Cf. KB. xxiii. 1.

[2] RV. viii. 101. 9, 10; 46. 25; iv. 46. 5, 6, 7; vii. 66. 10–12; 74. 1–3; viii. 3. 1–3; 27. 13–15; vii. 96. 1–3; ĀÇS. vii. 12. 7; ÇÇS. x. 6. 6.

[3] RV. viii. 63. 7; ĀÇS. vii. 12. 9; ÇÇS. x. 6. 8.

[4] RV. viii. 2. 4; 53. 5; i. 40. 1; iii. 20. 1; i. 91. 2; 64. 6; viii. 89. 1; ĀÇS. vii. 12. 9; AB. iv. 29; ÇÇS. x. 6. 9 differs.

[5] RV. viii. 86; ĀÇS. vii. 12. 9; ÇÇS. x. 6. 9.

[6] RV. i. 80; ĀÇS. vii. 12. 9; ÇÇS. x. 6. 9.

[7] RV. vi. 40; ĀÇS. vii. 12. 9; ÇÇS. differs.

[8] RV. viii. 76. 7–9; ĀÇS. viii. 3. 2; ÇÇS. x. 3. 6.

(the word) 'forward'; on the fifth day it is a symbol of the fifth day. They are Gāyatrī verses; Gāyatrī verses support the midday (pressing) of this set of three days; that metre is a support in which a Nivid is inserted; therefore in the Gāyatrī verses he inserts a Nivid.

v. 7 (xxii. 2). Here they chant the Mahānāmnī verses[1] to the Çākvara Sāman; on the Rathantara day, the fifth day, it is a symbol of the fifth day. By them Indra fashioned himself as great; therefore are they called Mahānāmnīs; moreover these worlds are the Mahānāmnīs and these are great. Having created these worlds Prajāpati had all power whatever there is here. In that having created these worlds Prajāpati had all power whatever there is here, therefore they become the Çakvarī verses; that is why the Çakvarīs have the name (powerful). Beyond the boundary he created them; so that he created them beyond the boundary, they became the Simās; that is why the Simās have their name. 'Of the sweet thus diffused', 'To our pressed drink with the dappled steeds', and 'Indra all made grow' are the antistrophe[2]; as containing (the words) 'strong', 'dappled' 'be drunk' and 'grow' on the fifth day it is a symbol of the fifth day. 'What he hath won' is the normal inserted verse[3]. In 'Towards thee, O hero, we utter praise' he makes to follow the basis[4] of the Rathantara; for this day is connected with the Rathantara in place. 'Not then any of thy worshippers' is the Pragātha of the Sāman;[5] as having an addition it is on the fifth day a symbol of the fifth day. 'This steed, god strengthened' is the normal Tārkṣya[6] (hymn).

v. 8 (xxii. 3). 'Thou hast furthered our prayer in the overcoming of Vṛtra' is the hymn[1]; as being in the Pañkti metre and having five Padas on the fifth day it is a symbol of the fifth day. 'Indra hath waxed for the drink' is the hymn[2]; as containing (the word) 'be drunk' and as being in the Pañkti metre and having five Padas on the fifth day it is a symbol of the fifth day. 'Ever for all men are thy drinkings' is the hymn,[3] containing (the word) 'be drunk' and in Triṣṭubh metre; with it with its feet supported he maintains the pressing; thereby it departs not from its place. 'Him Indra we strengthen' is the conclusion[4]; as being a symbol of cattle in 'May he become a strong bull' on the fifth day it is a symbol of the fifth day.

[1] Cp. above AB. iv. 4; KB. xxiii. 2. The mode of using the verses in the case of the Pṛṣṭha Stotra being in the Çākvara is given in ĀÇS. vii. 12. 10–14; ÇÇS. x. 6. 10–13.

[2] RV. i. 84. 10; viii. 93. 31; i. 111. 1; ĀÇS. vii. 12. 15. ÇÇS. differs here and in the rest.

[3] RV. x. 74. 6; see AB. iv. 29.

[4] RV. vii. 32. 22, 23; see AB. iv. 29.

[5] RV. vii. 32. 1 and 2; ĀÇS. vii. 3. 19.

[6] RV. x. 178; ĀÇS. vii. 1. 13.

[1] v. 8. RV. viii. 37; ĀÇS. vii. 12. 16. Cf. KB. xxiii. 3.

[2] RV. i. 8. 1; ĀÇS. vii. 12. 16.

[3] RV. vi. 36. 1; ĀÇS. vii. 12. 16.

[4] RV. viii. 93. 7–9; ĀÇS. viii. 8. 2; ÇÇS. x. 6. 16.

These are Gāyatrī verses; Gāyatrī verses support the midday (pressing) of this set of three days; that metre is a support in which a Nivid is inserted; therefore he inserts a Nivid in the Gāyatrī verses. 'That of Savitṛ we choose,' and 'To-day for us, O god Savitṛ' are the strophe and antistrophe [5] of the Vaiçvadeva; on the Rathantara day, the fifth day, it is a symbol of the fifth day. 'Up the god Savitṛ of the home' is (the hymn) to Savitṛ[6]; in 'May he instigate much that is desirable to the generous one' the desirable is a symbol of cattle; on the fifth day it is a symbol of the fifth day. 'The great ones, sky and earth, here the oldest' is (the hymn) to sky and earth[7]; in 'Roaring, the bull' there is a symbol of cattle; on the fifth day it is a symbol of the fifth day. 'To us Ṛbhus, Vibhvan, Vāja, Indra' is (the hymn) to the Ṛbhus[8]; cattle are Vāja (strength); as being a symbol of cattle on the fifth day it is a symbol of the fifth day. 'I praise the man, of good vows, with a new song' is (the hymn) to the All-gods[9]; as having an addition and being a symbol of cattle on the fifth day it is a symbol of the fifth day. 'The swelling oblation, unaging, in the finding of light' is the beginning of the Āgnimāruta[10]; as containing (the word) 'oblation' on the fifth day it is a symbol of the fifth day. 'Even to the wise let it be a wondrous thing' is (the hymn) to the Maruts[11]; as containing (the word) 'wonder' on the fifth day it is a symbol of the fifth day. 'To Jātavedas let us pour the Soma' is the normal (verse) to Jātavedas.[12] 'Agni is the Hotṛ, the householder, the king' is (the hymn) to Jātavedas[13]; as containing an addition and being a symbol of cattle on the fifth day, it is a symbol of the fifth day.

v. 9 (xxii. 4). The sixth day is a field of the gods; those who approach the sixth day approach a field of the gods. 'The gods dwell not in one another's houses, nor a season in the house of a season' they say. Therefore in due order the priests perform the sacrifice to the seasons, not handing them over (to others). Thus they arrange in order the seasons according to the season, and place in order communities.[1] They say 'No directions should be given with the Ṛtupraiṣas, nor should the *vaṣaṭ* call be said with the Ṛtupraiṣas. The Ṛtupraiṣas are speech; on the sixth day speech is made up.' If they

[5] RV. v. 82. 1–3 and 4–6; see AB. iv. 30.

[6] RV. vi. 71. 4–6; ĀÇS. viii. 8. 6; ÇÇS. x. 6. 18.

[7] RV. iv. 56. 1–4; ĀÇS. viii. 8. 6; ÇÇS. x. 6. 18.

[8] RV. iv. 34; ĀÇS. viii. 8. 6; ÇÇS. x. 6. 18.

[9] RV. vi. 49 (v. 8 is specially referred to); ĀÇS. viii. 8, 6; ÇÇS. x. 6. 18 differs.

[10] RV. x. 88; ĀÇS. viii. 8. 6; ÇÇS. x. 6. 19.

[11] RV. vi. 66; ĀÇS. viii. 8. 6; ÇÇS. x. 6. 19.

[12] RV. i. 99. 1; ĀÇS. vii. 1. 14.

[13] RV. vi. 15. 13–15; ĀÇS. viii. 8. 6; ÇÇS. x. 6. 19.

[1] The point is that in this case the Adhvaryu and the Yajamāna repeat their own Yājyās and do not leave that function to the Hotṛ as in the normal sacrifice to the seasons. GB. xi. 10 and 11 follow AB. v. 9–12. 4.

were to give directions with the Ṛtupraiṣas, if they were to say *vaṣaṭ* with the Ṛtupraiṣas, verily thus they would go to speech when made up, weary, with galled shoulders, groaning under the yoke. But if they were not to give directions with them, if they were not to say *vaṣaṭ* with them, they would depart from the norm of the sacrifice, from the sacrifice, from breath, from Prajāpati, from cattle they would go away. Therefore directions should be given only after that which contains a Ṛc, and the *vaṣaṭ* call said only after that which contains a Ṛc; then they do not go to speech when made up, weary, with galled shoulders, groaning under the yoke, nor do they depart from the norm of the sacrifice, nor from the sacrifice, breath, Prajāpati, cattle do they go away.[2]

v. 10 (xxii. 5). In the first two pressings he inserts (verses) by Parucchepa[1] before the offering verses for the Prasthita libations; the metre of the Parucchepa (verses) is the mounting; by it Indra mounted the seven worlds of heaven; he mounts the seven worlds of heaven, who knows thus. They say 'Seeing that (verses) of five Padas are a symbol of the fifth day, and (verses) of six Padas of the sixth, then why are (verses) of seven Padas recited on the sixth day?' By six Padas they make up the sixth day, cutting off as it were the seventh day; that they keep grasping by the seventh Pada. Verily thus they approach speech again, for continuity. With sets of three days, uninterrupted and continuous, they proceed who proceed knowing thus.

v. 11 (xxii. 6). The gods and the Asuras were in conflict over these worlds. The gods by the sixth day repelled the Asuras from these worlds; taking all the wealth that was within reach, they cast[1] it into the sea. Following up they rescued by this metre the wealth within reach; in that this Pada is a repeated Pada, it is a hook to fasten on. He secures the wealth of him who hates him, he repels him from all these worlds who knows thus.

v. 12 (xxii. 7). The sky as deity supports the sixth day, the Trayastriṅça Stoma, the Raivata Sāman, the Atichandas metre. With it according to the deity, the Stoma, the Sāman, the metre, he prospers who knows thus. That which has the same endings is a symbol of the sixth day, for the sixth day is a repetition of the third day. That which contains (the word)

[2] Here the point is that the normal rule of Praiṣa and Yājyā in Praiṣa form with *vaṣaṭ* call is to be observed, subject to the concluding of either with a Ṛc, the verses being given by Sāyaṇa as RV. ii. 36 and 37. See ĀÇS. viii. 1. 6–8 who prescribes *hotā yakṣat* + Praiṣa + Ṛc + *hotar yaja* for the Praiṣa and *ye yajāmahe* + yājyā + Ṛc + *vauṣaṭ* for the Yājyā. Cf. ÇÇS. x. 7. 8. *ṛgma* must be interpreted in the light of ĀÇS. and not as 'beginning with a Ṛc.'

[1] For them see ĀÇS. viii. 2. 2 and 4. The verses are RV. i. 139. 1–11; 130. 2–10. Cf. KB. xxiii. 4 and 5; ÇÇS. x. 7. 2. See also *Vait.* xxxi. 27; GB. xi. 10.

[1] v. 11. The passive *praupyanta* is an odd use, which, however, can hardly reasonably be corrected.

'horse', (the word) 'end', that which is repeated, that which is alliterated, that which contains (the word) 'stay', that which contains (the word) 'surround', that which contains (the word) 'three', that which is a symbol of the end, (the fact) that the deity is mentioned in the last Pada, (the fact) that yonder world is referred to, that which is connected with Parucchepa, that which has seven Padas, the Nārāçaṅsa, the Nābhānediṣṭha, the Raivata, the Atichandas metre, the past tense, that which is a symbol of the third day; these are the symbols of the sixth day. 'He is born in the ordinance of Manu' is the Ājya[1] of the sixth day; as being by Parucchepa, in Atichandas metre, and of seven Padas, on the sixth day it is a symbol of the sixth day. 'Come to our strewn grass for enjoyment,' 'Let the chariot with the steeds bear you hither for aid,' 'We have pressed with the stones; O come ye'; 'You pious men with praises, O Açvins,' 'Thou hast revealed the mighty, O Indra,' 'O strong Indra,' 'Be it so; let it be heard,' 'Hearken to us, O Agni; thou art praised,' 'The eleven gods in the sky,' and 'She gave the impetuous one, canceller of debts' are the Praüga[2]; as being by Parucchepa, in Atichandas metre, and of seven Padas, on the sixth day it is a symbol of the sixth day. 'He first of the great' is the beginning of the Marutvatīya[3]; the great is the end; the sixth day is the end; on the sixth day it is a symbol of the sixth day. 'Three Soma draughts for Indra,' 'O Indra, come near,' 'Forward now Brahmaṇaspati,' 'Agni the leader,' 'Thou, O Soma, with inspiration,' 'They swell the waters,' 'No one the chariot of Sudās' are the continuation[4], being the same as that of the third day; on the sixth day it is a symbol of the sixth day. 'The chariot which thou, O Indra, for the winning of the offering' is the hymn[5]; as being by Parucchepa, in Atichandas metre, and of seven Padas, on the sixth day it is a symbol of the sixth day. 'The strong with the strong in one dwelling' is (the hymn[6]); as having the same endings on the sixth day it is a symbol of the sixth day. 'O Indra with the Maruts here drink the Soma' is the hymn[7]; 'With them let him drink, the destroyer of Vṛtra' (he says); the destroyer is the end; the sixth day is the end; on the sixth day it is a symbol of the sixth day. It is in

[1] RV. i. 128. Cf. KB. xxiii. 6; ĀÇS. viii. 1. 9; ÇÇS. x. 8. 1.

[2] RV. i. 135. 1–3; 4–6; 135. 4–6; 137. 1–3; 139. 4–6; 133. 6, 7; 139. 6, 1, 7, 11; vi. 61. 1–3; ĀÇS. viii. 1. 12.

[3] RV. viii. 63. 1–3: Sāyaṇa says that the argument is either that *mahānām* ends the Pada or that a great thing has nothing after it. Haug suggests that *mahāntam* as the strong base is the explanation; but this is needless.

[4] RV. viii. 2. 7–9; 53. 5 and 6; i. 40. 5 and 6; iii. 20. 4; i. 91. 2; 64. 6; viii. 32. 10; ĀÇS. viii. 1. 14; see AB. v. 1.

[5] RV. i. 127; ĀÇS. viii. 1. 14.

[6] RV. i. 100: the refrain is *Marutvān no bhavatu Indra ūtī*; ĀÇS. viii. 1. 14.

[7] RV. iii. 51. 7: v. 9 contains the citation. It is noteworthy that this is not a hymn in the *Saṁhitā*, but begins at iii. 51. 7. ĀÇS. viii. 1. 14 calls it *tisraḥ*; ÇÇS. x. 5. 8 a *tṛca*. This use of *sūkta* is not rare.

Triṣṭubh; with it with feet supported he maintains the pressing; thereby it departs not from its place. 'This is he by whom this' is the conclusion[8]; 'sky was won with the Maruts' aid' (he says); won is the end; the sixth day is the end; on the sixth day it is a symbol of the end. These are Gāyatrī verses; Gāyatrī verses support the midday (pressing) of this set of three days; that metre is a support, in which a Nivid is inserted; therefore he inserts a Nivid in the Gāyatrī verses. 'Rich be ours in joint carouse' and 'Rich the praise of the rich' are the Raivata as Pṛṣṭha[9]; on the Bṛhat day, the sixth day, it is a symbol of the sixth day. 'What he hath won' is the normal inserted verse.[10] In 'Thee we invoke' he makes to follow the basis[11] of the Bṛhat, for this day is connected with the Bṛhat in place. 'Indra for divine service' is the Pragātha[12] of the Sāman; as containing alliteration on the sixth day it is a symbol of the sixth day. 'This steed, god strengthened' is the normal Tārkṣya[13] (hymn).

v. 13 (xxii. 8). 'O Indra, come to us from afar' is the hymn[1]; as being by Parucchepa, in the Atichandas metre, and of seven Padas, on the sixth day it is a symbol of the sixth day. 'The greatnesses of the great one' is the hymn[2]; as having the same endings on the sixth day it is a symbol of the sixth day. 'Thou hast become the one lord of wealth' is the hymn[3]; 'Stand on thy dread chariot, O thou of impetuous manhood' (he says); standing is the end; the sixth day is the end; on the sixth day it is a symbol of the end. It is in Triṣṭubh; with it with feet supported he maintains the pressing; thereby it departs not from its place. 'To our pressed drank with the steeds' is the conclusion[4]; as having the same endings on the sixth day it is a symbol of the sixth day. These are Gāyatrī verses; Gāyatrī verses support the midday (pressing) of this set of three days; that metre is a support in which a Nivid is inserted; therefore he inserts a Nivid in the Gāyatrī verses. 'To the god Savitṛ in the bowls' is the beginning of the Vaiçvadeva[5]; as being in the Atichandas metre, on the sixth day it is a symbol of the sixth day. 'That desirable of Savitṛ' (he says[6]); 'The evening hath come' is the antistrophe[7]; what has gone is the end; the sixth day is the end; on the sixth day it is a symbol of the

[8] RV. x. 65. 4–6; ĀÇS. viii. 8. 2; ÇÇS. x. 6. 9.

[9] RV. i. 30. 13–15; viii. 2. 13–15; ĀÇS. viii. 1. 16.

[10] RV. x. 74. 6; see AB. iv. 29.

[11] RV. vi. 46. 1 and 2; see AB. iv. 31.

[12] RV. viii. 3. 5 and 6; ĀÇS. vii. 3. 19; ÇÇS. x. 5. 18 (fourth day: here, x. 8. 8, it differs).

[13] RV. x. 178; ĀÇS. vii. 1. 18.

[1] RV. i. 130; ĀÇS. viii. 1. 17; ÇÇS. x. 8. 9. *Cf.* KB. xxiii. 7. 8.

[2] RV. ii. 15; ĀÇS. viii. 1. 17; ÇÇS. x. 8. 9.

[3] RV. vi. 31. v. 5 is referred to; ĀÇS. viii. 1. 17; ÇÇS. x. 6. 16 (6th day: here it differs).

[4] RV. viii. 93. 31–33; ĀÇS. viii. 8. 2; ÇÇS. x. 8. 9.

[5] See above AB. i. 19; ĀÇS. viii. 1. 18.

[6] RV. iii. 62. 10 and 11; these form the strophe with the preceding verse; see ĀÇS. viii. 1. 18; cf. ÇÇS. x. 8. 11–13.

[7] Cited in ĀÇS. viii. 1. 18.

end. 'Up the god Savitṛ for instigation' is (the hymn) to Savitṛ[8]; 'Forever he hath stood, the bearer intent on his work' (he says); standing is the end; the sixth day is the end; on the sixth day it is a symbol of the sixth day. 'Which is the first, which is the latter of these two?' is (a hymn) to sky and earth[9]; as having the same endings on the sixth day it is a symbol of the sixth day. 'Why hath the best, why hath the youngest come to us?' and 'To our sacrifice, O Vājas, O Ṛbhukṣans' are (a hymn[10]) to the Ṛbhus and one connected with Narāçaṅsa; as having (the word) 'three' on the sixth day it is a symbol of the sixth day. 'This dread thing he of glad speech' and 'Those who through the sacrifice are endowed with the fee' are the Vaiçvadeva.[11]

v. 14 (xxii. 9). He recites the Nābhānediṣṭha[1]; Nābhānediṣṭha Mānava when he was performing his studentship, his brothers deprived of any share (in his father's property). Having returned he said to them 'What have you allotted to me?' 'This judgement giver, the decider' they replied. Therefore now here the sons call the father 'The judgement giver, the decider.' He having gone to his father said 'O father, they have allotted thee to me.' To him said his father, 'Do not care for that, O my boy. These Aṅgirases are performing a sacrificial session for the world of heaven; they fall into confusion whenever they reach the sixth day; make them recite these two hymns on the sixth day; when they go to the world of heaven they will bestow on thee the thousand which is the gift at the session.' 'Be it so' (he said); he went to them (saying) 'Accept the Mānava, O wise ones[2]'. They replied to him, 'What dost thou desire when thou sayest this?' 'Let me reveal to you the sixth day,' he replied, 'And when ye go to the heaven, do you give me the thousand which is the gift at the session.' 'Be it so' (they said). Them he made to recite these two hymns on the sixth day; then indeed did they discern the sacrifice, the world of heaven. In that he recites these two hymns on the sixth day, (it is) to discern the sacrifice, to reveal the world of heaven. To him as they went to heaven they said 'This thousand is for thee, O Brahman.' As he was gathering it together, a man in black garments, coming from the north, said to him 'Mine is this; mine is what is left on the place (of sacrifice).' He said 'To me have they given it.' He replied 'Then let us question thy father.' He went to his father, to him his father said 'Did not

[8] RV. ii. 38; ĀÇS. viii. 8. 18; ÇÇS. x. 8. 14.

[9] RV. i. 185; ÇÇS. x. 8. 14; ĀÇS. vii. 7. 8.

[10] RV. i. 161. 1–13; iv. 37. 1–4; see ĀÇS. viii. 8. 6; ÇÇS. x. 1. 14; *nārāçaṅsam* in Sāyaṇa's view means 'in which heroes are praised', but cf. ZDMG. liv. 49–57.

[11] RV. x. 61 and 62. See AB. v. 14.

[1] Cf. TS. iii. i. 9. 4. The two hymns RV. x. 61 and 62 are the Nābhānediṣṭha. Cf. below AB. vi. 27; ĀÇS. viii. 1. 20–24; ÇÇS. x. 8. 14.

[2] This is taken verbally from RV. x. 62, not as suggested by Geldner *vice versa*; see Oldenberg, *Ṛgveda-Noten*, ii. 269, whose reconstruction of the legend is given, ibid. ii. 261, 262.

they give it to thee, O son?' 'They did give it,' he replied, 'but a man in black garments came from the north upon me and (saying) "Mine is this; mine is what is left on the place (of sacrifice)" has taken it away.' To him said his father, 'His it is, O my boy; but he will give it to thee.' Returning he said 'Thine is this, O blessed one, so my father tells me'. He replied 'I give it to thee who hast spoken the truth.' Therefore by one who knows thus should truth alone be spoken. The Nābhānediṣṭha is a speech to win a thousand; a thousand comes to him, with the sixth day he discerns the world of heaven, who knows thus.

v. 15 (xxii. 10). These they call accompaniments; the Nābhānediṣṭha, the Vālakhilyā,[1] the Vṛṣākapi,[2] and the Evayāmarut[3] (hymns). Them he should recite together. Whichever of them he should omit, that of the sacrificer he would omit. If the Nābhānediṣṭha, he would omit his seed; of the Vālakhilyās he would omit his breaths; if the Vṛṣākapi, he would omit his body; of the Evayāmarut, he would remove him from support, both divine and human. With the Nābhānediṣṭha he poured seed; that he discriminated by the Vālakhilyās; with (the hymn of) Sukīrti Kākṣīvata[4] he made (it) leave the womb (saying) 'That we may rejoice in thy broad protection, O Indra.' Therefore the embryo, being larger, yet does not harm the womb which is smaller; for it is made proper by the holy power. By means of the Evayāmarut he produces motion; by it set in motion all whatever there is here moves. 'The dark day and the bright day' is the beginning of the Āgnimāruta[5]; in 'day and day' is there repetition and alliteration; on the sixth day it is a symbol of the sixth day. 'Of the sweet juice, the Marut name, O holy ones' is (the hymn) to the Maruts[6] wherein is much to be uttered; much is the end; the sixth day is the end; on the sixth day it is a symbol of the end. 'To Jātavedas let us pour the Soma' is the normal (verse) to Jātavedas.[7] 'He born of old with strength' is (the hymn) to Jātavedas[8]; as having the same endings on the sixth day it is a symbol of the sixth day. 'They supported,' 'They supported,' he recites; he fears the slipping down of the end. Just as a man ties the end, twining it again and again intertwining it, or as one sticks in a peg at the end to keep (a skin) taut, so is it in that he recites 'They supported', 'They supported', for continuity. With sets of three days, uninterrupted and continuous, they proceed, who proceed knowing thus.[9]

[1] RV. viii. 49–59. See below AB. vi. 28.
[2] RV. x. 86. See below AB. vi. 29.
[3] RV. v. 87. See below AB. vi. 30 and 31.
[4] RV. x. 131. See below AB. vi. 29.
[5] RV. vi. 9. 1–3; ĀÇS. viii. 8. 9; ÇÇS. x. 8. 15 which differs for the rest.
[6] RV. vii. 57; ĀÇS. viii. 8. 9.
[7] RV. i. 99. 1; ĀÇS. vii. 1. 14.
[8] RV. i. 96: *dhārayan* is the refrain in *d* of each verse; ĀÇS. viii. 8. 9; wrongly attributed in the *Vedic Concordance*.
[9] This chapter appears to require the Hotṛ himself to perform all these recitations contrary to the view in vi that the

ADHYĀYA III

The Chandomas.

v. 16 (xxiii. 1). That which has (the words) 'hither' and 'forward' is a symbol of the seventh day, for the seventh day is a repetition of the first day. That which contains (the word) 'yoke', (the word) 'chariot', (the word) 'swift', (the word) 'drink', (the fact), that the deity is mentioned in the first Pada, (the fact) that this world is referred to, that which contains (the word) 'born', that which has no express mention (of the deity), the future tense, that which is a symbol of the first day; these are the symbols of the seventh day. 'From the ocean the aroma of sweetness hath arisen' is the Ājya[1] of the seventh day; as not containing any express mention of the deity, on the seventh day it is a symbol of the seventh day. The ocean is speech; speech wastes not away, the ocean wastes not away. In that this is the Ājya of the seventh day, verily thus from the sacrifice they extend the sacrifice; verily thus they again approach speech for continuity. With sets of three days, uninterrupted and continuous, they proceed who proceed knowing thus. The Stomas are obtained, the metres are obtained on the seventh day. Just as they smear with butter again the portions cut off to refresh them, so here they perform again the Stomas and the metres to refresh them, in that this is the Ājya of the seventh day. It is in Triṣṭubh; this set of three days has the Triṣṭubh at the morning pressing. 'O Vāyu, drinker of the pure, come hither to us,' 'With which thou dost come forward to the bounteous one,' 'To our sacrifice hither with hundreds of steeds,' 'The lively presser at the sacrifices hath arisen forward,' 'The draughts delighting Indra,' 'Thy hundred steeds, thy thousand,' 'When forward, O Mitra and Varuṇa, for you they struggle,' 'Hither, O Nāsatyas, with chariot rich in cattle,' 'Come hither to us, O god, O impetuous one,' 'Forward to you in the sacrifices the pious have sung,' and 'Forward she hasteneth with her nourishing stream' are the Praüga.[2] (The words) 'hither' and 'forward' on the seventh day are symbols of the seventh day. It is in Triṣṭubh; this set of three days has the Triṣṭubh at the morning pressing. 'Thee like a car for aid,' 'This Soma juice hath been pressed,

Vālakhilyās, the Vṛṣākapi and the Evayāmarut fell normally to the Hotrakas. See however vi. 21, whence *çaṅs* seems to have a looser sense than merely recite as it covers *çaṅsayāni*.

[1] RV. iv. 59; ĀÇS. viii. 9. 2; cf. ÇÇS. x. 9 which differs considerably; see KB. xxvi. 7, 8; BÇS. xvi. 6; ĀÇS. xxi. 8. 11, 12.

[2] RV. vii. 92. 1, 3, 5, 2, 4; 91. 6; vi. 67. 9-11; vii. 72. 1-3; 30. 1-3; 43. 1-3; 99. 1-3; ĀÇS. viii. 9. 2.

O bright one,' 'O Indra come near,' 'Let Brahmaṇaspati move forward,' 'Agni, the leader,' 'Thou, O Soma, with inspiration,' 'They swell the waters,' and 'Forward to Indra, the great' are the continuation,[3] being the same as that of the first day; on the seventh day it is a symbol of the seventh day. 'With what array, of one age, of one home' is the hymn;[4] as containing (the word) 'born' in 'Neither he that is being born nor he that is born shall attain' on the seventh day it is a symbol of the seventh day. It is the 'With what array (hymn); the 'With what array' hymn is one producing agreement and continuing (life). By it Indra and Agastya and the Maruts came to agreement; thus, in that he recites the 'With that array' (hymn), (it serves) to produce agreement. It is also life-giving; therefore for him who is dear to him he should perform the 'With what array' hymn. It is in Triṣṭubh; with it with feet supported he maintains the pressing; thereby it departs not from its place. 'That ram that winneth the light I glorify' is the hymn;[5] as containing (the word) 'chariot' in 'Like a strong steed the chariot hastening at the call' on the seventh day it is a symbol of the seventh day, It is in Jagatī; Jagatī verses support the midday (pressing) of this set of three days; that metre is a support in which a Nivid is inserted; therefore he inserts a Nivid in the Jagatī verses. Pairing hymns are recited, in Triṣṭubh and Jagatī; cattle are a pairing; the Chandomas are cattle; (they serve) to win cattle. 'Thee we invoke', and 'Do thou come to the worshipper', are the Bṛhat as Pṛṣṭha[6] on the seventh day; that is what belongs to the sixth day; the Rathantara is the Vairūpa, the Bṛhat the Vairāja; the Rathantara the Çākvara, the Bṛhat the Raivata; in that there is the Bṛhat as Pṛṣṭha, verily thus with the Bṛhat they support the Bṛhat, to avoid cleaving the Stomas. If it were to be the Rathantara, there would be a cleavage (of the Stomas). Therefore the Bṛhat only is to be used. 'What he hath won' is the normal inserted verse.[7] In 'Towards thee, O hero, we utter praise' he makes to follow the basis of the Rathantara,[8] for this day is connected with the Rathantara in place. 'Drink of the pressed draught rich in sap' is the Pragātha[9] of the Sāman; as containing (the word) 'drink' on the seventh day it is a symbol of the seventh day. 'This steed, god strengthened' is the normal Tārkṣya[10]. (hymn).

[3] RV. viii. 68. 1–3; 2. 1–3; 58. 5, 6; i. 40. 3, 4; iii. 20. 4; i. 91. 2; 64. 6; viii. 89. 3; see AB. iv. 29.

[4] RV. i. 165: v. 9 is cited; ĀÇS. viii. 6. 6; ÇÇS. x. 9. 11. For the legend cf. Sieg, *Sagenstoffe des Ṛgveda*, pp. 115 seq.; v. Schroeder, *Mysterium und Mimus*, pp. 91 seq., 102 seq.; Hertel, VOJ. xviii. 153; Oldenberg, *Ṛgveda-Noten*, i. 170.

[5] RV. i. 52; ĀÇS. viii. 6. 6; ÇÇS. x. 9. 12.

[6] RV. vi. 46. 1, 2; viii. 61. 7, 8; see AB. iv. 31.

[7] RV. x. 74. 6; see AB. iv. 29.

[8] RV. vii. 32. 22, 23; see AB. iv. 29.

[9] RV. vii. 3. 1, 2; see AB. iv. 29.

[10] RV. x. 178; ĀÇS. vii. 1. 18.

v. 17 (xxiii. 2). 'I shall proclaim the mighty deeds of Indra' is the hymn;[1] the word 'forward' (in 'proclaim') on the seventh day is a symbol of the seventh day. It is in Triṣṭubh; with it with feet supported he maintains the pressing; thereby it departs not from its place. 'Towards the ram, much invoked, worthy of praise' is the hymn;[2] 'towards' is equivalent to 'forward'; on the seventh day it is a symbol of the seventh day. It is in Jagatī; Jagatī verses support the midday (pressing) of the set of three days; that metre is a support in which a Nivid is inserted; therefore he inserts a Nivid in the Jagatī verses. Pairing hymns are recited in Triṣṭubh and in Jagatī; cattle are a pairing, the Chandomas cattle; (they serve) to win cattle. 'That of Savitṛ we choose,' and 'To-day, for us, O god Savitṛ' are the strophe and antistrophe of the Vaiçvadeva;[3] on the Rathantara day, the seventh day, it is a symbol of the seventh day. 'Towards thee, O god Savitṛ' is (the triplet) to Savitṛ.[4] 'Towards' is equivalent to 'forward'; on the seventh day it is a symbol of the seventh day. 'Let them come forward with weal for the sacrifice' is (the triplet) to sky and earth;[5] 'forward' on the seventh day is a symbol of the seventh day. 'This to the race divine' is (the triplet) to the Ṛbhus;[6] as containing (the word) 'born' on the seventh day it is a symbol of the seventh day. He recites (the verses) of two Padas,[7] 'Come hither with thy beauty'; man has two feet, cattle four feet; the Chandomas are cattle; (verily they serve) to win cattle; in that he recites (verses) of two Padas, verily thus he makes the sacrificer with two feet find support in four-footed cattle. 'Hither to our service, the songs, O Agni' is the (hymn) to the All-gods;[8] 'hither' on the seventh day is a symbol of the seventh day. These are Gāyatrī verses; this set of three days has the Gāyatrī at the third pressing. 'Vaiçvānara hath produced' is the beginning of the Āgnimāruta;[9] as having (the word) 'born' on the seventh day it is a symbol of the seventh day. 'Forward to you, the Triṣṭubh, food' is (the hymn) to the Maruts;[10] 'forward' on the seventh day is a symbol of the seventh day. 'To Jātavedas let us pour the Soma' is the normal (verse) to Jātavedas.[11] 'Your envoy, with all knowledge' is (the hymn) to Jātavedas;[12] as not having the deity mentioned on the seventh day it is a symbol of the seventh day. These are Gāyatrī verses; this set of three days has the Gāyatrī at the third pressing.

[1] RV. i. 32; ĀÇS. viii. 6. 12; not in ÇÇS. Cf. KB. xxvi. 9, 10.
[2] RV. i. 51; ĀÇS. viii. 6. 12; ÇÇS. x. 9. 13.
[3] RV. v. 82. 1-3; 4-6; see AB. iv. 29.
[4] RV. i. 24. 3-5; ĀÇS. viii. 9. 5.
[5] RV. ii. 91. 19-21; ĀÇS. viii. 9. 5; ÇÇS. x. 9. 16.
[6] RV. i. 20. 1-3; ĀÇS. viii. 9. 5; ÇÇS. x. 9. 16.
[7] RV. x. 172; ĀÇS. viii. 9. 6; ÇÇS. x. 9. 16.
[8] RV. i. 14; ĀÇS. viii. 9. 5.
[9] See ĀÇS. ii. 15. 2; ĀÇS. viii. 9. 7. Cf. ÇÇS. x. 9. 17; 10. 8.
[10] RV. viii. 7; ĀÇS. viii. 9. 7; ÇÇS. x. 9. 17.
[11] RV. i. 99. 1; ĀÇS. vii. 1. 14.
[12] RV. iv. 8; ĀÇS. viii. 9. 7.

v. 18 (xxiii. 3). That[1] which has not (the words) 'hither' and 'forward', that which has (the word) 'stand', is the symbol of the eighth day, for the eighth day is a repetition of the second day. That which contains (the word) 'upright', (the word) 'to', (the word) 'between', (the word) 'strong', (the word) 'grow', (the fact) that the deity is mentioned in the middle Pada, (the fact) that the atmosphere is referred to, that which has Agni twice, that which contains (the word) 'great', that which contains a double invocation, that which contains (the word) 'again', the present tense, that which is a symbol of the second day; these are the symbols of the eighth day. 'Agni for you the god in union with the flames' is the Ājya[2] of the eighth day; as containing Agni twice, on the eighth day it is a symbol of the eighth day. It is in Triṣṭubh; this set of three days has the Triṣṭubh at the morning pressing. 'Were not they who were made great with homage?,' 'Those rich of food, wealth gathering, the wise one,' 'The dawns with fair days, spotless have dawned,' 'Guardians infallible, eager envoys,' 'So far as the power of the body, so far as the might,' 'To you two at the rising of the sun with hymns,' 'The cow milking the desire of the ancient one,' 'To our prayers come, O Indra, knowing,' 'Agni, upright, hath established the favour of the bright one' and 'May Sarasvati for us rejoicing' are the Praüga;[3] as containing (the words) 'to', 'between', an invocation of two deities and 'upright' on the eighth day it is a symbol of the eighth day. It is in Triṣṭubh; this set of three days has the Triṣṭubh metre at the morning pressing. 'Lord of every man,' 'Indra is the Soma drinker only,' 'O Indra, come near,' 'Rise up, O Brahmaṇaspati,' 'Agni, the leader,' 'Thou, O Soma, with inspiration,' 'They swell the waters,' and 'Sing aloud to Indra' are the continuation[4] being the same as that of the second day; on the eighth day it is a symbol of the eighth day. 'I praise great Indra in whom all' is the hymn;[5] as containing (the word) 'great' on the eighth day it is a symbol of the eighth day. 'Even from great, O Indra, these that approach' is the hymn;[6] as containing (the word) 'great' on the eighth day it is a symbol of the eighth day. 'Drink the Soma, towards which, O dread one, thou hast penetrated' is the hymn;[7] as containing (the word) 'great', in 'The cattle stall, being greatly lauded, O Indra' on the eighth day, it is a symbol of the eighth day. 'Great is

[1] For the eighth or second Chandoma see KB. xxvi. 11–18.

[2] RV. vii. 3; ĀÇS. viii. 10. 1; ÇÇS. x. 8. 1. It differs in detail throughout.

[3] RV. vii. 91. 1, 3; 90. 4; 91. 2, 4, 5; 65. 1–3; iii. 58. 1–3; vii. 28. 1–3; 39. 1–3; 95. 4–6; ĀÇS. viii. 10. 1.

[4] RV. viii. 68. 6; 2. 4; 33. 5, 6; i. 40. 1, 2; iii. 20. 4; i. 41. 2; 64. 6; viii. 87. 1 and 2.

[5] RV. iii. 19; ĀÇS. viii. 7. 22.

[6] RV. i. 169; ĀÇS. viii. 7. 22.

[7] RV. vi. 17; AÇS. viii. 7. 22.

Indra, man-like, spreading over mortals' is the hymn;[8] as containing (the word) 'great' on the eighth day it is a symbol of the eighth day. It is in Triṣṭubh; with it with feet supported he maintains the pressing; thereby it departs not from its place. 'Him sky and earth of one mind' is the hymn;[9] as containing (the word) 'great' in 'When he went displaying his greatness, his power' on the eighth day it is a symbol of the eighth day. It is in Jagatī; Jagatī verses support the midday (pressing) of this set of three days; that metre is a support in which a Nivid is inserted; therefore he inserts a Nivid in the Jagatī verses. Pairing hymns are recited in Triṣṭubh and Jagatī; cattle are a pairing, the Chandomas are cattle; (verily they serve) to win cattle. Hymns containing (the word) 'great' are recited; the atmosphere is great; (verily they serve) to obtain the atmosphere. Five hymns are recited; the Pañkti has five Padas; the sacrifice is fivefold; cattle are fivefold; the Chandomas are cattle; (verily they serve) to win cattle. 'Towards thee, O hero, we utter praise' and 'Towards thee for the first drink' are the Rathantara as Pṛṣṭha[10] on the eighth day. 'What he hath won' is the normal inserted verse.[11] In 'Thee we invoke' he makes to follow the basis[12] of the Bṛhat, for this day is connected with the Bṛhat in place. 'Both may he hear for us' is the Pragātha of the Sāman;[13] 'that which is lasting and that which was yesterday' (he means); on the Bṛhat day, the eighth day, it is a symbol of the eighth day. 'This steed, god strengthened' is the normal Tārkṣya[14] (hymn).

v. 19 (xxiii. 4). 'Many not of old to him' is the hymn;[1] as containing (the word) 'great' in 'To the great, the hero, impetuous, eager' on the eighth day it is a symbol of the eighth day. 'This fame for thee, O bounteous one, though thy greatness' is the hymn;[2] as containing (the word) 'great' on the eighth day it is the symbol of the eighth day. 'Thou art great, O Indra, who by thy might' is the hymn;[3] as containing (the word) 'great' on the eighth day it is a symbol of the eighth day. 'Thou art great, O Indra; to thee the earth' is the hymn;[4] as containing (the word) 'great' on the eighth day it is a symbol of the eighth day. It is in Triṣṭubh; with it with feet supported he maintains the pressing; thereby it departs not from its place. 'Though the width of the sky is outspread' is the hymn;[5] as containing (the word) 'great' in 'Not Indra in greatness'

[8] RV. vi. 19; ĀÇS. vii. 9. 22.

[9] RV. x. 113; ĀÇS. vii. 9. 22; it precedes there RV. vi. 19.

[10] RV. vii. 32. 22, 23; viii. 3. 7, 8; see AB. iv. 29.

[11] RV. x. 74. 6; see AB. iv. 29.

[12] RV. vi. 46. 1 and 2; see AB. iv. 31.

[13] RV. viii. 61. 1 and 2; see AB. iv. 31.

[14] RV. x. 178; ĀÇS. vii. 1. 13.

[1] RV. vi. 32; ĀÇS. viii. 7. 23; ÇÇS. x. 10. 6. Cf. KB. xxiii. 12, 13.

[2] RV. x. 54; ĀÇS. viii. 7. 23; ÇÇS. x. 10. 6.

[3] RV. i. 63; ĀÇS. viii. 7. 23; ÇÇS. x. 10. 6.

[4] RV. iv. 17; ĀÇS. viii. 7. 23; ÇÇS. x. 10. 6.

[5] RV. i. 55; ĀÇS. viii. 7. 23: it precedes RV. iv. 17 there; not in ÇÇS.

on the eighth day it is a symbol of the eighth day'. It is in Jagatī; Jagatī verses support the midday (pressing) of this set of three days; that metre is a support in which a Nivid is inserted; therefore he inserts a Nivid in the Jagatī verses. Pairing hymns are recited, in Triṣṭubh and in Jagatī; cattle are a pairing, the Chandomas cattle; (verily they serve) to win cattle. Hymns containing (the word) 'great' are recited; the atmosphere is great; (verily they serve) to obtain the atmosphere. Two sets of five hymns are recited; the Pañkti has five Padas; the sacrifice is fivefold; cattle are fivefold; the Chandomas are cattle; (verily they serve) to win cattle. They are separate, five in one set, five in the other; they make up ten; the Virāj is a set of ten; the Virāj is food; cattle are food, the Chandomas cattle; (verily they serve) to win cattle. 'Let each man of the god that leadeth,' 'That desirable of Savitṛ' and 'God of all, lord of the good' are the strophe and antistrophe of the Vaiçvadeva.[6] On the Bṛhat day, the eighth day, it is a symbol of the eighth day. 'The golden-handed to aid' is (the triplet) to Savitṛ[7]; as containing (the word) 'upright' on the eighth day it is a symbol of the eighth day. 'May the two great ones, sky and earth, for us' is (the triplet) to sky and earth;[8] as containing (the word) 'great' on the eighth day it is a symbol of the eighth day. 'Youthful the parents again' is (the triplet) to the Ṛbhus;[9] as containing (the word) 'again' on the eighth day it is a symbol of the eighth day. He recites (verses) of two Padas,[10] 'These worlds let us subject'; man has two feet, cattle four feet; the Chandomas are cattle; (verily they serve) to win cattle. In that he recites (verses) of two Padas, verily thus he makes the sacrificer with two feet to find support among four-footed cattle. 'The great aid of the gods' is (the hymn) to the All-gods;[11] as containing (the word) 'great' on the eighth day it is a symbol of the eighth day. These are Gāyatrī verses; this set of three days has the Gāyatrī at the third pressing. 'The righteous, belonging to all men' is the beginning of the Āgnimāruta;[12] as containing (the word) 'great' in 'Agni, of all men, the great' on the eighth day it is a symbol of the eighth day. 'The sporting troop of the Maruts' is (the hymn) to the Maruts;[13] as containing (the word) 'grow' in 'With the taste of the sap it grew great' on the eighth day it is a symbol of the eighth day. 'To Jātavedas let us pour the Soma' is the normal (verse) to Jātavedas.[14]

[6] RV. v. 50. 1; 82. 7, 8; see AB. iv. 32.

[7] RV. i. 22. 5–7; ĀÇS. viii. 10. 2; ÇÇS. x. 10. 7.

[8] RV. i. 22. 13–15; ĀÇS. viii. 10. 2; ÇÇS. x. 10. 7.

[9] RV. i. 20. 4–6; ĀÇS. viii. 10. 2; ÇÇS. x. 10. 7.

[10] RV. x. 157; ÇÇS. x. 10. 7; ĀÇS. viii. 7. 24.

[11] RV. viii. 83; ĀÇS. viii. 10. 2; ÇÇS. x. 10. 7.

[12] In ĀÇS. viii. 10. 3; ÇÇS. x. 10. 8.

[13] RV. i. 37; ĀÇS. viii. 10. 3.

[14] RV. i. 99. 1; ĀÇS. vii. 1. 14.

'O Agni, be kind; thou art great' is (the hymn) to Jātavedas;[15] as containing (the word) 'great' on the eighth day it is a symbol of the eighth day. These are Gāyatrī verses; this set of three days has the Gāyatrī metre at the third pressing.

ADHYĀYA IV

The Chandomas (continued).

v. 20 (xxiv. 1). That[1] which has the same endings is a symbol of the ninth day; for the ninth day is a repetition of the third day. That which contains (the word) 'horse', (the word) 'end', that which is repeated, that which is alliterated, that which contains (the word) 'stay', (the word) 'surpass', (the word) 'three', that which is a symbol of the end, (the fact) that the deity is mentioned in the last Pada, (the fact) that yonder world is referred to, that which contains (the word) 'pure', (the word) 'true', (the word) 'dwell', (the word) 'gone', (the word) 'dwelling', the past tense, that which is a symbol of the third day; these are the symbols of the ninth day. 'We have gone with great praise to the youngest', is the Ājya[2] of the ninth day; as containing (the word) 'gone' on the ninth day it is a symbol of the ninth day. It is in Triṣṭubh; this set of three days has the Triṣṭubh metre at the morning pressing. 'Forward to thee the pure are offered boldly', 'They perceiving with true mind', 'Dwelling in the sky, from the atmosphere, on the earth', 'Come hither to us with all boons, O Açvins', 'The Soma, O Indra, is pressed for thee', 'The Brahmans, the Añgirases, will attain', 'Sarasvatī pious men invoke', 'Hither to us from the sky, from the great mountain' and 'O Sarasvatī lead us to prosperity' are the Praüga[3]; as containing (the words) 'pure', 'true', 'dwell', 'gone', and 'house', on the ninth day it is a symbol of the ninth day. It is in Triṣṭubh; this set of three days has the Triṣṭubh metre at the morning pressing. 'Him for great gain', 'Three Soma draughts for Indra', 'O Indra, come near' 'Forward now Brahmaṇaspati', 'Agni, the leader', 'Thou, O Soma, with inspiration', 'They swell the waters', and 'No one the chariot of Sudās' are the continuation[4], being the same as that of the third day; on the ninth day it is a symbol of the ninth day. 'Let Indra drink whose Soma, hail!'

[15] RV. iv. 9; ĀÇS. viii. 10. 3.

[1] For the ninth day see KB. xxvi. 14–17.

[2] RV. vii. 12; ĀÇS. viii. 11. 1; ÇÇS. x. 11. 1 with variants throughout.

[3] RV. vii. 90. 1, 5; 64. 1; 70. 1–3; 29. 1–3; 42. 1–3; x. 17. 7–9; v. 43. 11–13; vi. 61. 14–16; ĀÇS. viii. 11. 1; ÇÇS. x. 11. 4, 5.

[4] RV. viii. 68. 7–9; 2. 7–9; 53. 5, 6; i. 40. 5, 6; iii. 20. 4; i. 91. 2; 64. 6; vii. 32. 10. See AB. v. 1.

is the hymn[5]; the call of Hail! is the end; the ninth day is the end; on the ninth day it is a symbol of the end. 'Let him say the Sāman, springing forth as of a bird' is the hymn[6]; (containing) 'Let us sing that which becometh heavenlike'; the heaven is the end; the ninth day is the end; on the ninth day it is a symbol of the ninth day. 'Stand on the steeds being yoked to the chariot' is the hymn[7]; standing is the end; the ninth day is the end; on the ninth day it is a symbol of the ninth day. 'Those of many a poet' is the hymn[8], (containing) 'The hymns him that standeth on the chariot'; standing is the end; the ninth day is the end; on the ninth day it is a symbol of the ninth day. That is in Triṣṭubh; with it with its feet supported he maintains the pressing; thereby it departs not from its place. 'Sing ye forth to the glad one the song rich in food' is the hymn[9]; as having the same endings on the ninth day it is a symbol of the ninth day. It is in Jagatī; Jagatī verses support the midday (pressing) of this set of three days; that metre is a support in which a Nivid is inserted; therefore he inserts a Nivid in the Jagatī verses. Pairing hymns are recited, in Triṣṭubh and in Jagatī; cattle are a pairing; the Chandomas are cattle; (verily they serve) to win cattle. Five hymns are recited; the Pañkti has five Padas; the sacrifice is fivefold; cattle are fivefold; the Chandomas are cattle; (verily they serve) to win cattle. 'Thee we invoke' and 'Do thou come to the worshipper' are the Bṛhat as Pṛṣṭha[10] on the ninth day. 'What he hath won' is the normal inserted verse.[11] In 'Towards thee, O hero, we utter praise' he makes to follow the basis[12] of the Rathantara, for this day is connected with the Rathantara in place. 'O Indra, threefold protection' is the Pragātha of the Sāman[13]; as containing (the word) 'three' on the ninth day it is a symbol of the ninth day. 'This steed, god strengthened' is the normal Tārkṣya[14] (hymn).

v. 21 (xxiv. 2). 'In thee from of old the songs have gone together, O Indra' is the hymn[1]; as containing (the word) 'gone' on the ninth day it is a symbol of the ninth day. 'When shall our prayers dwell in the chariot' is the hymn[2]; as containing (the word) 'dwell' it is a symbol of the end; having gone to the end he dwells as it were; on the ninth day it is a symbol of the ninth day. 'May the true one come hither, the generous, he of the Soma lees' is the hymn[3]; as containing (the word) 'true' on the

[5] RV. iii. 50; ĀÇS. viii. 7. 28.
[6] RV. i. 173; AÇS. viii. 7. 23; ÇÇS. x. 11. 6.
[7] RV. iii. 35; ĀÇS. viii. 7. 23; ÇÇS. x. 11. 6.
[8] RV. vi. 21; ĀÇS. viii. 7. 28.
[9] RV. i. 101; ĀÇS. viii. 7. 28: it precedes RV. vi. 21 there; ÇÇS. x. 11. 6.
[10] RV. vi. 46. 1, 2; viii. 61. 7, 8; see AB. iv. 31.
[11] RV. x. 74. 6; see AB. iv. 29.
[12] RV. vii. 32. 22 and 23; see AB. iv. 29.
[13] RV. vi. 46. 9 and 10; see AB. v. 1.
[14] RV. x. 178; ĀÇS. vii. 1. 13.
[1] RV. vi. 34; ĀÇS. viii. 7. 24. Cf. KB. xxvi. 16, 17.
[2] RV. vi. 35; ĀÇS. viii. 7. 24.
[3] RV. iv. 16; ĀÇS. viii. 7. 24; ÇÇS. x. 11. 17.

ninth day it is a symbol of the ninth day. 'That highest power of thine is on high' is the hymn[4]; the highest is the end; the ninth day is the end; on the ninth day it is a symbol of the end. It is a Triṣṭubh; with it with feet supported he maintains the pressing; verily it departs not from its place. 'I am the first lord of wealth' is the hymn[5] (containing the words) 'I win wealth of every man'; what is won is the end; the ninth day is the end; on the ninth day it is a symbol of the ninth day. It is in Jagatī; Jagatī verses support the midday pressing of this set of three days; that metre is a support in which a Nivid is inserted; therefore he inserts a Nivid in the Jagatī verses. Pairing hymns are recited, in Triṣṭubh and in Jagatī; cattle are a pairing; the Chandomas are cattle; (verily they serve) to win cattle. Two sets of five hymns are recited; the Pañkti has five Padas; the sacrifice is fivefold; cattle are fivefold; the Chandomas are cattle; (verily they serve) to win cattle. They are separate, five in one set, five in the other; they make up ten; the Virāj is a set of ten; the Virāj is food; cattle are food; the Chandomas are cattle; (verily they serve) to win cattle. 'That of Savitṛ we choose' and 'To-day for us, O god Savitṛ' are the strophe and antistrophe of the Vaiçvadeva[6]; on the Rathantara day, the ninth day, it is a symbol of the ninth day. 'The evening hath come' is (the triplet) to Savitṛ[7]; what has gone is the end; the ninth day is the end; on the ninth day it is a symbol of the ninth day; 'Forward towards you mightily sky and earth' is (the triplet) to sky and earth[8]; as containing (the word) 'pure' in 'To the pure the praises' on the ninth day it is a symbol of the ninth day. 'Let Indra give for sap to us' and 'Give ye jewels' are (the triplet) to the Ṛbhus[9]; as containing (the word) 'three' in 'Three sevens to the presser' on the ninth day it is a symbol of the ninth day. He recites (verses) of two Padas[10], 'Brown is one, active, bounteous, youthful'; man has two feet, cattle four feet; the Chandomas are cattle; (verily they serve) to win cattle; in that he recites (verses) of two Padas, verily thus he makes the sacrificer with two feet find support in four-footed cattle. 'That are three over thirty' is (the hymn) to the All-gods[11]; as containing (the word) 'three' on the ninth day it is a symbol of the ninth day. These are Gāyatrī verses; this set of three days has the Gāyatrī metre at the third pressing. 'Vaiçvānara, to our aid' is the beginning[12] of the Āgnimāruta (containing) 'Let him come hither from

[4] RV. i. 103; ĀÇS. viii. 7. 24; ÇÇS. x. 11. 17.

[5] RV. x. 48; ĀÇS. viii. 7. 24: it precedes RV. i. 103 here; ÇÇS. x. 11. 7.

[6] RV. v. 82. 1–3; 4–6; see AB. iv. 30.

[7] See above AB. v. 18; ĀÇS. viii. 11. 3.

[8] RV. iv. 56. 5–7; ĀÇS. viii. 11. 3; ÇÇS. x. 11. 8.

[9] RV. viii. 93. 34; i. 20. 7 and 8; ĀÇS. viii. 11. 3; ÇÇS. x. 11. 8.

[10] RV. viii. 29; ĀÇS. viii. 7. 24; ÇÇS. x. 11. 8.

[11] RV. viii. 28; ĀÇS. viii. 11. 3; ÇÇS. x. 11. 8.

[12] See ĀÇS. viii. 11. 4; AV. vi. 35. 1: TS. i. 5. 11. 1 and its parallels.

afar'; from afar is the end; the ninth day is the end; on the ninth day it is a symbol of the end. 'O Maruts in whose dwelling' is the hymn[13] to the Maruts; as containing (the word) 'dwell' it is a symbol of the end; having gone to the end he dwells as it were; on the ninth day it is a symbol of the ninth day. 'To Jātavedas let us pour the Soma' is the normal (verse) to Jātavedas[14]. 'Forward to Agni, move your speech' is (the hymn) to Jātavedas[15]; as having the same endings in the ninth day it is a symbol of the ninth day. 'May he convey us beyond our foes, may he convey us beyond our foes' he recites; in the set of nine nights much is done that is forbidden; verily (this serves) for atonement. In that he recites[16] 'May he convey us beyond our foes; may he convey us beyond our foes', verily thus he releases them from all sin. These are Gāyatrī verses; this set of three days has the Gāyatrī metre at the third pressing.

The Tenth Day.

v. 22 (xxiv. 3). They[1] perform the Pṛṣṭhya Ṣaḍaha. As is the mouth, so is the Pṛṣṭhya Ṣaḍaha; as within the mouth are the tongue, palate, and teeth, so are the Chandomas; now that by which he makes speech distinct, by which he discerns sweet and not sweet, is the tenth day. As the two nostrils, so the Pṛṣṭhya Ṣaḍaha, as that within the nostrils, so the Chandomas; now that by which he discriminates scents is the tenth day. As is the eye, so is the Pṛṣṭhya Ṣaḍaha; as the black within the eye, so the Chandomas; now the pupil, by which he sees, is the tenth day. As is the ear, so is the Pṛṣṭhya Ṣaḍaha; as what is within the ear, so the Chandomas; now that by which he hears is the tenth day. The tenth day is prosperity; they attain prosperity who perform the tenth day (rite). Wherefore the tenth day is one on which corrections are not to be made (thinking) 'Let us not speak ill[2] of prosperity', for it is unwise to speak ill of a superior. They creep thence, they purify themselves, they enter the hut of the wives; of those he who knows this libation should say 'Hold ye on to one another'. He should offer with 'Here stay, stay ye here; here be support, here self support; O Agni; *vāṭ*! Hail! *vāṭ*!' In that he says 'Here stay' he

[13] RV. i. 86; ĀÇS. viii. 11. 4; ÇÇS. x. 11. 9.
[14] RV. i. 99. 1; ĀÇS. vii. 1. 14.
[15] RV. x. 187; ĀÇS. viii. 11. 4.
[16] In each verse of RV. x. 187.
[1] AB. v. 22-28 and KB. xxvii. deal with the tenth day following the nine (Chandomas and Pṛṣṭhya Ṣaḍaha); for the day, cf. ÇÇS. x. 13-21; BÇS. xvi. 6-9; ĀpÇS. xxi. 9-12; ĀÇS. viii. 12. 10-13. 2 for the rites here prescribed; for the *avivākya* character see TS. vii. 3. 1. 1; BÇS. xvi. 6; ĀpÇS. xxi. 9.
[2] Haug, contra Sāyaṇa, translates 'we shall not bespeak (the goddess of) wealth.'

makes them stay in this world; in that he says 'Stay ye here' he makes offspring stay in them. In that he says 'Here be support; here self-support', verily thus he confers speech and offspring upon the sacrificers. The Rathantara is 'O Agni, *vāṭ*!', the Bṛhat is 'Hail! *vāṭ*'. The Bṛhat and Rathantara are a pairing of the gods; verily thus by a pairing of the gods they win a pairing; by a pairing of the gods they are propagated in pairings; (therefore this serves) for propagation; he is propagated with offspring and cattle who knows thus. They creep thence; they purify themselves; they go to the Agnīdh's altar; of them he who knows this libation should say 'Hold ye on to one another'. He should offer with [3]

> 'Sending the sucking calf (to its mother),
> Himself a sucking calf sucking his mother,
> Increase of wealth, sap, and strength
> May he support in us; hail!'

Increase of wealth, sap and strength he wins for himself and the sacrificers when one knowing thus offers this libation.

v. 23 (xxiv. 4) They creep thence; they go to the Sadas; the other priests creep out severally according to their wont; the Udgātṛs creep together. They chant to the verses of the serpent queen. The serpent queen is this (earth), for this (earth) is the queen of what creeps; this (earth) in the beginning was bare; she saw this spell [1] 'The dappled bull hath come'; this dappled colour, of various forms, entered her; whither she desired, whatever there is here, plants, birds all forms (entered her). The dappled colour enters him with various forms, whatever he desires who knows thus. With mind he utters the prelude, with mind he sings, with mind he responds; with voice he recites. Speech and mind are a pairing of the gods, verily thus with a pairing of the gods they win a pairing, by a pairing of the gods they are propagated in pairings; (verily it serves) for propagation; he is propagated with offspring and cattle who knows thus. Then the Hotṛ recites [2] the Four Hotṛs; verily thus he accompanies in recitation the song. The Four Hotṛs are the sacrificial, secret name of the gods; in that the Hotṛ recites the Four Hotṛs, verily thus he reveals the sacrificial, secret name of the gods; that revealed reveals him. He is revealed who knows thus. 'That Brahman, to whom, though learned, fame does not come', he used to say, 'having gone into the wild should gather a bunch of Darbha grass, points upward, and, placing to his right

[3] Cf. VS. viii. 51. In both cases the ĀÇS. viii. 13. 1 and 2 merely has *juhoti* and Nārāyaṇa says that this or the Sūtra mode may be adopted.

[1] RV. x. 189; ĀÇS. viii. 13. 3-6; ÇÇS. x. 13. 26. Cf. KB. xxvii. 4; ÇB. iv. 6. 9. 17.

[2] Cf. below AB. v. 25. *Vyācakṣ* means 'expound' and the word has now a special propriety in its double force. See ĀÇS. viii. 13. 6-9; ÇÇS. x. 13. 27 and 15.

a Brahman, recite the Four Hotṛs; the Four Hotṛs are the sacrificial, secret name of the gods; if he were to recite the Four Hotṛs, he thus reveals the sacrificial, secret name of the gods; that revealed reveals him; he is revealed who knows thus.'

v. 24 (xxiv. 5) Then[1] they together lay hold of an Udumbara (branch) with 'Sap and strength I lay hold of'. The Udumbara is strength and proper food. In that the gods distributed sap and strength, thence the Udumbara came into being. Therefore thrice in a year it ripens. Thus in that they lay hold together of the Udumbara (branch), verily thus they lay hold together on sap and strength. They restrain their speech; the sacrifice is speech; verily thus they restrain the sacrifice. They suppress the day; the world of heaven is the day; verily thus they press down the world of heaven. They should not utter speech by day; if they were to utter speech by day they would leave the day over to a rival. They should not utter speech by night; if they were to utter speech by night, they would leave the night over to a rival; let the sun be half set; then should they utter speech; so much only of space do they leave over to a rival. Or rather, when the sun is set, should they utter speech; verily thus they make the rival who detests them have the darkness as his portion. Having gone round the Āhavanīya should they utter speech; the Āhavanīya is the sacrifice, the Āhavanīya the world of heaven; verily thus by the sacrifice as the world of heaven they go to the world of heaven. With

> 'What we have done here defective,
> What we have done in excess,
> To Prajāpati the father
> Let that go.'

they utter speech. Through Prajāpati are offspring born; Prajāpati is the support of what is defective and excessive; them neither defect nor excess harms. To Prajāpati they transfer defect and excess who knowing thus utter speech with this (verse). Therefore those who know thus should utter speech with this (verse)[2].

v. 25 (xxiv. 6) 'O Adhvaryu' he calls when about to speak out in the Four Hotṛs. This is the form of the Call. 'Yes, O Hotṛ; be it so, O Hotṛ' is the response of the Adhvaryu at each pause in the ten sentences.[1]

> 'Their offering spoon was thought.
> (Their) butter was intelligence.
> (Their) altar was speech.

[1] Cf. TS. vi. 6. 11. 6. Anup. iii. 12; LÇS. iii. 1. 18. For this passage cf. KB. xxvi. 5.

[2] For the ritual see ĀÇS. viii. 13. 22–26; ÇÇS. x. 21. 6 seq.; BÇS. xvi. 9.

v. 25. [1] This is part of the Caturhotṛ; see ĀÇS. viii. 13. 10; ÇÇS. x. 15. 5–7, where the Mantra differs. Here it is corrupt.

(Their) strew was learning.
(Their) Agni was insight.
(Their) Agnīdh was knowledge.
(Their) oblation was breath.
(Their) Adhvaryu was the Sāman.
(Their) Hotṛ was Vācaspati.
(Their) Upavaktṛ was mind.

They drew this cup (with)

"O Vācaspati, O worshipper, O name. Let us worship thy name. Do thou worship, with our name go to the sky. That prosperity with which the gods with Prajāpati as householder prepared, that prosperity shall we attain." '

Then he runs over the Bodies of Prajāpati and the riddle.

'Eater of food and mistress of food': the eater of food is Agni; the mistress of food Āditya.

'The fair and the beautiful': the fair is Soma, the beautiful is cattle.

'The unresting and the fearless': the unresting is Vāyu, for he never rests; the fearless is death, for all fear it.

'The unattained and the unattainable': the unattained is the earth; the unattainable is the sky.

'The unattackable and the irresistible': the unattackable is Agni; the irresistible is Āditya.

'That which has no prius and no rival': that which has no prius is mind; that which has no rival is the year.

These are the twelve Bodies of Prajāpati; this is the whole of Prajāpati, thus the whole of Prajāpati he obtains on the tenth day.

Then they say the riddle[2].

' "Agni is the householder" some say: he is the householder of the world.

"Vāyu is the householder" some say: he is the householder of the atmosphere.

"He who gives heat yonder is the householder" some say: he is the lord, the seasons are the house. The householders prosper, the sacrificers prosper, for whom there is as householder one knowing the god as householder. The householder smites away evil, the sacrificers smite away evil for whom there is as householder one knowing the god who most effectively has smitten away evil." O Adhvaryu we have won[3].'

[2] For the riddle here cf. KB. xxvii. 5; ĀÇS. viii. 13. 14; ÇÇS. x. 20; for the bodies of Prajāpati see KB. xxvii. 5; ĀÇS. viii. 13. 13; ÇÇS. x. 19 (in this case very elaborate). Both seem called Brahmodya in ÇB. iv. 6. 9. 20; cf. PB. iv. 9. 14; KÇS. xii. 4. 21; Eggeling, SBE. xxvi. 452, 453; ĀpÇS. xxi. 12 takes the view of PB. unfavourable to Prajāpati.

[3] This is used as Yājyā; see ĀÇS. viii. 13. 15, 16.

ADHYĀYA V

The Agnihotra.

v. 26 (xxv. 1) 'Take[1] out the Āhavanīya' he says on the afternoon; whatever good he does on the day, verily thus, by taking it out and bringing forward, he places in security. 'Take out the Āhavanīya' he says on the morning; whatever he does well by night verily thus, by taking it out and bringing it forward, he places in security. The Āhavanīya is the sacrifice, the Āhavanīya the world of heaven; verily thus in the sacrifice as the world of heaven, he places the world of heaven who knows thus. He who knows the Agnihotra as connected with the All-gods, of sixteen parts, and finding support in cattle, prospers with the Agnihotra, as connected with the All-gods, of sixteen parts, and finding support in cattle. When in the cow, it is Rudra's[2]; when allowed to drop, it is Vāyu's; when being milked, it is the Açvin's; when milked, it is Soma's; when put on the fire, it is Varuṇa's; when swelling up, it is Pūṣan's; when pouring over, it is the Maruts'; when bubbling, it is the All-gods'; when covered with a film, it is Mitra's; when removed, it is sky and earth's; when it is ready (for the Hotṛ), it is Savitṛ's; when it is being taken (for the oblation), it is Viṣṇu's; when put (on the altar), it is Bṛhaspati's; the first libation is for Agni; the next for Prajāpati; the offering is Indra's. This is the Agnihotra, connected with the All-gods, of sixteen parts, and finding support in cattle. With the Agnihotra, as connected with the All-gods, of sixteen parts and finding support in cattle he prospers who knows thus.

v. 27 (xxv. 2) (They ask) 'If the[1] Agnihotra cow, when united (with its calf) and being milked sits down, what is the expiation then?' He should address it with

> 'That from fear of which thou dost sit down
> Thence give us security;
> Guard all our cattle;
> Homage to Rudra, the bountiful.'

He should make her rise with[2]

[1] AB. v. 26–31 and KB. ii. deal with the Agnihotra. *Cf.* ĀÇS. iii. 11.

[2] Cf. ÇB. xi. 5. 3. 5: *samudantam* is found in ĀÇS. ii. 3. 8; TB. ii. 1. 7 and KÇS. xxv. 2. 8 have *udanta* and GB. iii. 12 *samudvāntam*. Weber (*Ind. Stud.* ix. 291) prefers *viṣpandamānam*, an obvious *v.l.*; see below AB. v. 27, n. 5.

v. 27. [1] Repeated with all down to paragraph iv in AB. vii. 3. See ĀÇS. iii. 11. 1; JB. i. 58. 1; TB. iii. 7. 8. 1; ÇB. xii. 4. 1. 9; ĀÇS. iii. 21; ĀpÇS. ix. 5. 1 *seq*; *Atharvaprāyaçcitta*, ii. 4 and 5.

[2] See ĀÇS. iii. 11. 2; TB. i. 4. 3. 1: MÇS. iii. 2. 1.

'The goddess Aditi hath arisen,
She hath bestowed life upon the lord of the sacrifice;
Making good fortune for Indra,
For Mitra and for Varuṇa.'

Then should he place on her udder and her mouth a pot of water, and then give her to a Brahman. That is the expiation in this case. 'If one's Agnihotra cow, when united and being milked, calls aloud, what is the expiation then' (they ask). She calls aloud foreseeing hunger for the sacrifices[3]; he should make her eat food, for expiation; food is expiation. (He says[4]) 'From eating the good pasture mayst thou be of good fortune'. That is the expiation in this case. 'If one's Agnihotra cow when united and being milked stumbles, what is the penance then?' (they ask). If she causes any (milk) to spill, he should touch it and mutter[5]

'That milk which to-day hath crept over the earth
That which hath crept over the plants, the waters
The milk in the house, the milk in the cow,
The milk in the calves, that milk be mine.'

He should offer with the remainder of the milk, if it be enough for an oblation. But, if all be poured out, then he should summon another (cow) and milk her and offer with it, but there must be an offering, even if only in faith.[6] That is the expiation in this case. All becomes for him suited for the strew, all is secured, who knowing thus offers the Agnihotra.

v. 28 (xxv. 3) The sacrificial post is yonder sun, the altar the earth, the strew the plants, the kindling wood the trees, the sprinkling waters the waters, the enclosing sticks the quarters. Whatever of his is lost, or dies, or men drive away, all of that comes to him in yonder world who knows thus to offer the Agnihotra, just as what is placed on the strew would come. Both sets, gods and men, reciprocally he leads as fees and all this whatever there is here. Men by the evening libation he leads as fees to the gods and all this whatever there is is here; they lie as it were relaxed and at home, when taken as fees for the gods. The gods by the morning libation he leads as fees to man and all this whatever there is here. They

[3] Sāyaṇa and Haug take this as 'to reveal her hunger to the sacrificer' but this is forcing the sense of *pratikhyāya*; cf. Weber, *Ind. Stud.* ix. 291. Cf. *Atharvaprāyaçcitta*, ii. 4 which has *saṁprakhyāya*.

[4] RV. i. 164. 40; AV. vii. 73. 11; ĀÇS. iii. 11. 4; ĀpÇS. ix. 5. 4.

[5] See ĀÇS. iii. 11. 7; TB. i. 4. 3. 3; ĀÇS. has *spandeta* which may be preferred; ĀpÇS. ix. 5. 6; MÇS. iii. 2. 1; JAOS. xxxiii. 115, n. 728; cf. ÇB. xii. 4. 1. 6; JB. i. 58. 1.

[6] The sense here, as given by Sāyaṇa, is that if all else fails he must offer faith only *ahaṁ çraddhāṁ juhomi*, not as Haug that he is to offer with faith in any case.

leap up[1] recognizing this as it were (saying) 'That shall I do; there shall I go'. The world which a man conquers by giving all this, that world he conquers who knowing thus offers the Agnihotra. By the evening libation for Agni he begins the Āçvina (Çastra); speech utters the response[2] in 'Speech, speech'. By Agni, by the night, is the Āçvina recited by him who knowing thus offers the Agnihotra. For Āditya by the morning libation he begins the Mahāvrata; breath utters the response in 'Food; food'; by Āditya, by the deity is the Mahāvrata recited by him who knowing thus offers the Agnihotra. Of this Agnihotra there are seven hundred and twenty evening libations in the year; there are also seven hundred and twenty morning libations in the year. So many are the bricks accompanied by Yajus verses of the fire[3]. By the year, by the fire fully does he sacrifice who knowing thus offers the Agnihotra.

v. 29 (xxv. 4) Vṛṣaçuṣma Vātāvata Jātūkarṇya said 'We shall declare this to the gods; the Agnihotra which used to be performed on both days is now performed on alternate days only'. This also said a maiden seized by a Gandharva 'We shall declare this to the fathers; the Agnihotra which used to be performed on both days is now performed on alternate days only.[1]' The Agnihotra is offered on alternate days in that one offers it on the evening after sunset and in the morning before sunrise. The Agnihotra is offered on both days in that one offers it in the evening after sunset and in the morning after sun rise. Therefore the offering should be made after sun rise. He who offers before sunrise obtains the world of the Gāyatrī in the twenty-fourth year; in the twelfth he who offers after sunrise. If he offers for two years before sunrise then he has really sacrificed for one only; he who sacrifices after sunrise with the year obtains the year, he who knowing thus offers after sunrise. Therefore should one offer after sunrise. He offers in the brilliance of day and night who offers in the evening after sunset and in the morning after sunrise. By Agni as brilliance the night is brilliant, by Āditya as brilliant the day is brilliant.

[1] The sense is clearly that the gods also act as fees; hence Weber's view (*Ind. Stud.* ix. 290) '*vivaddināḥ* is wrong. Sāyaṇa offers an alternative that the men are meant, having obtained the fees in the shape of divine favour.

[2] The point is that the opening to Agni of the Āçvina is compared with the offering to Agni at evening: the Pratigara is according to Sāyaṇa *vācā tvā hotrā*: see ĀpÇS. vi. 1. 2; and in the next case of the offering to Āditya *annaṁ payo reto 'smāsu dhehi*; see ĀpÇS. vi. 11. 5; ÇÇS. iv. 18. 1.

[3] Weber (*Ind. Stud.* ix. 291) refers them to 360 *yajuṣmatyaḥ* and 360 *pariçrit* bricks in ÇB. x. 4. 2. 2.

v. 29. [1] This is the reasonable sense and construction; cf. KB. ii. 9. The *yad* may be 'that', one *iti* being only usual to cover *vadca*, or it may be the relative, in which case there is a slight anacoluthon but the first view is perhaps the best.

In the brilliance of day and night does he offer who knowing thus offers after sunrise. Therefore should one offer after sunrise [2].

v. 30 (xxv. 5) Day and night are the wheels of the year; verily thus with them he goes through the year. If he offers before sunrise, that is as if one were to go with (a chariot with) a single wheel. But if he offers after sunrise, that is as if one were swiftly to perform a journey with (a chariot with) wheels on both sides. As to this the sacrificial verse is recited:

'This goeth yoked with Bṛhad and Rathantara,
All that hath been and is to be;
With them should he go who is wise taking the fires,
By day should he offer one, by night another.'

The night is connected with the Rathantara, the day with the Bṛhat; Agni is the Rathantara, Āditya the Bṛhat. Those deities make him attain the vault of the tawny one, the world of heaven, who knowing thus offers after sunrise. Therefore should one offer after sunrise. As to this, the sacrificial verse is recited

'As one may go with a single horse
Having nothing else for harnessing,
So many men go,
Who offer the Agnihotra before sunrise.'

The deity as it proceeds, all this whatever there is here follows upon it; of the deity all this whatever there is here is a follower; this deity is that which has followers. A follower he finds, a follower is his who knows thus. He is the one guest, he lives among the offerers. This is why there is in the world the following verse

'Let him heap blame on the blameless,
Or take away blame from the blameworthy,
The one guest at evening he turns away,
The thief who stole away the lotus fibres.' [1]

[2] Weber (*Ind. Stud.* ix. 292) points out that in the Avesta there is expressed a preference for the period from the first appearance of light to the sunrise as the proper time of sacrifice, while the time of the sunrise is the *daevayaçna*.

[1] *Yo* for *so* is an obvious correction suggested first by Weber and later by Geldner. The stanza was partly intelligible to Sāyaṇa, as he makes it said as an oath by one accused of stealing lotus fibres. The verse is clearly cited from a story of which we have divergent versions in the *Mahābhārata* (2 accounts; xiii. 4396–4546 and 4547–4600) and in the *Jātaka* no. 488, and in which the Ṛṣis in order to release themselves of the accusation of being guilty of the theft of lotus fibres swore frightful oaths, one of which is here recorded, but which has no parallel in the *Mahābhārata* or the *Jātaka*. See Charpentier, ZDMG. lxiv. 65 *seq.*; lxvi. 44 *seq.*; Geldner, lxv. 306, 307 (who overlooks Weber's suggestion of *yo*); Oldenberg, GGN. 1911, p. 464, n. 2 who suggests *ruṇaddhu* as a possibility, a very plausible conjecture.

He is the one guest, he dwells among offerers; this deity he turns away who being fit for the Agnihotra does not offer the Agnihotra. This deity being turned away turns him away from this world and from yonder, both of them, who being fit for the Agnihotra does not offer the Agnihotra. Therefore he who is fit for the Agnihotra should offer it. Therefore they say 'A guest at evening should not be turned away', knowing this Nagarin Jānaçruteya said as to Aikādaçākṣi [2] Mānutantavya 'In his offspring will we know him if he offer with knowledge or without knowledge'. Of Aikādaçākṣi the offspring became as kingly person; as a kingly person his offspring becomes, who knowing thus offers after sunrise. Therefore after sunrise should offering be made.

v. 31 (xxv. 6) Āditya on rising unites his rays with the Āhavanīya; if one offers before sunrise, that is as if one were to offer the breast to a child unborn or to a calf unborn. But, if he offers after sunrise, that is as if one were to offer the breast to a child born or a calf born.[1] Through his being united in both worlds proper food is offered both from this world and from yonder to him. If he offers before sunrise, that is as if one were to offer to a man or an elephant, without hand stretched out [2], if he offers after sunrise it is as if one were to offer to a man or an elephant, with hand stretched forth. He [3] having taken him with his hand and dragged him upwards places him in the world of heaven, who knowing thus offers after sunrise. Therefore one should offer after sunrise. Āditya as he rises leads forward all creatures; therefore they call him breath. In breath does he sacrifice who knowing thus sacrifices after sunrise; therefore one should sacrifice after sunrise. Speaking truth he offers in truth who offers in the evening after sunset and in the morning after sunrise. With *bhūḥ, bhuvaḥ, svar, om*; Agni is light, light is Agni' he offers in the evening; with '*bhūḥ, bhuvaḥ, svar, om*; Sūrya is light, light is Sūrya' in the morning. By him speaking truth in truth is the offering made, who knowing thus offers after sunrise; therefore should one offer after sunrise. As to this a sacrificial verse is sung:

[2] *Aikādaçākṣim* should probably be read as suggested by *tasya* below where *Aikādaçākṣe* as a locative is very difficult.

[1] Cf. ÇB. ii. 2. 1. 1.

[2] So Sāyaṇa and Haug: but of course *prayate* and *aprayate* may equally well be datives, and the sense be 'put into the hand of a man who is not coming', as Weber (*Ind. Stud.* ix. 298), prefers as in KB. ii. 9.

[3] Sāyaṇa consistently here and in the clause above *tam asmai pratidhīyamānam* takes the worshipper and the sun as the two persons though he renders the passive erroneously as an active. This seems correct, as the only real alternative is to assume that the sun and the sacrifice are meant which is very difficult in the second passage, as *tam* must correspond with *ya* since *eṣa* clearly is the sun.

'Every morning they tell falsehood
Who offer the Agnihotra before sunrise,
Declaring what is to be declared by day on what is not day,
"Sūrya is the light"; there is not then light for them.[3]'

Errors in the Sacrifice.

v. 32 (xxv. 7) Prajāpati[1] desired 'May I be propagated; may I be multiplied'. He practised fervour; having practised fervour he created these worlds; the earth, the atmosphere, the sky. He brooded over these worlds; from these worlds when brooded over these luminaries were born; Agni was born from the earth, Vāyu from the atmosphere, Āditya from the sky. He brooded over these luminaries. From these brooded over the three Vedas were born; the Ṛgveda was born from Agni, the Yajurveda from Vāyu, the Sāmaveda from Aditya. He brooded over these Vedas; from these (Vedas) when brooded over three pure (sounds) were born; *bhūḥ* from the Ṛgveda was born, *bhuvaḥ* from the Yajurveda, *svar* from the Sāmaveda. He brooded over these pure ones; from them when brooded over the three sounds were born; the letter *a*, the letter *u*, and the letter *m*. Them he brought together; that made (the word) *om*. Therefore with *om* does he say the Praṇava. *Om* is the world of heaven; *om* is he that yonder gives heat. Prajāpati extended the sacrifice; he took it; he sacrificed with it. He performed the Hotṛ's office with the Ṛc alone, the Adhvaryu's with the Yajus, the Udgātṛ's with the Sāman. He performed the Brahman's office with the pure (part) of the threefold knowledge. Prajāpati handed over the sacrifice to the gods; the gods extended the sacrifice; they took it, they sacrificed with it. They performed the Hotṛ's office with the Ṛc alone, the Adhvaryu's with the Yajus, the Udgātṛ's with the Sāman. They performed the Brahman's office with the pure (part) of the threefold knowledge. The gods said to Prajāpati 'If there be trouble in our sacrifice from the Ṛc, or from the Yajus, or from the Sāman, or an unknown (trouble) or a complete failure, what is the expiation?' To the gods said Prajāpati 'If there is trouble in your sacrifice from the Ṛc, do ye offer on the Gārhapatya, with '*bhūḥ*'; if from the Yajus, with '*bhuvaḥ*' on the Agnīdh's altar, or on the Anvāhāryapacana at oblation sacrifices[2]; if from the Sāman, with '*svar*' on the Āhavanīya; if (the trouble) is unknown or a complete

[3] The last words really give a further assertion of what is already said in *adivā*, which is based, of course, on *divā*; *sūryo jyotiḥ* is clearly a citation without *iti*.

[1] KB. xxvi. 3–6 has a Prāyaçcitta section, but only remotely similar. Cf. ÇB. xi. 5. 8; CU. iv. 17; ṢB. i. 5. 6–8; JB. i. 357, 358; JUB. iii. 15. 4–17. 10; Oertel, JAOS. xviii. 33, 34; *Trans. Conn. Acad.* xv. 155 *sq.*

[2] As opposed to the Soma sacrifice where alone there is an Agnīdh's altar.

failure, running through all '*bhūḥ, bhuvaḥ, svar*', do ye offer on the Āhavanīya only'. These exclamations are the internal fastenings of the Vedas; just as one may unite one thing with another[3], or joint with joint, or with a cord unite an object of leather or something which has come apart, so with these he unites whatever in the sacrifice has come apart. These exclamations are an expiation for all; therefore this expiation only should be performed in the sacrifice.

v. 33 (xxv. 8). Important sages say 'Since the Hotṛ's office is performed with the Ṛc, the Adhvaryu's with the Yajus, the Udgātṛ's with the Sāman, the threefold knowledge is taken up; how then is the Brahman's office performed?' 'With the threefold knowledge', he should say. He that blows here is the sacrifice; two paths it has, speech and mind, for by speech and by mind the sacrifice proceeds. Speech is this (earth), mind yonder (world); by speech as the threefold knowledge they make ready one side, by mind the Brahman makes (another) ready.[1] Now some Brahman priests, when the morning litany is begun, having muttered the Stomabhāgas[2], wait talking. As to this[3] a Brahman said, seeing the Brahman talking when the morning litany was begun, 'They have omitted half of this sacrifice'. Just as a man with one foot when going, or a chariot with a wheel on one side when moving, fails, so the sacrifice fails and through the failure of the sacrifice the sacrificer fails. Therefore the Brahman priest, when the morning litany is begun, should remain silent until the offering of the Upāñçu and Antaryāma (cups); when the Pavamānas have been begun, until the conclusion; again, in the case of Stotras accompanied with Çastras, he should be silent until their *vaṣaṭ* call. Just as a man with both feet when going, or a chariot with wheels on both sides when moving, does not come to any harm, so the sacrifice does not come to harm, and through the sacrifice being unharmed, the sacrificer is not harmed.

v. 34 (xxv. 9). They say 'Seeing that the fees are brought for the Adhvaryu (by the sacrificer thinking) 'He has drawn the cups for me, he has acted for me, he has offered the libations for me', for the Udgātṛ (thinking) 'He has sung for me', for the Hotṛ (thinking) 'He has said the invitatory verses for me, he has recited (the litanies) for me, he has said the offering verses for me', what has the Brahman priest done for the fees brought for him; or is it that without action he is to receive them?' The Brahman is the physician

[3] Sāyaṇa justifies the rendering by a reference to CU. iv. 17. 7, where cases of other things are given.

[1] CU. iv. 17. 1.

[2] For these cf. PB. i. 8, 9; TS. iii. 5. 2; iv. 4. 1; v. 3. 6; KS. xvii. 7; xxxvii. 7; MS. ii. 8. F; VS. xv. 6.

[3] See GB. iii. 2, 3.

of the sacrifice; he receives for making medicine for the sacrifice. Moreover in that (the Brahman) performs his function as Brahman with the greatest amount of holy power, with the sap of the metres, therefore is he the Brahman; in the beginning the Brahman was a sharer of half with the other priests; a half (of the holy power) was the Brahman's, a half the other priests. Therefore if there is trouble in the sacrifice from the Ṛc the Brahman should offer on the Gārhapatya with '*bhūḥ*'; if from the Yajus, on the Agnīdh's altar, or on the Anvāhāryapacana at oblation offerings with '*bhuvaḥ*'; if from the Sāman with '*svar*' on the Āhavanīya; if (the trouble) is unknown or a complete failure, he should run over all '*bhūḥ, bhuvaḥ, svar*' and offer on the Āhavanīya only. The Prastotṛ when the Stotra is being begun, says 'O Brahman,[1] shall we chant, O Praçāstṛ?'. At the morning pressing the Brahman should say '*bhūḥ*! with Indra do ye chant'; '*bhuvaḥ*' he should say at the midday pressing 'With Indra do ye chant'; '*svar*' he should say at the third pressing, 'With Indra do ye chant'. '*bhūḥ, bhuvaḥ, svar*' he should say at an Uktha or Atirātra, 'With Indra do ye chant'. In that he says 'With Indra do ye chant', and the sacrifice is connected with Indra, and the god of the sacrifice is Indra, verily thus he makes the chanting possessed of Indra, verily to them he says in effect 'Let it go not from Indra; with Indra do ye chant'.

[1] For this cf. ĀÇS. v. 2. 11-16; ÇÇS. vi. 8. 5, 6. For the Brahman's activity see KB. vi. 12. See also MÇS. iii. 1. 11 *seq.*; ĀpÇS. ix. 16. 4, 5. The absence of reference to the AV. is strongly in favour of the priority of the AB.; cf. Bloomfield, *Atharvaveda*, p. 4.

PAÑCIKĀ VI

THE SOMA SACRIFICE (*continued*).

The Recitations of the Hotrakas.

ADHYĀYA I

The Offices of the Subrahmaṇyā and Grāvastut.

vi. 1 (xxvi. 1). The[1] gods performed a Sattra at Sarvacaru;[2] they could not smite away evil. To them said Arbuda Kādraveya, the serpent seer, the maker of spells, 'One Hotṛ's office has not been performed by you, that will I perform for you; then will you smite away evil. They said 'Be it so'. At each midday he crept out for them; he praised the pressing stones; therefore at each midday they praise the pressing stones in imitation of him. The way by which he crept out is now called the creeping out of Arbuda. Them the king made drunk; they said 'It is a poisonous snake that looks at our king; come, with a turban let us bind his eyes'. 'Be it so' (they said); with a turban they bound[3] his eyes; therefore winding round a turban they praise the pressing stones in imitation of him. The king still made them drunk; they said 'With his own spell he praises the pressing stones; come, let us mingle the spell with other verses.' 'Be it so' (they said); with other verses they mingled his spell; then he did not make them drunk. In that they mingle his spell with other verses, verily (it serves) for expiation. They smote away evil; in accordance with their smiting away the serpents smote away evil; having smitten away evil they lay aside their old worn out skin and go on with a new one. He smites away evil who knows thus.

vi. 2 (xxvi. 2). They say 'With how many verses[1] should he praise?'

[1] For the activity of the Grāvastut see KB. xxix. 1; his part is described in full in ĀÇS. v. 12; ÇÇS. vii. 15. His special Arbuda hymn is RV. x. 94 with x. 76 and x. 175 before the last verse; these are preceded by RV. i. 24. 3; v. 81. 1; viii. 81. 1; 1. 1; Eggeling, SBE. xxvi. 331, 332; Cf. Lévi, *La doctrine du sacrifice*, pp. 142, 143.

[2] A place according to Sāyaṇa: Aufrecht supplies *yajñe*; a man, BR.

[3] *Apinahyus* is a wholly anomalous and incorrect form; probably merely a blunder.

vi. 2. [1] I. e. of the Pāvamānī verses which he is to use.

'With a hundred' they say; man has a hundred (years of) life, a hundred strengths, a hundred powers; verily thus he places him in life, in strength, in power. 'Or with thirty-three' they say; 'he smote away the evils of thirty-three gods; thirty-three were the gods for him.' With an unlimited number should he praise; Prajāpati is unlimited. The Hotr̥ function of the Grāvastut is Prajāpati's; in it all desires are won. In that he praises with an unlimited number, (it serves) to win all desires. All desires he wins who knows thus. Therefore should he praise with an unlimited number only. They say 'How is he to praise?' 'By syllables?' 'By sets of four syllables?' 'By Padas?' 'By half-verses?' 'By verses?' By verses does not fit, nor again does by Padas fit; as to by syllables or sets of four syllables, the metres would be broken up so, many syllables would so be omitted. By half verses only should he praise, for support. Man has two supports, cattle four feet; verily thus he makes the sacrificer with two supports find support in four-footed cattle. Therefore should he praise by half verses only. They say 'Since it is at the midday only that he praises the pressing stones, how is the praising at the other pressings performed by him?' In that he praises with Gāyatrī verses, and the morning pressing is in Gāyatrī, thereby (is the praise accomplished) at the morning pressing; in that he praises with Jagatī verses, and the third pressing is in Jagatī, thereby at the third pressing. So by him who knows thus, although he praises the pressing stones only at the midday, is praising accomplished in all the pressings. They say 'Seeing that the Adhvaryu directs the other priests, then why does he undertake this without a direction?' The office of the Grāvastut is mind; mind requires no direction; therefore he undertakes this without a direction.

vi. 3 (xxvi. 1). The Subrahmaṇyā[1] is speech; its calf is Soma the king; when Soma the king has been bought, they summon the Subrahmaṇyā, just as one summons a cow; with this as calf it milks all desires for the sacrificer. All desires speech milks for him who knows thus. They say 'Why has the Subrahmaṇyā its name?' 'It is speech', he should reply; 'speech is the holy power and the good holy power (*su-brahma*).' They say 'Why then do they call him that is male female as it were?' 'Because the Subrahmaṇyā is speech' he should reply, 'for that reason.' They say 'Seeing that the other priests perform their priestly functions within the altar, and the Subrahmaṇyā without the altar, how is his function performed within the altar?' 'From the altar they throw up the rubbish heap; in that standing on the heap he calls', he should reply, 'for that

[1] For the Subrahmaṇyā formula see ÇB. iii. 3. 4. 17 *seq.*; TĀ. i. 12. 3, 4; LÇS. i. 3; Caland and Henry, *L'Agniṣṭoma*, pp. 65 *seq.*; Oertel, JAOS. xviii. 34.

reason.' They say 'Then why does he stand on the heap when calling the Subrahmaṇyā?' The seers performed a sacrificial session; to the tallest[2] of them they said 'Do thou call the Subrahmaṇyā; from nearest wilt thou summon the gods.' Verily thus they make him the tallest; moreover thus he delights the whole of the altar. They say 'Why do they drive up a bull as the fee for him?' 'The bull is male, the Subrahmaṇyā female; that is a pair; for the propagation of this pair' (he should reply). Inaudibly[3] the Agnīdh utters the offering verse for the cup for (Tvaṣṭṛ) with the wives; the cup for (Tvaṣṭṛ) with the wives is seed; seed is poured inaudibly as it were. He does not say the second *vaṣaṭ* (thinking) 'The second *vaṣaṭ* call is a completion; let me not bring seed to completion.' The incomplete state of seed is perfect; therefore he does not say the second *vaṣaṭ*. Seated on the lap of the Neṣṭṛ he partakes; the Neṣṭṛ represents the wife;[4] Agni places seed in the wives for propagation; verily thus by Agni he places seed in the wives for propagation. He is propagated with offspring and cattle who knows thus. After the fees the Subrahmaṇyā is completed; the Subrahmaṇyā is speech; the fee is food; verily thus in proper food and speech at the end they establish the sacrifice.

ADHYĀYA II

The Çastras of the other Hotrakas at Sattras and Ahīnas.

vi. 4 (xxvii. 1). The[1] gods performed a sacrifice; as they were performing it the Asuras came up to them (saying) 'We will make a confusion of their sacrifice.' From the south they approached them, where they thought was the thinnest part of the sacrifice. The gods perceiving this put Mitra and Varuṇa around on the south; by means of Mitra and Varuṇa on the south at the morning pressing they smote away the Asuras and the Rakṣases. Verily thus also the sacrificers by means of Mitra and Varuṇa on the south at the morning pressing smite away the Asuras and the Rakṣases. Therefore the Maitrāvaruṇa recites (the litany) to Mitra and Varuṇa at the morning pressing, for by means of Mitra and Varuṇa the gods smote away the Asuras and the Rakṣases on the south at the morning pressing. Smitten off at the south the Asuras entered

[2] 'Eldest' Sāyaṇa and Haug, but 'tallest' above gives a reply to the question of the use of the Utkara.

[3] For the omission of the *anuvaṣaṭkāra* see ĀÇS. v. 5. 21.

[4] For this Sāyaṇa cites TS. vi. 5. 8. 6. Cf. also ÇB. iv. 4. 2. 17; ÇÇS. viii. 5. 3, 4.

[1] This chapter merely gives explanations of the origin of the several Çastras of the three Hotrakas.

the sacrifice in the middle. The gods perceiving this placed Indra in the middle; they with Indra in the middle smote away the Asuras and Rakṣases at the morning pressing. Verily thus also the sacrificers with Indra in the middle smite away the Asuras and the Rakṣases at the morning pressing. Therefore the Brāhmaṇācchaṅsin at the morning pressing recites (a litany) to Indra, for with Indra in the middle the gods at the morning pressing smote away the Asuras and the Rakṣases. The Asuras, smitten off in the middle, entered the sacrifice from the north. The gods, perceiving this, put Indra and Agni around on the north; with Indra and Agni on the north at the morning pressing they smote away the Asuras and the Rakṣases. Verily thus also the sacrificers with Indra and Agni on the north at the morning pressing smite away the Asuras and the Rakṣases. Therefore the Achāvāka at the morning pressing recites (a litany) to Indra and Agni, for with Indra and Agni on the north at the morning pressing the gods smote away the Asuras and the Rakṣases. The Asuras smitten off on the north ran round to the front in battle array. The gods perceiving this placed Agni around in front at the morning pressing; with Agni in front at the morning pressing they smote away the Asuras and the Rakṣases. Verily thus also the sacrificers with Agni in front at the morning pressing smite away the Asuras and the Rakṣases. Therefore the morning pressing is connected with Agni. He smites away evil who knows thus. The Asuras, smitten off in front, having gone round to the back entered. The gods, perceiving this, put the All-gods, as their self, around behind at the third pressing; they with the All-gods, as themselves, behind at the third pressing smote away the Asuras and the Rakṣases. Verily thus also the sacrificers with the All-gods, as themselves, behind at the third pressing smite away the Asuras and the Rakṣases. Therefore the third pressing is connected with the All-gods. He smites away evil who knows thus. So the gods smote away the Asuras from the whole of the sacrifice. Then the gods prospered, the Asuras were defeated. He prospers himself, the evil rival who hates him is defeated, who knows thus. The gods with the sacrifice so ordered smote away the Asuras, the evil, and conquered the world of heaven. He smites away the evil rival who hates him and conquers the world of heaven who knows thus and who knowing thus orders the pressings.

vi. 5 (xxvii. 2). They make the strophe the antistrophe of the strophe[1]

[1] The point is that the Çastras of the Hotrakas are made up at the morning pressing of the Stotriya (taken from the corresponding three Ājya Sāmans) and as Anurūpa the Stotriya of the next day. This cannot be done at the other pressings because the Stotras there (Pṛṣṭha and Uktha) do not from day to day remain in the same ritual form. The idea occurs in AB. vi. 17. See ĀÇS. vii. 2. 2 *seq.* Cf. GB. vii. 11.

at the morning pressing; verily thus they make one day the counterpart of the other; verily thus by the preceding day they lay hold of the subsequent day. But this is not the case at the midday (pressing); the Pṛṣṭhas are prosperity; they have not the position[2] for the purpose of making the strophe the antistrophe of the strophe. By reason of the same distinction they do not at the third pressing make the strophe the antistrophe of the strophe.

vi. 6 (xxvii. 3). Next as to the commencing verses.[1] 'With true guidance for us, let Varuṇa' is that of the Maitrāvaruṇa[2] (containing) 'Let Mitra lead us knowing'; the Maitrāvaruṇa is the leader of the Hotrakas; therefore this (verse) contains the word 'leader'. 'Indra for you on all sides' is that of the Brāhmaṇācchaṅsin,[3] (containing) 'We invoke for men'; verily with this (verse) day by day they invoke Indra. When they invoke in competition no other appropriates Indra, where a Brāhmaṇācchaṅsin knowing thus day by day recites this (verse). 'What time, when the Soma was pressed, men' is that of the Achāvāka;[4] 'invoked Indra and Agni' (it continues); verily with this (verse) day by day they invoke Indra and Agni. When they invoke in competition no other appropriates Indra and Agni, where an Achāvāka knowing thus recites this (verse) day by day. They are ships which carry over to the world of heaven; verily with these (verses) they cross to the world of heaven.

vi. 7 (xxvii. 4). Next as to the concluding verses. 'May we be thine, O god Varuṇa' is that of the Maitrāvaruṇa;[1] 'Sap and light may we obtain' (it ends); 'sap' is this world; 'light' is yonder world; verily with this (verse) they lay hold of both worlds. 'He hath traversed the atmosphere' is that of the Brāhmaṇācchaṅsin,[2] a triplet, containing the word 'apart'; verily with these he puts apart the world of heaven for them. 'In the joy of the Soma the worlds, when Indra broke Vala' (he says); the consecrated ones are eager to win; therefore this (verse) contains the word 'hole' (*vala*).

> 'He drove out the cows for the Aṅgirases,
> Revealing them that were in secret,
> Headlong he hurled Vala;'

verily with this (verse) he wins booty. 'By Indra the spaces of the

[2] Aufrecht with Sāyaṇa and Haug and the Ānand. ed. read *tatsthānāni*: Weber (*Ind. Stud.* ix. 295) suggests the alteration *tasthānāni*, quoting the precise parallel with *yad* in ÇB. xii. 5. 1. 1–8, but this is no doubt wrong: cf. Eggeling, SBE. xxvi. 242, n. 1; KB. xxvi. 8: *etatsthāne* . . . *çasyāya*.

[1] I. e. after the Stotriyas and Anurūpas of AB. vi. 5 in sacrifices of a series of days.

[2] RV. i. 90. 1; ĀÇS. vii. 2. 10; ÇÇS. xii. 2. 14.

[3] RV. i. 7. 10; ĀÇS. vii. 2. 10.

[4] RV. vii. 94. 10; ĀÇS. vii. 2. 10. Cf. ÇÇS. xii. 2. 19.

vi. 7. [1] RV. vii. 66. 9.

[2] RV. viii. 14. 7–9.

sky' (he says); the spaces of the sky are the world of heaven; by Indra (they)

'Are made firm and established
The firm are not to be moved away';

verily with this (verse) day by day they continue to find support in the world of heaven. 'I seek of those with Sarasvatī' is that of the Achāvāka;[3] Sarasvatī is speech; verily thus he says 'of those with speech'; 'Of Indra and Agni the aid' (he says); speech is the dear abode of Indra and Agni; verily thus he unites these two with their dear abode. With a dear abode does he prosper who knows thus.

vi. 8 (xxvii. 5). There are two kinds of concluding verses of the Hotrakas, at the morning and at the midday, those of the Ahīna and those of the one day rites. The Maitrāvaruṇa concludes with those of the one day rite only;[1] thereby he departs not from the world. With those of the Ahīna the Achāvāka,[2] to obtain the world of heaven. Both are used by the Brāhmanācchaṅsin;[3] thereby grasping both he goes to this and to yonder world; moreover he goes grasping both, the Maitrāvaruṇa and the Achāvāka, the Ahīna and the one day rite, the year and the Agniṣṭoma. Now at the third pressing the concluding verses of the Hotrakas are those of the one day rite only;[4] the one day (rite) is a support; verily thus at the end they establish the sacrifice on a support. Without taking a breath he should say the offering verse at the morning pressing; save for one or two (verses) he should not recite beyond the Stoma,[5] (thinking) 'That is as if one were to give quickly to one neighing and thirsting; moreover I shall swiftly give proper food and Soma drinking to the gods.' Swiftly he finds support in the world. (He uses) an unlimited number at the two latter pressings; the world of heaven is unlimited; (verily it serves) to obtain the world of heaven. At pleasure the Hotṛ may recite whatever the Hotrakas may recite on the previous day; or the Hotrakas

[3] RV. viii. 38. 10.

[1] I. e. at the two Savanas of morning and midday he uses the same concluding verse (the plural being *prayogabahutvāpekṣam*) they are RV. vii. 66. 9 and iv. 16. 21 (cf. AB. vi. 28). See ĀÇS. v. 10. 28; 16. 1; vi. 18. 5.

[2] RV. viii. 38. 10 and vii. 94. 9; RV. ii. 11. 21 (AB. vi. 23) and iii. 30. 22 are those for the Ahīna and Ekāha respectively.

[3] This means that at the morning pressing he used different verses in the Ekāha and Ahīna (RV. viii. 93. 3; 14. 9), but at the midday pressing the same (RV. vii. 23. 6).

[4] Viz. RV. vii. 84. 1; x. 43. 1; vi. 69. 1; see ĀÇS. viii. 2. 16; 3. 34; 4. 3.

[5] The sense as taken by Sāyaṇa and Haug seems that meant; cf. AB. vi. 23. 10 for the same use: Weber (*Ind. Stud.* ix. 296) objects on grammatical grounds to the wording and prefers the normal 'He should use one or two verses, but not over recite the Stoma'; but this is really not consistent with the context in vi. 23 and ĀÇS. vii. 18. 2 expressly says that there is *atiçaṅsana* in one or two verses.

what the Hotṛ may recite; the Hotṛ is the breath, the Hotrakas the limbs; in common does this breath go through the limbs. Therefore at pleasure the Hotṛ may recite what the Hotrakas recite on the previous day, or the Hotrakas what the Hotṛ (recites). The Hotṛ keeps concluding with the ends of the hymns. Moreover the concluding verses of the Hotrakas are the same at the third pressing; the Hotṛ is the body, the Hotrakas the limbs; the ends of the limbs are the same; therefore the concluding verses of the Hotrakas at the third pressing are the same.

ADHYĀYA III

The Çastras and other Recitations of the Hotrakas.

vi. 9 (xxviii. 1). 'Let[1] the bays carry thee hither' he recites at the morning pressing for the (goblets) being filled, (verses) containing (the words) 'strong', 'drink', 'pressed', and 'be drunk' and so perfect in form. They are (verses) to Indra which he recites; the sacrifice is connected with Indra. They are Gāyatrīs which he recites; the morning pressing is connected with the Gāyatrī. Nine small[2] (verses) he recites at the morning pressing; in what is small is seed poured; ten at the midday he recites; seed poured in the small having attained the middle part of the woman becomes most firm; nine small (verses) he recites at the third pressing: from what is small are offspring born. In that he repeats the whole of the hymns, verily thus he propagates the sacrificer as an embryo from the sacrifice as the womb of the gods. Some recite seven verses each, seven at the morning pressing, seven at the midday (pressing), seven at the third pressing; saying 'The offering verses should be as many as the invitatory verses;[3] seven eastward say the offering verses, seven say the *vaṣaṭ* call; these are the invitatory verses of those'. That he should not do so; they injure the seed of the sacrifice and morever the sacrificer himself, for the hymn is the sacrificer. By nine (verses) the Maitrāvaruṇa carries him from this world to the world of the atmosphere, by ten from the world of the atmosphere to yonder world, for the world of the atmosphere is the longest,[4] with nine from

[1] This chapter, in part, like KB. xxviii. 2 and 3 deals with the Maitrāvaruṇa's recitations at the three pressings, which are RV. i. 16 (ĀÇS. v. 5. 14), vii. 21, and iv. 35 complete in each case as against the alternative of sets of seven verses.

[2] The argument is that as ten is the norm, nine is small; or defective.

[3] I. e. at the Prasthita offering; see ĀÇS. v. 5. 15–18; ÇÇS. vii. 4. 2–10; Caland and Henry, *L'Agniṣṭoma*, pp. 209, 211, 212.

[4] Sāyaṇa treats this as if it were *antarikṣalokād dhi*: the world meant is in his view the *nākapṛṣṭha*.

yonder world to the world of heaven. They cannot bear the sacrificer to the world of heaven who recite sets of seven. Therefore as wholes should he recite the hymns.

vi. 10 (xxviii. 2). Further he says 'Seeing that the sacrifice is for Indra, then why do two only at the morning pressing use as offering verses for the Prasthita (libations) verses manifestly addressed to Indra, namely the Hotṛ and the Brāhmaṇācchaṅsin: 'This Soma drink for thee' is the offering verse of the Hotṛ,[1] 'O Indra, thee as a bull we' is that of the Brāhmaṇācchaṅsin.[2] The others use (verses) to various deities; how are their verses connected with Indra?' The Maitrāvaruṇa[3] uses as offering verse 'Mitra we hail'; 'Varuṇa for the Soma drinking' (he says); whatever Pada contains (the word) 'drink' is a symbol of Indra; thereby he delights Indra. The Potṛ[4] uses as offering verse 'O Maruts, in whose dwelling'; 'He is best protected of men' (he says); the protector is Indra; this is a symbol of Indra; thereby he delights Indra. 'O Agni, bring hither the wives' the Neṣṭṛ[5] uses as offering verse; 'Tvaṣṭṛ to the Soma drinking' (he says); Tvaṣṭṛ is Indra; this is a symbol of Indra; thereby he delights Indra. 'To him whose food is the ox, whose food the cow' the Agnīdh[6] uses as offering verse; 'Soma-backed, the creator' (he says); the creator is Indra; this is a symbol of Indra; thereby he delights Indra.

'Come hither with those that move at dawn,
The gods, ye that have excellent wealth,
Indra and Agni, to the Soma drinking';

is the offering verse of the Achāvāka,[7] being in itself perfect. So are these verses to Indra; in that they are addressed to various deities, thereby he delights the other deities. In that they are in Gāyatrī, thereby they are connected with Agni; these three with them he obtains.

vi. 11 (xxviii. 3). 'There[1] hath been pressed the divine Soma juice mingled with milk' he recites at the midday for (the goblets) being filled, (verses) containing (the words) 'strong', 'drink', 'pressed', and 'be drunk' and so perfect a form. (The verses) which he recites are addressed to Indra; the sacrifice is connected with Indra; they are Triṣṭubh verses which he recites;

[1] RV. viii. 65. 8; ĀÇS. v. 5. 18; ÇÇS. vii. 4. 3. Cf. KB. xxviii. 3; GB. vii. 20.
[2] RV. iii. 40. 1; ĀÇS. v. 5. 18; ÇÇS. vii. 4. 7.
[3] RV. i. 23. 4; ĀÇS. v. 5. 18; ÇÇS. vii. 4. 6.
[4] RV. i. 86. 1; ĀÇS. v. 5. 18; ÇÇS. vii. 4. 8.
[5] RV. i. 22. 9; ĀÇS. v. 5. 18; ÇÇS. vii. 4. 9.
[6] RV. viii. 43. 11; ĀÇS. v. 5. 18; ÇÇS. vii. 4. 10.
[7] RV. viii. 38. 7; AÇS. v. 7. 6; ÇÇS. vii. 7. 2.

vi. 11. [1] This chapter gives the hymn for the filling of the goblets and the Prasthita libations; for the former see ĀÇS. v. 5. 14; 18. 11; ÇÇS. vii. 17. 3; it is merely alluded to in KB. xxix. 2. The hymn is RV. vii. 21: the word *gorjika* is quite uncertain; 'dont la flèche est la vache' is Caland and Henry's rendering *L'Agniṣṭoma*, p. 284.

the midday pressing is connected with the Triṣṭubh. They say 'Seeing that (the word) "be drunk" is a symbol of the third pressing, then why does he recite verses containing (the word) "be drunk" and why do they use such verses as offering verses?' At the midday the gods become drunk as it were; they also at the third pressing become drunk together; therefore at the midday he recites (verses) containing the word 'be drunk' and they use such (verses) as offering verses. All of them at the midday use for the Prasthita libations [2] verses manifestly addressed to Indra. Some use verses containing (the words) 'penetrate towards'. The Hotṛ [3] uses as offering verse 'Drink the Soma towards which O dread one thou hast penetrated'. The Maitrāvaruṇa [4] uses as offering verse 'Drink it, thou that art impetuous, penetrating'. The Brāhmaṇācchaṅsin [5] uses as offering verses 'Do thou drink as of old; let it delight thee'. The Potṛ [6] uses as offering verse 'Come hither; Soma lover they call thee'. The Neṣṭṛ [7] uses as offering verse 'Thine is this Soma; do thou come hither'. The Achāvāka [8] uses as offering verse 'For Indra the Soma draughts found aforetime'. The Agnīdh [9] uses as offering verse 'Filled is his cup; hail!' Of these those contain (the words) 'penetrate towards'; Indra was not victorious at the morning pressing; with these (verses) he penetrated towards the midday pressing; in that he penetrated towards, therefore do these verses contain (the words) 'penetrate towards'.

vi. 12 (xxviii. 4). 'Come [1] hither, O sons of strength' he recites at the third pressing for (the goblet) being filled, (verses) containing (the words) 'strong', 'drink', 'press', and 'be drunk' and so perfect in form. They are addressed to Indra and the Ṛbhus. They say 'Since they do not chant (verses) to the Ṛbhus, then why do they call it the Ārbhava Pavamāna?' Prajāpati as father having made immortal the Ṛbhus being mortal gave them a share in the third pressing; therefore they do not chant (verses) to the Ṛbhus, but they call it the Ārbhava Pavamāna. Further he says 'Seeing that in the two first pressings he recites according to the metre, Gāyatrī verses at the morning pressing, Triṣṭubhs at the midday pressing, then why does he recite Triṣṭubh verses at the third pressing which is connected with the Jagatī?'

[2] For the Prasthitas, see ĀÇS. v. 5. 19; ÇÇS. vii. 17. 6–11; Caland and Henry, pp. 286, 287.

[3] RV. vi. 17. 1: this and the next two contain forms of *abhi-tṛd* ĀÇS. v. 5. 19; ÇÇS. vii. 17. 5. Cf. GB. vii. 21.

[4] RV. vi. 17. 2; ĀÇS. v. 5. 18; ÇÇS. vii. 17. 6.

[5] RV. vi. 17. 3; ĀÇS. v. 5. 19; ÇÇS. vii. 17. 7.

[6] RV. i. 104. 9; ĀÇS. v. 5. 19; ÇÇS. vii. 17. 8.

[7] RV. iii. 35. 6; ĀÇS. v. 5. 19; ÇÇS. vii. 17. 9.

[8] RV. iii. 36. 2; ĀÇS. v. 5. 19; ÇÇS. vii. 17. 10. ĀÇS. inverts the order of the preceding and this.

[9] RV. iii. 32. 15; ĀÇS. v. 5. 19; ÇÇS. vii. 17. 11.

[1] For the filling of the goblets to RV. iv. 35 see ĀÇS. v. 5. 14; ÇÇS. viii. 2. 3; Caland and Henry, *L'Agniṣṭoma*, pp. 345, 346. It is merely referred to in KB. xxx. 1. Cf. GB. vii. 22.

'The third pressing has the sap sucked out; the Triṣṭubh metre is one with the sap not sucked out but full of pure juice; (therefore it serves) to make it full of sap' should he reply; 'Moreover he thus gives Indra a share in the pressing'. Further he says 'Seeing that the third pressing is connected with Indra and the Ṛbhus, then why does he, the Hotṛ, alone at the third pressing use for the Prasthita libations[2] what is manifestly (a verse[3]) to Indra and the Ṛbhus "O Indra with the Ṛbhus, full of strength, the well blended", while the others use (verses) to various deities, and how are these (verses) connected with Indra and the Ṛbhus'. The Maitrāvaruṇa[4] uses as offering verse 'O Indra and Varuṇa, drinkers of the pressed this pressed (juice)'; in 'Your chariot the sacrifice for the enjoyment of the gods' he mentions many; that is a symbol of the Ṛbhus. The Brāhmaṇācchaṅsin[5] uses as offering verse 'With Indra, O Bṛhaspati, drink the Soma'; in 'Let the drops well formed enter you' he mentions many; that is a symbol of the Ṛbhus. The Potṛ[6] uses as offering verse 'May the steeds, swift speeding, bring you hither'; in 'Swiftly leaping, come ye forward on their backs' he mentions many; that is a symbol of the Ṛbhus. The Neṣṭṛ[7] uses as offering verse 'As at home come ye to us, swift to listen'; in 'Come ye' he mentions many; that is a symbol of the Ṛbhus. The Achāvāka[8] uses as offering verse 'O Indra and Viṣṇu drink of this sweet drink'; in 'The sweet Soma juices of you two have come' he mentions many; that is a symbol of the Ṛbhus. The Agnīdh[9] uses the offering verse 'This praise to Jātavedas who doth deserve it; in 'Like a chariot let us magnify with devotion' he mentions many; that is a symbol of the Ṛbhus. So are these verses addressed to Indra and the Ṛbhus. In that they are addressed to various deities, thereby he delights the other deities. In that they consist mainly of Jagatī verses,[10] and the third pressing is connected with the Jagatī, verily (they serve) to make perfect the pressing.

vi. 13 (xxviii. 5). Further he says 'Seeing that some of the Hotṛ's offices have litanies and others have no litanies, how are they all made by him to have litanies, and be equal and perfect?' In that naming them together[1] they call them Hotṛ's offices, thereby are they equal. In that some of the Hotṛ's offices have litanies and others not, thereby are they different. So they all become for him possessed of litanies, equal and perfect. Further

[2] For the Prasthita libations see ĀÇS. v. 5. 19; ÇÇS. viii. 2. 4–12; Caland and Henry, pp. 346–349.

[3] RV. iii. 60. 5; ĀÇS. v. 5. 19; ÇÇS. viii. 2. 5.

[4] RV. vi. 68. 10; ĀÇS. v. 5. 19; ÇÇS. viii. 2. 6.

[5] RV. iv. 50. 10; ĀÇS. v. 5. 19; ÇÇS. viii. 2. 7.

[6] RV. i. 85. 6; ĀÇS. v. 5. 19; ÇÇS. viii. 2. 8.

[7] RV. ii. 36. 3; ĀÇS. v. 5. 19; ÇÇS. viii. 2. 9.

[8] RV. vi. 69. 7; ĀÇS. v. 5. 19; ÇÇS. viii. 2. 10.

[9] RV. i. 94. 1; ĀÇS. v. 5. 19; ÇÇS. viii. 2. 11.

[10] Weber compares *prāya* in ÇÇS. vii. 26. 6.

[1] Weber (*Ind. Stud.* ix. 298) suggests as an alternative 'übereinstimmend'.

he says 'The Hotrakas recite at the morning pressing and recite at the midday pressing; how do they recite at the third pressing?' 'In that at the midday they recite two hymns apiece', he should reply, 'for that reason.' Further he says 'Seeing that the Hotṛ has two litanies, how have the Hotrakas two litanies?' 'In that they use as offering verses (verses) addressed to two deities', he should reply, 'for that reason.'

vi. 14 (xxviii. 6). Further he says 'Seeing that these three Hotṛ's offices are possessed of litanies, how have the others litanies?' The Ājya is the litany of the Agnīdh's office, the Marutvatīya of the Potṛ's, the Vaiçvadeva of the Neṣṭṛ's; these Hotṛ's offices contain the characteristics accordingly.[1] Further he says 'Seeing that some Hotrakas have one direction only given to them, then why has the Potṛ two directions given, and the Neṣṭṛ two[2]?' When the Gāyatrī yonder having become an eagle brought the Soma, Indra having cut off the litanies of these Hotṛ's offices gave them to the Hotṛ (saying) 'You have called to me; you have known this'. The gods said 'With speech let us strengthen these two Hotṛ's offices'. Therefore have they two directions. By speech they strengthened the Agnīdh's office; therefore his offering verses are one verse larger.[3] Further he says 'Seeing that the Maitrāvaruṇa gives directions to the Hotṛ with 'Let the Hotṛ say the offering verse; let the Hotṛ say the offering verse', then why does he give directions with 'Let the Hotṛ say the offering verse; let the Hotṛ say the offering verse' to the Hotrāçaṅsins who are not Hotṛs?' The Hotṛ is the breath; all the priests are the breath; verily thus he says in effect 'Let breath say the offering verse; let breath say the offering verse'. Then he says 'Is there a direction for the Udgātṛs, or is there not?' 'There is' he should reply. In that the Praçāstṛ, after muttering, says 'Do ye chant', this is their direction. Further he says 'Is there a choosing[4] of the Achāvāka? Or not?' 'There is' he should reply. In that the Adhvaryu says to him, 'O Achāvāka, say what is to be said by you', this is the choice of him. Further he says 'Seeing that at the third pressing the Maitrāvaruṇa recites (a litany) to Indra and Varuṇa, then why are the strophe and antistrophe addressed to Agni?' With Agni as their head the gods smote away the Asuras from the litanies; therefore its strophe and antistrophe are addressed to Agni.[5] Further he says 'Seeing that the Brāhmaṇācchaṅsin recites (a litany) to Indra and Bṛhaspati at the third pressing,

[1] The offering verses of the three priests contain references to Agni, the Maruts, and the All-gods.

[2] I. e. at the Ṛtuyājas of the twelve Praiṣas, the Potṛ number 2 and 8, the Neṣṭṛ 3 and 9. The text is given in full in Scheftelowitz, *Die Apokryphen des Ṛgveda*, as v. 7.

[3] The Agnīdh has an extra verse RV. iii. 6. 9; ĀÇS. v. 19. 7; ÇÇS. viii. 5. 1.

[4] There is no formal Pravara; see ĀÇS. v. 8. 12.

[5] RV. vii. 82 and 84 are the Çastra; vii. 16. 16–18; 19–21 are the Stotriya and Anurūpa.

and the Achāvāka one to Indra and Viṣṇu, how are their strophes and antistrophes addressed to Indra[6]?' Indra drove away the Asuras from the litanies; he said 'With me who?' With 'I' and 'I' the deities followed after; in that Indra was the first to drive away, therefore their strophes and antistrophes are addressed to Indra; in that with 'I' and 'I' the deities followed after, therefore do they recite to various deities.

vi. 15 (xxviii. 7). Further he says 'Seeing that the third pressing is connected with the All-gods, then why are these hymns to Indra in Jagatī recited as the commencement at the third pressing?' 'Verily laying hold of Indra by them they proceed' he should reply. Moreover in that the third pressing is connected with the Jagatī, it is for desire[1] of the Jagatī. Whatever metre is recited thereafter, it is all in the Jagatī if these hymns to Indra in Jagatī are recited as the commencement at the third pressing. Then at the end the Achāvāka recites a hymn in Triṣṭubh[2] 'With the rite'; the rite which is to be praised he refers to. 'With sap' (he says); sap is food; (verily it serves) to win proper food. 'With safe paths furthering us' (he says); verily thus he recites for safety day by day. Further he says 'Since the third pressing is connected with the Jagatī, then why have they concluding verses in Triṣṭubh?' The Triṣṭubh is strength; verily thus at the end they keep finding support in strength. 'This speech of mine hath reached Indra, Varuṇa' is that of the Maitrāvaruṇa;[3] 'May Bṛhaspati protect us around behind' that of the Brāhmaṇācchaṅsin;[4] 'Both have conquered' is that of the Achāvāka,[5] for they two are victorious; 'They are not conquered, he is not conquered' (he says), for neither of them has conquered.

'What time, O Viṣṇu, with Indra ye did strive
Then did ye two divide in three the thousand'

(he says). Indra and Viṣṇu fought with the Asuras; having conquered, them they said 'Let us make an arrangement'. The Asuras said 'Be it so'. Indra said 'So much as Viṣṇu three times traverses, so much be ours; let the rest be yours'. He traversed these worlds, then the Vedas, then speech.

[6] RV. i. 57; x. 68 and 48 are the Çastra; viii. 21. 1-2; 9-10 are the Stotriya and Anurūpa of the Brāhmaṇācchaṅsin; ii. 18; vii. 100; i. 156; vi. 69; and viii. 98. 7-9; 18. 4-6 are the verses of the Achāvāka referred to. All these are the Çastras of the Hotrakas at the third pressing in the Ukthya; see ĀÇS. vi. 1. 2; ÇÇS. ix. 1-4; AB. iii. 49, 50.

[1] *Cf.* KB. xxx. 2, 3 and see also *Vait.* xxxii. 35. The form *jagatkāmyā* is very abnormal; *mitrakṛtyā* in AB. iii. 4. 6 is not probably a parallel, but *bhūyaskāmyā* occurs in a Kaṇva passage of the ÇB., cited by Eggeling, SBE. xxvi. 42, n. 2.

[2] RV. vi. 69.

[3] RV. vii. 84. 5.

[4] RV. x. 43. 11 (not 42. 11 as Haug, the last hymn being x. 43).

[5] RV. vi. 69. 8; cf. ÇB. iii. 3. 1. 13; Eggeling, SBE. xxvi. 62, n. 2.

They say 'What is the thousand?' 'These worlds, these Vedas, moreover speech' he should reply. 'Did ye divide' the Achāvāka repeats in the Ukthya, for he is then the last; the Hotṛ at the Agniṣṭoma and the Atirātra, for he is then the last. 'Should he repeat at the Ṣoḍaçin? Or should he not repeat?' 'He should repeat' they say; 'Why should he repeat in the other days and not at this?' Therefore he should repeat.[6]

vi. 16 (xxviii. 8). Further he says 'Seeing that the third pressing is connected with the Nārāçaṅsa, then why does the Achāvāka at the end recite in the Çilpas verses without reference to the Nārāçaṅsa.[1] The Nārāçaṅsa (hymn) is a development; some seed is developed as it were; this is already developed and so propagated. Again the Nārāçaṅsa hymn is soft and slipping; but the Achāvāka is the last; (they think) 'We shall establish it in something firm for the sake of firmness'. Therefore the Achāvāka at the end in the Çilpas recites (verses) without reference to the Nārāçaṅsa (thinking) 'We shall establish it in something firm, for the sake of firmness'.

ADHYĀYA IV

The Sampāta and other Hymns.

vi. 17 (xxix. 1). The strophe of the next day they make the antistrophe, at the morning pressing[1] for the continuity of the Ahīna (sacrifice). Just as the one day (rite) pressing, so the Ahīna; just as the pressings of the one day (rite) as a pressing keep united, so the days of the Ahīna keep united. In that they make the strophe of the next day the antistrophe at the morning pressing for the continuity of the Ahīna, verily thus they continue the Ahīna. The gods and the seers planned 'With what is the same, let us continue the sacrifice; they saw this similarity in the sacrifice,

[6] The last four syllables are repeated; see ĀÇS. vii. 1. 12.

[1] Sāyaṇa explains the term Nārāçaṅsa as praise of men like the Ṛbhus or Aṅgirases. In vi. 32 the Nārāçaṅsī verses (Dānastutis) are mentioned. Cf. however the Nārāçaṅsa hymn, RV. x. 62 in AB. vi. 27; KB. xxiii. 8. There can be no real doubt that the real reference is to RV. x. 62 with its generative reference. The reply to the objection is twofold; in the first place the seed when developed needs no further aid and as the Achāvāka is late in the ritual it is developed when it reaches him. Secondly the hymn is soft and so a bad ending. The term Nārāçaṅsa occurs in yet another use of the cups of the libations (Caland and Henry, *L'Agniṣṭoma*, p. 220: the connexion with Nārāçaṅsa and the manes is discussed by Oldenberg, ZDMG. liv. 49 *seq.* and Hillebrandt, *Vedo Myth.* ii. 102), but this is not here in place.

vi. 17. [1] Cf. above AB. vi. 5.

the Pragāthas the same,[2] the beginnings[3] the same, the hymns[4] the same. Indra is a house frequenter; where Indra goes first, then he returns again; verily (it serves) to secure Indra in the sacrifice.

vi. 18 (xxix. 2). These Sampātas Viçvāmitra first saw; them seen by Viçvāmitra Vāmadeva created,[1] 'Thee, O Indra with the thunderbolt'; 'That which of ours Indra rejoiceth in and desireth', and 'How? of what Hotṛ hath he made great?' To them he swiftly moved; in that he swiftly moved (*samapatat*), that is why the Sampātas have their name. Viçvāmitra considered 'The Sampātas which I saw Vāmadeva has created; what hymns now can I create as counter Sampātas?' He created these hymns as Sampātas their counterparts.[2] 'Straightway on birth, the bull, the youngling,' 'Indra, breaker of citadels, overcame the Dāsa with his beams,' 'This offering do thou make attain,' 'Thy comrades, Soma-loving, desire thee,' 'Ordering the bearer hath gone to the grandson of the daughter', and 'Like a carpenter, have I fashioned a thought.' 'Who alone is to be invoked by mortals' Bharadvāja[3] (saw). 'With sharp horns, like a terrible wild beast', and 'Praises have been offered in desire of glory' Vasiṣṭha[4] (saw). 'To him the eager, the impetuous' Nodhas[5] (saw). Having recited at the morning pressing the strophes of the six-day (rite), at the midday they recite the Ahīna hymns. These are the Ahīna hymns; 'Let the true one come hither, the bounteous, he of the Soma lees' the Maitrāvaruṇa[6] (recites) containing (the word) 'true'. 'To him the eager, the impetuous' (this hymn) containing (the word) 'prayer' in 'To Indra the prayers most truly given' and 'O Indra, these prayers have the Gotamas made' the Brāhmaṇācchaṅsin[7] recites. 'Ordering the bearer' (this hymn) containing (the word) 'bearer' in 'They have produced the bearer' the Achāvāka[8] recites. They say 'Why does the Achāvāka recite this hymn containing (the word) "bearer" both in the days that go away and those that come up again?'

[2] See ĀÇS. vii. 4 6; see below AB. vi. 21.

[3] See ĀÇS. vii. 4. 7; below AB. vi. 22.

[4] Not the *ahīnasūktāni* as Sāyaṇa but the *aharahaḥçasyāni*; see ĀÇS. vii. 4. 8 and 9; AB. vi. 20. *Mokahadrī* he sees a cat.

[1] RV. iv. 19, 22, 23; ĀÇS. vii. 5. 20.

[2] RV. iii. 48, 34, 36, 30, 31, 38; ĀÇS. vii. 5. 20 omits iii. 48 and iii. 38; see AB. vi. 20.

[3] RV. vi. 22; ĀÇS. vii. 5. 20.

[4] RV. vii. 19, 23; ĀÇS. vii. 5. 20 omits vii. 23; see AB. vi. 20. It is really not a Sampāta proper.

[5] RV. i. 61; ĀÇS. vii. 4. 8; ÇÇS. xii. 4. 17, 18.

[6] RV. iv. 16; ĀÇS. vii. 4. 9; ÇÇS. xii. 8. 13, 14.

[7] RV. i. 61: 1 *d* and 16 are referred to.

[8] RV. iii. 31; ĀÇS. vii. 4. 9; ÇÇS. xii. 5. 16, 17. This is repeated both on the days of the Ṣaḍahas and also on the days, which once past do not recur, here specified; for its use on the Ṣaḍahas, see AB. vi. 19. 4. The term Ahīna is here a quite peculiar one, the days being single days *in se*. The order is (1) strophe and antistrophe; (2) the Kadvant Pragātha; (3) the *Āram bhaṇīya*; (4) the *aharahaḥçasya*; (5) the Ahīna for the Maitrāvaruṇa; (4) and (5) being inverted for the other two; see ĀÇS. vii. 4.

The knower of many Ṛcs is powerful; the hymn contains (the word) 'bearer'; the bearer bears the yoke to which it is yoked. Therefore the Achāvāka recites in both cases this hymn containing (the word) 'bearer', both in the days that go away and in those that come up again. These are on five days, the Caturviṅça, Abhijit, Viṣuvant, Viçvajit and Mahāvrata; these days are Ahīnas, for nothing in them is left out; these days go away without recurring; therefore they recite them on these days. In that they recite them, (they hope) 'Let us obtain the worlds of heaven without defect, with all forms, with all perfection. In that they recite them, they invite Indra with them, like a bull to a cow. In that moreover they recite them, it is for the continuity of the Ahīna; verily thus they continue the Ahīna.

vi. 19 (xxix. 3). These three Sampāta (hymns) the Maitrāvaruṇa recites one by one day by day, alternating their order;[1] on the first day (he recites) 'Thee O Indra, with the thunderbolt', on the second 'That which of ours Indra rejoiceth in and desireth', on the third 'How? of what Hotṛ hath he made great?' Three Sampātas the Brāhmaṇācchaṅsin recites one by one day by day, alternating their order,[2] on the first day 'Indra, breaker of citadels, overcame the Dāsa with his beams', on the second 'Who alone is to be invited by mortals', on the third 'With sharp horns, like a terrible wild beast'. Three Sampātas the Achāvāka recites one by one, day by day, alternating their order,[3] on the first day 'This offering do thou make attain', on the second 'Thy comrades, Soma-loving, desire thee', on the third 'Ordering the bearer hath gone to the grandson of the daughter'. These number nine; there are three to be recited every day;[4] these make up twelve; the year has twelve months; Prajāpati is the year; the sacrifice is Prajāpati; thus they obtain the year and Prajāpati; thus they continue day by day to find support in the year, in Prajāpati, in the sacrifice. Between them they should insert an insertion, Virāj verses and verses[5] by Vimada without repetition of *o* on the fourth day, Pañkti[6] verses on the fifth,

[1] RV. iv. 19; iv. 22; iv. 23. *viparyāsam* presumably means that on the last three days of the Ṣaḍaha they are repeated in the same order. These hymns replace the Ahīna hymns of the special days (AB. vi. 18, n. 8). See ĀÇS. vii. 5. 21, 22; cf. *Vait.* xxxi. 25.

[2] RV. iii. 34; vi. 22; vii. 19.

[3] RV. iii. 36; iii. 30; iii. 31.

[4] See for these AB. vi. 20.

[5] RV. vii. 22. 5–8; vii. 31. 10–12; see KB. xxix. 5 where they are called Çilpas. These are made into three triplets and inserted by the three priests on the fourth day of the Ṣaḍaha; the verses by Vimada are not an alternative as suggested by Sāyaṇa (*ekaḥ pakṣaḥ* . . . *pakṣāntaram*) but an addition, and the Ānand. ed. reads *vaimadīç ca caturthe* (which is of course palaeographically practically the same as the reading *vaimadīç caturthe*). The verses are RV. x. 23. 1–7; the first three verses in each case go to the Maitrāvaruṇa; the Brāhmaṇācchaṅsin has 3–5; the Achāvāka 5–7. See ĀÇS. vii. 11. 34 *seq.*; *Vait.* xxxii. 7.

[6] RV. i. 29. 1–7; ĀÇS. vii. 11. 39. Cf. ÇÇS. xii. 5. 12; *Vait.* xxxii. 8.

and verses by Parucchepa[7] on the sixth. Moreover on those days which have great Stomas the Maitrāvaruṇa[8] should insert 'What friend of man to-day, god-loving?', the Brāhmaṇācchaṅsin,[9] 'He who hath been placed as it were in the forest delighting,' and the Achāvāka[10] 'Come hither, standing on thy chariot seat'. These are the insertions; by means of these insertions the gods, the seers, conquered the world of heaven. Verily thus also the sacrificers by these insertions conquer the world of heaven.

vi. 20 (xxviii. 4) 'Straightway on birth the bull, the youngling' the Maitrāvaruṇa[1] recites day by day before the hymns. That hymn is heavenly; by this hymn the gods conquered the world of heaven, by this the seers. Verily thus also the sacrificers by this hymn conquer the world of heaven. It is by Viçvāmitra; Viçvāmitra was the friend of all; all becomes friendly to him who knows thus and to those for whom a Maitrāvaruṇa, knowing thus, recites this before the hymns day by day. It contains (the words) 'bull' and 'cattle'; (it serves) to win cattle. It is of five verses; the Pañkti has five Padas; food is the Pañkti; (it serves) to win proper food. 'Praises have been offered in desire of glory' the Brāhmaṇācchaṅsin[2] recites day by day the hymn containing (the word) 'praise' and so perfect. This hymn is heavenly; by this hymn the gods conquered the world of heaven, by this the seers. Verily thus also the sacrificers by this hymn conquer the world of heaven. It is by Vasiṣṭha; by it Vasiṣṭha went to the dear abode of Indra, he conquered the highest world. He goes to the dear abode of Indra, he conquers the highest world who knows thus. It has six verses; the seasons are six; (it serves) to win the seasons. He recites it after the Sampātas. Having obtained thus the world of heaven the sacrificers find support in this world. 'Like a carpenter have I fashioned a thought', the Achāvāka[3] recites day by day, containing (the word) 'towards' and a symbol of continuity. 'Pondering on the dear (days) to come' (he says); the days to come are dear; verily thus they proceed pondering on, laying hold of, them. The world of heaven is to come as compared with this world; verily thus he alludes to it. 'I long to see the sages, with wisdom' (he says), our seers who are departed are the sages; verily thus he refers to them. It is by Viçvāmitra; Viçvāmitra was the friend of all; all becomes friendly to him who knows thus. That which he recites has no deity mentioned and is connected with

[7] RV. i. 181. 1-7; ĀÇS. vii. 11. 40. Cf. ÇÇS. xii. 8. 12; *Vait.* xxxii. 9.

[8] RV. iv. 25; ĀÇS. vii. 12. 1; *Vait.* xxxiii. 18; GB. xi. 1. These are used for the Chandomas as the Stomas increase in size.

[9] RV. x. 29; ĀÇS. vii. 12. 1; *Vait.* xxxii. 10; GB. xi. 2.

[10] RV. iii. 48; ĀÇS. vii. 12. 1.

[1] RV. iii. 48. Cf. ĀÇS. vii. 4. 8

[2] RV. vii. 28. Cf. ĀÇS. vii. 4. 9; ÇÇS. xii. 4. 8.

[3] RV. iii. 38. Cf. ĀÇS. vii. 4. 9; ÇÇS. xii. 5. 8.

Prajāpati. Prajāpati is he whose name is not mentioned; (it serves) to obtain Prajāpati. Once[4] he mentions Indra; thereby he departs not from the Indra form. It is in ten verses; the Virāj has ten syllables; the Virāj is food; (it serves) to win food. As to its being of ten verses, the breaths are ten; verily thus they obtain the breaths, they place breaths in the body. He recites it after the Sampātas; verily thus having obtained the world of heaven, the sacrificers find support in this world.

vi. 21 (xxix. 5). 'Who, O Indra, him that hath thee as his wealth', 'What newest of praises', and 'What hath not been wrought by him' are the Pragāthas[1] containing the word 'who' which are recited day by day at the beginning. Prajāpati is Who; (verily they serve) to obtain Prajāpati. Moreover in that they contain (the word) 'who' and who is food, (they serve) to win food. Moreover as to their containing (the word) 'who', day by day they praise employing the Ahīna hymn, duly appeased, and it is by the Pragāthas containing (the word) 'who' that they appease them. Appeased they bring them prosperity (*ka*); appeased they carry them towards the world of heaven. The beginnings of the hymns which they recite should be in Triṣṭubh; these some recite before the Pragāthas, calling them inserted verses. That he should not do so. The Hotṛ is lordly power, the Hotrāçaṅsins are the people; verily thus they would make the people refractory to the lordly power which is a confusion. He should know 'These my hymn beginnings are Triṣṭubhs'. Just as men set sail on an ocean so set they sail who perform the year or a twelve day (rite); just as men desiring to reach the other shore mount a ship well found,[2] so do they mount the Triṣṭubhs. That metre having made them go to the world of heaven does not fail, for it is the strongest of all. He should not utter the call for these (verses) (thinking) 'The metre is the same; moreover let me not make them inserted verses.' In that they recite these (verses), (they think) 'Let us mount the hymns with the recognized beginnings of the hymns.' In that they recite these (verses), verily with them they summon Indra, like a bull to the cow. Moreover in that they recite them, (it serves) for the continuity of the Ahīna; verily thus they continue the Ahīna.

vi. 22 (xxix. 6). 'O Indra drive away all our enemies in front' the Maitrāvaruṇa[1] recites day by day before the hymns:

[4] RV. iii. 38. 10.

[1] RV. vii. 32. 14 and 15; viii. 3. 13 and 14; 66. 9 and 10. In this chapter the order of the various parts of the litanies agrees clearly with that in ĀÇS. vii. 4 (misinterpreted by Haug, ii. 412, n. 8); viz. the Pragāthas; then the Triṣṭubh verses; then RV. iii. 48; i. 61; iii. 31; then RV. iv. 16; vii. 23; iii. 38; then the concluding verses; AB. vi. 18, n. 8 explains the order of iii. 48 and iv. 16 (for the opposite order see AB. vi. 18 and 20). *Apāntāni* may be read.

[2] Cf. below AB. vii. 13; BR. vii. 1199.

vi. 22. [1] RV. x. 131. 1. Cf. ĀÇS. vii. 4. 7; ÇÇS. xii. 3. 5; KB. xxix. 4.

'Drive away those behind, O overpowering one,
Drive away those to the north, O hero, those below to the south
That we may delight in thy wide protection'

(he says); it is a symbol of freedom from fear; for he desires as he proceeds freedom from fear. 'Those yoked with prayer, I yoke with prayer' the Brāhmaṇācchaṅsin[2] recites day by day; in 'I yoke' it contains (the word) yoke, since the Ahīna is yoked as it were; (therefore) it is a symbol of the Ahīna. 'To wide space thou leadest us after knowing' the Achāvāka[3] recites day by day; since the Ahīna goes as it were, (the words) 'Thou leadest after' are a symbol of the Ahīna; (the words) 'Thou leadest' are a symbol of the proceeding of the sacrificial session. These are recited day by day. They should conclude with the same verses;[4] Indra is a home-goer as regards their sacrifice; as a bull to the cow, or as a cow to its well-known place of pasture, so does Indra come to their sacrifice. He should not conclude with the 'Prosperity let us invoke' verse[5] the Ahīna (hymn); the Kṣatriya departs from his kingdom; his rival he then summons.

vi. 23 (xxix. 7). Then follows the yoking and releasing of the Ahīna (rite), with[1] 'He traversed the atmosphere' he yokes; with 'So Indra' he releases; with[2] 'I of the two connected with Sarasvatī' and 'Surely this of thee' he yokes the Ahīna; with[3] 'Let us be thine, O god Varuṇa' and 'Chant ye' he releases. He is worthy to weave the Ahīna who knows how to yoke and to release it. In that they are yoked on the Caturviṅça day is the yoking; in that they are released before the concluding Atirātra is the releasing. If on the Caturviṅça day they were to conclude with (the verses) of the one day (rite), they would conclude the sacrifice, and would not make it an Ahīna; if they were again to conclude with the concluding verses of the Ahīna, the sacrifice would perish, just as one wearied and not being released perishes. With both sets should they conclude.[4] That is as if one were to go a long journey unyoking from time to time; the sacrifice becomes continuous, and yet they release (it). He should not over-recite the Soma by

[2] RV. iii. 35. 4. Cf. ĀÇS. vii. 4. 7; ÇÇS. xii. 4. 2.

[3] RV. vi. 47. 8. Cf. ĀÇS. vii. 4. 7; ÇÇS. xii. 5. 2.

[4] Viz. RV. iv. 16. 21 (Maitrāvaruṇa); vii. 23. 6 (Brāhmaṇācchaṅsin); ii. 11. 21 Achāvāka); see AB. vi. 23.

[5] RV. iii. 38. 10. See ĀÇS. vii. 4. 10.

[1] RV. viii. 14. 7–9; vii. 23. 6 (the Brāhmaṇācchaṅsin), for the morning and midday pressings as concluding verses. Cf. GB. xi. 5.

[2] RV. viii. 38. 10; ii. 11. 21 (the Achāvāka); the second refers to the release.

[3] RV. vii. 66. 9; iv. 16. 21 (the Maitrāvaruṇa); the first refers to the joining.

[4] I. e. the Maitrāvaruṇa with those of the one day rite only; the Achāvāka with those of the Ahīna; the Brāhmaṇācchaṅsin with those of the Ahīna in the morning and those of the one day rite at the midday pressing: above AB. vi. 8.

more than one or two verses at the two pressings[5]; when a Stoma is over-recited by many verses then come into existence long stretches of wild; he may use an unlimited number at the third pressing; the world of heaven is unlimited; (it serves) to obtain the world of heaven. He grasps the Ahīna continuous and firm who knowing thus performs the Ahīna.

vi. 24 (xxix. 8). The gods saw the cows in a cave; they sought to win them with the sacrifice; they obtained them with the sixth day. At the morning pressing with Nabhāka's (hymn) they tore open (*nabh*) the cave; in that they tore it open, verily thus they loosened it. On the third pressing having destroyed the cave with the Vālakhilyās as the thunderbolt and (the verse) of one Pada as the hammer of speech, they drove out the cows. Verily thus also the sacrificers tear open the cave at the morning pressing with Nabhāka's (hymn); in that they tear it open, verily thus they loosen it. Therefore the Hotrakas at the morning pressing recite triplets[1] by Nabhāka. 'When supporting the summits', the Maitrāvaruṇa, 'O Indra, ancient are thine addresses', the Brāhmaṇācchaṅsin; 'The middle of conflicts', the Achāvāka. At the third pressing having destroyed the cave with the Vālakhilyās as the thunderbolt and (the verse) of one Pada as the hammer of speech they obtain the cows. First he transposes by Padas[2] the six hymns of the Vālakhilyās, by half verses the second time, by verses the third time. When transposing by Padas he should place (a verse) of one Pada in each Pragātha; that is the hammer of speech. There are five (verses) of one Pada; four from the tenth day, one from the Mahāvrata. There are the Mahānāmnī Padas of eight syllables; he should recite as many of these as he requires to complete; he should disregard the others. When transposing by half verses he should recite these (verses) of one Pada, and these eight-syllable Padas of the Mahānāmnīs. When trans-

[5] Cf. AB. vi. 8. 5; here an unlimited number is allowed for the third pressing only, a view which really is not consistent with that view; cf. ĀÇS. vii. 12. 5 with comm.

[1] RV. viii. 41. 4–6; 40. 9–11; 3–5; ĀÇS. vii. 2. 17. They follow the Anurūpas or Triṣṭubhs.

[2] The mode of recitation is given by ĀÇS. viii. 2. 19–21. The first six hymns (RV. viii. 49–54) are recited by Padas, half verses, and verses; the order is first Pada of first verse of first hymn, then second Pada of second verse of second hymn; first Pada second verse second hymn, second Pada first verse first hymn and so forth. The Pragāthas are made up of two verses; this done, an eight-syllable verse is added, viz. *indro viçvasya gopatiḥ*; *indro viçvasya bhūpatiḥ*; *indro viçvasya rājati*; *indro viçvasya cetati*; *indro viçvaṁ virājati*; further the eight-syllable Padas of the Mahānāmnīs are added (from AĀ. iv. *pracetana pra cetaya*, &c.) so far as is needed to fill up the number of Pragāthas. The transposition of half verses follows in precisely the same way, thus viii. 49. 1 *a* and *b*; 50. 2 *c* and *d*; that by verses viii. 49. 1; 50. 2, &c. ĀÇS. viii. 2. 28 says that the Mahānāmnīs yield with the *puriṣas* 28 sets of eight syllables to fill up the 28 Pragāthas of the six Vālakhilyā hymns. Below in AB. vi. 28 two other ways of the recitation are referred to.

posing by verses, he should recite these (verses) of one Pada and these eight-syllable Padas of the Mahānāmnīs. In that he transposes for the first time the six hymns of the Vālakhilyās, verily thus he transposes breath and speech; in that for the second time, thus he transposes eye and mind; in that for the third, thus he transposes ear and self. Thus is the desire in the transposition obtained, in the Vālakhilyās as the thunderbolt, in (the verse) of one food as the hammer of speech, in the arrangement of the breaths. For the fourth time he recites the Pragāthas without transposition; the Pragāthas are cattle; (they serve) to win cattle. He should not here insert (the verse) of one Pada; if he were to insert (the verse) of one Pada, by the hammer of speech he would strike off cattle from the sacrificer. If a man were to say to him then 'You have struck off cattle from the sacrificer, you have made him without cattle', it would certainly be so. Therefore he should not insert (the verse) of one Pada. He inverts the last two hymns; this is their transposition. This to Saubala Sarpis Vātsi recited; he said 'I have secured [3] the most abundant cattle in this sacrifice; not the least will come to me.' To him he gave (fees) as to great priests. That recitation is rich in cattle and heavenly; therefore he recites it.

vi. 25 (xxix. 9). He mounts the difficult mounting; the explanation of this has been given.[1] In (a hymn) to Indra[2] should he mount for one desiring cattle; cattle are connected with Indra. It should be in Jagatī; cattle are connected with the Jagatī; it should be a great hymn; verily thus he establishes the sacrificer in most numerous cattle. In (a hymn) by Baru should he mount; it is a great hymn and in Jagatī. In (a hymn) to Indra and Varuṇa[3] should he mount for one desiring support. This Hotṛ's office has these as deities, and has support in these; in that (the offering verse is) addressed to Indra and Varuṇa,[4] verily thus he establishes it in its own support as the end. As to (his mounting) in (a hymn) to Indra and Varuṇa, there is here a Nivid; by a Nivid are desires obtained. If he mounts in (a hymn) to Indra and Varuṇa, it should be in (a hymn) by Suparṇa. Thus is obtained the desire in (the hymn) to Indra and Varuṇa, in (the hymn) by Suparṇa.

vi. 26 (xxix. 10). They say 'Should he recite together[1] on the sixth day?

[3] Cf. AB. vi. 35, n. 3.

[1] See AB. iv. 21; KB. xxx. 5. The Dūrohaṇa follows the Vālakhilyās and the subsequent hymn, before its last verse.

[2] RV. x. 96; it begins *pra vo mahe*; but Sāyaṇa sees here in *mahāsūkta* the same use as in AĀ. ii. 2. 2. Cf. ÇÇS. xi. 14. 10, 26.

[3] RV. viii. 59 by Suparṇa is clearly meant and not the hymn *pra dhārā yantu* (ĀGS. iii. 12. 14) given as an alternative by Sāyaṇa. This is given as the hymn in ĀÇS. viii. 2. 13–15 in which the Dūrohaṇa is to be performed (see AB. vi. 26). Cf. ÇÇS. xii. 11. 17.

[4] RV. vi. 68. 11; see ĀÇS. vi. 1. 2.

vi. 26. [1] I. e. the question is whether the ordinary Çastra is to be performed or not with the Dūrohaṇa. Cf. AB. vi. 36.

Or should he not recite together?' 'He should recite together' they say; 'Why should he recite together on the other days and why not recite together on this?' Or rather they say 'He should not recite together. The sixth day is the world of heaven; the world of heaven is not a place where all meet; only certain ones meet in the world of heaven'. If he were to recite together, he would make it common; in that he does not recite together, it is a symbol of the world of heaven. Therefore he should not recite together. Again as to his not reciting together, the strophe is the body, the Vālakhilyās the breaths; if he were to recite together, from these deities he would sever the breaths of the sacrificer; if one were to say of him then 'From these two deities he has severed the breaths of the sacrificer; breath will leave him', it would certainly be so. Therefore he should not recite together. If he should reflect 'I have recited the Vālakhilyās; let me recite together before the difficult mounting', he should not on any account so desire. But if pride seizes him, let him recite many hundreds after the difficult mounting; therein is obtained that in desire of which he does so. The Vālakhilyās are addressed to Indra; they have Padas of twelve syllables; therein is there obtained the desire that is in the Jagatī (hymn) to Indra.[2] Moreover there is this hymn to Indra and Varuṇa,[3] and a closing verse for Indra and Varuṇa; therefore he should not recite together. They say 'As is the Stotra, so the Çastra; the Vālakhilyās are recited transposed, is the Stotra transposed or not transposed?' 'Transposed' he should reply, 'A twelve-syllable within eight-syllable[4] (Padas).' They say 'As is the Çastra, so the offering verse; three deities are praised, Agni, Indra, Varuṇa, but he uses (a verse) to Indra and Varuṇa as offering verse; how is it that Agni is not omitted?' Varuṇa is Agni, this also is declared by a seer.[5] 'Since thou, O Agni, art born as Varuṇa'; thus in that he uses (a verse) to Indra and Varuṇa as offering verse, Agni is not omitted.

ADHYĀYA V

The Çilpas.

vi. 27 (xxx. 1). They recite the Çilpas.[1] These are the works of art of the gods; in imitation of these works of art here is a work of art accomplished; an elephant, a goblet, a garment, a gold object, a mule chariot are

[2] I.e. RV. iii. 51. 1–3 (ĀÇS. vi. 1. 2; ÇÇS. ix. 8. 3) is to be omitted in favour of the RV. vii. 84; see ĀÇS. viii. 2. 16. The sense of *vi + i* as sever (from) seems necessary; cf. PB. xiv. 6. 6.

[3] RV. vii. 84.

[4] The Stotra is prepared on the Dvipadā verses, RV. v. 24. 1–3.

[5] RV. v. 3. 1.

[1] Cf. KB. xxix. 5 for a different view of the word; the parallel is xxx. 4. They are said at the 3rd pressing normally on the 6th day of the Pṛṣṭhya Ṣaḍaha.

works of art; a work of art is accomplished in him who knows thus. As to these 'works of art' (Çastras), the Çilpas are a perfection of the self; verily by them the sacrificer perfects himself as composed of the metres. He recites the Nābhānediṣṭha [2] (hymn); the Nābhānediṣṭha (hymn) is seed; thus he pours seed; he recites it without mention (of the deity); without mention is seed secretly poured in the womb. He becomes mingled with seed: 'United with earth he sprinkled seed' (he says); verily (it serves) to perfect seed. He recites it with the Nārāçaṅsa [3] (hymn); man is offspring, praise speech; verily thus he places speech in offspring, therefore offspring are born speaking. Some recite it before saying 'Speech has its place in front'; others after saying 'Speech has its place behind'; in the middle should he recite it; speech has its place in the middle; in a place nearer the end; speech is nearer the back as it were. It the Hotṛ having poured in seed form hands over to the Maitrāvaruṇa,[4] (saying) 'Do thou provide the breaths for it'.

vi. 28 (xxx. 2). He recites the Vālakhilyās;[1] the Vālakhilyās are the breaths; verily thus he provides breaths for him. He recites them transposed; these breaths are transposed, expiration (linked) with inspiration, cross breathing with inspiration. He transposes by Padas the first two hymns, by half verses the second two, by verses the third two. In that he transposes the first two hymns, thus he transposes breath and speech; in that the second two, thus he transposes eye and mind; in that the third two, thus he transposes ear and self. Some transpose, putting Bṛhatī verses and Satobṛhatī verses in twos together; then the desire that is in transposition is obtained, but Pragāthas do not come about. He should transpose with intermingling; thus are Pragāthas produced. The Vālakhilyās are to be Pragāthas; therefore should he transpose with intermingling; as to his intermingling, the Bṛhatī is the body, the Satobṛhatī the breaths; he recites

[2] RV. x. 61; v. 5 is referred to. See ĀÇS. viii. 1. 20. Cf. above AB. vi. 16.

[3] RV. x. 62. It is inserted after RV. x. 61. 25; see ĀÇS. viii. 1. 20.

[4] The Çilpas of these priests have two forms, the *vihṛta* at the third pressing of the sixth day, at the Viçvajit, and if the Sāman chanters use Dvipadās at the third pressing of any Ukthya day; this is the form contemplated in AB., save in vi. 30, 31; in the case that the sixth day or the Viçvajit is an Agniṣṭoma or the Dvipadās are not used, then a simpler form of Çilpas appears at the midday pressing, the Achāvāka discontinuing his Evayāmarut and the Maitrāvaruṇa using only the Bṛhatī hymns; see ĀÇS. viii. 4. 4–12.

[1] ĀÇS. viii. 2. 5 *seq.* (cf. ÇÇS. xii. 6. 12 *seq.*) gives the modes of reciting here mentioned as two, the Mahāvālabhid, adopted in AB. vi. 24. 5 wherein all the six hymns are recited in the three ways, and the two Hauṇḍinas in which the hymns are divided into three sets of two each (so KB. xxx. 4); the first of the Hauṇḍina methods uniting the Bṛhatīs and the Satobṛhatīs in twos, while the other is here preferred, and unites on the basis of vi. 24.

the Bṛhatī, it is the body, then the Satobṛhatī, it is the breaths; then the Bṛhatī, then the Satobṛhatī; thus he continues to strengthen the body with the breaths around. Therefore should he transpose with intermingling. Again as to his intermingling, the Bṛhatī is the body, the Satobṛhatī cattle; he recites the Bṛhatī, it is the body, then the Satobṛhatī, it is cattle; then the Bṛhatī, then the Satobṛhatī; thus he continues to strengthen the body with cattle around. Therefore should he transpose with intermingling. He inverts the two last hymns;[2] this is their transposition. The Maitrāvaruṇa having made the breaths for it hands it over to the Brāhmaṇācchaṅsin (saying) 'Do thou propagate it'.

vi. 29 (xxx. 3). He recites the Sukīrti[1] (hymn); the Sukīrti hymn is a birthplace of the gods; thus he produces the sacrificer from the sacrifice as a divine birthplace. He recites the Vṛṣākapi[2] (hymn); the Vṛṣākapi is the body; verily thus he makes a body for it. He recites it with the sound *o*; the sound *o* is food; thus to it on birth he gives food as the breast to a child. It is in Pañktī verses; man is fivefold and arranged in five divisions, hair, skin, flesh, bone, marrow. As great as is man, so great does he make the sacrificer. Having produced him the Brāhmaṇācchaṅsin hands him over to the Achāvāka (saying) 'Do thou fashion a support for him'.

vi. 30 (xxx. 4). He recites the Evayāmarut[1] (hymn); the Evayāmarut (hymn) is a support; verily thus he makes a support for him. It he recites with the sound *o*; the sound *o* is food; verily thus he places food in him. It is in Jagatī or Atijagatī; all the world is connected with the Jagatī or Atijagatī. It is addressed to the Maruts; the Maruts are waters, food is water; verily thus in order he places proper food in him. These they call the accompanying (hymns), the Nābhānediṣṭha, the Vālakhilyās, the Vṛṣākapi, the Evayāmarut. These he should recite together or not recite together; if he recites them separately; that would be as if one were to divide in two a man or seed; therefore he should recite them together or not recite them together. Bulila Āçvatara Āçvi being Hotṛ at the Viçvajit meditated 'Of these Çilpas two are liable to be performed at the midday in the Viçvajit in the year (rite); come, let me here have recited the Evayāmarut (hymn)'. He then had recited the hymn. When it was being recited thus, Gauçla came up; he said 'O Hotṛ, how is that your Çastra is wandering without a wheel'. 'What has happened' (he

[2] AB. vi. 24. 15.

[1] RV. x. 131. Cf. KB. xxx. 5. It follows the strophe and antistrophe, RV. x. 157. 1–5; vi. 17. 5; see ĀÇS. viii. 3. 3; ÇÇS. xii. 13. 1.

[2] RV. x. 86. See ĀÇS. viii. 3. 4-6; ÇÇS. xii. 13. 1.

vi. 30. [1] RV. v. 87; see ĀÇS. viii. 4. 2; ÇÇS. xii. 26. 10. Cf. AB. v. 15.

replied). 'The Evayāmarut is being recited further on';[2] he replied, 'the midday is connected with Indra; why do you seek to draw Indra away from the midday?' 'I do not seek to draw Indra away from the midday; he said. 'But this text is not appropriate for the midday; it is Jagatī or Atijagatī; all this is connected with the Jagatī or Atijagatī; it also is addressed to the Maruts; do not recite it' (he replied). He said 'Stop, O Achāvāka'; then he sought instruction from him.[3] He said 'Let him recite (a hymn) to Indra[4] with a reference to Viṣṇu; then do thou, O Hotṛ, after the inserted verse to Rudra[5] and before (the hymn) to the Maruts insert this (Evayāmarut) hymn. He caused the recitation to be made so; now to-day it is thus performed.[6]

vi. 31 (xxx. 5). They say[1] 'Seeing that in the Viçvajit, in the Atirātra form,'[2] and so on the sixth day the sacrifice comes into order, the generation of the sacrificer comes into order, how is it that here, while the Nābhānediṣṭha hymn is not recited, the Maitrāvaruṇa recites the Vālakhilyās; they are the breaths; seed comes first and then breath. So the Brāhmaṇācchaṅsin: while the Nābhānediṣṭha is not recited, he recites the Vṛṣākapi; it is the body; seed is first, then the body; how then is the sacrificer produced? How are the breaths not confused?' 'By means of the whole sacrificial rite they prepare the sacrificer; like an embryo in the womb, so he lies growing. Not at once in the beginning does it come into being whole; separately each member comes into being as it comes into being' (is the reply). If they perform all on the same day, the sacrifice comes into order, the generation of the sacrificer comes into order. Moreover the Hotṛ recites at the third pressing the Evayāmarut (hymn); verily thus at the end he establishes him in a support.

vi. 32 (xxx. 6). When the metres had been obtained by the sixth day the sap poured over; Prajāpati was afraid 'This sap of the metres going away

[2] 'North' is Sāyaṇa's version, i. e. by the Achāvāka, whose altar is north of the Hotṛ's.

[3] Sāyaṇa takes *iṣe* = *ichāmi* and makes this a quotation obviously in error. Weber (*Ind. Stud.* ix. 308) corrects the version of Sāyaṇa which takes *çaṅsiṣṭa* as third person sing.

[4] RV. vi. 20: v. 2 refers to Viṣṇu; see ĀÇS. viii. 4. 10; ÇÇS. xii. 6. 14.

[5] RV. i. 43. 6; see Caland and Henry, *L'Agniṣṭoma*, pp. 373, 375.

[6] I. e. at the Viçvajit, the other two Çilpas being transposed to the midday; see ĀÇS. viii. 4. 7–9; ÇÇS. xi, 15. 10.

[1] This refers to the Viçvajit in a Sattra where the Nābhānediṣṭha of the Hotṛ is as usual in the Vaiçvadeva Çastra in the third pressing. The Çastras of the Maitrāvaruṇa and the Brāhmaṇācchaṅsin then loose their special predecessor; being transferred to the midday ritual, in the Agniṣṭoma form; cf. KB. xxv. 12–14. The answer is that all the Çilpas are performed though not in the same order, the Evayāmarut being also found in the Hotṛ's recitation.

[2] I. e. as an Ekāha, and also on the sixth day, an Ukthya (read *ukthyasaṁsthātvena* in comm.). Cf. ĀÇS. viii. 4. 5, 6.

will go over the worlds. It he grasped around from above with the metres, that of the Gāyatrī with the Nārāçansī, that of the Triṣṭubh with the Raibhī, that of the Jagatī with the Pārikṣitī, that of the Anuṣṭubh with the Kāravyā. Thus he placed again the sap in the metres. He sacrifices with metres full of sap, with metres full of sap he extends the sacrifice who knows thus. He recites the Nārāçansī (verses)[1]; men are offspring, praise is speech; verily thus he places speech in offspring; therefore offspring here are born speaking (for him), who knows thus. As to the Nārāçansīs, by reciting the gods and the seers went to the world of heaven; verily thus also the sacrificers by reciting go to the world of heaven. These he recites taking apart,[2] as (he recites) the Vṛṣākapi (hymn); for it is connected with the Vṛṣākapi; thus it follows the rule of the Vṛṣākapi. In them he should not say the sound *o*; he should accent specially,[3] for it is their sound *o*. He recites the Raibhī (verses)[4]; the gods and the seers making a noise went to the world of heaven; verily thus the sacrificers making a noise go to the world of heaven. These he recites taking apart, like the Vṛṣākapi, for it is connected with the Vṛṣākapi; thus it follows the rule of the Vṛṣākapi. In them he should not say the sound *o*; he should accent specially, for it is their sound *o*. He recites the Parikṣit[5] (verses); Parikṣit is Agni, for Agni dwells around (*pari kṣeti*) these creatures; for round Agni these creatures dwell; he attains union and identity of form and world with Agni who knows thus. As to these being Parikṣit (verses), Parikṣit is the year, for the year dwells round these creatures, for round the year these creatures dwell. He attains union and identity of form and world with the year who knows thus. These he recites taking apart, like the Vṛṣākapi, for it is connected with the Vṛṣākapi; thus it follows the rule of the Vṛṣākapi. In them he should not say the sound *o*; he should accent specially, for it is their sound *o*. He recites the Kāravyā[6] (verses). Whatever good thing they did, the gods obtained with the Kāravyās; verily thus also the sacrificers obtain with the Kāravyās whatever good thing they do. These

[1] All these are to be recited by the Brāhmaṇācchaṅsin (see AB. vi. 29). The whole is the Kuntāpa, referred by Sāyaṇa to a book called the Kuntāpa being a Khila. See AV. xx. 127. 1–3; RVKh. v. 8; ÇÇS. xii. 14. 1–3. See also ĀÇS. viii. 3. 10 *seq.*; *Vait.* xxxii. 19 *seq.* Cf. KB. xxx. 5–7.

[2] I. e. pausing at each Pada. In § 3 above the words *yad eva nārāçaṅsīḥ* should go with the next clause, as in §§ 13 and 14. For the Nārāçaṅsīs (distinct from the Nārāçaṅsa in AB. vi. 16 and 27) see *Vedic Index*, i. 445, 446; SBE. xlii. 690 *seq.*

[3] The Ninarda is a species of accent described in ĀÇS. viii. 3. 9 *seq.*; *Vait.* xxxii. 14–17. It affects the second vowel of the third Pada, the normal place of the Nyūṅkha. The first vowel is pronounced as *anudātta*, the second as *udātta*, the next *ekaçruti*. The Pratigara is *othāmo daivom.*

[4] AV. xx. 127. 4–6; RVKh. v. 9; ÇÇS. xii. 15. 1; 14. 4, 5. Cf. *Vait.* xxxii. 19.

[5] AV. xx. 127. 7–10; RVKh. v. 10; ÇÇS. xii. 17. 1. 1–4.

[6] AV. xx. 127. 11–14; RVKh. v. 11, ÇÇS. xii. 15. 2–4. v. 12 occurs in AB. viii. 11. 5.

he recites taking apart, like the Vṛṣākapi, for it is connected with the Vṛṣākapi; thus it follows the rule of the Vṛṣākapi. In them he should not say the sound *o*; he should accent specially, for it is their sound *o*. He recites the orderings of the quarters;[7] verily thus he puts in order the quarters; five he recites; these quarters are five, four transverse, one upwards. In these he should not say the sound *o*, nor should he accent specially[8] (thinking) 'Let me not make to move these quarters'. These he recites by half-verses, for support. He recites the man-ordering (verses);[9] the man-ordering (verses) are offspring; verily thus having put in order the quarters he establishes offspring in them. In these he should not say the sound *o* nor accent specially (thinking) 'Let me not make to move these offspring'. These he recites by half-verses, for support. He recites the Indragāthās[10]; by the singing against them of the Indragāthās, the gods overpowered the Asuras; verily thus also the sacrificers by singing the Indragāthās against the hated rival overpower him. By half-verses he recites these, for support.

vi. 33 (xxx. 7). He recites the prattle of Aitaça[1]; Aitaça, the sage, saw the life of Agni; 'the unwearied part of the sacrifice' say some. He said to his sons 'My boys, I have seen the life of Agni; I shall chatter it; whatever I say do not disregard'. He began 'These horses float up to Pratīpa Prātisatvana'; (his son) Abhyagni Aitaçāyana, having come, arriving at a wrong moment, seized his mouth (saying) 'Our father has become out of his mind'. He said to him 'Go hence; thou hast been a sluggard in spoiling my speech; I was about to make the cow of a hundred (years of) life, man of a thousand (years of) life; worst of all do I make thine offspring since thou here hast fastened on me'. Therefore they say 'The Abhyagnis Aitaçāyanas are the least of the Aurvas'. Some recite it of longer length; he should not prevent it; 'Recite as much as is desired' he should say; the prattle of Aitaçapa is life; verily thus he prolongs the life of the sacrificer who knows thus. As to there being the prattle of Aitaça; the prattle of Aitaça is the sap of the metres; verily thus he places sap in the metres. He sacrifices with metres full of sap and with metres full of sap he extends the sacrifice who knows thus. Again as to the prattle of Aitaça; the

[7] AV. xx. 128. 1–5; RVKh. v. 12; ÇÇS. xii. 20. 2. 1, 3, 2, 4, 5.

[8] *naivaiva* is read by Sāyaṇa but it is very odd to have two *eva's* thus used; it is natural to suppose *iva* is once meant as above it is always *ni viva nardet*.

[9] AV. xx. 128. 6–11; RVKh. v. 13; ÇÇS. xii. 21. 2. 1–6.

[10] AV. xx. 128. 12–16; RVKh. v. 14; 12, 13, and 15 occur in ÇÇS. xii. 15. 5; 16. 1.

[1] AV. xx. 129. 1 *seq.* See KB. xxx. 5; *Vait.* xxxii. 20; GB. xi. 12 *seq.* ĀÇS. viii. 3. 14 prescribes 70 Padas or 18, viz. 1–3 *a*; 15 *d*–17 *b*; 17 *d*; 18 *b*. See RVKh. v. 15; (17 × 4 + 2); ÇÇS. xii. 18. 2. 1–9; 1. 11–18 has eight of the verses. Cf. ĀÇS. viii. 3. 14 *seq.* for the following; Bloomfield, *Atharvaveda*, pp. 96 *seq.*

prattle of Aitaça is freedom from exhaustion and unfailingness; (he thinks) 'Let there be freedom from exhaustion in my sacrifice, unfailingness in my sacrifice'. He recites the prattle of Aitaça, taking it by Padas, like a Nivid. He says *om* with the last Pada as in the case of a Nivid. He recites the riddle verses.[2] The gods having confounded the Asuras with the riddles overcame them; verily thus also the sacrificers having confounded the hated rival with the riddles overcome him. These he recites by half verses, for support. He recites the Ājijñāsenyā (verses);[3] by means of the Ājijñāsenyā verses the gods recognizing the Asuras overcame them; verily thus also the sacrificers by means of the Ājijñāsenyā (verses) recognizing the hated rival overcome him. These he recites by half verses, for support. He recites the Pratirādha;[4] by the Pratirādha the gods overpowered the Asuras and overcame them; verily thus also the sacrificers overpower the hated rival and overcome him. He recites the Ativāda;[5] by means of the Ativāda the gods outspoke the Asuras and overcame them; verily thus also by means of the Ativāda the sacrificers outspeak the hated rival and overcome him. These by half verses he recites, for support.

vi. 34 (xxx. 8). He recites the Devanītha;[1] the Ādityas and Añgirases disputed as to the world of heaven. 'We shall go first, we'. The Añgirases first saw the Soma pressing on the next day for the world of heaven. They dispatched Agni—Agni is one of the Añgirases—(saying) 'Go, tell the Ādityas of our pressing to-morrow for the world of heaven'. The Ādityas having seen Agni saw the pressing on the same day for the world of heaven. To them he said on his arrival 'We announce to you the pressing to-morrow for the world of heaven'. They said 'But we announce to thee the pressing on this day for the world of heaven; with thee for Hotṛ we shall go to the world of heaven'. 'Be it so' he said and returned with his reply. They said 'Didst thou announce?' 'I announced' he replied; 'moreover they gave me a reply'. 'No: surely thou didst not respond?' (they said). 'I did respond' he replied; 'With fame he[2] approaches who approaches with the priestly function; if one were to refuse him, he would

[2] AV. xx. 133. 1–6; RVKh. v. 16; ÇÇS. xii. 22. 1–6; *Vait.* xxxii. 21. Govindasvāmin and Sāyaṇa take *pravalhya* as = cheating with fair words.

[3] AV. xx. 134. 1–4; RVKh. v. 17; ÇÇS. xii. 23. 1. In *Vait.* xxxii. 22 and 23 these and the next are confused.

[4] AV. xx. 135. 1–3; RVKh. v. 18; ÇÇS. xii. 23. 2.

[5] AV. xx. 135. 4; RVKh. v. 19; ÇÇS. xii. 23. 4; *Vait.* xxxii. 26 (*ativāda*).

[1] AV. xx. 135. 6 *seq.*; RVKh. v. 20; ÇÇS. xii. 19. 1–4; *Vait.* xxxii. 28; see ĀÇS. viii. 3. 25. Cf. KB. xxx. 6; Lévi, *La doctrine du sacrifice*, pp. 65, 66.

[2] The offerer, rather than as Sāyaṇa, the priest. *tam* is naturally masculine and *yajñam* is not very easily to be supplied. Cf. ÇB. iii. 5. 1. 13–17. *no . . . na* above is overlooked by Delbrück, *Altind. Synt.* p. 544.

refuse fame; therefore I did not refuse'. If one desire to refuse (to officiate at a sacrifice) on account of (another) sacrifice[3] should he refuse it. But if (the offerer) is one for whom it is not suitable to sacrifice, spontaneous refusal is appropriate.

vi. 35 (xxx. 9). The Aṅgirases sacrificed for the Ādityas; to them as sacrificing for them, they gave this earth full of fees; being accepted it caused them to burn; they cast her away; she becoming a lioness with gaping jaws assailed men. Of her as she burned came forth thin fissures which are now upon her; aforetime she was all even, as it were. Therefore they say 'He shall not accept a gift laid aside', (thinking) 'Let it not, being pierced with heat, pierce me with heat.' But if he should accept it, he should give it to a hated rival; he is ruined. Now as to yonder sun: he having taken the form of a white horse with its body bound with a horse halter went (to them) (saying) 'This we bring (as a fee) for you.' Thus is the Devanitha[1] recited,

> 'The Ādityas, O singer, brought a fee to the Aṅgirases;
> This, O singer, they did not approach';

for they did not approach the (earth).

> 'But this, O singer, they did approach'

for they did approach yonder (sun).

> 'This, O singer, they did not accept,'

for they did not accept this (earth).

> 'But this, O singer, they did accept,'

for they did accept yonder (sun).

> 'Lest the days be without discrimination'

he is the discriminator of the days.

> 'Without a leader[2] the sacrifices'

the fee is the leader of the sacrifices; just as in this world a wagon without a leader comes to harm, so the sacrifice without a fee comes to harm; therefore they say 'At the sacrifice a fee should be given, if but a small one.'

> 'White and swift of motion,
> And most rapid of foot,
> Swiftly it accomplisheth its purpose;
> The Ādityas, Rudras, Vasus praise thee,
> This gift do thou accept, O Aṅgiras';

[3] This must be the sense, as Sāyaṇa takes it: *asmāt = ārtvijyāt*.

[1] The text is the same in its variants save that ÇÇS. has *deta* and *yajñā*. The text is hopeless; Haug renders 'he being carried away', *neta(ḥ) = nītaḥ*. Weber (*Ind. Stud.* ix. 306) suggests *ned asann* 'that they may not be' in this and the next case.

[2] Again the text is hopeless. Haug as before renders 'he being carried away', the wise men were without a leader (from Sāyaṇa). Read below *atyalpikāpi*.

Verily thus they sought acceptance of their gift.

'This gift, great and broad,
Let the gods give as a boon,
Let that be pleasing to you,
Given be it day by day,
Do ye accept it.'

Verily thus they accepted [3] it. He recites this Devanītha taking it by Padas like a Nivid; he says *om* with its last Pada as in the case of a Nivid.

vi. 36 (xxx. 10). He recites the Bhūtechads [1]; by means of the Bhūtechads the gods assailed the Asuras with battle and with craft. The gods, having obscured by the Bhūtechads the might of the Asuras, overcame them; verily thus the sacrificers having obscured by the Bhūtechads the might of the hated rival overcame him. These he recites by half verses, for support. He recites the Āhanasyā (verses); [2] from this organ is seed poured, from seed offspring are born; verily thus he secures propagation. Ten he recites; the Virāj has ten syllables; the Virāj is food; from food is seed poured; from seed offspring are born; verily thus he secures propagation. In them he inserts the sound *o*; the sound *o* is food; from food is seed poured, from seed offspring are born; verily thus he secures propagation. In 'I have celebrated Dadhikrāvan' he recites the Dadhikrā (verse); [3] Dadhikrā is the divine filter; herein he has said a speech full of impurity; thus speech he purifies with the divine filter. It is in Anuṣṭubh; the Anuṣṭubh is speech; thus with its own metre he purifies speech. In 'The most sweet draughts are pressed' he recites (verses) to Soma, the purifying; [4] (verses) to Soma, the purifying are a divine filter; herein he has said a speech full of impurity; thus with the divine filter he purifies speech. They are in Anuṣṭubh; the Anuṣṭubh is speech; verily thus with its own metre he purifies speech. In 'The drop hath mounted Añçumatī' he recites a triplet to Indra and Bṛhaspati; [5]

'The hosts, godless, as they attacked,
With Bṛhaspati to aid, Indra overwhelmed'

[3] Sāyaṇa clearly read *ajagrabhaiṣan* which in sense is right, despite Aufrecht. In AB. vi. 24 occurs *paryagrahaiṣam*. The most probable reading is *ajigrabhīṣan* with ī as elsewhere (Whitney, *Sansk. Gr.* § 1081 *b*; cf. § 801 *i*), unless we allow *ai* as an abnormality for ī.

[1] AV. xx. 135. 11-13; RVKh. v. 21; ÇÇS. xii. 16. 4, 5, 8; *Vait.* xxxii. 30.

[2] AV. xx. 136. 1-10; RVKh. v. 22. 1-10; *Vait.* xxxii. 31; ĀÇS. viii. 3. 30-32; cf. KB. xxx. 6; ÇÇS. xii. 24. 2; 25. 1.

[3] AV. xx. 137. 3; RV. iv. 39. 6; RVKh. v. 22. 13; cf. KB. xxx. 8; *Vait.* xxxii. 33. The sense of *vyāhanasyām* is not quite certain, as though Sāyaṇa takes it *viçiṣṭa*, still *vi* 'without' might do.

[4] RV. ix. 101. 4-6; ĀÇS. viii. 3. 32 (reading *ca tisraḥ* for *catasraḥ*); ÇÇS. xii. 25. 2; *Vait.* xxxii. 33.

[5] RV. viii. 96. 13-15; AV. xx. 137. 7-9; AÇS. viii. 3. 33; ÇÇS. xii. 25. 2. *udācārya* is corrupt; Weber (*Ind. Stud.* ix. 307) suggests °*cāri*; BR. v. 1412 *udācarya*.

(he says); the Asura folk were rebellious towards the gods; Indra with Bṛhaspati as companion smote away the Asura hue when attacking; verily thus also the sacrificers by means of Indra and Bṛhaspati as aid smite away the Asura hue when attacking. They say 'Should he recite together[6] on the sixth day.[7] Or should he not recite together?' 'He should recite together' they say,[8] 'why should he recite together on the other days and not recite together on this?' Or rather they say 'He should not recite together; the sixth day is the world of heaven; the world of heaven is not a place where all meet; only certain people meet in that world. If he were to recite together, he would make it common. In that he does not recite together, that is a symbol of the world of heaven; therefore he should not recite together. Again as to his not reciting together; the litanies here are the Nābhānediṣṭha, the Vālakhilyās, the Vṛṣākapi and the Evayāmarut; if he were to recite together, he would loose the desire that is in these. The Vṛṣākapi is connected with Indra; the prattle of Aitaça is all the metres; herein is the desire obtained which is in (the hymn) in Jagatī to Indra; moreover the hymn is addressed to Indra and Bṛhaspati;[7] the concluding verse is addressed to Indra and Bṛhaspati; therefore he should not recite together.

[6] With the normal form, RV. i. 57; AB. iii. 50. This explains *Vait.* xxxii. 35 which Caland has not identified.

[7] I. e. RV. viii. 96 (n. 5).

[8] Cf. above AB. vi. 26.

PAÑCIKĀ VII

SUPPLEMENTARY MATTER AND THE RĀJASŪYA.

ADHYĀYA I

The Division of the Sacrificial Animal.

vii. 1 (xxxi. 1). Now[1] regarding the division of the sacrificial animal; we shall declare the division. The two jaws along with the tongue belong to Prastotṛ; the breast in eagle shape to the Udgātṛ, the palatal part of the throat to the Pratihartṛ, the right loin to the Hotṛ, the left to the Brahman, the right thigh to the Maitrāvaruṇa, the left to the Brāhmaṇācchaṅsin, the right side with the shoulder to the Adhvaryu, the left to the Upagātṛs, the left shoulder to the Pratipasthātṛ, the right lower foreleg to the Neṣṭṛ, the left to the Potṛ, the right foreleg to the Achāvāka, the left to the Agnīdh, the right upper foreleg to the Ātreya, the left to the Sadasya, the seat and spine to the householder, the two right feet[2] to the man who gives the fast milk to the householder, the two left feet to him who gives the fast milk to the wife of the householder,[3] the lip is common to the two; this the householder should leave over. They take the tail to the wives, but they should give it to a Brahman. The fleshy growth on the neck and three ribs belong to the Grāvastut; three ribs and half the flesh[4] to the Unnetṛ, the other half of the flesh and the lungs to the slaughterer; it he should give to a Brahman, if he is not a Brahman. The head belongs to the Subrahmaṇyā priest, the skin to him who declares the pressing on the next day;[5] the sacrificial food to all or to the Hotṛ. These thirty-six each

[1] The division is given in ĀÇS. xii. 9, the probably original source; it is borrowed from AB. in GB. iii. 18. The Upagātṛs are subordinate Sāman priests who accompany the chants of the Sāman singers; the Ātreya is not a normal priest, but he appears as specially privileged elsewhere, e. g. KÇS. x. 2. 21; KS. xxviii. 4. Cf. the part of the Ātreya in ÇÇS. xvi. 18, 19; Weber, *Ind. Stud.* x. 384. See for the division ÇB. iii. 8. 3; Schwab, *Das Altindische Thieropfer*, pp. 126–130.

[2] Sāyaṇa holds that the terms *doḥ* and *bāhu* exhaust the forelegs, but this seems unlikely; the term here is *pada* 'foot'.

[3] Apparently this sense is meant, and so with *enayoḥ*, but Sāyaṇa's comment is confused.

[4] The *vaikarta* is an unknown part, but apparently near the *kīkasā*, here perhaps the ribs.

[5] I. e. the Agnīdh; see ĀÇS. vi. 11. 16. Weber (*Ind. Stud.* ix. 308) cites PB. xvi. 18. 10; LÇS. i. 1. 9, 12; ÇÇS. xiv. 40. 21;

of one foot support the sacrifice; the Bṛhatī has thirty-six syllables; the worlds of heaven are connected with the Bṛhatī; verily thus they obtain the breaths and the worlds of heaven; verily thus they proceed finding support in the breaths and in the worlds of heaven. It is a heavenly victim for those who thus divide it. But those who do it otherwise, it is as if robbers or evildoers should rend an animal. This division of the victim Çrautarṣi Devabhāga knew; but he left the world without proclaiming it. But it is a superhuman being proclaimed to Girija Bābhravya; since that time on men study it.

ADHYĀYA II

Expiations for Errors in the Agnihotra, &c.

vii. 2 (xxxii. 1). They[1] say 'If one who has established the fires dies on the fast day, how is it with his sacrifice?' 'He should not sacrifice for him', they say, 'for he has not arrived at the sacrifice.' They say 'If one who has established the fires dies when the Agnihotra has been put on the fire or the Sāṁnāyya milk or the oblations, what is the expiation here?' He should put them all around so that they may all be burned together. That is the expiation here. They say 'If one who has established the fires dies when the oblations have been put in place, what is the expiation here?' (Saying) 'Hail!' to those deities for whom the libations were drawn he should offer them whole in the Āhavanīya. That is the expiation here. They say 'If one who has established the fires dies in absence, how is his Agnihotra to be performed?' He should offer with the milk of (a cow) with a calf to which it is to be won over;[2] the milk of (a cow) with a calf to which it is to be won over is different, as it were, the Agnihotra of the dead is different as it were. Or they may offer with milk from whatever source. Moreover they say 'They should keep kindled these fires, without offering, until the bones are collected.' If the bones cannot be found, having gathered three hundred and sixty leaf stalks,[3] and having made of them

41. 11. The presence of the Sadasya, who is not recognized by the Āçvalāyana school, but only by the Kauṣītaki, is another sign of later origin, as in the use of the word *vibhāga*; probably, as Lindner (*Pāṇini*, p. 79) suggests, an older account has been superseded by the Sūtra version.

[1] For the Prāyaçcittas cf. ÇB. xii. 5. 1 *seq.*; *Kauç.* xiv; ĀÇS. iii; Āp. ix; *Atharva-prāyaçcitta* (JAOS. xxxiii. 71 *seq.*). For this case cf. JB. i. 57. 1–8; ÇB. xii. 4. 2. 5.

[2] See TS. i. 8. 5. 1; TB. i. 6. 8. 4; Sāyaṇa's derivation from √*rā* is very bad: Nārāyaṇa on ĀÇS. iii. 10. 17 recognizes the root *van*; *Vedic Index*, i. 452.

[3] *paṣṭiḥ* is one of the extraordinary forms of the tradition: *ṣaṣṭim* must no doubt be read.

a human figure as it were, they should perform on it the usual round (of ceremonies) and thus after mingling, the (fires) with the bones gathered together remove them. A hundred and fifty should he place on the body, a hundred and forty on the thigh bones, fifty on the thighs, and the rest on the head. That is the expiation here.

vii. 3 (xxxii. 2). [As in AB. v. 27.[1]]

vii. 4 (xxxii. 3). They say 'If a man's Sāṁnāyya[1] milked in the evening becomes spoiled or some one carries it away, what is the expiation here?' Having divided into two the morning's milking, he should curdle one half of it and sacrifice with it. That is the expiation here. They say 'If the morning milking of the Sāṁnāyya becomes spoiled or some one carries it away, what is the expiation here? He should prepare in its place a cake for Indra or Mahendra and sacrifice with it. That is the expiation here. They say 'If the whole of his Sāṁnāyya becomes spoiled or some one carries it away, what is the expiation here. (He should offer) a cake for Indra or Mahendra just as above. That is the expiation here. They say 'If the whole of his oblation becomes spoiled or men take them away, what is the expiation then?' Having made them according to the deities out of butter, he should offer with a butter oblation and thus perform another offering without a flaw. The sacrifice is the expiation of the sacrifice.

vii. 5 (xxi. 4). They say 'If on to a man's Agnihotra when put on the fire something not fit for sacrifice falls, what is the expiation here?' Having poured it all into the offering spoon, and having gone east, he places the kindling stick on the Āhavanīya, and having taken off a hot coal from the north of the Āhavanīya he should pour the offering, either in silence or with a verse to Prajāpati.[1] That is both offered and not offered. If it happens when (the spoon) has been filled once or twice, the same procedure applies. If he can remove it, having poured off the spoilt portion, and having poured the unspoiled portion (into the offering spoon) he should offer it in the ordinary way.[2] That is the expiation here. They say 'If a man's Agni-

Weber (*Ind. Stud.* ix. 310) suggests *parṇasadaḥ* (cf. ÇÇS. xii. 28. 13). The parallel texts giving the rite have *palāçavṛntāni* (ÇÇS. iv. 15. 19; KÇS. xxv. 8. 15) or °*tsarūṇām* (*Kauç.* 83) or *pālāçatsarūṇi* (*Ath. Prāy.* iii. 8). For *viṅças* = *dvivíṅças* cf. Wackernagel, *Altind. Gram.* II. i. 30, 31.

[1] The only changes are the omission of the last sentence and the insertion of 'They say' before each hypothesis.

vii. 4. [1] I. e. the mixture of milk prepared at the evening and on the morning for the Agnihotra. The evening milk is made sour and mixed with the fresh milk. Cf. *Atharvaprāyaçcitta*, ii. 1.

vii. 5. [1] RV. x. 121. 10. Cf. ĀÇS. iii. 20. 28. TB. i. 55. 8 and SB. xii. 4. 2. 4 differ. See also *Atharvaprāyaçcitta*, i. 3 *seq.*

[2] I. e. in the usual mode of *unnayana*, pouring into the spoon; TB. ii. 1. 3. 5. The form *vyapanayitum* is very irregular; for parallels see Whitney, *Sansk. Gr.* § 968 *d*. Cf. JAOS. xxxiii. 78, n. 49. *sa yadi* is a sign of lateness.

hotra when put on the fire spills or pours over, what is the expiation here?' He should pour water on it for expiation; waters are expiation; then he touches (the rest) with his right hand and mutters. 'To the sky a third, to the gods the sacrifice hath gone; thence may wealth come to me; to the atmosphere, a third, to the fathers the sacrifice hath gone; thence may wealth come to me; to the earth a third, to me the sacrifice hath gone; thence may wealth come to me.' He then mutters (a verse) to Viṣṇu and Varuṇa,[3] 'By whose might the regions are established; Viṣṇu guards that of the sacrifice which is well sacrificed, Varuṇa that which is ill sacrificed; verily (it serves) to appease both of them. That is the expiation here. They say 'If, as he goes eastwards,[4] the Agnihotra which has been put on the fire spills or falls out, what is the expiation here?' If he were to fetch it again, he would turn the sacrifice away from the world of heaven; he should stay where he is and others should fetch to him the remains of the Agnihotra and he should offer it in the usual way. That is the expiation here. They say 'If the offering spoon splits, what is the expiation here?' He should fetch another spoon and offer; then he should put on the Āhavanīya the broken spoon; handle in front, bowl behind. That is the expiation here. They say[5] 'If there is fire on a man's Āhavanīya, but that on the Gārhapatya is extinguished, what is the expiation here?' If he were to take out (the fire) to the east, he would fall away from his abode; if to the west he would perform the sacrifices like the Asuras; if he were to kindle afresh he would produce a rival for the sacrificer; if he should make (the Āhavanīya) also go out, breath would forsake the sacrificer; verily having gathered the whole of it with the ashes he should put it in the place of the Gārhapatya and from it take out the Āhavanīya to the east. That is the expiation here.

vii. 6 (xxxii. 5). They say[1] 'If they take out a fire (and put it with)

[3] Above AB. iii. 38.

[4] The anacoluthon seems clear and Sāyaṇa so takes it. Weber (*Ind. Stud.* ix. 311) refuses to accept it, but does not explain *yasya* and the verbs do not suit that view.

[5] The Āhavanīya is normally taken out to the east from the Gārhapatya which alone remains in; the five alternative courses in the circumstances are (1) to to take as the Gārhapatya the Āhavanīya and then take out the Āhavanīya from it; (2) to take out the Gārhapatya from the Āhavanīya, like the Asuras (TB. i. 1. 4. 4); (3) to rekindle the fire; (4) to extinguish the Āhavanīya also, and (5) to remove the whole fire to the Gārhapatya and then take out the Āhavanīya. All the modes are allowed by ĀÇS. iii. 12. 21–25 in defiance of the Brāhmaṇa. The same result is arrived at by the ÇB. xii. 4. 3. 6–10 by somewhat different arguments. Cf. *Ath. Prāy.* i. 5; JB. i. 61. 3–7 which agrees closely with ÇB. (JAOS. xxiii. 343, 344).

[1] The readings (*abhyuddharet* and *abhyuddhareyuḥ*) of JB. i. 65. 2 and ÇB. xii. 4. 3. 4 suggest the rendering followed; the fire taken out being from the Gārhapatya;

a man's fire what is the expiation then?' If he can see it, removing the former (fire) he should put down the other; if however he cannot see it, he should offer a cake on eight potsherds to Agni with Agni; the invitatory and offering verses for it are[2] 'Agni by Agni is kindled' and 'For thou, O Agni, by Agni.' Or he should offer a libation in the Āhavanīya with 'To Agni with Agni hail!' That is the expiation here. They say 'If a man's Gārhapatya and Āhavanīya unite together what is the expiation here?' He should offer to Agni as delight a cake on eight potsherds; its invitatory and offering verses are[3] 'O Agni come for delight', and 'Who Agni for the delight of the gods.' Or he should offer a libation in the Āhavanīya with 'To Agni as delight hail!' That is the expiation here. They say 'If all a man's fires should unite together, what is the expiation here?' He should offer a cake on eight potsherds to Agni as discrimination; its invitatory and offering verses are[4] 'He hath shone like the sun at the breaking of the dawns' and 'Thee, O Agni the tribes of men praise.' Or he should offer a libation in the Āhavanīya with 'To Agni as discrimination hail!' That is the expiation here. They say 'If a man's fire unite with other fires, what is the expiation here?' He should offer a cake on eight potsherds to Agni the charred;[5] its invitatory and offering verses[6] are 'Agni hath roared like Dyaus thundering' and 'As our fathers of old.' Or he should offer a libation in the Āhavanīya with 'To Agni the charred hail!' That is the expiation here.

vii. 7. (xxxii. 6). They say 'If a man's fires are involved in a village fire, what is the expiation here?' He should offer a cake on eight potsherds to Agni, the spoiler; the invitatory and offering verses are[1] 'In our cattle fray' and 'Do not as in the great contest.' Or he should offer a libation in the Āhavanīya with 'To Agni, the spoiler, hail!' That is the expiation here. They say 'If a man's fires be united with a divine conflagration, what is the expiation here?' He should offer a cake on eight potsherds

else the sense might be, if people needlessly take out an Āhavanīya, where there is an Āhavanīya; then the old one if still recognizable is to be extinguished. The reading of Aufrecht *yady u* for *yadya* of the MSS. is essential.

[2] RV. i. 12. 6; viii. 43. 14; ĀÇS. iii. 13. 8, 12; cf. ÇÇS. iii. 4. 1; 5. 1; JB. i. 65. 3; ÇB. xii. 4. 3. 5.

[3] RV. vi. 16. 10; i. 12. 9; ĀÇS. iii 1 . 6, 12; cf. ÇÇS. iii. 4. 8; 5. 2; JB. . 65. 4.

[4] RV. vii. 10. 2; v. 8. 8; ĀÇS. iii. 13. 5, 12, where the offering verse is RV. vi. 6. 3; cf. ÇÇS. iii. 4. 4; 5. 3: JB. i. 64. 1; MÇS. iii. 4. 4, 5; ĀpÇS. ix. 3. 18; ÇB. xii. 4. 4. 2.

[5] *Kṣāmavant* is doubtful: cf. NS. i. 8. 9; Sāyaṇa takes it as = *kṣamāvant*, 'patient' or 'forgiving'; ĀpÇS. ix. 3. 17 has a different use of it; cf. *Ath. Prāy.* v. 4.

[6] RV. x. 45. 4; iv. 2. 16; ĀÇS. iii. 13. 4, 12 with different order of verses and a new sense; cf. ÇÇS. iii. 4. 13. For the whole cf. *Atharvaprāyaçcitta*, ii. 7; v. 4, 5.

[1] RV. viii. 75. 11 and 12; ĀÇS. iii. 13. 7, 12; ÇÇS. iii. 4. 5 5. 4; ÇB. xii. 4. 4. 3.

to Agni as in the waters; its invitatory and offering verses are[2] 'In the waters, O Agni, is thy seat' and 'The clever, of pure insight hath wrought a wondrous deed.' Or he should offer a libation in the Āhavanīya with 'To Agni as in the waters hail!' That is the expiation here. They say 'If a man's fires are united with the fire which burns a corpse, what is the expiation here?' He should offer a cake on eight potsherds to Agni, the pure; its invitatory and offering verses are[3] 'Agni of purest vows' and 'Up, O Agni, thy pure (rays).' Or he should offer a libation in the Āhavanīya with 'To Agni, the pure, hail!' That is the expiation here. They say 'If a man's fires are involved in a forest fire, what is the expiation here?' He should mount (the fires) on the two fire sticks[4] or take out a fire brand from the Āhavanīya or from the Gārhapatya; if he cannot so do, he should offer a cake on eight potsherds to Agni, the spoiler; its invitatory and offering verses have been given. Or he should offer a libation in the Āhavanīya with 'To Agni, the spoiler, hail!' That is the expiation here.

vii. 8 (xxxii. 7). They say 'If at the fast day one who has established the fires weeps, what is the expiation here?' He should offer a cake on eight potsherds to Agni, the supporter of vows; its invitatory and offering verses are[1] 'Thou, O Agni, art the supporter of vows, the pure' and 'Supporting vows, guardian of vows, undeceived.' Or he should offer a libation in the Āhavanīya with 'To Agni, supporter of vows, hail!' That is the expiation here. They say 'If one who has established the fires on the fast day should happen to commit a breach of his vow, what is the expiation here?' He should offer a cake on eight potsherds to Agni, the lord of vows; its invitatory and offering verses are[2] 'Thou, O Agni, art the guardian of vows' and 'If we have contravened your vows.' Or he should offer a libation in the Āhavanīya with 'To Agni, the lord of vows, hail!' That is the expiation here. They say 'If one who has established the fires should omit the offering at new or at full moon, what is the expiation here?' He should offer a cake on eight potsherds to Agni, the maker of ways; its invitatory and offering verses are[3] 'For thou knowest, O wise one, the ways' and 'We have come to the way of

[2] RV. viii. 43. 9; iii. 1. 8; ĀÇS. iii. 13. 8, 12 with viii. 43. 28 as second; cf. ÇÇS. iii. 4. 7; 5. 5; ÇB. xii. 4. 4. 4.

[3] RV. viii. 44. 21 and 17; ĀÇS. iii. 13. 4; ÇÇS. iii. 4. 6. No verses are given in ĀÇS. Cf. ÇB. xii. 4. 4. 5.

[4] Cf. ÇB. xii. 4. 3. 10; 4. 1; 5. 2. 1; xiii. 6. 2. 20; iv. 6. 8. 3; ÇÇS. ii. 17. 1–5; KÇS. v. 3. 1; xxi. 1. 17. Cf. also *Atharva-prāyaçcitta*, ii. 7 and 8.

[1] ĀÇS. iii. 12. 14; TB. ii. 4. 1. 11: ÇÇS. iii. 4. 12; 5. 9. Cf. JAOS. xxxiii. 85, n. 257.

[2] RV. viii. 11. 1; x. 2. 4; ĀÇS. iii. 13. 2, 12; cf. ÇÇS. iv. 4. 11.

[3] RV. vi. 16. 3; x. 2. 3; ĀÇS. iii. 10. 10–12; cf. ÇÇS. iv. 4. 2: 5. 7; JAOS. xxxiii. 80, n. 148.

the gods.' Or he should offer a libation in the Āhavanīya with 'To Agni, the maker of ways, hail!' That is the expiation here. They say 'If all a man's fires are extinguished, what is the expiation here?' He should offer a cake on eight potsherds to Agni, the fervid, connected with man, the purifying; its invitatory and offering verses are[4] 'O come with fervour among men' and 'Come to us with fervour among men.' Or he should offer a libation in the Āhavanīya with 'To Agni, the fervid, connected with men, the purifying hail!' That is the expiation here.

vii. 9 (xxxii. 8). They say 'If one who has established the fires eats new food without making the Āgrayaṇa offering, what is the expiation here?' He should offer a cake on twelve potsherds to Agni Vaiçvānara; its invitatory and offering verses are[1] 'Vaiçvānara hath produced' and 'Present in the sky, present Agni on earth.' Or he should offer a libation in the Āhavanīya with 'To Agni Vaiçvānara hail!' That is the expiation here. They say 'If one has established his fires and a potsherd be lost what is the expiation here?' He should offer a cake on two potsherds to the Açvins; its invitatory and offering verses[2] are 'O Açvins to our abode' and 'With chariot rich in cattle O Nāsatyas.' Or he should offer a libation in the Āhavanīya with 'To the Açvins hail!' That is the expiation here. They say 'If one has established the fires and the filter be lost, what is the expiation here?' He should offer a cake on eight potsherds to Agni with the filter; its invitatory and offering verses are[3] 'Thy filter is outstretched, O lord of prayer' and 'The filter of the burning one outstretched in the sky.' Or he should offer a libation in the Āhavanīya with 'To Agni with the filter hail!' That is the expiation here. They say 'If one has established the fires and the gold be lost, what is the expiation here?' He should offer a cake on eight potsherds to Agni with the gold; its invitatory and offering verses are[4] 'Golden haired in the expanse of the atmosphere' and 'The well winged ones strengthen in the ways.' Or he should offer a libation in the Āhavanīya with 'To Agni with the gold hail!' That is the expiation here. They say 'If one who has established the fires were to offer without having bathed in the morning, what is the expiation here?' He should offer

[4] RV. again has not this; see ĀÇS. iii. 12. 27. Agni as *janadvant* is one connected with the root *jan* seen in *janeṣu*. Sāyaṇa leaves it untranslated. Cf. MS. i. 8. 9.

[1] Above AB. v. 17; RV. i. 98. 2; only in ĀÇS. ii. 15. 2 in another ritual.

[2] RV. i. 92. 16; vii. 72. 1; not in ĀÇS. in this use.

[3] RV. ix. 83. 1 and 2; not in ĀÇS. in this use.

[4] RV. i. 77. 1 and 2; not in this sense in ĀÇS., which has it in the Kārīriṣṭi, ii. 13. 7.

a cake on eight potsherds to Agni as Varuṇa; its invitatory and offering verses are[5] 'Thou for us O Agni, knowing Varuṇa' and 'Thou O Agni be nearest with aid to us.' Or he should offer a libation in the Āhavanīya with 'To Agni as Varuṇa hail!' That is the expiation here. They say 'If one who has established the fires should eat the food of a woman with child, what is the penance here?' He should offer a cake on eight potsherds to Agni of the thread; its invitatory and offering verses are[6] 'Extending the thread of the atmosphere do thou follow the light' and 'Do ye, O Soma born, bind the axle strings.' Or he should offer a libation in the Āhavanīya with 'To Agni of the thread hail!' That is the expiation here. They say 'If one who has established the fires should live, hearing himself spoken of as dead,[7] what is the expiation here?' He should offer a cake on eight potsherds to Agni the fragrant; its invitatory and offering verses are[8] 'Agni as Hotṛ hath set down, good sacrificer' and 'True he hath made to-day our offering to the gods.' Or he should offer a libation in the Āhavanīya with 'To Agni, the fragrant, hail!' That is the expiation here. They say 'If one has established the fires and his wife or a cow produces twins, what is the expiation here?' He should offer a cake on thirteen potsherds to Agni with the Maruts; its invitatory and offering verses are[9] 'O Maruts in whose dwelling' and 'Like the spokes, none last, like the days.' Or he should offer a libation in the Āhavanīya with 'To Agni with the Maruts hail!' That is the expiation here. They say 'Should a man without a wife offer the Agnihotra? Or should he not offer it?' 'He should offer' they say; if he were not to offer he would be a mock man.[10] 'What is a mock man?' (they ask); 'One who (offers) neither to gods nor to the fathers nor to men.' Therefore, even if one has no wife, he should offer the Agnihotra. With regard to this a sacrificial verse[11] is recited

'Even one who has no wife and who drinks no Soma
Should sacrifice in the Sautrāmaṇī;
"Sacrifice to free thyself from debt to father and mother"
In accord with this command is this rule of scripture.'

Therefore should he make one, who is connected with the Soma, sacrifice.

[5] RV. iv. 1. 4 and 5; not in ĀÇS.

[6] RV. x. 53. 6 and 7. In ĀÇS. ix. 10. 15 the first verse is used otherwise; see below AB. vii. 12.

[7] The construction is so odd that *jīvet* seems obviously needed; ĀÇS. iii. 13. 11 has *yasmin jīve mṛtaçabdaḥ*. Cf. JAOS. xxxiii. 98, n. 498.

[8] RV. v. 1. 6; x. 53. 8; ĀÇS. iii. 13. 11 has *surabhaye* for *surabhimate*.

[9] RV. i. 86. 1; v. 58. 5; ĀÇS. has not these verses in this use.

[10] The *anaddhāpuruṣa* appears in a different connexion in the ÇB; see Eggeling, SBE. xli. 197, 206, 207.

[11] The verse is bad metre: *ayam* with *sautrā-*

[vii. 10 (xxxii. 9). They[1] say 'Why does a man without a wife offer at command the Agnihotra? 'If one has commenced[2] (the sacrifice), and his wife dies or disappears, how does he offer the Agnihotra?' 'Sons, grandsons, and great grandsons (he wins)' they say, 'in this and yonder world; in this world is yonder (world) of heaven, by that which is not heaven one mounts to the world of heaven.' He maintains the continuity of yonder world. Therefore they perform the piling for one without a wife. How does one without a wife perform the Agnihotra? 'The wife is faith, the sacrificer truth; faith and truth are the highest pair; by faith and truth as a pair he conquers the worlds of heaven' (he should reply).

vii. 11 (xxxii. 10). They[1] say, 'In that he fasts at the new and full moon, it is because the gods do not eat the oblation of one who does not keep his vow of fasting; therefore does he fast (thinking) 'May the gods eat my oblation.' 'On the first[2] full moon day should he fast' is the view of Paiñgya; 'on the second' that of Kauṣītaki. The first full moon day is Anumati, the second Rākā; the first new moon day is Sinīvālī, the second Kuhū. The period is that when (the sun) sets near or rises towards the moon. On the first full moon should he fast. In that he begins not having

manyā might do as a correction. Aufrecht points out that *anṛṇī* is really the origin of the gloss *anṛṇārthāt*. The construction seems to be abbreviated: the rule is laid down in the first line and the reason given in the second, and *çrutiḥ* strictly speaking requires *iti* in front of it. The Sautrāmaṇī is to be performed; *a fortiori* the Agnihotra. Sāyaṇa cites the rule of the three debts to the gods, fathers, Ṛṣis (TS. vi. 3. 10. 5), and Viṣṇu's rule that sacrifices are to be continued even on a wife's death using a substitute for the wife, for which he cites the Smṛti authority. On the other hand Manu (v. 168) prescribes the burning of a wife in the fires and a repiling, contrary to ĀGS. vi. 10. 9; Bhāradvāja and a Maitrāyaṇī Çruti. Cf. Yājñ. i. 88.

[1] Sāyaṇa, who explains this after the next chapter, expressly states that in some *deças* these two chapters were not read, and that his predecessors did not comment on them. This chapter is clearly in part at least corrupt.

[2] *niviṣṭa*, according to Sāyaṇa, refers to one who has commenced his duties as a householder including the Agnihotra. The repetition of *agnihotram* is as in § 4. The point of the sentence following is hopelessly obscure. Haug takes *āruroha* as a first person and, following Sāyaṇa, *yasyaiṣām patnīm naichet* as 'who does not wish for a (second) wife', but this is impossible unless *ya . . nechet* is read. Weber despairs of the passage; perhaps *yasyaiṣā patnī naçyet*.

vii. 11. [1] This is a mutilated and partially unintelligible version of KB. iii. 1; cf. Weber, *Jyotiṣha*, pp. 61, 62.

[2] This is clearly a reference to the doctrine of two (new and) full moon days (ÇÇS. i. 3. 3–6), one of which is when the sun and moon when full are visible together at sunset, and one when the full moon is only visible after sunset. Sāyaṇa, however, takes the sense that the time for the rite falls on the period between sunrise and sunset, which may be connected with the fourteenth and first days of the two halves of the month. Haug gets the same result by taking *tithi* as defined in terms of the setting and rising of the moon. But the sentence is a mere corruption of KB. iii. 1: *yām paryastamayam utsarped iti sa sthitiḥ*; the *tithi* is a conception of the Sūtra period only. For the names cf. Weber, *Ind. Stud.* v. 228, 229.

discerned the moon in the east at the new moon, and in that he sacrifices, thereby they purchase the Soma, thereby the second.[3] On the second should he fast; on the latter days Soma sacrifices in accord with Soma the deity[4]; the moon is the Soma of the gods; therefore should he fast on the second day.]

vii. 12 (xxxii. 11). They say,[1] 'If the sun rises or sets on a man's fire before it is taken out, or if being taken forward it dies out before the oblation, what is the expiation here?' He should put gold in front when taking it out in the evening; gold is a pure light, yonder sun is a pure light; verily thus gazing on the pure light he takes it out. Having interposed silver he should take it out in the morning; that is a symbol of the night. Before the blending of the shadows he should take out the Āhavanīya; the shadow is the darkness, death; verily thus with this light he crosses over the shadow, the darkness, death. That is the expiation here. They say, 'If a wagon or a chariot or a dog[2] come between the Gārhapatya and the Āhavanīya, what is the expiation here?' 'He should not pay heed to it,' they say, 'on his self are the (fires) placed[3].' If he should pay heed to it, he should draw a continuous stream of water from the Gārhapatya to the Āhavanīya with[4] 'Stretching the thread of the atmosphere do thou follow the light.' That is the expiation here. They say, 'When he is piling on fuel to the fires should he procure the Anvāhāryapacana? Or should he not procure it?' 'He should procure,' they say; he places the breaths in himself who piles the fires; the Anvāhāryapacana is the most fond of food of them; in it he offers the libation with 'Hail to Agni, the eater of food, the lord of food.' An eater of food, a lord of food, he becomes, he attains with his offspring proper food who knows thus. When about to offer he should move between the Gārhapatya and the Āhavanīya; when he moves by this way the fires know 'He is going to offer in us.' 'When he moves by this way the Gārhapatya and the Āhavanīya smite away his guilt; he with guilt smitten away goes aloft to the world of heaven'; so they quote a Brāhmaṇa. They say, 'How should one revere the fires when about to go away, or when having returned after absence or

[3] Sāyaṇa did not read *tena somaṁ krīṇanti* and the words are apparently corrupt; so after *tenottarām* something seems to be missing unless it be *yajanti* understood, which is poor sense. KB. has a a different reading with good meaning.

[4] The sense here is clearly imperfect, and, as KB. shows, corrupt.

[1] Cf. ÇB. xii. 4. 4. 6.

[2] *Açvā* in Aufrecht's edition is improbable though *açva* occurs in MÇS. iii. 4. 9, as the verb is singular and *çvā* seems clearly right, *açvāḥ* is also used by Haug; Sāyaṇa does not interpret, naturally enough. Cf. ĀÇS. iii. 10. 10–15 where *çvā* is mentioned. So ÇÇS. ii. 6. 13: *çvāpade gate*; ĀÇS. ix. 10. 15; ÇB. xii. 4. 1. 4; JB. i. 51. 4.

[3] *hi tā* apparently was read by Sāyaṇa and so the Ānand. ed. But *hitāḥ* is much better.

[4] RV. x. 53. 6; ĀÇS. iii. 10. 15; ÇÇS. ii. 6. 13.

day by day?' 'In silence,' they say; in silence men await a superior's orders. But also they say, 'Day by day they fear through the sacrificer's lack of faith removal or extinction. He should revere them with, 'Safety to you, safety to me.' Safety becomes his lot.[5]

ADHYĀYA III

The Legend of Çunaḥçepa.

vii. 13 (xxxiii. 1). Hariçcandra[1] Vaidhasa Aikṣvāka was the son of a king; a hundred wives were his, but he had no son from them. In his house dwelt Parvata and Nārada; he asked Nārada:

'Since[2] now men desire a son,
Both those that have and those that have not knowledge
What doth a man gain by a son?
Tell me that, O Nārada.'

He, asked in one verse, replied in ten:

'A debt he payeth in him,
And immortality he attaineth,[3]
That father who seeth the face
Of a son born living.
The delights in the earth,
The delights in the fire,
The delights in the waters of living beings,
Greater than these is that of a father in a son.
By means of a son have fathers ever[4]
Passed over the deep darkness;
The self is born from the self

[5] The ĀpÇS. vi. 27. 2 ascribes to a Bahvṛca Brāhmaṇa the use of a Mantra *namo vo 'stu pravatsyāmi* (or *prāvātsam*: so read for °*tsyam*) for one who is about to go and for one on his return. This does not agree with either the text or the KB. ii. 5, though the latter does not specify the Mantras, nor with ÇÇS. Cf. Keith, JRAS. 1915, pp. 493–498.

[1] The tale of Çunaḥçepa is to be repeated to the king after the anointing at the end of the Marutvatīya, by the Hotṛ sitting on a golden seat south of the Āhavanīya; the response of the Athvaryu to each Gāthā is *tathā*, to each Ṛc *om*, to the prose of course nothing; see ĀÇS. ix. 3. 9–16. The legend also occurs in ÇÇS. xv. 17 *seq.* It has been edited in both versions by Max Müller in his *History of Ancient Sanskrit Literature* (1859), pp. 573–588, by Fr. Streiter (Berlin, 1861), and translated also by Roth (IS. i. 457; ii. 112). A revised text is given in the 2nd ed. of Böhtlingk's *Chrestomathie*.

[2] *yan* = *yad* should be read, perhaps, though *yam* is good enough sense. ÇÇS. has *tan naḥ prabrūhi Nārada*.

[3] *vindate*, ÇÇS.

[4] Or 'the fathers passed assuredly'. For *sa īrāvati* which is the reading of all the MSS. in ÇÇS. also, Böhtlingk has *sairāvati*; see AB. vi. 21. In *c* there is in the MSS. of the ÇÇS. a variant *yajña* and so the *Mitākṣarā* cited by Max Müller.

The (son) is (a ship), well-found, to ferry over.
What is the use of dirt, what of the goat-skin?
What of long hair, and what of fervour?
Seek a son, O Brahmans,
This is the world's advice[5].
Food is breath, clothing a protection,
Gold an ornament, cattle lead to marriage,
A wife is a comrade, a daughter a misery,
And a son a light in the highest heaven.[6]
The father entereth the wife,
Having become a germ (he entereth) the mother,
In her becoming renewed,
He is born in the tenth month.[7]
A wife hath her name of wife,
Since in her he is born again
He is productive, she productive,
The seed is placed here.[8]
The gods and the seers
Brought her together as great brilliance;
The gods said to men
"This is your mother again."[9]
"A sonless one cannot attain heaven,"
All the beasts know this;
Therefore a son his mother
And his sister mounteth.
This is the broad and auspicious path
Along which men with sons fare free from sorrow;

[5] *vadāvadaḥ* is probably to be read as an intensive like *calācala*, *carācara*, cf. Wackernagel, *Altind. Gramm.* ii. 1. 147. Sāyaṇa has *avadāvadaḥ* as = not deserving blame, Roth (*Ind. Stud.* i. 458) rendered 'He is a blameless world'; so Streiter and Weber; 'he is undoubtedly the world' Max Müller. The comm. sees here a reference to the four *āçramas*, but without ground.

[6] The connexion of cattle and marriage is reasonable enough, and the conjecture accepted by Böhtlingk '*vivāhāḥ* is very unnatural. Böhtlingk also suggests *kanyā* for *duhitā metri causa*, but this is wholly unnecessary and in AB. viii. 22. 6 we have *āḍhyaduhitṛṇām* where *duhi*° = one syllable. He takes *annam*, as is natural, predicatively, but this is against the context.

[7] ÇÇS. has *atha* for *sa mātaram*. For the ten-month year of gestation cf. the old Roman year, Censorin. *de die natali*, c. 20; *Vedic Index*, ii. 159.

[8] The sense of *ābhūtir eṣā ābhūtiḥ* as is necessary for the metre is uncertain and obscure: Böhtlingk quite needlessly reads *ā bhūmir eṣā bhavati*. Hillebrandt suggests that the sense is 'She is procreation; the germ is procreation; it is hidden in her,' but it is more reasonable to assume that the two *ābhūti* forms are father and mother. Sāyaṇa renders as if *bhūtiḥ* and *ābhūtiḥ* were read. Max Müller has 'She is a mother, because she brings forth'.

[9] This verse is transposed in ÇÇS. with the next.

On it beasts and herds gaze
For it they unite even with a mother.[10]

Thus he told him.[11]

vii. 14 (xxxiii. 2). Then he said to him, 'Have recourse to Varuṇa, the king, (saying) 'Let a son be born to me; with him let me sacrifice to thee.' 'Be it so,' (he replied). He went up to Varuṇa, the king, (saying) 'Let a son be born to me; with him let me sacrifice to thee.' 'Be it so' (he replied). To him a son was born, Rohita by name. To him he said 'A son hath been born to thee; sacrifice to me with him.' He said 'When a victim is over ten days old then it becomes fit for sacrifice; let him become over ten days old; then let me sacrifice to thee with him.' 'Be it so' (he replied). He became over ten days old. He said to him 'He hath become over ten days old; sacrifice to me with him.' He said 'When the teeth of a victim appear, then it becomes fit for sacrifice; let his teeth appear; then let me sacrifice to thee (with him).' 'Be it so' (he replied). His teeth appeared; he said to him 'His teeth have appeared; sacrifice to me with him.' He said 'When the teeth of a victim fall, then it becomes fit for sacrifice; let his teeth fall; then let me sacrifice to thee.' 'Be it so' (he replied). His teeth fell; he said to him 'His teeth have fallen; sacrifice to me with him.' He said 'When the teeth of a victim appear again, then it becomes fit for sacrifice; let his teeth appear again; then let me sacrifice to thee.' 'Be it so' (he replied). His teeth appeared again; he said to him 'His teeth have appeared again; sacrifice to me with him.' He said 'When the Kṣatriya is fit to bear arms,[2] then is he fit for sacrifice; let him win his arms; then let me sacrifice to thee.' 'Be it so' (he replied). He won[3] his arms; he said to him 'He hath now won[4] his arms; sacrifice to me with him.' 'Be it so' he said and addressed[5] his son 'O my dear one, this one gave thee to me;

[10] ÇÇS. has *vitato devayānaḥ* in *a*, and in *b* *yenākramante putriṇo ye' viçokāḥ*; in *c* it omits *ca*; and in *d* ends *mithunaṁ caranti* and has *mātary api. tat te* is preferred by Böhtlingk, and *tasmāt* without *te* is also possible. The practice here referred to is reported of the Irish by Strabo iv. 5. 4; its prevalence in Iran (cf. Meyer, *Hist. de l'Antiq.* i. 38) is not in all probability here referred to, though, of course, it may be suggested that a reference is meant.

[11] *hāsmai* is, of course, necessary for the grammar. ÇÇS. omits it. Aufrecht (p. 431) prefers *ha smāsmā ākhyāya*; Böhtlingk (BKSGW. 15 Dec. 1900, p. 417), however, prefers *hāsmā*, as suggested by Weber, on the ground that *iti ha sma* does not elsewhere precede an absolute; for *atha* after an absolute see Delbrück, *Altind. Synt.* p. 409.

[1] The two verses here differ slightly: ÇÇS. omits the words at the end of AB. vii. 13 after *iti* and has *sa hovāca, sa vai me brūhi yathā me putro jāyeteti, taṁ hovāca*, &c.

[2] *saṁnāhaṁ prāpnoti* ÇÇS., clearly inferior. The form *sāṁnāhuka* is irregular for *saṁnāhuka*.

[3] *prāpat* in both versions must be *prāpa* as Böhtlingk points out.

[4] *prāpat* of ÇÇS. is clearly necessary.

[5] *cakre* ÇÇS., which is, of course, the older form; but contra below AB. vii. 16, n. 4.

come, let me sacrifice to him with thee.' 'No' he said and taking his bow went to the wild, and for a year he wandered in the wild.

vii. 15 (xxxiii. 3). Then Varuṇa seized Aikṣvāka; his belly swelled up. This Rohita heard; he went from the wild to the village. To him Indra came in human form and said

'"Manifold is the prosperity of him who is weary,"
So have we heard, O Rohita;
Evil is he who stayeth among men,
Indra is the comrade of the wanderer.[1]

Do thou wander[2]'. (Thinking) 'This Brahman hath bidden me "wander", he[3] wandered for a second year in the wild. He came from the wild to the village. To him came Indra in human form and said

'Flower-like the heels of the wanderer,
His body groweth and is fruitful;
All his sins disappear,
Slain by the toil of his journeying.[4]

Do thou wander'. (Thinking) 'This Brahman hath bidden me "wander", he wandered for a third year in the wild. He came from the wild to the village. To him came Indra in human form and said

'The fortune of him who sitteth also sitteth,
But that of him who standeth standeth erect;
That of him that reclineth lieth down;
The fortune of him that moveth shall move indeed.[5]

Do thou wander.' (Thinking) 'This Brahman hath bidden me "wander", he wandered for a fourth year in the wild. He came from the wild to the village. To him came Indra in human form and said

'Kali he becometh who lieth,
Dvāpara when he riseth,
Tretā when he standeth erect
And Kṛta when he moveth.[6]

[1] The reading is clearly right as *nānā*; Sāyaṇa recognizes as an alternative *nānāçrāntāya*. There is a *v. l. cana* for *janaḥ* ÇÇS. Weber (*Ind. Stud.* ix. 314) with Streiter renders as *nānā açrāntāya*. The curious *nṛṣadvara* Böhtlingk (on *Kaṭha Up.* v. 2) derives from *nṛṣad varasad* in RV. iv. 60. 5. ÇÇS. has *niṣadvarah*.

[2] *Rohita* is added in ÇÇS. here and throughout.

[3] *sa* in ÇÇS. throughout.

[4] ÇÇS. puts the verse after *Kaliḥ*, &c. It has *phalagrahiḥ* and *çerate 'sya*.

[5] *carāti* is not only certain, but clearly correct, both for metrical reasons and as more pointed than *carati*.

[6] ÇÇS. has *puruṣaḥ* for *bhavati*, and *utthitaḥ* for *uttiṣṭhan*. The throws of dice are clearly meant, not as Sāyaṇa, the four Yugas, despite the agreement of Max Müller *Anc. Sansk. Lit.* p. 412) and Weber (*Ind. Stud.* ix. 315): Manu, ix. 302 is no evidence for the AB. and the ages are not Vedic, as AV. x. 8. 39, 40 (cited by Jacobi, GGA. 1895, p. 210) is not thus to be understood.

Do thou wander.' (Thinking) 'This Brahman hath bidden me "wander", he wandered for a fifth year in the wild. He came from the wild to the village; to him Indra came in human form and said

> 'Wandering one findeth honey,
> Wandering the sweet Udumbara fruit,
> Consider the pre-eminence of the sun,
> Who wearieth never of wandering.''

Do thou wander.' (Thinking) 'This Brahman hath bidden me "wander", he wandered for a sixth year in the wild.[8] He found in the wild Ajīgarta Sauyavasi, a seer, overcome with hunger.[9] Three sons were his, Çunaḥpucha, Çunaḥçepa, and Çunolāñgūla. He said to him[10] 'O seer, I offer thee a hundred; let me redeem myself with one of these.' Keeping back the eldest son, he said 'Not this one'; 'nor this one' (said) the mother, (keeping back) the the youngest son. They made an agreement regarding the middle one, Çunaḥçepa. Having given a hundred for him[11], taking him, he went from the wild to the village. Going to his father he said, 'O father dear, come, let me redeem myself with this one.' He went[12] to Varuṇa, the king (saying) 'With this one let me sacrifice to thee.' 'Be it so' (he replied); 'A Brahman is higher[13] than a Kṣatriya' Varuṇa said. To him he proclaimed this sacrificial rite, the Rājasūya. On the day of anointing he took the man as victim.

vii. 16 (xxxiii. 4). For him Viçvāmitra was the Hotṛ, Jamadagni the Adhvaryu, Vasiṣṭha the Brahman, and Ayāsya the Udgātṛ.[1] When he had been brought up they could not find one to bind him; Ajīgarta Sauyavasi said 'Give me another hundred, and I shall bind him.' They gave him another hundred; he bound him. When he had been brought up, bound, and the Āprī verses had been said over and fire carried round him,[2] they could not find one to slaughter him; Ajīgarta Sauyavasi said 'Give me another hundred, and I shall slaughter him.' They gave him another hundred and he whetting[3] his knife went forward. Then Çunaḥçepa

[7] *Çramaṇam* is read by Hillebrandt in ÇÇS., where there is good MS. authority for *çrayamāṇam*.

[8] ÇÇS. has another verse and another year of wandering.

[9] ÇÇS. has the insertion of *putraṁ bhakṣ(y)amāṇam* and reads *açanāyāparītam*, which is a much better form.

[10] ÇÇS. varies the wording slightly and inverts the two clauses, reading *dadāni* and inserting *gavām*, both less primitive features.

[11] *tasya* may mean 'to him' as usually taken, but this is not necessary.

[12] ÇÇS. has *āmantrayāṁ cakre* which is inferior, and inserts *tathety uktvā* which is verbiage.

[13] *çreyān* ÇÇS.

[1] The transposition of the clause to second place in ÇÇS. is clearly a later trait.

[2] ÇÇS. omits *āprītāya*; above it has *niyuyoja* for AB. *niniyoja* which is absurd, and below *viçastāram*.

[3] *niḥçyānaḥ* ÇÇS. and Böhtlingk. *niḥçāna* is, of course, incorrect.

reflected[4] 'Like one that is not a man, they will slaughter me; come, let me have recourse to the deities.'[5] He had recourse to Prajāpati first of the deities with the verse[6] 'Of whom now, of which of the immortals?' To him said Prajāpati 'Agni is the nearest of the gods; do thou have recourse to him.' He had recourse to Agni with the verse[7] 'Of Agni first of the immortals we.' To him said Agni 'Savitṛ is the lord of instigations; do thou have recourse to him.' He had recourse to Savitṛ with the triplet[8] 'To thee O god Savitṛ.' To him Savitṛ said 'For Varuṇa, the king, art thou bound; do thou have recourse to him.' He had recourse to Varuṇa the king with the following thirty-one[9] (verses). To him said Varuṇa 'Agni is the first of the gods, the best friend[10]; praise him, and we shall deliver thee[11].' He praised Agni with the next twenty-two[12] (verses). To him said Agni 'Praise the All-gods, then we shall deliver thee.' He praised the All-gods with the verse[13] 'Homage to the great, homage to the small!" To him said the All-gods 'Indra[14] is the mightiest, most powerful, strongest, most real, and most effective of the gods; praise him and we shall deliver thee.' He praised Indra with the hymn[15] 'Whatever, O true one, the drinkers of Soma' and fifteen (verses) of the following one. To him Indra, delighted in mind with the praise,[16] gave a chariot of gold. He approached him with this[17] (verse) 'Ever Indra.' To him said Indra 'Praise now the Açvins, then shall we deliver thee.' He praised the Açvins with the following triplet.[18] To him said the Açvins 'Praise now Uṣas, then we shall deliver thee.' He praised Uṣas with the following triplet.[19] As each verse was said by him a bond was loosened[20] the belly of Aikṣvāka became smaller; when the very last verse was said[21] the (last) bond was loosened and Aikṣvāka became[22] free from disease.

vii. 17 (xxxiii. 5). To him the priests said 'Do thou devise for us the performance of the day.' Then Çunaḥçepa saw the immediate pressing; it

[4] *ikṣām āsa* ÇÇS. contra above AB. vii. 14, n. 5.

[5] *upadhāvāniti* ÇÇS. as above *dadāni* for AB. *dadāmi*. But after *hanta* the subj. is most natural and should be read.

[6] RV. i. 24. 1. Prajāpati's reply in ÇÇS. is *agner vai nediṣṭho 'si*.

[7] RV. i. 24. 2.

[8] RV. i. 24. 3–5.

[9] RV. i. 24. 6–25. 21.

[10] *Suhṛdayam* is read by Hillebrandt in ÇÇS.

[11] ÇÇS. has the singular here and elsewhere.

[12] RV. i. 26. 1–27. 12.

[13] RV. i. 27. 13.

[14] Omitted down to *tam*, with *indram* instead in ÇÇS.

[15] RV. i. 29; 30. 1–15.

[16] ÇÇS. omits *prītaḥ*.

[17] RV. i. 30. 16.

[18] RV. i. 30. 17–19.

[19] RV. i. 30. 20–22.

[20] *vitarām* is read by Roth, and Böhtlingk for *vi* because of *nitarām* in ÇÇS. But this is needless, and *nitarām* may easily be a correction by some one who could not understand the sense of *vi pāço mumuce*; Weber (*Ind. Stud.* ix. 316) suggests that the second *vipāço* is a compound, but this is very improbable.

[21] *uttamāyām ha sma* ÇÇS.

[22] *babhūva* ÇÇS.

he pressed with these four verses [1] 'Whatever thou in every house'. Then he carried it to the wooden tub with the verse [2] 'Take up what remaineth in the bowls'. Then as he took hold of him, he offered with the four preceding verses [3] with calls of Hail! Then he led him to the final bath with the two [4] (verses) 'Thou, O Agni, knowing Varuṇa'. Then he next made him pay reverence to the Āhavanīya [5] with 'Çunaḥçepa bound from a thousand'. Then Çunaḥçepa sat on the lap of Viçvāmitra. Ajīgarta Sauyavasi said 'O seer, give back to me my son'. 'No' said Viçvāmitra; 'the gods have given him to me'. He was Devarāta Vaiçvāmitra, and his descendants are the Kāpileyas and the Bābhravas.[6] Ajīgarta Sauyavasi said 'Come now; let us invite him [7]'. Ajīgarta Sauyavasi said

'Thou art an Āṅgiras by birth,
Famed as a sage, son of Ajīgarta;
O seer, thine ancestral line
Abandon not, return to me.'

Çunaḥçepa said

'They have seen thee knife in hand,
A thing they have not found even among Çūdras.
Three hundreds of kine didst thou,
O Āṅgiras, prefer to me [8].'

Ajīgarta Sauyavasi said

'Remorse it causeth me, dear one,
The evil deed done by me,
I would obliterate it in thine eyes;
Thine be the hundreds of kine [9].'

[1] RV. i. 28. 5–8. In this chapter slight verbal differences between the two versions increase.

[2] RV. i. 28. 9.

[3] RV. i. 28. 1–4.

[4] RV. iv. 1. 4, 5. The object is presumably Hariçcandra, not the preparation for the ceremony.

[5] RV. v. 2. 7.

[6] The clause *tasyaite* as omitted in ÇÇS., and Delbrück suspects the whole from *devā* on.

[7] *tvam v ehi* is clearly meant by Pāṇini, viii. 3. 33, as Böhtlingk points out. The two are not mother and father, as taken by Sāyaṇa and Max Müller, nor father and son. ÇÇS. has *tvaṁ vai vihvayāvahai* which Hillebrandt alters to *tam*, and the sense is really good, as it is the boy the two invite in turn, first the father talks to the son, and then Viçvāmitra as taken by Weber, *Ind. Stud.* ix. 316, 317.

[8] For *alapsata* (3rd plur. *s.* aor.) there is in ÇÇS. a variant *alipsata*, but the conditional is here in proper use and *alapsyata* seems a natural conjecture. The sense would be the same, since the generic singular is also possible.

[9] *nihnave* is the reading of the overwhelming authority of the MSS. of the AB., and though ÇÇS. has *nihnuve*, it is a mistake to insert it as is done in the Ānand. ed. of AB. *ā* may mean as rendered or 'go back' to the giver, as taken by Weber.

Çunaḥçepa said

'He who once doth what is evil
Would do that evil again;
Thou hast not abandoned thy Çūdra way;
What thou hast done is irreparable [10].'

At the word 'irreparable' Viçvāmitra joined in (the discussion [11]); Viçvāmitra said

'Dread indeed was Sauyavasi when,
Knife in hand, ready to slaughter;
He stood erect; be not his son;
Become thou a son of mine [12].'

Çunaḥçepa said

'As thou hast intimated to us,
So, O son of a king, tell
How being an Añgiras
I can become thy son [13].'

Viçvāmitra said

'Thou wouldst be the eldest of my sons,
Thy offspring would hold the highest place.
Accept my divine inheritance,
Unto this I invite thee [14].'

[10] ÇÇS. in some MSS. reads *enas*, but this is needless, and *enat* is found in the best MSS. there also. Sāyaṇa seems to recognize *enat*, while the comm. on ÇÇS. has *enas*. In *c* ÇÇS. has *māpagāḥ*: metrically *na apāgāḥ* must be read; in both cases there are variants of *çaudrān nyāyāt* which is certain and is recognized by Sāyaṇa. Max Müller has 'Thou wilt not abstain'.

[11] ÇÇS, inserts *vā avocad iti*; the sense given by Sāyaṇa of *upa papāda* is 'supported by proofs', but this is wrong, nor, as Haug and Max Müller, can the word *asaṁdheyam* be given to Viçvāmitra.

[12] ÇÇS. has *viçāçiṣat*.

[13] *jñapaya* is read in ÇÇS. Sāyaṇa renders *jñāyase* 'as a Brahman', but this is not possible, though Max Müller accepts it, and is not supported by a verse cited by him as expressing the sense: *purātmānaṁ nṛpaṁ vipra tapasā kṛtavān asi* which means that he had made himself a king by *tapas*, and not vice versa; apparently this verse took the sense as *jñapayā rājaputra* 'thou art known as a king's son'; clearly in view of the agreement of the MSS. (both Aufrecht's and those of the Ānand.) any alteration of this verse is incorrect, and also clearly it is only to be explained as above. *jñapayā* is, if it is to be taken as correct, a subj., and the sense must be 'tell us how thou wilt arrange', or something similar. It seems easier to read *'jñapayo* and render 'as thou hast said', referring to his offer made just above. Böhtlingk adds *'ham* before *sann*, *metri causa*.

[14] Here Viçvāmitra offers only *daivaṁ dāyam*, but in point of fact he allowed him succession to both; see AB. vii. 18. 9.

Çunahçepa said

'Bid these agree
For friendship and prosperity to me
That I may, O bull of the Bharatas,
Become thy son[15].'

Then Viçvāmitra addressed his sons

'Do thou, Madhuchandas, and do ye hearken,
Ṛṣabha, Reṇu, and Aṣṭaka
And all their brothers,
Do ye accept his superiority[16].'

vii. 18 (xxxiii. 6). Viçvāmitra had a hundred and one sons, fifty older than Madhuchandas, fifty younger. Those that were older did not think this right. Them he cursed (saying) 'Your offspring shall inherit the ends[1] (of the earth).' These are the (people), the Andhras, Puṇḍras, Çabaras, Pulindas, and Mūtibas,[2] who live in large numbers beyond the borders; most of the Dasyus are the descendants of Viçvāmitra. Madhuchandas with the other fifty said

'What our father agreeth to
That we accept;
We all place thee before us,
We are after thee.'[3]

Then Viçvāmitra, pleased, praised his sons

'O my sons, rich in cattle
And with heroic offspring, shall ye be,
Who, accepting my will,
Have made me possessed of heroic offspring.'[4]

[15] *brūyāḥ* is read in some MSS. of ÇÇS., but in most *brūyāt*, and Sāyaṇa as well as the MSS. have *brūyāt* at this place. It cannot be rendered satisfactorily as 'every one of your sons' with Sāyaṇa, nor as 'may the leader of the Bharatas say so, in the presence of his agreeing sons', and very possibly *saṁjñānam eṣu* should be read with Aufrecht. In *b* Böhtlingk restores *mama*, and Hillebrandt has *me* . . . *me* by conjecture, but this is not probable as the Pāda is independent and should not begin with an enclitic.

[16] ÇÇS. has *sthā* and *tiṣṭhadhvam*. Böhtlingk suggests *tiṣṭhata*, *metri causa*. Haug's interpretation of *sthana* as *stha na* is quite impossible.

[1] ÇÇS. has *antam*. Sāyaṇa renders *caṇḍālādirūpān nīcajātiviçeṣān*.

[2] ÇÇS. has no Pulindas, and reads *Mūcīpāḥ*. It also reads, very badly, *udañcaḥ*, and *bahudasyavaḥ*, and ends *ity udāharanti*, and extends the sentence regarding Madhuchandas. For the tribes mentioned, doubtless non-Aryan in the main, see *Vedic Index*, s.vv.

[3] ÇÇS. *purastāt*.

[4] *vīravantaḥ* is replaced by *prajāvantaḥ* in ÇÇS. It is possibly really a reference as in the next verse to the *vīra* Devarāta, and not to *prajā* generally.

With a hero to lead you,
With Devarāta, O Gāthinas,
Shall ye all prosper, O my sons;
He shall discern the truth for you.[5]
This is your hero, O Kuçikas,
Devarāta; him follow;
As inheritance from me shall he obtain you
And the knowledge which we know.[6]
In agreement the sons of Viçvāmitra,
All together joyously,
Accepted the control of Devarāta,[7]
And his pre-eminence, the Gāthinas.
Devarāta was granted
Both inheritances, the sage,
The overlordship of the Jahnus,
And the sacred lore of the Gāthinas.[8]

[5] *Gāthinā* in some MSS. of ÇÇS. is needless. ÇÇS. has in a majority of MSS. *rādhyās tu* and *eṣa vas tad vivācanaḥ*, while Hillebrandt with Streiter would read *sadvivācanaḥ*. The change is clearly needless.

[6] ÇÇS. has *copetām*. The sense is clearly as above; Sāyaṇa takes *dāyam* as subject, and *ca* he refers to Devarāta! Aufrecht suggests *yuṣme*, but the sense is not 'he shall inherit among you' but 'he shall inherit you' as becoming the head (*çreṣṭhin*) of the family. ÇÇS. has *yām uta* which is a less good reading. For *upetā* see Whitney, *Sansk. Gr.* § 137 *b*.

[7] ÇÇS. has *jyaiṣṭhye* and *çraiṣṭhye*; *sarātayaḥ* is, as Aufrecht points out, an artificial word on the basis of *arāti*, 'foe'.

[8] ÇÇS. ends *Jahnūnāṁ cādhitasthire daive vede ca Gāthināḥ*. This version cannot be made to mean anything else than a statement that the Gāthinas were prominent among the Jahnus and in sacred lore (cf. Weber, *Episches im vedischen Ritual*, pp. 16 *seq.*), the two *ca*'s being explained in this way (*daive* and *vede* cannot really, as by Weber, be made consistently contrasts). This view then treats the Jahnus as the whole and the Gāthinas a class of them, not necessarily rulers (even priestly), but as great priests. The AB. version must be regarded as an explanation of the *ubhayoḥ* and the term seems to need explanation, and therefore *a priori*, *pace* Weber, the AB. is the older version, as it normally is superior to the ÇÇS. Moreover the term *rājaputra* in AB. vii. 17. 6 points to royal claims on the part of Viçvāmitra (quite contrary to the *Ṛgveda* tradition, where he is the Purohita of Sudās, a view here also accepted from the tradition), and this agrees with the tradition of the PB. xxi. 12. 2 where Viçvāmitra is styled *Jāhnavo rājā*. The AB. version must therefore mean that Devarāta succeeded to the overlordship over the Jahnus and the divine lore of the Gāthinas at one time. Sāyaṇa's version treats the two inheritances, as is Weber's view and also that of Max Müller (*Anc. Sansk. Lit.* p. 418, n. 2), as that of the Ajīgarta family (Jahnus), and of Viçvāmitra, but there is to this the serious objection that the young man definitely leaves his connexion with Ajīgarta, and therefore cannot be said to succeed to the overlordship of that family in any sense, even if there were any other suggestion that the Ajīgarta family was called Jahnu, as there is not. *adhīyata* is no doubt from *dhā*, not, as Max Müller, from *adhi + i*. *Gāthinām* is merely, in all probability, a brief form of *Gāthinānām*, though a change of stem is conceivable; if the former, the use is rare; cf. Lanman, *Noun Infl.* p. 358; Macdonell, *Ved. Gramm.* p. 262.

This is the tale of Çunaḥçepa, with a hundred Ṛc verses as well as Gāthās.[9] This the Hotṛ tells to the king after the anointing. He tells it seated on a golden cushion; seated on a golden cushion he[10] responds; gold is glory; verily thus he makes him prosper by glory. *Om* is the response to a Ṛc, 'Be it so' to a Gāthā; *om* is divine, 'Be it so' human; verily thus with what is divine and what is human he frees him from evil[11] and from sin. Therefore a victorious[12] king should, even when not sacrificing, make him narrate this tale of Çunaḥçepa; not the least tinge of sin will be left over in him. A thousand should he give to the narrator, a hundred to him who makes the response; the seats and a white mule chariot[13] (should also be given) to the Hotṛ. Those who desire sons also should[14] have it narrated; they obtain sons.

ADHYĀYA IV

The Rājasūya.

vii. 19 (xxxiv. 1). Prajāpati created the sacrifice;[1] after the creation of the sacrifice the holy power and the lordly power were created; after the holy power and the lordly power both kinds of offspring were created, those who eat the oblations and those who do not eat the oblations; after the holy power those that eat the oblations, after the lordly power those that do not eat the oblations. The Brahmans are the offsping that eat the oblations; the Rājanya, Vaiçya, and Çūdras those that do not eat the oblations.[2] From them the sacrifice departed; it the holy power and the lordly power pursued; the holy power pursued with the weapons of the holy power; the lordly power with those of the lordly power. The weapons of the holy power are the weapons of the sacrifice; the weapons of the lordly

[9] ÇÇS. adds *aparimitam*. The number is 97 of Çunaḥçepa, three not by him, and thirty-one Gāthās. Weber's rendering (*op. cit.*, p. 10) 'über 100' is less probable than that of BR. adopted above.

[10] I.e. the Adhvaryu.

[11] ÇÇS. has *sarvasmād enasaḥ sampramuñcati* (with *v.ll. sampramucyate*, °*ete*, °*nte*).

[12] ÇÇS. has *rājā vijitī* understood by the comm. as *vijayāsamarthaḥ*. But this is not at all necessary and Nārāyaṇa on ĀÇS. ix. 3. 13 has clearly *yaḥ parabalaṁ yuddhena vijitavān* where *yudhe na* is not really possible, *pace* Hillebrandt. The *v. l.* in ÇÇS. *atha yajamānaḥ* is a bad one. Weber (*Ind. Stud.* ix. 318) prefers '*vijitī*, but Aufrecht retains the view of Sāyaṇa. In his *Rājasūya*, p. 8, n. 2, Weber renders *rājāvijitin* in the *Kāṭhaka* as 'von (anderen) Königen unbesiegt'.

[13] This sentence down to *hotuḥ* is not in ÇÇS. which divides the spoil less unfairly.

[14] Indic. in ÇÇS.

[1] Cf. TS. i. 6. 8. 2. Generally speaking, for the Rājasūya of the AB. there is no parallel elsewhere. ĀÇS. has only a few scattered sentences in ix. 3 and 4. The whole rite is elaborately dealt with by Weber, *Über den Rājasūya* (*Abh. Berl. Akad.* 1893).

[2] Cf. ÇB. iv. 5. 2. 16.

power are the horse chariot, the corslet, the bow and arrow. The lordly power returned without attaining it; from its weapons it turns away trembling. The holy power followed it and obtained it; having obtained it it kept blocking it from above; it being obtained and blocked from above standing, recognising its own weapons, went up to the holy power. Therefore even now the sacrifice finds support in the holy power and in the Brahmans. The lordly power then followed it; it said 'Do thou call upon me in this sacrifice'. 'Be it so' it replied; 'Lay aside thine own weapons, and with the weapons of the holy power, the form of the holy power, becoming the holy power, do thou come to the sacrifice'. 'Be it so' (it said). Thus the lordly power, having laid aside its own weapons, with the weapons of the holy power, with the form of the holy power, becoming the holy power, went to the sacrifice. Therefore now also the Kṣatriya, as sacrificer, having laid aside his own weapons, with the weapons of the holy power, with the form of the holy power, becoming the holy power, goes to the sacrifice.

vii. 20 (xxxiv. 2). Then comes the begging of a place of sacrifice. They say 'Seeing that a Brahman, a Rājanya, a Vaiçya, when about to consecrate himself asks a Kṣatriya for a place of sacrifice, whom is the Kṣatriya to ask?' 'He should ask the divine lordly power' they say. The divine lordly power is the sun; the sun is the overlord of these beings. On the day on which he is going to consecrate himself, on that day in the forenoon he should revere the rising sun; with [1]

'This is the best of lights, the highest light.'

With 'O god Savitṛ, give me a place of sacrifice for sacrifice to the gods' he asks for a place of sacrifice. In that being asked here he goes on his upward course,[2] 'Yes, I give it' he says in effect. No harm befalls him instigated by the god Savitṛ; ever increasing prosperity he attains; he attains lordship over offspring and supremacy, who having thus paid reverence, having asked for, having settled on a place of sacrifice, consecrates himself, being a Kṣatriya.[3]

vii. 21 (xxxiv. 3). Then comes the prevention of decay of the sacrifice and the gifts (to the priests) for a Kṣatriya as sacrificer. Before the consecration he should offer a libation of butter in four portions, in the Āhavanīya to prevent the decay of the sacrifice and the gifts, with

'Let Indra, the bounteous, restore to us
The holy power; let him give again the sacrifice, the gifts; hail!'

[1] RV. x. 170. 3.

[2] *uttarām* is adverbial as in AB. iii. 44: *abhitarām*; 24: *nicaistarām* and often.

[3] For the *devayajana* cf. ṢB. ii. 10; PB. xxiv. 18. 2; ÇB. iii. 1. 1. 4; Weber, *Ind. Stud.* x. 356, n. 3.

Then after the concluding formulas of the final offering of a cow[1]

> 'Let Agni, all knower, restore to us
> The lordly power; let him give again the sacrifice, the gifts; hail!'

These two libations are the prevention of decay of the sacrifice and the gifts for a Kṣatriya as sacrificer; therefore should they be offered.

vii. 22 (xxxiv. 4). As to this Saujāta Ārāḷhi used to say 'These two libations are not a winning again of what has decayed'. 'As he desires he may perform these two, who takes his instruction hence' (he said[1]); but the following he should certainly offer with

> 'I have recourse to the holy power; may the holy power guard me from the lordly power; to the holy power hail!'

'Thus, thus' (he said). He who has recourse to the sacrifice has recourse to the holy power; the sacrifice is the holy power; moreover from the sacrifice is he who consecrates himself born again. Him who has recourse to the holy power the lordly power does not oppress. 'May the holy power guard me from the lordly power' he says, in order that the holy power may guard him from the lordly power; 'To the holy power hail' (he says); thus he delights it. Thus it delighted guards him from the lordly power. Then after the concluding formulas of the final offering of a cow (he says)

> 'I have recourse to the lordly power; may the lordly power guard me from the holy power; to the lordly power hail!'

'Thus, thus' (he said). He who has recourse to the kingship has recourse to the lordly power, for the kingship is the lordly power. Him who has recourse to the lordly power the holy power does not oppress, 'May the lordly power guard me from the holy power' he says, in order that the lordly power may guard him from the holy power; 'To the lordly power hail!' (he says); thus he delights it. Thus it delighted guards him from the holy power. These[2] two libations are the prevention of decay of the sacrifice and the gifts; therefore they must be offered.

vii. 23 (xxxiv. 5). Now the Kṣatriya has Indra as his deity, the Triṣṭubh as his metre, the Pañcadaça as his Stoma, and is Soma in kingship, the Rājanya in relationship. Being consecrated he attains Brahmanhood in that he puts on the black antelope's skin, in that he performs the vow of one

[1] See TS. i. 4. 44. 3 for the *Samiṣṭayajūṅṣi*.

vii. 22. [1] The *iti* is a little awkward; but presumably it represents the views of Saujāta. Weber (*Ind. Stud.* ix. 320) does not indicate how he takes the clause, translating as if there was no *iti*. *tat tad iti* recurs in AB. vii. 25; viii. 6 and 9. BR. take *ajita*° as a Dvandva; Sāyaṇa treats *ajita* as *ajita*, both without point. *ito* refers to the view in vii. 21, not to Saujāta.

[2] i. e. = *ime* above.

consecrated, in that Brahmans come around him. As he is being consecrated Indra takes his power, the Triṣṭubh his strength, the Pañcadaça Stoma his life, the Soma his kingdom, the fathers his fame and renown, saying 'He is becoming other than we; he is becoming the holy power; he is joining the holy power'. He should offer a libation before the consecration and adore the Āhavanīya (saying)

> 'I depart not from Indra as my deity, nor from the Triṣṭubh metre, nor the Pañcadaça Stoma, nor Soma the king, nor my relationship with the fathers. Let not Indra take my power, nor the Triṣṭubh my strength, nor the Pañcadaça Stoma my life, nor Soma my kingdom, nor the fathers my glory and fame. With my power, strength, life, kingdom, glory, relationship, I approach Agni, the Gāyatrī metre, the Trivṛt Stoma, Soma the king; I have recourse to the holy power; I become a Brahman.'

Indra does not appropriate the power, nor the Triṣṭubh the strength, nor the Pañcadaça Stoma the life, nor Soma the kingdom, nor the fathers the glory and fame of him who having offered thus this libation and having adored the Āhavanīya consecrates himself, being a Kṣatriya.

vii. 24 (xxxiv. 6). Now the Kṣatriya has Agni for his deity, when consecrated, the Gāyatrī for his metre, the Trivṛt for his Stoma, and is the Brahman in relationship; when he concludes he assumes his Kṣatriya character; when he concludes Agni takes his brilliance, the Gāyatrī his strength, the Trivṛt Stoma his life, the Brahmans his glory and fame, saying 'He is becoming other than we; he is becoming the lordly power; he is joining the lordly power'. After the concluding formulas of the final offering of a cow he should offer a libation and adore the Āhavanīya with

> 'I depart not from Agni as my deity, nor from the Gāyatrī metre, nor from the Trivṛt Stoma, nor from the holy power as relation. Let not Agni take my brilliance, nor the Gāyatrī my strength, nor the Trivṛt Stoma my life, nor the Brahmans my holy power, glory, and fame. With brilliance, strength, life, the holy power, glory and fame, I approach Indra the deity, the Triṣṭubh metre, the Pañcadaça Stoma, Soma the king; I have recourse to the lordly power; I become a Kṣatriya.
>
> O gods, O fathers, O fathers, O gods, I offer being he who I am.
> This is my sacrifice, my gift, my toil, my offering.
> Be Agni here my witness, Vāyu my hearer, Āditya yonder my proclaimer;
> I who am I am I.'

Agni does not appropriate his brilliance, nor the Gāyatrī his strength, nor the Trivṛt Stoma his life, nor the Brahmans his holy power, glory and fame who having offered thus this libation and having adored the Āhavanīya concludes, being a Kṣatriya.

vii. 25 (xxxiv. 7). Then as to the announcement of the consecration. They say 'Seeing that they announce the consecration of a Brahman when consecrated with "The Brahman hath consecrated himself", how is one to announce (the consecration) of a Kṣatriya?' 'As in the case of a Brahman when consecrated they announce the consecration with "The Brahman hath consecrated himself", so should he announce (the consecration) of a Kṣatriya, with the Ṛṣi descent of his Purohita[1]' (they say); 'Thus, thus' (they say). Having laid aside his own weapons, with the weapons of the holy power, with the form of the holy power, having become the holy power, he resorted to the sacrifice. Therefore should they announce his consecration with the Ṛṣi descent of his Purohita; with the Ṛṣi descent of the Purohita they should perform the ancestral invocation.[2]

vii. 26 (xxxiv. 8). Then as to the share of the sacrificer. They say 'Should a Kṣatriya eat the sacrificer's share? Or should he not eat?' If he who is not an eater of the oblations were to eat, by eating the oblation he would become worse; if he were not to eat, he would shut himself out from the sacrifice; the share of the sacrificer is the sacrifice. It is to be handed over to the Brahman. The Brahman priest is in the relation of Purohita to the Kṣatriya; the Purohita is half the self of the Kṣatriya. Secretly verily it obtains the appearance of being eaten; it is not openly consumed by him. The Brahman is manifestly the sacrifice, for in the Brahman the whole sacrifice finds support, in the sacrifice the sacrificer. They place the sacrifice in the sacrifice, as water in water, fire in fire; thus it is not superfluous, thus it harms him not. Therefore should it be handed over to the Brahman. Some make an offering in the fire with

> 'Prajāpati's is the world named Vibhāt; in this I place thee with the sacrificer; hail!'

That he should not do so. The share of the sacrificer is the sacrificer; he places on the fire the sacrificer. If a man were here to say to him 'Thou hast placed the sacrificer on the fire; Agni will burn his breaths; the sacrificer will die', it would certainly be so. Therefore he should not desire this.

[1] For this rule see ĀÇS. i. 3. 3; xii. 15. 4.

[2] I.e. on the invocation of Agni by the ancestral names; cf. Weber, *Ind. Stud.* ix. 321–326. In this, as in the exclusion of the prince from the drinking of the Soma, the Brāhmaṇa shows its high claim for its caste.

ADHYĀYA V

The Proper Food of the King in lieu of Soma.

vii. 27 (xxxv. 1). Viçvantara Sauṣadmana, despising the Çyāparṇas, performed a sacrifice without the Çyāparṇas.[1] Perceiving this the Çyāparṇas went to the sacrifice and sat down within the altar. Seeing them he said 'There sit those doers of an evil deed, speakers of impure speech, the Çyāparṇas; remove them; let them not sit within my altar'. 'Be it so' (they replied). They removed them. They being removed cried aloud 'Heroes had the Kaçyapas among them in the Asitamṛgas who, at the sacrifice from which Janamejaya Pārikṣita excluded the Kaçyapas, won the Soma drinking from the Bhūtavīras. What hero have we among us who will win this Soma drinking?'[2] 'I am the hero for you', said Rāma Mārgaveya; Rāma Mārgaveya was a learned member of the Çyāparṇas. When they were rising up, he said 'Can it be that they are removing, O king, from the altar one who knows thus?' 'What is that thou knowest, O worthless Brahman' (he replied).

vii. 28 (xxxv. 2). 'When the gods excluded Indra (saying) 'He hath misused Viçvarūpa, son of Tvaṣṭṛ, he hath laid low Vṛtra, he hath given the Yatis to the hyaenas, he hath killed the Arurmaghas, he hath contended with Bṛhaspati',[1] then Indra was deprived of the Soma drinking, and in accordance with the deprivation of Indra the lordly power was deprived of the Soma drinking. Indra obtained later a share in the Soma drinking, having stolen the Soma of Tvaṣṭṛ, but to day even the lordly power is deprived of Soma drinking. How can they remove from the altar him who knows the food which belongs to the lordly power now that it is deprived of the Soma drink, and by which the holy power is made prosperous?' 'Dost thou know, O Brahman, this food?' (he asked) 'I know it' (he replied).

[1] Cf. Weber, *Ind. Stud.* x. 32, 33, who seeks to see in this a case of punishment for disloyalty, as in PB. xiv. 6. 8, where, however, the position is much clearer than here. The impure speech need not be more than a ritual defect of the priests, especially as it is made good by a point of ritual. Cf also ZDMG. lii. 787; liv. 611.

[2] Böhtlingk (BKSGW. 15 Dec. 1900, p. 419) suggests *asmāko*.

vii. 28. [1] Cf. the similar lists in KU. iii. 1; TS. ii. 5. 1; Weber, *Ind. Stud.* i. 409; *Rājasūya*, p. 109, n. 2. In *Bṛhaspateḥ pratyavadhīt* Sāyaṇa sees the sense *vākyam*, and this is apparently meant: he cites ĀpDS. ii. 2. 5. 11. The aorist is natural and proper and needs no special explanation (cf. Delbrück, *Altind. Synt.* p. 281). The Arurmaghas are connected by Eggeling (SBE. xii. 57, n. 1) hesitatingly with the demon Araru; cf. Weber, *Ind. Stud.* i. 411. The curious way in which Indra loses his place in favour of the priestly Bṛhaspati is noted by Weber, *Rājasūya*, p. 110.

'Do thou tell it to me, O Brahman' (he said). '(I shall tell it) to thee, O king' he said.

vii. 29 (xxxv. 3). 'They will bring one of three foods, the Soma or curds or water. If [1] the Soma (they bring up), that is the food of the Brahmans; with this food thou wilt strengthen the Brahmans; in thine offspring will be born one like a Brahman, an acceptor of gifts, a drinker (of Soma), a seeker of livelihood, one to be moved at will.[2] When evil happens to a Kṣatriya one like a Brahman is born in his offspring; the second or third from him may become a Brahman; he is fain to live as a sort of Brahman. If curds (they bring), it is the food of the Vaiçyas; with this food thou wilt strengthen the Vaiçyas; in thine offspring one like a Vaiçya will be born, tributary to another, to be eaten by another, to be oppressed at will. When evil happens to a Kṣatriya, there is born in his offspring one like a Vaiçya; the second or third from him may become a Vaiçya; he is fain to live as a Vaiçya. If water (they bring), it is the food of the Çūdras; with this food thou wilt strengthen the Çūdras; in thine offspring one like a Çūdra will be born, the servant of another, to be removed at will, to be slain at will. When evil happens to a Kṣatriya, there is born in his offspring one like a Çūdra; the second or third from him may become a Çūdra; he is fain to live as a Çūdra.'

vii. 30 (xxxv. 4). 'These are the three foods, O king', he said 'which a Kṣatriya as sacrificer should not desire. Now this is his proper food; he should press together [1] the descending growths and the fruits of the Nyagrodha and (the fruits of) the Udumbara, Açvattha and Plakṣa trees, and partake of them. This is his proper food. On the place whence by offering the sacrifice the gods went to the world of heaven they tilted over (*nyubjan*) the goblets; they became the Nyagrodha trees. Even to-day in Kurukṣetra they call them the Nyubjas. They were the firstborn of Nyagrodhas; from them are the others born. In that they grew downwards, therefore the Nyagroha grows downwards; its name is Nyagroha; it being Nyagroha the gods call Nyagrodha mysteriously, for the gods love mystery as it were.'

vii. 31 (xxxv. 5). 'The sap of the goblets which went downwards became

[1] Sāyaṇa needlessly takes *sa* as referring to an ignorant priest; very possibly this is the common use in ÇB. and less often elsewhere of *sa yadi* = *yadi*, or, of course, a second form or verb may be supplied.

[2] Sāyaṇa recognizes the passive sense of *yathākāmaprayāpyaḥ*, but Haug suggests 'roam about according to pleasure' which is impossible, though allowed by Weber (*Ind. Stud.* ix. 326; x. 14), who prefers 'dwelling everywhere' for *āvasāyī*; cf. *Vedic Index*, ii. 82.

vii. 30. [1] The construction is awkward; the nom. *avarodhāç ca phalāni ca* which, as AB vii. 31 shows, applies to the Nyagrodha, is altered to the acc. with *abhiṣuṇuyāt*.

the descending growths; that which went up the fruits. This Kṣatriya does not depart from his proper food, who eats the shoots and the fruits of the Nyagrodha. Mysteriously verily he obtains the Soma drinking; it is not consumed openly by him. The Nyagrodha is mysteriously Soma the king; mysteriously does the Kṣatriya assume the form of the holy power, through the Purohita, through the consecration, through the ancestral invocation. The Nyagrodha is the lordly power of the trees, the Rājanya is the lordly power, for the Kṣatriya here dwells fastened as it were to the kingdom, and supported as it were, and the Nyagrodha is fastened as it were by its descending growths to the ground, and supported as it were. In that the Kṣatriya as sacrificer eats the descending growths of the Nyagrodha and the fruits, verily thus he establishes in himself the lordly power of the plants and in the lordly power himself. In the lordly power, in himself he establishes the lordly power of the plants, like the Nyagrodha with its descending shoots in the earth, in the kingdom he finds support, dread becomes his sway and unassailable, who as a Kṣatriya when sacrificing eats thus this food.'[1]

vii. 32 (xxxv. 6). 'Now as to the (fruits) of Udumbara. The Udumbara tree was born from strength and proper food; this is the pre-eminence of the trees; verily thus he places in the lordly power strength, proper food, and the pre-eminence of the trees. Now as to the (fruits) of Açvattha. The Açvattha tree was born from brilliance; this is the overlordship of the trees; verily thus he places in the lordly power the brilliance and the overlordship of the trees. Now as to the (fruits) of Plakṣa. The Plakṣa tree was born of might; it is the self rule and the control of the trees; verily thus he places in the lordly power the self rule and the control of the trees. These are first of all prepared and then they buy Soma, the king. They proceed with the rites[1] according to the manner of the (sacrifice of Soma) the king up to the fast day; then comes the fast day. These things the Adhvaryu should make ready in advance; the skin for pressing, the two pressing boards, the wooden tub, the filter cloth, the pressing stones, the vessel for the pure Soma, the stirring vessel, the vessel, the drawing cup, and the goblet. When they press the king in the morning,

[1] The inferior position of the Kṣatriya here may be contrasted with the fact that LÇS. ix. 2. 4 allows him at the consecration to drink the Soma, and even KÇS. xv. 8. 19–21 reaches the same conclusion; see Weber, *Rājasūya*, pp. 80, 81, 109, 117, 134.

vii. 32. [1] *prativeçaiḥ* is not certain in sense: Sāyaṇa has *prasiddhaiḥ kriyāviçeṣaiḥ*, and this can be made to agree with the sense 'auxiliary' by referring it to the rites prior to the first day. Weber (*Ind. Stud.* ix. 327) has, instead, the rendering 'the fruits substituted for the Soma', but this is doubtful, for the ordinary Soma sacrifice is daily offered.

then he should divide these (fruits) in two; some he should press, the rest leave over for the midday pressing.'

vii. 33 (xxxv. 7). 'When they fill up the goblets, then he should fill up the goblet of the sacrificer; in it should have been cast two Darbha shoots. When the *vaṣaṭ* call has been uttered he should throw the first of them within the altar, with the verse[1] 'I have celebrated Dadhikrāvan' accompanied by the call of Hail! The second (he should throw) after the second *vaṣaṭ* call has been said with[2] 'Dadhikrā with his brilliance the five folks'. When they take up the goblets, then he should take up the goblet of the sacrificer. When they lift them up (to the mouth), then he should lift it up after them. When the Hotṛ invokes the sacrificial food, when he partakes of the food in the goblet, then he should partake of it with[3]

> 'That which is left over of the pressed juice rich in sap,
> Which Indra drank mightily,
> Here with auspicious mind this of him,
> I partake of Soma the king.'

Auspiciously to him this (food) from the trees is consumed with auspicious mind, dread is his sway, unassailable, who as a Kṣatriya when sacrificing partakes thus of this food. With

> 'Be thou kindly to our heart when drunk,
> Do thou extend our life, to live long, O Soma';[4]

the touching of himself (is accompanied). If not touched this (drink) is liable to destroy the life of man (thinking) 'An unworthy one is partaking of me'. In that he touches himself with it, verily thus he prolongs life. With the appropriate (verses[5]) 'Swell up, let them come together for thee' and 'Let the milk unite for thee, the strengths' he makes the goblet full; that which is appropriate in the sacrifice is perfect.'

vii. 34 (xxxv. 8). 'When they put the goblets in place, then he should put in place the sacrificer's goblet. When they move them forward, he should move it forward after them. Then he should take it and partake of it.

> 'O god Soma, of thee that art drunk by Narāçaṅsa, that findest the mind, that art partaken of by the fathers, the helpers, I partake',[1]

[1] RV. iv. 39. 6. Not in ĀÇS. in this use. But this and iv. 38. 10 occur in an Iṣṭi in ii. 12. 5 and this is used by the priests when they drink in vi. 12. 12.

[2] RV. iv. 38. 10.

[3] KS. xvii. 19; MS. ii. 3. 8; iii. 11. 7; TB. i. 4. 2. 8; ĀpÇS. xix. 3. 4. A variant with *riptam* occurs in the Sautrāmaṇī in ĀÇS. iii. 9. 5. Cf. AB. viii. 20. 4.

[4] A variant of RV. viii. 48. 4 with which *b* agrees, and which is used in ĀÇS. v. 6. 26 in the Agniṣṭoma.

[5] RV. i. 91. 16 and 18; ĀÇS. v. 6. 27 in the Agniṣṭoma.

vii. 34. [1] The nine Soma goblets when emptied and filled are the Narāçaṅsas (cf. MÇS. ii. 4. 2. 32); they belong rather to the fathers (cf. PB. i. 5. 9). The name is either is the partaking connected with Narāçaṅsa at the morning pressing; at the midday (pressing) 'the great' is used; at the third pressing 'the sages' is used (as epithet of the fathers). The fathers are helpers at the morning pressing, the great at the midday, and the sages at the third pressing; verily thus he makes the fathers immortal and sharers of the pressings. 'Every one is immortal', Priyavrata Somāpa used to say, 'who is a sharer in the pressings.' Immortal become his fathers and sharers in the pressings, dread his sway becomes and unassailable, who as a Kṣatriya when sacrificing partakes thus of this food. The touching of himself is the same and the same the filling up of the goblet. They should proceed at the morning pressing in the manner of the morning pressing, in that of the midday (pressing) at the midday, and in that of the third pressing at the third pressing.' This food Rāma Mārgaveya proclaimed to Viçvantara Sauṣadmana; when it had been proclaimed he said 'A thousand we grant to you, O Brahman; my sacrifice will be performed by the Çyāparṇas'. This also Tura Kāvaṣeya proclaimed to Janamejaya Pārikṣita; this Parvata and Nārada proclaimed to Somaka Sāhadevya, to Sahadeva Sārñjaya, Babhru Daivāvṛdha, Bhīma of Vidarbha, Nagnajit of Gandhāra;[2] this Agni proclaimed to Sanaçruta Ariṃdama and to Kratuvid Jānaki;[3] this Vasiṣṭha proclaimed to Sudās Paijavana. All of them attained greatness having partaken of this food. All of them were great kings; like Āditya, established in prosperity, they gave heat, obtaining tribute from all the quarters. Like Āditya, established in prosperity, he gives heat, from all the quarters he obtains tribute, dread his sway and unassailable, who as a Kṣatriya when sacrificing partakes thus of this food.

derived from the use here, or because Soma is addressed as Narāçaṅsa in the Mantra (ÇÇS. vii. 5. 21), or because the fathers are praised by men (Sāyaṇa on PB. *l. c.*). Cf. AB. vi. 16 for another use of Narāçaṅsa in a different connexion; ZDMB. liv. 49 seq.

[2] Sāyaṇa, who is hopelessly perverse in dissecting the names, tries to make out a succession of teachers; this is clearly wrong: the names are those of kings, not of sages.

[3] Agni is no doubt the god, not the imaginary sage of Sāyaṇa. This is a variant *proccāçniḥ* whence Weber (*Ind. Stud.* ix. 330) creates an Āçni, but this is no more than a misread *gn* as *çn*, though Weber (*Rājasūya*, p. 109) still keeps the other reading.

PAÑCIKĀ VIII

The Rājasūya

ADHYĀYA I

The Çastras and Stotras of the Soma Sacrifice.

viii. 1 (xxxvi. 1). Now regarding the Stotras and the Çastras. The morning pressing follows the one day (rite), the third pressing follows the one day (rite). The pressings which follow the one day (rite) are appeased, well ordered, and established; (they serve) for expiation, arrangement, support, and to prevent falling. The midday Pavamāna of the day with two Sāmans and the Bṛhat as its Pṛṣṭha has been described,[1] for both Sāmans are employed. 'Thee like a car for aid' and 'This juice hath been pressed, O bright one' are the strophe and antistrophe[2] connected with the Rathantara. The Marutvatīya is the litany of the Pavamāna; in the Pavamāna here they employ the Rathantara (tune), and the Bṛhat for the Pṛṣṭha to create a balance. The Rathantara when sung he follows in recitation with these (verses) as strophe and antistrophe. Now the Rathantara is the holy power, the Bṛhat the lordly power; the holy power is prior to the lordly power; (it is his wish) 'Let my sway, with the holy power before, be dread and unassailable.' Now the Rathantara is food; verily thus he places food before for him. Again the Rathantara is this earth; this earth is a support; verily thus he places a support in front for him. The invocation of Indra is the same, and unaltered; it is (that) of the days. (The Pragātha) addressed to Brahmaṇaspati contains (the word) 'up';[3] it is a symbol of that which has two Sāmans, for both Sāmans are performed. The inserted verses are the same and

[1] The form has been mentioned in so far as the verses are mentioned in AB. iv. 29, where also the Rathantara Sāman is mentioned. The rule is a rare one as two Sāmans, viz. Bṛhat and Rathantara, are rarely used together, the Abhijit and Viṣuvant days being the chief exceptions (others are given in ÇÇS. xi. 2. 1; 11. 2). The Rathantara is used for the Pavamāna, the Bṛhat for the Pṛṣṭha Stotra. See ĀÇS. ix. 3. 3.

[2] RV. viii. 68. 1–3; 2. 1–3; ĀÇS. v. 14. 4. For the invocation of Indra (RV. viii. 58. 5, 6), see AB. iii. 16.

[3] I. e. RV. i. 40. 1 and 2; above AB. iv. 31; the inserted verses are in iii. 18.

unaltered; they are (those) of the days. The Marutvatīya Pragātha[4] is that of the one day (rite).

viii. 2 (xxxvi. 2). 'Thou hast been born dread, for impetuous strength' is the hymn[1] containing (the words) 'dread' and 'strength'; this is a symbol of the lordly power. In 'Exalting, most mighty' it contains (the word) 'might'; that is a symbol of the lordly power; in 'Full of pride (*abhi-māna*)' it contains (the word) 'towards (*abhi*)'; this is a symbol of overpowering. It is of eleven verses; the Triṣṭubh has eleven syllables; the Rājanya is connected with the Triṣṭubh; the Triṣṭubh is might, power, strength; the Rājanya is might, the lordly power, strength; thus he makes him prosper with might, the lordly power, strength. It is by Gaurivīti; the Gaurivīti (hymn) is the perfect Marutvatīya; the explanation of it has been given. In 'Thee we invoke' it has the Bṛhat as Pṛṣṭha;[2] the Bṛhat is lordly power; verily thus he makes the lordly power prosper with the lordly power. Moreover the Bṛhat is the lordly power; the Niṣkevalya is the body of the sacrificer; in that it has the Bṛhat as Pṛṣṭha, and the Bṛhat is lordly power, verily thus he makes it prosper with the lordly power. Moreover the Bṛhat is the highest; verily thus he makes him prosper with the highest. Moreover the Bṛhat is the best; verily thus he makes him prosper with the best. In 'To thee, O hero, we utter praise' they make the Rathantara the antistrophe;[3] the Rathantara is this world; the Bṛhat yonder world; yonder world is the counterpart of this world; of yonder world this world is the counterpart. In that they make the Rathantara the antistrophe, verily thus they make both these worlds possessed of enjoyment for the sacrificer. Moreover the Rathantara is the holy power, the Bṛhat the lordly power; on the holy power is the lordly power established, on the lordly power the holy power; moreover (it serves) to secure the Sāman its birthplace. 'What he hath won' is the inserted verse;[4] the explanation of this has been given. 'Both let him hear for us' is the Pragātha[5] of the Sāman; it is a symbol of (the day) with both Sāmans, for both Sāmans are performed.

[4] RV. viii. 89. 3 and 4; above AB. iii. 19. The days are, of course, naturally taken by Weber and Haug as rites extending over several days, Ahīnas. But this is not the view of Sāyaṇa, and in fact the verses referred to are used at the day rite as well as the Ahīnas, and in the case where there is a divergence, the Pragātha for Bṛhaspati, the reference to the days is omitted.

[1] RV. x. 73. See also AB. iii. 19. 2; AÇS. v 4. 19.

[2] RV. vi. 46. 1 and 2; AÇS. v. 15. 3. See also v. 15. 16–18 for the order. *bṛhatpṛṣṭham* is here taken as a compound by Sāyaṇa, Weber, and Aufrecht, but it may not be so.

[3] RV. vii. 32. 22 and 23; AÇS. v. 15. 2.

[4] RV. x. 74. 6. See AB. iii. 22; ĀÇS. v. 15. 21.

[5] RV. viii. 61. 1 and 2. See AB. iv. 31; v. 18.

viii. 3 (xxxvi. 3). 'Praise him who hath force to overcome' is the hymn;[1] as containing (the word) 'to' it is a symbol of overcoming. In 'Unsupportable, dread, enduring' it contains (the words) 'dread' and 'enduring'; it is a symbol of the lordly power. It is in fifteen verses; the Pañcadaça (Stoma) is might, power, and strength; the Rājanya is might, the lordly power, and strength; thus he makes him prosper with might, the lordly power, and strength. It is by Bharadvāja; the Bṛhat is by Bharadvāja; by reason of the authorship it is similar.[2] That sacrifice of a Kṣatriya is perfect which has the Bṛhat for its Pṛṣṭha; therefore whenever a Kṣatriya sacrifices, the Bṛhat should be the Pṛṣṭha; that is perfect.

viii. 4 (xxxvi. 4). The Hotṛ offices are taken from the one day (rite); the Hotṛ offices as taken from the one day (rite) are appeased, well ordained, and supported; (they serve) for expiation, arrangement, support, and to prevent falling away. These are of all forms, all perfect (and serve) to secure all forms, all perfection; (they think) 'With the Hotṛ offices of all forms, all perfect, let us obtain all desires.' Therefore, whenever the one day (rites) have not all the Stomas and the Pṛṣṭhas, the Hotṛ offices of the one day (rite) should be used; that is perfect. 'This should be a fifteenfold Ukthya' they say[1]; 'the Pañcadaça (Stoma) is might, power, and strength; the Rājanya is might, the lordly power, and strength; thus he makes him prosper with might, the lordly power, and strength. It has thirty Stotras and Çastras; the Virāj has thirty syllables; proper food is the Virāj; verily thus he establishes him in the Virāj as proper food. Therefore should it be a fifteenfold Ukthya' they say. It should be a Jyotiṣṭoma of the Agniṣṭoma form. The Trivṛt of Stomas is the holy power, the Pañcadaça the lordly power; the holy power is prior to the lordly power; (it is his wish) 'May my sway with the holy power in front be dread and unassailable.' The Saptadaça is the people, the Ekaviñça the Çūdra class; verily thus they make the people and the Çūdra class obedient to him. Moreover the Trivṛt of Stomas is brilliance, the Pañcadaça strength, the Saptadaça generation, the Ekaviñça support; thus he makes him prosper with brilliance, strength, generation, and support at the end. Therefore it should be a Jyotiṣṭoma. It has twenty-four Stotras and Çastras; the year has twenty-four half months; in the year is all proper food; verily thus he establishes him in all proper food. Therefore it should be a Jyotiṣṭoma of the Agniṣṭoma form.

[1] RV. vi. 18.

[2] This is clearly the sense, and Sāyaṇa seems to have had it in mind on taking *saloma* = *saṃpūrṇaḥ*. Haug renders 'is in direct relationship with the ancestral fire' in accord with his theory of *ārṣeya*. Cf. Weber, *Ind. Stud.* ix. 331.

viii. 4. [1] So ĀÇS. ix. 8. 8, despite the decision here; in the very faintly parallel rite in ÇÇS. v. 12. 14 the *sutya* day is *ṣoḍaça*.

ADHYĀYA II

The Punarabhiṣeka.

viii. 5 (xxxvii. 1). Now as to the renewed anointing. His lordly power is consecrated, who being a Kṣatriya consecrates himself. When he concludes, after coming out of the concluding bath and having offered the final offering of a cow, then they again anoint him when the concluding offering has been completed. For him in advance the following preparation has been made: a throne of Udumbara[1]; its feet should be a span in size, the head (and foot) and the cross (boards) an ell in size, the cover seat of Muñja grass, the spread a tiger skin; a goblet of Udumbara; a branch of Udumbara. In this goblet are poured eight elements; curds, honey, melted butter, the waters of rain during heat, grass and green barley, liquor and Dūrvā grass. Where the line drawn by the sword on the south of the altar is, there he places the throne facing east. Two of its feet are within, two outside the altar. Prosperity is the (earth). What is within the altar is its limited form; what is without the altar is the unlimited space. In that its two feet are within the altar, two outside of the altar, (it serves) to obtain both desires, that which is within the altar and that without the altar.

viii. 6 (xxxvii. 2). He covers (it) with a tiger skin, skin uppermost, neck in front. The tiger is the lordly power of the wild animals, the Rājanya is the lordly power; thus he makes the lordly power prosper with the lordly power. From behind it he approaches it facing east bending the right knee, and taking hold of it with both hands he addresses it with

> 'May Agni in unison with the Gāyatrī metre mount thee; Savitṛ with the Uṣṇih, Soma with the Anuṣṭubh, Bṛhaspati with the Bṛhatī, Mitra and Varuṇa with the Pañkti, Indra with the Triṣṭubh, the All-gods with the Jagatī.'
>
> With 'After them I mount for kingship, for overlordship, for paramount rule, for self rule, for sovereignty, for supreme authority, for kingship,[1] for great kingship, for suzerainty, for supremacy, for preeminence.'

[1] For the throne cf. AV. xv. 3. 2 in the case of the Vrātya; *Vedic Index*, i. 71. The ĀÇS. and ÇÇS. have nothing of this or of the following rites. Sāyaṇa explains the Punarabhiṣeka as one following on that already performed by the Adhvaryu after the Māhendra Sāman, clearly referring to ĀpÇS. xviii. 15. 10: *māhendrasya stotraṁ praty abhiṣiñcati*. Āp. quotes in viii. 8. 7 a Bahvṛcabrāhmaṇa (read *trīṇi ṣaṣṭiçatāni*) which is not AB. or KB. Cf. Weber, *Rājasūya*, pp. 110 *seq.*; Goldstücker, *Sanscrit Dict.* pp. 279 *seq.*

viii. 6. [1] Weber (*Rājasūya*, p. 112, n. 3) suggests that the original list was *rājyāya* alone, since it twice occurs here.

He should mount the throne, with the right knee first, then the left. 'Thus, thus (is it to be performed)' (they say). The gods in unison with the metres increasing by four syllables mounted on the prosperity on which they now are established, Agni with the Gāyatrī, Savitṛ with the Uṣṇih, Soma with the Anuṣṭubh, Bṛhaspati with the Bṛhatī, Mitra and Varuṇa with the Pañkti, Indra with the Triṣṭubh, the All-gods with the Jagatī. These two are mentioned[2] in 'The Gāyatrī hath become the yoke fellow of Agni'. Fortune attends him, prosperity ever increasing he attains, he attains control and overlordship over people who, being a Kṣatriya, thus mounts this throne after those deities. Then being about to anoint him, he makes him recite the appeasing of the waters

'With eye propitious regard me, O waters;
With propitious body touch my skin;
All the Agnis that sit on the waters I invoke you;
Confer on me radiance, force and might,'

(thinking) 'Let not the waters, unappeased, strike away the strength of him when anointed.'[3]

viii. 7 (xxxvii. 3). Then he anoints him, placing the Udumbara branch between, with

'These waters are most auspicious,
These healing all,
These prosper the realm,
These support the realms and are immortal.
With these by which Prajāpati anointed Indra,
Soma the king, Varuṇa, Yama, Manu,
With these waters I anoint thee,
Do thou become here the overking of kings.
Thee great, of the great
People the ruler,
The lady, thy mother, bore
The noble lady, thy mother bore.

On the impulse of the god Savitṛ, with the arms of the Açvins, with the hands of Pūṣan, with the brilliance of Agni, with the radiance of the sun, with the power of Indra I anoint thee, for might, for prosperity, for glory, for the eating of food.'

With *bhūḥ* (he concludes) if he desire of him 'May he eat food'; with *bhūḥ, bhuvaḥ*, if he desire thus of him with two descendants;[1] with *bhūḥ*,

[2] RV. x. 180. 4.

[3] Cf. Lévi, *La doctrine du sacrifice*, p. 108.

[1] Weber (*Ind. Stud.* ix. 335) prefers to take *dvipuruṣa* as the sacrificer and his son, but Aufrecht prefers Sāyaṇa's version quoting *tripuruṣa*, 'with three assistants', of the Hotṛ. There is no reference to a temporary kingship.

bhuvaḥ, *svar* if he desire thus of him with three descendants, or without rivals. Some say 'These exclamations are an obtaining of all; by using too much it is performed by him for another.' He should anoint him with this (formula)

> 'On the instigation of the god Savitṛ, with the arms of the Açvins, with the hands of Pūṣan, with the brilliance of Agni, with the radiance of the sun, with the power of Indra I anoint thee, for might, for prosperity, for glory, for the eating of food.'

This again they reject. 'If he is anointed without the whole of speech, he is liable to depart before his day', Satyakāma Jābāla used to say, 'whom they do not anoint with these exclamations.' 'He is liable to live the whole of his life, and to obtain[2] all by conquest', Uddālaka Āruṇi used to say, 'whom they anoint with these exclamations. Him he should anoint with this (formula)

> 'On the instigation of the god Savitṛ, with the arms of the Açvins, with the hands of Pūṣan, with the brilliance of Agni, with the radiance of the sun, with the power of Indra I anoint thee, for might, for prosperity, for glory, for the eating of food; *bhūḥ*, *bhuvaḥ*, *svar*.'

These things have departed from a Kṣatriya who has sacrificed; the holy power and the lordly power, strength, the eating of food, the sap of the plants and the waters, splendour, refreshment,[3] growth and propagation; moreover, as this is a symbol of the lordly power, the sap of food, the lordly power of the plants and support. In that he offers beforehand these two libations, thus he confers on him the holy power and the lordly power.

viii. 8 (xxxvii. 4). In that the throne is of Udumbara, the goblet of Udumbara, and there is a branch of Udumbara, and the Udumbara is strength and the eating of food, verily thus he confers upon him strength and the eating of food. In that there is curd, honey, and ghee, and it is the sap of the plants and the waters, verily thus he confers upon him the sap of plants and the waters. In that there are waters of rain in sunshine, and the waters of rain in sunshine are brilliance and splendour, verily thus he confers on him brilliance and splendour. In that there are grass and green barley, and these are a symbol of refreshment and growth, and also of propagation, verily thus he confers upon him refreshment and growth and also propagation. In that there is Surā, and this is

[2] *Āpnot* is very strange in tense and probably impossible: *āptor* is a most simple correction: naturally misread and misunderstood as an unusual form.

[3] *irāpuṣṭiḥ* is taken as one word, *annasamṛddhiḥ*, by Sāyaṇa.

a symbol of the lordly power, and also the sap of food, verily thus he confers upon him the symbol of lordly power and also the sap of food. In that there is Dūrvā grass, the Dūrvā is the lordly power of the plants, the Rājanya is the lordly power, for the Kṣatriya dwelling in the kingdom is fastened here as it were, and supported as it were; the Dūrvā is fastened as it were to the ground with descending growths, and is supported as it were. Thus in that there is Dūrvā grass, verily thus he confers upon him the lordly power of the plants and also a support. Those that have departed from him after sacrificing he thus confers upon him; verily thus he makes him prosper with them. Then he places in his hand a bowl of Surā with [1]

> 'With thy sweetest, most intoxicating
> Stream be thou purified, O Soma,
> Pressed for Indra to drink.'

Having placed it with (this verse), he makes him recite the expiation

> 'Separate for you is the place made by the gods,
> Be ye not united in the highest heaven,
> Surā thou art, the impetuous; he is king Soma;
> Harm him not, when entering your own place of birth.' [2]

This is the discrimination of the drinking of Soma and of Surā. Having drank he should give it to him whom he deems generous, for that is a symbol of friendship; verily thus at the end he establishes it in a friend; for he thus finds support in a friend. He finds support who knows thus.

viii. 9 (xxxvii. 5). Then he descends towards [1] the Udumbara branch; the Udumbara is strength and the eating of food; verily thus he descends towards strength and the eating of food. Sitting down he places his feet on the earth and says the descent formula [2]

> 'I find support in the sky and the earth; I find support in expiation and inspiration; I find support in day and night; I find support in food and drink; in the holy power, in the lordly power, in these three worlds I find support.'

At the end he finds support with his whole self; in all this he finds support, prosperity ever increasing he attains, he attains sovereignty and overlord-

[1] RV. ix. 1. 1.

[2] See TB. i. 4. 2. 2; ĀÇS. iii. 9. 4; VS. xix. 7; ÇB. xii. 7. 3. 14; KÇS. xix. 2. 21.

viii. 9. [1] The branch is now placed on the ground and he descends down towards it.

[2] This is probably the sense as taken by Sāyaṇa in view of the instr. below. Otherwise it could be the gerund as Weber (*Ind. Stud.* ix. 387) thinks.

ship over people, who, anointed with the renewed anointing, being a Kṣatriya descends thus. Having descended with this descent formula he sits facing east, making a lap, and thrice pays honour to the holy power with 'Homage to the holy power! Homage to the holy power! Homage to the holy power.' Then he utters speech with 'A boon I give for conquest, for victory, for winning, for success.' In that he pays thrice homage to the holy power with 'Homage to the holy power! Homage to the holy power! Homage to the holy power!' verily thus the lordly power falls under the influence of the holy power. When the lordly power falls under the influence of the holy power, that kingdom is prosperous, rich in heroes; in it[3] a heir is born. In that he utters speech with 'A boon I give for conquest, for victory, for winning, for success', that is the conquest of speech in that he says 'I give'. Moreover as to the conquest of speech, (he thinks) 'Through this my rite shall be completed'. Having uttered speech, and having risen up he places a kindling stick on the Āhavanīya with

> 'Thou art a kindling stick; kindle thou,[4] with power, with strength, hail!'

Verily thus at the end with power and strength he makes himself to prosper. Having put on the kindling stick he steps out three strides north-east. (Saying)

> 'Thou art the orderer of the quarters,
> In me be ye ordered for the gods;
> Mine be good fortune
> Freedom from fear be mine,'[5]

he reveres the unconquered quarter, to secure the permanence of his conquest. 'Thus, thus (is it to be performed)' (they say).

viii. 10 (xxxvii. 6). The gods and the Asuras strove for these worlds; they strove for the eastern quarter; the Asuras drove them thence; they strove for the southern quarter; the Asuras drove them thence; they strove for the western quarter; the Asuras drove them thence; they strove for the northern quarter; the Asuras drove them thence; they strove for this inter-

[3] Or, as Sāyaṇa, 'to him'.

[4] For *sam v ēṅkṣva* Sāyaṇa has *indriyapāṭavena çarīrasāmarthyena ca saṁyojaya*; Aufrecht suggests *sam menīsva* as the original, with *īṅkṣva* for *intsva* like *avākṣam* for *avātsam* in i. 28 above (cf. Weber, *Ind. Stud* ix. 245). Böhtlingk (BKSGW. 15 Dec. 1900, p. 419) argues against *īṅkṣva* but accepts *mā* in place of *u*.

[5] Aufrecht suggests, after *diçām*, *diço me kalpantām*, but that is not good metrically: possibly *diçaḥ* should be added after *diçām*. *Kalpata* as active 2nd pl. is very strange, and Weber (*Ind. Stud.* ix. 338) suggests taking it as a 3rd pers. sing. injunct.

mediate quarter, the north-east; they thence defeated them. If, when two armies meet, a Kṣatriya runs up to him (saying) 'So do for me that I shall conquer that army', and if he reply 'Be it so', he should touch the body of his chariot with[1] 'O tree, be thou strong limbed' and then say to him

> 'Do thou mount, to this quarter for thee let the chariot, well tied, advance, to the north (let it advance), to the west, to the south, to the east, against the foe.'

With[2] 'With the attacking oblation' he should make him turn; then he should look at him with the Apratiratha,[3] Çāsa,[4] and Sauparṇa[5] hymns. He conquers that army. If again he runs up to him when about to engage in battle (saying) 'So do for me that I shall conquer in this battle', he should make him contend in this quarter; he conquers in this battle. If again he run up to him, being expelled from his kingdom (saying) 'So do for me that I may be restored to this kingdom', he should make him go away to this quarter; so does he again become restored to his kingdom. After the paying of reverence, he goes to the house saying (the verse) for the driving away of foes,[6] 'Drive away, O Indra, all my foes to the east'; from all sides freedom from foes and danger becomes his, prosperity ever increasing he attains, he attains sovereignty and overlordship over people who goes to the house saying thus this (verse) for the driving away of foes. Having gone to the house he sits down behind the household fire and holds on to the priest who at the end offers three butter libations to Indra, in four portions, with the bowl, in the Prapad way,[7] for freedom from distress, injury, loss, and danger.

viii. 11 (xxxvii. 7).

> 'Do[1] thou pour forth for the winning of strength; the foe around—
> *Bhūḥ*; the holy power, breath, immortality, this N. N. approacheth, protection, guarding, freedom from fear, for safety, with offspring, with cattle—
> overcoming:
> To overwhelm the foe thou movest like one taking payment for a debt; hail!

[1] RV. vi. 47. 26.
[2] RV. v. 174.
[3] RV. x. 103.
[4] RV. i. 152.
[5] See above AB. vi. 25. 7. Sāyaṇa here, however, gives *pra dhārā yantu* (ĀÇS. iii. 12. 14) as meant; cf. KB. xviii. 4; RVKh. i. 3.
[6] RV. x. 131. 1.
[7] I. e. in equal parts with insertions as in AB. viii. 11.

viii. 11. [1] The verses treated are RV. ix. 110. 1–3: the verses consist of Padas of 12 + 8 + 12 syllables respectively. The treatment accorded is to insert after 16 + 16, irrespective of the forms and metre, the insertion; thus in a sense the verses are reduced to normal Anuṣṭubh verses. The Prapad mode is defined in a verse cited by Sāyaṇa as—
pādā yasya tu yāvanto yāvadakṣarasaṃmitāḥ

In thee when pressed, O Soma, we delight, in the great—

Bhuvaḥ; the holy power, breath, immortality, this N. N. approacheth, protection, guarding, freedom from fear, for safety, with offspring, with cattle—

kingship of concourse;

For the booty, O purifying one, thou dost plunge; hail!

Thou hast brought to life, O purifying one, the sun; in the pail—

Svar; the holy power, breath, immortality, this N. N. approacheth, protection, guarding, freedom from fear, for safety, with offspring, with cattle—

with might the milk;

In eagerness with the milk that is thy living gift; hail!'

Free from harm and injury, unoppressed, protected on every side, by the form of the threefold knowledge he wanders through all the quarters, finding support in the world of Indra, for whom the priest at the end offers those three libations of butter in four portions with the bowl, in the Prapad manner. Then at the end he invokes propagation for cows, horses, and men with [2]

'Here ye cows, be ye propagated,
Here ye horses, here ye men;
Here with a thousand fees to give
Let the hero, the protector, sit down.'

He becomes multiplied with offspring and cattle who thus at the end invokes the propagation of cows, horses, and men. This Kṣatriya is never brought low, for whom those knowing thus sacrifice. But they bring him low for whom they sacrifice not knowing thus: just as outcasts,[3] or robbers, or evildoers, seizing a wealthy man in the wild, fling him into a pit and run away taking his wealth, so these priests fling the sacrificer into a pit and run away taking his wealth. Knowing this Janamejaya Pārikṣita used to say 'Those who know thus sacrifice for me who know thus; therefore I conquer the assailing host, I conquer with an assailing host. Me neither the arrows of heaven nor of men reach. I shall live all my life, I shall become lord of all the earth.' Him neither divine nor human arrows reach, he lives all his life, he becomes lord of all the earth, for whom men, knowing thus, sacrifice.

ṛcy adhyayanam eteṣāṁ prapadaṁ tad vidur budhāḥ.

[2] Cf. AV. xx. 127. 12; ÇÇS. xii. 15. 8 where Hillebrandt reads in *á 'pi pūṣā* against his MSS. which has *prātā*, a blunder for *trātā*; RVKh. v. 11. 2.

[3] For the Niṣādas see Weber, *Ind. Stud.* ix. 340; *Vedic Index*, i. 453, 454.

ADHYĀYA III

The Mahābhiṣeka of Indra.

viii. 12 (xxxviii. 1.) Now comes the great anointing of Indra. The gods with Prajāpati said 'He is of the gods the mightiest, the most powerful, the strongest, the most real, the best to accomplish; let us anoint him.' 'Be it so' (they replied). Thus (they did anoint) Indra. For him they brought together the throne called Ṛc; as its two front feet they made the Bṛhat and the Rathantara,[1] as its two back feet the Vairūpa and the Vairāja, as the head (and foot) (planks) the Çākvara and the Raivata, as the cross (planks) the Naudhasa and Kāleya, as the lengthwise ropes the Ṛc verses, as the cross-ties the Sāmans, as the holes the Yajuses, as the coverlet glory, as the pillow prosperity. Savitṛ and Bṛhaspati supported its front feet, Vāyu and Pūṣan the back feet, Mitra and Varuṇa the head (and foot) (planks), the Açvins the cross (planks). He mounted this throne with[2]

> 'Let the Vasus mount thee with the Gāyatrī metre, the Trivṛt Stoma, the Rathantara Sāman; after them I mount for overlordship. Let the Rudras mount thee, with the Triṣṭubh metre, the Pañcadaça Stoma, the Bṛhat Sāman; after them I mount for paramount rule. Let the Ādityas mount thee with the Jagatī metre, the Saptadaça Stoma, the Vairūpa Sāman; after them I mount for self rule. Let the All-gods mount thee with the Anuṣṭubh metre, with the Ekaviñça Stoma, the Vairāja Sāman; after them I mount for sovereignty. Let the Sādhya and the Āptya gods mount thee with the Pañkti metre, the Triṇava Stoma, the Çākvara Sāman; after them I mount for kingship. Let the Maruts and the Añgirases the gods mount thee with the Atichandas metre, the Trayastriñça Stoma, the Raivata Sāman; after them I mount for supreme authority, for great kingship, for suzerainty, for supremacy, for pre-eminence;'

he mounted the throne. When he was seated on the throne the All-gods said 'If Indra is not proclaimed he cannot display his strength; let us proclaim him.' 'Be it so.' Him the All-gods proclaimed (saying)

> 'Do ye proclaim him, O gods, as overlord and overlordship, as paramount ruler and father of paramount rulers, as self ruler and self rule, as sovereign and sovereignty, as king and father of kings, as supreme lord and supreme authority. The lordly power hath been born, the Kṣatriya

[1] See for the Sāmans above AB. iv. 18; for the throne AB. viii. 5.

[2] For the same series of metres cf. AĀ. v. 1. 4; ÇÇS. xvii. 16. 1.

hath been born, the suzerain of all creation hath been born, the eater of the folk hath been born, the breaker of citadels hath been born, the slayer of the Asuras hath been born, the guardian of the holy power hath been born, the guardian of the law hath been born.'

When he had been proclaimed Prajāpati, being about to anoint him, addressed him with the verse

viii. 13 (xxxviii. 2).

'Varuṇa within the waters[1]
Hath set him down, preserving order,
For overlordship, for paramount rule, for self rule, for sovereignty, for supreme authority, for kingship, for great kingship, for suzerainty, for supremacy, for pre-eminence, the wise one.'

Him when seated on the throne, Prajāpati, standing in front of him, facing west, anointed through a branch of Udumbara, dry but with leaves, and a golden strainer, to the accompaniment of the triplet[2] 'These waters are most auspicious', the Yajus formula '(On the instigation) of the god thee', and the exclamations *bhūḥ*, *bhuvaḥ*, *svar*.

viii. 14 (xxxviii. 3). Then the Vasus, the gods in the eastern quarter anointed him with six days with the Pañcaviñça,[1] and with this triplet and this Yajus and these exclamations, for overlordship. Therefore in this eastern quarter, whatever kings there are of the eastern peoples, they are anointed for overlordship; 'O Overlord' they style them when anointed in accordance with the action of the gods. Then in the southern quarter the Rudras, the gods, anointed him with six days with the Pañcaviñça, and with this triplet and this Yajus and these exclamations, for paramount rule. Therefore in this southern quarter, whatever kings there are of the Satvants, they are anointed for paramount rule; 'O paramount ruler' they style them when anointed in accordance with the action of the gods. Then in the western quarter the Ādityas, the gods, anointed him with six days with the Pañcaviñça, and with this triplet and this Yajus and these exclamations, for self rule. Therefore in this western quarter, whatever kings there are of the southern and western peoples, they are anointed for self rule; 'O self ruler' they style them when anointed in accordance with the action of the gods. Then in the northern quarter the All-gods anointed him with six days with

[1] This is RV. i. 25. 10 extended.

[2] See AB. viii. 7.

viii. 14. [1] Sāyaṇa has *ekatriñçatsv ahassu*, which is no doubt wrong. But Aufrecht in suggesting 6 × 25 = 150 seems unjustified: his reason is that there is no Pañcaviñça Stoma at the Rājasūya, but here we have direct evidence that it was used in that of the gods, and we need not go beyond that. There is no use of 150 days in the Rājasūya either, so that Aufrecht's own suggestion is equally out of place, and it is bad grammar.

the Pañcaviñça, and with this triplet and this Yajus and these exclamations, for sovereignty. Therefore in this northern quarter, the lands of the Uttara Kurus and the Uttara Madras, beyond the Himavant, their (kings)[2] are anointed for sovereignty; 'O sovereign' they style them when anointed in accordance with the action of the gods. Then in this firm middle established quarter the Sādhyas and the Āptyas, the gods, anointed him with six day with the Pañcaviñça, and with this triplet and this Yajus and these exclamations, for kingship. Therefore in this firm middle established quarter, whatever kings there are of the Kuru-Pañcālas with the Vaças and Uçīnaras, they are anointed for kingship; 'king'[3] they style them when anointed, in accordance with the action of the gods. Then in the upward quarter the Maruts and the Añgirases, the gods, anointed him with six days with the Pañcaviñça, and with this triplet and this Yajus and these exclamations, for supreme authority, for great kingship, for suzerainty, for supremacy, for pre-eminence. He became the supreme authority, as connected with Prajāpati. Anointed with this great anointment Indra won all victories, found all the worlds, attained the superiority, pre-eminence and supremacy over all the gods, and having won the overlordship, the paramount rule, the self rule, the sovereignty, the supreme authority, the kingship, the great kingship, the suzerainty in this world, self-existing, self-ruling, immortal, in yonder world of heaven, having obtained all desires he became immortal.

ADHYĀYA IV

The Mahābhiṣeka of Kings.

viii. 15 (xxxix. 1). If he who knows thus should desire of a Kṣatriya 'May he win all victories, find all the worlds, attain the superiority, pre-eminence and supremacy over all kings, and overlordship, paramount rule, self rule, sovereignty, supreme authority, kingship, great kingship, and suzerainty; may he be all encompassing, possessed of all the earth, possessed of all life, from the one end up to the further side of the earth bounded by the ocean, sole ruler', he should anoint him with this great anointing of Indra, after adjuring him

[2] The sense is clear, though the construction is careless: Haug, however, seeks to render the *janapadāḥ* as subject and as being 'without kings', which is wholly inconceivable.

[3] Here *rājā* is meant, and therefore the other names of no distinct form may be nom. or voc. as *bhoja* clearly is.

> 'From the night of thy birth [1] to that of thy death, for the space between these two, thy sacrifice and thy gifts, thy place, thy good deeds, thy life, and thine offspring let me take, if thou dost play me false.'

If a Kṣatriya who knows thus desire 'May I win all victories, find all worlds, attain the superiority, pre-eminence, and supremacy over all kings and overlordship, paramount rule, self rule, sovereignty, supreme authority, kingship, great kingship and suzerainty; may I be all encompassing, possessed of all the earth, possessed of all life, from the one end up to the further side of the earth bounded by the [2] ocean sole ruler', he should not doubt, but say with faith

> 'From the night of my birth to that of my death, for the space between these two, my sacrifice and my gifts, my place, my good deeds, my life, and mine offspring mayest thou take, if I play thee false.' [3]

viii. 16 (xxxix. 2). Then should he say 'Bring together four things of the trees, of the Nyagrodha, Udumbara, Açvattha, and Plakṣa'. The Nyagrodha is the lordly power of the trees; in that they bring together Nyagrodha (products), verily thus he confers on him the lordly power. The Udumbara is the paramount rule of the trees; in that they bring together Udumbara (products), verily thus he confers upon him the paramount rule. The Açvattha is the overlordship of the trees; in that they bring together Açvattha (products), verily thus he confers upon him overlordship. The Plakṣa is the self rule and sovereignty of the trees; in that they bring together Plakṣa (products), verily thus he confers upon him self rule and sovereignty. Then should he say 'Bring together the four things of the plants, in the shape of the green shoots of rice, large rice, panic seed and barley.' The rice is the lordly power of the plants; in that they bring together the green shoots of rice, verily thus he confers upon him the lordly power. Large rice is the overlordship of the plants; in that they bring together the green shoots of large rice, verily thus he confers upon him overlordship. Panic seeds are the paramount rule of the plants; in that they bring together the green shoots of panic seeds, verily thus he confers upon him paramount rule. Barley is the leadership of the plants; in that they bring together the green shoots of barley, verily thus he confers upon him leadership.

[1] *ajāyethāḥ* and *vṛñjīyam* are strange and really impossible blunders. For others in this book cf. AB. viii. 23: *avapadyeyam* and 28: *prajighyati*, °*tu*, *jāgriyāt*; Böhtlingk, BKSGW. 15 Dec. 1900, p. 414.

[2] Sāyaṇa sees in *parārdha* a term of time. Weber (*Ind. Stud.* ix. 348) suggests the rendering adopted.

[3] In *Kauç.* xvii. 4–8 the oath of priest and king is a mutual one, and very probably reflects a more primitive state of usage; cf. Weber, *Rājasūya*, pp. 142, 143.

viii. 17 (xxxix. 3). They then bring for him a throne of Udumbara; the explanation of it has been given. There is a goblet of Udumbara or a bowl, and a branch of Udumbara. Having collected these preparations, they should throw them together in the bowl or goblet of Udumbara, and, when these have been mixed together, he should put curds, honey, melted butter, and water of the rains with sunshine, and, setting them down, he should address the throne with [1]

'Let the Bṛhat and the Rathantara be thy two front feet, and the Vairūpa and the Vairāja thy back feet, the Çākvara and the Raivata the head (and foot) (planks), the Naudhasa and Kāleya the cross (planks), the Ṛc verses the lengthwise ropes, the Sāmans the cross-ties, the Yajuses the holes, glory the coverlet, prosperity the pillow. Let Savitṛ and Bṛhaspati support thy front feet, Vāyu and Pūṣan thy back feet, Mitra and Varuṇa the head (and foot) (planks), the Açvins the cross (planks).'

Then he should make him mount the throne. With

'Let the Vasus mount thee with the Gāyatrī metre, the Trivṛt Stoma, the Rathantara Sāman; after them do thou mount for overlordship. Let the Rudras mount thee with the Triṣṭubh metre, the Pañcadaça Stoma, the Bṛhat Sāman; after them do thou mount for paramount rule. Let the Ādityas mount thee with the Jagatī metre, the Saptadaça Stoma, the Vairūpa Sāman; after them do thou mount for self rule. Let the All-gods mount thee with the Anuṣṭubh metre, the Ekaviṅça Stoma, the Vairāja Sāman; after them do thou mount for sovereignty. Let the Maruts and the Aṅgirases, the gods, mount thee with the Atichandas metre, the Trayastriṅça Stoma, the Raivata Sāman; after them do thou mount for supreme authority. Let the Sādhya and the Āptya gods mount thee with the Pañkti metre, the Triṇava Stoma, the Çākvara Sāman; after them do thou mount for kingship, great kingship, suzerainty, supremacy, and pre-eminence';

he should make him mount the throne. When he is seated on the throne the king-makers should say 'The Kṣatriya if not proclaimed cannot show his strength; let us proclaim him'. 'Be it so' (they reply). Him the king-makers proclaim (saying)

'Him do ye proclaim, O men, as overlord and overlordship, as paramount ruler and father of paramount rulers, as self ruler and self rule, as sovereign and sovereignty, as supreme lord and supreme authority, as

[1] See above AB. viii. 12. The slight variant is presumably deliberate, two clauses being inverted in order. Weber (*Rājasūya*, p. 116) points out that the number of materials of the ointment is much less (cf. AB. viii. 5) than the number (17) of the Yajus ritual, and sees in this a sign of the old character of the simple *punarabhiṣeka* at least (*ibid.* p. 113).

king and father of kings. The lordly power hath been born, the Kṣatriya hath been born, the suzerain of all creation hath been born, the eater[2] of the folk hath been born, the slayer of foes hath been born, the guardian of the Brahmans hath been born, the guardian of the law hath been born.'

When he has been proclaimed one knowing thus, being about to anoint him, should address him with this verse

viii. 18 (xxxix. 4).

'Varuna[1] within the waters
Hath sat him down, preserving order,
For overlordship, for paramount rule, for self rule, for sovereignty, for supreme authority, for kingship, for great kingship, for suzerainty, for supremacy, for pre-eminence, the wise one.'

Him when seated on the throne one who knows thus standing in front, facing west, anoints through a branch of Udumbara, dry but with leaves, and a golden strainer, to the accompaniment of the triplet 'These waters are most auspicious', the Yajus '(On the instigation) of the god thee', and the exclamations *bhūḥ*, *bhuvaḥ*, *svar*.

viii. 19 (xxxix. 5).

'In the[1] eastern quarter let the Vasus, the gods, anoint thee with six days with the Pañcaviṅça, and with this triplet and this Yajus and these exclamations, for overlordship.

In the southern quarter let the Rudras, the gods, anoint thee with six days with the Pañcaviṅça, and with this triplet and this Yajus and these exclamations, for paramount rule.

In the western quarter let the Ādityas, the gods, anoint thee with six days with the Pañcaviṅça, and with this triplet and this Yajus and these exclamations, for self rule.

In the northern quarter let the All-gods anoint thee with six days with the Pañcaviṅça, and with this trip nd this Yajus and these exclamations, for sovereignty.

In the upright quarter let the Maruts and Aṅgirases, the gods, anoint thee with six days with the Pañcaviṅça, an d with this triplet and this Yajus and these exclamations, for supreme authority.

In this firm middle established quarter let the Sādhya and the Āptya gods anoint thee with six days with the Pañcaviṅça, and with this triplet and this Yajus and these exclamations, for kingship, for great kingship, for suzerainty, for supremacy, and for pre-eminence.'

[2] For this common description cf. Weber, *Ind. Stud.* x. 8, 14; *Rājasūya*, pp. 66, n. 2, 116, n. 2.

[1] See above AB. viii. 13.

viii. 19. [1] See above AB. viii. 14.

He becomes the supreme authority, as connected with Prajāpati. The Kṣatriya anointed with this great anointing of Indra wins all victories, finds all worlds, attains the superiority, pre-eminence, and supremacy over all kings, and having won overlordship, paramount rule, self rule, supreme authority, kingship, great kingship and suzerainty in the world, self-existing, self-ruling, immortal, in yonder world of heaven having obtained all desires he becomes immortal, whom as a Kṣatriya he anoints with this great anointing of Indra, after adjuring him.

viii. 20 (xxxix. 6). Curds is power in this world; in that he anoints him with curds, verily thus he confers power upon him. Honey is the sap in plants and in trees; in that he anoints with honey, verily thus he confers sap upon him. Ghee is the brilliance of animals; in that he anoints with ghee, verily thus he confers brilliance upon him. Waters are the immortal in the world; in that he anoints with water, thereby he confers immortality upon him. Being anointed he should give gold to the Brahman who anoints; a thousand should he give, a field and quadrupeds; moreover they say 'He should give an uncounted, an unlimited, guerdon; the Kṣatriya is unlimited; (it serves) to attain the unlimited.' Then he places in his hand a bowl of Surā (saying [1])

> 'With thy sweetest, most intoxicating
> Stream be thou purified, O Soma,
> Pressed for Indra to drink.'

He should drink it (saying [2])

> 'That which is left over of the pressed juice, rich in sap
> Which Indra drank mightily
> Here with auspicious mind this of him,
> I partake of Soma, the King.
> To thee, O bull (the Soma) being pressed,
> I offer the pressed juice to drink;
> Rejoice and make thyself glad.'

The Soma drink which is in the Surā is what is drunk by the Kṣatriya when anointed by this great anointing of Indra; not the Surā. Having drunk it he should address it with [3] 'We have drunk the Soma' and 'Be thou propitious to us.' Just as in the world a dear son touches a father or a dear wife a husband pleasantly and auspiciously up to decay,[4] even so Surā or Soma or any other food in the case of a Kṣatriya anointed by the great anointing of Indra touches him auspiciously and pleasantly up to decay.

[1] See above AB. viii. 8.

[2] See above AB. vii. 33 and RV. viii. 45. 22.

[3] RV. viii. 48. 3; x. 87. 10.

[4] Probably until old age, cf. Sāyaṇa's version *dehapātaparyantam*.

viii. 21 (xxxix. 7). With this great anointing of Indra Tura Kāvaṣeya anointed Janamejaya Pārikṣita. Therefore Janamejaya Pārikṣita went round the earth completely, conquering on every side, and offered the horse in sacrifice. Regarding this a sacrificial verse[1] is sung

'At Āsandīvant a horse, grass eating,
Adorned with gold and a yellow garland,
Of dappled hue, was bound
By Janamejaya for the gods.'

With this great anointing of Indra Cyavana Bhārgava anointed Çāryāta Mānava. Therefore Çāryāta Mānava went around the earth completely, conquering on every side, and offered the horse in sacrifice; at the sacrificial session of the gods he was the householder. With the great anointing of Indra Somaçuṣman Vājaratnāyana anointed Çatānīka Sātrājita. Therefore Çatānīka Sātrājita went round the earth completely, conquering on every side, and offered the horse in sacrifice. With the great anointing of Indra Parvata and Nārada anointed Āmbāṣṭhya. Therefore Āmbāṣṭhya went round the earth completely, conquering on every side, and offered the horse in sacrifice. With this great anointing of Indra Parvata and Nārada anointed Yudhāṁçrauṣṭi Augrasainya. Therefore Yudhāṁçrauṣṭi Augrasainya went round the earth completely, conquering on every side, and offered the horse in sacrifice. With this great anointing of Indra Kaçyapa anointed Viçvakarman Bhauvana. Therefore Viçvakarman Bhauvana went round the earth completely, conquering on every side, and offered the horse in sacrifice. The earth sang, they tell[2]

'No man whatsoever ought to give me,
O Viçvakarman Bhauvana, thou hast been fain to give me;
I shall plunge into the middle of the water;
Vain was this thy compact with Kaçyapa.'

With this great anointing of Indra Vasiṣṭha anointed Sudās Paijavana. Therefore Sudās Paijavana went round the earth completely, conquering on every side, and offered the horse in sacrifice. With this great anointing of Indra Saṁvarta Āñgirasa anointed Marutta Āvikṣita. Therefore Marutta Āvikṣita went round the earth completely, conquering on every side, and offered the horse in sacrifice. Regarding this, this verse is sung[3]

[1] See also ÇB. xiii. 5. 4. 2; ÇÇS. xvi. 9. 1, with the reading *abadhnād açvaṁ sāraṅgam*.

[2] Cf. ÇB. xiii. 7. 1. 15 where *manda āsitha* replaces *didāsitha*, *upamaṅkṣyati syā* and *mṛṣaiṣa te saṁgaraḥ Kaçyapāya*; ÇÇS. xvi. 16. 3 has *ā* as in ÇB. and *upamaṅkṣye* but otherwise agrees with AB.

[3] So ÇB. xiii. 5. 4. 6 with *Āvikṣitasyāgniḥ kṣattā*, ÇÇS. xvi. 9. 16 agrees with ÇB. These texts deal with the horse sacrifice. Cf. Oldenberg, ZDMG. xxxvii. 80, 81.

'The Maruts as attendants
Dwelt in the house of Marutta;
Of Āvikṣita Kamapri
The All-gods were the assessors.'

viii. 22 (xxxix. 8). With this great anointing of Indra Udamaya Ātreya anointed Añga. Therefore Añga went round the earth completely, conquering on every side, and offered the horse in sacrifice. He whose limbs were not defective said 'Ten thousands of elephants, ten thousands of female slaves, I offer to thee. O Brahman; invite me to the sacrifice.' Regarding this these verses are sung

'Of the cows for which Udamaya
The Praiyamedhas aided in his sacrificing[1]
Two thousand of the myriads (day by day)
Ātreya gave at the middle (of the offering).
Eight and eighty thousand
White horses, Vairocana,
Side steeds,[2] loosing them,
Gave when his Purohita was sacrificing.
Of those brought from each country,
All daughters of wealthy men,
Ten thousands he gave,
Ātreya, with necklaces on their necks.
Ten thousands of elephants,
Ātreya, having given at Avacatnuka,
Wearied, sought for attendants,[3]
By reason of the gift of Añga, the Brahman.
"A hundred to you, a hundred to you,"
So saying he grew weary;
By saying "A thousand to you"
He got back his breath.'

viii. 23 (xxxix. 9). With this great anointing of Indra Dīrghatamas Māmateya anointed Bharata Dauḥṣanti. Therefore Bharata Dauḥṣanti went round the earth completely, conquering on every side, and offered the horse in sacrifice. Regarding this these verses are sung[1]

[1] This seems to be the sense accepted by Sāyaṇa, Colebrooke, and Weber; assuming the Praiyamedhas to be Ṛṣis, as it seems they were from the other references to their ancestors, as seers of RV. viii. 1–40, &c. Otherwise the more natural way would be to treat them as princes who gave fees, but the plur. is against this.

[2] *prasti* is here as usual of doubtful sense and possibly is more generally merely 'leading horses'; *Vedic Index*, ii. 515.

[3] To give the gifts away.

viii. 23. [1] See ÇB. xiii. 5. 4. 11 *seq.*

'Covered with golden trappings,
Beasts black with white tusks,
As Maṣṇāra Bharata gave,
A hundred and seven myriads.
This is the fire of Bharata Dauḥṣanti
Piled at Sācīguṇa,
At which a thousand Brahmans
Divided cows in myriads.[2]
Eight and seventy did Bharata
Dauḥṣanti on the Yamunā,
On the Gaṅgā for the slayer of Vṛtra he bound
Five and fifty steeds.
A hundred and thirty-three steeds,
The king having bound for the sacrifice,
Dauḥṣanti surpassed all other kings,
In craft, the more crafty.[3]
The great deed of Bharata,
Neither men before or after,
As the sky a man with his hands
The five peoples have not attained it.'

This great anointing of Indra Bṛhaduktha the seer proclaimed to Durmukha, the Pāñcāla. Therefore Durmukha Pāñcāla, being a king,[4] by this knowledge went round the earth completely, conquering on every side. This great consecration of Indra Vāsiṣṭha Sātyahavya proclaimed to Atyarāti Jānaṁtapi. Therefore Atyarāti Jānaṁtapi, though not a king, through his knowledge went round the earth completely, conquering on every side. Vāsiṣṭha Sātyahavya said 'Thou hast conquered entirely the earth on every side: do thou make me great.' Then said Atyarāti Jānaṁtapi 'When I conquer, O Brahman, the Uttara Kurus, then thou wouldst be king of the earth, and I should be thy general.' Vāsiṣṭha Sātyahavya replied 'That is a place of the gods; no mortal man may conquer it. Thou hast been false to me; therefore I take this from thee.'[5] Then Amitratapana Çuṣmiṇa Çaibya, a king, slew Atyarāti Jānaṁtapi, whose strength

[2] *badva* as a hundred *koṭis* is given by Sāyaṇa; *sahasram* is taken by Weber with *gāḥ* and *badvaçaḥ* as 'by flocks', but this makes the number too low.

[3] ÇB. has *Saudyumnir atyaṣṭhād anyān amāyān* and Aufrecht suggests *amāyino* as better sense and metre. Weber (*Ind. Stud.* ix. 346) reads *'māyān*.

[4] *rājā* is read by Sāyaṇa, but the parallelism below certainly suggests *'rājā*, as taken by Haug.

[5] *ā ta* (i. e. *te*) must of course be read; Weber, *Rājasūya*, p. 118, n. *adrukṣaḥ* is an odd form, for which Liebich (*Pāṇini*, p. 77) would restore *adhrukṣaḥ*, but Whitney (*Sansk. Gramm.* § 920 *f*) accepts the form.

had been taken away and who had lost his power. Therefore one should not play false with a Brahman who knows thus and has done thus (thinking) 'Let me not loose my kingdom,[6] nor let breath forsake me.'

ADHYĀYA V

The Purohitaship.

viii. 24 (xl. 1). Now as to the Purohitaship. The gods eat not the food of a king without a Purohita. Therefore a king when about to sacrifice should select as Purohita a Brahman (wishing) 'May the gods eat my food.' The king in appointing a Purohita takes out the fires that lead to heaven. The Purohita is the Āhavanīya, his wife the Gārhapatya, his son the Anvāhāryapacana. What he does to the Purohita, verily thus he offers in the Āhavanīya; what he does to his wife, verily thus he offers in the Gārhapatya; what he does to his son, verily thus he offers in the Anvāhāryapacana. They, being appeased in body, having received the offerings and propitiated, carry him to the world of heaven, to the lordly power, might, the kingdom, and the people. They, if not appeased in body, not having received the offering and not being propitiated, repel him from the world of heaven, from the lordly power, might, the kingdom, and the people. The Purohita is Agni Vaiçvānara, possessed of five missiles; in his speech is one missile, in his feet one, in his skin one, in his heart one, in his organ one. With these flaming and blazing he approaches the king. In that he says 'Where, O blessed one, hast thou been dwelling? Bring ye grass for him', thereby he appeases that missile of his that is in his speech. In that they bring to him water for the feet, thereby he appeases that missile of his that is in his feet. In that they adorn him, thereby he appeases that missile of his that is in his skin. In that they delight him, thereby he appeases that missile of his that is in his heart. In that he dwells unimpeded in his dwelling, thereby he appeases that missile of his which is in his organ. He, having been appeased in his body, and having received offering and being delighted, carries him to the world of heaven, the lordly power, might, the kingdom, and the people. He also, if not appeased in body, and not offered to and delighted, repels him from the world of heaven, from the lordly power, might, the kingdom, and the people.

viii. 25 (xl. 2.) The Purohita is Agni Vaiçvānara with five missiles; with these he keeps enveloping the king as the ocean the earth. His kingship perishes not in its youth, life leaves him not before his time, up to old age

[6] For *avapadyeyam* cf. AB. viii. 15, n. 1. The constr. with *ned* is unparalleled. See Delbrück, *Altind. Synt.* p. 545. *jahat* may be subj. or inj.; *ibid.* p. 359.

he lives, he lives a full life, he dies not again,[1] who has for Purohita to guard the kingdom a Brahman with this knowledge.[2]

By the lordly power he conquereth the lordly power,
By might he attaineth might,
Who hath for Purohita to guard the kingdom
A Brahman with this knowledge,
For him are his people in harmony,
With one aspect and one mind,
Who hath for Purohita to guard the kingdom
A Brahman with this knowledge.

viii. 26 (xl. 3). This is also declared by a seer[1]

'The king all hostilities
With his onset, his might, doth overcome',

Hostilities are the rivals who vie with and hate him; verily thus he overcomes them with his onset and his might.

'Who supporteth Bṛhaspati in comfort',

Bṛhaspati is the Purohita of the gods; analogues of him are the other Purohitas of human kings. In that he says 'Who supporteth Bṛhaspati in comfort', verily he says in effect 'Who supporteth a Purohita in comfort'.

'Who treateth him kindly, and maketh welcome the first sharer',

(he says); verily thus he mentions honour for him.

'He dwelleth in ease in his own abode'[2]

(he says); the abode is the house; verily thus he dwells at ease in his own house.

'For him fare is ever plentiful'

(he says); fare is food; verily thus for him food is ever full of strength.

'To him the peoples of themselves pay homage'

(he says); the peoples are the kingdoms; verily thus spontaneously the kingdoms pay him homage.

'In whose reign the Brahman goeth first',

(he says); verily thus he refers to the Purohita.

'Unsurpassed he winneth wealths'[3]

[1] This is the only occurrence of the idea in AB. Cf. Lévi, *La doctrine du sacrifice*, pp. 96 *seq.* *ayuvamāri* (not *ayuvam*) is clearly right. Weber has 'free from death of young men'.

[2] The true character of the passage now becomes distinct: as below in AB. viii. 27. 2 and 3.

viii. 26. [1] RV. iv. 50. 7.

[2] RV. iv. 50. 8.

[3] RV. iv. 50. 9.

Wealths are kingdoms; them he wins unsurpassed.

'Of his foe as of his kin'

(he says); the foe are the rivals that vie with and hate him; them he conquers unsurpassed. In that he says

'Who maketh wide room for him that seeketh aid,'

verily he says in effect 'Who maketh riches for the poor.'

'The king for the Brahman, him the gods aid',

(he says); verily thus he refers to the Purohita.

viii. 27 (xl. 4). He who knows the three Purohitas and the three appointers, that Brahman is to be made Purohita. He should say for the Purohitaship

> 'Agni is the Purohita, the earth the appointer; Vāyu is the Purohita, the atmosphere the appointer; Āditya is the Purohita, the sky the appointer.'

He who knows this is chosen as Purohita, he who does not know this is rejected.

A king is the friend of him,
He repulseth the foe
Who hath for his Purohita to guard the kingdom
A Brahman with this knowledge.
By the lordly power he conquereth the lordly power,
By might he attaineth might
Who hath for his Purohita to guard the kingdom
A Brahman with this knowledge.
For him are his people in harmony,
With one aspect and one mind,
Who hath for his Purohita to guard the kingdom
A Brahman with this knowledge.

Bhūḥ, bhuvaḥ, svar, om.[1]

I am that, thou art this; thou art this, I am that. I am sky, thou art earth. I am the Sāman, thou the Ṛc. Let us two unite. Save us from great danger.[2]

Thou art the body; protect my body.
The plants whose king is Soma,
Manifold, with a hundred forms,
In this seat do ye to me

[1] The ceremony of selection is here described on the exact lines of a marriage (Weber, *Ind. Stud.* v. 216, 332, 348, 368; Whitney on AV. xiv. 2. 71) to which *saṁvahāvahai* refers, though Sāyaṇa does not recognize the force, and endeavours to construe it with *purāṇi* as villages in the kingdom. Weber (*Ind. Stud.* x. 160) suggests *tāv ehi*; *saṁvivahāvahai* is possible, but the text may mean 'let us fare together'; cf. Oldenberg, *Rel. des Veda*, p. 376.

[2] *purāṇi* appears corrupt (*pur* is the old form); possibly it might be an irregular form, 'let me escape from', but, as no special danger is mentioned, it may be an old error for *pārayā ṇo* (glossed *asmān*).

Accord unfailing protection.[2]
The plants whose king is Soma,
Which are scattered over the earth,
In this seat do ye to me
Accord unfailing protection.
In this kingdom I make prosperity to dwell,
Then I behold the waters divine.[3]
I purify my right foot; I place power in this kingdom.
I purify my left foot; I increase power in this kingdom.
First one, then another, I purify my two feet,
O gods, for the protection of the kingdom, to win security from danger.
Let the waters for the foot-washing burn away my foe.

viii. 28 (xl. 5). Now comes the dying round the holy power. He who knows the dying round the holy power, round him the rivals that vie with and hate him die. He who blows here is the holy power; round him die these five deities, the lightning, the rain, the moon, the sun, the fire. The lightning after lightening enters into the rain; it is concealed; then men do not perceive it. When a man dies, then he is concealed, then men do not perceive him. He should say at the death of the lightning 'Let my enemy die, let him be concealed, may they not perceive him.' Swiftly they perceive him not. The rain having rained enters into the moon; it is concealed; then men do not perceive it. When a man dies, then he is concealed, then men do not perceive him. He should say at the death of the rain 'Let my enemy die, let him be concealed, may they not perceive him.' Swiftly they perceive him not. The moon at the conjunction enters into the sun; it is concealed; men do not perceive it. When a man dies, then he is concealed, then men do not perceive him. He should say at the death of the moon 'Let my enemy die, let him be concealed, may they not perceive him.' Swiftly they perceive him not. The sun on setting enters into the fire; it is concealed; men do not perceive it.[1] When a man dies, then he is concealed, then men do not perceive him. He should say at the death of the sun 'Let my enemy die, let him be concealed, may they not perceive him.' Swiftly they perceive him not. The fire, breathing forth, enters into the wind; it is concealed; men do not perceive it. When a man dies, then he is concealed, then men do not perceive him. He should say at the death of the fire 'Let my enemy die, let him be concealed, may they not perceive him.' Swiftly they perceive him not. Thence are these deities born again; from the wind is born the fire, for from breath it is

[2] *rājadattaviṣṭarābhimantraṇam* according to Sāyaṇa.

[3] This is used for the water brought up for the ceremony of feet washing which is accompanied by the following Mantras.

[1] Cf. TB. ii. 1. 2. 9.

born, being kindled by strength. Having seen it he should say 'Let the fire be born; let not my enemy be born; far hence may he hasten[2] away.' Far hence he hastens away. From the fire is the sun born; having seen it he should say 'Let the sun be born; let not my enemy be born; far hence may he hasten away.' Far hence he hastens away. From the sun is the moon born. Having seen it he should say 'Let the moon be born; let not my enemy be born; far hence may he hasten away.' Far hence he hastens away. From the moon is rain born. Having seen it he should say 'Let the rain be born; let not my enemy be born; far hence may he hasten away.' Far hence he hastens away. This is the dying round the holy power. This dying round the holy power Maitreya Kauṣārava proclaimed to Sutvan Kairiçi Bhārgāyaṇa the king. Round him died five kings; then Sutvan attained greatness. His vow is 'One should not sit down before the foe; if he think him to be standing, he should stand also. Nor should he lie down before the foe; if he think him to be sitting he should sit also. Nor should he go to sleep before the foe; if he think him awake, he should keep awake also. Even if his enemy has a head of stone,[3] swiftly he lays him low.'

[2] These forms are of doubtful value and reality: cf. *jāgriyāt* here and above AB. viii. 15, n. 1. Liebich (*Pāṇini*, p. 76) takes them as 3rd plural of the 3rd class of *hi* and as act. with *parā* adverbial.

[3] A helmet like stone is Sāyaṇa's version, but this seems needless; cf. Colebrooke, *Essays*, ii. 41.

TRANSLATION OF THE

KAUṢĪTAKI BRĀHMAṆA

ADHYĀYA I

The Establishing of the Fires.

i. 1. In[1] this world both the gods and men were. The gods going to the world of heaven said to Agni 'Be thou for us the overseer of this world.' To them replied Agni 'But, since I am he among you whose contact is most dangerous, and men do not pay honour (to me), how will that become yours which is among men?' The gods said 'The dread forms of thee as such we will deposit apart, and then wilt thou be here for man with that form of thine which is auspicious, helpful, and worthy of sacrifice.' Then in the waters they placed (his form as) blowing, in the wind (his form as) purifying, in the sun (his form as) bright. Then with his auspicious, helpful, and sacrificial form he burned here for men. These indeed are the forms of Agni. In that he offers to these deities, then Agni becomes delighted with his limbs and with his forms. These are three; three indeed are these worlds; verily thus he obtains these worlds. The full-moon offering is the model of the first (sacrifice), the new-moon offering of the second; thereby does he commence the new- and full-moon (offerings). The invitatory and offering verses[2] of the first contain (the words) 'praise' and 'bearer of the oblation'; that is the form of the invitatory and invoking verses. Those of the second[3] have (the word) 'Agni' twice, for he offers to two Agnis. The third has seventeen Sāmidhenī verses; the Iṣṭi and

[1] In i. 1-2 the establishing of the three sacrificial fires is very briefly dealt with. In the Sūtras, though the establishing is a necessary preliminary to any rite of the Çrauta ritual, the establishing does not come first in order but is relegated to the treatment of the new- and full-moon sacrifices which, as is also here stated, serve as the groundwork or model (*tantra*) of all Iṣṭis. For the ritual see ĀÇS. ii. 1. 9 *seq.*; ÇÇS. ii. 1 *seq.*; BÇS. ii. 12-20; MÇS. i. 5. 15; ĀpÇS. v. 1 *seq.*; KÇS. iv. 7-10; LÇS. iv. 9. 10 *seq.*; 12. 6. *seq.*; *Vait.* v, vi. The point here dealt with is the making of offerings to the three forms of Agni; there is no parallel in AB., but cf. KS. vii. 10; viii. 1, 3-5, 10; MS. i. 6; TB. i. 1. 2-10; ÇB. ii. 2. 1. 6 *seq.* See Hillebrandt, *Rituallitteratur*, § 59; Eggeling, SBE. xii. 274, 275.

[2] I. e. the Yājyā and Puronuvākyā for the offering to Agni Sviṣṭakṛt. The verses referred to are RV. v. 14. 3 and iv. 8. 5, which contain *īḍate* and *havyāya voḍhave* and *havyadātibhiḥ*.

[3] I. e. the verses used are RV. i. 12. 2 and 6, which both have the word Agni twice.

Paçubandha offerings have seventeen Sāmidhenī verses;[4] therefore he obtains the Iṣṭi and Paçubandha offerings. The offerings of the butter[5] portions have (the word) 'be'; (with the desire) 'Let me be', he establishes the fires; 'May I be' he desires. He, even if being very contemptible as it were he establishes the fires, quickly prospers; he attains enjoyableness, who makes them possessed of (the word) 'be'. The invitatory and offering verses are Virāj verses;[6] prosperity and proper food are the Virāj, (and so they serve) for the winning of the Virāj as prosperity and proper food. These are Gāyatrī verses;[7] Agni is connected with the Gāyatrī and has the Gāyatrī for his metre; verily thus with his own metre he establishes the fires. They are uttered inaudibly; the establishing of the fires is an outpouring of seed; inaudibly is seed outpoured. They are appropriate what in the sacrifice is appropriate, that is perfect; (so they serve) for the perfection of the sacrifice. Twelve (cows) should he give; the year has twelve months; verily (they serve) to make up the year. He gives a horse as thirteenth, to make up the thirteenth month.

i. 2. The gods and the Asuras were in conflict over[1] these worlds. From them Agni departed, and entered the seasons. The gods, having been victorious and having slain the Asuras, sought for him; Yama and Varuṇa discerned him. Him (the gods) invited, him they instructed, to him they offered a boon. He chose this as a boon, '(Give) me the fore-offerings and the after-offerings for my own, and the ghee of the waters and the male of plants.' Therefore they say 'Agni's are the fore-offerings and the after-offerings; Agni's is the butter.' Then indeed did the gods prosper, the Asuras were defeated. He prospers himself, his foe is defeated, who knows thus.

i. 3. They[1] say, 'In which season should he re-establish (the fires)?' 'In

[4] At the new- and full-moon sacrifices there are used 15, Hillebrandt, *Neu- und Vollmondsopfer*, pp. 74–79; 17 at the animal sacrifice, Schwab, *Das altindische Thieropfer*, pp. 82, 88. For 17 as the characteristic number as an Iṣṭi see ÇB. i. 6. 2. 12.

[5] RV. v. 18. 14 which has *asi* and i. 91. 9 which has *santi*. We must read *yadi ha* and *svaiṣāvīra iva*; Vināyaka has *svaiṣā vīra* but this is nonsense; see Weber, *Ind. Stud.* i. 228; x. 158, n. 1; Keith, JRAS. 1915, p. 501.

[6] These are RV. vii. 1. 8 and 18; see ÇB. i. 6. 2. 12.

[7] I. e. the other verses used are in the Gāyatrī metre; cf. ÇB. ii. 2. 1. 17.

[1] The locative is one of what is fought for, as with *spṛdh*, AB. vi. 34. 2; Delbrück, *Altind. Synt.* p. 119. The construction appears in Sanskrit in the well-known example *carmaṇi dvīpinaṁ hanti dantayor hanti kuñjaram* (*Kāçikā* on Pāṇini, ii. 3. 36) which need not be traced to Pāli as Kielhorn (JRAS. 1898, p. 19) was inclined to do.

i. 3. [1] This chapter with i. 4 and 5 deals briefly with the Punarādheya of the fires; there is nothing parallel in AB., but cf. TS. i. 5. 1 *seq.*; KS. viii. 14–ix. 8; KapS. viii. 2–6; MS. i. 7. 1–5; ÇB. ii. 2. 3. 2–6. For the ritual see ĀÇS. ii. 8. 4 *seq.*; ÇÇS. ii. 5. 1; BÇS. iii. 1–3; MÇS. i. 6. 5; v. 1. 2. 6 *seq.*; ĀpÇS. v. 26; KÇS. iv. 11; *Vait.* viii. 8; Hillebrandt, *Rituallitteratur*, § 60.

the rains' some say; in the rains are all desires; verily (it serves) to obtain all desires. In the middle of the rains, with regard to the Nakṣatra, the Punarvasūs, he should re-establish (the fires) (saying) 'May riches and wealth again come to me.' Thus (it serves) for the winning of a repeated desire. In this period (the new moon) does not in the first half (of the month) come into conjunction with the Punarvasūs. On the new moon which follows after (full moon) in the Aṣāḍhās[2] should he re-establish; it is in conjunction with the Punarvasūs. The desire is obtained that is in the new moon, there is obtained that in the rains, there is obtained that in the Punarvasūs; therefore on that day should he re-establish. The cake is offered on five potsherds;[3] the Pañkti has five feet; the sacrifice is fivefold; (so it serves) to obtain the sacrifice.

i. 4. With discriminations[1] he offers the fore-offerings and the after-offerings; the fore-offerings and the after-offerings are the seasons; thus does he gather him from the seasons. The discriminations are the head words of these Ṛcs, 'O Agni, come for enjoyment'; 'Agni we choose as messenger'; 'By Agni Agni is kindled'; 'May Agni smite the foes'; 'Of Agni the praise we meditate'; 'To Agni that mortal who doth service.' They are six; the seasons are six; verily from the seasons for a second time he gathers him. The last fore-offering and after-offering are unaltered. Thus he does not depart from the fore-offerings and the after-offerings. The first butter-portion is connected with the slaying of Vṛtra;[2] verily (it serves) for the destroying of the evil one. Thus he does not depart from the model of the full-moon sacrifice. 'He should make the first (butter-portion) for Agni, the wise, (saying) "Agni do ye awaken with the praise",'[3] some say, 'the

[2] The date fixed is a refinement on that of TS. and ÇB. ii. 1. 2. 10 which prescribe merely the Punarvasūs. BÇS. iii. 1 fixes the date as on the new moon in the Punarvasūs preceding the full moon in the Aṣāḍhās, a variance in view possibly because of the duplicate nature of the Nakṣatra Aṣāḍhās as the 18th and 19th Nakṣatras, while Punarvasūs is the fifth. Cf. Caland, *Ueber das rituelle Sūtra des Baudhāyana*, pp. 36, 37.

[3] This refers to the fact that in place of the three Iṣṭis of i. 1 a cake is offered to Agni on five Kapālas; the verses of the offering are in Pañkti metre, viz. RV. iv. 10. 2 and 4, and for the Sviṣṭakṛt offering, iv. 10. 4 and 1.

[1] The point is that in the case of the first four fore-offerings and the first two after-offerings the normal forms are changed by the addition, after the word denoting the object of offering, of a case of the word Agni; the other two are left unaltered. According to Eggeling (SBE. xii. 317, n. 4) and Hillebrandt, *vibhaktayaḥ* directly denote the 'cases' of the word Agni, but this is not, it seems, precisely the sense, but rather (cf. TS. i. 5. 2. 2) they are 'discriminations' between the ordinary forms of the fore- and after-offerings. The sense 'cases' cannot here be regarded as natural. The verses cited are RV. vi. 16. 10; i. 4. 1; 12. 6; vi. 16. 34; v. 13. 2; vi. 14. 1. Cf. ZDMG. xxxvii. 25.

[2] Because it has the words (RV. vi. 16. 34) *Agnir vṛtrāṇi jañghanat*; see Hillebrandt, *Neu- und Vollmondsopfer*, pp. 102 *seq.*

[3] RV. v. 14. 1. So ÇB. ii. 2. 3. 21.

fire of him who removes the fire is asleep as it were, verily so does he again awaken it.' But that connected with the slaying of Vṛtra is the approved one. 'O Agni, thou purifiest lives'[4] is the invitatory verse of the second (butter-portion). 'Thou purifiest' is the symbol of Soma, for the sacrificial offering is wholly for Agni; in that he makes mention of the purifying, so he departs not from the butter-portion for Soma. The offering and the invitatory verses are Padapañktis; the Pañkti has five feet; the sacrifice is fivefold; verily (they serve) to obtain the sacrifice.

i. 5. (The verses) are intertwined[1] (on the ground that) 'Intertwined as it were these breaths support the self.' The whole (offering) is performed including the kindling verses in a low tone up to the first two after-offerings. After the (word) butter the discriminations are interwoven; further all desires are in the discriminations; therefore they are uttered in a low tone, for the obtaining of all desires. Aloud he sacrifices with the last after-offering, aloud he utters the Sūktavāka and the Çaṁyorvāka.[2] Just as a man makes to appear what is lost (saying) 'I have found', so he makes to appear his desires (saying) 'I have obtained.' Some, however, perform three (parts) in a low tone, the discriminations, the second butter-portion, and the oblation (on the ground that), 'So much is there which is adventitious.'[3] The (offering) is both uttered in a low tone and uttered aloud;[4] Agni has two forms, the expressly declared and that which is not expressly declared; thereby he obtains that (characteristic) of him. Some make it with Agni all through, but that he should not do. The sacrificial fee is a bad chariot, resown, with an old wrapper, renewed, a draft ox, or gold, for this is a renewed ceremony. The second (offering) is for Aditi;[5] Aditi is a support; verily (it serves) for support.

[4] RV. ix. 66. 19. This is given as an alternative in ÇB. ii. 2. 3. 22. Normally the second Ājyabhāga is offered to Soma, and in this indirect way the fact is here reflected. Cf. Hillebrandt, *op. cit.* pp. 106, 107; Eggeling, SBE. xii. 318 *seq.*

[1] For the intertwining see ÇÇS. ii. 5. 18 where RV. iv. 10. 1 and 3 are for the oblation itself, and iv. 10. 2 and 4 for the Sviṣṭakṛt.

[2] See Hillebrandt, *Neu- und Vollmondsopfer*, pp. 142 *seq.*, 147 *seq.*

[3] The reading of both edd. *etāvadhyāgantu* is clearly a blunder for *etāvad dhy āgantu*, which, indeed, is probably read by M., though in a Grantha MS. before *y* consonants like *dh* are normally doubted. But *āgantu* is uncertain in sense, and a Sūtra word like others in this Brāhmaṇa. The simplest view is to take the reference as to the new matter of this rite, as opposed to the ordinary form, which does comprise precisely the three in question.

[4] This must be the sense here of *niruktā* as contrasted with *upāṅçu*. Cf. KB. iii. 6.

[5] The offering for Aditi breaks the predominance of Agni; it is put in slightly different places in the different Sūtras.

ADHYĀYA II

The Agnihotra.

ii. 1. In[1] that (there is performed) the Agnihotra the cauldron here is heated. Now he who makes heat yonder is yonder cauldron; verily him thus he delights. He offers in the evening and in the morning, to Agni in the evening, to Sūrya in the morning; the day is connected with Sūrya, the night with Agni; verily thus at the beginning he delights day and night. With milk should he offer; milk is the sap of all the plants; verily so with all kinds of sap he delights the fires. As to this they say: 'He may offer any kind of food; all this is Agni's food; so with their own food he delights the fires. Having put (it) over the Gārhapatya, he should offer in the Āhavanīya; the Gārhapatya is the fire for cooking, the Āhavanīya that for offering; therefore having put (it) over the Gārhapatya, he should offer in the Āhavanīya. He makes the embers have their ends apart;[2] verily thus he severs these two worlds; therefore these two worlds though being together are as it were separate. Now in that he lights up (the fire) after putting (the milk) over it, thus he makes it cooked. In that he brings up the waters, and the waters are complete,[3] all the oblations become complete; verily (they serve) to complete the oblation. In that a second time he lights up, verily thus he cooks the waters. Thrice he sets down the vessel for the offering and removes it northwards,[4] to make a threefold characteristic, for threefold is the performance for the gods. Without spilling[5] should he take (it); thus the sacrificer is not likely to fall into ruin. Then with the poking-stick he touches the embers

[1] The second Adhyāya deals with the Agnihotra, and has a vague parallel in AB. v. 26–31; cf. for the Agnihotra, and especially the Agnyupasthāna which is connected with it, TS. i. 5. 5 *seq.*; KS. vi. 9 *seq.*; KapS. iv. 8; MS. i. 5. 1 *seq.*; ÇB. ii. 2. 3. 1 *seq.* For the ritual see ĀÇS. ii. 2–5; ÇÇS. ii. 7–12; BÇS. iii. 4–9; MÇS. i. 6. 1–3; ĀpÇS. vi; *Vait.* vii; Hillebrandt, *Rituallitteratur*, § 61.

[2] *vyanīān* (which is read *pr. m.* in M., but with a correction by a later hand to *dvy°*) is Caland's necessary correction of Lindner's text; see VOJ. xxiii. 61; so the Ānand ed.; cf. ĀpÇS. vi. 5. 6; and often in BÇS. e.g. iii. 5.

[3] Lindner's text must be corrected, and the insertion of *kṛtsnāḥ* before *kṛtsnāni* is easy and gives fairly good sense. Caland (VOJ. xxiii. 62) suggests omitting *sarvāṇi* (as a gloss) and replacing it by *kṛtsnāni*, which is very good sense but a less easy corruption. M. has *avadyotayati*.

[4] *udag* is probably not compounded with *homīyam* which must refer to the vessel in which the oblation is carried.

[5] *ucchindan* is adopted by Lindner as explaining the variant readings of the other MSS. (*chinnann iva*; *chindant iva* (M. *chinnant* corrected to *chindant*)); it is plainly correct, and the sense must be as rendered. The Ānand. has ridiculously *anucchinnaṁ nivaharet*.

on the south side (saying) 'Homage to the gods!', for the gods are not above the paying of homage. He should arrange the embers broadly; thus not even the outermost (of his offering) is wasted. Four times should he ladle out; fourfold is all this (universe); verily (it serves) for the obtaining of all this. Five times should he ladle out; the sacrifice is fivefold; verily (it serves) to obtain the sacrifice.

ii. 2. The settings down in the Agnihotra must be explained. Having ladled out he sets down to the north of the Gārhapatya; thus he obtains this world. In the Āhavanīya (he sets down) for the second time when about to offer; thus he obtains the world of the atmosphere. After offering (he sets down) for the third time; thus he obtains yonder world. He puts on a kindling stick of *Butea frondosa*; the *Butea frondosa* is Soma; this is the first Soma libation. It is a span in measure, for these breaths are a span over[1] the body. Making two finger breadths of the kindling stick jut over and making a knot as it were,[2] he offers over it; in two finger breadths of the mouth here food is placed. When it smokes, in it should he offer for one who desires a village; when it flames, for one who desires radiance; in the embers, for one who desires cattle. But the established practice is after putting it on, for then (they say)[3] all these desires are obtained. Having offered the two libations, he mutters 'May the blessing of the sacrifice as successful be successful for me.' The blessing of the sacrifice as successful belongs to the sacrificer. He should offer the libations over one another; verily thus he obtains the worlds of heaven over one another. He touches the embers with the base of the offering ladle; verily thus he places the sacrificer in the world of heaven. Twice he holds out the offering ladle to the north; verily thus having pleased Rudra in his own quarter he lets (him) go. Therefore one should not stand to the north of the offering as it is made, lest he be in the vicinity of this dread god. In the evening he rubs it on the north side as it points west; thus he makes the sun to set. In the morning (he rubs it) on the south side as it points upwards; thus he leads upwards the sun. That which he rubs the first time he smears on the mat; thereby he delights the plants; in that

[1] *adhi*, the reading of M., seems the only possible one to be accepted. With *abhi* the acc. sing. would be inevitable. The Ānand. ed. has *abhiprāṇād*, a mere error.

[2] The *samidh* above referred to must be meant: it is therefore impossible to render *samidhaḥ* as plural, as apparently it is taken by PW. and MW. The idea is that in some way the two finger breadths of the *samidh* are made into an outline of a human mouth, as the next words clearly prove. The Ānand. ed. has *atiritya*.

[3] The rule laid down is that the offering should be made on the *samidh* as soon as it is put on, and the reason is evidently given here by *iti*, though no word of quotation of opinion is included. The term *abhyādhā* refers to the laying of the *samidh* on the fire, not to the placing of the offering on the *samidh*.

(he rubs) the second time, he lays down his outstretched hand to the south of the mat; thereby he delights the fathers. In that he twice eats by means of his forefinger, with the first he delights foetuses; therefore though not eating, foetuses draw breath; with the second birds; therefore birds eat very multifarious[4] matter as it were, but exude what is white as it were. In that he eats with the offering ladle, thereby he delights what has been and what will be. In that he licks the offering ladle, thereby he delights the serpents, the god folk. In that he cleanses the offering ladle, thereby he delights the Rakṣases, the god folk. In that he pours forth the waters to east and north,[5] thereby he delights the Gandharvas and the Apsarases. In that he directs the offering ladle to east and north,[5] verily thus he places Rudra in his own quarter; thus with the Agnihotra he delights all creatures.

ii. 3. 'In the Āhavanīya only should he offer' some say, but he should offer in all, for they are established for the offering. Four (are offered) in the Gārhapatya, four in the Anvāhāryapacana, two in the Āhavanīya; these make up ten;[1] the Virāj consists of series of ten; the Virāj is prosperity and proper food; (they serve) for obtaining the Virāj as prosperity and proper food. He who offers the Agnihotra with the Virāj thus included obtains all desires.

ii. 4. In that, after offering, he pays reverence to the fires, verily thus having given pleasure, at the end he declares his purpose among the gods. In that also he touches the calf, therefore there is the hymn of Vātsaprī;[1] thus cattle are not liable to stray away from the sacrificer. In that he releases his vow, after sipping water, verily in the waters he places the vow; they guard his vow until his next offering.

ii. 5. In[1] that when about to go on a journey or having gone on a journey he pays reverence to the fires, this is an address to the deity, in

[4] The reading *kiṁ ca kiṁ cid iva*, which is also in M., is open to grave suspicion of the duplication of *kiṁ ca*. *prasrāpayanti* is clearly to be read, as *prasrāvayanti* is an easy corruption of it. Cf. however AB. vi. 16: *kim iva ca vai kim iva ca reto vikriyate*. *sarpadevajanān* and *rakṣodevajanān* seem best taken as appositive, not Dvandva, compounds.

[5] The reading of M. *prācīr udīcīr* and below *prācīm udīcīm* seems to deserve preference over the *prāgudīcīr prāgudīcīm* of the ordinary MSS. In the latter case we have been only told above *udīcīm*, but it is now rendered more precise to accord with the general view of the north-east as Rudra's quarter. The compound is found in the Sūtras only, sometimes as in MÇS. i. 1. 1. 12 with variants as here (Wackernagel, *Altind. Gramm.* II. i. 171).

[1] ÇB. ii. 3. 1. 18 has a quite different series of ten to make up the Virāj.

ii. 4. [1] The play on *vatsaṁ spṛçati* and *Vātsapram* is quite untranslatable. The Vātsapra is RV. x. 45.

ii. 5. [1] For this rite see ÇÇS. ii. 14. 1 *seq.*; MÇS. i. 6. 3. 1 *seq.*; ĀpÇS. vi. 24. 1 *seq.* The Mantras of the rite are in TS. i. 5. 10. 1; VS. i. 5, 6; ÇB. ii. 4. 4. 3 *seq.* AB. vii. 12 is only vaguely similar; cf. ĀÇS. ii. 5. 1 *seq.*

that there is a going out.[2] Verily also thus he confides himself to the fires, and those that follow after him.

ii. 6. In that he causes the fires to mount on the two Aranis,[1] and the two Aranis are a chariot of the gods, verily he causes them to mount on a chariot of the gods, and he with this chariot of the gods attains in safety the world of heaven. In that also he repeatedly churns out (the fire), thereby verily by him is the re-establishment (of the fires) obtained.

ii. 7. All the joys that are in food, in drink, in union, verily these are made, together, without break, from the night. For them the sieve is the night; whatever joys there are are all born of food. The gods said 'How now shall we accept these joys from one like ourselves?' They pushed upwards the sap of the waters; it became the plants and the trees. They pushed upwards the sap of the plants and the trees; it became fruit. They pushed upwards the sap of fruit; it became food. They pushed upwards the sap of food; it became seed. They pushed upwards the sap of food; it became man. Man here, in that he breathes out or breathes in, does not say by means of expiration or inspiration, 'Thus have I breathed out or breathed in'; by speech only does he say this. Thus expiration and inspiration enter into speech, and become composed of speech. Again, in that he sees with the eye, he does not say by means of the eye, 'Thus have I seen'; by speech only does he say this. Thus the eye enters into speech, and becomes composed of speech. Again, in that he hears with the ear, he does not say by means of the ear, 'Thus have I heard'; by speech only does he say this. Thus the ear enters into speech, and becomes composed of speech. Again, in that he resolves with the mind, he does not say by means of the mind, 'Thus have I resolved'; by speech only does he say this. Thus mind enters into speech, and becomes composed of speech. Again, in that he touches with his limbs something pleasant or unpleasant to lie upon, he does not say by means of the limbs, 'Thus have I touched what is pleasant or unpleasant to lie upon'; by speech only does he say this. Thus the whole self enters into speech, and becomes composed of speech. That is set forth in a Ṛc,[1] 'Not without Indra is any form made pure'; Indra is speech; for not without speech is any form made pure. He offers in the evening (saying),[2]

ii. 8. 'The light is Agni, Agni is the light.' Him that is light he calls 'Light'; he speaks the truth; his self here, being composed of speech, becomes composed of truth; the gods also are composed of truth. Again,

[2] This seems the sense of the curious neuter *utkāçam*.

[1] Cf. AB. vii. 7; ÇÇS. ii. 17. 1 *seq.*

ii. 7. [1] RV. ix. 69. 6; *Nir.* vii. 2.

[2] ÇÇS. ii. 9. 1; ĀÇS. ii. 3. 16.

he offers with 'Hail!' This offering of him of true offering the gods accept. At the head of night he speaks truth; if indeed even henceforth he speaks falsely, still truth is uttered by him,[1] for at the head of night he speaks truth. He offers in the morning (saying) 'The light is the sun, the sun is the light.' Him that is light he calls light; he speaks the truth; his self here, being composed of speech, becomes composed of truth; the gods also are composed of truth. Again, he offers with 'Hail!' This offering of him of true offering the gods accept. At the head of day he speaks truth; if indeed even henceforth he speaks falsely, still truth is uttered by him, for at the head of day he speaks truth. The fire here offers itself in the rising sun; yonder sun, when setting, offers itself in the fire at evening; the night also (offers itself) in day, the day in night; the expiration also offers in inspiration, the inspiration in expiration. These six sacrifice themselves, each in the other; he who knows these six in the sacrificer, by him even if he sacrifices not is offering made; and if he does sacrifice twice is offering made by him who knows thus. If indeed even from a very small portion,[2] knowing thus, he offers the Agnihotra, these two offerings of his the gods accept, and he whose (offerings) the gods once eat, from that time he is immortal. Composed of truth and immortality does he become who knows thus. Just as is the offering of a man who has faith as his deity,[3] who speaks the truth, and is full of fervour, such is the offering of him who, knowing thus, offers the Agnihotra. Therefore (they say) one knowing thus should offer the Agnihotra.

ii. 9. 'Should[1] the offering be made when the sun has risen, or before it is risen?' they debate. He who offers when the sun has risen thus offers hospitality to the great god when gone on a journey. He who offers when the sun has not risen, thus offers hospitality to the great god when close at hand. Therefore the offering should be made when the sun has not risen.

[1] *sa yadi* corresponds with the *sa yadi* of the ÇB.; cf. *sa yaḥ* KB. ii. 9. The sentence is best begun here.

[2] *suriçāt*, the reading of most MSS. is meaningless, and the variants, of which M.'s *suruçāt* is the most important, render no help. The Ānand. ed. has *suriçānenevam*. The reading adopted for trans. is the conjecture *sureçāt* = *suleçāt*, *leça*, a small portion.

[3] For this exception see Lévi, *La doctrine du sacrifice*, p. 114; Sāyaṇa on TS. vii. 1. 8. 2. The view of BR., that *çraddhādeva* is 'one who believes in god', is now generally abandoned.

ii. 9. [1] There is an earlier version of this discussion in AB. v. 29 which resolves that the time after the rising of the sun is the proper time in the morning, so that the performance is daily, not only in effect once in two days. In this version the rôle of the two authorities has been curtailed, the antithesis of gods and fathers being suppressed, and as a result the *kumārī* is left with a rather meaningless opinion. ĀÇS. ii. 4. 24 and ÇÇS. ii. 7. 8, 4 have *upodayaṁ vyuṣita udite vā* which Nārāyaṇa takes as a threefold choice; ÇB. ii. 3. 1. 9, 36 and KÇS. iv. 14. 1; 15. 1 agree with KB. Cf. Weber, *Ind. Stud.* ii. 293–298; BÇS. iii. 4; MÇS. i. 6. 1. 8.

Thus also declared Vṛṣaçuṣma Vātāvata, one of the men of old, when lying worn out, having seen these two offerings being offered at night, 'At night verily they offer the two offerings.' 'For it is at night (they offer)' he said, 'and we shall proclaim,[2] having gone to yonder world, to the fathers, and they will believe us in it, that the Agnihotra which used to be performed on successive days is now performed on one day out of two, in the night only.' That also declared the maiden seized of the Gandharva, 'In the night verily they offer both offerings'. 'For it is at night (they offer)' she declared. At the twilight should he offer. Night and day are the flood that takes all; the two twilights are the fordable crossings of it; just as a man may cross the flood by the two fordable crossings, so is it in that he offers at the twilight. Again night and day are the missile of the god that goes on its way eager to kill; the two twilights are the two wings; just as with wings[3] it may swiftly perform a journey, so is it in that he offers at the twilight. Again, night and day are the encircling arms of death; just as a man, who is about to grasp[4] with encircling arms, may be evaded in the interval (between the arms), so is it in that he offers at the twilight. Kauṣītaki used to declare 'In the evening, after sunset, before the darkness, at this time should he offer; this is the time of the going to the gods; grasping it he reaches safely the world of heaven. In the morning, before sunrise, when the darkness has been smitten away, at this time should he offer; this is the time of the going to the gods; grasping it he reaches safely the world of heaven. He that at another time offers the Agnihotra, the dark and the dappled[5] rend apart his Agnihotra; the dappled is day,

[2] For *nv sva yam* we must, of course (JRAS. 1915, pp. 498–500) read *nvai vayam* (a *pluralis maiestatis*). The periphrastic future here has perhaps a sense of fixed intention of future action, but Whitney, (*Sansk. Gramm.* § 949) thinks that the parallel AB. passage is merely an equivalent of the future. Cf. Delbrück, *Altind. Synt.* p. 296. The comm. has Vādhāvata ($\sqrt{}$*dhāv*) and as a *v. l. pidṛbhyo*, corrected by Benfey (GGA. 1852, p. 184) to °*dṛbhmaḥnaḥ* is necessary with B below for *na* and perhaps *enan* for *enam*. Caland (VOJ. xxiii. 62) reads *nv sva vayam*, ignoring Aufrecht's previous correction (AB. p. 442).

[3] *pakṣau* may very possibly here mean two side horses, which gives excellent sense, while 'wings' is rather absurd: *pakṣa*, however, has not this sense for certain anywhere else (cf. Keith, JRAS. 1914, p. 1085). *pakṣasi* is generally taken with BR. as the wings of an army, but *sená* here rather seems to be a 'missile' and the *pakṣasi* its feathers, as wings, a view which of course may explain the use of *pakṣau* if that is 'wings'; cf. KB. vii. 7. For the metaphor of the ford, cf. the Çailāli Brāhmaṇa in ĀpÇS. vi. 4. 7.

[4] The form *parijigrahiṣyan* (read also in M) cannot be correct and must be replaced by *parijigrahiṣan* (desid.) or possibly *parigrahiṣyan*. Weber (*Ind. Stud.* ii. 418) suggests a pass. part. of the desid. with active termination. *ṣ* and *ṣy* are constantly interchanged.

[5] For the two dogs cf. Bloomfield, JAOS. 1893, pp. 163 *seq.*; Macdonell, *Vedic Mythology*, p. 173. The Ānand. ed. has the impossible *viṣidataḥ*; M. has the necessary *vikhidataḥ*.

the dark night. He who offers in the midnight,[6] the dark rends apart his Agnihotra; he who offers in the afternoon, the dappled rends apart his Agnihotra. Therefore assuredly whenever he may offer he should have regard to the prosperity of the offering.'

ADHYĀYA III

The New and Full Moon Offerings.

iii. 1. In[1] that he fasts at the new and full moon it is because the gods do not eat the oblation of him who does not perform the fast. Therefore he fasts (desiring) 'May the gods eat my oblation'. 'On the first full moon (day) should he fast' is the view of Paiñgya; 'on the second' that of Kauṣītaki; 'that on which (the moon) appears (full) about the setting of the sun' is the rule;[2] he should fast on the second full moon day.

[6] Here *mahārātra* and *mahāhna* seem really to mean when night or day is fully set in as opposed to the times decided on, which are to be really twilights.

[1] In this Adhyāya a comparatively brief account of the new and full moon sacrifice is given; the Mantras of the Adhvaryus are given in TS. i. 1; KS. i; KapS. i; MS. i, and the Brāhmaṇa elaborately in TS. i. 6 and 7; ii. 5 and 6; KS. v; MS. i. 4; ÇB. i. Of these TS. ii. 5. 7-11; 6. 7-10, and ÇB. deal with a good deal of the Hotṛ's functions. For the ritual see ĀÇS. i. 1; ÇÇS. i. 4-15; BÇS. i; MÇS. i. 1-8; ĀpÇS. ii-iv; *Vait.* i-iv; Hillebrandt, *Neu- und Vollmondsopfer*. There is a corrupt version of this chapter in AB. vii. 11; cf. KS. xii. 8.

[2] The distinction between the two full moon days is given by ÇÇS. i. 3. 5 as *yām paryastamayaṁ pūrṇa udiyāt* and *yām cāstamite*, and of the new moon days (i. 3. 6) as *çvo na draṣṭeti yad ahaç ca na dṛçyeta*. This distinction seems in accord with that in ĀpÇS. (xxiv. 2. 21, 22: *yad ahaḥ purastāc candramāḥ pūrṇa utsarpet tāṃ paurṇamāsīm upavaset, çvaḥ pūrita iti vā*; 24, 25: *yad ahar na dṛçyeta tad ahar amāvāsyā, çvo na draṣṭāra iti vā*) so far as the new moons are concerned, but as regards the full moons, the relation is uncertain. The definition in GGS. i. 5. 10 agrees with the Brāhmaṇa as interpreted by Oldenberg (SBE. xxx. 26), in the opinion of that scholar, and Weber also (*Über den Vedakalender*, p. 62) treats the Brāhmaṇa as agreeing with the ÇÇS. Yet, as is clear, the Brāhmaṇa as it stands makes the second the day on which the moon appears full about sunset, while the Sūtras make that day the first. This discrepancy suggests that it is quite probable that the second set, the new moons, do not correspond with those of the Sūtras either, and in point of fact it seems natural to hold that *çvo na draṣṭā* cannot be paralleled by *anirjñāya purastād amāvāsyāyāṁ candramasam* which is rather *yad ahaç ca na dṛçyeta*. The Brāhmaṇa in fact would put its days each one day further back or on than the Sūtras. The only way to produce agreement with the Sūtras would be to assume that *yām paryastamayam utsarpet* is either misplaced or a mere gloss, or less probably that it explains the Paiñgyan view, the conclusion beginning with *sā sthitiḥ*. *purastāt* is difficult: possibly it = before the sunset, not before the next day (cf. SBE. xxx. 333). 'In the east' is, however, alone probable; in *Atharvaprāyaçcitta*, ii. 3, it seems to have this sense, and the same

In that he fasts on the new moon day not discerning the moon in the east, thereby he delights the first (new moon day); in that he sacrifices, thereby the second. He should fast on the second; on the second the ocean swells in accordance with the moon, its deity. The moon is the truth of the gods; therefore should he fast on the second.

iii. 2. In that before the kindling verses he mutters, verily thus he makes a benediction. After uttering the sound *hiñ* he repeats the kindling verses; the sound *hiñ* is a thunderbolt; verily thus with a thunderbolt he smites the misfortune of the sacrificer. Three times he utters the sound *hiñ*; the thunderbolt is threefold; verily thus he produces a thunderbolt. By this threefold thunderbolt the gods drove away the Asuras from these worlds, and verily so the sacrificer with this threefold thunderbolt drives away the enemies who hate him from these worlds. He repeats eleven kindling verses; the Triṣṭubh has eleven syllables; Indra is connected with the Triṣṭubh; thus both Indra and Agni he obtains. The first he thrice repeats, the last thrice; they make up fifteen; the days of the first and the second halves of the month are fifteen; thus by the kindling verses he obtains the first and the second halves of the month. Again, the kindling verses are a thunderbolt; the thunderbolt is fifteenfold; verily thus by a thunderbolt he smites the misfortune of the sacrificer. In that (he repeats) the first thrice and the last thrice, verily thus he ties the two ends of the sacrifice for firmness and to avoid slipping. There are three hundred and sixty syllables in these (verses); three hundred and sixty are the days of the year; thus by the kindling verses he obtains the days of the year. They are Gāyatrī verses; Agni is connected with the Gāyatrī, and has the Gāyatrī as his metre; verily thus he praises Agni with his own metre. They are appropriate; what in the sacrifice is appropriate is perfect; verily (they serve) for the perfection of the sacrifice. With the *om* in the third uttering of the last (verse) he connects the address, 'O Agni, thou art great, O Brāhmaṇa, O Bhārata[1].' Agni is Bhārata; he bears (*bharati*) the oblation to the gods. In that he utters the Ṛṣi descent[2] of the sacri-

sense appears in KB. iv. 2. In his commentary on AB. vii. 11 Sāyaṇa renders 'in the eastern quarter'. The double kind of *amāvāsyā* and *paurṇamāsī* may reflect a confusion of dating due to the alternative commencement of day with night or morning; cf. Hirt, *Die Indogermanen*, ii. 540 with Fleet, JRAS. 1915, p. 218; Keith, 1916, pp. 143-146. The version in AB. has the term *tithi*, which alone would show that the passage is corrupt, as the *tithi* is an idea wholly unknown to any text earlier than the Sūtras and is there mainly a late passage of the *Gṛhya Sūtras*.

[1] Agni of the Bharatas is clearly meant, but the misunderstanding is obviously very old, and perhaps deliberate. Cf. Macdonell and Keith, *Vedic Index*, ii. 96 *sq.*

[2] See Weber, *Ind. Stud.* ix. 323; Hillebrandt, *Neu- und Vollmondsopfer*, p. 81, n. 1. ÇÇS. i. 4. 15–18 requires three ancestors to be cited, or six in the case of a son of two Gotras (an adopted son); if the sacri-

ficer, it is because the gods do not eat the oblation of one who has not descent from a Ṛṣi. Therefore he utters his descent from a Ṛṣi. He connects the address of fifteen elements; it is the Nivid[3] of the kindling verses; therefore has it fifteen elements; for the kindling verses are fifteen. It is not in metre; all this is twofold, metrical and not in metre; (he says it thinking), 'With all this let me praise Agni.' Having connected seven elements he should stop; the metres are seven; verily (they serve) to obtain all the metres. Then (come) four, then four; all this is fourfold; verily (they serve) to obtain all this.

iii. 3. In[1] that he summons the deities severally, it is because the oblations are taken separately for them. In that he summons Agni through Agni, the form of Agni which bears the oblation is his sacrificial form. It is what there over yonder sun shines like light; therefore the sun (appears) to every man. Thus in that he says 'O Agni bring Agni', verily thus he says 'That (form) bring.' In that he invites the gods that drink the butter, thus he invites the fore-offerings and the after-offerings. In that he invites Agni for the Hotṛ's function, thus he invites the Sviṣṭakṛt (offering). In that he invites his own greatness, thus he invites Vāyu; Agni's own greatness is Vāyu, for by him he acquires and attains greatness. In that he recites by order, and sacrifices by order, thereby verily sacrifice is made to his own greatness. 'Bring, O All-knower, and offer with good sacrifice', (with these words) he says to him, 'Bring the gods, O All-knower, and offer to the gods with good sacrifice.' In that he mutters before the kindling verses, and the kindling verses are a thunderbolt, verily thus he appeases him both before and after. In that he takes up the two ladles with the verse for taking up the ladles,[2] verily thus he yokes a chariot of the gods, being about to bestow the oblation upon the gods. With this chariot of the gods he attains safely the world of heaven.

iii. 4. He[1] offers the fore-offerings. The fore-offerings are the seasons; verily thus he delights the seasons. They are five; with them he obtains whatever there is fivefold pertaining to the self or to the gods. He offers to the kindling sticks; verily (thus he delights) the spring; in the spring all

ficer is not a Brahman then the Hotṛ's ancestors may be named, or in all cases *mānava* may be used.

[3] The fifteen *pada* character of the Nivid must be made up by the use of some addition. MÇS. v. 1. 4. 12 has *mānuṣa*, giving fifteen syllables, and TB. iii. 5. 8. 1 *asāv asau*. The fifteen additional words are given in sets of 7, 4, and 4, in ÇÇS. i. 4. 19–21.

[1] For the *devatānām āvāhana* see ÇÇS. i. 4. 22 *seq.*; Hillebrandt, p. 84. The Sandhi in *devāň ājyapāň* is due to quotation of the words of the summons.

[2] The phrase is found also in ÇÇS. i. 14. 22; the *srucau* are the *juhū* and the *upabhṛt*; cf. ĀÇS. ii. 2. 4; Hillebrandt, p. 85. The verse is given in ÇÇS. i. 6. 16. It precedes the fore-offerings.

iii. 4. [1] For the five fore-offerings see ÇÇS. i. 7; Hillebrandt, pp. 96–101. *yaj* is strictly = 'say the offering verse for'.

this is kindled. He offers to Tanūnapāt; verily (thus he delights) the hot season, for the hot season heats the body. He offers to the sacrificial food; verily (thus he delights) the rains, for through the rains sacrificial food arises. He offers to the strew; verily (thus he delights) the autumn, for in the autumn the plants on the strew grow best. He offers at the end to the making of Hail!; verily (thus he delights) the winter, for in the winter over all this is Hail! made. They say 'Seeing that there are five fore-offerings and six seasons, where does he offer to the sixth season?' In that in the fourth fore-offering he mingles (the butter),[2] thus he gives it a share in the others. Again, in that in the last fore-offering he mixes together the gods, he makes them sharers in the fore-offerings. Just as Agni has a share in all oblations, so he makes the deities sharers in the share of Agni. He does not say here[3] 'Agni from the Hotṛ's office' (thinking), 'The fore-offerings are cattle; the Sviṣṭakṛt is Rudra; let me not bring the cattle of the sacrifice into contact with Rudra.' Some[4] say 'Hail! May the gods, drinking the butter, rejoicing, O Agni, enjoy this butter.' He should not so do. The butter is one half of the sacrifice, the oblation is the other half; if he were to say one only of these, then one half of the sacrifice would have an accompaniment, the other half not. Therefore he should say 'Hail! May the gods, drinking the butter, rejoicing, O Agni, enjoy this butter, this oblation.'

iii. 5. In[1] that the butter portions at the full moon offering contain references to the slaying of Vṛtra, it is because Indra slew Vṛtra with the full moon offering. In that they have references to growth at the new moon offering, it is because then the moon becomes destroyed and verily thus does he cause it to swell up and to increase The offering verses in these offerings contain the word 'rejoicing', for they include the same oblations as the fore-offerings. Now 'rejoicing' is the holy power; verily thus by the holy power he offers the oblation to the gods. These offerings are threefold, *ye yajāmahe*, the Nigada, the sound *vaṣaṭ*[2]; the butter portions

[2] This refers to the putting of butter from the *upabhṛt* into the *juhū*; see BÇS. i. 16; Hillebrandt, p. 94, n. 4.

[3] This is a reference to the form of the Mantra given in MS. iv. 10. 3 and it confirms von Schroeder's reading there of *hotrāt* for the erroneous *hotrān* of the MSS. The Pratīka has been overlooked in the *Vedic Concordance*; cf. also TB. iii. 6. 2. 2.

[4] This form is found in MS. iv. 10. 3; 13. 5, which is doubtless (as in n. 3) the text referred to; KS. xv. 13; VS. xxviii. 11 has *indra* for *agna*.

[1] This section deals with the two butter portions which differ in their formation at new and full moon, the verses used being RV. viii. 44. 12 and vi. 16. 34 respectively; see ÇÇS. i. 8; Hillebrandt, pp. 102 *seq.*

[2] The Nigada is the material part in the offering verse, which runs in ĀÇS. i. 5. 34: *ye 3 yajāmaha agnim agnir juṣāṇa ājyasya vetū 3 vau 3 ṣaṭ.* The rules for Pluti in the sacrifice are given by ÇÇS. i. 2. 2 *seq.*, who gives as the Nigada *haviṣaḥ* as well as above in KB. iii. 4 *ad fin.*

are the eye; the eye is threefold, white, black, and red. These offerings he does not perform in the animal or Soma sacrifice (thinking), 'Through the animal offering the Soma sacrifice is possessed of eyes; let me not make the sacrifice four-eyed and loathsome.' In that the invitatory verses contain the words 'to' and 'offered',[3] and the offering verses the words 'forward', that is, 'given', verily thus having sacrificed he gives the oblation to the gods. These (verses) are Gāyatrī and Triṣṭubh; the Gāyatrī is the holy power; the Triṣṭubh is lordly power; verily thus with the holy and lordly power he gives the oblation to the gods. So great is the extension of the metre; verily thus with the whole extension of the metre he gives the oblation to the gods. At the end of the Ṛc he utters the sound *vaṣaṭ*; so do all his offering verses become beautiful. With *ṣaṭ* he utters *vaṣaṭ*; the seasons are six; verily thus he pleases the seasons. He should utter *vaṣaṭ* as connected with the Bṛhat and the Rathantara,[4] with a long in front and short behind; the short is the Rathantara, the long the Bṛhat; again, the Rathantara is this (earth); the Bṛhat is yonder (sky); verily thus in these two he finds support. So great is the extension of speech; verily thus with the whole extension of speech he gives the oblation to the gods. '*bhūr bhuvaḥ*'[5] he mutters before *ye yajāmahe*, 'Strength is might, might is strength; light' after the sound *vaṣaṭ*: the sound *vaṣaṭ* is a thunderbolt; verily thus he quietens it, both in front and behind. Strength and might are the two most dear forms of the sound *vaṣaṭ*; verily with them he quietens it.

iii. 6. In[1] that he offers to Agni first of the deities, and because Agni is the mouth (beginning) of the gods, verily thus at the beginning he delights the gods. Now as to his sacrificing to Agni and Soma at the full moon offering, Agni and Soma were within Vṛtra; with regard to them Indra could not hurl his bolt; for them he arranged the portion at the full moon

[3] *ā-hutaḥ* occurs in RV. vi. 16. 34; *pra*, here explained as it seems by *pratta*, only in the Yājyās of the main offering to Indra and Agni, RV. i. 109. 6 and at the Sāṁnāyya, x. 180. 1.

[4] Cf. Ānartīya on ÇÇS. i. 2. 18, where this sentence is cited by Suyajña, the reputed author. *vaṣaṭ* is to be made *vau 3 ṣaṭ*.

[5] See ÇÇS. i. 1. 38 for the standing rule of the use of this formula.

[1] This chapter deals with the chief oblation (*pradhānahaviṣi*) of the two sacrifices: as here treated they clearly are for the full moon (1) a cake for Agni; (2) an Upāṅçuyāja; (3) a cake for Agni and Soma; for the new moon (1) a cake for Agni; (2) an Upāṅçuyāja; (3) a cake for Indra and Agni *or* a milk offering (Sāṁnāyya) for Indra. In the case of the second alternative under (3) the Sāṁnāyya is divided into two parts by the extension of the Upāṅçuyāja. This is in general accord with ÇÇS. i. 13–18 which, however, is less explicit as to the position of the Upāṅçuyāja and which specifies the duties of the Upāṅçuyājas as Agni and Soma normally, but in the case of no Sāṁnāyya Viṣṇu. The other Sūtras agree generally, but vary in detail; see Hillebrandt, pp. 111–115. The last paragraph of the chapter deals with the offering to Agni Sviṣṭakṛt.

sacrifice; the two are offered to inaudibly, and in a higher tone, to prevent sameness. In that he sacrifices inaudibly, thereby he delights Soma; in that (he sacrifices) in a higher tone, thereby (he delights) Agni. In that he sacrifices to Indra and Agni at the new moon sacrifice, it is because Indra and Agni are supports; verily (the offering serves) for a support. In that, mingling, he sacrifices to Indra at the new moon sacrifice, that is the light of the new moon sacrifice, for the moon is not then seen. In that, without mingling,[2] he offers the butter of the inaudible (sacrifice) between the two cakes, it is for preventing sameness. In that, mingling, he offers the butter of the inaudible (sacrifice) in the midst of the milk offering (*sāṁnāyya*), the explanation of that has been given.[3] In that he sacrifices at the end to Agni Sviṣṭakṛt, it is because he gives the oblation to the gods; he who divides out food tastes it himself last. Again Sviṣṭakṛt is Rudra and he enjoys at the end. Therefore to him at the end he sacrifices. In that (offering) the invitatory and offering verses are of the same metre, but the Nigada differs; though this sameness is avoided. After saying *vaṣaṭ*, he touches water; the waters are healing and medicine; verily thus are healing and medicine produced at the end in the sacrifice.

iii. 7. In[1] that he smears on the lower lip the first anointing of the sacrificial food on the forefinger, the lower lip is this world, the upper lip is yonder world, what is between the lips is the atmosphere here; therefore in that he eats, verily thus he delights these worlds continuously. In that he invokes the sacrificial food, verily thus he seeks renown among all beings. Again, the sacrificial food is food; verily thus he places food in himself; again the sacrificial food is cattle; verily (the invocation) serves to obtain cattle. On it four times he breathes; all this (universe) is fourfold; verily (it serves) to obtain all this (universe). Again, in that after invoking the sacrificial food he smells it and the sacrificial food is cattle, verily thus he confers cattle upon himself. Again, in that the Adhvaryu makes the cake to sit on the strew, verily thus he delights the fathers. Again, in that he eats the second[2] portion of the sacrificial food with

[2] *saṁnayan* is the technical term which expresses the central act of the Sāṁnāyya or offering of milk to Indra.

[3] I. e. it is to avoid sameness, as in the case of the intervention of the offering between the two cakes.

[1] This chapter gives explanation of the details of the invocation of the sacrificial food (*iḍā*), for which see ÇÇS. i. 10, 11; Hillebrandt, pp. 125 *seq.* Then came notes on the *anvāhārya*, a mess of food cooked with rice which is the fee for the priests and the recitation over the kindling stick which is prescribed in ÇÇS. i. 12.

[2] *uttareḍā* (also in KB. xiii. 7) is the portion of the Hotṛ of the five portions into which the *iḍā* proper is divided. It may be called 'second' as being the second part out, or, because it is held in the left hand, perhaps 'left' is meant; cf. Ānartīya on ÇÇS. i. 10. 4. The AB. has *avāntareḍā*; see Weber, *Ind. Stud.* ix. 225, 226; AÇS. ii. 9. 7.

muttering, and the muttering is the holy power; verily thus with the holy power he appeases it. Again, in that they cleanse themselves on that (part of the strew) where the strainers are, and the waters are healing and medicine, verily thus at the end in the sacrifice are healing and medicine made. Again, in that they bring up the mess of food, it is because the new and full moon sacrifices have that as the sacrificial fees; therefore they bring up the mess of food. Again, in that he addresses[3] the kindling stick, it is because it alone is left over of the kindling fuel; therefore he celebrates it.

iii. 8. In[1] that he offers three after-offerings, and these worlds are three, verily thus he obtains these worlds. In that he says all last, and the Sviṣṭakṛt is a support, verily (it serves) for a support. In that he says the Sūktavāka, and the Sūktavāka is a support, verily (it serves) for a support. In that he makes mention of earth and sky, and earth and sky are supports, verily (it serves) for a support. Some say 'Agni hath rejoiced in this oblation'. This he should not do;[2] the deity to whom he is sacrificing comes forward thinking 'It is a renewed sacrifice; again will he give me the oblation', and takes away the blessings of the sacrificer; therefore 'He hath rejoiced in oblation, he hath rejoiced in oblation' only should he say. The deities to whom he sacrifices in the beginning, verily in the end through them he finds support. In that in the Sūktavāka he mentions the name[3] of the sacrificer, it is because it is the divine self of the sacrificer which the priests make ready; therefore he mentions his name; for here is he born. He should mention it aloud, even if he be a teacher; thus is the sacrificer not likely to fall into ruin. Five[4] blessings he utters; there are three in the sacrificial food; they make up eight; by them the gods attained all attainments (*iṣṭīḥ*); verily thus does the sacrificer by means of them attain all attainments. Having placed his clasped hands pointing east on the strew he mutters 'For homage', for the gods are not superior to homage. In that he says the Çaṁyuvāka, and the Çaṁyuvāka is a support, verily (it serves) for a support; again Çaṁyu Bārhaspatya appeased all sacrifices; therefore he utters the Çaṁyuvāka.

[3] The Ānand. ed. has *anumantrayeta*.

[1] This chapter briefly touches on the three after-offerings and the Sūktavāka and the Çaṁyuvāka, which here is called Çaṁyorvāka and attributed to Çaṁyu Bārhaspatya: see ÇÇS. i. 12. 13–14. 24; Hillebrandt, pp. 134–149.

[2] The point is *idam*, which is found with *agnir* in TS. ii. 6. 9. 6; TB. iii. 5. 10. 2; MS. iv. 13. 9 (cf. MS. v. 1. 4. 28); ÇB. i. 9. 1. 9 and even in ĀÇS. i. 9. 1 (without *Agnir*). But the god's name is apparently also to be omitted contrary to ÇÇS. unless we are to understand that merely *idam* is to be rejected, as is reasonable.

[3] *nāmani* has Çāñkhāyana, explained as the personal and Nākṣatra name; see Hillebrandt, p. 145, n. 1.

[4] Viz. *uttarāṁ devayajyāṁ bhūyaḥ haviṣkaraṇam āyuḥ suprajāstvaṁ divyaṁ dhāma*, ÇÇS. i. 14. 17.

In that he touches the waters, and the waters are healing and medicine, verily thus at the end in the sacrifice are healing and medicine produced.

iii. 9. In[1] that they perform in the Gārhapatya the sacrifices to the wives with (the gods), the wives share the Gārhapatya, the sacrificer the Āhavanīya; therefore they perform the sacrifices for the wives with (the gods) in the Gārhapatya. They are four in number; up to four (degrees), are pairing, union, propagation; (they serve) for generation.[2] They are performed inaudibly; the sacrifices to the wives with (the gods) are a pouring of seed; inaudibly is seed poured; they are appropriate; what in the sacrifice is appropriate is perfect; verily (they serve) for the perfection of the sacrifice. He sacrifices to Soma, Tvaṣṭṛ, the wives of the gods; and Agni, lord of the house; these deities are the controllers of unions; them here he delights; they here being delighted confer unions. To Soma first he sacrifices; thus he pours seed; to Tvaṣṭṛ second, Tvaṣṭṛ transmutes the seed that is poured; then to the wives, for these are joint sacrifices for the wives; in that he sacrifices last to Agni, lord of the house, the wives are those of him that makes the sacrifice well performed; therefore he sacrifices to him at the end. In that he mutters the Ṛc, verily thus he procures a blessing. In that he invokes the sacrificial food, in that he purifies himself, in that he utters the Çaṁyuvāka, the explanation of that has been given.[3] In that he causes the wife to speak on the grass bundle, and the grass bundle is male and the wife female, verily thus he confers union upon women; therefore the wife puts between her thighs blades of the grass bundle. In that he strews the grass bundle, thereby the new and full moon offerings are continued by him; verily also thereby the strew for his Agnihotra is spread. In that he pays reverence to the remnant of the grass bundle, verily thus he utters a prayer for blessing; in that he pays reverence to the Āhavanīya, verily thus having delighted (them) he speaks at

[1] This chapter deals with the four Patnīsaṁyājas, which appear to be offerings to the gods including the wives of the gods, being really offerings to Soma, Tvaṣṭṛ, and Agni, and one to the wives; see ÇÇS. i. 15. 1-8; Hillebrandt, pp. 151 *seq.* Then come references to the muttering of a Ṛc (iv. 12. 6); the invocation of the sacrificial food; the cleansing; the Çaṁyuvāka; the speech of the sacrificer's wife while standing on the grass bundle; the spreading of the bundle of grass; the reverence of the remnant of the bundle and of the Āhavanīya; and the touching of water, for which see ÇÇS. i. 15. 9-18; Hillebrandt, pp. 162 *seq.*

[2] Possibly the four nouns express the four things exemplified in the four sacrifices, the dative in the last case being natural enough; it is also possible to stop at *mithunam* and make *prajananaṁ prajātyai* the description of the effort of the four, but in that case *eva* would be expected. More probable, however, is the version of the text; cf. MS. i. 7. 3; Schol. on Pāṇ. viii. 1. 15; the reference may be to the limits of human marriage; cf. ÇB. i. 8. 3. 6, *ā* being exclusive (cf. AB. iv. 24), not animal mating. Possibly it only means a pair union, and propagation make up four; cf. viii. 2, n. 6.

[3] I. e. in iii. 7 and 8.

the end his purpose to the gods; in that he touches the waters, and the waters are healing and medicine, verily thus at the end in the sacrifice are healing and medicine produced.

ADHYĀYA IV

Special Sacrifices.

iv. 1. By[1] means of the supplementary offering the gods smote away the Asuras; verily so also does the sacrificer by the supplementary offering smite away the foes that hate him. He offers to Indra, driver away of enemies, a cake on eleven potsherds. Indra is the smiter away of enemies; verily he smites away his enemies. Again, he adds on the new moon ceremonial. In that at the full moon sacrifice he offers to Indra, therein the sacrificer has the new and full moon sacrifices completed[2]; if he were to incur a disaster in the second half of the month, there would not be a dragging apart of his sacrifice. In that in the new moon sacrifice he offers to Aditi, it is to balance the sacrifice. From the invitatory and offering verses it is possessed of the characteristic of driving away enemies.[3]

iv. 2. Next[1] as to the Abhyuditā sacrifice. He wanders from the path of the sacrifice at whose fast the moon is seen in the east. He offers to Agni, the giver, a cake on eight potsherds; Agni is the giver; verily he gives the sacrifice to him. (He offers) to Indra, the bestower, curds milked in the evening; Indra is the bestower; verily he bestows the sacrifice upon him. (He offers) to Viṣṇu Çipiviṣṭa[2] a pap in milk milked in the morning; Viṣṇu is the sacrifice; verily he gives to him the sacrifice. In that he sacrifices to these deities, (it is because he thinks) 'Let me not wander from the path of the sacrifice.' The sacrificial fee is a bow with three arrows; that is a symbol of a safe journey.

[1] This chapter deals with a special variant of the new and full moon sacrifices, the Anunirvāpyā Iṣṭi, details of which occur in ÇÇS. iii. 1. The chief features are offerings to Indra and Aditi at the end of the full and new moon rites respectively, the rites being based on the new and full moon rites.

[2] The ordinary offerings may end with a milk offering to Indra.

[3] The *saṁyājyās* of the offering to Vaimṛdha are used for the Sviṣṭakṛt in the offering after the new moon offering to Aditi which is thus connected with *vimṛdh*. The Ānand. ed. has absurdly *saṁyājyā 'to*.

iv. 2. [1] This chapter (cf. *Atharvaprāyaçcitta*, ii. 2 and 3) deals with the case when a new moon offering is begun before the actual time acc. to ÇÇS. iii. 2, *purastāt* presumably meaning 'before new moon', and in iii. 3 *paçcāt* 'after new moon'. But the terminology of the Brāhmaṇa can hardly be so interpreted and the sense seems to be as above; cf. KB. iii. 1. The distinction is thus one of degree of lateness, as suggested by the expression *abhyud* in both cases.

[2] For this epithet see Keith, *Taittirīya Saṁhitā*, p. 622, n. 3.

iv. 3. Next [1] as to the Abhyuddṛṣṭā sacrifice. He wanders from the path of the sacrifice at whose fast the moon is seen in the west. He offers to Agni, maker of paths, a cake on eight potsherds; Agni is the maker of paths; verily he sets him again [2] on the path of the sacrifice. To Indra, slayer of Vṛtra, (he offers a cake) on eleven potsherds; Indra is the slayer of Vṛtra; verily he sets him again on the path of the sacrifice. To Vaiçvānara (he offers a cake) on twelve potsherds; he who yonder gives heat is Vaiçvānara; verily he sets him again on the path of the sacrifice. In that he sacrifices to these deities, (it is because he thinks) 'Let me not wander from the path of the sacrifice.' The sacrificial fee is a pair of shoes and a staff; that is the symbol of fearlessness.

iv. 4. Next as to the Dākṣāyaṇa sacrifice.[1] He who means to proceed with the Dākṣāyaṇa sacrifice begins on the full moon night in the Phalgunīs; the full moon night in the Phalgunīs is the beginning of the year; therefore on it the proceedings of the unconsecrated are begun. Now Dakṣa Pārvati, having sacrificed with this sacrifice, obtained all desires; in that he sacrifices with the Dākṣāyaṇa sacrifice, verily (it serves) for the obtaining of all desires. He should not take pleasure in eating [2]; 'Soma, the king, the moon I eat', thus thinking in his mind should he eat; now the moon is Soma, the king, the wise; it on the second half of the month the gods press out. In that on the second half of the month he performs the vows of the Dākṣāyaṇa sacrifice, (it is because he wishes) 'Let me share in the Soma drinking of the gods.' In that during the fast day [3] he offers a cake on eleven potsherds to Agni and Soma, thereby he obtains the victim for

[1] This chapter deals with the case where the new moon sacrifice commences after the new moon acc. to ÇÇS. iii. 8. The MSS. vary between °*dṛṣṭā* and °*draṣṭā*.

[2] *apipāthayati* is clearly the correct term, and is read by the Ānand. ed.; the variants *abhipāthayati* and *apipātayati* both pointing to it.

iv. 4. [1] This important offering is to be performed for fifteen years or every year according to Çāñkhāyana, taking the place of the new and full moon offerings of which it is an elaborated variant. It is a substitute for the Sattras of the Soma sacrifices with which in this chapter its details are equated. The offerings are (1) day before full moon, the usual full moon offerings including cakes to Agni and Agni and Soma; (2) full moon, cake to Agni and milk for Indra, which of course is the usual new moon offering and hence is here so called (*āmāvāsya*); (3) day before new moon, the usual offerings of a cake to Agni and a cake to Indra and Agni; (4) new moon, a cake to Agni and *payasyā* for Mitra and Varuṇa; see ÇÇS. iii. 8, which has a further offering for the steeds, here ignored. The Dākṣāyaṇa is also dealt with by Hillebrandt, *Neu- und Vollmondsopfer*, pp. 177–185; cf. Eggeling, SBE. xii. 374 *seq.*

[2] *āpsti*, which Lindner reads, is wrong; the *āpayita* of M (*āpaiti* other MSS.) is the correct reading which the scribes have misunderstood. The Sūtra (iii. 8. 14) has *na sauhityaṁ prāpnuyāt* which shows what it read. The Ānand. ed. has *āpayati*.

[3] The ordinary rite has an *upavasatha* day before the actual offering day. This rite has for that day a special performance of the ordinary offerings, giving up the next day to the special offerings.

Agni and Soma which is offered on the fast day of the Soma (sacrifice). In that he sacrifices in the morning with the new moon offerings, and the pressing day is Indra's, thus he obtains the pressing day. In that at the new moon offering on the fast day he offers a cake on twelve potsherds to Indra and Agni and the third pressing belongs as regards its Sāman to Indra and Agni, thus he obtains the third pressing. In that there is a milk mess for Mitra and Varuṇa, and the offering (of a cow) is for Mitra and Varuṇa, thus he obtains the offering of a cow. Thus Soma is present, having penetrated the Haviryajñas; therefore though unconsecrated he performs the vows of the consecrated.

iv. 5. Next[1] as to the Iḍādadha sacrifice. He who means to proceed with the Iḍādadha sacrifice begins on the same full moon night; the explanation of it has been given. It is a sacrifice for one desiring cattle or desiring proper food. With it should one desiring cattle or one desiring proper food sacrifice; verily in it thus also does he perform the vows, for it is a combination of the Dākṣāyaṇa sacrifice.

iv. 6. Next[1] as to the Sārvaseni sacrifice. He who means to proceed with the Sārvaseni sacrifice begins on the same full moon night; the explanation of it has been given. It is a sacrifice for one desiring propagation; with it should one desiring propagation sacrifice. In that the Adhvaryu produces the oblation, that is the symbol of propagation.

iv. 7. Next[1] as to the Çaunaka sacrifice. He who means to proceed with the Çaunaka sacrifice begins on the same full moon night; the explanation of this has been given. It is a sacrifice for one desiring to lay low (his enemies); with it should one desiring to lay low sacrifice; he who desires 'May I lay low the rival who hates me', should sacrifice with this; he lays him low indeed.

[1] According to ÇÇS. iii. 9 the four days have the following offerings, (1) cake for Agni, pap for Sarasvatī; (2) cake for Agni and Soma with the Upāṅçuyāja, and milk for Indra; (3) cake for Agni, pap for Sarasvant; (4) cake for Indra and Agni, and milk mess for Mitra and Varuṇa. He adds the *vājina* offerings as in the Dākṣāyaṇa. The sacrifice is just mentioned in AB. iii. 40. 9; ĀÇS. ii. 14. 11; ĀpÇS. iii. 17. 12.

iv. 6. [1] According to ÇÇS. iii. 10 the point of distinction in this rite is the combination of the new and full moon offerings at full moon and their omission *in toto* at new moon. Cf. AB. iii. 40. 7; AÇS. ii. 14. 7–10; ÇB. ii. 4. 4. 4; xi. 1. 2; ĀpÇS. iii. 17. 12.

iv. 7. [1] According to ÇÇS. iii. 10. 7 there is no distinction in this case for the Hotṛ as compared with the normal model. Ānartīya points out that the Anunirvāpyās are to be performed in this case, and that the rule of *prakṛti* and *vikāra* which usually holds is not applicable to these rites. Cf. ĀpÇS. iii. 17. 12. The mention of Çaunaka is probably a piece of evidence for the later date of the KB., as the family appears to have been prominent in the late Brāhmaṇa epoch, as indicated by the citations in *Vedic Index*, ii. 396.

iv. 8. Next[1] as to the Vasiṣṭha sacrifice. He who means to proceed with the Vasiṣṭha sacrifice begins on the new moon in the Phalgunis (thinking) 'The full moon night is the holy power; the new moon night is the lordly power; this sacrifice is, as it were, the lordly power. By means of the lordly power let me overcome my foes.' Vasiṣṭha desired, when his sons were slain, 'May I be propagated with offspring, with cattle, may I overcome the Saudāsas.' He saw this sacrificial rite, the Vasiṣṭha sacrifice; he grasped it and sacrificed with it; having sacrificed with it, he was propagated with offspring, with cattle; he overcame the Saudāsas. Verily thus also the sacrificer, in that he sacrifices with the Vasiṣṭha sacrifice, is propagated with offspring, with cattle; he overcomes the rivals who hate him.

iv. 9. Next[1] as to the Sākaṁprasthāyya sacrifice. He who means to proceed with the Sākaṁprasthāyya begins on the same new moon night; the explanation of it has been given. It is a sacrifice for one desiring pre-eminence, desiring heroism; with it should one desiring pre-eminence, desiring heroism, sacrifice. In that together they move forward, together they sacrifice, together they eat, therefore is it called Sākaṁprasthāyya (moving forward together).

iv 10. Next[1] as to the Munyayana. He who means to proceed with the Munyayana begins on the same full moon night; the explanation of it has been given. It is a sacrifice for one desiring all; with it should one desiring all sacrifice.

iv. 11. Next[1] as to the Turāyaṇa. He who means to proceed with the Turāyaṇa begins on the same full moon night; the explanation of this has been given. It is a sacrifice for one desiring heaven; with it should one

[1] According to ÇÇS. iii. 11. 1-3 this offering follows the model of the Sārvaseni sacrifice, but with all the offerings combined on the new moon, instead of the full moon as in that case. For Vasiṣṭha and the death of his sons see TS. vii. 4. 7. 1; Muir, OST. i.[2] 328; Macdonell and Keith, *Vedic Index*, ii. 275. Cf. ĀpÇS. iii. 17. 12.

iv. 9. [1] Like the Çaunaka sacrifice (iv. 7) this is discussed in ÇÇS. iii. 10. 7 as being like the new and full moon offerings.

iv. 10. [1] According to ÇÇS. iii. 11. 7-10 the sacrificer sacrifices to Agni and Agni and Viṣṇu every time save at the Parvan, i.e. the new and full moon offering, the four monthly offerings, the Ayana (animal), and the Year (Soma) offerings. Two different Munyayanas are given in BÇS. xvi. 30.

iv. 11. [1] According to ÇÇS. iii. 11. 11-15 the characteristics of this Ayana are a cake for Agni and Indra and a pap for the All-gods. But while the former is based on the full moon sacrifice, the latter follows the new moon as its model and includes the imitation of the Dīkṣā for the Soma sacrifice in the use of a black antelope's skin. Both are to last a year, ÇÇS. iii. 11. 16. Cf. ĀÇS. ii. 14. 4-6. For the name Weber compares Pāṇ. v. 1. 72, and suggests (*Ind. Stud.* ii. 312) a possible relation to Tura Kāvaṣeya.

desiring heaven sacrifice. In that he puts on a black antelope's skin, and the black antelope's skin is the holy power, verily thus he unites the sacrifice with holy power. There are three oblations; these worlds are three; verily thus he obtains these worlds.

iv. 12. Next [1] as to the Āgrayaṇa. He who desires proper food should sacrifice with the Āgrayaṇa. In the rains when the millet harvest has come, he gives orders to pluck millet. The new moon night which coincides with that time, on it should he sacrifice and then offer this sacrifice. If he is a full moon sacrificer, he should sacrifice with this and then offer the full moon sacrifice. If again he desires [2] a Nakṣatra, he should in the first half of the month look out for a Nakṣatra and offer under the Nakṣatra [3] which he desires. There are seventeen kindling verses in this sacrifice, the butter portions [4] contain the word 'being'; the invitatory and offering verses (of the Sviṣṭakṛt offering) are Virāj verses [5]; the explanation of that has been given [6]. There is a pap for Soma; Soma is the king of the plants; thus he delights him with his own subjects. In that he gives the honey drink, it is because this is the sap of the forest things.

iv. 13. When [1] spring has come and the bamboo seeds are ripe, he gives orders to pluck bamboo seeds. Of this (sacrifice) there is the same time, the same model, the same deity, the same fee, the same explanation. Some perform (the offering) for Agni, or Varuṇa, or Prajāpati, but with the same model and the same explanation.

iv. 14. When [1] the rice harvest or the barley harvest has come, he gives orders to pluck (grains) for the Āgrayaṇa: of this (sacrifice) there is the same time, the same model. In that there is (a cake) on twelve potsherds for

[1] This and the next two rites are dealt with together by ÇÇS. iii. 12: the chief rites are beside the Soma offering of *çyāmāka* or *veṇuyavas*, in the case of the *vrīhiyava* form a cake for Indra and Agni or Agni and Indra, a pap for the All-gods, and a cake for sky and earth, these last being Upāṅçuyājas; ÇÇS. iii. 12. 10. Cf. BÇS. iii. 12; MÇS. i. 64. ĀpÇS. vi. 31. 13 quotes a different practice from a Bahvṛcabrāhmaṇa.

[2] *upepset* is preferable to Rs. *apepset*, the corruption being easy.

[3] M inserts *kalyāṇe*, but this looks like a mere gloss.

[4] I.e. RV. iv. 13. 4 (*asi*); i. 91. 9 (*santi*).

[5] I.e. RV. vii. 1. 3 and 10.

[6] See KB. i. 1. There is a calf as the fee of the Indra and Agni offering as opposed to the honey mixture (*dadhi* and *madhu*) for the Soma offering.

iv. 13. [1] To this account ÇÇS. iii. 12 adds nothing, but Ānartīya on iii. 12. 10 cites this passage.

iv. 14. [1] This is the full form of the Āgrayaṇa where rice and barley are offered with three oblations for Indra and Agni, the All-gods and earth and sky, and with a number of simpler variants. For the various forms of the ritual see ĀÇS. ii. 9; BÇS. iii. 12; ĀpÇS. vi. 29, 30; *Vait.* viii. 4; Hillebrandt, *Rituallitteratur*, § 65. The offering is not so much, as Lindner (*Festgruss an Böhtlingk*, pp. 79 *seq.*) suggests, a thank-offering, as an offering to secure the fruitfulness of the new crop as this Brāhmaṇa shows (Oldenberg, *Die Religion des Veda*, p. 305).

Indra and Agni, and Indra and Agni are the beginning of the gods, verily thus at the beginning he delights the gods. In that there is a pap for the All-gods, and the All-gods are all the gods, verily (it serves) to delight all the gods. In that there is (a cake) on one potsherd for sky and earth, (it is because) sky and earth are the preparers of the harvest, and earth is a support, and by the flooding yonder (sky) co-operates.[2] In that he sacrifices to these deities, (it is because he thinks) 'By these deities shall I eat food made calm.' In that he gives an ox of the first birth, it is because this is a first ceremony. If he is wearied of this (sacrifice),[3] he should offer the oblation of the full or the new moon, with the new (plants)[4] to obtain both. Or again he may employ the oblations at the full moon or the new moon (sacrifice) to secure the presence of the deities. Or again he may offer in the morning and in the evening the Agnihotra with barley gruel of the new (plants), to obtain both. Or again having cooked milk in a pot on the Gārhapatya he should make an offering of the new (plants) in the Āhavanīya to the gods of the Āgrayaṇa, with Sviṣṭakṛt for a fourth (saying) 'To N.N. hail. To N.N. hail!' to secure the presence of the deities. Or again having made the Agnihotra cow to eat the new (plants), he should offer in the morning and in the evening the Agnihotra with its milk, to obtain both. These are so many possibilities; he may offer with whichever he may desire, but the established rule is that of three oblations. Three are these worlds; verily thus he obtains these worlds.

ADHYĀYA V

The Four-Monthly Sacrifices

The Vaiçvadeva

v. 1. Next[1] as to the four-monthly sacrifices. He who prepares the four-monthly sacrifices begins on the full moon night in the Phalgunīs.

[2] *odmandsām*, the version of the MSS., with a variant *odmandsāv*, read in M, in the comm. is difficult and obscure. The instr. is probably to be understood and reference may be to the swelling of the grain, but *āsām* is unexpected, as *vrīhi* and *yava* are masculine. The gen. with *anuveda* is not unnatural if not paralleled. *āsām* is, however, an attempt to explain away *āsāv* which has been misinterpreted. *asau* is the sky which co-operates or sympathizes with earth, *anuveda* being used absolutely.

[3] For the dative see Delbrück, *Altind. Synt.* p. 142. The Ānand ed. has *[śyāt*.

[4] *navānām* apparently goes with *kurvīta* not *ubhayasya*; cf. ÇÇS. iii. 12. 14.

[1] The first two chapters deal with the Vaiçvadeva, the first of the four-monthly sacrifices; then the next two with the Varuṇapraghāsas, the second; then the next with the Sākamedhas, the last, and

The full moon night is the Phalgunīs in the beginning of the year; the latter two Phalgus are the beginning, the two former the end. Just as the two ends of what is round may unite, so these two ends of the year are connected. In that he sacrifices with the Vaiçvadeva sacrifice on the full moon night in the Phalgunīs, verily thus at the beginning he delights the year. Again the four-monthly sacrifices are sacrifices of healing; therefore are they performed in the joinings of the seasons, for in the joinings of the seasons pain is born. There are eight oblations, the oblations of four full moon days amount to eight; the Vaiçvadeva is a compound of four full moon days. In that Agni is kindled, it is because the Vaiçvadeva is propagation; therefore he generates this divine embryo. As to there being seventeen kindling verses, the butter portions containing the word 'being', the invitatory and offering verses being Virāj verses, the explanation of that has been given.[2] In that there are nine fore-offerings and nine after-offerings,[3] eight oblations and the offering for the steeds as the ninth, thus he obtains the brilliance of the Nakṣatras.

v. 2. In[1] that he sacrifices to Agni and Soma first of the deities, it is because these are the deities of the new and full moon sacrifices; therefore to them first he sacrifices. In that he sacrifices to Savitṛ, and Savitṛ is lord of instigations, (it serves) for the creation of instigation by Savitṛ. In that he sacrifices to Sarasvatī, and Sarasvatī is speech, verily thus he delights speech. In that he sacrifices to Pūṣan and Pūṣan is he who yonder gives heat, verily thus he delights him. In that he sacrifices to the Maruts as impetuous, and the Maruts as impetuous are terrible, verily thus he makes healing. In that there is a milk mess for the All-gods, and the All-gods are all these gods, verily (it serves) to delight all the gods. In that there is (a cake) on one potsherd for the sky and earth, and sky and earth are supports, verily (it serves) for support. In that he gives an ox of the first birth, it is because that is a first ceremony. In that before or after the Çaṁyuvāka, he sacrifices to the steeds uninvited, and the steeds are the horses of the gods, verily thus he delights these steeds.

eight to ten with the Çunāsirīya rite which is connected with these sacrifices. The AB. has nothing to correspond, but the rites are explained in the Yajur texts, TS. i. 8. 2–7; KS. ix. 4–7; xv. 2; KapS. viii. 7–11; MS. i. 10. 1–4; ii. 6. 8; VS. iii. 44–61; ix. 35–8; ÇB. ii. 5 and 6. For the ritual see ĀÇS. ii. 15–20; ÇÇS. iii. 13–18; BÇS. v; MÇS. i. 7 and 8; v. 1. 3, 4; ĀpÇS. viii; KÇS. v; *Vait.* viii. 8 *seq.*; Hillebrandt, *Ritualliteratur*, § 64; Eggeling, SBE. xii. 383 *seq.* For Phalgunī as the beginning of the year cf. Hopkins, JAOS. xxiv. 20; Macdonell and Keith, *Vedic Index*, i. 424 *seq.*

[2] See i. 1.

[3] I. e. four more between the fourth and the fifth, and six between first and second, ÇÇS. iii. 13. 19 *seq.*

[1] The offerings here are enumerated in ÇÇS. iii. 18. 6–11; the *vājina* offering is described in iii. 8. 20–27 in connexion with the Dākṣāyaṇa.

Therefore the gods with their horses become delighted. Now the steeds are also the seasons; verily thus he delights the seasons. In that he sacrifices afterwards with the full moon offering, thus by him in the first half[2] of the month is the Vaiçvadeva offered.

The Varuṇapraghāsas

v. 3. By[1] means of the Vaiçvadeva sacrifice Prajāpati created offspring; they, being created, not born, ate the barley of Varuṇa; Varuṇa grasped them with Varuṇa's nooses. The offspring having gone ran up to their father Prajāpati, 'Do thou devise that sacrificial rite by which we may sacrifice and be set free from the nooses of Varuṇa, from all ill.' Then Prajāpati saw this sacrificial rite, the Varuṇapraghāsas; he grasped it, and sacrificed with it; having sacrificed with it he delighted Varuṇa; Varuṇa being delighted, freed offspring from the nooses of Varuṇa and from all evil. From the nooses of Varuṇa and from all evil are freed the offspring of him who knowing thus sacrifices with the Praghāsas. In that they bring forward the fire, verily thus do they bring forward yonder fire which they kindle at the Vaiçvadeva. In that the fire is kindled, the explanation of that has been given. In that there are seventeen kindling verses, the butter portions contain the word 'being' and the invitatory and offering verses are Virāj verses, the explanation of that has been given. In that there are nine fore-offerings and nine after-offerings, and nine oblations, thus he obtains the brilliance of the Nakṣatras; the five accompanying oblations ending with that to Pūṣan are the same; the explanation of them has been given.

v. 4. In that there is (a cake) on twelve potsherds for Indra and Agni, and Indra and Agni are supports, verily (it serves) for support. Indra is in the middle; therefore to him in the middle he sacrifices. In that there is a milk mess for Varuṇa, (it is because) Varuṇa is Indra, and he has milk as his portion; therefore there is a milk mess for Varuṇa. In that there is a milk mess for the Maruts, (it is because) the Maruts are situated in the waters; therefore with milk he sacrifices to them, for milk is the waters. Moreover the Maruts are Indra's, milk is Indra's; therefore is there a milk mess for the Maruts. In that there is (a cake) on one potsherd for Ka,

[2] This clearly shews that the full moon for this part of the Brāhmaṇa was in the middle of the month; yet in v. 1 the full moon begins the year, one of the many inconsequences of the Brāhmaṇas. So iv. 4.

[1] For the offerings here and in v. 4 see ÇÇS. iii. 14. The two fires are taken forward from the Āhavanīya and there is an offering to Varuṇa at the closing bath.

and Ka is Prajāpati, verily thus he delights him; moreover the word Ka is a name of happiness; verily thus he confers happiness upon himself. In that he gives two pairing cattle, that is the symbol of propagation. In that he sacrifices to the steeds, the explanation of that has been given. In that he sacrifices to Varuṇa in the waters, verily thus he delights him in his own home. In that afterwards he sacrifices with the full moon sacrifice, thus in the first half of the month does he sacrifice with the Varuṇapraghāsas.

The Sākamedhas

v. 5. The[1] Sākamedhas are a sacrificial rite for Indra. Just as a great king placing in front the advance guard of his army, pursues his way in safety, verily so does he sacrifice in front to the gods. Just as there is that Mahāvrata in the Soma sacrifice, even so is this a Mahāvrata in the Iṣṭi sacrifice. In that he offers to Agni of the front first of the deities, and Agni is the beginning of the gods, thus at the beginning he delights the gods. In that at midday he sacrifices to the Maruts, the heaters, (it is because) it is hot at midday; therefore at the midday he sacrifices to the Maruts, the heaters. Moreover, the Maruts are Indra's, the midday is Indra's; therefore at the midday he sacrifices to the Maruts, the heaters. In that in the evening they proceed with the householder's sacrifice and the householder's sacrifice is a rite for prosperity, and prosperity is in the evening, therefore he offers the butter portions with the word 'prosperity';[2] verily thus he makes the sacrificer to prosper. In that in the morning they proceed with a full ladle, verily thus he unites the ceremony in the morning with the ceremony on the previous day. In that he sacrifices to the Maruts, the playful, and the Maruts, the playful, are Indra's, therefore he sacrifices to them in conjunction with Indra. In that they bring forward the fire, that it is kindled, the explanation of that has been given. In that there are seventeen kindling verses, the butter portions contain the word 'being', and the invitatory and offering verses (of the Sviṣṭakṛt) are Virāj verses, the explanation of that has been given.[3] In that there are nine fore-offerings, nine after-offerings, eight oblations and the Sviṣṭakṛt as ninth, thus he obtains the brilliance of the Nakṣatras. The six accompanying oblations ending with that to Indra and Agni are the same, the explanation of them

[1] ÇÇS. iii. 15 gives the offerings thus referred to. Only one fire is taken forth, and there is no *vājina* offering or final bath as in the Varuṇapraghāsas, and the fee is only a bull.

[2] Viz. RV. i. 1. 3 (*póṣam*) and 91. 12 (*puṣṭi-várdhanaḥ*). The offering is to the Maruts as householders (*gṛhamedhinaḥ*).

[3] KB. i. 1; v. 1.

has been given.[4] In that he sacrifices at the end to Mahendra, (it is because) the leader[5] occupies the end; therefore at the end he sacrifices to him. In that there is (a cake) on one potsherd for Viçvakarman, and he yonder that gives heat is Viçvakarman, verily thus he delights him. In that he gives a bull, (it is) because the sacrificial rite is Indra's.

v. 6. In[1] that in the afternoon they proceed with the sacrifice to the fathers, (it is because) the fathers have the waning as their portion; therefore in the afternoon they proceed with the sacrifice to the fathers. They say 'Seeing that the fathers have the second half as their portion, then why do they sacrifice to them on the first half (of the month)?' The fathers are connected with the gods; therefore they sacrifice to them on the first half of the month. In that he recites one kindling verse only[2], it is because the fathers are one (offering) as it were, therefore he recites one kindling verse only. It is an Anuṣṭubh verse; the Anuṣṭubh is speech; the fathers are turned away; verily thus with the Anuṣṭubh as speech he causes them to come. In that he does not recite the Ṛṣi descent of the sacrificer, (it is because he thinks) 'Let me not place the sacrificer in the fire'. He recites this Nigada; the explanation of it has been given.[3] In that he invites Soma with the fathers, or the fathers with Soma, the fathers sitting on this strew, and the fathers made ready by Agni[4], (it is because) the fathers are connected with the gods; therefore he unites them. In that he invites Agni, bearer of the oblations, (it is because) the fathers are Sviṣṭakṛt's; therefore he invites him. Some do not invite his greatness, saying 'This is the greatness of the sacrificer'; but the rule is 'He should invite', for it is the greatness of Agni.

v. 7. In[1] that from the fore-offerings and the after-offerings he leaves out the two for the strew, (it is because he thinks) 'The strew is offspring; let me not cast offspring in the fire.' They are six; the seasons are six; the fathers are the seasons; verily thus he delights the fathers. In that he offers the butter portions[2] with the word 'living', verily thus he causes the sacrificer to live. In that there are three[3] for each oblation, (it is because) there are three oblations, and he cuts off from them together; therefore

[4] That is the five of the Vaiçvadeva (KB. v. 2) and the Indra and Agni offering of the Varuṇapraghāsas.

[5] For the *çreṣṭhin* see *Vedic Index*, ii. 262, 403.

[1] The ritual of the offering to the Pitṛs is given by ÇÇS. iii. 16. The offerings are not eaten but smelt and then given to the fathers.

[2] Viz. RV. x. 16. 12.

[3] See KB. iii. 2.

[4] *iti* here is probably not merely enumerative, but is a quotation of the actual words of invitation preceded by *ā,vaha*.

v. 7. [1] This chapter completes the Sākamedhas; the two offerings to the straw are omitted, reducing the fore-offerings to four and the after-offerings to two; see ÇÇS. iii. 16 and 17.

[2] I. e. RV. i. 79. 9; 91. 7.

[3] Three for each set of offering, viz. two Puronuvākyās and one Yājyā, see ÇÇS. iii. 16. 4–9.

there are three for each oblation. Moreover thus he discriminates the rite for the fathers from the rite for the gods. Now the fathers are at a great distance; verily he summons them with the first, brings them with the second, and offers with the third. In that he sacrifices at the end to Agni, bearer of the oblation, (it is because) the fathers are Sviṣṭakṛt's; therefore he sacrifices to him at the end. In that after invoking the sacrificial food and smelling it they do not eat it, (it is because they think) 'The sacrificial food is cattle; let us not cast the sacrificer's cattle in the fire'. In that the Adhvaryu gives to the fathers, verily thus he delights the fathers. In that they cleanse themselves (in the place) where the filters are, and the waters are healing and medicine, verily thus at the end in the sacrifice are healing and medicine produced. In that they mutter the Ṛc, verily thus they produce a benediction. In that having gone north they reverence the Gārhapatya and the Āhavanīya, verily thus having given delight, they declare at the end their purpose to the gods. Moreover the sacrifice to the fathers is terminated in the south; verily thus they make it terminated in the north. In that having gone eastwards[4] they reverence the sun, and the sun is the world of the gods, and the fathers are the world of the fathers, verily thus they ascend from the world of the fathers to the world of the gods. In that in the Sūktavāka he does not mention the name of the sacrificer, (it is because he thinks) 'Let me not cast the sacrificer in the fire.' In that they do not perform the offering to the wives with (the gods), (it is because they think) 'Let us not cast the wives in the fire.' In that having gone north they perform the offerings to Tryambaka[5], verily thus they delight Rudra in his own quarter. Moreover, the sacrifice to the fathers is terminated in the south; verily thus they make it terminated in the north. In that at the end having sacrificed he sacrifices with an Iṣṭi, (it is because) the Sākamedhas terminate in that; therefore at the end having sacrificed he sacrifices with an Iṣṭi. In that afterwards he sacrifices with the full moon offering, thus in the first half of the month he sacrifices with the Sākamedhas.

v. 8. He[1] obtains the thirteenth month in that he sacrifices with the

[4] *prāñca(ḥ)* seems almost inevitable as a correction of *prāñcam* and so the Ānand ed. (cf. *Vait.* vii. 18 with Caland's note), and it is actually read in M, though Lindner ignores it.

[5] The offerings to Tryambaka are described in full detail in ĀpÇS. viii. 18; BÇS. v. 16, 17.

[1] This chapter gives the ritual of the Çunāsīrīya rite which is described in ÇÇS. iii. 18. It may be treated either as a Vaiçvadeva modification or as merely a modification of the full moon sacrifice, and its characteristics are the offerings to Çunāsīrau, to Vāyu and to Sūrya. Çunāsīrau are apparently the ploughshare (*çuna*) and the plough (*sīra*); see Macdonell, *Vedic Mythology*, p. 155. Cf. Weber, *Naxatra*, ii. 334.

Çunāsīrya sacrifice; so great is the year as the thirteenth month; in that there is the thirteenth month, verily thus here is the whole year obtained. If the fire is kindled, the model is the framework of the Vaiçvadeva; if it is not kindled, then the model is the full moon sacrifice; the full moon sacrifice is a support; verily (it serves) for support. In that the fire is kindled, the explanation of that has been given. In that there are seventeen kindling verses, the butter portions contain the word 'being', and the invitatory and offering verses are Virāj verses, the explanation of that has been given. In that there are nine fore-offerings, nine after-offerings, eight oblations and the Sviṣṭakṛt as the ninth, thus he attains the brilliance of the Nakṣatras. The five accompanying oblations ending with that for Pūṣan are the same; the explanation of them has been given. In that he sacrifices to Çunāsīrau, and Çunāsīrau are healing and medicine, verily thus at the end in the sacrifice are healing and medicine produced. In that he sacrifices to Vāyu, and Vāyu is breath, verily thus he delights breath. In that there is (a cake) on one potsherd for Sūrya, and he yonder that gives heat is Sūrya, verily thus he delights him. In that the sacrificial fee is a white (cow[3]), verily thus he delights him; verily thus is his form produced.

v. 9. In[1] that they perform the expiations and the substitutions, in that they offer the libations, verily thus do they produce a benediction, for the healing of the sacrifice and the medicine of the sacrificer.

v. 10. In that they lay to rest the sacrificer with his own fires[1], and the fires are a chariot of the gods, verily thus they lay him to rest on a chariot of the gods; he with this chariot of the gods goes to the world of heaven, where is the world of those who do good.[2]

[3] This is an interesting case of the Sūtra not following the Brāhmaṇa, as the cow is only optional there, the ox being specified first.

[1] ÇÇS. iii. 19. 1, 2 explains that expiations are in the case of disregard of rules, and substitutions in the absence of the proper material. The expiatory verses are given with directions for the libations in iii. 19. 3–8, and in 20 much regarding substitutes.

v. 10. [1] There is a reference to this topic in AB. vii. 2. He is burnt with his sacred fires.

[2] The last words make a Triṣṭubh and the phrase is clearly poetic.

ADHYĀYA VI

THE BRAHMAN PRIEST.

The Creative Activity of Prajāpati.

vi. 1. Prajāpati, being desirous of propagation, underwent penance; from him when heated were born five, Agni, Vāyu, Āditya, Candramas, and Uṣas as fifth. He said to them, 'Do ye also practise fervour.' They consecrated themselves; then when they had consecrated themselves and had acquired fervour, Uṣas, offspring of Prajāpati, taking the form of an Apsaras, came out in front of them; to her their minds inclined; they poured out seed; they went to Prajāpati, their father, and said, 'We have poured out seed; let it not remain here[2]'. Prajāpati made a golden bowl, an arrow breadth in height and similar in breadth; in it he poured the seed; then arose he of a thousand eyes, of a thousand feet, with a thousand fitted (arrows).

vi. 2. He grasped[1] his father Prajāpati; he said to him, 'Why dost thou grasp me?' He replied, 'Give me a name, for without a name assigned I shall not eat food here.' He answered, 'Thou art Bhava.' Since the waters are Bhava, thereby Bhava harms him not, nor his offspring, nor his cattle, nor any one claiming to be his. He who hates him becomes worse, not he who knows thus; his vow is 'A wet garment should one wear.'

vi. 3. A second time he grasped him; he said to him, 'Why dost thou grasp me?' He replied, 'Give me a second name, for with one name only I shall not eat food here.' He answered, 'Thou art Çarva.' Since the fire is Çarva, thereby Çarva harms him not, nor his offspring, nor his cattle nor any one claiming to be his. He who hates him becomes worse, not he who knows thus. His vow is 'All (*sarva*[1]) one should not eat[2].'

[1] Chapters 1–9 give unimportant legends of Prajāpati.

[2] *amuyā bhūt* thus means 'be lost', but not directly. *asicāmahā* in Lindner's ed. is read in the Ānand. ed. as *asiñcāma hā*. The form is, of course, not correct, and is presumably a blunder. In any event the aorist is essential. M reads *retova asicāmahai*; this suggests *reto vā asicāmahi* (with lengthening of *-i* in prolongation misunderstood) which is obviously better, and which Lindner has overlooked.

vi. 2. [1] *abhyāyachat* is rather odd and *abhyāgachat* is an obvious correction, but hardly necessary; M has the former reading.

vi. 3. [1] The play of words on Çarva and Sarva is obvious, and early evidence for that similarity in sound which accounts for the constant doubt as to the real first letter of many words in Sanskrit lexicography (cf. Wackernagel, *Altind. Gramm.* i. 226 *seq.*).

[2] *nāçnīyād* is the obvious reading and is in M. *nāçrīyāt* in Lindner is a mere misprint.

vi. 4. A third time he grasped him; he said to him, 'Why dost thou grasp me?' He replied, 'Give me a third name, for with two names only I shall not eat food here. He answered, 'Thou art the lord of cattle.' Since Vāyu is the lord of cattle, the lord of cattle harms him not, nor his offspring, nor his cattle, nor any one claiming to be his. He who hates him becomes worse, not he who knows thus. His vow is 'One should not speak ill of a Brahman.[1]'

vi. 5. A fourth time he grasped him; he said to him, 'Why dost thou grasp me?' He replied, 'Give me a fourth name, for with three names only I shall not eat food here.' He answered, 'Thou art the dread god.' Since the plants and trees are the dread god, thereby the dread god harms him not, nor his offspring, nor his cattle, nor any one claiming to be his. He who hates him becomes worse, not he who knows thus. His vow is 'One should not look at the cavity of a woman.'

vi. 6. A fifth time he grasped him; he said to him, 'Why dost thou grasp me?' He replied, 'Give me a fifth name, for with four names only I shall not eat food here.' He answered, 'Thou art the great god.' Since the sun is the great god, thereby the great god harms him not, nor his offspring, nor his cattle, nor any one claiming to be his. He who hates him becomes worse, not he who knows thus. His vow is 'One should not look at him on his rising or on his setting.'

vi. 7. A sixth time he grasped him; he said to him, 'Why doest thou grasp me?' He replied, 'Give me a sixth name, for with five names only I shall not eat food here.' He answered, 'Thou art Rudra.' Since the moon is Rudra, thereby Rudra harms him not, nor his offspring, nor his cattle, nor any one claiming to be his. He who hates him becomes worse, not he who knows thus. His vow is 'What is deformed one should not eat, nor the narrow.'

vi. 8. A seventh time he grasped him; he said to him, 'Why dost thou grasp me?' He replied, 'Give me a seventh name, for with six names only I shall not eat food here.' He answered, 'Thou art Īçāna.' Since food is Īçāna, thereby Īçāna harms him not, nor his offspring, nor his cattle, nor any one claiming to be his. He who hates him becomes worse, not he who knows thus. His vow is 'One should not repulse one who desires food only.'

vi. 9. An eighth time he grasped him; he said to him, 'Why dost thou grasp me?' He replied, 'Give me an eighth name, for with seven names only I shall not eat food here.' He answered, 'Thou art the thunderbolt.' Since Indra is the thunderbolt, thereby the thunderbolt harms him not, nor his offspring, nor his cattle, nor any one claiming to be his. He who hates

[1] *parivadet* presumably has the full sense of 'speak ill of' or perhaps 'revile', not merely 'speak about'. *brāhmaṇam* is prob. masc. but the neut. is possible.

him becomes worse, not he who knows thus. His vow is 'Let him speak truth only, and let him bear gold.' This is the great god of eight names, distributed eightfold; up to the eighth generation his offspring eats food; ever more brilliant is a son born in the offspring of him who knows thus.

The Function of the Brahman Priest.

vi. 10. Prajāpati practised fervour; he, having practised fervour, developed from his expiration this world, from his inspiration the world of the atmosphere, from his cross-breathing yonder world. He practised fervour over these three worlds; from this world he created Agni, from the world of the atmosphere Vāyu, from the sky Āditya. He practised fervour over these three lights; from Agni he created the Ṛc verses, from Vāyu the Yajus formulae, from Āditya the Sāmans. He practised fervour over the threefold lore; he stretched out the sacrifice; he recited with the Ṛc, he proceeded with the Yajus, he sang with the Sāman. He developed the sap of the brilliance of this threefold lore, for the healing of these Vedas; he developed *bhūḥ* of the Ṛcs, *bhuvaḥ* of the Yajuses, and *svar* of the Sāmans.[1] On the south side of Ka was the Brahman, the sacrifice of Ka ended as broader to the south and sloping to the north; his sacrifice ends as broader to the south and sloping to the north, whose is a Brahman who knows thus.

vi. 11. They[1] say 'Since it is by the Ṛc that the Hotṛ becomes Hotṛ, by the Yajus that the Adhvaryu becomes Adhvaryu, by the Sāman that the Udgātṛ becomes Udgātṛ, by what does the Brahman become Brahman?' That sap of brilliance which he developed from the threefold lore, by that the Brahman becomes Brahman. They say 'What should he know and what his metre whom he should choose as Brahman?' 'An Adhvaryu', some say, 'he knows the places for moving about.' 'A Chandoga,' some say, 'so are his Haviryajñas[2] performed with the three Vedas.' 'A Bahvṛca' is however the rule, 'The other two Vedas are attendants of that (the

[1] In ÇÇS. iii. 21. 1-6 it is explained that the Brahman priest offers the expiations at all Iṣṭis, the animal and the Soma sacrifices and the expiations for the faults in the three Vedas are given as above. Cf. ĀÇS. i. 12. In AB. v. 32-34 there is some parallel material; see also LÇS. iv. 9. 1-v. 12. 25: KÇS. xi. 1. 1 *seq.*; xxv. 14. 35; Weber, *Ind. Stud.* x. 136.

[2] *Kena* and *Kasya* are presumably as less obvious the correct reading, as referring to Prajāpati, not as the interrogative.

vi. 11. [1] This chapter is important in its support of the Brahman and its assigning of him to the Bahvṛcas. Cf. Bloomfield, *Atharvaveda*, pp. 29 *seq.* For the relation of the Vedas cf. Max Müller, *Anc. Sansk. Lit.* p. 457; Muir, OST. ii.[2] 192.

[2] I. e. the Sāman is thus introduced indirectly into the Haviryajñas.

Ṛgveda), and on it very many Hotṛ's functions[3] depend.' With Ṛcs the cups are drawn, to Ṛcs the Sāmans are sung; therefore should he be a Bahvṛca. They say, 'How much of the sacrifice does the Brahman perform? How much the other priests?' 'A half' should he reply. There are two tracks of the sacrifice; one is performed with speech, the other with the mind; that which is performed with speech the other priests do; that which (is performed) with the mind, the Brahman does; therefore so long as they perform with the Ṛc, the Yajus, the Sāman, so long should the Brahman sit, for he performs a half of the sacrifice.

vi. 12. When they say to him,[1] 'O Brahman, shall we bring forward?' 'O Brahman, shall we proceed?' 'O Brahman, shall we set forth?' 'O Brahman, shall we praise?' he should instigate (them) with the word *om* only; that one syllable is a counterpart for the threefold lore; thus by him with the threefold lore is instigation given. In the Brahman the sacrifice finds support. Whatever blunder or flaw there is in the sacrifice, that they report to the Brahman; that he remedies with the threefold lore. If there be any flaw in the Ṛc, having taken the butter in four portions, he should offer in the Gārhapatya the expiatory libation, with *bhūḥ svāhā*; thus he places the Ṛc in the Ṛc; with the Ṛc in the Ṛc he makes expiation. If there be any flaw in the Yajus, having taken the butter in four portions, he should offer in the Anvāhāryapacana[2] the expiatory libation with *bhuvaḥ svāhā* in the case of the Haviryajña; in the Agnīdh's fire at the Soma sacrifice; thus he places the Yajus in the Yajus; with the Yajus in the Yajus he makes expiation. If there be a flaw in the Sāman, having taken the butter in four portions, he should offer in the Āhavanīya the expiatory libation with *svaḥ svāhā*; thus he places the Sāman in the Sāman; with the Sāman in the Sāman he makes expiation. If there be a flaw which cannot be identified, having taken the butter in four portions, he should offer in the Āhavanīya only the expiatory libation with *bhūr bhuvaḥ svar*. He completes the imperfect part of the sacrifice who makes expiation with these exclamations. He should not say, when appealed to,[3] 'I know not this,' when he knows these exclama-

[3] Or Hotrakas. The reference is clearly to the multiplicating of the priestly functions falling on the Hotṛ and those who assist him; cf. Caland and Henry, *L'Agniṣṭoma*, p. 8. The Ānand. ed. has *atra na*, which is nonsense.

[1] These are a selection of addresses to the Brahman; the two last are given in ÇÇS. iv. 7. 16 in the singular; vi. 8. 5 respectively. The first is paralleled in AÇS. i. 12. 12 by *brahmann apaḥ praṇeṣyāmi*, the second is dubious in reading, *pra variṣyāmaḥ* being found in b as well as *tvariṣyāmaḥ* w, *tariṣyāmaḥ* OL, but *cariṣyāmaḥ* is found in other non-Ṛgvedic texts (ÇB. xiv. 1. 3. 2; TĀ. iv. 5. 1, &c.). Of the other details in 13 and 14 here mention is made in ÇÇS. iii. 21 and iv. 6 and 7. The Ānand. ed. has *pra ca tariṣyāmaḥ*.

[2] I. e. the southern fire used for cooking the Anvāhārya mess.

[3] *upasṛtaḥ* must have this sense; *upaçrutaḥ* of Ob and Max Müller's MS. is not possible.

tions. All indeed does he know who knows these exclamations. Just as there may be a string or leather fastening of wood,[4] so these exclamations are the fasteners of the threefold lore.

vi. 13. In[1] that he casts away a blade of grass from the seat of the Brahman, verily thus he purifies it. Then he takes his place (saying) 'Here I sit down on the seat of Arvāvasu; Arvāvasu is the Brahman of the gods; verily thus he makes him sit down first (saying) 'May he continue uninjured the sacrifice.' Then, having taken his place, he mutters 'Bṛhaspati the Brahman'; Bṛhaspati is the Brahman of the gods; verily thus from him he seeks approval. When the Praṇītā waters are being brought forward, he keeps silence until the uttering aloud of (the word) *haviṣkṛt*. That is the door of the sacrifice; thus he makes it not vacant. (He keeps silence) after the Sviṣṭakṛt sacrifice has been offered until the instigation of the after-offerings. That is the second door of the sacrifice; thus he makes it not vacant. When the gods performed the sacrifice they kept the Brahman's portion for Savitṛ; it cleft his two hands; to him they gave instead two golden ones; therefore is he celebrated as 'Golden handed'. They kept it for Bhaga; it destroyed his eyes; therefore they say 'Bhaga is blind'. They kept it for Pūṣan[2]; it knocked out his teeth; therefore they say 'Pūṣan is toothless and an eater of gruel.' The gods said,

vi. 14. 'Indra is the most forcible, most mighty, of the gods; for him keep it.' They kept it for him; he appeased it with the holy power; therefore he says 'Indra the Brahman.'[1] He gazes on it (saying), 'With the eye of Mitra I gaze on thee'; verily thus with the eye of Mitra he appeases it; he accepts it (saying) 'On the instigation of the god Savitṛ, with the arms of the Açvins, with the hands of Pūṣan I take thee'; verily with these deities he appeases it. Then separating the blades of grass he places (the vessel containing the Brahman's portion) with handle pointing east on the bare earth (saying) 'On the navel of earth I set thee, in the lap of Aditi'; the earth is the appeaser of foods; verily thus he appeases it. Taking thence he eats (saying) 'With the mouth of Agni I eat thee'; Agni is the appeaser of foods; verily thus he appeases it. Then he sips water (saying) 'Thou art healing'; the waters are healing and medicine; verily

[4] *dāruṇaḥ* must of course be read as in ÇĀ. ii. 1, and in the Ānand. ed. For *çleṣman* here BR. vii. 407 suggests 'deim'.

[1] See ÇÇS. iv. 6 and 7 (and i. 6. 9 which is incorporated in iv. 6 by reference). The Mantra *ariṣṭaṁ yajñaṁ tanutāt* is not, however, given in the Sūtras, but recurs in GB. ii. 1. 1. For the breaking of silence with *haviṣkṛt* see ÇÇS. iv. 7. 2; VS. i. 15 (*háviṣkṛd éhi*); the use of the term in this sense is common in ĀpÇS. i. 16. 7; 19. 9. &c.

[2] Cf. ÇB. i. 7. 4. 5–8; TS. ii. 6. 8. 3; GB. ii. 1. 2, which uses KB.; Lévi, *La doctrine du sacrifice*, pp. 125, 126.

vi. 14. [1] *Indro brahmā* is clearly meant on the model of *Bṛhaspatir brahmā* above, but the variant is not in ritual use.

thus at the end in the sacrifice are healing and medicine produced. He touches his vital airs; whatever of the breaths has been ill used or injured, verily thus he makes it to fill up, he heals it. At the end he touches his navel (saying), 'In the belly of Indra I place thee', for Indra thus appeased it. In that he instigates with a muttered prayer for Savitṛ,[3] and Savitṛ is the instigator, verily (it serves) to instigate the rite.

The Characteristics of the Haviryajñas.

vi. 15. Prajāpati is the creator of the sacrifice[1]; by the establishment of the fire he created seed, gods, men, and Asuras[2] by the Agnihotra, by the new and full moon offerings Indra he created. For them he has created food and drink in the Haviryajñas and the Soma sacrifice. Moreover, whatever desire they had, that they obtained by these proceedings (*ayana*), and proper food by the Āgrayaṇa. They say, 'Why are they proceedings?' They are goings to every desire and to the world of heaven; by the four-monthly sacrifices they obtained the worlds of heaven, all desires, all attainments, all immortality. The four-monthly sacrifices are Prajāpati here, the twentyfour-fold year; the Vaiçvadeva is, as it were, his mouth; the new and full moon sacrifices his joints; the days and nights his bones and marrow; the Varuṇapraghāsas his two arms; the three Iṣṭis his expiration, inspiration, and cross-breathing; the great oblation his body; the other Iṣṭis the deities within him, and the Çunāsīrīya[3] sacrifice his support. The four-monthly rites are Prajāpati here, the twentyfour-fold year; Prajāpati is all; the four-monthly sacrifices are all; thus by all all he obtains who knows this.

[3] The Mantra is given in ÇÇS. iv. 7. 17.

[1] The mixture of perfects and imperfects is so complete that it is uncertain if any real attempt can be made to distinguish the force.

[2] *iti* here and below is enumeratory only.

[3] Çunāsīrya in KB. v. 8.

ADYĀYA VII

The Soma Sacrifice.

The Consecration.

vii. 1. The[1] consecration is speech, for by speech is he consecrated. The consecrated is breath; by the consecration as speech, by the consecrated as breath, the gods, having encompassed all desires on both sides, conferred them upon themselves. So verily also the sacrificer, by the consecration as speech, by the consecrated as breath, having encompassed all desires on both sides, confers them upon himself. He offers a cake on eleven potsherds to Agni and Viṣṇu; Agni is of the lower end of the gods, Viṣṇu of the upper end; verily through the two who are of the lower end and the upper end of the gods having encompassed the gods, he obtains identity of world with them. Therefore he who first has consecrated himself will attain his desire, for by him first are the gods encompassed. He consecrates himself with incorporeal breath consecrations; the fore-offerings are expirations, the after-offerings inspirations. In that they proceed with the fore-offerings and the after-offerings, thus expirations and inspirations are consecrated; in that (they proceed) with an oblation, thus the body (is consecrated). He with the body being consecrated obtains all desires; with expirations and inspirations being consecrated, identity of world and union with all the deities.

vii. 2. He recites fifteen kindling verses; the kindling verses are a thunderbolt and the thunderbolt is fifteenfold. The butter portions refer to the slaying of Vṛtra; the butter portions referring to the slaying of Vṛtra are a thunderbolt. The invitatory and offering verses of the oblation are Triṣṭubh verses; the Triṣṭubh is a thunderbolt; by this thrice-formed thunderbolt the gods pushed away the Asuras from these worlds. Verily thus also the sacrificer with this thrice-formed thunderbolt pushes away the rivals who hate him from these worlds. The butter portions refer to the slaying of Vṛtra; they have been described. Next as to the invitatory and offering verses[2] of the oblation, the former contains (the word) 'to', 'Let your tongue move up to the ghee'; that is the symbol of the invitatory

[1] For the consecration see AB. i. 1–6. The mystic version is an advance on the primitive conception of that rite.

vii. 2. [1] The Dīkṣaṇīyeṣṭi is described in ÇÇS. v. 8: it is based on the full moon sacrifice with a cake for Agni and Viṣṇu as its component offering.

[2] See ÇÇS. ii. 4. 8 for the verses. For *caraṇyat* TS. i. 8. 22. 1 has *caraṇyet*; AV. vii. 29. 1 *caraṇyāt*.

verse. The latter contains the word 'out', 'Let your tongue move out towards the ghee'; that is the symbol of the offering verse. The invitatory and offering verses are Triṣṭubh verses; the Triṣṭubh is might and strength; verily thus he confers upon the sacrificer might and strength. 'The conclusion of the approving formula' he says at the sacrificial food offering and at the Sūktavāka; when the cake for Agni and Viṣṇu is offered then he says 'Consecrated'; therefore he should say only 'The conclusion of the approving formula.'[3] Just as in the case of the consecrated, he does not utter the name of the sacrificer in the Sūktavāka; the consecrated is a divine embryo; they give no name to an embryo unborn; therefore he does not utter his name.

vii. 3. He[1] does not make the wife (of the sacrificer) speak on the grass bundle; he does not strew it (thinking) 'In that it is a Soma sacrifice, this sacrifice is not here complete as it were; let me not conclude the Soma sacrifice before its time.' They say 'Why do others not utter the name of the consecrated?' He who is consecrating himself consecrates himself as Agni; in that others do not utter his name, (it is because they think), 'Let us not sit down in Agni.' Again, in that he does not utter the name of another, (it is because he thinks) 'Let me not, having become Agni, burn him.' If he hate a man, he should mumble his name when consecrated; verily thus, having become Agni, he burns him. If he desire a man, he should utter[2] his name with a clear voice; that is the expiation here; the clear is the eye; for with the eye he sees clearly. But this exclamation is the speech of the consecrated, and it is verily truth. 'He who speaks truth, he is consecrated,' so used he to say. They say 'Why do they not eat the food of the consecrated?' In that he consecrates himself, he becomes an oblation; it would be as one might eat of the undivided oblation. He may eat at pleasure when there is continuous pressing; that would be as one might eat of the oblation when fresh.[3] They say 'Why does the consecrated not offer the Agnihotra?' The Asuras offered (it) in themselves without fire which was blown out; they were defeated, when they sacrificed in what had no fire; then the gods appropriated this breath, Agni. In that in the evening and in the morning the fast drink is bestowed, the Agnihotra is offered continuously and without a break in this breath, Agni.

[3] The usual formulae are (*upahūto*) '*yaṁ yajamāno 'sya yajñasyāgura udṛcam açīya*, but this rule omits the reference to the sacrificer for the reason given.

[1] This chapter contains a discussion of some minor points in the Dīkṣā and an explanation of the omission of the Agnihotra on that day, which is represented by the fast food (milk) of the consecrated.

[2] The Ānand. ed. inserts *na*.

[3] So the edd. reading *ayātayāmasya*; much more probable than the sense 'used' if the *a* is not kept.

This is the continuity of the Agnihotra in the consecrations.[4] They proceed (with the ceremony) on the Upasads. What is there to discuss as to the day of pressing?

vii. 4. Next the consecration of Keçin. Keçin Dārbhya, not being consecrated,[1] sat down. To him flew up a golden bird and said 'Thou hast not been consecrated; I know the consecration; let me tell it to thee; I have[2] sacrificed once; I am afraid of it perishing; thou dost know the imperishableness of that which once has been offered; it do thou (tell) to me.' He said 'Yes'; they two discussed together. It was he, or Ula Vārṣṇivṛddha or Iṭant Kāvya or Çikhaṇḍin Yājñasena or whoever it was, it was he. He said 'The bodies are consecrated by that sacrifice; but the man is consecrated indeed whose gods within are consecrated', so he used to say. Where the Adhvaryu offers the uplifting offerings, then the sacrificer should offer five libations, the first with 'May mind for me with mind be consecrated; hail!'; the second with 'May speech for me with speech be consecrated; hail!'; the third with 'May breath for me with breath be consecrated; hail!' The breath (he mentions) in the middle, for breath is in the middle. The fourth (he offers) with 'May the eye for me with the eye be consecrated; hail!'; the fifth with 'May the ear for me with the ear be consecrated; hail!' But Kauṣītaki used to say 'These offerings should not be made; if they were made the libations would be superabundant; he should merely take hold of the Adhvaryu as he offers and pronounce as accompaniment the commencement (of the verses), first 'May mind for me with mind be consecrated'; second, 'May speech for me with speech be consecrated'; third, 'May breath for me with breath be consecrated'; fourth, 'May the eye for me with the eye be consecrated'; fifth, 'May the ear for me with the ear be consecrated.' Verily also he consecrates the deities in man, and the libations which are superfluous are not offered. Now the imperishableness of what has once been offered is faith; he who sacrifices with faith, his sacrifice perishes not. Imperishableness is the waters, both those which are in these worlds, and those which are about the self. He who knowing 'In me there is imperishableness,' sacrifices, his

[4] There are any number of Dīkṣās if desired; see ÇÇS. v. 4. 7. The next clause seems to denote that on the Upasad days the practice of using *vrata* food is also equivalent to Agnihotra, and on the *sutyā* day the question does not arise.

[1] *dīkṣitaḥ* in Lindner's and the Ānand. texts and in the comm. (Weber, *Ind. Stud.* ii. 308) contradicts the statement of the golden bird, and presumably the obvious correction *'dīkṣitaḥ* should be adopted. Dālbhya is read in the Ānand. ed. and the comm., which has *āgatya*. For Keçin cf. *Vedic Index*, i. 186, 187.

[2] *ayaje* is very odd, and *yaje* perhaps should be read. The Ānand. ed. has *ayajet*. Lévi omits the words in his translation, *La doctrine du sacrifice*, p. 108; *aho* may be interrog., as Lévi, but this seems improbable. His observation (p. 109, n. 1) as to a difference of Weber's and Lindner's texts is erroneous.

sacrifice perishes not. This imperishableness of what has once been offered Keçin Dārbhya proclaimed to the golden bird. In the afternoon he consecrates himself; in the afternoon he commingles all creatures; further the beams go over him[3]; therefore making red as it were he goes to his setting. He who consecrates himself consecrates himself as him who yonder gives heat; therefore on the afternoon he consecrates himself, to obtain all desires.

The Introductory Sacrifice.

vii. 5. The[1] gods obtained expiration by the introductory sacrifice[2], breathing out by the concluding sacrifice; verily thus also the sacrificer by the introductory sacrifice obtains expiration and by the concluding sacrifice breathing out; the introductory and concluding sacrifices are expiration and breathing out; therefore those who are priests for the introductory sacrifice should also act for the concluding sacrifice, for expiration and breathing out are alike.

vii. 6. The gods having reached the world of heaven by means of the introductory sacrifice could not discern the quarters. To them said Agni, 'Do you offer to me one libation of butter; then shall I discern one quarter.' To him they offered; he discerned the eastern quarter; therefore they lead Agni forward to the east; the sacrifice is extended eastwards, sitting eastwards they offer in it (the fire), for this was the quarter discerned by him. Then said Soma, 'Do you offer to me one libation of butter; then shall I discern one quarter'. To him they offered; he discerned the southern quarter; therefore they carry round in the south[1] the Soma when purchased; standing in the south he praises; standing in the south he concludes; sitting in the south they press it, for this was the quarter discerned by him. Then said Savitṛ, 'Do ye offer to me one libation of butter; then shall I discern one quarter'. To him they offered; he discerned the western quarter; Savitṛ is he yonder who gives heat; therefore him men see day by day going westwards, not eastwards, for this was the quarter discerned by him. Then said Pathyā Svasti, 'Do ye offer to me one libation of

[3] *raçanāḥ* is clearly correct (*rajatā* M; *rajanā* BK and Ānand. ed.), but the metaphor is not certain; the idea may be that the rays make a red glow as the sun sinks to his setting.

[1] For the introductory offering (KB. vii. 5–9), made on the first Upasad day, see AB. i. 7–11. The ritual is very briefly given in ÇÇS. v. 5; it consists of butter offerings to Pathyā Svasti, Agni, Soma, and Savitṛ, a pap for Aditi; there are no butter portions.

[2] A mere play on *prāyaṇīya* and *udayanīya* with *prāṇa* and *udāna*, for which see *Vedic Index*, i. 86; ii. 47.

vii. 6. [1] *dakṣiṇā* is, as usual in the Brāhmaṇa style, adverbial; so in the parallel TS. vi. 1. 5. 1, 2; cf. MS. iii. 7. 1; ÇB. iii. 2. 3. 14–19; AB. i. 17.

butter; then shall I discern one quarter.' To her they offered; she discerned the northern quarter; Pathyā Svasti is speech; therefore in the northern quarter is speech uttered with more discernment, and northwards go men to learn speech; he who comes thence, to him men hearken, so he used to say,[2] for this was the quarter discerned by speech. Then said Aditi, 'Do ye offer to me one libation of food; then shall I discern one quarter.' To her they offered; she discerned the zenith; Aditi is this (earth); therefore on this (earth) plants grow upright, trees upright, men upright, Agni is kindled upright, whatever there is on this (earth) that stretches upright, for this was the quarter discerned by her.

vii. 7. Thus[1] did the gods discern by means of the introductory sacrifice the world of heaven; verily thus also does the sacrificer by the introductory rite discern the world of heaven. The introductory and concluding sacrifice should be alike. The sacrifice is a chariot of the gods; the introductory and concluding sacrifices are the two sides[2] of it; he who makes them alike, just as one can perform a journey as desired by driving on in a chariot with two sides, so safely he attains the world of heaven. He who makes them unlike, just as one cannot perform a journey as desired by driving on in a chariot with one side only, so he does not safely attain the world of heaven. Therefore the introductory and the concluding sacrifices should be alike, the introductory ending with the Çaṁyuvāka, and the concluding sacrifice ending with the Çaṁyuvāka.

vii. 8. He sacrifices first at the introductory sacrifice to Pathyā Svasti, then to Agni, then to Soma, then to Savitṛ, then to Aditi; he advances with the introductory sacrifice to the world of heaven. In that he sacrifices to Pathyā Svasti in front, verily thus he produces a benediction, for the attainment of the world of heaven. To Agni first he sacrifices in the concluding sacrifice, then to Soma, then to Savitṛ, then to Pathyā Svasti, then to Aditi; he goes with the concluding sacrifice to this world. In that behind he offers sacrifices to Pathyā Svasti, verily thus he produces a benediction, for the attainment of this world. To those five deities he sacrifices; with these

[2] The extent of the quotation is not certain. For the north as a specially important place see Keith, TS. pp. 408, 442, n. 1. Weber (*Ind. Stud.* i. 153) and Muir (OST. ii.[2] 323, 329) cite this passage in connexion with the northern origin of the Aryans, and it is clearly evidence of speech cultivation in the north (*Vedic Index*, ii. 279), perhaps, as Vināyaka holds, Kashmir (cf. Franke's theory of the cultivation of Sanskrit there; *Pāli und Sanskrit*, pp. 87–9). *āha* cannot be taken as referring to *tasya* as taken by Muir; the lack of *iti* is in the context fatal.

[1] This chapter reinforces the doctrine of KB. vii. 5 of the identity of the two sacrifices.

[2] Or 'side-horses' (cf. Keith, JRAS. 1914, pp. 1084, 1085). But the use of such phrases as *ubhayataçcakra* (AB. v. 33. 4) renders this uncertain and indeed improbable. Cf. above, ii. 9.

deities he obtains all that is fivefold regarding the deities and regarding the self. Of these the invitatory and offering verses [1] contain (the words), 'safe', 'path', 'bring across', 'forward', and 'lead'. The Maruts, the subjects of the gods, enjoying the atmosphere, have the power to confound the sacrifice of the sacrificer as he goes to the world of heaven. In that they contain (the words) 'safe', 'path', 'bring across', 'forward', and 'lead', verily the Maruts, the subjects of the gods, harm him not; safely he attains the world of heaven. Them he inverts; the invitatory verses in the introductory sacrifice he makes the offering verses in the concluding sacrifice, the offering verses (he makes) the invitatory verses.

vii. 9. He falls away as it were from this world who advances with the introductory sacrifice; in that he inverts (the verses), thus he finds support in this world on a support which cannot be moved. Moreover the metres are the breaths; verily thus in the self he intertwines the breaths, to prevent severance; therefore these breaths though blowing in diverse directions do not blow out.[1] 'Thee, O thou of most varied fame,' 'What is best, that to Agni,' are the Anuṣṭubh invitatory and offering verses [2] (of the Sviṣṭakṛt offering). The introductory sacrifice is the continuance of the sacrifice, the concluding sacrifice is speech; the Anuṣṭubh is speech; with speech the sacrifice is continued. These two he does not invert, (thinking) 'The invitatory and offering verses are supports; let me not intertwine two supports.' (The sacrifice) ends with the Çaṁyuvāka; that is the symbol of approach. It is as if having advanced one should dwell in the vicinity of the world of heaven. Again, as to (the sacrifice) ending with the Çaṁyuvāka, all the deities unite in the introductory sacrifice; he who would here cause joint offering to be made to the wives with (the gods), it would be as if he were to bring the wives of the gods to the place of their assembling; then it would be as if a man there were to say of him, 'This (fellow) has brought the wives of the gods to the place of their assembly; his wife will be following him to the assembly'.[3] Therefore it ends with the Çaṁyuvāka, to prevent the coming together of the deities.

[1] RV. x. 63. 15 and 16 both contain *svasti* or *svastiḥ*; i. 189. 1 and 2 (for Agni) have *naya* and *pāraya*; i. 91. 1 (Soma) has *pra*; x. 63. 15 has *pathyāsu*.

vii. 9. [1] The reading of M *vānto na nirvānti* clearly is right against the text of the other MSS. *vāñco nunirvāñci*, kept in the Ānand. ed.

[2] RV. i. 45. 6; v. 25. 7.

[3] For the idea see *Vedic Index*, ii. 427. The Ānand. ed. has *abhyava iṣyasi* The acc. denotes the person spoken of; Hopkins' view (JAOS. xxviii. 404 *seq.*) that even when the 3rd person is used, as here, the sense 'say to' can be intended is clearly impossible; in BAU. i. 4. 8, cited by him, *sa yo 'nyam ātmanaḥ priyaṁ bruvāṇaṁ brūyāt priyaṁ rotsyatīti* must mean 'say of him "he will lose"', not 'say to him'. *saṁgatām* if correct must be a gen. pl., a very remarkable form in prose; *saṁgatim* or *saṁgatam*, as a noun, is possible.

The Purchase of the Soma.

vii. 10. The[1] Asuras in this quarter obstructed the gods. Being in the north-east quarter they anointed Soma in the kingship, they with Soma as king pushed away the Asuras from these worlds. Verily thus also the sacrificer with Soma the king pushes away his rivals who hate him from these worlds. Him he buys with four things, a cow, gold, a garment, a female goat; up to four (degrees) are pairing, union, propagation; (they serve) for generation.[2] The moon yonder is Soma the king, the discerning; it enters into him when bought; in that he buys Soma the king, (it is because he thinks) 'The moon yonder as Soma, the king, the discerning, be it pressed out.' Nine verses he recites for him when bought; these vital airs are nine; verily thus he confers vital airs on the sacrificer, for completeness of life in this world and for immortality in yonder world. 'From good to better do thou advance forward,' (this verse[3]) containing the word 'forward' he recites for him being brought forward, 'Let Bṛhaspati be thy harbinger'; Bṛhaspati is the holy power; (thus it serves) for the winning of the glory of holiness. He recites two Triṣṭubh[4] verses to Varuṇa, 'This prayer of the seeker, O god,' 'Within the woods he hath extended the atmosphere'; the Triṣṭubh is the lordly power; Varuṇa is the Triṣṭubh; (thus it serves) for the winning of the glory of lordliness. He recites four Gāyatrī verses[5] to Soma, 'O Soma, thy wondrous'; the Gāyatrī is the holy power; Soma is the lordly power; (thus it serves) for the winning of the glory of holiness and the glory of lordliness. He pauses after uttering the half of the last verse; the verse is immortality; thus he enters immortality. Moreover the verse is the holy power; verily thus he makes a defence on both sides in the holy power and the half verses. Wherever he stops at a half verse or a quarter verse, this is the explanation. He recites the verse,[6] 'Thine abodes which they worship with oblation,' containing (the word) 'forward', for him as he starts forward. He concludes with (the verse[7]), 'He hath come, the god, with the seasons, let him prosper the house,' containing the words 'come' and 'season'; 'Soma, the king, is the year,' used to say Kauṣītaki, 'He, coming, with the seasons approaches.' He repeats (verses) which are appropriate; what in the sacrifice is appropriate, that is perfect; verily (it serves) for the

[1] For the buying of the Soma see AB. i. 12–14. For the ritual see ÇÇS. v. 6.

[2] The same phrase occurs above in KB. iii. 9; below, xxix. 8.

[3] Quoted in full in ÇÇS. v. 6. 2.

[4] RV. viii. 42. 3; v. 85. 2.

[5] RV. i. 91. 9–12.

[6] RV. i. 91. 19.

[7] RV. iv. 53. 7.

perfection of the sacrifice. Nine[8] he recites; the explanation of them has been given; thrice (he repeats) the first, thrice the last; they make up thirteen; the year has twelve months; verily (it serves) to win the year. In that he recites a thirteenth, (it is because) there is a thirteenth month, supplementary and distinct as it were; (thus it serves) for its obtainment.[9]

ADHYĀYA VIII

The Soma Sacrifice (*continued*).

The Guest Reception.

viii. 1. By[1] means of the guest reception (to Agni) the gods obtained both biped and quadruped animals; verily thus also the sacrificer by means of the guest reception obtains both biped and quadruped animals. When the oblation for the guest reception is brought up, they kindle the fire; the guest reception is the head of the sacrifice; Agni is the breath; verily thus he places breath in the head. He recites twelve (verses) for the kindling of the fire;[2] the year has twelve months; verily (it serves) to obtain the year. He recites first (a verse[3]) to Savitṛ, 'To thee, O god Savitṛ', to secure instigation by Savitṛ; to one instigated by Savitṛ no possible injury happens; (verily it serves) to secure freedom from injury. He recites to sky and earth (the verse[4]), 'May the two great ones, sky and earth, for us'; sky and earth are supports; verily (it serves) for support. He recites for him as he is kindled the three verses[5] containing (the word) 'kindle', 'Thee, O Agni from the lotus'; for him when born (the verse[6]) containing (the word) 'born', 'Let men say'; for him when borne in the hand (the verse[7]) containing (the word) 'hand', 'Whom with the hand like a quoit'; for him when being taken forward (the verse) containing (the word[8]) 'forward', 'Forward the god to the feast for the gods'; for him

[8] i. e. 8 Ṛgveda verses and the one in note 3.

[9] The KB. insists with peculiar emphasis on the 13th month; hence *vijñātaḥ* is probably correct and not *'vijñātaḥ*. On intercalation, cf. *Vedic Index*, ii. 162, 412, 413.

[1] For the guest offering to Soma see AB. i. 15–17. For the ritual see ÇÇS. v. 7. The verses for the kindling by friction of the fire are given in iii. 13. 15–17.

[2] These are the verses which follow and which are made up to sixteen.

[3] RV. i. 24. 3.

[4] RV. i. 22. 13.

[5] RV. vi. 16. 13–15.

[6] RV. i. 74. 3.

[7] RV. vi. 16. 40.

[8] RV. vi. 16. 41: it and the next vi. 16. 42 are classed together in ÇÇS.

when being summoned (the verse[9]) containing (the word) 'hither', 'Hither born in the All-knower'; for him when being lighted, 'Agni is lighted by Agni' and 'For thou, O Agni, by Agni', two (verses[10]) containing the word 'lighted'. 'They cleanse him with keen insight', he says in conclusion, with (a verse[11]) ending 'The strong steed in his own abodes'; the abode is the end; the concluding verse is the end; in the end he places the end. (He recites) the first thrice, the last thrice; they make up sixteen; (all this universe) has sixteen parts; verily (it serves) to obtain all this (universe).

viii. 2. With this (verse he concludes) here and in the four-monthly sacrifices; when an animal is offered, after reciting this first[1] he concludes with a Triṣṭubh, 'By the sacrifice the gods sacrificed the sacrifice'; cattle are connected with the Triṣṭubh; verily (it serves) to obtain cattle. (He recites) the first thrice, the last thrice; they make up seventeen; Prajāpati is seventeenfold; that rite is beneficial which is commensurate with Prajāpati. He recites seventeen kindling verses; Prajāpati is seventeenfold; that rite is beneficial which is commensurate with Prajāpati. The two butter portions contain references to the slaying of Vṛtra; verily (they serve) for the slaying of evil; moreover he does not depart from the model of the full moon sacrifice. Some[2] make them contain the word 'guest'; but the rule is that they should contain references to the slaying of Vṛtra. Some say 'They should have Ṛc verses as the offering verses,' stating 'These deities have Ṛc verses as the offering verses[3] in the Upasads.' But the rule is that they should have offering verses with the word 'delighting'. To him that is Soma he sacrifices as Viṣṇu;[4] in that being bought he enters this (universe) as it were, that is his form as Viṣṇu. In that, further, he offers sacrifice to him that is Soma as Viṣṇu, here what in this name is Viṣṇu is to be eaten in yonder name of Soma. Therefore they offer saying 'Soma'; so do they eat. The invitatory and offering verses of the oblation are Triṣṭubh verses; the Triṣṭubh is might and strength; verily thus he confers might and strength upon the sacrificer. The invitatory and offering verses (of the Sviṣṭakṛt offering) are Triṣṭubh verses,[5] addressed to Agni, containing (the words) 'guest' and 'chariot', 'The Hotṛ of the sacrifice, of brilliant

[9] RV. vi. 16. 42.

[10] RV. i. 12. 6; viii. 43. 14.

[11] RV. viii. 84. 8.

[1] *paridhim*, i. e. when the last verse (RV. i. 164. 50) is added it is the *paridhi*.

[2] A reference to the AB. view.

[3] The Yājyā verse normally and here is a Mantra in prose containing the term *juṣāṇa*.

[4] M reads *Viṣṇur iti*, but it is doubtful if this can be accepted as it is an obvious correction and *Viṣṇum iti* occurs again below.

[5] RV. x. 1. 5; iv. 4. 10.

chariot', and 'Who thee, of good horses, of good gold, O Agni.' That is like what is fourfold and complete.[6] The chariot comes to him who uses these two. (The sacrifice) ends with the sacrificial food; that is the symbol of approach; it is as if having advanced one should dwell in the vicinity of the world of heaven.[7] The oblations in these sacrifices, that of consecration, the introductory, the guest offering and the Upasads, are performed inaudibly; these sacrifices are a pouring of seed; inaudibly is seed poured. They proceed, ceasing (the various) rites; the consecration sacrifice ends with the joint sacrifice for the wives with (the gods); the introductory sacrifice ends with the Çaṁyuvāka; the guest reception with the sacrificial food; in the Upasads he sacrifices to the gods. Ceasing with these rites Prajāpati went to the world of heaven; verily thus also the sacrificer ceasing with these rites proceeds to the world of heaven.

The Pravargya.

viii. 3. The[1] Mahāvīra is the head of the sacrifice; he should not at the first sacrifice place it on the fire; the second sacrifice condescends to him who does not place it on the fire in the first sacrifice. Nevertheless for him who is a learned Brahman[2] he may place it in the fire. It is the self of the sacrifice; verily thus with the self he completes the sacrifice. The Mahāvīra is he yonder that gives heat; verily thus he delights him. Him should he praise with a hundred and one (verses); at a hundred leagues hence he gives heat;[3] with a hundred he attains the journey of a hundred leagues; the hundred and first is the world of the sacrificer; of this self the sacrificer becomes master. The man of whom men speak in the sun is Indra, is Prajāpati, is the holy power; thus herein the sacrificer attains identity of world and union with all the deities. Without taking in breath, should he praise, for the continuity of the breaths, for these breaths are continuous as it were. Both aloud and audibly should he praise; the praise is the breaths, for it is expressed, for it has speech as its deity. He utters in praise verses to Savitṛ first, to secure instigation by Savitṛ; to one instigated by Savitṛ no possible injury happens; (verily thus it serves) to secure freedom from injury.

[6] The complete character of four appears not to be meant in the repeated phrase *âcaturam*, iii. 9; vii. 10; but the sense here is clear. The number 4 as the *kṛta* number in dicing may be cited (see *Vedic Index*, i. 4).

[7] So above KB. vii. 9.

[1] For the Pravargya (KB. viii. 3–7) see AB. i. 18–22. For the ritual see ÇÇS. v. 9 and 10.

[2] This is cited in ĀpÇS. xi. 2. 10 with the omission of *syāt* from the Bahvṛcabrāhmaṇa. Cf. KB. xii. 7.

[3] For this estimate cf. Weber, *Ind. Stud.* ix. 349 *seq.*

viii. 4. 'The holy power born first in the east[1]' (he says); the holy power born first in the east is yonder where yonder (sun) gives heat; verily thus here he places the sacrificer. He utters in praise two appropriate verses[2] containing the words 'anoint' and 'sit', 'Whom extending as it were the sages anoint' and 'Sit down; great art thou.' He utters in praise three appropriate (verses[3]), containing the word 'burn', 'Be thou well disposed to us, O Agni, at our approach,' 'Burn thou well, O Agni, the foes that are near,' and 'The foe who secretly may attack us, O Agni'; what in the sacrifice is appropriate, that is perfect; verily (it serves) for the perfection of the sacrifice. He utters in praise (verses[4]) referring to the slaying of Rakṣases, 'Make thou thy brilliance, like a broad net,' for the smiting away of the Rakṣases; Agni is the smiter away of the Rakṣases; they are five; by the symbol of the quarters from the quarters he smites them off. Moreover, the number of spans the Adhvaryu measures, those he accompanies with these (verses). He utters in praise two appropriate (verses[5]) addressed to Indra, 'Around thee, O singer, the songs,' and 'In the two hast thou placed the word of praise'; verily with these two he accompanies the call of Hail! to Indra. Moreover, the number of splinters the Adhvaryu gathers round, those he accompanies with the first, the last which he deposits with the last. He utters in praise two appropriate (verses[6]) to Pūṣan and to Rudra, 'Pure is one of them, worthy of sacrifice one,' and 'Worthily dost thou bear the missiles and the bow'; verily with these two he accompanies the call of Hail! to Pūṣan and to Rudra. Moreover the two golden chips which the Adhvaryu makes of gold and silver, those two with these two he accompanies. 'The bird anointed by the craft of the Asura' (he says[7]); the bird is breath; breath is Vāyu; verily thus with these (verses) he accompanies the call of Hail! to Vāyu. 'I beheld thee perceiving with thy mind,' this[8] he should utter in praise in the house of him who desires offspring. Moreover both (should he utter) when there is something unaccomplished.

viii. 5. 'They of the sounding drop have sounded at the rim' is a whole (hymn) and 'The strainer for thee is outspread, O Brahmaṇaspati' are two verses.[1] 'What time the Dhiṣaṇās spread out the strainer' is one

[1] See ÇÇS. v. 9. 5. The verse occurs in AV. iv. 1. 1, where see Whitney's notes, and see AB. i. 19. The verses in v. 9. 6 and 7 are no doubt also meant as used in view of the use of *sāvitrīḥ* in viii. 3.

[2] RV. v. 43. 7 used *bile 'jyamāne*, ÇÇS. v. 9. 8, and RV. i. 36. 9, used *sādyamāne*, ÇÇS. v. 9. 9.

[3] RV. iii. 18. 1 and 2; vi. 5. 4, used when the coals are put on, ÇÇS. v. 9. 10.

[4] RV. iv. 4. 1–5.

[5] RV. i. 10. 12; 38. 3.

[6] RV. vi. 58. 1; ii. 33. 10.

[7] RV. x. 177, three verses in all.

[8] RV. x. 183, also three verses. *ubhe* refers to both hymns. Çāñkh. ignores this.

viii. 5. [1] RV. ix. 73 and 83. 1 and 2.

verse;[2] they make up twelve (verses) for (Soma) the purifying; verily with these he accompanies the call of Hail! for Soma. 'May Vena impel those born of Pṛçni' (he says); Vena is Indra; verily with these verses[3] he accompanies the call of Hail! for Indra. Of this (hymn) one verse, 'The eagle flying in the vault,' he omits; this is the radiance of the self; this (verse) he inserts in the later (verses), thereby it is not removed. For one who is spoken ill of on both sides of the Vena (hymn) he should utter in praise (the verses) for (Soma) the purifying; Vena is the self; (the verses) for (Soma) the purifying are a purifier; verily thus he purifies him. He utters in praise verses for Brahmaṇaspati[4] which are appropriate, 'Thee, lord of hosts, we invoke'; that is the head; Brahmaṇaspati is the holy power; verily by the holy power he perfects the head. When he approaches (the verse[5]) 'May we speak aloud in the assembly with good sons,' he should think of a son for one desiring a son; she obtains a son. 'What offering will win your favour, O Açvins?' these are nine aimless verses.[6] The aimless verses are as it were of the Gāyatrī metre; breath is connected with the Gāyatrī; the aimless verses are breath. (He utters) three Anuṣṭubh verses,[7] 'Hither with all aids'; that is speech. 'Let Viṣṇu form the womb,' that (hymn[8]) should he utter in praise in the house of him who desires offspring. Moreover both (should he utter) when there is something unaccomplished.

viii. 6. 'Make sacrifice to the two who move in the morning first,' (he utters) in the forenoon this hymn;[1] 'Agni shineth, the forefront of the dawns' in the afternoon.[2] They are Triṣṭubh (hymns), of five verses; that is the eye. 'I praise sky and earth for first inspiration' is in Jagatī,[3] of twenty-five verses; that is the ear. That is the head; that head is complete in which there is breath, speech, the eye and the ear. Thus them in it he places. When it is said, 'Glowing is the pot,' he utters in praise this appropriate (verse[4]), containing (the word) 'glow', 'The tawny one, the chief, hath made the dawns to glow.' He concludes with (a verse[5]) containing (the word) 'around', 'With days and with nights guard us around.' He utters in praise appropriate (verses); what in the sacrifice is appropriate, that is perfect; verily (it serves) for the perfection of the sacrifice. They make up

[2] Given in full in ÇÇS. v. 9. 16.
[3] RV. x. 123, omitting verse 6.
[4] RV. ii. 23, the whole hymn.
[5] RV. ii. 23. 19 d.
[6] RV. i. 120. 1–9. *akūdhryañc* (also in KB. xviii. 4) is of quite uncertain sense, but cf. *mā́kudryak* in RV. x. 22. 12, and *akūtrā* in RV. i. 120. 7; Oldenberg, *Ṛgveda-Noten*, i. 117.
[7] RV. vii. 24. 4–6.
[8] RV. x. 184, the whole hymn. Not noticed in ÇÇS.
[1] RV. v. 77.
[2] RV. v. 76.
[3] RV. i. 112.
[4] RV. ix. 88. 3.
[5] RV. i. 112. 25.

a hundred and one verses; the explanation of these has been given. In that he touches the waters, and the waters are healing and medicine, verily thus at the end in the sacrifice are healing and medicine produced. In that he pays reverence with the 'opening' verses,[6] and the openings are the breaths, verily thus he places the breaths in himself. In that he touches the waters, and the waters are healing and medicine, verily thus at the end in the sacrifice are healing and medicine produced. The latter set are thirty-three;[7] all the deities are thirty-three; they should support that; from them is all that taken out.

viii. 7. He utters in praise appropriate (verses) for the milking;[1] what in the sacrifice is appropriate, that is perfect; verily (it serves) for the perfection of the sacrifice. He utters in praise the two appropriate (verses[2]), containing (the word) 'pour', 'In the pressed pour the admixture' and 'Now hath the Ṛṣi for the Açvins.' He utters in praise the appropriate (verse[3]), 'Up the god Savitṛ with the golden,' containing the word 'lift up' as (the pot) is being lifted up. He utters in praise an appropriate (verse[4]) addressed to Brahmaṇaspati, containing (the word) 'forward' as they move forward, 'Let Brahmaṇaspati move forward.' As they go he utters in praise (the verse[5]) appropriate in containing (the word) 'flying', 'The eagle flying in the vault.' With two (verses[6]) should he utter the offering prayer; strength is a pair; (verily it serves) to win strength; with a Triṣṭubh in the verses on the forenoon, for it, being connected with the Triṣṭubh, keeps supporting the three worlds; with a Jagatī in the verses in the afternoon, for it is connected with the Jagatī, for as it goes to rest all the world (*jagat*) goes to rest with it. 'Inverting the two verses from the Saṁhitā should he utter the call of *vaṣaṭ*,' some say, but the rule is to follow the traditional text. He utters in praise subsequent (verses) which are appropriate; what in the sacrifice is appropriate, that is perfect; verily (they serve) for the perfection of the sacrifice. 'O thou rich in oblation, oblation, the mighty seat of the gods' (he says[7]) before the accomplishment of the libation; verily thus he makes it with renewed oblation and unexhausted. He concludes with (a verse[8]) containing a benediction, 'From eating the good pasture mayest thou be of good fortune'; verily thus he pronounces a benediction for cattle; so are cattle not liable to stray from the sacrificer. In that he

[6] Of the Adhvaryu, ÇÇS. v. 9. 31.

[7] i. e. the verses for the milking referred to in KB. viii. 7.

[1] For these 33 verses see ÇÇS. v. 11. 1 *seq.*

[2] RV. viii. 72. 13; 9. 7.

[3] RV. vi. 71. 1.

[4] RV. i. 40. 3.

[5] RV. x. 123. 6.

[6] The two verses used together (*samasta*) at the morning Pravargya are RV. i. 46. 15 (Gāyatrī) and a special verse in ÇÇS. v. 11. 18 (Triṣṭubh), in the afternoon, RV. viii. 5. 14, and a verse in ÇÇS. v. 11. 21 (Jagatī).

[7] RV. ix. 83. 5.

[8] RV. i. 164. 40.

touches the waters, and the waters are healing and medicine, verily thus at the end in the sacrifice are healing and medicine produced. Now they say 'After the pressing[9] should it be put on the fire'; when the Bahiṣpavamāna (Stotra) has been sung, they invoke the two Açvins, the gods; at that moment should they put it on the Agnīdh's fire; just as there in the Upasads, so here on the pressing day the procedure is without taking breath. Then after due performance (the pot) is put on, and the animal sacrifice is undertaken; the Mahāvīra terminates[10] at midday; in that with it they proceed at midday, and the Mahāvīra is he yonder that gives heat, verily thus they delight him; verily thus his symbol is produced.

The Upasads.

viii. 8. The Asuras made citadels[1] in these worlds, iron in this, silver in the world of the atmosphere golden yonder in the sky they made; the gods when these worlds were invested[2] saw the fifteenfold thunderbolt; three kindling verses repeated together make up nine, the invitatory and offering verses six; they make up fifteen. By means of this fifteenfold thunderbolt the gods pushed away the Asuras from these worlds; verily thus also the sacrificer with this fifteenfold thunderbolt pushes away the rivals who hate him from these worlds. In the forenoon he should repeat the three verses,[3] 'To the bounteous one, to him to be attended'; for these are the Upasads. That rite is successful over which the first (three verses) are said, (for, they say), 'This day is as it were to be attended on by yonder sun.' 'This kindling-stick of mine, O Agni' (he says[4]) in the afternoon; that is the symbol of night, (for they say) 'In the evening they sit round this fire kindled as it were.' Then on the second day (he says) in the forenoon 'This kindling-stick of mine, O Agni'; that is the symbol of day, (for they say) 'This day is kindled as it were by yonder sun.' (He says) in the afternoon 'To the bounteous one, to him to be attended'; that is the symbol of night, (for they say) 'They sit round in the evening this fire which is to be attended as it were.' Both these symbols are recognized;

[9] This is a variant mode of the Pravargya where the two performances take place on the *sutyā* day, one after the morning Stotra and one after the midday Stotra.

[10] The Ānand. ed. has *madhyaṁdino (ne) sargas.*

[1] For the Upasads see AB. i. 23–6. For the ritual see ÇÇS. v. 11. The Upasads here must be fortifications of the Asuras against the worlds to hold them from the gods. *Upasadaḥ* at the beginning is probably the title of the section, and is clearly so taken in M, which punctuates after it; so below, KB. xxiv. 1; xxvii. 4.

[2] *pariçr̥teṣu* is clearly preferable to either °*str̥teṣu* W, or °*svr̥teṣu* O w μ, or *pariçruteṣu* Ānand. ed.

[3] RV. vii. 15. 1–3: these (like the next) are the Sāmidhenī verses.

[4] RV. ii. 6. 1–3.

therefore day by day in alternation should he repeat (hoping) 'Let both symbols, both desires be attained.' He should repeat without taking breath, for the continuity of the breaths; for continuous as it were are these breaths. Thrice each one should he repeat; these worlds are three; verily thus he obtains these worlds. They repeated together make up nine; the seasons are six; these worlds are three; verily thus they make up that. He should not say this Nigada[5] in the kindling verses; the Nigadas are omitted; it would be repetition if one were to say this Nigada. 'He should not invite at all,' some say; 'But how without inviting can he say the offering verse for a deity?' (For this reason). After the Ṛc he should invite with (the invitatory verses), 'Bring Agni, bring Soma, bring Viṣṇu.' For these three gods he says the offering verses; these worlds are three; verily thus he makes these worlds full of light.

viii. 9. The two verses[1] for Agni are Gāyatrī verses; this world is connected with the Gāyatrī; thus he obtains this world. Those for Soma are Triṣṭubh verses; the world of the atmosphere is connected with the Triṣṭubh; thus he obtains the world of the atmosphere. Those for Viṣṇu are Jagatī verses; yonder world is connected with the Jagatī; thus he obtains yonder world. These he inverts; those which in the forenoon were invitatory verses he makes offering verses in the afternoon; those which were offering verses he makes invitatory verses, to avoid exhaustion, (thinking) 'The Ṛc becomes exhausted through the *vaṣaṭ* call; let me perform the *vaṣaṭ* call with (verses) unexhausted on the same day'.[2] In that he inverts also, (it is) for the strength of the neck; therefore the joints of the neck are as it were intertwined. The gods have butter as their oblation, the sacrificer has milk as his fast food; that is in accord. He should treat them as broader above; on the first day (he should milk) three teats, then two, then one;[3] verily thus he makes the worlds mutually broader. He should not take out; they advance to the world of heaven who undertake the Upasads; the world of heaven is twelve journeys away; he who takes out once, it is with him as if one should follow after those with one object sent on a single

[5] The point of this, if *ṛca* = *ṛcaḥ*, is that he is not to use the usual formula (Nigada) *Agne mahān asi* (ÇÇS. i. 4. 44) and the terms *ā vaha devān yajamānāya*, but merely after the last Praṇava of the preceding Ṛc to use the three invitatory formulae given; if *ṛca* = *ṛce* then the translation is less easy; it seems most probable that *kim u* begins a new clause, answering the previous, though it might = 'but rather'. *caned* read by Lindner and the Ānand. ed. is really impossible. *caneti* should be read with WM.

[1] For the verses see ÇÇS. v. 11. 7: they are RV. vi. 16. 34 and 39 for Agni; i. 91. 2 and 21 for Soma; i. 156. 2 and 3 for Viṣṇu. They follow the invitatory formulae.

[2] The offering verses end with *vauṣaṭ*, but not the invitatory verses.

[3] The discussion evidently touches on the usual question of possible mitigations of the unpleasantness of fasting.

night before. If he takes out twice, it is as if the time were two nights; through a third (taking) he loses the world of heaven, he cannot attain it. 'He may however follow,' used to say Paiñgya. 'But he should not take out; wherever he wishes, there first should he go in the world of heaven and stop: such a completion is better,' used Kauṣītaki to say. In the case of (need of) eating his compeers[4] may bring curds for him, but not in the time of the fast food; curds is Soma; his food becomes unobstructed; he obtains it. If they purchase (the Soma) together, the others should proceed for two days with the middle Upasad, for it is an insertion, being in position the world of the atmosphere: so without conflict[5] he proceeds.

ADHYĀYA IX

The Soma Sacrifice (*continued*).

The Bringing forward of the Fire.

ix. 1. Agni[1] is the holy power; in that on the fast day they bring forward the fire, with the holy power do they strike away the evil of the sacrificer, in front with the Āhavanīya, behind with the Gārhapatya, on the north with the Āgnīdhrīya, on the south with the Mārjālīya, in the middle with those within the Sadas. Therefore on the fast day they lead forward the fire to the east, they take out the fires of the priests; verily (they serve) to smite away the evil of the sacrificer. The gods being about to consecrate themselves had recourse to speech, 'Thou hast much and varied experience; but we wish to be compact of truth, compact of restraint.' She desired a portion in the consecration, but the gods would not give her a share therein. She (desired a share) in the introductory sacrifice, and they would not (give) her (a share) therein; in the sale, and they would not (give) her (a share) therein; in the guest reception, and they would not (give) her (a share) therein. She did not at all approach the Upasads being as it were vexed; therefore there should they proceed inaudibly so that they can just hear one another. She came when the fire was being brought forward on the fast day; the gods gave her a share therein; therefore there first should he recite aloud, so that they may know that she has arrived and has been given a share in the sacrifice.

[4] *kṛtavādyapeyāḥ*, comm.; otherwise *samrāj* is Soma, the king.

[5] It may be 'it' proceeds: there is no certainty: *asamāram* would be more simple, but the concurrence of the MSS. including M establishes this text. Cf. KB. vii. 9.

[1] For the Agnipraṇayana see AB. i. 27 and 28. For the ritual see ÇÇS. v. 12. 5; iii. 14. 8–14.

ix. 2. He recites for him as he is taken forth the three verses[1] containing 'forth', 'Forth the god with the thought divine.' 'Thee in the footstep of the sacrificial food', he says[2]; the sacrificial food is this (earth), for in it he praises (*īṭṭe*) all. He praises him when deposited with the half verse[3] containing (the word) 'deposit', 'O All-knower, we deposit thee.' He praises him when he has sat down with (the verses[4]) containing (the word) 'sit', 'O Agni, of fair face, with all the gods'; 'Sit, O Hotṛ, in thine own place, discerning', and 'The Hotṛ in the Hotṛ's seat, well knowing.' He concludes with (a verse[5]) containing the word 'herald', 'Thou art a herald; thou also our protector from afar.' He recites appropriate verses; what in the sacrifice is appropriate, that is perfect; verily (it serves) for the perfection of the sacrifice. Eight he recites; the Gāyatrī has eight syllables; Agni is connected with the Gāyatrī, and has the Gāyatrī as his metre; verily thus with his own metre they bring Agni forward. (He recites) the first thrice, the third thrice; they make up twelve; the year has twelve months; verily (they serve) to obtain the year. They repeated together make up eighteen Gāyatrī verses; verily by the metre it is connected with Agni. Of whatever even metre there are six[6], they make up a Gāyatrī; of whatever there are seven, an Uṣṇih, of whatever there are eight an Anuṣṭubh, of whatever there are nine a Bṛhatī, of whatever there are ten a Pañkti, of whatever there are eleven a Triṣṭubh, of whatever there are twelve (syllables) a Jagatī.

The Moving forward of the Soma Carts.

ix. 3. The[1] two oblation holders are speech and mind; in speech and in mind is all this (universe) placed. In that they move forward the two oblation holders, verily (it serves) to obtain all desires. The oblation holders are two, the cover as the third they deposit; with them he obtains all that which is threefold regarding the gods or the self. He recites for them as they are moved forward (a verse[2]) containing (the word) 'forward', 'Let the two come forward with weal for the sacrifice', 'May sky and earth for us this', and 'Rich in ghee is their milk' he says[3]; the first (verse) contains a benediction; the second mentions two deities: the libation which

[1] RV. x. 176. 2–4.

[2] RV. iii. 29. 4, when the kindling wood is being placed on, ÇÇS. iii. 14. 11.

[3] RV. iii. 29. 4 c.

[4] RV. vi. 15. 16; iii. 29. 8; ii. 9. 1.

[5] RV. ii. 9. 2.

[6] Four Pādas are absurdly assumed, it would appear.

ix. 3. [1] For the moving forward of the two carts which held the oblations see AB. i. 29. For the ritual see ÇÇS. v. 13.

[2] RV. ii. 41. 19 (also cited in KB. xxvi. 10).

[3] RV. i. 22. 14.

the Adhvaryu offers in the track of the two oblation holders he accompanies with the first (verse); in that they move forward the two oblation holders, that he accompanies with the latter. He praises the two oblation holders with the appropriate (verse[4]), 'What time ye came like twins striving.' 'Let men in service to the gods' (he says[5]), for many drag the two. 'In the two hast thou placed the word of praise' and 'All forms the sage doth assume', (he says)[6]; in that they put on the cover third, that he accompanies with the first, in that they enclose the two oblation holders, that with the latter.

ix. 4. Moreover (he accompanies) with the latter the offering on the front[1]. When he thinks of the two, 'They will not move them there', when they make them standing in the middle, then (should he say[2]) 'To your lap, O ye that deceive not'; when there is rest, then a lap[3] is made. He concludes with (a verse[4]) containing (the word) 'around', 'Around thee, O singer, the songs.' He recites appropriate (verses); what in the sacrifice is appropriate, that is perfect; verily (they serve) for the perfection of the sacrifice. They make up eight; with them the gods attained all attainments; verily thus also with these the sacrificer attains all attainments. (He recites) the first thrice, the last thrice; they make up twelve; the year has twelve months; verily (they serve) to obtain the year. Further, in that (he recites) the first thrice and the last thrice, verily thus he ties the two ends of the sacrifice, for firmness and to avoid slipping. Then they say to the Hotṛ 'Do thou, O Hotṛ, act so that there may be freedom from fear.' Thus exhorted, before pronouncing the Ṛc, he pushes a clod westwards with the fore part of his right foot (saying[5]),

'From hence the fear from men and from others than men, O Vṛtra slayer.

Away the wheels have rolled';

Hence is there risk from the wheels; thus for this region there is freedom from fear. He[6] should resort to the left track of the right

[4] RV. x. 18. 2.

[5] RV. x. 18. 2 *b*.

[6] RV. i. 88. 8 (above KB. viii. 4); v. 81. 2.

[1] This offering of the Adhvaryu is described in Caland and Henry, *L'Agniṣṭoma*, p. 89.

[2] RV. ii. 41. 21. The meaning of *nabhyastha* is not quite clear; cf. Caland and Henry, p. 86.

[3] *upasthaḥ* alludes, no doubt, to the fact that in sitting (*kṣema* in the case of a man) then an *upastha* can be formed by crossing the limbs; see Hillebrandt, *Neu- und Vollmondsopfer*, p. 92.

[4] RV. i. 10. 12 (cited also in KB. viii. 4).

[5] The translation of this verse is conjectural but makes sense; it occurs in variant versions in MS. i. 2. 9; TB. iii. 7. 7. 14. The Ānand. ed. has *jajñam* and *anyajajñam*.

[6] *prācyam* is possible, but odd. M. has apparently *prāñayan* (*prāñ yan* ?), *ayāni* in M. agrees, and suggests this use of *yan*; Lindner's *pratidadhyāt* is nonsense, and M and the Ānandāçrama ed. have the certain *paridadhyāt*. Cf. Caland, VOJ. xxiii. 62, who compares ÇÇS. v. 18. 5 *anusaṁyan*, but does not suggest *yan* here.

oblation holder, which is facing east, (thinking) 'The right oblation holder is this world; this world is a support; let me be unmoved in going on this support.' He should not move to right or left from the place where he stands as he says the final verse. If he should move from it to right or left, and if some one were to say of him, 'He shall fall away', so would it be. After concluding, having wheeled round on his right arm, keeping silence, have gone as he came, having stood where standing he has uttered the first (verse), both in the rite and in the taking forth of the fires,[7] he should go to his place.

The Bringing forward of Agni and Soma.

ix. 5. Agni[1] is the holy power; Soma the lordly power; in that on the fast day they lead forward Agni and Soma, verily thus by the holy power and by the lordly power, they smite away the evil of the sacrificer. They say 'Sitting the Hotṛ should recite this first (verse); all beings move forward with the leading forward of Soma, the king; in that sitting the Hotṛ recites this Ṛc, verily thus[2] he restrains all beings in their due place.' 'Do thou pour forth, O god, for the first the father', this verse[3] for Savitṛ he first recites, to secure instigation by Savitṛ; to one instigated by Savitṛ no possible injury happens; (verily it serves) to secure freedom from injury. (With the verse[4]), 'Rise up, O Brahmaṇaspati', he causes (the fire) to be removed; (with the verse[5]), 'Let Brahmaṇaspati move forward' he leads (it) forward. He recites two appropriate (verses) for Brahmaṇaspati; Brahmaṇaspati is the holy power; verily thus by the holy power he makes the sacrifice successful. 'The Hotṛ, the god, the immortal' and 'To thee, O Agni, day and day', these sets of three verses[6] for Agni alone he recites, for Agni they take first. These contain (the word) 'go', for he praises Agni as he is taken. When he comes to (the words[7]), 'The embryo of beings I take up', then he should think of an embryo for one who desires an embryo; she obtains an embryo. In the Agnīdh's altar they put down the fire. When the Adhvaryu offers the libation, then should he repeat this (verse[8]), 'O Agni, rejoice; be glad in this prayer.' This is the offering verse for this (libation), being appropriate as containing the words 'rejoice' and 'be glad'.

[7] The Ānand. ed. has, absurdly, *agniḥ praharaṇa.*

[1] For the leading forward of Agni and Soma see AB. i. 30. For the ritual see ÇÇS. v. 14.

[2] *tad eva* and *yathāyatanam* in M are decidedly superior to the readings *tad* and *yathāyatham* of the other MSS.

[3] Given in full in ÇÇS. v. 14. 8.

[4] RV. i. 40. 1. According to ÇÇS. v. 14. 9 it is said *uttiṣṭhatu.* Cited also in KB. xx. 3.

[5] RV. i. 40. 3.

[6] RV. iii. 27. 7–9 and i. 1. 7–9.

[7] RV. iii. 27. 9.

[8] RV. i. 144. 7.

ix. 6. Then they lead Soma alone eastwards; therefore he recites verses[1] for Soma alone, 'Soma goeth, who knoweth the way.' Reciting the three verses, which contain a reference to 'going', he follows on. There the Adhvaryu offers again a libation in the Āhavanīya; then he should recite this (verse[2]), 'To the dear one, the strengthener.' This is the offering verse for this (libation), being appropriate as containing (the word) 'increasing the libation'. Then they cause the king to enter by the eastern door; as he is made to enter, he recites for him made to enter (the verse[3]), 'This of him King Varuṇa, this the Açvins,' which is appropriate in having (the words), 'This stall doth Viṣṇu, with his companions, reveal.' For him when he has arrived he recites (the verse[4]) 'Within hast thou come forward; thou shalt be Aditi', which contains (the word) 'forward'. He praises him when seated with the verses[5] containing (the word) 'sit', 'Like an eagle his nest, the seat wrought with devotion', 'Thee, lord of hosts, we invoke', and 'He hath established the sky, the Asura, all-knower.' He concludes with (a verse[6]) containing a benediction, 'Do thou welcome Varuṇa the great.' He recites appropriate verses; what in the sacrifice is appropriate, that is perfect; verily (they serve) for the perfection of the sacrifice. He recites twenty verses; they make up the Virāj; Soma is connected with the Virāj; the Virāj is food; Soma is food; thus by food he causes proper food to abound. (He recites) the first thrice and the last thrice; they make up twenty-four; the half months of the year are twenty-four; verily (they serve) to obtain the year. If they cause the king to enter by the eastern door thus is it; but if they (cause him to enter) by the western (door) the Hotṛ should follow after[7] (thinking) 'The Hotṛ is the body of the sacrificer; Soma is the breath; let me not sever the body from the breath.' He concludes standing facing south to the north (of the oblation holder); Soma the king is glory; proper food from thence onwards he confers and glory upon himself.

1 RV. iii. 62. 13–15.
2 RV. ix. 67. 29.
3 RV. i. 156. 4.
4 RV. viii. 48. 2.
5 RV. ix. 71. 6; ii. 23. 1 (cited above KB. viii. 5); viii. 62. 1.
6 RV. viii. 62. 2.
7 *anusamīyāt* is paralleled by *īyuḥ*, KB. xxx. 6; it is read in M.

ADHYĀYA X

The Animal Sacrifice.

x. 1. The[1] sacrificial post is a thunderbolt. In that they erect the post on the fast day, verily thus with a thunderbolt they smite away the evil of the sacrificer. It should not be bent, as it were, for to be bent in the stomach is the symbol of one hungry. Again it should be turned towards the Āhavanīya; that is the symbol of one well fed; his wives[2] are not like to be hungry, who makes a post so formed. One of Palāça wood he should make who desires splendour, of Bilva wood he who desires proper food, and of Khadira he who desires heaven. It should be three cubits with the symbol of these worlds, four cubits with the symbol of cattle, five cubits with the symbol of the Pañkti, six cubits with the symbol of the seasons, seven cubits with the symbol of the metres, eight cubits with the symbol of the Gāyatrī, nine cubits with the symbol of the Bṛhatī, ten cubits with the symbol of the Virāj, eleven cubits with the symbol of the Triṣṭubh, twelve cubits with the symbol of the Jagatī. These measures are suitable forms for the post. One suitable form should he produce and make the post. They say[3], however, 'One should not measure the post; let it be unmeasured; the measured by the measured one wins; the unmeasured by the unmeasured; (therefore it serves) to win the incommensurable.' 'Both for the post and the altar (he should choose[4]) the size which he considers in his mind suitable', (Kauṣītaki) used to say. Mind is Prajāpati; Prajāpati is the sacrifice; the sacrifice itself rejoices in the sacrifice when mind in mind. The post in the Vājapeya alone is determined as of seventeen cubits. It is placed in with eight corners, for the attainment of all desires. Then they wash it; thus what of it has here been harshly treated as it were with the axe and hewn as it were, that of it verily he makes whole, that he heals. Then they[5] anoint it; thus the waters which are in man, these they place in it; well anointed himself should the sacrificer make it; so does the sacrificer become not rough as it were.

[1] For the animal offering of the Soma sacrifice see AB. ii. 1-14. For the ritual see ÇÇS. v. 15-20. The Adhyāya is trans. by R. Löbbecke, who gives the commentary in full (*Über das Verhältnis von Brāhmaṇas und Çrautasūtras*; Leipzig dissertation, 1906), on which see W. Caland, VOJ. xxiii. 68.

[2] *bhāryā bhavanti* is to be read with W w b M μ K, not *bhavati*.

[3] The quotation is not marked but no doubt ends at *avaruddhyai*. Cf. KB. x. 8, n. 2.

[4] M. adds *tai kurvīta*, a mere gloss but a correct one. The opinion is, of course, Kauṣītaki's.

[5] *añjati* as a singular is an anomaly which can be excused only by the proximity of *añjanti* in x. 2. But I think *añjanti* should be restored and so read; as in the case of *praṇenijati* a plural is natural.

x. 2. For it when being anointed he recites the appropriate (verse[1]) containing the word 'anoint', 'They anoint thee at the sacrifice, pious men'. For it when being placed erect he recites (verses[2]) containing the words 'erect' and 'up', 'Rise erect, O lord of the forest', 'Rising before the kindled', 'Born he is born in the fairness of the days', 'Aloft to our aid', and 'Aloft do thou guard us from tribulation with thy ray'. He concludes with (a verse[3]) containing the word 'covered round', 'The youth, well clad, covered round, hath come.' He recites appropriate verses; what in the sacrifice is appropriate, that is perfect; verily (it serves) for the perfection of the sacrifice. He recites seven (verses); the metres are seven; verily (they serve) to obtain all the metres. (He recites) the first thrice and the last thrice; they make up eleven; the Triṣṭubh has eleven syllables; cattle are connected with the Triṣṭubh; verily (they serve) to obtain cattle. So is (the ceremony) in the case of one victim and one post. If at one post they should deal with eleven victims, then in the case of each victim the Adhvaryu gives directions, in the case of each victim there is the same concluding (verse), 'The youth, well clad, covered round, hath come'; it is (recited) for it as it is being covered round. 'So in the case of one post, but how in the case of eleven posts?' (they ask). The same seven verses he should recite for them up to ten; in the case of the last post they set up he should apply the remainder of the hymn, before the Pragātha[4], 'Then like horns of the horned they appeared.' Verily all he accompanies; there is the same concluding verse, 'The youth, well clad, covered round, hath come'; it is (recited) for it as it is being covered round. 'It', they say, 'he should throw along; the post is the sacrificer; the Āhavanīya is the world of heaven; verily thus he makes him go to the world of heaven; that is heavenly'. But they say 'Let it stand; in that this is the place of the splinter of the post, the Asuras and the Rakṣases could drink after if this were not so[5]; therefore this (post) should stand erect as a thunderbolt on the place of sacrifice, smiting away the Asuras and the Rakṣases, and repressing them, and also guarding the sacrifice and the sacrificer.' One is suited for the post, one is rich in wood, one is fitted for a hole. That which has its rind downwards, that is fitted for a hole; such a one[6] he should not wish; that which has its rind pointing up, and is rich in wood[7],

[1] RV. iii. 8. 1.

[2] RV. iii. 8. 3; 2; 5; i. 36. 13; 14.

[3] RV. iii. 8. 4.

[4] RV. iii. 8. 10.

[5] For the construction see Delbrück, *Altind. Synt.* p. 87.

[6] This (cf. AB. iii. 46; vii. 26, 30) is the most probable sense of *āçā* here. The Ānand. ed. has *āsānyeyāt*!

[7] *sa dravyaḥ* seems almost certainly to be read, though only by conjecture. *kāmam* is not certain in sense but most probably may be taken as above: he *may* use it. For *prasavyāḥ* cf. *prasavi*, x. 8, for which BR. (iv. 1094) suggest °*salavi*; the sense is certain.

is that connected with man; he may use it if he desires; the tree, whose rind grows from left to right in accord with the course of the sun, is that suited for the post and is heavenly. (The tree), which stands alone, unrivalled, or is covered up to the root with shoots, is not bare; it is connected with cattle; it one desiring cattle should use.[8]

x. 3. He who is consecrated enters the jaws of Agni and Soma; in that on the fast day he offers a victim to Agni and Soma, this is a buying off of himself[1]; with this buying off of himself he becomes free from debt and then sacrifices. So he should not eat of it, for it is man in counterfeit. But they say 'Every oblation is a buying off of oneself; he would not eat of any oblation, if he were not willing to eat because it is a buying off of oneself. Therefore at will should one eat[2].' Agni and Soma are day and night; in that by day they proceed with (the offering of) the omentum, thereby is day pleased. In that the offering to Agni is carried out during the night, thereby is the night as connected with Soma pleased. 'That is the final setting free of day and night' (they say); by the sacrifice are day and night set free; they do not obtain him, who knowing thus offers this victim. They say 'It should be two coloured; white and black with the symbols of day and night; or white and red with the symbols of Agni and Soma.' There are eleven fore-offerings and eleven after-offerings, and eleven supplementary offerings; these are thirty-three; all the gods are thirty-three; verily (they serve) to delight all the gods. The fore-offerings are expirations, the after-offerings inspirations; therefore are they alike, for the expirations and the inspirations are similar. They say 'Why does he sacrifice with a Ṛc in the fore-offerings and with the opening words only in the after-offerings?' 'The fore-offerings are seed to be poured, the after-offerings are seed to be deposited; therefore with a Ṛc he sacrifices in the fore-offerings, and with the opening words in the after-offerings.' In that he says the last whole, verily thus he places the sacrificer in the world of heaven. He invokes with the Āprī verses; with the whole self, with the whole mind, he gathers together the sacrifice, who sacrifices. The self of him becomes empty as it were; he fills it up for him with these (verses). In that he fills it up, therefore are they

[8] The position of *vā* makes it clear that it contrasts the tree with shoots and that with no other trees near it, and calls both *paçavya* as contrasted with the merely *svargya* tree. It is quite clear that '*bhrātṛvyaḥ* is to be read and taken with *ekasthaḥ*. The Ānand. ed. here is very careless, having *svayūpyasya*, and like Lindner it reads *bhrātṛvyaḥ*. Caland (VOJ. xxiii. 68) remarks on the obscurity of the passage, but offers no help.

[1] For this idea cf. Schwab, *Das altindische Thieropfer*, p. xix; Keith, *Taittirīya Saṁhitā*, pp. cvi *seq.* See AB. ii. 3.

[2] There is no *iti* to make clear the end of the argument, but it is doubtless here. Cf. KB. x. 1, n. 3; xii. 7, n. 6; xvii. 1; xxiv. 8; xxv. 8.

called Āprīs (fillers). He surrounds the animal with fire, to smite away the Rakṣases; Agni is the smiter away of the Rakṣases; he carries the fire round thrice from left to right; that is as if Agni were to put three forts. Therefore, 'Go round again' he should say to the Agnīdh, if he desire of a man, 'May he not fall away.'

x. 4. 'O ye divine slayers and ye human make ready; bring (the victim) to the doors of the sacrifice, ordaining the sacrifice for the two lords of the sacrifice'; regarding this[1] some say, 'The lord of the sacrifice is the sacrificer.' 'What man (is the lord)?' he should say, 'the lord of the sacrifice is the deity only.' 'Its bends are twenty-six', (he says); the bends are the ribs. On both sides of the blood he breathes down, (thinking) 'The Rakṣases have the blood as their share; let me not set away the share of the gods with the share of the Rakṣases.' It is the Adhrigu (formula). The instruction is 'Do not mutilate the limbs.' What is unspoilt is the oblation of the gods; they do not eat the oblation which is spoilt. Nine times does he breathe down in the Adhrigu; the breaths are nine; verily thus he places breaths in the sacrificer, to secure full life in this world and immortality in yonder world. Thrice[2] he utters the concluding verse, to avoid non-recurrence. He says one before; the fathers are one as it were; the victim has as it were the fathers for its deity when it is being offered. In that he says three after, and among the gods (things are) thrice, verily thus he makes it have the gods as its deities, and renews it. Having concluded he mutters inaudibly, 'Both and he that is not evil'; the slayer of the gods is not evil;[3] to him verily does he hand it over, for he knows the gods.

x. 5. Then he recites (the verses) accompanying the drops;[1] verily with them he makes the drops suitable for Agni. These are the invitatory verses for them, these the offering verses. Therefore they are appropriate. Having proceeded with the (offering to the) calls of Hail! they proceed with the (offering of the) omentum; verily thus they make the fore-offerings sharers in the victim. He should not utter speech between the (offering to the) calls of Hail! and the (offering of the) omentum,

[1] For the Mantra see Schwab, pp. 102 *seq.*; ÇÇS. v. 17. 1–9. There are nine Mantras for the Hotṛ in the Adhrigu. The account in AB. ii. 6, 7 is fuller.

[2] *adhrigo çamīdhvaṁ suçami çamīdhvaṁ çamīdhvam adhrigo 3*, ÇÇS. v. 17. 10.

[3] Haug's ingenious view that *apāpa* = *apa*, *apa* addressed to the slaughterer, though in consonance with probability, is not supported by any real evidence, and the explanation of the word as a symbol of deprecation of sin in the slayer is equally good, and accords with the use of such terms as *çamitṛ* and *saṁjñapaya*.

x. 5. [1] For the ritual see ÇÇS. v. 18. 1–19. 12. The Puroḍāça offering follows the norm of the Iṣṭis, i. e. the new and full moon sacrifices, and the Sviṣṭakṛt offering is one of a cake.

(thinking) 'The calls of Hail! are the breaths; the omentum is the body; let me not separate the breaths and the body by anything.' In that the invitatory verses of the victim for Agni and Soma are Anuṣṭubh verses, (it is because) the Anuṣṭubh is the Gāyatrī and the metre of Agni is the Gāyatrī; in that the offering verses are Triṣṭubh verses, it is because the Triṣṭubh is the metre of the lordly power, and Soma is the lordly power. Thus according to the metre he delights the two deities. During the offering of the victim a cake is offered;[2] the cake is the sap of animals; verily thus he makes (the victim) full of sap and fit for sacrifice. Where a cake in connection with the victim is offered, the Sviṣṭakṛt of the cake (offering) is permanent; the Sviṣṭakṛt is Agni (the unmoved);[3] therefore it becomes permanent. Having recited (a verse) of Viçvāmitra, as the invitatory verse for the cake Sviṣṭakṛt, he recites (a verse) of Viçvāmitra as the offering verse; the cake is the continuity of the sacrifice; Viçvāmitra is speech; by speech the sacrifice is continued.

x. 6. Then he recites the Manotā.[1] All the deities gather towards the victim as it is offered, (thinking) 'He will utter my name; he will utter my name.' The minds of all these are woven in the victim; these he delights herein; so it is not in vain that all these have assembled together. They say 'Since the victims are offered to diverse deities, then why does he accompany that for Agni alone?' 'Three are the Manotās of the gods; Agni is the Manotā of the gods, for in him the minds of the gods are woven. Moreover, speech is the Manotā of the gods, for in it are their minds woven. Moreover, the cow is the Manotā of the gods, for in her are their minds woven. All the Manotās are Agni; in Agni the Manotās unite; therefore he accompanies that for Agni only' (is the answer). They make up thirteen; thirteen are the cuttings of the victim; these he accompanies.[2] (He recites) the first thrice and the last thrice; they make up seventeen; Prajāpati is seventeenfold; that rite is beneficial which is commensurate with Prajāpati. He recites seventeen kindling verses; Prajāpati is seventeenfold; that rite is beneficial which is

[2] The construction as the sentence stands is an accusative absolute, but it is obvious, as Lindner points out, that *'nunirupyate* must be read. Curiously enough the same change is not suggested by Lindner below, where it is certain as *nunirupyate* is found in OLC, *na nirupyate* in Ānand. ed. and W w B K, and *na nirupyata* in b, and the reading *nirupyate* which he adopts only in M. *na nirupyate* could be rendered, but the sense is not better than that given by *'nunirupyate*.

[3] *acyutaḥ* (cf. KB. x. 6) goes with the preceding words, but it also applies to Agni, who is the connecting link in the argument. Read *puroḍāçasviṣṭakṛt*.

[1] RV. vi. 1; see ÇÇS. v. 9. 18. Cf. also KB. xii. 8.

[2] This is doubtless the real force of *samavadyati*: he shares in the making portions (*avadyati*) of the victim by his recitation.

commensurate with Prajāpati. When the victim is offered, then the lord of the forest is unmoved; the lord of the forest is Agni, he bestows the oblation on the gods; therefore he becomes unmoved; he also has milk as his portion; so Agni becomes a sharer in all the oblations. They say 'Since the gods possess the solid[3], then why does the lord of the forest possess the liquid as his share?' 'The gods shared the solid of the sacrifice, the fathers the liquid; the victim has, as it were, the fathers as its deities; the milk has the fathers as its deities; therefore is it', he should reply. They say 'Why in the Soma sacrifice do they offer two libations for the choosing[4] (of priests), and not in the Haviryajña?' 'The Haviryajña is an incomplete sacrifice; the Soma sacrifice is a complete sacrifice; therefore at the Soma sacrifice alone do they offer the two libations for the choosing and not at the Haviryajña' (is the answer). He offers in the first case with the call of Hail! 'Acceptable to speech may I become, acceptable to the lord of speech; O divine speech, what of thy speech is sweetest, in that us may he[5] to-day place; hail to Sarasvatī.' Thus he releases speech; therefore hence onwards speech being released supports the sacrifice; with the mind (he accompanies) the second (libation); for by mind is mind delighted.

ADHYĀYA XI

The Soma Sacrifice (*continued*)

The Prātaranuvāka.

xi. 1. Next[1] comes the morning litany. In that he recites it in the morning, that is why the morning litany has its name. In that he mutters the formulae of recourse, in that he offers the libations, verily thus he produces a benediction. After uttering the sound *hiñ* he recites the morning litany; the sound *hiñ* is a thunderbolt; verily thus with a thunderbolt he smites the evil of the sacrificer. He should recite aloud in a clear tone. The clear is the one part of speech which is not infested by evil; therefore in a clear tone should he recite, to smite away the evil of the sacrificer. By half verses should he recite; these worlds are com-

[3] *dhāma* and *pāthaḥ* here seem necessarily to have some such sense (*pā* 'drink' explaining *pāthaḥ*); read *abhajanta*. Cf. ZDMG. liv. 608.

[4] For these libations see ÇÇS. vi. 9. 16–18; Caland and Henry, *L'Agniṣṭoma*, p. 186.

[5] See TS. iii. 1. 10. 1 with Keith's note.

[1] For the morning litany see AB. ii. 15–18. For the ritual see ÇÇS. vi. 2 *seq.* The formulae of recourse are a series *bhūḥ prapadye*, &c., said before the Agnīdh's altar.

mensurate with the Ṛc; the first half verse is this world, the second yonder world; what is between the two half verses is the atmosphere here. In that he recites by half verses, verily thus he makes the sacrificer to prosper with these worlds; verily thus he places the sacrificer in these worlds.

xi. 2. 'Now the Pañkti has five feet; how is it recited by half verses?' (they ask). The syllable *om* is the third with the last two; so is it recited by half verses. He recites the service[2] to Agni; thus he obtains this world; he recites that to Uṣas; verily thus he obtains the world of the atmosphere; he recites that to the Açvins; verily thus he obtains yonder world. He recites a Gāyatrī; the Gāyatrī is the mouth; he recites an Anuṣṭubh; the Anuṣṭubh is speech; thus he places speech in the mouth; by the mouth he utters speech. He recites a Triṣṭubh; the Triṣṭubh is might and strength; verily thus he places might and strength in the sacrificer. He recites a Bṛhatī; the Bṛhatī is cows and horses; he recites a Uṣṇih; the Uṣṇih is sheep and goats; he recites a Jagatī; the Jagatī is might and strength; the Triṣṭubh is might and strength in the front; the Jagatī is might and strength behind;

xi. 3. in the middle are cattle connected with the Bṛhatī and the Uṣṇih; verily thus with might and strength he encircles the cattle on both sides and confers them upon the sacrificer. So from the sacrificer cattle are not likely to depart. Just as in this world men eat cattle, just as they enjoy them, so in yonder world cattle eat men, so they enjoy them. He wins them here with the morning litany; won here they eat him not in yonder world, they enjoy him not in requital. Just as he eats them in this world, just as he enjoys them, so in yonder world he eats them, so he enjoys them. He recites a Pañkti verse; the Pañkti is a support; verily thus in all creatures he makes the sacrificer find support.

xi. 4. Now all the gods resort to the Hotṛ as he is about to recite the morning litany, expecting 'With me will he commence, with me will he commence.' If he were to commence indicating one deity, he would fall a victim to the other deities. He commences with (a verse) not addressed (to one deity); thereby he does not fall a victim to any deity. (With the verse),[1] 'O waters, the rich ones' he commences; all the deities are the waters; verily thus with all the deities he commences. 'Advancing

[1] The recitation ends with *o 3*, which counts here as the sixth Pāda; ÇÇS. vi. 8. 10.

[2] For these see ÇÇS. vi. 4–6.

xi. 3. [1] A rare and interesting passage on moral retribution, regarded as usual ritually: cf. the vision of Bhṛgu in the ÇB. xi. 6. 1; JB. i. 44–48 (Oertel, JAOS. xv. 234–238; xxvi. 196); Lévi, *La doctrine du sacrifice*, pp. 100–102.

xi. 4. [1] RV. x. 30. 12.

forward up to the sacrifice', (with this)[2] he continues. 'Up' is the symbol of this world, 'advancing' is that of yonder (world); 'up' is the symbol of Agni, 'advancing' is that of yonder sun; so in all the formulae of recourse, in all the services to Agni, to Uṣas, and to the Açvins the first utterance is the symbol of Agni, the second that of yonder sun. There are varied metres and between them pits as it were; these two are the strongest, the uninjured, the untroubled, deities; with these two he commences. With the one hymn[3] should he mount; that is the symbol of mounting without falling into a pit and is heavenly. When there occurs in the one hymn a difference of authorship, then without taking breath should he step over. Breath is immortality; thus by immortality he passes by death; just as one steps over a pit by means of a beam or a roller,[4] so with the Praṇava he steps over; the Praṇava is holy power; verily thus with the holy power he continues the holy power.

xi. 5. The Praṇava[1] should be uttered pure for those who desire offspring, with *m* at the end for those who desire support. 'The Praṇava should have *m* at the end', some say, but the rule is that it should be used pure. The Praṇava is investigated as to the fact that 'Here it is pure, here it is in full form'. 'The Praṇava should be pure in the middle of Çastras and of recitations', Kauṣītaki used to say. Thus is continuity. It should have *m* at the end for the sake of a pause; the pause is a support; verily (it serves) for a support. Verily (the two serve) to obtain both desires. These are the carryings of the metres; they carry the subsequent over the preceding metre. No harm[2] befalls him, who by the metre is carried over[3] the metre. 'When he is passing over, he should pierce with his mind as it were him whom he hates; in the fractures of the metre he either goes to ruin or is crushed,' so he used to say. The Pañktis at the end of the offerings he recites with the same endings; the end is sap, the metres are cattle; verily thus the metres end in sap; cattle ending as it were rejoice in the good grass. This is a Virāj with one syllable short; with one twice repeated it is exactly a Virāj; with one thrice repeated there is one over the Virāj.

[2] RV. i. 74. 1 (also in KB. xxii. 1).

[3] The three *kratus* have parts in Gāyatrī, Anuṣṭubh, Triṣṭubh, Bṛhatī, Uṣṇih, Jagatī, Pañkti. Hence there are breaks in the metre; but in the case of the *samdrohaṇīya* verses they are all to be treated as in a single hymn, disregarding differences of hymn (*ārṣeya*). On this plan the occurrence of *gartas* is avoided. For the verses which are reduced to 360 by some see Ānartīya on ÇÇS. vi. 6. 89 *seq.*

[4] Something flat, like a board, is clearly meant. The Ānand. ed. reads *martyena.*

[1] i. e. *o 3* not *o 3 m*.

[2] *āptiḥ* is read in the Ānand. ed.

[3] The sense is doubtful, but nothing better seems possible as the text stands in the MSS. and edd.

xi. 6. Three desires are there in the sacrifice, that in its completion, that in its deficiency, that in its superabundance. The complete part of the sacrifice is heavenly, the defective food, the superabundant serves for generation. Verily thus here the sacrificer obtains all desires. He concludes with (a verse) containing a benediction[1], 'Uṣas with her ruddy kine hath appeared'; verily thus he utters a benediction for cattle. So cattle are not likely to stray from the sacrificer. At this verse he lets out his voice[2]; thus he announces him to the gods, 'He has been born,' for in it is he born. He repeats (the verse[3]) of two Padas, 'With this let us win the prize set by the gods'; the metres increasing by four (syllables) are cattle; (the verses) with two Padas are the sacrificer's metre; verily thus he places the sacrificer in command of cattle; man stands over cattle, as it were. He recites the thrice seven metres of the services; that makes up twenty-one; the fourfold Stoma, the highest of the Stomas, is the twenty-onefold; thus he obtains the highest of the Stomas. In that there are twenty-one, the months are twelve, the seasons five, these worlds three, and the sun yonder the twenty-first, verily thus he fixes the sacrificer in unity of world with him.

xi. 7. They say 'Seeing that there are these kindling verses of the Haviryajña or the animal sacrifice, then what are those of the Soma sacrifice?' 'The morning litany', he should reply, for by the syllables of the others he seeks to obtain the year, by the Ṛcs here. A hundred[1] only should he recite; man has a hundred (years of) life; verily thus he confers life upon him. He should recite a hundred and twenty; the days of a season are one hundred and twenty; thus he obtains the season; by the season the year, and the desires that are in the year. He should recite three hundred and sixty; the days of the year are three hundred and sixty; verily (they serve) to obtain the year. He should recite seven hundred and twenty; seven hundred and twenty are there of the days and nights of the year; thus he obtains the days and nights of the year. A thousand should he recite; a thousand is all, the morning litany is all; thus all he obtains with all, who knows thus. But Kauṣītaki used to say 'The morning litany is Prajāpati; Prajāpati is incommensurable; who ought to measure it?' This is the rule.

xi. 8. They say 'Since the hymns are recited in the Sadas, then why does he recite the morning litany at the two oblation holders?' The two

[1] RV. v. 75. 9.
[2] i. e. he goes from the middle to the highest tone, ÇÇS. vi. 6. 15.
[3] RV. vi. 17. 15.
xi. 7. [1] The 100 verse form is given in the Aitareya tradition from a Prayoga by Caland and Henry, p. 181; the 120 and 360 and 720 verse forms in Ānartīya's commentary on ÇÇS. v. 6. 41 in lieu of the 1,000 verse form laid down in the Sūtra itself.

oblation holders are the head of the sacrifice; the metres are the breaths; thus he places breath in the head. In the Sadas the hymns are recited; the Sadas is the stomach; the hymns are food; proper food is suited for the stomach. As is a cart, so is the sacrifice in counterfeit; as the corn, so the morning litany; as the vessels, so the hymns. If a man recites a little just as vessels come together (in a cart) with a little corn only, so his hymns come together, and on account of the coming together of the hymns tottering is liable to befall the sacrificer; therefore should he repeat many; thus he makes strong the hymns. (He says) 'Let the benediction of the sacrifice as successful be obtained for me'; the benediction of the sacrifice as successful is the sacrificer's. Three are these sets of a thousand in the sacrifice, the morning litany, the Açvins' litany, and the great litany.[1] He should begin when night is far advanced,[2] before the emission of speech, before the time when cattle, men, and birds take up speech; speech these creatures make to swell, in that they lie silent (thinking) 'Let us first prosper on speech, swollen, not dissipated.' Between the morning litany and the Upāñçu and Antaryāma cups he should not set free his speech (thinking) 'The Upāñçu and Antaryāma cups are expiration and inspiration; the morning litany is speech; let me not separate expiration and inspiration and speech by any other thing.' Some begin with 'O waters, ye wealthy ones', after muttering (thinking) 'This is a yoking of the metres[3]'; but the rule is 'He should not insert anything before the words 'O waters, ye wealthy ones', to prevent him being laid low.

ADHYĀYA XII

THE SOMA SACRIFICE (*continued*).

The Aponaptrīya.

xii. 1. The[1] waters are the sacrifice; in that they come to the waters, verily thus they come to the sacrifice. Moreover the waters are strength and sap.[2] Verily thus they unite the sacrifice with strength and sap.

[1] The reading of M. *mahāvratam iti etad uktham* is a good example of the glosses which are found here and there in that MS.

[2] *mahārātram* in W w O b μ is a common error before *u* (*pakuryāt*), and is kept in the Ānand. ed.

[3] These words seem (despite the silence of the *Vedic Concordance*) to be intended to be the matter muttered, unless it is a title of some text, or unless we take it as 'having muttered (thinking) "This is a yoking of the metres".'

xii. 1. [1] For the Aponaptrīya see AB. ii. 19, 20. For the ritual see ÇÇS. vi. 7. 1–10.

[2] The reading is certainly *ūrjaiva* despite the errors of the MSS., *ūrjenaiva* (so the

Moreover, the waters are immortality; verily thus he confers immortality upon himself. Now aforetime the Rakṣases, confounders of the sacrifice, used to watch the waters at the fords; then whosoever came to the waters they killed them all; then Kavaṣa saw this hymn of fifteen verses,[3] 'Forth among the gods let there be speeding for the Brahman'; he recited it; thereby he smote away the confounders of the sacrifice, the Rakṣases, from the fords; thence since then they return in safety and uninjured from the sacrifice.[4] Yonder in the waters the Adhvaryu offers a libation; then should he accompany this (with the verse [5]), 'Send forth our sacrifice with divine offering.' This is the offering verse for this (libation), being appropriate by containing (the word) 'offering'. (He recites [6]) 'Winding hitherward, those of two streams,' when (the waters) are being brought; 'What time the waters are seen coming forward,'[7] when they are discerned; 'Some come together; others come up,'[8] as they come up; some waters come, others come up; 'Like the waters divine, they come up to the vessel of the offering',[9] as they are poured down into the Hotṛ's bowl; 'May the cows with milk eager for the end',[10] the cows are the waters, for the waters impel all this (universe). The Adhvaryu stands turned towards the Hotṛ; the Hotṛ asks him, 'O Adhvaryu, hast thou found the waters?' 'Hast thou found the sacrifice?' verily thus he says to him. 'They have indeed condescended'[11] he replies; 'We have found what we have sought in these waters; for this they have condescended,' verily thus he says to him. Being answered the Hotṛ begins the Nigada; the Nigada is strength and sap; verily strength and sap he places in the oblation by means of the Nigada.

xii. 2. 'The mothers go with the paths' (he recites [1]); the mothers are the waters, for he praises the waters as they go. 'They have come, rich, with living gifts' (he recites [2]) when they have come up. He concludes with

Ānand. ed.) *anurjenaiva* (M), *ūrjam eva*. This episode, according to Weber (*Ind. Stud.* x. 158, n. 1), may refer to attacks by the aborigines on the Aryan invaders. The reading of M *'ccha yanti* is obviously to be restored in the text for *ucchrayanti*; cf. Caland, VOJ. xxiii. 63.

[3] RV. x. 30.

[4] *svastir iṣṭyāḥ* is hardly correct, as *svastiḥ* as nom. is not natural since it leaves no qualification of the sentence *iṣṭyāḥ*, &c.; the readings of M *svasty ariṣṭā* and K *svasty ariṣṭyā* point to a possible original *svasty ariṣṭā iṣṭyāḥ*. The Ānand. ed. has *svasti riṣṭyāḥ*.

[5] RV. x. 30. 10.

[6] RV. x. 30. 11.

[7] RV. x. 30. 13.

[8] RV. ii. 35. 3. The waters mixed are the Vasatīvarī's with those in the Maitrāvaruṇa's bowl.

[9] RV. v. 43. 1.

[10] RV. v. 43. 1.

[11] M has *tad ālotem anannamur iti*. AB. ii. 20. 12 has *anamnamuḥ*, and *avaḥ* in the question in the Mantra, glossed by *avidaḥ*, the two imperfects being natural.

[1] RV. i. 23. 16.

[2] RV. x. 30. 14.

(a verse [3]) containing the word 'across', 'The waters have arrived, eager, to this strew.' He recites appropriate (verses); what in the sacrifice is appropriate, that is perfect; verily (they serve) for the perfection of the sacrifice. The morning litany had been recited, the hymns had not been obtained [4]; at this conjunction the Asuras went against them; the gods, perceiving in fear, saw this thriceforged thunderbolt; 'The waters' is the first form of the thunderbolt; 'Sarasvati' is the second form of the thunderbolt [5]; this [6] is a hymn of fifteen verses, that is the third form of the thunderbolt. The gods with the thriceforged thunderbolt pushed away the Asuras from these worlds; verily thus also the sacrificer pushes away with this thriceforged thunderbolt the rivals who hate him from these worlds.

xii. 3. The [1] Mādhyamas performed a session on the Sarasvatī. Then Kavaṣa sat down in the midst, they said to him, 'Thou art the son of a female slave; we will not eat with you.' He rushing on in anger praised the Sarasvatī with this hymn; she followed after him; thereupon they felt themselves free from passion [2]; they went after him and said 'O seer, homage be to thee; harm us not; thou art of us the best, seeing that she follows after thee.' Thus they informed him; they removed his anger. This is the greatness of Kavaṣa and the founder of the hymn (is he). In that they go with their wives, (it is because) the Gandharvas as commissioners [3] in the waters guard the Soma of Indra. They love women, and they turn their minds towards them; so it is as if one might take the sacrifice of careless persons. The sacrifice condescends to him who knows thus. He recites twenty (verses); they make up the Virāj; the waters are connected with the Virāj, the Virāj is food, the waters are food; thus by food he causes proper food to abound. (He recites) the first thrice, and the last thrice; they make up twenty-four; the Gāyatrī has twenty-four syllables; the Gāyatrī supports the morning pressing; thus the waters contain the symbol of the morning pressing. So much for the Aponaptrīya.

[3] RV. x. 30. 15.

[4] *aprāptā* is read in the Ānand. ed. as well as in the MSS., except M, used by Lindner, but as an active it is doubtful; and it is difficult to trust the MSS. and M is very often right. Cf. Delbrück, *Altind. Synt.*, pp. 382 *seq.*; KB xxix. 8, n. 3.

[5] RV. x. 30. 12.

[6] i. e. RV. x. 30.

[1] For the Mādhyama Ṛṣis see ĀGS. iii. 4. For this chapter see AB. ii. 19; cf. the Chāgaleya Upaniṣad, Weber, *Ind. Stud.* ix. 42–46.

[2] *nirāgā iva* is rendered by Haug (*Aitareya Brāhmaṇa*, ii. 112, n. 1) as if *nirāgā* (sinless) *iti* were read of Kavaṣa, but this cannot very naturally be so taken.

[3] *pratyāhitāḥ* in M is a clear case of a gloss ousting the text; cf. AJP xxxvi. 257, 258. Like *nirāga*, the word is late.

The Upāñçu and Antaryāma Cups.

xii. 4. The[1] Upāñçu (cup) is expiration; as it is offered he should breathe forth along it (saying) 'Protect my expiration, quicken my expiration; hail! Thee of fair birth to the sun!' This is its call of *vaṣaṭ* and its call of Hail! These libations go not to the gods over which the *vaṣaṭ* call or the call of Hail! is not pronounced. Inspiration is the Antaryāma (cup); as it is offered he should breathe down along it (saying) 'Protect my inspiration, quicken my inspiration; hail! Thee of fair birth to the sun!' This is its call of *vaṣaṭ*, and its call of Hail! These libations go not to the gods over which the *vaṣaṭ* call or the call of Hail! is not pronounced. The Upāñçu and Antaryāma are expiration and inspiration; one of these they offer when the sun has risen, the other before the sun has risen; verily thus they separate expiration and inspiration; therefore expiration and inspiration, though being together, are separate as it were. 'In that they offer one when the sun has risen and the other before the sun has risen, verily thus from day and night they obstruct[2] the Asuras, for on both sides of yonder sun are day and night, and the sacrificer (obstructs) evil,' so he used to say.[3] He for whom they offer both (cups) after the sun has risen or before the sun has risen is a sacrificer with water, not a sacrificer with Soma; he for whom these two are offered in their order is a real sacrificer with Soma.[4] So for the Upāñçu and Antaryāma (cups).

The Sarpaṇa.

xii. 5. 'Should[1] the Pavamāna be followed up or not?' (they ask). 'It should not be followed up,' they say. The abode of the Ṛc is where the Hotṛ stands; that of the Sāman where they yonder sing the Sāman. He who follows up removes[2] the Ṛc from its own abode, and makes the Ṛc a follower of the Sāman. Therefore he should not follow up, (thinking) 'Let me not remove the Ṛc from its own abode' and 'Let me not make the

[1] For the two cups see AB. ii. 21. For the ritual see ÇÇS. vi. 8. 1 and 2.

[2] All the MSS. of Lindner and the Ānand. ed. have *antarayanti*, a denominative form not found certainly before the classical period.

[3] *vā* is possibly = *vai* here, but *vā* may be 'or'. Cf. KB. xvi. 9, n. 5.

[4] The reading of all MSS. but M, and of the Ānand. ed. *somayājīti* may be correct, the first *iti* being a dictum of Kauṣītaki as above, but the simpler reading of M is perhaps better, as often; so the comm.

xii. 5. [1] For this rule regarding the participation of the Hotṛ in the movement of the other priests to the place for the performance of the Sāman and the eating there of a *caru* see AB. ii. 22. ÇÇS. vi. 8. 3–18 gives the ritual for the Bahiṣpavamāna and in 14 the Mantra for the Hotṛ as here.

[2] For *cyāvayati* (in M also) there is a parallel in PB. and it need not therefore be corrected.

Ṛc a follower of the Sāman.' But, if (the sacrificer) be also the Hotṛ, he should follow up, for to him falls the duty of a chorister, (thinking) 'The Svarasāman[3] is the world of heaven; let me place myself in the Svarasāman, the world of heaven.' Then (they ask) 'All the gods rejoice together in the morning in the Pavamāna; how then is it not then completely consumed?' When the Pavamāna has been sung, he should mutter the following, 'Invoked are the gods for the eating of this Soma, the purifying, the discerning; let the gods invoke me for the eating of this Soma, the purifying, the discerning; with mind thee I eat; with speech thee I eat; with breath thee I eat; with the eye thee I eat; with the ear thee I eat.' This is the joint invocation with the gods. So by him yonder Soma, the king, the discerning, the moon, the food, is eaten, that food yonder which the gods eat.

The Animal Sacrifice (continued).

xii. 6. Now[1] as to the victim. The victim is clearly Soma, for if it were not offered it would be as it were a water drinking; thereby he makes firm the pressings. In that they proceed with the omentum, thereby is the morning pressing made firm; in that they cook, in that they proceed with the cake at the animal sacrifice, thereby is the midday pressing made firm; in that they proceed with this (victim) at the third pressing, thereby is the third pressing made firm. This is the making firm of the pressings. The deities who drink the Soma and those who share the victim—there are thirty-three Soma drinking deities who depend on the Soma libations, eight Vasus, eleven Rudras, twelve Ādityas, Indra as the thirty-second, Prajāpati as the thirty-third; then also thirty-three who share the victim—both of these sets are delighted. Of this (victim) which is offered some say 'It should be for Indra and Agni', saying 'All the gods are Indra and Agni; thus by it he delights all the gods.' But others say 'This (victim) should be for Agni, the cakes are for Indra; thus Indra and Agni have equal shares.' 'Agni's is the morning pressing, this (victim) is offered at the morning pressing; they take for another that which is Agni's who make it have another for its deity; it is as if one were to take for another what is another's; further the year is alone for those who perform a session of a year, (the victim) is for Agni only; it should not change,' so some say. In the teaching (of Kauṣītaki) (the victim) is determined as for Agni:

[3] The Svarasāman is properly the Sāman of the three days before and after the Viṣuvant or central day in the Gavām Ayana, the great sacrificial session, here contemplated (cf. KB. xii. 6). This or a similar passage is cited in ĀpÇS. xii. 17. 2 from the Bahvṛcabrāhmaṇa.

[1] For the ritual see ÇÇS. vi. 9.

xii. 7. The offering verse[1] for the omentum of the victim contains (the word) 'become', 'Thou hast become the leader of the sacrifice and the region'; that[2] for the cake contains (the word) 'pure',' Forward to the pure radiance do ye bear'; that[3] for the oblation contains (the word) 'oblation' 'The singers urged by thought'. 'The set of eleven[4] they should arrange in order' is the rule. If (the sacrifice) is accompanied with Pṛṣṭhyas[5], in the invitation he issues invitations for the morning pressing (with the words), 'Bring the gods to the sacrificer; bring Agni, O Agni; bring the lord of the forest; bring Indra with the Vasus'; he issues invitations for the midday pressing (with the words), 'Bring Indra with the Rudras'; he issues invitations for the third pressing (with the words), 'Bring Indra with the Ādityas, with the Ṛbhus, with the Vibhus, with Vāja, with Bṛhaspati, with the All-gods.' Some include the lord of the forest in this invitation, saying 'At the end should (the lord of the forest) be invited, for they sacrifice to him at the third pressing.' As to this they say[6] 'The victim is the body, the lord of the forests the breath; if one there were to say of him, "He hath separated the body from the breath, he shall not live", it would be so. Therefore in connexion with the victim the lord of the forest should be invited.' The victim has been discussed.

xii. 8. Prajāpati[1], having created offspring, felt himself empty as it were; he pondered, 'How now can I sacrifice with such a sacrificial rite that by sacrificing with it I shall obtain my desires and win proper food?' He saw the set of eleven (victims); he grasped it and sacrificed with it; having sacrificed with it he obtained his desires and won proper food; verily thus also the sacrificer having sacrificed with this set of eleven obtains his desires, and wins proper food. Of this set of eleven the invitatory and offering verses are distinct and those for the oblation to Manotā, but the rest is the same. The first is for Agni; Agni is the holy power; (it serves) to win the glory of the holy power. The second is for Sarasvatī; Sarasvatī is speech; by speech is food made sweet and eaten; (it serves) to obtain proper food. The third is for Soma; Soma is the lordly power; (it serves) to win the glory of the lordly power. The fourth is for Pūṣan; Pūṣan is food; (it serves) to obtain proper food. The fifth is for Bṛhaspati; Bṛhaspati is the holy power; (it serves) to win the glory of the holy power. The

[1] RV. x. 8. 6.

[2] RV. vii. 4. 1 (cited also in KB. xxvi. 8).

[3] RV. iii. 6. 1.

[4] *ekādaçinīm*, the reading of the comm., is clearly correct, Anusvāra being easily omitted and °*nīs* of M being a facile correction.

[5] *pṛṣṭhyopāyam* is perhaps more probable than *pṛṣṭhopāyam*, as it thus refers naturally to a Sattra (cf. KB. xii. 6).

[6] As often no *iti* ends the quotation; cf. KB. x. 1, 8; xvii. 1; xxiv. 8.

xii. 8. [1] ÇÇS. vi. 10 has the verses for the eleven victims which differ. For the Manotā oblation see KB. x. 6.

sixth is for the All-gods; of all forms is food eaten; (it serves) to obtain proper food. The seventh is for Indra; Indra is the lordly power; (it serves) to win the glory of the lordly power. The eighth is for the Maruts; the Maruts are the waters; the waters are food; (it serves) to obtain proper food. The ninth is for Indra and Agni; Indra and Agni are the holy and the lordly powers; (it serves) to win the glory of the holy power and the glory of the lordly power. The tenth is for Savitṛ; instigated by Savitṛ is this food eaten; (it serves) to win proper food. The eleventh is for Varuṇa; Varuṇa is the lordly power; (it serves) to win the glory of the lordly power. Thus Prajāpati, by the holy power and the lordly power and by the lordly power and the holy power, kept encircling on both sides and winning proper food. Verily thus also the sacrificer, by the holy power and the lordly power and by the lordly power and the holy power, keeps encircling on both sides and winning proper food.

ADHYĀYA XIII

THE SOMA SACRIFICE (*continued*).

The Creeping to the Sadas.

xiii. 1. The[1] sacrifice is Prajāpati; in it are all desires, all immortality; the altars are the protectors; to them as he creeps[2] to the Sadas he pays homage, 'Homage, homage', for the gods are not above receiving homage. They, having homage paid, let the Hotṛ pass on. He proceeds to this Prajāpati, the sacrifice; thus herein the sacrificer obtains all desires.

The Set of Five Oblations.

xiii. 2. Then[1] they proceed with the set of five oblations. The set of five oblations is cattle; verily (they serve) to obtain cattle. There are five oblations, curds, fried grains, groats, the cake, the milk mess. The Pañkti has five Padas; the sacrifice is fivefold; cattle are fivefold; man is fivefold; for obtaining the sacrifice and cattle this is offered, also for the encircling of cattle and the making firm of the pressings. Breath is the set of five[2]

[1] For the ritual see ÇÇS. vi. 12 and 13.

[2] The Ānand. ed. has *prasṛpsyan*.

xiii. 2. [1] For the *haviṣpañkti* see AB. ii. 24. For the ritual see ÇÇS. vii. 1.

[2] Çāñkh. more correctly notes that the formal beginnings of the verses must be changed to alter a *praiṣa* into a *yājyā*.

oblations; therefore the Hotṛ utters as the offering verse the same formulae as the Maitrāvaruṇa for his directions; for breath is the same. They say 'The Ṛc which he uses in the morning as offering verse is wearied for that day; then how is it fresh in all the pressings?' In that he continues to carry on with the pressings, (saying) 'In the morning, (the cakes) of the morning pressing', at the morning pressing, 'Those of the midday pressing', at the midday pressing, 'Those of the third pressing', at the third pressing, thereby is it fresh[3]. They say[4] 'Why in the morning only is there a milk mess, and not in the midday or at the third pressing?' 'The Maitrāvaruṇa is the sacrifice; the sacrifice is born at the morning pressing; a young boy's portion is milk; this is as if one should give the breast to a child on birth; it is old at the other two pressings; when one grows one is past the breast then. Therefore in the morning only is there a milk mess, and not in the midday nor at the third pressing' (is the answer).

The Cakes.

xiii. 3. 'O[1] Agni, enjoy the oblation,' he says at each pressing as the offering verse of the Sviṣṭakṛt offering of the cake. Avatsāra Prāsravaṇa[2] was the Hotṛ of the gods. To him in that glory death attached itself; death is Agni; having delighted Agni by the oblation (saying), 'O Agni, enjoy the oblation,' he was set free. Verily thus also a Hotṛ, who knowing thus delights Agni by the oblation (saying) 'O Agni, enjoy the oblation, is set free. Through these intermediate spaces the gods went to the world of heaven; to them in that glory death attached itself; death is Agni; they having delighted Agni by the oblation (saying) 'O Agni, enjoy the oblation,' were set free. Verily thus also a Hotṛ who knowing thus delights Agni by the oblation (saying) 'O Agni, enjoy the oblation,' is set free. (The words), 'O Agni, enjoy the oblation,' have six syllables; this body has six members and is sixfold; thus ransoming the self by the self, having become free of debt, he sacrifices. This is the Mantra of Avatsāra Prāsravaṇa; he should not think 'By which now, by which shall I sacrifice?'; he should know 'Let me sacrifice by the Mantra made by a Ṛṣi, the Ṛc.'

[3] The variants of the *yājyās* according to the pressing make the decisive difference. The *praiṣas* are given in Scheftelowitz, *Die Apokryphen des Ṛgveda*, p. 145, where *prātaḥsāvasya* (cf. p. 147) occurs for *prātaḥsavanasya* here; so in the Prayogas and Ānand. ed.

[4] For this see AB. ii. 22.

[1] For the cakes of the pressings see AB. ii. 23. For this point in the ritual, the *yājyā* of the Sviṣṭakṛt offering, ÇÇS. vii. 1. 8.

[2] The v. l. Prāçravaṇa is supported by W w B b M K, the Ānand. ed., and by Max Müller's MS. at least once. There is the same variation in the name of the Plakṣa Prāsravaṇa (*Vedic Index*, s.v.).

xiii. 4. Now we have called the victim Soma; and so the cakes. Ten are they, shoots of Soma; the old shoot, which they press here; the glad shoot, the waters; the sap shoot, rice; the male shoot, barley; the bright shoot, milk; the living shoot, the victim; the immortal shoot, gold; the Ṛc shoot; the Yajus shoot; the Sāman shoot; these are the ten Soma shoots; when all these unite, then is there Soma, then the pressed (Soma).

The Cups for two Deities.

xiii. 5. Having[1] proceeded with the cakes, they proceed with (the cups) for two deities. The cakes are the body of the sacrificer, (the cups) for two deities the breaths; in that having proceeded with the cakes, they proceed with (the cups) for two deities, verily thus they place[2] the breaths in the sacrificer, to secure fullness of life in this world and immortality in yonder world. So the sacrificer lives his full life in this world, he obtains immortality, imperishableness in the world of heaven. The first is for Indra and Vāyu; Indra is speech, Vāyu is breath; that for Mitra and Varuṇa is the eye; that for the Açvins is the ear; those for two deities are these breaths. Therefore without taking breath he utters the offering verse, for the continuity of the breaths, for these breaths are continuous as it were; he does not utter the second *vaṣaṭ* (thinking) 'Those for two deities are the breaths, the second *vaṣaṭ* call marks the completion; let me not before the time make the breaths completed', for these breaths are yoked as it were. He places that for Indra and Vāyu on the front side, for it of these breaths is designated as of the front side; closer together as it were[3] around the other two behind he deposits, for the eye and the ear are around this as it were. Them he continues to hold (thinking) 'Let them not start forward[4].' He does not cover (thinking) '(The cups) for two deities are the breaths; let me not cover the breaths.'

xiii. 6. 'This sweet Soma drink for thee' is the offering verse[1] of the Prasthitas, which distil sweetness, containing (the word) 'sweet'. He utters a second *vaṣaṭ*, for the appeasing of the libations, for the support of the libations. Then the Hotrakas sacrifice together; verily thus they

[1] For these cups, to Indra and Vāyu, Varuṇa and Mitra, and the Açvins, see AB. ii. 25–28, 30. For the ritual see ÇÇS. vii. 2 and 3.

[2] *dadhāti* is not so probable although it is possible, and has strong MS. support (W w O B K, Ānand. ed., and Max Müller's MS.). Cf. below, xiii. 9.

[3] So *abhidhānatare* is taken by Vināyaka and it is probably thus to be rendered: *abhidhānataḥ* is less likely and does not explain the variant.

[4] *pravartantai* is odd (Whitney, *Sansk. Gr.* § 737).

xiii. 6. [1] For the Prasthitas and the Hotrakas' offerings and the eating of the libations see ÇÇS. vii. 4 and 5.

release the sacrificer from indebtedness.[2] The first eating is that of (the cups) for two deities, then the sacrificial food, then the Hotṛ's goblet. The cakes are the body of the sacrificer, (the cups) for two deities are the breaths; the sacrificial food is cattle and food; by food are the breaths and the body combined. Therefore the first eating is of (the cups) for two deities, then sacrificial food, then the Hotṛ's bowl. Them he gives to the Adhvaryu; he does not let go (thinking) '(The cups) for two deities are breaths; let me not let go the breaths.' Twice he eats of (the cup) for Indra and Vāyu, for twice he utters the *vaṣaṭ* call for it; once of (the cup) for Mitra and Varuṇa, once for that for the Açvins. Turning it round on all sides he eats of that for the Açvins, for by the ear he hears on all sides. The dregs he pours down on the Hotṛ's bowl; verily thus he makes them sharers in the sacrificial food.

xiii. 7. Then[1] he invokes the sacrificial food; carrying in his right hand the second (portion of the) sacrificial food he in the left holds together, but without allowing to touch, the Hotṛ's bowl and the cup (thinking) 'The butter is a thunderbolt; Soma is seed; let me not harm seed by the thunderbolt.' He does not speak the formula of pouring[2] into it, he does not utter benedictions. Having invoked the sacrificial food and having sniffed it he pauses; he eats the second (portion of the) sacrificial food; then having sipped water he eats of the Hotṛ's bowl. The Soma is the highest kind of proper food; verily thus all, having invoked the highest kind of proper food, eat of it.

xiii. 8. Next[1] the response of the Achāvāka. 'These dear songs the sacrificer, the pourer, hath seized; the Upavaktṛ is a support, the cows are invited by us (he should say), if he does not desire to invite; 'He also is invited' he adds, if he desires to invite. The Achāvāka in response to the invitation should run over as many verses as he can of the hymn,[2] 'Do ye stay, go not away.' Or a Hotṛ (may do so) to an unwilling[3] Achāvāka. That is the expiation here.

[2] *anṛṇatāyai* of M is possible as a dative of purpose, but is clearly a conjectural emendation.

[1] See above AB. iii. 7, n. 2.

The sense of *sunvat* is very doubtful, and the phrase may be corrupt.

xiii. 8. [1] For the response of the Achāvāka see ÇÇS. vii. 6, where, however, the verse, RV. x. 19. 1, is attributed to the Achāvāka if not invited. The use of *pratyupahava* is odd.

[2] The reading of the KB. is certain but the sense most obscure; Henry (*L'Agniṣṭoma*, p. 221) suggests *pratiṣṭhatotopavakta* (ÇÇS. has °*opavakta*), but this is improbable. The rendering given assumes the reading *pratiṣṭhopavakta*; for the Sandhi see ÇÇS. i. 4. 5; vii. 14. 9.

[3] Cf. KB. xv. 3, n. 4. Read perhaps *vā prati prati*°.

The Seasonal Cups.

xiii. 9. The[1] offerings to the seasons are the breaths; in that they proceed with the offerings to the seasons, verily thus they place the breaths in the sacrificer. Breath is in three ways ordered, expiration, inspiration, cross-breathing. Six (priests) sacrifice (saying) 'With the season,' verily thus they place expiration in the sacrificer; four 'With the seasons'; verily thus they place inspiration in the sacrificer; twice (they sacrifice) afterwards, (saying) 'With the season'; verily thus they place cross-breathing in the sacrificer,[2] to secure fullness of life in this world and immortality in yonder (world). So the sacrificer lives a full life in this world and obtains immortality and imperishableness in the world of heaven. The offerings to the seasons are these breaths; therefore without taking in breath they utter the offering verses, for the continuity of the breaths, for these breaths are continuous as it were. They do not say the second *vaṣaṭ* (thinking) 'The offerings to the seasons are the breaths; the second *vaṣaṭ* call marks the completion; let me not before the time make the breaths completed', for these breaths are yoked as it were. They say 'Why does he give directions to all (the priests) (in the words), 'Let the Hotṛ utter the offering verse, let the Hotṛ say the offering verse.' The Hotṛ is speech; he says in effect, 'Let speech utter the offering verse, let speech utter the offering verse.' The seven Hotṛs moreover are all these; further it is said in a Ṛc,[3] 'The seven Hotṛs sacrifice according to due seasons.' In that he arranges two afterwards, it is to avoid repetition. There are twelve; the year has twelve months; verily (it serves) to obtain the year. If he should eat then, and any one should say of him, 'Food over which no second *vaṣaṭ* has been said is unwholesome; it has penetrated through his breaths,[4] he will not live,' so would it be. If he does not eat, and any one were to say of him, 'Food is breath; he has separated himself from breath, he will not live,' so also would it be. He should smear as it were, and sniff it, both here and in the case of (the cups) for two deities; this is the rule which they proclaim. In that these two Adhvaryus cross each other and neither interferes with the other, therefore season interferes not with season.

[1] For the offerings to the seasons see AB. ii. 29. For the ritual see ÇÇS. vii. 8.

[2] For *dadhātu* see KB. xiii. 5.

[3] See VS. xxiii. 58 *d*; the allusion here is omitted in the *Vedic Concordance*.

[4] *prāṇān* with *vyagāt* is difficult but not impossible. There is no obvious correction save, of course, *prāṇāt* as with *prāṇāt* below, and possibly that should be read. On the other hand the acc. is found in AB. several times, apparently as 'separate' and so destroy.

ADHYĀYA XIV

The Soma Sacrifice (*continued*).

The Ājya Çastra.

xiv. 1. Next[1] as to the Ājya (Çastra). By the Ājya the gods conquered all desires, all immortality; verily thus also the sacrificer by the Ājya conquers all desires, all immortality. The Ājya is sixfold, the silent muttering, the silent praise, the Puroruc, the hymn, the strength of the hymn, and the offering verse. The year is sixfold in having six seasons; by this sixfold Ājya the gods obtained the sixfold year with its six seasons, and by the year all desires, all immortality. Verily thus also the sacrificer by this sixfold Ājya obtains the sixfold year with its six seasons, by the year all desires, all immortality. In that he mutters in front the silent muttering, (it is because) the sacrifice is the world of heaven; thus, in that he mutters the silent muttering in front, verily thus he produces a benediction, for the attainment of the world of heaven. Then he recites inaudibly the silent praise, to obtain all desires. 'Agni, light, light, Agni,' (he says); thus he obtains this world of worlds, the morning pressing of the sacrifice. 'Indra, light, light, Indra,' (he says); thus he obtains the world of the atmosphere of worlds, the midday pressing of the sacrifice. 'Sun, light, light, sun,' (he says); thus he obtains yonder world of worlds, the third pressing of the sacrifice. He who yonder gives heat is the Nivid, for he keeps announcing all this. It is placed in front of the hymn at the morning pressing, for (the sun) then is in front; in the middle of the hymn at the midday pressing, for it is then in the middle; leaving over the last in the third pressing, for then it has gone round to the west. Thus he keeps placing[2] the Nivid according to its appearance. They say 'Coloured[3] (steeds) draw the morning pressing, white-backed the midday pressing, those with a white gloss the third pressing.' Because of the sun also he recites the Puroruc in twelve sentences; the year has twelve months; verily (it serves) to obtain the year.

xiv. 2. Then he recites the seven-versed Ājya[1]; the metres are seven;

[1] For the Ājya Çastra see AB. ii. 31–41. For the ritual ÇÇS. vii. 9.

[2] *dadhad eti* is certain, but beside the comm. is read only by M and W of Lindner's MSS. The Ānand. ed. has *dadhateti*.

[3] *añjayaḥ* is rarely used as an epithet of colour by itself, but this seems the sense here.

xiv. 2. [1] RV. iii. 13. The mode of recitation presumes that the second half-verse is to be pronounced *samasta* with the usual Praṇava at the end, while there is a pause at the end of the first half-verse, which is recited as two Padas but without breathing in. Cf. AB. ii. 35.

verily (it serves) to obtain all the metres. It is in Anuṣṭubh verses; the Anuṣṭubh is speech; whatever is described by speech, the Anuṣṭubh, all that he obtains. He separates the two Padas; that is a symbol of generation; a man takes apart as it were (the limbs) of his wife. Further, in that he takes apart, that is a symbol of support. Now that between these two Padas is the face of death; if a man say of one who breathes in at this place, 'He has entered the face of death, he will not live', so would it be. Therefore without drawing in breath should he pass over; breath is immortality; thus by immortality he crosses death. He utters the Praṇava at the end of the whole half-verse; verily thus he hurls a thunderbolt at his evil rival. They make up ten Gāyatrī verses, for the tenth Pada has eight syllables. The Anuṣṭubh is the Gāyatrī; the metre of Agni is the Gāyatrī; ten cups the Adhvaryu draws at the morning pressing; to nine (verses) they sing with the Bahiṣpavamāna (Stotra), the tenth is the call *hiñ*; these ten they taking separately make up the Virāj; the Virāj is all proper food; having procured that they deposit it in the sacrificer. Thrice (he recites) with the first, thrice with the last; they make up eleven; the twelfth is the offering verse; the year has twelve months; verily (they serve) to obtain the year. They, recited together, make up sixteen Gāyatrīs; thus the Ājya becomes converted into Gāyatrī verses. He utters as offering verse one to Agni and Indra; verily thus he makes Indra a half-sharer in the pressing. 'In the offering verse give the deities a portion,' Kauṣītaki used to say. The Virāj has thirty-three syllables; the gods are thirty-three; he makes the gods sharers in the syllables. 'O Agni, with Indra, in the home of the generous one,' leaving over this Pada,[2] he breathes in at the half-verse of the Virāj; the Virāj is prosperity and proper food; thus on the Virāj as prosperity and proper food he finds support. With the second half of the Virāj he utters the *vaṣaṭ* call; verily thus in the world of heaven he places the sacrificer; he utters the second *vaṣaṭ*, for the healing of the libations, for the support of the libations.

xiv. 3. 'Let us two recite[1],' he calls out at the morning pressing; in that they make the Praṇava pure, it is a symbol of this world; in that they make it end in *m*, it is one of yonder (world). In that they make the Praṇava pure, (it is thinking) 'Turned away is yonder world; let us not go turning away.' Moreover, this world is generation; verily (it serves) for generation; this world is a support; verily (it serves) for support. 'Let us recite, O divine one,' the Adhvaryu (replies). These are eight syllables. 'The hymn hath been uttered,' the Hotṛ should say inaudibly at the

[2] RV. iii. 25. 4.

[1] For the Āhāvas and responses see AB. iii. 12; Caland and Henry, *L'Agniṣṭoma*, p. 232.

morning pressing; 'Reciter of hymns', the Adhvaryu (replies). These are eight. Having begun the pressing with the Gāyatrī they have found support in the Gāyatrī. 'O Adhvaryu, let us two recite,' he calls out at the midday pressing. 'Let us recite, O divine one,' the Adhvaryu (replies). These are eleven syllables. 'The hymn hath been uttered to Indra', the Hotṛ should say inaudibly at the midday pressing. 'Reciter of hymns', the Adhvaryu (replies). These are eleven. Having begun the pressing with the Triṣṭubh they have found support on the Triṣṭubh. 'O Adhvaryu, let, let us two recite,' he calls out towards (him) at the third pressing. 'Let, let us recite, O divine one,' the Adhvaryu (replies). There are twelve syllables roughly,[2] thirteen. 'The hymn hath been uttered to Indra, to the gods,' the Hotṛ should say inaudibly at the third pressing. 'Reciter of hymns', the Adhvaryu (replies). These are twelve exactly. Having begun the pressing with the Jagatī they have found support on the Jagatī. This is what is placed in the middle. If he uses here a transposed metre, still the metres are in order and carry the sacrifice of him who knows thus. 'Moreover the following verse has been declared', he used to say, 'That the Gāyatrī is deposited on the Gāyatrī, or that they fashioned the Triṣṭubh from the Triṣṭubh, or that the Jagatī Pada is placed on the Jagatī, they who know this obtain immortality.' In that these deities are fixed on these worlds, Agni as connected with the Gāyatrī here is fixed in this world of the Gāyatrī, Vāyu as connected with the Triṣṭubh is fixed in the world of the atmosphere connected with the Triṣṭubh; yonder sun as connected with the Jagatī is fixed in yonder world connected with the Jagatī.

The Praüga Çastra.

xiv. 4. Having recited the Ājya, he recites the Praüga.[1] The Ājya is the body of the sacrificer, the Praüga the breaths; in that having recited the Ājya he recites the Praüga, verily thus he places breaths in the sacrificer, to secure fullness of life in this world and immortality in yonder world. So the sacrificer lives a full life in this world, and obtains immortality and imperishableness in the world of heaven. When the Pavamāna has been sung, he recites the Ājya. When the Ājya (Stotra) has been sung, (he

[2] M has *lomaçena*; the sense is conjectural, but plausible. The number of syllables is thirteen instead of twelve, to correspond with the Jagatī metre of the third pressing. The number 9 is only arrived at in *avācindrāyokthaṁ devebhyaḥ* by leaving in operation the full Sandhi, contrary to the usage of the AB. Cf. Oldenberg, *Prolegomena*, pp. 378 *seq.*

[1] For the Praüga Çastra see AB. iii. 1–4. This chapter deals with the seven Triças of which it is composed (RV. i. 2. 1–3; 4–6; 7–9; 3. 1–3; 4–6; 7–9; 10–12) and the relation to the Grahas. For the relationship of Ājya and Praüga see Weber, *Ind. Stud.* x. 373, 374.

recites) the Praüga. The Praüga is the hymn of the Pavamāna; the Ājya is the hymn of the Ājya. Thus he transposes the two; it is as if one were to intertwine the outer reins of a chariot. 'Thus he accompanies the cups', Kauṣītaki used to say; yonder cup for Vāyu and Indra and Vāyu (he accompanies) by that (recitation) for Vāyu and for Indra and Vāyu; that for Mitra and Varuṇa with that for Mitra and Varuṇa; that for the Açvins with that for the Açvins; in that he utters the offering verses for the Prasthitas, that (he accompanies) with that for Indra; in that the Hotrakas sacrifice together, that with that for the All-gods. Sarasvatī is speech in all the pressings. He yonder who makes heat is the Puroruc, for he shines in front; again breath is the Puroruc, while the hymn is the body; the body is the Puroruc and the hymn is cattle and offspring; therefore he should not utter any call between the Puroruc and the hymn [2]. Reciting the hymn with the Puroruc, he calls aloud for each Puroruc; 'Vāyu, proceeding in front' is the symbol of expiration; 'O Vāyu' is the symbol of inspiration. He recites the Praüga as Gāyatrī; thereby the morning pressing is obtained; (he recites it) as addressed to Indra; thereby the midday pressing is obtained; (he recites it) as addressed to the All-gods; thereby the third pressing is obtained.

xiv. 5. Then [1] he recites a Puroruc addressed to the All-gods. It is of six feet; the seasons some call it. The seasons are six; he recites each two feet of it separately; therefore the seasons are united in pairs and called 'Summer, the rains, and winter.' Some recite the Puroruc for Sarasvatī; he should not do so; it is superfluous; speech has of itself radiance; speech is the Puroruc. 'O Vāyu, come hither, O lovely one' and 'O Açvins, sacrificial food', these two (hymns) are the Praüga; (they are) of nine verses and of twelve verses; these make twenty-one; the four (verse) Stoma, the highest of Stomas, is twenty-onefold; thus he obtains the highest Stoma; in that, further, there are twenty-one, and the months are twelve, the seasons five, these worlds three, and yonder sun the twenty-first, verily thereby he places the sacrificer in identity of world with (the sun). There are seven triplets; the metres are seven; verily (they serve) to obtain all the metres. Moreover with these the gods appropriated the seven heptads of the Asuras; verily thus also the sacrificer appropriates the seven heptads of the rival who hates him. In the beginning the morning pressing was Agni's, the midday pressing Indra's, the third pressing the All-gods'. Agni desired 'Let me have a share in the midday pressing, also in the third pressing.'

[2] The hymn has at the beginning only a Puroruc and then the first verse; afterwards before each new triplet it has an Āhāva, with the response of the Adhvaryu, before the Puroruc.

[1] For the ritual see ÇÇS. vii. 10. There a Puroruc for Sarasvatī, here forbidden, is given without qualification.

Indra desired 'Let me have a share in the morning pressing, also in the third pressing.' The All-gods desired, 'Let us have a share in the midday pressing, also in the morning pressing.' These deities thenceforward extended the morning pressing from the third pressing; in that they extended (*abhiprāyuñjata*), that is why the Praüga has its name. Therefore many deities are praised at the Praüga; therefore all the pressings have all the deities. Having recited the hymn [2], 'With all the sweet Soma drink', he utters the offering verse for the All-gods, for the hymn is for the All-gods; in Gāyatrī, the morning pressing is connected with the Gāyatrī. He should recite the second *vaṣaṭ*.[3]

ADHYAYA XV

The Soma Sacrifice (*continued*).

Preliminary Rites.

xv. 1. The[1] Gods having praised the pressing stones with the Arbuda (hymn [2]) and the verses for (Soma), the purifying, obtained immortality, obtained truth and resolve. Verily thus also the sacrificer in that he praises the pressing stones with the Arbuda (hymn) and the verses for (Soma), the purifying, obtains immortality, obtains truth and resolve. When the Pavamāna has been sung, they proceed with the pot of milk, for this is the time for it; moreover (it serves) to give the pressing sap. Then they proceed with the set of five oblations; the explanation of this has been given. At the midday he utters a verse of Bharadvāja's as the offering verse for the Prasthitas; at the midday Bharadvāja gave Soma to Indra. It is a Triṣṭubh verse, addressed to Indra; the midday pressing is connected with Indra and the Triṣṭubh. He says the second *vaṣaṭ*, for the healing of the libations, for the support of the libations. Then the Hotrakas sacrifice together; the explanation of these (offerings) has been given; then come the sacrificial food and the Hotṛ's bowl; the explanation of that has been given. When the Dakṣiṇā offerings have been made, the fees are taken, for then the pressing stops. Moreover he ransoms himself in that the fees are taken; moreover with the fees he makes strong the sacrifice; in that with the fees he makes strong (*dakṣayati*) the sacrifice, therefore has the fee its name. The Sattra has the self as the Dakṣiṇā; therefore day by day should they mutter, 'Here let me take myself as a fee for fair fame, for the world of heaven,

[3] The subj. is strange and doubtful; cf. p. 87.

[1] For the ritual see ÇÇS. vii. 15–19.

[2] RV. x. 94. For the Pāvamānīs to be used see Ānartīya on ÇÇS. vii. 15. 16. Cf AB. vii. 1 and 2.

for immortality'; verily thus they take themselves as a fee for fair fame, for the world of heaven, for immortality. Having recited (a verse[3]) by Viçvāmitra as the invitatory (verse) of the cup for the Maruts, he utters (a verse[4]) by Viçvāmitra as the offering verse; the cup for the Maruts is the continuity of the pressing; Viçvāmitra is speech; by speech the sacrifice is continued. These are two Triṣṭubhs addressed to Indra; the midday pressing is connected with Indra and the Triṣṭubh. He says the second *vaṣaṭ*, for the healing of the libations, for the support of the libations.

The Marutvatīya Çastra.

xv. 2. Then[1] he recites the sixfold Marutvatīya; the year has six seasons; verily (it serves) to obtain the year. He recites the six metres, Anuṣṭubh, Gāyatrī, Bṛhatī, Uṣṇih, Triṣṭubh, and Jagatī. Therefore is it sixfold. With an Anuṣṭubh[2], 'Thee like a car for aid', he begins the Marutvatīya. The Marutvatīya is the hymn of the Pavamāna; the metre of Soma is the Anuṣṭubh. The explanation of the transposition of the Padas has been given. He recites Gāyatrī verses; Gāyatrī verses are breath; verily thus he places breath in himself. 'This drink, O bright one, is pressed' is the antistrophe[3], containing the words 'pressed' and 'drink', for it is the hymn of the Pavamāna. 'O Indra, come nearer' is a Pragātha[4] inviting Indra. 'Nearer let us approach', the Maruts said to him encouraging him; he said 'Having conquered and slain Vṛtra, this is my Soma drinking along with you.' This is his Soma drinking along with them. 'Forward now, Brahmaṇaspati' is (a Pragātha) addressed to Brahmaṇaspati[5] and contains (the word) 'Forward'. 'Smite', Brahman said to him, encouraging him; he said, 'Having conquered and slain Vṛtra, this is my Soma drinking along with you.' This is the Soma drinking of Brahman. 'In it give the gods a share', Kauṣītaki used to say. 'In which Indra, Varuṇa, Mitra, Aryaman, the gods, made their homes', in this[6] are the gods given a share. They say 'In that in there is no strophe nor antistrophe, but an invitation to Indra and (a triplet) addressed to Brahmaṇaspati, then why are they recited repeating them and making them into Kakubh (verses)?' The Sāman singers sing with repetition in the Pavamāna; verily thus is a symbol of it produced. 'Agni, like Bhaga, is leader of the folk' and 'Thou with insight art keen of

[3] RV. iii. 51. 7.

[4] RV. iii. 47. 2.

[1] For the Marutvatīya Çastra of the midday pressing, see AB. iii. 12–21. For the ritual see ÇÇS. vii. 9. 6–25.

[2] RV. viii. 68. 1 (also cited xix. 8; xx. 2; xxiv. 2; xxv. 3).

[3] RV. viii. 2. 1–3 (also cited xix. 8; xx. 2; xxiv. 2; xxv. 3).

[4] RV. viii. 53. 5 and 6.

[5] RV. i. 40. 5 and 6.

[6] RV. i. 40. 5 c.

insight, O Soma' are addressed to Agni and Soma.[7] Agni and Soma were within Vṛtra; Indra was unable to hurl his bolt against them; they went out for this share and for that which is theirs in the full moon sacrifice. The Marutvatīya is a hymn connected with the slaying of Vṛtra; by it Indra slew Vṛtra.

xv. 3. 'The Maruts, rich in dew, swell the waters' is the water-swelling (verse);[1] the water-swelling (verse) is the waters; in that over Vṛtra slain the waters went apart, in that they swelled, thus it is (called) the water-swelling. It is a Jagatī verse; through it all the pressings are Jagatī. 'Thou hast been born, dread, for impetuous strength' is the Marutvatīya[2] containing the word 'born'. Indra is born, in that he slew Vṛtra; thus he who sacrifices is born. At the first (verse) of it the Adhvaryu responds once with (a response) containing the form *mad*;[3] here Indra for the first time was drunken (*amādyat*). The Marutvatīya is a hymn, winning battles; thereby Indra won battles. In the middle of it he places a Nivid; in the middle of the body is food placed; then he recites Nivids; the Nivids are the breaths; verily thus he places the breaths in himself. Each quarter verse of these he recites taking it separately; verily thus each breath he places in himself; with the last he utters the Praṇava; thus he lets go this breath; therefore all the breaths breath along this breath. Now they say 'The Nivids are food'; therefore should he recite them quietly, for not hastening as it were he eats unpleasant[4] food. 'Those who magnified thee, O bounteous one, at the slaying of the dragon', having recited the hymn, (this verse[5]) he utters as the offering verse. 'Who in the affair with Çambara, who in the fight for cattle, O lord of the bays', (he says);[5] with them he performed these heroic deeds; with them is this his Soma drinking. The verse is a Triṣṭubh addressed to Indra, for the midday pressing is connected with Indra and the Triṣṭubh. He says the second *vaṣaṭ*, for the healing of the libations, for the support of the libations. The first Anuṣṭubh is speech; after it follow five Gāyatrīs; the invitation to Indra is the mind[5]; (the couplet) addressed to Brahmaṇaspati is the ear; the three of common character[6] are expiration, inspiration, and cross-breathing; the hymn is the body; the Nivid what is within the body; the concluding verse a support; the offering verse food.

[7] RV. iii. 20. 4; i. 91. 2.

[1] RV. i. 64. 6.

[2] RV. x. 73 (also cited in KB. xxi. 2; xxiv. 2; xxv. 8). *ajāyata* is not necessary.

[3] i.e. *mad* in *çoñsāmo daiva*. See KB. xvi. 8, n. 5.

[4] PW. takes this as 'unpleasant', and in KB. xiii. 8 *vā pratikāminam* should be read, and so in ÇÇS. vii. 6. 9; as *annādya* is normally neuter the form is a transfer to the *a* class.

[5] RV. iii. 47. 4.

[6] The Dhāyyās, RV. iii. 20. 4; i. 91. 2; 64. 6.

The Niṣkevalya Çastra.

xv. 4. (Next)[1] the Niṣkevalya. Both before and after are many gods mentioned in recitation; but the Niṣkevalya is Indra's only; that is why the Niṣkevalya has its name. In that he begins with a Bṛhatī, and he who gives heat here is connected with the Bṛhatī, thus he makes him to prosper with his own symbol. He makes two into three by repetition; that is the symbol of generation; two as it were are there at first, then they are propagated. Having recited the strophe, he recites the antistrophe; the strophe is the self; the antistrophe the offspring; therefore he should make the antistrophe to be corresponding in form; a corresponding one is born in his offspring, not one who does not correspond. He recites a supplementary verse; the supplementary verse is breath; verily thus in himself he places breath. He recites a Pragātha; the Pragātha is cattle; verily (it serves) to obtain cattle. Moreover the Bṛhatī Pragātha is expiration and inspiration; verily thus he places expiration and inspiration in himself. 'I shall proclaim the manly deeds of Indra' is the Niṣkevalya of fifteen verses;[2] the thunderbolt is fifteenfold; verily thus with the thunderbolt he smites the evil of the sacrificer. In the middle of it he places a Nivid; in the middle of the body is food placed; then he recites Nivids; the Nivids are the breaths; verily thus he places the breaths in himself. Each quarter verse of these he recites, taking it separately; verily thus each breath he places in himself; with the last he utters the Praṇava; thus he lets go this breath; therefore all the breaths breathe along this breath. Now they say 'The Nivids are food'; therefore should he recite them quietly, for not hastening as it were he eats unpleasant food. He should recite the concluding verse in a lower tone; so is his wife unlikely to fall away. (He should recite) in still lower a tone;[3] so does his wife become as it were not uplifted in her mind. In that he gives a horse, and the horse is Indra, for the hymn is connected with Indra, verily thus he delights Indra. The strophe is the self; the antistrophe offspring; the supplementary verse the wife; cattle the Pragātha; the hymn the body; the Nivid what is within the body; the concluding verse a support; the offering verse food.

xv. 5. When[1] the Pavamāna was being sung, death clung to the Hotṛ; he removed it by the Ājya (Çastra) except from the strophe;

[1] For the Niṣkevalya Çastra see AB. iii. 22–24. For the ritual ÇÇS. vii. 20; viii. 17.

[2] RV. i. 32 (also cited in KB. xx. 4; xxiv. 2).

[3] *anuddyitataram* is read in M and the Ānand. ed. The sense must be as translated, but the reading is uncertain.

xv. 5. [1] Cf. AB. iii. 14.

when the Ājya[2] Stotra (was being sung) it clung (to him); he removed it by the Praüga except from the strophe; when the Mādhyaṁdina Pavamāna (was being sung) it clung to him; he removed it by the Marutvatīya except from the strophe. In the Niṣkevalya he begins with the strophe; that is as one in freedom from fear having removed death, like one having been set free.[3] They say, 'There is a Niṣkevalya here, and a Niṣkevalya there in the Mahāvrata. There are recited there (metres) increasing by four; how here are they obtained?' There are even more realized here; the strophe and antistrophe, recited together, make up the seven increasing by four, and there is a four-syllable foot left over. They are cattle; these cattle he confers upon the sacrificer. The Agniṣṭoma is the Virāj; they make up a hundred and ninety strophes; he attains clearly the symbol of the Agniṣṭoma in that he uses a Virāj as offering verse. 'Drink the Soma, O Indra, let it delight thee', having left over this quarter verse he takes breath in at the half verse of the Virāj; the Virāj is prosperity and proper food; thus he finds support in the Virāj as prosperity and proper food. He says *vaṣaṭ* with the second half verse of the Virāj; verily thus he places the sacrificer in the world of heaven. He says the second *vaṣaṭ*, for the healing of the libations, for the support of the libations.

ADHYĀYA XVI

The Soma Sacrifice (*continued*).

The Āditya Cup.

xvi. 1. The[1] morning pressing belongs to the Vasus, the midday pressing to the Rudras, the third pressing to the Ādityas. In that he commences the third pressing with the Āditya cup, verily thus he begins with its own deity. Moreover this pressing has the sap extracted, in that it is the third pressing. The Āditya cup is full of sap; thereby verily he makes the third pressing possessed of sap. Having recited a Triṣṭubh as the invitatory verse for the Āditya cup, he utters a Triṣṭubh as the offering verse; the Triṣṭubh is might and strength; verily thus he confers might and strength upon the sacrificer. He does not say the second *vaṣaṭ* (thinking) 'The Āditya cup is the continuity of the pressing; the

[2] *sāmājye* looks like a gloss on *ājye*, but possibly the first *ājye* is to be taken with *strotriyāt*. The expression is awkward.

[3] Possibly a gloss.

[1] For the Āditya cup and the other offerings here mentioned, see ÇÇS. viii. 1 and 2; Caland and Henry, *L'Agniṣṭoma*, pp. 330–332.

second *vaṣaṭ* call is the completion; let me not before the time complete the pressing.' The offering verse[2] contains (the words) 'be drunk', for the third pressing is connected with 'be drunk'. Then when the Pavamāna has been sung, they proceed with the victim, for this is the time for it; moreover (it serves) to confer sap on the pressing. Then they proceed with the five-oblation (sacrifice); the explanation of this has been given. He recites at the third pressing verses to Indra and the Ṛbhus[3] for the filling (of the bowls). When the Ṛbhus attained the love of Prajāpati, then Indra gave them a share in the Soma drinking. Therefore they do not sing to verses to the Ṛbhus; but they call it the Ārbhava Pavamāna. At the third pressing he uses as offering verse for the Prasthitas (a verse)[4] addressed to Indra and the Ṛbhus; verily thus he makes Indra a half-sharer in the pressing; in Jagatī metre, for the third pressing is connected with the Jagatī; containing (the words) 'be drunk', for the third pressing is connected with 'be drunk'. He says the second *vaṣaṭ*, for the healing of the libations, for the support of the libations. Then the Hotrakas sacrifice together; the explanation of these (offerings) has been given. Then the sacrificial food, then the Hotṛ's bowl; the explanation of this has been given. At the third pressing they offer cakes for the fathers; verily thus they delight the fathers.

The Sāvitra Cup.

xvi. 2. Then[1] they proceed with the cup for Savitṛ. At first they offered to him at the morning pressing; offspring were not born; then at the midday pressing; they were not born even then; then at the third pressing they offered to him; then offspring were born. Therefore at the third pressing is Savitṛ fixed. Moreover Savitṛ is one of the Ādityas; the third pressing belongs to the Ādityas; therefore they offer to him at the third pressing. Having recited a Triṣṭubh[2] as the invitatory verse for the cup for Savitṛ, he utters a Jagatī[3] as the offering verse; the Triṣṭubh is might and strength; the Jagatī is cattle; verily thus at the end he finds support in might, in strength, and in cattle. He does not say for it the second *vaṣaṭ* (thinking) 'The cup for Savitṛ is breath; the second *vaṣaṭ* call is the completion; let me not before the time complete breath', for breath here is yoked as it were. The offering verse contains (the words) 'be drunk', for the third pressing is connected with 'be drunk'.

[2] The verse is RV. vii. 51. 2.

[3] RV. iv. 35.

[4] RV. iii. 60. 5.

[1] For the ritual see ÇÇS. viii. 3. 1–4; Caland and Henry, *L'Agniṣṭoma*, pp. 352, 353. Cf. AB. iii. 29.

[2] RV. iv. 54. 1.

[3] Given in ÇÇS. viii. 3. 4.

The Vaiçvadeva Çastra.

xvi. 3. He[1] begins the Vaiçvadeva with Savitṛ; on the instigation of Savitṛ the gods brought together the third pressing; therefore the strophe and antistrophe and hymn[2] are all Savitṛ's. He begins the Vaiçvadeva with an Anuṣṭubh, 'That of Savitṛ we choose.' The Vaiçvadeva is the hymn of the Pavamāna; the metre of Soma is the Anuṣṭubh. The explanation of the division of the quarter verses has been given. He recites Gāyatrī verses; Gāyatrī verses are breath; verily thus he places breath in himself. He recites a hymn to Savitṛ, for a cup has been drawn for Savitṛ; verily therewith he accompanies it. He recites (a verse) for Vāyu;[3] (the verse) for Vāyu is breath; verily thus he places breath in himself. In the recitation of this he releases (the cups) for two deities in Vāyu, the breaths in the breath. He recites (the hymn[4]) to sky and earth; sky and earth are supports; verily (it serves) for support. In this the Adhvaryu responds with (a formula containing the word[5]) *mad*, for the third pressing is connected with 'be drunk' (*mad*). He recites (the verse[6]) 'Maker of fair forms'; that which has a fair form is food; verily thus he places food in himself. Moreover this is the Soma drinking of the forms; verily thus he places form in himself. He recites (a hymn[7]) to the Ṛbhus, for then Prajāpati made preparation for them; therefore (the hymn) to the Ṛbhus is recited here. Then he recites (verses)[8] to Vena, to the Ādityas, and to Bṛhaspati; with these he accompanies the Çukra and Manthin cups and the Āgrayaṇa cup; moreover this is the Vaiçvadeva Çastra,[9] (so it serves) to secure that none of the deities are excluded. He recites the Vaiçvadeva, for the Vaiçvadeva cup has been drawn; verily therewith he accompanies it. The concluding verse[10] he recites twice by quarter verses, the third time by half verses; it makes up a Virāj; the Virāj is prosperity and proper food; (verily it serves) to obtain the Virāj as prosperity and proper food. Four hymns he recites in the Vaiçvadeva; the Vaiçvadeva is cattle; cattle are fourfold, and also four-footed; verily (they serve) to obtain cattle. Therefore he should recite it abidingly; with him cattle abide.

xvi. 4. He recites the Vaiçvadeva with sixteen calls;[1] all this is of sixteen

[1] For the Vaiçvadeva Çastra see AB. iii. 25-32. For the ritual see ÇÇS. viii. 3. 5-19.

[2] RV. v. 82. 1-3; 4-6; iv. 54.

[3] Not in RV. Given in full at ÇÇS. viii. 3. 10.

[4] RV. i. 159.

[5] i. e. *çoṅsāmo daiva*, treated as *çoṅsā modaiva*.

[6] RV. i. 4. 1.

[7] RV. i. 111.

[8] RV. x. 123. 1; 63. 3; iv. 50. 6.

[9] RV. i. 89.

[10] RV. i. 89. 10.

xvi. 4. [1] That is, it occurs sixteen times; see Caland and Henry, *L'Agniṣṭoma*, p. 355. Cf. Weber, *Ind. Stud.* ix. 111, n. 1.

parts; verily (it serves) to obtain all this. It is seventeenfold; eleven deities, four Nivids, the strength of the litany, and the offering verse; Prajāpati is seventeenfold; that rite is beneficial which is commensurate with Prajāpati. Having recited the litany, he says an offering verse[2] for the All-gods, 'O All-gods, hearken to this my call', for the litany is for the All-gods; containing (the words) 'be drunk', for the third pressing is connected with 'be drunk'; in Triṣṭubh metre; the Triṣṭubh is might and strength; verily thus he places might and strength in the sacrificer. He says the second *vaṣaṭ*, for the healing of the libations, for the support of the libations. The first Anuṣṭubh yonder is speech; five Gāyatrī verses follow the Anuṣṭubh; (the hymn) to Savitṛ is mind; (the verse) to Vāyu is breath; (the hymn) to earth and sky is the eyes; there is the breath here which is not distinct in (the verse), 'Maker of fair forms'; (the hymn) to the Ṛbhus is the ear; the three isolated verses are expiration, inspiration, and cross-breathing; the hymn is the body; the Nivid what is within the body; the concluding verse a support; the offering verse is food. They say 'Why are the holy power and the lordly power unstable, the subjects stable'. 'The morning pressing is the holy power, the midday pressing the lordly power, the third pressing is the subjects; in that at the morning pressing and the midday pressing he concludes just as it may occur, therefore the Brahmans[3] rule the people insecurely, insecurely also the Kṣatriyas; in that the concluding verse of the third pressing is stable, therefore are the subjects stable' (is the reply).

xvi. 5. 'Say[1] the offering verse for the ghee' and 'Say the offering verse for the Soma drink', he says; by ghee and by Soma is the sacrifice carried on; these here he delights (thinking) 'They delighted shall support the sacrifice.' Inaudibly he says the offering verse for the ghee; ghee is a pouring of seed; inaudibly is seed poured. In that he says the offering verse aloud for the Soma drink, (it is because) Soma is the moon, and the moon is distinct. 'After it he should not perform any additional offering,' they say, 'So do they yonder from yonder look[2] back on this (world)'. But the rule is, 'Let him perform'. The butter is the world of the gods, the Soma the world of the fathers; verily thus they arise from the world

[2] RV. vi. 52. 13.

[3] *brāhmaṇāḥ* must be read. The Ānand. ed. has *brāhmaṇyaprajāḥ*.

[1] The question here discussed is whether a third offering should be made to Viṣṇu after the two for Agni and Soma, the first of butter, the latter of a *saumya caru*. The answer here is in the affirmative, but ÇÇS. viii. 4 treats it as optional. Cf. Caland and Henry, *L'Agniṣṭoma*, pp. 362–4.

[2] *paryāvartantīti* in O marg. is a natural but needless correction; so the comm. in causative sense.

of the fathers to the world of the gods[3]. 'Moreover thus they delight the fathers only in that they proceed with the Soma drink; moreover thus the Upasads are left over,' they say. In the Upasads he sacrifices to Agni, Soma, and Viṣṇu and to match this here also to Agni, Soma, and Viṣṇu. They take the Soma drink to the Sadas; the Hotṛ takes it and deposits it; then he looks at himself in the melted butter in it and with two fingers touches the melted butter; (with the words) 'Thou art the guardian of the eye, guard mine eye,' he should rub his eyes; verily thus he guards his eyes. It he hands over to the Udgātṛs.

The Pātnīvata Cup.

xvi. 6. Then[1] they proceed with the Pātnīvata cup; verily thus they make the wives of the gods sharers in the Āhavanīya. He does not say for it the second *vaṣaṭ*, for it is mixed with butter, and butter has no share in the second *vaṣaṭ* call. Inaudibly he says the offering verse; the Pātnīvata cup is a pouring of seed; inaudibly is seed poured. He does not say the second *vaṣaṭ* (thinking) 'The Pātnīvata cup is a pouring of seed; the second *vaṣaṭ* is completion; let me not before the due time complete the pouring of seed.' The offering verse[2] contains (the words) 'be drunk', for the third pressing is connected with 'be drunk'. They say 'Since this is the offering verse of the Neṣṭṛ, then why does the Āgnīdhra say it as an offering verse?' 'This offering verse is connected with Agni; the Āgnīdhra is connected with Agni; therefore the Āgnīdhra uses it as an offering verse; moreover, thus the *vaṣaṭ* calls of these unuttered become the same' (is the reply).

The Āgnimāruta Çastra.

xvi. 7. He[1] recites the Āgnimāruta with twenty-one calls; the four-verse Stoma, the highest of Stomas on which support is to be found, is twenty-onefold; verily (it serves) for a support. The (Çastra) is twenty-fourfold; there are twenty joinings; these make forty-four; the Triṣṭubh has forty-four syllables; the Triṣṭubh is might and strength; verily thus he places might and strength in the sacrificer. He recites (a hymn[2]) to Vaiçvānara, for a cup for Vaiçvānara has been drawn; verily therewith he accompanies

[3] Perhaps this is the division of the sentence best to be adopted. Cf. below KB. xvi. 8.

[1] The Pātnīvata cup is one for Agni with the wives of the gods (*patnīvant*); see ÇÇS. viii. 5; Caland and Henry, *L'Agniṣṭoma*, pp. 366, 367.

[2] RV. iii. 6. 9.

xvi. 7. [1] For the Āgnimāruta Çastra see AB. iii. 32–38. For the ritual see ÇÇS. viii. 5 and 6. For the calls in this Çastra see the rules in ÇÇS. viii. 7; Caland and Henry, *L'Agniṣṭoma*, p. 378.

[2] RV. iii. 3.

it. He recites (a verse[3]) to Rudra; Rudra is dread; verily thus he makes medicine; moveover his share is at the end; therefore in the end Çastra he recites it. He recites (a hymn[4]) to the Maruts; Rudra has them as his horde; verily thus he makes him prosper with his own horde. Then come the strophe and antistrophe of the Yajñāyajñīya[5]; these two he recites in the middle to frighten, for in the middle of the body is the womb placed to frighten. He recites (a hymn[6]) to Jātavedas; thereby is it called the Āgnimāruta (Çastra). Therefore should he recite it quickly, just as one escaping a forest fire. He recites (verses[7]) with the waters as deities; the waters are healing and medicine; verily thus at the end in the sacrifice are healing and medicine produced. Therefore should he recite them slowly, just as one spraying himself in the waters. He recites 'the Dragon of the Deep'[8]; the dragon of the deep is Agni; him with it he makes to glow; moreover, with it he accompanies the altars. He recites 'the wives of the gods'[9] and 'Rākā'[10]; verily with these he accompanies the Pātnīvata cup; moreover, the wives have their portion at the end; therefore in the end Çastra he recites these verses.

xvi. 8. He recites the Akṣarapañktis[1]; the Akṣarapañktis are cattle; verily (they serve) to obtain cattle; moreover, the Akṣarapañktis are expiration and inspiration; thereby then he places expiration and inspiration in himself; moreover (they serve) to secure the presence of Indra in the Çastra. He recites (verses) to the fathers[2] and to Yama[3]; verily thus he accompanies the Nārāçaṅsa cups; moreover the fathers have their portion at the end; therefore he recites these (verses) in the end Çastra. He recites (the verses[4]) 'Sweet indeed is he'; verily with them he makes sweet the Soma for Indra; moreover, Indra is the world of the gods, Yama the world of the fathers; verily thus he arises from the world of the fathers to the world of the gods. To them the Adhvaryu responds with (a formula containing the word) '*mad*', for the third pressing is connected with 'be drunk'. He recites (a verse) to Viṣṇu and Varuṇa[5]; the sacrifice is

[3] RV. ii. 33. 1.
[4] RV. i. 87.
[5] RV. vi. 48. 1, 2; vii. 16. 11, 12 (made into three verses in each case). The Ānand. ed. has *iti* absurdly.
[6] RV. i. 143. The variant °*mokṣyamāṇaḥ* of M is an easy variation, but not necessary nor so probable as the text, which shows *mokṣa* as a desiderative basis without the sense of spiritual freedom.
[7] RV. x. 9. 1–3.
[8] RV vi. 50. 14. Here, as in the next case, either the names are made up of the first words of the verses, or *çaṅs* means 'celebrate'. The first is clearly the case in *Ahir budhnyam çaṅsati*.
[9] RV. v. 46. 7, 8.
[10] RV. ii. 32. 4, 5.
[1] RV. vi. 44. 7–9.
[2] RV. x. 15. 1–3.
[3] RV. x. 14. 4, 3 and 5.
[4] RV. vi. 47. 1–3. For the last words of the sentence cf. above KB. xvi. 5.
[5] Not in RV. AV. vii. 25. 1 has one version, ĀÇS. v. 20 another.

connected with Viṣṇu and Varuṇa; whatever mistake or error there is in the sacrifice, that with this he remedies; verily this is medicine. He recites (a verse) to Viṣṇu [6] and (a verse) to Agni [7]; of the gods Agni and Viṣṇu are those whose portions are at the end; therefore these he recites in the end Çastra. He concludes with (a verse) to Indra,[8] for he is Indra's; verily him Indra at the end establishes.[9]

xvi. 9. 'What is the deity of the Soma?' [1] Madhuka asked Gauçra. He, after running over (the words) 'Soma becometh pure', replied 'There may be different ones.' 'As with the Bahvṛcas [2], it should be connected with Indra' was the rule of Paiñgya. 'It should be connected with Indra and Agni' is Kauṣītaki's view. 'By Agni it begins in that (it begins) with the Ājya; with Indra it ends (in) this concluding verse [3]; therefore it should be connected with Indra and Agni.' 'This is the Agniṣṭoma; this is taken for every desire. He who offers with any other sacrifice without having sacrificed with this [4] prepares for himself a pitfall, he comes to ruin [5]', he used to say. This Agniṣṭoma begins with the Ājya (Çastra) and ends with the Āgnimāruta. What has to be recited makes up three hundred and sixty Ṛc verses; three hundred and sixty are the days of the year; verily (it serves) to obtain the year.[6] After reciting the litany he uses as offering verse,[7] 'O Agni, with the Maruts, resplendent, loud singing', addressed to Agni and the Maruts, for this litany is addressed to Agni and the Maruts; in Jagatī metre, for the third pressing is connected with the Jagatī; containing (the words) 'be drunk', for the third pressing is connected with 'be drunk'. He says the second *vaṣaṭ*, for the healing of the libations, for the support of the libations.

[6] RV. i. 154. 1.

[7] RV. x. 53. 6.

[8] RV. iv. 17. 20.

[9] M alone has the necessary causative, the comm. and the other MSS. and the Ānand. ed. having the simple.

[1] It is not clear to what this refers. *Somaḥ pavate* is the Pratīka of RV. ix. 96. 5, and if anything more than these two words are meant then the reference ought to be to a RV. text. On the other hand they are also the Pratīka of VS. vii. 21, and the *Vedic Concordance* treats this verse as repeated in the Soma sacrifice at the Bahiṣpavamāna; Caland and Henry (*L'Agniṣṭoma*, p. 174), however, thinks that there also merely the words themselves are meant, and this may be the case here also. The sense clearly is that Gauçra treated the Soma as having, as deity, diverse gods.

[2] Apparently the contrast is with a special school name Bahvṛcas, as in the wider sense of that term it covers Paiñgya. Cf. the Bahvṛcabrāhmaṇa of Āpastamba; Keith, JRAS. 1915, pp. 493–498.

[3] The construction is rather *ad sensum*.

[4] KÇS. x. 9. 25; PB. xvi. 1. 2 agrees with this.

[5] For this phrase cf. KB. xxv. 14: *vā* may be alternative, or merely assertive. Cf. KB. xii. 4; xi. 4.

[6] M has *tat saṁvatsarasyāhāny āpnoti*.

[7] RV. v. 60. 8.

The Sautrāmaṇī.

[xvi. 10. Having[1] sacrificed with Soma he should sacrifice with the Sautrāmaṇī who desires prosperity, offspring, and the Virāj. The Sautrāmaṇī is a sacrificial rite for Indra; the third victim is the body of the sacrifice, two victims the arms; therefore the arms are about the body; therefore the two should be at each side about the body; in that, after saying the second *vaṣaṭ* over the cups of Surā and Soma, all[2]; therefore having sacrificed with Soma let him perform the Sautrāmaṇī; he who knowing thus, having sacrificed with Soma, sacrifices with the Sautrāmaṇī, obtains prosperity, offspring, and the Virāj, and so he also who knows thus. The Virāj is prosperity and proper food; (verily it serves) to obtain the Virāj as prosperity and proper food. He goes to the final bath, as at the Soma sacrifice. Or he may if he will offer a milk mess to Mitra and Varuṇa.]

The Ukthya Sacrifice.

xvi. 11. The[1] litanies of the Ukthya are addressed to Indra and Agni; all the gods are Indra and Agni; the third pressing is connected with the All-gods; verily (they serve) to delight all the gods. In (verses) to Agni they give the lead for the Maitrāvaruṇa, in (verses) to Indra in the other two cases; thereby these are addressed to Indra and Agni. They recite four hymns each; the litanies are cattle; cattle are fourfold; moreover,

[1] For the Sautrāmaṇī see ÇÇS. xiv. 13 (where the three victims for the Açvins, Sarasvatī and Indra are specified), cf. xv. 15 (where the Surā is specified). The form here is that called elsewhere the Kaukilī, an independent rite, while that connected with the Rājasūya is the Caraka; see Weber, *Ind. Stud.* x. 349–358; Eggeling, SBE. xliv. 213, 214; Hillebrandt, *Ritual-litteratur*, p. 159. See also MÇS. v. 2. 8 and 11; BÇS. xvii. 31–38.

[2] These victims are offered (comm.); the text is corrupt. The bad text and the fact, not mentioned by Lindner, that M omits the whole section, taken in conjunction with the unnatural insertion of this paragraph at this juncture, and with the fact that the ÇÇS. shows no knowledge of this portion of the text, justify us in the belief that the chapter is an interpolation. Moreover, the term *tripaçu* naturally denotes here the third victim, not a set of three victims, and in either case is an odd form without an early parallel; the apparently similar *tridiva* hardly means simply the 'third heaven' as taken by MW.; it is rather a collective formed in the normal way (Wackernagel, *Altind. Gramm.* II. i. 304 *seq.*) from *tri* and *dyu*, meaning a collection of three heavens, and is due to the Vedic triplication of the heaven, which again arose from the triplication of the universe (cf. Macdonell, *Vedic Mythology*, p. 9). BR.'s view that it refers to the inner space of the highest heaven is likewise implausible.

xvi. 11. [1] For the three additional Çastras of the Hotrakas after the Āgnimāruta Çastra in the Ukthya rite, see AB. iii. 49, 50. The Çastras are given in detail in ÇÇS. ix. 1–4.

cattle are four-footed; verily (they serve) to obtain cattle. They make up twelve; the year has twelve months; verily (they serve) to obtain the year. The Çastras contain four calls; the litanies are cattle; cattle are fourfold; moreover cattle are four-footed; verily (they serve) to obtain cattle. The offering verses of the litanies are addressed to two deities; the sacrificer has two feet; (therefore they serve) for support. They make up four;[2] the litanies are cattle; cattle are fourfold; moreover, cattle are four-footed; verily (they serve) to obtain cattle. That of the Maitrāvaruṇa[3] is addressed to Indra and Varuṇa, for his litany is addressed to Indra and Varuṇa; that of the Brāhmaṇācchaṅsin[4] to Indra and Bṛhaspati, for his litany is addressed to Indra and Bṛhaspati; that of the Achāvāka[5] to Indra and Viṣṇu, for his litany is connected with Indra and Viṣṇu. The first and last contain (the words) 'be drunk', for the third pressing is connected with 'be drunk'. They make up three; these worlds are three; verily thus they obtain these worlds. They are Triṣṭubh verses; the Triṣṭubh is might and strength; verily thus they place might and strength in the sacrificer. They say the second *vaṣaṭ*, for the healing of the libations, for the support of the libations.

ADHYĀYA XVII

The Soma Sacrifice (*continued*).

The Ṣoḍaçin.

xvii. 1. The[1] Ṣoḍaçin is a thunderbolt composed of the Anuṣṭubh; in that they undertake the Ṣoḍaçin, they smite away the evil of the sacrificer with the thunderbolt composed of the Anuṣṭubh. It refers to the 'bay steeds'; the bay is breath, for it draws; therefore it refers to the 'bay steeds'. The Ṣoḍaçin is he yonder that gives heat; verily thus they delight him. There is a sixteenth Stotra, a sixteenth Çastra; therefore is it called the Ṣoḍaçin. In that they undertake the Ṣoḍaçin, and all this (universe) is of sixteen parts, verily (it serves) to obtain all this. Moreover, the Ṣoḍaçin is Indra; therefore it refers to the 'bay steeds', for Indra's bay steeds are praised. 'O Indra rejoice, bring forward, come hither, O hero,

[2] i.e. deities, Indra, Varuṇa, Viṣṇu, Bṛhaspati.

[3] RV. vi. 68. 11.

[4] RV. vii. 97. 10.

[5] RV. vi. 69. 8.

[1] For the Ṣoḍaçin rite see AB. iv. 1–4. For the ritual see ÇÇS. ix. 5. M reads *anuṣṭubho* which is possibly correct.

of the bay steeds' these (verses)[2] have twenty-five syllables and one by one have nine syllables added. The self is twenty-fivefold, what is added is offspring and cattle; verily thus he adds to himself in offspring, cattle, servants, and proper food. These make up thirty-four; whatever is of thirty-four syllables, that metre is the Svarāj; verily thereby he obtains self rule. Repeated together they make up five Anuṣṭubh verses and a ten-syllable quarter verse is left over, two syllables for each verse. 'Of such a one as thou, O thou of much light', this Gāyatrī verse[3] he recites next, for the completion of these syllables; moreover along with it they make up a strophe of six Anuṣṭubh verses; therefore he recites it, for completion. To match it some make an antistrophe; but as to this they say[4] 'The Ṣoḍaçin is he yonder that gives heat; there is none other to be a counterpart of him; if he were to make a counterpart and one were to say of him, "The rival who is hateful will reject him", so would it be. Therefore he should not trouble about a counterpart.'

xvii. 2. Thereafter he transposes the metres which follow; the metres are the breaths; verily thus in the body he interweaves the breaths, to prevent separation; therefore these breaths, though breathing in different directions, do not blow out.[1] Moreover the Ṣoḍaçin is connected with the Anuṣṭubh; verily thus he brings all the metres into relation with the Anuṣṭubh. He transposes Gāyatrī and Pañkti verses;[2] the Pañkti is the metre of the sacrificer; the Gāyatrī is brilliance and splendour; verily thus he places brilliance and splendour in the sacrificer. He transposes Uṣṇih and Bṛhatī verses;[3] the Uṣṇih is the metre of the sacrificer; the Bṛhatī is cattle; verily thus he confers cattle as connected with the Bṛhatī upon the sacrificer. He transposes a verse of two Padas containing twenty syllables and a Triṣṭubh;[4] the verse of two Padas

[2] These verses are given in full in ÇÇS. ix. 5. 2; AV. ii. 5. 1; SV. ii. 302–304; ĀÇS. vi. 3. 1. *hariha* of ÇÇS. *l. c.* and of SV. is absurd. ĀÇS. has *harī iha* as trisyllabic (no doubt) and this is presumably the source of *hariha*. AV. has *haribhyām*. The verses consist of 5 pentads and after each of the first three syllables are added (here *pra vaha*, *hariha*).

[3] RV. viii. 46. 1.

[4] The quotation is not finished by *iti*; cf. KB. xii. 3, n. 2.

[1] As in KB. vii. 9 all the MSS. save M and the Ānand. ed. read *vāñco 'nunirvāñcy*.

[2] RV. i. 16. 1–3 and i. 84. 10–12. The *viharaṇa* consists in placing a Pada of the Pañkti after each of the Padas of the Gāyatrī and pausing after the first two, saying *om* after the second two, pausing after the third pair and saying *om* after the two remaining Padas of the Pañkti, each by itself.

[3] RV. viii. 98. 1–3 and iii. 45. 1–3. The Padas are put together by two's with alternate pause and *om*; the two eight-syllable feet are made into one followed by a pause, then the two sets of four syllables over are united and combined with the last Bṛhatī foot into a single verse followed by *om*.

[4] RV. vii. 34. 4 and vi. 47. 8. The combination is effected by dividing the Dvipadā into four sets of five syllables.

is the metre of the sacrificer; the Triṣṭubh is might and strength; verily thus he confers might and strength upon the sacrificer. He transposes verses of two Padas containing sixteen syllables and Jagatī verses;[5] verses of two Padas are the metre of the sacrificer; the Jagatī is cattle; verily thus he confers cattle as connected with the Jagatī on the sacrificer. He recites Gāyatrī verses; Gāyatrī verses are breath; verily thus he places breath in himself. He recites a verse of seven Padas; the metres are seven; verily (it serves) to obtain all the metres; moreover, with it the Gāyatrī verses make up four Anuṣṭubh verses;[6] therefore he recites it, for completion.

xvii. 3. Then he recites Anuṣṭubhs[1] of normal type; the Ṣoḍaçin is connected with the Anuṣṭubh; thus he causes it to prosper by its own symbol. They make up eight; by these (verses) the gods attained all attainments; verily thus also with these the sacrificer attains all attainments. With the last verse thrice repeated they make up ten; the Virāj consists of tens; the Virāj is prosperity and proper food; (they serve) to obtain the Virāj as prosperity and proper food. He concludes with 'When up to the place of the bright one'; yonder is the place of the bright one where he yonder gives heat; verily thus he places the sacrificer there. Three times[2] he utters the call for the Ṣoḍaçin, in the strophe, for the Nivid, for the concluding verse; the Ṣoḍaçin is threefold; verily thus with a threefold thunderbolt he smites the evil of the sacrificer. These are the fame, the sounds, the strengths of the litanies. Famous, resounding, strong, renowned does he become who knows thus the strengths of the litanies. They recited together make up forty Anuṣṭubhs; the Pañkti has forty syllables; the Pañkti is a support; verily thus in all creatures he establishes the sacrificer.

xvii. 4. Some say 'He should use an interpolated Triṣṭubh as offering verse'.[1] 'For indeed the courser.—Thou hast drunk of the ancient draughts, O lord of the bays.—For the courser is a courser.—Now let this pressing be thine only.—The courser is a bearer.—Drink the Soma rich in honey, O Indra.—For the courser is active.—Do thou ever, O strong one, pour into thy belly.' But the rule is not to interpolate. The offering verses are duly prepared dishes for the gods; verily thus with a duly

[5] The Dvipadās are given in ÇÇS. ix. 6. 6; and RV. x. 96. 1-3. The former are divided into four sets of four syllables.

[6] RV. i. 84. 13-15 with RV. x. 133. 1 make up Anuṣṭubhs by recital by two's and two's with pause and *om*.

[1] ÇÇS. ix. 6. 14-19 prescribes RV. viii. 69. 1-3, 10, 13-15, and 17, all Anuṣṭubh verses. These are *nitya* as offered to the artificial Anuṣṭubhs above arrived at. The Nivid comes in before RV. viii. 69. 15.

[2] This is repeated in ÇÇS. ix. 6. 17. The variation in construction is noteworthy.

xvii. 4. [1] RV. x. 96. 18. ÇÇS. ix. 6. 18 ignores the option, for which cf. AB. iv. 4.

prepared dish for the gods he tenders the oblation to the gods. He should not undertake it at night;[2] the Ṣoḍaçin is Indra; there is nothing above Indra; much is accomplished at night, the rounds as it were, and the Āçvina[3] (Çastra); therefore he should undertake it on the fourth[4] day; that is the abode of the Ṣoḍaçin; that day concludes with the Ṣoḍaçin as its end. But they say 'Let him undertake it'; the Ṣoḍaçin is the day and night complete; in that they undertake the Ṣoḍaçin it is to make day and night complete.

The Atirātra.

xvii. 5. In[1] that they undertake the Atirātra, (it is because) the year is as great as day and night; in that they undertake the Atirātra, (it serves) to obtain the year. Moreover, all this (universe) is twofold, unguent and brilliance; both of these are obtained by day and night. In that they undertake the Atirātra, (it is) for the obtaining of unguent and brilliance.

xvii. 6. They recite strophes and antistrophes[1] in Gāyatrī; the Gāyatrī is light; night is the evil, the darkness; thus thereby they smite away the evil, the darkness. They recite with repetitions, for so do the Sāman chanters sing; (they say) 'According as it is sung, is it recited.' Then they say 'Why after the final Pratīhāra do they call and link the Çastra with the Sāman?'

xvii. 7. The sacrifice is a man; of him the oblation holders are the head, the Āhavanīya the face, the Sadas the stomach, the litanies the food, the Mārjālīya and the Āgnīdhrīya the arms, the altars within the Sadas the internal divinities; the Gārhapatya and (the fire) for cooking the fast milk the support. Again, of him the Brahman priest is the mind, the Udgātṛ the expiration, the Prastotṛ the inspiration, the Pratihartṛ the cross-breathing, the Hotṛ the speech, the Adhvaryu the eye, the Sadasya

[2] The argument is clearly one as to the place of the Ṣoḍaçin if used in connexion with an Atirātra as it is assumed to be used in this school. Is it to be said at night after the threefold carousal of the Atirātra begins, or is it to be said on the morning of the day after the carousal? The answer first suggested is the latter view. *bahurātryām* may be a cpd. as taken by the edd., but this is unnecessary.

[3] Cited in *Nirukta* i. 9 as equivalent to *āçvinaṁ ca paryāyāç ca*, where the reading as in M has only one *tvad*. But this is very strange, *tvad ata* or *tvai tata* may be read. The Āçvina Çastra is to be recited up to sunrise; see ÇÇS. ix. 20. 19 *seq.*

[4] i. e. the Ṣoḍaçin is the suitable rite for the fourth day in a continuous offering; see ÇÇS. x. 2. 11.

[1] For the Atirātra see AB. iv. 5 and 6. For the ritual see ÇÇS. ix. 7–19 for the Çastras of the priests at the three Paryāyas.

xvii. 6. [1] The explanation follows in KB. xvii. 7. The point is not that the correspondence of Çastra and Stotra is modified by the Çastra beginning after the Pratīhāra of the Sāman and not after the Nidhana, but merely, it seems, to explain the parallelism.

generation,[1] the sacrificer the body, the Hotrāçaṅsins the limbs. In that the Adhvaryu starts the Stotra, verily thus he unites the eye with the breaths; moreover, verily thus he connects inspiration with the mind. In that the Prastotṛ addresses the Brahman with 'O Brahman, shall we begin the praise, O Praçāstṛ?' (it is because they think), 'Mind is the leader of these breaths; impelled by mind let us sing the Stoma'; moreover, verily thus he connects inspiration with the mind. In that the Brahman approves the Stotra, verily thus he unites the mind with the breaths; moreover, verily thus he connects inspiration with the mind. In that the Prastotṛ begins the praise, verily thus he places inspiration in expiration. In that the Udgātṛ sings, verily thus he places expiration in cross-breathing. In that the Pratihartṛ utters his part, verily thus he places cross-breathing in expiration. So all these deities find support in expiration. In that the Hotṛ connects the Çastra with the Sāman, and the Hotṛ is speech, verily thus he unites speech with the breaths; moreover, verily thus he connects inspiration with mind. In that the Hotrāçaṅsins make a continuity with the Sāman, verily thus they connect the limbs with the breaths. In that the sacrificer sings in accompaniment to the Stotra, and the singers are the breaths, verily thus he places the breaths in himself. Therefore the sun should not set on him outside the altar place,[2] nor should it rise on him, nor should he make preparations, nor utter the invitation, nor say the *vaṣaṭ*, nor should (the sun) heat (him) when in what is not an altar,[3] (thinking) 'Let me not sever the body from the breaths.'

xvii. 8. In that in the first rounds they repeat[1] in the first Padas, verily thus from the first night they smite away the Asuras; in that in the middle rounds they repeat in the middle Padas, verily thus from the middle night they smite away the Asuras; in that in the last rounds they repeat in the last Padas, verily thus from the last night they smite away the Asuras. Just as one can by separate repetition[2] and by repeating severally smite away evil again and again, so with these strophes and antistrophes from day and night they smite away the Asuras.

xvii. 9. They recite the beginnings of the litanies in Gāyatrī verses; the Gāyatrī is brilliance and splendour; verily thereby they place brilliance

[1] The Ānand. ed. has *prajāpatiḥ* for *prajātiḥ*, but merely, it is clear, by an error.

[2] The whole emphasis is placed on *bahirvedi*.

[3] Cf. *Vait.* xii. 8 where *pratapet* is normal as against *pratapeta*; perhaps heating implements is meant.

xvii. 8. [1] The reference is to the repetition of the first Padas in the Stotras and the Çastras. The use of *ninartayanti* in this sense points to the union of song and recitation and dancing.

[2] *abhyāgāram* is doubtful: BR. gave it as 'besprechen', B. as 'in the house'; this is possible, but MW.'s rendering is followed: if *abhyāgāram* is taken as by B. then there may be a reference to a magic dance as a popular rite.

and splendour in the sacrificer. Having recited Gāyatrī verses, they recite Jagatī verses; between the Gāyatrī and Jagatī verses they insert the calls; verily thus they make the metres of varied strength. Having recited Jagatī verses, they conclude with Triṣṭubh verses. The Triṣṭubh is might and strength, the Jagatī cattle; verily thus in might and strength at the end and in cattle they find support. The offering verses[1] are in Triṣṭubh, and contain (the words) 'Soma juice', 'be drunk', and 'drink' as their characteristics and are perfect; that is the symbol of night. They should keep awake through the night; keeping awake is the light; the night is the dark, the evil; thereby by the light they cross the dark, the evil. So long as there is no singing or reciting, so long are the Rakṣases able to drink after;[2] therefore 'Do ye lighten up the kindled Āhavanīya, the Āgnīdhriya, the Gārhapatya and the altars' they should say aloud; they should lighten up, it should be light as it were, they should lie snoring; them the evil does not attack (perceiving) 'They are in motion';[3] they smite away the evil.

ADHYĀYA XVIII

THE SOMA SACRIFICE (*continued*).

The Āçvina Çastra.

xviii. 1. The[1] Āçvina (Çastra) is (a sacrifice) wherein there is a redundancy of Soma; wherein in the sacrifice there is a redundancy, thereby the rival of the sacrificer is energetic against him. In that afterwards he sacrifices to the Açvins, and the Açvins are the physicians of the gods, verily thus he makes medicine. Now when Savitṛ gave Sūryā to Soma, the king, he made over to his daughter whether she was Prajāpati's[2] (or his own) on

[1] These are for him and twelve offering verses; it is clear that *andhas* is by the *Brāhmaṇa* connected with 'darkness'. The Yājyās are for the first night RV. ii. 14. 1; vi. 44. 15; vi. 24. 1; vi. 44. 16; for the second night, ii. 19. 1; vi. 44. 14; x. 112. 2; x. 112. 6; for the third night, iii. 35. 1; ii. 15. 1; vi. 37. 2; x. 104. 8.

[2] See above KB. x. 2.

[3] M has clearly *tān vi tat ceṣṭanti nvai* (misread by Lindner), K. has the same without *vi*, and BL. nearly the same. The reading must certainly be *ceṣṭanti*. The Ānand. ed. has *taṁ ceṣṭiṁ tanvā*. It, however, has correctly *ujjvalayateti bhāṣeran* for Lindner's *ujjvalayata 'tibhāṣeran*. *samindhvam* is possible, not necessary.

xviii. 1. [1] For the Āçvina Çastra see AB. iv. 7–11. For the ritual see ÇÇS. ix. 20.

[2] This seems the reasonable sense of the interpolation of these words. Prajāpati figures as the giver and Savitṛ as the father of the girl in AB. iv. 7, and *Prajāpatis* is, of course, an easy correction; the genitive cannot well be meant as = a dative (*Nir.* xii. 8), as this is contrary to the usual version. The Ānand. ed. has *purastāt*, erroneously.

marriage this thousand (of verses) that was in the possession of these deities; they said 'Let us run a race for this thousand'; they ran the race; then the Açvins were victorious by means of the ass. Therefore are many gods celebrated, and yet it is called the Āçvina. Hence, moreover, the ass does not run with his full speed, considering himself worn out (because) 'I have done my running.'[3] A thousand should he recite, for a thousand they too won.

xviii. 2. They say 'Seeing that the Pṛṣṭhas depend on the Bṛhatī, then why does he begin with a Triṣṭubh?' Thrice repeated it makes three Bṛhatī verses and one Gāyatrī. The three Bṛhatī verses are the symbol of union, the Gāyatrī the symbol of the first. In that he produces the Bṛhatī, (it is because) it is with regard to the Bṛhatī that the vow is produced.[1] In that of the strophes in Bṛhatī he recites the first Pragātha, repeating it and making it into Kakubh form, (it is because) the Sāman chanters sing with repetitions; verily thus the symbol of this is produced. He recites the service for Agni; thus he obtains this world. He recites that for Uṣas; thus he obtains the world of the atmosphere. He recites that for the Açvins; thus he obtains yonder world. He recites the service for Sūrya; there is a fourth world of the gods, the waters; verily thereby he obtains it. He recites a Pragātha; the Pragātha is cattle; verily (it serves) to obtain cattle. Moreover the Pragātha in Bṛhatī is expiration and inspiration; verily thus he places expiration and inspiration in himself; also (it serves) to secure the presence of Indra in the Çastra. He recites (a hymn) to sky and earth; sky and earth are supports; verily (it serves) for support. He recites (a verse) of two Padas; (the verse) of two Padas is a metre in which to find support; verily (it serves) for support. He concludes with (a verse) to Bṛhaspati; Bṛhaspati is the holy power; verily thus in the holy power at the end he finds support. Now this is the completion.

xviii. 3. Three[1] hundred Gāyatrī verses are two hundred Bṛhatī verses;

[3] This seems the sense of M's reading *sṛtam*; the other MSS. and the comm. have *çritam*, while the Ānand. ed. has *çritaṁ nayeti*.

[1] The Ānand. ed. has *bṛhati* and *saṁpadyante* absurdly.

xviii. 3. [1] The Āçvina Çastra according to Çāñkh. is composed as follows, as a *vikṛti* of the Prātaranuvāka: it commences with RV. vi. 15. 13–15 (to Agni) in place of x. 30. 12; of the Gāyatrī verses 19 are omitted, of the Anuṣṭubh two, of the Triṣṭubhs 113; the hymns by Kakṣīvant (i. 116–118) and Agastya (i. 180, 181, 183, 184) stand, but after i. 116 is placed i. 120. 1–9; after i. 184 come 108 verses of the Suparṇa or in place another 108 to the Açvins (given by Ānartīya); then in the Prātaranuvāka, RV. x. 150. 1–3 is omitted; all of i. 47. 1–8 is said (not only 1, 3, 5); 11 verses of the Uṣṇih section disappear and 11 of the Agni section in Jagatī; sunrise is to take place at the last Pañkti Pada, and then the Sūrya hymns begin, viz. i. 50. 1–9; i. 115; x. 37; the Pragātha, vii. 32. 26, 27; i. 22. 13–15; a Dvipadā

seventy Anuṣṭubh and seventy Paṅkti verses are one hundred and forty Bṛhatī verses; deducting a hundred Gāyatrī from three hundred Triṣṭubh verses there are three hundred Bṛhatī verses; the hundred Gāyatrī verses and a hundred Jagatī verses are two hundred Bṛhatī verses; fifty Triṣṭubh and fifty Uṣṇih verses make up a hundred Bṛhatī verses; then there are fifty-seven Bṛhatī verses actually found; the fifty-first and fifty-second Triṣṭubh verses and (the verse) of two Padas are three Bṛhatī verses; thus a thousand Bṛhatīs are made up from a thousand of varied metres. 'He should not recite over a thousand, nor less than a thousand' is the rule;[2] the expansion of the Āçvina is however conspicuous. This is a service for Agni; verily he should not fall away from the service for Agni; if he should pass over the service for Agni before the due time, he should apply there whatever in the Āçvina is addressed to two gods in the Ṛcs; in the service for Sūrya (he should use) (the verses) for Soma, the purifying, according to metre, Gāyatrī in Gāyatrī, Triṣṭubh in Triṣṭubh, Jagatī in Jagatī; all that is connected with Sūrya[3] in the place of (the service) for Sūrya; all Pragāthas to Indra in the place of the Pragātha; all to sky and earth in the place of (the hymn) to sky and earth; all (verses) of two Padas in the place of (the verse) of two Padas; all addressed to Bṛhaspati before the final verse. That is whatever of the Ṛcs is not set forth.[4]

xviii. 4. The Āçvina is like (a wagon) with wheels; the two Ālambanas[1] are the wheels, the aimless verses the axle, (the verse[2]) 'Hither your chariot, O Açvins, with the speed of the falcon' the seat; the four Agastya hymns the yokes. This is the chariot of the gods. With this chariot of the gods he attains in safety the world of heaven. (The Çastra) should include the Suparṇa; the Suparṇa is a bird; like it becoming a winged one, a bird, so he attains in safety the world of heaven. Twice he utters the call for the Āçvina, for the introduction and for the concluding verse; that is as when one, not being covered, makes a covering by an obstruction.[3] Now comes the question of the conclusion. Whenever the sun creeps over on to the front (of the oblation holder), whenever the Hotṛ himself can discern it,

(12+8); as finale ii. 23. 15 (to Bṛhaspati). The invitatory verse is given in ÇÇS. ix. 20. 31.

[2] It is clear that the text encourages the use of extra verses which it goes on to enumerate. The last verse being addressed to Bṛhaspati explains the nature of the insertion allowed before it. The comm. takes *pro* as a *paramata*, and *stad vai* as *svamata*.

[3] *sūryanyañgam* of M is clearly to be read, against *sauryaṁ nyañgam* of the edd.

[4] The sense of this clause is doubtful; *yat* seems needed before *kiṁcit*.

[1] The sense of *ālambana* is clearly some part of the Āçvina Çastra, viz. the two supporting parts. For *akūdhryañc* see KB. viii. 5, n. 6.

[2] RV. i. 118. 1. For Suparṇa cf. Oldenberg, GGA. 1907, p. 229, n. 6; AB. viii. 10. n. 5.

[3] The constr. is curious in the absence of an expressed object.

whenever its ruddiness comes on,[4] whenever all its rays move out towards him, that is the time for the conclusion; for at this time he is freed from evil, severed from evil. He smites away evil, he is severed from evil, who concludes at this time. If there is rain, that is the form of him by which he supports offspring; this breath in the self is one with it; 'It is not concealed[5] from me',

xviii. 5. so regarding it, he should conclude. He should offer a libation to the shining one, when the sun cannot be discerned, he who is unsuited[1]; he becomes then revealed to them. With two (verses) should he sacrifice, for by reason of two it is called the Āçvina. Having recited the Gāyatrī without breathing in, he takes in breath at the half verse of the Virāj; the Virāj is prosperity and proper food; verily thus he finds support in the Virāj as prosperity and proper food. With the second half verse of the Virāj he says the *vaṣaṭ* call; verily thus he places the sacrificer in the world of heaven. 'He should use the Virāj only as offering verse', Kauṣītaki used to say; the Virāj has thirty-three syllables; the gods are thirty-three; the gods he makes to share the syllables. 'O Açvins, ye of keen insight, with Vāyu', is, however,[2] the rule, namely a Triṣṭubh to the Açvins, containing (the words) 'Kept over night', for the Somas are kept over night. Moreover, the Triṣṭubh is might and strength; verily thus he places might and strength in the sacrificer. He says the second *vaṣaṭ*, for the healing of the libations, for the support of the libations. When the Sāman chanters have finished, he offers the two libations of the offering for the choosing (of priests) (thinking) 'Speech and mind being delighted shall support[3] the great Çastra.'

The Hāriyojana.

xviii. 6. They[1] proceed with the offering to the yoker of bays; verily thus they delight the two bays; therein the gods with their horses are delighted. Having recited a Triṣṭubh as invitatory verse, he uses a Jagatī as offering verse; the Triṣṭubh is might and strength; the Jagatī is cattle; verily thus in might and strength at the end and in cattle he

[4] *āpiyāt* is odd and *apīyāt* (comm.) seems natural.

[5] The identity of the breath and the sun is clearly indicated. The Ānand. ed. has *atilohito mad* which is clearly an error due to *lohitam* above. It has also *yad abhram*, and, with M, *pratyutperan*. M runs on the sentence, as is essential.

[1] *anupayuktaḥ* can hardly apply to the sun, but is rather used to denote one whom the sun does not oblige by his presence.

[2] Kauṣītaki's rule is here disregarded in favour of a different rule. ÇÇS. ix. 20. 32 gives the rule as a compound of RV. i. 46. 15 and vii. 68. 2. The rule here is to use RV. iii. 58. 7.

[3] The Ānand. ed. has the form *udyatsāte*; cf. VOJ. xxiii. 70. M has *udyacchātam iti*.

xviii. 6. [1] For the Hāriyojana see ÇÇS. viii. 8. The verses are RV. iii. 58. 2; i. 82. 6.

finds support. The offering verse contains (the words) 'be drunk', for the third pressing is connected with 'be drunk'. He says the second *vaṣaṭ* for the healing of the libations, for the support of the libations. He should take the most of the grains; the grains are cattle; verily thus he confers a multitude of cattle upon himself. In that they mutter the Ṛc, in that they offer the libation, verily thus they produce a benediction, for the healing of the sacrifice, and for the curing of the sacrificer. They cast them down on the ash border of the Āhavanīya; the Āhavanīya is the birthplace[2] of cattle; verily thus he places them in a secure fold.

The Çākalas.

xviii. 7. Then[1] they offer the Çākalas. Just as a snake is rid of its old skin, or the stem from reed grass, so are they set free from all evil.

The Conclusion of the Jyotiṣṭoma.

xviii. 8. Then[1] turning to the left, they approach the Somas in the waters; they place them here within the altar, for that is the abode of the Soma; they distribute the branches of Darbha grass; when the waters and the plants come together, then the Soma is complete. With a verse to Viṣṇu[2] they pour them down; Viṣṇu is the sacrifice; verily thus they establish them at the end in the sacrifice. Then they stroke the vital organs; verily thus they make whole whatever here has been ill-treated or injured of the vital organs, they cure it. They make enclosures for the food; verily thus the food of the gods they sever from the food of man.

The Final Bath.

xviii. 9. The[1] final bath (is described). Him who yonder gives heat they seek by these pressings to obtain; the rising by the morning pressing, (the sun) in the middle (of his course) by the midday pressing, (the sun) as he sets by the third pressing. He, having entered the waters, becomes Varuṇa; therefore he offers to Varuṇa a cake on one potsherd; prosperity is solitary; Varuṇa is prosperity; verily thus he finds support at the end in prosperity. They depart between the pit and the mound, for that is

[2] *jyotiḥ* is clearly a very inferior reading: it is accepted by the Ānand. ed.

[1] For these offerings see ÇÇS. viii. 9, 1; Caland and Henry, *L'Agniṣṭoma*, p. 388.

xviii. 8. [1] This chapter continues the Jyotiṣṭoma; see ÇÇS. viii. 9. 2–9.

[2] RV. vii. 36. 9.

xviii. 9. [1] For the Avabhṛtha see ÇÇS. viii. 10; Caland and Henry, *L'Agniṣṭoma*, pp. 393 *seq.*

the proper path of the sacrifice, named Āpnāna. That is declared in a Ṛc,[2] 'Who here hath proclaimed the Āpnāna passage?' Having approached the sacrifice by this passage, they obtained all desires. Verily thus also the sacrificer by this passage having approached the sacrifice obtains all desires.

xviii. 10. Turning[1] to the region in which are the waters, they proceed (with the rite); it is the eastern quarter in which the deities are. He offers four fore-offerings, omitting that for the strew;[2] that for the strew he omits, for the strew is not strewn here. The butter portions contain a reference to the slaying of Vṛtra, for the slaying of evil; moreover, thus he does not depart from the model of the full moon sacrifice. Some make them contain (the words)[3] 'in the waters', but the rule is that they should refer to the slaying of Vṛtra. In that he sacrifices to Varuṇa in the waters, verily thus he delights him in his own abode. In that he sacrifices to Agni and Varuṇa, therein Agni becomes a sharer in all the oblations. He offers two after-offerings, omitting that for the strew; he leaves out that for the strew, (thinking) 'The strew is offspring; let me not cast offspring into the waters.' There are a hundred and one fore-offerings and after-offerings; man has a hundred (years of) life, has a hundred joints, has a hundred strengths, has a hundred powers; the hundred and first is the body. This is the way of the Añgirases; he sets out by this way, he obtains identity of world and union with the Añgirases.[4] The six or eight *vaṣaṭ* calls are the way of the Ādityas; he sets out by this way, he obtains identity of world and union with the Ādityas.

The Anūbandhyā.

xviii. 11. The Anūbandhyā[1] (is explained). The offering of the cow is the fourth pressing; therefore is it immovable, for it is the fourth of the pressings. It is offered to Mitra and Varuṇa, for (the victim) for Agni and Soma has been offered before; therefore is it for Mitra and Varuṇa, to secure the equipoise of the sacrifice. Moreover, in that he sacrifices to Varuṇa in the waters, therein is Mitra neglected;[2] therefore is it for Mitra and Varuṇa, to secure Mitra also.

[2] RV. x. 114. 7 *a*.

[1] See for the offering to Varuṇa and the other rites ÇÇS. viii. 11.

[2] *ṛtebarhiṣkān* and *ṛtebarhiṣkam* must, of course, be read; so xviii. 12 *arakṣohatam*; xix. 5 *tredhāvihito*; xv. 1; xvi. 1; xxix. 2; and xxx. 1 *aivakālo* (Caland, VOJ. xxiii. 63) is certain.

[3] RV. viii. 48. 9 and i. 23. 20.

[4] See ÇB. iv. 4. 5. 19, 20; KÇS. x. 8. 30; for the Ādityas see ÇB. iv. 4. 5. 18, 19, which allows only six offerings in all: cf. Weber, *Ind. Stud.* x. 393.

xviii. 11. [1] For the Anūbandhyā offering see ÇÇS. viii. 12. 5–14; Caland and Henry, *L'Agniṣṭoma*, pp. 406–8.

[2] *hi no* is absurdly read in the Ānand. ed.

xviii. 12. If the victim has been brought up but before being prepared for sacrifice dies, he should cause it to be given to the priests; then they should offer another, of the same form and of the same deity.[1] When the Āprīs have been said over it and the fire carried round it, they should lead it northwards and should dispose of it. In the manner of it they should take another. Having forced out their omenta separately and cooked them separately, they should offer them, cutting off portions separately, with one *vaṣaṭ* call. Having cooked separately the cakes for the victims, and having made portions separately, they should offer them with one *vaṣaṭ* call. Having cooked separately the oblations and having made portions separately, they should offer them with one *vaṣaṭ* call. So with the thirds of the intestines, so with the hind portions. 'Even if, however, but one of the Āprīs has been said, with it should they proceed' is the rule.[2] The Āprīs are the breaths; verily thus he places the breaths in it. Now (they ask) 'If (the victim) is eight-footed, how shall it be?' Having cooked on the slaughtering fire from the skin of the embryo (a portion) shaped like the omentum and from chaff of the pounded grains an embryo itself, they should offer on the slaughterer's fire to the *vaṣaṭ* calls of the other.[3] The Rakṣases go to the sacrifice when such a thing occurs; them thereby he smites away; that is not smitten by Rakṣases. So now if that which is to be offered is an animal, but if it is a milk mess (it is because) the milk mess is Mitra and Varuṇa's own oblation, for it is the rule that to Mitra and Varuṇa the milk mess is offered.

xviii. 13. If the victim is a cow, (it is because) Mitra and Varuṇa are praised with the cow; therefore the victim is a cow. The offering verse[1] for the omentum is 'Ye two are clothed in garments of fatness'; 'fatness' is the symbol of the fat of the omentum. That[2] of the cake is 'What is most abundant, not to be pierced, O ye rich in dew'; 'most abundant', (he says), for the cake is abundant as it were. 'Do ye stretch forth your arms for life for us' is that[3] of the oblation; 'arms' is the symbol of the members of the oblation.

xviii. 14. He[1] concludes facing north, for north is the world of the living. Having concluded facing north, he offers a full libation with a verse to Viṣṇu; Viṣṇu is the sacrifice; verily thus he grasps the sacrifice. The

[1] See ÇÇS. xiii. 2. 1.

[2] I. e. go on with the offering; see ÇÇS. xiii. 3. 1.

[3] See ÇÇS. xiii. 3. 5, which verbally quotes. The phrase *phalīkaraṇānām phālikaraṇān* 'scrapings of polished rice grains' (comm.) is curious, and probably corrupt: as M reads the much more simple *phālīkaraṇāt* (not recorded by Lindner), I have translated it, the other reading being very probably a gloss interpolated in the text. Cf. *Atharvaprāyaçcitta*, ii. 5.

xviii. 13. [1] RV. i. 152. 1.

[2] RV. v. 62. 9.

[3] RV. vii. 62. 5.

xviii. 14. [1] For the ritual see ÇÇS. viii. 13.

cake is offered on five potsherds, for the Pañkti has five Padas; the sacrifice is fivefold; verily (it serves) to obtain the sacrifice. But, if it is offered on eight potsherds, verily this is the model of the full moon sacrifice; the full moon sacrifice is a support; verily (it serves) for support. In that the invitatory and offering verses are Padapañkti verses, this is obviously the symbol of the re-establishment (of the fires). So also are they interwoven.[3] When this has been completed, the sacrificer offers the Agnihotra, for on the completion of the establishment of the fires the Agnihotra is offered; therefore, when this is completed, the sacrificer should offer the Agnihotra, (so they say).

ADHYĀYA XIX

THE SOMA SACRIFICE (*continued*).

The Caturviñça Day.

xix. 1. They[1] being about to consecrate themselves gather together the fires; verily thus they place might and strength in one place in themselves. Then they perform the gathering together sacrifice; they offer a cake on eight potsherds to Agni of the holy power, to Agni of the lordly power one on eleven potsherds, to Agni, supporter of the lordly power, one on twelve potsherds. Verily thus the sacrificers mount on the holy power and the lordly power; verily thus with them in safety they pass over[2] the year. Of many who are about to pile (the fire) this is the gathering together (offering), connected with the bringing together of the firepan;[3] for one who is about to consecrate himself it is the same.

xix. 2. Then[1] they sacrifice with a victim for Prajāpati, (thinking) 'Instigated by Prajāpati,[2] in safety let us attain this year.' Some make the cake

[3] The verses are RV. iv. 10. 1–4; 1 and 3 are used as invitatory and offering verses for the oblation, 2 and 4 for the Sviṣṭakṛt; hence they are interwoven. See ÇÇS. viii. 18. 4; ii. 5. 18, being taken from the Punarādheya.

[1] For the Caturviñça see AB. iv. 12–14. For the ritual see ÇÇS. ix. 22.

[2] *caranti* is only an obvious correction, though read in the Ānand. ed.

[3] For *ukhā saṁbharaṇīyā, ukhāsaṁ°* is to be read, though both edd. separate. The two words probably go together and the new sentence begins at *sā*. The whole clause after *taranti* is omitted by M, which explains perhaps its continuing with *ta etena*.

xix. 2. [1] For the ritual see ÇÇS. ix. 23. The date of the Dīkṣā is dealt with in ÇÇS. xiii. 19: it has been repeatedly discussed in connexion with the parallel passages TS. vii. 4. 8; PB. v. 9; see Weber, *Naxatra*, ii. 341 *seq.*; Thibaut, *Ind. Ant.* xxiv. 89 *seq.*; Whitney, JAOS. xvi. lxxxvi *seq.*; *Vedic Index*, i. 420–427. See also ĀpÇS. xxi. 15. 4–6; BÇS. xvi. 18.

[2] The Ānand. ed. and M have *prajāpatiḥ prasūtā*, which error—a transposition of the *ḥ*—points to the use by Ānand. of a MS. with affinities with M though not of its tradition.

for it for Vāyu (saying), 'Vāyu is clearly the symbol of Prajāpati.' Others again make it for Agni as desire; Agni as desire is lord of the gods; verily (it serves) to delight all the gods. Some make the cake for the victim for Vaiçvānara; Vaiçvānara is he yonder that gives heat; verily thus they delight him. They make ready beforehand the Soma pressings[3] for the consecration. 'They should consecrate themselves on one day after the new moon of Taiṣa or of Māgha,' they say; both of these views are current, but that as to Taiṣa is the more current[4] as it were. They obtain this thirteenth additional month; the year is as great as this thirteenth month; in it verily the whole year is obtained.

xix. 3. On the new moon of Māgha he rests, being about to turn northwards; these also rest, being about to sacrifice with the introductory Atirātra; thus for the first time they obtain him; on him they lay hold with the Caturviñça; that is why the laying hold rite has its name. He goes north for six months; him they follow with six-day periods in forward arrangement. Having gone north for six months he stands still, being about to turn southwards; these also rest, being about to sacrifice with the Viṣuvant day; thus for the second time they obtain him. He goes south for six months; him they follow with six-month periods in reverse order. Having gone south for six months he stands still, being about to turn north; these also rest, being about to sacrifice with the Mahāvrata day; thus for the third time they obtain him. In that they obtain him thrice, and the year is in three ways arranged, verily (it serves) to obtain the year. With regard to this this sacrificial verse is sung,

> Ordaining the days and nights,
> Like a cunning[1] spider,
> For six months south constantly,[2]
> For six north the sun goeth.

For six months he goes north, six south. They should not consecrate themselves at this time; the corn has not arrived, the days are short; shivering they come out from the final bath. Therefore they should not consecrate themselves at this time. They should consecrate themselves one day after the new moon of Caitra; the corn has come, the days are long, not shivering do they come out from the final bath. Therefore that is the rule.

[3] °*prasuvān* in Bo is hardly a real word (as taken by BR., MW.), but only a misreading.

[4] This is certainly the sense, not that Taiṣa is disapproved.

[1] The comm. reads *jūryaḥ* which in the MSS. O o appears as a v. l.

[2] The *dakṣiṇādityaḥ* of M is a simple blunder.

xix. 4. Then [1] in the piling of the fire some offer this consecration sacrifice consisting of five oblations; the Pañkti has five Padas; the sacrifice is fivefold; verily (it serves) to obtain the sacrifice. Then some offer this guest reception sacrifice, consisting of five oblations; the Pañkti has five Padas; the sacrifice is fivefold; verily (it serves) to obtain the sacrifice. Then he recites these many fire (verses); for they carry forward many fires; they are four; all this (universe) is fourfold; verily (they serve) to obtain all this. (He recites) the first thrice and the last thrice; they make up eight; the Gāyatrī has eight syllables; Agni is connected with the Gāyatrī and has the Gāyatrī as metre; verily thus with their own metre they carry forward the fires. Then they pile for so much of the day [2] as they wish. Then they celebrate it when piled with Sāmans. Then they say to the Hotṛ, 'Mutter the Agni litany'; (the fire) when piled becomes Rudra, the unappeased one of the gods; him verily thus he appeases. He says the offering verse for Vaiçvānara distinctly, for he becomes distinct when they carry forward the fires.

xix. 5. Thereafter is as the one-day rite; the moving forward of the oblation holders, the carrying forward of Agni and Soma, the victim for Agni and Soma. The explanation of this has been given. Following on the cake for the victim for Agni and Soma, they offer oblations for the divine instigators; these deities are the lords of the pressings; them herein they delight; they being [1] delighted herein instigate the offerings; therefore are they instigators. They are eight; by them the gods attained all attainments (*aṣṭīḥ*); verily thus also the sacrificers by them attain all attainments. Here some offer the oblation of (the sacrifice) with all the Pṛṣṭhas, (thinking) 'The fire piling is all; by all all let us obtain'; there are ten oblations; the Virāj consists of sets of ten; the Virāj is prosperity and proper food; (verily it serves) to obtain the Virāj as prosperity and proper food. Then they press (Soma) for as much of the day [2] as they wish.

xix. 6. When [1] (the offering of) the omentum of the Anūbandhyā (cow)

[1] The rites here given are prescribed in ÇÇS. ix. 24 and 25. Characteristically the direction for the Agni litany is *anuçaṅsa* not *anujapa*. The rule is that he should recite the silent praise of the Ājya with the silent muttering of that Çastra also. The silent praise is the Agnyuktha (Anartīya on ÇÇS. ix. 25. 2).

[2] This seems the only possible sense of *yāvad-aham*, not recognized in the Lexx. So in KB. xix. 5 *ad fin.*: any other rendering is open to grave objections.

xix. 5. [1] For these two rites see ÇÇS. ix. 26 and 27. Weber (*Rājasūya*, p. 29, n. 2) suggests that originally *devasū* meant 'King impeller', *deva* in the sense of King. But this is most improbable.

[2] Cf. KB. xix. 4, n. 2.

xix. 6. [1] For this offering see ÇÇS. ix. 27. 4–7, who allows an offering of butter in the form of the animal sacrifice as a substitute.

has been completed, they proceed with the victim for Tvaṣṭṛ; that for Tvaṣṭṛ is a pouring of seed; in the hut of the wife they proceed; in wives is seed poured. Inaudibly they proceed; (the victim) for Tvaṣṭṛ is a pouring of seed; inaudibly is seed poured. After surrounding it with fire they let it go; they do not dispose of it, (thinking) '(The victim) for Tvaṣṭṛ is a pouring of seed; let us not dispose of seed poured before the time.' They say 'Seeing that he invites these two deities, Tvaṣṭṛ and the lord of the forest, in what place are these two sacrificed to by him?' In the fore-offerings he sacrifices to these two deities; then are these two sacrificed to by him.

xix. 7. Following[1] on the cake for the victim in the Anūbandhyā rite, they offer the oblations to the minor deities. The metres of him who offers the Soma sacrifice become exhausted; the minor deities are the metres; in that they offer oblations to the minor deities, thus (his metres) become unexhausted and fresh. The metres of him who offers the Soma sacrifice lose their sap; the minor deities are the metres; in that they offer oblations to the minor deities, verily (it serves) to confer sap on the metres. Now these are deities (*devī*) and Prajāpati is Ka; therefore are they minor deities (*devikā*). There are five oblations; the Pañkti has five Padas; the sacrifice is fivefold; verily (it serves) to obtain the sacrifice. Here some offer oblations to the female deities, (thinking) 'The fire piling is all; by all all let us obtain.' There are ten oblations; the Virāj consists of sets of ten; the Virāj is prosperity and proper food; (verily it serves) to obtain the Virāj as prosperity and proper food. Here some perform the offerings to appease the quarters, (thinking) 'The fire piling is all; by all all let us obtain.' There are six oblations; the year has six seasons; verily (it serves) to obtain the year. When the concluding rite has been completed, he should sacrifice with a milk mess to Mitra and Varuṇa; the explanation of this has been given. 'No piler of the fire should indulge in sexual union without having offered this sacrifice,' (they say).

xix. 8. The Caturviñça[1] is the beginning of the year; therefore it is an Agniṣṭoma, for the Agniṣṭoma is the beginning of the sacrifices; verily thus at the beginning they delight the year. Some make it an Ukthya, for the equipoise of the sacrifice. It has the Caturviñça Stoma; the half months of the year are twenty-four; verily (it serves) to obtain the year. There are in it three hundred and sixty Stotriyās;[2] three hundred and sixty are the days of the year; verily (they serve) to obtain the year.

[1] For these rites see ÇÇS. ix. 28.

xix. 8. [1] For the ritual see ÇÇS. xi. 2.

[2] Each of the fifteen triplets is made into twenty-four according to the Caturviñça Stoma rule: hence 15 × 24 = 360.

The Pṛṣṭha (Stotra) in it is the Bṛhat (Sāman); this is the second of the days; the Bṛhat is the second of the Pṛṣṭhas; therefore is its Pṛṣṭha the Bṛhat. Again the Mahāvrata is fixed there where they approach the Caturviñça; the Bṛhat is in its place the Pṛṣṭha of the Mahāvrata; therefore (they say) 'Let the Bṛhat be the Pṛṣṭha of this (day).' It has the word 'together'; the year is uttered around about. There are in its verses the following symbols. 'The Hotṛ is born, the wise' is the Ājya [3] of eight verses in Gāyatrī metre; the Stoma is in Gāyatrī metre; that Çastra is perfect which accords with the Stoma. The Praüga is of Madhuchandas; it is perfect; in its model are other Praügas shaped, (thinking) 'May I have accomplished a rite successful from the beginning.' 'Thee like a car for aid' is the strophe [4] of the Marutvatīya; 'This drink, O bright one, is pressed' is the antistrophe.[5] This is the regular one-day form; the explanation of it has been given.

xix. 9. 'With what array, of one age, of one home?' is the Marutvatīya.[1] The ninth (verse) is 'Thou canst not be overthrown, O generous one, no one'; with it he concludes, having recited in front of it the later verses, for they are verses to the Maruts, and this is connected (with Indra) only. There is in this (Çastra) 'The Maruts are joined together' containing [2] (the word) 'together'; thus he refers to the year; this is the symbol of this day. 'That was the highest in the worlds' is the Niṣkevalya,[3] of Bṛhaddiva; here the Hotṛ pours seed with the Bṛhaddiva, (thinking) 'That he propagates [4] yonder with the Mahāvrata day.' After each year the pouring of seed is fruitful. In this there is 'Together they sing to thee, brought forward at the carouses,' containing [5] (the word) 'together'; thus he refers to the year; this is the symbol of this day. 'That of Savitṛ we choose' and 'To-day for us, O god Savitṛ' are the normal strophe [6] and antistrophe [7] of the Vaiçvadeva; the explanation of these two has been given. 'That desirable greatness of Savitṛ, the god' is the Savitṛ (hymn) [8]; it contains [9] (the word) 'together' in 'Wealth with offspring for us together

[3] RV. ii. 5 (cited also in KB. xxi. 2).
[4] RV. viii. 6. 1-3; see above KB. xv. 2.
[5] RV. viii. 2. 1-3; see above KB. xv. 2.
RV. i. 165. Throughout, as in KB. xix. 8, the point is that the second day coincides with the Mahāvrata day as falling really a year later at the end of the year Sattra before the final Atirātra, after the Daçarātra which concludes the last month of the year Sattra (see Hillebrandt, *Rituallitteratur*, p. 157).
[1] RV. i. 165. 1.
[3] RV. x. 120 (also cited in KB. xxv. 11).
[4] *janayati* expresses what it normally does, and so probably this sentence is to be given to the actor, not treated as a remark of the Brāhmaṇa. See for the idea AB. iv. 14.
[5] RV. x. 120. 2 *d*.
[6] RV. v. 82. 1 (also cited in KB. xvi. 3).
[7] RV. v. 82. 4 (also cited in KB. xxii. 2; xxv. 9).
[8] RV. iv. 53 (also cited in KB. xxi. 2, 4; xxii. 2).
[9] RV. iv. 53. 7 *d*.

may he instigate'; thus he refers to the year; this is the symbol of this day. 'They two, sky and earth, all weal producing' is (the hymn) to sky and earth;[10] it contains[11] (the word) 'together' in 'Force to be glorified may ye together instigate for us'; thus he refers to the year; this is the symbol of this day. 'Why hath the best, why hath the youngest come to us?' is (the hymn[12]) to the Ṛbhus; 'Thus in the year to-day did ye discern' (it contains[13]); thus openly he refers to the year; this is the symbol of this day. 'The charioteer of the sacrifice, the lord of the folk' is the Vaiçvadeva hymn[14] of Çaryāta; it contains[15] (the word) 'together' in 'Together have Indra, Mitra, and Varuṇa pondered'; thus he refers to the year; this is the symbol of this day. 'To Vaiçvānara the praise, increasing holy order' is (the hymn) to Vaiçvānara[16]; it contains[17] (the word) 'together' in 'With skill, as (a carpenter's) axe a car, he brings together'; thus he refers to the year; this is the symbol of this day. 'To the strong host, majestic, pious' is (the hymn) to the Maruts[18]; it contains[19] (the word) 'together' in 'Together I adorn the words, powerful in the assemblies'; thus he refers to the year; this is the symbol of this day. 'With the sacrifice make to increase the All-knower' is (the hymn) for Jātavedas;[20] it contains[21] (the word) 'together' in 'Together giving riches shine among us'; thus he refers to the year; this is the symbol of the day. These are the Āgnimāruta hymns; these are the hymns of this day. So the day is either an Agniṣṭoma or an Ukthya; 'an Agniṣṭoma is it' is the view of Paiñgya, 'an Ukthya is it' is the view of Kauṣītaki.

xix. 10. Some Sāman chanters make this day have all the Stomas, (saying) 'By this day they obtained the six-day period, by the six-day period the year and the desires in the year; the whole year is the six-day period.' If they do this he should make the Çastra composed of the six-day period. The Ājya should be the Ājya of the first day; the Praüga the Praüga of the second day; the Marutvatīya the Marutvatīya of the third day; the Niṣkevalya the Niṣkevalya of the fourth day; the Vaiçvadeva the Vaiçvadeva of the fifth day; the Āgnimāruta the Āgnimāruta of the sixth day. Then collecting all the verses of the Pṛṣṭha Stotras and making them into Pragāthas he should recite them after the Pragātha, to obtain the six-day period. Just as by this day the Sāman chanters obtain the six-day period

[10] RV. i. 160 (also cited in KB. xx. 3; xxi. 2; xxv. 9).

[11] RV. i. 160. 5 *d*.

[12] RV. i. 161 (also in KB. xxi. 4; xxiii. 8; xxv. 9).

[13] RV. i. 161. 8 *d*.

[14] RV. x. 92 (also cited in KB. xxii. 2).

[15] RV. x. 92. 4 *a*.

[16] RV. iii. 2 (also in KB. xx. 4; xxi. 4; xxii. 5; xxv. 9).

[17] RV. iii. 2. 1 *d*.

[18] RV. i. 64 (also in KB. xx. 3; xxii. 2).

[19] RV. i. 64. 1 *d*.

[20] RV. ii. 2 (also in KB. xx. 3).

[21] RV. ii. 2. 6 *b*.

and by the six-day period the year and the desires in the year, so by this day the Hotṛ obtains the six-day period, and by the six-day period the year and the desires in the year. Indicating that he used to say, 'This is confusion.' 'Whatever Stoma the Sāman chanters resort to, that he should not regard; the Çastra which we have here already considered,[1] from that he should not depart; the two hymns[2] "With what array" and "That was" are Stoma subduing; verily he should not fall away from these two' (he used to say).

ADHYĀYA XX

THE SOMA SACRIFICE (*continued*).

The Abhiplava Ṣaḍaha.

xx. 1. The[1] year is a revolving wheel of the gods; that is immortality; in it is the there sixfold proper food, wild animals, domesticated animals, plants, trees, that which goes in the waters and that which swims. Mounted on this the gods move round all the worlds, the world of the gods, the world of the fathers, the world of the living, the world of Agni without water,[2] the world of Vāyu, established in moral order, the world of Indra, unconquerable, the world of Varuṇa over the sky, the world of death the highest sky, the world of Brahman the welkin, the most real[3] of worlds the vault. In that they perform the Abhiplava, verily thus the sacrificers mount on the year; in it they obtain this sixfold proper food, wild animals, domesticated animals, plants, trees, that which goes in the waters and that which swims. Twice they perform the Jyotis (Stoma); thereby they obtain a double portion of proper food, wild animals and domesticated animals. Twice they perform the Go; thereby they obtain a double portion of proper food, plants and trees. Twice they perform the Āyus; thereby they obtain a double portion of proper food, that which goes in the waters and that which swims.

[1] M has *prāvocāma* but this is not essential. The Ānand. ed. has the regular blunder *aikṣyāma*; it has *pratiçya* for *pradiçya*, suggestive of *prati* as glossed by *pradiçya*.

[2] RV. i. 164; x. 120.

xx. 1. [1] For the Abhiplava Ṣaḍaha of the Sattra see AB. iv. 15-17. The six days have the six forms of Jyotis, Go, Āyus, Go, Āyus, and Jyotis, the first and last being Agniṣṭomas, the rest Ukthyas, and the Sāmans being Rathantara and Bṛhat; see ÇÇS. xi. 4. 1-7. AB. has only a few remarks on it in iv. 15; cf. ĀÇS. vii. 5-7.

[2] The Ānand. ed. has *upodakam*.

[3] *saptamam* is read in the Ānand. ed. and in a marg. note in O from the *bhāṣya*. It is clearly wrong.

xx. 2. They perform the Jyotis as the first day; it has the same symbols in its verses as the first day. 'Forward to the god Agni' is the Ājya,[1] containing (the word) 'forward'; what contains 'forward' is a symbol of the first day. The Praüga is by Madhuchandas; when the Rathantara Sāman was created, the Praüga by Madhuchandas was created after it; thus he makes the rite successful with its symbol; that rite is likely to cause success which is successful with its symbol. 'Thee like a car for aid' is the strophe of the Marutvatīya;[2] 'This drink, O bright one, is pressed' is the antistrophe;[3] this is the normal one-day form; the explanation of it has been given. 'Indra maketh for the car a way forward' is the Marutvatīya,[4] containing (the word) 'forward'; what contains forward is a symbol of the first day. 'Come hither, standing on thy chariot seat' is the Niṣkevalya,[5] containing (the word) 'hither'; what contains 'hither' is a symbol of the first day. 'That of Savitṛ we choose' and 'To-day for us, O god Savitṛ' are the normal strophe and antistrophe of the Vaiçvadeva;[6] the explanation of these two has been given. 'They yoke their minds, they also yoke their thoughts' is (the hymn) to Savitṛ,[7] containing (the word) 'yoke'; what contains 'yoke' is a symbol of the first day. 'Forward sky and earth, increasing holy order, with the sacrifices' is (the hymn) to sky and earth,[8] containing (the word) 'forward'; what contains 'forward' is a symbol of the first day. 'Here, here in mind is your relationship, O heroes' is (the hymn) to the Ṛbhus,[9] containing (the word) 'to' in 'Desiring they came to these with wealth'; that is the symbol of the Rathantara. 'How, of what one of the gods, in this service?' is (the hymn) to the All-gods,[10] containing the word 'hither' in 'Which one with aid will come hitherward?'; what contains 'hither' is a symbol of the first day. 'To Vaiçvānara with broad radiance bards' is (the hymn) to Vaiçvānara,[11] containing (the word) 'forward'; what contains 'forward' is a symbol of the first day. 'Forward pressing, mighty and resounding' is (the hymn) to the Maruts,[12] containing (the word) 'forward'; what contains 'forward' is the symbol of the first day. 'The Hotṛ goeth forward to the sacrifice with the power of him' is (the hymn) to Jātavedas,[13] containing (the word) 'forward'; what contains 'forward' is the symbol of

[1] RV. iii. 13 (also cited in KB. xxii. 1; xxiv. 1; xxv. 8).
[2] RV. viii. 68. 1–3 (also cited in KB. xv. 2).
[3] RV. viii. 2. 1–3 (also cited in KB. xv. 2).
[4] RV. v. 31; ÇÇS. xi. 4. 8.
[5] RV. iii. 43; ÇÇS. xi. 4. 9.
[6] RV. v. 82. 1 and 4 (also cited in KB. xix. 9).
[7] RV. v. 81 (also cited in KB. xxii. 1; xxv. 9).
[8] RV. i. 159 (also cited in KB. xxii. 1).
[9] RV. iii. 60 (also cited in KB. xxii. 1).
[10] RV. x. 64 (also cited in KB. xxi. 8); ÇÇS. xi. 4. 10.
[11] RV. iii. 33 (also cited in KB. xxi. 2; xxii. 1).
[12] RV. i. 87.
[13] RV. i. 144; ÇÇS. xi. 4. 13.

the first day. This world they move up to with the first day, Agni the god, the name the supreme[14] essence of the deities; they confer speech upon themselves.

xx. 3. They perform the Go as the second day; the symbols in its verses are those of the second day. 'Thou hast a glory of rule' is the Ājya[1] containing (the word) 'apart' in 'Thou, O active one (*vicarṣaṇe*), fame'; this is the symbol of this atmosphere; for this atmosphere is wide apart as it were. The Praüga is by Gṛtsamada;[2] when the Bṛhat Sāman was created, the Praüga by Gṛtsamada was created after it; thus he makes the rite successful with its symbol; that rite is likely to cause success which is successful with its symbol. 'Lord of every man' is the strophe[3] of the Marutvatīya, containing the word 'apart'; the explanation of this has been given. 'Indra alone is the drinker of Soma' is the antistrophe,[4] containing (the word) 'apart' in 'Indra, drinker of the pressed juice, of all life'; the explanation of this has been given. 'Rise up, O Brahmaṇaspati' is addressed to Brahmaṇaspati,[5] and contains (the word) 'up'; there is 'up' in 'Rise up'; the second day has 'up'. 'These thee of many a poet' is the Marutvatīya,[6] containing (the word) 'up'; the explanation of this has been given. 'Thou art mingled with the pressed drink, O Indra' is the Niṣkevalya,[7] containing (the word) 'up' in 'The Stoma, the prayer, the hymn being recited'; the explanation of this has been given. 'Every man of the god that leadeth' is the strophe[8] of the Vaiçvadeva, containing (the word) 'apart'; the explanation of this has been given. 'The god of all, lord of the good' is the antistrophe,[9] containing (the word) 'apart'; the explanation of this has been given. There are two strophes for the Vaiçvadevas, two antistrophes; the year has six seasons and is sixfold; sky and earth are two; these supports are two; this body has six members; day and night are two: these, expiration and inspiration, are two; thus they depart not from the completion of the year, nor from the perfection of the body, nor the perfection of the breaths. 'The god Savitṛ hath appeared, to be praised by us now' is (the hymn) to Savitṛ,[10] containing (the word) 'up'; the explanation of this has been given. 'They two, sky and earth, all weal producing' is (the hymn) to sky and earth,[11] containing (the word) 'apart'; the explanation of this has

[14] *adhibhūtam* means that the name (or force in KB. xx. 8; form, xx. 4) is the essence of the deities.

[1] RV. vi. 2. Here and repeatedly below the *vi* or *ud* is made up artificially.

[2] See ÇÇS. x. 8. 4, 5.

[3] RV. viii. 68. 4–6.

[4] RV. viii. 2. 4–6.

[5] RV. i. 40. 1, 2 (cited also in KB. ix. 5).

[6] RV. vi. 21; ÇÇS. xi. 5. 1.

[7] RV. vi. 23; ÇÇS. xi. 5. 2.

[8] RV. v. 50. 1–3.

[9] RV. v. 82. 7–9.

[10] RV. iv. 54.

[11] RV. i. 160 (cited already in KB. xix. 9).

been given. 'My work hath been stretched, now is it stretched again' is (the hymn) to the Ṛbhus,[12] containing the word 'up'; the explanation of this has been given. 'I hail the gods, of great fame, for security' is (the hymn) to the All-gods,[13] containing the word 'up'; the explanation of this has been given. 'The might of the swift, strong, ruddy one' is (the hymn) to Vaiçvānara,[14] containing (the word) 'strong'; Indra is strong, the Triṣṭubh is strong; therefore it contains 'strong'. 'To the strong host, majestic, pious' is (the hymn) to the Maruts;[15] the explanation of this has been given. 'By the sacrifice make to increase the All-knower' is (the hymn) to Jātavedas[16] containing 'up' in 'Kindled, well fed, hero of heaven'; the explanation of this has been given. The world of the atmosphere with the second day they obtain, Indra the god, force the supreme essence of the deities; they confer breath upon themselves.

xx. 4. They perform the Āyus as the third day; the symbols in its verses are those of the third day. 'Thou, O Agni, the Vasus here' is the Ājya;[1] self collected is that metre which accords with the symbol of the day; there is (the word) 'thou' in 'O thou of the ruddy steeds, singer, bring hither the three and thirty'; that is the symbol of the third day. The Praüga is in Uṣṇih verses by Viçvamanas;[2] when the Rathantara Sāman was created, the Praüga in Uṣṇih by Viçvamanas was created after it; thus he makes the rite successful with its symbol; that rite is likely to cause success which is successful with its symbol. 'Him for great gain' is the strophe of the Marutvatīya;[3] at 'him'[4] there is a repetition; the third day is the end; having gone to the end he repeats as it were, for hence whitherward should he go? 'Three Soma draughts for Indra' is the antistrophe.[5] This is the symbol of the third day. 'Let Brahmaṇaspati move forward', containing (the word) 'forward', is addressed to Brahmaṇaspati[6]; there is repetition[7] in 'Forward let the kindly goddess move'; the third day is the end; having gone to the end he repeats as it were; for hence whitherward should he go? There are three strophes of the Marutvatīyas, three antistrophes, three (Pragāthas) for Brahmaṇaspati;

[12] RV. i. 110 (cited also in KB. xxi. 3); ÇÇS. xi. 5. 4.

[13] RV. x. 66 (cited also in KB. xxiv. 9; xxv. 9); ÇÇS. xi. 5. 6.

[14] RV. vi. 8 (cited also in KB. xxi. 3; xxii. 2).

[15] RV. i. 64 (cited already in KB. xix. 9).

[16] RV. ii. 2 (cited already in KB. xix. 9); ÇÇS. xi. 5. 7.

[1] RV. i. 45 (cited also in KB. xxii. 3).

[2] RV. viii. 26. 23–25 (cf. ÇÇS. xi. 6. 2); iv. 46. 3–5; viii. 25. 1–3; 26. 4–6; 24. 1–3; 25. 10–12; vi. 61. 10–12.

[3] RV. viii. 68. 7–9.

[4] I. e. in *táṁ tam* of RV. viii. 68. 7.

[5] RV. viii. 2. 7–9.

[6] RV. i. 40. 3, 4 (a Pragātha).

[7] RV. i. 40. 3. *ninṛtti* denotes repetition of a word or part (e. g. xxi. 4). Cf. AB. v. 1 and 12, and the classical Anuprāsa.

these worlds are three; verily thus they obtain these worlds. 'Stand on the bays being yoked to the car' is (the hymn[8]) containing (the word) 'stand'; it is the symbol of the end; the third day is the end; having gone to the end he stands as it were, for hence whitherward should he go. 'I shall proclaim the manly deeds of Indra' is the Niṣkevalya;[9] it contains the symbol of ending in the reference to what has been; 'He slew the dragon, he penetrated the waters' is about what has been as it were. 'Hitherwards the god Savitṛ with the golden' is (the hymn) to Savitṛ;[10] it contains (the word) 'ghee' in 'With ghee both hands he imbueth, the sacrificer'; the ghee has many deities; the third pressing has many deities; therefore it contains (the word) 'ghee'. 'In ghee sky and earth enveloped' is (the hymn) to sky and earth,[11] containing (the word) 'ghee'; the explanation of this has been given. 'They have wrought the car well covered, skilled workers' is (the hymn) to the Ṛbhus;[12] there is repetition in 'They have wrought the two steeds, that bear Indra, strong in riches'; the third day is the end; having come to the end he repeats as it were, for hence whitherward should he go? 'To us from all sides may favouring powers come' is (the hymn) for the All-gods;[13] there is repetition in 'Unfailing guardians day by day'; the third day is the end; having gone to the end, he repeats as it were, for hence whitherward should he go? 'To Vaiçvānara, the praise, increasing holy order' is (the hymn) to Vaiçvānara;[14] in 'Like purified ghee to Agni we present' it contains (the word) 'ghee'; the explanation of this has been given. 'The Rudras, with Indra, accordant' is (the hymn) to the Maruts;[15] it contains the words 'from the sky' in 'Like springs of water from the sky for a thirsty man'; this is the symbol of yonder world. 'Thee, O Agni, the righteous have kindled' is (the hymn) to Jātavedas,[16] beginning with the same word 'Thee' (in each verse); just as that with the same end, so that with the same beginning is a symbol of the end. They obtain yonder world with the third day, Āditya the god, the form the supreme essence of the deities; they confer sight upon themselves.

[8] RV. iii. 35 (cited also in KB. xxvi. 16); ÇÇS. xi. 6. 3.

[9] RV. i. 32 (cited already in KB. xv. 4).

[10] RV. vi. 71.

[11] RV. vi. 70. 4–6 (also cited in KB. xxi. 4); ÇÇS. xi. 6. 5.

[12] RV. i. 111 (also cited in KB. xxii. 2).

[13] RV. i. 89.

[14] RV. iii. 2 (already cited in KB. xix. 9).

[15] RV. v. 57; ÇÇS. xi. 6. 8.

[16] RV. v. 8; ÇÇS. xi. 6. 8.

ADHYĀYA XXI

THE SOMA SACRIFICE (*continued*).

The Abhiplava Ṣaḍaha (*continued*).

xxi. 1. The gods, desirous of smiting away death, the evil, and desiring identity of world and union with Brahman, saw this Abhiplava six-day (rite); by this Abhiplava they approach, and having smitten away death, the evil, obtained identity of world and union with Brahman;[1] verily thus also the sacrificers approach by the Abhiplava, and having smitten away death, the evil, obtain identity of world and union with Brahman. Having approached with the first set of three days, they sacrificed on the fourth day with the Go, for going; they performed the Āyus as the fifth day, to secure full life; the Jyotis as the sixth day they put around behind again, to prevent evil following after.

xxi. 2. They perform the Go as the fourth day; the symbols in its verses are those of the fourth day. 'The Hotṛ is born, the wise' is the Ājya,[1] containing (the word) 'born'; that which contains (the word) 'born' is a symbol of the fourth day. The Praüga is by Medhātithi;[2] as the Bṛhat Sāman was created, the Praüga by Medhātithi was created after it; thus he makes the rite successful with its symbol; that rite is likely to cause success which is successful with its symbol. 'Thou hast been born dread, for impetuous strength' is the Marutvatīya,[3] containing (the word) 'born'; that which contains 'born' is a symbol of the fourth day. 'He hath been born dread for strength, possessed of will' is the Niṣkevalya,[4] containing (the word) 'born'; that which contains (the word) 'born' is a symbol of the fourth day. 'That desirable greatness of the god Savitṛ' is (the hymn) to Savitṛ,[5] containing (the word) 'born' in 'Savitṛ hath made to be born the hymn of good will'; that which contains (the word) 'born' is a symbol of the fourth day. 'They two, sky and earth, all weal producing' is (the hymn) to sky and earth,[6] containing (the word) 'born' in 'Between the two presses of noble birth he goeth';[7] that which contains (the word) 'born' is a symbol of the

[1] Cf. PB. xxv. 18. 6; TĀ. x. 15; ÇB. xi. 4. 4. 2–7; NTU. i. 1. 7; Weber, *Ind. Stud.* i. 396–408; ix. 87, 88.

xxi. 2. [1] RV. ii. 5 (already cited in KB. xix. 8); ÇÇS. xi. 7. 1.

[2] RV. i. 23. 1; see ÇÇS. xi. 7. 2.

[3] RV. x. 73 (already cited in KB. xv. 3).

[4] RV. vii. 20; ÇÇS. xi. 7. 7.

[5] RV. iv. 53 (already cited in KB. xix. 9).

[6] RV. i. 160 (already cited in KB. xix. 9).

[7] RV. i. 160. 1 c; *dhiṣaṇe* is of disputed sense; see Hillebrandt, *Ved. Myth.* i. 177; *Vedic Index*, i. 399, 400; ii. 476.

fourth day: 'Born without steed, without reins, worthy of praise' is (the hymn) to the Ṛbhus,[8] containing (the word) 'born'; that which contains (the word) 'born' is a symbol of the fourth day. 'Agni, Indra, Varuṇa, Mitra, Aryaman' is (the hymn) to the All-gods,[9] containing (the word) 'born' in 'Having caused the sacrifice to be born they wipe their bodies'; that which contains (the word) 'born' is a symbol of the fourth day. 'To Vaiçvānara with broad radiance bards' is (the hymn) to Vaiçvānara,[10] containing (the word) 'hither' in 'In him the sacrificer looks hither for favour'; that which contains (the word) 'hither' is a symbol of the fourth day as an opening ceremony, for the fourth day is a repetition of the opening ceremony.[11] In 'Born thou didst fill the worlds, the two firmaments', it contains (the word) 'born'; that which contains (the word) 'born' is a symbol of the fourth day. 'Those that shine forth, like women, the racers' is (the hymn) to the Maruts,[12] containing (the word) 'born'; that which contains (the word) 'born' is a symbol of the fourth day. 'He hath been born, guardian of men, wakeful' is (the hymn) to Jātavedas,[13] containing (the word) 'born'; that which contains (the word) 'born' is a symbol of the fourth day. Food with the fourth day they obtain, the moon the god, the quarters the supreme essence of the deities; the ear they confer upon themselves.

xxi. 3. They perform the Āyus as the fifth day; the symbols in its verses are those of the fifth day. 'O Agni, bring the mightiest' is the Ājya,[1] containing (the word) 'wealth' in (the word) 'wealth' in 'Forward for us with wealth, with abundance'; containing (the word) 'wealth' is a symbol of this (day); it also contains an addition;[2] this is the symbol of the Pañkti. The Praüga is one to be gathered together;[3] when the Rathantara Sāman was created, the Praüga which is to be gathered together was created after it; thus he makes the rite successful with its symbol; that rite is likely to cause success, which is successful with its symbol. 'Where is this hero, who hath seen Indra?' is the Marutvatīya,[4] containing (the word) 'wealth' in (the word) 'wealth' in 'The bearer of the bolt seeking the pressed Soma with wealth'; containing (the word) 'wealth' is the symbol of this. 'Come, let us approach Indra, seeking for cows' is the Niṣkevalya,[5] containing (the word) 'cattle' in 'seeking for cows'; con-

[8] RV. iv. 36 (also cited in KB. xxii. 5).
[9] RV. x. 65 (also cited in KB. xxiv. 9); ÇÇS. xi. 7. 10.
[10] RV. iii. 3 (already cited in KB. xx. 2).
[11] RV. iii. 3. 3 *d* and 10 *c*.
[12] RV. i. 85; ÇÇS. xi. 7. 12.
[13] RV. v. 11.
[1] RV. v. 10; ÇÇS. xi. 8. 1.
[2] The last verse of RV. v. 10 (as also v. 4) has an extra Pada: hence *adhyāsa*.
[3] The actual composition is given in ÇÇS. xi. 8. 2, 3.
[4] RV. v. 30 (also cited in KB. xxiv. 5; xxvi. 12); ÇÇS. xi. 8. 4.
[5] RV. i. 33; ÇÇS. xi. 8. 5.

taining (the word) 'cattle' is the symbol of this. 'Hitherward the god Savitṛ with the golden' is (the hymn) to Savitṛ,[6] containing (the word) 'ghee' in 'With ghee both hands he imbueth, the sacrificer'; in 'ghee' it contains (the word) 'cattle'; containing (the word) 'cattle' is a symbol of this. 'Rich in ghee, encompassing the worlds' is (the hymn) to sky and earth,[7] containing (the word) 'ghee'; the explanation of this has been given. 'My work hath been stretched; now is it stretched again' is (the hymn) to the Ṛbhus,[8] containing (the word) 'ghee' in 'As ghee with the ladle let us offer with knowledge'; the explanation of this has been given. 'How, of what one of the gods, in this service?' is (the hymn) to the All-gods,[9] containing (the word) 'cattle' in 'Winners of thousands' in 'Winners of thousands in the attainment of the offering, by themselves';[10] containing (the word) 'cattle' is the symbol of this. 'The might of the swift, strong, ruddy one' is (the hymn) to Vaiçvānara,[11] containing (the word) 'cattle' in 'the bulls' in 'The bulls seized them in the lap of the waters';[12] containing (the word) 'cattle' is the symbol of this. 'Your spy hath called to you to accord favour' is (the hymn) to the Maruts,[13] containing (the word) 'cattle' in 'as of kine' in 'As of kine the lofty born for splendour';[14] containing (the word) 'cattle' is the symbol of this. 'Wonderous is the growth of the tender young one' is (the hymn) to Jātavedas,[15] containing (the word) 'strong' in 'To the most strong, the mighty, O thou of a good father';[16] this is a symbol of this day; it contains an addition. Cattle by the fifth day they obtain, Rudra the god, fame the supreme essence of the deities; they confer strength upon themselves.

xxi. 4. They perform the Jyotis as the sixth day; the symbols in its verses are those of the sixth day. 'O friends, together the seemly' is the Ājya;[1] 'O friends' is the symbol of all; the sixth day has the symbol all; therefore in 'O friends' he refers to all. The Praüga[2] is one to be gathered together; when the Bṛhat Sāman was created, the Praüga which is to be gathered together was created after it; thus he makes the rite successful with its symbol; that rite is likely to cause success which is successful with its symbol. 'Great is Indra, manlike, spreading over mortals' is the Marutvatīya;[3] there is repetition in 'He hath become broad, wide,

[6] RV. vi. 71 (already cited in KB. viii. 7).
[7] RV. vi. 70 (also cited in KB. xxiii. 5).
[8] RV. i. 110 (already cited in KB. xx. 3).
[9] RV. x. 64 (already cited in KB. xx. 2).
[10] RV. x. 64. 6 c.
[11] RV. vi. 8 (already cited in KB. xx. 3).
[12] RV. vi. 8. 4.
[13] RV. v. 59; ÇÇS. xi. 8. 7.
[14] RV. v. 59. 3.
[15] RV. x. 115; ÇÇS. xi. 8. 7.
[16] RV. x. 115. 6. The addition is the last Çakvarī verse.
[1] RV. v. 7; ÇÇS. xi. 9. 1.
[2] For the composition see ÇÇS. xi. 9. 2, 3.
[3] RV. vi. 19 (also cited in KB. xxvi. 12); ÇÇS. xi. 9. 4.

well made by the makers'; the sixth day is the end; having gone to the end, he repeats as it were, for hence whitherward should he go? 'He who is born the first, the wise' is the Niṣkevalya;[4] it contains a symbol of ending in the reference to what has been; 'He who hath in secret depressed the hostile colour' is about what has been as it were. It has the same ending; that is a second symbol of the end. 'That desirable greatness of Savitṛ, the god' is (the hymn) to Savitṛ;[5] there is 'of the sky' in 'Prajāpati, supporter of the sky, of the earth'; this is the symbol of yonder world. 'With ghee sky and earth enveloped' is (the hymn) to sky and earth,[6] containing (the word) 'ghee'; ghee has all as its deity; the sixth day has all as its deity; therefore it contains (the word) 'ghee'. 'Why hath the best, why hath the youngest come to us?' is (the hymn) to the Ṛbhus;[7] there is repetition in 'the best, the youngest'; the sixth day is the end; having gone to the end, he repeats as it were, for hence whitherward should he go? 'These fires with Indra have awakened' is (the hymn) to the All-gods;[8] in that it has the same ending it is a symbol of the end. 'To Vaiçvānara the praise, increasing holy order' is (the hymn) to Vaiçvānara;[9] containing (the word) 'ghee' in 'Like pure ghee to Agni we accord'; the explanation of this has been given. 'Rich in showers, the Maruts of daring might' is (the hymn) to the Maruts;[10] there is repetition in 'rich in showers'; the sixth day is the end, having gone to the end, he repeats as it were, for hence whitherward should he go? 'Thou, O Agni, with the days, the shining' is (the hymn) to Jātavedas;[11] in 'Thou' it has the same beginning; just as that with the same end, so that with the same beginning is a symbol of the end. The waters by the sixth day they obtain, Prajāpati the god, brilliance the supreme essence of the deities; the immortal they confer on themselves.

xxi. 5. They[1] say 'Why are (the litanies) for the All-gods expanded, and not those for one deity or for two deities?' No exhaustion arises through that for one deity or that for two deities, but exhaustion does arise through that for the All-gods; therefore those for the All-gods only are expanded, to secure the might of these days, to prevent exhaustion of the Abhiplavas. They perform the Jyotis as the first day, with the symbol of the one day (rite), for the one day (rite) is the light of the other days; the Go as the

[4] RV. ii. 12 (also cited in KB. xxii. 4); ÇÇS. xi. 9. 5.

[5] RV. iv. 53 (already cited in KB. xix. 9).

[6] RV. vi. 70. 4-6 (already cited in KB. xx. 4).

[7] RV. i. 161 (already cited in KB. xix. 9). The *ninṛtti* is in the *sthaḥ*.

[8] RV. x. 35; ÇÇS. xi. 9. 7.

[9] RV. iii. 2 (already cited in KB. xix. 9).

[10] RV. ii. 34 (also cited in KB. xxii. 5); ÇÇS. xi. 9. 8.

[11] RV. ii. 1.

[1] Cf. AB. iv. 16.

second day, for they go by it; the Āyus as the third day, for they move by it. The first and last days are Agniṣṭomas, in the middle are four Ukthyas; the Agniṣṭoma is the holy power; the Ukthyas are cattle; verily thus by the holy power having surrounded cattle on both sides they confer them upon themselves. Of these four Ukthyas there are a thousand verses in the Stotras; cattle are connected with a thousand; a thousandfold prosperity he obtains who knows thus. Hence they perform sets of four Abhiplavas, ending with a Pṛṣṭhya; the Abhiplavas are cattle; the Pṛṣṭhyas are prosperity; verily thus having encompassed prosperity on both sides with cattle they confer it upon themselves. From the Viçvajit they perform sets of four Abhiplavas beginning with a Pṛṣṭhya; the Abhiplavas are prosperity; the Pṛṣṭhyas are cattle; verily thus with prosperity having encompassed cattle on both sides they confer them upon themselves.

xxi. 6. The Abhiplava is a definitely arranged (sacrifice) with definite metres. The Nivids inserted in a sacrificial rite which has definite metres are all in Jagatī at the third pressing. So duly are the Nivids inserted; they being duly inserted place them duly in all worlds and in all desires. In that the Nivids are inserted all in Jagatī at the third pressing, thereby is there obtained whatever is desired in a third pressing all of Jagatí (verses). Again, in that day by day these Triṣṭubh verses from the model are recited, thereby is there obtained whatever is desired in a third pressing all of Triṣṭubh (verses). Again, in that day by day this Gāyatrī[1] from the model, 'Maker of fair forms', is recited, thereby is there obtained whatever is desired in a third pressing all of Gāyatrī. In that this six-day (rite) repeatedly approaches (*abhiplavate*), therefore is it called Abhiplava, for by it the sacrificers approach the world of heaven.

ADHYĀYA XXII

THE SOMA SACRIFICE (*continued*).

The Pṛṣṭhya Ṣaḍaha.

xxii. 1. The first day is this world in abode, Agni, the Gāyatrī, the Trivṛt Stoma, the Rathantara Sāman, the base by Tanva.[1] It has the following symbols in its verses: the future tense with the god mentioned in the first Pada—that which is to be is the future tense—(the word) 'hither', (the

[1] RV. 1. 4. 1; see ÇÇS. viii. 8. 13.

xxii. 1. [1] The enumeration of the facts in this catalogue shape is a precursor of the regular style of introduction of spells of all sorts in the Tantra literature as in Buddhist texts. Cf. the end for the full form. Tanva (cf. *Ind. Stud.* iii. 217; *Puṣpa Sūtra*, v. 252, with Simon's note) must be a man here, though not so taken by Lindner. For the contents see AB. iv. 29 and 30; ÇÇS. x. 2.

word) 'forward', (the word) 'this', (the word) 'go', (the word) 'adorn', (the word) 'yoked', (the word) 'yoking', (the word) 'light', (the word) 'bright'. 'Advancing forward up to the sacrifice' is the Ājya,[2] containing (the word) 'forward'; that which contains 'forward' is a symbol of the first day; it is in Gāyatrī, for this set of three days has the Gāyatrī at the morning pressing. So in the transposed form.[3] Taking out that, 'Forward to the god, Agni' is used in the conjunct form;[4] the explanation of this has been given. The Praüga is by Madhuchandas;[5] the explanation of this has been given. 'Let Indra come hither to aid us' is the Marutvatīya,[6] containing (the word) 'hither'; that which contains (the word) 'hither' is a symbol of the first day; there is a reference to the Maruts in it in 'From the realm of light, with the Maruts, to aid us'.[7] 'Hither to us, Indra, hither to us from afar, from near' is the Niṣkevalya,[8] containing (the word) 'hither'; that which contains 'hither' is a symbol of the first day. The Niṣkevalya and the Marutvatīya are contiguous (hymns) on the first day; by the contiguous (hymns) the gods flew up to the world of heaven together; therefore these two are recited first as being heavenly. In that the Niṣkevalya and the Marutvatīya are contiguous (hymns) on the first day, verily (they serve) to obtain the world of heaven. 'They yoke their minds, they also yoke their thoughts[9],' 'Forward sky and earth, increasing holy order, with the sacrifices[10],' and 'Here, here in mind is your relationship, O heroes[11]'; (the last) is (the hymn) to the Ṛbhus;' with it he restrains; on the first day are recited hymns containing (the word) 'yoked' as well as (the word) 'forward'; in that he uses as (the hymn) to the Ṛbhus, 'Here, here is your,' it is a symbol of restraint, of preventing falling away. 'Like a skilled steed, he hath yoked himself to the pole' is (the hymn) to the All-gods,[12] containing (the word) 'yoked'; that which contains (the word) 'yoked' is a symbol of the first day. The last two (verses) of it he omits. (Now they ask) 'Shall these two prescribed be recited in the Āgnimāruta?' Kauṣītaki used to say 'He should recite (them), to avoid breaking up the hymn; the Ṛc is not exhausted by the litany nor by the supplementary repetition; it is by the *vaṣaṭ* call alone that it becomes exhausted on one day.' 'To Vaiçvānara with broad radiance bards' is (the hymn) to Vaiçvā-

[2] RV. i. 74 (already cited in KB. xi. 4).
[3] See ÇÇS. x. 2. 2 with Ānartīya, who quotes the Brāhmaṇa as usual: the rendering transposed is conventional: 'altered' would do, but for the contrast with *samūḍha* below.
[4] RV. iii. 13 (already cited in KB. xx. 2).
[5] ÇÇS. x. 2. 2 and vii. 10. 3 *seq.*
[6] RV. iv. 21; ÇÇS. x. 2. 4.
[7] RV. iv. 21. 3 c.
[8] RV. iv. 20; ÇÇS. x. 2. 5.
[9] RV. v. 82; see above KB. xx. 2.
[10] RV. i. 159; see above KB. xx. 2; ÇÇS. x. 2. 7.
[11] RV. iii. 60; see above KB. xx. 2; ÇÇS. x. 2. 7.
[12] RV. v. 46; ÇÇS. x. 2. 7.

nara,[13] containing (the word) 'forward'; that which contains (the word) 'forward' is a symbol of the first day. 'Forward to the horde of the Maruts, self-radiant' is (the hymn) to the Maruts,[14] containing (the word) 'forward'; that which contains (the word) 'forward' is a symbol of the first day. 'Forward the strong, new, hymn to Agni' is (the hymn) to Jātavedas,[15] containing (the word) 'forward'; that which contains (the word) 'forward' is a symbol of the first day. This world with the first day they obtain, the Gāyatrī metre, the Trivṛt Stoma, the Rathantara Sāman, the eastern quarter, the spring of seasons, the Vasus the gods, Agni, born of the gods, the overlord.

xxii. 2. The second day is the world of the atmosphere in its abode, Indra, the Triṣṭubh, the Pañcadaça Stoma, the Bṛhat Sāman, the basis by Tanva. It has the following symbols in its verses: the present tense with the god mentioned in the middle Pada—the present is what is before the eyes, but not tangible—(the word) 'deities', (the word) 'thunderbolt', (the word) 'slaying Vṛtra', (the word) 'strong', (the word) 'apart', (the words) 'stand', 'him', and 'thou'. 'Agni we choose as envoy' is the Ājya,[1] containing the word 'apart' in 'The Hotṛ of all knowledge'; the explanation of this has been given. It is in Gāyatrī, for this set of three days has the Gāyatrī at the morning pressing. So in the transposed form. Taking out that, 'For thou hast a glory of rule' is used in the conjunct form; the explanation of this has been given. The Praüga is by Gṛtsamada;[2] the explanation of this has been given. 'O Indra, drink this Soma, O lord of the Soma' is the Marutvatīya,[3] containing (the word) 'thunderbolt' in 'At the midday pressing, O thou with the thunderbolt in thy hand'; this is a symbol of this day. 'Thy nearest, farthest, help' is the Niṣkevalya,[4] containing (the word) 'slaying Vṛtra' in 'With these thou hast helped us in slaying Vṛtra'; this is a symbol of this day. 'That desirable greatness of Savitṛ, the god' is (the hymn) to Savitṛ,[5] containing 'Three times the atmosphere Savitṛ with his greatness'; this is openly the symbol of the atmosphere. 'They two, sky and earth, all weal producing' is (the hymn) to sky and earth,[6] containing (the word) 'apart'; the explanation of this has been given. 'They have wrought the car well covered, skilled workers' is (the hymn) to the Ṛbhus,[7] containing (the word) 'strong' in 'They have wrought the two steeds, that bear Indra, strong in riches'; the explanation of this has been given. 'The

[13] RV. iii. 3 (already cited in KB. xx. 2).

[14] RV. v. 54; ÇÇS. x. 2. 8.

[15] RV. i. 143.

[1] RV. i. 12 (already cited in KB. i. 4), or vi. 2 (already cited in KB. xx. 3); ÇÇS. x. 3. 2, 3. Cf. AB. iv. 31, 32.

[2] See KB. xx. 3; ÇÇS. x. 3. 4, 5.

[3] RV. iii. 32; ÇÇS. x. 3. 6.

[4] RV. vi. 25 (also cited in KB. xxiv. 2); ÇÇS. x. 3. 9.

[5] RV. iv. 53 (already cited in KB. xix. 9); ÇÇS. x. 3. 14.

[6] RV. i. 160 (already cited in KB. xix. 9); ÇÇS. x. 3. 14.

[7] RV. i. 111 (already cited in KB. xx. 4).

charioteer of the sacrifice, the lord of the folk' is (the hymn) to the All-gods by Çaryāta,[8] containing (the word) 'strong' in 'The strong banner, the holy one, hath attained the sky'; the explanation of this has been given. 'The might of the swift, strong, ruddy one' and 'To the strong host, majestic, pious' are (two hymns) containing (the word) 'strong'; the explanation of them has been given.[9] 'The immortal, born of strength, doth penetrate' is (the hymn) to Jātavedas,[10] containing (the word) 'apart' in 'What time he became a messenger of Vivasvant'; the explanation of this has been given. The last verse of it is 'Early and soon at the prayer may the bright one come'; verily thus he refers to the next day;[11] 'Verily thus they keep taking hold of the next day' Kauṣītaki used to say. The world of the atmosphere with the second day they obtain, the Triṣṭubh metre, the Pañcadaça Stoma, the Bṛhat Sāman, the southern quarter, the summer of the seasons, the Maruts the gods, Indra, born of the gods, the overlord.

xxii. 3. The third day is yonder world in its abode, Varuṇa, the Jagatī, the Saptadaça Stoma, the Vairūpa Sāman, the basis by Tanva; it has the following symbols in its verses: the past tense with the mention of the god in the last Pada—the past is what refers to what has happened—(the word) 'horse', (the word) 'cow', (the word) 'chariot', (the word) 'go', (the word) 'stand', (the word) 'end', the same ending, the lack of definite mention (of the deity), the same beginning. 'Yoke thou those best fit to invoke the gods' is the Ājya.[1] They say 'Seeing that the third day is the end, then why does the Ājya contain (the word) "yoke"?' 'By this day the gods went to the world of heaven; yoked thither they went; therefore (it contains "yoke")' should he reply. It contains (the word) 'chariot' in 'The steeds, O Agni, like a charioteer'; this is a symbol of this day. It is in Gāyatrī, for this set of three days has the Gāyatrī at the morning pressing. So in the transposed form. Taking out that, 'Thou, O Agni, the Vasus here' is used in the conjunct form.[2] The explanation of this has been given. The Praüga is in Uṣṇih verses by Atri;[3] the third day is connected with the Jagatī; in that the Praüga is in Uṣṇih verses by Atri for the third day, thus the Jagatī enjoys the third pressing.

xxii. 4. 'Three friendships hath man's worship' is the Marutvatīya;[1] (the word) 'three' is a symbol of the third day. 'If a hundred skies, O Indra, were thine' is the strophe of the Vairūpa;[2] there is repetition in 'and

[8] RV. x. 92 (already cited in KB. xix. 9).

[9] RV. vi. 8 (already cited in KB. xx. 8) and i. 64 (already in KB. xix. 9); ÇÇS. x. 8. 15.

[10] RV. i. 58; ÇÇS. x. 8. 15.

[11] Because of *prātar. parame vai tat*, Ānand.

[1] RV. viii. 75; ÇÇS. x. 4. 2. Cf. AB. v. 1, 2.

[2] RV. i. 45 (already cited in KB. xx. 4); ÇÇS. x. 4. 3.

[3] See ÇÇS. x. 4. 4 and 5.

xxii. 4. [1] RV. v. 29 (also cited in KB. xxvi. 16); ÇÇS. x. 4. 8. The sense of *tryaryamā* is doubtful.

[2] RV. viii. 70. 5, 6 (also cited in KB. xxv. 6); ÇÇS. x. 4. 9.

a hundred earths also'; the third day is the end; having gone to the end, he repeats (as it were); for hence whitherward should he go? 'O Indra, as many as thou' is the antistrophe;[3] there is repetition in 'Day by day would I obey the mighty'; the third day is the end; having gone to the end, he repeats as it were, for hence whitherward should he go? 'O Indra, threefold protection' is the Pragātha of the Sāman,[4] containing in 'threefold' (the word) 'three'; this is a symbol of the third day. 'I was the first lord of wealth' is (the hymn) to Indra;[5] in 'I' and 'I' it has the same beginning; just as that which has the same ending, so that which has the same beginning is a symbol of the end. In the Triṣṭubh (hymn), 'He who is born the first, the wise,' he inserts a Nivid.[6] That hymn is the body of Indra. 'Placing in it a Nivid, Gṛtsamada Bhārgava[7] went to the dear abode of Indra' (they say). He goes to the dear abode of Indra, he conquers the other world, who places a Nivid in this hymn. It contains a symbol of ending in the reference to what has been; 'He who in secret hath depressed the hostile colour' is about what has been as it were. It has the same ending; this is a second symbol of the end.

xxii. 5. 'Towards thee, O god Savitṛ' is the antistrophe,[1] containing the word 'towards'. They say 'In that the third day is the end, then why has the antistrophe (the word) "towards"?' 'By this day the gods went to the world of heaven; desiring towards it they went; therefore (it has "towards")' he should reply. 'Hitherward the god Savitṛ with the golden' and 'Rich in ghee, encompassing the worlds' are (two triplets[2]) containing (the word) 'ghee'; the explanation of these has been given. 'Born, without steed, without reins, worthy of praise' is (the hymn) to the Ṛbhus;[3] there is the word 'with three wheels' in 'The chariot of three wheels circleth round the atmosphere'; this is a symbol of the third day. 'Those who from afar would assume kinship' is (the hymn) to the All-gods;[4] (it contains the word) 'from afar'; from afar is the end; the third day is the end; in the end he places the end. These hymns end in half-verses, some in Padas, some in half-Padas; this ends with a third of a Pada; this is a symbol of the third day. 'To Vaiçvānara the praise, increasing holy order' is (the

[3] RV. vi. 32. 18, 19; ÇÇS. x. 4. 9.

[4] RV. vi. 46. 9; ÇÇS. x. 4. 10.

[5] RV. x. 48 (also cited in KB. xxvi. 16); ÇÇS. x. 4. 11.

[6] RV. ii. 12 (already cited in KB. xxi. 4); ÇÇS. x. 4. 11.

[7] M's reading *Bābhravaḥ* and so the Ānand. ed.

[1] RV. i. 24. 3–5 (already cited in KB. viii. 1); ÇÇS. x. 4. 13.

[2] RV. vi. 71 (already cited in KB. viii. 7; xx. 4; xxi. 3) and 70 (already in xxi. 3). The whole hymn is not meant, but only three verses as in ÇÇS. x. 4. 14, in each case. But 'hymn' is regularly applied to such cases in the Brāhmaṇas.

[3] RV. iv. 36 (already in KB. xxi. 2); ÇÇS. x. 4. 14.

[4] RV. x. 63; ÇÇS. x. 4. 14.

hymn) to Vaiçvānara,[5] containing (the word) 'ghee' in 'Like pure ghee to Agni we accord'; the explanation of this has been given. 'Rich in showers, the Maruts, of daring might' is (the hymn) to the Maruts;[6] in 'Rich in showers' there is repetition; the third day is the end; having gone to the end, he repeats as it were, for hence whitherward should he go? 'Thou O Agni, the first Añgiras, the Ṛṣi,' is (the hymn) to Jātavedas;[7] it has the same beginning in 'thou' and 'thou'; just as that which has the same ending, so that which has the same beginning is a symbol of the end. Yonder world with the third day they obtain, the Jagatī metre, the Saptadaça Stoma, the Vairūpa Sāman, the western quarter, the rains of the seasons, the Ādityas the gods, Varuṇa, born of the gods, the overlord.

xxii. 6. The third day is the end; the gods having gone to the end desired the fourth day; therefore it contains (the word) 'desire'; having sacrificed they found it; therefore it contains (the word) 'yoke'. They say 'Since the third day is the end, then why on the fourth day does he insert the sound *o*?' The fourth day is the abode of speech; the Virāj is food; the sound *o* is food; verily thus he places food in the sacrifice and in the sacrificers. Moreover by the third day is speech obtained; verily thus on the fourth day he expands it; this is as when one expands heated metal;[1] this (serves) to expand speech. It has the following symbols in its verses, (the word) 'ruling', (the word) 'self-ruling', (the word) 'Virāj', (the word) 'born', (the word) 'aid', (the word) 'delight', (the word) 'around', (the word) 'towards', (the word) 'up to'. 'With offerings for ourselves Agni' is the Ājya[2] by Vimada. By means of Vimada('s hymn) the gods confused[3] the Asuras; in that (the hymn of) Vimada is recited both in the middle and in the recitations of the Hotrakas, from each limb the sacrificers expel in confusion evil. It contains (the word) 'born' in 'Agni brought to birth by Atharvan'; this is a symbol of this day.

xxii. 7. They make up ten Jagatī verses, for this set of three days has the Jagatī at the morning pressing. They are twenty Gāyatrīs, the Gāyatrī bears the morning pressing; thus he departs not from the symbol of the morning pressing. So in the transposed form. Taking out that, 'Agni men with praise from the fire sticks' is used in the conjunct form.[1] The Ājya is in Virāj metre; the Pṛṣṭha is in Virāj; that is accordant.

[5] RV. iii. 2 (already cited in KB. xix. 9); ÇÇS. x. 4. 15.

[6] RV. ii. 34 (already cited in KB. xxi. 4); ÇÇS. x. 4. 15.

[7] RV. i. 31; ÇÇS. x. 4. 15.

[1] Presumably *yathāyas* is to be read, but *yathāyas* is also possible.

[2] RV. x. 21; ÇÇS. x. 5. 2. Cf. AB. v. 4, 5.

[3] *vimadan* of OoBLK is perhaps a mere error; it is found as *vimadas* in the Ānand ed., possibly an error for *vimadus*.

xxii. 7. [1] RV. vii. 1 (also cited in KB. xxv. 11; xxvii. 1); ÇÇS. x. 5. 2.

The Ājya is by Vasiṣṭha; the Pṛṣṭha is by Vasiṣṭha; that is accordant. It contains (the word) 'born' in 'By the movements of the hands they have made the famed one to be born'; this is a symbol of this day. The Praüga[2] is in Anuṣṭubh verses; the fourth day is connected with the Anuṣṭubh; verily thus he makes it to succeed with its own metre. With 'Thee with the sacrifices we invoke', which contains the word 'sacrifice', he begins the Marutvatīya;[3] the sacrifice has to be taken up again on the fourth day; verily thus he takes up again the sacrifice. 'Hear our call, O Indra, harm us not' is the Marutvatīya.[4] These Triṣṭubh verses have a Virāj tinge; they are employed here, for they are endowed with the symbol of the day. 'O Indra, with the Maruts here drink the Soma' is (a triplet) in normal Triṣṭubh[5] and supports the pressing; these in normal Triṣṭubh that support the pressing do not depart from the midday (pressing). Indra is connected with the Triṣṭubh and Indra has his abode in the midday pressing; in that these in normal Triṣṭubh which support the pressing do not depart from the midday (pressing) even with transposed metres, (it is because he thinks) 'Indra is connected with the Triṣṭubh; let me not cause Indra to depart from his own abode.' 'When born the gods did adorn thee' contains (the word) 'born'; this is a symbol of this day. 'Him the cunning I invoke' is the Marutvatīya;[6] it is in Gāyatrī, for this set of three days has the Gāyatrī at the midday pressing.

xxii. 8. Then (they ask) 'Should he utter the sound *o* here or here?' The sound *o* is intended for the strophe and the antistrophe and for (the verses) commencing litanies. That he should not trouble about; the strophe is the body, the antistrophe offspring, the Virāj food, the sound *o* food; verily he places food in the body and in offspring. 'The sound *o* as connected with the Anuṣṭubh should he utter' some say; the fourth day is connected with the Anuṣṭubh; verily thus he makes it successful with its own metre.[1] 'The sound *o* as connected with the Virāj should he utter' is the rule; the Virāj is food, the sound *o* food; verily thus he places food in the body and in offspring. At the middle Pada should he utter *o*; the first Pada is the body, the last offspring, the middle Pada the middle, in the middle of the body is food placed; it is as when one eats food, swallowing it piece by piece. 'Indra to the divine service' is the Pragātha of the Sāman,[2] by which Indra is attained; by it the gods

[2] ÇÇS. x. 5. 3, 4.

[3] RV. viii. 68. 10–12; ÇÇS. x. 5. 6.

[4] RV. ii. 11; ÇÇS. x. 5. 8.

[5] RV. iii. 51. 7–9; ÇÇS. x. 5. 8.

[6] RV. viii. 76. 1–3; ÇÇS. x. 5. 8.

[1] The phrase *vairājanyūākha* occurs in ÇÇS. xii. 13. 4. For the mode see x. 5. 23 with Ānartīya's comm. The *o* is repeated twelve times after the second syllable of the middle Pada, the vowel of which it absorbs, every fourth being Pluti. Cf. AB. v. 3.

[2] RV. viii. 3. 5 and 6; ÇÇS. x. 5. 13.

attained all attainments; verily thus also the sacrificers by it attain all attainments. 'Where is Indra famed, in what to-day?' are the 'Where famed' verses;[3] they are Virāj or Anuṣṭubh; they are employed here, for they are endowed with the symbol of the day. 'Of thee, the warrior, the bull, self-ruling' is in normal Triṣṭubh[4] and supports the pressing; the explanation of this has been given; it contains in 'self-ruling' (the word) 'self-ruling'; containing 'self-ruling' is a symbol of this (day). 'Him of you, ever enduring' is the Niṣkevalya,[5] containing (the word) 'hither' in 'In all speech outstretched hither'; that which contains (the word) 'hither' is a symbol of the fourth day as introductory, for the fourth day is a second introduction; it is in Gāyatrī, for this set of three days has the Gāyatrī at the midday pressing.

xxii. 9. 'The golden handed for aid' is the antistrophe,[1] containing (the word) 'aid'; it has (the word) 'aid' in 'for aid'; containing (the word) 'aid' is a symbol of this (day). 'Let the god Savitṛ with fair jewels come hither', 'Forward the sky and earth with sacrifices, with homage', 'Forward to the Ṛbhus like a messenger shall I speed my speech',[2] and 'Forward the bright, the divine, hymn' (are used); either 'hither' or 'forward' is a symbol of introduction; therefore on the fourth day the hymns are recited containing (the words) 'hither' and 'forward', for the fourth day is a second introduction. Verses of two Padas are recited; by having two feet one is able to ascend; this is a symbol of ascent; it is as if one having advanced should rest in the vicinity of the world of heaven. 'Praise of the ruling, the Asura' is (the hymn) to Vaiçvānara[3] containing (the word) 'ruling' in 'of the ruling'; containing (the word) 'ruling' is a symbol of this (day). 'Who are these men revealed together?' is (the hymn) to the Maruts; the explanation of this is that of the (hymn)[4] 'Forward the bright.' 'For you I hail the glorious, the effulgent' is (the hymn) to Jātavedas;[5] the explanation of this is that of the Marutvatīya. 'Let the strong go forward, the flames with might' are three additional verses[6] in the conjunct form. 'Hither for aid we come to the brilliant, the dread' contains (the word) 'hither'; that which contains (the word) 'hither' is a symbol of this fourth day as introductory, for the fourth day is a second introduction. 'I praise him of valiant might like the bright one' is (the hymn) to Jātavedas;[7] containing (the word)

[3] RV. x. 22; ÇÇS. x. 5. 20.
[4] RV. iii. 46; ÇÇS. x. 5. 20.
[5] RV. viii. 92. 7-9; ÇÇS. x. 5. 20.
[1] RV. i. 22. 5-7 (also cited in KB. xxvi. 18; ÇÇS. x. 5. 22.
[2] RV. vii. 45; vi. 53; iv. 33; and vii. 34; ÇÇS. x. 5. 23.
[3] RV. vii. 6; ÇÇS. x. 5. 24.
[4] RV. vii. 56; *praçukrīya* is vii. 34 (n. 2); ÇÇS. x. 5. 24.
[5] RV. ii. 4: ÇÇS. x. 5. 24.
[6] RV. iii. 26. 4-6. The reading of LoK and Ānand. ed. *samūḷhā* cannot be supported.
[7] RV. x. 122.

'hither' in 'Clothed in ghee further the way for the prayer hither';[8] that which contains (the word) 'hither' is a symbol of the fourth day as introductory, for the fourth day is a second introduction. Having performed the litanies, having crept along, they perform the Ṣoḍaçin; all this (universe) is sixteenfold; verily (it serves) to obtain all this. Food with the fourth day they obtain, the Anuṣṭubh metre, the Ekaviñça Stoma, the Vairāja Sāman, the northern quarter, the autumn of seasons, the Sādhya and the Ājya gods,[9] Bṛhaspati and the moon, born of the gods,[10] the overlords.

ADHYĀYA XXIII

The Soma Sacrifice (*continued*).

The Pṛṣṭhya Ṣaḍaha (*continued*).

xxiii. 1. The fifth day is cattle; the basis by Tanva is the Pañkti, the Pañkti is cattle, (they say). It has the following symbols in its verses: (the word) 'bull', (the word) 'cow', (the word) 'milk', (the word) 'ghee', (the words) 'be drunk', (the word) 'wealth', (the word) 'strong', having an addition. 'This guest of yours, waking at dawn', is the Ājya,[1] containing (the word) 'wealth' in 'wealths' in 'Wealths, O son of strength, among mortals'; containing (the word) 'wealth' is a symbol of this (day); it has an addition; this is a symbol of the Pañkti; it is in Jagatī, for this set of three days has the morning pressing in Jagatī. So in the transposed form. Having taken out this, 'Him I deem Agni who is bright' is used in the conjunct form.[2] It is in Pañkti; the fifth day is the Pañkti; these are the fifth day. 'To whom the cows go home' (it contains); containing (the word) 'cow' is a symbol of this (day). The Praüga is in Bṛhatī;[3] the fifth day is cattle; cattle are connected with the Bṛhatī; verily (it serves) to obtain cattle. The strophe of the Marutvatīya[4] has (the word) 'of the five peoples' in 'When with the folk of the five peoples'; this is a symbol of the fifth day. 'Thus in the Soma, in the drink' is in Pañkti[5] and contains (the words) 'be drunk'; the explanation of this has been given. 'Thou art the helper of him who poureth offering, with the strew spread'

[8] RV. x. 122. 2 *c*.

[9] For these deities (clearly based on Sādhyas) cf. ÇB. xiii. 4. 2. 16; Lévi, *La doctrine du sacrifice*, p. 62.

[10] *devajāte* is curious as °*jātau* seems necessary: it may be neuter, but this is hardly likely; an error is probable enough. Cf. below KB. xxviii. 1, n. 8.

[1] RV. vi. 15 (also cited in KB. xxiii. 3); ÇÇS. x. 6. 2. Cf. AB. v. 6.

[2] RV. v. 6; ÇÇS. x. 6. 2–4.

[3] For its composition see ÇÇS. x. 6. 5 and 6.

[4] RV. viii. 63. 7–9; ÇÇS. x. 6. 8.

[5] RV. i. 80; ÇÇS. x. 6. 9.

are verses of six Padas; the year has six seasons; verily (they serve) to obtain the year. 'They are to be recited as Gāyatrī verses', Kauṣītaki used to say; the reciting as Gāyatrī makes full completion;[6] in that with each set of eight syllables he says the Praṇava, that is the Gāyatrī form. 'Indra with the Maruts, the bull, for joy' is in normal Triṣṭubh and supports the pressing.[7] The explanation of this has been given. It contains (the word) 'bull' in 'The bull, for joy'; this is a symbol of this day. 'He by whom this' is the Marutvatīya;[8] it is in Gāyatrī, for this set of three days has the Gāyatrī at the midday pressing.

xxiii. 2. The Mahānāmnīs[1] are the Pṛṣṭha; by the Mahānāmnīs Indra slew Vṛtra; him having slain Vṛtra the gods met as he went; before they had retreated away from him and stood in terror. Him Prajāpati asked, 'Hast thou been able to slay?' 'Yes, yes' he replied, without mention (of his name), for Prajāpati is he whose (name) is not mentioned; this is a symbol of Prajāpati. Him Agni asked, 'Hast thou been able to slay?' 'Yes, O Agni' he replied. Him his own greatness asked, 'Hast thou been able to slay?' Before it had retreated from him and stood in terror. 'Yes, O Indra' he replied. Him Pūṣan asked, 'Hast thou been able to slay?' 'Yes, O Pūṣan' he replied. Him the All-gods asked, 'Hast thou been able to slay?' 'Yes, O All-gods' he replied. These five Padas are recited as 'mortar'; it is the boundary of the Ṛc; they are the strong ones; by them Indra had strength to slay Vṛtra; in that by them he had strength to slay Vṛtra, therefore are they the strong ones, for they are strengths. 'To him athirst', 'Who is most wealthy, O wealthy one' and 'Him for you who injureth not' are three sets of three verses;[2] he makes as tenth the Bṛhatī[3] 'To him, to him of the drink.' 'Yea, thou art the powerful' is, however, the rule,[4] having the same utterance as the 'mortar' (verses); so it becomes equal with or even superior to the strophe. 'Whether, O Indra, among the tribes of Nahus' is the Pragātha of the Sāman;[5] 'Or of the five folks' contains (the word) 'five'; this is a symbol of the fifth day. It contains (the words) 'be drunk' in 'Indra hath waxed to be drunk'; it is in Pañkti; the explanation of this has been given. 'Thou hast furthered our prayer in the overcoming of Vṛtra' are verses of six Padas;[6] the explanation of them has been given. 'Thou hast become the

[6] M's reading *atisamṛddham* is good sense but is probably a gloss.

[7] RV. iii. 47; ÇÇS. 6. 9.

[8] RV. viii. 76. 4–6; ÇÇS. x. 6. 9.

[1] AĀ. iv; ÇÇS. x. 6. 10–13. Cf. AB. v. 7. The KB. version of the Purīṣapadas seems to have differed from AĀ. by omitting that to Viṣṇu; cf. BD. viii. 102; Scheftelowitz, ZDMG. lix. 423, 424.

[2] RV. vi. 42. 1–3 (also cited in KB. xxviii. 7); 44. 1–3; and 44. 4–6; ÇÇS. x. 6. 14.

[3] RV. vi. 42. 4; ÇÇS. x. 6. 14.

[4] RV. viii. 92. 28; ÇÇS. x. 6. 14 (*iti vā* simply).

[5] RV. vi. 46. 7, 8; ÇÇS. x. 6. 15.

[6] RV. viii. 37; ÇÇS. x. 6. 16.

only wealth-lord of wealth' is in normal Tristubh[7] and supports the pressing; the explanation of this has been given. In 'wealth-lord of wealth' it contains (the word) 'wealth'; containing (the word) 'wealth' is a symbol of this (day); it contains an addition; this is a symbol of the Paṅkti. 'Him Indra we strengthen' is the Niṣkevalya[8] containing (the word) 'bull' in 'May he become a strong bull'; this is a symbol of this day. It is in Gāyatrī, for this set of three days has the Gāyatrī at the midday pressing.

xxiii. 3. 'That desirable of Savitṛ' is the antistrophe[1] by Viçvāmitra, to secure variety of the Pṛṣṭhyas. 'Strengthening by their thought'[2] contains (the word) 'strength'; this is a symbol of this day. 'Up the god Savitṛ of the home' is (the hymn) to Savitṛ,[3] containing (the word) 'cattle' in 'prosperity' in 'Prosperity to-day, O Savitṛ, prosperity also to-morrow'; containing (the word) 'cattle' is a symbol of this (day). 'The great ones, sky and earth, here the eldest' is (the hymn) to sky and earth,[4] containing (the word) 'cattle' in 'steer' in 'Rousing the steer, in far-reaching courses'; containing (the word) 'cattle' is a symbol of this day. 'To us Ṛbhu, Vibhvan, Vāja, Indra' is (the hymn) to the Ṛbhus,[5] containing (the word) 'cattle' in 'possessing cows' in 'Who that which possesseth cows, strength, of good heroes'; containing (the word) 'cattle' is a symbol of this (day). 'Who now, O Mitra and Varuṇa, pious one' is (the hymn) for the All-gods,[6] containing (the word) 'cattle' in 'for bestowing of cattle' in 'To the pious strength as it were for the bestowing of cattle'; containing (the word) 'cattle' is a symbol of this (day). It contains an addition; this is a symbol of the Paṅkti. 'The swelling oblation, unaging, in the finder of light' is (the hymn) to Vaiçvānara[7]; 'swelling' is a symbol of the fifth day. 'Even to the wise let it be a wondrous thing' is (the hymn) to the Maruts,[8] containing (the word) 'cattle' in 'cow' in 'That owneth the common name of cow'; containing (the word) 'cattle' is a symbol of this (day). 'Agni is the Hotṛ, the householder, the king' is (the hymn) to Jātavedas,[9] containing (the word) 'strength' in 'Help us, O bountiful one, in the winning of strength'; this is a symbol of this day. It contains an addition; this is a symbol of the Paṅkti. So in the transposed form. In the conjunct form, 'The head of the sky, the messenger of the earth' is (the hymn) to

[7] RV. vi. 31 (also cited in KB. xxv. 8); ÇÇS. x. 6. 16.

[8] RV. viii. 93. 7–9; ÇÇS. x. 6. 16.

[1] RV. iii. 62 10–12; ÇÇS. x. 6. 18. Cf. AB. v. 8.

[2] RV. iii. 62. 12 c.

[3] RV. vi. 71. 4–6; ÇÇS. x. 6. 18.

[4] RV. iv. 56. 1–4; see ÇÇS. x. 6. 18.

[5] RV. iv. 34; ÇÇS. x. 6. 18.

[6] RV. v. 41; ÇÇS. x. 6. 18.

[7] RV. x. 88; ÇÇS. x. 5. 12.

[8] RV. vi. 66; ÇÇS. x. 6. 19.

[9] AV. vi. 15. 13–15; ÇÇS. x. 6. 19.

Vaiçvānara[10]; in 'The navel of the sacrifices, the seat of wealth' it contains (the word) 'wealth'; containing (the word) 'wealth' is a symbol of the (day). 'Hither the Rudras with Indra in unison' is (the hymn) to the Maruts,[11] containing (the word) 'cattle' in 'having cars and having heroes' in 'Having cows, having horses, having cars, and of good heroes'; containing (the word) 'cattle' is a symbol of this day. 'This guest of yours waking at dawn' is (the hymn) to Jātavedas[12]; the explanation of this has been given. Cattle with the fifth day they obtain, the Pañkti metre, the Triṇava Stoma, the Çākvara Sāman, the zenith[13] quarter, the winter of seasons, the Maruts the gods, Rudra, born of the gods, the overlord.

xxiii. 4. The fifth day is cattle; the sixth day is man; Prajāpati is man, being before all this (universe). Prajāpati is beyond the normal metres; this is a symbol of Prajāpati. An Asura woman approached[1] Indra making *muṣkas* at every joint; Indra, desirous of subduing her, at every joint made *çepas*; Indra indeed is Parucchepa ('having in joints *çepas*'); all does Indra seek to conquer. With her he had union; with him was she angry[2] with the cunning of the Asuras; he saw these (verses) with repeated Padas; with them from every limb, from every joint, from all evil was he set free. In that the Parucchepa (text) is recited, in the middle and in the recitations of the Hotrakas, the sacrificers are set free from every limb, from every joint, from all evil. Placing first the normal offering verses, they use the (verses) of Parucchepa as offering verses; in that on this day they do not say *vaṣaṭ* with them, thereby are they left out; in that they do not omit[3] them, (it is because they think) 'Let us not omit the unfailing part of the sacrifice, what is dear to the gods.' Having performed first the normal seasonal offering (verses), they use (verses) of Gṛtsamada as offering verses[4]; in that on this day they do not say *vaṣaṭ* with them, thereby are they left out; in that they do not omit them, (it is because they think) 'Let us not omit the unfailing part of the sacrifice, what is dear to the gods.' Thereby they become above the normal metre; thus with (verses) of seven Padas they perform the *vaṣaṭ* call. Now as to this Kauṣītaki used to say,[5] 'The metres with the

[10] RV. vi. 7; ÇÇS. x. 6. 26.

[11] RV. v. 57 (already cited in KB. xx. 4); ÇÇS. x. 6. 20.

[12] RV. vi. 15 (also cited in KB. xxiii. 1); vv. 1–9 are meant; see ÇÇS. x. 6. 20.

[13] M has *ūrdhvām*.

[1] For the *pratyutkramata* of BLK and the Ānand. ed. cf. in KB. xxii. 6 the *v. l. vimadan* of the same MSS. and Oo. For the story here cf. AB. v. 10, 11.

[2] *ahṛṇāt* is very uncertain in sense; possibly 'charmed him' may be meant. The Ānand. ed. has *arhaṇāt*, which is nonsense.

[3] The MSS. and the comm. recognize here *nāntarayanti* only. The verses for the different priests are given in ÇÇS. x. 7. 2–6. BK and the Ānand. ed. have *utsṛjati*.

[4] I. e. RV. ii. 36 and 37 give the offering verses for the offerings after the Praiṣas; see ÇÇS. x. 7. 7.

[5] It is clear from KB. xxiii. 5 that the rule of Kauṣītaki is rejected.

Virāj as the eighth guard him who yonder gives heat. That concord they disturb who use (verses) over the normal metre as offering verses.

xxiii. 5. Therefore assuredly they should use (the verses) of the one-day rite as offering verses, to prevent disturbance of the path that leads to the gods.' As to this Aṇicin Mauna asked the Jābāla householders, having glided up to them when they were performing a sacrificial session, 'Have ye departed from the day, are ye Parucchepas?'[1] Then were they silent; then from the north half of the Sadas Citra Gauçrāyaṇi, or Gauçra, made reply, 'We have not indeed left the day; we are not Parucchepas; in our litany the Parucchepa has already been added in the day[2] (rite); with (the verses) for the one-day (rite) have we sacrificed; therefore we have not departed from the day.' One after another should they say the offering verses; the sixth day is an abode of the gods; if on that day the Hotṛ alone should say *vaṣaṭ*, the Hotṛ would commingle the abode of the gods of the Adhvaryu and the householder.[3] A race they run for the world of heaven by the sixth day; he who completes it without drawing in breath wins the world of heaven; but, if he should draw in breath, let him ever and again pushing forward[4] try (to complete it).

xxiii. 6. 'He is born in the ordinance of Manu' is the Ājya,[1] with no deity mentioned by name in 'he'; Prajāpati is he (whose name is) not mentioned; this is a symbol of Prajāpati. They are beyond the normal metres, having seven Padas, and have repeated Padas; in that it is this day, they are thus. He should not draw in breath between the Pada and the repeated Pada; the Pada is the body, the repeated Pada the breaths; if one should say of him who breathes in at this point, 'He has separated the body from the breath; he will not live', so would it be. Therefore he should not draw in breath between the Pada and the repeated Pada. The Praüga is in a metre beyond the normal; the sixth day is connected with a metre beyond the normal; verily thus he makes it successful with its own metre. 'He first of the great' is the strophe of the Marutvatīya[2]; in 'he' no deity is mentioned by name; Prajāpati is he (whose name is) not mentioned; this is a symbol of Prajāpati. 'The chariot which thou, O Indra, for the

[1] *ahno 'gātā* must be read to make sense. The Ānand. ed. has *papracchānno gātā*. The sense is perhaps literally 'by having *çepas* at the joints'; a reference to the addition of verses after the normal offering verses. *Parucchepāt* in M is a bad correction, like *tasmād vaikāhikībhiḥ* just above.

[2] *na* might be read as in BK. and as suggested by the obvious blunder *çastreṇāhan* in BC and the Ānand. ed. which has, like OoC (*ahar* LBK), *'hnāyatiṣvaikāhikībhir*. But *naḥ* (M, Burnell MS.) seems better.

[3] This is explained by ÇÇS. x. 7. 9 and 10; cf. AB. v. 9.

[4] *pratisdram* may mean 'recurring' to the work as BR. take it.

xxiii. 6. [1] RV. i. 128; cp. ÇÇS. x. 8, which gives in 2 and 8 the Praüga. Cf. AB. v. 12.

[2] RV. viii. 63. 1-3; ÇÇS. x. 8. 5.

winning of the offering' is by Parucchepa[3]; the explanation of this has been given. In 'He who with heroes winneth the light' there is a reference to the Maruts in 'with heroes'. 'He who strong with the strong in one dwelling' is in normal Triṣṭubh[4] and supports the pressing; the explanation of this has been given. There is repetition in 'Strong with the strong'; the sixth day is the end; having gone to the end, he repeats as it were, for hence whitherward should he go? 'O Indra, generous, with the Maruts' is the Marutvatīya[5]; it is in Gāyatrī, for this set of three days has the Gāyatrī at the midday pressing.

xxiii. 7. 'Rich be ours in joint carouse', and 'Rich the praiser of the rich', thus[1] the Vāravantīya is imposed on the foundation of the Raivata. The Sāman is addressed to Agni, with verses to Indra; it makes a pairing, a symbol of generation. 'Praise naught else' is the Pragātha of the Sāman[2]; in 'O friends' in 'O friends, come not to harm' it is the symbol of all; the sixth day is the symbol of all; therefore in 'O friends' he refers to all. 'O Indra, come to us from afar' is by Parucchepa[3]; the explanation of this has been given. (It contains) 'from afar'; from afar is the end; the sixth day is the end; he places the end in the end. 'The greatnesses of this great one' is the normal Triṣṭubh support of the pressing[4]; the explanation of this has been given. There is repetition in 'The greatnesses of this great one'; the sixth day is the end; having gone to the end, he repeats as it were, for hence whitherward should he go? 'With the bay steeds to our pressed (drink)' is the Niṣkevalya.[5] There is repetition in 'Come, O lord of the draughts, to us with the bay steeds'; the sixth day is the end; having gone to the end, he repeats as it were, for hence whitherward should he go? It is in Gāyatrī, for this set of three days has the Gāyatrī at the midday pressing.

xxiii. 8. 'To the god Savitṛ in the bowls, the sage', with this (verse) in a metre beyond the normal he begins the Vaiçvadeva[1]; the sixth day is connected with a metre beyond the normal; the metre beyond the normal thus attains the third pressing. Moreover the sixth day is connected with Prajāpati; Prajāpati is beyond the normal metre; this is a symbol of Prajāpati. The antistrophe[2] contains (the word) 'towards'; the explanation of this has been given. 'Up this god Savitṛ for instigation' is (the hymn)

[3] RV. i. 129; ÇÇS. x. 8. 6.
[4] RV. i. 100; ÇÇS. x. 8. 6.
[5] RV. viii. 76. 7–9; ÇÇS. x. 8. 6.
[1] RV. i. 30. 13–15 and viii. 2. 13–15. The verses of the Raivata are then sung to the Vāravantīya Sāman; ÇÇS. x. 8. 7. Cf. AB. v. 12, 13.
[2] RV. viii. 1 and 2; ÇÇS. x. 8. 8.
[3] RV. i. 130; ÇÇS. x. 8. 9.
[4] RV. ii. 15; ÇÇS. x. 8. 9.
[5] RV. viii. 98. 31–33; ÇÇS. x. 8. 9.

xxiii. 8. [1] For the text see ÇÇS. v. 9. 7; x. 8. 10.
[2] It is taken from the third day, ÇÇS. x. 8. 13.

to Savitṛ[3]; there is repetition in 'Savitṛ for instigation'; the sixth day is the end; having gone to the end, he repeats as it were; for hence whitherward should he go? 'Which is the first, which the latter of these two?' is (the hymn) to sky and earth[4]; there is repetition in 'first' and 'latter'; the sixth day is the end; having gone to the end, he repeats as it were, for hence whitherward should he go? 'Why hath the best, why hath the youngest come to us?' is (the hymn) to the Ṛbhus[5]; there is repetition in 'best' and 'youngest'; the sixth day is the end; having gone to the end, he repeats as it were, for hence whitherward should he go? 'This dread thing be of glad speech' is (the hymn) to the All-gods[6], containing (the word) 'stand' in 'When making his parents, standing firm on liberality'; this is a symbol of the end; the sixth day is the end; having gone to the end, he stands still as it were, for hence whitherward should he go? Having left over the last two (verses), he throws in (the hymn) to Narāçaṅsa,[7] 'Those who through the sacrifice are adorned with the fee.' The hymn is the body, (the hymn) to Narāçaṅsa is offspring and cattle; verily thus in the middle in the body he places both sets, offspring and cattle. 'The dark day and the bright day' is (the hymn) to Vaiçvānara[8]; there is repetition in 'and the bright day'; the sixth day is the end; having gone to the end, he repeats as it were, for hence whitherward should he go? 'Forward the Maruts, devoted, with gleaming lances' is (the hymn) to the Maruts[9]; in that it has the same endings it is a symbol of the end. 'This praise to Jātavedas who doth deserve it' is (the hymn) to Jātavedas[10]; in that it has the same endings it is a symbol of the end. 'Let us not be harmed; let us not be harmed' at the end is a symbol of freedom from harm. The waters with the sixth day they obtain, the Atichandas metre, the Trayastriṅça Stoma, the Raivata Sāman, the zenith quarter, the cool of the seasons, the All-gods, Prajāpati, born of the gods, the overlord.

ADHYĀYA XXIV

The Soma Sacrifice (*continued*).

The Abhijit.

xxiv. 1. The[1] Abhijit (is explained). By the Abhijit the gods conquered these three worlds; therefore has it three turns and four endings. With

[3] RV. ii. 38; ÇÇS. x. 8. 14.
[4] RV. i. 185; ÇÇS. x. 8. 14.
[5] RV. i. 161 (already cited in KB. xix. 9); ÇÇS. x. 8. 14.
[6] RV. x. 61: verse 1 is of doubtful sense; ÇÇS. x. 8. 14.
[7] RV. x. 62; ÇÇS. x. 8. 14.
[8] RV. vi. 9; ÇÇS. x. 8. 15.
[9] RV. v. 55; ÇÇS. x. 8. 15.
[10] RV. i. 94; ÇÇS. x. 8. 15.
[1] For the Abhijit see ÇÇS. xi. 10; AÇS. viii. 5. 1–9. The use of the nom. twice, which

the Viçvajit they conquered these four quarters; therefore it has four turns and three endings. The Abhijit (is explained). By the Abhijit the gods conquered; what was left unconquered clung on as it were; that they conquered by the Viçvajit; the Viçvajit is so called (because they said) 'All have we conquered.' The Abhijit and the Viçvajit are these two, Indra and Agni; the Abhijit is Agni, for Agni conquered all this (universe); the Viçvajit is Indra, for Indra conquered all this wholly. The Abhijit has both Sāmans and all the Stomas; therefore both sets of hymns, those connected with the Bṛhat and the Rathantara, are recited. The two hymns,[2] 'Forward to the god, Agni' and 'What is best, that to Agni'[3] are its Ājya; 'Forward' is a symbol of the Rathantara; 'aloud' in 'Sing aloud, O thou of wide radiance' is (a symbol) of the Bṛhat. The two Praügas of Madhuchandas and Gṛtsamada should he interweave; having recited the Puroruc to Vāyu, then (he should insert) two triplets to Vāyu; then, having recited the Puroruc to Indra and Vāyu, two triplets to Indra and Vāyu; the Puroruc, then the two triplets, the Puroruc and then the two triplets; thus should he interweave. This he should not regard; he makes the triplets of Madhuchandas first, those of Gṛtsamada second. As to this they say 'Why should he interweave the two (Praügas)? This he should not regard; the Praüga being that of Madhuchandas only, he should put on (the triplet) to the All-gods of Gṛtsamada above (the triplet) to the All-gods of Madhuchandas[4]; there is one (hymn) with the Bṛhat character expressed.

xxiv. 2. 'O ye All-gods, come hither; hear this my call; sit on this strew[1]. (The word) "strew" is a symbol of the Bṛhat.' Then (comes) (the triplet) to Sarasvatī of Madhuchandas[2]. 'Let him conclude with the last verse of it; so let the morning pressing be in the one-day form' is the rule. The Abhijit is a one-day (rite); the one-day (rite) is a support; verily (it serves) for support. 'Thee like a car for aid' is the strophe of the Marutvatīya[3]; 'This drink, O bright one, is pressed' is the antistrophe[4]; this is the normal one-day form; the explanation of it has been given. 'Thou hast been born dread for impetuous strength', having recited this of Gaurivīti[5] first, he inserts a Nivid in the five-verse hymn of Bṛhatī verses,[6]

is also in M, is odd: the reading *hānv iveva* (not *ivaiva* as stated by Lindner) of M is clearly correct; the Ānand. ed. has *ha nv ivaiva* with OoBC. M has *ṣaṣañje*.

[2] RV. iii. 13 (already cited in KB. xx. 2); ÇÇS. xi. 10. 2.

[3] RV. v. 25. 7–9 (already cited in KB. vii. 9); ÇÇS. xi. 10. 2.

[4] RV. i. 3. 7–9. Cf. ÇÇS. xi. 10. 3, 4, 5, for the different possibilities, which in xxiv. 2 end in the acceptance of the one-day form after all. *iti* is omitted below.

[1] RV. ii. 41. 13–15 (also cited in KB. xxvi. 17).

[2] RV. i. 3. 10–12.

[3] RV. viii. 68. 1–3 (also cited in KB. xv. 2).

[4] RV. viii. 2. 1–3 (already cited in KB. xv. 2).

[5] RV. x. 73 (already cited in KB. xv. 3).

[6] RV. vi. 60; ÇÇS. xi. 10. 7.

'O Indra, drink; for thee it hath been pressed for delight.' 'I shall proclaim the manly deeds of Indra', this of Hiraṇyastūpa[7] having recited first, he inserts a Nivid in the hymn of nine Bṛhatī verses,[8] 'Thy nearest, thy furthest aid.' So if the Pṛṣṭha be the Rathantara. 'But, if it be the Bṛhat, having recited the two of Bṛhatī verses first he should place Nivids in the two from the one-day (rite),' (they say). 'The Niṣkevalya and the Marutvatīya should be each of one hymn only' is the rule. 'Drink the Soma towards which, O dread one, thou hast penetrated' and 'Praise him who hath might to overcome' are (two hymns [9]) containing (the word) 'towards'; this is the symbol of the Abhijit. 'The third pressing should follow the normal one-day (rite)' is the rule; the Abhijit is a one-day (rite); the one-day (rite) is a support; verily (it serves) for support.

The Svarasāmans.

xxiv. 3. Svarbhānu, an Asura, pierced with[1] darkness the sun; the Atris were fain to smite away its darkness; they performed, before the Viṣuvant, this set of three days, with the Saptadaça Stoma. They smote away the darkness in front of it; that settled behind[2]; they performed the same three-day (rite) after the Viṣuvant; they smote away the darkness behind it. Those who perform, knowing thus, this three-day (rite) with the Saptadaça Stoma on both sides of the Visuvant, verily those sacrificers smite away evil from both worlds. They call them the Svarasāmans; by them the Atris rescued (*apaspṛṇvata*) the sun from the darkness; in that they rescued, therefore are they Svarasāmans. This is declared in a Ṛc,

xxiv. 4. 'The sun which Svarbhānu
The Asura pierced with darkness,
The Atris found it.
None other could do so.'

By this the Svarasāmans are mentioned. The Marutvatīyas have (the word) 'who'; the Pragāthas of the Niṣkevalyas have (the word) 'who'. Prajāpati is 'Who'; the Svarasāmans are Prajāpati; they have Anuṣṭubh Nivids inserted. The Anuṣṭubh is the waters; the Svarasāmans are the waters, for all this (universe) is surrounded with the waters, for on both sides of yonder sun there are waters below and above. This is declared in a Ṛc,

[7] RV. i. 32 (already cited in KB. xv. 4.)

[8] RV. vi. 25 (already cited in KB. xxii. 2); ÇÇS. xi. 10. 8.

[9] RV. vi. 17, and vi. 18 (also cited in KB. xxv. 6; xxvi. 9); ÇÇS. xi. 10. 9.

[1] The legend of Svarbhānu is common; see Macdonell, *Vedic Mythology*, pp. 145, 160.

[2] *parastād* seems meant, and is read in the Ānand. ed., not *purastāt* as in Lindner's text. Cf. AB. iv. 19. M has *parastād asīdat ta etam . . . tasyopariṣṭāt . . . vidvāṅsam ubhayato viṣuvantam ubhayamiti* and inserts after *apajaghnuḥ* and before *tad ya* the words *tat parastād asīdat*.

xxiv. 5. 'The waters that stand above and below,
In the realm of the sun.'[1]

'O god, the mortal with sacrifice hither' is the Ājya[2] of the first Svarasāman (day), containing the word 'hither' and connected with the Rathantara. 'Great strength in the beam' is (the Ājya[3]) of the second, (containing the word) 'great', and connected with the Bṛhat. 'O Agni, bring hither the most mighty' is (the Ājya) of the third, containing (the word) 'hither', and connected with the Rathantara.[4] The Praüga of the first Svarasāman is by Madhuchandas, that of the second by Gṛtsamada, and that of the third in Uṣṇih verses by Atri; the explanation of these has been given. The strophe and antistrophe of the Marutvatīyas, the verses to Brahmaṇaspati, follow the model of the three-day (rite); the explanation of them has been given. 'Where is this hero who hath seen Indra'? is the Marutvatīya[5] of the first Svarasāman, containing (the word) 'who' in 'where'. 'With what array, of one age, of one home?' is (the Marutvatīya[6]) of the second, containing (the word) 'who' in 'what'. 'Let him sing the Sāman springing forth as of a bird' is (the Marutvatīya[7]) of the third, containing (the word) 'who' in 'work (*ka-rma*)' in 'Those works most welcome to him'; Prajāpati is 'Who'; the Svarasāmans are Prajāpati. 'When thou wast born, O unequalled one'; on this strophe[8], which has a Bṛhatī as the third verse, some daily bring in the Svaras; if they do so, the strophe and antistrophe and the inserted verse are the same.[9] 'What newest of praisers?' is the Pragātha[10] containing (the word) 'who'; the explanation of this has been given.

xxiv. 6. Then the basis of the Rathantara (is recited). 'Which thou, O Indra, dost support' is a couple of verses,[1] to avoid isolation; (it is used, thinking) 'Let not that Bṛhatī have been recited by itself alone as it were'. 'O Indra, O generous one, to thee we have turned' is the normal Triṣṭubh[2] (triad) which supports the pressing; the explanation of this has been given. 'That most effectual for aid (power) of them' is the

[1] RV. iii. 22. 3 *c*.

[2] RV. v. 17. 1–4; ÇÇS. xi. 11. 7.

[3] RV. v. 16. 1–4; ÇÇS. xi. 11. 7.

[4] The hymn is RV. v. 10. 1–6; see ÇÇS. xi. 11. 7. *rathantaram* is probably an error for *rāthantaram* as above, and the Ānand. ed. actually has *rāth*°.

[5] RV. v. 30 (already cited in KB. xxi. 3); ÇÇS. xi. 11. 9. For the Praügas see xi. 11. 8.

[6] RV. i. 165; ÇÇS. xi. 11. 9.

[7] RV. i. 173; ÇÇS. xi. 11. 9.

[8] RV. viii. 89. 5–7. *bṛhatītṛtīye* is essential as a compound. Cf. KB. xviii. 10.

[9] This must be the sense, that all these are to be the same for all days; ÇÇS. xi. 11 *seq.*, gives variants, but Ānartīya recognizes the rule here as intended to have this sense.

[10] RV. viii. 3. 13, 14.

xxiv 6. [1] RV. viii. 97. 2 and 3. The Anand. ed. has *çastvā*. They are Bṛhatī verses and match the Bṛhatī of the Stotriya; ÇÇS. xi. 12. 4.

[2] RV. vi. 44. 10–12; ÇÇS. xi. 12. 5.

Niṣkevalya in Anuṣṭubhs,[3] containing (the word) 'hither' in [4] 'O Indra, do thou hither bear that power,' and connected with the Rathantara. 'What hath not been wrought by him?' is the Pragātha containing (the word) 'who'; the explanation of this has been given.

xxiv. 7. Then the basis of the Bṛhat (is recited). 'They call thee, men, when (the juice) is pressed' is a couplet,[1] to avoid isolation; (it is used, thinking) 'Let not that Bṛhatī have been recited by itself alone as it were.' 'O Adhvaryu, O hero, to the mighty the pressed (juices)' is the normal Triṣṭubh [2] (triplet) which supports the pressing; the explanation of this has been given. 'The singers sing thee' is the Niṣkevalya [3] in Anuṣṭubhs, containing (the word) 'up' in 'Up with a rod they have raised thee', and connected with the Bṛhat. 'These thee, O thou of much light' is the Pragātha,[4] containing (the word) 'who (*ka*)' in *kavarṇa* in 'of pure hues (*pāvakavarṇāḥ*)'; the explanation of this has been given.

xxiv. 8. Then the basis of the Rathantara (is recited), then that of the Bṛhat. 'Bounding as a wild elephant' is a couplet,[1] to avoid isolation; (it is used, thinking) 'Let not that Bṛhatī have been recited by itself alone as it were'. 'This bowl with the drink for Indra' is the normal Triṣṭubh [2] (triplet) which supports the pressing; the explanation of this has been given. 'Indra all have caused to grow' is the Niṣkevalya in Anuṣṭubhs,[3] containing (the word) 'towards' in 'Towards thee we sing our praise'; this is a symbol of the Rathantara. They say [4] 'He should not place the Nivid in the Anuṣṭubh (hymns), he confuses the arrangement of metres at the midday (performance).' Having recited the Anuṣṭubhs first for the obtaining of desire, he inserts a Nivid in the Triṣṭubh (hymns); thus in due order is the Nivid inserted; it being inserted in due order places them in due order in all the worlds and in all desires. 'Hither thy car with every boon, O dread one'; (he inserts a Nivid) in (this hymn [5]), containing (the word) 'hither' and connected with the Rathantara on the first day. 'He hath drunk hence, most marvellous and up for us', (he inserts a Nivid) in (this hymn [6]) containing (the word) 'up', and connected with the Bṛhat on the second (day). 'In thee from of old the songs have gone together, O Indra', (he inserts a Nivid) in (this hymn [7]), containing (the word) 'go' and being a symbol of the end on the third (day). If the Pṛṣṭhas are the Svaras the Sāman

RV. v. 35. 1-7; ÇÇS. xi. 11. 12; 12. 5. 7; 6 gives an alternative.
[4] RV. viii. 66. 9 and 10; ÇÇS. xi. 11. 11.
[1] RV. viii. 33. 2 and 3; ÇÇS. xii. 12. 4.
[2] RV. vi. 44. 13–15; ÇÇS. xii. 12. 5.
[3] RV. i. 10; ÇÇS. xii. 11. 12; 12. 5, 9; 6 gives an alternative.
RV. viii. 3 and 4; ÇÇS. xii. 11. 11.

xxiv. 8. [1] RV. viii. 33. 8 and 9; ÇÇS. xi. 12. 4.
[2] RV. vi. 44. 16–18; ÇÇS. xi. 12. 5.
[3] RV. i. 11; ÇÇS. xi. 11. 12.
[4] *iti* omitted as not rarely; cf. n. 3.
[5] RV. vi. 37; ÇÇS. xi. 11. 12.
[6] RV. vi. 38; ÇÇS. xi. 11. 12.
[7] RV. vi. 34; ÇÇS. xi. 11. 12.

chanters use the Bṛhat and the Rathantara in the Pavamānas, but, if the Pṛṣṭhas are the Bṛhat and the Rathantara, then the Sāman chanters use the Svaras in the Pavamānas. 'But the Pṛṣṭhas should be the Svaras only,' Kauṣītaki[8] used to say; 'for they are the Svarasāmans; by the Pṛṣṭhas the gods have touched the world of heaven; the Pṛṣṭhas are the Svaras, for the touching of the world of heaven.'

xxiv. 9. The strophes (used) are those of the Vaiçvadeva (litanies) of the first three days of the Pṛṣṭha Ṣaḍaha in conjunct form. The third pressings with the antistrophes are the third pressings of the second three days. The Vaiçvadeva (hymns) there are taken out and other crypto-Vaiçvadevas,[1] without mention (of the deities), connected with Prajāpati, are inserted, 'This drink to you, O swift to wrath,' 'Him of old, aforetime, at all times, now,' and 'What vessel here of those that are pious?' in place of (the hymn) of Nābhānediṣṭha. There should, however, be used the open Vaiçvadevas, 'Agni, Indra, Varuṇa, Mitra, Aryaman' on the first day,[2] containing (the word) 'who' in 'Having established (*s-ka-bhitvī*) the sky'; 'I hail the gods of great fame for security' on the second,[3] containing (the word) 'who' in 'Light making (*jyotiṣkṛtaḥ*).' 'Dawn and night (*uṣāsā naktā*) the great ones, of fair form' on the third[4] (day), containing (the word) 'who' in 'night'. Prajāpati is 'Who'; the Svarasāmans are Prajāpati. They are made up as Agniṣṭomas or Ukthyas; 'As Agniṣṭomas' (is) Paiṅgya's view; they become possessed of splendour who perform Agniṣṭomas. 'Let them be Ukthyas,' Kauṣītaki used to say. The Ukthya is a successful form of sacrifice, for it has fifteen Stotras, fifteen Çastras; they make thirty Stotras and Çastras; it makes up the Virāj; the Virāj is prosperity and proper food; (it serves) for the winning of the Virāj as prosperity and proper food.

ADHYĀYA XXV

The Soma Sacrifice (*continued*).

The Viṣuvant

xxv. 1. The[1] waters practised fervour; after practising fervour they

[8] *iti* is probably to be understood (cf. KB. x. 8, n. 2) after *spṛçyai*, which explains probably Svara and its connexion with Pṛṣṭha; only thus can *aspṛkṣan* as aorist be easily explained. For Kauṣītaki's view see ÇÇS. xi. 11. 8. The other view gives the first a Rathantara in its Pṛṣṭha, the second a Bṛhat, the third both.

[1] RV. i. 122; v. 44; i. 121 (the latter replaces RV. x. 61 (the Nābhānediṣṭha); see KB. xxiii. 8); ÇÇS. xi. 12. 13.

[2] RV. x. 65; ÇÇS. xi. 12. 14; on the fourth day, 7. 10; KB. xxi. 2.

[3] RV. x. 66; ÇÇS. xi. 12. 16; on the fifth (second), 5. 6; KB. xx. 3.

[4] RV. x. 36; ÇÇS. xi. 12. 17; on the sixth (third), 9. 10.

xxv. 1. [1] For the Mahādivākīrtya and the Viṣuvant day in the middle of the year Sattra see AB. iv. 18-22. For the ritual see ÇÇS. xi. 13 and 14; ĀÇS. viii. 6.

conceived; thence was this sun born on the sixth month; therefore on the sixth month the performers of a session perform the Divākīrtya. It goes north for six months, then for six reversed; therefore the performers go for six months forward, then for six months reversed. Without it are hunger and repeated death; they conquer hunger and repeated death who perform the Viṣuvant day. It has these symbols in its verses: (the word) 'sun', (the word) 'blaze', (the word) 'light', (the word) 'ornament', (the word) 'shine', (the word) 'delight'. 'From the ocean the wave rich in sweetness hath arisen' is the Ājya[2]; for from the ocean, from the waters he comes out. It contains (the word) 'sun' in 'Indra one, the sun one hath produced'; this is a symbol of this day. These (verses) recited together make up twenty-one Anuṣṭubhs; he who gives heat here is twenty-onefold; thus he makes it successful with its own symbol. The Praüga is in Triṣṭubh[3]; this is the middle of the days; the Triṣṭubh is the middle of metres. Thus he makes it successful with its own metre.

xxv. 2. 'Were not they who were made great with homage?' is (the triplet) to Vāyu,[1] containing (the word) 'sun' in 'They made bright the dawn with the sun'; this is a symbol of this day. The succeeding triplet is addressed to Indra and Vāyu,[2] 'So far as the power of the body, so far as the might', with the symbol (of the day) in 'So far as men with the eye may discern'. 'Up the eye of you two, O Varuṇa, fair of aspect' is (the triplet) to Indra and Varuṇa,[3] containing (the word) 'sun' in 'The sun goeth extending of the pious one'; this is a symbol of this day. 'Hither, O Nāsatyas, with chariot rich in cattle' is (the triplet) to the Açvins[4]; the third (verse) contains (the word) 'blaze' in 'The god Savitṛ hath raised aloft the blaze'; this is a symbol of this day. 'Come hither to us, O impetuous god, with might' is (the triplet) to Indra,[5] containing (the word) 'sun' in 'Heroes for life for the gaining of the sun'[6]; this is a symbol of this day. 'Let the prayer go forward from the abode of holy order' is (the triplet) to the All-gods,[7] containing (the word) 'sun' in 'The sun hath created the kine with his rays'; this is a symbol of this day. 'May Sarasvatī for us rejoicing' is (the triplet) to Sarasvatī,[8] with the symbol in 'O happy one, thou hast unbound the doors of holy order.' This is the Praüga of Vasiṣṭha arranged in triads of Triṣṭubh verses, and containing (the word) 'sun'. Vasiṣṭha is Prajāpati; verily in Prajāpati they succeed in all their desires.

[2] RV. iv. 58; ÇÇS. xi. 13. 11.
[3] ÇÇS. xi. 13. 12 *seq.* gives the composition.
[1] RV. vii. 91. 1–3. Cf. ÇÇS. x. 10. 4; xi. 13. 13.
[2] RV. vii. 91. 4–6; ÇÇS. x. 10. 4.
[3] RV. vii. 61. 1–3 (also cited in KB. xxvi. 8); ÇÇS. x. 9. 4; xi. 13. 14.
[4] RV. vii. 72. 1–3 (also cited in KB. xxvi. 8); ÇÇS. x. 9. 4; xi. 13. 14.
[5] RV. vii. 30. 1–3; (also cited in KB. xxvi. 8); ÇÇS. x. 9. 4; xi. 13. 14.
[6] RV. vii. 30. 2.
[7] RV. vii. 36. 1–3; ÇÇS. xi. 13. 16.
[8] RV. vii. 95. 4–6 (also cited in KB. xxvi. 11); ÇÇS. x. 10. 4; xi. 13. 17.

xxv. 3. They[1] say 'The morning pressing should not be in Triṣṭubh; he disturbs the beginning of the sacrifice from its appointed metre; let it be the one-day (form) only'. The one-day (rite) is light; he who here gives heat is light; verily thus they cause light to prosper with light. 'Forward to the god, to Agni' and 'Thou hast glory of rule', these two are the Ājya.[2] These (verses) recited together make up twenty-one Anuṣṭubhs; the explanation of these has been given. The Praüga is by Madhuchandas; the explanation of this has been given. 'Thee like a car for aid' is the strophe of the Marutvatīya[3]; 'This drink, O bright one, is pressed' is the antistrophe[4]; this is the normal one-day form; the explanation of this has been given. 'With what array, of one age, of one home?' is the Marutvatīya,[5] with the symbol (of this day) in 'brightness' in 'array' (*çubhā*). 'That ram that winneth the light I glorify' is in Jagatī,[6] containing (the word) 'sun' in 'Thou didst support the sun in the sky to see'; this is a symbol of this day. 'Thou hast been born dread for impetuous strength,' in this Triṣṭubh (hymn[7]) he inserts a Nivid. (The hymn[8] has) the symbol (of this day) in 'Dispel the darkness, fill full our vision'. Two sets, Triṣṭubhs and Jagatīs, are recited, for the sun here gives heat, resting on the Triṣṭubh and the Jagatī; thus openly they obtain it.

xxv. 4. 'The Bṛhat should be the Pṛṣṭha of this day' some hold, saying 'He who here gives heat is connected with the Bṛhat; the Bṛhat gives heat; moreover, the Mahādivākīrtya is not a Pṛṣṭha, the Bṛhat and Rathantara are openly Pṛṣṭhas; therefore the Bṛhat alone should be the Pṛṣṭha of this day.' If they should perform the Bṛhat on a Pragātha containing (the word) 'sun' and Pragāthas containing 'sun', (it is) with the symbol of this day.[1] 'Indra hath knowledge for the hearing of this' is the beginning of the litany,[2] containing (the word) 'sun' in 'He is the lively pathmaker for the sun'; this is the symbol of this day. 'The Mahādivākīrtya alone should be the Pṛṣṭha of this day' is the rule. The Mahādivākīrtya is openly a Sāman; thus with its own Sāman they make it success-

[1] As often the *iti* is omitted. This chapter gives an alternative view of the day; ÇÇS. xi. 13. 17.

[2] RV. iii. 13 (already cited in KB. xx. 2) and vi. 2 (also in KB. xx. 3); ÇÇS. xi. 13. 18.

[3] RV. viii. 68. 1-3 (already cited in KB. xv. 2).

[4] RV. viii. 2. 1-3 (already cited in KB. xv. 2).

[5] RV. i. 165 (already cited in KB. xix. 9); ÇÇS. xi. 13. 20.

[6] RV. i. 52 (also cited in KB. xxvi. 9); ÇÇS. xi. 13. 20.

[7] RV. x. 73 (also cited in KB. xv. 3); ÇÇS. xi. 13. 20.

[8] In its last verse which as usual follows the Nivid, as the construction of the sentence shows.

xxv. 4. [1] The apodosis is doubtless the following clause; cf. ÇÇS. xi. 14. 3, 4; for the case here the recitation is RV. viii. 99. 3, 4; 70. 5, 6; vi. 46. 3, 4; see ÇÇS. xi. 13. 21, 22, 31.

[2] RV. x. 111. 3; ÇÇS. xi. 14. 3.

ful. Now some perform it on Triṣṭubh verses [3]; he who here gives heat is connected with the Triṣṭubh; thus it with its own metre they make successful. 'Let it be performed on Bṛhatī verses' some say; he who here gives heat is connected with the Bṛhatī; thus with its own metre they make it successful. But the rule is 'Let it be performed on Jagatī verses'; he who here gives heat is connected with the Jagatī; thus with its own metre they make it successful.

xxv. 5. 'May the radiant one drink the great Soma-made mead' is the strophe triplet,[1] containing in 'All radiant, brilliant, great, the sun to see' (the words) 'apart (*vi*)', 'radiance', and 'sun'; this is a symbol of this day. 'The sun hath loosened apart his car in the middle of the sky' is the antistrophe,[2] containing (the words) 'apart' and 'sun'; the common metre is Jagatī, but the rule [3] is (the triplet) to Sūrya, 'For all love thee, of one mind, one countenance', with the symbol of the sun in 'Long living may we see, O sun'. 'Assuredly thou art great, O sun' is the Pragātha of the Sāman,[4] containing (the word) 'sun'; this is a symbol of this day. Here he recites the bases of the Bṛhat and the Rathantara; 'Indra hath knowledge for the hearing of this' is the beginning of the litany,[5] containing (the word) 'sun' in 'He is the lively pathmaker for the sun'; this is a symbol of this day, but the rule is (a verse[6]) to Sūrya, 'Be favourable to us with thine eye, favourable to us with the day', containing the symbol of the sun in 'Give us, O sun, this wealth varied.' 'Who alone is to be invoked by mortals' is (a hymn [7]) in Triṣṭubh, with the symbol 'The divine atmosphere thou didst make to shine.' So if they make the Mahādivākīrtya the Pṛṣṭha, but, if they perform the Bṛhat on its own basis, having recited the extension of the Bṛhat, he recites the basis of the Rathantara [8]; 'Indra hath knowledge for the hearing of this' is the beginning of the litany,[9] containing (the word) 'sun' in 'He is the lively pathmaker for the sun'; this is a symbol of this day.

xxv. 6. 'As the sky surpasseth the earth, O Indra, that which our foes' is (the hymn) [1] in Triṣṭubh, containing (the word) 'sun' in 'Indra to Kutsa in the winning of the sun'; this is a symbol of this day. If they do not (perform it) on its own basis, 'Turning as it were to the sun' is the

[3] For the alternatives see ÇÇS. xi. 13. 23 *seq.* Those rejected are RV. i. 115. 1-3, 4, 5; vii. 62. 1 and viii. 101. 11, 12; vii. 66, 14, 15.

[1] RV. x. 170. 1-3; ÇÇS. xi. 13. 28.

[2] RV. x. 188. 3-5; ÇÇS. xi. 13. 28.

[3] RV. x. 37. 7-9; ÇÇS. xi. 13. 29 (merely *vā*).

[4] RV. viii. 101. 11; ÇÇS. xi. 13. 30.

[5] RV. x. 111. 3 (already cited in KB. xxv. 4); ÇÇS. xi. 14. 3.

[6] RV. x. 37. 10; ÇÇS. xi. 14, 4.

[7] RV. vi. 22; ÇÇS. xi. 14. 6, 7.

[8] See ÇÇS. xi. 13. 32.

[9] See KB. xxv. 4.

xxv. 6. [1] RV. vi. 30 (also cited in KB. xxvi. 16); ÇÇS. xi. 14. 5.

strophe,[2] containing (the word) 'sun'; this is a symbol of this day. 'If, O Indra, a hundred skies were thine' is the antistrophe,[3] containing (the word) 'sun' in 'a thousand suns'; this is the symbol of this day. 'Who most active, ever slayeth' is the Pragātha[4] of the Sāman, containing (the word) 'sun' in 'In bodies, in the waters, the sun'; this is a symbol of this day. Then he recites the bases of the Bṛhat and the Rathantara. 'Indra hath knowledge for the hearing of this' is the beginning of the litany;[5] the explanation of this has been given. 'Who alone is to be invoked by mortals' is (the hymn[6]) in Triṣṭubh; the explanation of this has been given. So now if they perform the Bṛhat on its own basis or on a different basis. If they perform without the two Sāmans, it is the same up to the beginning of the litany; he should take out the bases of the Bṛhat and the Rathantara. 'Praise him who hath might to overcome' is (the hymn[7]) in Triṣṭubh, with the symbol in 'Increase with praises the bull of mortals.' The next is the same. 'The ram, much invoked, worthy of praise' is (the hymn[8]) in Jagatī, containing (the word) 'sun' in 'Thou didst indeed mount the sun in heaven to see'; this is a symbol of this day. Both sets, Triṣṭubh and Jagatī, are recited; the sun here gives heat, resting established on the Triṣṭubh and the Jagatī; thus it openly they touch.

xxv. 7. 'I shall proclaim at the great assembly thy two bays', having recited nine verses of this (hymn[1]) and having uttered the call, he inserts a Nivid. It contains (the word) 'sun' in 'Reveal to the bright one, the sun';[2] this is a symbol of this day. He then recites four verses of the 'All-bay' hymn. 'May the true one come hither, the generous, he of the Soma lees' has twenty-one verses,[3] with the symbol (of this day) in 'What time at the dawn they made to shine the great light.' These make up twenty-five. 'To the all conquering, the booty conquering, the light conquering' is six Jagatī verses,[4] with the symbol (of this day) in 'To Indra the Soma, to him worthy of sacrifice the delightful.' These make up thirty-one. In these Jagatīs he performs the difficult mounting;[5] he who here

[2] RV. viii. 99. 3, 4; ÇÇS. xi. 13. 21. This explains above KB. xxv. 4.

[3] RV. viii. 70. 5, 6 (already cited in KB. xxii. 4); ÇÇS. xi. 13. 22.

[4] RV. vi. 46. 3, 4; ÇÇS. xi. 13. 31.

[5] RV. x. 118. 3; above KB. xxv. 4 and 5; ÇÇS. xi. 14. 3. For the two bases, see ÇÇS. xi. 13. 33.

[6] RV. vi. 22; above KB. xxv. 5; ÇÇS. xi. 14. 6.

[7] RV. vi. 18 (already cited in KB. xxiv. 2); ÇÇS. xi. 14. 8.

[8] RV. i. 51 (also cited in KB. xxvi. 9); ÇÇS. xi. 14. 9. For the six alternative ways see Ānartīya on ÇÇS. xi. 14. 2.

[1] RV. x. 96. 1–9; ÇÇS. xi. 14. 10.

[2] RV. x. 96. 11. He recites after the Nivid x. 96. 10–13, as usual with Nivids.

[3] RV. iv. 16; ÇÇS. xi. 16. 11.

[4] RV. ii. 21. 1–6 (also cited in KB. xxvi. 16); ÇÇS. xi. 14. 12.

[5] According to ÇÇS. xi. 14. 12–14 the *dūrohaṇa* is performed on RV. iv. 40. 5. Cf. AB. iv. 20, 21. The sense of *kevalīṁ sa āvapaḥ* is suggested by *anavānam* in ÇÇS. and by *kevalyā* in AB. iv. 21. 3.

gives heat is connected with the Jagatī, the difficult mounting is the sacrificers; verily thus the sacrificers mount him. By Padas he mounts first; thus they obtain this world; by half verses for the second time; thus they obtain the world of the atmosphere; by three Padas for the third time; thus they obtain yonder world; the entrance is by performance as one unit; then by three Padas, by half verses, by Padas (he descends); thus he rests in this world, on a support immovable. This difficult mounting verse being recited together makes up seven. These are thirty-eight in all. 'For his full oblations', (these) are six (verses) in Jagatī,[6] containing (the word) 'sun' in 'Indra it waiteth on as the sun on the dawn'; this is a symbol of this day. These make up forty-four. 'The bird anointed by the craft of the Asura', (these) are three (verses [7]), with the symbol (of this day) in 'This radiant sun-like prayer'. These are forty-seven. With the concluding verse [8] thrice repeated, 'Lead us to a wide space, wise one', with the symbol (of this day) in 'The heaven, the light, freedom from danger', they make up fifty. Those preceding are fifty-one; they make up a hundred and one verses; man has a hundred (years of life), a hundred forms, a hundred strengths, a hundred powers; the hundred and first verse over is the world of the sacrificer; thus here they make ready the sacrificers; thus here having made ready the sacrificers at the beginning, he propagates them with the Mahāvrata day. So the total as made up by Paiṅgya.[9]

xxv. 8. Then (the computation) of Kauṣītaki. It is the same up to the beginning of the litany. If one removes the Bṛhat and the Rathantara, the Ṛjujanitrīya [1] (is used); eleven (verses) of it (are used, if the Bṛhat is performed) on its own basis, nine otherwise, with the symbol (of this day) in 'Now allotting the forms, now the works one goeth.'[2] 'O Indra, come hither with thy bays', (these) are fifteen verses,[3] with the symbol (of this day) in 'With those of fair form do thou come to us'. Having recited eleven (verses) of (the hymn of) Baru [4] or of the 'All-bay' hymn,[5] (he recites) a Nivid in the middle of the hundred and one verses; having recited fifty-one he recites the two (remaining verses) of the Baru (hymn) or of the 'All-bay' (hymn). 'May the true one come hither, the generous, he of the Soma lees', (these) are twenty-one verses.[6] These make up

[6] RV. i. 56.

[7] RV. x. 188 (already cited in KB. viii. 4); ÇÇS. xi. 14. 17.

[8] RV. vi. 47. 8 (also cited in KB. xxv. 8; xxix. 4); ÇÇS. xi. 14. 6.

[9] ÇÇS. xi. 14. 19.

[1] I. e. RV. ii. 13. The reading above *Kauṣītakeḥ* of M is needless, and its insertion of *trayodaçarcam* here is a sign of its tendency to interpolate, just as with *Tārkṣyaḥ* below. Lindner needlessly queries *okthamukhīyāyā*.

[2] RV. ii. 13. 3: the sense is speculative; see ÇÇS. xi. 14. 22–24.

[3] RV. viii. 34. 1–15; ÇÇS. xi. 14. 25.

[4] RV. x. 96 (cited by Pratīka in KB. xxv. 7); ÇÇS. xi. 14. 26.

[5] RV. x. 96, a variant name from its content.

[6] RV. iv. 16 (already cited in KB. xxv. 7); ÇÇS. xi. 14. 11.

twenty-three. 'To the all-conquering', (these) are six verses.[7] These make up twenty-nine. The 'difficult mounting' verses are seven. These make up thirty-six. 'Thou art alone the lord of wealth' is a Triṣṭubh (hymn) of five verses,[8] containing (the word) 'sun' in 'Thou didst destroy at the rising of the sun';[9] this is a symbol of this day. These make up forty-one. 'This strong one, god speeded', (these) are three (verses),[10] with the symbol (of this day) in 'As the sun with light, he hath stretched out the waters'. These make up forty-four. The bird (hymn[11]) is three (verses); these make up forty-seven. 'Lead us to wide space, wise one', with this concluding verse thrice repeated, they make up fifty; the preceding are fifty-one. They make up a hundred and one verses; the explanation of these has been given.

xxv. 9. 'That of Savitṛ we choose' and 'To-day for us, O god Savitṛ' are the normal strophe and antistrophe[1] of the Vaiçvadeva; the explanation of these two has been given. 'They yoke their minds, they also yoke their thoughts' is (the hymn[2]) to Savitṛ, containing (the word) 'sun' in 'Thou dost shine forth with the rays of the sun'; this is a symbol of this day. 'They two, sky and earth, all weal producing' is (the hymn) to sky and earth,[3] containing (the word) 'sun' in 'The god, the bright sun, between the goddesses in accord with law'; this is a symbol of this day. 'Why hath the best, the youngest come to us?' is (the hymn) to the Ṛbhus[4] with the symbol (of the day) in 'He discerned' in 'What time he discerned the four beakers they had made.' 'I hail the gods of great fame, for security' is (the hymn) for the All-gods,[5] containing (the words) 'sun' and 'light' in 'Those who obtained a share of the light of the sun'; this is a symbol of this day. 'To Vaiçvānara, the praise, increasing holy order' is (the hymn) for Vaiçvānara,[6] containing (the words) 'shining', 'radiance', and 'light' in 'Shining with radiance, with light in greatness';[7] this is a symbol of this day. 'Forward the Maruts, devoted, with gleaming lances' is (the hymn) to the Maruts,[8] containing (the word) 'sun' in 'The shining rays of the sun';

[7] RV. ii. 21 (already cited in KB. xxv. 7); ÇÇS. xi. 14. 12.

[8] RV. vi. 31 (already cited in KB. xxiii. 2); ÇÇS. xi. 14. 27.

[9] RV. vi. 31. 3: sense conjectural, *daça* being unintelligible as it stands.

[10] RV. x. 178; ÇÇS. xi. 14. 28.

[11] RV. x. 177: Lindner's conjecture *patañgam iti* is quite needless in view of the frequent formation of names like *patañga*, seen also in ÇÇS. xi. 14. 28.

[1] RV. v. 82. 1 (already cited in KB. xvi. 3) and 4 (already cited in KB. xix. 9); ÇÇS. xi. 14. 30.

[2] RV. v. 81 (already cited in KB. xx. 2); ÇÇS. xi. 14. 30.

[3] RV. i. 160; ÇÇS. xi. 14. 31; x. 3. 14.

[4] RV. i. 161 (already cited in KB. xix. 9); ÇÇS. xi. 14. 32; x. 8. 13.

[5] RV. x. 66 (already cited in KB. xx. 3); ÇÇS. xi. 14. 33.

[6] RV. iii. 2 (already cited in KB. xix. 9); ÇÇS. xi. 14. 34; x. 4. 15.

[7] RV. iii. 2. 9.

[8] RV. v. 55 (already cited in KB. xxiii. 8); ÇÇS. xi. 14. 32; x. 8. 15.

this is a symbol of this day. 'To him who sitteth on the altar, with a dear abode, of fair radiance' is (the hymn) to Jātavedas,[9] with the symbol (of this day) in 'The light, the car, of bright hue destroying the darkness.' These are the hymns of the Āgnimāruta (Çastra). These are the hymns of this day. It is an Agniṣṭoma. The Agniṣṭoma is light; he who here gives heat is light; verily thus they make light successful with light; immortality they obtain who perform the Viṣuvant day.

xxv. 10. Before the setting of the sun should they seek to complete (the rite of) this day; the day has its morning litany, to be recited by day. They should seek to complete with this day including its morning litany and the offerings to the wives (with the gods) before the setting of the sun. 'Agni, I deem father, Agni friend', with this (verse[1]) the Hotṛ begins the morning litany on this day, with the symbol of the 'rich waters' verse[2] in 'friend (*āpim*)'. It contains (the word) 'sun' in 'In the sky the bright, worthy of sacrifice, of the sun'; this is a symbol of this day. As to this Kauṣītaki used to say,[3] 'The morning litany is Prajāpati, and is not connected with the darkness; verily in due order should he commence it; that is its prosperity; so in due order are offered the Upāṅçu and the Antaryāma (cups); that is their prosperity.' The Āprī hymn[4] is by Vasiṣṭha, containing (the word) 'sun' in 'Overspread thyself with the rays of the sun'; this is a symbol of this day. 'The Hotṛ for this day should be white, with red eyes' some say; with this day they seek to obtain him who yonder gives heat; this is as if one should approach a superior with a gift.[5] But the rule is 'Just as it may happen to be'. With the Çastra alone should he seek to produce the symbol of this day.[6] A victim to the sun should be offered (in addition) to the usual victim for the pressing. It is offered inaudibly; if a man should utter aloud (the recitation) for it, then if one were to say of him, 'He will become afflicted with skin disease, a leper'[7] it would be so. Four victims only are offered inaudibly; that to the sun, that to Savitṛ, that to Prajāpati, and that whose divinity is speech; the others are offered aloud. Then they perform three Svarasāman (days) reversed; the explanation of these has been given.

[9] RV. i. 140; ÇÇS. xi. 14. 86.

[1] RV. x. 7. 3–5; ÇÇS. xi. 13. 5.

[2] RV. x. 30. 12; as in the normal form, ÇÇS. vi. 8. 11.

[3] The point seems to be that the observance of this order is the really important thing: *tamasaḥ* or *tamase* may be meant.

[4] RV. vii. 2; ÇÇS. xi. 13. 7.

[5] *āharan* in having white and red, both sun symbols.

[6] M has *saṁpādayiṣyaḥ* (*saṁpādayiṣeyuḥ*), but it is a marvellous form, like *saṁsthāpayiṣyuḥ* above, and not necessary.

[7] *kilāsī* is enough as in MK; *kilāsīt* is simply an obvious error, and *kilāsīti* of Lindner is a mistaken conjecture. *bhaviṣyasīti* of the Ānand. ed., L, and the comm. is another easy blunder, but against the regular usage of KB. It is most improbable that in *kilāsīt* we can see the particle *id*: *kilāsī*, a rare word, was thought of as *kila āsīt*.

The Viçvajit.

xxv. 11. They obtain this thirteenth month in that they perform the Viçvajit; the thirteenth month is as great as the year; here verily the whole year is made up. Of it they say 'The six-day (rite) is the one-day (rite)', for whatever is done each day in the six-day (rite) that is done on the one-day (rite), the Viçvajit. Much and varied is done on the Viçvajit, in that all the Pṛṣṭhas, and all the various Stomas are together put in it. Its Pṛṣṭha is openly the Vairāja, the Rathantara at the midday Pavamāna, the Bṛhat at the third Pavamāna is performed, the Çākvara as the Maitrāvaruṇa's, the Vairūpa as the Brāhmaṇācchaṅsin's, the Raivata as the Achāvāka's. They obtain this thirteenth supernumerary month, for that is thirteenth, as they perform the Pṛṣṭhas; 'Agni men with praise from the fire sticks' is the Ājya[1] of this (day) in Virāj verses; the explanation of this has been given. The Praüga is by Madhuchandas; the explanation of this has been given. 'Thee like a car for aid' is the strophe of the Marutvatīya;[2] 'This drink, O bright one, is pressed' is the antistrophe.[3] This is the normal one-day form; the explanation of it has been given. 'With what array, of one age, of one home? is the Marutvatīya;[4] the 'What array' hymn contains the word 'who'; the Viçvajit as Prajāpati is 'Who'.[5] The strophe and antistrophe of the Vairāja are the strophe and antistrophe; in them he inserts a repeated *o* just as yonder in the fourth day (rite);[6] for as it is in Virāj it is not the place to omit the repetition of *o*; then there is the inserted verse, then the Pragātha in which Indra is attained; then he recites the bases of the Bṛhat and the Rathantara. 'That was the best in the worlds' is the Niṣkevalya;[7] the sacrifice is the best in the worlds; the Viçvajit as Prajāpati is the sacrifice. Then, if[8] the third pressing of the sixth day is the third pressing, (it is because) the sixth day is connected with Prajāpati, the Viçvajit is Prajāpati. The strophe is from the one-day (rite); the Viçvajit is a one-day (rite); the one-day (rite) is a support; verily (it serves) for support. The antistrophe contains the word 'towards'; the explanation of this has been given.

xxv. 12. They say 'Why in the Viçvajit with all the Stomas as a one-

[1] RV. vii. 1 (already cited in KB. xxii. 7); ÇÇS. xi. 15. 2.

[2] RV. viii. 68. 1–3 (already cited in KB. xv. 2).

[3] RV. viii. 2. 1–3 (already cited in KB. xv. 2).

[4] RV. i. 165 (already cited in KB. xix. 9).

[5] *viçvajit* is uncertain in sense; it may be a noun and subject, or an adj. Cf. for the first interpretation ÇÇS. xv. 2. 10, 13, 20.

[6] See above KB. xxii. 8.

[7] RV. x. 120 (already cited in KB. xix. 9).

[8] *yadi* is unnatural: *yad* would be adequate.

xxv. 12. [1] I.e. as in AB. vi. 30, 31 the two Viçvajits are distinguished.

day rite are the Çilpas[2] recited at the third pressing? Why (in it) as an Agniṣṭoma at the midday pressing?' The Çilpas are the lower breaths; the sacrifice is man; the morning pressing is the upper breaths; the midday is the body; the third pressing the lower; these are the Çilpas; therefore the Çilpas are performed at the third pressing, for this is their abode. Then why are the Çilpas recited at the midday pressing in the Viçvajit as an Agniṣṭoma in a year-long sacrificial session? The Pṛṣṭhas are the body; the Çilpas are the breaths; the breaths are not known without the body, nor without the breaths the body; assuredly the two are not severable. Therefore are the Çilpas recited at the midday pressing in the Viçvajit as an Agniṣṭoma, (for they think) 'Let me not separate the body from the breaths.' Moreover, the Viçvajit is Prajāpati; as Prajāpati the Viçvajit[3] is all; therefore all the Pṛṣṭhas are performed, all the Çilpas; the Viçvajit as Prajāpati is all; with all he obtains all he who knows thus.

xxv. 13. In the Āgnimāruta (Çastra) the Hotṛ having recited the Rudra verse, recites the Evayāmarut hymn[1] in Pañkti form; the sacrifice is fivefold; verily (it serves) to obtain the sacrifice. 'Let me not,' (he thinks), 'obstract the Çilpa of the Achāvāka.' Moreover Rudra is the oldest and best of the gods, the Atichandas of metres, the Viçvajit of one-day rites. Thus he makes it successful with its own symbol. At three verses of it should he repeat *o*;[2] if he desire to repeat *o* he should do it at all. The repetition of *o* is food; the breaths are food; the Çilpas are the breaths; verily thus he places the breath in the breaths. Moreover by the Viçvajit Prajāpati propagated all offspring, and conquered all. Thus is it the Viçvajit. Now is he born who sacrifices with the Viçvajit; therefore does he repeat *o*. Stumbling[3] as it were does he move as he seeks to walk for the first time. Thus him from the immortal metre he propagates to immortality. They obtain immortality who perform the Viçvajit.

xxv. 14. The Viçvajit of the year-long session is composed as an Agniṣṭoma with all the Stomas and all the Pṛṣṭhas; the Agniṣṭoma is a support; verily (it serves) for support. If the Viçvajit is a one-day (rite), or the middle day of a night session,[1] it should be an Atirātra. The Atirātra is the complete Viçvajit; half of the Viçvajit is performed by day, half by night. The (Viçvajit), which is performed apart from a case

[2] The Çilpas are correctly given by ÇÇS. xii. 8. 1 *seq.* in the Hotrakas' portion of his work.

[3] See KB. xxv. 12, n. 5.

[1] RV. v. 87; ÇÇS. xi. 15. 10. *Cf.* KB. xvi. 7.

[2] ÇÇS. xi. 15. 11–13 gives these alternatives, as Jagatī without Nyūñkha, as Pañkti with or without. *dṛ* is unique, read perhaps *dhriyeta*.

[3] The term recurs in KB. xxv. 8 and is unique.

xxv. 14. [1] See ÇÇS. xiii. 13. 1, 2 for the *ekāha*, and 14. 9 (ĀÇS. xi. 6) for the Rātrisattras (12–24 days).

when all one's property is given or a session, is one which brings all ruin. It is a loss of all if a man gives all[2] without a Viçvajit. If there is a Viçvajit (he should give) all; if (he gives) all, it (should be) a Viçvajit. 'If a man does not give all, saying "Let me give all," he prepares for himself a pitfall,[3] he comes to ruin,' he used to say. 'Or a thousand makes this up,' Kauṣītaki used to say, 'The thousand is all; the Viçvajit is all; by all may I obtain all,' (so thinking he gives a thousand).

xxv. 15. He should put round a calfskin; bare as it were becomes the body of him who gives all. (He puts round thinking) 'Cattle desire a calf; let cattle again desire me.' He should dwell in an Udumbara wood; the Udumbara is strength and proper food; (verily it serves) to obtain strength and proper food. He should dwell with a Naiṣāda; the Naiṣāda is the minimum of proper food; (verily it serves) to obtain the minimum of proper food. He should dwell with a Vaiçya; the Vaiçya prospers; (verily it serves) to obtain the proper food which is with a Vaiçya. He should dwell with a Kṣatriya; the Kṣatriya is the maximum of proper food; (verily it serves) to obtain the maximum of proper food. He should dwell with a Brahman of the same family, to obtain the proper food which is with a Brahman of the same family. For a year should he wander, lying on the ground, accepting only uncultivated (fruits),[1] not asking for food, clothed in what is given. With that he clothes himself. 'Having done this for twelve nights he may devote himself to another desire,' Kauṣītaki used to say, 'the year has twelve months, this is an image of the year.' The Ājya (Çastras) of the Hotrakas are addressed to Prajāpati, as having no deity mentioned. The strophes[2] of this day (of these priests) are 'Do ye two aid us to terrestrial,' 'They yoke the tawny ruddy one,' and 'Them they ever praise' or 'Praise him who with his light.' The strophes of the sixth day they should make the antistrophes; the sixth day is connected with Prajāpati; the other five are Prajāpati as the Viçvajit the litanies they conclude[3] with the ending sets of verses; the ending verses are a support; verily (they serve) for support.

[2] This seems the most reasonable sense if the reading is correct.

[3] As above in KB. xvi. 9.

[1] *aphālakṛṣṭāṅç ca pratigṛhṇan* is really 'not accepting what grows on ploughed land', a construction favoured in the Sūtra-period (Wackernagel, *Altind. Gramm.* II. i. 78). For Naiṣāda cf. *Vedic Index*, i. 458.

[2] RV. v. 68. 3–5; i. 6. 1–3; vii. 94. 5–7 or vi. 60. 10–12; see ÇÇS. xiii. 1. 3–5, with Ānartīya.

[3] Read *tad uktham* with M.

ADHYĀYA XXVI

The Soma Sacrifice (continued)

The Order of the Gavām Ayana.

xxvi. 1. The first month has thirty-two (days), the last thirty-two; the Anuṣṭubh has thirty-two syllables; the Anuṣṭubh is speech; thus with speech they advance, in speech they conclude. There are two months of twenty-eight days on both sides of the Viṣuvant (day); the Uṣṇih has twenty-eight syllables; the neck is connected with the Uṣṇih. Now the Viṣuvant is the head of the sacrifice; verily thus having produced a neck they fit the head upon it. They say 'Of which of the two sets of days is it (the head), of the previous or the subsequent?' 'Neither of the previous nor of the subsequent,' they say.[1] Of both sets of days is it (the head); both sets of days are its. They say 'How many sets of six days are in the year?' There are sixty six-day sets; thus the course of the year by six-day sets is unbroken. Those who yoke thus the days of the year, they attain those desires which are in the year. Those who yoke them otherwise than that, they attain not those desires which are in the year. Now some perform the months in the forward order only, and the days in the forward order, (saying) 'We are mounting the year in the forward direction in both ways.' 'The months alone should be reversed, not the days,' some (hold), saying 'The months are reversed in that this Pṛṣṭhya Ṣaḍaha comes round again from the back.' Others say 'The Trivṛt and the Trayastriṅça Stomas are characterized by being at a great distance; it is as if from a mountain peak one should fall into a pit;[2] that is a cleaving of the Stomas, therefore the days alone should be reversed, and not the months, to prevent cleaving of the Stomas.'[3]

xxvi. 2. Then (follows) the discussion of the Go and Āyus.[1] They should

[1] See ÇÇS. xiii. 19. 7 *seq.*

[2] M has *kartam* and °*skandeva* by haplology.

[3] *stomakṛntatāyai* will hardly do (cf. KB. xxviii. 4), as the normal dative of purpose is practically essential: perhaps *stomā*° or *astoma*° (cf. AB. v. 16) should stand. The days are, of course, the individual days (ÇÇS. xiii. 19. 12); the proximity is caused by a Pṛṣṭhya being now placed in the beginning of the second set of the months. The first normal day of the Pṛṣṭhya has the Trivṛt and the sixth the Trayastriṅça; see ÇÇS. x. 2. 1; 7. 1. But ÇÇS. xiii. 19. 12 and ĀÇS. xi. 7. 9 agree in inverting the days as well as the Ṣaḍahas; in xi. 7. 19, however, the two cases here given are mentioned.

xxvi. 2. [1] The Go and Āyus days precede the last ten days of the last month of the Sattra. They form also the second and third days of the normal Abhiplava Ṣaḍaha; see KB. xx. and xxi; ÇÇS. xi. 4. The order here is Āyus, then Go, hence *vihṛte*; see ÇÇS. xiii. 19. 16, which does not note the variant here in favour of the normal order as in ĀÇS. xi. 7. 11.

perform the Go and Āyus as inverted; the Go and Āyus are day and night; day and night are inverted towards each other; moreover the Go and Āyus are sky and earth; sky and earth are inverted towards each other; moreover the Go and Āyus are expiration and inspiration; expiration and inspiration, being inverted, find support in each other.[2] Some perform them in the forward order, saying 'The Go and Āyus should be performed in the forward direction; the Abhiplava Stomas are reversed, and the Pṛṣṭhya Stomas in the ten-night (period).' They say 'The Go and Āyus are the second and the third day.'

Expiations of Errors.

xxvi. 3. Now[1] they discuss (this question), 'Supposing some one in carelessness makes a blunder in a Çastra or a recitation or if there is doubt, should one, thinking that the error has passed unnoticed[2], mentally considering the (place of) occurrence, having gone back and remedied the error, proceed immediately from the (place of) occurrence (of the error)?' Now Paiñgya used to say 'Superfluous would be a Mantra repeated twice when not prescribed; therefore he should not proceed immediately.' So used Paiñgya to say. Now Kauṣītaki used to say 'These rites in which the number of Mantras employed is limited have limited fruits. Those in which an unlimited number of Mantras is employed have unlimited fruits; the unlimited is mind; mind is Prajāpati, Prajāpati is the sacrifice; the sacrifice rejoices in the sacrifice itself as mind in mind; therefore should he proceed immediately.' So used Kauṣītaki to say.[3] 'By the limited he conquers the limited, the unlimited by the unlimited; (it serves) for the winning of the unlimited; in that there is no flaw', so used Kauṣītaki to say. He should not offer a libation. So the sacrificer obtains the worlds of heaven, all desires, all attainments, and all immortality, and acquires the pre-eminence, rule, and overlordship of all creatures, for whom it is done thus.

xxvi. 4. 'Now if after the conclusion or after the Praṇava or *vaṣaṭ* call of the invitatory and offering verses, (an error) is perceived, by that time the flaw has been passed over',[1] Prāgahi used to say. 'Therefore the priest in

[2] The Ānand. ed. has *vikṛte* and *pratyatiṣṭhata*.

[1] There is no real parallel in AB. v. 32–34 which deals with the Brahman's part as correcting errors (cf. ÇÇS. iii. 21), nor, what is more noteworthy, is there any parallel in ÇÇS. The exact sense of the passage is not certain as *ānantaryātprayogaḥ* is not unambiguous and may have the sense of necessity rather than immediacy.

[2] *abuddham* may refer to the case of *vicikitsā* and be a subject; or it may be object—'passed unnoticed'.

[3] LK and the Ānand. ed. insert *Paiñgyo 'tha ha smāha*, which will not do.

xxvi. 4. [1] This sense seems required to explain

the Sadas should not call attention to a flaw passed over at this time', Paiñgya used to say; 'he knocks into a pillar or falls into a pit or is put into one or perishes', he used to say. 'If the priest in the Sadas should call attention to a flaw passed over, there must not be repetition of what has been done,' Āruṇi used to say; 'There is loss of a secondary element,' said Çvetaketu.[2] 'Therefore the priest in the Sadas should not call attention to a flaw passed over,' Paiñgya used to say. 'It is a tribulation to the sacrifice if the priest in the Sadas calls attention to a flaw passed over'. 'Therefore the priest in the Sadas should not call attention to a flaw passed over,' Paiñgya used to say.[3]

xxvi. 5. Further he used to say[1] this. Daivodāsi Pratardana having gone to a sacrificial season of the Naimiṣīyas and having glided up asked a question on this point of doubt, 'If the priest in the Sadas should call attention to a flaw passed over or any one of the priests should note it, how would you remove the flaw?' They were silent; Alīkayu Vācaspata was their Brahman priest; he said 'I know that not; but will ask Jātūkarṇya,[2] the aged teacher of those formerly.' Him he asked, 'If the performer himself should note a flaw passed over or another should call attention to it, how is that flaw to be made flawless? By repetition of the Mantra or by an oblation?' 'The Mantra should be recited again', Jātūkarṇya said. Him Alīkayu again asked, 'Should one recite in full the Çastra or recitation or Nigada or offering verse or whatever else it be?' 'So much as is erroneous only need be repeated, a verse, or half verse, or quarter verse, or word, or letter,' Jātūkarṇya replied. But Kauṣītaki used to say,[3] 'He should not repeat the Mantra, nor offer a libation; there is no flaw', for, whatever flaw the Hotṛs make in the sacrifice through inattention, all that Agni as divine Hotṛ makes flawless. This is declared in a Ṛc,

xxvi. 6. 'If that in poverty of mind, with feeble intellect,

the reason for neglecting the flaw, the view of Paiñgya. The alternative is to take the statement of Prāgahi as laying down the problem only, *bhavanti* thus going with *budhyeta* (which is of active sense). The comm. supplies *prāyaçcittāhutiḥ*.

[2] It is noteworthy that Çvetaketu appears in close contact with Jātūkarṇya in ÇÇS. xvi. 29. 6, where his father and he are mentioned. *guṇalopa* is late.

[3] LK. and the Ānand. ed. add *haika āhus* before *tasmāt*, and this is slightly better sense. The chapter, however, like KB. xxvi. 5, is probably confused in text.

[1] Presumably Paiñgya's view is meant, as at the end. For the Sadasya cf. ÇÇS. v. 1. 8 with comm.; ĀGS. i. 23. 5; Weber, *Ind. Stud.* x. 144. The use of this priest is condemned in ÇB. xii. 4. 1. 19.

[2] Jātūkarṇya appears in a similar light in ÇÇS. iii. 20. 19, and is mentioned in i. 2. 17; iii. 16. 14. He became Purohita of the Kāçyas, Videhas, and Kausalyas, xvi. 29. 5; he was envied by Çvetaketu. For Pratardana see *Vedic Index*, ii. 29, 30.

[3] Cf. KB. xxvi. 2, where the correction is done, not merely *manasā*, as it seems, but also by actual repetition.

Men think not of the sacrifice,
Then Agni the Hotṛ skilled in the offering, well knowing,
Most skilled to offer, to the gods shall offer in due season.'[1]

In that also, when the sacrifice is completed, he says 'The All-knower hath offered the sacrifice,'[2] he says 'The All-knower hath offered this sacrifice.' In that he says 'Having sat down before us,' he says 'Agni, as divine Hotṛ, having sat down before the human Hotṛ sacrifices.' Verily with the second half verse or[3] the first verse he utters a benediction.

The Chandomas.

xxvi. 7. On[1] the sixth day the gods obtained the Stomas and the months; having obtained these Stomas they compressed these same Stomas in couples, being the Stomas of the Pṛṣṭhya, for whence could they have obtained another Stoma? The Trivṛt and the Pañcadaça Stomas becoming the Caturvinça Stoma support the seventh day; the Saptadaça and the Triṇava Stomas, becoming the Catuçcatvārinça Stoma, support the eighth day; the Ekavinça and the Trayastrinça Stomas, becoming the Aṣṭācatvārinça Stoma, support the ninth day. Of them the first is measured by the Gāyatrī, the second by the Triṣṭubh, the third by the Jagatī; in that they are measured by the metres, therefore are they Chandomas. The six Stotriyā verses which are over the Aṣṭācatvārinça Stoma, these they call the seasons; the seasons are six; by these the tenth day is performed.

xxvi. 8. The sixth day is the end; the seventh day is a repeated extension (of the rite); therefore on the seventh day are recited hymns containing the word 'extend', and with the symbols of the introductory (rite), for the seventh day is a second introduction. 'Forward to the pure radiance do ye bear' is the Ājya,[1] containing (the word) 'forward'; that which contains (the word) 'forward' is a symbol of the first day. 'Forward to you, the pure, are offered boldly' is (the triplet) to Vāyu,[2] containing (the word) 'forward'; that which contains 'forward' is a symbol of the first day. The next triplet is addressed to Mitra and Vāyu,[3] 'They perceiving with true mind'; it contains (the word) 'yoke' in 'Yoked with their own insight they bear'; that which contains (the word) 'yoke' is a symbol of the first day. 'Up the eye of you two, O Varuṇa, fair of aspect' is (the triplet)

[1] RV. x. 2. 5.

[2] This and the next line occur in ÇÇS, i. 15. 17; ĀpÇS. iii. 18. 1; KÇS. ii. 2. 38, but not in this connexion, though in an

[3] The Ānand. ed. has *carā*.

analogous way. *aśman*, a *v. l.* in O and comm., is clearly right.

xxvi. 7. [1] For the Chandomas see AB. v. 16–21. For the ritual see ÇÇS. x. 9–11.

xxvi. 8. [1] RV. vii. 4 (already cited in KB. xii. 7); ÇÇS. x. 9. 2

[2] RV. vii. 90. 1–3; see ÇÇS. x. 9. 3, 4 for this and nn. 3–8.

[3] RV. vii. 90. 4–6.

to Mitra and Varuṇa [4]; containing (the word) 'extend' in 'The sun goeth, extending of the pious one'; that which contains (the word) 'extend' is a symbol of the seventh day. 'Hither, O Nāsatyas, with chariot rich in cattle' [5], 'Come hither to us, O impetuous god, with might,' [6] 'Forward to you in the sacrifices the pious have sung,' [7] and 'Forward she hath come forth with fostering current' [8] (are the other triplets); the symbols of the introductory (day) are (the words) 'hither' or 'forward'; therefore on the seventh day are recited hymns containing (the words) 'hither' and 'forward' with the symbols of the introductory (day), for the seventh day is a second introduction. They say 'Whatever metre may be used in the morning pressing, the recitation of it is by half verses, with the symbol of the Gāyatrī, and thus moreover with the symbol of the morning pressing.' But as to this Kauṣītaki used to say, 'The Triṣṭubh and Jagatī are not suitable to be recited [9] by half verses; even if they be employed at the morning pressing, they are to be recited by Padas only.' So is the rule. The Pṛṣṭha is the Bṛhat and the Çastra is connected with the Rathantara; this is a pairing, a symbol of generation. The strophes and antistrophes of the Marutvatīyas and (the Pragāthas) to Brahmaṇaspati are in accord with the form of the third day (rite); the explanation of these has been given.

xxvi. 9. 'With what array, of one age, of one home?' is the Marutvatīya [1]; that is called the 'prosperity hymn'. With it Indra and the Maruts came to an accord. The pre-eminence of him who knows thus men accept. It contains (the word) 'hither' in 'With what mind have they come hither, and whence?', and is connected with the Rathantara. 'That ram that winneth the light I glorify' is a Jagatī,[2] containing (the word) 'hither' in 'Hither Indra would I turn for aid with good offerings', and is connected with the Rathantara. They say, 'Seeing that the Rathantara is normally the Pṛṣṭha of the seventh day, then why is the Bṛhat performed daily?' These days have great Stomas; therefore daily is the Bṛhat performed, to confer equality of might on these days, to secure inequality of might of these Stomas.[3] Having recited the extension of the Bṛhat he recites the basis of the Rathantara. 'Our father did not teach us any recitation [4] of the basis; each stood alone', Kauṣītaki used to say, 'But whenever the Sāmans fall together on the same day then he should recite also the basis of the one or the other'.

[4] RV. vii. 61. 1–3 (already cited in KB. xxv. 2).

[5] RV. vii. 72. 1–3 (already cited in KB. xxv. 2).

[6] RV. vii. 30. 1–3 (already cited in KB. xxv. 2).

[7] RV. vii. 48. 1–3.

[8] RV. vii. 95. 1–3 (also cited in KB. xxvi. 15).

[9] *staisthāne* hardly means 'in that place', but is comparable with the use in AB. vi. 5.

RV. i. 165 (already cited in KB. xix. 9); ÇÇS. x. 9. 12.

[2] RV. i. 52 (already cited in KB. xxv. 3); ÇÇS. x. 9. 12.

[3] M has *chandomānām*, but this is not essentially required. *asamabalatāyan* is strange.

[4] For the mode of *anuçaṅsana* see ÇÇS. vii. 21. 1–5; x. 9. 14. The sense seems as given, but the text looks corrupt.

'But, if they use the Rathantara of Kaṇva,[5] then he should not recite also the basis, for the basis of other Pṛṣṭhas is not to be recited', Kauṣītaki used to say. 'Praise him who hath might to overcome', and 'Towards this ram much invoked, worthy of praise' are hymns[6] in Triṣṭubh and Jagatī, both containing (the word) 'towards'; this is a symbol of the Rathantara. Two hymns each are recited in the Niṣkevalya and the Marutvatīya of the first Chandoma; the sacrificer has two feet; (they serve) for support. They make up four; the Chandomas are cattle; cattle are fourfold; moreover, they are four-footed; (they serve) for the obtaining of cattle.

xxvi. 10. 'That desirable of Savitṛ' is (the triplet) to Savitṛ,[1] containing (the word) 'forward' in 'May he forward our prayers'; that which contains (the word) 'forward' is a symbol of the first day. 'Let the two come forward with weal for the sacrifice' is (the triplet) to sky and earth,[2] containing (the word) 'forward'; that which contains (the word) 'forward' is a symbol of the first day. 'This to the race divine' is (the triplet) to the Ṛbhus,[3] containing (the word) 'hither' in 'The hymn by the sages with their mouth (*āsayā*)'; that which contains (the word) 'hither' is a symbol of the first day. 'With straight leading for us, O Varuṇa' is a five-verse (hymn) to the All-gods,[4] containing (the word) 'lead'; that which contains (the word) 'lead' is a symbol of the seventh day. 'Come hither with thy beauty' is (a hymn) in verses of two Padas[5]; it contains (the word) 'hither'; that which contains (the word) 'hither' is a symbol of the first day. 'Dread, supporting the people' is (the hymn) to the All-gods,[6] containing (the word) 'hither' in 'O ye All-gods, come hither'; that which contains (the word) 'hither' is a symbol of the first day. It is in Gāyatrī, for this set of three days has the Gāyatrī at the third pressing. 'Vaiçvānara to our aid' is (the hymn) to Vaiçvānara;[7] containing (the word) 'hither' in 'Hither, hither come forward from afar'; that which contains (the word) 'hither' is a symbol of the first day. 'Forward to you the Triṣṭubh, food' is (the hymn) to the Maruts,[8] containing (the word) 'forward'; that which contains (the word) 'forward' is a symbol of the first day. 'Singing, thee we invoke' is (the hymn) to Jātavedas,[9] containing (the words) 'extend' in 'With thee they extend the sacrifice'; that which contains (the word)

[5] The Ānand. ed. has absurdly *yady uka eva*. For the Kaṇvarathantara see *Ind. Stud.* iii. 212; PB. xiv. 3. 15; xviii. 4. 7, 9.

[6] RV. vi. 18 (already cited in KB. xxiv. 2) and i. 51 (already cited in KB. xxv. 6); ÇÇS. x. 9. 18.

[1] RV. iii. 62. 10-12 (already cited in KB. xxiii. 3); ÇÇS. x. 9. 16.

[2] RV. ii. 41. 19-21 (already cited in KB. ix. 3); ÇÇS. x. 9. 16.

[3] RV. i. 20. 1-8; ÇÇS. x. 9. 16.

[4] RV. i. 90. 1-5; ÇÇS. x. 9. 16.

[5] RV. x. 172; ÇÇS. x. 9. 16.

[6] RV. i. 3. 7-9; ÇÇS. x. 9. 16.

[7] See ÇÇS. ii. 5. 3; AV. vi. 35. 1; ÇÇS. x. 9. 17.

[8] RV. viii. 7. 1-15 or 1-9 (ÇÇS. x. 9. 17).

[9] RV. v. 13; ÇÇS. x. 9. 17.

'extend' is a symbol of the seventh day. It is in Gāyatrī, for this set of three days has the Gāyatrī at the third pressing. These are the hymns of the Āgnimāruta. These are the hymns of this day. It is an Ukthya. It obtains what the first day obtains.

xxvi. 11. The first Chandoma is this world, the second the world of the atmosphere, the last yonder world; therefore on the middle day are recited hymns containing (the word) 'great', for the atmosphere is great. 'Moreover, they should contain (the word) "begun"; verily thus he refers to the next day, verily thus they keep taking hold of the next day', Kauṣītaki used to say. 'Agni for you the god, in unison with the flames' is the Ājya;[1] in 'When he hath stood out from the great enclosure' it contains (the word) 'great' and also contains (the idea) 'begun'. 'Were not they who were made great with homage?' is (the triplet) to Vāyu,[2] containing (the word) 'great'; that which contains (the words) 'made great' contains (the word) 'great', for this day contains (the word) 'great'. The following triplet [3] is addressed to Indra and Vāyu, 'So far as the power of the body, so far as the might', containing (the idea) 'begun' in 'So far as men can discern with the eye.' 'To you two at the rising of the sun with hymns' is (the triplet) to Mitra and Varuṇa,[4] containing (the word) 'great' in 'I invoke Mitra, Varuṇa of pure strength', and also (the idea) 'begun'. 'From her sister dawn night doth retreat' is (the triplet) to the Açvins,[5] containing (the word) 'great' in 'With great guerdon in horses, in cows, let us invoke you', and also (the idea) 'begun'. 'This Soma hath been pressed for you, O Indra' is (the triplet) to Indra,[6] containing (the idea) 'begun' in 'O Brahman, O hero, rejoicing in the making of prayer.' 'Let the Brahmans, the Aṅgirases, come forward' is (the triplet) to the All-gods,[7] containing the idea) 'begun' in 'Let the noise of the cloudy one have knowledge.' 'May Sarasvatī for us rejoicing' is (the triplet) to Sarasvatī[8] containing (the word) 'great' in 'make great' in 'Make great, O beauteous one, to thy praiser accord strength', for this day contains (the word) 'great'. The Pṛṣṭha is connected with the Rathantara, the Çastra with the Bṛhat; this is a pairing, a symbol of generation.

xxvi. 12. 'Great is Indra, manlike, spreading over mortals' is the first[1] of the Marutvatīyas in Triṣṭubh, containing (the word) 'great', for this day

[1] RV. vii. 8: *abhyārabdha* is nowhere found as word, but only as an idea, ÇÇS. x. 12. 2. Read *param svaitad* as in KB. xxii. 2.

[2] RV. vii. 91. 1–3 (already cited in KB. xxv. 2); ÇÇS. x. 10. 3, 4 for this and nn. 3–8.

[3] RV. vii. 91. 4–6 (already cited in KB. xxv. 2).

[4] RV. vii. 65. 1–3.

[5] RV. vii. 71. 1–3.

[6] RV. vii. 29. 1–3.

[7] RV. vii. 42. 1–3.

[8] RV. vii. 95. 4–6 (already cited in KB. xxv. 2).

xxvi. 12. [1] RV. vi. 19. 1–13 (already cited in KB. xxi. 4); ÇÇS. x. 10. 5.

contains (the word) 'great'. 'These thee of many a poet' is the second,[2] containing (the word) 'great' in 'Call thee that art to be invoked, O hero', and also (the idea) 'begun'. 'Where is this hero, who hath seen Indra?' is the third[3] containing (the word) 'great' in 'Going with the bays on a fair chariot', and also (the idea) 'begun'. 'Even from great, O Indra, thou those that approach' is the fourth,[4] containing (the word) 'great' in 'Even from great misfortune thou art the protector', and also (the idea) 'begun'. 'Him sky and earth of one mind' is the fifth[5] in Jagatī, containing (the word) 'great' in 'What time he went revealing greatness and power', and also (the idea) 'begun'. 'Thou art great, O Indra; to thee the earth' is the first[6] in Triṣṭubh of the Niṣkevalyas, containing (the word) 'great', for this day contains (the word) 'great'. 'Thou art great, O Indra, who by thy might' is the second,[7] containing (the word) 'great' and also (the idea) 'begun'. 'Many not of old to him' is the third,[8] containing (the word) 'great', in 'To the great, the hero, impetuous, eager', and also (the idea) 'begun'. 'This fame for thee, O bounteous one, through thy greatness' is the fourth,[9] containing (the word) 'great' and (the idea) 'begun'. 'This prayer to thee I offer, the great one' is the fifth in Jagatī,[10] containing (the word) 'great' and (the idea) 'begun'. Five hymns each are recited in the Niṣkevalya and the Marutvatīya in the middle Chandoma; the Chandomas are cattle; cattle are fivefold; verily (they serve) to obtain cattle.

xxvi. 13. 'The golden handed for aid' is (the hymn) to Savitṛ,[1] containing (the idea) 'begun' in 'The son of the waters for aid'. 'May the two great ones, sky and earth, for us' is (the triplet) to sky and earth,[2] containing (the word) 'great', for this day contains (the word) 'great'. 'Youthful the parents again' is (the triplet) to the Ṛbhus,[3] containing (the idea) 'begun' in 'With Indra with the Maruts and the Ādityas, the kings.' 'The great aid of the gods' is a nine-verse (hymn) to the All-gods.[4] In 'Favour be ours, O Aryaman, favour, O Varuṇa, to be celebrated', it contains (the word) 'great', and (the idea) 'begun'. 'These worlds let us subject' is a hymn in verses of two Padas,[5] containing (the idea) 'begun' in 'Indra and the All-gods'. 'All-gods increasing holy order' is (the hymn) to the All-gods,[6] containing

[2] RV. vi. 21 (already cited in KB. xx. 3); ÇÇS. x. 10. 5.
[3] RV. v. 30. 1-12 (already cited in KB. xxi. 3); ÇÇS. x. 10. 5.
[4] RV. i. 169; ÇÇS. x. 10. 5.
[5] RV. x. 113; ÇÇS. x. 10. 5.
[6] RV. iv. 17; ÇÇS. x. 10. 6.
[7] RV. i. 63; ÇÇS. x. 10. 6.
[8] RV. vi. 32; ÇÇS. x. 10. 6.
[9] RV. x. 54; ÇÇS. x. 10. 6.
[10] RV. i. 102; ÇÇS. x. 10. 6.
[1] RV. i. 22. 5-8; see ÇÇS. x. 10. 7.
[2] RV. i. 22. 13-15 (already cited in KB. xiii. 1); ÇÇS. x. 10. 7.
[3] RV. i. 20. 4-6; ÇÇS. x. 10. 7.
[4] RV. viii. 83; ÇÇS. x. 10. 7.
[5] RV. x. 157; ÇÇS. x. 10. 7.
[6] RV. vi. 52. 10-12; ÇÇS. x. 10. 7.

(the word) 'great' in the word 'increase', for this day contains (the word) 'great'. It is in Gāyatrī, for this set of three days has the Gāyatrī at the third pressing. 'Vaiçvānara hath produced' is (the hymn) to Vaiçvānara,[7] containing (the word) 'great' in 'waxing great' in 'Waxing great with might on the earth', for this day contains (the word) 'great'. 'What now, when as a dear?' is (the hymn) to the Maruts,[8] containing (the idea) 'begun'. 'The messenger of you, of all knowledge' is (the hymn) to Jātavedas.[9] Or 'O Agni, be merciful; thou art great', an eight-verse hymn for the eighth day,[10] but the former is the rule. It contains (the word) 'great' in 'He great the recess of the sky', for this day contains (the word) 'great'. It is in Gāyatrī, for this set of three days has the Gāyatrī at the third pressing. These are the hymns of the Āgnimāruta. These are the hymns of this day. It is an Ukthya. It obtains what the second day obtains.

xxvi. 14. Going is the end; so yonder sky, yonder world, and the ninth day; therefore at the ninth day are recited hymns containing (the word) 'go'. 'We have gone with great praise to the youngest' and 'Me, the strong, O Agni, of the Soma', these two (hymns) are the Ājya, containing (the word) 'go' in 'We have gone'; this is a symbol of the end; the ninth day is the end; he returns as it were, having gone to the end, for hence whitherward should he go? It contains (the word) 'stand' in 'Here stand the cows, fattening'; this is a symbol of the end; the ninth day is the end; having gone to the end, he stands as it were, for hence whitherward should he go? '"We have gone with great praise to the youngest", this triplet alone should form the Ājya,'[1] Paiñgya used to say. It contains (the word) 'go' in 'We have gone'; this is a symbol of the end; the ninth day is the end; he returns as it were, having gone to the end, for hence whitherward should he go? 'How can a triplet make up the Aṣṭācatvāriṅça Stoma?' Kauṣītaki used to say. 'Me the strong, O Agni, of the Soma'[2] he should also recite; this contains a symbol of ending in its reference to what has taken place; 'We have brought forward the sacrifice' and 'From the sky they have learned'[3] are regarding what has taken place as it were. 'Here however,[4] the Stoma is not pervaded' Paiñgya used to say, 'since by verses alone the Stoma cannot be pervaded'. 'The verse by means of syllables makes up the Stoma, with syllables the Nivid or Puroruc the verse; the Stoma is pervaded then when either a Nivid or a Puroruc is recited.

7 Given in full in ÇÇS. x. 10. 8.

8 RV. i. 38; ÇÇS. x. 10. 8.

9 RV. iv. 8; ÇÇS. x. 10. 8.

10 RV. iv. 9; ÇÇS. vi. 4. 1, who, however, does not even mention this as a variant here.

1 RV. vii. 121-3; ÇÇS. x. 11. 2, 3, which allows both or one.

2 RV. iii. 1.

3 RV. iii. 1. 2.

4 *nvā api* of M is clearly correct, *nvāpi* of the comm. and most MSS. (K has *nvābhi*, read also in the Ānand. ed.) being an obvious blunder.

Therefore[5] yonder triplet alone should be the Ājya' (they say). 'Yonder' is according to the order of Paiñgya.[6] But the rule is 'both'. By it Viçvāmitra and Vasiṣṭha came into accord; they grant accord to the pre-eminence of him who knows thus. Therefore should both be the Ājya, first that of Vasiṣṭha, then that of Viçvāmitra.

xxvi. 15. 'O Vāyu, come to us, drinker of the pure' is (the triplet) to Vāyu and to Indra and Vāyu,[1] containing (the word) 'go' in 'gone'[2]; this is a symbol of the end; the ninth day is the end; he returns as it were, being gone to the end, for hence whitherward should he go? In 'The lively pourer hath stood at the sacrifices',[3] it contains (the word) 'stand'; this is a symbol of the end; the ninth day is the end; having gone to the end, he stands as it were, for hence whitherward should he go? 'Dwelling in the sky, from the atmosphere, on the earth' is (the triplet[4]) to Mitra and Varuṇa, containing (the word) 'dwell' in 'dwelling'; this is a symbol of the end; the ninth day is the end; having gone to the end, he dwells as it were, for hence whitherward should he go? 'Come hither to us with all boons, O Açvins' is (the triplet) to the Açvins,[5] containing (the word) 'stand' in 'That standing place hath been proclaimed for you on earth'; this is a symbol of the end; the ninth day is the end; having gone to the end, he stands as it were, for hence whitherward should he go? 'Indra men invoke in the conflict' is (the triplet) to Indra;[6] 'That he may make our prayers effective', (in this) 'effective' denotes the highest; this is a symbol of the end; the ninth day is the end; in the end he places the end. 'Agni, erect, hath established the favour of the bright one' is (the triplet) to the All-gods,[7] containing (the word) 'establish'; this is a symbol of the end; the ninth day is the end; having gone to the end he establishes as it were, for hence whitherward should he go? 'Forward she hath come forth with fostering current' is (the triplet) to Sarasvatī.[8] In 'Forcing forward' there is repetition; the ninth day is the end; having gone to the end, he repeats as it were, for hence whitherward should he go? These are the Praügas by Vasiṣṭha, arranged in triplets; Vasiṣṭha is Prajāpati; he is the extender of

[5] M seems to have had, before *tṛcam*, *tasmād vyāpyata eva tasmād ada eva*, of which the second clause has dropped out. The first is not essential and may be a gloss.

[6] M has *vacased* for which *vacasa* may be an unusual Sandhi. The sense is apparently as rendered, in which case the previous clause can hardly be given to Paiñgya; but as they refer to the Tṛca he approves, *adas* becomes a suitable description. The Ānand. ed. has, absurdly, *varcasa*.

[1] RV. vii. 92. 1, 3, 5, according to ÇÇS. xii. 5, and vii. 92. 2. 4, and vii. 90. 5. See for the next nos. 2–8 ÇÇS. xii. 5.

[2] RV. vii. 92. 5.

[3] RV. vii. 92. 2.

[4] RV. vii. 64. 1–3.

[5] RV. vii. 70. 1-3.

[6] RV. vii. 27. 1-3.

[7] RV. vii. 39. 1–3.

[8] RV. vii. 95. 1-3 (already cited in KB. xxvi. 8).

the sacrifice; he is renewed at the repeated extension of the sacrifice; verily in Prajāpati they attain all their desires. The Pṛṣṭha is the Bṛhat, the Çastra connected with the Rathantara; this is a pairing, a symbol of generation.

xxvi. 16. 'Three friendships hath man's worship' is the first of the Marutvatīyas in Triṣṭubh,[1] containing (the word) 'three'; it is a symbol of the third day. 'Indra maketh for the car a way forward' is the second,[2] containing (the word) 'stand' in 'hath stood upon' in 'Which in strength the generous one hath stood upon'; this is a symbol of the end; the ninth day is the end; having gone to the end, he stands as it were, for hence whitherward should he go? 'Stand on the bays being yoked to the car' is the third,[3] containing (the word) 'stand' in 'stand'; this is a symbol of the end; the ninth day is the end; having gone to the end, he stands as it were, for hence whitherward should he go? 'Let him sing the Sāman springing forth as of a bird' is the fourth[4]; (the word) 'Sāman' is a symbol of yonder world. 'Sing ye forth to the glad one the song rich in food' is the fifth[5] in Jagatī; in that it has the same ending, it has the symbol of the end. 'May the true one come hither, the generous, he of the Soma lees' is the first of the Niṣkevalyas in Triṣṭubh.[6] There is repetition in 'Let loose, O hero'; the ninth day is the end; having gone to the end, he repeats as it were, for hence whitherward should he go? 'To him the strong, the impetuous' is the second,[7] having the same beginning in 'To him', and 'To him'; just as that which has the same ending, so that which has the same beginning is a symbol of the end. 'As the sky surpasseth the earth, O Indra, that which our foes' is the third[8]; (the word) 'sky' is a symbol of yonder world. 'That highest power of thine is on high' is the fourth[9]; there is repetition in 'highest on high'; the ninth day is the end; having gone to the end, he repeats as it were, for hence whitherward should he go? 'I was the first lord of wealth' and 'To the all conquering, the booty conquering, the light conquering' are two (hymns) in Jagatī[10]; in 'I' and 'I' there is the same beginning; just as that which has the same ending, so that which has the same beginning is a symbol of the end; in 'conquering' and 'conquering' there is repetition; the ninth day is the

[1] RV. v. 29 (already cited in KB. xxii. 4); ÇÇS. x. 11. 6.
[2] RV. v. 31 (already cited in KB. xx. 2); ÇÇS. x. 11. 6.
[3] RV. iii. 35 (already cited in KB. xx. 4); ÇÇS. x. 11. 6.
[4] RV. i. 173 (already cited in KB. xxiv. 5); ÇÇS. x. 11. 6.
[5] RV. i. 101; ÇÇS. x. 11. 6.
[6] RV. iv. 66 (already cited in KB. xxv. 7); ÇÇS. x. 11. 7.
[7] RV. i. 66; ÇÇS. x. 11. 7.
[8] RV. vi. 20 (already cited in KB. xxv. 6); ÇÇB. x. 11. 7.
[9] RV. i. 103; ÇÇS. x. 11. 7.
[10] RV. x. 48 (already cited in KB. xxii. 4) and ii. 21 (already cited in KB. xxv. 7); ÇÇS. x. 11. 7.

end; having gone to the end he repeats as it were; for hence whitherward should he go? In the Marutvatīya are recited five hymns in the last Chandoma; the Chandomas are cattle; cattle are fivefold; verily (they serve) to obtain cattle. Six at the end (are recited) in the Niṣkevalya; the year has six seasons; verily (they serve) to obtain the year.

xxvi. 17. 'Towards thee, O god Savitṛ' is (the triplet) to Savitṛ[1]; yonder world is turned towards (this) as it were; this is a symbol of yonder world. 'Forward towards you, mightily, sky and earth' is (the triplet) to sky and earth;[2] there is repetition in 'Mightily, sky and earth, towards'; the ninth day is the end; having gone to the end, he repeats as it were, for hence whitherward should he go? 'Let Indra give for food to us' is one (verse[3]); 'Give ye jewels' are two; these are (the triplet) to the Ṛbhus; there is repetition in 'one one' in 'Each one each one with wise direction'; the ninth day is the end; having gone to the end he repeats as it were, for hence whitherward should he go? Then the Vaiçvadeva is composed of the whole of Manu's (hymns[4]); Manu is life; verily thus he places life in the sacrifice and in the sacrificers. Here are (the verses) with two Padas; the explanation of them has been given. 'O ye All-gods, come hither' is (the triplet) to the All-gods,[5] containing (the word) 'go' in 'come hither'; this is a symbol of the end; the ninth day is the end; he returns as it were, having gone to the end, for hence whitherward should he go? It is in Gāyatrī, for this set of three days has the Gāyatrī at the third pressing. 'Present in the sky he shone' is to Vaiçvānara;[6] 'in the sky' is a symbol of yonder world. 'O Maruts, in whose dwelling' is (the hymn[7]) to the Maruts, containing (the word) 'dwell' in 'dwelling'; this is a symbol of the end; the ninth day is the end; having gone to the end, he dwells as it were, for hence whitherward should he go? 'Agni is the Hotṛ, the Purohita' is (the hymn) to Jātavedas,[8] containing (the word) 'dwell' in 'The dwelling, O thou of pure radiance'; this is a symbol of the end; the ninth day is the end; having gone to the end, he dwells as it were, for hence whitherward should he go? It is in Gāyatrī, for this set of three days has the Gāyatrī at the third pressing. These are the hymns of the Āgnimāruta. These are the hymns of this day. It is an Ukthya. It obtains what the third day obtains. Daily in all the

[1] RV. i. 24. 3-5 (already cited in KB. viii. 1); ÇÇS. x. 11. 8.

[2] RV. iv. 56. 5-7; ÇÇS. x. 11. 8.

[3] RV. viii. 93. 34 and i. 20. 7 and 8; ÇÇS. x. 11. 8.

[4] RV. viii. 27-31; ÇÇS. x. 11. 8, omitting viii. 28. 4.

[5] RV. ii. 41. 13-15 (already cited in KB. xxiv. 2); ÇÇS. x. 11. 8.

[6] The verses are given in ÇÇS. x. 11. 9.

[7] RV. i. 86 (also cited in KB. xxviii. 3); ÇÇS. x. 11. 9.

[8] RV. iii. 11; ÇÇS. x. 11. 9.

Chandomas (the verses) of two Padas are recited; the Chandomas are cattle; (the verses) with two Padas are the metre of the sacrificer; verily thus he places the sacrificers in the overlordship of cattle; man stands over cattle as it were.

ADHYĀYA XXVII

The Soma Sacrifice (*continued*).

The Tenth Day of the Daçarātra.

xxvii. 1. 'The tenth day [1] is that which is above in the sky' Kauṣītaki used to say; therefore it is what is not to be explained, for no one knows this clearly. 'Let me not explain ignorantly' (he thinks). The tenth day is a limited divine rite; it is the Anuṣṭubh; he who explains it makes a surplus; stumbling is liable to befall him who explains. As to this they say 'Let him explain; the sacrifice rejoices at the approach of a wise man, "What [2] is to become successful in me, that will he cause to be successful."' If any person inadvertently makes an error, then he who observes it should aside repeat the passage as a self study, or the householder or one of the priests should creep up, and he aside should recite the passage as a self study.[3] If he does not think this proper, he should at once explain.[4] The Anuṣṭubh is released on the tenth day; the Anuṣṭubh is speech; now speech having borne the burden becomes as it were the bearer of a dread thing.[5]

[1] For the tenth day of the Daçarātra which ends the twelfth month of the year Sattra see AB. v. 22–25. For the ritual see ÇÇS. x. 12. For the non-use of the Anuṣṭubh see BÇS. xvi. 6.

[2] As cited by Ānartīya on ÇÇS. x. 12. 5 the reading is the more simple one *yato 'samṛddham*, but it is very unlikely that this could have been changed into the reading of the text. The Ānand. ed. has *'yaṁ me*.

[3] This is the sense as taken by Ānartīya on ÇÇS. *l. c.* M curiously inserts *yas taṁ tatra brūyāt* after *adhīyāt*.

[4] The lack of a concluding *iti* as often renders uncertain the point at which the text of the view cited stops.

[5] M has *krūravahena* and this in view of *tadohuṣī* is clearly correct, though the comm. has *krūraravena*. M has (*vāg*)*vṛ* (*tadohuṣī*) in a correction. This Anuṣṭubh verse, despite its clear character and the particles, has escaped the vigilance of the edd. and of the *Vedic Concordance*. The words *tad enām*, for which M has the far simpler and probably certain *tad etan* (ignored by Lindner), appear to me to be prefixed to fit the verse, which seems to be a relic of old Indian Nīti literature, in order to adopt the sense to the Anuṣṭubh which is the subject of the comparison. M has the excellent reading *prasisṛkṣāmi*. The verse is, of course, in very free Anuṣṭubh form and *me 'sti* may be read in *d* for the sake of the metre. M has *puṅçalyāyanam me 'stīti* which is best taken as a cpd. (*puṅçalyāyanam*) and not as hyper sandhi. It is best to read *asti* and take *iti* as quoting the whole verse, and not as part of the verse. *saṁpādayati* is read by M and Ānand., and is preferable to the plural in Lindner.

Therefore is it released, (as they think) 'Let us not consort with speech.' Now all the metres here he converts into the Anuṣṭubh; there is this (verse)

> 'Her I touch not as being a Çūdrā;
> Yet will I not let her go;
> Nowhere else do I go;
> To a courtesan is my approaching,'

for on the tenth day here the Anuṣṭubh is sung around.

They say, 'He should not abandon the abode of the Anuṣṭubh; there should he recite Virāj verses; the Virāj and the Anuṣṭubh are the same metre, for not by one syllable is a metre made different, nor yet by two.' Of these two triplets there are six syllables over, and six of the strophe and antistrophe of the Agniṣṭoma Sāman; these twelve syllables the Hotṛ should make up in the morning litany. He need not trouble as to this; it is made up here. 'There is an Uṣṇih additional,' we hold,[6] 'or a Gāyatrī; that he should make up at the morning litany.' He need not trouble about this; it is made up here.

xxvii. 2. 'O Agni, this to-day as a steed with praises' is the Ājya.[1] That being created for the tenth day he need not make up. He need not trouble as to this; it is made up here. The Praüga is by Madhuchandas; the explanation of this has been given. With an Atichandas (verse), 'In the three bowls the bull that mixed with barley, he of strong power,' he begins the Marutvatīya.[2] It made up amounts to sixty-four syllables; these make up two Anuṣṭubhs. 'Sing aloud to Indra' and 'Forward to Indra, the great', these two Pragāthas[3] he recites along with the 'Water swellers' before the hymn[4]; so is it made up. 'Thou hast been born dread, for

Lindner treats it as prose, and so also Aufrecht (ZDMG. xxxiv. 75, 76), who renders 'Deshalb will ich einerseits sie weder berühren, weil ich mich mit keinem (lärmenden) Çūdra-weibe befassen will; noch gehe ich zu einer ganz verschiedenen Form über, sonst würde man von mir sagen, ich gliche einer lockeren Dirne'. But this necessitates the reading of *prasisakṣāṇi* (*prasañgenechāmi* in comm.), ignores the metre, and takes the *iti* as part of the quotation. For *yāmaki* see *Mahābhāṣya* on Pāṇ. v. 3. 68; *Kāçikā* on v. 3. 77. The Ānand. ed. has *vāhevābhimṛçe* and *yāmaka* (so M). Cf. also Keith, JRAS. 1915, pp. 502, 503. Böhtlingk (BKSGW. Apr. 23, 1897), also ignoring the metre, reads *yāmi kiṁ*, but this is impossible.

[6] The mysterious and unusual *menimahe* occurring here and recognized also by Ānartīya in his citation of the passage yields only this sense. The making up of the number of syllables of an Uṣṇih or Gāyatrī is given by Ānartīya as the result of three recitings, 12 + 6 + 6 = 24 = the Gāyatrī. If 2 Virāj triads replace two of Anuṣṭubh then there are clearly six extra syllables, Virāj = 33, and Anuṣṭubh = 32 syllables. M has *udaiti*, which is preferable.

[1] RV. iv. 40; ÇÇS. x. 13. 1.

[2] RV. ii. 22. 1; ÇÇS. x. 13. 8, 9 (the remainder of the strophe is viii. 68. 2, 3).

[3] RV. viii. 89. 1 and 2; 3 and 4, with i. 64. 16 without any call intervening; hence *saṁçaṅsati*; see Ānartīya on ÇÇS. x. 13. 10.

[4] I. e. RV. x. 73; ÇÇS. x. 13. 10.

impetuous strength' is the Marutvatīya[5] of the one-day (rite); the one-day (rite) is a support; verily (it serves) for support. 'With what hath he come, the brilliant one?' and 'With what aid thou to us?', on the basis[6] of the Vāmadevya is imposed the Rathantara. The Sāman is for Agni and is performed on Indra verses; this is a pairing, a symbol of generation. There are as many Uṣṇih triads as Pragāthas; one verse of two Padas forms the inserted verse, another the seventeenth of the hymn; this is made up. 'I shall proclaim the manly deeds of Indra' is the Niṣkevalya[7] of the one-day (rite); the one-day (rite) is a support; the tenth day is a support; the two (verses of) two Padas are a metre on which to find support; verily (they serve) for support. 'To the god Savitṛ in the bowls the sage,' with this Atichandas verse he begins the Vaiçvadeva;[8] it made up amounts to sixty-four syllables; these make up two Anuṣṭubhs; the antistrophe contains (the word) 'towards'; the explanation of this has been given. Then, before the 'Prosperity to us' hymn,[9] he recites the 'Forward the bright' hymn[10]; the one-day (rite) is a support; the tenth day is a support; (the verses) of two Padas are a metre on which to find support; verily (they serve) for support. The Agniṣṭoma Sāman as the Vāmadevya is performed on Virāj verses[11]; the Virāj is prosperity and proper food; (verily they serve) to obtain the Virāj as prosperity and proper food. Moreover the Vāmadevya is healing and medicine; verily thus at the end in the sacrifice are healing and medicine produced.

xxvii. 3. In that they perform the additional litany[1] of the conjunct (form), thereby they obtain the additional litany. Now this is the milking of the tenth day; they must make up the day so that there may be a thousand and fifteen Anuṣṭubhs; taking out fifteen, then of each hundred four he takes out; thus are fifty-five taken out. Then the rest make up thirty sets of thirty-two. Now this is the Anuṣṭubh of the Stomas and the syllables; the Gāyatrī has eight syllables; the Stoma is the twenty-fourfold; so the Anuṣṭubh of the Stoma and the syllables has thirty-two parts. Now there is the Anuṣṭubh of the Padas; there are six Padas in the Gāyatrī and Uṣṇih; three in the Virāj; these make nine; four in the Bṛhatī; these make thirteen; five in the Pañkti; these make eighteen; four in the Triṣṭubh; these make twenty-two; in the Jagatī and Atichandas eight; these make thirty; two in the verse of two Padas; these make

[5] RV. x. 73 (already cited in KB. xv. 3).

[6] RV. iv. 31. 1–3 and viii. 93. 19–21; see ÇÇS. vii. 22. 2, and for the Rathantara, &c., x. 18 11.

[7] RV. i. 32 (already cited in KB. xv. 4). The Dvipadās are RV. vii. 34. 4; viii. 29. 4; ÇÇS. x. 18. 13.

[8] Cited above KB. xxiii. 7.

[9] RV. i. 89 (already cited in KB. xx. 4); ÇÇS. x. 18. 18

[10] RV. vii. 34 (already cited in KB. xxii. 9); ÇÇS. x. 18. 18.

[11] RV. vii. 1. 1–6.

[1] For this see ÇÇS. x. 18. 21–25.

thirty-two; so the Anuṣṭubh of the Padas becomes of thirty-two parts. Now there is the Anuṣṭubh of the gods[2]; eight Vasus, eleven Rudras, twelve Ādityas, Indra as the thirty-second; so the Anuṣṭubh of the deities becomes of thirty-two parts. Now the fifty-five taken out are forty-four Pañkti verses; the forty of these are the udder, the four over the teats; thus the Anuṣṭubh of the Stoma and the syllables with this udder and these teats pours over this body of Indra, the fast day; by reason of the pouring over[3] of it the Chandomas increase both as regards Stomas and Çastras; he who knows it becomes composed thereof; he who knows thus before his life (is over) becomes master of this body of Indra, the fast day[4]; him this Anuṣṭubh of the Stoma and the syllables with this udder, these teats, with all flavours, all delights, all proper food, all immortality besprinkles, who recites the tenth day (rite) as thus made up. 'Therefore should he recite the tenth day (rite) as thus made up,' (they say).[5]

xxvii. 4. In that they perform the additional litany of the transposed[1] (form), verily thus they delight mind. That with all the sacrifices they recite, for this is the measure of mind. When the tenth day is over, before the offerings to the wives (with the gods), at this moment they creep forward, saying 'The wives are unworthy of sacrifice, for they are outside the altar.' But the rule is (that they do so) when the offerings to the wives have been completed. 'Here a little space is left over for rivals,' (thinking thus) they creep forward together and sing with the verses of the serpent queen;[2] the serpent queen is this (earth), for she is the queen of what creeps; the serpent queen is speech, for speech is the queen of what creeps; moreover, the serpent queen is the cow, for the cow is the queen of what creeps. 'The spotted bull hath come', this triplet[3] he should not omit, to prevent the omission of the strophe. 'In us place manliness' (he says); manliness is food; verily thus he places food in the sacrifice and in

[2] *devatyā* in M is equally isolated as a form with *devakyā*.

[3] *vyakṣareṇa* is an extraordinary and impossible form; possibly *abhikṣareṇa* may be intended, but M has *vikṣareṇa*.

[4] The Ānand. ed. has *pratyam ahar* twice and so M, which after the first *abhikṣarati* inserts *sarveṇānnādyena sarvai rasais sarvaiḥ kāmais sarveṇāmṛtatvenābhikṣarati*. It also has *yad u vai veda* and *sa ya evaṁvid asyā°* (which is suggested by the reading of the Ānand. also) and at the end it omits *sarvai rasaiḥ* and inserts *sarvaiḥ kāmaiḥ* after *annādyena*.

[5] The composition of the number of verses is given by Ānartīya on ÇÇS. xi. 12 (ii. 68–79, ed. Hillebrandt).

[1] *vyūḍhasya* is omitted in M and may be an interpolation. For the *atiriktoktha* of the *samūḍha* see ÇÇS. x. 13. 21–25.

[2] *sārparājñī* (°*rājñyarkṣu* by hyper sandhi; p. 71) is a curious form for *sarparājñī*, and may be a mere error; *per contra sarparājñīnām* is used in ĀpÇS. xxi. 10. 5 of the verses. The verses are *sārparājñī*, as Ānartīya on ÇÇS. x. 13. 29 says. Cf. AB. v. 23. M has the short vowel of *vāc*.

[3] RV. x. 189. 1–3; ÇÇS. x. 13. 26. Garbe, ĀpÇS. iii. 475, incorrectly identifies the ref. in ĀpÇS. xxi. 10. 5.

the sacrificers. 'O breath obtainer, that hear the call' (he says);[4] the breath obtainer is Indra, for he having obtained the breath goes round seeking bodies. (Now the) Adhvaryu; he offers in the Gārhapatya two libations to Prajāpati, without mention (of the deity); the Gārhapatya is Prajāpati; the Stotra and Çastra end with the two libations; the Stotra is completed; the Çastra is completed; the discussion of the Brahman is completed. Moreover they may[5] if they will offer a sacrifice, and take food. Here is Vena.[6] These are obviously the bodies of Prajāpati; them let the Hotṛ recite.

xxvii. 5. 'Eater of food and mistress of food' (is one form[1]); the eater of food is this (earth); the mistress of food yonder (sky). 'The fair and the beautiful' (is a second): the fair is the Soma; the beautiful is cattle. 'The unresting and the fearless' (is a third); the unresting is Vāyu, for he never rests; the fearless is death, for he has no fear. 'The unattained and the unattainable' (is a fourth); the unattained is this earth; the unattainable yonder sky. 'The unattacked and the unattackable' (is a fifth); the unattacked is Agni here; he unattackable yonder Āditya. 'That which has no prius and no rival'; that which has no prius is the mind; that which has no rival the year. Now[2] he yonder who gives heat is yonder householder, for he is a lord of houses, his houses are the seasons; he is a lord and he is also a god from whom evil has been smitten away. The Adhvaryu runs northward; they close the doors of the Sadas and also of the shed.[3]

xxvii. 6. They[1] lay hold of the branch of Udumbara; the Udumbara is strength and proper food; (it serves) for the obtaining of strength and proper food. The Hotṛ should make his two hands the highest (thinking),

[4] M inserts before *vātāper* the words *ātmānaṁ pūrvam āha tathā hānyātmānantaritā bhavati.* The verse is the last Pāda of a verse in ÇÇS. x. 17. 6, where *vātāpe* is read as here also in OoC and the Ānand. ed. but not in M; in MS. i. 9. 1 it occurs with *vātāpayaḥ* 'fermenting' (of the Soma drink), and in TĀ. iii. 8. 1 with *vātāpeḥ*, which is apparently a genitive with *havanaçrutaḥ*. The preceding words are found in MS. *l. c.*; TĀ. iii. 1. 1; ÇÇS. x. 14. 6 in a different context. OoC and the Ānand. ed. have the absurd reading *vātam ātmā* (K has *vācam*).

[5] M has the excellent reading *ato nv evāpi* which is much better than *anye* of the other MSS. and the Ānand. ed., and involves only a change of a letter. Ānartīya, on ÇÇS. x. 19. 1, has *anye*, and observes that the option of a sacrifice here is not accepted in the Sūtra. M has also *anirukte saṁsthe.*

[6] The Vena hymn is RV. x. 123 (already cited in KB. viii. 5), but that it should occur here (M clearly has the same reading, after a lacuna) is strange and not very probable, nor is the form of citation usual. The comm. takes it as Vena is *kama.* AB. i. 20. 2 (cf. KB. xxviii. 9) has the same phrase in the sense 'The Vena (vital air) is here (in the navel)' which is intelligible with regard to *bhakṣayuḥ*.

[1] See ÇÇS. x. 19. 1; AB. v. 25.

[2] This is the Brahmodya according to AB. v. 25. KB. omits all mention of the different Daçahotṛ, Caturhotṛ, Pañcahotṛ, Ṣaḍhotṛ, and Saptahotṛ recitations given in ÇÇS. x. 14–18, and referred to in ĀpÇS. xxi. 10. BÇS. xvi. 7 refers only to the Caturhotṛs.

[3] The verses are at this juncture three; see ÇÇS. x. 21. 10. M has *dvārau çālāyāç ca.*

xxvii. 6. [1] The ritual of this chapter and of the last sentence of the preceding chapter is given in ÇÇS. x. 21. Cf. AB. v. 24.

'Let me be the highest'; the highest does he become. In silence, with closed eyes, they sit until the Nakṣatras appear; speech do they make to grow strong in that they sit in silence, (thinking) 'Speech grown strong and poured upon may we obtain at the end.' Near the Mārjālīya, when the Nakṣatras (appear), they open their eyes; the Nakṣatras are light; verily thus they place light in themselves. They enter the two oblation holders by the western door; then the Adhvaryu approaching the pole of the northern oblation holder says 'Do thou sing the Prosperity of the Sacrificial Session'; he sings the 'Prosperity of the Sacrificial Session'; thus they obtain the prosperity of the sacrificial session. All perform the finale of the Sāman; the finale is a support; verily (it serves) for support. They creep beneath the axle of the northern oblation holder, muttering an Atichandas verse to Indra[2]; verily thus by the Atichandas verse the sacrificers smite away evil under the axle. 'We go round (them) to the north', Kauṣītaki used to say, 'following the path of the sacrifice, not being concealed from the Seven Ṛṣis.' Having taken up their places in front of the oblation holders they think of what they desire; whatever they desire 'Let this desire be fulfilled for us,' this desire for them is fulfilled; those who have many desires should mutter the three exclamations, *bhūḥ*, *bhuvaḥ*, *svar*. Having gone out to the east and to the north they vie in invoking speech, (thinking) 'Let not speech be averted.' They release the speech of the Subrahmaṇyā[3]; the Subrahmaṇyā is the holy power; verily thus with the holy power do they utter speech. They go to the Āgnīdhrīya along with the king; this is as if men should conduct the king, or his vicegerent,[4] when wearied to an abode; Soma the king they day by day, having taken down from the oblation holders, conduct to the Agnīdh's altar; at the Āgnīdhrīya they settle down with the king.

xxvii. 7. In[1] that they perform the Daçarātra in its conjunct form, verily (it serves) to obtain all desires. In that they perform it in its transposed form, verily (it serves) to obtain all the metres. In that they perform both the transposed and the conjunct forms, verily (it serves) to confer variety on the Daçarātra. The conjunct form was alone in the beginning. The metres desired one another's place, (thinking) 'Let us all be first, all be in the middle, and all at the end.' Moreover thus he makes all the metres

[2] The verse is RV. i. 132. 6. The rite is one with many parallels; cf. Henry, *La magie dans l'Inde*, pp. 132, 133.

[3] ÇÇS. x. 21. 17 has *subrahmaṇyāpratīkam abhivyāhṛtya*. See also *Jaiminīya Çrauta Sūtra*, iii. The AB. v. 3 deals much more fully with the Subrahmaṇyā priest and formula.

[4] According to BR. this term denotes any one having a claim to the rank; it occurs again in ÇÇS. xvii. 5. 3, 4; 15. 3.

[1] This chapter explains the use of the two forms *samūḍha* and *vyūḍha*, the details of which have been given above. The variation of metres at the several Tryahas is added.

sharers in all the pressings. The first set of three days has the Gāyatrī at the morning pressing, the Triṣṭubh at the midday, and the Jagatī at the third pressing. The second set of three days has the Jagatī at the morning pressing, the Gāyatrī at the midday, and the Triṣṭubh at the third pressing. The third set of three days has the Triṣṭubh at the morning pressing, the Jagatī at the midday, and the Gāyatrī at the third pressing. The tenth day has the Gāyatrī at the morning pressing; thus from the same metre to the same metre they proceed. Again in that they transform the tenth day into Anuṣṭubh verses, and this day is speech, and the Anuṣṭubh is speech, verily thus they establish speech in speech. Immortality they obtain who perform the tenth day (rite).

ADHYĀYA XXVIII

THE SOMA SACRIFICE (*continued*).

The Recitations of the Hotrakas at the Morning Pressing.

xxviii. 1. Prajāpati [1] created the sacrifice; with it when created the gods sacrificed; having sacrificed with it they obtained all desires. One half of it they deposited, namely the Praiṣas and the Nigadas. With the other (half of the) sacrifice the Ṛṣis sacrificed; they observed [2] 'With an incomplete sacrifice are we sacrificing; we do not obtain all desires.' They toiled; they saw the Praiṣas and Nigadas. Having sacrificed with the sacrifice with the Praiṣas and Nigadas they obtained all desires, (thinking) 'The Praiṣas and the Nigadas are so much [3] of the sacrifice as is not made up by the Ṛc verses. Thus with them shall we make up the whole.' These Praiṣas and Anupraiṣas [4] Viçvāmitra saw, and also the Praiṣas for the cake offering; then other Ṛṣis (saw) others. As to this they say 'Why does the Maitrāvaruṇa alone give directions to all?' The deities ran a race regarding the Praiṣas; the race Mitra and Varuṇa won; therefore the Maitrāvaruṇa [5] alone gives directions to all. He gives directions standing, (thinking) 'Standing is one strongest, standing also is one most easily heard; let me utter speech full of strength and resorting to the gods'.

[1] There is no precise parallel to this in the AB. With the views here given may be contrasted the statement quoted in Ānartīya's comm. on ÇÇS. viii. 15. 15 that all Nivids, Purorucs, and Praiṣas are Viçvāmitra's, and all other Mantras in Brāhmaṇas or Kalpas are Vāmadeva's. Cf. below, KB. xxviii. 8; RVKh. Anukramaṇī in Scheftalowitz, p. 181.

[2] *vijajñuḥ* is clearly to be read; see Gaastra, VOJ. xxiii. 64.

[3] M's *stāvate* points to *stāvanto* as the correct reading; cf. in KB. xxii. 9 *devajāte* apparently for °*jātau*.

[4] *praiṣān* only is read by M, but probably not correctly.

[5] See ÇÇS. v. 16. 1 *seq.*

xxviii. 2. 'Leaning forward like one slightly bent should he recite; thus is Parjanya likely to rain' Kauṣītaki used to say. Now the Asuras and the Rakṣases used to impede[1] the oblations; then Vāmadeva saw the appropriate (verses[2]), 'Agni the Hotṛ at our sacrifice'; with them they led Agni round. Therefore these Rakṣases, the destructive, they smote away. He recites an appropriate (verse[3]), containing (the word) 'accept', 'Accept our most extending', (thinking) 'Let me utter speech appropriate and containing (the word) "accept" among the gods.' 'Set this sacrifice for us among the immortals', with these (verses[4]) Viçvāmitra makes acceptable the drops. These are their invitatory verses, these their offering verses; therefore are they appropriate. A verse of Viçvāmitra's he recites as the invitatory verse[5] for the Sviṣṭakṛt offering in (the sacrifice of) the cake; the explanation of this has been given. Verses of Viçvāmitra's he recites in each pressing as invitatory verses for the cakes; Viçvāmitra saw these Praiṣas for the cakes; (verily they serve) for correspondence. Two appropriate verses of Madhuchandas[6] he recites as invitatory verses for the first of those for two deities; Madhuchandas saw these Praiṣas for these two deities; (verily they serve) for correspondence. A verse by Gṛtsamada[7] and a verse by Medhātithi[8] he recites, being appropriate, for the second two. Verses by Medhātithi[9] he recites at the morning pressing for (the goblets) being filled; Medhātithi at the morning pressing proclaimed the Soma to Indra; these (verses) contain (the words) 'hither' and 'bay steeds' with the symbols of the invitatory verses; they are addressed to Indra, for the sacrificial rite is Indra's; they are Gāyatrī verses; the morning pressing is in Gāyatrī. Nine verses he recites; nine goblets do they fill.

xxviii. 3. Six[1] some repeat at the morning pressing for (the goblets) being filled; (six the Maitrāvaruṇa) himself, the Achāvāka the seventh; seven each at the second and third pressings, saying 'Seven seated eastwards perform the *vaṣaṭ* call.' As to this they say 'According to the hymn should he recite, for these are the invitatory verses of the Hotṛ, for these goblets they fill up goblet by goblet as the Hotṛ's; therefore should he recite according to the hymn.' Then the Hotrakas sacrifice together; the explana-

[1] M has the common word *vimathnate*, needlessly. For *kuvakra = prahāṇa* cf. ÇÇS. v. 16. 4.

[2] RV. iv. 15. 1-3; see ÇÇS. v. 16. 8; they are said for the *paryagni* by the Maitrāvaruṇa.

[3] RV. i. 75; see ÇÇS. v. 18. 1. It and the next are for the *stokas*.

[4] RV. iii. 21.

[5] RV. iii. 28. 1; see ÇÇS. vii. 1. 6.

[6] RV. i. 2. 1; and i. 2. 4; see ÇÇS. vii. 2. 2, for the Indra-Vāyu cup.

[7] RV. ii. 41. 4; see ÇÇS. vii. 2. 8 for the Mitra-Varuṇa cup.

[8] RV. i. 22. 1; see ÇÇS. vii. 2. 8 for the Açvin cup.

[9] RV. i. 16. 1-9; see ÇÇS. vii. 4. 1.

xxviii. 3. [1] For this chapter see AB. vi. 9. The nine verses here are reduced to seven because of the seven offering verses enumerated in the rest of the chapter said by the seven priests, Hotṛ and Hotrakas.

tion of this has been given. The Maitrāvaruṇa uses (a verse) to Mitra and Varuṇa,[2] 'Mitra we hail,' to secure that the beginning of the sacrifice shall be provided with its own deity. 'Indra thee as a bull we', (this verse) to Indra[3] the Brāhmaṇācchaṅsin (uses), for the sacrificial rite is connected with Indra. 'O Maruts in whose dwelling', (this verse) to the Maruts[4] the Potṛ (uses); when the Maruts purified Indra, then Indra gave them a share in the Soma drinking; therefore is it (a verse) addressed to the Maruts that the Potṛ uses as offering verse at the first and at the last. 'O Agni bring hither the wives', (this verse[5]) which contains (the words) 'O Agni, with the wives' and (the word) 'Tvaṣṭṛ,' the Neṣṭṛ uses at the first and at the last; Agni is the one of the gods who is connected with (the words) 'with the wives', the Neṣṭṛ is the one of the priests (so connected); therefore it is (a verse) which contains (the words) 'Agni with the wives' and (the word) 'Tvaṣṭṛ' that the Neṣṭṛ uses as offering verse at the first and at the last. 'To him whose food is the ox, whose food the cow', (this verse) to Agni[6] is used by the Agnīdh; he kindles the fires; therefore the Agnīdh uses (this verse) to Agni as offering verse at the first and at the last. They repeat the second *vaṣaṭ*, for the healing of the libations, for the support of the libations. Then comes the sacrificial food, then the bowl of the Hotṛ; the explanation of this has been given.

xxviii. 4. When Nābhānediṣṭha Mānava sought an invitation from the Aṅgirases, he saw this Hotṛ function of the Achāvāka; he came when the sacrificial food had been invoked; therefore one does not select him.[1] He came from this eastern intermediate region; therefore seated in this region the Achāvāka awaits his invitation. They say 'Why do they keep a fragment of the cake for the Achāvāka?' Alīkayu Vācaspata was the Brahman at the consecration and Upasads of the Naimiṣīyas; he performed the Achāvāka's function when the pressing had been done. They said 'We have hitherto kept the Brahman's portion for him; for whom shall we keep it?' Then said they 'For him do ye keep it.' They kept it for

[2] RV. i. 23. 4; ÇÇS. vii. 4. 6. The phrase *anavarārdhyai* offers great difficulty of interpretation (cf. *anavārdhya* in xxv. 15), and seems an error for *anavarāddhyai*. The Hotrakas' performance is the so-called Prasthita libations. *yajanti* has, of course, the precise sense of 'say the offering verses'.

[3] RV. iii. 40. 1; ÇÇS. vii. 4. 7.

[4] RV. i. 86. 1 (already cited in KB. xxvi. 17); ÇÇS. vii. 4. 8.

[5] RV. i. 22. 9; ÇÇS. vii. 4. 9. The sense of *āgnipātnīvatyā* must be thus, that is, as in MW., a verse containing the words *agne patnīr*, the compound adj. being a natural device to get over the difficulty of saying 'containing Agni and *patnī*'. M has the variant *Tvaṣṭā vai*, which is clearly bad.

[6] RV. viii. 43. 11; ÇÇS. vii. 4. 10.

[1] The point here is the late place of the Achāvāka in the Soma offering which he only later, it is clear, attained; see Caland and Henry, *L'Agniṣṭoma*, p. 220; Oldenberg, *Religion des Veda*, pp. 384, n. 2; 397, n. 2. Cf. KB. vi. 13, 14.

him. This is the Brahman's portion. Moreover the other goblets share in the sacrificial food; therefore they keep for the Achāvāka the fragment of the cake, to prevent the goblet having none of the sacrificial food.[2]

xxviii. 5. Then the Adhvaryu says to him 'O Achāvāka, say what thou hast to say'; verily thus he says to him 'O Achāvāka, expect an invitation.' 'Hither Agni for help for you', (these verses) to Agni he recites; the morning pressing is connected with Agni; they are Anuṣṭubh verses; the Anuṣṭubh is the Gāyatrī; the metre of Agni is the Gāyatrī. They are three; Agni is threefold, coals, flame, and smoke. At the third saying with the Praṇava of the last verse, he unites the Nigada,[1] 'O sacrificer, O Hotṛ, O Adhvaryu, O Agnīdh, O Brahman, O Potṛ, O Neṣṭṛ, and thou also, O Upavaktṛ.' The Upavaktṛ is the Praçāstṛ; it is said in a Ṛc,[2] 'The Upavaktṛ of men.' 'Be forcible with force, strong with strength' (he says); 'Force as food, strength as food with food do ye unite,' in effect, he says to them. 'To you may the kin, may those that are not kin yield (he says); 'Whatever is kin, and whatever is not kin, may that yield to you,' verily thus he says to them. This is declared in a Ṛc,[3]

xxviii. 6. 'Kin or no kin, crush the foes.' 'The rivals beaten down in the way' (he says); 'Your rivals are destroyed in battle', verily thus he says to them. 'Conquer the attacking, conquer with the attacking'[1] (he says); the attacking is an army; 'With an army an army conquer,' verily thus he says to them. 'May Indra hear, may Agni hearken to you' (he says); 'Let Indra hear you, let Agni hear', verily thus he utters this benediction. 'Standing forth, do ye proclaim the Soma to Indra and Agni, and do ye, O Brahmans, invite[2] us who are Brahmans,' verily thus he requires an invitation from all. 'This Brahman here, or Achāvāka, desires an invitation', the Adhvaryu says, 'O Hotṛ, do thou invite him.' Him the Hotṛ invites, for he is the chief sharer of them; 'Whomever his chief invites, he indeed is invited' Kauṣītaki used to say.

xxviii. 7. 'To him athirst[1]' the Achāvāka recites for (the goblet) being

[2] The sense of *aparīdattyai* is clear, and while *parīdittyai* would be simpler, the sense of *pari* as 'apart from' is possible.

[1] See ÇÇS. vii. 6. 1 *seq.* The Mantra is printed in ÇÇS. vii. 6. 8 as *iṣepayadhvam*: and so in the *Vedic Concordance*, and this is, if taken from *iṣayate* as a denominative, correct, as *iṣaiṣayadhvam* would be necessary from √*iṣ* as causative; an instr. *iṣā* is more probable than *iṣe* as first element, but it is possible that *iṣe ṣayadhvam* misunderstood as two words may explain the *sayate*, go, of *Dhātupāṭha*, xiv. 8. Probably therefore *iṣeṣ°* should be read with *ūrjorj°* in place of Lindner's *ūrjo 'rjayadhvam*, which is also found in the Ān and. ed. In *b* read *jihatām*.

[2] RV. iv. 9. 5.

[3] RV. iv. 4. 5 *d*.

xxviii. 6. [1] Though ÇÇS. vii. 6. 8 also has *abhītvaryāḥ*, it is a *vox nihili* and *abhitvaryā* is actually found in ĀÇS. v. 7. 8, which has *jayata* for the rare *jeṣatha*.

[2] *vocatopo* must be read as in ÇÇS. vii. 6. 8.

xxviii. 7. [1] RV. vi. 42 (already cited in KB. xxiii. 2); the four verses contradict the one verse of KB. xxviii. 3. See ÇÇS. vii. 7. 1.

filled; these are four; all this (universe) is fourfold; verily (it serves) to obtain all this (universe). They are Anuṣṭubh verses, for reciting together. The last is a Bṛhatī; the Bṛhatī is prosperity; verily thus at the last he finds support in prosperity. 'Come with those that move at dawn,' with (this verse[2]) to Indra and Agni he offers, for his litany is addressed to Indra and Agni. It is in Gāyatrī; the morning pressing is in Gāyatrī. He says the second *vaṣaṭ*, for the healing of the libations, for the support of the libations. 'Without taking in breath should they say the offering verses at the morning pressing,' Paiñgya used to say, (thinking) 'Swiftly shall we give the oblation to the gods.' 'By half verses' Kauṣītaki (used to say). The half verse is the joint of the metres; verily thus by joints they give the oblation to the gods.[3]

xxviii. 8. Then[1] comes the consideration of the Praiṣas for the season (sacrifices). Kaṇva it was who saw the Praiṣas for the seasonal (sacrifices); and Medhātithi the offering verses[2]; Medhātithi is a descendant of Kaṇva. With this the two smote away[3] evil. He who desires 'May I smite away death, the evil,' should sacrifice with these.

xxviii. 9. The[1] sacrifice is a man; the Ājya is his speech; speech is one only; therefore he recites the Ājya with one deity only. The Praüga is the breaths; the breaths are many; therefore many deities are celebrated at the Praüga. The Maitrāvaruṇa and the Achāvāka are the two arms; these are twofold; therefore they recite (verses) for two deities at the morning pressing. The Brāhmaṇācchaṅsin is the middle as this navel suture[2]; therefore the Brāhmaṇācchaṅsin at the morning pressing recites (verses) to one deity. The midday (pressing) is the body; it is one only; therefore at the midday the Hotrā reciters recite (verses) to one deity; and the Hotṛ himself the Niṣkevalya. The Maitrāvaruṇa and the Achāvāka are the two thighs; these are twofold; therefore they recite at the third pressing (verses) to one deity. The Brāhmaṇācchaṅsin is the middle as this organ of generation; therefrom two forms arise, female and male; therefore the Brāhmaṇācchaṅsin at the third pressing recites (verses) to two deities. The Brāhmaṇācchaṅsin recites most (verses); the Brāhmaṇācchaṅsin is the body; therefore this middle of the body is the thickest.

xxviii. 10. In that the strophes and the antistrophes contain (the word)

[2] RV. viii. 38. 7; ÇÇS. vii. 7. 2.

[3] See ÇÇS. vii. 7. 3.

[1] See ÇÇS. vii. 8 with Ānartīya's comm.

[2] See Anartīya on ÇÇS. vii. 8. 5 where the verses are given.

[3] *apajighnāte* (so M) is impossible, and obviously *°jaghnāte* must be read, as suggested by D. Gaastra (no. x of her *Stellingen* issued with her *Jaiminīya Çrauta Sūtra*).

xxviii. 9. [1] AB. vi. 4 differs wholly from this account.

[2] This sense of *venā sevanī* seems to follow from AB. i. 20. 2 and iii. 37. 2, though *venā* has escaped the dictionaries.

'hither', this is a symbol of the first day. The strophes of the Maitrāvaruṇa and the Achāvāka are by Viçvāmitra,[1] the two nine-versed conclusions by Vasiṣṭha[2]; verily thus they two make the two ends alike. Having recited the strophes, they make as the antistrophes the strophes of the next day, to secure the form of the Ahīna, for the continuity of the Ahīna; verily thus they make day conformable to day; day indeed is conformable to day. They say 'Why is the Stotra followed in recitation? Why do they recite beyond the Stoma?' That is not indeed sung which is not followed in recitation; that Stoma goes not to the gods which is not recited beyond;[3] therefore is the Stotra followed in recitation; therefore do they recite beyond the Stoma. The Çastras have four calls; the litanies are cattle; cattle are fourfold; moreover they are four-footed; verily (they serve) to obtain cattle. The offering verses of the litanies are from the one-day (rite); the one-day (rite) is a support; verily (it serves) for support. They say the second *vaṣaṭ*, for the healing of the libations, for the support of the libations.

ADHYĀYA XXIX

The Soma Sacrifice (*continued*).

The Recitation of the Hotrakas at the Midday Pressing.

xxix. 1. When the gods at Sarvacaru performed the sacrifice, Arbuda Kādraveya came up to them at the midday (pressing) and said to them, 'One Hotṛ's office is not being performed for you, that of the Grāvastut; let me perform it for you, do ye invite me.' They said 'So be it'; they invited him; he saw these appropriate (verses) of the Grāvastut, namely, 'Let them call forth; let us call forth,' when they call forth,[2] for they call forth indeed; then when (they say) 'mightily mightily' (the verse containing 'mightily' is used), 'They speak out mightily with the strong exhilarating (drink)'; 'Set free the thought of him that hath pressed' (is the verse) when they set free.[3] They are fourteen; the fingers are ten, the pressing stones are four; they make up this (number). They are Jagatī verses; the stones are connected with the Jagatī. In that he concludes

[1] RV. iii. 62. 16–18 and iii. 12. 1–3; see ÇÇS. xii. 1. 3 and 5.

[2] RV. vii. 66. 7–9 and vii. 94. 7–9; ÇÇS. xii. 2. 4, and 8.

[3] See ÇÇS. xii. 2. 10 with Ānartīya's comm.; AB. vi. 8. In AB. vi. 5, 17 the use of strophe and antistrophe is dealt with.

xxix. 1. [1] The Arbuda hymn is RV. x. 94; see ÇÇS. vii. 15. Cf. AB. vi. 1, 2; Lévi, *La doctrine du sacrifice*, pp. 142, 143; Caland and Henry, *L'Agniṣṭoma*, pp. 269 *seq.*

[2] The verses are appropriate to the actions described as the part of the stones and the priests. For *yatra bṛhat* see ÇÇS. vii. 15. 11; RV. x. 94. 4. The action of the pressers is referred to; the verse is to be used when they say *bṛhad bṛhat*.

[3] RV. x. 94. 14 *c*.

with a Triṣṭubh,[4] thereby at the midday (pressing) is the Triṣṭubh secured. He praises, standing; the stones stand as it were. He praised wearing a turban, and with eyes tied up; therefore now also wearing a turban (the priest) praises the stones. Moreover they say 'The eye came[5]; it was a serpent; thus did poison come to the priests; he used these (verses) connected with (Soma) the purifying,[6] and repelling poison, in praise; in that he uses these (verses) connected with (Soma) the purifying and repelling poison, verily (it serves) for the healing of the sacrifice and the curing of the sacrificers.'[7]

xxix. 2. When the Pavamāna has been sung, they proceed with the pot of milk, for this is the time for it; moreover (it serves) to secure the sap of the pressing. Then they proceed with the sacrifice of five oblations; the explanation of this has been given. (Verses) by Vasiṣṭha[1] he repeats for (the goblets) being filled at the midday (pressing); Vasiṣṭha it was who proclaimed the Soma to Indra at the midday. They contain (the words) 'hither' and 'bay steeds', with the symbols of the invitatory verses. They are Triṣṭubh verses to Indra, for the midday pressing is connected with Indra and the Triṣṭubh. Ten he recites; ten goblets do they fill here. Then the Hotrakas sacrifice together; the explanation of this has been given. Triṣṭubh verses to Indra they use as offering verses for the Prasthitas at the midday (pressing), for the midday pressing is connected with Indra and the Triṣṭubh. They say the second *vaṣaṭ*, for the healing of the libations, for the support of the libations. Then comes the sacrificial food, then the goblet of the Hotṛ; the explanation of this has been given; when the Dakṣiṇā offerings have been made,[2] the sacrificial fees are taken; the explanation of these has been given. He recites (a verse) by Viçvāmitra[3] as the invitatory verse for the cup for the Maruts; the explanation of this has been given.

xxix. 3. The[1] Pṛṣṭha for the Maitrāvaruṇa is the Vāmadevya; the Vāmadevya is healing and medicine; verily thus are healing and medicine produced in the sacrifice. That of the Brāhmaṇācchaṅsin is the Naudhasa; that has a finale; the finale is a support; verily (it serves) for support. That of the Achāvāka is the Kāleya; that they perform as the Aiḍa on Bṛhatī verses; the sacrificial food is cattle; the Bṛhatī is cattle; cattle are connected with the Bṛhatī; verily (it serves) to obtain cattle. They recite

[4] RV. x. 94. 14.

[5] M has *cakṣur hāha*, K *cakṣur hāsa*. The sense is dubious, but apparently the idea is the eye was an evil eye.

[6] ÇÇS. vii. 15. 15.

[7] No *iti* at the end.

[1] RV. vii. 21; see ÇÇS. vii. 17. 3, most of the ritual is the same as in the first pressing; see ÇÇS. vii. 16, 17. Cf. AB. vi. 11.

[2] See ÇÇS. vii. 18.

[3] RV. iii. 51. 7; ÇÇS. vii. 19. 2.

xxix. 3. [1] For the Sāmans, &c., see ÇÇS. vii. 22–24. Lindner has Aiḍa, and so throughout, where AB. has ḷ.

the Pragāthas of the Sāman; thus they depart not from the Hotṛ's rule. The beginnings of the litanies of the Maitrāvaruṇa and Achāvāka are of five verses, the conclusions are of eleven verses; verily thus they make the two ends alike. The Maitrāvaruṇa recites (verses) by Viçvāmitra[2] and Vāmadeva,[3] for his conclusion is by Vāmadeva. The Brāhmaṇācchaṅsin recites (verses) by Viçvāmitra[4] and Vasiṣṭha,[5] for his conclusion is by Vasiṣṭha. The Achāvāka recites (verses) by Bharadvāja[6] and Viçvāmitra,[7] for his conclusion is by Viçvāmitra. They recite (verses) by four Ṛṣis; up to four (degrees) are pairing, union, propagation; (they serve) for generation.[8] The beginnings of the litanies of the Maitrāvaruṇa and Brāhmaṇācchaṅ sin are by Viçvāmitra, and so is the conclusion of the Achāvāka; Viçvāmitra is speech; verily thus with speech on all sides they extend the sacrifice. This is the explanation of the introductory and concluding rites and of the one day form.

xxix. 4. Day by day the Pṛṣṭha for the Maitrāvaruṇa is the Vāmadevya; the Vāmadevya is healing and medicine; verily thus are healing and medicine day by day produced in the sacrifice. Then day by day they recite these Pragāthas containing (the word) 'who'; Prajāpati is Who; verily thus day by day they continue finding support in Prajāpati. Moreover they continue employing the varied hymns, the Ahīnas (by name), unappeased; verily they continue to appease them day by day with the Pragāthas[1] containing (the word) 'who'. Then these regular Triṣṭubh verses are recited day by day as the strophes of the litanies; the Triṣṭubh is might and strength; verily thus day by day they continue finding support in might and strength. '(Drive) all our enemies away, O Indra,' the Maitrāvaruṇa[2] (recites) this verse by Sukīrti, containing (the word) 'drive away', for the driving away of the evil. By the same Ṛṣis as are the two hymns are the two beginnings of the litanies of the other two. 'Those yoked with prayer I yoke with prayer' and 'Lead us to a wide space, wise one' are the beginnings[3] of the litanies, containing (the words) 'prayer' and 'wide'; verily thus day and day they continue finding support in the prayer and in the wide goer.

xxix. 5. Then the Çilpas[1] are recited in the middle three days, for the

[2] RV. iii. 48; ÇÇS. vii. 22. 4; read *Kuruḍaḥ*.
[3] RV. iv. 19; ÇÇS. vii. 22. 5.
[4] RV. iii. 34; ÇÇS. vii. 23. 6. He allows also the Çyaita on a Bṛhatpṛṣṭha.
[5] RV. vii. 23; ÇÇS. vii. 23. 8.
[6] RV. vi. 30; ÇÇS. vii. 24. 4.
[7] RV. iii. 36; ÇÇS. vii. 24. 5.
[8] See above KB. iii. 9; vii. 10.
[1] See ÇÇS. vii. 22. 3; 23. 5; 24. 3, for the originals and for the new ones of the second two, xii. 4. 1; 5. 1.
[2] RV. x. 131. 1; ÇÇS. xii. 3. 5.
[3] RV. iii. 35. 4 and vi. 47. 8; ÇÇS. xii. 4. 2; 5. 2.
xxix. 5. [1] See for other Çilpas KB. xxx. 3. For the ritual see ÇÇS. xii. 8. 15 *seq.* Here the Çilpas are triplets recited on the three days of the second triad of the Dvādaçāha. For the verses cf. AB. vi. 19.

middle (set of) three days contains the Çilpas. Virāj[2] verses and verses by Vimada (are used) on the first day, for the fourth day is connected with the Virāj. Pañkti and great Pañkti[3] verses (are used) on the fifth day, for the fifth day is connected with the Pañkti. Atichandas[4] verses (are used) on the sixth day, for the sixth day is connected with the Atichandas. Moreover that which is performed without the Bṛhatī is not a Pṛṣṭha; the Pṛṣṭhas here fall away from the Bṛhatī; verily thus day by day they continue finding support in the Çilpas. Moreover the middle (set of) three days is the atmosphere; the atmosphere is without base or support; verily thus day by day they continue finding support in the Çilpas. They are triplets; the Çilpa is threefold, dancing, music, and singing. Verily thus day by day they continue finding support in them. 'Praise nought else' and 'Let us not fear, let us not be troubled' is the Pṛṣṭha for the Maitrāvaruṇa[5] on the tenth day by Medhātithi, for his Pṛṣṭha is not performed on Bṛhatī verses before the tenth day; prosperity is solitary; the Bṛhatī is prosperity; verily thus at the end he finds support in prosperity. Having recited (verses) of two Padas,[6] they recite (the hymn) of the one day (rite); the one day (rite) is a support; the tenth day is a support; (the verses) of two Padas are the metre in which support can be found; verily (they serve) for support.

xxix. 6. The Naudhasa is (the Pṛṣṭha) for the Brāhmaṇācchaṅsin; the explanation of this has been given. In Gāyatrī[1] verses they give the lead for the Brāhmaṇācchaṅsin on the sixth day with the symbol of the Raivata, of the day, to secure the form of the Ahīnas, for the continuity of the Ahīnas, (thinking) 'Undiminished (*ahīnān*) we secure all desires,' for here is nothing taken away. 'Prayers they have offered up through seeking glory' is the conclusion[2] day by day; the 'Prayers up' hymn is the seasons; verily thus day by day they continue finding support in the seasons. They are six (verses); the seasons are six; verily thus day by day they continue finding support in the seasons.

xxix. 7. The Kāleya is (the Pṛṣṭha) for the Achāvāka; the explanation of this has been given. In (verses) of six Padas[1] they give the lead to the Achāvāka on the sixth day, with the symbol of the sixth day. 'Having with thought, like a carpenter, a hymn' is the conclusion[2] day by day; the

[2] RV. vii. 31. 10–12; x. 23. 1–3; ÇÇS. xii. 3. 3; for the other two priests see 4. 10; 5. 9. LoK read *vai madhyas* and so Ānart. on ÇÇS. xii. 3. 3 as ed. by Hillebrandt.

[3] ÇÇS. xii. 3. 10; 4. 13; 5. 12.

[4] ÇÇS. xii. 3. 12; 4. 16; 5. 15 (one triplet each).

[5] RV. viii. 1. 1, 2; 4 7, 8; ÇÇS. xii. 3. 22.

[6] ÇÇS. xii. 3. 23; 4. 24; 5. 23.

[1] I. e. the Stotriya and Anurūpa on RV. i. 4. 1–6; the Raivata is also in Gāyatrī, i. 30. 13–15; viii. 2. 13–15.

[2] See ÇÇS. xii. 5. 3; RV. vii. 23.

xxix. 7. [1] RV. viii. 99. 1, 2; 66. 7, 8; ÇÇS. xii. 5. 4.

[2] See ÇÇS. xii. 5. 3; RV. iii. 38. 1–3.

'carpenter like' hymn is Prajāpati; verily thus they continue day by day finding support in Prajāpati. That (hymn) has no (deity) mentioned; Prajāpati is he (whose name is) not mentioned; verily thus they continue day by day finding support in Prajāpati. There is one (verse) alone [8] with (the deity) expressed; Prajāpati is one alone; verily thus they continue day by day finding support in Prajāpati. Of them the following are unchanged, the Maitrāvaruṇa's Pṛṣṭha, and the conclusions of the other two; verily thus they continue day by day finding support in them.

xxix. 8. It is of ten verses [1]; these breaths are ten; verily thus he places these breaths in the sacrifice and in the sacrificers; the midday (performances) of the Hotrakas consist of two hymns, to counterpoise the Hotṛ's two litanies. Moreover, the Hotṛ is the year, the Hotrakas the seasons; in that the seasons being united in couples are called summer, the rains, and winter, therefore the midday (performances) of the Hotrakas consist of two hymns. Moreover, the Hotṛ is the body, the Hotrakas the limbs; in that the limbs are twofold, therefore the midday (performances) of the Hotrakas consist of two hymns. Having recited at the morning pressings the over recitation of the Stomas, they recite the Ahīna [2] hymns at the midday (pressings) on the Caturviṅça, Abhijit, Viṣuvant, Viçvajit and Mahāvrata days, for these days [3] are not deficient. Having recited the Ahīna hymns (on these days) those of the one day (rite) they recite. These days are turned away and not returning; in that having recited the Ahīna hymns, they recite those of the one day (rite), and the one day (rite) is a support, verily (they serve) for support. Five hymns each time the Maitrāvaruṇa recites in all the Chandomas [4]; the Chandomas are cattle; cattle are fivefold; verily (they serve) to obtain cattle. Four each the Brāhmaṇācchaṅsin and the Achāvāka; the Chandomas are cattle; cattle are fourfold and also four-footed; verily (they serve) to obtain cattle. The Çastras have five calls; the litanies are cattle; cattle are fivefold; verily (they serve) to win cattle. The offering verses of the litanies are from the one day (rite); the one day (rite) is a support; verily (they serve) for support. They say the second *vaṣaṭ*, for the healing of the libations, for the support of the libations.

[8] RV. iii. 38. 10.

[1] See RV. iii. 38.

[2] For these cf. AB. vi. 18; ÇÇS. xii. 6. 7; viz. RV. iv. 16 (ÇÇS. xii. 8. 18); i. 61 (xii. 4. 17); iii. 31 (xii. 5. 17).

[3] *ahīnaḥ* (also in M) is strange in the masc.; and, in view of the parallelism of AB. vi. 18, *ahīnāni* must be read. Cf. KB. xii. 2, n. 4.

[4] ÇÇS. xii. 8. 17–19 for the five; the others have the normal number of four, but with variants.

ADHYĀYA XXX

The Soma Sacrifice (continued)

The Litanies of the Hotrakas at the Third Pressing.

xxx. 1. The morning pressing is the Vasus', the midday pressing the Rudras', the third pressing the Ādityas'. In that he begins the third pressing with the Āditya cup, verily thus he begins with its own deity. Moreover, the third pressing is a pressing which has the sap sucked out; the Āditya cup is a cup rich in sap; verily thereby he makes the third pressing rich in sap. He recites a Triṣṭubh as invitatory verse for the Āditya cup; the explanation of this has been given. Then, when the Pavamāna has been sung, they proceed with the animal victim, for this is the time for it; moreover (it serves) to confer sap on the pressing. Then they proceed with the sacrifice of five oblations; the explanation of this has been given. He recites (verses) by Vāmadeva[1] at the third pressing for (the goblets) being filled, for Vāmadeva it was who proclaimed the Soma to Indra at the third pressing. They contain (the words) 'hither' and 'bay steed', with the symbol of the invitatory verses; they are Triṣṭubhs addressed to Indra and the Ṛbhus; verily thus he makes Indra a half-sharer in the pressing. Nine he recites; ten goblets do they fill here, but the concluding is as the introductory rite. The Hotrakas sacrifice together; the explanation of this has been given. The offering verses[2] are Jagatī verses, containing (the words) 'draught', 'be drunk', and 'drunk', for the third pressing is connected with the Jagatī; they contain (the word) 'be drunk', for the third pressing contains (the word) 'be drunk'. They say a second *vaṣaṭ* for the healing of the libations, for the support of the libations. Then comes the sacrificial food,[3] then the Hotṛ's goblet; the explanation of this has been given. Then they offer the cakes (for the Pitṛs) at the third pressing; the explanation of these has been given. Then they proceed with the cup for Savitṛ[4]; the explanation of this has been given. He recites one Triṣṭubh as invitatory verse for the cup for Savitṛ; the explanation of this has been given. Again in that between the two litanies the Agnīdh says the offering verses for the cup for the wives,[5] thereby the two reach the Hotṛ.

[1] RV. iv. 35; see ÇÇS. viii. 2. 3.

[2] ÇÇS. viii. 2. 5 *seq.*

[3] ÇÇS. viii. 2. 13.

[4] ÇÇS. viii. 3. 2 gives the Triṣṭubh as RV. iv. 54. i, which is given in the *Anukramaṇī* as Jagatī. This precedes the Vaiçvadeva Çastra.

[5] I. e. between the Vaiçvadeva and the Agnimāruta Çastras; see Caland and Henry, *L'Agniṣṭoma*, p. 366.

xxx. 2. The litanies of the Ukthya are addressed to Indra and Agni; the explanation of these has been given. These to Indra in Jagatī they recite day by day[1]; the Jagatī is cattle; cattle are connected with the Jagatī; verily (they serve) to obtain cattle. 'These should be unchanged' some state, saying 'These are the supporters of the pressing.' But the rule is 'They should be varied,' for one day, then another, they approach. (Recitations) to Varuṇa, to Bṛhaspati, and to Viṣṇu they recite; their metre is the Jagatī; Indra's the Triṣṭubh; in that the metres are inverted, it is to secure the characteristic of the deities. (Recitations[2]) to Indra and Varuṇa, to Indra and Bṛhaspati, to Indra and Viṣṇu they recite; verily with these they accompany the cups, for so are the cups drawn.

xxx. 3. 'Holder of the people, the generous, worthy of praise' the Maitrāvaruṇa[1] (says); the explanation of this has been given. The conclusion[2] is by Vasiṣṭha day by day; Vasiṣṭha saw the third pressing for the Maitrāvaruṇa's function; therefore day by day the conclusion is by Vasiṣṭha. In Kakubh verses they give the lead to the Maitrāvaruṇa[3] on the third day; thereby he falls into the power of the Brāhmaṇācchaṅsin. On the fourth day they give the lead to each in his own metre; verily thus each in his own metre they continue finding support. In Gāyatrī verses[4] they give the lead to the Maitrāvaruṇa, in Uṣṇih verses to the Brāhmaṇācchaṅsin, in Anuṣṭubh verses to the Achāvāka, to secure a progressive increase. So their metres increase with four syllables each. In Paṅkti verses[5] they give the lead to the Maitrāvaruṇa on the fifth day, for the fifth day is connected with the Paṅkti; in (verses) of two Padas[6] they give the lead on the sixth day, for the sixth day is connected with (verses) of two Padas. Moreover they perform the Sāmans, Gūrda, Bhadra, Udvaṅçaputra;[7] moreover the Çilpas are accompanied by (verses) of two feet; therefore here the Çilpas are recited, (thinking) 'Let us not depart from the Çilpas.'

xxx. 4. With the Nābhānediṣṭha[1] the Hotṛ sprinkles seed; it he hands to the Maitrāvaruṇa; it he develops with the Vālakhilyās; these Vālakhilyās he recites as divided; by Padas the first two hymns he divides; verily thus

[1] See Ānartīya on ÇÇS. xii. 10. 1 and 2. Cf. AB. vi. 15, and 14.

[2] See RV. vii. 82 (ÇÇS. xii. 11. 15); x. 48 (ibid. 12. 6); vi. 69. 1–8 (ibid. 26. 5) for the seventh day; for the offering verses ÇÇS. ix. 2. 6; 3. 3; 4. 7, on the Ukthya; for the litanies, x. 2. 4; 3. 4; 4. 6.

xxx. 3. [1] RV. iii. 51. 1–3; ÇÇS. ix. 2. 3.

[2] RV. vii. 84. 1–3 (ÇÇS. ix. 2. 5; xii. 10. 5) 85. 1–3; ÇÇS. xii. 10. 6.

[3] ÇÇS. xii. 10. 7; RV. viii. 103. 8, 9; 19. 30, 31. See ÇÇS. xii. 12. 7 for the similar verses.

[4] Quoted summarily by Ānartīya on ÇÇS. xii. 10. 9; 12. 9 (ix. 3. 2); see also xii. 26. 7.

[5] ÇÇS. xii. 10. 12.

[6] ÇÇS. xii. 11. 1.

[7] For these cf. *Ind. Stud.* iii. 224, 226, 209; PB. xiii. 12. 6 *seq.*

xxx. 4. [1] RV. x. 61; see ÇÇS. xii. 11. 5–9; for the Vālakhilyās cf. AB. vi. 27, 28.

by joints he gathers him together; by half verses the second two; man consists of two portions; verily thus he unites them; verse by verse the third two hymns; verily thus he gathers him whole; he should invert in the Nārāçaṅsa[2]; therefore foetuses are born inverted.

xxx. 5. In the Tārkṣya[1] he mounts the difficult mounting; Tārkṣya is Vāyu; Vāyu is breath verily thus he places breath in him; him he hands over to the Brāhmaṇācchaṅsin. Him he receives in the womb of the Sukīrti (hymn[2]); for him born he recites in Pañkti form with repetition of *o* the Vṛṣākapi[3] (hymn); the repetition of *o* is food; verily thus born he finds support in proper food. Then he recites the Kuntāpa[4] according to the metres, for the obtaining of all desires; viz. the Nārāçaṅsīs,[5] the Raibhīs,[6] the Kāravyās,[7] the Indragāthās,[8] the Bhūtechads,[9] the Parikṣit verses,[10] and the prattle of Etaça.[11] Etaça, the sage, saw[12] the life of the sacrifice. He said to his sons 'My boys, I have seen the life of the sacrifice; that I shall prattle forth; think me not mad.' They said 'Be it so.' Then he prattled[13] it forth; his eldest son, creeping up, stopped his mouth, (saying) 'Our father has become mad.' To him he said 'Be gone; fie on thee, O fool; I make[14] thine offspring the worst; hadst thou not, O fool, stopped[15] my mouth, I had made the cow of a hundred (years of) life, and man of a thousand.' Therefore the descendants of Etaça being the Ājāneyas are the worst of the Bhṛgus, for they are under curse by a father, their own deity, their own Prajāpati.[16]

xxx. 6. (The verses) of the Ādityas and Añgirases[1] he recites next. The Ādityas and the Añgirases were at variance, 'We shall go first to the world

[2] RV. x. 12.

[1] RV. x. 178; see ÇÇS. xii. 11. 12.

[2] RV. x. 181; see ÇÇS. xii. 13. 1. Cf. AB. vi. 29; *jātam* represents an elliptical clause.

[3] RV. x. 86; see ÇÇS. xii. 13. 1, where the form of the Nyūñkha is given.

[4] RV. xx. 127–36; see ÇÇS. xii. 13. 7; AB. vi. 32, 33.

[5] RV. xx. 127. 1–3; see ÇÇS. xii. 14; RVKh. v. 8.

[6] RV. xx. 127. 4–6; see ÇÇS. xii. 15. 1; 14. 4, 5, where see Hillebrandt's crit. notes; RVKh. v. 9.

[7] RV. xx. 127. 11–14; see ÇÇS. xii. 15. 2–4; RVKh. v. 11

[8] AV. xx. 128. 12–16; see ÇÇS. xii. 15. 5; 16. 1; RVKh. v. 14.

[9] AV. xx. 135. 11–13; see ÇÇS. xii. 16. 4, 5, 8; RVKh. v. 21.

[10] AV. xx. 127. 7–10; see ÇÇS. xii. 16. 2; 17. 1. 1–4; RVKh. v. 10.

[11] AV. xx. 129; see ÇÇS. xii. 18; RVKh. v. 15. The story is given also in AB. vi. 33.

[12] BOoLK and the Ānand. ed. have the absurd *adarçat*.

[13] BLK have *apilalāpa*.

[14] Oo and the Ānand. ed. have *abhijagrāha*, which is, no doubt, correct.

[15] M. has needlessly *kariṣyāmi*.

[16] The exact force of these words which are probably best taken as in apposition to *pitrā*, who can be regarded as their *prajāpati*, is uncertain. The curse was not by any deity apparently. The alternative is to connect with the next clause, but that is unlikely.

xxx. 6. [1] AV. xx. 135. 6 *seq.*; see ÇÇS. xii. 19; RVKh. v. 20; AB. vi. 34 has a much longer version for which cf. Caland, *Jaiminīya Brāhmaṇa*, pp. 158–61, and ÇÇS. xiv. 40 has a variant version.

of heaven' (said) the Āditya; 'we' the Añgirases. The Añgirases sent to the Ādityas (saying) 'Ours is the pressing day to-morrow; do ye cause us to sacrifice.' Agni was their envoy; the Ādityas said 'Ours is the pressing day to-day; and thou art[2] the Hotṛ for us here, Bṛhaspati the Brahman, Ayāsya the Udgātṛ, Ghora Āñgirasa the Ādhvaryu.' Them they rejected; him they desired to please with these (verses); thus they repeat these (verses). They brought a white horse as sacrificial fee,[3] that one which here gives heat; therefore the Ādityas went to heaven; he goes to heaven who knows thus.

xxx. 7. He recites the orderings of the quarters[1]; the quarters are in order for him. He recites the man-ordering (verses)[2]; men are in order for him. He says the riddles,[3] the Pratirādhas,[4] the Atīvādā,[5] the Āhanasyās,[6] all forms of speech. Therefore a man speaks all forms of speech, but other animals one only. They are eight; by them the gods attained all attainments; so verily also the sacrificers by them attain all attainments. 'The Kapṛth, O men, the Kapṛth extend,' and 'What time forward ye came' are two (verses[7]); thus they become perfect[8]. They make up ten; the Virāj consists of sets of ten; the Virāj is prosperity and proper food; verily (they serve) to obtain the Virāj as prosperity and proper food.

xxx. 8. He recites the Dadhikrā (verse[1]); the Dadhikrā (verse) is speech; verily thus he places speech in him; he recites (the verses) to Soma the purifying[2]; (the verses) to Soma the purifying are a filter; verily thus he purifies him. Him he hands over to the Achāvāka; him he with the

[2] *hotāsi* is made certain (against *hotāsa* in BLK and Ānand. ed.) by the parallels ÇB. iii. 5. 1. 13–17; GB. ii. 6. 14. For *çiçikṣuḥ* cf. *Nir.* ii. 10; 'present' (BR.) is here impossible.

[3] *dakṣiṇā* in the Ānand. ed. is a mere error: *abhitadantaḥ* in OoK is an easier reading, but with *te* following is not probable.

[1] AV. xx. 128. 1–5; ÇÇS. xii. 20. 2; RVKh. v. 12.

[2] AV. xx. 128. 6–11; see ÇÇS. xii. 21. 2. 1–6; RVKh. v. 13.

[3] AV. xx. 133. 1–4 must be meant; see ÇÇS. xii. 21. 3; in xii. 22 are given all six verses of that hymn (cf. RVKh. v. 16), no doubt the last two in error, and some add the seventh verse, probably because they thought that 22 contained the seven (4 and 3) verses of ÇÇS. xii. 21. 3. In AB. vi. 33 the number six is probably meant as is accepted by Sāyaṇa. *Per contra* Ānartīya ignores the whole of 22 and regards as the Pravalhikā AV. xx. 134, which in AB. is the Ājijñāsenyās (RVKh. v. 17); the confusion seems to have arisen from the omission of that special category. The statement of the *Vedic Concordance* that Pravalhikā applies to AV. xx. 134 is erroneous, as is Scheftelowitz's view, ZDMG. lix. 425.

[4] AV. xx. 135. 1–3; see ÇÇS. xii. 23, 2; RVKh. v. 18; Pratirādha in AB. vi. 33.

[5] AV. xx. 135. 4; see ÇÇS. xii. 23. 4; RVKh. v. 19; Ativāda in AB. vi. 33.

[6] AV. xx. 136; see ÇÇS. xii. 24. 1; RVKh. v. 22.

[7] RV. x. 101. 12 and x. 155. 4; see ÇÇS. xii. 24. 2.

[8] *ānākṣipyaḥ* is apparently corrupt; the word rendered is *anākṣepyāḥ*, which, however, is not at all probable as a correction.

xxx. 8. [1] RV. iv. 39. 6; see ÇÇS. xii. 25. 1. Cf. AB. vi. 36.

[2] RV. ix. 101. 4–6; ÇÇS. xii. 25. 2; AB. vi. 36.

Evayāmarut (hymn[3]) makes to move when born; he repeats *o*; stumbling as it were one moves when first desirous to walk; verily thus from the immortal metre he propagates him for immortality; they obtain immortality who perform the sixth day (rite). Having recited the strophe and antistrophe, he recites the Vālakhilyās; the strophe and antistrophe are the body, the Vālakhilyās the breaths; these breaths are not separated (from the body). They say 'Why are they (called) Vālakhilyās?' That which is not in contact in two fields,[4] they call Khila; these breaths are a hair (*vāla*) in breadth and are not separated; therefore are they Vālakhilyās.

xxx. 9. 'In the Tārkṣya he mounts the difficult mounting,' it has been said.[1] In Gāyatrī verses they give the lead for the Brāhmaṇācchaṅsin on the second day, thereby he falls into the power of the Maitrāvaruṇa. 'Forward to the most generous, the great, born of great wealth' is a six verse (hymn[2]), twice as great as that of the Maitrāvaruṇa. The conclusion day by day is by Kṛṣṇa[3]; Kṛṣṇa Āñgirasa saw this third pressing for the Brāhmaṇācchaṅsin's office; therefore day by day the conclusion is by Kṛṣṇa. In Anuṣṭubhs they give the lead for the Achāvāka on the third day; thereby he falls into the power of the Brāhmaṇācchaṅsin. The 'season mother' (hymn[4]) has thirteen verses; it is twice as great as that of the Brāhmaṇācchaṅsin and there is one verse over. The conclusion day by day is by Bharadvāja[5]; Bharadvāja saw this third pressing for the Achāvāka's office; therefore day by day the conclusion is by Bharadvāja. The Achāvāka alternates the two Viṣṇu (hymns[6]), the conclusions the other two. The Maitrāvaruṇa and the Brāhmaṇācchaṅsin have two conclusions; the Achāvāka has one conclusion. In that the Achāvāka has an unchanging conclusion, the Achāvāka is a support; verily (it serves) for support.

xxx. 10. Thirty-six (verses) the Maitrāvaruṇa recites at the Caturviñça,[1] forty the Brāhmaṇācchaṅsin, and forty-four the Achāvāka. These are a hundred and twenty. A hundred and twenty are the days of the season; thus he obtains the season, with the season the year and the desires that are in the year. Five hymns the Maitrāvaruṇa recites on all the Chandoma days; the Chandomas are cattle; cattle are fivefold; verily (they

[3] RV. v. 87; see ÇÇS. xii. 26. 10; AB. vi. 30; the rendering of *nyūṅkhamānaka* in JAOS. xxxi. 331 is erroneous.

[4] See Pischel and Geldner, *Ved. Stud.* ii. 205; Oldenberg, *Ṛgveda-Noten*, i. 385, 386. The idea seems to be that the space between the fields in which they do not come into contact is the Khila, as Oldenberg takes it, but the word *asaṁbhinna* is very curious; the comm. suggests 'unploughed'.

[1] Above KB. xxx. 5.

[2] RV. i. 57; see ÇÇS. xii. 26. 4. The Stotriya and Anurūpa are RV. viii. 92. 28–30; i. 8. 8–10; ÇÇS. xii. 12. 1.

[3] RV. x. 42. 1–3 and 43. 1–3; see ÇÇS. xii. 12. 5 and 6.

[4] RV. ii. 13; see ÇÇS. xii. 26. 22. For the Stotriya and Anurūpa see RV. i. 11. 1–3; 8. 6, 7; ÇÇS. xii. 26. 1.

[5] RV. vi. 69. 1–3; see ÇÇS. xii. 26. 5.

[6] RV. vii. 100 and i. 154. 1–6; see ÇÇS. xii. 26. 2 and 3.

xxx. 10. [1] See ÇÇS. xii. 27. 1 with Ānartīya's note.

serve) to obtain cattle. Four hymns the Brāhmaṇācchaṅsin[2] recites in the first Chandoma; the Chandomas are cattle; cattle are fourfold, and also fourfooted; verily (they serve) to obtain cattle. Five hymns the Achāvāka[3] recites in the first Chandoma; the Chandomas are cattle; cattle are fivefold; verily (they serve) to obtain cattle. Six (they recite) in the second and third; the year has six seasons; verily (they serve) to obtain the year. The Çastras have four calls; the litanies are cattle; cattle are fourfold, and also fourfooted; verily (they serve) to obtain cattle. On the sixth day that of the Maitrāvaruṇa has five calls; the litanies are cattle; cattle are fivefold; verily (they serve) to obtain cattle. The offering verses of the litanies are from the one day (rite); the one day (rite) is a support; verily (they serve) for support. They say the second *vaṣaṭ*, for the healing of the libations, for the support of the libations.

xxx. 11. Five metres they recite at night, Anuṣṭubh, Gāyatrī, Uṣṇih, Triṣṭubh and Jagatī; these are the metres of night. The night has five calls, and so the additional litany of the Vājapeya. 'The night goes beyond the Uktha;[1] verily thus from metre to metre they call' Kauṣītaki used to say, to prevent sameness. In that he uses a Triṣṭubh containing the word 'over the night' as invitatory verse for the Açvin litany[2] cup, (it is because) the Praiṣa contains (the word) 'over the night', for the Somas are left over the night. Moreover, the Triṣṭubh is might and strength; verily thus might and strength he places in the sacrificer. The additional litanies of the Āptoryāma have four calls; the litanies are cattle; cattle are fourfold, and also fourfooted; verily (they serve) to obtain cattle. They use as concluding verses (verses) to the lord of the field, (thinking) 'The field is this earth; in it undepressed shall we find support at the end'; verily thus in it undepressed do they find support at the end. In that the offering verses are Triṣṭubhs containing (the word) 'over the night', (it is) because the Somas are left over the night. Moreover, the Triṣṭubh is might and strength; verily thus might and strength he places in the sacrificer. They say the second *vaṣaṭ*, for the healing of the libations, for the support of the libations. They then proceed with (the cup) for the yoker of the bays; the

[2] See ÇÇS. xii. 25. 4–7.

[3] See ÇÇS. xii. 26. 2, 12 *seq.*

[1] The sense must be as indicated, but *atigraha* is first found here in it. *Ukthasya* as read in the edd. with the MSS. is probably thus to be taken of the number of calls, five against four. It is not sufficient to assume the sense to be that the night has an extra Uktha, for in point of fact the night rite (i. e. the Atirātra) adds 12, while the Vājapeya adds one to the Ṣoḍaçin. For *āhvayante* the Ānand. ed. has *āhūyante*: the sense remains the same. *chandasaç chandasa* is ambiguous, and may mean from metre to metre, i. e. as bridging over the separation, or simply from each metre, but the former (*chandase*) is seemingly better.

[2] See ÇÇS. ix. 20. 30 and 31.

explanation of this has been given. He recites a Triṣṭubh as invitatory verse for (the cup) for the yoker of the bays [3]; the explanation of this has been given. In that he recites an invitatory verse [4] for the Atipraiṣa, (it is because) without strength is the Praiṣa which has no invitatory verse. Moreover there are invitatory verses in the case of (the cups) for two deities, and in the case of all the Prasthitas; therefore he recites an invitatory verse for it. 'In that he recites an Atipraiṣa, verily thus he refers to the next day, verily thus they keep taking hold of the next day' Kauṣītaki used to say.[5]

[3] See RV. i. 177. 4; ÇÇS. x. 1. 10.

[4] Both are given in ÇÇS. x. 1. 11 as RV. iii. 58. 5 (or 4) and *iha mada iha maghavan.*

[5] See KB. xxii. 2; xxvi. 11.

GENERAL INDEX

Abhijit day of the Sattra, 23, 26, 51, 52, 211, 480-482, 523.
Abhiplava Ṣaḍaha, 23, 51, 52, 58, 209, 457-466.
Ābhipratāriṇa Vṛddhadyumna, a king, 196.
Abhiṣecanīya day of Rājasūya, 67.
Abhiṣeka, 67.
Abhyagnis Aitaçāyanas, the least important of the Aurvas, 284.
Abhyuddṛṣṭā sacrifice, 366.
Abhyuditā sacrifice, 365.
Ablative, use of, 83.
Absolute case, 83; apparent use of accusative absolute, 407, n. 2, 421, n. 3, 526, n. 2.
Accents, absence of in Brāhmaṇas of the Ṛgveda, 96.
Accusative, uses of, 81, 82, 107; with *brū*, 388, n. 3; apparently absolute, 407, n. 2, 421, n. 3, 526, n. 2.
Achāvāka, priest, 32, 160, 173, 197, 262, 263, 264, 266, 267, 269, 270, 281, 282, 289, 421, 489, 493, 494, 515, 516, 517, 518, 521, 522, 523, 528.
Adhrigu, formula, 406.
Adhrigu, priest, 140.
Adhvaryu, priest, 115, 116, 121, 128, 132, 156, 256, 257, 258, 289, 308, 309, 310, 362, 375, 379, 385, 398, 400, 401, 404, 413, 422, 442, 512, 517.
Adhyāyas, 30 or 40 in the Aitareya Brāhmaṇa, 35.
Aditi, 112, 123, 184, 387.
Āditya cup, 431, 432, 524.
Adityas, 114, 119, 126, 147, 186, 209, 244, 285, 286, 311, 329, 338, 416, 511, 525; conflict with Aṅgirases, 22, 285-287, 526, 527.
Adverbial forms, anomalous, 78.
Adverbs, uses of, 89.
After-offerings, included in introductory sacrifice, 114.
Age, of the two Brāhmaṇas *inter se*, 26-28; absolutely, 42-50.
Ages, of the world, not Vedic, 302, n. 6.
Agni, 187, 256, 268, 295, 296, 304, 305, 311, 323; nearest of gods, 107, 304, 388; three forms of, 347; as death, 419; *and see* Jātavedas, Vaiçvānara.
Agni and the Maruts, 296, 487.
Agni and Soma, 401, 405, 453.
Agni and Varuṇa, 449.
Agnicayana, human sacrifice at, 63.
Agnīdh, priest, 160, 267, 268, 269, 289, 516, 517.
Āgnīdhra priest, 125, 248, 485.
Āgnīdhrīya, 398.
Agnihotra, 31, 33, 51, 190, 251-256, 290-296, 353-357, 370, 451.
Āgnimāruta Çastra, 174, 185-189, 485-487, 456, 467, 492, 494, 501, 504, 524, n. 2.
Agnipraṇayana, 128-131, 398, 399.
Agniṣṭoma, 31, 189, 190, 270, 431, 437, 454, 456, 466, 485, 492.
Agniṣṭoma Sāman, 509.
Agnisvāmin, views of on Kauṣītaki school, 42.
Āgrayaṇa, 369, 370; cup, 60, 295, 433.
Āhanasyā, verses (AV. xx. 136. 1-10), 287, 527.
Aharahahçasya, 272.
Āhavanīya, 249, 256, 258, 290, 296, 298, 305, 310, 312, 339, 353, 364, 370, 375, 398, 408, 442.
Āhāvas, 424, 425, 483, 484, 489, 529.
Ahi budhnya, the dragon of the deep, as name of a verse (RV. vi. 50. 14), 486.
Ahīna, 52, 59, 264, 271, 272, 320, 521, 522, 523.
Aiḍa Sāman, 520.
Aikādaçākṣi (cf. JB. ii. 229) Mānutantavya, his royal offspring, 255.
Aikṣvāka Hariçcandra Vaidhasa, 299.
Ailūṣa, Kavaṣa, excluded from sacrifice, 148, 413.
Aindravāyava cup, order of, 59.
Aitareya, cited tacitly, 169, 170, 185.
Aitareya Āraṇyaka, 36, 38.
Aitareya Brāhmaṇa, contents of with parallels in the Kauṣītaki Brāhmaṇa, 1-13; relation to Kauṣītaki, 22-26; comparative age, 26-28; composition, 28-36; date of, 42-50; ritual of, 51-61; Rājasūya and legend of

Çunaḥçepa, 61–68; language, 69–96; style, 96–98; metre, 98–101; idea of Punarmṛtyu, only in latest part, 340, n. 1; borrowing of vii. 11 from KB. iii. 1, 49, 50, 297, n. 2.
Aitaçapralāpa, hymn (AV. xx. 129. 1 *seq.*), 22, 284, 285, 288; Etaçapralāpa, 526.
Ājāneyas, descendants of Etaça, 526.
Ajīgarta Sauyavasi, a seer, father of Çunaḥçepa, 68, 64, 303, 304.
Ājijñāsenyā, verses (AV. xx. 134. 1–4), 285, 527, n. 3.
Ājya Çastra, 158–164, 193, 423–425, 455, 456, 458, 459, 460, 462, 463, 464, 467, 468, 469, 471, 474, 478, 481, 483, 486, 487, 493, 499, 502, 504, 509, 518.
Ājya Stotra, 425, 480, 431.
Ākhyāna theory, 65, 66.
Akṣarapañkti, 486.
Ākṣyant days, 209.
Ālambana, 446.
Alīkayu Vācaspata, a Naimiṣīya priest, 498.
All-gods, 126, 134, 251, 304, 329, 333, 371, 418, 426, 458, 459, 460, 461, 464, 465, 467, 468, 470, 475, 476, 480, 491, 501, 503, 507.
Alliteration, 80.
Āmbāṣṭhya, performs the horse sacrifice, 336.
Amitratapana Çuṣmiṇa Çaibya, a king, 338.
Anacoluthon, 292.
Ānartīya, commentator on the Çāñkhāyana Çrauta Sūtra, cites with different reading KB. xxvii. 1, 508, n. 2.
Ancestral seer of sacrificer (or his priest), use of verses by (*yathārṣi*) for the Āprīs recommended, 188, *and see* Ārṣeya.
Andhras, 65, 307.
Añga Vairocana, performs the horse sacrifice, 337.
Āñgirasa, Ghora, a mythical sage, 527.
Āñgirasa, Hiraṇyastūpa, author of RV. i. 32, 180.
Āñgirasa, Kṛṣṇa, author of RV. x. 42, 43, 528.
Āñgirasa, Saṁvarta, 336.
Añgirases, 119, 124, 186, 209, 263, 286, 288, 329, 333, 449, 516; conflict with Ādityas, 22, 285–287, 526, 527.
Aṇīcin Mauna, a sage, 478.
Animal sacrifice, 134–145, 403–408.
Animals, contrasted with men in mode of generation, 161, 162; commit incest, 300.
Anointing of the sacrificial post, 404.
Anointment of king, 23.
Añçumati, 287.
Antaryāma cup, 150, 257, 412, 415, 492.
Anūbandhyā, offering, 449–451.
Anumati, first full-moon day, 195, 297.
Anunirvāpyā Iṣṭi, 365.
Anupraiṣas, 514.
Anuṣṭubh, 173, 199, 329, 333, 399, 407, 424, 428, 440, 508, 509, 511, 514, 518, 528; treatment of in the Aitareya Brāhmaṇa, 99, 100.
Anvāhāryapacana, 256, 258, 298, 389, 353.
Aorist indicative, use of, 85, 86, 314, n. 1, 385, n. 2, 418, n. 11, 485, n. 8; irregular forms of, 76.
Āpastamba, date of, 48.
Āpastamba Çrauta Sūtra, relation to the Kauṣītaki Brāhmaṇa, 48; date of, 48, 49; ritual in, 55, 57.
Apiçarvara, etymology and meaning of, 201.
Āpnāna passage, 449.
Āpohiṣṭhīya, hymn (RV. x. 9), 187.
Aponaptrīya, 148–150, 412–414.
Apratiratha, hymn (RV. x. 103), 327.
Āprī verses, 187, 188, 405, 450.
Apsarases, 184, 358.
Aptoryāma, 33, 54, 55, 191; Āptoryāma, 529.
Āptya gods, 329, 333, 474.
Ārāḷhi Saujāta (cf. JB. iii. 37), 311.
Araṇis, 354.
Araru, a demon, 314 (vii. 28), n. 1.
Ārbhava Pavamāna, 54, 267, 432.
Arbuda, hymn (RV. x. 94), 79, 427, 428.
Arbuda Kādraveya, a serpent seer, 259, 519.
Arindama Sanaçruta, 318.
Arithmetic, division of a thousand by three, 271.
Arrow, parts of, 126.
Ārṣeya, invocation of Agni by ancestral names, 313, n. 2, 321, n. 2, 358, n. 2, 410, n. 3.
Āruṇi, Uddālaka, 324, *and see* Āruṇi.
Āruṇi, views on expiations of errors in the sacrifice, 41, 498.
Arurmaghas, destroyed by Indra, 314.
Arvāvasu, the Brahman priest of the gods, 381.
Aryans, attacks on by aborigines possibly referred to, 413.
Açani, epithet of Rudra, 25, 378.
Āçramas, alleged reference to doctrine of, 300, n. 6.
Āçvalāyana, probable date of, 44.
Āçvalāyana Gṛhya Sūtra, 36.
Āçvalāyana Çrauta Sūtra, relation to the Aitareya Brāhmaṇa, 32, 33, 44; date of, 44; ritual in, 51–53, 57, 61, 67
Açvamedha, 40, 52, 336.
Açvatara Āçvi, Buliḷa, 281
Açvattha, tree, 315, 316, 332.
Āçvina Çastra, 253, 444–447, 528.

Açvins, 121, 145, 251, 295, 364, 381, 394, 409, 421, 426, 445.
Aṣṭācatvāriṅça Stoma, 206, 499.
Āsandīvant, a place of performance of the Açvamedha, 336.
Asitamṛgas, a branch of the Kaçyapas, 314.
Ass, virility of destroyed, 203, 204, 445.
Assembly, comradeship in, 116; women not to go to, 333.
Assimilation of sibilants, 84.
Asura woman, and Indra, 477.
Asuras, 117, 121, 125, 126, 133, 261, 270, 285, 288, 334, 396, 414, 415, 443, 485, 515.
Atharvan, 118.
Atharvaveda, not recognized in the Ṛgveda Brāhmaṇas, 47.
Atichandas, 480, 494, 509, 510, 518.
Atipraiṣa, 530.
Atirātra, 33, 51, 52, 53, 54, 191, 201, 202, 250, 271, 281, 442-444, 494.
Ativāda, verse (AV. xx. 135. 4), 285, Atīvādā, 527.
Atmosphere, 292; Maruts' place in, 113; life of victim sent to, 139.
Ātreya, portion of victim assigned to an, 289.
Ātreya, Udamaya, a sacrificer, 337.
Atris, 469; the Atris rescue the sun, 483.
Atyagniṣṭoma, form of Jyotiṣṭoma, 54.
Atyarāti Jānaṁtapi, performs, though not a king, the horse sacrifice, 338.
Aufrecht's edition of the AB., 101, 102; view as to authorship of Ṛgvedic hymns, 64.
Augment, omission of, in imperfect indicative, 74, 75.
Augrasainya, Yudhāṁçrauṣṭi, 336.
Aupāvi, 127, n. 4.
Avabhṛtha, 448, 449.
Avacatnuka, a place, 337.
Avatsāra, a seer, 158; Prāsravaṇa (v. l. Prāçravaṇa), a Hotṛ, 419.
Avesta, proper time of sacrifice in, 254.
Āvikṣita, Marutta, 336.
Avoidance, of daughter-in-law for father-in-law, 24, 178, 179.
Axe (*paraçu*), shape of, 160.
Ayāsya, Udgātṛ at the sacrifice of Çunahçepa, 308; at the Ādityas' sacrifice, 527.
Āyus, special form of rite, 206, 457, 462, 463, 466.

Bābhrava, v. l. for Bhārgava, 470, n. 7.
Bābhravas, descendants of Devarāta Vaiçvāmitra, 305.
Bābhravya, Girija, 290.
Babhru Daivāvṛdha, a sacrificer, 318.
Bahiṣpavamāna Stotra, 151, 160, 165, 173, 396.
Bahvṛca, 379.
Bahvṛcabrāhmaṇa, evidence of existence of a text other than AB. or KB., 22, 48, 299, n. 5, 392, n. 2, 416, n. 5, 437, n. 2.
Baida (Veda, JB. ii. 278), Hiraṇyadant, 168.
Bamboo seeds, 369.
Bārhaspatya, Çaṁyu, 368.
Barley harvest, 369.
Barren cow, offered to Fathers, 185.
Baru, hymn of (RV. x. 96), 79, 490.
Bath, expiation for omission of morning, 295.
Baudhāyana Çrauta Sūtra, 40, 57.
Bhadra Sāman, 525.
Bhaga, 381.
Bhāllavika form of Gavām Ayana, 57.
Bharadvāja, 196, 272, 321, 427, 528.
Bharadvāja Çrauta Sūtra, uses the Aitareya Brāhmaṇa, 145.
Bharata Dauḥṣanti, performs the horse sacrifice, 45, 337, 338.
Bharatas, 45; Agni of the, 120, 359; claim of their charioteers to a fourth part of the booty won in their raids on the Satvants, 153, 154.
Bhāratī, 152.
Bhārgava, Cyavana, 336; Gṛtsamada, 470.
Bhārgāyaṇa, Sutvan Kairiçi, 348.
Bhāṣā, of Pāṇini, 42.
Bhāṣikasūtra, statement as to accent of texts, 96.
Bhāsa Sāman, 211.
Bhauvana, Viçvakarman, a sacrificer, seeks to give away land, 336.
Bhava, epithet of Rudra, 25, 377.
Bhīma Vaidarbha, 318.
Bhṛgu, as adopted son of Varuṇa, 136; vision of, 409, n. 1.
Bhṛgus, Ājāneyas worst of, 526.
Bhūtapati, as name of Rudra, 135.
Bhūtavīras, a priestly family, 314.
Bhūtechads, verses (AV. xx. 135. 11-13), 287, 526.
Bilva wood, use of, 134, 403.
Bird, golden, discusses Dīkṣā with Keçin Dārbhya, 385, 386.
Bird hymn (RV. x. 177), 491.
Birds, mouthpiece of Nirṛti (dissolution), 145, 146.
Black antelope skin, 109, 117, 133.
Black, garments of Rudra, 286; as a symbol of night, 405.
Black Yajurveda, priority of Mantras in to prose, 47.
Blood, of sacrificial victim, used to propitiate Rakṣases, 139, 406.
Bodies of Prajāpati, a form of litany, 250, 512.

Böhtlingk, O., criticisms on Aufrecht's edition of the AB., 102.
Bṛhaddiva, name of RV. x. 120, 79; Niṣkevalya of, 455.
Bṛhaduktha, a priest, 888.
Bṛhaspati, 115, 121, 126, 186, 269, 814, 819, 829, 888, 389, 417, 471, 525, 527.
Bṛhat Sāman, 122, 211, 254, 819, 829, 888, 861, 899, 408, 416, 468, 481, 482, 488, 484, 485, 487, 488, 489, 498, 500, 502.
Bṛhatī, 178, 199, 201, 322, 899, 408, 409, 428, 480, 440, 445, 474, 488, 510, 520, 522.
Brahman (neuter), resolution of all into the, 80, 342, 848.
Brahman (personal) found only in KB., 27, 428, 457.
Brahman, priest, 81, 121, 124, 201, 256, 257, 258, 879, 442, 516, 517; as Purohita of the king, 818, 889.
Brāhmaṇa, higher than a Kṣatriya, 308; alone eater of oblations, 309; asks Kṣatriya for a place of sacrifice, 310; mode of announcing consecration of, 818; status of, 815; not to be spoken ill of, 878; position insecure as regards the people, 484; to receive slaughterer's share of victim, if the latter is not a Brāhmaṇa, 289; insistence on purity of descent, 148, 414; accusation of not being, 119, 147, 414.
Brāhmaṇa, variation from Sūtra, 876, n. 2.
Brāhmaṇācchaṅsin, priest, 82, 58, 197, 262, 263, 264, 266, 267, 268, 269, 270, 281, 282, 289, 489, 493, 516, 518, 520, 521, 522, 523, 525, 528.
Brahmaṇaspati, 121, 122, 174, 898, 429; identical with Brahman, 428.
Brahmanical self-assertion, prominent in AB. vii. 18–viii. 28, 29.
Brahmodya, 512, n. 2.
Breach of vows, expiation for, 294.
Breaths, 120, 122.
Bringing forward of Agni and Soma, 181–188, 401, 402.
Bringing forward of the fires, 128–131, 898, 899.
Bulila Āçvatara Āçvi, a Hotṛ priest, views on performance of Çilpas, 281, 282, x.
Burnell's MS. of the KB., 103.
Butter portions, in the new and full moon sacrifices, 360.
Buying of the Soma, 115–117, 889, 890.

Caitra, Dīkṣā in, 452.
Cake offering, at animal sacrifice, purpose of and equivalence to the animal victim, 141, 148, 407; at the Soma sacrifice, 151, 152.
Calls, number of, 529.
Candramas, 877, 474.
Carrying forward of the Soma, 115, 889.
Cases, syntax of, 81–88.
Caste, high claims for Brahmans, 29, 818.
Catalogue style, precursor of Tantra, 466, n. 1.
Cattle, become thin and shaggy in cool season, 216; connected with the Jagatī metre, 128; necessity of house for, 180.
Caturhotṛs, recited by the Hotṛ, 248, 249; not in KB., 512, n. 2.
Cāturmāsya, offerings, 108, n. 1, 870–876.
Caturviñça day, 26, 51, 52, 209, 451–457, 528.
Catuçcatvāriñça Stoma, 499.
Catuṣṭoma, 426; derivation of from Catustoma, a mystery, 192.
Causal use of relative clauses, 91.
Chandoga, 379.
Chāndogya Upaniṣad, 28.
Chandomas, 26, 51, 52, 238, 499–508, 528, 529.
Change of text, to avoid use of the word Rudra, 186, n. 3.
Chariot, mode of management of reins of horses of, 160, 426; metaphor from, 887.
Charioteers, of Bharatas, claim a fourth share of booty from raids on the Satvants, 158, 154.
Child, development of intelligence in, 166; mode of obtaining, 401.
Chip, or splinter of sacrificial post, use of, 186, 898.
Citadels of the Asuras, 896.
Citra Gauçrāyaṇi, or Gauçra, a sage, 478.
Club (*daṇḍa*), shape of, 160.
Colour of the Hotṛ, 492; of the animal victim, 186, 405.
Commentaries on the Brāhmaṇas, 102, 108.
Comparative relative clauses, 91.
Comparison, clauses of, 94, 95.
Competing sacrifice (*saṁsava*), 109, 398, 451.
Compounds, anomalies in formation of, 78; denoting direction, 47.
Concord, rules of, 81, 474, n. 10.
Conditional, use of, 92.
Conditional clauses, 92.
Conditional relative clauses, 91, 92.
Conjunct form, of Çastras, 59, 60, 476, 511, 518.
Connective particles, use of, 90.
Consecration sacrifice, 107–111, 888–886, 451.
Consonantal stems, irregularities in declension of, 78, 74.

Conversion, of Anuṣṭubh verses into Gāyatrī verses, 161.

Corpse, pollution of fires by contact with fire of cremation, 294.

Corruption of text, hopeless, 286, n. 1, 297.

Cow, barren, killed for a guest, 118; offered to Agni, 251, 252; to Fathers, 185.

Creeping to the Sadas, 418.

Crime, of incest, 185.

Cups, order of at pressings, 59, 60.

Cups for two deities, 153–157, 420, 421.

Curds, as food of the Vaiçya, 315.

Cyavana Bhārgava, a priest, 336.

Dadhikrā, verse, 527.

Dadhikrāvan, 287, 317.

Daivāvṛdha, Babhru, 318.

Daivodāsi, Pratardana, asks questions, 45, 498.

Dakṣa Pārvati, a sacrificer, 366.

Dākṣāyaṇa sacrifice, 190, 366.

Dakṣiṇā offerings, 427, 520.

Dancing, one of three Çilpas, 522.

Darbha grass, 108, 248, 317, 448.

Dārbhya, or Dālbhya, Keçin, a sage, 385, 386.

Daçahotṛ, 512, n. 2.

Daçapeya, rite in Rājasūya, 67.

Date of the Dīkṣā, 451, 452; of the AB. and the KB., 42–50.

Dative, uses of, 82.

Daughter, not desired, 300; Prajāpati's incest with his, 185.

Daughter-in-law, avoidance of father-in-law, 24, 179.

Dawn, 137, 145, 185, 304, 377, 409, 445.

Day, white as a symbol of, 405.

Death of the sacrifice, 121; expiation for presumption of during life, 296; produced by the *vaṣaṭ* call, 169, 170; *see also* Animal sacrifice, Soma.

Debt of man, to father and mother, 296.

Deprecation of anger of relatives of dead animal victim, 139.

Desiderative, anomalous forms of, 77, 78, 226, n. 3, 492, n. 6.

Devabhāga, Çrautarṣi, an ancient teacher, 290.

Devanītha verses (AV. xx. 135. 6 *seq.*), 285, xi.

Devikās, 196, 454.

Dhānaṁjayya, view of as to Kauṣītaki school, 42.

Dhātṛ, 195.

Dhiṣaṇās, 122, 393.

Dice, throws of, 302, n. 6, 392, n. 6.

Dīkṣā, 107–111, 333–336, 451.

Dīrghajihvī ('long-tongue'), an Asura woman, licks the sacrifice, 151.

Dīrghatamas Māmateya, a priest, 337.

Disjunctive particles, 90.

Disloyalty, punishment of, 314, n. 1.

Divākīrtya, 210, 486.

Divine, as opposed to human, 309.

Divine Hotṛs, two, 137.

Division, of a thousand by three, 271.

Division of sacrificial victim, 289, 290.

Divisions of time, 125, 126.

Dogs, two, of Yama, 356, n. 5.

Door of world of heaven, opened by Agni, 191.

Double negative in question, 90.

Durmukha Pāñcāla, performs the horse sacrifice, 338.

Dūrohaṇa, a certain mode of recitation, 32, 218, 278, 489, 526.

Dūrvā grass, 325.

Dvādaçāha, 26, 51, 52, 55, 56, 214–218, 499–514.

Dvāpara, throw at dice, 301.

Dyaus, 292, 293, *and see* Sky.

Eagle, and the Gāyatrī, 269.

Earth, 123, 286, 292; prohibition of giving, 336; *see also* Sky.

East, villages plentiful in, 93.

Eating of the victim, Soma, 366, 389, 416, 434.

Editions of the Brāhmaṇas, 101–103.

Eight-footed victim, 450.

Ekadhanā waters, 149, 150.

Ekāha, 264.

Ekaviṅça Stoma, 191, 192, 311, 312, 329, 333, 411, 426, 474, 499.

Elephants, as sacrificial fees, 337, 338.

Embryo, condition of, 109; process of generation of, 282; offering of victim with, 450; born inverted, 526.

Embryology, 170, 171.

Empire, unknown to AB. or KB., 45.

Errors in sacrifice, Viṣṇu's care of, 189; mode of remedying, 256–258, 497–499; in the choice of sacrificial priests, 194.

Etaça, 526; *see also* Aitaçapralāpa.

Evayāmarut, a hymn (RV. v. 87), 58, 79, 237, 281, 288, 494, 528.

Evil eye, 520.

Exclamation, accusative of, 82.

Expiation of sacrificial errors, 256–258, 497–499; in choice of priests, 194, 195; Viṣṇu's part in making good errors, 189; for extinction of fires, 292.

Extinction of fires, expiation for, 292.

Eye, of victim sent to the sun, 139; *see also* Evil eye.
Eyesight, mode of retaining until old age, 177.

Fame, spell to obtain for Brahman, 248, 249.
Fasting, at the Upasad rite, remedy for, 397, 398.
Fat, victim should be, 136.
Father-in-law, relation to daughter-in-law, 24, 179.
Fathers, 374, 436; receive sacrifice before the gods, 174; have liquid as opposed to solid offerings, 408; are the deity of the victim when it is offered, 406; offering of barren cow to, 135.
Fees, sacrificial, 286; Dakṣiṇā offerings, 427, 520.
Female slaves, from various countries, 337; Kavaṣa Ailūṣa's descent from, 148, 414.
Fields, unploughed land between, 528.
Finale (*nidhana*), 180.
Finding, as root of property, 182.
Fire, carrying round of, effect in deterring Asuras and Rakṣases from attacking the sacrifice, 142.
Five peoples, definition of, 184.
Five portions, making of in animal sacrifice, 145.
Fivefold composition of man, hair, skin, flesh, bone, marrow, 145, 281.
Foetus, *see* Embryo.
Food, breath dependent on, 300.
Forests, of western country, 193.
Forms of Agni, three, 347.
Four, as a complete number, 392, n. 6.
Full moon, days of, 297; time of, 357, 358; does not begin the month, 370, n. 1, 372, n. 1.
Future, anomalies of, 77; uses of, 87; definition and name of (*kariṣyat*), 466, 467.

Gāndhāra, Nagnajit, 318.
Gandharva, maiden seized by a, 28.
Gandharvas, 124, 128, 184, 358, 414.
Gaṅgā, 338.
Gārhapatya, 256, 258, 290, 294, 298, 389, 358, 364, 370, 375, 398, 442.
Gāthās, antiquity of linguistic forms of, 68; of metre of, 50.
Gaupalāyana, Çucivṛkṣa, a priest, 196.
Gauramṛga, 140.
Gaurivīta Sāman, 198.
Gaurivīti Çāktya, 176; hymn of, 481.
Gauḍa, views on performance of Çilpa Çastras, 281.
Gauçra, 487; *alias* Gauçrāyaṇi, 478.
Gavām Ayana, 51, 52, 56, 59, 209-211, 496, 497, x, xi.
Gaya Plāta, a seer, 225.
Gayal, 136.
Gāyatrī, 110, 128, 129, 178, 180, 181, 265, 270, 277, 312, 322, 329, 333, 358, 361, 389, 399, 403, 407, 409, 414, 424, 425, 428, 440, 445, 466, 514, 525.
Generation, symbol of, 159, 424; contrast between quadrupeds and bipeds in method of, 161, 162.
Genitive, use of, 88, 370, nn. 2, 3.
Gerund, forms of, 77.
Gerundive, forms of, 77.
Gestation, duration of, 300, n. 11.
Gesture, use of, 120, n. 6.
Ghora Āṅgirasa, Adhvaryu at the Ādityas' sacrifice, 527.
Gift, not to be accepted in certain circumstances, 286; of land, 336.
Girija Bābhravya, expounds doctrine of division of sacrificed animal, 290.
Go, 208, 457, 459, 462, 465.
Goat, fit for sacrifice, 140.
Gods, number of as 33, 114, 395; as 32, 311; receive solid part of offerings, 408; competition of for sacrifice, 409.
Gold, 145; as the sun, 298.
Golden bird, dialogue of with Keçin Dārbhya, 385, 386.
Gopatha Brāhmaṇa, relation to the Aitareya and Kauṣītaki Brāhmaṇas, 45, x.
Govindasvāmin's commentary on the AB., 102, 285, n. 2.
Gṛtsamada Bhārgava (*v.l.* Bābhrava), 224, 459, 468, 470, 477, 481, 488.
Graha, 170-172.
Grammatical terms, 79, 80.
Grāvastut priest, use of Arbuda hymn by, 22, 259, 260, 289, 519, 520.
Guest reception of Soma, 118-120, 390-392.
Gujarat, home of Kauṣītaki school, 42.
Gūrda Sāman, 525.

Haplology, 496, n. 2.
Hariçcandra Vaidhasa Aikṣvāka, 63, 64, 65, 299.
Hāriyojana, 447, 448, 529, 530.
Haviryajña, 367, 379, 382, 408, 411.
Haug, Dr. Martin, edition of the AB, 101, 102.

Heat of the sun, stages of development of, 198.
Heaven, distance of, from earth, 147, 397, 398.
Hiatus, probable occurrence of, in *me astu*, 508, n. 5.
Himavant, Uttara Kurus dwell beyond, 331.
Hiraṇyadant Baida (cf. JB. ii. 278), a sage, 168.
Hiraṇyastūpa, author of RV. i. 32, 180, 482.
Homage, gods desire, 418.
Horns, the way in which the cows obtained or did not obtain, 209.
Horse, unfit for sacrifice, 140; journey of, as unit of measurement of distance of heaven from earth, 147; created by the gods at the sacrifice, and suitable gift for reciter of Nivids, 171; Agni's form as a, 197.
Hotṛ, 400, 401, 418, 419, 421, 471, 495, 512, 515, 520, 524, 525; suggested rule for colour of, 492.
Hotrakas, 58, 160, 421, 426, 427, 528.
Hotrāçaṅsins, 448.
Householder, share of sacrificial victim, 289.
Human sacrifice, alleged traces of in tale of Çunaḥçepa, 62, 63, 66.
Hymn, use of term, 470, n. 2.
Hyper-Sandhi, possible case of in *pañçalyāyanam*, 508, n. 5.

Iḍā, 362, 421.
Iḍādadha, offering, 191, 367.
Imperfect indicative, anomalous forms in, 75; as narrative tense, 27, 28, 84, 85; confused with aorist, 377, n. 2, 382, n. 1, 385, n. 2; used with perfect, 88.
Inaudible performance of sacrifice, to defeat Rakṣases, 139, 350, n. 4.
Incest of Prajāpati with his daughter, 185.
Indefinite pronoun, 84.
Indefinite relative clauses, 91.
Indra, 126, 127, 174, 263, 268, 282, 302, 303, 304, 311, 314, 317, 329-331, 360, 361, 372, 373, 416, 475, 524.
Indra and Bṛhaspati, 287, 439, 525.
Indra and Varuṇa, 525.
Indra and Vāyu, 421, 426, 481, 486.
Indra and Viṣṇu, 439, 525.
Indragāthās, verses (AV. xx. 128. 12-16), 284, 526.
Infinitive, more varied use of, in AB. than in KB., 27; forms of, 77; uses of, 88.
Inheritance, division of, among sons, 285; of Çunaḥçepa, 306, n. 14, 308, n. 8.
Injunctive, forms of, 76; uses of, 88, 94, xii.
Instrumental, form in *ebhiḥ*, 72; uses of, 82; doubtful sense of *artha* with, 128, n. 2.
Intercalary month, 376, 390, 452, 498.
Interpolations, in AB. 35, (vii. 10 and 11) 297, 298; in KB. 42, (xvi. 10) 438.
Interrogative pronouns, 84; sentences, 90.
Introductory sacrifice, 111-115.
Īçāna, epithet of Rudra, 25, 26, 27, 378.
Iṣu Trikāṇḍā, the three-pointed arrow, a constellation, 185.
Itant Kāvya, a sage (cf. JB. iii. 110), 385.
Itarā, legendary mother of Aitareya, 28.

Jābāla, Satyakāma, 324.
Jagatī, 110, 123, 178, 180, 181, 267, 270, 322, 329, 330, 408, 409, 425, 428, 441, 466, 514, 529.
Jahnus, 308.
Jaiminīya Brāhmaṇa, relation to the Aitareya, 46, x, xi.
Jaiminīya Brāhmaṇa Upaniṣad, 28.
Jānaki, Kratuvid, 318.
Janamejaya Pārikṣita, a king, 28, 29, 45, 217, 314, 318, 336.
Janamejayaka, 79.
Jānaṁtapi, Atyarāti, 333.
Jānaçruteya, Nagarin, 255.
Jānaçruteya, Upāvi, 127.
Jātaka, legend of lotus theft in, 254.
Jātavedas, Agni as, 436, 451, 458, 460, 461, 463, 464, 465, 467, 469, 471, 473, 476, 477, 480, 492, 501, 504, 507.
Jātūkarṇya, a teacher, 498.
Jātūkarṇya, Vṛṣaçuṣma Vātāvata, 258.
Journey, reverence of fire in connexion with a, 353, 354.
Jyotis, 208, 457, 462, 464, 465.
Jyotiṣṭoma, 192.

Ka, 178, 378, 454, 483, 484, 521.
Kādraveya, Arbuda, a serpent seer, 259, 519.
Kairiçi, Sutvan Bhārgāyaṇa, 348.
Kakṣīvant, 122.
Kākṣīvata, Sukīrti, 287.
Kakubh, 428, 445, 525.
Kāleya Sāman, 329, 333, 520, 521.
Kali, throw at dice, 302.
Kāmapri, Marutta Āvikṣita, 337.
Kaṇva, as author of Praiṣas, 518.
Kaṇvarathantara, 501.
Kāpileyas, descendants of Devarāta Vaiçvāmitra, 305.
Kāravyā, verses (AV. xx. 127. 11-14), 283, 526.
Kārīrīṣṭi, 295.
Kaçyapa, anoints Viçvakarman Bhauvana, 336; Kaçyapas and Janamejaya, 314.
Kashmir, cultivation of Sanskrit in, 387, n. 2.
Kaṭha Upaniṣad, later than verses of AB., 50.

Kāṭhaka Saṁhitā, infrequent use of narrative perfect in, 28.
Kātyāyana, grammarian, date of, x.
Kātyāyana Çrauta Sūtra, date of, 48, 49.
Kaukilī Sautrāmaṇī, 488, n. 1.
Kauṣārava Maitreya, 348.
Kauṣītaki, 24. 25, 37, 297, 357, 385, 389, 398, 410, 411, 424, 426, 437, 456, 467, 469, 475, 477, 485, 490, 495, 497, 498, 500, 501, 502, 504, 508, 518, 530.
Kauṣītaki Brāhmaṇa, contents of, with parallels in the Aitareya Brāhmaṇa, 13–21; relation to Aitareya, 22–26; comparative age, 26–28; composition of, 36–42; date of, 42–50; ritual of, 51–61; language, 68–96; style, 96–98; metre, 101; mentions Çaunaka, 367, n. 1.
Kauṣītakins, 42.
Kavaṣa Ailūṣa, story of, 25, 28, 148, 418.
Kāvaṣeya, Tura, 318, 336.
Kāvya, Iṭant, a sage, 385.
Keçavapanīya, rite in Rājasūya, 67.
Keçin Dārbhya, a sage (cf. JB. ii. 53, 54), 385, 386, xi.
Khārgali, Luçākapi, 42.
Khila, unploughed land between arable, 528.
King, defeat of gods through lack of, 117; paying of honour to as a guest, 118; precedence of, 188; needs a Purohita, 339–348; alleged temporary kingship, 328, n. 1.
Kṛçānu, a Soma guardian, 181.
Kṛṣṇa Āñgirasa, a sage, 528.
Kṛta, throw at dice, 302, 392, n. 6.
Kratuvid Jānaki, a king, 318.
Kṣatrasya Dhṛti rite, 41.
Kṣatriya, when fit to bear arms, 301; inferior to the Brāhmaṇa, 308; not an eater of the oblations, 309; grants place of sacrifice, 310; converted by consecration into a Brāhmaṇa, 311; chooses a Brahman priest as Purohita, 313, 339; proper food of in lieu of Soma, 314–318; his rule insecure, 434; rich in food, 495.
Kuhū, second new moon day, 195, 297.
Kuntāpa, hymns, 58, 526; collation of, referred to by Sāyaṇa, 283.
Kurus, curse on, 41; *see also* Uttara Kurus.
Kurukṣetra, expulsion of Kurus from, 41.
Kuru-Pañcālas, in AB., 45, 331, xi.

Lāñgalāyana, Brahman Maudgalya, 226.
Language, of Mantras, 68–70; of prose, 70–97; study of, in the north, 387.
Lengthening of final vowels, 72.
Life of man, a hundred years, 490, 526.
Limits of marriage among men, 364, n. 2; among animals, 364.
Lindner, B., edition of the KB., 102, 103.
Lioness, earth as a, 286.
Locative, use of, 83; of thing contended for, 348, n. 1.
Lord of the forest, 408.
Lord of the sacrifice, definition of, as sacrificer or as deity, 133.
Lords and people, discord between, 176, 177.
Loss of gold, expiation for, in sacrifice, 295.
Lotus theft, allusion to the legend of, 254, 255.
Luçākapi Khārgali, 42.

Madhuchandas, 64, 65, 455, 458, 467, 481, 483, 487, 509, 515.
Madhuka, 437.
Mādhyamas, seers, 414.
Mādhyaṁdina Pavamāna, 54, 173.
Māgha, Dīkṣā in, 452.
Magic, used against sacrificer, 169, 176; in the Brāhmaṇas, 178.
Magic powers of the priesthood, recognized in Aitareya Brāhmaṇa, 23, 24.
Magic rites to injure the sacrificer, available for use by the priest, 166, 167.
Mahābalabhid, mode of recitation of Vālakhilyās, 32.
Mahābhārata, legend of lotus theft in, 254.
Mahābhiṣeka of Indra, 329–31; of kings, 331–343.
Mahādeva or Mahān Deva, epithet of Rudra, 25, 27, 378.
Mahādivākīrtya Sāman, 213, 437, 488.
Mahaitareya, 36, 38.
Mahākauṣītaka, or Mahākauṣītaki, 36, 38, 41.
Mahākauṣītaki Brāhmaṇa, 41.
Mahānāmnīs, 231, 475.
Mahāvīra, pot, 392, 396.
Mahāvrata, 207, 208, 431, 432, 528.
Mahendra, origin of name, 178, 291, 374.
Mahidāsa Aitareya, reputed author of the AB., 28.
Maitrāvaruṇa, priest, 32, 58, 138, 197, 261, 263, 264, 266, 269, 270, 281, 282, 419, 438, 498, 514, 515, 518, 521, 523, 525, 528, 529.
Maitrāyaṇī Saṁhitā, spurious section referring to Mahādeva, 27; little use of perfect in narrative in, 28.
Maitreya, Kauṣārava, a priest, 348.
Māmateya, Dīrghatamas, 337.
Man, posture of in generation, 159, 161; alone goes to the Assembly, 388.
Mānava Nābhānediṣṭha, 286, 287, 516.

Mānava Çrauta Sūtra, 40, n. 1.
Man-ordering verses, a recitation, 284, 527.
Manotā, 141, 142, 407.
Manu, 189, 328; hymns of (RV. viii. 27–31), 507.
Manuscripts of the KB., 108, n. 2.
Mānutantavya, Aikādaçākṣi, 255.
Mārgaveya, Rāma, 314, 318.
Mārjālīya, 398, 442.
Marriage, cattle as bringing, 300; between close kin, 300, 301; limits of degrees, 364, n. 2; polyandry disapproved, polygamy sanctioned, 179.
Maruts, 118, 132, 174, 177, 282, 371, 372, 373, 418, 429, 456, 458, 460, 461, 463, 464, 465, 467, 469, 471, 473, 476, 477, 480, 491, 501, 504, 507.
Marutta Āvikṣita, performs the horse sacrifice, 336.
Marutvatīya Çastra, 172–178, 319, 428, 429, 455, 456, 458, 459, 460, 462, 463, 464, 465, 467, 468, 469, 472, 474, 478, 482, 488, 487, 493, 500, 502, 506, 509, 510.
Maṣṇāra, a place, 338.
Mātariçvan, 141.
Mātalī, 180.
Maudgalya Lāñgalāyana Brahman, 226.
Mauna Aṇicin, a sage, 478.
Medhātithi, 462, 515, 518, 522.
Men, dependence of, on Agni, 187.
Metempsychosis, not referred to in AB. or KB., 44; Punarmṛtyu only in KB. xxv. 1 and latest part of AB. (viii. 25), 27, 47, 340, n. 1, 486.
Metres, do not differ merely because of excess by one or two syllables, 110; difference of syllable in same, 161; normal and varied orders of, in the Prātaranuvāka, 147; of the three pressings, 178; interrelations of, 181, 182, 513.
Metrical parts of the Brāhmaṇas, metre of, 98–101.
Middle voice, users of, 84, 85, 158.
Milk, for a child, not for an adult, 419.
Milk mess, 152, 438, 450.
Millet harvest, 369.
Mind, acts without a direction, 260; instigates speech, 188.
Misdivision of words, 502, n. 1.
Mitra, 123, 329, 381.
Mitra and Varuṇa, 421, 426, 449, 514.
Mock man, definition of as one who offers neither to gods, fathers, nor men, 296.
Month, beginning of with new moon, 372, n. 1; thirteenth, 376, 390, 452, 498.
Moon, as the Soma of the gods, 298; concealed at the conjunction, 342.
Mother, incest with, 300, 301; with daughter, 185.
Motion of the sun, 198.
Moving forward of the Soma carts, 130, 131, 399–401.
Mṛgavyādha, 'piercer of the deer', a constellation, 185.
Muñja grass, 322.
Munyayana, 368.
Music, one of the three Çilpas, 522.
Mūtibas, or Mūcīpas, a tribe, 307.
Mutilation, of limbs of victim to be avoided, 139, 140.
Mystery, loved by the gods, 192.
Mysticism, in last section of Aitareya Brāhmaṇa, 24.

Nābhānediṣṭha, a hymn (RV. x. 61), 32, 58, 79, 234, 237, 281, 288, 485, 525.
Nābhānediṣṭha Mānava, legend of, 22, 236, 237, 516.
Nagarin Jānaçruteya, a priest, 255.
Nagnajit Gāndhāra, a king, 318.
Nahus, 475.
Naimiṣīyas, in KB., 45, 498, 516.
Naiṣāda, 495; see also Niṣāda.
Nakṣatras, origin of list of, 49; preference for a special, 369; referred to, 513; name from, 363, n. 3.
Names of hymns, forms of, 79; of men, formed from connexion with Nakṣatras, 363, n. 3.
Nānada Sāman, 198.
Nārada, a sage, 66, 299, 318, 336.
Narāçaṅsa, fore-offering to, 137, 172, 317.
Nārāçaṅsa, a hymn (RV. x. 62), 32, 58, 79, 234, 271, 280, 480, 526.
Nārāçaṅsa cups, 152, 172, 271, n. 1, 317.
Nārāçaṅsī, verses (AV. xx. 127. 1–3), 271, n. 1, 288, n. 1.
Nārmedhasa Sāman, 197.
Nāsatyas, 295; and see Açvins.
Naudhasa Sāman, 217, 329, 338, 520, 522.
Necklaces, worn by women, 337.
Negative particles, use of, 90; in dependent clauses, 94.
Neṣṭṛ, priest, 261, 267, 268, 269, 289, 435, 516, 517.
New moon, days of, 297; time of, 357, 358.
New and full moon offerings, 50, 357–365.
Newly-born, milk as food of, 419; stumbling gait of, 494, 528.
Nigada, 360, n. 2, 397, 418, 498, 514.
Night, 137; black as a symbol of, 405.

Nigrabhītṛa, priests, 140.
Nihnavana, ceremony of, 127, 128.
Ninarda, species of accent, 283, n. 3.
Nirṛti, 145.
Nirūḍhapaçu, offering, time of, 108, n. 1.
Niṣādas, 328; *and see* Naiṣāda.
Niṣkevalya Çastra, 320, 430, 431, 455, 456, 458, 459, 461, 462, 463, 467, 468, 473, 476, 479, 482, 493, 501, 502, 506, 509, 510.
Nivid, 158, 201, 285, 286, 353, 423, 429, 430, 466, 470, 487, 489, 490, 504; all ascribed to Viçvāmitra, 514, n. 1.
Nominative, uses of, 81.
North, as home of correct speech, 387, xi; connexion of Rudra with, 286.
North-eastern quarter, that of victory, 117.
North-west monsoon referred to, 112.
Number of gods, thirty-three given as, 114, 161; of sacrificial posts used at animal sacrifice, 404.
Numerals, irregular forms of, 74.
Nyagrodha, tree, 332; for Nyagroha, 315.
Nyubja, name at Kurukṣetra of the Nyagrodha, 315.
Nyūñkha, 226, 472.

Oath, of priest and king in the Rājasūya, 332.
Obscurity, gods fond of, 315.
Offal, at sacrifice buried in ground as connected with plants, 139, 143.
Oldenberg, Prof. Hermann, Ākhyāna theory discussed, 65, 66.
Omentum, forced out for offering essential part of animal sacrifice, 139, 143, 144, 406, 407.
Omission of offering at new or full moon, expiation for, 294.
Optative, anomalous forms of, 75; use of, in main clauses, 88; in relative clauses, 91, 92; in conditional clauses, 92; in clauses of comparison, 92, 93; in clauses of occasion, 93; in purpose clauses with *iti*, 93, 94; with *ned*, 339, n. 6.
Order of words, 96.
Orderings of the quarters, a recitation, 284, 527.
Orthoepic diaskeuasis of RV., unknown to AB., 43, 44.
Owl, the screech of compared with the wail of mourners, 140.
Ox, fit for sacrifice, 140; killed for a guest, 118.

Padapañkti, 451.
Paijavana, Sudās, 318, 366.
Paiñgi Brāhmaṇa, 87.
Paiñgya, 24, 25, 37, 297, 357, 393, 437, 456, 485, 490, 492, 497, 504, 518.
Pākayajñas, 190.
Palāça, double sense of word as (1) Parṇa, (2) generic term for foliage, 135; tree, 403.
Pañcadaça Stoma, 311, 312, 329, 333, 468, 469, 499.
Pañcahotṛ, 512, n. 2.
Pāñcāla, Durmukha, 333.
Pañcaviñça Brāhmaṇa, infrequent use of narrative perfect in, 98; possibly later than the Aitareya (i–xxiv), 46; reference to Viçvāmitra as a king (as in the later part of the Aitareya), 67.
Pāṇini, knowledge of Aitareya and Kauṣītaki Brāhmaṇas, 35, 38, 42; of Kātyāyana Çrauta Sūtra, 49; date of, x.
Pañkti, 110, 199, 281, 329, 333, 399, 403, 409, 446, 472, 475, 510, 522, 525.
Pantheism, of Agni as identified with all the gods, 167.
Parikṣit, as Agni, 288.
Pārikṣita, Janamejaya, 314, 318.
Pārikṣitī, verses (AV. xx. 127. 7–10), 283, 526.
Parisāraka, place name, 143.
Parjanya, 148, 176.
Participial forms, anomalies in, 76, 77.
Participles, uses of, 89.
Parucchepa, insertion of verses by, in certain hymns, 59, 233, 234, 477, 478, 479, xi, xii.
Parvata, a sage, 66, 299, 318, 336.
Pārvati, Dakṣa, a sacrificer, 366.
Paçupati, epithet of Rudra, 25, 185, n. 2, 378.
Passive, anomalous forms of, 77.
Past tense, appropriate as symbol of certain rites, 469.
Patañga, hymn (RV. x. 177), 79, 409, n. 11.
Pathyā Svasti, 113, 387, 388.
Pātnīvata cup, 435.
Pavamānas, 202, 257, 319, 415, 425, 428, 430, 435.
Pāvīravī, as speech, 133.
People and lords, discord between, 176, 177.
Perfect, anomalous forms of, 76.
Perfect indicative, as narrative tense, 27, 28, 34, 36, 46, 86, 87.
Periphrastic future, only regular forms, 77; use of, 87, 356, n. 2.
Periphrastic perfect, 76.
Phalgunīs, 366, 368, 370, 371.
Physicians of the gods, the Açvins, 444.
Piling of the fires, 347–350.

Piṇḍapitṛyajña, 51.
Pitudāru tree, 186.
Place, arguments against changing during recitation, 461.
Place, construction of clauses of, 95.
Plakṣa, tree, 315, 316, 332.
Plāta, Gaya, a seer, 225.
Play on words, resulting in false form, 72.
Plural, of majesty, 81; *prayogabahutvāpekṣam*, 264.
Pluti, use of, 95, 96.
Poison, result of evil eye, 520.
Polishings, of rice and grain (*phalīkaraṇa*), as distinct from the husks (*tuṣa*), 139, 141.
Political references, in AB. and KB., 44, 45.
Polyandry disapproved, 179.
Polygamy sanctioned, 179.
Potṛ, priest, 266, 267, 268, 269, 289, 516, 517.
Potsherds, use of, at sacrifice, 151.
Pṛçni, 122, 184, 394.
Pṛṣṭhas, 54, 319, 458, 482, 487, 498, 502.
Pṛṣṭhya, 417.
Pṛṣṭhya Ṣaḍaha, 26, 51, 52, 209, 218–236, 466–474.
Prāgahi, cited in KB., 41, 497.
Praiṣas, 170, 514, 515, 530.
Praiyamedhas, priests, 337.
Prajāpati, 108, 114, 117, 122, 304, 309, 318, 329, 330, 372, 378, 377–379, 391, 407, 411, 416, 417, 432, 444, 451, 465, 477, 478, 485, 486, 498, 505, 523, 526, *and see* Ka.
Prajāvant Prājāpatya, reputed seer of RV. x. 183, possible origin of tradition as to, 122.
Prākritic form, 447, n. 3.
Prākritisms in text, 46, 72.
Pramaṅhiṣṭhīya Sāman, 197.
Praṇava, 410, 424.
Praṇītā waters, 381.
Prapad, 327, 328.
Praçāstṛ, 258, 443.
Prāçravaṇa, a. v.l. for Prāsravaṇa, 419.
Praçukrīya, hymn (RV. vii. 34), 473, n. 4.
Prāsahā, wife of Indra, cajoles her husband, 179.
Prāsravaṇa, Avatsāra, a Hotṛ, 419.
Prasthita libations, 59, 266, 267, 268, 421, 427, 520, 530.
Prastotṛ, 289, 442.
Prātaranuvāka, 145–148, 408–412, 492.
Pratardana Daivodāsi, a king, 45, 496.
Pratihāra, 442.
Pratihartṛ, 289, 442.
Pratīpa Prātisutvana, a king, 284.
Pratiprasthātṛ, priest, 132, 154, 289.
Pratirādha, 285; Pratirādhas, 527.
Prātisutvana, Pratīpa, a king, 284.
Prattle of Aitaça, a recitation, 284, 526.
Praüga Çastra, 160, 165–168, 425–427, 455, 456, 458, 459, 460, 462, 463, 464, 467, 468, 469, 472, 474, 478, 481, 483, 486, 487, 493, 499, 502, 505, 509.
Pravalhikā, verses (AV. xx. 133. 1–6), 285, 527, n. 3.
Pravargya, 121–125, 190, 392–396.
Prāyaṇīya, 386–388.
Prāyaçcittas, for errors in the sacrifice, 51, 290–296.
Precative, forms of, 75; use of, 93.
Prefixes, separation of, from verb, 78; from infinitive, 89.
Prepositions, uses of, 83, 84.
Present indicative, uses of, 85, 455, n. 4, 468.
Pressing stones, praise of, by Grāvastut, 260.
Priests, errors in choice of, 194, 195.
Priyamedhas, seers, referred to in RV., 177.
Priyavrata Somāpa, a priest, 318.
Pronoun, anomalies in inflexion of, 74; uses of, 84.
Propagation, mode of, 159.
Property acquired by finding, 182.
Proverb, cited, 88.
Pulindas, a tribe, 65, 307.
Punarabhiṣeka, 67, 322–328.
Punarādheya, 50.
Punarmṛtyu, in KB. xxv. 1, 27, 47, 486; idea only (*na punar mriyate*) in the latest part of AB. (viii. 25), 340, n. 1.
Puṇḍras, a tribe, 307.
Purchase of Soma, 389, 390.
Purīṣapadas, 475, n. 1.
Puritanical spirit, traces of in Çāṅkhāyana school, 24.
Purohita, 318, 337, 339–345.
Puronuvākyā, 170, 201.
Puroruc, 162, 163, 423, 426, 481, 504; all ascribed to Viçvāmitra, 514, n. 1.
Purpose clauses, 94, 95.
Puruṣamedha, 52.
Pūṣan, 329, 333, 371, 376, 381, 393, 417.

Quadrupeds, habits of, contrasted with those of man, 161.
Quarters, ear of the animal victim sent to, 139.
Questions, form of simple, 90.

Ṛbhukṣan, 286.
Ṛbhus, 183, 220, 222, 243, 267, 268, 432, 433, 456, 458, 460, 461, 463, 464, 465, 467, 470, 473, 476, 480, 491, 501, 503, 507, 524.

Ṛc, 329, 333, 379, 415, 419, 420; relation of, to Sāman, 151, 179.
Ṛgveda, legend of Çunaḥçepa in, 63, 64; born of Agni, 256.
Ṛjujanitrīya, hymn (RV. ii. 13), 490.
Ṛṣi descent, 358, 359; ascribed to Kṣatriya at the Rājasūya offering, 313.
Race, use of, to decide question, 153, 202, 203.
Raibhī, 283, 526.
Rain, continuous as opposed to sporadic, 149; from the moon, 343; produced by attitude of Maitrāvaruṇa, 515.
Raivata Sāman, 207, 233, 234, 329, 333, 479, 480, 522, n. 1.
Rājanya, 128, 309, 316, 321; asks Kṣatriya for a place of sacrifice, 310.
Rājasūya, 29, 50, 61, 68.
Rākā, a goddess, 187, 188, 436, second full moon day, 297.
Rakṣases, 118, 122, 261, 404, 406, 418, 444, 450, 515.
Rāma Mārgaveya, a contemporary of Janamejaya and priest of the Çyāparṇa family, 23, 314, 318.
Rathantara Sāman, 122, 204, 211, 254, 319, 329, 333, 361, 455, 464, 468, 469, 481, 484, 485, 487, 488, 489, 493, 500, 502.
Rātrisattra, 494.
Red, a symbol of the sun, 492, n. 5; of Agni, 405.
Redemption, of self by sacrifice, 136, 405.
Refusal to sacrifice for a patron, when justifiable, 285, 286.
Reins, of chariot-horses, mode of holding, 160, 426.
Relative clauses, use of, 91, 92.
Relays, use of in the case of horses or oxen for journeys, 217.
Repeated death, one reference to in the later Aitareya, 340, n. 1; in KB. 27, 47, 486.
Repetitions in the AB., 82; of particles, 90; of omitted passages, 497.
Reported speech, 95.
Revenge, practised by person deprived of due portion (i. e. Rakṣases) on person depriving, 139.
Ribs, of the animal victim, 26 in number, 189.
Rice, use of, for sacrifice, 143.
Rice harvest, 369.
Riddle, a part of the ritual service, 250.
Right arm, turning upon, 401.
Rivalry of sacrificers, 135, 398; of the gods for the sacrifice, 407.
Rivers, westward course of many, 112.
Rohiṇī, a constellation, 136.
Rohita, 30, 63, 64, 65, 301.
Roller (*matya*), for use in treating ploughed land, 139.
Rope, tying of knots at end of, 115.
Royal titles, in various parts of the country, 330, 331.
Rudra, 135, 282, 353, 360, 362, 375, 378, 393, 464, 477; prominence of, in period of the Brāhmaṇas, 25–27.
Rudras, 114, 126, 147, 286, 329, 333, 416, 481, 511, 524.

Çabaras, a tribe, 307.
Çaibya, Çuṣmiṇa Amitratapana, 333.
Çākala, a Vedic school ritual, 192, x.
Çākalas, offering of, 23, 448.
Çākalya, relation of Brāhmaṇas to, 43, 44.
Çāktya, Gaurivīti, a sage, 176.
Çākvara Sāman, 207, 229, 329, 333, 477.
Çakvarī, 231.
Çaṁyu Bārhaspatya, a mythic sage, 363.
Çaṁyuvāka, 363, 371, 387, 388, 392.
Çāṅkhāyana Āraṇyaka, 36, 38, 51.
Çāṅkhāyana Gṛhya Sūtra, 36.
Çāṅkhāyana Çrauta Sūtra, story of Çunaḥçepa in, 29, 30; Mahāvrata section (xvii and xviii), 36; relation to the Kauṣītaki Brāhmaṇa, 38–41, 44; date of, 44; ritual in, 50, 51, 52, 53, 54, 55, 61, 67.
Çarva, epithet of Rudra, 25, 377.
Çāryāta Mānava, 222, 456, 469; performs the horse sacrifice, 336.
Çāsa, hymn (RV. x. 103), 327.
Çastra, 410, 443, 498, 523, 529.
Çatānīka Sātrājita, performs the Açvamedha, 336.
Çatapatha Brāhmaṇa, position of Rudra in, 26; relation to Kauṣītaki, 27, 37, 45, 47, 48; use of narrative perfect in, 23, 34, 49; of *anyo 'nya*, 46, 47; disapproves use of a Sadasya priest, 48.
Çāṭyāyanaka form of Gavām Ayana, 57.
Çaunaka sacrifice, 367.
Çikhaṇḍin Yājñasena, a sage, 385.
Çilpas, special Çastras, 32, 58, 271, 281, 494, 525; special verses, 521, 522.
Çrautarṣi Devabhāga, knew the division of the sacrificial victim, 290.
Çrotriya, ugliness of, mentioned, 127.
Çucivṛkṣa Gaupalāyana, a priest, 196.
Çūdras, low character of, 305, 306, 315.
Çukra cup, 60.
Çukra and Manthin cups, 433.
Çūlagava, 51.
Çunaḥpucha, 303.

Çunaḥçepa, 29, 40, 61–68, 303–309.
Çunakas, use of fore-offering to Narāçaṅsa, 187.
Çunāsīrau, 376.
Çunāsīrīya or Çunāsīrya sacrifice, 375, 376.
Çunolāṅgūla, youngest son of Ajīgarta, 303.
Çuṣmiṇa, Çaibya Amitratapana, 338.
Çvetaketu, not referred to in AB., but in KB., 47, 48, 498.
Çyaita Sāman, 217.
Çyāparṇas, a priestly family, 314.

Ṣaḍhotṛ, 512, n. 2.
Ṣoḍaçin, 38, 51, 52, 58, 191, 198–201, 439–442.

Sācīguna, a place, 338.
Sacrifice, offered to itself by the gods, 119; relation of Viṣṇu and Varuṇa to, 139; victim to be eaten of by the sacrificer, 186, 187, 405; accompanied by surrender of all one's property, 495; must be accompanied by a fee, 286; eating of the god, Soma, in, 366, 416, 484; death of, 121; as a redemption of self, 136, 405.
Sacrificer, relation of priest to, 23, 24, 166, 169, 285, 286; burning on his own fires, 376, n. 2.
Sacrificial food (*iḍā*) as cattle, 141.
Sacrificial post, treatment of, 134–136, 403–405.
Sadas, 125, 248, 411, 442; fire in to be derived from altar of Agnīdh, 160.
Sadasya priest, used by Kauṣītakins, 48, 290, 442, 498, n. 1.
Sādhya gods, 329, 333, 474.
Sahadeva Sārñjaya, a king, 318.
Sāhadevya Somaka, a king, 318.
Sākamaçva Sāman, 197.
Sākamedhas, 373–375.
Sākaṁprasthāyya sacrifice, 368.
Sāman, relation to Ṛc, 151; union of, with three Ṛc verses, 179; referred to, 357, 415, 420, 448, 447.
Sāmaveda, born from Āditya, 256.
Sāmidhenī verses, number of, in certain rites, 347, 348, 411.
Sāṁnāyya, 291, 362, n. 2.
Saṁpāta hymns, 58, 59, 219, 220, 271, 467.
Saṁvarta Āṅgirasa, a priest, 336.
Sanaçruta Arindama, 318.
Sandhi, peculiarities of, 71, 72.
Sandhi Sāman, 191.
Saptadaça Stoma, 191, 192, 210, 223, 329, 333, 469, 471, 485, 499.
Saptahotṛ, 512, n. 2.
Sarasvatī, 152, 244, 264, 323, 371, 406, 414, 417, 426, 486.
Sarasvatī, river, 148, 414.
Sārñjaya, Sahadeva, 318.
Sarpaṇa, 151.
Sarparājñī, verses of, 248, 511.
Sarpis Vātsi, a sage, 278.
Sarvacaru, place (?), 259, 519.
Sarvamedha, 40, 58.
Sārvaseni sacrifice, 367.
Satobṛhatī, metre, 281.
Sātrājita, Çatānīka, 336.
Sattra, 26, 51, 206–214; Rātrisattra, 494.
Satvants, raided by Bharatas, 158; kings of, 330.
Sātyahavya Vāsiṣṭha, 338.
Satyakāma Jābāla, a sage, 324.
Saubala, a sage, 278.
Saubhara Sāman, 197.
Saudāsas, overcome by Vasiṣṭha, 368; *see also* Sudās.
Saujāta Ārāḍhi, 311.
Sauparṇa Ākhyāna, 180, 181.
Sauparṇa hymn, 327; *see* Suparna.
Sauṣadmana, Viçvantara, 314.
Sautrāmaṇī, 438.
Savitṛ, 113, 116, 304, 310, 329, 333, 371, 381, 382, 459, 460, 462, 464, 465, 468, 470, 473, 476, 480, 501, 503, 507, 524, *and see* Sūryā.
Sāvitra cup, 482.
Sāyaṇa's commentary on the AB., 102.
Season, suitable for consecration, 216.
Seasonal cups, 156, 422.
Secondary conjugations, anomalous forms of, 77.
Seed, analogy with omentum, 144; mode of emission, 161, 162.
Seeds, must be of ten months' or a year's growth, 218.
Set of five oblations, 152, 418, 419.
Seven, metres used in the Prātaranuvāka, 410, 411, offering verses, at Prasthita libations, 515, n. 1.
Seven Ṛṣis, a constellation, 518.
Seventeen, kindling verses, 407, 408.
Siege, use of to reduce great citadels, 125.
Sight, superior to hearing as evidence, 111.
Silent Praise, 157, 158.
Silver, as night, 298.
Sin, of the father visited on children and grandchildren, 139, 140.
Sindhu, 123.
Singing, one of the three Çilpas, 522.
Singular, and plural confused, 508, n. 5.
Sinīvālī, first new moon day, 195, 297.
Sister, inferiority of, to wife of brother, 187, 188.
Skin, serpent's change of, 259.

Sky, 123, 185; and Earth, 458, 461, 462, 464, 465, 467, 468, 470, 476, 480, 491, 501, 503, 507.

Slaughterer, share in sacrificial victim, 289.

Slavewoman, son of, rejected as a Brahman, 148, 414.

Slaying of Soma in the sacrifice, 185; *see also* Soma.

Solstice, 452.

Soma, 111, 180-182, 267, 298, 311, 317, 361, 364, 527; eaten as the moon, 366, 389, 416, 484; slain in the pressing, 185.

Soma shoots, ten metaphorically described, 420.

Somaka Sāhadevya, a king, 318.

Somāpa Priyavrata, a sage, 313.

Somaçuṣman Vājaratnāyana, a priest, 336.

Son, value of, 299, 300.

South, early ripening of plants in and trade with, 111.

Speech, 354, 398; bartered for Soma by the gods, 128; relation to mind, 188, 245; of successful man imitated by others, 145; as the holy power, 146; sevenfold, 147; of Rakṣases, 139, 140.

Spell, for defeat of an opposing army, 24, 178, 179.

Stomas, order of, in Pṛṣṭhya Ṣaḍaha, 55; in Abhiplava Ṣaḍaha, 58.

Stooping, in seeking for what is lost, 170.

Stotra, 443, 447, 512, 519; correspondence of, with Çastra, 160, 161.

Strainer, golden, used at Mahābhiṣeka, 330, 332.

Style of the Brāhmaṇas, 96-98.

Subjunctive, anomalous form of, 75, 76; uses of in main clauses, 87, 88, 427, n. 2; in purpose clauses with *iti*, 93, 94.

Subrahmaṇyā, priest and formula, 260, 261, 289, 513.

Sudās Paijavana, a king, 318, 336; *see also* Saudāsa.

Sukīrti Kākṣīvata, a seer, 287.

Sukīrti, a hymn (RV. x. 131), 58, 281, 521, 526.

Sūkta, uses of, 284, 470, n. 2.

Sūktavāka, 363, 375, 384.

Sun, theory of motion of, 193; born from fire, 348; distance from, 392; eye of victim sent to, 139; as a horse, 286, 376.

Sun-maiden, 202, 444.

Sunrise, period of offering the Agnihotra before or after, 253-255.

Suparṇa (RVKh. i. 6 or i. 3), 278, 327, 446; *see also* Sauparṇa.

Superlative, with double ending, 74.

Surā, as substitute for Soma, 335, 438.

Sūryā Sāvitrī, 202, 444.

Sūtra style, 89.

Suture, in man's *çiçna*, placed there by Rākā, 188; in head of man, 213.

Sutvan Kairiçi Bhārgāyaṇa, a king, 343.

Suyajña Çāñkhāyana, age of, 44.

Svarasāmans, 23, 26, 51, 210, 211, 416, 482-485, 492.

Svarbhānu, an Asura, eclipses the sun, 482, 483.

Svasti, Pathyā, 337, 338.

Sviṣṭakṛt, offering, 124, 360, 362, 369, 370, 375, 407.

Taboo, of father-in-law in regard to daughter-in-law, 179.

Taiṣa, Dīkṣā in, 452.

Taittirīya Brāhmaṇa, relation to the Aitareya, 46, 47.

Taittirīya Saṁhitā, rare use of narrative perfect in, 28; possibly later than the Aitareya (i-xxiv), 46.

Tame animals, seven in number, 147.

Tāṇḍaka form of Gavām Ayana, 57.

Tanūnapāt, fore-offering for, 137.

Tānūnaptra, rite of covenant between sacrificer and priests, 126.

Tanva, Nidāna of, 466, n. 1.

Tārkṣya, as the wind, 212.

Tārkṣya, hymn, 212, 213, 224, 228, 235, 242, 245, 526.

Tenth Day of the Daçarātra, 508.

Thank-offering, Āgrayaṇa not to be regarded as a, 369, n. 1.

Threefold knowledge, the instrument of the Brahman priest, 257.

Three steps of Viṣṇu, 271.

Thirteen, cuttings of the victim, 407.

Thirteenth month, 376, 390, 452, 493.

Thirty-three gods, 114, 395, 405; Soma drinkers, and the same number not, 147, 148.

Thousand, division by three, 271.

Throne, at the Rājasūya, 329, 333.

Thunderbolt, shape of the, 160.

Time for offering the Agnihotra, 253-255.

Time, clauses of, 95.

Tone of recitation, 193.

Torch, carried before animal victim at sacrifice as symbol of Agni, 142, 143.

Touching the earth, rite prescribed at end of Āgnimāruta Çastra, 189.

Tradition, inferior, of AB. vi-viii, 34.

Transfer of gift wrongly taken to a rival, 286.

Transposed form, of Çastras, 476, 513.

Trayastriṅça Stoma, 283, 329, 333, 480, 496.
Tretā, throw at dice, 302.
Triṇava Stoma, 229, 329, 333, 477, 499.
Triçañku, legend of, 66.
Triṣṭubh, 110, 128, 178, 180, 181, 199, 267, 270, 311, 312, 322, 329, 333, 350, 361, 383, 389, 399, 403, 407, 409, 425, 428, 440, 466, 514, 524, 529; treatment of the metre in the Brāhmaṇas, 101.
Trivṛt Stoma, 191, 192, 218, 329, 333, 461, 463, 496, 499.
Truth, relation to falsehood, 355.
Tryambaka, 375.
Tura Kāvaṣeya, priest of Janamejaya, 45, 217, 318, 336, 363.
Turāyaṇa sacrifice, 363.
Turban, bound over eyes of Grāvastut during his recitation, 259, 520.
Tūṣṇiṁçaṅsa, 161.
Tvaṣṭṛ, 137, 314, 364, 454.
Twins, expiation on occurrence of birth of, 296.

Udamaya Ātreya, a priest, 337.
Udayanīya, 336–338.
Uddālaka Āruṇi, a priest, 324.
Udgātṛ, 151, 248, 256, 257, 258, 269, 289, 303, 379, 435, 442, 527.
Udumbara, tree, 249, 315, 316, 332, 333, 495, 512.
Udvaṅçaputra Sāman, 525.
Ugra Deva, epithet of Rudra, 25, 378.
Uktha, 206, 529, n. 1.
Ukthya, 28, 33, 51, 52, 58, 191, 250, 271, 321, 438, 439, 454, 456, 466, 485.
Ula Vārṣṇivṛddha, a sage, 335.
Uniting of fires, expiation for, 298.
Unnetṛ priest, 289.
Upagātṛ, share of sacrificial victim, 289.
Upaniṣads, position of metrical, 50.
Upāṅçu cup, 150, 257, 412, 415, 492.
Upasads, 125-128, 175, 185, 194, 385, 391, 392, 396, 398, 485.
Upavaktṛ, priest, 421, 517.
Upāvi Jānaçruteya, a sage, 127.
Uçīnaras, a people in AB., 45, 331.
Uṣas, 137, 145, 185, 304, 377, 409, 445.
Uṣṇih, 110, 199, 322, 399, 409, 428, 440, 458, 469, 510, 525, 529.
Utkara, 260, 261.
Uttara Kurus, beyond the Himavant, 331; unconquerable, 338.
Uttara Madras, 331.

Vācaspata, Alikayu, a Naimiṣīya priest, 496.
Vādhāvata, v. l. for Vātāvata, 356, n. 2.
Vaidarbha, Bhīma, 318.
Vaidhasa, Hariçcandra Aikṣvāka, 299.
Vairāja Sāman, 207, 228, 329, 333, 474, 498.
Vairūpa Sāman, 207, 283, 329, 333, 469, 471.
Vaiçvadeva, Çastra, 174, 433–435, 455, 456, 458, 459, 479, 485, 491, 507, 524, nn. 4, 5.
Vaiçvadeva sacrifice, 370–372.
Vaiçvānara, Agni as, 339, 435, 456, 458, 460, 461, 463, 464, 465, 467, 470, 473, 476, 477, 480, 491, 501, 504, 507.
Vaiçya, and cattle, 129; asks Kṣatriya for a place of sacrifice, 310; position of stable, 484.
Vāja, a Ṛbhu, 282, 417.
Vājapeya, peculiarities of, 38, 54, 55, 191, 403, 529.
Vājaratnāyana, Somaçuṣman, 336.
Vala, 263.
Vālakhilyā, hymns, 32, 58, 237, 281, 288, 522, 525, 528.
Vāmadeva, 521, 524.
Vāmadevya Sāman, 195, 510, 520, 521.
Vāravantīya Sāman, 479.
Vārṣṇivṛddha, Ula, a sage, 335.
Varuṇa, 116, 123, 126, 136, 251, 263, 268, 301, 304, 305, 328, 329, 372, 373, 389, 418, 448, 449, 457, 469, 525.
Varuṇapraghāsas, 372, 373.
Vaças, a people, in AB., 45, 331.
Vasatīvarī waters, 149, 150, 413, n. 3.
Vasiṣṭha, 122, 308, 521, 525; overcomes the Saudāsas, 363.
Vāsiṣṭha, Sātyahavya, a priest, 333.
Vasiṣṭhas, use of Narāçaṅsa as deity of fore-offering, 137.
Vasiṣṭhayajña, 363.
Vasus, 114, 147, 286, 329, 333, 416, 431, 463, 511, 524.
Vātāvata (v. l. Vādhāvata) Vṛṣaçuṣma Jātūkarṇya, 263, 356; Vātavāta, x.
Vātsapra, a hymn, 353.
Vātsi, Sarpis, 278.
Vāyu, 212, 329, 376, 377, 378, 393, 426, 433, 452, 457, 512, 526.
Vedi, 170.
Vena, as the central breath, 122, 124, 133, 394, 433, 512.
Verse, disguised as prose, 68.
Vibhāt, a world of Prajāpati, 313.
Vibhus, 417.
Vibhvan, a Ṛbhu, 282.
Victim, the division of among priests, 30, 289.
Victims, succession of, in sacrifice, 140.
Vikarṇa Sāman, 211.

Villages of eastern country, 193.
Vimada, 227, 471, 522.
Vināyaka's commentary on the KB., 102, 103.
Virāj, 114, 206, 287, 321, 353, 372, 373, 402, 410, 414, 424, 431, 441, 447, 471, 472, 493, 509, 510, 522, 527.
Viçvajit, 23, 26, 51, 52, 211, 231, 493–495, 523.
Viçvakarman, 374.
Viçvakarman Bhauvana, performs the horse sacrifice, 336.
Viçvamanas, Praüga of, 460.
Viçvāmitra, 63, 64, 122, 272, 303, 305, 407, 423, 520, 523.
Viçvantara Sauṣadmana, a Kṣatriya, 314.
Viçve devāḥ, *see* All-gods.
Viṣṇu, 107, 118, 120, 126, 269, 282, 365, 388, 397, 435, 448, 450, 525; *see also* Indra and Viṣṇu.
Viṣṇu and Agni, 437.
Viṣṇu and Varuṇa, 292, 436.
Viṣuvant, 26, 51, 52, 210–213, 485–492, 523.
Vṛddhadyumna Ābhipratāriṇa, a king, 41, 196.
Vṛṣākapi, a hymn (RV. x. 86), 58, 79, 237, 231, 238, 526.
Vṛṣaçuṣma Vātāvata Jātūkarṇya, views on the time of offering the Agnihotra, 28, 253, 356.
Vṛtra, 127, 137, 174, 177, 214, 314, 361, 383, 391, 429, 449, 475.
Vyāhṛtis, 330, 513.
Vyuṣṭi form of Dvyaha rite, 67.

Wailing, by mourners for the dead, 140.
Warp, decorations inserted in, 171.
Water, as food of the Çūdra, 315.
Weber, A., review of Haug's edition of the AB., 102.
West, forests abundant in, 193.
White, as a symbol of the sun, 497, n. 5; of Soma, 405.
White horse, sun as a, 286.
Wife of the sacrificer, 334; not to become too uplifted in mind, 430; share in sacrificial victim, 289; relation to husband and child, 300; question as to offering of Agnihotra by a man without a, 296, 297; *see also* Women.
Wind, breath of the animal victim sent to, 139.
Winter solstice, at new moon of Māgha, 49.
Wives of the gods, 137, 138, 364.
Women, mode of cajoling husbands, 178; impurity of food connected with, when with child, 296; not to go to the assembly, 338; share in propagation, 159, 364, 424; *see also* Daughter, Marriage, Mother, Sister, Wife.
Word formation, 79, 80.
Worlds, broader above, narrower below, 126, 397; of different deities, 204, 457.
Writing, question of use of, in tradition of the Brāhmaṇas, 24.

Yajñagāthās, metre of, 101.
Yajñāyajñīya Stotra, 174.
Yājñasena, Çikhaṇḍin, a sage, 335.
Yajurveda, born of Vāyu, 256.
Yajus, 256, 329, 333, 379, 420.
Yājyās, spoken exceptionally by Adhvaryu and Yajamāna, 282.
Yama, 138, 323, 436.
Yamunā, 338.
Yāska, knowledge of Aitareya and Kauṣītaki Brāhmaṇas, 42, 48.
Yatis, given to hyaenas by Indra, 314.
Year, of ten months, 300; beginning of, with full moon in Phalgunī, 370, n. 1, 372, n. 1; on the new moon of Māgha, 452; *and see* Sattra.
Yudhāṁçrauṣṭi Augrasainya, performs the horse sacrifice, 336.
Yugas, doctrine of, post-Vedic, 302, n. 6.

Zenith, 430.

SANSKRIT INDEX

a, confused with *u* in MSS., 78, 209, 298, 367, n. 2, 407, n. 2; with *i*, 527, n. 2.
a, stems, irregularities of, 72; gen. plural in *-ām*, 384, n. 3 (prose); 308, n. 8 (verse).
a, Sandhi of, before *ṛ*, 71.
aṅcā, dual in a Mantra, 69.
akar, 2nd person, 76.
akarat, 70.
akarta, 69.
akūdhricyaḥ (RV. i. 120. 1–9), 79, 394, n. 6.
akṣarapaṅktyaḥ, as accusative, 73.
agni, v. l. *açni*, 318, n. 3.
acyuta, 407, n. 3.
acha yanti, to be restored for *ucchrayanti*, 418.
ajagrabhaiṣan, anomalous form, 76, 287, n. 3.
ajāyathāḥ, 34, 69, 75.
ajigrahīṣan, probable reading for *ajagrabhaiṣan*, 287, n. 3.
ajitapunarvaṇya, 311, n. 1.
ajñāsam, 76.
añc, declension of stems in, 78.
añjati, 3rd singular, 108, 403, n. 5.
añjayaḥ, as adjective, 423, n. 1.
ati, with accusative, 83.
atigraha, with gen., 529, n. 1.
atibhāṣeran, w. r. for *°eti bhāṣeran*, 444, n. 3.
atimumucānaḥ, 77.
atimokṣamāṇaḥ, 78, 436, n. 6.
atimokṣyamāṇa, v. l., 436, n. 6.
atiriktoktha, 61, 511, n. 1.
atiçaṅs, construction with, 82.
atiçaṅsana of *Stoma*, 32, 264, n. 5.
atī, 72.
atrakāla, as compound, 449, n. 3.
atha, following a gerund, 89, 301, n. 11.
atho . . . u vai, 90.
adarçat, wrong reading, 526, n. 12.
adarçaḥ, 69.
adīdet, 75.
adrukṣaḥ, w. r. for *adhrukṣaḥ*, 76, 338, n. 5.
adhi, with accusative and ablative, 83, 84; with genitive (*adhitasthire*), 308, n. 8.
adhibhūtam, 459, n. 1.
adhīyata, 308, n. 8.
adhyāsa, 468, n. 2.
an, declension of stems in, 78.
an, alleged use of, as a negative prefix to a finite verbal form, 78.
an : abhyapānet, *prāṇet*, 75.
anaddhā puruṣa, 296.
anamnamuḥ, 85, 418, n. 11.
anavarāddhyai (or *anapa°*), to be replaced for *anavarārdhyai*, 516, n. 2.
anucchindan, 351, n. 5.
anujapa, 458, n. 1.
anutsāram (v. l. *anūtsāram*), 77, 194.
anudāyitatarām, 430, n. 3.
anunirupyate, 407, n. 2.
anuparyāguḥ, 76.
anupravadiṣma, 76.
anuvaṣaṭkāra, use of, 155, 188, 261.
anuvaṣaṭkṛ, with genitive, 83.
anuvādiṣma, 76.
anuveda, with genitive, 370, n. 1.
anuçaṅsa, 453, n. 1; *anuçaṅsana*, 500, n. 4.
anuṣṭhyā, 112, n. 4.
anusamīyāt, 402, n. 7.
anusmasi, 68, 75.
anūtsāram, w. r. for *anutsāram*, 77, 194.
anṛṇatāyai, 421, n. 2.
anorathāḥ, correct reading for *manorathāḥ*, 102, 202, n. 2.
antarayanti, 77, 415, n. 2 477, n. 3.
antavat, 80.
andhas, 444, n. 1.
anyatra, with ablative, 84.
anyo 'nya, 46, 47, 78.
apajighnāte, w. r. for *apajaghnāte*, 103, 518, n. 3.
apariḍatāyai, meaning of, 517, n. 2.
apaspṛṇvata, 75.
apaharāt, in a Mantra, 69.
apāpa, euphemism for slayer of victim, 406, n. 3.
apāhata, doubtful form, 75.
api, v. l. for *abhi*, 504, n. 4.
api yadi, 92.
apidadhuḥ, imperfect or perfect, 87.
apinahyuḥ, doubtful reading, 34, 96, 259.
apiçasaḥ, infinitive with *purā*, 77.
apepset, w. r. for *upepset*, 369, n. 2.
aporevatyai, verse (RV. x. 30. 12), 79.
apracutyām, 73.
aprayate, doubtful sense, 255, n. 2.
aprāptāḥ, active sense doubtful, 89, 414, n. 1.
aphālakṛṣṭān, 495, n. 1.
abrāhmaṇa, 119, n. 13, 147.
abrāhmaṇokta, 119, n. 13, 147.
abhi, with accusative, 84; apparently with ablative, 84.
abhigrāsam, 77.
abhitarām, 78.
abhidhānatare, 74.
abhivānyavatsā, derivation of, 290.

abhivi-jñā, with participle, 89; *abhivyajānīmaḥ*, w. r., 85.
abhiçastāt, in a Mantra, 69.
abhiṣiṣicāna, perfect participle, 77.
abhisaṁ-jñā, with dative, 82.
abhisaṁ-pad, with accusative, 83.
abhītvaryāḥ, w. r. for *abhītvaryā*, 517, n. 1.
abhyasuṣavuḥ, 75.
abhyahanat, 75.
abhyāgāram, 443, n. 2.
abhyāyachat, v. l. *abhyāgachat*, 377, n. 1.
abhyārabdha, 502, n. 1.
am, gerund in, 89.
amāvāsyā, properly time of conjunction, popularly rendered 'new moon', 357, n. 2.
amuyā bhūt, 377, n. 2.
ayāṅsi, 76.
ayuvamāri, correct reading in AB. viii. 25, 340, n. 1.
arakṣohata, as a compound, 449, n. 3.
arājā, v. l. for *rājā*, 333, n. 4.
arjātai, 75, 87.
arjayadhvam, w. r. for *ūrjayadhvam*, 517, n. 1.
arjasi, doubtful reading for *arjasva* or *arjāsi*, 75, 83, 192.
arvāk, with ablative, 84.
arṣavat, 80.
alapsata, 69, 305.
alipsata, v. l. for *alapsata*, 305.
avadyolayati, v. l. for *avajyolayati*, 77.
avapadyeyam, wrong reading for *avapadyeya*, 84, 69, 75.
avapādāt (AB. iv. 18 has *avapātāt*), 210.
avarodhana, 208.
ava-vad, with genitive, 83.
avākṣam, play on *vāc* for *avātsam*, 72, 129, n. 5, 326, n. 4.
avāntaredā, 156.
avijiti, or *vijiti*, 309, n. 12.
avijñātaḥ, or *vijñātaḥ*, 390, n. 9.
avivākya, 247, n. 1.
avikṛta, 199, n. 3.
avoḥ, 85, 418, n. 11.
avyūḍha, form of Dvādaçāha, 60.
aç, with genitive of owner, 83.
açanayāparita, 80, 84, 79.
açayat, 175.
açni, v. l. for Agni, 318, n. 3.
açraddhayāçrūgāni, doubtful reading, 209, n. 1.
açvāḥ, w. r. for *çvā*, 228, n. 2.
aṣṭi, play on *aṣṭau*, 453.
aṣṭhīvantā, 69.
as, subjunctive forms of, 75, 76.
asakthāḥ, 76.
asamaram, 398, n. 5.
asaṁbhinnam, doubtful sense, 528, n. 4.
asaṁmugdhyai, 78.
asicāmahai, w. r. for *asicāmahi*, 76, 377, n. 2.
asiñcāma ha, w. r., 377, n. 2.
asunvan or *asanvan*, 209.
asmāka, genitive in a Mantra, 74.
asyāthāḥ, 75.
ah, with dative infinitive, 88.
aha, 90.
ahaiva, 90; after negative, 90.
ahan, *ahani*, 73.
aharahaḥçasya, hymns, 58.
ahirbudhnya, as name of passage, 486.
ahṛṇāt, doubtful form, 75, 477, n. 2.
aho, possibly interrogative, 385, n. 2; *kiṁ svid . . . aho svid*, 90.

ā, with accusative and ablative, 83, 214, n. 1, 364, n. 2.
ā stems, irregularities of, 72.
ā, irregular Sandhi of, 71, 421, n. 2.
ākṣyant, of days (perhaps for *ākṣiyant* or *ārkṣyant*), 209.
āgam, force of, 116, n. 5.
āgantu, sense doubtful, 350, n. 3.
āgur, 155, n. 1.
āgnipāvanīvati, 516, n. 5.
ācaturam, 364, n. 2, 392, n. 6.
ājarasam, 83.
ā-dṛ, use of in AB., 81.
ānantaryātprayoga, doubtful sense of, 497, n. 1.
ānākṣipyaḥ (comm. *pūrṇāḥ*), impossible form, 527, n. 3.
āntam, 83.
āpati, 76.
ā-pad, middle of, 85.
āpayita, 75, 366, n. 2.
āpaḥ, accusative, 73.
āpiyāt, w. r. for *apiyāt*, 447, n. 1.
āptoḥ, probable restoration for *āpnot*, 324, n. 2.
āpriyaḥ, nominative, 73.
ābhūtiḥ, doubtful sense, 308, n. 3.
āmanirayām cakre, 308, n. 12.
āyāṅsi, w. r. in Sāyaṇa for *ayāṅsi*, 163, n. 3.
āratam, 83.
ārpaya, 313, n. 2, 321, n. 2, 358, n. 2, 410, n. 3.
ālambana, 446, n. 1.
ālulobhayiṣāt, 78.
āsām, 46, 74.
ā-vṛç, with dative, 82.
āsade, infinitive, 77.
āhuti, etymology of, 108.
āhvayita, 75.
ā-hve, use of middle, 85, 529.

i, declension of stems in, 73.
i, with participle, 423, n. 2; *upaprāyata*, 75.
iṅkṣva, doubtful form, 326, n. 4.
iḍayati, 77.
iḍā, 362, n. 1, 421.
iti, construction of clauses with 93–95, 109, n. 6; in enumeration, 81, 332, n. 2; omitted at end of quotation, 170, n. 2, 297, 405, n. 2, 417, n. 6, 440, n. 4, 484, n. 4, 485, n. 3, 487, n. 1, 508, nn. 4 and 5, 520, n. 7; in a Mantra, 256, n. 3; alleged omission of, 387, n. 2, 414, n. 2; uncertain meaning, 127, n. 4, 158, n. 4, 311, n. 1, 415. n. 4.
iti nvai, 89.
iti ha sma, doubtful use preceding gerund, 301, n. 11.
intsva, possible reading for *iṅkṣva*, 72, 326, n. 4.
irāpuṣṭiḥ, w. r. for *irā puṣṭiḥ*, 324, n. 3.
iva, almost = *eva*, 89.
iṣayate, 517, n. 1.

iṣṭīḥ, nominative, 78.
iṣṭyāḥ, ablative, 78, 418, n. 4.
iṣvai, 78.

ī, declension of stems in, 72, 78.
ī in optative for *e*, 75.
ī in cpds. with *kṛ*, 78.
īkṣata, 74.
īkṣām āsa, 804, n. 4.
īps, with *upa* (v. l. *apa*), 869, n. 2.
īyuḥ. 75, and see *anusamīyāt*.
īṣ, 75, misinterpreted by Sāyaṇa, 282.
īçvara, with infinitive equivalent to a futural expression, 92; *yadi na*, 88, 404, n. 5, xi; construed with a plural, 81; with genitive, 81, 89.

u, confused with *a* in MSS., 78, 209, 293, 869, n. 2, 457, n. 2.
u, declension of stems in, 78.
u, Sandhi of in *tam v ehi*, 805, n. 7; *sam v ūñkṣva*, 826, n. 4.
u, uses of, 90; *u cet*, 92; *u tv eva*, 90; *u ha . . . u ha*, 90; *kim u*, 90.
u tv eva, 90.
ukhāsaṁbharaṇīyā, 451, n. 8.
uccakrāmat, w. r. for *uccakrāma*, 76.
ujjvalayate 'ti, w. r. for *ujjvalayata + iti*, 444, n. 8.
uta, 90; *uta vā*, 90.
utkāçam, 854, n. 1.
uttaravedinābhi, 72.
uttarām, 810, n. 2.
uttareḍā, 862, n. 2.
utthitaḥ, v. l. for *uttiṣṭhan*, 802, n. 6.
utpāthayati, 77.
utsṛṣṭvā, w. r. for *utsṛṣṭā*, 477, n. 8.
udañcaḥ, w. r. for *udanīyāḥ*, 807, n. 2, xi.
udaprapatat, doubtful form, 74, 75, 185.
udayanīya, 886, n. 2.
udācārya, corrupt reading, 287.
udāna, 208, 886, n. 2.
uddāyitnitarām, v. l. *uddāyi nitarām*, 78, 480, n. 8.
udūhya, 77.
ud-dhartavai, with *ah*, 77.
udyatsāle, 447, n. 8.
udyāsam, 75.
udrodhana, 208.
unnayana, mode of performing, 291.
unmūla, 46.
upabhṛt, 859, n. 1, 860, n. 2.
upavakta, v. l. *upavaktar*, 421, n. 2.
upadhāvāni, v. l. for *upadhāvāmi*, 86, 804, n. 5.
upa-pad, 806, n. 11.
upasamagṛbhṇāt, 75.
upasṛtaḥ, v. l. for *upaçrutaḥ*, 880, n. 8.
upastha, 400, n. 8.
upāṅçu, sense of as contrasted with *nirukta*, 850, n. 4.
upāṅçuyāja, 861, n. 4.
upāptataraṇi, 74.
upālambhya, with genitive, 88.
upetā, irregular form, 69, 808, n. 6.
upepset, correct reading for *apepset*, 869, n. 2.
upodaka, v. l. for *apodaka*, 447, n. 2.
ubhayataçcakra, 887, n. 2.
urūka, 'owl' (for correspondence with *ravitā ravat*), 72, 140, n. 1.

ū, declension of stems in, 78.
ū, 72.
ūti, 108.
ūrjayadhvam, to be restored for *arjayadhvam*, 517, n. 1.
ūrjena, w. r., 408, n. 2.
ūh: perhaps seen in *udūhya*, *nirūhya*, 77.
ūhuṣī or *ohuṣī* (*ā* + *ūhuṣī*, rather than *tadā* + *ūhuṣī*), 77.

ṛtebarhiṣkām, 79, 449, n. 8.
ṛdh, with accusative, 82, 107, n. 8; with accusative and locative, 88.

e and *o* confused, 514, n. 8; and *ai* confused, 144, n. 2.
ekaçruti, 49.
ekaika, 47, 78.
eñkṣva (*ā-iñkṣva*), doubtful reading, 72, 826, n. 4.
etaiṣṭhāna, with dative, 82, 500, n. 9.
etavai, infinitive, 77.
ed, with accusative of exclamation, 82, 89, 144, n. 2.
enat, as nominative, 74.
eva, use of, in sentence construction, 95, 97.
eṣavat, 80.

aikādaçākṣe, doubtful reading, 255, n. 2.
aikṣyāma, 457, n. 1.
ait or *ed*, 89.

o, use of in recitation (*nyūñkha*), 281, 288, 494, 526.
odman, 870, n. 2.
om, 256, 409; contrasted with *tathā*, 809.

au, Sandhi of, 71.

ka, use of as affix, 79, misunderstood by Sāyaṇa, 217, n. 4; as an infix, 69, 509.
ka, apparently indefinite in *na vai kam*, 84; indefinite effect in *kaḥ svid*, 84.
ka, as Prajāpati, 178, 878, 879, n. 2, 454, 488, 484, 521.
katiṣaḍaha, 79.
kadvant pragātha, 58, 521.
karavat, subj. with *vaṣaṭ* in prose, 427.
kariṣyat, 'future', 80.
kartṛ: *rājakartāraḥ*, 79.
kalpata, doubtful form, 826, n. 5.
kalpayiṣan, w. r. *vāci kalpayiṣan* for *avācikalpayiṣan*, 74, 188, n. 1.
kavaṣorū (*kavaṣā-ūrū*), 189.
kaç cit, indefinite, 84.
kaçyapā, dual in a Mantra, 69.
kāmayīta, 75.
kim iva ca, 84, 858, n. 1.
kim u, 90.
kimpuruṣa, 140.
kilāsī, misread in MSS. and edd., 492, n. 7.
kīkasā, 289.
kīrtayati, with genitive, 88.

kurvat, 'present', 80.
kṛṇvantha, in a Mantra, 69.
kṛta, 'past', 80; throw in dicing, 302, 392, n. 6.
kṛdhi, repeated from a Mantra, 70.
kram: *uccakrāmat*, 76; *atikrāmāt*, 75.
krūraravā, v. l. for *krūravahā*, 508, n. 5.
klapsyete, 77.
kṣāmavant, as an epithet of Agni, 293.
kṣeti, with *pari*, as etymology of Parikṣit, 74, 288.

kh and *ṣ*, confused in MSS., 356, n. 5.
khyā, *prati-*, 'foresee', 252.

g and *ç*, confused in MSS., 318, n. 3.
gachān, 78; *samgachātai*, 73.
gatavat, 80.
gā, with ablative, 478, n. 2; *anuparyāguḥ*, 76.
Gāthinām, gen. pl., 70, 308, n. 8.
guṇalopa, 498, n. 2.
guptyai, 73.
gṛbhītaḥ, 77.
gṛh, forms in *bh*, 75.
goäyuṣī, 79.
gorjīka, 266.
gras: *abhigrāsam*, 77.
glāvaḥ, acc. of *glau*, 88.
glai, with dative, 370, n. 3.

c and *j*, confused in MSS., 302, n. 1.
ca . . . *ca*, 308, n. 8.
cakṛvat, 'past', 80.
cakṣ, *vyā-*, 248, n. 2.
catuḥṣaṣṭim, in nominative, 74.
canasita, used in address, 111.
caraṇyat, v. ll. *caraṇyet*, *caraṇyāt*, 385, n. 3.
carāti, 69, 99, 302, n. 5.
ced, *u ced*, 92.
ceṣṭ, 444, n. 3.
cyavayati, 103, 415, n. 2.

chid, *uc-chindan*, 351, n. 5.

j, confused with *c* in MSS., 302, n. 1; with *ç*, 386, n. 3; *jñ* with *ny*, 400, n. 5.

jagatkāmyā (instr.), 72.
jaghnāte, *apa-*, to be read in KB. xxviii. 3, 518, n. 3.
janadvant, epithet of Agni, 295.
Janamejayaka, diminutive form, 79.
janaḥ, v. l. for *cana*, 302, n. 1.
janitoḥ, active infinitive, 127, n. 3.
jas, causitive gerund of (*nijāsya*), 187.
jāgriyāt, doubtful reading for *jāgṛyāt*, 84, 75, 348, n. 2.
jāmi and *jāmī*, at end of compounds, 78.
ji: *vijigyāna*, *jijyūṣita*, *jigīṣita*, 77.
jighnāte, *apa-*, incorrect reading, 518, n. 3.
jighyati, 34, 74, 348, n. 2.
jijyūṣitaḥ, 77.
jīve, misreading for *jīvet*, 296.
juṣ, with genitive, 88.
juhavātha, 75.
juhū, 359, n. 2, 360, n. 2.
jūrya, v. l. for *dhīrya*, 452, n. 1.
jeṣatha, rare form in a Mantra, 517, n. 1.
jñapayā, doubtful form, 69, 306, n. 18.
jñā, *sam-*, with dative and locative, 88; *abhivi-*, with participle, 89; *prajñātha*, 78.
jy and *dy*, confusion of, 77.
jyoktamām, 78.

ṇa, irregular Sandhi, 71.

t and *th*, confused in MSS., 224, n. 7.
tat, *yatra-tat*, 98.
tat tad iti 3 ñ, 34, 311, n. 1.
tatsthāna, with dative, 82; see also *staitsthāna*.
tad etat, introducing a quotation, 103, n. 3, 508, n. 5.
tanvaḥ, accusative, 73.
tariṣyāmaḥ, v. l. for *cariṣyāmaḥ*, 380, n. 1.
tasmāt, use in sentence construction, 95.
tāṣṭi, in an etymology, 74.

tithi, not known to Brāhmaṇas, 297.
tiraçciḥ, nominative, 73.
tiṣṭhadhvam, doubtful reading, 307, n. 16.
tustūrṣamāṇa, 77.
tūṣṇīṁçaṅsa, 157, 258.
trayastriṅçatyā, 74.
trayī vidyā, meaning of, 47.
tridiva, 438, n. 2.
tripaçu, 438, n. 2.
tripuruṣa, 328, n. 1.
tredhāvihita, 449, n. 3.
tryanīkā, form of Dvādaçāha, 60.
tryaryamā, 469, n. 1.
tvad, used once only (cf. JB. ii. 374), 442, n. 3.
tvariṣyāmaḥ, v. l. for *cariṣyāmaḥ*, 380, n. 1.

th and *t*, confused in MSS., 224, n. 7.

dakṣiṇā, derivation from *dakṣ*, 427.
dakṣiṇā, adverbial, 386, n. 1; misreading for *dakṣiṇām*, 527, n. 2.
dā, with genitive, 83.
dādhāra, 76.
dīkṣitaḥ, or *adīkṣitaḥ*, 385, n. 1.
didāsitha, in a Mantra, 69.
dīdhāya, 76.
duruktokta, 117, n. 13.
duhitṝṇām, scansion of, 100.
duhe, 75.
dṛ, or *dhṛ*, 494, n. 2.
dṛpta, 139.
dṛbh, alleged root, 356, n. 2.
dṛç: *adrāk*, 74.
deva, 'king', 453, n. 3.
devajāte, 474, n. 10.
devatyā or *devakyā*, anomalous form, 79, 511, n. 3.
devayajana, 310, n. 3.
devavarman, 127, n. 1.
devasū, 453, n. 1.
daiva veda, 308, n. 8; *dāya*, 306, n. 14.
doṣaṇi, in a Mantra, 69.
dy, confused with *dhy*, 522, n. 3; with *jy*, 77.
dyāvā, nom. feminine, 73, 318.
dravya, 404, n. 7.

drupada, 68.
dvyantān, w. r. for *vyantān*, 451, n. 2.
dvandva, construction of, 47.
dvāpañcāçyau, 74.

dh, variant for *t* in *Vādhāvata*, 356, n. 2.
dhāpayati, with instrumental only, 82.
dhāma, as opposed to *pāthas*, 408, n. 1.
dhī : *dīdhāya*, 76.
dhṛ : *dādhāra*, 74 ; or *dṛ*, 494, n. 2.
dhṛtyai, 78.
dhvāt, in imperative, 69.

na, use of, 90, 94 ; v. l. for *naḥ*, 356, n. 2, 478, n. 2.
na, among gods = *om*, 135.
nabhayanti, 77.
nabhyastha, 400, n. 2.
namnamuḥ, v. l. for *anamnamuḥ*, 75.
nah : *apinahyuḥ*, 76.
nānā çrāntāya, uncertain sense, 302, n. 1.
nābheḥ, artificial explanation of, 76, 122, n. 2.
nāhaiva, beginning a sentence, 90.
nijāsya, causative gerund of *nijas*, 137.
ninyuḥ, incorrect reading, 72.
niniyoja, wrong reading for *niyuyoja*, 30, 34, 76, 308, n. 2.
nirṛtia, 225, n. 11.
nirṛti, 80, n. 2, 225, n. 11, 465, n. 7.
nisrocati, 33.
nirāgāḥ, doubtful sense, 414, n. 2.
nirukta, contrasted with *upāṅçu*, 350, n. 4.
nirūhya, 77.
nir-mā, with accusative and nominative, 81.
niṣadvara, v. l. for *nṛṣadvara*, 302, n. 1.
niṣkakaṇṭh(i)yaḥ, scansion of, 100.
nihnave, 74, 128, n. 3, 305, n. 9.
nihnavate, w. r. for *nihnuvate*, 74, 128, n. 3.

ni-hnu, 128, n. 3, 305, n. 9.
nihçāna, doubtful reading, 30, 34, 76, 308, n. 3.
nihçyāna, correct reading for the preceding, 308, n. 3
nī : *samnayan*, 362, n. 2.
nī, 72, 284, n. 3.
nicaistarām, 78.
nu, 90.
nṛṣadvara, 302, n. 1.
netaḥ, impossible reading in AB. vi. 35, 286, n. 1, xi.
ned, construction with, 94, 140, n. 1, 339, n. 6, xii ; perhaps to be read in AB. vi. 35, 286, n. 1.
nediyastā, 79.
naivaiva, 90, 286, n. 3.
no . . . na, 90, 285, n. 2.
nyubjan, 74.
nyūṅkham, gerund of *nyūṅkh*, 77.
nyūṅkhayati, 77.
nyūṅkhamānaka, present participle of *nyūṅkh* with affix *ka*, 79, 494, n. 3, 528, n. 3.
nv svāpi, 512, n. 5.
nvai, 89, to be restored in AB. ii. 9, 356, n. 1 ; in KB. xvii. 9, 444, n. 3.

p and *bh*, confused in MSS., 504, n. 4 ; and *y*, confused, 251, n. 2.
pakṣa, *pakṣas*, sense of, 356, n. 3, 387, n. 2.
paṅktiḥ, as nominative, 78.
pat : *āpati*, 76.
pataṅga, name of a hymn (RV. x. 177), 491.
patnyaḥ, as accusative, 78.
pad, *abhisam-*, with accusative, 83.
pada, ' word ', 80.
padāvagrāham, 80.
payasyā, 152.
parastat, or *purastāt*, 482, n. 2.
parācī, 391, n. 1.
parāñ, neuter, 73 ; adverbial, 348, n. 1.
parāñcin, 74.
pari, sense of in *aparidilāyai*, 517, n. 2.
parigāta, with *mā*, 76.

parigrahīṣyan, suggested reading for the following, 356, n. 4.
parijigrahīṣyan, wrong form for *parijigrahīṣan*, 356, n. 4.
parininyuḥ, doubtful reading, 72.
pari-vad, 378, n. 1.
parivāpa, 152, n. 3.
pariçrit, bricks in the Agnicayana, 258.
pariçrita, 396, n. 2.
pariçriyete, doubtful form, 77.
pariçaya, 72.
Parucchepāt, w. r. for *parucchepāḥ*, 478, n. 1, xi.
parṇaçar, alleged stem, 74, 291.
parṇaçrkā, dual in a Mantra, 69.
paryagrahaiṣam, irregular and doubtful form, 76.
paryajet, 72.
paryat, 72.
paryastavat, 80.
paryāṇa, 72.
paçcā, 78.
paçcāt, doubtful sense of, 357, n. 3.
pāthas, as opposed to *dhāma*, 408, n. 1.
pāthayati, *api-*, 366, n. 2.
pidṛbhyo, w. r., 356, n. 2.
pibavat, 80.
puṅçcalyāyanam, probable reading in KB. xxvii. 1, 508, n. 5.
putraka, 79.
punarāvṛttam, 80.
punarninṛttam, 80.
punarmṛtyu, only in KB. xxv. 1, 27, 47, 486 ; cf. in latest part of AB. (viii. 25), *na punar mriyate*, 340, n. 1.
purastāt, variant for *puras*, 307, n. 3 ; doubtful sense, 357, n. 2 ; w. r. for *parastāt*, 482, n. 2.
purā, with ablative, 34 ; with present indicative, 35 ; with infinitive, 88.
puruṣa, insertion of syllables of, in RV. iv. 31. 3, 195.
peçāḥ, *peças*, alternating in one passage, 171.

paurṇamāsī, definition of, 357, n. 2.
pragrāham, 80.
pracārīḥ, 76, 116, n. 4.
prajanayan, 75, n. 1, 76.
prajāpati, confusion with *prajāti*, 448, n. 1; doubtful sense of, 526, n. 16.
prajighyati, 34, 74, 348, n. 2.
pra-ṇī, with locative, 82.
pratapeta, unusual reading, 448, n. 3.
pratamām, 78.
prati, apparent omission of before *prati*°, 421, n. 3.
pratikāmina, neuter, 81, 429, n. 4.
prati-khyāya, 'foresee', 252.
pratidadhyāt, wrong reading for *paridadhyāt*, 400, n. 6.
pratirundhet, 75.
prati-vadh, with genitive, 314 (vii. 28), n. 1.
prativeṣa, 316 (vii. 32), n. 1.
pratiṣya, wrong reading for *pradiṣya*, 457.
pratiṣṭhānīya, 77.
pratisāram, 77, 478, n. 4.
pratyakṣatamāt, 78.
pratyagṛbhṇan, 75.
pratyaraudsi, 76.
pratyavarūhya, 77.
pratyutkramata, 477, n. 1.
pratyuttabhnuvan, 74.
pratyupahava, of Achāvāka, 421, n. 1.
pradhānahavīṃṣi, 361, n. 1.
prapad, formulae of recourse, 408, n. 1.
prayata, doubtful sense, 255, n. 2.
pravartantai, doubtful form, 76.
pravalhya, 285, n. 2.
pravibhāvayiṣanti, w. r. for °*bibhāvayiṣanti*, 78 (misprinted), 226, n. 3.
pravṛtāhuti, 408.
pravlīyeran, doubtful reading, 77.
praçastṛ, 189.
praçukrīya, name of a hymn (RV. vii. 34), 478, n. 4.
praṣṭi, 387, n. 2.
prasavi, or *prasalavi*, 404, n. 7.
prasavya, sense of, 404, n. 7.
prasisakṣāṇi, wrong reading, 509.
prasisṛkṣāṇi, 69, 508, n. 5.
prasisṛkṣāmi, 508, n. 5.
pranevān, false reading, 452, n. 3.
prasṛpsyan, false reading, 418, n. 2.
prasrāvayanti, or *prasrāpayanti*, 77, 358, n. 4.
prahāṇa, 515, n. 1.
prāk, with ablative, 84.
prāgudīcī, late form, 47, 358, n. 5.
prācīr udīcīḥ, 358, n. 5.
prācya, probably false reading, 400, n. 6.
prāñcaḥ, to be restored for *prāñcam*, 375, n. 4.
prāṇa, 386, n. 2.
prāṇat, 75.
prāpat, w. r. for *prāpa*, 76.
prāyaṇīya, 386, n. 2.
prāvartanta, 209.
prāvārkṣīḥ, 76.
pluti, 95, 96, 134, n. 2.

ph, confused with *bh*, *viribhita*, 227.
phalīkaraṇa, 450, n. 3.
phālakṛṣṭān, 79.
phālīkaraṇa, 450, n. 3.

badva, 338, n. 2.
baliṣṭhatama, 74.
bahu, 'plural', 80.
bahura, in a Mantra, 72.
bahurātri, doubtful reading, 442, n. 2.
bibhāya, 76, 86.
bṛhatītṛtīya, a compound, 433, n. 3.
bṛhatpṛṣṭham, doubtful if compound, 221, n. 11, 320, n. 2.
brahmaṇaḥ parimara, 342, 343.
brāhmaṇa, 'explanation' of a ceremony, 34, 127, 373, n. 1.
brū, with acc. of person spoken of, 384, n. 3.
brūyāḥ, v. l. for *brūyāt*, 70, 506, n. 14.

bh and *p*, confused in MSS., 504, n. 4; and *y*, 408, n. 1.
bhakṣ, with genitive, 83.
bhakṣiṣṭa, 75.
Bharatarṣabha, 72.
Bharatām, (?gen. pl.), 70, n. 1.
bhī: *bibhāya*, 76.
bhū: *prabibhāvayiṣanti*, 78, 226.
bhūtiḥ, doubtful reading and sense, 300, n. 3.
bhūmi, forms of, 78.
bhūḥ, *bhuvaḥ*, *svar*, use of these formulae, 157, 161, 255.
bhṛ: *saṃjabhruḥ*, 74.
bhrātṛvyahā, as neut. nom., 75.
bhrātṛvyaḥ, or (*a*)*bhrātṛvyaḥ*, 405, n. 3.

m and *n*, variation of in readings, 303, n. 10, 304, n. 5, 508, n. 5; *māpagāḥ*, 306, n. 10; omission of, 414, n. 4.
maiya, 189, 410, n. 4.
mad, represented by *modaiva*, 429, n. 3, 433, n. 5.
man, with participle, 89; with adjective, 414, n. 2.
manuṣyarājñām, 79.
manorathāḥ, w. r. for *anorathāḥ*, 102, 202, n. 2.
martya, w. r. for *matya*, 410, n. 4.
mahāṇagni, w. r. for °*nagnī*, 71.
mahārātra, 357, n. 6.
mahāhna, 357, n. 6.
mā, with injunctive, 75, 88, 90, 93; variant for *na*, 306, n. 10.
mā: *mimet*, 75.
mitrakṛtyā, instrumental, 72.
mimet, 75.
muc: passive forms from, 77; see also *atimokṣamāṇa*.
muṣṭī kṛ, 78.
Mūcipa, v. l. for *Mūtiba*, 307, n. 2.
medh(*i*)*yda*, scansion of, 100.
menimahe, 509, n. 6.
meṣyan, 212.

y and *j*, confused in MSS., 299, n. 4, 400, n. 5; and *p*, confused in MSS., 251, n. 2.

ya, construction of clauses with, 81.
yaj, middle and active, &c., 85.
yajuṣmatyaḥ, bricks, 258.
yat, sense of, 117, n. 2.
yat kiṁcitkam, 84.
yatra, denoting occasion, 98.
yathā, in clauses of comparison, 69, 92, 93; possibly with a relative (*yathā yas* or *yathāyas*), 98, 471, n. 1.
yathākāmaprayāpyaḥ, 77, 315, n. 2.
yathāyatham, v. l. for *yathāyatanam*, 401, n. 2.
yathopapādam, 77.
yad, constructions with, 92, 94, 95, 96, 97, 299, n. 2.
yadi, 92; curious use of, 493, n. 3; *sa yadi*, 89, 315, n. 1, 355, n. 1; *yadi na*, 88, xi.
yady a, a misreading for *yady u*, 78, 298.
yaças kīrtim, in a Mantra, 72.
yasmāt . . . hi, 127, n. 4.
yā: *yathākāmaprayāpya*, 77.
yātayan, 76, 88, 116, n. 4.
yāmaki, 508, n. 5.
yāvatkāmam, 89.
yāvadaham, 458, n. 2.
yuktavat, 80.
yuj: *niniyoja*, 74.
yuñjānavat, 80.
yuvam, 74.
yuṣme, unnecessary conjecture for *yuṣmān*, 308, n. 6.
yeyajāmahaḥ, 78.
ye yajāmahe, 360, 361.
yoni, forms of, 78.
yoṣan, 'feminine', 80.

r, preference for in AB., 72; lingualizing effect, 71.
rakṣobhāṣaḥ, 189.
rajatāḥ, v. l. for *raçanāḥ*, 386, n. 3.
ratavat or *rathavat*, 80, 224, n. 7.
rathantaram, w. r. for *rāthantaram*, 488, n. 4.
rarāṭyā, 181.
raçanāḥ, v. l. for *rajatāḥ*, 386, n. 3.
rājakartāraḥ, 79.
rājaputra, 306, n. 18.
rājamātra, 27.
rājā, v. l. for *arājā*, 338, n. 4; *manuṣyarājñām*, 79.
rāthantaram, correct reading for *rathantaram*, 488, n. 4.
riricāna, perfect participle, 77.
ru, 'cry' and 'cut', 69, 140.
rudriya, substituted for *rudra*, 186, n. 3.
rudh: *pratirundhet*, 75.
rebhati, 127, n. 4.
romāṇi, 72.

l and *r* confused, 425, n. 1, 447, n. 5.
lajjamāna, 46.
lipsitavyam, 77.
lokete, 46.
lomaçna (M; cf. *ālobhantaḥ* in KB. xvii. 9), or *romaçna*, 425, n. 1.

vacasā, 505, n. 6.
vad: *ava-*, with genitive, 83; *pari-*, with accusative, 378, n. 1; *udyāsam*, 75; *anupravadiṣma*, *anuvādiṣma*, 76.
vadatyaḥ, 76.
vadāvada, probably intensive in sense, 300.
vadh, with *prati*, 314, n. 1.
vayam, plural of majesty, 356, n. 2.
variṣyāmaḥ, v. l. for *cariṣyāmaḥ*, 380, n. 1.
varṇa, 'letter', 80.
vaṣaṭ call, 168, 206, 361, n. 4, 523, 525.
vaṣaṭkaravat, 427, n. 2.
Vaṣaṭkāra, as a deity, 147.
vas, with locative, 83.
vah: *ūhuṣī*, 77; *saṁvahārahai*, 341, n. 1.
vā, 'or', 90, 405, n. 3, 415, n. 3, 437, n. 5.
vā = *vai*, 89, 415, n. 3, 437, n. 5.
vājavant, 149, n. 7.
vājina, offerings, 367, n. 1, 371, n. 1.
vāṭ, 247, 248.
vātāpi, 512, n. 4.
vānto na nirvānti, correct reading of *avāñco 'nunirvāñci*, 338, n. 1.
vārayadhvāt, in a Mantra, 69.
vāva, 89.
vāvātā, 173, n. 2.
vi-gā, with accusative, 422, n. 4.
vicakṣaṇa, used in address, 111.
vichandāḥ, neuter, 78.
vijajñuḥ, necessary correction in KB. xxviii. 1, 514, n. 2.
vijigyāna, perfect participle, 77.
vijiti, or *avijiti*, 309.
vijñātaḥ, or *avijñātaḥ*, 390, n. 9.
vitarām, needless conjecture for *vi*, 304, n. 20.
vidmasi, in a verse, 69.
vidre, 76.
vibhaktayaḥ, force of, 349, n. 1.
vibhāga, in lieu of *vibhakti*, a sign of later date, 290.
vimathnate, v. l. for *vibadhnate*, 515, n. 1.
vimadan, 75, 471, n. 3, 477, n. 1.
vimṛdh, 365, n. 3.
viriphitam, 80.
viribhita (cf. M's reading *ālobhantaḥ* in KB. xix. 7), 227, n. 2.
vivācana, 308, n. 5.
vividāna, perfect participle, 77, 258, n. 1.
viçeṣa, 225, n. 11.
viṣpandamānam, v. l. for *viṣyandamānam*, 251, n. 2.
visraṁsata, 74.
viharaṇa, 440, n. 2.
viharanta, 74.
vihṛte, 496, n. 1.
vi-hve, 305, n. 7.
vīva, 72, 90.
vṛj: *prāvārkṣīḥ*, 76; see also *vṛñjīyam*.
vṛdhanvat, 80.
vṛñjīyam, doubtful form, 34, 69, 75.
vṛṣan, 'masculine', 80.
veda daiva, 308, n. 3.
vedī, in cpd., 72; *vedeḥ*, abl., 78.
venā sevanī, 518, n. 2.
vai, construction of clauses with, 95, 97.

vau = yonder sun, 169.
vauṣaṭ, 361, n. 4, 397, n. 2.
vyakṣareṇa, w. r. for *vikṣareṇa*, 79, 511, n. 3.
vyantān, to be restored for *dyantān*, 351, n. 2.
vyapanayitum, doubtful form, 34, 77, 291.
vyā-cakṣ, 248.
vyāhanasyā, used of verses, 287.
vyāhāvam, 188.
vyāhvayita, 75.
vyūḍha, form of Dvādaçāha, 59-61, 467, n. 3, 511, n. 1, 513, n. 1.
vyūḍhachandas, 59.
vyūha, 217, n. 1.
vlī : *pravlīyeran*, 77.

ç and *j*, confused in MSS., 386, n. 3.
çaṅs, sense of, 187, n. 1, 436, n. 3.
çaṅsāmo daivam, as *āhāva*, 172, 189, n. 2.
çaṅsiṣṭa, 81, taken as 3rd person singular by Sāyaṇa, 282.
çaṅstavya, 77.
çaṅstvā, w. r. for *çastvā*, 77.
çatāyu, variant of *çatāyus*, 78.
çanaiṣṭarām, 78.
çamitṛ, euphemistic use of, 406, n. 3.
çayāsai, 78.
çarabha, 140.
çalā, dual in a Mantra, 69, 189, n. 3.
çalya, part of arrow, 126.
çaçvat, 90, 120, n. 2.
çastvā, w. r. for *çastā* (cf. *uçṛṣṭā*), 433, n. 1; correct reading for *çaṅstvā*, 77.
çithirāṇi, 72.
çī : *çere*, *çayāsai*, *açayat*, 75.
çunāsīrau, 375, n. 1.
çuçruma, 69.
çuṣma or *çuṣman*, at end of compounds, see Somaçuṣman, 386; Vṛṣaçuṣma, 356.
çepas, 477.
çere, 69, 75.
ço : *niḥç(y)āna*, 76.
çaṅsāmo daiva, 429, n. 3, 433, n. 5.
çocatyaḥ, 76.
çraddhādeva. 355, n. 3.
çramaṇam, v. l. for *çremaṇam*, 303, n. 7.
çri : *pariçriyate*, 77.
çrita, v. l. for *sṛta*, 445, n. 3.
çritavat, 80.
çrī, forms of, 78.
çreṣṭhin, 303, n. 6, 374, n. 2.
çraiṣṭhya, 303, n. 3.
çvā, or *açvā*, 293, n. 2.

ṣ and *kh*, interchange of, 356, n. 5.
ṣ and *ṣy*, interchange of (cf. *s* and *sy*, 299, n. 6), 303, n. 9, 356, n. 4.
ṣayadhvam, w. r. in Lindner's text, 517, n. 1.
ṣaṭ = the six (seasons), 169.
ṣaṭtriṅçatam, 74.
ṣaṣṭiḥ, as accusative, 74, 290.

s and *sy*, confused in MSS., 299, n. 6.
sa, as *quasi* particle, 84; resuming subject in anacoluthon, 81; contraction in a verse, 100; *so*, erroneously read for *yo*, 254, n. 1; omitted, 404, n. 7.
sa yadi, 84, 315, n. 1, 355, n. 1.
saṁyājye, 110, n. 1, 365, n. 3.
saṁlokate, 46.
saṁvahāvahai, 341, n. 1.
saṁ-çaṅs, 509, n. 3.
saṁsthāpayan, 74; *saṁsthāpayiṣyuḥ*, 492, n. 6, xii.
saṁgatām, doubtful form, 334, n. 3.
saciva, 46.
saṁjabhruḥ, 75.
saṁjñapaya, euphemistic use of, 406, n. 3.
saṁ-jñā, with dative and locative, 83.
saṁjñānāneṣu, w. r. for *saṁjñānam eṣu*, 70, 307, n. 15.
sattamam, v. l. *saptamam*, 457, n. 3.
Sattrasya ṛddhi, 518.
saptatim, apparently as nominative, 74.
samagṛbhṇāt, 75.
samavadyati, 407, n. 2.
samindhvam, possible reading for *samiddham*, 444, n. 3.
samiṣṭayajūṅṣi, 311, n. 1.
samudantam, 251, n. 2.
samūḍha, form of Dvādaçāha, 59-61, 511, n. 1, 513, n. 1; *samūḷhā*, w. r., 473, n. 6.
saṁ-pā, middle of, with instrumental, 86.
saṁpādayiṣyuḥ, an impossible form (cf. *pravibhāvayiṣanti*), 492, n. 6.
samrāj, used probably of fellow sacrificers, 398, n. 4.
sarātayaḥ, origin of, 303, n. 7.
sayate, 'go', Dhātupāṭha root, possible source of, 517, n. 1.
sarparājñī, irregular use of, 511, n. 2.
Sarvacaru, perhaps a place name, 259, 519.
sarvasvajaina, 67, n. 7.
sarvahari, a hymn (RV. x. 96), 79.
saloma, 321, n. 2.
sasṛjāna, 77.
sahasrāyu, variant of *sahasrāyus*, 78.
sādhu, 188, n. 7.
sāṁnāyya, 361, n. 1.
sāma, *sāman*, derivative of, 179.
sāmājye, doubtful reading, 431, n. 2.
sāṁnāhuka, irregular form (JAOS. xxxi. 105), 30, 34, 79.
sārparājñī, irregular form, 511, n. 2.
sic : *abhiṣiṣicāna*, 77; *asicāmahai*, 76.
siṣāsatyaḥ, 76.
sira, 375, n. 1.
su, use of, 79.
sudhāyām, 38, 190, n. 2, 195, n. 2.
sunvat, doubtful sense, 421, n. 2.
su mat pad vag de, 152.
subrahmaṇyā, 513, n. 3.
suruçāt, doubtful word, 355, n. 2.

suleṣāt, conjectural restoration, 355, n. 2.
suhṛdayam, 304, n. 10.
sūryanyaṅga, 446, n. 3.
sṛ: *pratisāram*, 77; *sṛta*, v. l. for *çrita*, 445, n. 3.
sṛj: *prasisṛkṣāṇi*, 509.
sairāvatī, suggested reading for *sa irāvatī*, 299, n. 4.
sevanī, 518, n. 2.
startavai, infinitive, 77.
stomakṛntatraitāyai, doubtful sense, 496, n. 3.
stomebhiḥ, unique form for prose, 72.
sthana, 69.
sthā, with double dative, 70, 82; *pratitiṣṭhāt*, *saṁtiṣṭhātai*, 75.
sthitavat, 80.
spand or *syand*, 252.
spṛdh, with locative, 348, n. 1.
smasi, in *anusmasi*, 68, 75.
srucau, 359, n. 2.
svadayati, 77.
svaraviçeṣa, sense of, 80, n. 2, 225, n. 11.
svid, in *kaḥ svid*, 84; *kiṁ svid* . . . *aho svid*, 90.

h and *s*, confused in MSS., 520, n. 6.
ha vā api (misprinted *iha vā api* in Lindner's ed.), 89.
ha sma, with present indicative, 85; with imperfect and perfect, xi; with *iti*, preceding a gerund, 301, n. 11.
han: *nirhaṇan*, 75; *ahanat*, 75; *apa-jaghnire*, misread *jajñire*, xii.
hanta, with subjunctive, 86, 304, n. 5.
haratai, doubtful reading for *harātai*, 75.
hariṣṭha, wrong reading, 440, n. 2.
haviṣkṛt, 381, n. 1.
haviṣpaṅkti, sacrifice of five oblations, 152, 418, n. 1.
hi, repeated, 90; *yad* . . . *hi*, 95; *yasmāt* . . . *hi*, 127, n. 4.
hinaḥ, misreading for *hīnaḥ*, 449, n. 2.
hiṅ, 358, 403.
hṛ: *ahṛṇāt*, 75, 477, n. 2.
hṛ: *saṁjabhruḥ*, 75.
hotṛ, etymology of the word, 110.

HARVARD ORIENTAL SERIES

Founded in 1891 by CHARLES ROCKWELL LANMAN and HENRY CLARKE WARREN.

Edited, with the coöperation of various scholars, by CHARLES ROCKWELL LANMAN, A.B. and LL.D. (Yale), LL.D. (Aberdeen), Professor of Sanskrit (since 1880: Wales Professor since 1903) at Harvard University (founded, 1636);

Member of the American Philosophical Society (founded, 1727); Fellow of the American Academy of Arts and Sciences (1780); President (1890) of the American Philological Association (1869); President (1908, 1920) of the American Oriental Society (1842);

Honorary Fellow of the Asiatic Society of Bengal (Calcutta, 1784); Honorary Member of the Société Asiatique (Paris, 1822), the Royal Asiatic Society (London, 1823), and the Deutsche Morgenländische Gesellschaft (Leipzig, 1845);

Honorary Member of the North-China Branch of the Royal Asiatic Society (Shanghai), the Finnish-Ugrian Society (Helsingfors), the India Society (London); Honorary Correspondent of the Archæological Department of the Government of India; Foreign Member of the Bohemian Society of Sciences (Prague, 1759); Member of the Colonial Society of Massachusetts; Corresponding Member of the Academy of Sciences of the Institute of Bologna (1712), of the Society of Sciences at Göttingen (1751), of the Russian Academy of Sciences (Petrograd, 1725), and of the Académie des Inscriptions et Belles-Lettres (1663) of the Institute of France.

Published by the Harvard University Press, Cambridge, Massachusetts, U.S. of America. The home office of the Press is at Randall Hall, Cambridge. The Agent of the Press in Great Britain is Humphrey Milford, Oxford University Press, Amen Corner, London, E.C., England.

Direct application for books of this Series may be made, with remittance, to the Harvard University Press at Cambridge, Massachusetts. The volumes will then be sent by mail or parcel-post direct to the buyer.

The list-prices are subject to a trade-discount. No extra charge is made for postage. This list is here revised up to date of December, 1920. Prices of previous revisions are cancelled.

Descriptive List. A bound volume, containing a list of the volumes of this Series, and a brief Memorial of HENRY CLARKE WARREN, joint-founder, will be sent free upon application to the Harvard University Press, Cambridge, Massachusetts.—The list tells the general nature and contents of each work of the Series, and the uses which that work is designed to serve. The List gives also extracts from critical notices of those works, taken from various periodicals of high standing.

Externals of the volumes. The books of this Series are all printed on paper of a quality and tensile strength very far above the average. They are all bound durably in full buckram. The edges are cut, but the margins are ample; and the tops are gilded, not for ornament, but to make cleaning easy. The backs are properly lettered. No work is issued until it is complete. Volume 10 is royal quarto (32 cm.); volumes 7 and 8 are super-royal octavo (28 cm.); the rest are royal octavo (26 cm.).

HARVARD ORIENTAL SERIES

Volume 1. Jātaka-Mālā. Stories of Buddha's former incarnations. By Ārya Çūra. Critically edited in the original Sanskrit (Nāgarī letters) by HENDRIK KERN, Professor in the University of Leiden, Netherlands. 1891. Second issue, 1914. Pages, 270. Royal 8°. Price, $3. (Translation by Speyer, London, 1895, Frowde.)

Volume 2. Sānkhya-Pravachana-Bhāshya, or Commentary (Bhāshya) on the Exposition (Pravachana) of the Sānkhya philosophy. By Vijñāna-Bhikshu. Edited in Sanskrit (Roman letters) by RICHARD GARBE, Professor in the University of Tübingen, Germany. 1895. Pages, 210. Royal 8°. Price, $3. (Translated by Garbe, Leipzig, 1889, Brockhaus.)

Volume 3. Buddhism in Translations. Passages selected from the Buddhist sacred books, and translated from the original Pāli into English, by HENRY CLARKE WARREN, late of Cambridge, Massachusetts. 1896. Sixth issue, 1915. Pages, 540. Royal 8°. Price $1.20. (In accordance with the author's wish, the original price was set extremely low, at $1.20. In spite of economic conditions now prevailing, the original price has been maintained unaltered.)

The first chapter gives the picturesque and touching Buddha-legend; the last treats of the monastic order; the other three give the fundamental doctrines of Buddhism. Warren's material is drawn straight from the fountain-head. It is this fact that gives his book an abiding importance and value. It has been widely circulated in America and Europe and the Orient. Nearly half of the work is included in The Harvard Classics, of which over a quarter of a million sets have been sold. A memorial of Henry Warren as a scholar is appended to the Descriptive List mentioned above.

Volume 4. Karpūra-Mañjarī. A drama by the Indian poet Rājaçekhara (900 A. D.). Critically edited in the original Prākrit (Nāgarī letters), with a glossarial index and an essay on the life and writings of the poet, by STEN KONOW, Professor of Indic Philology at the University of Christiania, Norway, and Epigraphist to the Government of India. And translated into English with introduction and notes, by C. R. LANMAN. 1901. Pages, 318. Royal 8°. Price, $3.

Volumes 5 and 6. Bṛhad-Devatā (attributed to Çāunaka), a summary of the deities and myths of the Rig-Veda. Critically edited in the original Sanskrit (Nāgarī letters), with an introduction and seven appendices (volume 5), and translated into English with critical and illustrative notes (volume 6), by Professor ARTHUR ANTHONY MACDONELL, University of Oxford. 1904. Pages, 234 + 350 = 584. Royal 8°. Not sold separately. Price, $6.

Volumes 7 and 8. Atharva-Veda. Translated, with a critical and exegetical commentary, by WILLIAM DWIGHT WHITNEY, late Professor of Sanskrit in Yale University, Editor-in-Chief of The Century Dictionary, an Encyclopedic Lexicon of the English Language.—Revised and brought nearer to completion and edited by C. R. LANMAN. 1905. Pages, 1212. Super-royal 8°. Not sold separately. Price, $10.

The work includes critical notes on the text, with various readings of European and Hindu mss.; readings of the Kashmirian version; notices of corresponding passages in the other Vedas, with report of variants; data of the scholiasts as to authorship and divinity and metre of each stanza; extracts from the ancillary literature concerning ritual and exegesis; literal translation; elaborate critical and historical introduction.

Volume 9. **The Little Clay Cart** (Mṛc-chakaṭika). A Hindu drama attributed to King Çūdraka. Translated from the original Sanskrit and Prākrits into English prose and verse by ARTHUR WILLIAM RYDER, Instructor in Sanskrit in Harvard University. 1905. Pages, 207. Royal 8°. Price, $2.

A Hindu masterpiece, reproduced with truth and literary finish. 'The champagne has been decanted, and has not lost its fizz.' Noble typography, magnificent paper, dignified binding. Most volumes of the Series are for technical study. This one, like Warren's Buddhism, is for the 'general reader', for whom it might often be happily chosen as a gift-book.

Volume 10. **Vedic Concordance**: being an alphabetic index to every line of every stanza of the published Vedic literature and to the liturgical formulas thereof, that is, an index (in Roman letters) to the Vedic mantras, together with an account of their variations in the different Vedic books. By Professor MAURICE BLOOMFIELD, Johns Hopkins University, Baltimore. 1906. Pages, 1102. Royal 4°. Price, $15.

The Concordance enables us to find with ease: 1. where a given mantra occurs, if it occur but once; 2. if more than once, in what places; and 3. if with variants, what those variants are. Being in one volume, it is thus the most convenient register of Vedic variants available. It is also by far the most comprehensive. It covers such great texts as the Rig-Veda and Atharva-Veda exhaustively (these two alone require about 50,000 entries); and, exhaustively or selectively, it covers over 100 other texts. The book was printed, not from electrotype plates, but from type, and in an edition of 1000 copies, now half exhausted. The cost in money and labour was so great that the prospect of a new edition is very remote. For many decades it will maintain its value, an enduring monument to the industry and learning and resolute will of Professor Bloomfield.

Volume 11. **The Pañcha-tantra**: a collection of ancient Hindu tales, in the recension (called Pañchākhyānaka, and dated 1199 A. D.) of the Jaina monk, **Pūrṇabhadra**, critically edited in the original Sanskrit (in Nāgarī letters: and, for the sake of beginners, with word-division) by Dr. JOHANNES HERTEL, Professor am königlichen Realgymnasium, Doebeln, Saxony. 1908. Pages, 344. Royal 8°. Volumes 11 and 12 and 13 are not sold separately. Price for the three, $4.

Volume 12. **The Pañchatantra-text of Pūrṇabhadra**: critical introduction and list of variants. By Dr. HERTEL. 1912. Pages, 246. Royal 8°. Price, see above.

Volume 13. **The Pañchatantra-text of Pūrṇabhadra**, and its relation to texts of allied recensions, as shown in **Parallel Specimens**. By Professor HERTEL. 1912. Pages, 10: and 19 sheets, mounted on guards and issued in atlas-form. Royal 8°. Price, see above.

Volume 14. **The Pañchatantra**: a collection of ancient Hindu tales, in its oldest recension, the Kashmirian, entitled **Tantrākhyāyika**. The original Sanskrit text (in Nāgarī letters), editio minor, reprinted from the critical editio major which was made for the Königliche Gesellschaft der Wissenschaften zu Göttingen, by Professor HERTEL. 1915. Pages, 160. Royal 8°. Price, $2.

The Pañchatantra. For two thousand years and more, the tales of the Pañchatantra have instructed and delighted the Hindus. It was the Pañchatantra that formed the basis of the studies of the immortal pioneer in the field of comparative literature,

Theodor Benfey. From the Pañchatantra, through translations of translations, have come some of the most notable books of mediæval Europe, such as the Directorium (1270) of John of Capua, the Buch der Beispiele (1483), and so on, down to that gem of racy Tudor English, the translation (1570) of Doni by Sir Thomas North (reprinted by J. Jacobs, London, 1888).—The Hindus have a way of emboxing a second story into the first, a third into the second, and even a fourth into the third. The result is confusing. These emboxments are here shown in an ingenious and self-explaining way, by putting into the margin vertical wavy lines, single or double or triple, as the case may be. Thus the continuation of an interrupted story is found at a glance.

Volume 15. Bhāravi's poem Kirātārjunīya or Arjuna's combat with the Kirāta. Translated from the original Sanskrit into German and explained by CARL CAPPELLER, Professor at the University of Jena. 1912. Pages, 231. Royal 8°. Price, $2.

The subject-matter is taken from the Mahā-Bhārata. The Kirāta or mountaineer is the god Shiva in disguise. A valuable introduction and various other useful additions are given.

Volume 16. The Çakuntalā, a Hindu drama by Kālidāsa: the Bengālī recension critically edited in the original Sanskrit and Prākrits by RICHARD PISCHEL, late Professor of Sanskrit at the University of Berlin.

The masterpiece of the literature of India. Pischel died in 1908. Under many difficulties, the book (all except a couple of sheets) was beautifully printed by Kohlhammer of Stuttgart. Then came the world-conflagration. We may yet hope to complete and issue the book.

Volume 17. The Yoga-system of Patañjali, or the ancient Hindu doctrine of concentration of mind: embracing the Mnemonic Rules (Yoga-sūtras) of Patañjali, the Comment (Bhāshya) attributed to Vyāsa, and the Explanation (Tattva-vāiçāradī) of Vāchaspati-Miçra: translated from the original Sanskrit by JAMES HAUGHTON WOODS, Professor of Philosophy at Harvard University. 1914. Pages, 422. Royal 8°. Price $4.

The Comment is the oldest systematic exposition of Yoga-doctrine, written in Sanskrit, that we possess. Although the book consists of three separate works, these are so distinguished, one from another, by differences of type and other devices, that the general impression is one of admirable clearness.

Volumes 18 and 19. The Veda of the Black Yajus School, entitled Tāittirīya Saṁhitā. Translated from the original Sanskrit prose and verse, with a running commentary. By ARTHUR BERRIEDALE KEITH, D.C.L. (Oxford), of the Inner Temple, Barrister-at-law, and of His Majesty's Colonial Office, sometime Acting Professor of Sanskrit at the University of Oxford, Author of 'Responsible Government in the Dominions'. Volume 18, kāṇḍas I-III; volume 19, kāṇḍas IV-VII. 1914. Pages, 464 + 374 = 838. Royal 8°. Price, $7. Not sold separately.

This work, in spite of its large extent, is notable for its well-rounded completeness. The entire text is translated. The commentary runs *pari passu* with the version, and is presented with the utmost typographical perspicuity. An elaborate introduction is given, treating of the relation of this text to kindred texts, its contents, language style, and date ('about 600 B.C.'), and the religious ritual of ancient India.

Volumes 20 and 24. Rig-Veda Repetitions. The repeated verses and distichs and stanzas of the Rig-Veda in systematic presentation and with critical discussion. By Professor MAURICE BLOOMFIELD, of the Johns Hopkins University, Baltimore. Volume 20 contains Part 1: The repeated passages of the Rig-Veda, systematically presented in the order of the Rig-Veda. Volume 24 contains Part 2: Comments and classifications from metrical and lexical and grammatical points of view, and from the point of view of the themes and divinities of the repeated passages. 1916. Pages, 508+206=714. Royal 8°. Price, $5. Not sold separately.

This work is the first of three natural sequels to Bloomfield's great Vedic Concordance: 1. The Rig-Veda Repetitions; 2. The Reverse Concordance; 3. The Vedic Variants. A draft of the second has been actually prepared by Bloomfield. And he and Edgerton have in hand the first draft of the third, a systematic presentation and critical discussion of the variant readings of the Vedic texts. The aim of this work on the Repetitions is to help us to understand the oldest religious document of Indo-European antiquity.

Volumes 21 and 22 and 23. Rāma's Later History, or Uttara-Rāma-Charita, an ancient Hindu drama by Bhavabhūti. Critically edited in the original Sanskrit and Prākrit, with an introduction and English translation and notes and variants, &c. By SHRIPAD KRISHNA BELVALKAR, Graduate Student of Harvard University. (Now, 1920, Professor of Sanskrit at Deccan College, Poona, India.)

Dr. Belvalkar, when returning to India in 1914 from his studies at Harvard, shipped his manuscript-collations and other papers and his books by the German freighter, Fangturm. In August, 1914, the Fangturm was interned at the port of Palma, Balearic Islands. In 1919, she was released. In May, 1920, Dr. Belvalkar recovered his papers.

Volume 21 was issued in 1915, complete.

Of volume 22, the first 92 pages, containing the text of the whole play, have been in print since January, 1915, awaiting for over five and one half years the recovery of the material for the rest of the book.

Of volume 23, the material included collation-sheets giving the readings of manuscripts from widely-separated parts of India, from Nepal to Madras, from Calcutta to Bombay. In spite of the generous assistance of His Majesty's Secretary of State for India in Council, the work of getting the loan of these mss. was so great that it seemed best not to try to do it again, but to await the release of the Fangturm.—There is hope now that volumes 22 and 23 may be issued.

Volume 21. Rāma's Later History, &c. Part 1. Introduction and translation. (Prefixed is a convenient synoptic analysis of the play. The introduction treats of Bhavabhūti's life and date and works, and includes a summary of the Rāma-story as given by the Rāmāyaṇa. Lanman adds an essay entitled 'A method for citing Sanskrit dramas.' The method is very simple and practical.) 1915. Royal 8°. Pages, 190. Price, $2.

Volume 22. Rāma's Later History, &c. Part 2. The text, with index, glossaries, &c. (This was printed at Bombay, with the exquisitely beautiful type, newly cast for this work, of Jāvajī's Nirṇaya Sāgara Press, and upon paper made at Oxford for this edition. Each Prākrit speech is followed by the Sanskrit version in immediate sequence.) See above.

Volume 23. Rāma's Later History, &c. Part 3. Explanatory and critical epilogue. (Critical account of the Manuscripts. Running expository comment. The variant readings of the mss. The typographical 'make-up' of Comment and Variants into pages is such that they go *pari passu*. These epilegomena close with an essay on the two text-traditions of the play, a time-analysis, a note on the Hindu stage, &c.) See above.

Volume 24. Rig-Veda Repetitions. Parts 2 and 3. By Professor BLOOMFIELD. Described above, with volume 20.

Volume 25. Rig-Veda Brāhmaṇas: The Aitareya and Kauṣītaki Brāhmaṇas of the Rig-Veda. Translated from the original Sanskrit. By ARTHUR BERRIEDALE KEITH, D.C.L., D. Litt., of the Inner Temple, Barrister-at-law, Regius Professor of Sanskrit and Comparative Philology at the University of Edinburgh. 1920. Pages, 567. Royal 8°. Price, $5.

The Vedic literature falls into three clearly sundered groups: the Vedic hymns or Mantras; the Brāhmaṇas, 'the priestlies' or 'priestly (discourses)'; and the Sūtras. Keith thinks that the Aitareya is not later than 600 B.C. The plan of the work is like that of volumes 18–19: elaborate introduction; translation; running comment on the same page. The skill of the priestly story-tellers is at its best in the splendid legend of Çunaḥçepa (threatened sacrifice of son by father: cf. Isaac, Iphigeneia, Phrixos). Despite the pseudo-profundity and puerility of the Brāhmaṇas, they are of genuine significance to the student of Hindu antiquity, social and religious. And they are in fact the oldest Indo-European prose extant.

Volumes 26 and 27. Vikrama's Adventures, or The Thirty-two Tales of the Throne. A collection of stories about King Vikrama, as told by the Thirty-two Statuettes that supported his throne. Edited in four different recensions of the Sanskrit original (Vikrama-charita or Siṅhāsanadvātriṅçaka) and translated into English with an introduction, by FRANKLIN EDGERTON, Assistant Professor of Sanskrit at the University of Pennsylvania. Nearly ready.

Vikrama's Adventures is one of the most famous story-books of mediæval India. Vikrama is a kind of Hindu King Arthur, an example for real kings. Edgerton hopes that his work may prove suggestive as a model for students of comparative literature. The text of each of the four recensions is printed in horizontally parallel sections, so that each page contains those parts which correspond to each other in substance. And the translation is treated in like manner. Comparisons are thus facilitated to a degree never before attained in a work of this kind.

From all this, Edgerton reconstructs, with some detail, and with reasonable certainty, the original work from which the current versions are derived. This he presents in the form of a Composite Outline, the concrete solution of a problem in literary genetics.

Volumes 28 and 29 and 30. Buddhist Legends. Translated from the original Pāli text of the Dhamma-pada Commentary, by EUGENE WATSON BURLINGAME, Fellow of the American Academy of Arts and Sciences, sometime Harrison Fellow for Research at the University of Pennsylvania and Johnston Scholar in Sanskrit at the Johns Hopkins University and Lecturer on Pāli at Yale University. 1921. Pages, 362 + 370 + 378 = 1110. Royal 8°. Not sold separately. Price, $15.

Dhamma-pada, or Way of Righteousness, is the name of one of the canonical books of the Buddhist Sacred Scriptures. It consists of 423 stanzas. These are reputed to be the very words of the Buddha himself. The Dhamma-pada Commentary, composed by an unknown author in Ceylon about 450 A. D., purports to tell the circumstances under which Buddha uttered each one of these stanzas. In telling them, it narrates 299 stories or legends. These stories are the preponderating element of the Commentary, and it is these which are here translated.

In style and substance the tales resemble those of the famous Jātaka Book, the Buddhist Acta Sanctorum, a counterpart of the Legends of the Christian Saints. And they present many parallels to well-known stories of mediæval literature, Oriental and European. For comparative study of such parallels (a most inviting task), Doctor Burlingame's Synopses, clear and brief, will prove a very great convenience. His vigorous diction suggests familiarity with such 'wells of English undefyled' as the Bible and the Book of Common Prayer. The work gives a vivid picture of the everday life of the ancient Buddhists—monks, nuns, lay disciples. It is thus, incidentally, an admirable preparative for the study of the more difficult Buddhist books in the original. As especially attractive stories may be cited: Lean Gotamī seeks mustard-seed to cure her dead child; Murder of Great Moggallāna; Buddha falsely accused by Chinchā; the Hell-pot. A critical and historical introduction is prefixed. At the end is an *intelligent* index.